REAL WORLD APPLICATION | Are Fixed Costs Dragging Major League Baseball Teams Down?

Although actual costs and revenues of major league baseball teams are not available to the public, *USA Today* hired a baseball expert to estimate the profitability of each team. The expert reported that half the teams are profitable and the other half are losing money.

After looking at the following data, baseball teams clearly have significant fixed costs, especially in the area of player payrolls. In fact, for the Kansas City Royals, player payroll (including payroll taxes and pension costs) is *higher* than total revenues. It should come as no surprise that the Royals had the biggest loss of all 28 teams. In contrast, the Colorado Rockies is the most profitable team with player payroll amounting to 35 percent of total revenues. (The Rockies have also shown that success does not require high player payrolls.)

	Colorado Rockies	Kansas City Royals
Revenues		
Ticket sales	$36,000,000	$19,800,000
Concessions	9,500,000	5,200,000
TV/Radio fees	11,000,000	12,000,000
Spring training income	11,000,000	700,000
Other revenues	10,800,000	8,300,000
Total revenues	78,300,000	46,000,000
Variable Costs	8,750,000	8,100,000
Fixed Costs		
Player payroll (including payroll taxes and pension costs)	27,400,000	46,500,000
Administrative payroll	7,500,000	6,000,000
Stadium	5,000,000	3,500,000
Other fixed costs	4,400,000	4,450,000
Total fixed costs	44,300,000	60,450,000
Net income	$25,250,000	($22,550,000)

Source: Morten Stone, "Baseball's Bucks: Owners Should Open Books," *USA Today,* October 20, 1994, pp. 8c and 9c.

(page 40)

REAL WORLD APPLICATION | How Stanford Got into Trouble with its Cost Assignment Methods

Stanford University is one of the leading research universities in the United States. The Office of Naval Research paid Stanford hundreds of millions of dollars for research performed from 1981 through 1992. Research contracts, which are jobs, entitled Stanford to be reimbursed for 100 percent of its direct costs and its indirect costs based on a negotiated percentage of direct costs. This percentage is negotiated based on several items, including the university's past record of indirect costs as a percentage of direct costs.

In reviewing Stanford's indirect costs assigned to funded research, Paul Biddle, a representative of the Office of Naval Research, identified inappropriate expenses, including flowers for the president's home and depreciation on a 72-foot university-owned yacht. Stanford subsequently reviewed its records and was chagrined to find many expenses inadvertently allocated to funded research. As a result of an investigation performed by the Office of Naval Research, Stanford's indirect cost reimbursement rate decreased from 70 percent of direct costs to 58.3 percent. In addition, it repaid more than $3 million to the government.

Source: William Celis III, "Navy Settles a Fraud Case on Stanford Research Costs," *New York Times,* October 19, 1994; and S. Huddart, "Stanford University Indirect Cost Recovery," Stanford University School of Business, 1992.

(page 99)

See these and numerous other examples throughout the book . . .

Adding value to your course!

COST ACCOUNTING

Creating Value for Management

Fifth Edition

THE IRWIN SERIES IN UNDERGRADUATE ACCOUNTING

Ainsworth, Deines, Plumlee and Larson
Introduction to Accounting: An Integrated Approach

Ansari (Editor—Modular Series)
Management Accounting: A Strategic Focus

Bernstein
Financial Statement Analysis: Theory, Application and Interpretation
Fifth Edition

Bernstein and Maksy
Cases in Financial Statement Reporting and Analysis
Second Edition

Boatsman, Griffin, Vickrey and Williams
Advanced Accounting
Eighth Edition

Boockholdt
Accounting Information Systems
Fourth Edition

Booker, Caldwell, Galbreath, and Rand
Praxis Ready Slides
Praxis Ready Shows
Praxis Ready Notes
Power Point Classroom Presentation Products

Carse and Slater
Payroll Accounting
1997 Edition

Danos and Imhoff
Introduction to Financial Accounting
Second Edition

Dyckman, Dukes and Davis
Intermediate Accounting
Third Edition

Engler, Bernstein and Lambert
Advanced Accounting
Third Edition

Engstrom and Hay
Essentials of Accounting for Governmental and Not-for-Profit Organizations
Fourth Edition

Epstein and Spalding
The Accountant's Guide to Legal Liability and Ethics

Ferris
Financial Accounting and Corporate Reporting: A Casebook
Fourth Edition

Garrison and Noreen
Managerial Accounting
Eighth Edition

Hay and Wilson
Accounting for Governmental and Nonprofit Entities
Tenth Edition

Hermanson and Edwards
Financial Accounting: A Business Perspective
Sixth Edition

Hermanson, Edwards and Maher
Accounting: A Business Perspective
Sixth Edition

Hermanson and Walker
Computerized Accounting with Peachtree Complete® Accounting, Version 8.0

Hoyle
Advanced Accounting
Fourth Edition

Larson
Essentials of Financial Accounting: Information for Business Decisions
Seventh Edition

Larson and Chiappetta
Fundamental Accounting Principles
Fourteenth Edition

Larson, Spoede and Miller
Fundamentals of Financial and Managerial Accounting

Libby, Libby and Short
Financial Accounting

Maher
Cost Accounting: Creating Value for Management
Fifth Edition

Mansuetti and Weidkamp
Introductory/Intermediate Practice Set Series
Fourth Edition

Marshall and McManus
Accounting: What the Numbers Mean
Third Edition

Miller, Redding and Bahnson
The FASB: The People, the Process and the Politics
Third Edition

Morris
Short Audit Case
Seventh Edition

Morse and Zimmerman
Managerial Accounting

Mueller, Gernon and Meek
Accounting: An International Perspective
Fourth Edition

Pasewark and Louwers
Real World Accounting Series
    Athletronics, Inc.
    Shoe Business, Inc.
    Understanding Corporate Annual Reports

Pany and Whittington
Auditing
Second Edition

Peters and Peters
College Accounting
Second Edition

Peters, Peters and Yacht
Computerized College Accounting

Pratt and Kulsrud
Corporate, Partnership, Estate and Gift Taxation
1997 Edition

Pratt and Kulsrud
Federal Taxation
1997 Edition

Pratt and Kulsrud
Individual Taxation
1997 Edition

Rayburn
Cost Accounting: Using a Cost Management Approach
Sixth Edition

Robertson
Auditing
Eighth Edition

Schrader
College Accounting: A Small Business Approach
Second Edition

Van Breda and Hendriksen
Accounting Theory
Sixth Edition

Whittington and Pany
Principles of Auditing
Eleventh Edition

Yacht
Computer Accounting with Peachtree® for Microsoft® Windows® Release 3.0/3.5

Yacht and Terry
Computer Accounting for Microsoft® Windows®

COST ACCOUNTING

Creating Value for Management   *Fifth Edition*

MICHAEL MAHER
University of California, Davis

IRWIN
Chicago • Bogotá • Buenos Aires • Caracas
London • Madrid • Mexico City • Sydney • Toronto

McGraw-Hill

A Division of The **McGraw·Hill** Companies

Chapter opening photo credits: **Chapter 1,** © Dan Bosler/Tony Stone Images. **Chapter 2,** © Alan Levenson/Tony Stone Images. **Chapter 3,** © Charles Thatcher/Tony Stone Images. **Chapter 4,** © Mitch Kezar/Tony Stone Images. **Chapter 5,** Seth Resnick/Light Sources. **Chapter 6,** Courtesy of Honda North America, Inc. **Chapter 7,** © Charles Gupton/Tony Stone Images. **Chapter 8,** Courtesy of Deere & Company. **Chapter 9,** © Boris Pittman/Courtesy of United Parcel Service. **Chapter 10,** © David Austein/Tony Stone Images. **Chapter 11,** © Dennis O'Clair/Tony Stone Images. **Chapter 12,** © Jim Cambon/Tony Stone Images. **Chapter 13,** © Andy Sacks/Tony Stone Images. **Chapter 14,** © Craig Schmitman/Tony Stone Images. **Chapter 15,** Paul Damien/Tony Stone Images. **Chapter 16,** © Jim Pickerell/Tony Stone Images. **Chapter 17,** © Mark Segal/Tony Stone Images. **Chapter 18,** © Robert Torez/Tony Stone Images. **Chapter 19,** © L.L.T. Rhodes/Tony Stone Images. **Chapter 20,** © J.P. Williams/Tony Stone Images. **Chapter 21,** © Jon Riley/Tony Stone Images. **Chapter 22,** © Robert E. Daemmrich/Tony Stone Images. **Chapter 23,** © Eric Berndt/Unicorn Stock Photos. **Chapter 24,** © Tom McCarthy/Unicorn Stock Photos. **Chapter 25,** © Bettmann. **Chapter 26,** © Chuck Keeler/Tony Stone Images.

Interior photo credits: **p. 4,** © Dan Bosler/Tony Stone Images. **p. 12,** Courtesy of Southwest Airlines. **p. 13,** © Walter Hodges/Tony Stone Images. **p. 30,** © John Terence Turner/FPG International. **p. 31,** © Ed Pritchard/Tony Stone Images. **p. 33,** (*top*) © Kaluzny/Thatcher/Tony Stone Images, (*bottom*) © Chip Henderson/Tony Stone Images. **p. 39,** © Alan Levenson/Tony Stone Images. **p. 67,** © Charles Thatcher/Tony Stone Images. **p. 70,** © Ken Fisher/Tony Stone Images. **p. 85,** © Mitch Kezar/Tony Stone Images. **p. 89,** © Jon Riley/Tony Stone Images. **p. 96,** © Billy E. Barnes/Tony Stone Images. **p. 100,** © Kaluzny/Thatcher/Tony Stone Images. **p. 126,** © Telegraph Color Lab/FPG International. **p. 162,** © David R. Frazier/Tony Stone Images. **p. 166,** © Keith Wood/Tony Stone Images. **p. 171,** © Dennis O'Clair/Tony Stone Images. **p. 189,** © Charles Gupton/Tony Stone Images. **p. 204,** © Charles Gupton/Tony Stone Images. **p. 233,** Courtesy of Domino's Pizza. **p. 235,** © Jim Pickerell/Tony Stone Images. **p. 272,** © Bruce Forster/Tony Stone Images. **p. 277,** Courtesy of Chrysler Corporation. **p. 506,** © D E Cox/Tony Stone Images. **p. 516,** © Robert E. Daemmrich/Tony Stone Images. **p. 585,** Courtesy of Toyota Motor Mfg. U.S.A., Inc.

COST ACCOUNTING: CREATING VALUE FOR MANAGEMENT.

This book was printed on recycled paper containing 10% postconsumer waste.

1 2 3 4 5 6 7 8 9 0 VH VH 9 0 9 8 7 6

ISBN 0-256-17001-0

Publisher: *Michael W. Junior*
Sponsoring editor: *Mark Pfaltzgraff*
Development editor: *Tracy Klein Douglas/Burrston House, Ltd.*
Editorial assistant: *Marc Chernoff*
Marketing manager: *James Rogers*
Project supervisor: *Jim Labeots*
Production supervisor: *Pat Frederickson*
Cover Designer: *Michael Warrell*
Interior Designer: *Maureen McCutcheon*
Prepress buyer: *Charlene R. Perez*
Photo research: *Randall Nicholas*
Photo research coordinator: *Keri Johnson*
Compositor: *Shepard Poorman Communications*
Typeface: *10/12 Times Roman*
Printer: *Von Hoffmann Press, Inc.*

Library of Congress Cataloging-in-Publication Data

Maher, Michael, (date)
    Cost accounting: creating value for management / Michael Maher.—5th ed.
      p. cm.—(The Irwin series in undergraduate accounting)
    Includes bibliographical references and index.
    ISBN 0-256-17001-0
    1. Cost accounting. I. Title. II. Series.
HF5686.C8D24   1997
657'.42—dc21   96–44028

http://www.mhcollege.com

To Miriam, Krista, and Andrea for teaching me so much.

PREFACE

HOW THE FIFTH EDITION IS DIFFERENT

Our goal in writing the fifth edition was to make this book much more valuable for users. To learn what would make it more valuable required input from many people. The development process that provided that input to this project was extensive and thus, we believe, instrumental in making this text and package truly market-driven. In virtually every instance where preferences were at stake, we deferred to the suggestions of our colleagues and their students. We will attempt to thank everyone involved in the acknowledgments, but first we wanted to provide a brief overview of the market-driven process which guided the development of this edition.

THE DEVELOPMENT STORY

In August of 1994, the author and publisher met with eight cost accounting instructors from around the country at a focus group where we discussed the topics and issues most important to them when teaching this course. Following this, we had eight users of our fourth edition text provide detailed chapter-by-chapter comments in user diaries as they taught from the book in the fall of 1994. Concurrent to this, 12 nonusers of the book provided extensive chapter-by-chapter suggestions comparing the book to their existing text materials. From this initial market research, we drafted a plan and revised table of contents for this new edition that was shared with over 50 instructors who provided us feedback to this plan via detailed survey responses. This information drove the writing of the first draft of the fifth edition manuscript.

As I wrote this first draft, we had 12 cost accounting professors provide detailed chapter-by-chapter feedback on the entire first draft manuscript. We were able to incorporate all of this extensive and extremely helpful input into shaping a final draft that we feel best meets the needs of our intended audience. In summary, *over 70 professors* participated in this development process. The tremendous feedback provided by each of them helped shape our vision into developing numerous differences and advantages we believe distinguish this book from other offerings.

WHAT OUR RESEARCH DISCOVERED

This market research stated that we should attempt to accomplish the following three objectives:

- Provide more coverage of contemporary topics such as nonfinancial performance measures, quality management, and strategic uses of cost analysis.
- Give the book a particular focus of providing value to customers both of the organization and of cost accounting.
- Emphasize managerial uses and critical analysis.

Here are the steps that we took to accomplish these objectives.

Contemporary Topics

- *New chapters.* First, we added three new chapters: (1) Chapter 9, *Activity-Based Management,* which together with Chapter 8, *Activity-Based Costing,* provides two chapters on these important cost management topics; (2) Chapter 16, *Managing Quality and Time;* and (3) Chapter 22, *Nonfinancial Performance Measures.*
- *New topics integrated into existing chapters.* Second, we integrated new topics into existing chapters. These include discussions of the value chain, using the value chain to develop more useful income statements, benchmarking, continuous improvement, theory of constraints, *Kaizen* costing, target costing, customer costing and profitability analysis, expanded discussion of just-in-time, and strategic uses of cost management. In addition, the topics in the new chapters are integrated throughout the book. For example, several reviewers thought the inclusion of activity-based costing in Chapter 18's discussion of cost variances was a major strength of that chapter.

Focus of the Book: Adding Value to Customers

Introduction to the Student   We added an introduction to the student that emphasizes how important it is to use cost accounting and management to add value in the organization. We tell the students that

REAL WORLD APPLICATION   **The Accountant as a Communicator**

Although accounting is often called the language of business, it is a foreign language to most businesspeople. According to Joseph Barra, a division controller at Lever Brothers Co., the solution may lie with accountants. "I have enc̲_____ accountants who were excellent _____ really knew their field but could _____ management and get the messag_____ present basic accounting inform_____

Communication with nonacco_____ portant because of the interactio_____ and users of information. Accord_____ people at Lever Brothers look to _____ mation about distribution costs f_____ management decides to change _____ work with people in purchasing t_____ the company is considering a ne_____ and estimation of the cost is con_____

right from the beginning. . . . Ideally, this process results in a combination of the disciplines. The marketing people make the estimates of what they think sales will be and also calculate what happens if the estimates are missed."

FOCUSING ON CUSTOMERS

L.O. 4: Identify the users or "customers" of cost accounting information.

To communicate with nonaccountants, accountants must get out where products are made and customers are served. Here an accountant communicates with her "customers"—people from production, engineering, and management. (© Walter Hodges/Tony Stone Images.)

the major purpose in writing this book is to help them add value to the organizations in which they will work during their careers. The book also points out the importance of working in teams—employees will add more value to the organization if they understand the entire business, not just the accounting function, as demonstrated by the picture above and the accompanying discussion.

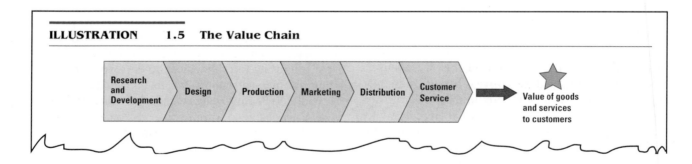

ILLUSTRATION   1.5   The Value Chain

Research and Development → Design → Production → Marketing → Distribution → Customer Service → Value of goods and services to customers

Value Chain   We use the value chain to demonstrate ways to add value in the organization.

Value Income Statements   We demonstrate how to prepare reports and provide analyses that go beyond traditional presentations. Examples of these reports and analyses include the value income state-

ment shown below, the comparison of resources used to resources supplied under activity-based management in Chapter 9, the profit variance analysis in Chapter 18, and several reports and analyses in the new chapters on quality and time management (Chapter 16) and nonfinancial performance measures (Chapter 22).

ILLUSTRATION 2.12	Value Income Statement

UNIQUE DENIMS: NEW JACKETS
Value Income Statement
For the Year Ending December 31, Year 3

	Nonvalue-Added Activities	Value-Added Activities	Total
Sales revenue		$400,000	$400,000
Variable manufacturing costs			
Materials used in production		80,000	80,000
Materials waste	$ 10,000		10,000
Labor used in production		40,000	40,000
Labor used to rework products	20,000		20,000
Manufacturing overhead used in production		45,000	45,000
Manufacturing overhead used to rework products	5,000		5,000
Variable marketing and administrative costs			
Marketing and administrative services used to sell products		25,000	25,000
Marketing and administrative services used to process returned products	5,000		5,000
Contribution margin	(40,000)	210,000	170,000
Fixed manufacturing			
Fixed manufacturing costs used in production		40,000	40,000
Salaries of employees reworking products	10,000		10,000
Fixed marketing and administrative costs			
Marketing and administrative services used to sell products		15,000	15,000
Marketing and administrative services used to process returned products	5,000		5,000
Operating profit	$(55,000)	$155,000	$100,000

Emphasize Managerial Uses and Critical Analysis

Critical Analysis and Discussion Questions

We have added critical analysis and discussion questions in each chapter. These questions are designed to be used in classroom discussion or assigned as homework. They can be used as either group or individual assignments. A particularly effective collaborative classroom learning experience is to divide the class into groups to work on these questions. Assign each group to give a brief oral report or put their answers in writing. Some of these questions require students to conduct interviews of managers, such as the following questions from Chapter 4 *(Job Costing)*.

4.11 Interview the manager of a construction company (for example, a company that does house construction, remodeling, landscaping, or street or highway construction) about how the company bids on prospective jobs. Does it use cost information from former jobs that are similar to prospective ones, for example? Does it have a specialist in cost estimation who estimates the costs of prospective jobs? Write a report to your instructor summarizing the results of your interview.

4.12 Interview the manager of a campus print shop or a print shop in the local area about how the company bids on prospective jobs. Does it use cost information from former jobs that are similar to prospective ones, for example? Does it have a specialist in cost estimation who estimates the costs of prospective jobs? Write a report to your instructor summarizing the results of your interview.

Managerial Report Writing   Many of the problems include an assignment to report the results of the analysis to management, such as the following problem from Chapter 6 *(Spoilage and Quality Management).*

6.29   Cost of Spoilage   Oregonian, Inc., uses weighted-average costing to compute product costs. At the beginning of the period, it had 200 units in beginning inventory that were complete 100 percent with respect to materials and 40 percent with respect to conversion costs. All units in beginning inventory were good units. During the period, the company started 4,800 units; it produced 4,000 good units but lost 1,000 to spoilage.

Oregonian's production people detect spoilage after the application of 20 percent of conversion costs and 100 percent of materials costs. Of the 4,000 good units, 3,600 were transferred out to Finished Goods Inventory. The remaining 400 units were in ending WIP inventory, complete 100 percent with respect to materials and 50 percent with respect to conversion costs. From the accounting records, we find the following costs:

	Beginning Inventory	Current Period Costs	Total
Materials	$10,000	$190,000	$200,000
Conversion costs	4,000	196,000	200,000

Required   Management is concerned that so many units were spoiled and has asked you to determine the cost of spoiled units. Compute the cost of spoiled units and write a report to management recommending whether further action should be taken to reduce spoilage, which management will take if the cost of spoilage exceeds 10 percent of the cost of good units transferred out.

Pictures and Real World Applications. One of the major challenges in teaching cost accounting is providing students with an understanding of real world problems. Unlike our financial accounting counterparts, we cannot rely on published financial reports for classroom examples. Like many other textbooks in cost and managerial accounting, this book contains numerous examples and surveys of practice. We have gone further to make these more provocative by using pictures as pedagogical devices to get students to think about the issues discussed in the text and by presenting managerial applications that provoke students to think hard about ways to add value to organizations. Here are some examples.

REAL WORLD APPLICATION   **Recalling Products to Provide Good Service to Customers**

 Automobile companies, drug manufacturers, and others have frequently attempted to recall and replace defective products before they reached the customers. The best example we have seen of recalling products to provide good service to customers was that of a newspaper publisher in a community in Kansas. Shortly after the papers were delivered to people's homes, they were soaked by a sudden unexpected downpour as they lay on porches, sidewalks, and lawns. So the publisher ordered the entire press run of 100,000 newspapers to be repeated. Why? He was attempting to provide a high level of service to readers and advertisers.

Source: M. Fitzgerald, "Kansas Community 'Recalls' Entire Press Run," *Editor & Publisher* 128, no. 33, p. 27.

REAL WORLD APPLICATION | Will L.A. Cut Costs by Eliminating Wasteful Activities?

Note to readers: We include "real world applications" of cost accounting throughout the book. Our purpose is to describe some of the many cost accounting issues that occur in the real world. These brief applications are based on article... who describe their experiences or re... world problems. We hope you will find... enjoyable and informative.

Los Angeles Mayor Richard J. Riordan... make L.A.'s motor pool maintenance o... cient. By eliminating some nonvalue-a... ciated with fleet operations, Mayor Ri... increase efficiency and reduce costs.

One nonvalue-added activity was t... tion truck drivers during normal trash...

Sanitation truck drivers add value when they are picking up trash, not when they are idle. They were idle during their normal working hours because their trucks had bro-ken down and were being fixed. This problem was traced...

Strategic Cost Analysis

Using the value chain and information about... identify strategic advantages in the market p...
eliminate...
duce cos...
product...
compan...
tomers, ...
petitors.
resources...
added ac...
customers...

By eli...
Southw...
around t...
means t...
airplane f...
This redu...
Southwes...
tage in lo...

The id...
that do n...
money t...
will save...
more com...

Southwest Airlines has been one of the fastest growing airlines in U.S. history. Part of its success has been due to its ability to eliminate nonvalue-added activities. How does eliminating vonvalue-added activities lead to success? (See text on this page for the answer.) (Courtesy of Southwest Airlines)

ORGANIZATION AND USE OF THE BOOK

This book is intended to be used in a cost or managerial accounting course in which students have had a course in accounting principles or financial accounting. This prerequisite assures that students understand basic accounting terminology and the financial reporting system. *It is not necessary that students have had a previous course in managerial or cost accounting.*

Users of the book should have a knowledge of elementary algebra. Although previous coursework in statistics, operations research, computer sciences, and other similar disciplines is not required, such work can enrich the student's experience with this book.

We have built flexibility into this text in two ways. First, some instructors prefer to cover major topic areas in a difference sequence than presented in this book. For example, some instructors prefer to cover decision-making topics or planning and control topics before covering cost accounting systems. This book is designed so that any major part, or "module," can be covered after Part 1, which presents all of the background concepts necessary for continuing to any of the three major topic modules. Adopters have used the book in class with each of the following sequences of the three major parts:

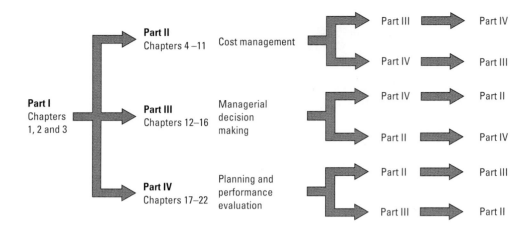

Second, chapters are self-contained. Therefore, instructors can skip chapters or rearrange the sequence of chapters. Adopters of previous editions were able to skip chapters or change the sequence as appropriate. We have put special emphasis on making this easier in the present edition. End-of-chapter materials that cover topics from more than one chapter (e.g., integrative cases) are clearly labeled to facilitate flexibility.

COMPLETE LEARNING PACKAGE

Study Guide   The Study Guide prepared by the author contains a number of useful references for the student. Each chapter includes the following: Overview of Chapter, Restatement of Learning Objectives, Chapter Outline, and Questions and Exercises including those which require the student to match key terms and concepts with definitions and numerical exercises and problems with worked-out solutions.

Instructor's Resource Guide   Authored by Mark Nigrini of St. Mary's University, the Instructor's Resource Guide contains the following items by chapter to provide additional support for the instructor: sample course outlines, assignment charts showing topic coverage and degree of difficulty for exercises and problems, chapter outlines, chapter overviews, discussion of chapter objectives, lecture transparency masters, and self-tests with solutions.

Solutions Manual   The Solutions Manual has been prepared by the author and carefully reviewed for accuracy by outside sources. This contains solutions to all assignment material and is available in electronic format as well.

Solutions Transparencies   These transparencies are set in large, boldface type to maximize their effectiveness in large classrooms.

Ready Shows, Ready Slides, Ready Notes
These teaching enhancement packages were prepared by Jon A. Booker, Charles W. Caldwell, Susan C. Galbreath, and Richard S. Rand, all of Tennessee Technological University.

Ready Shows. This is a package of multimedia lecture enhancement aids that uses PowerPoint7 software to illustrate chapter concepts.

Ready Slides. These selected four-color teaching transparencies are printed from the PowerPoint7 Ready Shows.

Ready Notes. This booklet of Ready Show screen print-outs enables students to take notes during Ready Show or Ready Slide presentations.

SPATS (Spreadsheet Applications Template Software)   This includes Lotus 1-2-3 and Excel templates for selected problems and exercises from the text. The templates gradually become more complex, requiring students to build a variety of formulas. "What if" questions are added to show the power of spreadsheets and a simple tutorial is included. Instructors may request either a free master template for students to use or copy, or shrinkwrapped versions are available to students for a nominal fee. Both DOS and Windows versions are available.

Check Figures   A list of check figures gives key answers to selected problem assignment materials. These check figures are available in bulk.

Test Bank   Prepared by Robert Gruber of the University of Wisconsin-Whitewater, the Test Bank contains multiple-choice, true-false, matching and completion questions, and short problems requiring analysis and written answers. The testing material is coded by type of question and level of difficulty.

Computest A computerized version of the manual testbank for more efficient use is available in Macintosh, Windows, or DOS versions. The extensive features of this test generator program include random question selection based on the user's specification of learning objectives, type of question, and level of difficulty.

Teletest By calling a toll free number, users can specify the content of exams and have a laser-printed copy of the exams mailed to them.

Virtual Manager This Windows-based multimedia software program acts as a vehicle for simulating various cost accounting concepts and tasks. The Virtual Manager provides an interactive means of gathering information pertaining to the many different scenarios facing a manager in today's business world. The Virtual Manager interface allows students to launch tutorial software to enhance subject knowledge, to document their analysis by launching macro-driven spreadsheet, word processing, and intranet-based applications, and to explore a simulated cost/managerial accounting environment.

Richard D. Irwin Managerial/Cost Video Library These short, action-oriented videos provide the impetus for lively classroom discussion. The *Managerial/Cost Video Library* includes videos on international and service examples to go along with numerous manufacturing examples.

ACKNOWLEDGMENTS

Throughout the process of writing this text, many people stepped forward with tremendous efforts that allowed us to accomplish our revision goals. We would like to recognize the sincere and devoted efforts of the many people who added their imprint to the process of developing this edition. As stated above in the "Development Story" section, we received invaluable advice and suggestions regarding previous edition feedback as well as throughout the entire draft process of this edition's manuscript. For this assistance, we thank the following colleagues:

Willie D. Adamson
California Polytechnic University-Pomona

Nasrollah Ahadiat
California Polytechnic University-Pomona

Tarek S. Amer
Northern Arizona University

Janice Ammons
New Mexico State University

Onker Basu
University of Akron

James P. Bedingfield
University of Maryland

Marinus J. Bouwman
University of Arkansas

Annhenrie Campbell
California State University-Stanislaus

Le Cao
George Mason University

Al Y. Chen
North Carolina State University

Peter Cheng
Purdue University

Peter J. Clarke
University College-Dublin

B. Douglas Clinton
University of South Alabama

Jeffrey Cohen
Boston College

Michael F. Cornick
UNC-Charlotte

Randolph S. Coyner
Florida Atlantic University

Karen Cravens
University of Tulsa

Reba Love Cunningham
University of Texas-Dallas

James W. Damitio
Central Michigan University

Peggy deProphetis
University of Pennsylvania

James M. Emig
Villanova University

James R. Emore
University of Akron

Gail Eynon
DePaul University

Charles Fazzi
Robert Morris College

Steven A. Fisher
California State University-Long Beach

Dana Forgione
University of Baltimore

James M. Fremgen
Naval Postgraduate School

Margaret L. Gagne
University of Colorado-Colorado Springs

Donald W. Gribbin
Southern Illinois University-Carbondale

Robert Gruber
University of Wisconsin-Whitewater

Joseph Guardino
Kingsborough Community College

John Hardy
Brigham Young University

Richard Houser
Northern Arizona University

Sung-Kyoo Huh
California State University-San Bernardino

Sharon J. Huxley
Teikyo Post University

Rudolph Jacob
Pace University

Fred Jacobs
Michigan State

Lal C. Jagetia
Cleveland State University

Philip Jagolinzer
University of Southern Maine

Fred R. Jex
Macomb Community College

Phillip A. Jones, Sr.
University of Richmond

Robert Jordan
University of Wisconsin-Superior

Robert C. Kee
University of Alabama

David E. Keys
Northern Illinois University

Zafar U. Khan
Eastern Michigan University

Il-woon Kim
University of Akron

Ilene Kleinsorge
Oregon State University

Leslie Kren
University of Wisconsin-Milwaukee

Wallace R. Leese
California State University-Chico

Robert Lin
California State University-Hayward

Marlys Lipe
University of Colorado-Boulder

Patrick B. McKenzie
Arizona State University

C. Michael Merz
Boise State University

Mark Nigrini
Saint Mary's University

Fred Nordhauser
University of Texas-San Antonio

August Petersen
University of Texas-Austin

Joseph R. Razek
University of New Orleans

Jane L. Reimers
Florida State University

Harold P. Roth
University of Tennessee

Jeffrey Schatzberg
University of Arizona

Ragnor Seglund
California State University-Sacramento

Shirish B. Seth
California State University-Fullerton

Wendy Jones Shanks
University of Illinois

Terrance R. Skantz
Florida Atlantic University

David Skougstad
Metro State College-Denver

Lanny Solomon
University of Texas-Arlington

Chris D. Stenberg
Robert Morris College

Michael Trubnick
California State University-San Bernardino

David E. Wallin
Ohio State University

Benson Wier
Virginia Commonwealth University

Neil Wilner
University of North Texas

Massoud Yahyazadeh
Penn State University

In addition, we are deeply indebted to the following individuals who helped develop, critique, and shape the extensive ancillary package: Jon Booker, Tennessee Technological University; Charles Caldwell, Tennessee Technological University; Paul Dierks, Wake Forest University; Susan Galbreath, Tennessee Technological University; Robert Gruber, University of Wisconsin-Whitewater; Paul Juras, Wake Forest University; Richard Rand, Tennessee Technological University; and Jack Terry, ComSource, Inc.

Finally, the extraordinary efforts of a talented group of individuals at Irwin made all of this come together. I would especially like to thank my Sponsoring Editor, Mark Pfaltzgraff; my Marketing Managers, Jim Rogers and Heather Woods; Marc Chernoff, Tracey Douglas, and Stephen Isaacs for editorial support and developmental editing; Michael Warrell, for outstanding design work; Jim Labeots, the project editor; Pat Frederickson, the production manager; Charlene Perez, the pre-press buyer; and Glenn Turner, Cathy Crow, and the staff at Burrston House, for outstanding marketing research support and feedback. Throughout the project various members of Irwin's editorial management team, in particular Mike Junior, were always available to provide guidance, direction, and additional support.

I thank Krista and Andrea Maher for their forthright criticism and help in editing this manuscript. Vanetta Van Cleave provided excellent help in all phases of the work on this edition. Finally, Kurt Heisinger simply made it possible to get this edition done. It would not have been possible without your help, Kurt.

Michael Maher

CONTENTS IN BRIEF

CONTENTS

PART TWO

(© Charles Gupton/Tony Stone Images)

COST MANAGEMENT

Chapter Three

Cost System Design: An Overview

Chapter Four

Job Costing

P A R T   T H R E E

(© Bill Bachmann/Tony Stone Images)

MANAGERIAL DECISION MAKING

C h a p t e r   T w e l v e

Cost Estimation   345

Chapter Thirteen

Cost-Volume-Profit Analysis 381

Chapter Fourteen

Differential Cost and Revenue Analysis 417

Chapter Fifteen

Using Differential Analysis for Production Decisions

Chapter Sixteen

Managing Quality and Time   484

P A R T F O U R

(© J. P. Williams/Tony Stone Images)

PLANNING AND PERFORMANCE EVALUATION

Chapter Seventeen

Planning and Budgeting

Chapter Eighteen

Flexible Budgeting and Performance Evaluation

Chapter Nineteen

Performance Evaluation: Cost Variances

Chapter Twenty

Performance Evaluation in Decentralized Organizations

Chapter Twenty-One

Transfer Pricing

Chapter Twenty-Two

Nonfinancial Performance Measures

PART FIVE

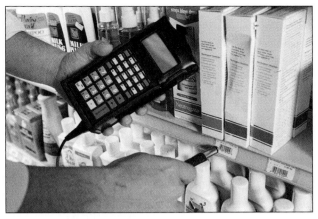

(© Tom McCarthy/Tony Stone Images)

SPECIAL TOPICS

Chapter Twenty-Three

Capital Investment Decisions

Chapter Twenty-Four

Inventory Management

Chapter Twenty-Five

Management Ethics and Financial Fraud

Chapter Twenty-Six

Revenue, Mix, and Yield Variances

INTRODUCTION TO STUDENTS

Welcome to the study of cost accounting. A famous economist once commented, "Cost accounting is like broccoli. Whether you like it or not, it surely is good for you." This same economist observed that what the new market-oriented economies in Eastern Europe needed was not more economists but more cost accountants.

This economist's point is that cost accounting adds value to us as individuals, to the organizations in which we work, and to the economies in which those organizations function. It adds value by helping all of us understand how to manage our resources wisely.

During your careers, you will be expected to add value to the organizations in which you work. As a former student said, "The best way to ensure job security is to make yourself valuable to your organization—so valuable that it can't afford to fire you!" The major purpose in writing this book is to help you add value to the organizations in which you currently work or will work in the future.

CAREER PATHS

Cost accounting is used in many careers. It is one of the largest growth areas in consulting today. The growth of consulting in the Big Six public accounting firms far exceeds the growth of auditing. Much of this growth is in cost accounting and related areas such as information systems.

Meanwhile, opportunities in industry are growing rapidly because more and more companies need excellent cost management to be successful. Basic industries such as the automobile and computer industries are well aware of the need for excellent cost management. Other fields that are rapidly recognizing the need for cost management include health care, public utilities, and financial institutions. Even educational and governmental organizations are *beginning* to see the need for improved cost management.

Excellent opportunities exist in cost accounting, which also supports many other fields. People going into auditing, financial reporting, and commercial taxation (particularly cost allocation and transfer pricing) simply must know cost accounting. Commercial lawyers find that much of their work deals with disputes over the application of cost concepts such as cost allocation and with calculations of damages, which rely on cost concepts.

Marketing people need expertise in cost accounting to understand product costs and to decide whether products are profitable. Engineering, production, and general managers all need to understand cost accounting to manage resources wisely. Even doctors are returning to school to learn more about cost management in the new health care environment in which they practice.

In short, today more than ever, knowledge of cost accounting helps you add value to organizations.

PROFESSIONAL ENVIRONMENT

The accounting profession includes many types of accountants: external auditors, consultants, controllers, internal auditors, tax experts, and so forth. Because accounting positions carry great responsibility, accountants must be highly trained and well informed about new developments in their fields. Here are some of the organizations and certification programs for accountants.

Organizations and Professional Certifications

The Institute of Management Accountants (IMA) in the United States and its counterparts in other countries (such as the Society of Management Accountants in Canada, the Japanese Industrial Management and Accounting Institute, and the Chartered Institute of Management Accountants in the United Kingdom) are the main professional organizations concerned with the topics in this book. The IMA has more than 100,000 members who work in management accounting. It publishes the journal *Management Accounting,* issues numerous policy statements, and commissions research studies on accounting issues.

The IMA also sponsors the program that leads to the Certificate in Management Accounting (CMA). For people working in industry and consulting, the CMA is the counterpart to the auditor's certified public accountant (CPA) certificate or license. According to a recent employment study, having a CMA added

$10,000 per year to the salaries of experienced financial people.[1] Your instructor or the Institute of Management Accountants, 10 Paragon Drive, Montvale, NJ 07645 (telephone: 800-638-4427) can give you more information about this valuable certification.

The American Institute of Certified Public Accountants (AICPA) in the United States and its counterparts in other countries (for example, the Canadian Institute of Chartered Accountants and the Australian Society of Certified Practicing Accountants) focus on external reporting, management consulting services, and auditing. Cost accounting issues appear particularly in management consulting practices of public accounting firms, which is a rapidly growing segment of public accounting firms' business. Cost accounting topics appear on the CPA examination in the United States and on the professional certification examinations in other countries. The AICPA publishes the *Journal of Accountancy*.

The Institute of Internal Auditors is an organization of internal auditors. It publishes a periodical called the *Internal Auditor* and numerous research studies on internal auditing. It also sponsors the Certificate in Internal Auditing program.

---

[1]*Management Accounting*, January 1995, p. 20.

The Association of Government Accountants is an organization of federal, state, and local government accountants. It publishes the *Government Accountants Journal*.

In addition to the journals listed, the *Journal of Cost Management*, the *Journal of Management Accounting Research*, and general-interest journals such as *The Wall Street Journal, Business Week,* and the *Harvard Business Review* contain many articles that will help you keep up with current developments in cost accounting.

LEARNING COST ACCOUNTING

You are undoubtedly a good student or you wouldn't be this far in your academic career. We won't insult your intelligence by stating obvious things like the need to study, do homework, and so forth. As in other areas in accounting, answering questions and working exercises and problems is essential for learning cost accounting. We particularly encourage you to work the self-study problems in each chapter. They are short and to the point and are designed to make sure that you are comprehending the material that you read.

All of us who helped develop this book wish you well in your study of cost accounting and in your careers.

COST ACCOUNTING
Creating Value for Management

Cost Accounting: How Managers Use Cost Accounting Information

LEARNING OBJECTIVES

After reading this chapter, you should be able to:

1. Identify the key financial players in the organization.

2. Explain how accounting is used for decision making and performance evaluation in organizations.

3. Explain how cost accounting information can add value to an organization.

4. Identify the users or "customers" of cost accounting information.

5. Understand ethical issues faced by accountants and ways to deal with ethical problems that you may face in your career.

We start this chapter by identifying the key financial people in an organization. It's important to start here to emphasize that *people* get the job done in organizations. No matter how sophisticated our systems, nothing happens without people making it happen.

Next we discuss how managers use information and how accounting information adds value to the organization. We focus on uses of **cost accounting,** which is the field of accounting that measures, records, and reports information about costs. After studying cost accounting, you will be able to add value to users of accounting information—users who can be thought of much like customers. Finally, we alert you to ethical issues that you will have to deal with if you provide or use accounting information. The sooner you are aware of these issues, the better you will be able to deal with them in your careers.

cost accounting
The field of accounting that measures, records, and reports information about costs.

KEY FINANCIAL PLAYERS IN THE ORGANIZATION

L.O. 1: Identify the key financial players in the organization.

Illustration 1.1 shows a part of du Pont de Nemours & Company's organization chart. Several financial jobs are highlighted. If you work in the accounting or finance function in an organization, you are likely to have one of these jobs. If you are an auditor or consultant, you will work with these people. If you work in marketing, operations, or management, you will work in teams with these people. Whatever your job, you will work in cross-functional teams of people from many areas such as engineering, production, marketing, finance, and accounting. Cross-functional teams are necessary for several reasons, including these:

* To bring a variety of expertise and perspectives to a problem.
* To ensure that the product is appropriate for its customer base (requiring interaction between engineering and marketing).

ILLUSTRATION   1.1   Partial Organization Chart, E. I. du Pont de Nemours & Company

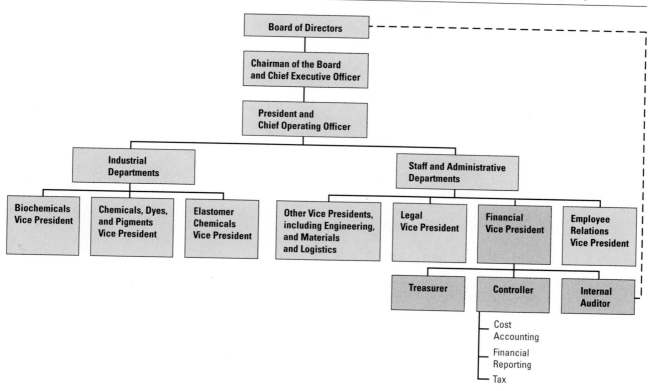

- To give production a chance to formulate an efficient production process (requiring interaction between engineering and production).
- To obtain financing for the project (requiring interaction between all groups, including finance and accounting).
- To determine whether the project is economically feasible (requiring interaction between all functions).

Clearly, finance and accounting personnel play an integral role in making the company a success. The following sections describe what key financial people do.

Financial Vice President

The top financial person is usually a senior vice president in the company. This person is in charge of the entire accounting and finance function and is typically one of the three most influential people in the company. (The other two are the president and the chief executive officer.)

Treasurer

If you have been treasurer of an organization, such as a club, you have an idea what this position involves. The treasurer is responsible for managing liquid assets (cash and short-term investments), handling credit reviews, and collecting receivables. The treasurer conducts business with banks and other financial sources and oversees public issues of stock and debt.

Controller

In most organizations, the individual in charge of accounting is called the *controller,* a name that sounds as though he or she controls things. In fact, the controller is involved in planning, decision making, designing information systems and incentive systems, helping managers make operating decisions, and various other things. The controller is a senior member of the management team.

Internal Auditor

Internal auditors are part of an internal audit department, which provides a variety of consulting and auditing services. At some companies, such as General Electric,

An internal auditor presents her findings to senior managers. Why do internal auditors have access to senior management? (Answer: There are two reasons: (1) their findings are important and (2) they must have independence from middle managers who are often their auditees.)

internal auditing is an important training ground for managers. At Alcoa and many other companies, internal auditors are essentially internal consultants who identify good ideas from their experience in various parts of the company. They learn something, for example, from their audit of department A that they can also use in department B. These internal auditors learn much and teach managers. Top managerial people around the company notice internal auditors—something that's very good for one's career prospects. Internal auditors also assist external auditors examining external financial reports and reviewing companies' internal control systems.

Notice that the internal auditor reports to the controller's superior at du Pont, as is true in many companies. That's because the controller is in charge of accounting systems while the internal auditor audits those systems. An internal auditor who reports to the controller would be auditing his or her boss. You can imagine how that would stifle the internal auditor's activities. The dotted line in Illustration 1.1 between Internal Audit and the Board of Directors signifies that internal auditors often report directly to the board or to the audit committee composed of certain of the board's members. That allows internal auditors to "blow the whistle" on anybody in the company—even the president—if they believe it's necessary to do so.

Cost Accountants

Cost accountants record, measure, determine, and analyze costs. They also work in teams of people from marketing who decide whether to keep or drop products (because of product profitability, for example). They work with people from operations to find ways to redesign products to save money. For example, cost accountants worked with elementary school principals and staff in a school district to find ways to reduce costs. They changed certain schools from grades K–6 to grades K–3 and others to grades 4–6 to use specialized teachers and school facilities more efficiently. For example, by combining the grades 4–6 from two schools into one school, the new school could afford a full-time science teacher, a full-time computer teacher, and laboratories in sciences and computers. The district saved money and actually saw quality improve because each school focused on the needs of a more homogeneous set of students.

The key to successful cost accounting is for cost accountants to have a good knowledge of the business. They also should constantly look for ways to add value to their organizations. Merely keeping records is only the beginning of a cost accountant's job. Cost accountants must constantly analyze operations and costs to find ways to improve operations and product quality while reducing costs. This may sound difficult, but when you work in organizations, you will find many ways to add value. Just look.

SELF-STUDY QUESTION

1. Who are the key financial players in organizations? Name one important thing that each type of key financial player does.

The solution to this question is at the end of this chapter on page 25.

COST DATA FOR MANAGERIAL PURPOSES

This book covers many topics in the use of cost data for managers. The following sections provide examples of these topics.

L.O. 2: Explain how accounting is used for decision making and performance evaluation in organizations.

Costs for Decision Making

One of the most difficult tasks in calculating the financial consequences of alternatives is to estimate how costs (or revenues or assets) will differ among the alternatives. Suppose the management of a department store is considering expanding its operations and store size to include several new product lines. Another option is to open a new outlet in a different location. The key is to determine which would be most profitable: remain the same size, expand operations in the current location, or open a new outlet.

For example, suppose that Jennifer's Sandwiche Shoppe has been open for lunch only, Monday through Friday, from 11 AM to 2 PM. The owner-manager, Jennifer Everhart, is considering expanding its hours by opening Monday through Friday evenings from 5 to 8. Now Jennifer has a difficult task. She has to estimate how revenues and costs will change if she expands to stay open in the 5 to 8 PM time period. She uses her work experience and knowledge of the company's costs to estimate cost changes, and she identifies **cost drivers,** which are factors that cause costs. For example, to make sandwiches requires labor. Therefore, the number of sandwiches made is a cost driver that causes, or drives, labor costs. To estimate the effect of opening from 5–8 PM on sandwich-making costs, Jennifer estimates how many additional sandwiches would be made if she stayed open in the 5 to 8 PM time period. Based on that estimate, she determines the additional costs and revenues to the company that selling additional ones would generate.

This type of analysis is both fun and challenging. In business, nobody knows for certain what will happen in the future, yet in making decisions, managers constantly must try to predict what will happen. Cost accounting has little to do with recording costs of the past but much to do with estimating costs in the future. For decision making, information about the past is a means to an end; it helps us predict what will happen in the future.

To complete the example, assume that Jennifer figures that her revenues, food costs, labor, and utilities would increase 50 percent, rent per month would not change, and other costs would increase by 25 percent if she opens in the evening. Her present and estimated costs, revenues, and profits are shown in columns 1 and 2 of Illustration 1.2. The costs shown in column 3 are the differences between those in columns 1 and 2.

cost driver
A factor that causes, or "drives," costs.

ILLUSTRATION 1.2	Differential Costs, Revenues, and Profits for One Week		
JENNIFER'S SANDWICHE SHOPPE Projected Income Statements For One Week			
	(1) Baseline Open 11 AM–2 PM	(2) Alternative Open 11 AM–2 PM and 5 PM–8 PM	(3) Difference (2) − (1)
Sales revenue	$2,200	$3,300[a]	$1,100
Costs			
Food	1,000	1,500[a]	500
Labor	400	600[a]	200
Utilities	160	240[a]	80
Rent	500	500	—
Other	120	150[b]	30
Total costs	2,180	2,990	810
Operating profits	$ 20	$ 310	$ 290

[a]50 percent higher than baseline.

[b]25 percent higher than baseline.

differential costs
Costs that change in response to a particular course of action.

differential revenues
Revenues that change in response to a particular course of action.

We use a particular term to refer to the costs and revenues that appear in column 3: differential costs and differential revenues. **Differential costs** and **differential revenues** are the costs and revenues, respectively, that change in response to a particular course of action. The costs in column 3 of Illustration 1.2 are differential costs because they are the costs that differ if Jennifer decides to open from 5 to 8 PM.

The analysis shows a $290 increase in operating profits if the shop is open in the evening. Based on it, Jennifer decides to expand her hours to the evening. Note that only differential costs and revenues figure in the decision. For example, rent does not change, so it is irrelevant to the decision.

Costs for Planning and Performance Evaluation

responsibility center
A specific unit of an organization assigned to a manager who is held accountable for its operations and resources.

An organization divides responsibility for specific functions among its employees. A maintenance group, for example, is responsible for maintaining a particular area of an office building. A Wal-Mart store manager is responsible for most operations of a particular store, and the president of the company is responsible for the entire company. A **responsibility center** is the specific unit of an organization assigned to a manager who is held accountable for its operations and resources.

Consider Jennifer's Sandwiche Shoppe. When she first opened it, she managed the entire operation herself. As the enterprise became more successful, she added a catering service. She then hired two managers: Sam Watts to manage the restaurant and Carol Capocci to manage the catering service. Jennifer, as general manager,

ILLUSTRATION 1.3	Responsibility Centers, Departmental Costs, and Revenues

General Manager Jennifer

Sandwich Department Manager Sam

Catering Manager Carol

JENNIFER'S SANDWICHE SHOPPE
Income Statement
Month Ending October 31

	Sandwich Department	Catering	Total
Sales revenue	$17,000	$11,000	$28,000
Department costs			
Food	7,000	3,000	10,000
Labor[a]	3,000	5,000	8,000
Total department costs	10,000	8,000	18,000
Department margin[b]	$ 7,000	$ 3,000	$10,000
General and administrative costs			
Utilities			$ 1,500
Rent			2,500
Other			900
General manager's salary (Jennifer)			4,000
Total general and administrative costs			8,900
Operating profit			$ 1,100

[a]Includes department managers' salaries but excludes Jennifer's salary.

[b]The difference between revenues and costs attributable to a department.

oversaw the entire operation. The top part of Illustration 1.3 shows the shop's organization chart.

Each manager is responsible for the revenues and costs of his or her department. Jennifer's own salary, rent, utilities, and other costs are shared by both departments. She is directly responsible for these shared costs; the department managers are not.

Illustration 1.3 shows departmental income statements. The Total column is for the entire company. Note that the costs at the bottom of the income statement are not assigned to the departments; they are the costs of running the company. These costs are not the particular responsibility of either Sam or Carol. Consider rent. Jennifer, not Sam or Carol, is responsible for negotiating rent terms with the owner of the building, so she manages this cost as part of her responsibility to run the entire organization. Sam and Carol, on the other hand, focus on managing food and labor costs (other than their own salaries) and departmental revenues.

Budgeting

You have probably had to budget—for college, a vacation, or living expenses. Even the wealthiest people should budget to get the best use of their resources. Budgeting is very important to the financial success of individuals and organizations.

budget

A financial plan of the revenues and resources needed to carry out the responsibility center's tasks and meet financial goals.

Each responsibility center in an organization typically has a **budget.** This budget is its financial plan for the revenues and resources needed to carry out the center's tasks and meet financial goals. Budgeting helps managers decide whether their goals can be achieved and, if not, what modifications will be necessary.

Managers are responsible for achieving the targets set in the budget. The resources that a manager actually uses are compared with the amount budgeted to assess the responsibility center's and the manager's performance. For example, managers in a department store compare the daily sales to a budget every day. (Sometimes that budget is the sales achieved on a comparable day in the previous year.) Every day, managers of airlines compare the percentage of their airplanes' seats filled to a budget. Every day, managers of hotels and hospitals compare their occupancy rates to their budgets. By comparing actual results with the budgets, managers can do things to change their activities or revise their goals and plans.

As part of the planning and control process, managers prepare budgets containing expectations about revenues and costs for the coming period. At the end of the period, they compare actual results with the budget to see whether changes can be made to improve future operations. Illustration 1.4 illustrates the type of statement

ILLUSTRATION 1.4	**Budget versus Actual Data**	
JENNIFER'S: SANDWICH DEPARTMENT		
Department Budget versus Actual Data		
Month Ending October 31		
Department	**Budget**	**Actual**
Food		
Bakery.........................	$1,100	$ 1,050
Meat.......................	2,500	2,700
Fish......................	1,500	1,750
Dairy.....................	1,500	1,500
Total food	6,600	7,000
Labor		
Manager and chef	2,000	2,000
Counter	800	1,000
Total labor.................	2,800	3,000
Total sandwich costs	$9,400	$10,000
Number of sandwiches sold..........	4,100	4,100

used to compare actual results with the planning budget for Jennifer's Sandwich Department.

For instance, Sam observes that the Sandwich Department sold 4,100 sandwiches as budgeted but that actual costs were higher than budgeted. Costs that appear to need follow-up are the cost of fish, meat, and counter labor. Should Sam inquire whether there was waste in using fish or meat? Did the cost per pound rise unexpectedly? Were customers given larger portions than expected? Was there unexpected overtime for the counter staff? These are just a few of the questions that the information in Illustration 1.4 would prompt.

DIFFERENT NEEDS REQUIRE DIFFERENT DATA

One of the principles of cost accounting is that different needs often require different cost data. "One size fits all" does not apply to cost accounting.

Each time you are faced with an accounting problem in your careers, you should first learn whether the data will be used for managerial or financial purposes. Are the data needed to value inventories in financial reports to shareholders? Are they for managers' use in evaluating performance? Are the data to be used for decision making? The answers to these questions will guide your selection of the most appropriate accounting data.

Cost Accounting and GAAP

generally accepted accounting principles (GAAP) The rules, standards, and conventions that guide the preparation of financial accounting statements for shareholders.

The primary purpose of financial accounting is to provide investors (for example, shareholders) or creditors (for example, banks) information regarding company and management performance. The financial data prepared for this purpose are governed by **generally accepted accounting principles** (GAAP), which provide consistency in accounting data used for reporting purposes from one company to the next.

In contrast to cost data for financial reporting to shareholders, cost data for managerial use (that is, within the organization) need not comply with GAAP. Management is free to set its own definitions for cost information. Indeed, the accounting data used for external reporting are often entirely inappropriate for managerial decision making. For example, managerial decisions deal with the future, so estimates of future costs are more valuable for decision making than are the historical and current costs that are reported externally.

Many organizations have tried to modify their financial accounting systems a little for managerial uses. The results are often disastrous. This approach is like using a fork to eat soup: People can do it, but it is far from effective.

Many proponents of improvements in business have been highly critical of cost accounting practices in companies. One such critic even produced a film titled "Cost Accounting: Enemy Number One of Productivity"![1] In fact, this critic identified important problems with cost accounting that companies should address, although he exaggerated them. The most serious problems with accounting systems appear to occur when managers attempt to use accounting information that was developed for external reporting for decision making. Decision making often requires different information than that provided in financial statements to shareholders.

It is important that companies realize that different uses of accounting information require different types of accounting information.

SELF-STUDY QUESTIONS

2. Suppose that *all* of the costs for Jennifer's Sandwiche Shoppe (Illustration 1.2) had been differential and increased proportionately with sales revenue. What would have been the impact on profits of increasing the hours by staying open in the 5 to 8 PM time period?

3. Give two managerial uses of estimated costs.

The solutions to these questions are at the end of this chapter on page 25.

---

[1]This film was produced in 1983 by Elihu Goldratt, Avraham Y. Goldratt Institute, New Haven, Connecticut.

CREATING VALUE IN ORGANIZATIONS

L.O. 3: Explain how cost accounting information can add value to an organization.

The Value Chain

value chain
The linked set of activities that increases the usefulness (or value) of the goods or services of an organization.

value-added activities
Those activities that customers perceive as adding utility to the goods or services they purchase.

Most organizations operate under the assumption that each step of the development, production, and distribution processes add value to the product or service. Before product ideas are formulated, no value exists. Once an idea is established, however, value is created. When research and development of the product begins, value increases. As the product reaches the design phase, value continues to increase. Each step of the process adds value to the product or service.

The **value chain** describes the linked set of activities that increases the usefulness (or value) of an organization's products or services. These **value-added activities** are those that customers perceive as adding utility to the goods or services they purchase. The value chain comprises activities from research and development through the production process to customer service. These activities are evaluated as to how they contribute to the final product's service, quality, and cost. In general, these activities include the items shown in Illustration 1.5 and described here.

- **Research and development.** The creation and development of ideas related to new products, services, or processes.
- **Design.** The detailed development and engineering of products, services, or processes.
- **Production.** The collection and assembly of resources to produce a product or deliver a service.
- **Marketing.** The process that informs potential customers about the attributes of products or services and leads to their sale.
- **Distribution.** The process established to deliver products or services to customers.
- **Customer Service.** The support activities provided to customers concerning a product or service.

For example, suppose your accounting professor assigns you a research paper. You would begin at the left side of the value chain and work toward the right, starting with your *research*, *developing* your ideas, *designing* the paper (for example, outlining topics), and *producing* a draft of the paper. These steps are analogous to the first three functions in the value chain in Illustration 1.5.

Next you *market* and *distribute* the paper by rewriting it to meet the customer's specifications (your professor's requirements for typing, length, and so forth) and turning it in. Finally, *customer service* involves answering your professor's questions about your work and perhaps responding to criticisms.

Each step of the process adds value (measured in terms of a grade) to your research paper—from the research and development phase to the customer service phase.

You may have noticed that administrative functions are not shown as part of the value chain in Illustration 1.5. They are included in *every* business function of the

ILLUSTRATION   1.5   The Value Chain

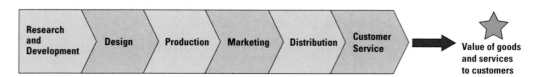

value chain. For example, human resource management is involved in hiring employees for all business functions of the value chain. Cost accounting personnel use cost information from each business function to help management evaluate employee and departmental performance. Many administrative areas cover each business function of the value chain.

Using Cost Information to Increase Value

Using the value chain as a reference, how can cost accounting information add value to the organization? The answer to this question depends on whether the accounting information provided improves managers' decisions. Suppose a production process was selected based on cost information indicating that the process would be less costly than all other options. Clearly, the accounting information added value to the process and its products, and the measurement and reporting of costs was a value-added activity. Suppose cost information was irrelevant to managers because it was received too late to help make a decision. Such information would not add value.

Finding and Eliminating Activities That Don't Add Value

nonvalue-added activities
Activities that do not add value to the good or service.

In their quest to continually improve the production process, companies seek to identify and eliminate nonvalue-added activities. **Nonvalue-added activities** are activities that do not add value to the good or service. They often result from the current product or process design. If a poor facility layout exists and work in process must be moved during the production process, the company is likely performing nonvalue-added activities.

Why do managers want to eliminate nonvalue-added activities? An important concept in cost accounting is that *activities cause costs*. Moving inventory is a nonvalue-added activity that causes costs (for example, wages for employees moving the inventory and costs of equipment used to move the goods). In general, if activities that do not add value to the company can be eliminated, then costs associated with them will also be eliminated.

Nonvalue-added activities are not necessarily easily eliminated. A steel plant that we studied had hundreds of miles of railroad track to haul things from one place to another. Once during a blizzard, the trains in the plant were slow, causing some blast furnaces to shut down because they did not have enough raw materials to work on. After that, the plant kept considerable raw materials inventory near the blast furnaces so it would not have to shut down because of transportation problems. Of course, the actual problem was poor plant layout that required hundreds of miles of railroad tracks just to move things around.

To correct the problem of poor facility layout, the production process must be reengineered. This can be a costly process and may take several years to implement. The steel company that we studied decided not to change the facility layout after considering the costs and the projected savings (or benefits) resulting from the change.

cost-benefit analysis
The process of comparing benefits (often measured in savings or increased profits) with costs associated with a proposed change within an organization.

Companies are constantly comparing the costs and benefits related to proposed changes within the organizational structure all along the business functions of the value chain. Ideas often sound reasonable, but if their benefits (typically measured in savings or increased profits) do not outweigh the costs, management will likely decide against them. The concept of considering both the costs and benefits of a proposal is **cost-benefit analysis.** Managers should do cost-benefit analyses to assess whether proposed changes in an organization are worthwhile. For example, managers should use cost-benefit analysis to determine whether to implement a new cost accounting system.

Strategic Cost Analysis

Using the value chain and information about the costs of activities, companies can identify strategic advantages in the market place. For example, if a company can eliminate nonvalue-added activities, it can reduce costs without reducing the value of the product to customers. By reducing costs, the company can reduce the price it charges customers, giving it a cost advantage over competitors. Or the company can use the resources saved from eliminating nonvalue-added activities to provide better service to customers.

By eliminating nonvalue-added activities, Southwest Airlines has reduced airplane turnaround time at the gate. Reduced turnaround means the number of passengers flown in an airplane for a given time period can increase. This reduces the cost per passenger, helping Southwest Airlines gain a competitive advantage in low ticket prices.

The idea here is simple. Look for activities that do not add value. If the company can save money by eliminating them, then do so. You will save your company money and make it more competitive.

Southwest Airlines has been one of the fastest growing airlines in U.S. history. Part of its success has been due to its ability to eliminate nonvalue-added activities. How does eliminating vonvalue-added activities lead to success? (See text on this page for the answer.)

Global Strategies

Another approach to gain a strategic advantage is to identify where on the value chain your company has invested resources that make it difficult for competitors to match. Many software companies that have invested heavily in research and development are using global strategies to take advantage of their competitive advantages. They reason as follows. Potential competitors must make large investments in research and development to provide products that can compete with theirs. Since they have already incurred those costs, they can charge relatively low prices, which makes it difficult for new market entrants to be profitable.

REAL WORLD APPLICATION | Will L.A. Cut Costs by Eliminating Wasteful Activities?

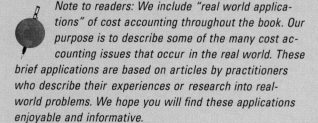

Note to readers: We include "real world applications" of cost accounting throughout the book. Our purpose is to describe some of the many cost accounting issues that occur in the real world. These brief applications are based on articles by practitioners who describe their experiences or research into real-world problems. We hope you will find these applications enjoyable and informative.

Los Angeles Mayor Richard J. Riordan was determined to make L.A.'s motor pool maintenance operation more efficient. By eliminating some nonvalue-added activities associated with fleet operations, Mayor Riordan was able to increase efficiency and reduce costs.

One nonvalue-added activity was the idleness of sanitation truck drivers during normal trash pick-up hours.

Sanitation truck drivers add value when they are picking up trash, not when they are idle. They were idle during their normal working hours because their trucks had broken down and were being fixed. This problem was traced to failure of sanitation fleet drivers to inspect their trucks at the end of their shifts. Consequently, trucks needing repairs were not fixed at night when they were idle. If this had been done, they would be ready to go the next morning, preventing drivers from being idle.

To create an incentive for drivers to get their trucks fixed at night, the mayor threatened to privatize trash collection. As a result, the drivers checked the trucks more closely and more regularly, reducing the out-of-service rate during normal working hours from 30 to 18 percent.

Source: Jeff Bailey, "How Can Government Save Money? Consider the L.A. Motor Pool," *The Wall Street Journal*, July 6, 1995, p. A1.

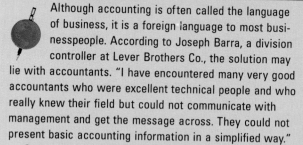

REAL WORLD APPLICATION   **The Accountant as a Communicator**

Although accounting is often called the language of business, it is a foreign language to most businesspeople. According to Joseph Barra, a division controller at Lever Brothers Co., the solution may lie with accountants. "I have encountered many very good accountants who were excellent technical people and who really knew their field but could not communicate with management and get the message across. They could not present basic accounting information in a simplified way."

Communication with nonaccountants is particularly important because of the interaction between accountants and users of information. According to Mr. Barra, marketing people at Lever Brothers look to the accountants for information about distribution costs for established products. If management decides to change a product, the accountants work with people in purchasing to obtain new materials. If the company is considering a new product, "the analysis and estimation of the cost is controlled by the controller

right from the beginning. . . . Ideally, this process results in a combination of the disciplines. The marketing people make the estimates of what they think sales will be and also calculate what happens if the estimates are missed."

What is required for effective communication with nonfinancial people? Mr. Barra lists four basic ground rules:

1. Keep examples simple.
2. Avoid technical jargon.
3. Show an understanding of marketing and production issues.
4. Avoid lessons in bookkeeping.

Good communication is self-serving. By making managers aware of financial issues, accountants will find their services in greater demand.

Source: A classic article by Joseph A. Barra, "Marketing the Financial Facts of Life," *Management Accounting,* March 1983, p. 29.

Many analysts thought software companies had matured by the mid-1990s because they had saturated North American markets. These analysts had not counted on global strategies based on good cost-benefit and value-chain analyses.

FOCUSING ON CUSTOMERS

L.O. 4: Identify the users or "customers" of cost accounting information.

To communicate with nonaccountants, accountants must get out where products are made and customers are served. Here an accountant communicates with her "customers"—people from production, engineering, and management.

See "The Accountant as a Communicator" and the text on this page for discussion of the importance of good communication between accountants and users of accounting information.

Of all the facets of the business that management must consider, the most important is the customer. Without customers, the organization loses its ability to exist; customers provide the organization with its focus. The days of producing a product or providing a service and hoping customers will appear are over. Instead, companies are now identifying customers' needs before designing and producing products.

Users of Cost Accounting

Who uses cost accounting information? Who are the "customers" of cost accounting? At the production level, where products are assembled or services are performed, information is needed to control and improve operations. This information is provided frequently and is used to track the efficiency of the activities being performed. For example, if a machine is assembled in 1.5 hours on average and data show that the previous day's average assembly time was 2 hours, production-level employees would use this daily information to identify what caused the delay and correct the problem.

At the middle management level, where managers supervise work and make operating decisions, cost accounting is used to send a warning signal if some aspect of operations is different from expectations. At the executive level, financial information is used to assess the company's overall performance. This information is more strategic in nature and typically is provided on a monthly, quarterly, or annual basis.

Cost accountants must work with their users (or customers of cost accounting information) to provide the best possible information for managerial purposes. As noted in the Real World Application, "The Accountant as a Communicator," your ability to communicate financial issues and concepts to nonfinancial people will be valuable both to you and them.

TRENDS IN COST ACCOUNTING

Cost accounting is experiencing dramatic changes. Developments in computer systems have nearly eliminated manual bookkeeping. Emphasis on cost control is increasing in hospitals, industries producing computers and automobiles, airlines, and many other organizations that have traditionally not focused on cost control. Cost accounting has become a necessity in virtually every organization, including banks, fast-food outlets, professional organizations, and government agencies.

Cost Accounting in High-Tech Production Settings

Many companies have installed computer-assisted methods to manufacture products, merchandise products, or provide services. These new technologies have had a major impact on cost accounting.

For example, robots and computer-assisted manufacturing methods have replaced humans for some jobs. Labor costs have shrunk from 20 to 40 percent of product costs in traditional manufacturing settings to less than 5 percent in many highly automated settings. Cost accounting in traditional settings requires much more work to track labor costs than current systems do. On the other hand, in highly automated environments, cost accountants have had to become more sophisticated at determining the causes of manufacturing costs because these costs are no longer driven by labor.

Just-in-Time Method

just-in-time method
In production or purchasing, each unit is purchased or produced just in time for its use.

The development of the **just-in-time** (JIT) production and purchasing method also affects cost accounting systems. Using just-in-time methods, units are produced or purchased just in time for use, keeping inventories at a minimum. If inventories are low, accountants can spend less time on inventory valuation for external reporting and more time on managerial activities. For example, a Hewlett-Packard plant eliminated 100,000 journal entries per month after installing just-in-time production methods and adapting the cost accounting system to the new production methods. Just-in-time inventory freed up two additional staff people to assist managers in running the business.[2]

Lean Production

Just-in-time production is a part of a "lean production" philosophy that has been credited for the success of many Japanese companies and such U.S. companies as Lincoln Electric. Using lean production, Lincoln Electric is eliminating inventories between production departments, making the quality and efficiency of production the highest priority, providing the flexibility to change quickly from one product to another, and emphasizing training and worker skills. Companies that do not have

---

[2]Rick Hunt, Linda Garrett, and C. Mike Merz, "Direct Labor Cost Not Always Relevant at H-P," *Management Accounting,* February 1985, pp. 58–62.

these characteristics find it difficult to implement the just-in-time production method.

Emphasis on Quality

total quality management
A management method by which the organization seeks to excel on all dimensions, with the customer ultimately defining quality.

Many companies have adopted the concept of **total quality management (TQM),** which means that the organization is managed to excel on all dimensions and the customer ultimately defines quality. The customers determine the company's performance standards according to what is important to them (which is not necessarily what is important to product engineers, accountants, or marketing people).

This exciting and sensible idea affects accountants who measure and report on people's performance. Under TQM, performance measures are likely to include such things as product reliability and service delivery. Traditional accounting measures of performance can thwart managers' efforts to achieve high quality.

Benchmarking and Continuous Improvement

benchmarking
The continuous process of measuring one's own products, services, and activities against the best levels of performance.

A recurring theme in the new approach to management is the combination of benchmarking and continuous improvement. **Benchmarking** is the continuous process of measuring one's own products, services, and activities against the best levels of performance. These levels may be found either inside or outside one's own organization. Continuous improvement means managers do not treat benchmarking as a one time event, but continuously strive to improve.

For example, managers at the University of Chicago Hospital benchmarked departmental efficiency against best practices in other teaching hospitals to find ways to improve their own performance. Managers compared the hospital's own surgery practice with that at other hospitals considered to be tops in surgery. Then they compared the hospital's own internal medicine department with the departments at other hospitals that were tops in internal medicine, and so forth, for all of the hospital's departments. By benchmarking best practices elsewhere, the University of Chicago Hospital managers found ways to improve their own practices.

Toyota Motor Company gets much of the credit for applying the concept of benchmarking and continuous improvement, a movement that many other companies have joined. These include Chrysler and Xerox, whose managers were shocked to find how poor its performance was compared to its Fuji-Xerox subsidiary in Japan. Benchmarking and continuous improvement is often called "the race with no finish" because managers and employees are not satisfied with a particular performance level but seek ongoing improvement. Organizations that adopt this philosophy find that they are able to achieve performance levels previously thought to be unattainable.

Theory of Constraints

theory of constraints
A management method that focuses on maximizing profits by identifying capacity constraints and increasing capacity.

According to the **theory of constraints,** every organization must have at least one bottleneck that limits production. Otherwise, it would produce an infinite amount of whatever it strives for (for example, profits).

The theory of constraints views a business as a sequence of processes linked like a chain. If the weakest link is strengthened, the chain is strengthened. If some other link is strengthened, however, you do not strengthen the chain.

For example, if the person taking the orders at a drive-through fast-food restaurant is the bottleneck, having the people making hamburgers and shakes work faster to build up inventory does little good. The focus should be on ways to increase the capacity at the drive-through window (for example, by improving the order-taker's language skills or by opening a second drive-through window).

Traditional accounting performance measures generally do not distinguish between bottlenecks and nonbottlenecks. Traditional accounting measures would encourage the burger and shake makers to build up inventory. The sensible thing, however, would be for the burger and shake makers just to keep pace with the order-taker until his or her capacity is increased. We discuss these issues in more depth in later chapters.

Activity-Based Costing and Management

activity-based costing (ABC)
A costing method that assigns the costs of making a product to the activities that are needed to make a product and then sums the cost of those activities to determine the cost of making the product.

Activity-based costing is a product costing method that is becoming more widely used, particularly in industries where competition is keen and direct labor costs are low. **Activity-based costing (ABC)** is a costing method that assigns costs of activities needed to make a product, such as quality testing, machine repair, product engineering, and distribution to customers, and then sums the cost of those activities to compute a product's cost. This costing method is more detailed and complicated than conventional costing methods, but it can provide more accurate cost numbers.

ABC assigns costs to products based on several different activities, whereas traditional costing methods assign costs to products based on only one or two different activities. In general, ABC provides more detailed cost information, enabling managers to make more informed decisions.

Activity-based management builds on ABC by using the information about the cost of activities. This information helps managers identify activities that do not add value but consume resources. ABC information also prompts managers to redesign costly production methods to save their companies money.

We devote two chapters to ABC and activity-based management later in the book, and we discuss the topic in several other chapters. Those of you who plan careers in consulting and industry will likely have an opportunity to use the material on activity-based costing and management in this book to help companies develop and install activity-based costing and management systems.

Creating Value in the Organization

These changes in the way organizations do business create exciting times in cost accounting and excellent future opportunities for you to make important contributions to organizations. Keep in mind that these new methods are not ends in themselves, they are tools to help you add value to organizations and their employees, customers, shareholders, and communities.

SELF-STUDY QUESTION

4. What are the major causes of changes in cost accounting systems in recent years?

The solution to this question is at the end of this chapter on page 25.

CHOICES: ETHICAL ISSUES FOR ACCOUNTANTS

What Makes Ethics So Important?

L.O. 5: Understand ethical issues faced by accountants and ways to deal with ethical problems that you may face in your career.

Accountants report information that can have a substantial impact on the careers of managers. Managers are generally held accountable for achieving financial performance targets, and failure to achieve these targets can have serious negative consequences for these managers, including losing their jobs. If a division or company is having trouble achieving financial performance targets, accountants may find themselves under pressure by management to make accounting choices that will improve performance reports.

For example, division managers have been known to record sales before the revenue was earned. This early revenue recognition usually occurs just before the end of the reporting period, say, in late December for a company using a December 31 year-end. Management might rationalize the early revenue recognition on the grounds that the sale will probably be made in January anyway; this practice just moved next year's sale (and profits) into this year.

Despite such rationalization, this practice is wrong and has resulted in many legal actions by the Securities and Exchange Commission and others against accountants and business executives.

As a professional accountant or businessperson, you will face ethical situations on an everyday basis. Therefore, it stands to reason that you, as students, should have some preparation to face these upcoming predicaments. The following discussion, the Real World Application, "A Company That Takes Its Conduct Seriously," and the management accountants' code of conduct in Illustration 1.6 are meant to help prepare you for the decisions you will face.

REAL WORLD APPLICATION   **A Company That Takes Its Conduct Seriously**

Johnson & Johnson has a corporate code of conduct and believes in it! This belief in the company's code of conduct may explain why this pharmaceutical and household products company is so highly regarded.

Johnson & Johnson's code emphasizes the company's responsibility to its community, employees, customers, and society as a whole, as well as to its stockholders. Many companies publish a corporate code of conduct. When you look at the way executives are rewarded, however, you find considerable emphasis on short-term profits at the expense of the idealistic statements in the corporate code of conduct. At Johnson & Johnson, however, executives are rewarded in a way that is consistent with the statements in the code of conduct.

Source: Authors' research and the Johnson & Johnson Credo.

Your personal ethical choices can affect not only your own self-image but also others' perception of you. Ultimately, the ethical decisions you make directly influence the type of life you are likely to lead. You should confront ethical dilemmas bearing in mind the type of life that you would like to lead.

In an attempt to influence the accounting profession, many of its professional organizations such as the Institute of Management Accountants (IMA), Institute of Internal Auditors (IIA), and the American Institute of Certified Public Accountants (AICPA) have developed codes of ethics to which their members are expected to adhere. Similarly, businesses such as Johnson & Johnson generally use these codes as a public statement of their commitment to certain business practices with respect to their customers and as a guide for their employees.

Throughout this book, we include discussions of ethical issues. Our aim is to make you aware of potential problems that you and your colleagues will face in your careers. Many accountants and businesspeople have found themselves in serious trouble because they did many small things, none of which appeared seriously wrong, only to find that these small things added up to big trouble. If you know the warning signs of potential ethical problems, you will have a chance to protect yourself and set the proper moral tone for your company and your profession at the same time.

The IMA code of conduct appears in Illustration 1.6. In its code of conduct, "Standards of Ethical Conduct for Management Accountants," the IMA states that management (and cost) accountants have a responsibility to maintain the highest levels of ethical conduct. They also have a responsibility to maintain professional competency, refrain from disclosing confidential information, and maintain integrity and objectivity in their work. These standards recommend that accountants faced with ethical conflicts follow the established policies that deal with them. If the policies do not resolve the conflict, accountants should consider discussing the matter with superiors, potentially as high as the audit committee of the board of directors. In extreme cases, the accountant may have no alternative but to resign.

Many people believe that the appropriate way to deal with ethical issues is not by requiring employees to read and sign codes of ethics but to rely on more fundamental concepts of right and wrong. Codes of conduct look good on paper, but ultimately much of ethical behavior comes from an individual's personal beliefs. We are certain that you will be faced with important ethical choices during your career, and we wish you well in making the right choices.

What Should You Do If You Discover Unethical Conduct?

In applying the standards of ethical conduct, cost accountants may encounter problems in identifying unethical behavior or in resolving an ethical conflict. When faced with significant ethical issues, cost accountants should follow the organization's established policies bearing on the resolution of such conflict. If these policies do not

ILLUSTRATION 1.6	Institute of Management Accountants: Standards of Ethical Conduct for Management Accountants

Management accountants have an obligation to the organizations they serve, their profession, the public and themselves to maintain the highest standards of ethical conduct. In recognition of this obligation, the IMA has promulgated the following standards of ethical conduct for management accountants; adherence to them is integral to achieving the objectives of management accounting. Management accountants shall not commit acts contrary to these standards, nor shall they condone the commission of such acts by others within their organizations.

Competence
Management accountants have a responsibility to:

- Maintain an appropriate level of professional competence by ongoing development of their knowledge and skills.
- Perform their professional duties in accordance with relevant laws, regulations, and technical standards.
- Prepare complete and clear reports and recommendations after appropriate analyses of relevant and reliable information.

Confidentiality
Management accountants have a responsibility to:

- Refrain from disclosing confidential information acquired in the course of their work except when authorized, unless legally obligated to do so.
- Inform subordinates as appropriate regarding the confidentiality of information acquired in the course of their work and monitor their activities to assure the maintenance of that confidentiality.
- Refrain from using or appearing to use confidential information acquired in the course of their work for unethical or illegal advantage either personally or through third parties.

Integrity
Management accountants have a responsibility to:

- Avoid actual or apparent conflicts of interest and advise all appropriate parties of any potential conflict.
- Refrain from engaging in any activity that would prejudice their ability to carry out their duties ethically.
- Refuse any gift, favor, or hospitality that would influence or would appear to influence their actions.
- Refrain from either actively or passively subverting the attainment of the organization's legitimate and ethical objectives.
- Recognize and communicate professional limitations or other constraints that would preclude responsible judgment or successful performance of an activity.
- Communicate unfavorable as well as favorable information and professional judgments or opinions.
- Refrain from engaging in or supporting any activity that would discredit the profession.

Objectivity
Management accountants have a responsibility to:

- Communicate information fairly and objectively.
- Disclose fully all relevant information that could reasonably be expected to influence an intended user's understanding of the reports, comments, and recommendations presented.

Source: National Association of Accountants, *Statement No. 1B*, "Statements on Management Accounting: Objectives of Management Accounting" (New York, June 17, 1982). These standards are reprinted with the permission of the Institute of Management Accountants.

resolve the ethical conflict, cost accountants should consider the following courses of action.

Discuss such problems with the immediate superior except when it appears that the superior is involved, in which case the problem should be presented initially to the next higher managerial level. If satisfactory resolution cannot be achieved when the problem is initially presented, submit the issues to the next higher managerial level.

Most operational, quality control, and ethical problems in organizations are faced by workers such as these. Wise managers and accountants stay in touch with workers to resolve such problems.

If the immediate superior is the chief executive officer or equivalent, the acceptable reviewing authority may be a group such as the audit committee, executive committee, board of directors, board of trustees, or owners. Contact with levels above the immediate superior should be initiated only with the superior's knowledge if the superior is not involved with the problem.

Clarify relevant concepts by confidential discussion with an objective advisor to obtain an understanding of possible courses of action.

If the ethical conflict still exists after exhausting all levels of internal review, the cost accountant may have no other recourse than to resign from the organization and to submit an informative memorandum to an appropriate representative of the organization.

SUMMARY

This chapter discusses the use of cost accounting in its two primary managerial uses: decision making and performance evaluation. The following summarizes key ideas tied to the chapter's learning objectives. For example, LO1 refers to the first learning objective in the chapter.

LO1: Key financial players. The key financial players in organizations are:

- The vice president of finance, who is in charge of all finance and accounting activities in the organization.
- The treasurer, who is responsible for managing liquid assets, doing business with banks, and overseeing public issues of stock and debt.
- The controller, who is in charge of accounting.
- The internal audit department, which provides various consulting and auditing services inside the organization.
- Cost accountants, who record and analyze costs.

LO2: Managerial uses of accounting. Accounting information can be used for decision making by assessing differential costs associated with alternative courses of action. Accounting information also can be used to evaluate performance by comparing budget amounts to actual results.

LO3: Adding value. The value chain is a useful tool in assessing the value-added and nonvalue-added activities within an organization. The value chain consists of several primary business functions including research and development, design, production, marketing, distribution, and customer service. Cost accounting adds value by helping managers of all these business functions make good decisions.

LO4: Users or "customers" of cost accounting. Cost accounting information is frequently used by a variety of employees in an organization including production personnel, middle management, and executives.

LO5: Ethical issues. Ethical standards exist for management accountants. These standards are related to competence, confidentiality, integrity, and objectivity.

KEY TERMS

activity-based costing, 16

benchmarking, 15

budget, 8

cost accounting, 3

cost-benefit analysis, 11

cost drivers, 6

differential costs, 6

differential revenues, 6

generally accepted accounting principles
(GAAP), 9

just-in-time (JIT) method, 14

nonvalue-added activities, 11

responsibility center, 7

theory of constraints, 15

total quality management, 15

value-added activities, 10

value chain, 10

REVIEW QUESTIONS

1.1 Column 1 lists three decision categories. Column 2 lists three accounting costs and a corresponding letter. Place the letter of the appropriate accounting cost in the blank next to each decision category.

Column 1	Column 2
Analyzing divisional performance	A. Costs for inventory valuation
Costing for income tax purposes	B. Costs for decision making
Determining how many units to produce in the coming weeks	C. Costs for performance evaluation

1.2 Describe the six business functions in the value chain.

1.3 Distinguish between value-added and nonvalue-added activities.

CRITICAL ANALYSIS AND DISCUSSION QUESTIONS

1.4 A manager once remarked, "All I need are the differential costs for decision making; don't bother me with information about any other costs. They aren't relevant." Give examples of other costs useful to management. Comment on this remark.

1.5 You are considering sharing your living quarters with another person. What costs would you include if you decide to split them? What costs would differ if another person were to move in with you? Discuss the agreement options available.

1.6 Would you support a proposal to develop a set of "generally accepted" accounting standards for managerial performance evaluation? Why or why not?

1.7 A telephone company established discounts for off-peak use of telephone services. A 35 percent discount is offered for calls placed in the evenings during the week, and a 60 percent discount is offered for late-night and weekend calls. Because the telephone company would probably not be profitable if these discounts were offered all the time, explain what cost considerations may have entered into management's decision to offer them at these times.

1.8 A critic of the expansion of the role of the accountant has stated, "The controller should have enough work filling out tax forms and the paperwork required by the bureaucracy without trying to interfere with management decision making. Leave that role to those more familiar with management decisions." Comment.

1.9 For a corporation organized according to the organization chart in Illustration 1.1, what potential conflicts might arise between production managers and the controller's staff? How might these potential conflicts be resolved with a minimum of interference from the chief executive officer?

1.10   Refer to the Real World Application, "The Accountant as a Communicator," on page 13. Why is it important for accountants at Lever Brothers Co. to communicate effectively with marketing people?

1.11   Refer to the Real World Application, "Will L.A. Cut Costs by Eliminating Wasteful Activities," on page 12. What was the cause of the nonvalue-added activity—idle workers during normal trash pickup hours? How do you suppose Mayor Riordan's threat to privatize trash collection created incentives to eliminate wasteful activities?

1.12   Refer to the Real World Application, "A Company That Takes Its Conduct Seriously," on page 17. Why is it important for Johnson & Johnson to reward its executives in a way that is consistent with its corporate code of conduct?

EXERCISES

1.13   **Cost Data for Managerial Purposes (L.O. 2)[3]**

During your first day as a member of the controller's staff, you are asked to report on a contemplated change in the use of a new type of material in production for next year. The new material is expected to result in a 15 percent reduction in materials costs but no changes in any other costs. This year, materials costs are $6 per unit produced. Other costs are $9 per unit produced. The company can sell as many units as it can manufacture.

Required

a.   Identify the differential costs for the decision to use the new material next year. What would be the cost savings per unit if the company were to use the new material instead of the old one next year?

b.   Describe how management would use the information in (*a*) and any other appropriate information to proceed with the contemplated use of the new material.

1.14   **Cost Data for Managerial Purposes (L.O. 2)**

Management of the Microwave Division of Technology, Inc., wants to know whether to continue operations in the division. The division has been operating at a loss for the past several years as indicated in the accompanying divisional income statement. If the division is eliminated, corporate administration is not expected to change, nor are any other changes expected in the operations or costs of other divisions.

Required

What costs are probably differential for the decision to discontinue this division's operations?

TECHNOLOGY, INC., MICROWAVE DIVISION
Divisional Income Statement
For the Year Ending December 31

Sales revenue	$430,000
Costs	
Advertising	17,500
Cost of goods sold	215,000
Divisional administrative salaries	29,000
Selling costs	41,000
Rent	90,500
Share of corporate administration	47,500
Total costs	440,500
Net loss before income tax benefit	(10,500)
Tax benefit at 40% rate	4,200
Net loss	$ (6,300)

---

[3]Each exercise in this book is keyed to one or more learning objectives. The key L.O. 2 refers to the second learning objective on the title page of the chapter.

1.15   Value Chain and
Classification of
Costs
(L.O. 3)

Compaq incurs the following costs:

* Transportation costs for shipping computers to retail stores.
* Utilities costs incurred by the facility assembling Compaq computers.
* Salaries for personnel developing the next line of computers.
* Cost of Compaq employee's visit to a major customer to illustrate computer capabilities.
* Payment for design of packaging material for computers.
* Cost of advertising.

Required   Classify each of these cost items into one of the business functions on the value chain.

1.16   Value Chain and
Classification of
Costs
(L.O. 3)

Johnson & Johnson, a pharmaceutical company, incurs the following costs:

* To redesign drug containers to make them more tamperproof.
* To promote materials sent to doctors.
* For equipment purchased by a scientist to conduct experiments on drugs yet to be approved by the government.
* To pay quarterly bonuses to salespeople.
* For postage to send drugs to hospitals.
* For labor costs of workers in the packaging area of a production facility.

Required   Classify each of these cost items into one of the business functions of the value chain.

1.17   Ethics and Altering
the Books
(L.O. 5)

Amos & Associates, a closely held accounting services group, has been very successful over the past three years. Bonuses for top management have ranged from 50 percent to 100 percent of base salary. Top management, however, holds only 35 percent of the common stock, and recent industry news indicates that a major corporation may try to acquire Amos. Top management fears that they might lose their bonuses, not to mention their employment, if the takeover occurs. Management told the controller at Amos to make a few changes to several accounting policies and practices, thus making Amos a much less attractive acquisition. Elizabeth Chan, the controller, knows that these changes are not in accordance with GAAP. She also has been told not to mention these changes to anyone outside the top-management group.

Required
a. From the viewpoint of the "Standards of Ethical Conduct for Management Accountants," what are Elizabeth's responsibilities?
b. What steps should she take to resolve this problem?

(CMA adapted)

PROBLEMS

1.18   Responsibility for
Ethical Action

Paul Martinez recently joined Toxic, Inc., as assistant controller. Toxic processes chemicals to use in fertilizers. During his first month on the job, Paul spent most of his time getting better acquainted with those responsible for plant operations. In response to Paul's questions as to the procedure for disposing of chemicals, the plant supervisor responded that he was not involved in the disposal of waste and that Paul would be wise to ignore the issue. Of course, this just drove Paul to investigate the matter further. He soon discovered that Toxic was dumping toxic waste in a nearby public landfill late at night. He also discovered that several members of management appeared to be involved in arranging for this dumping. He was unable however, to determine whether his superior, the controller, was involved. Paul considered three possible courses of action. He could discuss the matter with the controller, anonymously release the information to the local newspaper, or discuss the situation with an outside member of the board of directors whom he knows personally.

Required
a. Does Paul have an ethical responsibility to take a course of action?
b. Of the three possible courses of action, which are appropriate and which inappropriate?

(CMA adapted)

1.19 Ethics and Inventory Obsolescence

Angioplasty Corporation's external auditors are currently performing their annual audit of the company with the help of Linda Joyner, assistant controller. Several years ago Angioplasty developed a unique balloon technique for opening obstructed arteries in the heart, which utilizes an expensive component that Angioplasty purchases from a sole supplier. Until last year, Angioplasty maintained a monopoly in this field.

During the past year, however, a major competitor developed a technically superior product that uses an innovative, less costly component. The competitor was granted FDA approval, and Angioplasty is expected to lose market share as a result. Angioplasty currently has several years' worth of expensive components essential for manufacturing its balloon product. Linda knows that these components will decrease in price due to the introduction of the competitor's product. She also knows that her boss, the controller, is aware of the situation. The controller, however, has informed the chief financial officer that there is neither any obsolete inventory nor need to reduce inventories to net realizable values. Linda is aware that the chief financial officer's bonus plan is tied directly to corporate profits.

In signing the auditor's representation letter, the chief financial officer acknowledges that all relevant information has been disclosed to the auditors and that all accounting procedures have been followed according to GAAP. Linda knows that the external auditors are unaware of the inventory problem, and she is unsure what to do.

Required

a. Has the controller behaved unethically?

b. How should Linda resolve this problem? Should she report this inventory overvaluation to the external auditors?

(CMA adapted)

1.20 Cost Data for Managerial Purposes

Wegrow Fruits, Inc., agreed to sell 40,000 cases of Fang, a dehydrated fruit drink, to NASA for use on space flights at "cost plus 10 percent." Wegrow Fruits operates a manufacturing plant that can produce 120,000 cases per year, but it normally produces 80,000. The costs to produce 80,000 cases are as follows:

	Total	Per Case
Materials	$ 960,000	$12.00
Labor	1,520,000	19.00
Supplies and other costs that will vary with production	640,000	8.00
Costs that will not vary with production	440,000	5.50
Variable marketing costs	160,000	2.00
Administrative costs (all fixed)	160,000	2.00
Totals	$3,880,000	$48.50

Based on these data, company management expects to receive $53.35 (that is, $48.50 × 110 percent) per case for those sold on this contract. After completing 10,000 cases, the company sent a bill (invoice) to the government for $533,500 (that is, 10,000 cases at $53.35 per case).

The president of the company received a call from a NASA representative, who stated that the per case cost should be

Materials	$12
Labor	19
Supplies and other costs that will vary with production	8
	$39

Therefore, the price per case should be $42.90 (that is, $39 × 110 percent). NASA ignored marketing costs because the contract bypassed the usual selling channels.

Required

What price would you recommend? Why? (*Note:* You need not limit yourself to the costs selected by the company or by the government agent.)

1.21   Cost Data for Managerial Purposes

Ante Division is part of a large corporation. It normally sells to outside customers but, on occasion, sells to another division of its corporation. When it does, corporate policy states that the price must be cost plus 20 percent. Ante received an order from Beta Division for 5,000 units. Ante's planned output for the year had been 25,000 units before Beta's order. Ante's capacity is 37,500 units per year. The costs for producing those 25,000 units follow.

	Total	Per Unit
Materials	$ 20,000	$ .80
Direct labor.	100,000	4.00
Other costs varying with output	10,000	.40
Fixed costs	90,000	3.60
Total costs	$220,000	$8.80

Based on these data, Ante's controller, who was new to the corporation, calculated that the unit price for Beta's order should be $10.56 ($8.80 × 120 percent). After producing and shipping the 5,000 units, Ante sent an invoice for $52,800. Shortly thereafter, Ante received a note from the buyer at Beta stating that this invoice was not in accordance with company policy. The unit cost should have been

Materials	$ .80
Direct labor.	4.00
Other costs varying with output	.40
Total	$5.20

The price would be $6.24 ($5.20 × 120 percent) per unit.

Required

If the corporation asked you to review this intercompany policy, what policy would you recommend? Why? (*Note:* You need not limit yourself to Beta Division's calculation or to current policy.)

1.22   Cost Data for Managerial Purposes

Amanda's Coffee, Inc., operates a small coffee shop in the downtown area. Its profits have been declining, and management is planning to expand and add ice cream to the menu. The annual ice cream sales are expected to increase revenue by $40,000. The cost to purchase ice cream from the manufacturer is $20,000. The coffee shop and ice cream shop will be supervised by the present manager. Due to expansion, however, the labor costs and utilities would increase by 50 percent. Rent and other costs will increase by 20 percent.

AMANDA'S COFFEE, INC.
Annual Income Statement
Before Expansion

Sales revenue.	$38,000
Costs	
Food	15,000
Labor.	12,000
Utilities	2,000
Rent	4,000
Other costs.	2,000
Manager's salary	6,000
Total costs.	41,000
Operating profit (loss)	$ (3,000)

Required

a. Prepare a report of the differential costs and revenues if ice cream is added. (*Hint:* Use format of Illustration 1.2)

b. Should management open the ice cream shop?

1.23 Cost Data for Managerial Purposes

Change Management Corp. helps companies adapt organizational structures to current industry trends. Recently, one of its officers was approached by a representative of a high-tech research firm, who offered a contract to Change Management for some help in reorganizing the company. Change Management reported the following costs and revenues during the past year.

CHANGE MANAGEMENT CORP.
Annual Income Statement

Sales revenue.	$1,200,000
Costs	
Labor.	570,000
Equipment lease.	84,000
Rent	72,000
Supplies	54,000
Officers' salaries	350,000
Other costs.	38,000
Total costs	1,168,000
Operating profit	$ 32,000

If Change Management decides to take the contract to help the company reorganize, it will hire a full-time consultant at $134,000. Equipment lease will increase by 5 percent because of the need to buy certain computer equipment. Supplies will increase by an estimated 10 percent and other costs by 15 percent. The existing building has space for the new consultant. In addition, management believes that no new officers will be necessary for this work.

Required

a. What are the differential costs that would be incurred as a result of taking the contract?

b. If the contract will pay $150,000 in the first year, should Change Management accept it?

c. What considerations, other than costs, are necessary before making this decision?

SOLUTIONS TO SELF-STUDY QUESTIONS

1. Major financial offices or departments in organizations are

- Financial vice president: Is in charge of accounting and finance functions of the company.
- Treasurer: Manages liquid assets, credit reviews, and receivables.
- Controller: Is in charge of accounting.
- Internal auditor: Provides consulting and auditing services.
- Cost accountant: Records, measures, determines, and analyzes costs.

2. All costs in Illustration 1.2 would increase 50 percent. Total costs would increase from $2,180 in the baseline to $3,270 (150% × $2,180). Profits would increase from $20 in the baseline to $30 ($3,300 revenues − $3,270 costs). Jennifer's profits increase compared to the baseline but not as much as in Illustration 1.2 because some of the costs do not increase proportionately with sales revenue.

3. Managerial purposes of estimated costs:

- Decision making.
- Performance evaluation.

4. Causes of changes include (but are not limited to) the following:

- Accounting has become more computerized, thus reducing manual bookkeeping.
- Increased competition in many industries, including automobiles and electronic equipment, has increased management's interest in managing costs.
- Developments of more highly technical production processes have reduced emphasis on labor and increased emphasis on overhead cost control.
- Developments in new management techniques have affected accounting. For example, by reducing inventory levels, JIT methods have reduced the need to compute costs of inventory.

Cost Concepts and Behavior

LEARNING OBJECTIVES

After reading this chapter, you should be able to:

1. Explain the basic concept of cost.

2. Explain how costs are presented in financial statements.

3. Understand how materials, labor, and overhead costs are added to a product at each stage of the production process.

4. Define basic cost behaviors including variable, fixed, semivariable, and step costs.

5. Identify the components of a product's costs.

6. Provide managers with traditional, contribution margin, and value-based financial statements.

This chapter provides the basic terms and concepts that you need to understand how to use cost accounting. Accounting is often called the *language of business.* Think of this chapter as providing the basic grammar for the cost accounting language.

We start by presenting fundamental concepts in cost accounting and showing how these costs appear on the financial statements. Next we show how costs are added to a product at each stage of production, using a jeans manufacturer as our example. We explain the types of costs that managers use in making decisions. Finally, we present several diagrams that will help you track the different components of a product's cost.

Illustration 2.13 on page 47 near the end of the chapter summarizes the most important cost concepts in this chapter; it will serve you well when you review for exams or need a quick reference.

WHY IT'S IMPORTANT TO KNOW COST CONCEPTS

For many of you, this chapter presents information most often used in your work. Many companies are getting "back to basics" in understanding and managing their costs. To be competitive, we must understand fundamental cost concepts and manage companies and governmental units to keep costs under control and use resources wisely. This chapter provides the building blocks for successful cost management.

Knowing cost concepts is particularly important if you are paid or pay others based on costs. Disputes, including costly litigation, often arise when people are (1) paid based on profit sharing, (2) reimbursed for costs, and (3) sharing costs with others.

The movie *Forrest Gump* provides a good example. In the movie, Forrest refers to life as a box of chocolates; you never know what you'll get. The same could be said of people who agree to a profit-sharing arrangement or cost-based reimbursement without understanding basic cost concepts. The coproducers, novelist, and screen writer for the movie all agreed to share in its profits. Imagine their surprise when this box office hit still had not made a profit nearly a year after its release! (See the Real World Application, "Gump Accounting.")

The key lesson from "Gump Accounting" is that the party who keeps the books controls the information. (In this case, Paramount Studio controls the information about the revenues from and costs assigned to *Forrest Gump.*) This party has much flexibility in determining what the numbers are. This is not necessarily illegal or wrong; it is simply a fact that when parties to a contract act in their own interests, the results may displease other parties to it. Before entering any agreement based on sharing costs or profits, be sure you know how each and every cost will be measured.

This is an important way that you can add value to your customers (for example, managers of your company or your clients).

WHAT IS A COST?

cost
A sacrifice of resources.

A **cost** is a sacrifice of resources. In going about our daily affairs, we buy many different things: clothing, food, books, a desk lamp, perhaps an automobile, and so on. The price of each item measures the sacrifice we must make to acquire it. Whether we pay immediately or agree to pay at a later date, the cost is actually established by that price.

IMPORTANT DISTINCTIONS

Costs versus Expenses

expense
A cost that is charged against revenue in an accounting period.

outlay cost
A past, present, or future cash outflow.

opportunity cost
The forgone benefit from the best (forgone) alternative course of action.

It is important to distinguish cost from expense. An **expense** is a cost charged against revenue in an accounting period; hence, expenses are deducted from revenue in that accounting period. A *cost* is a sacrifice of resources, regardless of whether it is accounted for as an asset or an expense. If it is recorded as an asset (for example, prepaid rent for an office building), it becomes an expense when the asset has been consumed (i.e., the building has been used for a period of time after making the prepayment). In this book, we use the term *expense* only when referring to external financial reports.

The focus of cost accounting is on costs, not expenses. Generally accepted accounting principles (GAAP) and regulations such as the income tax laws specify when costs are to be treated as expenses. Although the terms *cost* and *expense* are sometimes used as synonyms in practice, we use *cost* in this book for all managerial purposes.

The two major categories of costs are outlay costs and opportunity costs. An **outlay cost** is a past, present, or future cash outflow. Consider the cost of a college education; clearly, the cash outflows for tuition, books, and fees are outlay costs. Cash is not all that many college students sacrifice; they also sacrifice their time to get a college education. This sacrifice of time is an opportunity cost. **Opportunity cost** is the forgone benefit that could have been realized from the best forgone alternative use of a resource. For example, many of you gave up jobs to take the time to earn a college degree. The forgone income is part of the cost of getting a college degree and is the forgone benefit that could be realized from an alternative use of a scarce resource—time. These are other examples of opportunity costs:

- The opportunity cost of funds that you invest in a bank certificate of deposit is the forgone interest you could have earned on another security, assuming that both securities were equal in risk and liquidity.
- Tower Records started in a drug store in Sacramento, California. The opportunity cost of using the drug store to sell records was the forgone profits that could have been earned from selling other products or from renting out the space to someone else.
- The opportunity cost of time spent working on one question on an examination is the forgone benefit of time spent working on another question.

Of course, no one can ever know all the possible opportunities available at any moment. Hence, some opportunity costs are undoubtedly not considered. Accounting systems typically record outlay costs but not opportunity costs. Unfortunately, managers sometimes incorrectly ignore opportunity costs in making decisions. As a cost accountant, one way you can add value to your customers (or users of cost information) is to remind them of the opportunity costs that they may have ignored in decision making.

COSTS IN FINANCIAL STATEMENTS

operating profit
The excess of operating revenues over the operating costs necessary to generate those revenues.

L.O. 2: Explain how costs are presented in financial statements.

Unless otherwise stated, assume that income statements are prepared for internal management use, not for external reporting. We focus on **operating profit,** which for internal reporting purposes is the excess of operating revenues over the operating costs incurred to generate those revenues. This figure differs from net income, which is operating profit adjusted for interest, income taxes, extraordinary items, and other adjustments required to comply with GAAP or regulations.

Financial statements presented for managerial use will often be the product of your work. Of course, these statements are just a means to an end; the final products are managerial decisions and actions that result from the information presented in those financial statements. The following sections present some examples of how cost information appears in financial statements prepared for managers. These are basic statements that we build on. As we proceed through the book, we show you how to improve these basic statements to make them more informative.

Service Organizations

Service companies generally provide customers with an intangible product. For example, public accounting firms provide audit services and tax services. Labor costs tend to be the most significant cost category for most service organizations.

The costs associated with Audit Write, a public accounting firm, are shown in the income statement in Illustration 2.1. The line item cost of services sold includes the costs of billable hours, which are the hours billed to clients plus the cost of other things billed to clients (for example, charges for an information search or for printing financial statements). Costs not part of services billable to clients are included in the line marketing and administrative costs.

Retail and Wholesale Companies

Retail and wholesale organizations, like supermarkets, clothing stores, furniture stores, and motorcycle distributors, have a tangible product. These companies both offer a service, namely marketing the goods, and have tangible products. The income statement for these companies includes revenue and cost items like those in service companies, but they add a category of cost information (called *cost of goods sold*) to track the tangible goods they buy and sell.

Masthead Records is a retail company that sells CDs, tapes, and other items (for example, CD holders). The company's income statement and cost of goods sold statement are shown in Illustration 2.2. The cost of goods sold statement shows how the cost of goods sold was computed. The one in Illustration 2.2 shows the following information for Masthead:

- It had a $100,000 beginning inventory on January 1. This represents the cost of the tapes, CDs, and other salable items on hand at the beginning of the year.
- The company purchased $600,000 of goods during the year and had transportation-in costs of $30,000. Therefore, its total cost of goods purchased

ILLUSTRATION 2.1	Income Statement for a Service Company

AUDIT WRITE
Income Statement
For the Year Ended December 31, Year 2

Revenues	$1,000,000
Cost of services sold	600,000
Gross margin	400,000
Marketing and administrative costs	290,000
Operating profits	$ 110,000

ILLUSTRATION 2.2	Income Statement for a Merchandise Company

MASTHEAD RECORDS
Income Statement
For the Year Ended December 31, Year 2

Sales revenue	$1,000,000
Cost of goods sold (see statement below)	530,000
Gross margin	470,000
Marketing and administrative costs	200,000
Operating profit	$ 270,000

Cost of Goods Sold Statement
For the Year Ended December 31, Year 2

Beginning inventory	$ 100,000
Cost of goods purchased	
Merchandise cost	600,000
Transportation-in costs	30,000
Total cost of goods purchased	630,000
Cost of goods available for sale	730,000
Less cost of goods in ending inventory	200,000
Cost of goods sold	$ 530,000

Record company managers know the importance of monitoring inventory turnover. In some cases, hit songs are off the charts in just a few weeks.

was $630,000 ($630,000 = $600,000 for the purchases + $30,000 for the transportation costs).

- Based on the information so far, Masthead had $730,000 cost of tapes, CDs, and other items available for sale ($730,000 = $630,000 total cost of goods purchased + $100,000 available from beginning inventory). The $730,000 is cost of the goods that the company *could* have sold.

- At the end of the year, the company still had inventory on hand costing $200,000. Therefore, Masthead sold tapes, CDs, and other items costing $530,000.

The income statement summarizes Masthead's operating performance with the following information:

- Sales revenue for the year was $1,000,000.
- The cost of goods sold amount, $530,000, came from the cost of goods sold statement. Therefore, the gross margin (the difference between sales revenue and cost of goods sold) is $470,000 ($470,000 = $1,000,000 sales revenue − $530,000 cost of goods sold). If you were Masthead's manager, you would know that, on average, every $1 of sales gave you $.47 to cover marketing and administrative costs and earn a profit.

* The income statement also shows that marketing and administrative costs were $200,000 and operating profits were $270,000 ($270,000 = $470,000 gross margin − $200,000 marketing and administrative costs).

cost of goods sold
The cost assigned to products sold during a period.

The term **cost of goods sold** is intended to be self-descriptive. It includes only the actual costs of the goods that were sold. It does not include the costs of selling them, such as the salaries of salespeople, which are marketing costs, or the salaries of top executives, which are administrative costs.

What do we learn from a statement like that in Illustration 2.2? First, Masthead is making a profit. Second, it is earning an operating profit of $.27 on every dollar of sales, relatively high for a retailer, even one in the music business. (Don't leave school to set up a record store assuming that you will make this level of profits.) This implies that Masthead has some special success from perhaps hot new products and/or a great location. Third, compare the income statement for Masthead Records with that for the service company, Audit Write (Illustration 2.1). Like other retail and wholesale organizations, Masthead has an entire category of amounts that do not appear in a service company's income statement. This category appears in the cost of goods sold statement, which accounts for the inventories, purchases, and sales of tangible goods. By contrast, the service company does not "purchase" anything to be held in inventory until sold. Service companies are generally most interested in measuring the cost of providing services.

Manufacturing Companies

A manufacturing company has a more complex income statement than service or retail/wholesale companies. Whereas the retailer/wholesaler *purchases* goods for sale, the manufacturer *makes* them. For decision making, it is not enough to know how much was paid for a good; the manufacturer must also know the different costs associated with making it.

The manufacturer purchases materials (for example, unassembled parts), hires workers to convert the materials to a finished good, and then offers the product for sale. There are three major categories of manufacturing costs:

direct materials
Those materials that can feasibly be identified directly with the product.

direct labor
Work that actually transforms materials into finished products during the production process.

manufacturing overhead
All production costs except direct labor and direct materials.

1. **Direct materials** that can feasibly be identified directly with the product. (To the manufacturer, purchased parts, including transportation-in, are included in direct materials.) Direct materials are also called *raw materials*. Materials that cannot be identified with a specific product (for example, glue or grease) are included in category 3.

2. **Direct labor** of workers who transform the materials into a finished product.

3. All other costs of transforming the materials to a finished product, often referred to in total as **manufacturing overhead.** Some examples of manufacturing overhead follow.

   a. Indirect labor, the cost of workers who do not work directly on the product yet are required for the factory to operate, such as supervisors, maintenance workers, and inventory storekeepers.

   b. Indirect materials, such as lubricants for the machinery, polishing and cleaning materials, repair parts, and light bulbs, which are not a part of the finished product but are necessary to manufacture it.

   c. Other manufacturing costs, such as depreciation of the factory building and equipment, taxes on the factory assets, insurance on the factory building and equipment, heat, light, power, and similar expenses incurred to keep the factory operating.

The salaries of these supervisors is an example of overhead costs.

Although we use *manufacturing overhead* in this book, common synonyms used in practice are *factory burden, factory overhead, burden, factory expense,* and the unmodified word, *overhead.*

Prime Costs and Conversion Costs

prime costs
The sum of direct materials and direct labor.

conversion costs
The sum of direct labor and manufacturing overhead.

You are likely to encounter the following two categories of costs in manufacturing companies: prime costs and conversion costs. **Prime costs** are the direct costs, namely, direct materials and direct labor. In some companies, such as Hewlett-Packard's Networks Division in Roseville, California, managers give prime costs much attention because they represent 80 to 90% of total manufacturing costs. Just as Willie Sutton robbed banks because "that's where the money was," managers might focus nearly all of their attention on prime costs because "that's where nearly all the costs are."

In other cases, managers give most of their attention to conversion costs. **Conversion costs** are the costs to convert direct materials into the final product, namely, costs for direct labor and manufacturing overhead. Managers who focus on conversion costs use a controllability argument: "We can manage conversion costs. Direct materials costs are mostly outside of our control."

Generally, companies with relatively low manufacturing overhead focus on managing prime costs. Companies that have high direct labor and/or manufacturing overhead tend to be more concerned about conversion costs. In practice, you should figure out what cost information decision makers need to manage effectively.

Illustration 2.3 summarizes the relationship between conversion costs and the three elements of manufactured product cost: direct materials, direct labor, and manufacturing overhead.

Nonmanufacturing Costs

marketing costs
The costs required to obtain customer orders and provide customers with finished products, including advertising, sales commissions, and shipping costs.

Nonmanufacturing costs have two elements: marketing costs and administrative costs. **Marketing costs** are the costs required to obtain customer orders and provide customers with finished products. These include advertising, sales commissions, shipping costs, and marketing departments' building occupancy costs. **Administrative costs** are the costs required to manage the organization and provide staff support, including executive and clerical salaries; costs for legal, financial, data processing, and accounting services; and building space for administrative personnel.

Nonmanufacturing costs are expensed in the period incurred for financial accounting purposes. For managerial purposes, managers often want to see nonmanufacturing costs assigned to products; this is particularly true for commissions and

---

ILLUSTRATION   2.3   Components of Manufactured Product Cost

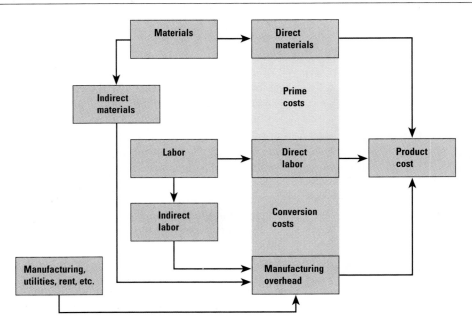

administrative costs
The costs required to manage the organization and provide staff support, including executive salaries, costs of data processing, and legal costs.

Is the professor's salary a direct or indirect cost of a course?
(Answer: Direct cost)

advertising related to a specific product. For example, managers at PepsiCo want the cost of advertising Diet Pepsi assigned to that product.

Sometimes distinguishing between manufacturing costs and nonmanufacturing costs is difficult. For example, are the salaries of accountants who handle factory payrolls manufacturing or nonmanufacturing costs? What about the rent for offices for the manufacturing vice president? There are no clear-cut classifications for some of these costs, so companies usually set their own guidelines and follow them consistently.

Direct versus Indirect Costs

direct cost
Any cost that can be directly related to a cost object.

indirect cost
Any cost that *cannot* be directly related to a cost object.

cost object
Any end to which a cost is assigned. Examples include a product, a department, or a product line.

Is the cost of the library a direct or indirect cost of a course? (Answer: Indirect cost)

Any cost that can be directly related to a cost object is a **direct cost** of that cost object. Those that cannot be directly related to a cost object are **indirect costs.** A **cost object** is any end to which a cost is assigned, for example, a unit of inventory, a department, or a product line. Earlier we distinguished between direct and indirect labor costs.

Accountants use the terms *direct cost* and *indirect cost* much as a nonaccountant might expect. One difficulty is that a cost may be direct to one cost object and indirect to another. For example, the salary of a supervisor in a manufacturing department is a direct cost of the department but an indirect cost of the individual items the department produces. So when someone refers to a cost as either direct or indirect, you should immediately ask, "Direct or indirect with respect to what cost object? Units produced? A department? A division?" (When we use *direct* and *indirect* to describe labor and materials the cost object is the unit being produced.)

cost allocation
The process of assigning indirect costs to cost objects.

Many indirect costs result from several departments sharing facilities (buildings, equipment) or services (data processing, maintenance staff). If you share an apartment with someone, the rent is an indirect cost to each person sharing the apartment. Usually, some method must be devised for assigning a share of indirect costs to each user. This process of assigning indirect costs is called **cost allocation.** We discuss implications of allocating costs throughout this book.

STAGES OF PRODUCTION

Suppose you suddenly find yourself a consultant to Unique Denims, a company that produces denim products, such as jeans and jackets. (It's a real company with a name change to disguise it.) Imagine the three stages in which materials might exist:

L.O. 3: Understand how material, labor, and overhead costs are added to a product at each stage of the production process.

work in process
Product in the production process but not yet complete.

finished goods
Product fully completed, but not yet sold.

inventoriable costs
Costs added to inventory accounts.

1. First, you would see direct materials that have not yet been put into production, most likely rolls of denim.
2. Next, you would find on the production line products being worked on—**work in process.**
3. Finally, somewhere past the end of the production process, perhaps in the shipping area, you would find **finished goods** ready for sale.

Cost accounting systems have three major categories of inventory accounts, one category for each of these three stages: Direct Materials Inventory, Work in Process Inventory, and Finished Goods Inventory.

Each inventory account is likely to have a beginning inventory amount, additions (debits) and withdrawals (credits) during the period, and an ending inventory based on what's still on hand at the end of the period. Those costs added (debited) to inventory accounts are called **inventoriable costs.**

To show how this works, here's a simplified version of the actual production process at Unique Denims. Illustration 2.4 shows the stages of production from receipt of materials through manufacturing to the finished goods warehouse. Unique Denims receives denim at its Direct Materials Receiving Department. The people in this department are responsible for checking each order to be sure that it meets quality specifications and that the goods received are what was ordered.

If Unique Denims uses just in time (JIT), people in Direct Materials Receiving send the materials—denim—to the manufacturing departments immediately. If Unique does not use JIT, people in this department send the denim to a materials warehouse until it is needed for production. Any product that has been purchased but not yet transferred to manufacturing departments will be part of direct materials inventory on the balance sheet at the end of the accounting period.

When the production process begins, the Cut, Make, and Trim (CMT) Department cuts the denim to size and then sends it to sewing stations where it is sewn into jeans and trim is added.

From there, the jeans are sent to the Wash and Inspect (WI) Department where they are washed to meet customer specifications and inspected for fabric or sewing flaws. Note that both the CMT and WI Departments are part of work in process. Any product still in these departments at the end of an accounting period is part of work in process inventory on the balance sheet.

ILLUSTRATION 2.4   Unique Denims—Departmental Responsibilities

Direct materials receiving	Cut, make, and trim (CMT)	Wash and inspect (WI)	Finished goods—shipping
	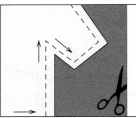	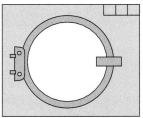	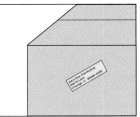

- Receive raw materials.
- Ensure that correct amount is received.
- Inspect materials.
- Release materials to manufacturing as needed.

- Make pattern to conform with customer specifications for fit and size distribution.
- Cut denim into individual parts for sewing.
- Sew garments.
- Apply buttons, zippers, and labels.

- Wash garments to customer specifications.
- Inspect garments for fabric or sewing flaws.

- Pack finished garments to customer specifications for size and style, and ship garments.

After the goods are inspected, the Finished Goods—Shipping Department ships them immediately to customers under a just-in-time system; otherwise they are shipped to a warehouse that holds finished goods until they are shipped to customers. Any product that is finished but not yet sold to customers is included in finished goods inventory at the end of an accounting period.

REPORTING COSTS AND REVENUES

Income Statements

Next we use a numerical example to show how to report Unique Denims' revenues and costs. The result is a typical income statement for a manufacturing company (see Illustration 2.5). The income statement shows that Unique Denims generated sales revenue of $4,500,000, had cost of goods sold of $2,810,000, and incurred marketing and administrative costs of $1,440,000 for the year.

Cost of Goods Sold Statement

We now demonstrate how to derive the cost of goods sold amount on the income statement from the company's activities. The resulting statement is the cost of goods sold statement, which appears in Illustration 2.6. You will be able to see how these items appear in the cost of goods sold statement if you trace each amount in the following example to Illustration 2.6.

Direct Materials

- Assume the company's direct materials inventory on hand January 1 was $200,000.
- Purchases of denim during the year cost $800,000.
- Ending inventory on December 31 was $150,000.
- Therefore, the cost of direct materials put into production during the year was $850,000, computed as follows:

Beginning direct materials inventory, January 1	$ 200,000
Add purchases during the year	800,000
Direct materials available during the year	1,000,000
Less ending direct materials inventory, December 31	150,000
Cost of direct materials put into production	$ 850,000

Work in Process

- The Work in Process Inventory account had a beginning balance on January 1 of $350,000, as shown in Illustration 2.6.
- Illustration 2.6 shows that costs incurred during the year from the preceding schedule of direct materials costs were $850,000 in direct materials, $700,000 in direct labor costs, and $1,850,000 in manufacturing overhead. The sum of

ILLUSTRATION 2.5 Income Statement

UNIQUE DENIMS
Income Statement
For the Year Ending December 31, Year 2

Sales revenue	$4,500,000
Cost of goods sold (see Illustration 2.6)	2,810,000
Gross margin	1,690,000
Less: Marketing and administrative costs	1,440,000
Operating profit before taxes	$ 250,000

ILLUSTRATION	2.6	**Cost of Goods Sold Statement**

UNIQUE DENIMS
Cost of Goods Sold Statement
For the Year Ending December 31, Year 2

Beginning work in process inventory, January 1			$ 350,000
Manufacturing costs during the year:			
Direct materials:			
Beginning inventory, January 1	$ 200,000		
Add purchases.	800,000		
Direct materials available	1,000,000		
Less ending inventory, December 31	150,000		
Direct materials put into production.		$ 850,000	
Direct labor.		700,000	
Manufacturing overhead		1,850,000	
Total manufacturing costs			
incurred during the year			3,400,000
Total cost of work in process during the year.			3,750,000
Less ending work in process inventory,			
December 31.			400,000
Cost of goods manufactured during the year			3,350,000
Beginning finished goods inventory, January 1			920,000
Finished goods inventory available for sale			4,270,000
Less ending finished goods inventory,			
December 31.			1,460,000
Cost of goods sold			$2,810,000

materials, labor, and manufacturing overhead costs incurred, $3,400,000, is the total manufacturing costs incurred during the year. Managers in production and operations give careful attention to these costs. Companies that want to be competitive in setting prices must manage these costs diligently.

• From here on it seems complicated, but it's not really so hard if you realize that accountants are just adding and subtracting inventory values. Adding the $350,000 beginning work in process inventory to the $3,400,000 total manufacturing costs gives $3,750,000, the total cost of work in process during the year. This is a measure of the resources that have gone into production. Some of these costs were in the work in process inventory on hand at the beginning of the period (that's the $350,000 in beginning inventory) and much has been incurred this year (that's the $3,400,000 total manufacturing costs).

• At year-end, the work in process inventory has a $400,000 cost, which is subtracted to arrive at the cost of goods manufactured during the year: $3,350,000 (= $3,750,000 − $400,000). This $3,350,000 represents the cost of denim clothes finished during the year. Production departments usually have a goal for goods completed each period. Managers would compare the cost of goods manufactured to that goal to see whether the production departments were successful in meeting it.

Finished Goods Inventory

The work finished during the period is transferred from the production department to the finished goods storage area or it is shipped to customers. If goods are shipped to customers directly from the production line, no finished goods inventory exists. Unique Denims had a finished goods inventory, however. Here's how the amounts appear on the financial statements:

- Illustration 2.6 shows that Unique Denims had $920,000 of finished goods inventory on hand at the beginning of the year (January 1). From the discussion about work in process, we know that Unique Denims completed $3,350,000, which was transferred to finished goods inventory. Therefore, Unique Denims had $4,270,000 finished goods inventory available for sale, in total.

- Of the $4,270,000 available, Unique Denims had $1,460,000 finished goods still on hand at the end of the year. That means that the cost of goods sold was $2,810,000 (= $4,270,000 available − $1,460,000 in ending inventory).

Cost of Goods Sold Statement

As part of its internal reporting system, Unique Denims prepares a cost of goods sold statement. Cost of goods sold statements are for managerial use; you will rarely see one published in external financial statements. As noted, this statement appears in Illustration 2.6. It incorporates and summarizes information from the preceding discussion.

Manufacturing companies typically prepare a cost of goods sold statement to summarize and report manufacturing costs such as those discussed for Unique Denims, most often for managers' use. Some companies have experimented with preparing these statements for production workers and supervisors, who in some cases have found them effective communication devices once these people learn how to read them. For example, management at Unique Denims might use the cost of goods sold statement to communicate the size of manufacturing overhead and inventories to stimulate creative ideas for reducing the size of these items.

The cost of goods sold statement in Illustration 2.6 has three building blocks. The darkest area reports the cost of direct materials. The medium shaded area reports the Work in Process account with its beginning balance, costs added during the period, ending balance, and cost of goods manufactured. The last item in the lightest area reports the beginning and ending finished goods inventory and cost of goods sold.

These financial statements are presented in a standard format that you will find used by many companies and on the CPA and CMA examinations. Please be aware that we discuss many variations in this book, and many more exist in practice. It is important that financial statements effectively present the information that best suits the needs of your customers or users of the information (for example, managers of your company or your clients). For managerial purposes, it is important that the format of financial statements be tailored to what users want (or to what you want if you are the user of financial information).

SELF-STUDY QUESTIONS

1. The following items appeared in the records of Shoreline Products, Inc., for the last year:

Administrative costs	$ 304,000
Depreciation, manufacturing	103,000
Direct labor	482,000
Finished goods inventory, January 1	160,000
Finished goods inventory, December 31	147,000
Heat, light, and power plant	87,000
Marketing costs	272,000
Miscellaneous manufacturing costs.	12,000
Plant maintenance and repairs	74,000
Direct materials purchases	313,000
Direct materials inventory, January 1	102,000
Direct materials inventory, December 31	81,000
Sales revenue	2,036,000
Supervisory and indirect labor	127,000

Supplies and indirect materials.	14,000
Work in process inventory, January 1	135,000
Work in process inventory, December 31	142,000

Prepare an income statement with a supporting cost of goods sold statement. Refer to Illustrations 2.5 and 2.6.

2. Using the data from Question 1 place dollar amounts in each box in Illustration 2.3.

The solutions to these questions are at the end of this chapter on page 58.

COST BEHAVIOR

L.O. 4: Define basic cost behaviors including variable, semi-variable, and step costs.

The previous section dealt with financial statements, which are like pictures of a child's birthday party. They provide some indication of what happened, but they don't show all of the preparation that went into the party, and they only partly capture the feeling of what happened.

This section discusses cost analysis. Cost analysis is the behind-the-scenes work leading to decisions that result in activities causing the costs that appear in the financial statements. Activities cause costs, so for management to make informed decisions regarding costs, they must first know what activities cause them.

Cost behavior deals with the way costs respond to changes in activity levels. Throughout this book we refer to the idea of a cost driver. As defined in Chapter 1, a cost driver is a factor that causes, or "drives," costs. For example, the cost driver for the cost of lumber for the activity of building a house could be the number of board feet of lumber used. The cost driver for direct labor costs could be the number of labor hours worked.

Managers need to know how costs behave to make informed decisions about products, to plan, and to evaluate performance. Fundamentally, managers need to know cost behavior for four basic categories: fixed, variable, semivariable, and step costs as discussed next.

Fixed versus Variable Costs

Suppose that management contemplates a change in the volume of a company's activity. Some questions different managers might ask follow:

- A production manager at Saturn Corporation: "How much will our costs decrease if the volume of production is cut by 1,000 automobiles per month?"
- A manager of Marriott Corporation's campus food service: "How much will our costs increase if we serve 200 more meals per day?"
- A university president: "How much will costs increase if the number of students enrolled in the university increases by 10 percent?"

variable costs
Costs that change in direct proportion with a change in volume within the relevant range of activity.

fixed costs
Costs that are unchanged as volume changes within the relevant range of activity.

To answer questions such as these, we need to know which costs are **variable costs** that change in direct proportion with the change in volume of activity and which costs are **fixed costs** that are unchanged as the volume of activity changes.

Variable manufacturing costs typically include direct materials, certain manufacturing overhead (for example, indirect materials, materials-handling labor, energy costs), and direct labor in some cases (such as temporary workers). Certain nonmanufacturing costs such as distribution costs and sales commissions are typically variable. Much of manufacturing overhead and many nonmanufacturing costs are typically fixed costs.

Direct labor has traditionally been considered a variable cost. Today the production process at many firms is very capital intensive. In a setting where a fixed amount of labor is needed only to keep machines operating, direct labor is probably best considered to be a fixed cost.

The salary of each additional cook in this kitchen is a step cost.

ILLUSTRATION   2.7   Four Cost Patterns

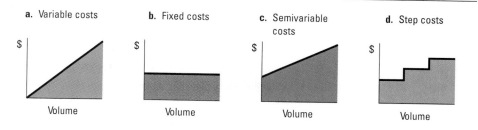

In merchandising, variable costs include the cost of the product and some marketing and administrative costs. All of a merchant's product costs are variable. In manufacturing, a portion of the product cost is fixed. In service organizations, variable costs typically include certain types of direct labor (such as temporary employees), supplies, and copying and printing costs. Illustration 2.7 depicts variable cost behavior—item (a)—and fixed cost behavior—item (b). Note that in the graph volume is on the horizontal axis, and total costs (measured in dollars) are on the vertical axis. Item (a) shows that total variable costs increase in direct proportion to changes in volume. Thus, if volume doubles, total variable costs also double. Item (b) shows that fixed costs are at a particular level and do not increase as volume increases.

The identification of a cost as fixed or variable is valid only within a certain range of activity. For example, the manager of a restaurant in a shopping mall increased the capacity from 150 to 250 seats, requiring an increase in rent costs, utilities, and many other costs. Although these costs are usually thought of as fixed, they change when activity moves beyond a certain range. This range within which the total fixed costs and unit variable costs do not change is called the **relevant range.**

relevant range
The activity levels within which a given total fixed cost or unit variable cost will be unchanged.

The Real World Application on page 40, "Are Fixed Costs Dragging Major League Baseball Teams Down?" presents an example of organizations that have high fixed costs. Sports franchises typically commit to leases for facilities and player contracts for one year or more. If interest in the team is low, the owners stand to lose a lot of money. Nevertheless, major league sports franchises sell for a lot of money.

REAL WORLD APPLICATION | **Are Fixed Costs Dragging Major League Baseball Teams Down?**

Although actual costs and revenues of major league baseball teams are not available to the public, *USA Today* hired a baseball expert to estimate the profitability of each team. The expert reported that half the teams are profitable and the other half are losing money.

After looking at the following data, baseball teams clearly have significant fixed costs, especially in the area of player payrolls. In fact, for the Kansas City Royals, player payroll (including payroll taxes and pension costs) is *higher* than total revenues. It should come as no surprise that the Royals had the biggest loss of all 28 teams. In contrast, the Colorado Rockies is the most profitable team with player payroll amounting to 35 percent of total revenues. (The Rockies have also shown that success does not require high player payrolls.)

	Colorado Rockies	Kansas City Royals
Revenues		
Ticket sales	$36,000,000	$19,800,000
Concessions	9,500,000	5,200,000
TV/Radio fees	11,000,000	12,000,000
Spring training income	11,000,000	700,000
Other revenues	10,800,000	8,300,000
Total revenues	78,300,000	46,000,000
Variable Costs	8,750,000	8,100,000
Fixed Costs		
Player payroll (including payroll taxes and pension costs)	27,400,000	46,500,000
Administrative payroll	7,500,000	6,000,000
Stadium	5,000,000	3,500,000
Other fixed costs	4,400,000	4,450,000
Total fixed costs	44,300,000	60,450,000
Net income	$25,250,000	($22,550,000)

Source: Morten Stone, "Baseball's Bucks: Owners Should Open Books," *USA Today,* October 20, 1994, pp. 8c and 9c.

Three aspects of cost behavior complicate the task of classifying costs into fixed and variable categories. First, not all costs are strictly fixed or variable. For example, electric utility costs may be based on a fixed minimum monthly charge plus a variable cost for each kilowatt-hour in excess of the specified minimum usage. Such a **semivariable cost** has both fixed and variable components. Semivariable costs, also called *mixed costs,* are depicted in Illustration 2.7, item (c).

Second, some costs increase with volume in "steps." **Step costs,** also called *semifixed costs,* increase in steps as shown in item (d) in Illustration 2.7. For example, one supervisor might be needed for up to four firefighters in a fire station, two supervisors for five to eight, and so forth as the number of firefighters increases. The supervisors' salaries represent a step cost.

Third, as previously indicated, the cost relationships are valid only within a relevant range of activity. In particular, costs that are fixed over a small range of activity are likely to increase over a larger range.

semivariable cost
A cost that has both fixed and variable components; also called *mixed cost.*

step cost
A cost that increases with volume in steps. Also called *semifixed cost.*

COMPONENTS OF PRODUCT COSTS

L.O. 5: Identify the components of a product's cost.

By now you realize that various concepts of costs exist. The diagrams in this section have been used in practice to explain cost concepts. Starting with Illustration 2.8, assume that Unique Denims estimates the cost to produce jackets during year 3. The **full cost** to manufacture and sell one jacket is estimated to be $30, as shown on the left side of Illustration 2.8. The unit cost of manufacturing the jacket is $25, also shown on the left side of the illustration. (One unit is one jacket.) This full cost of manufacturing the one unit is known as the **full absorption cost.** It is the amount of inventoriable cost for external financial reporting according to GAAP. The full absorption cost "fully absorbs" the variable and fixed costs of manufacturing a product.

The full absorption cost excludes nonmanufacturing costs, however, so marketing and administrative costs are not inventoriable costs. These nonmanufacturing costs equal $5 per unit, which is the sum of the two blocks at the bottom of Illustration 2.8.

ILLUSTRATION 2.8 Unique Denims—Product Cost Components

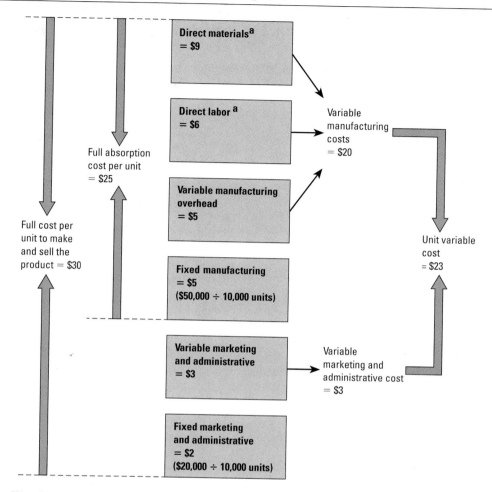

[a]Direct labor and direct materials are assumed to be variable costs for this illustration. Direct labor is classified as a fixed cost in many cases, particularly in highly automated companies.

full cost
The sum of all costs of manufacturing and selling a unit of product (includes both fixed and variable costs).

full absorption cost
All variable and fixed manufacturing costs; used to compute a product's inventory value under GAAP.

The variable costs to make the product are variable manufacturing costs, $20 per unit, and variable nonmanufacturing costs, $3 per unit. Variable nonmanufacturing costs could, in general, be either administrative or marketing costs. For Unique Denims, variable nonmanufacturing costs are selling costs and the costs of distributing products. In other cases, variable administrative costs could include costs of data processing, accounting, or any administrative activity that is affected by volume.

Illustration 2.8 also includes unit fixed costs. The unit fixed costs are valid only at one volume—10,000 units per year for Unique Denims. By definition, total fixed costs do not change as volume changes (within the relevant range, of course). Therefore, a change in volume results in a change in the unit fixed cost, as demonstrated by the self-study question that follows on page 42.

You should use unit fixed costs very carefully. Many managers fail to realize that they are valid at only one volume. The next section shows how unit fixed costs can lead to wrong thinking and incorrect decisions.

Unit Fixed Costs Can Be Misleading for Decision Making

When fixed costs are allocated to each unit, accounting records often make the costs appear as though they are variable. For example, allocating some of factory rent to each unit of product results in including rent as part of the "unit cost" even though the total rent does not change with the manufacture of another unit of product. Cost data that include allocated common costs therefore may be misleading if used incorrectly. The following example demonstrates the problem.

Superstar, Inc., manufactures ski boots that have a unit manufacturing cost of $80 ($50 per unit variable manufacturing cost + $30 per unit fixed manufacturing cost), computed as follows (each pair of boots is one unit):

Variable manufacturing costs per unit	$50
Fixed manufacturing costs	
$\text{Unit cost} = \dfrac{\text{Fixed manufacturing cost per month}}{\text{Units produced per month}}$	
$= \dfrac{\$600,000}{20,000 \text{ units}}$	$30
Total unit cost used as the inventory value	
for external financial reporting	$80

Superstar received a special order for 1,000 pairs of ski boots at $75 each. These units could be produced with currently idle capacity. Marketing, administrative, and the total fixed manufacturing costs of $600,000 would not be affected by accepting the order, nor would accepting this special order affect the regular market for it.

Marketing managers believed the special order should be accepted as long as the unit price of $75 exceed the cost of manufacturing each unit. When the marketing managers learned from accounting reports that the inventory value was $80 per unit, their initial reaction was to reject the order because, as one manager stated, "We are not going to be very profitable if our selling price is less than our production cost!"

Fortunately, some additional investigation revealed the variable manufacturing cost to be only $50 per unit. Marketing management accepted the special order, which had the following impact on the company's operating profit:

Revenue from special order (1,000 units × $75)	$75,000
Variable costs of making special order	
(1,000 units × $50)	50,000
Contribution of special order to operating profit	$25,000

The moral of this example is that it is easy to interpret unit costs incorrectly and make incorrect decisions. In this example, fixed manufacturing overhead costs had been allocated to units, most likely to value inventory for external financial reporting and tax purposes. The resulting $80 unit cost appeared to be the cost to produce a unit. Of course, only $50 was a per unit variable cost; the $600,000 per month fixed cost would not be affected by the decision to accept the special order.

SELF-STUDY QUESTION

3. Refer to the Unique Denims example in Illustration 2.8 that is based on a volume of 10,000 units per year. Assume the same total fixed costs and unit variable costs but a volume of only 8,000 units. What is the fixed manufacturing cost per unit and the fixed marketing and administrative cost per unit?

The solution to this question is at the end of this chapter on page 58.

---

gross margin
Revenue − Cost of goods sold on income statements. Per unit, the gross margin equals Sales price − Full absorption cost.

Illustrations 2.9 and 2.10 are designed to clarify definitions of gross margin, contribution margin, and operating profit. You recall from your financial accounting courses that the **gross margin** appears on external financial statements as the difference between revenue and cost of goods sold. We refer to this format as a *traditional income statement*. Cost of goods sold is simply the full absorption cost per unit times the number of units sold. Illustration 2.9 presents the gross margin per unit for the jacket that Unique Denims produces and sells for $40 each.

ILLUSTRATION 2.9 Unique Denims—Gross Margin per Unit

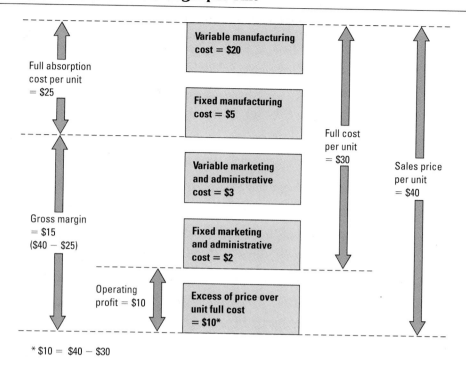

* $10 = $40 − $30

ILLUSTRATION 2.10 Unique Denims—Contribution Margin per Unit

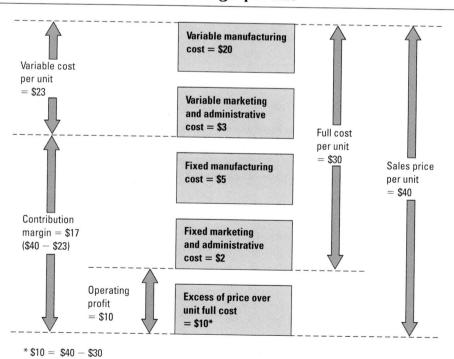

* $10 = $40 − $30

Recall from Illustration 2.8 that each jacket is estimated to have a $25 full absorption cost. Therefore, the gross margin per unit is $15 ($40 − $25). The operating profit per unit is the difference between the sales price and the full cost of making and selling the product. For Unique Denims, Illustration 2.9 shows the operating profit per unit to be $10 ($40 sales price − $30 full cost).

contribution margin
Sales price − Variable costs.

Illustration 2.10 also shows the contribution margin per unit. On a per unit basis, the **contribution margin** is the difference between the sales price and the variable cost per unit. Think of the contribution margin as the amount available to cover fixed costs and earn a profit.

The contribution margin is important information for managers because it allows them to assess the profitability of products before factoring in fixed costs (which tend to be more difficult to change in the short run). For example, assume that you own an ice cream and yogurt shop. You sell one pint of ice cream for $2.00 and one pint of yogurt for $2.50. Which product contributes more per unit to profits? Answer: We don't know until we know the contribution margin per unit for each product. Suppose that the variable cost per pint is $.75 for ice cream and $1.50 for yogurt. Then the contribution margins (per unit) are as follows:

* Ice cream $1.25 (= $2.00 sales price − $.75 variable cost)
* Yogurt $1.00 (= $2.50 sales price − $1.50 variable cost)

Although the yogurt sells for more, the ice cream provides a higher contribution per unit toward covering fixed costs and earning a profit. We refer to this format as a *contribution margin income statement.*

SELF-STUDY QUESTION

4. Refer to the Unique Denims' examples in Illustrations 2.9 and 2.10.
   a. Assume that the variable marketing and administrative cost is $6 per unit; all other cost numbers remain the same. What are the new gross margin, contribution margin, and operating profit amounts?
   b. Assume that the fixed manufacturing cost dropped from $50,000 to $40,000 in total, or from $5 to $4 per unit. All other cost numbers remain the same as in Illustrations 2.9 and 2.10. What are the new gross margin, contribution margin, and operating profit amounts?

The solution to this question is at the end of this chapter on pages 58 and 59.

HOW TO MAKE COST INFORMATION MORE USEFUL FOR MANAGERS

L.O. 6: Provide managers with traditional, contribution margin, and value-based financial statements.

product costs
Costs that can be attributed to a product.

period costs
Costs that can be attributed to time intervals.

Cost accountants divide costs into product or period categories. In general, **product costs** are costs more easily attributed to products; **period costs** are more easily attributed to time intervals. Once product costs are defined, all other costs are assumed to be period costs. It is important to note, however, that the determination of product costs varies, depending on the approach used. Three common approaches are outlined here.

* **Full absorption costing (traditional income statement).** Under this approach required by GAAP, all fixed and variable manufacturing costs are product costs. All other costs are period costs.
* **Variable costing (contribution margin income statement).** Using this approach, only variable manufacturing costs are product costs. All other costs are period costs.
* **Managerial costing.** This approach assumes that management determines which costs are associated with the product and should be considered product costs. Management asks whether adding a product will incur new costs. Any new costs are considered *product costs.* For example, management may decide that promotional campaigns associated with a new product are product costs. Under the other two approaches, promotional costs would be period costs. Clearly, the managerial costing approach to defining product costs is subjective and depends on management's use of cost information.

ILLUSTRATION 2.11	Traditional versus Contribution Margin Income Statements

UNIQUE DENIMS: NEW JACKETS
Traditional Income Statement
versus
Contribution Margin Income Statement

Traditional Income Statement		Contribution Margin Income Statement	
Revenue	$400,000	Revenue	$400,000
Variable manufacturing costs	200,000	Variable manufacturing costs	200,000
Fixed manufacturing costs	50,000	Variable marketing and administrative costs	30,000
Gross margin	150,000	Contribution margin	170,000
Variable marketing and administrative costs	30,000	Fixed manufacturing costs	50,000
Fixed marketing and administrative costs	20,000	Fixed marketing and administrative costs	20,000
Operating profit	$100,000	Operating profit	$100,000

Traditional versus Contribution Margin Income Statements

A traditional income statement using full absorption costing (the first approach in the list) and a contribution margin income statement using variable costing (the second approach) for the new line of jackets are shown in Illustration 2.11. The data come from Illustrations 2.9 and 2.10, but unit costs are multiplied by 10,000 jackets to give total amounts for year 3. Net income is the same for each approach because total units produced equal total units sold, but note the difference in product costs on each statement. We do not provide an income statement example for the third point because the treatment of product costs using this approach varies from one company to the next.

The product costs assigned to inventory are carried in the accounts as assets. When the goods are sold, the costs flow from inventory to the income statement. At that time, these previously inventoried costs become expenses.

Developing Financial Statements Around Value Concepts

Given the importance of identifying value-added activities, companies should consider developing financial statements that classify costs into value-added or nonvalue-added categories. To manage costs, an organization must manage its activities. Remember that activities cause costs! By classifying activities as value added or nonvalue added, managers are better able to reduce or eliminate nonvalue-added activities and therefore reduce costs.

Suppose that the president of Unique Denims wants to know which costs add value. The controller reviews production activities and related costs in detail and prepares the value income statement shown in Illustration 2.12 (the data come from Illustration 2.11). However, costs are shown in greater detail and separated into nonvalue-added and value-added categories. For example, variable marketing and administrative costs of $30,000 from Illustration 2.11 are shown as two line items under variable marketing and administrative costs in Illustration 2.12: marketing and administrative services used to sell products totaling $25,000 and marketing and administrative services used to process returned products totaling $5,000. The value income statement outlines costs linked to three segments of the value chain: production, marketing, and distribution. Remember, the primary idea of the value chain is that value is added to the product in each business function. The goal is to maximize value-added activities (those activities that add value to the product) and minimize nonvalue-added activities (those that do not add value to it).

The controller identifies nonvalue-added activities associated with two areas, materials waste and reworked products. Materials waste refers to material that was thrown away because of incorrect cuts or defective material. Reworked products consist of products that had been assembled incorrectly (for example, missing a zipper or stitches on a pocket) and had to be fixed (or reworked). Costs to rework products are generally incurred by the production, marketing, and administration

ILLUSTRATION 2.12	Value Income Statement

UNIQUE DENIMS: NEW JACKETS
Value Income Statement
For the Year Ending December 31, Year 3

	Nonvalue-Added Activities	Value-Added Activities	Total
Sales revenue.		$400,000	$400,000
Variable manufacturing costs			
Materials used in production.		80,000	80,000
Materials waste	$ 10,000		10,000
Labor used in production		40,000	40,000
Labor used to rework products	20,000		20,000
Manufacturing overhead used in production		45,000	45,000
Manufacturing overhead used to rework products	5,000		5,000
Variable marketing and administrative costs			
Marketing and administrative services			
used to sell products.		25,000	25,000
Marketing and administrative services			
used to process returned products	5,000		5,000
Contribution margin	(40,000)	210,000	170,000
Fixed manufacturing			
Fixed manufacturing costs used in production.		40,000	40,000
Salaries of employees reworking products	10,000		10,000
Fixed marketing and administrative costs			
Marketing and administrative services			
used to sell products.		15,000	15,000
Marketing and administrative services			
used to process returned products	5,000		5,000
Operating profit	$(55,000)	$155,000	$100,000

departments. Marketing gets involved because detection sometimes does not occur until the customer returns the goods. Thus, nonvalue-added activities are not limited to production.

Assume that the company sold 10,000 units in year 3, and the controller uses the per unit costs outlined in Illustration 2.10. The controller's value income statement shows total nonvalue-added activities to be $55,000. This amount is only 18 percent of total costs but is 55 percent of operating profit. Clearly, reducing nonvalue-added activities could significantly increase profits.

Reducing nonvalue-added activities is not a simple task. For example, how should the production process be changed to reduce materials waste? Should higher quality materials be purchased, resulting in higher direct materials costs? Or should production personnel be trained and evaluated based on materials wasted? As you can see, the answer is not always clear. The value income statement is an important starting point for management, but it does not guarantee the reduction of nonvalue-added activities.

SUMMARY

The term *cost* is ambiguous when used alone; it has meaning only in a specific context. The adjectives used to modify *cost* constitute that context. Illustration 2.13 summarizes definitions of the word. It is important to consider how the use of these terms in cost accounting differs from common usage. For example, in common usage, a variable cost may vary with anything (geography, temperature, and so forth). In cost accounting, variable cost depends solely on volume.

The following summarizes key ideas tied to the chapter's learning objectives.

ILLUSTRATION 2.13 | Summary of Definitions

Concept	Definition
Nature of Cost	
Cost	A *sacrifice* of resources.
Opportunity cost	The benefit that could be realized from the best forgone alternative use of a resource.
Outlay cost	Past, present, or near-future cash outflow.
Expense	The cost charged against revenue in a particular accounting period. We use the term *expense* only when speaking of external financial reports.
Cost Concepts for Cost Accounting Systems	
Product costs	Costs that can be more easily attributed to products; costs that are part of inventory.
Period costs	Costs that can be more easily attributed to time intervals.
Full absorption costs	Costs used to compute a product's inventory value for external reporting according to GAAP.
Direct costs	Costs that can be directly related to a cost object.
Indirect costs	Costs that cannot be directly related to a cost object.
Additional Cost Concepts Used in Decision Making	
Variable costs	Costs that vary, in total, with the volume of activity.
Fixed costs	Costs that do not vary, in total, with the volume of activity.

LO1: Concept of cost. A cost is a sacrifice of resources and an expense is a cost charged against revenue in an accounting period, typically used for external reporting purposes.

LO2: Presentation of costs in financial statements. Cost of goods sold in a merchandising organization simply includes the costs associated with purchasing and transporting the goods. Cost of goods sold for manufacturing organizations is much more complicated and includes raw materials (direct materials), direct labor, and manufacturing overhead. Cost of goods (i.e., services) sold in a service organization primarily includes labor and overhead.

LO3: How products incur costs. Manufacturing organizations have three stages of production: raw materials, work in process, and finished goods. All items not sold at the end of the period are included in inventory as an asset on the balance sheet. All finished goods sold at the end of the period are included as cost of goods sold in the income statement.

LO4: Cost behavior. Cost behavior can be classified in one of four ways: fixed, variable, semivariable, or step costs. Definitions of these four terms appear on pages 38 to 40.

LO5: Components of a product's costs.
* Variable cost per unit.
* Full absorption cost per unit, which is the inventoriable amount under GAAP.
* Full cost per unit of making and selling the product.
* Gross margin, which equals sales price minus full-absorption cost.
* Contribution margin, which equals sales price minus variable cost.
* Profit margin, which equals sales price minus full cost.

LO6: Comparison of traditional, contribution margin, and value-based income statements. The traditional income statement format is used primarily for external reporting purposes and the contribution margin income statement format is used more for internal decision-making and performance evaluation purposes. A third alternative is the value approach, which categorizes costs into value- and nonvalue-added activities.

KEY TERMS

administrative costs, 33	indirect cost, 33
contribution margin, 44	inventoriable costs, 34
conversion costs, 32	manufacturing overhead, 31
cost, 28	marketing costs, 32
cost allocation, 33	operating profit, 29
cost object, 33	opportunity cost, 28
cost of goods sold, 31	outlay cost, 28
direct cost, 33	period costs, 44
direct labor, 31	prime costs, 32
direct materials, 31	product costs, 44
expense, 28	relevant range, 39
finished goods, 34	semivariable cost, 40
fixed costs, 38	step cost, 40
full absorption cost, 41	variable costs, 38
full cost, 41	work in process, 34
gross margin, 42	

REVIEW QUESTIONS

2.1   What is the difference between the meanings of the terms *cost* and *expense*?

2.2   What is the difference between product costs and period costs?

2.3   Is cost of goods sold an expense?

2.4   What are the similarities between the Direct Materials Inventory account of the manufacturer and the Merchandise Inventory account of the merchandiser? Are there any differences between the two accounts? If so, what are they?

2.5   What are the three categories of product cost in a manufacturing operation? Describe each element briefly.

2.6   What do the terms *step* and *semivariable costs* mean?

2.7   What do the terms *variable* and *fixed costs* mean?

CRITICAL ANALYSIS AND DISCUSSION QUESTIONS

2.8   "Prime costs are always direct costs, and overhead costs are always indirect." What is your opinion of this statement?

2.9   Unit costs represent the average cost of all units produced. If you want to know the cost to produce an extra amount of product, why not just multiply the unit average cost by the extra quantity you want?

2.10   How does the accounting for marketing and administrative costs in a manufacturing organization compare with the way those costs are treated in a merchandising organization?

2.11   In this chapter's Real World Application, "Gump Accounting," why was it important how Paramount assigns costs?

2.12   For a local fast-food restaurant, what is one example of each of the following types of costs: direct materials, direct labor, and overhead?

2.13   Pick a college department or school (for example, English Department or School of Business). What is one example of a direct labor cost and one example of an overhead cost?

EXERCISES

2.14 Basic Concepts (L.O. 1)

For each of the following costs incurred in a manufacturing operation, indicate whether the costs are fixed or variable (F or V) and whether they are period costs or product costs (P or R) under full absorption costing.

a. Transportation-in costs on materials purchased.

b. Assembly line workers' wages.

c. Property taxes on office buildings for administrative staff.

d. Salaries of top executives in the company.

e. Overtime pay for assembly workers.

f. Sales commissions.

g. Office rent for sales personnel.

h. Salaries for sales supervisors.

i. Controller's office rental.

j. Administrative office heat and air conditioning.

2.15 Basic Concepts (L.O. 1)

For each of the following costs incurred in a manufacturing operation, indicate whether they are included in prime costs (P), conversion costs (C), or both (B).

a. Factory heating and air conditioning.

b. Production supervisor's salary.

c. Transportation-in costs on materials purchased.

d. Assembly line worker's salary.

e. Raw materials used in production process.

f. Indirect materials.

2.16 Basic Concepts (L.O. 1)

Place the number of the appropriate definition in the blank next to each concept.

Concept	Definition
_____ Period costs	1. Costs that vary with the volume of activity.
_____ Indirect costs	2. A sacrifice of resources.
_____ Fixed costs	3. The cost charged against revenue in a particular accounting period.
_____ Opportunity costs	4. Costs that are part of inventory.
_____ Outlay costs	5. Costs that can more easily be attributed to time intervals.
_____ Direct costs	6. Past, present, or near-future cash flow.
_____ Expense	7. The lost benefit from the best forgone alternative.
_____ Cost	8. Costs used to compute inventory value according to GAAP.
_____ Variable costs	9. Costs that *cannot* be directly related to a cost object.
_____ Full absorption cost	10. Costs that can be directly related to a cost object.
_____ Product costs	11. Costs that do not vary with the volume of activity.

2.17 Basic Concepts (L.O. 1)

For each of the following costs incurred in a manufacturing operation, indicate whether the costs are fixed or variable (F or V) and whether they are period costs or product costs (P or R) under full absorption costing.

a. Factory security personnel.

b. Utilities in controller's office.

c. Factory heat and air conditioning.

d. Power to operate factory equipment.

e. Depreciation on furniture for company executives.

2.18 Prepare Statements for a Merchandising Company (L.O. 2)

PC, Inc., sells computers. On January 1 this year, it had a beginning merchandise inventory of $500,000, including transportation-in costs. It purchased $2,600,000 of merchandise, had $260,000 of transportation-in costs, and had marketing and administrative costs of $1,600,000 during the year. The ending inventory of merchandise on December 31 this year was $300,000, including transportation-in costs. Revenue was $5,000,000 for the year.

Required   Prepare an income statement with a supporting cost of goods sold statement.

2.19 Prepare Statements for a Manufacturing Company (L.O. 2)

The following balances appeared in the accounts of Sebastian Company (a manufacturing company) during the current year.

	January 1	December 31
Direct materials inventory	$12,250	$13,600
Work in process inventory	16,150	14,500
Finished goods inventory	2,250	3,250
Direct materials used	–0–	23,850
Cost of goods sold	–0–	28,000

Required   Reconstruct a cost of goods sold statement and fill in the following missing data:

a. Cost of direct materials purchased during the year.

b. Cost of goods manufactured during the year.

c. Total manufacturing costs incurred during the year.

2.20 Prepare Statements for a Manufacturing Company (L.O. 2)

The following balances appeared in the accounts of Nishimoto Machine Tool Company during the current year.

	January 1	December 31
Direct materials inventory	$32,800	$ 36,600
Work in process inventory	36,200	35,400
Finished goods inventory	14,600	15,000
Direct materials used	–0–	173,200
Cost of goods sold	–0–	600,000

Required   Reconstruct a cost of goods sold statement and fill in the following missing data:

a. Cost of direct materials purchased during the year.

b. Cost of goods manufactured during the year.

c. Total manufacturing costs incurred during the year.

2.21 Prepare Statements for a Manufacturing Company (L.O. 2)

The following information appears in Alexis Company's records for last year:

Administrative costs	$ 88,600
Manufacturing building depreciation	54,000
Indirect materials and supplies	12,600
Sales commissions	30,400
Direct materials inventory, January 1	36,800
Direct labor	71,200
Direct materials inventory, December 31	38,000
Finished goods inventory, January 1	21,800
Finished goods inventory, December 31	18,000
Direct materials purchases	44,600
Work in process inventory, December 31	26,200
Supervisory and indirect labor	28,800
Property taxes, manufacturing plant	16,800
Plant utilities and power	47,000
Work in process inventory, January 1	30,800
Sales revenue	420,800

Required   Prepare an income statement with a supporting cost of goods sold statement.

2.22 Prepare Statements for a Manufacturing Company (L.O. 2)

The following information appears in Tots' Toy Factory records for last year:

Administrative costs	$21,550
Manufacturing building depreciation	12,500
Indirect materials and supplies	2,150
Sales commissions	7,100
Direct materials inventory, January 1	8,200
Direct labor	16,300
Direct materials inventory, December 31	9,000
Finished goods inventory, January 1	4,450
Finished goods inventory, December 31	4,050
Direct materials purchases	10,150
Work in process inventory, December 31	5,550
Supervisory and indirect labor	6,200
Property taxes, manufacturing plant	3,700
Plant utilities and power	10,750
Work in process inventory, January 1	6,600
Sales revenue	97,200

Required

Prepare an income statement with a supporting cost of goods sold statement.

2.23 **Prepare Statements for a Manufacturing Company (L.O. 2)**

The following information appears in Carey's Cakes records for last year:

Sales revenue	$131,150
Work in process, January 1	7,700
Work in process, December 31	6,210
Direct materials inventory, January 1	8,600
Direct materials inventory, December 31	8,050
Finished goods inventory, January 1	3,550
Finished goods inventory, December 31	4,950
Direct materials transportation-in	1,150
Direct materials purchased	11,560
Direct labor	19,350
Supervisory and indirect labor—plant	10,950
Administrative salaries	18,000
Supplies and indirect materials—plant	1,450
Heat, light, and power (77.6% for plant)	12,500
Depreciation (80% for plant)	15,000
Property taxes (75% for plant)	4,200
Cost of goods manufactured during the year	71,350
Other administrative costs	4,350
Marketing costs	16,350

Required

Prepare an income statement with a supporting cost of goods sold statement.

2.24 **Cost Behavior for Decision Making (L.O. 4)**

Excalabur Company manufactured 1,000 units of product last year and identified the following costs associated with the manufacturing activity (variable costs are indicated with V, fixed costs with F):

Direct materials used (V)	$35,200
Direct labor (V)	66,500
Supervisory salaries (F)	31,100
Indirect materials and supplies (V)	8,000
Plant utilities (other than power to run plant equipment) (F)	9,600
Power to run plant equipment (V)	7,100
Depreciation on plant and equipment (straight-line, time basis) (F)	4,800
Property taxes on building (F)	6,500

Required   Unit variable costs and total fixed costs are expected to remain unchanged next year. Calculate the unit cost and the total cost if 1,400 units are produced next year.

2.25   Cost Behavior
(L.O. 4)   Refer to the information in Exercise 2.24.

Required   Construct graphs of fixed and variable costs. (See Illustration 2.7.)

2.26   Components of
Full Costs
(L.O. 5)   Illustration 2.8 shows basic relationships among costs. Given the following facts, complete the requirements that follow:

Sales price.	$400 per unit
Fixed costs	
Marketing and administrative	48,000 per period
Manufacturing overhead	72,000 per period
Variable costs	
Marketing and administrative	16 per unit
Manufacturing overhead	18 per unit
Direct labor.	70 per unit
Direct materials	120 per unit
Units produced and sold	1,200 per period

Required   Determine each of the following unit costs (see Illustration 2.8):

a. Variable manufacturing cost.

b. Variable cost.

c. Full absorption cost.

d. Full cost.

2.27   Components of
Full Costs
(L.O. 5)   For external financial reporting, all costs of manufacturing the product are product costs (that is, they are inventoriable).

Required   Using the data from Exercise 2.26, what are the following?

a. Product costs per unit.

b. Period costs for the period.

2.28   Components of
Full Costs
(L.O. 5, 6)   The following cost, price, and volume data apply to Young Company for a particular month:

Sales price.	$650 per unit
Fixed costs	
Marketing and administrative	65,000 per period
Manufacturing overhead	75,000 per period
Variable costs	
Marketing and administrative	40 per unit
Manufacturing overhead	100 per unit
Direct labor.	150 per unit
Direct materials	175 per unit
Units produced and sold	1,000 per period

Required   **a.** Determine each of the following unit costs (see Illustration 2.8):
   (1) Variable manufacturing cost.
   (2) Variable cost.
   (3) Full absorption cost.
   (4) Full cost.

b. Determine each of the following unit margins (see Illustrations 2.9 and 2.10):
   (1) Profit margin.
   (2) Gross margin.
   (3) Contribution margin.

2.29 Components of Full Costs (L.O. 5)

Joe's Tax Service provides tax services to various individuals and organizations. For a particular month, it had the following costs and revenues:

Hours worked and billed to customers	20,000
Price charged per hour	$35
Variable costs per hour	$20
Fixed costs for the month	$55,000

Required

a. What is the full cost per unit of providing the service?

b. Determine the following unit margins:
   (1) Profit margin.
   (2) Contribution margin.

2.30 Value Income Statement (L.O. 6)

A Top Videos store manager wants you to prepare a value income statement based on the following data for the month of August:

Sales revenue.	$200,000
Cost of merchandise	
Goods sold	110,000
Defective goods destroyed	10,000
Employee salaries and wages	40,000[a]
Rent, utilities, and other store costs	20,000
Supervisory salaries.	10,000[a]

[a]20 percent of these costs were related to goods destroyed.

Required

a. Using the traditional income statement format, prepare a value income statement.

b. What might the store manager do to reduce nonvalue-added activities?

2.31 Value Income Statement (L.O. 6)

A restaurant manager of Atul's Restaurant wants you to prepare a value income statement based on the following data for the month of November:

Sales revenue.	$130,000
Cost of food and beverages	
Food and beverages	34,000
Food returned by patrons.	3,000
Food rejected in kitchen.	2,000
Employee salaries and wages	60,000[a]
Supervisory salaries.	12,000[a]
Rent, utilities, and other store costs	16,000

[a]15 percent of these costs were related to food returned by patrons and food rejected by the chef.

Required

a. Using the traditional income statement format, prepare a value income statement.

b. What might the restaurant manager do to reduce nonvalue-added activities?

2.32 Value Income Statement (L.O. 6)

A manager of Tastee Ice Cream Shop wants you to prepare a value income statement based on the following data for July:

Sales revenue.	$60,000
Cost of ice cream	22,000[a]
Employee salaries and wages	8,000[b]
Supervisory salaries.	12,000[b]
Rent, utilities, and other store costs	9,000

[a]20 percent of this cost was related to spoiled ice cream as the result of a power outage during the month.

[b]25 percent of these costs were related to cleaning up spoiled ice cream.

Required

a. Using the traditional income statement format, prepare a value income statement.

b. What might the ice cream shop manager do to reduce nonvalue-added activities?

PROBLEMS

2.33 Cost Concepts:
Multiple Choice

Items (a) through (e) are based on the following data pertaining to Pacific Company's manufacturing operations:

Inventories	April 1	April 30
Direct materials	$ 9,000	$ 7,500
Work in process	4,500	3,000
Finished goods	13,500	18,000

Additional information for the month of April:

Direct materials purchased	$21,000
Direct labor costs	15,000
Manufacturing overhead	20,000

a. For the month of April, prime costs were
   (1) $37,500.
   (2) $34,500.
   (3) $22,500.
   (4) $19,500.

b. For the month of April, conversion costs were
   (1) $15,000.
   (2) $20,000.
   (3) $35,000.
   (4) $36,000.

c. For the month of April, total manufacturing costs were
   (1) $59,000.
   (2) $57,500.
   (3) $56,000.
   (4) $54,500.

d. For the month of April, cost of goods manufactured was
   (1) $59,000.
   (2) $57,500.
   (3) $56,000.
   (4) $54,500.

e. For the month of April, cost of goods sold was
   (1) $59,000.
   (2) $57,500.
   (3) $56,000.
   (4) $54,500.

(CPA adapted)

2.34 Cost Concepts:
Multiple Choice

Items (a) through (j) are based on the following data for a product manufactured by Eastern Company:

Sales price	$160 per unit
Fixed costs	
Marketing and administrative	$20,000 per period
Manufacturing overhead	$15,000 per period
Variable costs	
Marketing and administrative	$5 per unit
Manufacturing overhead	$30 per unit
Direct labor (manufacturing)	$10 per unit
Direct materials (manufacturing)	$40 per unit
Number of units produced and sold during the period	1,000 units

Required

Answer each question with the correct amount per unit.

a. How much is the variable **manufacturing cost** per unit?

    (1) $35.
    (2) $85.
    (3) $80.
    (4) $120.
    (5) Some other amount.

b. How much is the **full cost** per unit?
    (1) $160.
    (2) $85.
    (3) $80.
    (4) $120.
    (5) Some other amount.

c. How much is the **variable cost** per unit?
    (1) $35.
    (2) $85.
    (3) $80.
    (4) $50.
    (5) Some other amount.

d. How much is the **full absorption cost** per unit?
    (1) $95.
    (2) $85.
    (3) $100.
    (4) $120.
    (5) Some other amount.

e. How much is the **prime cost** per unit?
    (1) $40.
    (2) $50.
    (3) $80.
    (4) $95.
    (5) Some other amount.

f. How much is the **conversion cost** per unit?
    (1) $30.
    (2) $35.
    (3) $40.
    (4) $55.
    (5) Some other amount.

g. How much is the **profit margin** per unit?
    (1) $10.
    (2) $40.
    (3) $75.
    (4) $65.
    (5) Some other amount.

h. How much is the **contribution margin** per unit?
    (1) $40.
    (2) $75.
    (3) $65.
    (4) $120.
    (5) Some other amount.

i. How much is the **gross margin** per unit?
    (1) $35.
    (2) $40.
    (3) $75.
    (4) $65.
    (5) Some other amount.

j. If the number of units increases from 1,000 to 1,100, which is within the relevant range, will the **fixed manufacturing cost** per unit
    (1) Decrease?
    (2) Increase?
    (3) Stay the same?

2.35   Find the Unknown
Account Balances

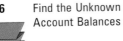

Each column below is independent and for a different company. Use the data given, which refer to one year for each company, to find the unknown account balances.

Account	Company 1	Company 2	Company 3
Direct materials inventory, January 1	$ 24,600	$ 8,000	$ 45,000
Direct materials inventory, December 31	20,000	12,400	(d)
Work in process inventory, January 1	11,600	12,560	(e)
Work in process inventory, December 31	12,000	12,560	85,200
Finished goods inventory, January 1	254,200	2,800	334,480
Finished goods inventory, December 31	(a)	4,600	367,400
Purchases of direct materials	262,000	(c)	248,400
Cost of goods manufactured during this year	679,200	58,000	1,518,220
Total manufacturing costs	679,600	1,658,000	1,526,800
Cost of goods sold	760,000	56,200	(f)
Gross margin.	328,000	13,400	1,874,600
Direct labor.	173,000	23,200	(g)
Direct materials used	(b)	15,000	234,200
Manufacturing overhead	240,000	19,800	430,600
Sales revenue	1,088,000	69,600	3,359,900

2.36   Find the Unknown
Account Balances

Each column below is independent and for a different company. Use the data given, which refer to one year for each example, to find the unknown account balances.

Account	Company 1	Company 2	Company 3
Direct materials inventory, January 1	(a)	$ 3,500	$ 16,000
Direct materials inventory, December 31	$ 3,600	2,900	14,100
Work in process inventory, January 1	2,700	6,720	82,400
Work in process inventory, December 31	3,800	3,100	76,730
Finished goods inventory, January 1	1,900	(d)	17,200
Finished goods inventory, December 31	300	4,400	28,400
Purchases of direct materials	16,100	12,000	64,200
Cost of goods manufactured during this year	(b)	27,220	313,770
Total manufacturing costs	55,550	23,600	308,100
Cost of goods sold	56,050	27,200	302,570
Gross margin.	(c)	16,400	641,280
Direct labor.	26,450	3,800	124,700
Direct materials used	15,300	(e)	66,100
Manufacturing overhead	13,800	7,200	(g)
Sales revenue	103,300	(f)	943,850

2.37 Reconstruct Financial Statements

The following data appeared in Garcia Mesa Company's records on December 31 of last year:

Direct materials inventory, December 31	$ 42,500
Direct materials purchased during the year	180,000
Finished goods inventory, December 31	45,000
Indirect labor	16,000
Direct labor	200,000
Plant heat, light, and power	18,600
Building depreciation (7/9 is for manufacturing)	40,500
Administrative salaries	25,700
Miscellaneous factory cost	15,950
Marketing costs	18,500
Maintenance on factory machines	6,050
Insurance on factory equipment	9,500
Distribution costs	800
Taxes on manufacturing property	6,550
Legal fees on customer complaint	4,100
Direct materials used	191,050
Work in process inventory, December 31	12,300

On January 1, at the beginning of last year, the Finished Goods Inventory account had a balance of $40,000, and the Work in Process Inventory account had a balance of $12,950. Sales revenue during the year was $812,500.

Required

Prepare a cost of goods sold statement and an income statement.

2.38 Analyze the Impact of a Decision on Income Statements

You have been appointed manager of an operating division of Micro, Inc., a manufacturer of products using the latest developments in microprocessor technology. Your division manufactures the chip assembly, CH-1. On January 1 of this year, you invested $1 million in automated processing equipment for chip assembly. At that time, your expected income statement for this year was as follows:

Sales revenues	$1,600,000
Operating costs	
Variable (cash expenditures)	200,000
Fixed (cash expenditures)	750,000
Equipment depreciation	150,000
Other depreciation	125,000
Total operating costs	1,225,000
Operating profits (before taxes)	$ 375,000

On November 15 of this year, a sales representative for the Hanimoto Machine Company approaches you. Hanimoto wants to rent to your division a new assembly machine that would be installed on December 31 for an annual rental charge of $230,000. The new equipment would enable you to increase your division's annual revenue by 10 percent. The more efficient machine would decrease fixed cash expenditures by 5 percent. You will have to write off the cost of the automated processing equipment this year because it has no salvage value. Equipment depreciation shown in the income statement is for the automated processing equipment.

Your bonus is determined as a percentage of your division's operating profits before taxes. Equipment losses are included in the bonus and operating profit computation.

Ignore taxes and any effects on operations on the day of installation of the new machine. Assume that the data given in your expected income statement are the actual amounts for this year and next year if the current equipment is kept.

Required

a. What is the difference in this year's divisional operating profit if the new machine is rented and installed on December 31 of this year?

b. What would be the effect on next year's divisional operating profit if the new machine is rented and installed on December 31 of this year?

c. Would you rent the new equipment? Why or why not?

SOLUTIONS TO SELF-STUDY QUESTIONS

1.

SHORELINE PRODUCTS, INC.
Income Statement
For the Year Ended December 31

Sales revenue	$2,036,000
Cost of goods sold (see following statement)	1,239,000
Gross margin.	797,000
Less	
Marketing costs	272,000
Administrative costs	304,000
Operating profit	$ 221,000

Cost of Goods Sold Statement
For the Year Ended December 31

Beginning work in process inventory, January 1		$ 135,000
Manufacturing costs during the year		
Direct materials		
Beginning inventory, January 1.	$102,000	
Add purchases	313,000	
Direct materials available.	415,000	
Less ending inventory, December 31.	81,000	
Direct materials put into production.	$334,000	
Direct labor	482,000	
Manufacturing overhead		
Supervisory and indirect labor	127,000	
Supplies and indirect materials.	14,000	
Heat, light, and power—plant	87,000	
Plant maintenance and repairs.	74,000	
Depreciation—manufacturing.	103,000	
Miscellaneous manufacturing costs. . . .	12,000	
Total manufacturing overhead		417,000
Total manufacturing costs incurred during the year		1,233,000

Total cost of work in process during the year	1,368,000
Less ending work in process inventory, December 31	142,000
Cost of goods manufactured during the year	1,226,000
Beginning finished goods inventory, January 1	160,000
Finished goods inventory available for sale	1,386,000
Less ending finished goods inventory, December 31	147,000
Cost of goods manufactured and sold.	$1,239,000

2.

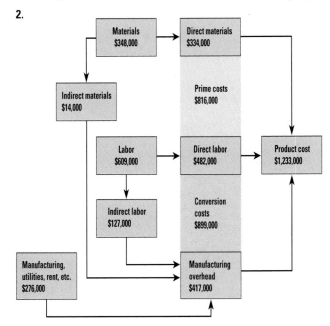

3. Fixed manufacturing = $6.25 (= $50,000/8,000)
Fixed marketing and administration = $2.50
(= $20,000/8,000)

4. **a.** Gross margin = Sales price − Full absorption cost
                = Sales price − (Variable manufacturing + Fixed manufacturing)
                = $40 − ($20 + $5)
                = $15

Contribution margin = Sales price − Variable costs
= Sales price − (Variable manufacturing + Variable marketing and administrative)
= $40 − ($20 + $6)
= $14

Operating profit = Sales price − Full cost to make and sell product
= Sales price − (Variable manufacturing + Fixed manufacturing + Variable marketing and administrative + Fixed marketing and administrative)
= $40 − ($20 + $5 + $6 + $2)
= $7

Note: The gross margin does not change from Illustration 2.9 because marketing and administrative costs are subtracted after gross margin.

b. Gross margin = $40 − ($20 + $4)
= $16

Contribution margin = $40 − ($20 + $3)
= $17

Operating profit = $40 − ($20 + $4 + $3 + $2)
= $11

Note: The contribution margin does not change from Illustration 2.10; however, the gross margin changes from Illustration 2.9.

Cost System Design:
An Overview

LEARNING OBJECTIVES

After reading this chapter, you should be able to:

1. Explain how different accounting systems are designed for different production systems.

2. Use the basic cost flow model.

3. Understand the just-in-time method of production.

4. Compare and contrast traditional sequential costing and backflush costing.

5. Explain the concept of customer costing and profitability analysis.

6. Know the fundamental themes underlying the design of cost systems.

This chapter provides an overview of alternative cost systems that are discussed in more detail in later chapters. It explains why different types of companies use different types of cost systems. Fundamental to the design of cost systems are the ideas that the cost system should be oriented to the needs of the decision makers (that is, users of the information) and that cost systems be designed so that the system's benefits exceed its costs.

DIFFERENT COMPANIES HAVE DIFFERENT PRODUCTION AND COSTING SYSTEMS

job costing
An accounting system that traces costs to individual units or to specific jobs, contracts, or batches of goods.

process costing
An accounting system used when identical units are produced through a series of uniform production steps.

continuous flow processing
Systems that generally mass produce a single, homogeneous output in a continuing process.

A **job costing** system (discussed in Chapter 4) records costs and revenues for each individual job. By contrast, **process costing** (discussed in Chapter 5) does not separate and record costs for each unit. The next time you have a soft drink, consider whether the manufacturer kept track of the cost of the liquid you are drinking. Not likely! Soft drink manufacturers and other companies that produce in continuous flow processes use process costing. Process costing is an accounting system used when identical units are produced through uniform production steps.

During your career, you may audit, consult for, or be employed by some companies that produce jobs, others that produce using continuous process production methods, and still others that use a combination of jobs and processes. It will be important that you first understand the company's production methods before you can understand how to account for costs.

Illustration 3.1 shows a continuum of production methods ranging from those requiring job costing to those needing process costing. Companies using job costing include construction companies such as Morrison-Knudsen, defense contractors such as Lockheed and Northrop, hospitals such as the Mayo Clinic (where the jobs would be called *cases*), moviemakers such as Universal Studios, public accounting firms such as Arthur Andersen & Co. and Price Waterhouse (where the jobs are often called *clients*), and Richard D. Irwin, the publisher of this textbook. These companies produce customized products.

Continuous flow processing is at the opposite end of the spectrum from job shops. Process systems generally mass produce a single, homogeneous product in a continuing process. Process systems are used in manufacturing chemicals, grinding flour, and refining oil. Companies with continuous flow processing use process costing methods.

ILLUSTRATION 3.1 Production Methods and Accounting Systems

Accounting system	Job costing (Chapter 4)	Operation costing[a] (Chapter 5)	Process costing (Chapter 5)
Type of production	Jobs shops • Construction • Movie studios • Hospitals	Batch production • Clothing • Automobiles • Computer terminals	Continuous flow processing • Oil refinery • Paper • Paint
Type of product	Customized product	Different batches of products, but standardized within a batch	Standardized product

[a]Operation costing is a hybrid of job and process costing.

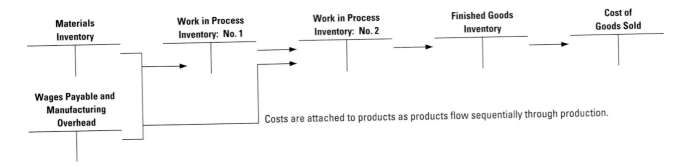

Costs are attached to products as products flow sequentially through production.

Many organizations use job systems for some projects and process systems for others. A home builder might use process costing for standardized homes with a particular floor plan. The same builder might use job costing when building a custom-designed home for a single customer. Honeywell, Inc., a high-tech company, uses process costing for most of its furnace thermostats but job costing for specialized defense and space contracting work.

operation costing
A hybrid costing system often used in manufacturing of goods that have some common characteristics plus some individual characteristics.

operation
A standardized method or technique that is repetitively performed.

Many companies use a hybrid of job and process costing, called **operation costing.** An **operation** is a standardized method of making a product that is performed repeatedly in production. Companies using operation costing produce goods using standardized production methods, like companies using process costing, but materials can be different for each product or batch of products as indicated in Illustration 3.1.

For example, Nissan manufactures a variety of models of cars and trucks on one assembly line in its manufacturing plant near Nashville, Tennessee. Each car or truck goes through the same work stations, for example, the same painting station. Each vehicle type has a different set of materials, however. For example, trucks have a different body from cars.

Operation costing is discussed in the appendix to Chapter 5 after you have learned more about the two methods at the extremes of the continuum—job costing and process costing.

THE BASIC COST FLOW MODEL

L.O. 2: Use the basic cost flow model.

The fundamental framework for recording costs is the basic cost flow model. You have applied this model in your previous accounting classes; we repeat it here because it is so important and helpful in assigning costs to jobs. The model is

Beginning balance (BB)	Transfers + in (TI)	Transfers − out (TO)	Ending = balance (EB)

Application

This model helps you solve for unknown amounts in accounts, which is very useful for both accountants and managers who frequently find that they are missing key accounting information. For example, suppose that Hurricane George has just wiped out the inventory of fine clothes in your Uncle Chuck's store. The insurance company will pay for the cost of the destroyed inventory, but you have to prove the cost of the inventory, which is nowhere to be found. Unfortunately, nobody bothered to count the inventory before the storm hit.

The basic accounting model comes to your rescue. Now you find from last year's financial statements that the ending inventory at the end of the year was $500,000,

REAL WORLD APPLICATION | **Using the Basic Cost Flow Model to Detect Fraud**

A senior official at Doughties Foods became curious about the high levels of inventory reported on the divisional financial statements of the Gravins Division. Based on Gravins' purchases (transfers in) and cost of goods sold (transfers out), the amount of ending inventory seemed high compared to other divisions in the company. When asked about the high inventory levels, the division manager confessed that he had overstated the inventory numbers to make his divisional profits look better than they really were.

Overstating the ending balance in the inventory understates cost of goods sold, which overstates gross margin and profits. In equation form,

$$BB + TI - (EB + F) = TO - F$$

where *F* is the amount of overstatement from the financial fraud, *EB* is the correct ending inventory amount, and *TO* is the correct transfer out of inventory, which is also cost of

goods sold. As the manager of the Gravins Division discovered to his dismay, the ending inventory for period 1 is the beginning inventory for period 2. Thus, the beginning inventory on the books carried an overstated amount, which had to be matched by an equal amount of overstatement at the end of period 2.

As time passed, the manager of the Gravins Division continued to make increasing overstatements of ending inventory to continue to look good to his superiors. He must have felt considerable personal pressure because, when an official from corporate headquarters arrived, the division manager confessed, handed over a notebook where he had kept track of the overstatement, and resigned. The Securities and Exchange Commission subsequently filed a formal complaint charging the division manager and the auditors with committing financial fraud.

Source: Based on the authors' research.

which was also the beginning inventory this year. From your uncle's suppliers, you find that he purchased $1,200,000 of clothes so far this year, and you find from sales records that he has sold clothes that cost $1,400,000. Therefore, you know the beginning balance to be $500,000, the amount transferred in to inventory to be $1,200,000, and the amount transferred out of inventory to be $1,400,000. Using the basic cost flow model,

$$BB + TI - TO = EB$$
$$\$500,000 + \$1,200,000 - \$1,400,000 = EB$$
$$\$300,000 = EB$$

Your uncle can report that inventory costing $300,000 was lost in the storm.

In practice, auditors use the cost flow models frequently to perform reasonableness checks on the data they receive from clients. For example, a client may report that ending inventory is $500,000 based on a count of the inventory. If you know from the basic cost flow model that the inventory should be $400,000 (i.e., $BB + TI - TO = \$400,000$), you know something is wrong.

Many financial frauds are discovered when an auditor finds that the amounts based on the basic cost flow model are different from those the client reported. The Real World Application, "Using the Basic Cost Flow Model to Detect Fraud," describes a case in which the basic cost flow model helped management discover fraudulent inventory reporting in one of its divisions.

Application to Manufacturing and Service Organizations

Service and manufacturing organizations have both Work in Process and Finished Goods Inventory accounts. The basic cost flow model ties these accounts together as shown in Illustration 3.2. Note that the *transfer-out (TO)* of work in process inventory is the *transfer-in (TI)* to finished goods inventory. The *transfer-out (TO)* of finished goods inventory is the cost of goods sold.

ILLUSTRATION	3.2	Basic Cost Flow Model, Work in Process, and Finished Goods

Work in Process Inventory Account	Finished Goods Inventory Account	
BB		Beginning **Work in Process Inventory**
+		plus
TI		**Manufacturing Costs** incurred during the period
−		minus
EB		Ending **Work in Process Inventory**
=		equals
TO ⟶	TI	**Cost of Goods Manufactured** during the period
	+	plus
	BB	Beginning **Finished Goods Inventory**
	−	minus
	EB	Ending **Finished Goods Inventory**
	=	equals
	TO	**Cost of Goods Sold** during the period

SELF-STUDY QUESTIONS

1. Classify each of the following products as either a job or the output of a process:
   a. Work for a client on a lawsuit by lawyers in a law firm.
   b. Diet cola.
   c. Patient care in an emergency room for a college basketball player.
   d. House painting by a company called Student Painters.
   e. The paint used by Student Painters.

2. Fill in the missing item for each of the following inventory accounts:

	A	B	C
Beginning balance	$40,000	_____	$35,000
Ending balance	32,000	$16,000	27,000
Transfers-in	_____	8,000	8,000
Transfers-out	61,000	11,000	_____

The solutions to these questions are at the end of this chapter on page 78.

Perpetual versus Periodic Inventories

perpetual inventory method
Method of accounting for inventory that keeps a continuous record of inventory additions and reductions.

periodic inventory method
Method of accounting for inventory that does not keep a continuous record but requires a physical count of inventory.

The **perpetual inventory method** requires an ongoing record of transfers in and transfers out of inventory accounts. Using the perpetual inventory method requires that inventory levels be updated continuously. For example, using the perpetual inventory method, Macy's Department Store records the reduction in inventory for each item of merchandise it sells. Management knows the level of inventory for each item without taking a physical inventory count.

In contrast to the perpetual inventory method, the **periodic inventory method** does not continually update inventory levels. Instead of maintaining continuous records of transfers in or out of inventory accounts, people must take a physical inventory. Then they derive the amount sold or transferred from one inventory account to another using the basic cost flow model.

For example, consider the sale of Super Sweet tennis rackets at Martha's Sport Shop in March. Beginning inventory was 10 rackets. Management counted the ending inventory on March 31 and found 15 rackets. Based on records of purchases, management knew that 40 rackets had been purchased during March. All rackets cost $10 each, so the cost amounts are:

Beginning inventory (10 rackets at $10) $100
Ending inventory (15 rackets at $10) 150
Purchases (40 rackets at $10) 400

Using the basic cost flow model,

$$BB + TI - TO = EB$$

management solves for the unknown cost of goods sold, or *TO*, as follows:

$$TO = BB + TI - EB$$
$$TO = \$100 + \$400 - \$150$$
$$TO = \$350$$

A perpetual inventory provides more data than a periodic inventory does. For example, with a perpetual system, up-to-date inventory balances and cost of goods sold are always available. But with a periodic system, these data are available only after taking a physical inventory count. Perpetual inventory also is useful for control purposes because the clerical record of transfers out can be compared with a physical count to check for theft, spoilage, and other problems. However, the perpetual method requires more expensive data maintenance systems.

With the expanded use of bar codes and other computerized inventory systems, nearly all large organizations use perpetual inventories. Periodically—say, every six months—they may take a physical inventory to check for shortages, theft, and clerical accuracy and to satisfy internal or external auditors. They often use the periodic method for office supplies and small merchandise.

Traditional costing systems use sequential tracking to record product costs. That is, as a product goes through its production steps, the costing system tracks it and attaches costs at each step. Panel A of Illustration 3.3 shows the flow of costs through T-accounts using a traditional costing system. This sequential tracking required for traditional costing systems is time consuming and expensive, not only for accountants but also for workers and managers who must keep records of labor time and other costs incurred at each step.

JUST-IN-TIME PRODUCTION SYSTEMS AND BACKFLUSH COSTING

just-in-time production
A system designed to obtain goods just in time for production and to provide goods just in time for sale.

L.O. 3: Understand the just-in-time method of production.

L.O. 4: Compare and contrast traditional sequential costing and backflush costing.

Recent innovations in inventory management and production methods have the potential to revolutionize both inventory management and the way accounting is done. Perhaps the most important innovation is the **just-in-time production** philosophy, which was discussed in Chapter 1. The objective of just-in-time (JIT) production systems is to obtain materials just in time for production and to provide goods just in time for sale. A JIT system has three important characteristics:

- Inventory on hand is reduced because materials are obtained just in time for production rather than stockpiled in a warehouse. Looking back at the value chain, remember that we are trying to reduce nonvalue-added activities. Storing inventory is a nonvalue-added activity. By implementing a JIT system, we are able to substantially reduce inventory levels.

- The production process tends to be refined as the focus shifts to improving quality and reducing nonvalue-added activities. A JIT production system requires that processes resulting in defective units be corrected immediately because there is no inventory where defective units can be sent to await reworking or scrapping.

- The time required to produce a product is typically reduced, enabling users of a JIT production system to be more flexible in meeting customer demands and reduce the amount of work in process at any point in time.

ILLUSTRATION   3.3   Comparison of Traditional Sequential Tracking of Costs with Backflush Costing

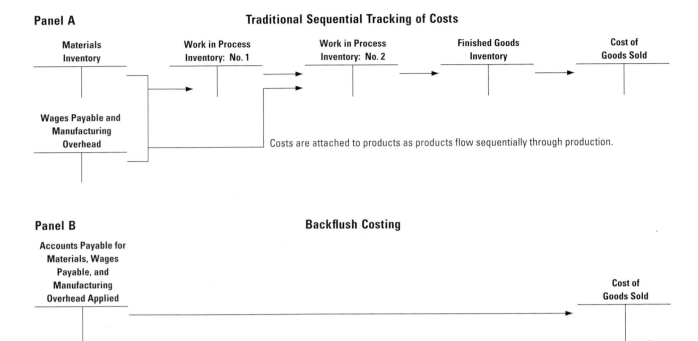

Each element of the process results in several financial benefits. By decreasing inventory levels, companies no longer need to tie up cash in inventory or in warehouse space to store inventory. The emphasis on eliminating nonvalue-added activities and improving the production process results in reduced production costs. Also, the risk of producing inventory that becomes obsolete—especially important in the computer industry—is eliminated.

In theory, a JIT system eliminates the need for inventories because no production takes place until it is known that the item will be sold. JIT requires reliable suppliers who deliver a quality product on time. The Real World Application on page 67, demonstrates what happened to General Motors' plants when a strike shut down their supplier.

Companies using JIT also normally have a backlog of orders for their finished product so they can keep their production operations going continuously. The benefits of the JIT system are lost if a company has to shut down its operations for lengthy periods of time while awaiting receipt of a new order.

Implementing a JIT system requires the highly efficient coordination of purchasing, production, and marketing functions. Companies that have consistent problems with any of these functions should not implement JIT until the problems have been resolved.

REAL WORLD APPLICATION | The Effect of Labor Disputes on Just in Time

Like many other manufacturers, General Motors (GM) has increased its use of just-in-time (JIT) production methods. During March 1996, one of GM's two brake parts plants went on strike over a dispute concerning GM's use of outside suppliers instead of its own plants. As a result, limited brake parts inventories ran out, and GM was forced to shut down its car and truck plants throughout North America at an estimated cost of $50 million a day in forgone pretax earnings.

Keeping the labor force working is a critical component of any company, especially one that implements JIT. As evidenced by GM's total production shutdown, to be effective, JIT requires that all components of the production process be reliable. If any one part of the process falters, JIT loses its efficiencies.

Source: Bill Vlasic, "Bracing for the Big One," *Business Week,* March 25, 1996, pp. 34–35.

Flexible Manufacturing

flexible manufacturing
A computer-based manufacturing system that allows companies to make a variety of products with minimal setup time.

To achieve just-in-time objectives, many companies install a flexible manufacturing system. **Flexible manufacturing** is a computer-based manufacturing system that allows companies to make a variety of products with minimal setup time. A company using flexible manufacturing can minimize its inventories while making products with small production runs. For example, Ford Motor Company installed flexible manufacturing so it could produce numerous different types of valves for the various engines that go into its cars and trucks.

Backflush Costing

backflush costing
A costing method that works backward from cost of goods sold to assign costs to inventories.

Companies that implement a JIT production system are not so concerned with tracking costs for inventory valuation because inventory levels are generally insignificant at any point in time. However, managers are still interested in the cost of products for decision-making purposes. As managers grapple with the problem of trying to use old cost accounting systems with JIT, a new streamlined costing approach has been developed.

This alternative to sequentially tracking costs (as traditional costing systems do) is to record all manufacturing costs directly in the Cost of Goods Sold account. This saves considerable time and effort and reduces computational errors. At the end of the accounting period, if the accountants learn that the company has some inventory, they can use backflush costing to record inventory values.

Backflush costing is a costing method that works backward from the cost of goods sold to assign manufacturing costs to work in process inventories. The term *backflush* probably arose because costs are "flushed back" through the production process to the points at which inventories remain. Illustra-

This company is implementing just-in-time inventory. Although inventory is low, it is not entirely eliminated.

tion 3.3 compares the traditional method of sequential costing with the backflush approach. Costs are initially recorded at the end of the production process in Cost of Goods Sold on the grounds that little or no inventories exist at the end of the period.

If no inventories exist at the end of the period, the company does not need to record the backflow of costs. (The backflow of costs is indicated by the arrows pointing to the left and up in Panel B of Illustration 3.3.) If there are inventories, the company must backflush costs from the end of the production process (for example, from Cost of Goods Sold) to the inventories, as demonstrated by the following example.

Example

Denton Biotechnics Corp., which uses the JIT system, sells diagnostic kits for medical use. Direct materials cost $5 per kit. The company received an order for 10,000 kits in January, which was its only business in January. It had no beginning inventory that month. Materials costs of $50,000 were incurred as were conversion costs of $94,000. Materials costs were credited to Accounts Payable as they were purchased. Of the conversion costs, $54,000 was credited to Manufacturing Overhead and $40,000 to Wages Payable, as incurred. Using backflush costing and charging the costs directly to Cost of Goods Sold, the journal entries for January are

Cost of Goods Sold.	50,000	
Accounts Payable		50,000
To record the purchase and use of materials.		
Cost of Goods Sold.	94,000	
Wages Payable.		40,000
Manufacturing Overhead.		54,000
To record conversion costs.		

This example presents the extreme version of JIT production by charging all manufacturing costs to Cost of Goods Sold as they were incurred. Other versions charge labor and overhead costs to the account Conversion Costs and then assign these conversion costs to Finished Goods Inventory or Cost of Goods Sold. Whatever peculiarity you encounter in practice, remember the principle that accountants normally do not need to track costs in work in process inventories for external reporting if the company has no work in process at the end of the accounting period.

If Denton Biotechnics Corp. had sold all 10,000 kits and had no inventories at the end of January, there would be no need for additional entries. If the company had inventories at the end of January, however, it must assign costs to those inventories. To demonstrate, we assume that the company had the following inventories at the end of January:

Work in process inventory. 1,000 units complete as to materials costs and 40 percent complete as to conversion costs.

Finished goods inventory. 1,000 units completed but not yet shipped.

The company further computes its conversion costs to be $10 for each completed kit. In addition, direct materials of $5 per kit are incurred at the beginning of work in process. Based on this information, the cost of each ending inventory is computed as follows:

Work in process inventory. (1,000 units × $5 for materials) + (40% stage of completion × 1,000 units × $10 per unit for conversion costs) = $5,000 + $4,000 = $9,000

Finished goods inventory. 1,000 units × ($5 for materials + $10 for conversion costs) = $15,000.

ILLUSTRATION   3.4   Comparison of Traditional Cost Flows to Backflush Costing

Panel A   **Traditional Costing**

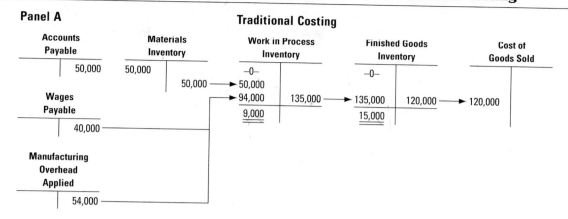

Panel B   **Backflush Costing**

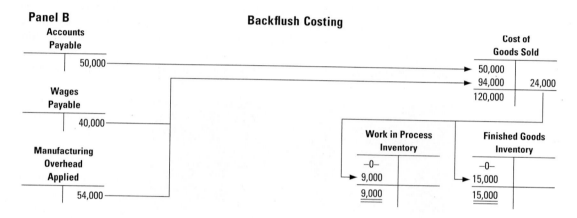

The entries to backflush the costs of inventories out of Cost of Goods Sold follow:

Work in Process Inventory	9,000	
Finished Goods Inventory	15,000	
Cost of Goods Sold		24,000
To record inventories.		

If the costs of these kits had been charged to the accounts using traditional sequential costing, we would have recorded materials in Materials Inventory when they were purchased. As materials were used and conversion costs were incurred, these costs would have been recorded in Work in Process and Finished Goods and, finally, in Cost of Goods Sold. Illustration 3.4 compares diagrams of the cost flows, first using the traditional method (Panel A) and then using backflush costing (Panel B).

What happens to the beginning inventory next period? The company can either use traditional sequential costing to record the movement of costs and products out of the inventory accounts, or it can reverse the backflush entry. By reversing the backflush entry, the company credits the inventory accounts and debits Cost of Goods Sold, thus recreating the situation that appeared before making the backflush entry. (If you recall how adjusting and reversing entries work, the backflush entry can be treated as an adjusting entry at the end of a period that is reversed at the beginning of the next period.)

3. Metro Media produces commercials. For the month of January, it incurred costs of $100,000 in making commercials. Of those costs $10,000 was tied up in one commercial for a real estate company that was not complete at the end of the month, and $20,000 had been assigned to one commercial for a clothing store that was finished but not yet recorded in Cost of Goods Sold. Show the flow of costs through T-accounts using (a) traditional costing and (b) backflush costing. The company has no Materials Inventory account, one Work in Process Inventory account, and one Finished Goods Inventory account. Assume that the credit entries for these costs when they were recorded during the month were 60 percent to Accounts Payable and 40 percent to Wages Payable. The company has no beginning inventories and no other business in January.

The solution to this question is at the end of this chapter on page 79.

The solution to this question is at the end of this chapter on page 79.

CUSTOMER COSTING AND PROFITABILITY ANALYSIS

L.O. 5: Explain the concept of customer costing and profitability analysis.

Managers use costing techniques to help control costs and learn more about them to better estimate future costs. Marketing managers also use cost information by customer. By comparing the costs of serving a customer to the revenues generated from that customer, marketing managers can assess the profits generated by the customer. After performing a profit and loss analysis by customer, many companies have found that a small number of customers provided most of the profits while the remaining customers provided little or no profits. Some customers even generated losses, after considering all of the hassles in dealing with them.

Keeping records of the revenues and costs for major customers helps this jewelry store target customers for repeat business. Certain customers buy expensive jewelry several times per year and do not require a lot of employee time.

The task of assigning costs to customers is a challenge. A system must be in place that enables the company to identify which customers are using customer support services and how frequently they do so. How much time must the marketing department spend on a customer to make the sale and to provide ongoing services? These costs are in addition to the cost of making the product or providing a service for the customer.

For example, Mesa Design Company specializes in designing commercial office space for several different customers. Suppose that Mesa's president reviewed the income statement shown in Illustration 3.5 and noticed that operating profits were below her expectations. She had a hunch that certain customers were not profitable for the company and asked the controller to perform a customer analysis showing profitability by customer for the month of January.

The controller provided the customer profitability graph shown in Illustration 3.5. It ranks each customer based on operating income; clearly customers 5 and 6 are not profitable for Mesa. The president and her management team must now decide how to proceed. Do they drop these customers? Do they raise prices for them? Do they cut costs and services for them to become profitable? Do they expect to become profitable with these customers by selling additional consulting services at a higher rate in the future? The purpose of the customer analysis is not to provide management with the answers to these questions, but to give management additional information to help with the decision-making process.

ILLUSTRATION   3.5   Customer Profitability Analysis

MESA DESIGN COMPANY
Income Statement
For the Month Ended January 31

Sales revenue	$300,000
Cost of services billed	255,000
Gross margin	45,000
Marketing and administrative costs	30,000
Operating profit	$ 15,000

MESA DESIGN COMPANY
Customer Profitability
For the Month Ended January 31

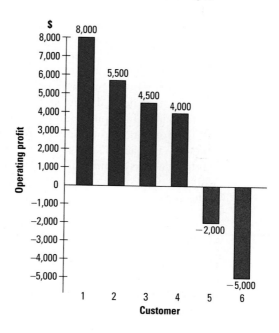

It is important not to be too quick to eliminate unprofitable customers. Companies often develop customer relationships over long time horizons by offering low prices and a high level of service up front. As the relationship develops, however, the customer may not require the same level of service and might be willing to pay a premium. The analysis shown in the graph of Illustration 3.5 helps management to see the financial picture for each customer, and it can use this information to help establish a strategic plan for the coming months, quarters, or years. Management may decide that it is worth keeping the unprofitable customers now for potential future profits.

FUNDAMENTAL THEMES UNDERLYING THE DESIGN OF COST SYSTEMS FOR MANAGERIAL PURPOSES

As we continue through this text, you will notice key themes that are critical to designing a cost system for managerial purposes. Before undertaking the design of a new cost system, we must first ask several important questions. How will managers use the information our system is designed to provide? What type of decisions will be made using the cost information? Will benefits of improved decision making outweigh the costs of implementing the new cost system? These are valid and important questions to ask. The following three points outline the fundamental themes related to designing a new cost system for managerial purposes.

- **Cost systems should have a decision focus.** Cost systems must meet the needs of the decision makers. Remember that the decision makers are the customers (or users) of cost accounting. In the previous section, the president of a company was provided with a customer profitability analysis. The decision focus was on which customers were most profitable. If the cost system had not been designed to provide these data, it would not have met the president's needs. Clearly, it is important to design the cost system to facilitate the decision making of the user of the cost data provided by the cost system.

- **Different cost information is used for different purposes.** What works for one purpose will not necessarily work for another purpose. For example, financial reporting requires the use of cost information from the past. Managerial decision makers, however, require information about the future. Cost information is often used to assess departmental profitability; other information is used to review customer profitability. As you can see, the cost information must provide the appropriate data for its intended purpose.

- **Cost information for managerial purposes must meet the cost-benefit test.** Cost information can always be improved. However, the benefits of improvements (i.e., better decision making) must outweigh the costs to make the improvements. For example, if customer profitability analyses are used for informational purposes only but do not provide the president with additional information needed to make better decisions, the costs of preparing this information may outweigh the benefits. However, if the president uses this information to decide where to focus her marketing efforts—whereas before she had no such information—the benefits *may* outweigh the costs. Cost information systems can be very costly to implement, so one basic question should be asked before establishing a new system: Will the benefits outweigh the costs?

SUMMARY

This chapter introduces cost systems used for different production systems: job costing, process costing, and operations costing. In designing a cost system for managerial purposes, we must consider the needs of the decision makers (or users of the information) and ensure that the benefits outweigh the costs to implement a cost system.

The following summarizes the key ideas tied to the chapter's learning objectives.

LO1: Comparing job and process costing. A job costing system records costs and revenues for each individual job or batches of goods. By contrast, process costing averages costs across units because identical units are produced through a series of uniform production steps.

LO2: Basic cost flow model. The basic cost flow model serves as the fundamental framework for recording costs. The model is $BB + TI - TO = EB$. The model can be used to solve for unknown amounts in accounts and can help to detect fraud.

LO3: Just-in-time method of production. The objective of just-in-time (JIT) production systems is to obtain materials just in time for production and to provide finished goods just in time for sale. The result is low inventory carrying costs, improved production techniques, and shorter production time.

LO4: Comparing traditional sequential costing and backflush costing. Traditional costing systems use sequential tracking to record product costs. As a product goes through its production steps, the costing system tracks the product and attaches costs at each step. Backflush costing is used in companies that utilize just-in-time production methods. They initially record manufacturing costs in the Cost of Goods Sold account and assign them back to Work in Process Inventory at the end of the accounting period.

LO5: Customer costing and profitability analysis. Customer costing focuses on the profitability of individual customers rather than products or departments.

LO6: Fundamental themes underlying the design of cost systems. Three important themes provide the foundation for designing a cost system for managerial purposes: (a) cost systems should have a decision focus, (b) different cost information is used for different purposes, and (c) cost information systems should meet the cost-benefit test.

KEY TERMS

backflush costing, 67	operation, 62
continuous flow processing, 61	operation costing, 62
flexible manufacturing, 67	periodic inventory method, 64
job costing, 61	perpetual inventory method, 64
just-in-time production, 65	process costing, 61

REVIEW QUESTIONS

3.1 What are the characteristics of the following three costing systems: (a) job costing, (b) process costing, and (c) operation costing?

3.2 What is continuous flow processing? Give at least three examples of products that might use continuous flow processing.

3.3 What is each component of the basic cost flow model? Describe each component.

3.4 What is the difference between perpetual and periodic inventories?

3.5 How does backflush costing work and in what production environment is it typically used?

3.6 What is a traditional costing system?

3.7 What are three important characteristics of a just-in-time production system?

CRITICAL ANALYSIS AND DISCUSSION QUESTIONS

3.8 Describe the concept of customer costing. Why is customer costing important?

3.9 When designing a cost system, what points should you consider before starting the design?

3.10 When is the basic cost flow model used? Give an example.

3.11 Suppose that you work for a new sporting goods store and your manager is considering whether to use the perpetual or periodic inventory method. She asks you to draft a memo explaining the difference between these two methods and to make a recommendation. What would you say in the memo?

3.12 Bill Hinson, a cost accountant, prepares a customer profitability report for John Griffin, the marketing manager. Much to Bill's surprise, almost one-third of the company's customers are not profitable. Bill says, "John, it looks like we will have to stop doing business with one-third of our customers to improve overall company profits. It's a good thing we decided to look at profitability by customer!"

Do you think John will agree with this approach? If so, why? If not, why not?

3.13 Suppose that you are the lead cost accountant for a company that manufactures computers. Your manager has just come from a just-in-time production seminar and asks you to meet with her. She says, "From what I can tell, JIT is the way to go. The benefits are incredible; we can reduce inventory and related carrying costs, our production process will improve, and best of all, our accounting system can be simplified and accounting staff reduced. Let's convert to a JIT system starting next month!"

How would you respond to this suggestion?

3.14   Refer to the Real World Application, "The Effect of Labor Disputes on Just in Time," on page 67. Why did a strike against the brake manufacturing plants cause such a widespread shutdown? How did JIT contribute to this problem?

3.15   How does a just-in-time philosophy result in better control over goods spoiled or lost in production?

3.16   How does flexible manufacturing work to support the just-in-time philosophy?

3.17   Using the information from the Real World Application, "Using the Basic Cost Flow Model to Detect Fraud," on page 63, explain how to use the cost flow model to detect fraudulent overstatement of inventory.

EXERCISES

3.18   Basic Cost
Flow Model
(L.O. 2)

Singh Company experienced the following events during the current year:

1.   Incurred $125,000 in marketing costs.
2.   Purchased $400,000 of merchandise.
3.   Paid $10,000 for transportation-in costs.
4.   Incurred $200,000 of administrative costs.
5.   Took a periodic inventory at year end and learned that goods costing $125,000 were on hand. This compared with a beginning inventory of $150,000 on January 1.
6.   Determined that sales revenue during the year was $1,000,000.

All costs incurred were debited to the appropriate account and credited to Accounts Payable. All sales were for cash.

Required

Give the amounts for the following items in the Merchandise Inventory account:

a.   Beginning Balance (*BB*).
b.   Transfers-in (*TI*).
c.   Ending Balance (*EB*).
d.   Transfers-out (*TO*).

3.19   Basic Cost
Flow Model
(L.O. 2)

Assume that the following events occurred at a division of Boeing Company for the current year.

1.   Purchased $180 million in direct materials.
2.   Incurred direct labor costs of $104 million.
3.   Determined that manufacturing overhead was $164 million.
4.   Transferred 70 percent of the materials purchased to work in process.
5.   Completed work on 60 percent of the work in process. Costs are assigned equally across all work in process.

The inventory accounts have no beginning balances. All costs incurred were debited to the appropriate account and credited to Accounts Payable.

Required

Give the amounts for the following items in the Work in Process account:

a.   Transfers-in (*TI*).
b.   Transfers-out (*TO*).
c.   Ending balance (*EB*).

3.20   Basic Cost
Flow Model
(L.O. 2)

Fill in the missing items for the following inventories:

	(A)	(B)	(C)
Beginning balance	$34,000	$14,200	$ 78,000
Ending balance	_____	12,400	64,000
Transferred in	32,000	_____	140,000
Transferred out	38,000	44,000	_____

3.21 Basic Cost Flow Model (L.O. 2)

Fill in the missing items for the following inventories:

	(A)	(B)	(C)
Beginning balance	$136,000	$ 56,800	$312,000
Ending balance	_____	49,600	256,000
Transferred in	128,000	_____	560,000
Transferred out	152,000	176,000	_____

3.22 Basic Cost Flow Model (L.O. 2)

Fill in the missing items for the following inventories:

	(A)	(B)	(C)
Beginning balance	$170,000	$ 71,000	$390,000
Ending balance	_____	62,000	320,000
Transferred in	160,000	_____	700,000
Transferred out	190,000	220,000	_____

3.23 Basic Cost Flow Model (L.O. 2)

Assume that the following T-accounts represent data from a division of Tower Design's accounting records. Find the missing amounts represented by the letters. (*Hint:* Rearrange accounts to conform with flow of costs.)

Costs of Goods Sold

41,000

Direct Materials Inventory

BB	(a)	Transferred out	10,500
Purchases	9,000		
EB	3,750		

Finished Goods Inventory

BB	23,200	(d)
	(c)	
EB	(f)	

Work in Process Inventory

BB	3,000	29,300
Mat'ls	(b)	
Labor	8,500	
Overhead	(e)	
EB	4,850	

3.24 Basic Cost Flow Model (L.O. 2)

Assume that the following T-accounts represent data from a division of Bridal Wear Corporation's accounting records. Find the missing amounts represented by the letters. (*Hint:* Rearrange accounts to conform with flow of costs.)

Costs of Goods Sold

123,000

Direct Materials Inventory

BB	(a)	Transferred out	31,500
Purchases	27,000		
EB	11,250		

Finished Goods Inventory

BB	69,600	(d)
	(c)	
EB	(f)	

Work in Process Inventory

BB	9,000	87,900
Mat'ls	(b)	
Labor	25,500	
Overhead	(e)	
EB	14,550	

3.25 Customer Profitability Analysis (L.O. 5)

Powertools, Inc., makes custom tools for three customers, Larry, Curly, and Moe. The following is Powertool's income statement the most recent year.

POWERTOOLS, INC.
Income Statement
For the Most Recent Year Ended December 31

Sales revenue	$200,000
Cost of goods sold	120,000
Gross margin.	80,000
Marketing and administrative costs	35,000
Operating profit	$ 45,000

In reviewing each customer, Powertool noticed that each made up the following percentages of Powertool's total revenue, cost of goods sold, and marketing and administrative costs.

	Larry	Curly	Moe
Sales revenue	20%	10%	70%
Cost of goods sold	40	5	55
Marketing and administrative costs	25	30	45

Required

Prepare income statements for each customer.

3.26 Customer Profitability Analysis (L.O. 5)

Custom Trailers, Inc., makes custom trailers for three customers (Trail Rite, Trail Ways, UTrail). The following is its income statement the most recent year.

CUSTOM TRAILERS, INC.
Income Statement
For the Most Recent Year Ended December 31

Sales revenue	$600,000
Cost of goods sold	360,000
Gross margin.	240,000
Marketing and administrative costs	105,000
Operating profit	$135,000

In reviewing each customer, Custom Trailer noticed that its three customers made up the following percentages of total revenue, cost of goods sold, and marketing and administrative costs.

	Trail Rite	Trail Ways	UTrail
Sales revenue	60%	5%	35%
Cost of goods sold	65	10	25
Marketing and administrative costs	75	10	15

Required

Prepare income statements for each customer.

3.27 Backflush Costing (L.O. 4)

Carson Biotech, Inc., manufactures medical devices and uses a JIT system. It received an order for 600 devices. To fill this order, materials costing $14,000 were purchased on account. Manufacturing costs of $48,000 were incurred, of which $16,000 was paid in cash, $12,000 was credited to Wages Payable, and the balance was credited to Manufacturing Overhead Applied.

While production was in progress, it was necessary for financial statement purposes to compute an inventory value for this order. The company has only one production division. The work in process inventory cost was estimated at $3,160. There was no finished goods inventory.

Required

Prepare journal entries for these transactions using backflush costing.

3.28 Backflush Costing (L.O. 4)

Interplay Systems, Inc., manufactures computer disk drives. It received an order for 500 drives. Materials costing $25,000 were ordered on account. Additional manufacturing costs were $94,000, of which $50,000 was accounts payable and the balance was wages payable. At the end of the accounting period, $8,200 of goods were not yet completed and were in the company's sole processing area. There was no finished goods inventory.

Required

Prepare journal entries to show the flow of costs using backflush costing.

3.29	Comparing Backflush and Traditional Sequential Costing (L.O. 4)	Refer to the data for Exercise 3.27 for Carson Biotech, Inc. Show the flow of costs through T-accounts using both traditional sequential costing and backflush costing.
3.30	Comparing Backflush and Traditional Sequential Costing (L.O. 4)	Refer to the data for Exercise 3.28 for Interplay Systems, Inc. Show the flow of costs through T-accounts using both traditional sequential costing and backflush costing.

PROBLEMS

3.31	Customer Costing and Profitability Analysis	Refer to the data in Exercise 3.25. If you were the marketing manager for Powertool, Inc., and had reviewed the income statements for each customer, what would you do?
3.32	Customer Costing and Profitability Analysis	Refer to the data in Exercise 3.26. If you were the marketing manager for Custom Trailers, Inc., and had reviewed the income statements for each customer, what would you do?
3.33	Backflush Costing	Creative Designers, Inc., uses JIT production in producing designs for dresses. For the month of June, the company incurred costs of $250,000 in making designs. Assume that the credit entries for these costs when they were recorded during the month were 40 percent to Accounts Payable and 60 percent to Wages Payable. Ten percent of those costs were tied up in one design for an Italian dressmaker that was not complete at the end of the month, and 20 percent of the costs had been assigned to one design for a dressmaker in Japan that was finished but not yet sold. Creative Designers had no Materials Inventory account.
	Required	Prepare journal entries to show the flow of costs using backflush costing.
3.34	Comparing Backflush and Traditional Sequential Costing	Refer to the data for Exercise 3.33 for Creative Designers, Inc. Show the flow of costs through T-accounts using both traditional sequential costing and backflush costing.
3.35	Just-in-Time Inventory	Interview the manager of a retail (or wholesale) store such as a music store, an automobile parts store, the automobile parts department of an automobile dealership, or the parts department of an appliance dealership. Ask him or her how items are ordered to replace those sold. For example, does he or she order based on observing inventory levels or each time a customer buys an item? Does he or she appear to use just-in-time inventory? Write a report to your instructor summarizing the results of your interview.
3.36	Compare Backflush and Traditional Sequential Cost Flows	River City Quality Instruments produces sensitive heat measurement devices. The units are produced in three manufacturing stages: (a) meter assembly, (b) case assembly, and (c) testing. The company has a large backlog of orders and had no beginning inventories because all units in production last year were sold by the end of the year. At the start of this year, it received an order for 4,000 meters. The company purchased $260,000 of materials on account. The Meter Assembly Division used $210,000 of the materials in production, the Case Assembly Division used $40,000, and the Testing Division used $10,000.

    Direct labor costs of $640,000 were incurred. These costs were assigned as follows: Meter Assembly, $200,000; Case Assembly, $350,000; Testing, $90,000. Overhead costs of $1,040,000 were charged to departments based on materials used ($210,000/$260,000 × $1,040,000 to Meter Assembly, for example).

    Ninety percent of the costs charged to Meter Assembly were transferred to Case Assembly during the period; 95 percent of the costs charged to Case Assembly (including the costs transferred in from Meter Assembly) were transferred to Testing. All of the costs charged to Testing were transferred to finished goods, and all of the finished units were delivered to the buyer. |
| | *Required* | **a.** Use T-accounts to show the flow of costs under a traditional costing system. |
| | | **b.** Use T-accounts to show the flow of costs using a backflush system. |

3.37 Compare Backflush and Traditional Cost Flows

Davis Agriproducts, Inc., sells specialty hybrid seed packets for agricultural use. The packets are processed through two work in process departments, Culturing and Packaging. Direct materials cost $1.50 per packet ($1.30 in Culturing and $.20 in Packaging). Conversion costs are $.80 for Culturing and $.30 for Packaging. The company received an order for 20,000 packets. Materials costs of $29,600 were incurred as were conversion costs of $21,400.

Assume that 2,000 units are left at the end of the Culturing operation and 1,000 units at the end of Packaging when financial reports are prepared. The units are 100 percent complete within the respective operations.

Required

a. Use T-accounts to show the flow of costs using a backflush system.

b. Use T-accounts to show the flow of costs under a traditional costing system.

3.38 Customer Costing and Profitability Analysis

Quality Lawn Care, Inc., specializes in commercial landscape maintenance. Each of its five clients pays a fixed monthly fee (based on size of each client's site). Quality keeps records of the time that maintenance workers spend at each client as well as the cost of the equipment used to perform the maintenance. Quality recently decided to compute profitability for each customer. The following data are for the month of July.

	Client Revenues	Client Costs
Sierra University	$130,000	$ 91,000
Davis Agriproducts Inc.	90,000	92,000
American River Restaurant	40,000	37,000
Brown and Associates	38,000	54,000
Ott Investment Advisers	186,500	115,500
Totals	$484,500	$389,500

Required

a. Calculate the operating income for each customer.

b. What should Quality Lawn Care do, if anything, given these data?

c. What problems might exist with estimating costs for each customer?

SOLUTIONS TO SELF-STUDY QUESTIONS

1. **a.** Lawsuit—job.
   b. Diet cola—process.
   c. Emergency room care—job.
   d. House painting—job.
   e. Paint—process.

2. For each case, start with the formula:

$$BB + TI - TO = EB$$

   a. $TI = TO + EB - BB$
      $= \$61,000 + \$32,000 - \$40,000$
      $= \$53,000$
   b. $BB = TO + EB - TI$
      $= \$11,000 + \$16,000 - \$8,000$
      $= \$19,000$
   c. $TO = BB + TI - EB$
      $= \$35,000 + \$8,000 - \$27,000$
      $= \$16,000$

3.

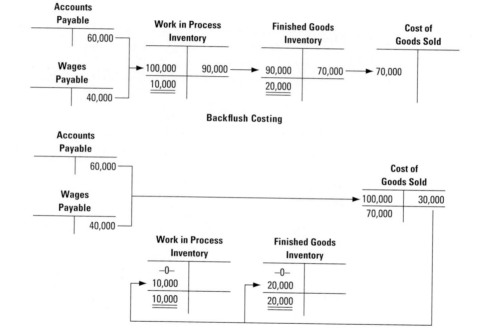

Job Costing

LEARNING OBJECTIVES

After reading this chapter, you should be able to:

1. Assign costs in a job cost system.

2. Account for overhead using predetermined rates.

3. Apply job costing methods in service organizations.

4. Understand how improprieties in job costing make managing job costs difficult.

5. Describe the difference between jobs and projects.

WHY IT'S IMPORTANT TO KNOW THE COST OF JOBS

jobs
Units of a product that are easily distinguishable from other units.

When you see construction sites where people are constructing new homes, repairing highways, remodeling office buildings, or building rapid transit systems, you are seeing job costing at work. **Jobs** are units of a product that can be easily distinguished from other units. If you or your family remodel or build a home, the construction work is called a *job* because it can be easily distinguished from other construction jobs.

Tracking the cost of each job is important for three reasons:

- Managers use their knowledge of the cost of jobs to estimate the costs of prospective jobs. Good cost estimates on future jobs help them prepare good bids. Construction contractors, for example, know that if they bid too high, they will not win the job. If they bid too low, on the other hand, they will lose money on it. Construction contractors and other people who bid on jobs need to have a good estimate of the costs of prospective jobs so they can prepare bids that are low enough to win but high enough to make money.

- Managers compare actual job costs to the estimated (sometimes called *budgeted*) job costs to control costs. A contractor once pointed out that if she did not have job cost information, she could be experiencing huge cost overruns without knowing it. For example, on one job she estimated the cost of lumber at a certain level. Then a hurricane hit the southeastern United States, causing lumber prices to double. She did not realize that the lumber shipped to the job was at the higher posthurricane prices until she got the job cost information. Based on it, she redesigned the job to use less lumber in places where it was not essential.

- Managers can use job cost information to renegotiate contracts with customers. Jobs often turn out different than originally specified. Sometimes these changes are inexpensive, and the contractor does the extra work as part of good customer service. Other times the changes are expensive and the customer and contractor need to negotiate who will pay for them. Good cost information helps the contractor know (1) whether the changes are expensive or inexpensive and (2) what the changes cost so the bid can be renegotiated.

Having provided an overview of alternative production methods and costing systems in Chapter 3, we now discuss how to account for costs in organizations that use job costing.

Job costing is important for pricing and cost control. Prospective customers always ask for estimates, and they frequently award jobs on a competitive cost basis. Consequently, suppliers must be able to estimate costs accurately if they are to be competitive and profitable.

source document
A basic record in accounting that initiates the entry of an activity into the accounting system.

job cost record
The source document for entering costs under job costing; sometimes referred to as a *job cost sheet, job cost file,* or *job card.*

For example, management of Public Consultants, a firm that customizes accounting systems for government agencies, recently completed jobs for two municipalities. The job for Gotham City, a large metropolis, required 7,000 hours of staff time and several sophisticated computer applications. The job for Smallville, a modest farming community, required 70 hours of staff time and one very simple computer application. To charge each municipality the same price by averaging the estimated total costs for the two jobs would obviously be incorrect. Job costing allowed Public Consultants to accurately estimate the costs for each job separately. Thus, they were able to submit a competitive bid and still make a reasonable profit on each job.

TRACKING COSTS

L.O. 1: Assign costs in a job cost system.

In job operations, managers estimate and control costs by keeping separate records of costs for each job. The source document for a job is a **job cost record,** called a *job cost sheet, card,* or *file.* **Source documents** are basic records that accountants use to initiate an accounting entry.

Illustration 4.1 presents a printout of a job cost record for Job 102 for New Abilities Manufacturing Company, which makes customized health care equipment for

REAL WORLD APPLICATION | Accounting for Flops

Movies and television shows are jobs. Some are successful; some are not. Studios must decide what to do with the cost of unsuccessful ones, the flops. Some studios have been criticized for assigning the cost of flops to successful shows, which in turn reduces profits available under profit-sharing agreements with actors, actresses, directors, and others associated with the successful show.

One studio carried the cost of flops in inventory, thereby overstating assets and understating expenses. When investors learned about this practice, the company's stock price plummeted.

Source: Based on the author's research.

ILLUSTRATION   4.1 | Job Cost Record

NEW ABILITIES MANUFACTURING

Job number:	102	Customer:	D. Bell
Date started:	Jan 8	Date Finished:	Jan 26
Description:	Manufacture custom equipment		
	according to customer specifications		

Assembly Department

Direct Materials			Direct Labor			Manufacturing Overhead	
Date	Requisition Number	Cost	Date	Employee Number	Cost	Date	Cost
Jan 8	102-A1	$20,000	Jan 8–14	88	$980	Jan 31	$48,000
Jan 13	102-A2	4,000	Jan 12–18	67	720		
			(Many more employees were added to this list. In total, $40,000 direct labor cost was incurred.)				

Total Costs

Direct materials	$24,000	
Direct labor	40,000	
Manufacturing overhead	48,000	$112,000

Transferred to Finished Goods Inventory on Jan 26

Total job costs:

Direct materials	$ 24,000
Direct labor	40,000
Manufacturing overhead	48,000
Total	$112,000

Explain any unusual items below:

None

Note: Data and comments are assumed for purposes of this illustration.

people with physical limitations. Note that this record shows detailed calculations for the direct materials, direct labor, and manufacturing overhead charged to the job.

As noted on the job cost record, the actual costs accumulated for the job are compared with estimated costs to evaluate employee performance in controlling costs and to provide information for negotiating price increases with the customer. The comparison of actual and estimated job costs also provides feedback on the accuracy of the cost estimation, which is important for pricing.

Recording Job Costs in the Accounts

subsidiary ledger
Detailed information used to support a general ledger account.

Most companies with jobs follow the basic steps presented in this section. We show the journal entries to record cost flows using New Abilities Manufacturing Company as an example. Work in Process Inventory is a control account because it is supported by records in the subsidiary ledger. Costs associated with each job are recorded on each job cost record as shown in Illustration 4.1. Thus, job cost records serve as **subsidiary ledgers** to the Work in Process Inventory (WIP) account. This enables management to identify the costs for a single job by reviewing its job cost record.

New Abilities had one job in process on January 1, Job 101. After some minor work, it was completed and shipped to a customer in January. The costs for New Abilities' second job, Job 102, were presented on the job cost record in Illustration 4.1. It was started in January and moved to finished goods inventory on January 26. At January 31, it awaited shipment to a customer. The third job, Job 103, was started in January and was still in process on January 31.

Beginning Inventories

Illustration 4.2 shows the flow of costs through accounts. Materials Inventory on hand January 1 was $10,000. Beginning Work in Process Inventory on January 1 was Job 101, which had incurred the following costs:

Direct materials	$14,000
Direct labor	22,000
Manufacturing overhead	25,000
Total	$61,000

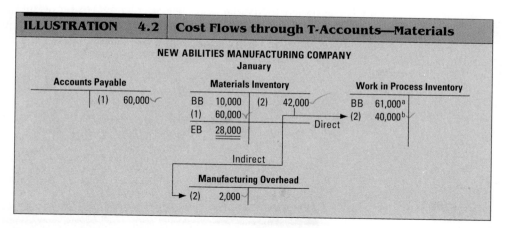

ILLUSTRATION   4.2 | Cost Flows through T-Accounts—Materials

NEW ABILITIES MANUFACTURING COMPANY
January

Accounts Payable	Materials Inventory	Work in Process Inventory
(1) 60,000	BB 10,000 (2) 42,000	BB 61,000ᵃ
	(1) 60,000	(2) 40,000ᵇ
	EB 28,000	

Direct

Indirect

Manufacturing Overhead

(2)   2,000

Note: BB = Beginning balance; EB = Ending balance. Numbers in parentheses correspond to journal entries presented in text.

ᵃBeginning inventory is composed of

Direct material	$14,000
Direct labor	22,000
Manufacturing overhead	25,000
Total	$61,000

ᵇ$40,000 = $24,000 for Job No. 102 + $16,000 for Job No. 103.

Hence, the Work in Process Inventory account balance on January 1 was $61,000.

Note the difference between Materials Inventory, $10,000, that has not yet been sent to production departments, and the materials component of beginning Work in Process Inventory, $14,000. The latter has already been sent to production.

These beginning balances are shown in Illustration 4.2. There was no beginning Finished Goods Inventory.

Accounting for Materials

Assume that in January, New Abilities purchased $60,000 of direct and indirect materials and accumulated the costs in one account. This purchase was recorded as follows:

(1)	Materials Inventory	60,000
	Accounts Payable	60,000

When the supplier sends an invoice or bill for the shipment, the payable is recorded as shown in entry (1). Subsequent payment is recorded with a debit to Accounts Payable and a credit to Cash.

materials requisition
An authorization to obtain materials from a storeroom; may be a paper document or an authorization card.

A job supervisor or other authority requisitions the materials needed for a job using a **materials requisition** form. It is the source document for the entry transferring materials from Materials Inventory to the job.

No materials were requisitioned for Job 101 in January. Job 102 had requisitions for materials totaling $24,000 (see Illustration 4.1). The entry to record this transfer of direct materials follows:

(2a)	Work in Process Inventory	24,000
	Materials Inventory	24,000
	To record the requisition of materials.	

Direct materials of $16,000 were requisitioned for Job 103 and recorded in entry (2b). Materials inventory is also used for indirect materials and supplies that are not assigned to specific jobs but are charged to the Manufacturing Overhead account. For New Abilities, the $2,000 of indirect materials requisitioned in January were recorded in the following entry.

(2b)	Work in Process Inventory	16,000
	Manufacturing Overhead	2,000
	Materials Inventory	18,000
	To record direct materials costs of $16,000 assigned to Job 103 and indirect materials costs of $2,000 charged to Manufacturing Overhead.	

Note that journal entries (2a) and (2b) are combined into one journal entry—journal entry (2)—in Illustration 4.2.

Note that Illustration 4.2 presents the ending materials inventory balance, which can be found from the facts given by solving the basic cost flow equation:

Beginning balance (BB)	+	Transfers in (TI)	−	Transfers out (TO)	=	Ending balance (EB)

$$\$10,000 + \$60,000 - \$42,000 = EB$$
$$\$28,000 = EB$$

Accounting for Labor

Production workers are usually paid an hourly rate and account for their time each day on time cards, time sheets, or other records. The time record provides space for them to account for the hours spent on the job during the day and is the basis for the company's payroll.

The salary paid to this maintenance worker is an indirect cost.

The total cost to the company includes gross pay plus the employer's share of social security and employment taxes, employer's contribution to pension and insurance plans, and any other benefits that the company pays for the employee. In general, these costs range from about 15 percent to about 70 percent of the wage rate, depending on a company's fringe benefit plans. Companies commonly add their fringe benefit costs to the wage rate to assign costs to jobs, although fringe benefits also may be part of overhead.

New Abilities' payroll department recorded accumulated costs of $110,000 for manufacturing employees. Of the $110,000 total, $80,000 was attributed to direct labor costs, including employee benefits and taxes. The $80,000 is charged (debited) to Work in Process Inventory and assigned to the specific jobs worked on during the period. Based on time cards, Job 101 was charged with $10,000 in January, Job 102 was charged with $40,000 as in the job cost record in Illustration 4.1, and Job 103 with $30,000.

The remaining $30,000 is indirect labor and charged to Manufacturing Overhead. This indirect labor includes the costs of supervisory, janitorial, maintenance, security, and timekeeping personnel, as well as idle time and overtime premiums paid to direct laborers.

The following entry records labor costs in January.

(3) Work in Process Inventory   80,000
        Manufacturing Overhead   30,000
            Wages Payable (or Accrued Factory Payroll)   110,000
        To record direct labor costs of $80,000 assigned to jobs and indirect labor costs of
        $30,000 charged to Manufacturing Overhead.

The flow of labor costs through the T-accounts is shown in Illustration 4.3.

Accounting for Manufacturing Overhead

Accounting for manufacturing overhead tends to be much more difficult than accounting for direct labor and direct materials. Manufacturing overhead costs are typically pooled together into one account and allocated to individual jobs based on a relatively arbitrary overhead base (for example, machine hours or direct labor hours). Management must make subjective decisions in establishing the process of allocating manufacturing overhead to each job. We discuss the process of creating predetermined overhead rates later in the chapter.

Indirect manufacturing costs, including indirect materials and indirect labor, are usually accumulated in the Manufacturing Overhead account. Each department typically has its own Manufacturing Overhead Summary account so each department manager can be held accountable for departmental overhead costs. This helps top management evaluate how well department managers control costs. This stage of cost allocation is to allocate costs from the accounts in which they were initially

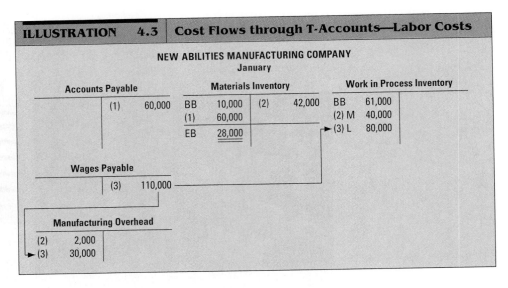

| ILLUSTRATION | 4.3 | Cost Flows through T-Accounts—Labor Costs |

NEW ABILITIES MANUFACTURING COMPANY
January

Note: M = Materials; L = Labor.

entered to responsibility centers. In this case, the responsibility centers are departments.

For example, in January, New Abilities charges indirect materials costs of $2,000 and indirect labor costs of $30,000 to the Manufacturing Overhead account as described in entries (2) and (3). Utilities and other overhead costs credited to Accounts Payable were $46,000. The portion of prepaid taxes and insurance applicable to the period, $7,000, is included in the actual overhead, as is depreciation of $19,000. These items total $72,000 and represent the actual overhead incurred during the period.

The journal entry to record manufacturing overhead follows:

(4)	Manufacturing Overhead.............................	72,000	
	Accounts Payable...........................		46,000
	Prepaid Expenses...........................		7,000
	Accumulated Depreciation		19,000

To record actual manufacturing overhead costs other than indirect labor and indirect materials.

This entry is labeled (4) in the T-account diagram in Illustration 4.4.

USE OF PREDETERMINED OVERHEAD RATES

predetermined overhead rate
An amount obtained by dividing total estimated overhead for the coming period by the total estimated overhead allocation base for the coming period.

L.O. 2: Account for overhead using predetermined rates.

Companies generally use predetermined overhead rates to allocate manufacturing overhead to jobs. The **predetermined overhead rate** is usually established before the year in which it is to be used and is used for the entire year.

By using a predetermined overhead rate, a company normalizes overhead applied to jobs. Over time, manufacturing overhead costs can be quite erratic. Preventive maintenance costs are often higher in months when activity is low. Utility costs in cold climates are higher in winter than in summer; the opposite is true in warm climates. A job in some months is assigned more overhead than it is in other months if actual overhead costs are assigned to jobs. In addition, a company might not know its actual overhead costs until the close of an accounting period. Management can prepare financial statements and use product cost data for managerial purposes based on a good estimate of product costs by using predetermined overhead rates.

Predetermined overhead rates "normalize" the application of manufacturing overhead to jobs; hence, the resulting product costs are called *normal costs*, and the accounting method is called **normal costing.** Predetermined overhead rates can be established by following a five-step approach. This approach is presented here using New Abilities Manufacturing as an example.

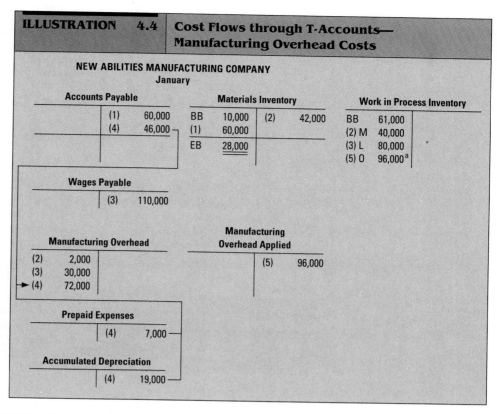

ILLUSTRATION 4.4 | **Cost Flows through T-Accounts— Manufacturing Overhead Costs**

Note: M = Direct materials; L = Direct labor; O = Manufacturing overhead.

[a]Overhead application rate = $120 per machine hour = $\dfrac{\text{Estimated manufacturing overhead for year}}{\text{Estimated machine hours for year}} = \dfrac{\$1,200,000}{10,000 \text{ machine hours}}$

normal costing
An accounting system that charges direct materials and direct labor to objects at actual costs and applies manufacturing overhead using predetermined rates.

Step 1. Identify the costs to be included as indirect costs. New Abilities has developed a detailed list of cost items included as manufacturing overhead. The total of these costs represents its total manufacturing overhead.

Step 2. Estimate the costs for each cost item identified in step 1. If the budget period is one year, budgeted (i.e., estimated) manufacturing overhead costs for New Abilities total $1,200,000, based on last year's actual manufacturing overhead adjusted for anticipated changes this year.

Step 3. Select the cost allocation base(s). Operating personnel at New Abilities have determined that the number of machine hours is the major driver of manufacturing overhead costs. That is, manufacturing overhead costs are primarily a function of the number of machine hours incurred. Machine hours are chosen as the cost allocation base as a result of this cause-and-effect relationship.

Step 4. Estimate the amount of the cost allocation base identified in step 3. New Abilities anticipates using 10,000 machine hours during the year based on expected customer demand for its products.

Step 5. Compute the predetermined overhead rate. This calculation follows.

$$\text{Predetermined rate} = \frac{\text{Estimated manufacturing overhead for the year}}{\text{Estimated machine hours for the year}}$$

$$= \frac{\$1,200,000}{10,000 \text{ machine hours}}$$

$$= \$120 \text{ per machine hour}$$

New Abilities used its predetermined rate to charge manufacturing overhead to individual jobs as follows.

	Actual Machine Hours Used		Predetermined Overhead Rate		Manufacturing Overhead Applied
Job 101	100	×	$120 per mh	=	$12,000
Job 102	400	×	120	=	48,000
Job 103	300	×	120	=	36,000
Total	800		120	=	$96,000

The entry to record the allocation of manufacturing overhead to jobs using a predetermined overhead rate is

(5) Work in Process Inventory.	96,000	
Manufacturing Overhead Applied		96,000
To record application of manufacturing overhead to jobs.		

Illustration 4.4 shows a separate account for Manufacturing Overhead Applied. Two overhead accounts may be used to separate actual and **applied overhead.** We title the account that records actual overhead *Manufacturing Overhead* and call the new account that records applied overhead *Manufacturing Overhead Applied.*[1] These accounts are closed at the end of the period, as described later in this chapter. The flow of these costs through T-accounts is illustrated in Illustration 4.4.

applied overhead
Overhead applied to a cost object using a predetermined overhead rate.

SELF-STUDY QUESTION

1. Lynn's Landscaping Company worked on three jobs during November. Job 1 was in process on November 1, with total charges of $11,000. During the month, the following additional transactions occurred.

   a. Purchased $20,000 worth of new materials.

   b. Charged materials to jobs as follows: $2,000 to Job 1, $8,000 to Job 2, $6,000 to Job 3, and $4,000 as indirect materials.

   c. Charged labor to jobs as follows: $2,000 to Job 1, $6,000 to Job 2, $4,000 to Job 3, and $2,000 as indirect labor.

   d. Incurred indirect expenses including depreciation totaling $20,000. Utilities and other expenses credited to Accounts Payable were $12,000. Depreciation was $8,000.

   e. Allocated manufacturing overhead for November to work in process based on materials used in each job. The predetermined rate was based on expected materials of $160,000 and expected overhead of $240,000 for this year.

Show the journal entries to record these transactions. Show the flow of costs using T-accounts as in Illustration 4.4.

The solution to this question is at the end of this chapter on page 116.

COMPLETING THE OPERATING CYCLE

Transfers to Finished Goods Inventory

When jobs are transferred out of production to the finished goods storage area, an entry is made transferring the costs of the jobs from the Work in Process Inventory account to the Finished Goods Inventory account. For example, New Abilities completed Jobs 101 and 102 in January and transferred them to the Finished Goods Inventory account. The journal entry is

(6) Finished Goods Inventory	195,000	
Work in Process Inventory.		195,000
To transfer completed jobs to the finished goods storage area.		

---

[1]Companies can combine the overhead into one account. In such a setting, the left side of the account is basically overhead "incurred" and the right side is overhead "applied."

Note that the amount transferred includes costs incurred in both the current period and previous periods. For example, the transfer for Job 101 includes $61,000 from beginning work in process inventory and $22,000 of costs incurred in January to complete the job.

Transfers to Cost of Goods Sold

When the goods are sold, they are transferred from the Finished Goods Inventory account to the Cost of Goods Sold account. For example, New Abilities sold Job 101 in January for $120,000 on account. When it was sold, the journal entry to record the cost of goods sold was

(7)	Cost of Goods Sold	83,000	
	Finished Goods Inventory		83,000
	Accounts Receivable	120,000	
	Sales Revenue		120,000
	To transfer finished goods inventory to cost of goods sold and to record corresponding sales revenue.		

When these goods are moved from the production area to finished goods storage, accountants make a journal entry such as journal entry (6) on page 88.

Manufacturing overhead accounts are temporary accounts. At the end of an accounting period, the actual and applied overhead accounts are closed. Usually this is not done until the end of the year when the books are closed. For illustrative purposes, however, we assume that New Abilities closes its books for January.

Under normal costing, the amount debited to the Manufacturing Overhead account (the actual manufacturing overhead) is unlikely to equal the amount applied (based on budgeted overhead). The difference between the actual and the applied manufacturing

overhead variance
The difference between actual and applied overhead.

overhead is the **overhead variance.** We use a Manufacturing Overhead Variance account to record the variance as follows.

Assume that $96,000 was credited to Manufacturing Overhead Applied (based on budgeted overhead) and $104,000 was debited to Manufacturing Overhead (actual overhead) during January, as shown in Illustration 4.5. In that case, the entry to close the actual against applied overhead for New Abilities is

---

ILLUSTRATION 4.5 | Closing Entries for Manufacturing Overhead

Overhead: Normal Costing

Manufacturing Overhead		Manufacturing Overhead Applied		Work in Process Inventory
104,000	(8) 104,000ª	(8) 96,000ª	96,000 ⟶	96,000

Manufacturing Overhead Variance	
(8) 8,000ª	

ªRefers to closing entry.

(8) Manufacturing Overhead Applied.   96,000
     Manufacturing Overhead Variance   8,000
          Manufacturing Overhead   104,000
     To close actual and applied overhead accounts.

This entry is shown in Illustration 4.5. We discuss methods to "dispose" of the manufacturing overhead variance later in this chapter.

SELF-STUDY QUESTION

2. Refer to the data for Lynn's Landscaping Company in Self-Study Question 1. Suppose that the following additional transactions occurred:
    a. Completed and charged the following jobs to Finished Goods: Job 1 for $18,000; Job 2 for $26,000.
    b. Sold Job 1 for $24,000 and Job 2 for $30,000.
    c. Closed actual and applied manufacturing overhead. Recall that actual manufacturing overhead for the month was $26,000.

Show journal entries and T-accounts for these transactions. Include the entry to close the manufacturing overhead accounts to Manufacturing Overhead Variance for the month of November.

The solution to this question is at the end of this chapter on page 117.

THE WHOLE PICTURE: SUMMARY OF JOB COST FLOWS

The flow of all manufacturing costs from buying materials to sale of product appears in Illustration 4.6. Note that the cost of goods sold statement in Illustration 4.7 presents the data from T-accounts in Illustration 4.6. You should cross-reference each item in the statement in Illustration 4.7 to the T-accounts in Illustration 4.6.

Marketing and Administrative Costs

Marketing and administrative costs do not flow through inventory accounts. These are expenses that are recorded in accounts to be closed at the end of the accounting period. For example, New Abilities' marketing and administrative costs (all on account) were $10,000 in January. The entry to record these costs is

Marketing and Administrative Costs.   10,000
     Accounts Payable   10,000
     To record marketing and administrative costs incurred in January.

We do not show T-accounts for this entry but note that the costs appear on the income statement in Illustration 4.7.

What Does the Overhead Variance Mean?

underapplied overhead
The excess of actual overhead costs incurred over applied overhead costs.

overapplied overhead
The excess of applied overhead costs incurred over actual overhead during a period.

The $8,000 amount in the Manufacturing Overhead Variance account in Illustration 4.6 appears in the income statement in Illustration 4.7 as underapplied manufacturing overhead. **Underapplied overhead** occurs when actual overhead exceeds applied overhead. New Abilities' underapplied overhead is shown as a debit to the Manufacturing Overhead Variance account. **Overapplied overhead** occurs when actual overhead is less than applied overhead. Overapplied overhead is shown as a credit to the Manufacturing Overhead Variance account.

Why does actual overhead typically differ from applied overhead? Remember that applied overhead is based on some predetermined overhead rate (i.e., estimates). As outlined earlier in this chapter, a five-step approach is used to establish the predetermined rate. New Abilities *estimated* total overhead manufacturing costs of $1,200,000 and machine hours of 10,000. Thus, for every machine hour incurred, $120 in manufacturing overhead is "applied" to WIP. Because this application of overhead is clearly based on budgeted amounts, total applied overhead will not equal actual overhead at the end of the accounting period (unless, of course, budgeted amounts are the same as actual amounts).

ILLUSTRATION 4.6 Summary of Job Costs

NEW ABILITIES MANUFACTURING COMPANY
January

Accounts Payable

(1)	60,000
(4)	46,000

Materials Inventory

BB	10,000	(2)	42,000
(1)	60,000		
EB	28,000		

Work in Process Inventory

BB	61,000	(6)	195,000
(2) M	40,000		
(3) L	80,000		
(5) O	96,000		
EB	82,000		

Finished Goods Inventory

BB	–0–	(7)	83,000
(6)	195,000		
EB	112,000		

Cost of Goods Sold

(7)	83,000

Wages Payable

(3)	110,000

Manufacturing Overhead Applied

		(5)	96,000
(8)	96,000		

Manufacturing Overhead Variance

(8)	8,000

Manufacturing Overhead

(2)	2,000	(8)	104,000
(3)	30,000		
(4)	72,000		

Prepaid Expenses

(4)	7,000

Accumulated Depreciation

(4)	19,000

| ILLUSTRATION | 4.7 | **Income Statement** |

NEW ABILITIES MANUFACTURING COMPANY
Income Statement
For the Month Ended January 31

Sales revenue.	$120,000
Cost of goods sold (see statement below)	83,000
Underapplied manufacturing overhead	8,000[a]
Gross margin	29,000
Less marketing and administrative costs.	10,000
Operating profit	$ 19,000

Cost of Goods Sold Statement
For the Month Ended January 31

Beginning work in process inventory, January 1		$ 61,000
Manufacturing costs during the month		
Direct materials		
Beginning inventory, January 1	$10,000	
Add purchases	60,000	
Materials available	70,000	
Less ending inventory, January 31	28,000	
Total materials used.	42,000	
Less: Indirect materials used	2,000	
Direct materials put into process.	$40,000	
Direct labor	80,000	
Manufacturing overhead.	96,000	
Total manufacturing costs incurred during the month		216,000[b]
Total costs of work in process during the month		277,000
Less work in process inventory, January 31		82,000
Cost of goods manufactured during the period		195,000[c]
Beginning finished goods inventory, January 1		–0–
Less ending finished goods inventory, January 31		112,000
Cost of goods sold		$ 83,000[d]

[a]This is the amount of manufacturing overhead underapplied during the month.
[b]This amount equals the total debits made to Work in Process Inventory during January (not counting the beginning balance).
[c]This amount equals the total debits to Finished Goods Inventory during January.
[d]This amount equals the total credits to Finished Goods Inventory during January.

For example, budgeted overhead manufacturing costs (the numerator in calculating a predetermined overhead rate) of $1,200,000 may have been based on prior year costs and, thus, not adjusted for increases in utility rates, rent, or other overhead costs.

How to Report This Information to Management

At year-end, the manufacturing overhead variance is either (1) prorated to Work in Process Inventory, Finished Goods Inventory, and Costs of Goods Sold or (2) assigned in total to Cost of Goods Sold. Illustration 4.8 recaps the costs of jobs before proration at New Abilities Manufacturing.

Method 1: Prorate the Overhead Variance

If the variance is prorated to Work in Process Inventory, Finished Goods Inventory, and Cost of Goods Sold, the cost of each job is adjusted to approximate actual cost. For New Abilities, the status and cost of each job before prorating the overhead

---

ILLUSTRATION   4.8

NEW ABILITIES MANUFACTURING COMPANY
Costs of Jobs before Prorating the Manufacturing Overhead Variance

Job No.	Beginning Inventory	Direct Materials	Direct Labor	Manufacturing Overhead Applied in January	Total Costs Charged to Jobs	Status of Job at End of Month
101	$61,000	–0–	$10,000	$12,000	$ 83,000	Cost of Goods Sold
102	–0–	$24,000	40,000	48,000	112,000	Finished Goods Inventory
103	–0–	16,000	30,000	36,000	82,000	Work in Process Inventory
	$61,000	$40,000	$80,000	$96,000	$277,000	

ILLUSTRATION   4.9

NEW ABILITIES MANUFACTURING COMPANY
Prorating Variances

Job		Account	(1) Manufacturing Overhead Applied in January[a]	(2)	(3) Percentage of Total Overhead Applied in January[b]	(4) Overhead to Be Prorated	(5) Prorated Variance
101		Cost of Goods Sold		$12,000	12.5 ×	$8,000 =	$1,000
102		Finished Goods Inventory		48,000	50.0 ×	8,000 =	4,000
103		Work in Process Inventory		36,000	37.5 ×	8,000 =	3,000
				$96,000	100.0		$8,000

[a]$120 per machine hour.
[b]12.5% = $12,000 ÷ $96,000; 50.0% = $48,000 ÷ $96,000; 37.5% = $36,000 ÷ $96,000.

---

variance are shown in Illustration 4.8. The variance is prorated so that each account and job bears a share of the $8,000 manufacturing overhead variance. For our example, this share is proportional to the overhead applied to the account during the month as shown in Illustration 4.9. Other methods for allocating the overhead variance are used also, including the total cost of jobs before the allocation.

The following entry is made to prorate the variance:

```
Cost of Goods Sold . . . . . . . . . . . . . . . . . . . . . . . . . . . . . . . . . . . . . . . . . . . . . . . . .   1,000
Finished Goods Inventory . . . . . . . . . . . . . . . . . . . . . . . . . . . . . . . . . . . . . . . . . . . .   4,000
Work in Process Inventory . . . . . . . . . . . . . . . . . . . . . . . . . . . . . . . . . . . . . . . . . . .   3,000
    Manufacturing Overhead Variance. . . . . . . . . . . . . . . . . . . . . . . . . . . . . . . . .          8,000
```

Method 2: Assign the Variance to Cost of Goods Sold

Many companies do not prorate the manufacturing overhead variance to inventories and Cost of Goods Sold; instead they transfer the entire variance to Cost of Goods Sold for both internal and external reporting using the following journal entry:

Cost of Goods Sold 8,000
    Manufacturing Overhead Variance. 8,000

In a company with many kinds of products and inventories, proration can be complicated. If the amounts to be prorated are immaterial relative to net income for external reporting or do not affect managerial decisions, proration may not be necessary (note that proration is generally required, however, for financial reporting and tax purposes). The difference in net income between prorating the variance and assigning it to Cost of Goods Sold is a matter of timing. Any difference between actual and applied overhead will eventually be expensed (or credited to expense), even if a company prorates. Prorating the overhead variance merely defers expensing the portion allocated to inventories until they are sold. For managerial purposes, one must ask how useful it is to revalue work in process and finished goods inventories to actual cost. A large overhead variance may affect some cost control, performance evaluation, pricing, and other decisions, but if the variance is small, proration is probably not worthwhile.

However the variance is disposed of, the key managerial issue is to understand causes of the difference between actual and applied overhead. Management may need to revise overhead rates, impose new cost control procedures, or take other action.

SELF-STUDY QUESTION

3. Refer to the information regarding Lynn's Landscaping Company in Self-Study Questions 1 and 2. Dispose of the manufacturing overhead variance by (1) prorating the variance to Work in Process Inventory and Cost of Goods Sold based on the applied overhead in jobs and (2) charging the entire variance to Cost of Goods Sold.

    Show journal entries for these transactions.

The solution to this question is at the end of this chapter on page 117.

Interim Reporting

When normal costing is used and the overhead accounts are not closed monthly, how do you report the balance in the Manufacturing Overhead Variance account on financial statements? There are two ways. It can be reported on the income statement, for example, as a line item below cost of goods sold, or carried on the balance sheet as an adjustment to inventory. The first option treats the adjustment as a period cost, the second as a product cost.

Managers generally do not want to be bothered with this variance unless they believe that it indicates a problem. Regardless of managers' interest in this number, we recommend reporting it as a separate line item on the income statement so they will notice it and take appropriate action (if any).

ACTUAL, NORMAL, OR BUDGETED COSTING: WHAT'S THE DIFFERENCE?

Suppose that New Abilities Manufacturing had used only actual costs to compute job costs, not a predetermined overhead rate. Then management would have waited until the actual overhead costs were known and allocated them to jobs based on the actual machine hours worked. Sometime in February, management would know that the actual overhead costs for January were $104,000. These would be allocated to jobs based on the actual machine hours (mh) worked on each job, as follows:

$$\frac{\text{Actual manufacturing overhead costs}}{\text{Actual machine hours used}} = \frac{\$104,000}{800 \text{ mh}}$$

$$= \$130 \text{ per mh}$$

The actual manufacturing overhead applied to each job in January is

	Machine Hours Used		Actual Overhead Rate		Manufacturing Overhead Applied
Job 101	100	×	$130	=	$ 13,000
Job 102	400	×	$130	=	52,000
Job 103	300	×	$130	=	39,000
Total	800	×	$130	=	$104,000

actual costing
The accounting method that assigns overhead based on actual overhead costs incurred.

budgeted costing
The accounting method that assigns costs to products using a predetermined or budgeted rate for *both direct (e.g., direct materials) and indirect (e.g., overhead) costs.*

Actual costing is the accounting method that assigns only actual cost to the products. **Budgeted costing** is the method that uses a predetermined (or budgeted) rate for *both direct and indirect costs* to allocate costs to the product. (Compare this to normal costing, which uses a predetermined or budgeted rate for indirect costs only.) The following compares actual, normal, and budgeted costing:

	Actual Costing	Normal Costing	Budgeted Costing
Direct costs	Actual rate × Actual inputs	Actual rate × Actual inputs	Predetermined rate × Actual inputs
Indirect costs	Actual rate × Actual inputs	Predetermined rate × Actual inputs	Predetermined rate × Actual inputs

The trade-offs among these three systems essentially involve the speed, convenience, and accuracy of the information. *Budgeted costing* provides the quickest feedback about product costs and is the most convenient but is the least accurate. *Actual costing* requires management to wait until actual costs are known but provides more accurate information. The information delay to get actual costs is usually short for direct materials and direct labor but is considerably longer for manufacturing overhead. For example, the costs of energy estimated for a particular day's activities won't be known until the utility bill is received. Even then, assigning the utility bill's amounts to a particular day of the month and to a particular piece of equipment is difficult, if not impossible. *Normal costing* is a reasonable compromise that uses estimates only for indirect costs, not for direct costs.

If managers complain that they are not getting cost information quickly enough, consider using normal or budgeted costing. The latter can provide cost information as soon as actual input (for example, the number of hours a machine runs) is known. Generally, you can learn the actual input in real time, meaning that you could provide cost information almost as fast.

CHOICE OF OVERHEAD APPLICATION BASE

Our example used machine hours to apply overhead to jobs for New Abilities Manufacturing. For now, make a mental note that organizations use a variety of bases to apply overhead to products, including the number of machine hours, the number of direct labor hours, and the amount of direct labor costs on each job. The choice of allocation base for applying overhead is an important and complex topic and is discussed in much greater detail later in this text. (See the Real World Application for a survey of actual practices on page 96.)

JOB COSTING IN SERVICE ORGANIZATIONS

You will frequently find job operations in service organizations, such as architectural firms, consulting firms, moving companies, and accounting firms. The job costing procedure is basically the same in both service and manufacturing organizations except that service firms generally use less direct materials than manufacturing firms do.

L.O. 3: Apply job costing methods in service organizations.

Both lawyers and the court treat each case as a separate job. The lawyers keep detailed records of the time they spend on each case. These records are used for billing the clients when clients pay hourly fees.

An accounting firm's audit department, for example, is very interested in the profitability of each job (referred to as a *client*). Bids to obtain or retain a client are typically based on projected costs, estimated based on actual results for comparable jobs. Therefore, job costing provides management the information necessary to assess job profitability and to use historical cost data to estimate costs for bidding purposes.

As we discussed in Chapter 3, customer costing assesses the profitability of each customer (or client). Accounting firms regularly review the profitability of each customer by using a job costing system.

Take the example of a service organization that uses job costing. The cost flows through T-accounts for our example are shown in Illustration 4.10. Assume that Priceless Peat Accounting Company has the following information for January (the first month of its fiscal year):

- Beginning work in process $94,000
  (represents one job in process,
  Job 501: $44,000 direct labor, $50,000
  service overhead)
- Beginning finished goods   0
- The payroll department recorded $220,000 in payroll costs for the month: $160,000 was attributed to direct labor costs and charged to work in process (Job 501, $20,000; Job 502, $80,000; and Job 503, $60,000). The remaining $60,000 was indirect labor and charged to Service Overhead.
- Indirect supplies costs of $4,000 were charged to Service Overhead.
- Utilities and other costs credited to Accounts Payable were $92,000. The portion of prepaid taxes and insurance applicable to the period, $14,000, is included in the actual overhead, as is depreciation of $38,000. These items total $144,000 and represent the actual overhead incurred during the period (debited to service overhead).

ILLUSTRATION 4.10 Cost Flows through T-Accounts—Service Organization

PRICELESS PEAT ACCOUNTING COMPANY
January

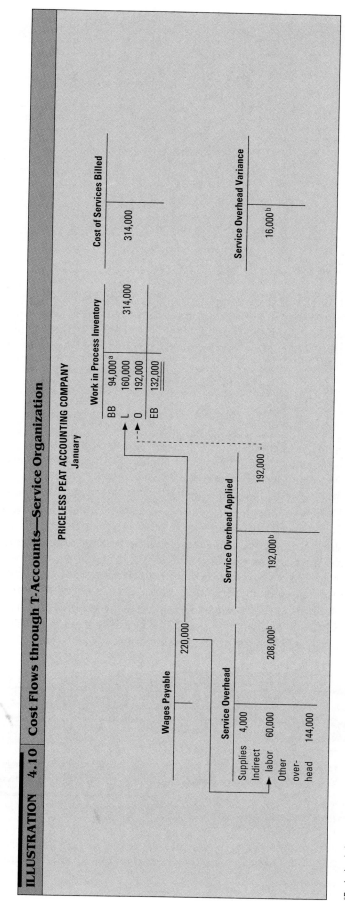

Wages Payable

220,000

Service Overhead

Supplies	4,000	
Indirect labor	60,000	208,000[b]
Other overhead	144,000	

Service Overhead Applied

192,000[b]

Work in Process Inventory

BB	94,000[a]	314,000	
L	160,000		
O	192,000		
EB	132,000		

Cost of Services Billed

314,000

Service Overhead Variance

16,000[b]

192,000

[a]Beginning balance represents contract work in process but not billed. It is composed of $44,000 for direct labor and $50,000 for service overhead incurred in previous periods on Job 501.
[b]Closing entry.

97

ILLUSTRATION 4.11	**Income Statement—Service Organization**

PRICELESS PEAT ACCOUNTING COMPANY
Income Statement
For the Month Ended January 31

Sales revenue	$400,000
Cost of services billed	314,000
Underapplied service overhead . .	16,000
Gross margin	70,000
Marketing and administrative costs	40,000
Operating profit	$ 30,000

- Using the five-step approach outlined earlier in the chapter, Priceless Peat established a predetermined overhead rate based on estimated annual overhead costs of $2,400,000 and 20,000 labor hours. This resulted in a rate of $120 per labor hour. The company incurred actual labor hours for each job in January as follows:

  Job 501: 200

  Job 502: 800

  Job 503: 600

  Thus, a total of $192,000 [(200 + 800 + 600) × $120] in service overhead was applied to work in process in January as shown in the Service Overhead Applied T-account in Illustration 4.10.

- Because each job was "sold" before Priceless Peat began work, there are no finished goods. Instead, costs associated with all completed jobs are transferred out of the Work in Process account into the Cost of Services Billed account. Jobs 501 and 502 were completed by January 31 and thus were transferred out of Work in Process. Costs for Jobs 501 and 502 totaled $138,000 and $176,000, respectively, totalling $314,000 which appears as a credit to the Work in Process account and a debit to the Cost of Services Billed account.

- Service overhead was underapplied by $16,000 ($208,000 actual overhead − $192,000 applied overhead). The closing entry for Service Overhead and Service Overhead Applied resulted in a $16,000 debit to Service Overhead Variance.

As you can see from comparing these data and Illustration 4.10 to our manufacturing company example (New Abilities), job costing is similar for both manufacturing and service organizations. The three primary differences are

1. Service organizations generally use fewer direct materials than manufacturing companies do.
2. Service companies' overhead accounts have slightly different names (*service* overhead, *service* overhead applied, and *service* overhead variance).
3. Service companies' finished goods (or services) are charged to Cost of Services Billed rather than to Cost of Goods Sold.

Illustration 4.11 shows an income statement for Priceless Peat, assuming $400,000 in sales and $40,000 in marketing and administrative expenses.

REAL WORLD APPLICATION | **How Stanford Got into Trouble with its Cost Assignment Methods**

Stanford University is one of the leading research universities in the United States. The Office of Naval Research paid Stanford hundreds of millions of dollars for research performed from 1981 through 1992. Research contracts, which are jobs, entitled Stanford to be reimbursed for 100 percent of its direct costs and its indirect costs based on a negotiated percentage of direct costs. This percentage is negotiated based on several items, including the university's past record of indirect costs as a percentage of direct costs.

In reviewing Stanford's indirect costs assigned to funded research, Paul Biddle, a representative of the Office of Naval Research, identified inappropriate expenses,

including flowers for the president's home and depreciation on a 72-foot university-owned yacht. Stanford subsequently reviewed its records and was chagrined to find many expenses inadvertently allocated to funded research. As a result of an investigation performed by the Office of Naval Research, Stanford's indirect cost reimbursement rate decreased from 70 percent of direct costs to 58.3 percent. In addition, it repaid more than $3 million to the government.

Source: William Celis III, "Navy Settles a Fraud Case on Stanford Research Costs," *New York Times,* October 19, 1994; and S. Huddart, "Stanford University Indirect Cost Recovery," Stanford University School of Business, 1992.

APPLYING THE VALUE CHAIN TO JOB COSTING

L.O. 4: Understand how improprieties in job costing make managing job costs difficult.

The value chain shown above is a useful management tool in calculating costs associated with an organization's different business functions. As indicated, these business functions are part of the value chain: research and development, design, production, marketing, distribution, and customer service.

It is important for companies to collect cost data for each part of the value chain. For example, tax accounting firms must continually invest in developing state-of-the-art tax research and preparation techniques. These expenditures are typically classified as research and development or design costs in the value chain. Marketing is also an essential component of tax accounting firms in their quest for new clients.

MANAGING JOBS: HOW TO KEEP JOB COSTS FROM GETTING OUT OF CONTROL

Many organizations have been criticized for improprieties in assigning costs to jobs. For example, major defense contractors have been accused of overstating the cost of jobs for which they were being reimbursed. Several universities have been accused of overstating the cost of research projects (which are jobs for costing purposes). Improprieties in job costing generally are caused by one or more of the following actions: misstating the stage of completion, charging costs to the wrong jobs or categories, or simply misrepresenting the cost.

Stage of Completion

Management needs to know the stage of completion of projects to evaluate performance and control costs. If the expenditures on a job are 90 percent of the amount estimated to be spent on the project but the job is only 70 percent complete, management needs to know as soon as possible that the job will require higher costs than estimated. Job supervisors who report the stage of completion of their jobs may be tempted to overstate it.

Charging Costs to the Wrong Jobs

To avoid the appearance of cost overruns on jobs, job supervisors sometimes ask employees to charge costs to the wrong jobs. If you work in consulting or auditing, you may encounter superiors who ask you to allocate your time spent on jobs that are in danger of exceeding cost estimates to other jobs that are not in such danger. At a minimum, this practice misleads managers who rely on accurate cost information for pricing, cost control, and other decisions. At worst, it cheats people who are paying for a job on a cost-plus-a-fee basis that does not really cost as much as claimed.

Misrepresenting the Cost of Jobs

These issues are part of the problem of misrepresenting the cost of jobs. Job costs also can be misrepresented in other ways. Sometimes managers know the correct cost of a job but intentionally deceive a customer to obtain a larger payment. Sometimes they deceive a banker to obtain a larger loan for the job or for other reasons. Many people insist on audits of financial records to avoid such deception. Government auditors generally work on-site at defense contractors, universities, and other organizations that have contracts with the government for large jobs.

MANAGING PROJECTS

L.O. 5: Describe the difference between jobs and projects.

project
A complex job that often takes months or years to complete and requires the work of many different departments, divisions, or subcontractors.

Complex jobs (for example, bridges, shopping centers, complex lawsuits) that often take months or years to complete and require the work of many different departments, divisions, or subcontractors are called **projects.**

Jobs can be evaluated relatively quickly, typically within a reporting period, but projects are more difficult to evaluate. Consider the job of painting a small house. The painter might establish an estimate of his costs and bid on the job accordingly. A week later, when the job is complete, he can compare estimated costs to actual costs and evaluate the job's profitability. In contrast, consider a contractor building a hospital, which will take more than two years to complete. The contractor must find a way not only to bid on the project but also to evaluate it at specified intervals.

The contractor must first establish a budget of costs to be incurred throughout the project at various stages of completion (described in percentages). Then, as the project progresses, the contractor evaluates two critical areas, budgeted cost of work performed to date versus actual cost of work performed to date and budgeted percentage of completion versus actual percentage of completion. The two graphs shown in Illustration 4.12 are simple examples of how the evaluation of costs and scheduling can be performed.

Assuming that the contractor is 40 percent complete in the 10th month of construction, the budget indicates that costs should be $2 million, as shown by panel A of Illustration 4.12. The actual costs line indicates, however, that actual costs were $2.5 million. Thus, at this stage of completion, cost overruns of $500,000 have been incurred.

The construction of this bridge is classified as a "project."

Although we know that cost overruns have occurred, we do not know whether the project is on schedule. Panel B of Illustration 4.12 shows that the project should be 35 percent complete by month 10. Because the contractor is 40 percent complete by month 10, the project is ahead of schedule.

ILLUSTRATION 4.12 Project Evaluation Graphs

Panel A

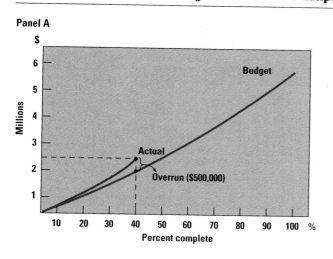

Panel B

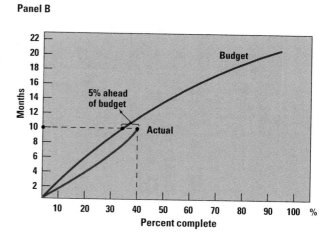

Given the complex nature of projects, it may be necessary to revise budgeted costs and budgeted stages of completion at certain intervals throughout the project to reflect changes. (Most major projects require changes due to their inherent uncertainty.) Thus, the graphs shown in Illustration 4.12 may be updated to reflect revised budgets. This allows managers to be evaluated by comparing actual results against the revised budget.

SUMMARY

This chapter introduces the method to account for inventory in a job costing system. Job costing concepts are used when products are easily identifiable as individual units or batches of identical units. Job costing data can be used to bid and price, control costs, and evaluate performance. The flow of cost diagrams in Illustrations 4.6 and 4.10 summarize our discussion of cost flows in the chapter.

The following summarizes key ideas tied to the chapter's learning objectives.

LO1: Assigning costs to jobs. Direct materials, direct labor, and manufacturing overhead costs (including indirect materials and indirect labor) are assigned to each job. This provides management with information useful for planning and evaluation purposes.

LO2: Using predetermined rates to apply overhead to jobs. Manufacturing overhead includes all manufacturing costs other than direct materials and direct labor. A predetermined rate is established to assign manufacturing overhead costs to jobs.

LO3: Apply job costing methods in service organizations. Service organizations also use job costing, and apply costs to jobs much like manufacturing companies do.

LO4: Improprieties in job costing. Improprieties in job costing generally are caused by one or more of the following actions: misstating the stage of completion of jobs, charging costs to the wrong jobs or categories, or simply misrepresenting the cost of jobs.

LO5: Describe the difference between jobs and projects. A job is a unit of product that is easily distinguishable from other units. Projects are large and complex jobs whose evaluation is typically based on a percentage of completion at a given point in time.

KEY TERMS

actual costing, 95

applied overhead, 88

budgeted costing, 95

job cost record, 81

jobs, 81

materials requisition, 84

normal costing, 87

overapplied overhead, 90

overhead variance, 89

predetermined overhead rate, 86

project, 100

source document, 81

subsidiary ledger, 83

underapplied overhead, 90

REVIEW QUESTIONS

4.1 What are the characteristics of companies that are likely to use a job cost system?

4.2 Refer to the Real World Application "Manufacturing Overhead Cost Allocation Bases Used in the United States" on page 96. What are the most common allocation bases used in the United States? Why do you suppose they are used more than others?

4.3 What is the difference between the Manufacturing Overhead account and the Manufacturing Overhead Applied account?

4.4 What documents are used to obtain materials for production?

4.5 How is job costing in service organizations (for example, consulting firms) different from job costing in manufacturing organizations?

4.6 What are the costs of a product using normal costing?

4.7 Refer to the Real World Application about Stanford University on page 99. Why was Stanford's indirect cost rate reduced?

CRITICAL ANALYSIS AND DISCUSSION QUESTIONS

4.8 On the first day of the job, a member of the management training program remarked, "The whole procedure of applying overhead and then spending a lot of time adjusting the Inventory and Cost of Goods Sold accounts back to the actual numbers looks like a complex solution to a simple problem. Why not simply charge the actual overhead to production and be done with it?" How would you reply to this comment?

4.9 Why is control of materials important from a managerial planning perspective?

4.10 Refer to the Real World Application about the cost of movie flops on page 82. What would you do with the cost of flops?

4.11 Interview the manager of a construction company (for example, a company that does house construction, remodeling, landscaping, or street or highway construction) about how the company bids on prospective jobs. Does it use cost information from former jobs that are similar to prospective ones, for example? Does it have a specialist in cost estimation who estimates the costs of prospective jobs? Write a report to your instructor summarizing the results of your interview.

4.12 Interview the manager of a campus print shop or a print shop in the local area about how the company bids on prospective jobs. Does it use cost information from former jobs that are similar to prospective ones, for example? Does it have a specialist in cost estimation who estimates the costs of prospective jobs? Write a report to your instructor summarizing the results of your interview.

4.13 Would a dentist, an architect, a landscaper, and a lawyer use job costing or process costing? Explain.

4.14 For costing purposes, was the O. J. Simpson trial a job?

EXERCISES

 4.15   **Assigning Costs**
         to Jobs
         (L.0. 1)

The following transactions occurred in January at Apex, Inc., a job order custom manufacturer of furniture:

1. Purchased $10,000 of materials.

2. Issued $500 of supplies from the materials inventory.

3. Purchased $7,000 of materials.

4. Paid for the materials purchased in transaction (1).

5. Issued $8,500 in direct materials to the production department.

6. Incurred direct labor costs of $12,500, which were credited to Payroll Payable.

7. Paid $13,250 cash for utilities, power, equipment maintenance, and other miscellaneous
    items for the manufacturing plant.

8. Applied overhead on the basis of 125 percent of $12,500 direct labor costs.

9. Recognized depreciation on manufacturing property, plant, and equipment of $6,250.

Required   Prepare journal entries to record these transactions.

4.16   **Assigning Costs**   Refer to the data in Exercise 4.15. The following balances appeared in the accounts of Apex,
         to Jobs   Inc., for January:
         (L.0. 1)

	Beginning	Ending
Materials inventory	$18,525	
Work in process inventory	4,125	
Finished goods inventory	20,750	$17,900
Cost of goods sold	32,925	

Required   Prepare T-accounts to show the flow of costs during the period from materials inventory
                 purchases through cost of goods sold.

 4.17   **Assigning Costs**   Partially completed T-accounts and additional information for the Avian Company for the
         to Jobs   month of March follow.
         (L.0. 1)

Materials Inventory		
BB 3/1	2,000	
	8,000	6,400

Work in Process Inventory		
BB 3/1	4,000	
Direct labor	6,000	

Finished Goods Inventory		
BB 3/1	6,000	
	12,000	8,000

Cost of Goods Sold	

Manufacturing Overhead	
5,200	

Manufacturing Overhead Applied	

Additional Information
- Labor wage rate was $24 per hour.
- Manufacturing overhead is applied at $20 per direct labor hour.
- During the month, sales revenue was $18,000, and selling and administrative costs were
  $3,200.
- This company has no indirect materials or supplies.

Required
a. What was the amount of direct materials issued to production during March?

b. What was the amount of manufacturing overhead applied to products during March?

c. What was the cost of products completed during March?

d. What was the balance of the Work in Process Inventory account at the end of March?

e. What was the manufacturing overhead variance during March?

f. What was the operating profit for March?

4.18   Predetermined Overhead Rates (L.O. 2)

Kustom-Kraft, Inc., manufactures one product and accounts for costs using a job order cost system. You have obtained the following information from the corporation's books and records for the year ended December 31, year 1:

- Total manufacturing cost during last year (called *cost to manufacture*) was $500,000 based on actual direct material, actual direct labor, and applied manufacturing overhead on the basis of actual direct labor dollars.
- Manufacturing overhead was applied to work in process at 75 percent of direct labor dollars. Applied manufacturing overhead for the year was 33 percent of the total manufacturing cost during the year.

Required   Compute actual direct material used, actual direct labor, and applied manufacturing overhead. (Hint: The total of these costs is $500,000.)

4.19   Predetermined Overhead Rates (L.O. 2)

Xavier Corporation estimates its manufacturing overhead to be $44,000 and its direct labor costs to be $80,000 for year 1. The actual direct labor costs were $20,000 for Job 1, $30,000 for Job 2, and $40,000 for Job 3 during year 1; the actual manufacturing overhead was $52,000. Manufacturing overhead is applied to jobs on the basis of direct labor costs using predetermined rates.

Required
   a. How much overhead was assigned to each job during year 1?
   b. What was the manufacturing overhead variance for year 1?

4.20   Applying Overhead Using a Predetermined Rate (L.O. 2)

Paige Printing uses a job order cost system. The following debits (credits) appeared in the Work in Process account for May:

	Description	Amount
May 1	Balance	$ 5,000
Entire month	Direct materials	30,000
Entire month	Direct labor	20,000
Entire month	Factory overhead	16,000
Entire month	To finished goods	(60,000)

Paige Printing applies overhead to production at a predetermined rate of 80 percent based on direct labor cost. Job 75, the only job still in process at the end of May, has been charged with direct labor of $2,500.

Required   What was the amount of direct materials charged to Job 75?
   (1) $3,125.
   (2) $3,750.
   (3) $6,500.
   (4) $8,500.

(CPA adapted)

4.21   Calculating Overhead Variance (L.O. 2)

Owings Co. uses a predetermined factory overhead rate based on direct labor hours. For October, Owings' budgeted overhead was $600,000 based on a budgeted volume of 100,000 direct labor hours. Actual overhead amounted to $650,000 with actual direct labor hours totaling 110,000.

Required   How much was overhead overapplied or underapplied?
   (1) $10,000 overapplied.
   (2) $10,000 underapplied.
   (3) $60,000 overapplied.
   (4) $60,000 underapplied.

(CPA adapted)

4.22 Prorate Under-
or Overapplied
Overhead
(L.O. 2)

Refer to the information in Exercise 4.19. Prepare an entry to prorate the overhead variance as follows:

Work in process inventory	10%
Finished goods inventory	25
Cost of goods sold	65

4.23 Compute Job Costs
for a Service
Organization
(L.O. 3)

At the beginning of the month, Terne Corporation had two jobs in process that had the following costs assigned from previous months:

Job No.	Direct Labor	Applied Overhead
X-10	$1,280	?
Y-12	840	?

During the month, Jobs X-10 and Y-12 were completed but not billed to customers. The completion costs for X-10 required $1,400 in direct labor. For Y-12, $4,000 in labor was used.

During the month, a new job, Z-14, was started but not finished. No other new jobs were started. Total direct labor costs for all jobs amounted to $8,240 for the month. Overhead in this company refers to the cost of work that is not directly traced to particular jobs, including copying, printing, and travel costs to meet with clients. Overhead is applied at a rate of 50 percent of direct labor costs for this and previous periods. Actual overhead for the month was $4,000.

Required

a. What are the costs of Jobs X-10 and Y-12 at (1) the beginning of the month and (2) when completed?

b. What is the cost of Job Z-14 at the end of the month?

c. How much was the manufacturing overhead variance for the month?

4.24 Job Costing in a
Service
Organization
(L.O. 3)

For September, Ernest Peat & Company worked 600 hours for client A and 1,400 hours for client B. Ernest Peat bills clients at the rate of $140 per hour; labor cost for its audit staff is $70 per hour. The total number of hours worked in September was 2,000, and overhead costs were $20,000. Overhead is applied to clients at $12 per labor hour. In addition, Ernest Peat had $84,000 in marketing and administrative costs. All transactions are on account. All services were billed.

Required

a. Show labor and overhead cost flows through T-accounts.

b. Prepare an income statement for the company for September.

PROBLEMS

4.25 Estimate Hours
Worked from
Overhead Data

Grault Company had projected its fixed overhead costs at $120,000. Direct labor was estimated to total 30,000 hours during the year, and the direct labor hours would be used as a basis for applying overhead. During the year, all fixed overhead costs were exactly as planned ($120,000). There was $4,000 in overapplied overhead.

Required

How many direct labor hours were worked during the period? Show computations.

4.26 Assigning Costs—Missing Data

Materials Inventory

BB 10/1	16,000		
	(a)	8,600	
EB 10/31	19,400	(b)	

Finished Goods Inventory

BB 10/1	28,400		(f)
	(e)		
EB 10/31	(g)		

Work in Process Inventory

BB 10/1	44,600		
	361,000		
	242,000		
	188,000		
EB 10/31	35,400	(e)	

Cost of Goods Sold

805,600	

Manufacturing Overhead Applied

	(d)

Wages Payable

		BB 10/1	248,600
	324,000		(c)
			72,400
		EB 10/31	239,000

Manufacturing Overhead

242,000	
8,600	
72,400	
63,200	
6,400	

Accounts Payable—Materials Suppliers

	200,000

Accumulated Depreciation—Manufacturing Property, Plant, and Equipment

	BB 10/1	408,200
		(h)
	EB 10/31	471,400

Prepaid Insurance

BB 10/1	48,600		(i)
EB 10/31	42,200		

Required

Compute the missing amounts indicated by the letters (a) through (i).

The following T-accounts are to be completed with the missing information.

4.27 Assigning Costs—Missing Data

Materials Inventory

EB 9/30 28,200	

Work in Process Inventory

BB 9/1 16,300	
Direct materials 43,100	

Finished Goods Inventory

EB 9/30 50,500	

Cost of Goods Sold

Manufacturing Overhead

(Actual)	

Manufacturing Overhead Applied

	132,000

Wages Payable

Sales Revenue

	362,700

Additional Data

- Materials of $56,800 were purchased during the month, and the balance in the inventory account increased by $5,500.
- Overhead is applied at the rate of 150 percent of direct labor cost.
- Sales are billed at 180 percent of cost of goods sold before overhead variance is prorated.
- The balance in the Finished Goods Inventory account decreased by $14,300 during the month.

- Total credits to the Wages Payable account amounted to $101,000 for direct and indirect labor.
- Factory depreciation totaled $24,100.
- Overhead was underapplied by $12,540. Overhead other than indirect labor and depreciation was $99,240, which required payment in cash. Underapplied overhead is to be prorated.
- The company has decided to allocate 25 percent of underapplied overhead to Work in Process Inventory, 15 percent to Finished Goods Inventory, and the balance to Cost of Goods Sold. Balances shown in T-accounts are before proration.

Required

Complete the T-accounts.

4.28

Analysis of Overhead Using a Predetermined Rate: Multiple Choice

Sparkle Corporation uses a job costing accounting system for its production costs. A predetermined overhead rate based on direct labor hours is used to apply overhead to individual jobs. An estimate of overhead costs at different volumes was prepared for the current year as follows:

Direct labor hours	50,000	60,000	70,000
Variable overhead costs	$350,000	$420,000	$490,000
Fixed overhead costs	216,000	216,000	216,000
Total overhead	$566,000	$636,000	$706,000

The expected volume is 60,000 direct labor hours for the entire year. The following information is for November, when Jobs 50 and 51 were completed.

Inventories, November 1	
Raw materials and supplies.	$ 10,500
Work in process (Job 50)	54,000
Finished goods.	112,500
Purchases of raw materials and supplies	
Raw materials	135,000
Supplies	15,000
Materials and supplies requisitioned for production	
Job 50	45,000
Job 51	37,500
Job 52	25,500
Supplies	6,000
	$114,000
Factory direct labor hours (DLH)	
Job 50	3,500 DLH
Job 51	3,000 DLH
Job 52	2,000 DLH
Labor costs	
Direct labor wages (all hours @ $8).	$ 68,000
Indirect labor wages (4,000 hours).	17,000
Supervisory salaries	36,000
Building occupancy costs (heat, light, depreciation, etc.)	
Factory facilities	6,500
Sales and administrative offices	2,500
Factory equipment costs	
Power	4,000
Repairs and maintenance	1,500
Other	2,500
	$ 8,000

Required

Answer the following multiple-choice questions.

a. The predetermined overhead rate (combined fixed and variable) to be used to apply overhead to individual jobs during the year is
   (1) $7.00 per DLH.
   (2) $9.38 per DLH.
   (3) $10.10 per DLH.
   (4) $10.60 per DLH.
   (5) None of these.
   Note: Without prejudice to your answer to requirement (a), assume that the predetermined overhead rate is $9 per direct labor hour. Use this amount in answering requirements (b) through (e).

b. The total cost of Job 50 when it is finished is
   (1) $104,500.
   (2) $151,500.
   (3) $158,500.
   (4) $161,300.
   (5) None of these.

c. The factory overhead costs applied to Job 52 during November were
   (1) $18,000.
   (2) $47,500.
   (3) $46,500.
   (4) $8,000.
   (5) None of these.

d. The total amount of overhead applied to jobs during November was
   (1) $58,500.
   (2) $76,500.
   (3) $94,500.
   (4) $112,500.
   (5) None of these.

e. Actual factory overhead incurred during November was
   (1) $67,500.
   (2) $73,500.
   (3) $76,000.
   (4) $77,500.
   (5) None of these.

f. At the end of the year, Sparkle Corporation had the following account balances:

Overapplied Overhead	$ 1,000
Cost of Goods Sold	980,000
Work in Process Inventory	38,000
Finished Goods Inventory	82,000

What would be the most common treatment of the overapplied overhead, assuming that it is not material?
   (1) Prorate it between Work in Process Inventory and Finished Goods Inventory.
   (2) Prorate it between Work in Process Inventory, Finished Goods Inventory, and Cost of Goods Sold.
   (3) Carry it as a credit on the balance sheet.
   (4) Carry it as miscellaneous operating revenue on the income statement.
   (5) Credit it to Cost of Goods Sold.

(CMA adapted)

4.29 Finding Missing Data

A hysterical I. M. Dunce corners you in the hallway 30 minutes before accounting class. "Help me, help me!" I. M. pleads. "I woke up this morning and discovered that my pet German Shepherds Fifo and Lifo ate my homework, and these shredded pieces are all that I have left!" Being a kind and generous soul, you willingly declare, "There's no need to fear! I'm a real whiz at accounting and will be glad to help you." A relieved I. M. Dunce hands you the following torn homework remnants.

	Page 1
Direct labor hours used	375
Direct labor rate—$5 per hour	
Direct materials purchased	$ 5,250
Direct materials beginning inventory	$ 1,400

	Page 2
Manufacturing overhead (actual = applied)	$ 750
Beginning work in process inventory	1,500
Cost of goods manufactured	8,000
Ending finished goods inventory	3,000

	Page 3
Job remaining in ending work in process inventory	
Labor	$ 500
Direct materials	1,300
Overhead ($2 per labor hour)	200
Ending work in process inventory	$ 2,000
Total revenue	$13,500
Gross margin	4,000
Marketing and administrative costs	
Operating profit	1,000

Required

a. Prepare T-accounts to show the flow of costs and determine each of the following:
   (1) Marketing and administrative costs.
   (2) Cost of goods sold.
   (3) Beginning finished goods inventory.
   (4) Direct materials used.
   (5) Ending direct materials inventory.

b. Prepare an income statement.

4.30   Finding Missing Data

After a dispute concerning wages, Steve W. Ozniak contaminated the computerized accounting system at Czech Company with a virus that destroyed most of the company records. The computer experts at the company could recover only a few fragments of the company's factory ledger, as shown:

Direct Materials Inventory			Manufacturing Overhead	
BB 4/1	30,000			

Work in Process Inventory			Accounts Payable	
BB 4/1	9,000			
			EB 4/30	18,000

Finished Goods Inventory			Cost of Goods Sold	
EB 4/30	22,000			

Further investigation and reconstruction from other sources yielded the following additional information.

- The controller remembers clearly that actual manufacturing overhead costs are recorded at $6 per direct labor hour. (The company assigns actual overhead to WIP Inventory.)
- The production superintendent's cost sheets showed only one job in work in process inventory on April 30. Materials of $5,200 had been added to the job, and 300 direct labor hours had been expended at $12 per hour.
- The Accounts Payable are for direct materials purchases only, according to the accounts payable clerk. He clearly remembers that the balance in the account was $12,000 on

April 1. An analysis of canceled checks (kept in the treasurer's office) shows that payments of $84,000 were made to suppliers during the month.

- The payroll ledger shows that 5,200 direct labor hours were recorded for the month. The employment department has verified that there are no variations in pay rates among employees (this infuriated Steve, who believed that his services were underpaid).

- Records maintained in the finished goods warehouse indicate that the finished goods inventory totaled $36,000 on April 1.

- The cost of goods manufactured for April was $188,000.

Required   Determine the following amounts:

a. Work in process inventory, April 30.

b. Direct materials purchased during April.

c. Actual manufacturing overhead incurred during April.

d. Cost of goods sold for April.

4.31 Cost Accumulation: Service

White and Brite Dry Cleaners has five employees and a president, Hexter Strength. Hexter and one of the five employees manage all the marketing and administrative duties. The remaining four employees work directly on operations. White and Brite has four service departments: dry cleaning, coin washing and drying, special cleaning, and repairs. A time card is marked, and records are kept to monitor the time each employee spends working in each department. When business is slow, there is idle time, which is marked on the time card. (It is necessary to have some idle time because White and Brite promises 60-minute service, and it is necessary to have direct labor hours available to accommodate fluctuating peak demand periods throughout the day and the week.)

Some of the November operating data are as follows

	Idle Time	Dry Cleaning	Coin Washing and Drying	Special Cleaning	Repairs
Sales revenue		$4,625	$5,250	$2,000	$625
Direct labor (in hours)	25	320	80	125	90
Direct overhead traceable to departments					
Cleaning compounds		$500	$250	$400	$–0–
Supplies		125	200	175	140
Electric usage		250	625	100	25
Rent		200	500	90	10

Other Data

- The four employees working in the operating departments all make $8 per hour.

- The fifth employee, who helps manage marketing and administrative duties, earns $1,500 per month, and Hexter earns $2,000 per month.

- Indirect overhead amounted to $512 and is assigned to departments based on direct labor hours used. Because there are idle hours, some overhead will not be assigned to a department.

- In addition to salaries paid, marketing costs for such items as advertising and special promotions totaled $400.

- In addition to salaries, other administrative costs were $150.

- All revenue transactions are cash, and all others are on account.

Required   Management wants to know whether each department is contributing toward the company's profit. Prepare an income statement for November that shows the revenue and cost of services for each department. Write a short report to management about departmental profitability. No inventories were kept.

4.32 Job Costs: Service

For the month of May, Wehelp Consultants worked 1,000 hours for Nocando Manufacturing, 300 hours for Sails, Inc., and 500 hours for Original John's Restaurants. Wehelp bills clients at $80 an hour; its labor costs are $30 an hour. A total of 2,000 hours were worked in May with 200 hours not billable to clients. Overhead costs of $30,000 were incurred and were assigned to clients on the basis of direct labor hours. Because 200 hours were not billable, some overhead was not assigned to jobs. Wehelp had $20,000 in marketing and administrative costs. All transactions were on account.

Required	**a.** What are the revenue and cost per client?
	b. Prepare an income statement for May.

4.33 Job Costs in a Service Company

On June 1, two jobs were in process at McHale Painters, Inc. Details of the jobs follow:

Job No.	Direct Materials	Direct Labor
A-15	$174	$64
A-38	32	84

Materials inventory (for example, paint and sandpaper) on June 1 totaled $920, and $116 in materials were purchased during the month. Indirect materials of $16 were withdrawn from materials inventory. On June 1, finished goods inventory consisted of two jobs, Job A-07, costing $392, and Job A-21, with a cost of $158. Both of these jobs were transferred to Cost of Goods Sold during the month.

Also during June, Jobs A-15 and A-38 were completed. To complete Job A-15 required an additional $68 in direct labor. The completion costs for Job A-38 included $108 in direct materials and $200 in direct labor.

Job A-40 was started during the period but was not finished. A total of $314 of direct materials was used (excluding the $16 indirect materials) during the period, and total direct labor costs during the month amounted to $408. Overhead has been estimated at 150 percent of direct labor costs, and this relation has been the same for the past few years.

Required Compute costs of Jobs A-15 and A-38 and balances in the June 30 inventory accounts.

4.34 Tracing Costs in a Job Company

The following transactions occurred at Arrow Space, Inc., a defense contractor that uses job costing:

1. Purchased $71,600 in materials on account.
2. Issued $2,000 in supplies from the materials inventory to the production department.
3. Paid for the materials purchased in (1).
4. Issued $34,000 in direct materials to the production department.
5. Incurred wage costs of $56,000, which were debited to Payroll, a temporary account. Of this amount, $18,000 was withheld for payroll taxes and credited to Payroll Taxes Payable. The remaining $38,000 was paid in cash to the employees. See transactions (6) and (7) for additional information about Payroll.
6. Recognized $28,000 in fringe benefit costs, incurred as a result of the wages paid in (5). This $28,000 was debited to Payroll and credited to Fringe Benefits Payable.
7. Analyzed the Payroll account and determined that 60 percent represented direct labor; 30 percent, indirect manufacturing labor; and 10 percent, administrative and marketing costs.
8. Paid for utilities, power, equipment maintenance, and other miscellaneous items for the manufacturing plant totaling $43,200.
9. Applied overhead on the basis of 175 percent of *direct* labor costs.
10. Recognized depreciation of $21,000 on manufacturing property, plant, and equipment.

Required **a.** Prepare journal entries to record these transactions.

b. The following balances appeared in the accounts of Arrow Space, Inc.:

	Beginning	Ending
Materials inventory	$74,100	—
Work in process inventory	16,500	—
Finished goods inventory	83,000	$ 66,400
Cost of goods sold	—	131,700

Prepare T-accounts to show the flow of costs during the period.

4.35 Cost Flows through Accounts

Leevies Pants, Inc., employed 20 full-time workers at $5 per hour. Since beginning operations last year, it had priced the various jobs by marking up direct labor and direct material costs 20 percent. Despite operating at capacity, however, last year's performance was a great disappointment to the managers. In total, 10 jobs were accepted and completed, incurring the following total costs:

Direct materials	$103,540
Direct labor.	400,000
Manufacturing overhead	104,000

Of the $104,000 manufacturing overhead, 30 percent was variable overhead and 70 percent was fixed.

This year Leevies expects to operate at the same activity level as last year, and overhead costs and the wage rate are not expected to change.

For the first quarter of this year, Leevies had just completed two jobs and was beginning the third. The costs incurred follow:

Jobs	Direct Materials	Direct Labor Costs
111.	$13,720	$49,000
112.	9,300	31,240
113.	9,400	19,760
Total factory overhead		27,120
Total marketing and administrative costs		11,200

You are a consultant associated with Reengineering Management Consultants, which Leevies has asked for help. Its senior partner has examined Leevies' books and has decided to divide actual factory overhead by job into fixed and variable portions as follows:

	Actual Factory Overhead	
Jobs	Variable	Fixed
111	$2,990	$10,400
112	2,750	8,820
113	460	1,700
	$6,200	$20,920

In the first quarter of this year, 40 percent of marketing and administrative costs were variable and 60 percent were fixed. You are told that Jobs 111 and 112 were sold for $85,000 and $55,000, respectively. All over- or underapplied overhead for the quarter is expensed on the income statement.

Required

a. Present in T-accounts the full absorption, actual manufacturing cost flows for the three jobs in the first quarter of this year.

b. Using last year's overhead costs and direct labor hours as this year's estimate, calculate predetermined overhead rates per direct labor hour for variable and fixed overhead.

c. Present in T-accounts the full absorption, normal manufacturing cost flows for the three jobs in the first quarter of this year. Use the overhead rates derived in part (b).

d. Prepare income statements for the first quarter of this year under the following costing systems:
   (1) Full absorption, actual.
   (2) Full absorption, normal.

4.36

Show Flow of Costs to Jobs

Bright Equipment Company assembles light and sound equipment for installation in various entertainment facilities. An inventory of materials and equipment is on hand at all times so that installation may start as quickly as possible. Special equipment is ordered as required. On September 1, the Materials and Equipment Inventory account had a balance of $48,000. The Work in Process Inventory account is maintained to record costs of installation work not yet complete. There were two such jobs on September 1, with the following costs:

	Job 46 Wheels and Spokes Country Music Hall	Job 51 Stars Theater
Materials and equipment	$32,000	$95,000
Technician labor	6,500	9,700
Overhead (applied)	4,800	14,250

Overhead has been applied at 15 percent of the costs of materials and equipment installed. During September, two new installations were begun. Additional work was carried out on Jobs 46 and 51, with the latter completed and billed to Stars Theater. Details on the costs incurred on jobs during September follow:

		Job		
	46	51	55	56
Materials and equipment	$3,200	$14,200	$17,000	$6,200
Technician labor (on account)	1,800	1,200	3,100	900

Other Period Events

- Received $25,000 payment on Job 55 delivered to customer.
- Purchased materials and equipment for $18,700.
- Billed Stars Theater $175,000 and received payment for $100,000 of that amount.
- Determined that payroll for indirect labor personnel totaled $1,300.
- Issued supplies and incidental installation materials for current jobs costing $310.
- Recorded overhead and advertising costs for the installation operation as follows (all cash except equipment depreciation):

Property taxes.	$1,100
Showroom and storage area rental.	1,350
Truck and delivery cost	640
Advertising and promotion campaign	1,200
Electrical inspections	400
Telephone and other miscellaneous.	650
Equipment depreciation	900

Required

a. Prepare journal entries to record the flow of costs for the installation operation during September.

b. Calculate the amount of over- or underapplied overhead for the month. This amount is debited or credited to Cost of Goods Sold.

c. Determine inventory balances for Materials and Equipment Inventory and Work in Process Inventory.

4.37   Reconstruct Missing Data

Disaster struck the only manufacturing plant of Badomen Equipment, Inc., on December 1. All the work in process inventory was destroyed, but a few records were salvaged from the wreckage and from the company's headquarters. The insurance company has stated that it will pay the cost of the lost inventory if adequate documentation can be supplied. The insurable value of work in process inventory consists of direct materials, direct labor, and applied overhead.

The following information about the plant appears on the October financial statements at the company's headquarters:

Materials inventory, October 31.	$ 49,000
Work in process inventory, October 31	86,200
Finished goods inventory, October 31	32,000
Cost of goods sold through October 31	348,600
Accounts payable (materials suppliers) on October 31	21,600
Manufacturing overhead through October 31 . . .	184,900
Payroll payable on October 31	–0–
Withholding and other payroll liabilities on October 31	9,700
Overhead applied through October 31.	179,600

A count of the inventories on hand November 30 shows

Materials inventory.	$43,000
Work in process inventory	?
Finished goods inventory	37,500

The accounts payable clerk tells you that outstanding bills to suppliers totaled $50,100 and that cash payments of $37,900 were made to them during the month.

The payroll clerk informs you that the payroll costs last month for the manufacturing section included $82,400 of which $14,700 was indirect labor.

At the end of November, the following balances were available from the main office:

Manufacturing overhead through November 30 . . . . . . $217,000
Cost of goods sold through November 30   396,600

Recall that each month there is only one requisition for indirect materials. Among the fragments of paper, you located the following information:

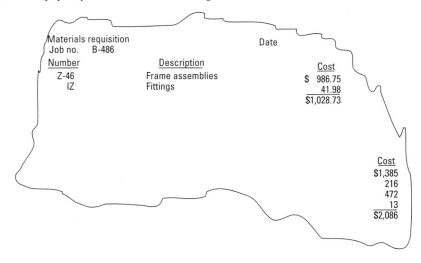

Materials requisition
Job no.   B-486   Date

Number	Description	Cost
Z-46	Frame assemblies	$ 986.75
IZ	Fittings	41.98
		$1,028.73

Cost
$1,385
216
472
13
$2,086

You also learn that the overhead during the month was overapplied by $1,200.

Required Determine the cost of the work in process inventory lost in the disaster.

4.38 Deriving Overhead Rates

Premier Pasta Company prepares, packages, and distributes six frozen pasta entrees in two different size containers. It prepares the different pastas and different sizes in large batches. It uses a normal costing job order costing system. Manufacturing overhead is assigned to batches by a predetermined rate on the basis of machine hours. The company incurred manufacturing overhead costs during two recent years (adjusted for changes using current prices and wage rates) as follows:

	Year 1	Year 2
Machine hours worked	1,380,000	1,080,000
Manufacturing overhead costs incurred		
Indirect labor	$11,040,000	$ 8,640,000
Employee benefits	4,140,000	3,240,000
Supplies	2,760,000	2,160,000
Power	2,208,000	1,728,000
Heat and light	552,000	552,000
Supervision	2,865,000	2,625,000
Depreciation	7,930,000	7,930,000
Property taxes and insurance	3,005,000	3,005,000
Total manufacturing overhead costs	$34,500,000	$29,880,000

Premier Pasta expects to operate at a level of 1.15 million machine hours in year 4. Using the data from the two recent years, write a report to management that shows the fixed and variable overhead rates used to assign manufacturing overhead to its products. (*Hint:* The variable rate can be found by comparing the change in costs to the change in hours.)

(CMA adapted)

4.39 Incomplete Data— Job Costing

Paige Printing, Inc., is a rapidly growing company that has not been profitable despite increases in sales. It has hired you as a consultant to find ways to improve the situation. You believe that the problem results from poor cost control and inaccurate cost estimation on jobs. To gather data for your investigation, you turn to the accounting system and find that it is almost nonexistent. However, you piece together the following information for April:

- Production:
    1. Completed Job 101.
    2. Started and completed Job 102.
    3. Started Job 103.
- Inventory values:
    1. Work in process inventory:

    March 31: Job 101
    Direct materials $2,000
    Labor (960 hours × $10) 9,600
    April 30: Job 103
    Direct materials $11,600
    Labor (1,040 hours × $10) 10,400

    2. Each job in work in process inventory was exactly 50 percent completed as to labor hours; however, all of the direct materials necessary to do the entire job were charged to each job as soon as it was started.
    3. There were no direct materials inventories or finished goods inventories at either March 31 or April 30.
- Actual manufacturing overhead was $20,000.
- Cost of goods sold (before adjustment for over- or underapplied overhead):

    Job 101
    Materials . . . . . . $ 2,000
    Labor . . . . ?
    Overhead . . . . . . ?
    Total $30,800

    Job 102
    Materials . . . . . . ?
    Labor . . . . ?
    Overhead . . . . . . ?
    Total . . . . ?

- Overhead was applied to jobs using a predetermined rate per labor dollar that has been used since the company began operations.
- All direct materials were purchased for cash and charged directly to Work in Process Inventory when purchased. Direct materials purchased in April amounted to $4,600.
- Direct labor costs charged to jobs in April were $32,000. All labor costs were the same per hour for April for all laborers.

Required

Write a report to management to show:

a. The cost elements (material, labor, and overhead) of cost of goods sold before adjustment for over- or underapplied overhead for each job sold.

b. The value of each cost element (material, labor, and overhead) for each job in work in process inventory at April 30.

c. Over- or underapplied overhead for April.

4.40 Job Costing and Ethics

Suzie Garcia, an accountant for a consulting firm, had just received the monthly cost reports for the two jobs she supervises: one for Arrow Space, Inc., and one for the U.S. government. She immediately called her boss after reading the figures for the Arrow Space job.

"We're going to be way over budget on the Arrow Space contract," she informed her boss. "The job is only about three-fourths complete, but we've spent all the money that we had budgeted for the entire job."

"You'd better watch these job costs more carefully in the future," her boss advised. "Meanwhile, charge the rest of the costs needed to complete the Arrow Space job to your U.S. government job. The government won't notice the extra costs. Besides, we get reimbursed for costs on the government job, so we won't lose any money on this problem you have with the Arrow Space contract."

Required   **a.** What should Suzie do?

               b. Does it matter that Suzie's company is reimbursed for costs on the U.S. government contract? Explain.

SOLUTIONS TO SELF-STUDY QUESTIONS

1. **a.** Materials Inventory   20,000
               Accounts Payable   20,000
        b. Work in Process Inventory   16,000
               Manufacturing Overhead   4,000
               Materials Inventory   20,000
        c. Work in Process Inventory   12,000
               Manufacturing Overhead   2,000
               Wages Payable   14,000
        d. Manufacturing Overhead   20,000
               Accounts Payable   12,000
               Accumulated Depreciation   8,000

e. Predetermined overhead   Estimated manufacturing overhead costs
        ───────────────────── = ──────────────────────────────────────
           application rate   Estimated direct materials used

$$= \frac{\$240{,}000}{\$160{,}000}$$

$$= \$1.50 \text{ per dollar of direct material}$$

The amount of overhead applied to each job is

        Job 1: $2,000 × $1.50 = $ 3,000
        Job 2: $8,000 × $1.50 = 12,000
        Job 3: $6,000 × $1.50 =   9,000
                                 $24,000

The journal entry to record this is

        Work in Process Inventory 24,000
          Manufacturing Overhead
          Applied   24,000

Accounts Payable			Materials Inventory					Work in Process Inventory		
	(1)	20,000	(1)	20,000	(2)	20,000	BB	11,000	
	(4)	12,000					(2)	16,000	
							(3)	12,000	
							(5)	24,000	

Wages Payable		
	(3)	14,000

Manufacturing Overhead			Manufacturing Overhead Applied		
(2)	4,000			(5)	24,000
(3)	2,000				
(4)	20,000				

Accumulated Depreciation		
	(4)	8,000

2. a. Finished Goods Inventory 44,000
  Work in Process Inventory   44,000
b. Cost of Goods Sold 44,000
  Finished Goods Inventory   44,000
  Accounts Receivable 54,000
  Sales Revenue   54,000
c. Manufacturing Overhead Applied 24,000
  Manufacturing Overhead Variance 2,000
   Manufacturing Overhead   26,000

Work in Process			Finished Goods			
	(1)	44,000	(1)	44,000	(2)	44,000

Accounts Receivable			Cost of Goods Sold		
(2)	54,000		(2)	44,000	

Manufacturing Overhead			Manufacturing Overhead Applied			Sales Revenue		
	(3)	26,000	(3)	24,000			(2)	54,000

Manufacturing Overhead Variance		
(3)	2,000	

3. (1) Overhead is prorated according to the amount of manufacturing overhead applied during the month. The amount can be calculated as follows:

Job	Manufacturing Overhead Applied in November	Percentage of Total[a]		Manufacturing Overhead Variance		Prorated Overhead
1	$ 3,000	12.5	×	$2,000	=	$ 250
2	12,000	50.0	×	2,000	=	1,000
3	9,000	37.5	×	2,000	=	750
	$24,000	100.0%				$2,000

   [a]12.5% = $3,000 ÷ $24,000, etc.

Jobs 1 and 2 were sold during the month. Only Job 3 remained in work in process inventory at the end of the month. The journal entry to prorate the overhead variance is

Cost of Goods Sold 1,250
Work in Process Inventory 750
  Manufacturing Overhead Variance   2,000

(2) If the entire variance is charged to Cost of Goods Sold, the journal entry is

Cost of Goods Sold 2,000
  Manufacturing Overhead Variance   2,000

Process Costing

LEARNING OBJECTIVES

After reading this chapter, you should be able to:

1. Explain the purpose of process costing.

2. Assign costs to products using the five-step process given two simple scenarios.

3. Assign costs to products using weighted-average costing.

4. Prepare and analyze a production cost report.

5. Assign costs to products using first-in, first-out costing.

6. Analyze the accounting choice between first-in, first-out, and weighted-average costing.

7. Know when to use process or job costing.

8. Compare and contrast operation costing with job costing and process costing (appendix).

ILLUSTRATION   5.1   **Comparison of Job and Process Costing**

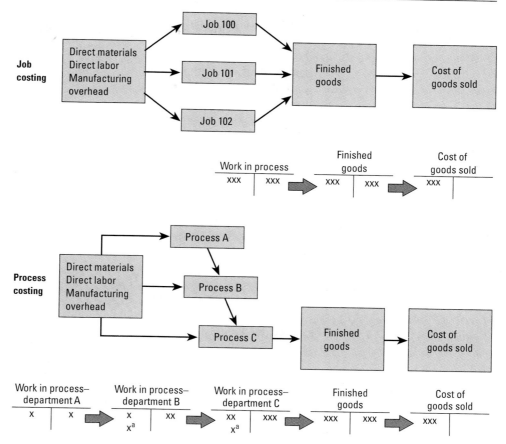

aDirect materials, labor, and manufacturing overhead added in production in the department.

L.O. 1: Explain the purpose of process costing.

process costing
A costing method that assigns costs equally to homogeneous units within a particular time period; used in continuous flow production settings.

Chapter 3 presented an overview of different production methods and accounting systems, and Chapter 4 focused on organizations that produce jobs. This chapter focuses on process costing methods. **Process costing** is used in companies having continuous flow production such as Coca-Cola (cola concentrate), Sherwin-Williams (paint), Shell (petroleum), and Dow Chemical (chemicals).

In job shops, costs are recorded for specific jobs. In continuous flow production, costs are first recorded for each department and then are assigned to the units (for example, gallons of cola concentrate) passing through the department. We show this distinction between job costing and process costing in Illustration 5.1; note that for process costing, at the bottom, costs are added to the product as it passes through each department. (Although the illustration shows the product passing through each department sequentially, some products might skip departments in practice. In some cases, products could even recycle back through departments if the work wasn't done right the first time.)

**WHY IT'S
IMPORTANT
TO HAVE COST
INFORMATION
TO MANAGE
PROCESSES**

Imagine that the consulting firm that hires you after graduation has sent you to help the manager of a Kellogg's cereal division. This manager is concerned that competitors that produce generic cereals are pricing their products substantially below Kellogg's prices. (In this case, the generic cereals are sold under a store's name, such as Safeway or IGA, or as generic cereal without a brand name.) Kellogg's expects to charge a premium because of its well-known brand name, but it knows it will lose market share if the generic cereals are much cheaper.

The manager of the Kellogg's division wants to cut prices to compete with generic cereals. He is concerned, however, that he might drop prices below costs. Your first task is to help the division improve its cost system so it will know how much each cereal product costs. That's what this chapter is about—learning the costs of products in a process (for items such as cereal).[1]

The costs assigned to products are commonly used to help set prices, particularly in periods of severe competition or economic downturn. These product costs also are used to identify which products appear to be too costly and should be redesigned or dropped.

Costs assigned to products are also used to determine inventory value for financial reporting purposes and to evaluate the efficiency of production operations.

ASSIGNING COSTS TO PRODUCTS

All Units Fully Completed (No Beginning or Ending WIP Inventory)

L.O. 2: Assign costs to products using the five-step process given two simple scenarios.

This chapter begins with two simple scenarios. The first one has no beginning or ending work in process (WIP) inventory. This is common when a company is successful at just-in-time production. Some companies schedule production so that they will have no inventory at the end of a day because work in process could deteriorate or spoil. (Consider a fast-food restaurant leaving partially completed hamburgers, french fries, and milkshakes overnight.)

Spirit Beverages produces a soft drink syrup. It sells this syrup to bottlers or to the fountain market (for example, restaurants or convenience stores). During October, the Blending Department, which had no beginning inventory, started 8,000 units (measured in gallons). The following were the plant's manufacturing costs for October:

Direct materials	$16,000
Conversion costs	5,600
Total costs to be assigned	$21,600

Spirit Beverages' process costing system has two cost categories: direct materials and conversion costs. Conversion costs represent direct labor and manufacturing overhead. All units placed into production in October were completed at the end of the month. The unit cost of goods completed is $21,600/8,000 = $2.70. Broken into components, manufacturing unit costs are as follows:

Direct materials ($16,000/8,000)	$2.00
Conversion costs ($5,600/8,000)	0.70
Manufacturing unit cost of a completed unit	$2.70

As shown, process costing systems do not track costs for each individual unit. Instead, they average the period's costs over its production. Consequently, managers should realize that if they have experienced large cost increases (or decreases) during the month, the average unit costs are probably out of line with the unit costs they face at the end of the month.

Some Units Not Fully Completed (Ending WIP Inventory Exists)

The facts for the second scenario are the same as for the first one with the exception that at the end of October, only 6,000 of the 8,000 units started had been completed and transferred out of production. These units were either sold or are still in the finished goods warehouse at the end of October. All direct materials had been added to each unit still in process, but on average only 20 percent of the conversion costs had been incurred for the 2,000 units in ending WIP inventory. How should the

---

[1]For examples of cost management in process companies, see "Targeting Costs in Process and Service Industries," *Harvard Business Review* 74, no. 1 (January/February 1996), p. 93.

Blending Department calculate for October (1) the cost of completed units and (2) the cost of WIP inventory not yet completed?

We assign costs to ending WIP inventory and to units completed (transferred out of WIP inventory) in five steps. These steps are as follows:

1. Summarize the flow of physical units.
2. Compute the equivalent number of units produced.
3. Summarize the total costs to be accounted for; these are the sum of the costs in beginning inventory and the costs incurred in the department during the period.
4. Compute costs per equivalent unit.
5. Assign costs to goods transferred out (completed) and to ending inventory (not completed).

For *step 1,* the flow of physical units, use the basic cost flow model to help account for units:

Beginning inventory + Transfers in − Transfers out = Ending inventory

In this case, there is no beginning inventory. Transfers in (or units started) total 8,000 units and transfers out (to finished goods) total 6,000 units. Thus, ending WIP inventory is 2,000 units (= 0 units at the beginning + 8,000 units started − 6,000 units transferred out).

equivalent units
The amount of work actually performed on products with varying degrees of completion, translated to the work required to complete an equal number of whole units.

Step 2 requires us to understand the concept of **equivalent units**, which is one of the keys to process costing. According to this concept, if two units were started at the beginning of a month and each was 50 percent finished at the end of the month, the cumulative work done on the two units that were each half done would be considered equivalent to the work done on one whole unit. Thus, for process costing purposes, the two half-finished units equal one equivalent unit. The equivalent unit concept is shown in Illustration 5.2, where two glasses of water one-half full are equivalent to one full glass.

The equivalent unit (E.U.) concept is common in many organizations. For example, university administrators often count the number of students in a department in terms of *full-time equivalents.* Two half-time students are considered to be one full-time equivalent.

Now we perform step 2 for Spirit Beverages. All direct materials had been added to each unit still in process, and only 20 percent of conversion costs (direct labor + manufacturing overhead) had been incurred.

- E.U. for direct materials totaled 8,000.
- E.U. for conversion costs totaled 6,400 units [6,000 completed and transferred to finished goods + 400 remaining in work in process (400 = 2,000 × 20% complete for conversion costs)].

ILLUSTRATION   5.2   Equivalent Unit Concept

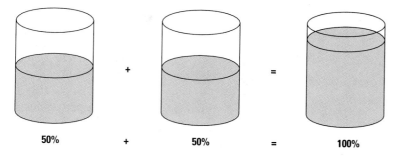

| 50% | + | 50% | = | 100% |

ILLUSTRATION 5.3	Equivalent Units		
		(Step 2) Equivalent Units	
Flow of Units	(Step 1) Physical Units	Direct Materials	Conversion Costs
Units to be accounted for			
Beginning work in process inventory	–0–		
Units started this period	8,000		
Total units to account for	8,000		
Units accounted for			
Completed and transferred out	6,000	6,000	6,000
In ending work in process inventory	2,000	2,000	400[a]
Total units accounted for	8,000	8,000	6,400

[a]2,000 units × 20% complete.

ILLUSTRATION 5.4	Production Costs		
Flow of Costs	Total	Direct Materials	Conversion Costs
Costs to be accounted for (Step 3)			
Costs in beginning work in process inventory	–0–	–0–	–0–
Current period costs	$21,600	$16,000	$5,600
Total costs to be accounted for	$21,600	$16,000	$5,600
Costs per equivalent unit (Step 4)		$ 2[a]	$0.875[b]
Costs accounted for (Step 5)			
Costs assigned to units transferred out	$17,250	$12,000[c]	$5,250[d]
Cost of ending inventory	4,350	4,000[e]	350[f]
Total costs accounted for	$21,600	$16,000	$5,600

[a]$2 = $16,000 ÷ 8,000 E.U. from Illustration 5.3.

[b]$0.875 = $5,600 ÷ 6,400 E.U. from Illustration 5.3.

[c]$12,000 = $2 × 6,000 E.U. from Illustration 5.3.

[d]$5,250 = $0.875 × 6,000 E.U. from Illustration 5.3.

[e]$4,000 = $2 × 2,000 E.U. from Illustration 5.3.

[f]$350 = $0.875 × 400 E.U. from Illustration 5.3.

Illustration 5.3 summarizes steps 1 and 2 for Spirit Beverages.

Note that direct materials just happen to be 100 percent complete with respect to ending WIP inventory in this example. In reality, direct materials might be added throughout the production process and therefore be partially complete for ending WIP inventory. If so, materials are treated like the conversion costs in this example.

Steps 3, 4, and 5 provide managers with the key cost information that appears in Illustration 5.4 for Spirit Beverages.

- Step 3 shows no beginning WIP inventory. Current period costs are separated into direct materials and conversion costs.
- Step 4 shows that total current period costs are divided by equivalent units to determine costs per equivalent unit. These unit costs are useful for managers to use in pricing and making decisions whether to keep or drop products. This

information would be helpful to the manager in your consulting job for Kellogg discussed at the beginning of the chapter.

- Step 5 shows costs assigned to units transferred out and costs assigned to units in WIP ending inventory. This information helps managers know how much money is tied up in inventory at the end of the period.

Now that you have learned how to account for costs in a process costing system under two relatively simple scenarios—one with no beginning and ending WIP inventory and the other with no beginning WIP inventory—we now discuss the more complex task of accounting for costs when beginning *and* ending work in process inventory exists.

ASSIGNING COSTS USING WEIGHTED-AVERAGE COSTING

L.O. 3: Assign costs to products using weighted-average costing.

weighted-average costing
The inventory method that for product costing purposes combines costs and equivalent units of a period with the costs and the equivalent units in beginning inventory.

Companies generally use one of two methods to assign costs to inventories in process costing when they have beginning inventory: first-in, first-out (FIFO) or weighted average. You probably have heard these terms before in other accounting classes. The basic idea here is the same.

Weighted-average costing combines the costs in beginning inventory with costs incurred during the period to compute unit costs. Many regard the weighted-average method as easier to learn and apply in practice, so we discuss it first.

To illustrate accounting for process costing using weighted-average costing, let's use the Spirit Beverages example but make a few changes in the facts. The new facts are shown in panel A of Illustration 5.5, which also shows a diagram of unit flows for the Blending Department for the month of December. Here are the facts:

- The department had 2,000 units in beginning WIP inventory, which it finished during the month.
- Of the 12,000 units that were started in December, 8,000 were finished, and the remaining 4,000 units were left in ending WIP inventory, partially completed.

For weighted-average costing, we do not have to know which of the finished units were from beginning inventory and which were started and finished in the current period. This saves considerable time and effort both in textbook problems and in real world applications.

Panel B of Illustration 5.5 shows the costs to be as follows:

- Beginning inventory $ 3,000
- Costs incurred in December   27,000

So the manager of the Blending Department has $30,000 to account for in December ($30,000 = $3,000 in beginning inventory + $27,000 in costs incurred during December).

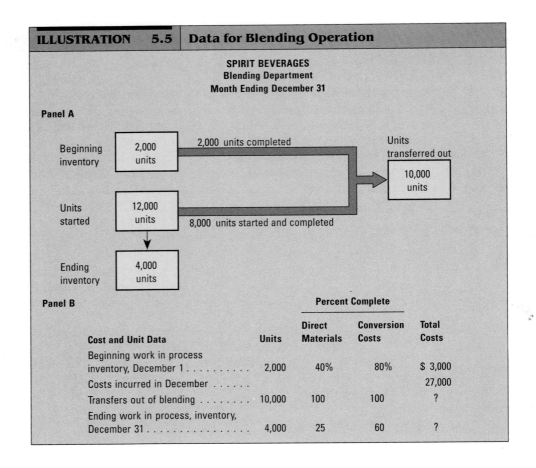

ILLUSTRATION 5.5 Data for Blending Operation

SPIRIT BEVERAGES
Blending Department
Month Ending December 31

Panel A

Beginning inventory — 2,000 units

2,000 units completed

Units started — 12,000 units

8,000 units started and completed

Ending inventory — 4,000 units

Units transferred out — 10,000 units

Panel B

Cost and Unit Data	Units	Direct Materials	Conversion Costs	Total Costs
Beginning work in process inventory, December 1	2,000	40%	80%	$ 3,000
Costs incurred in December				27,000
Transfers out of blending	10,000	100	100	?
Ending work in process, inventory, December 31	4,000	25	60	?

(Percent Complete spans Direct Materials and Conversion Costs columns)

Our problem is indicated by the question marks in Panel B of Illustration 5.5. How much of the $30,000 should be assigned to the 10,000 units transferred out and how much to the partially complete 4,000 units in the Blending Department's ending WIP inventory on December 31?

The Basic Idea: Applying the Basic Cost Flow Model

The basic cost flow model provides the underlying framework for solving the problem: How much of the cost incurred in the period to assign to units transferred out versus how much to assign to ending inventory.

$$\text{Beginning balance} + \text{Transfers in} - \text{Transfers out} = \text{Ending balance}$$
$$(BB) \qquad\qquad (TI) \qquad\qquad (TO) \qquad\qquad (EB)$$

The basic cost flow model can also be stated as follows:

$$BB + TI = TO + EB$$

We know that BB = $3,000 and TI = $27,000. By following the five-step process outlined earlier in this chapter, we are able to determine how much of these costs should be assigned to units transferred out and how much to units in ending inventory.

REAL WORLD APPLICATION	Canning Production Cycle for Coca-Cola®

The direct materials required for canning Coca-Cola are syrup, carbonated water, and cans. The bottler purchases syrup or a concentrate that it converts to syrup from the Coca-Cola Company and combines it with carbonated water in the first stage of production to make the liquid that is to be canned. At this point, materials costs are the costs of carbonated water and syrup.

In a separate process, empty cans are delivered to the plant where they are inspected and rinsed. They are filled with Coke® in the second stage, which requires only conversion costs. Tops are placed on the cans in the third stage, and then the filled cans are formed into cases of cans and packaged. This completes their journey through work in process. The product enters finished goods inventory when it is shipped to a warehouse. Cases of Coke become cost of goods sold when they are distributed to retail outlets.

Sources: Based on the authors' research and information provided by The Coca-Cola Company.

The Five Key Steps

Because this example is more complex than those used earlier in the chapter, we discuss the five-step process in detail here.

Step 1: Summarize the Flow of Physical Units

This step identifies the flow of physical units regardless of their stage of completion. This step has two parts: (1) units to be accounted for and (2) units accounted for. We identify these units for Spirit Beverages, as follows:

1. Units to account for
   - Units in beginning WIP inventory 2,000
   - Units started this period 12,000
   - Total units to account for 14,000

2. Units accounted for
   - Units transferred out 10,000
   - Units in ending WIP inventory 4,000
   - Total units accounted for. 14,000

This step indicates that we must account for the costs of 14,000 units, of which 2,000 were in beginning inventory and 12,000 were started during December. Of those 14,000 units, 10,000 were transferred out and 4,000 remained in ending inventory at December 31. The following summarizes the flow of physical units in terms of the basic cost flow model:

From 1.		From 2.
$BB + TI$	$=$	$TO + EB$
$2,000 + 12,000$	$=$	$10,000 + 4,000$

Step 2: Compute the Equivalent Units Produced

Some people find this step to be the most difficult part of process costing. We intend to make it as straightforward as possible.

Because Spirit Beverages' WIP inventories are at different stages of completion for direct materials and conversion costs, equivalent units must be calculated separately for direct materials and for conversion costs. Units transferred out are 100 percent completed (or they would not be transferred out!). Stages of completion for direct materials and conversion costs in ending inventory are given in Panel B of Illustration 5.5: Ending WIP inventory is 25 percent complete with respect to direct materials and 60 percent complete with respect to conversion costs.

Thus, equivalent units of work completed in December are computed as follows:

	Direct Materials	Conversion Costs
Units transferred out	10,000	10,000
Units in ending WIP inventory		
Materials: 4,000 × 25%	1,000	
Conversion: 4,000 × 60%		2,400
Total equivalent units	11,000	12,400

Managers review production reports such as the one we develop starting on page 128 to manage costs and production output. These reports are prepared at least once per month and sometimes weekly or even daily.

Note that these numbers indicate the equivalent units *completed* during the month. In general, it is possible that almost all work was done in previous periods, but the finishing touches were applied this period. These numbers don't tell managers how much work was done in the period, but they do tell the equivalent work *completed*. Of course, we know from the facts in this particular example that most of the work was done in December, but giving the equivalent units of work completed based on the weighted-average method would not have told the manager how much of the work equivalently completed in December was actually done in December compared to how much was done in November (or previous months). This lack of information about production in December would be a problem for a manager who wants information about worker productivity.

Step 3: Summarize the Total Costs to Be Accounted For

This step is easy. The total costs to be accounted for are those in beginning inventory plus those incurred during the period as shown in Panel B of Illustration 5.5. Assume that total costs are separated into direct materials and conversion costs as follows:

	Total Costs	Direct Materials	Conversion Costs
Costs to be accounted for			
Costs in beginning WIP inventory	$ 3,000	$ 2,000	$1,000
Current period costs.	27,000	20,000	7,000
Total costs to be accounted for	$30,000	$22,000	$8,000

This information indicates that $30,000 must be assigned either to products transferred out of the department or to ending WIP inventory.

Step 4: Compute Costs per Equivalent Unit

Costs per equivalent unit are calculated for direct materials (total costs = $22,000; equivalent units = 11,000) and conversion costs (total costs = $8,000; equivalent units = 12,400). The calculation is straightforward; simply divide total costs to be accounted for by equivalent units for each cost category as shown:

	Direct Materials	Conversion Costs
Total costs to be accounted for (from step 3)	$22,000	$ 8,000
Equivalent units (from step 2)	11,000	12,400
Cost per equivalent unit	$ 2.00	$ 0.645

This cost information helps managers make pricing and other managerial decisions.

Step 5: Assign Costs to Goods Transferred Out and to Ending Inventory

Now we have the data and computations needed to complete the task: divide the costs to be accounted for between goods transferred out and those in ending WIP inventory. To perform step 5, we multiply the cost per equivalent unit (computed in step 4) by the number of equivalent units in ending WIP inventory and transferred out for the period shown in step 2.

Costs accounted for as follows:

Transferred out	
Direct materials (10,000 units × $2)	$20,000
Conversion costs (10,000 units × $0.645)	6,450
Total transferred out	$26,450
Ending work in process, December 31	
Direct materials (1,000 E.U. × $2)	$ 2,000
Conversion costs (2,400 E.U. × $0.645)	1,550 (rounded)
Total work in process	$ 3,550
Total costs accounted for	$30,000

How to Check Our Work   Note the following equality:

$$\text{Total costs accounted for} = \text{Total costs to be accounted for}$$
$$\text{[Step 5]} \qquad\qquad\qquad \text{[Step 3]}$$

This equality must hold in every case (note that rounding may cause small discrepancies). Why must costs accounted for equal costs to be accounted for? Recall the principle of the basic cost flow model:

$$BB + TI = TO + EB$$

Costs to be accounted for represent the left side of the equation, $BB + TI$. The costs accounted for represent the right side of the equation, $TO + EB$.

How This Looks in T-Accounts

Although the computations do not require T-accounts, you may find it helpful for understanding the big picture if you see how costs flow through T-accounts. Illustration 5.6 shows the flow of costs through the WIP Inventory T-account for the Blending Department. The top panel shows the T-account as of the end of December after the costs incurred during the month were known but before completing the five steps to assign costs to ending inventory and transfers out. The bottom panel shows the T-account after completing step 5.

ILLUSTRATION   5.6   Cost Flows—Weighted Average

SPIRIT BEVERAGES
Blending Department
Month Ending December 31

Work in Process Inventory—Blending			Finished Goods Inventory or Next Department in Work in Process
Beginning inventory	3,000		
		Costs transferred out ? ⟶ ?	
Current period costs	27,000		
Ending inventory	?		

Work in Process Inventory—Blending			Finished Goods Inventory or Next Department in Work in Process
Beginning inventory	3,000		
		Costs transferred out 26,450 ⟶ 26,450	
Current period costs	27,000		
Ending inventory	3,550		

Reporting this Information to Managers: The Production Cost Report

L.O. 4: Prepare and analyze a production cost report.

production cost report
A report that summarizes production and cost results for a period; generally used by managers to monitor production and cost flows.

The **production cost report** summarizes the production and cost results for a period. It is an important document to managers for monitoring the flow of production and costs. Using this report, managers can determine whether inventory levels are getting too high, costs are not low enough, or the number of units produced is too low.

Illustration 5.7 presents a production cost report for the Blending Department of Spirit Beverages for December. Although it may look complex, you will soon see that this report simply includes the five steps for assigning costs to goods transferred out and to ending WIP inventory that we described earlier. To help relate the production cost report to those five steps, we present the report in five sections, each of which corresponds to a step.

Sections 1 and 2: Managing the Physical Flow of Units

Sections 1 and 2 of the production cost report correspond to steps 1 and 2 of the cost flow model. Section 1 summarizes the flow of physical units and shows 14,000 units to be accounted for, 10,000 as transfers out and 4,000 in ending inventory. Section 2 shows the equivalent units for direct materials and conversion costs separated into equivalent units transferred out and equivalent units remaining in WIP inventory.

Sections 3, 4, and 5: Managing Costs

Sections 3, 4, and 5 provide information about costs. Corresponding to step 3, section 3 shows the costs to be accounted for, $3,000 in beginning inventory and

| ILLUSTRATION | 5.7 | Production Cost Report—Weighted Average |

SPIRIT BEVERAGES
Blending Department
Month Ending December 31

	(Section 1) Physical Units	(Section 2) Equivalent Units	
		Direct Materials	Conversion Costs
Flow of Units			
Units to be accounted for			
Beginning WIP inventory	2,000		
Units started this period	12,000		
Total units to account for	**14,000**		
Units accounted for			
Completed and transferred out	10,000	10,000	10,000
In ending WIP inventory	4,000	1,000[a]	2,400[b]
Total units accounted for	**14,000**	**11,000**	**12,400**

	Costs (Sections 3 through 5)		
	Total	Direct Materials	Conversion Costs
Flow of Costs			
Costs to be accounted for (Section 3)			
Costs in beginning WIP inventory	$ 3,000	$ 2,000	$1,000
Current period costs	27,000	20,000	7,000
Total costs to be accounted for	**$30,000**	**$22,000**	**$8,000**
Costs per equivalent unit (Section 4)		$ 2.00[c]	$0.645[d]
Costs accounted for (Section 5)			
Costs assigned to units transferred out	$26,450	$20,000[e]	$6,450[f]
Cost of ending WIP inventory	3,550	2,000[g]	1,550[h]
Total costs accounted for	**$30,000**	**$22,000**	**$8,000**

[a]Ending inventory is 25 percent complete. 1,000 E.U. = 25% × 4,000 units.

[b]Ending inventory is 60 percent complete. 2,400 E.U. = 60% × 4,000 units.

[c]$2.00 = $22,000 ÷ 11,000 E.U.

[d]$0.645 = $8,000 ÷ 12,400 E.U.

[e]$20,000 = 10,000 E.U. × $2 per E.U.

[f]$6,450 = 10,000 E.U. × $0.645 per E.U.

[g]$2,000 = 1,000 E.U. × $2 per E.U.

[h]$1,550 (rounded) = 2,400 E.U. × $0.645 per E.U. + $2 rounding error.

$27,000 incurred during December. Section 4 shows how we computed the cost per equivalent unit for direct materials ($2.00) and conversion costs ($0.645). Finally, section 5 shows the cost assignment performed in step 5 for direct materials and conversion costs.

We now have assigned costs to units, shown cost flows through T-accounts and reported the steps performed on the production cost report. Having followed the five-step procedure in the text, you now have an opportunity to assign costs in the self-study question.

SELF-STUDY QUESTION

1. Green Earth Cleaners makes an environmentally sound household cleaner. The following data are available for the month of April:

	Units	Percent Complete	Costs
Beginning WIP inventory, April 1	1,000		
Direct materials.		75%	$ 3,200
Conversion costs.		70	1,450
Units started in April.	6,000		
Costs incurred in April			
Direct materials.			16,000
Conversion costs.			5,800
Ending WIP inventory	3,000		
Direct materials.		80	
Conversion costs.		60	

Using weighted-average process costing,
a. Derive the number of units transferred out.
b. Compute the amounts needed for each of the five steps described in the text.
c. Show the flow of costs through WIP Inventory T-account.
d. Prepare a production cost report.

The solution to this question is at the end of this chapter on page 156.

ASSIGNING COSTS TO PRODUCTS USING FIRST-IN, FIRST-OUT COSTING

What Are the Differences between FIFO and Weighted-Average Costing?

L.O. 5: Assign costs to products using first-in, first-out costing.

first-in, first-out costing
The inventory method whereby the first goods received are the first ones charged out when sold or transferred.

A disadvantage of weighted-average costing is that it mixes current period costs with the costs of products in beginning inventory, making it impossible for managers to know how much it cost to make a product *this period.* **First-in, first-out (FIFO) costing** assumes that the first units worked on are the first units transferred out of a production department. Whereas weighted-average costing mixes current period costs and costs from prior periods that are in beginning inventory, FIFO separates current period costs from those in beginning inventory. In FIFO costing, the costs in beginning inventory are transferred out in a lump sum (assuming that the units in beginning inventory were completed during the current period), not mingled with current period costs.

FIFO gives managers better information about the work done in the current period. Managers benefit from this separation of current period costs from costs in beginning inventory because they can identify and manage current period costs.

If the production process is a FIFO process, the inventory numbers are more likely to reflect reality under FIFO costing than under weighted-average costing because the units in ending inventory are likely to have been produced in the current period. FIFO costing assigns current period costs to those units, but weighted-average costing mixes current and prior period costs in assigning a value to ending inventory.

To illustrate accounting for process costing using FIFO, we use the data from the Spirit Beverages example. This enables you to compare FIFO and weighted-average costing and to see how the results differ. Recall the following facts:

	Units	Costs Direct Materials	Conversion Costs
Beginning WIP inventory	2,000	$ 2,000	$1,000
Current period	12,000	20,000	7,000
Transferred out	10,000	?	?
Ending WIP inventory	4,000	?	?

Remember that Panel B of Illustration 5.5 indicates that *beginning* WIP inventory is 40 percent complete for direct materials and 80 percent complete for conversion costs. It is also important to note that *ending* WIP inventory is 25 percent complete for direct labor and 60 percent complete for conversion costs.

The Five Key Steps   We combine the five-step procedure with the five sections of the production cost report to reduce redundancy in the presentation.

Step 1: Summarize the Flow of Physical Units

This step identifies the flow of physical units regardless of their stage of completion and is the same for both FIFO and weighted-average costing. Section 1 of the production cost report in Illustration 5.8 summarizes the flow of physical units, showing 14,000 units to be accounted for, 10,000 as transfers out of the Blending Department, and 4,000 units remaining in ending inventory.

Step 2: Compute the Equivalent Units Produced

Computing equivalent units is different in FIFO costing than in weighted-average costing. Recall that FIFO costing separates what was in beginning inventory from what occurs this period. The FIFO equivalent unit computation is confined only to what was produced this period. Under FIFO, we compute equivalent units in three parts for both direct materials and conversion costs:

1. Equivalent units to complete beginning WIP inventory.
2. Equivalent units of goods started and completed during the current period.
3. Equivalent units of goods still in ending WIP inventory.

For Spirit Beverages, 2,000 units in beginning inventory were 40 percent complete for direct materials and 80 percent complete for conversion costs at the beginning of the period. Completing the beginning inventory required 1,200 equivalent units for direct materials [(100% − 40%) × 2,000 units], and 400 equivalent units for conversion costs [(100% − 80%) × 2,000 units].

The units started and completed can be derived by examining the physical flow of units. Because 12,000 units were started and 4,000 of them remain in ending inventory, according to the FIFO method, the remaining 8,000 were completed. Thus, 8,000 units were started and completed. Another way to get the same result is to observe that of the 10,000 units completed during December, 2,000 came from beginning inventory (according to the FIFO method), so the remaining 8,000 units completed must have been started during December.

Either way you view the physical flow, 8,000 units were started and completed. Because these 8,000 units are 100 percent complete when transferred out of the department, the units started and completed represent 8,000 equivalent units produced during the current period for both direct materials and conversion costs.

Finally, we have the equivalent units of production in ending inventory.[2] Ending inventory of 4,000 units is 25 percent complete with respect to direct materials and 60 percent complete for conversion costs. Thus, there are 1,000 equivalent units (25% × 4,000) for direct materials in ending WIP inventory and 2,400 equivalent units (60% × 4,000) for conversion costs in ending WIP inventory. These equivalent unit results appear in section 2 of the production cost report in Illustration 5.8.

---

[2]For our examples, units in ending inventory come from the current period production. Although it is unlikely, you may encounter cases in practice when the inventory levels are so high relative to current period production that some of the beginning inventory is still in ending inventory. In that case, you should keep separate the costs and units in ending inventory that come from beginning inventory. Having separated those costs and units, you can perform the computations described in the text for the current period costs.

ILLUSTRATION	5.8	Production Cost Report—FIFO

SPIRIT BEVERAGES
Blending Department
Month Ending December 31

Flow of Units	(Section 1) Physical Units	(Section 2) Equivalent Units Direct Materials	Conversion Costs
Units to be accounted for			
Beginning WIP inventory	2,000		
Units started this period	12,000		
Total units to account for	**14,000**		
Units accounted for			
Units completed and transferred out			
From beginning WIP inventory	2,000	1,200[a]	400[b]
Started and completed currently	8,000	8,000	8,000
Total	10,000	9,200	8,400
Units in ending WIP inventory	4,000	1,000[c]	2,400[d]
Total units accounted for	**14,000**	**10,200**	**10,800**

Costs (Sections 3 through 5)

Flow of Costs	Total	Direct Materials	Conversion Costs
Costs to be accounted for (Section 3)			
Costs in beginning WIP inventory	$ 3,000	$ 2,000	$1,000
Current period costs	27,000	20,000	7,000
Total costs to be accounted for	**$30,000**	**$22,000**	**$8,000**
Costs per equivalent unit (Section 4)		1.961[e]	0.648[f]
Costs accounted for (Section 5)			
Costs assigned to units transferred out			
Costs from beginning WIP inventory	$ 3,000	$ 2,000	$1,000
Current costs added to complete beginning WIP inventory	2,612	2,353[g]	259[h]
Total costs from beginning WIP inventory	5,612	4,353	1,259
Current costs of units started and completed	20,872	15,688[i]	5,184[j]
Total costs transferred out	26,484	20,041	6,443
Cost of ending WIP inventory	3,516	1,959[k]	1,557[l]
Total costs accounted for	**$30,000**	**$22,000**	**$8,000**

[a]60 percent of costs must be added to complete beginning WIP inventory.

[b]20 percent of costs must be added to complete beginning WIP inventory.

[c]Ending WIP inventory for direct materials is 25 percent complete.

[d]Ending WIP inventory for conversion costs is 60 percent complete.

[e]$1.961 = $20,000 ÷ 10,200 E.U.

[f]$0.648 = $7,000 ÷ 10,800 E.U.

[g]$2,353 = 1,200 E.U. × $1.961 per E.U.

[h]$259 = 400 E.U. × $0.648 per E.U.

[i]$15,688 = 8,000 E.U. × $1.961 per E.U.

[j]$5,184 = 8,000 E.U. × $0.648 per E.U.

[k]$1,959 = (1,000 E.U. × $1.961 per E.U.) − 2 rounding error.

[l]$1,557 = (2,400 E.U. × $0.648 per E.U.) + 2 rounding error.

You will note that the equivalent units under FIFO are less than or equal to those under weighted average because the FIFO computations refer to this period's production only. Weighted-average equivalent units consider all units in the department, whether produced this period or in a previous period. (If the department has no beginning inventory, the weighted-average and FIFO equivalent units are equal.)

Step 3: Summarize the Total Costs to Be Accounted For

The total costs to be accounted for under FIFO costing are the same as in weighted-average costing. Whatever our assumption about cost flows, we must account for all costs in the department, composed of those in beginning inventory plus those incurred during the period. For Spirit Beverages, these costs are as follows:

	Total Costs	Direct Materials	Conversion Costs
Costs to be accounted for			
Costs in beginning			
WIP inventory	$ 3,000	$ 2,000	$1,000
Current period costs.	27,000	20,000	7,000
Total costs to be accounted for	$30,000	$22,000	$8,000

These costs are shown in section 3 of the production cost report in Illustration 5.8.

Step 4: Compute Costs per Equivalent Unit

Under FIFO, the costs per equivalent unit are confined to the costs incurred this period, $27,000, and the equivalent units produced this period, which were computed in step 2 (10,200 for direct materials and 10,800 for conversion costs). In formula form,

$$\text{Cost per equivalent unit} = \frac{\text{Current period costs}}{\text{Equivalent units of production this period}}$$

Note that only current period costs are included in the numerator. The FIFO method excludes the beginning WIP costs from the cost per equivalent unit calculation. Instead, beginning WIP inventory is assumed to be completed during the period and transferred out to finished goods.

For Spirit Beverages, the cost per equivalent unit under FIFO is calculated here. *Direct materials:*

$$\begin{aligned}\text{Cost per equivalent unit} &= \$20,000/10,200 \text{ equivalent units}\\ &= \$1.961 \text{ per equivalent unit}\end{aligned}$$

Conversion costs:

$$\begin{aligned}\text{Cost per equivalent unit} &= \$7,000/10,800 \text{ equivalent units}\\ &= \$0.648 \text{ per equivalent unit}\end{aligned}$$

The cost per equivalent unit appears in section 4 of the production cost report.

Step 5: Assign Costs to Goods Transferred Out and to Ending WIP Inventory

The cost of goods transferred out comprises the following components:

Costs in beginning WIP inventory (at beginning of period)	$ 3,000
Costs to complete beginning inventory	2,612
Cost of the 8,000 units started and completed this period	20,872
Cost of ending WIP inventory	3,516
Total costs accounted for.	$30,000

ILLUSTRATION   5.9   Cost Flows—FIFO

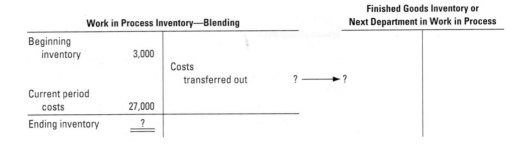

SPIRIT BEVERAGES
Blending Department
Month Ending December 31

Work in Process Inventory—Blending			Finished Goods Inventory or Next Department in Work in Process	
Beginning inventory	3,000	Costs transferred out ? ⟶ ?		
Current period costs	27,000			
Ending inventory	?			

Work in Process Inventory—Blending			Finished Goods Inventory or Next Department in Work in Process	
Beginning inventory	3,000	Beginning inventory costs transferred out ⟶ 3,000		
Current period costs	27,000	Current period costs transferred out ⟶ 23,484	26,484	
Ending inventory	3,516			

These results appear in section 5 of the production cost report. Note that the costs to be accounted for in section 3, $30,000, equal the costs accounted for in section 5, $30,000.

How This Looks in T-Accounts

Illustration 5.9 shows the flow of costs through the WIP Inventory T-account for the Blending Department using FIFO. The top panel shows the T-accounts as they appear before computing cost of goods transferred out and ending WIP inventory amounts. (Note the question marks, which indicate unknown amounts.) After the computations shown in the production cost report in Illustration 5.8, we complete the T-accounts as shown in the bottom panel of Illustration 5.9. It is helpful to use T-accounts to keep the big picture in mind when working on detailed computations such as those reported in Illustration 5.8.

SELF-STUDY QUESTION

2. We continue the example from Green Earth Cleaners. The data for April are repeated here. We have included the stage of completion of beginning inventory, which is needed to compute equivalent units using the FIFO method.

	Units	Percent Complete	Costs
Beginning WIP inventory, April 1	1,000		
Direct materials.		75%	$ 3,200
Conversion costs.		70	1,450
Units started in April.	6,000		
Costs incurred in April			
Direct materials.		80	16,000
Conversion costs.		60	5,800
Ending WIP inventory	3,000		

Using FIFO costing,

a. Determine the number of units transferred out.
b. Compute the amounts needed for each of the five steps described in the text.
c. Show the flow of costs through a T-account.
d. Prepare a production cost report.

The solution to this question is at the end of this chapter on page 157.

WHICH IS BETTER: FIFO OR WEIGHTED AVERAGE?

L.O. 6: Analyze the accounting choice between first-in, first-out, and weighted-average costing.

Weighted average costing does not separate beginning inventory from current period activity. Unit costs are a weighted average of the two, whereas under FIFO costing, unit costs are based on current period activity only. FIFO is typically advantageous when the number of units in beginning WIP inventory is large relative to the number of units started during the period. If this is not the case, beginning WIP inventory has little influence on the average unit cost using the weighted-average approach.

Illustration 5.10 compares the unit costs, costs transferred out, and ending WIP inventory values under the two methods for Spirit Beverages. Although either weighted-average or FIFO costing is acceptable for assigning costs to inventories and cost of goods sold for external reporting, the weighted-average method has been criticized for masking current period costs. Thus, using weighted-average costing, the unit costs reported for December are based not only on December's costs but also on the costs of previous periods that were in December's beginning inventory. For a company like Phillips Petroleum, which experiences changing crude oil prices, managers' decisions require knowledge of current period costs. If computational and recordkeeping costs are about the same under both FIFO and weighted average, FIFO costing is generally preferred.

TIME OUT: A SUMMARY OF THE FIVE KEY STEPS IN ASSIGNING COSTS TO UNITS

Illustration 5.11 summarizes the steps for assigning costs to units in process costing using FIFO and weighted-average costing. Notice how the steps correspond to the production cost report used by management to monitor production unit and cost flows.

COSTS TRANSFERRED IN FROM PRIOR DEPARTMENTS

Accounting for Transferred-In Costs

prior department costs
Manufacturing costs incurred in some other department and transferred to a subsequent department in the manufacturing process.

Our discussion so far has assumed a single department. Usually products pass through a series of departments, however. As the product passes from one department to another, its costs must follow.

The costs of units transferred out of one department and into another are called **prior department costs** or *transferred-in costs.* The costs of processing cereal at Kellogg is a prior department cost to the Packaging Department. Equivalent whole units are 100 percent complete in terms of prior department costs, so cost computations for prior department costs are relatively easy.

Let's go back to Spirit Beverages and change the assumptions to allow for prior department costs. Assume that the Blending Department's beginning WIP inventory came from another department. In this example, all the facts remain the same as in the previous one except that we include additional costs from the prior department and show these data under a new column, Prior Department's Costs. This column includes the prior department's costs associated with beginning WIP inventory of $5,000 and current costs (for goods transferred in from the prior department during the month) of $52,000. All other costs and physical units remain the same as in our original example. The following (bottom of page 136) summarizes the data. The new information is in bold.

ILLUSTRATION 5.10	Comparison of Weighted-Average and FIFO Costing	
	Weighted-Average (from illustration 5.7)	**FIFO** (from Illustration 5.8)
Equivalent unit costs		
Direct materials	$ 2.00	$ 1.961
Conversion costs	0.645	0.648
Cost of goods transferred out	26,450	26,484
Ending WIP inventory	3,550	3,516

ILLUSTRATION 5.11	Summary of Steps for Assigning Process Costs to Units

Step 1: Summarize the flow of physical units.

Step 2: Compute the equivalent units produced for direct materials and conversion costs.

Weighted average: E.U. produced = Units transferred out + E.U. in ending WIP inventory

FIFO: E.U. produced = E.U. to complete beginning WIP inventory + Units started and finished during the period + E.U. in ending WIP inventory

Step 3: Summarize the total costs to be accounted for.

Total costs to be accounted for = Costs in beginning WIP inventory + Costs incurred this period

Step 4: Compute costs per equivalent unit.

Weighted-average:

$$\text{Weighted-average unit cost} = \frac{\text{Costs in beginning WIP inventory} + \text{Current period costs}}{\text{Units transferred out} + \text{E.U. in ending WIP inventory}}$$

$$\textbf{FIFO:} \text{ Unit cost of current period work} = \frac{\text{Current period costs}}{\text{E.U. of current work done}}$$

Step 5: Assign costs to goods transferred out and to ending WIP inventory.

Weighted-average: Using weighted average, the cost of goods transferred out equals the total units transferred out times the weighted-average unit cost computed in step 4.

Using weighted average, the cost of goods in ending WIP inventory equals the equivalent units in ending WIP inventory times the weighted-average unit cost computed in step 4.

FIFO: Using FIFO, the cost of goods transferred out equals the sum of the following three items:

a. The costs already in beginning WIP inventory at the beginning of the period.

b. The current period cost to complete beginning WIP inventory, which equals the equivalent units to complete beginning WIP inventory from step 2 times the current period unit cost computed for FIFO in step 4.

c. The costs to start and complete units, calculated by multiplying the number of units started and finished from step 2 times the cost per equivalent unit computed for FIFO in step 4.

Using FIFO, the cost of goods in ending WIP inventory equals the equivalent units in ending WIP inventory from step 2 times the cost per equivalent unit computed for FIFO in step 4.

SPIRIT BEVERAGES
Blending Department
Month Ending December 31

| | | Prior Department's | Blending Department's Costs | |
| | | | Direct | Conversion |
	Units	Costs	Materials	Costs
Physical flow				
Beginning inventory	2,000	**100% complete**	40% complete	80% complete
Ending inventory	4,000	**100% complete**	25% complete	60% complete
Units started (**transferred in**)	12,000	**100% complete**		
Started and completed	8,000	**100% complete**	100% complete	100% complete
Costs incurred				
Beginning inventory		**$ 5,000**	**$ 2,000**	$1,000
Current costs		**52,000**	20,000	7,000

ILLUSTRATION 5.12	Production Cost Report with Prior Department Costs

SPIRIT BEVERAGES
Blending Department
Month Ending December 31

	(Section 1) Physical Units[a]	(Section 2) Equivalent Units		
		Prior Department Costs	Materials[a]	Conversion Costs[a]
Flow of Production Units				
Units to account for				
Beginning work in process inventory	2,000			
Units started this period	12,000			
Total units to account for	**14,000**			
Units accounted for				
Units completed and transferred out				
From beginning inventory	2,000	–0– [b]	1,200[b]	400[b]
Started and completed, currently	8,000	8,000	8,000	8,000
Units in ending WIP inventory	4,000	4,000	1,000	2,400
Total units accounted for	**14,000**	**12,000**	**10,200**	**10,800**

	Total Costs	Prior Department Costs	Materials[a]	Conversion Costs[a]
Flow of Costs				
Costs to be accounted for (Section 3)				
Costs in beginning WIP inventory	$ 8,000	$ 5,000	$ 2,000	$1,000
Current period costs	79,000	52,000	20,000	7,000
Total costs to be accounted for	**$87,000**	**$57,000**	**$22,000**	**$8,000**
Cost per equivalent unit (Section 4)				
Prior department costs ($52,000 ÷ 12,000) . .		$ 4.333		
Materials ($20,000 ÷ 10,200)			$ 1.961	
Conversion costs ($7,000 ÷ 10,800)				$0.648

Illustration continued on page 138.

Illustration 5.12 is a FIFO cost of production report that summarizes these data. As you review this report, notice that the prior department's costs are treated exactly as direct materials added at the beginning of a production process. Illustration 5.13 shows the flow of costs through the Blending Department using FIFO. You should be able to relate the costs in the production cost report to the T-accounts shown in Illustration 5.13.

Who Is Responsible for Costs Transferred In from Prior Departments?

An important question for performance evaluation is whether a department manager should be held accountable for all costs charged to the department. The answer is usually no. A department and its people are usually evaluated on the basis of costs added by the department relative to the good output from the department. Prior department's costs are often excluded when comparing actual department costs with a standard or budget. We discuss this point more extensively in later chapters on performance evaluation, but we mention it here to emphasize that different information is needed for different purposes. Assigning costs to units for inventory valuation requires that prior department's costs be included in department product cost

ILLUSTRATION 5.12 (concluded)	Production Cost Report with Prior Department Costs			
	Total Costs	Prior Department Costs	Materials[a]	Conversion Costs[a]
Flow of Costs				
Costs to be accounted for (Section 5)				
Costs assigned to units transferred out				
Costs from beginning WIP inventory	$ 8,000	$5,000	$2,000	$1,000
Current costs added to complete beginning WIP inventory				
Prior department costs	–0–	–0–		
Materials	2,353		2,353	
Conversion costs	259			259
Total costs to complete beginning inventory	2,612			
Costs of units started and completed				
Prior department costs (8,000 × $4.333)	34,664	34,664		
Materials	15,688		15,688	
Conversion costs	5,184			5,184
Total costs of units started and completed	55,536			
Total costs transferred out	66,148			
Costs assigned to ending WIP inventory				
Prior department costs	17,336	17,336[c]		
Materials	1,959		1,959	
Conversion costs	1,557			1,557
Total cost of ending WIP inventory . .	20,852			
Total costs accounted for	**$87,000**	**$57,000**	**$22,000**	**$8,000**

[a]See Illustration 5.8 for calculations.

[b]E.U. required to complete beginning inventory.

[c]Rounding error of $4 included in prior department's costs [$17,336 = (4,000 × $4.333) + $4 rounding error].

calculations. However, assigning costs to departments for performance evaluation usually requires that prior department's costs be excluded from departmental costs.

CHOOSING BETWEEN JOB AND PROCESS COSTING

L.O. 7: Know when to use process or job costing.

In job costing, costs are collected for each unit produced, as discussed in Chapter 4. For example, a print shop collects costs for each order, a defense contractor collects costs for each contract, and a custom home builder collects costs for each house. In process costing, costs are accumulated in a department for an accounting period (for example, a month) and then are spread evenly, or averaged, over all units produced that month. Process costing assumes that each unit produced is relatively uniform. The following example demonstrates a comparison of cost flows under each method.

Assume that Hobbes Company makes a customized product. In June, three jobs were started and completed (there were no beginning inventories). The manufacturing cost of each job follows:

ILLUSTRATION 5.13   Cost Flows with Prior Department Costs—FIFO Method

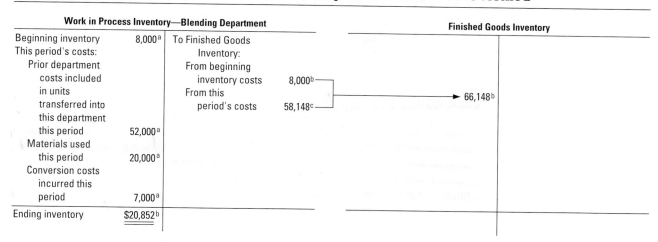

Work in Process Inventory—Blending Department			
Beginning inventory	8,000[a]	To Finished Goods Inventory:	
This period's costs:		From beginning inventory costs	8,000[b]
Prior department costs included in units transferred into this department this period	52,000[a]	From this period's costs	58,148[c]
Materials used this period	20,000[a]		
Conversion costs incurred this period	7,000[a]		
Ending inventory	$20,852[b]		

Finished Goods Inventory

66,148[b]

[a] See section 3 in the production cost report (Illustration 5.12).

[b] See section 5 in the production cost report (Illustration 5.12).

[c] Sum of total costs of units started and completed plus costs added to complete beginning WIP inventory.

ILLUSTRATION 5.14   Comparative Flow of Costs: Job and Process Costing

HOBBES COMPANY
June

Job Costing

Direct materials, direct labor, and manufacturing overhead	Work in Process Inventory		Finished Goods Inventory		Cost of Goods Sold	
	16,000	16,000	16,000	16,000	16,000	
	12,000	12,000	12,000			
	14,000	14,000	14,000			

Process Costing

Direct materials, direct labor, and manufacturing overhead	Work in Process Inventory		Finished Goods Inventory		Cost of Goods Sold	
	42,000	42,000	42,000	14,000[a]	14,000	

[a] $14,000 = \dfrac{1\ job}{3\ jobs} \times \$42,000.$

Job 10	$16,000
Job 11	12,000
Job 12	14,000
Total.	$42,000

Job 10 was sold; hence, the cost of goods sold in June is the cost of Job 10—$16,000. This flow of costs is shown in the top part of Illustration 5.14.

Suppose that Hobbes Company had used process costing. For convenience, assume that each job is defined to be a single unit of product. Total manufacturing costs were $42,000, so each unit is assigned a cost of $14,000. One unit was sold; hence, the cost of goods sold under process costing is the average cost of all three jobs—$14,000. This flow of costs is shown in the bottom part of Illustration 5.14.

Note that with process costing, Hobbes Company does not maintain a record of the cost of each unit produced. Process costing has less detailed recordkeeping; hence, if a company were choosing between job and process costing, it would generally find lower recordkeeping costs under process costing. Of course, process costing does not provide as much information as job costing because it does not record the cost of each unit produced. The choice of process versus job costing systems involves a comparison of the costs and benefits of each system. The production process being utilized is also a major factor in choosing a cost system.

A Cost-Benefit Comparison of Job and Process Costing

Consider a house builder. Under job costing, the costs must be accumulated for each house. It is not sufficient to record the total lumber delivered to several houses; records also must be kept of the amount subsequently returned from each house. If laborers work on several houses, they must keep track of the time they spend on each house. Process costing, however, simply requires recording the total costs incurred on all jobs. For the home builder, process costing records the average cost of all houses built. A custom home builder probably uses job costing. A developer might consider each development a job but use process costing for houses within each development.

Under process costing, the actual cost incurred for a particular unit is not reported. If all units are homogeneous, this loss of information is probably minimal. Is it important for Intel to know whether the cost of the 10,001st microprocessor chip is different from the 10,002nd? Probably not, particularly if the unit cost is calculated primarily to value inventory for external financial reporting. Cost control and performance evaluation take place by department, not by unit produced, in process systems. For companies like Intel making homogeneous units, the additional benefits of job costing do not justify the additional recordkeeping costs.

What if recordkeeping costs were equal under job and process systems for the units in a product line? Then we would say that job systems are better because they provide all of the data that process systems do, and more. As a general rule, job systems are usually more costly than process systems, however. Thus, managers and accountants must decide whether there are enough additional benefits (for example, better decisions) from knowing the actual cost of each unit, which is available in a job costing system, to justify additional recordkeeping costs. For companies producing relatively large, heterogeneous items, the additional benefits of job costing usually justify the additional costs.

SELF-STUDY QUESTION

3. FlyingFast, Inc., manufactures tennis rackets in two departments: frames and strings. Rackets are formed in the frames department. The completed frames are sent to the strings department where the rackets are strung and packaged for shipment to sporting goods stores. Six thousand frames were transferred to the strings department this month.

Because the rackets are homogeneous and manufactured in a continuous process, the company uses a process costing accounting system to assign costs to rackets. The following information is available for the strings department during October:

STRINGS DEPARTMENT
October

| | | Prior Department's Costs | This Department's Costs | |
	Units		Direct Materials	Conversion Costs
Physical flow				
Beginning inventory	1,000	100% complete	60% complete	75% complete
Ending inventory	2,700	100% complete	80% complete	45% complete
Transferred in	6,000	100% complete		
Costs incurred				
Beginning inventory		$ 7,100	$ 600	$ 420
Current costs		43,200	2,500	6,475

a. Prepare a production cost report for the strings department using FIFO.

b. Use a T-account to show the cost flows in the strings department using FIFO.

The solution to this question is at the end of this chapter on page 159.

SUMMARY

Process costing is used when it is not possible or practical to identify costs with specific lots or batches of product. The two most common methods of process costing are first-in, first-out (FIFO) costing and weighted-average costing. FIFO costing separates current period costs from the beginning inventory costs. The weighted-average method makes no distinction between beginning inventory and current period costs. As a result, weighted-average computations are simpler. The FIFO method is potentially more informative, however, because it tracks current and previous period costs separately.

Illustration 5.11 summarizes the steps required to assign costs to units. In comparing the weighted-average and FIFO methods, note the importance of matching costs with units. Weighted-average costing includes beginning inventory (that is, work done in a previous period) in computing both equivalent units and unit costs; FIFO costing excludes beginning inventory in computing equivalent units and unit costs.

Process costing systems accumulate costs for each production department but do not maintain separate records of costs for each unit produced. When comparing job and process costing, companies generally find that job costing provides more data but has higher recordkeeping costs. Managers and accountants must decide whether the additional data available under job costing justify these higher costs. For companies that produce relatively homogeneous units in a continuous process, cost-benefit analysis generally favors process costing.

The following summarizes key ideas tied to the chapter's learning objectives.

LO1: Purpose of process costing. Process costing is a costing method used for continuous flow production settings in which homogeneous units are produced within a specific time period.

LO2: Five-step process with no WIP inventory. Two simple scenarios—no beginning and no ending WIP inventory—allow us to compute product costs without having to select a method. Using these two examples, the five-step process is relatively simple.

LO3: Weighted-average costing. When beginning WIP inventory exists, we must choose between the weighted-average and FIFO costing methods. The five-step process is crucial in helping allocate production costs to finished goods inventory and ending WIP inventory.

LO4: Production cost report. The product cost report summarizes the costs allocated to finished goods inventory and ending WIP inventory. Managers use this report to monitor production and cost flows.

LO5: FIFO costing. The FIFO costing method assumes that all beginning WIP inventory is completed and transferred out during the period. Costs are tracked accordingly. The five-step process is also used for the FIFO method.

LO6: Choice between FIFO and weighted-average costing. Weighted-average costing does not separate beginning inventory from current period activity. Unit costs are a weighted average of the two, whereas under FIFO costing, unit costs are based on current period activity only. If computational and recordkeeping costs are about the same under both methods, FIFO costing is generally preferred.

LO7: Choosing between process or job costing. In general, job costing systems are more costly (and more accurate) than process costing systems. In deciding which system to use, accountants and managers must decide whether the benefits of implementing a job costing system outweigh the costs associated with such a system.

LO8: Operation costing (appendix). Operation costing is a hybrid of job and process costing and is typically implemented when different materials are used in the same production process.

KEY TERMS

equivalent units, 121	prior department costs, 135
first-in, first-out (FIFO) costing, 130	process costing, 119
operation,* 142	production cost report, 128
operating costing,* 142	weighted-average costing, 123

*Term appears in the appendix.

APPENDIX

L.O. 8: Compare and contrast operation costing with job costing and process costing (appendix).

operation costing
A hybrid costing system used in manufacturing goods that have some common characteristics and some individual characteristics.

operation
A standardized method of making a product that is repeatedly performed.

Operation Costing

Operation costing is a hybrid of job and process costing, as shown by Illustration 5.15. It is used in manufacturing goods that have some common characteristics plus some individual characteristics. An **operation** is a standardized method of making a product that is repeatedly performed. For example, an automobile assembly plant makes several models on the same assembly line. Each model has seat covers installed; installing them is an operation.

A company using operation costing typically uses a variety of different materials for products that pass through the same operation. Some automobiles have leather seats, others cloth seats. Whether the material is leather or cloth, the car passes through the same seat cover installation operation.

Companies such as Nike (shoes) and Volvo (automobiles) use operation costing. Van Heusen, a shirtmaker, has a cutting operation and a stitching operation for each shirt, although the materials (cotton, wool, polyester) for each type of shirt may differ.

Product Costing in Operations

The key difference between operation costing and the two methods discussed in this chapter and the previous chapter, job and process costing, is that for each work order

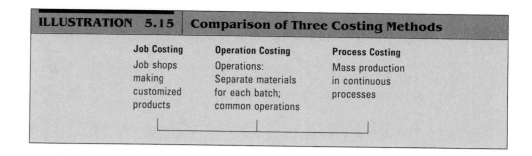

ILLUSTRATION   5.16   **Overview of Operation Costing**

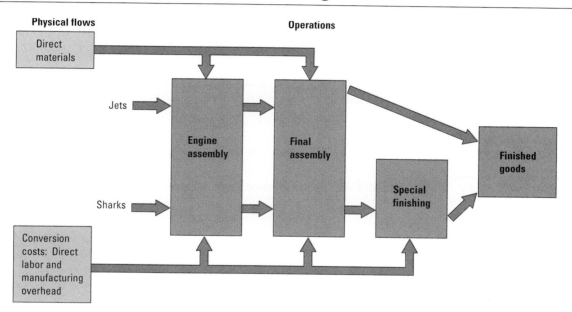

or batch passing through a particular operation, direct materials are different but conversion costs (direct labor and manufacturing overhead) are the same.

For example, assume that Yahonzi Motorcycle Company makes two models of motorcycles, Jets and Sharks. The Shark has a larger engine and generally more costly direct materials than the Jet. Illustration 5.16 shows the flow of products through departments (assume that each department has one operation). Note that Jets pass through only the first two departments, where operations are identical for both types of motorcycles, but Sharks pass through all three departments. Direct materials costs are added to both models in Engine Assembly and Final Assembly, but none are added to Sharks in Special Finishing. Conversion costs are added to Jets in the first two departments and to Sharks in all three departments. In principle, direct materials costs could be added in any operation. In this example, the direct materials costs are higher for Sharks.

Illustration of Operation Costing
Assume that Yahonzi Motorcycle Company management gave the following production work order for the month of March. Each work order is also called a *batch*.

YAHONZI MOTORCYCLE COMPANY

	Work Order 101	Work Order 102
Number and model of motorcycles	1,000 Sharks	2,000 Jets
Work order costs		
Direct materials		
Engine parts	$150,000	$200,000
Motorcycle parts, other than engines	200,000	300,000
Conversion costs (direct labor and manufacturing overhead)		
Engine assembly.	50,000	100,000
Final assembly	100,000	200,000
Special finishing	50,000	
Total costs.	$550,000	$800,000

Note that the materials costs per unit are more for Sharks than for Jets, but the conversion costs per unit are the same for the two operations that both models pass through. For example, engine assembly conversion costs are $50 per motorcycle for both models ($50 = $50,000/1,000 units for Sharks and $50 = $100,000/2,000 units for Jets).

Illustration 5.17 shows the flow of these costs through T-accounts to Finished Goods Inventory. In practice, direct labor and manufacturing overhead could be

---

ILLUSTRATION   5.17   Cost Flows through T-Accounts for Operation Costing

YAHONZI MOTORCYCLE COMPANY

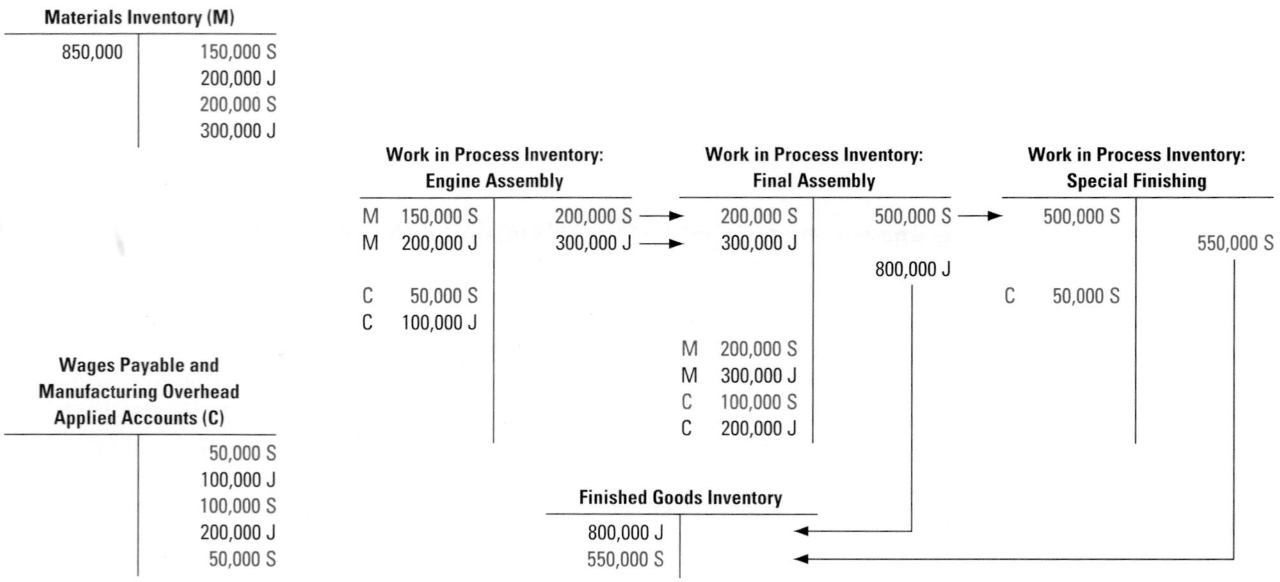

S = Sharks.

J = Jets.

M = Direct materials, credit to Materials Inventory.

C = Conversion costs, credit to Wages Payable and Manufacturing Overhead Applied Accounts.

Note: Amounts for Sharks are in color.

combined as they were in a Japanese motorcycle company that the author studied. Direct labor and manufacturing overhead could be charged separately to production as well. In many companies, direct labor is such a small portion of the total product cost that the accountants classify direct labor as part of manufacturing overhead. For example, in numerous high-tech companies, such as Hewlett-Packard, direct labor is less than 5 percent of total manufacturing costs in many operations.

Transactions The journal entries for applying costs to the Sharks follow; they are shown in color in Illustration 5.17. The same entries (with different numbers, of course) are used for the Jets, except that no entry is made for Work in Process Inventory: Special Finishing because Jets skip that operation.

1. First, direct materials are requisitioned for engine assembly as shown by the following entry debiting Work in Process (WIP) Inventory: Engine Assembly (the top amount on the debit side of the account in Illustration 5.17):

WIP Inventory: Engine Assembly	150,000	
Materials Inventory		150,000

2. Conversion costs for Engine Assembly are recorded as follows:

WIP Inventory: Engine Assembly	50,000	
Wages Payable and Manufacturing Overhead Applied Accounts		50,000

3. After assembly the engines are sent to Final Assembly where they are combined with other components to build the motorcycle. The costs transferred are the sum of entries 1 and 2. The transfer of the costs of assembled engines from Engine Assembly to Final Assembly is

WIP Inventory: Final Assembly	200,000	
WIP Inventory: Engine Assembly		200,000

   This entry is shown in Illustration 5.17 as the top numbers on the debit side of WIP Inventory: Final Assembly and the credit side of WIP Inventory: Engine Assembly.

4. The materials added in Final Assembly are recorded as follows:

WIP Inventory: Final Assembly	200,000	
Materials Inventory		200,000

5. The conversion costs incurred in Final Assembly to assemble motorcycles are as follows:

WIP Inventory: Final Assembly	100,000	
Wages Payable and Manufacturing Overhead Applied Accounts		100,000

6. After the Sharks are assembled, they are transferred to Special Finishing. A total of $500,000 costs has been accumulated in Final Assembly for Work Order 101, which is the total of the costs recorded in entries 3, 4, and 5. The entry to reflect the transfer of the motorcycles in Work Order 101 in Special Finishing is

WIP Inventory: Special Finishing	500,000	
WIP Inventory: Final Assembly		500,000

7. Work Order 101 requires $50,000 of conversion costs and no direct materials costs in Special Finishing. The entry to record these conversion costs is

WIP Inventory: Special Finishing	50,000	
Wages Payable and Manufacturing Overhead Applied Accounts		50,000

8. Now the entire manufacturing cost of Work Order 101 has been incurred, and the following entry transfers it to Finished Goods Inventory:

Finished Goods Inventory	550,000	
WIP Inventory: Special Finishing . .		550,000

Companies generally apply manufacturing overhead using predetermined overhead rates. As noted in previous chapters, when using predetermined rates, overhead can be overapplied or underapplied compared to actual manufacturing overhead. The over- or underapplied overhead is treated as an expense or allocated to inventories if the goods are still in inventory, as explained in Chapter 4.

Comparison of Job Costing, Process Costing, and Operation Costing

We have discussed how to account for product costs in three types of organizations: job shops, like construction companies, that use job costing; organizations with continuous flow processing, like soft drink syrup manufacturers, that use process costing; and companies with operations, like automobile manufacturers, that use operation costing. Operation costing combines the aspect of job costing that assigns materials separately to jobs (also called *work orders* or *batches* in operation costing) with the aspect of process costing that assigns conversion costs equally to each operation. Thus, in our motorcycle example, Sharks had different per unit materials costs but the same operations costs per unit for the two operations that both models passed through.

In practice, you are likely to find elements of all three production methods, and thus you will find elements of all three costing methods. Also, you will find that every company has its own unique costing methods that do not precisely fit any textbook description. Having studied these three basic costing methods will enable you to figure out the variations on the methods presented here.

SELF-STUDY QUESTION

4. Show the journal entries for the Jets motorcycles (Work Order 102) using the data given in the example in the text.

The solution to this question is at the end of this chapter on page 160.

REVIEW QUESTIONS

5.1 Why are equivalent units computed for process costing?

5.2 A manufacturing company has records of its current activity in WIP inventory and of its ending work in process inventory; however, the record of its beginning inventory has been lost. What data are needed to compute the beginning inventory? Express it in equation form.

5.3 If costs change from one period to another, costs that are transferred out of one department under FIFO costing will include units with two different costs. Why?

5.4 What is the distinction between equivalent units under the FIFO method and equivalent units under the weighted-average method?

5.5 It has been said that prior department's costs behave similarly to direct materials costs. Under what conditions are the costs similar? Why account for them separately?

5.6 Assume that the number of units transferred out of a department is unknown. What is the formula to solve for units transferred out using the basic cost flow model?

CRITICAL ANALYSIS AND DISCUSSION QUESTIONS

5.7 Management of a company that manufactures cereal is trying to decide whether to install a job or process costing system. The manufacturing vice president has stated that job costing gives them the best control because it is possible to assign costs to specific lots of goods. The controller, however, has stated that job costing requires too much recordkeeping. Would a process costing system meet the manufacturing vice president's control objectives? Explain.

5.8 Farleigh O. Tuvit is a new member of the controller's staff in your company. Farleigh has just completed a report that urges the company to adopt the last-in, first-out (LIFO) method for inventory accounting. The controller is concerned about the recommendation because the cost records are maintained on a FIFO basis. Indeed, the controller has not even heard of using LIFO for process cost accounting. Can you suggest how the controller might resolve the problem?

5.9 Refer to the Real World Application on page 125. What are the materials and the conversion process at each stage of production for canning such soft drinks? Describe them.

5.10 Under which of the following conditions will the first-in, first-out method of process costing produce the same cost of goods manufactured as the weighted-average method?
(1) When goods produced are homogeneous.
(2) When there is no beginning inventory.
(3) When there is no ending inventory.
(4) When beginning and ending inventories are each 50 percent complete.

(CPA adapted)

5.11 An error was made in the computation of the percentage of completion of the current year ending WIP inventory. The error resulted in assigning a lower percentage of completion to each component of the inventory than actually was the case. Assume that there was no beginning inventory. What is the effect of this error upon
a. The computation of total equivalent units?
b. The computation of costs per equivalent unit?
c. Costs assigned to cost of goods transferred out for the period?

Choose one of the four options in the following table for each of the three items above:

	a.	b.	c.
(1)	Understate	Overstate	Overstate
(2)	Understate	Understate	Overstate
(3)	Overstate	Understate	Understate
(4)	Overstate	Overstate	Understate

(CPA adapted)

5.12 In computing the cost per equivalent unit, the weighted-average method considers
(1) Current costs only.
(2) Current costs plus costs in beginning WIP inventory.
(3) Current costs plus cost of ending WIP inventory.
(4) Current costs less costs in beginning WIP inventory.

(CPA adapted)

5.13 When using the FIFO method of process costing, total equivalent units produced for a given period equal the number of units:
(1) Started and completed during the period, plus the number of units in beginning WIP, plus the number of units in ending WIP.
(2) In beginning WIP plus the number of units started during the period, plus the number of units remaining in ending WIP times the percentage of work necessary to complete the items.
(3) In beginning WIP times the percentage of work necessary to complete the items, plus the number of units started and completed during the period, plus the number of units started this period and remaining in ending WIP times the percentage of work necessary to complete the items.

(4) Transferred out during the period plus the number of units remaining in ending WIP times the percentage of work necessary to complete the items.

(5) None of these.

(CPA adapted)

EXERCISES

5.14 Compute Equivalent Units—Weighted-Average Method (L.O. 3)

A company that makes shampoo shows the following information concerning its work in process:

1. Beginning inventory, 3,500 partially complete units.
2. Transferred out, 9,000 units.
3. Ending inventory (materials are 10 percent complete; conversion costs are 15 percent complete).
4. Started this month, 12,000 units.

Required
a. Compute the equivalent units for materials using the weighted-average method.
b. Compute the equivalent units for conversion costs using the weighted-average method.

5.15 Compute Equivalent Units—FIFO Method (L.O. 5)

Refer to the data in Exercise 5.14. Assume that beginning inventory is 20 percent complete with respect to materials and 15 percent complete with respect to conversion costs.

Required
a. Compute the equivalent units for materials using FIFO.
b. Compute the equivalent units for conversion costs using FIFO.

5.16 Compute Equivalent Units—Weighted-Average Method (L.O. 3)

Tom & Jerry's Ice Cream Company shows the following information concerning the WIP at its plant:

1. Beginning inventory was partially complete.
2. Transferred out, 30,000 units.
3. Ending inventory, 10,000 units (materials are 25 percent complete; conversion costs are 15 percent complete).
4. Started this month, 35,000 units.

Required
a. Compute the equivalent units for materials using weighted average.
b. Compute the equivalent units for conversion costs using weighted average.

5.17 Compute Equivalent Units—FIFO Method (L.O. 5)

Refer to the data in Exercise 5.16. Assume that beginning inventory is 55 percent complete with respect to materials and 70 percent complete with respect to conversion costs.

Required
a. Compute the equivalent units for materials using FIFO.
b. Compute the equivalent units for conversion costs using FIFO.

5.18 Compute Equivalent Units—Weighted-Average Method (L.O. 3)

Keanu Co. adds materials at the beginning of the process in Department K. The following information pertains to Department K's work in process during April:

	Units
Work in process, April 1 (60% complete as to conversion costs)	6,000
Started in April	50,000
Completed	40,000
Work in process, April 30 (75% complete as to conversion costs)	16,000

Required

Under the weighted-average method, the equivalent units for conversion costs are
a. 52,000.
b. 50,000.

c. 48,400.

d. 43,600.

(CPA adapted)

5.19

Compute
Equivalent Units—
FIFO Method
(L.O. 5)

Alyssa Co. has a process costing system using the FIFO cost flow method. All materials are introduced at the beginning of the process in Department 1. The following information is available for the month of January.

	Units
Work in process, January 1 (40% complete as to conversion costs)	250
Started in January	1,000
Transferred to Department 2 during January	1,050
Work in process, January 31 (25% complete as to conversion costs)	200

Required

What are the equivalent units of production for the month of January?

	Materials	Conversion
a.	1,250	1,100
b.	1,250	850
c.	1,000	1,100
d.	1,000	1,000

(CPA adapted)

5.20

Compute Costs per
Equivalent Unit—
Weighted-Average
Method
(L.O. 3)

The following information pertains to Alexis Co.'s plant for the month of May:

	Number of Units	Cost of Materials
Beginning work in process	60,000	$11,000
Started in May	160,000	35,200
Units completed	170,000	
Ending work in process	50,000	

All materials are added at the beginning of the process.

Required

Using the weighted-average method, the cost per equivalent unit for materials is

a. $0.21.

b. $0.24.

c. $0.42.

d. $0.44.

e. Some other answer.

(CPA adapted)

5.21

Compute
Equivalent Units—
FIFO Method
(L.O. 5)

Department A is the first stage of Juan Co.'s production cycle. The following information is available for conversion costs for the month of April:

	Units
Beginning work in process (60% complete)	40,000
Started in April	680,000
Completed in April and transferred to Department B	640,000
Ending work in process (40% complete)	80,000

Required

Using the FIFO method, the equivalent units for the conversion cost calculation are

a. 640,000.

b. 648,000.

c. 672,000.

d. 720,000.

(CPA adapted)

5.22 Compute Costs per Equivalent Unit— Weighted-Average Method (L.O. 3)

Assume that a Pepsi-Cola bottling plant uses the weighted-average method to account for its WIP inventories. The accounting records show the following information for a particular day:

Beginning WIP inventory	
Direct materials	$488
Conversion costs	136
Current period costs in work in process	
Direct materials	$5,720
Conversion costs	3,322

Quantity information is obtained from the manufacturing records and includes the following (each unit equals 24 cans of Pepsi-Cola):

Beginning inventory.	150 units (partially complete)
Current period units started	1,000 units
Ending inventory.	300 units
Percent of completion	
Direct materials 40%	
Conversion costs 20%	

Required

Compute the cost per equivalent unit for direct materials and conversion costs.

5.23 Assign Costs to Goods Transferred Out and Ending Inventory— Weighted-Average Method (L.O. 3)

Refer to the data in Exercise 5.22. Compute the cost of goods transferred out and the ending inventory using the weighted-average method.

5.24 Compute Costs per Equivalent Unit— FIFO Method (L.O. 5)

Using the data in Exercise 5.22, compute the cost per equivalent unit for direct materials and for conversion costs using the FIFO method. Assume that beginning inventory is 60 percent complete with respect to materials and 30 percent complete with respect to conversion costs.

5.25 Assign Costs to Goods Transferred Out and Ending Inventory— FIFO Method (L.O. 5)

Refer to the data in Exercises 5.22 and 5.24. Compute the cost of goods transferred out and the ending inventory using the FIFO method.

5.26 Compute Costs per Equivalent Unit— Weighted-Average Method (L.O. 3)

Creative Paints Co. had beginning WIP inventory of $124,160 on October 1. Of this amount, $50,820 was the cost of direct materials, and $73,340 were conversion costs. The 8,000 units in the beginning inventory were 30 percent complete with respect to both direct materials and conversion costs.

During October, 17,000 units were transferred out and 5,000 remained in the ending inventory. The units in the ending inventory were 80 percent complete with respect to direct materials and 40 percent complete with respect to conversion costs. Costs incurred during the period amounted to $390,600 for direct materials and $504,640 for conversion.

Required

Compute the cost per equivalent unit for direct materials and for conversion costs using the weighted-average method.

5.27 Assign Costs to Goods Transferred Out and Ending Inventory— Weighted-Average Method (L.O. 3)

Refer to the data in Exercise 5.26. Compute the costs of goods transferred out and the ending inventory using the weighted-average method.

5.28 Compute Costs per Equivalent Unit—FIFO Method (L.O. 5)

Refer to the data in Exercise 5.26. Compute the cost per equivalent unit for direct materials and for conversion costs using the FIFO method. Are these unit costs higher or lower under weighted average compared to FIFO? Why?

5.29 Assign Costs to Goods Transferred Out and Ending Inventory—FIFO Method (L.O. 5)

Refer to the data in Exercise 5.26. Compute the cost of goods transferred out and the cost of ending inventory using the FIFO method. Is the ending inventory higher or lower under weighted average compared to FIFO? Why?

5.30 Prepare a Production Cost Report—FIFO Method (L.O. 4, 5)

The following information appears in the records of the Overland Company:

WIP inventory—Department 2
Beginning inventory
Prior department costs ...... $14,500   3,000 units (100% complete)
Department 2 costs......... 3,906   20% complete
Current work
Prior department costs 32,900   7,000 units (100% complete)
Department 2 costs......... 74,340

The ending inventory has 1,000 units, which are 45 percent complete with respect to Department 2 costs and 100 percent complete for prior department costs.

Required   Prepare a production cost report using FIFO.

5.31 Prepare a Production Cost Report—Weighted-Average Method (L.O. 3, 4)

Refer to the information in Exercise 5.30.

Required

a. Prepare a production cost report using the weighted-average method.

b. Is the ending inventory higher using FIFO or weighted average? Why?

PROBLEMS

5.32 Compute Equivalent Units

Select the best answer for each of the following independent multiple-choice questions.

a. Spinelli Corporation's production cycle starts in the First Department. The following information is available for April:

	Units
Work in process, April 1 (30% complete)	25,000
Started in April	120,000
Work in process, April 30 (40% complete)	12,500

Materials are added at the beginning of the process in the First Department. Using the weighted-average method, what are the equivalent units of production for the month of April?

	Materials	Conversion
(1)	120,000	130,000
(2)	145,000	137,500
(3)	132,500	132,500
(4)	140,000	135,000
(5) None of the above.		

b. Second Department is the second stage of Hurley Company's production cycle. On May 1, beginning work in process contained 50,000 units, which were 80 percent complete as to conversion costs. During May, 320,000 units were transferred in from the first stage of the production cycle. On May 31, ending WIP contained 40,000 units, which were 90 percent complete as to conversion costs. Materials are added at the end of the process. Using the weighted-average method, the equivalent units produced on May 31 were as follows:

	Prior Dept Costs	Materials	Conversion Costs
(1)	320,000	330,000	366,000
(2)	370,000	330,000	326,000
(3)	370,000	330,000	370,000
(4)	370,000	330,000	366,000

(5) None of the above.

c. Department A is the first stage of Drax Corporation's production cycle. The following information is available for conversion costs for the month of April:

	Units
Beginning WIP (60% complete)	16,000
Started in April	272,000
Completed in April and transferred to Department B	256,000
Ending WIP (40% complete)	32,000

Using the FIFO method, the equivalent units for the conversion cost calculation are
(1) 256,000.
(2) 259,200.
(3) 268,800.
(4) 288,000.
(5) None of the above.

d. Dressler Corporation computed the physical flow of units for Department A for the month of April as follows:

Units completed:	
From WIP on April 1	10,000
From April production	35,000
Total	45,000

Materials are added at the beginning of the process. Units of WIP at April 30 were 8,000. As to conversion costs, WIP at April 1 was 70 percent complete and at April 30 was 50 percent complete. What are the equivalent units produced for the month of April using the FIFO method?

	Materials	Conversion Costs
(1)	43,000	42,000
(2)	43,000	43,000
(3)	53,000	50,000
(4)	53,000	51,000

(5) None of the above.

(CPA adapted)

5.33   Multiple Choice— FIFO Method

The following questions are based on the Grease Department of the Spirit Petroleum Corporation. Conversion costs for this department were 80 percent complete as to beginning WIP and 50 percent complete as to ending WIP. Information about conversion costs for January is as follows:

	Units	Conversion Costs
WIP at January 1 (80% complete)	50,000	$ 86,000
Units started and costs incurred during January	270,000	484,000
Units completed and transferred to next department during January	200,000	—

The company uses FIFO in the Grease Department.

Required

a. What was the conversion cost of WIP in the Grease Department at January 31?
(1) $121,000.
(2) $130,000.
(3) $132,000.
(4) $155,000.
(5) None of the above.

b. What were the conversion costs per equivalent unit produced last period and this period, respectively?
(1) $2.15 and $2.59.
(2) $2.15 and $2.20.
(3) $2.20 and $2.20.
(4) $2.20 and $2.59.
(5) None of the above.

(CPA adapted)

5.34

Prepare a
Production
Cost Report—
Weighted-Average
Method

Baja Corporation is a manufacturer that uses the weighted-average process costing method to account for costs of production. Baja manufactures a child's car seat produced in three separate departments: Molding, Assembling, and Finishing. The following information was obtained for the Assembling Department for the month of June.

Work in process, June 1—1,000 units made up of the following:

	Amount	Degree of Completion
Prior department costs transferred in from the Molding Department.	$32,000	100%
Costs added by the Assembling Départment		
Direct materials	$20,000	100
Direct labor.	7,200	60
Manufacturing overhead	5,500	50
	32,700	
Work in process, June 1	$64,700	

During the month of June, 5,000 units were transferred in from the Molding Department at a prior department cost of $160,000. The Assembling Department added the following $150,000 of costs:

Direct materials	$ 96,000
Direct labor.	36,000
Manufacturing overhead	18,000
	$150,000

Four thousand units were completed and transferred to the Finishing Department.

At June 30, 2,000 units were still in WIP. The degree of completion of WIP at June 30 was as follows:

Direct materials	90%
Direct labor.	70
Manufacturing overhead	35

Required

a. Prepare a production cost report using the weighted-average method.

b. Management would like to decrease the costs of manufacturing the car seat. In particular, it has set the following per unit targets for this product in the Assembling Department: Materials—$20, labor—$10, and manufacturing overhead—$4.50. Has the product achieved management's cost targets in the Assembling Department? Write a short report to management stating your answer(s).

(CPA adapted)

5.35 Prepare a Production Cost Report— FIFO Method

5.36 Prepare a Production Cost Report and Adjust Inventory Balances— Weighted-Average Method

Refer to the facts in Problem 5.34.

a. Prepare a production cost report using FIFO.

b. Answer requirement (b) in Problem 5.34.

Lakeview Corporation's unaudited records show the following ending inventory balances, which must be adjusted to actual costs:

	Units	Unaudited Costs
Work in process inventory	300,000	$ 660,960
Finished goods inventory	200,000	1,009,800

As the auditor, you have learned the following information. Ending work in process inventory is 50 percent complete with respect to conversion costs. Materials are added at the beginning of the manufacturing process, and overhead is applied at the rate of 60 percent of the direct labor costs. There was no finished goods inventory at the start of the period. The following additional information is also available:

		Costs	
	Units	Direct Materials	Direct Labor
Beginning inventory (80% complete as to labor)	200,000	$ 200,000	$ 315,000
Units started	1,000,000		
Current costs		1,300,000	1,995,000
Units completed and transferred to finished goods inventory.	900,000		

Required

a. Prepare a production cost report for Lakeview Corporation using weighted-average. (Hint: You will need to calculate equivalent units for 3 categories—materials, labor, and overhead.)

b. Show the journal entry required to correct the difference between the unaudited records and actual ending balances of Work in Process Inventory and Finished Goods Inventory. Debit or credit Cost of Goods Sold for any difference.

c. If the adjustment in requirement (b) had not been made, would the company's income and inventories have been overstated or understated?

(CPA adapted)

5.37 Show Cost Flows—FIFO Method

Bran-U-Flake Company uses continuous processing to produce cereals and FIFO process costing to account for its production costs. It uses FIFO because costs are quite unstable due to the volatile price of materials. The cereals are processed through one department. Overhead is applied on the basis of direct labor costs, and the application rate has not changed over the period covered by the problem. The WIP Inventory account showed the following balances at the start of the current period:

Direct materials	$ 65,500
Direct labor	130,000
Overhead applied	162,500

These costs were related to 26,000 units that were in the process at the start of the period.

During the period, 30,000 units were transferred to finished goods inventory. Of the units finished this period, 70 percent were sold. After units have been transferred to finished goods inventory, no distinction is made between the costs to complete beginning WIP inventory and the costs of goods started and completed in WIP this period.

The equivalent units for materials this period were 25,000 (using FIFO). Of these, 5,000 were equivalent units with respect to materials in the ending WIP inventory. Materials costs incurred during the period totaled $150,200.

Conversion costs of $643,500 were incurred this period for 31,250 equivalent units (using FIFO). The ending inventory consisted of 11,000 equivalent units of conversion costs. The actual manufacturing overhead for the period was $330,000.

Required

Prepare T-accounts to show the flow of costs in the system. Any difference between actual and applied overhead of the period should be debited or credited to Cost of Goods Sold.

5.38   Prepare a
Production
Cost Report
and Show Cost
Flows through
Accounts—
FIFO Method

Required

Malcolm Corporation has devised a process for converting garbage into liquid fuel. The direct materials costs are zero, but the operation requires the use of direct labor and overhead. The company uses a process costing system and tracks the production and costs of each period. At the start of the current period, 1,000 units in WIP inventory were 40 percent complete and were carried at a cost of $840.

During the month, costs of $36,000 were incurred, 9,000 units were started and 500 units were still in process at the end of the month. The ending units were 20 percent complete.

a.   Use FIFO to prepare a production cost report.

b.   Show the flow of costs through T-accounts. Assume that current period conversion costs are credited to Various Payables.

c.   Management is concerned that production costs are rising and would like to see them held to less than $4 per unit. Has the company achieved management's target? Write a short report to management stating your answer.

5.39   Solving for
Unknowns—
FIFO Method

For each of the following independent cases, use FIFO costing to determine the information requested.

a.   Beginning inventory amounted to 500 units. This period 2,250 units were started and completed. At the end of the period, the 1,500 units in inventory were 30 percent complete. Using FIFO costing, the equivalent production for the period was 2,800 units. What was the percentage of completion of the beginning inventory?

b.   The ending inventory included $8,700 for conversion costs. During the period, 4,200 equivalent units were required to complete the beginning inventory, and 6,000 units were started and completed. The ending inventory represented 1,000 equivalent units of work this period. FIFO costing is used. What were the total conversion costs incurred this period?

c.   In the beginning inventory, 1,000 units were 40 percent complete with respect to materials. During the period, 8,000 units were transferred out. Ending inventory consisted of 1,400 units that were 70 percent complete with respect to materials. How many units were started and completed during the period?

d.   At the start of the period, 8,000 units were in the work in process inventory and 6,000 units were in the ending inventory. During the period, 19,000 units were transferred out to the next department. Materials and conversion costs are added evenly throughout the production process. FIFO costing is used. How many units were started this period?

5.40   Solving for
Unknowns—
Weighted-Average
Method

For each of the following independent cases, determine the units or equivalent units requested (assuming weighted-average costing).

a.   In the beginning inventory 4,100 units were 40 percent complete with respect to conversion costs. During the period, 3,500 units were started. In the ending inventory, 3,250 units were 20 percent complete with respect to conversion costs. How many units were transferred out?

b.   The beginning inventory consisted of 4,000 units with a direct materials cost of $14,200. The equivalent work represented by all of the direct materials costs in the WIP Inventory account amounted to 18,000 units. There were 6,000 units in ending inventory that were 20 percent complete with respect to materials. The ending inventory had a direct materials cost assigned of $4,500. What was the total materials cost incurred this period?

c.   The WIP Inventory account had a beginning balance of $1,900 for conversion costs on items in process and during the period $18,100 in conversion costs were charged to it. Also during the period, $19,200 in costs were transferred out. There were 400 units in the beginning inventory, and 4,800 units were transferred out during the period. How many equivalent units are in the ending inventory?

d.   During the period, 1,050 units were transferred to the department. The 1,600 units transferred out were charged to the next department at an amount that included $3,360 for direct materials costs. The ending inventory was 25 percent complete with respect to direct materials and had a cost of $630 assigned to it. How many units are in the ending inventory?

SOLUTIONS TO SELF-STUDY QUESTIONS

1. a. From the basic cost flow model, $BB + TI - TO = EB$, solve for TO:

$$BB + TI - TO = EB$$
$$1,000 + 6,000 - TO = 3,000$$
$$TO = 1,000 + 6,000 - 3,000$$
$$TO = 4,000 \text{ units}$$

b. Step 1: Summarize the flow of physical units:

Units to account for	
Units in beginning WIP inventory	1,000
Units started this period	6,000
Total units to account for	7,000
Units accounted for	
Units transferred out	4,000
Units in ending WIP inventory	3,000
Total units accounted for	7,000

Step 2: Compute the equivalent units produced.

	Direct Materials	Conversion Costs
Units transferred out	4,000	4,000
Units in ending WIP inventory		
3,000 × 80%	2,400	
3,000 × 60%		1,800
Total equivalent units	6,400	5,800

Step 3: Summarize the total costs to be accounted for.

	Total Costs	Direct Materials	Conversion Costs
Costs to be accounted for			
Costs in beginning WIP inventory	$ 4,650	$ 3,200	$1,450
Current period costs.	21,800	16,000	5,800
Total costs to be accounted for	$26,450	$19,200	$7,250

Step 4: Cost per equivalent unit:

	Direct Materials	Conversion Costs
Total costs to be accounted for (from step 3)	$19,200	$7,250
Equivalent units (from step 2)	6,400	5,800
Cost per equivalent unit.	$ 3.00	$ 1.25

Step 5: Assign costs to goods transferred out and to ending inventory:

Costs accounted for as follows	
Transferred out	
Direct materials (4,000 × $3.00)	$12,000
Conversion costs (4,000 × $1.25)	5,000
Total transferred out	$17,000
Work in process, December 31	
Direct materials (2,400 × $3.00)	$ 7,200
Conversion costs (1,800 × $1.25)	2,250
Total work in process	$ 9,450
Total costs accounted for	$26,450

c. Cost flows through T-account

Work in Process Inventory

Beginning inventory	4,650			
		Transfers out	17,000 →	to Finished Goods Inventory
Current period costs	21,800			
Ending inventory	9,450			

d. Production cost report—weighted average:

	(Section 1)	(Section 2) Equivalent Units	
Flow of Units	Physical Units	Direct Materials	Conversion Costs
Units to be accounted for			
Beginning WIP inventory	1,000		
Units started this period.	6,000		
Total units to account for.	7,000		
Units accounted for			
Completed and transferred out. . .	4,000	4,000	4,000
In ending WIP inventory . . .	3,000	2,400	1,800
Total units accounted for	7,000	6,400	5,800

Flow of Costs	**Total**	**Direct Materials**	**Conversion Costs**
Costs to be accounted for (Section 3)			
Costs in beginning WIP inventory . . .	$ 4,650	$ 3,200	$1,450
Current period costs.	21,800	16,000	5,800
Total costs to be accounted for . .	$26,450	$19,200	$7,250
Costs per equivalent unit (Section 4)		$ 3.00	$ 1.25
Costs accounted for (Section 5)			
Costs assigned to units transferred out. . .	$17,000	$12,000	$5,000
Cost of ending WIP inventory . . .	9,450	7,200	2,250
Total costs accounted for	$26,450	$19,200	$7,250

2. **a.** The physical flow of units is the same using either the weighted-average or FIFO method. The calculations are as follows. From the basic cost flow model, $BB + TI - TO = EB$, solve for TO:

$$BB + TI - TO = EB$$
$$1,000 + 6,000 - TO = 3,000$$
$$TO = 1,000 + 6,000 - 3,000$$
$$TO = 4,000 \text{ units}$$

b. Step 1: Summarize the flow of physical units: (Same as Step 1 in solution for weighted average.)

Step 2: Compute the equivalent units produced this period:

	Direct Materials	**Conversion Costs**
Units completed and transferred out:		
From beginning WIP inventory (100% − 75%) × 1,000 units	250	
(100% − 70%) × 1,000 units		300
Started and completed currently	3,000	3,000
Total.	3,250	3,300
Units in ending WIP inventory		
3,000 × 80%.	2,400	
3,000 × 60%.		1,800
Total equivalent units	5,650	5,100

Step 3: Summarize the total costs to be accounted for:

	Total Costs	**Direct Materials**	**Conversion Costs**
Costs to be accounted for			
Costs in beginning WIP inventory	$ 4,650	$ 3,200	$1,450
Current period costs.	21,800	16,000	5,800
Total costs to be accounted for	$26,450	$19,200	$7,250

Step 4: Cost per equivalent unit: Costs to be accounted for (current costs from step 3) ÷ Equivalent units (from step 2):

Direct materials:

$$\text{Cost per E.U.} = \$16,000/5,650 \text{ E.U.}$$
$$= \$2.832 \text{ per E.U.}$$

Conversion costs:

$$\text{Cost per E.U.} = \$5,800/5,100 \text{ E.U.}$$
$$= \$1.137 \text{ per E.U.}$$

Step 5: Assign costs to goods transferred out and to ending inventory:

	Total	**Direct Materials**	**Conversion Costs**
Costs in beginning WIP inventory (at beginning of period).	$ 4,650	$ 3,200	$1,450
Costs to complete beginning inventory			
250 E.U. × $2.832 per E.U.	708	708	
300 E.U. × $1.137 per E.U.	341		341
Cost of units started and completed			
3,000 units × $2.832 per E.U.	8,496	8,496	
3,000 units × $1.137 per E.U.	3,411		3,411
Subtotal (Finished Goods)	17,606		
Cost of ending WIP inventory			
2,400 E.U. × $2.832 per E.U.	6,797	6,797	
1,800 E.U. × $1.137 per E.U.	2,047		2,047
Subtotal (Ending WIP inventory) . . .	8,844		
Total costs accounted for	$26,450	$19,201	$7,249

c. Cost flows through T-account (amounts rounded to whole dollars):

Work in Process Inventory

Beginning inventory	4,650	Transfers out 17,606 →	to Finished Goods Inventory
Current period costs	21,800		
Ending inventory	8,844		

d. Production cost report—FIFO:

	(Section 1) Physical Units	(Section 2) Equivalent Units	
		Direct Materials	Conversion Costs
Flow of Units			
Units to be accounted for			
Beginning WIP inventory . . .	1,000		
Units started this period	6,000		
Total units to account for . . .	7,000		
Units accounted for			
Units completed and transferred out			
From beginning WIP inventory . .	1,000	250	300
Started and completed currently	3,000	3,000	3,000
Total	4,000	3,250	3,300
Units in ending WIP inventory . .	3,000	2,400	1,800
Total units accounted for	7,000	5,650	5,100

	Total	Direct Materials	Conversion Costs
Flow of Costs			
Costs to be accounted for (Section 3)			
Costs in beginning WIP inventory . . .	$ 4,650	$ 3,200	$1,450
Current period costs	21,800	16,000	5,800
Total costs to be accounted for . .	$26,450	$19,200	$7,250
Costs per equivalent unit (Section 4). . . .		$ 2.832	$1.137
Costs accounted for (Section 5)			
Costs assigned to units transferred out			
Costs from beginning WIP inventory . .	$ 4,650	$ 3,200	$1,450
Costs to complete beginning WIP inventory . .	1,049	708	341
Total costs from beginning WIP inventory . . .	5,699	3,908	1,791
Current costs of units started and completed	11,907	8,496	3,411
Total costs transferred out	17,606	12,404	5,202
Cost of ending WIP inventory . .	8,844	6,797	2,047
Total costs accounted for	$26,450	$19,201	$7,249

3. a. Production cost report—FIFO:

FLYINGFAST, INC.
Strings Department
Month Ending October 31

Flow of Production Units	(Section 1) Physical Units	(Section 2) Equivalent Units		
		For Prior Department Costs	For Materials	For Conversion Costs
Units to account for				
Beginning work in process inventory	1,000			
Units started this period	6,000			
Total units to account for	7,000			
Units accounted for				
Units completed and transferred out:				
From beginning inventory	1,000	–0–[a]	400[a] (40%[b])	250[a] (25%[b])
Started and completed, currently	3,300[c]	3,300	3,300	3,300
Units in ending WIP inventory	2,700	2,700	2,160 (80%[d])	1,215 (45%[d])
Total units accounted for	7,000	6,000	5,860	4,765

Flow of Costs	Total Costs	Prior Department Costs	Materials	Conversion Costs
Costs to be accounted for (Section 3)				
Costs in beginning WIP inventory	$ 8,120	$ 7,100	$ 600	$ 420
Current period costs	52,175	43,200	2,500	6,475
Total costs to be accounted for	$60,295	$50,300	$ 3,100	$ 6,895
Cost per equivalent unit (Section 4)				
Prior department costs ($43,200 ÷ 6,000)		$7.2000		
Materials ($2,500 ÷ 5,860)			$0.4266	
Conversion costs ($6,475 ÷ 4,765)				$1.3589
Costs accounted for (Section 5)				
Costs assigned to units transferred out				
Costs from beginning WIP inventory	$ 8,120	$ 7,100	$ 600	$ 420
Current costs added to complete beginning WIP inventory				
Prior department costs	–0–	–0–		
Materials (400 × $0.4266)	171		171	
Conversion costs (250 × $1.3589)	340			340
Total costs to complete beginning inventory	511			
Costs of units started and completed				
Prior department costs (3,300 × $7.20)	23,760	23,760		
Materials (3,300 × $0.4266)	1,408		1,408	

Continued on next page.

[a]Equivalent units required to complete beginning inventory.

[b]Percent required to complete beginning inventory.

[c]Units in beginning inventory + Units started and completed + Units in ending inventory = Total units accounted for. 1,000 + X + 2,700 = 7,000; X = 7,000 − 2,700 − 1,000 = 3,300.

[d]Stage of completion.

	Total Costs	Prior Department Costs	Materials	Conversion Costs
Conversion costs (3,300 × $1.3589)	4,484			4,484
Total costs of units started and completed	29,652			
Total costs transferred out.	38,283			
Costs assigned to ending WIP inventory				
Prior department costs (2,700 × $7.20)	19,440	19,440		
Materials (2,160 × $.4266)	921		921	
Conversion costs (1,215 × $1.3589)	1,651			1,651
Total cost of ending WIP inventory	22,012			
Total costs accounted for	$60,295	$50,300	$3,100	$6,895

b.   Cost flows—FIFO:

Work in Process Inventory—Strings Department				Finished Goods Inventory
Beginning Inventory	8,120ᵃ	To Finished Goods Inventory:		
This period's costs:		From beginning		
Prior department		inventory costs	8,120ᵇ	
costs included in		From this		→ 38,283ᵇ
units transferred		period's costs	30,163ᶜ	
into this department				
this period	43,200ᵃ			
Materials used				
this period	2,500ᵃ			
Conversion costs				
incurred this period	6,475ᵃ			
Ending inventory	$22,012ᵇ			

ᵃSee section 3 in the production cost report.

ᵇSee section 5 in the production cost report.

ᶜSum of total costs of units started and completed plus costs added to complete beginning WIP inventory.

4.   Entries for the Jets follow:

a.   Direct materials requisitioned for engine assembly are recorded as follows:

```
WIP Inventory: Engine
  Assembly. . . . . . . . . . . . . . .   200,000
    Materials Inventory . . . . . .            200,000
```

b.   Conversion costs for Engine Assembly are recorded as follows:

```
WIP Inventory: Engine
  Assembly. . . . . . . . . . . . . . .   100,000
    Wages Payable and
    Manufacturing Overhead
    Applied Accounts . . . . . . .            100,000
```

c.   The transfer of the costs from Engine Assembly to Final Assembly is

```
WIP Inventory: Final Assembly . .   300,000
  WIP Inventory:
    Engine Assembly. . . . . . . .            300,000
```

d.   The materials added in Final Assembly are accounted for in the following entry:

```
WIP Inventory: Final Assembly . .   300,000
  Materials Inventory . . . . . .            300,000
```

e.   The conversion costs incurred in Final Assembly are recorded as follows:

```
WIP Inventory: Final Assembly . .   200,000
  Wages Payable and
  Manufacturing Overhead
  Applied Accounts . . . . . . .            200,000
```

f.   Now the entire manufacturing cost of Work Order 101 has been incurred. This cost is transferred to Finished Goods Inventory in the following entry:

```
Finished Goods Inventory. . . . . .   800,000
  WIP Inventory:
    Final Assembly . . . . . . . .            800,000
```

6

Spoilage and Quality Management

LEARNING OBJECTIVES

After reading this chapter, you should be able to:

1. Differentiate between "normal" and "abnormal" spoilage.

2. Demonstrate how to account for abnormal spoilage.

3. Account for normal spoilage in process costing using the weighted-average method.

4. Account for normal spoilage using a job costing system.

5. Add value to companies by identifying spoilage at the beginning of the value chain.

6. Account for normal spoilage in process costing using the FIFO method (appendix).

If you have ever worked on a project that you discarded and started then on a new one, you understand the concept of spoilage. From your experience, you understand that spoilage, whether a discarded term paper, meal, or college application, is costly. Sometimes spoilage is a necessary part of doing the job right. Doing something that did not turn out right can be part of the learning experience. If you have learned a sport, a dance, or to play a musical instrument, you know that no matter how much instruction you get, at some point you just have to go out and learn from your mistakes.

At other times, spoilage occurs because people are not well trained, work with poor materials, or have faulty equipment. If so, managers can fix the spoilage problem if they choose to do so.

Managers face these key problems concerning spoilage:

- Identifying whether it exists.
- Determining whether and how it can be eliminated. For example, spoilage can often be reduced by spending more time training employees.
- Deciding whether eliminating it is worthwhile. For example, is eliminating spoilage worth the cost of employee training?

TOTAL QUALITY MANAGEMENT AND SPOILAGE

Companies implementing total quality management focus on the concept of continuous improvement. Continuous improvement is applicable to products and product features, and every facet of the value chain, including the production process, is continuously improved.

A current theme in business today is that "quality is free." The belief is that if quality is built into the product, the resulting benefits in customer satisfaction, reduced reworking and warranty costs, and other important factors far outweigh the costs of improving quality. Cost-benefit analyses are no longer the primary focus in improving quality. Instead, the emphasis is on improving quality with the understanding that quality is free in the long run.

Detecting Poor Quality before It Reaches the Customer

Quality has become an increasingly important factor in measuring customer satisfaction. Customers often switch brands if they purchase a product with poor quality. For example, many loyal car buyers in the United States opted for foreign imports because the quality of imported cars was superior to U.S. automobiles. U.S. car companies are just beginning to recover from lost market share as a result of relatively poor quality.

This is just one example of the negative impact of producing poor quality products or failing to detect poor quality before it reaches the customer. As a counterexample, the Real World Application "Recalling Products to Provide Good Service to Customers" on page 163, is a good example of making sure that customers do not get defective products. Another negative impact of producing poor quality products is the cost of the goods that are damaged or do not meet specifications. Not only is there a cost of losing customers due to poor quality, the company must pay for materials that have been

It is important to detect poor quality before it gets to the customer. If this customer takes home dairy products that are spoiled, she may simply switch brands or shop at another store.

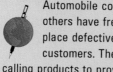

REAL WORLD APPLICATION

Recalling Products to Provide Good Service to Customers

Automobile companies, drug manufacturers, and others have frequently attempted to recall and re-place defective products before they reached the customers. The best example we have seen of re-calling products to provide good service to customers was that of a newspaper publisher in a community in Kansas. Shortly after the papers were delivered to people's homes,

they were soaked by a sudden unexpected downpour as they lay on porches, sidewalks, and lawns. So the pub-lisher ordered the entire press run of 100,000 newspapers to be repeated. Why? He was attempting to provide a high level of service to readers and advertisers.

Source: M. Fitzgerald, "Kansas Community 'Recalls' Entire Press Run," *Editor & Publisher* 128, no. 33, p. 27.

spoilage
Goods that are damaged, do not meet specifications, or are otherwise not suitable for further processing or sale as good output.

wasted during the production process—referred to as **spoilage.** By improving quality early in the production process, quality improves and costs can be lowered by elim-inating or reducing defective products later in production. As a result, customers can receive higher quality products at reduced prices.

Using Spoilage Cost Information to Reduce Costs

By measuring the costs of spoilage and the costs to reduce it (such as the costs to train employees and to use higher quality materials), managers are able to make informed decisions to improve quality and reduce costs.

NORMAL VERSUS ABNORMAL SPOILAGE: IS SPOILAGE EVER NORMAL?

L.O. 1: Differentiate between "normal" and "abnormal" spoilage.

L.O. 2: Demonstrate how to account for abnormal spoilage.

Lost units during the regular operations of the production process are called **normal spoilage.** Normal spoilage is expected as part of the production process as shown in the left panel of Illustration 6.1. Some may not consider this to be normal spoilage, however, and strive to eliminate all spoilage. **Abnormal spoilage** occurs if units are lost for unusual or abnormal reasons, as shown in the right panel of Illustration 6.1. For abnormal spoilage, the debit in the journal entry is made to an account such as Abnormal Spoilage, which writes off the costs as an expense for the period.

ILLUSTRATION   6.1   Normal versus Abnormal Spoilage

Normal spoilage

Abnormal spoilage

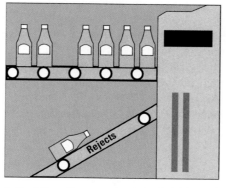

In the left section, some bottled soft drinks are rejected because the bottling process did not sufficiently fill the bottles. Although not desirable, the company considers this "normal" spoilage. In the right section, an accident has created "abnormal" spoilage.

lost units
Goods that evaporate or otherwise disappear during a production process.

normal spoilage
Spoiled goods that are a result of the regular operation of the production process.

abnormal spoilage
Spoilage due to reasons other than the usual course of operations of a process.

To illustrate the accounting for abnormal spoilage, assume managers of a Coca-Cola bottling plant discovered that it had received a shipment of defective plastic bottles. These bottles, which had already been filled with soft drink, had to be destroyed at a cost of $8,000. The journal entry to record the transfer of this spoilage out of Work in Process Inventory is

Abnormal Spoilage	8,000	
Work in Process Inventory		8,000

Abnormal spoilage is an expense for the period and appears in the income statement. Managers watch the Abnormal Spoilage account closely to identify causes of spoilage and to prevent it from occurring in the future.

Companies that have a zero defects policy might treat *all* spoilage as abnormal. They probably would not consider the left panel of Illustration 6.1 to be normal.

PROCESS COSTING: CONTROLLING SPOILAGE COSTS

L.O. 3: Account for normal spoilage in process costing using the weighted-average method.

The Five Key Steps

good output
Units completed and suitable for further processing or for sale at the end of a production process.

Cost information regarding spoilage can be very helpful to management. Normal spoilage is typically accounted for separately so management can track costs associated with it and make production process decisions accordingly.[1] Accounting for normal spoilage is illustrated using the five-step approach used in Chapter 5. (If you did not cover Chapter 5 or have forgotten the five steps, don't worry; they will become self-evident as you go through them in this chapter.)

Suppose that a department had no beginning inventory and started 3,000 units. These units cost $24,000 ($9,000 for materials and $15,000 for conversion costs). It produced only 2,500 units of **good output** and lost 500 units (normal spoilage) which were detected to be spoiled at the end of the production process. There is no ending WIP inventory.

The same five steps used to assign costs to products in a process costing environment are also used to account for spoilage. Note that we do not distinguish between the weighted-average or FIFO costing methods in the following example because both methods yield the same result when there is no beginning WIP Inventory account balance.

1. **Summarize the flow of physical units.** From the basic cost flow model (beginning inventory + transfers in − transfers out = ending inventory), we can perform this step. Beginning inventory is 0 and 3,000 units were transferred in (or started). All units started were transferred out either to finished goods (2,500) or spoilage (500), and no units remain in ending WIP inventory.

2. **Compute the equivalent units produced.** This calculation is relatively simple for this example because no beginning inventory existed and all units started were either completed or treated as spoilage. The equivalent units of good units produced totaled 2,500 for both direct materials and conversion costs. The equivalent units for spoilage totaled 500 for both direct materials and conversion costs. Thus, there are 3,000 equivalent units in total.

3. **Summarize the total costs to be accounted for.** Again, given the simplicity of this example, total costs are easily summarized. Beginning WIP inventory is 0, $9,000 was spent on materials, $15,000 in conversion costs were incurred, and all inventory was transferred out of WIP inventory at the end of the period. Thus, costs totaled $24,000.

---

[1] Another approach that is often used in practice buries the cost of spoilage in the cost of good units produced. We do not advocate using this approach, however, because it does not provide management with useful cost information associated with spoilage.

4. **Compute costs per equivalent unit.** This calculation is summarized:

	Direct Materials	Conversion Costs
Total costs to be accounted for (from step 3)	$9,000	$15,000
Equivalent units (from step 2)	3,000	3,000
Cost per equivalent unit	$ 3.00	$ 5.00

5. **Assign costs to goods transferred out and to ending inventory.** Costs for the good units are assigned as follows:

Direct materials (2,500 × $3.00)	$ 7,500
Conversion costs (2,500 × $5.00)	12,500
Total transferred out	$20,000

Costs for spoiled units are assigned as follows:

Direct materials (500 × $3.00)	$1,500
Conversion costs (500 × $5.00)	2,500
Total spoiled units.	$4,000

At the end of the period, the $4,000 cost of the 500 lost units is assigned to WIP inventory, finished goods inventory, or cost of goods sold, depending on the status of the good units. For example, if 1,000 of the good units were in ending finished goods inventory and the remaining 1,500 units were sold, the entry is

Finished Goods Inventory—Spoiled Goods (1,000/2,500 × $4,000).	1,600	
Cost of Goods Sold—Spoiled Goods (1,500/2,500 × $4,000).	2,400	
WIP Inventory—Spoiled Goods		4,000

This method of accounting for spoilage provides managers with data that clearly identify the cost of spoilage. The flow of costs is diagrammed in Illustration 6.2.

This example assumes that no inspections were performed during the production process to identify bad or defective units, therefore 100% of direct materials

---

ILLUSTRATION   6.2   Cost Flows for Normal Lost Units

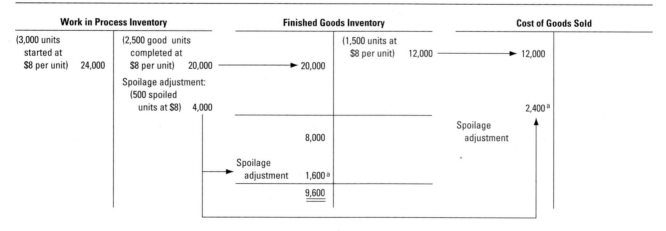

ᵃAllocate spoilage costs proportional to good units costs.

$1,600 = $8,000/$20,000 × $4,000 to Finished Goods Inventory.

$2,400 = $12,000/$20,000 × $4,000 to Cost of Goods Sold.

and conversion costs were incurred before inspecting the products. As a result, the company likely wasted a significant amount of resources completing what were already bad units.

The timing of inspections has a direct impact on the amount of normal and abnormal spoilage the firm incurs. In the previous example, suppose inspections had been performed at the 20 percent, 40 percent, or 60 percent stage of comple-

Inspections During the Process

In this factory, inspection is part of a training and feedback process. How does this help build quality into the entire purchasing and production process? (© Keith Wood/Tony Stone Images)

tion rather than after 100 percent completion. Clearly, defective products would have been identified earlier in the production process, saving the department in additional direct materials and conversion costs—assuming that both costs are incurred throughout the production process.

Spoilage Is Detected During the Process

What if spoilage occurs and is detected during the process? For example, starting with the following facts from the previous example:

Materials, *all added at the beginning of the process* . . . . $ 9,000
Conversion costs, *added evenly throughout the process*   15,000

Spoilage of 500 units occurs and is detected when the process is 40 percent complete (but after all materials have been added).

Using the five-step process, costs are allocated to good units and to spoiled units as follows:

1. **Summarize the flow of physical units.**

   Units to account for:

   Units in beginning WIP inventory   0
   Units started this period   3,000
   Total units to account for   3,000

   Units accounted for:

   Units transferred out to:
     Finished goods (good units)   2,500
     Spoilage   500
   Units in ending WIP inventory   0
   Total units accounted for   3,000

2. **Compute the equivalent units produced.**

	Direct Materials	Conversion Costs
Units transferred out to:		
Finished goods (good units)........	2,500	2,500
Spoilage		
(500 × 100%)	500	
(500 × 40%)		200
Units in ending WIP inventory........	0	0
Total equivalent units..............	3,000	2,700

The equivalent units of goods spoiled for conversion costs is only 200 (40 percent x 500 units spoiled) because spoilage occurred and was detected at the 40 percent stage. Consequently, the total equivalent units produced for conversion costs, including equivalent units of goods spoiled, equals 2,700.

Spoilage occurred after all materials were added, however, so the equivalent units spoiled for materials costs equal 500 units; the total equivalent units produced, including spoiled goods, equal 3,000.

3. **Summarize the total costs to be accounted for.**

	Total Costs	Direct Materials	Conversion Costs
Costs to be accounted for			
Costs in beginning WIP inventory ...	$ –0–	$ –0–	$ –0–
Current period costs...........	24,000	9,000	15,000
Total costs to be accounted for	$24,000	$9,000	$15,000

4. **Compute costs per equivalent unit.**

	Direct Materials	Conversion Costs
Total costs to be accounted for (from step 3).................	$9,000	$15,000
Equivalent units (from step 2)	3,000	2,700
Cost per equivalent unit (rounded)	$3.000	$5.556

5. **Assign costs to goods transferred out (good and spoiled) and to ending inventory.**

Costs accounted for as follows:		
Transferred out to finished goods:		
Direct materials (2,500 × $3).........	$ 7,500	
Conversion costs (2,500 × $5.556)	13,889	
Subtotal....................		$21,389
Transferred out to scrap (spoilage):		
Direct materials (500 × $3)..........	$ 1,500	
Conversion costs (200 × $5.556)	1,111	
Subtotal....................		2,611
Total transferred out..............		$24,000
Work in process, December 31		0
Total costs accounted for..............		$24,000

Computing Equivalent Units and Spoilage Costs When Companies Have Beginning and Ending Inventories

The previous example assumed no beginning or ending work in process inventories. Adding WIP inventories complicates the calculations, but it does not affect the general principles.

Weighted-Average Process Costing

Suppose that a company uses weighted-average costing to compute product costs. At the beginning of the period, it had 200 units in beginning inventory that were 100 percent complete with respect to materials and 35 percent complete with respect to conversion costs; all were good units. During the period, the company produced 2,500 good units and lost 500 units to spoilage. Management is concerned that so many units were spoiled and wants us to determine their cost.

To determine the cost of spoiled units, we must allocate all costs (beginning inventory and current period costs) to finished goods inventory, spoilage, and ending WIP inventory. We learn that production people detect spoilage at the 30 percent stage of production, that is, after 30 percent of conversion costs and 100 percent of materials costs had been applied. Of the 2,500 good units, we learn that 2,100 were transferred out to Finished Goods Inventory. The remaining 400 units were in ending work in process inventory, 100 percent complete with respect to materials and 20 percent complete with respect to conversion costs.

From the accounting records, we find the following cost data:

	Total	Beginning Inventory	Current Period Costs
Materials	$30,000	$2,000	$28,000
Conversion costs	46,600	2,400	44,200

Once again, we can use the five-step process to allocate costs. This process is summarized below.

1. **Summarize the flow of physical units.**

   Units to account for:

Units in beginning WIP inventory	200
Units started this period	2,800
Total units to account for	3,000

   Units accounted for:

Units transferred out to:	
Finished goods (good units)	2,100
Spoilage	500
Units in ending WIP inventory	400
Total units accounted for	3,000

2. **Compute the equivalent units produced.**

	Direct Materials	Conversion Costs
Units transferred out to:		
Finished goods (good units)	2,100	2,100
Spoilage		
(500 × 100%)	500	
(500 × 30%)		150
Units in ending WIP inventory		
(400 × 100%)	400	
(400 × 20%)		80
Total equivalent units.	3,000	2,330

3. Summarize the total costs to be accounted for.

	Total Costs	Direct Materials	Conversion Costs
Costs to be accounted for:			
Costs in beginning WIP inventory . . .	$ 4,400	$ 2,000	$ 2,400
Current period costs.	72,200	28,000	44,200
Total costs to be accounted for	$76,600	$30,000	$46,600

4. Compute costs per equivalent unit.

	Direct Materials	Conversion Costs
Total costs to be accounted for (from step 3)	$30,000	$46,600
Equivalent units (from step 2)	3,000	2,330
Cost per equivalent unit.	$ 10	$ 20

5. Assign costs to goods transferred out (good and spoiled) and to ending inventory.

Costs accounted for as follows		
Transferred out to finished goods		
Direct materials (2,100 × $10)	$21,000	
Conversion costs (2,100 × $20)	42,000	
Subtotal.		63,000
Transferred out to spoilage		
Direct materials (500 × $10)	$5,000	
Conversion costs (150 × $20)	3,000	
Subtotal.		8,000
Total transferred out		$71,000
Work in process		
Direct materials (400 × $10)	$4,000	
Conversion costs (80 × $20)	1,600	
Total in ending WIP inventory		$ 5,600
Total costs accounted for		$76,600

In general, the earlier we can detect spoilage, the less costly it is to the company. If spoilage cannot be prevented, it should be detected as early as possible.

SELF-STUDY QUESTION

1. A company using the weighted-average costing method maintains a Spoilage Expense account for spoiled goods. The cost of units spoiled in process is charged to this account. At the beginning of the period, 1,000 units in beginning inventory were 70 percent complete with respect to materials and 60 percent complete with respect to conversion costs. All units in beginning inventory were good units. During the period, the company started 8,000 units. 5,000 units passed quality control inspection, 1,500 units were lost to spoilage, and 2,500 units had not reached the inspection point.

Production people detect spoiled goods at the point that 40 percent of conversion costs and 55 percent of materials costs had been incurred. 5,000 units were transferred out to Finished Goods Inventory. The 2,500 units in ending WIP inventory were 30 percent complete with respect to materials, and 20 percent complete with respect to conversion costs.

The accounting records show the following information for the activities in the WIP Inventory account:

	Total	Beginning Inventory	Current Period Costs
Materials	$ 50,000	$10,000	$40,000
Conversion costs	100,000	20,000	80,000

Using the five-step process, allocate costs to the appropriate categories (finished goods inventory, spoilage, and ending WIP inventory).

The solution to this question is at the end of this chapter on page 183.

JOB COSTING: CONTROLLING SPOILAGE COSTS ON JOBS

L.O. 4: Account for normal spoilage using a job costing system.

Spoilage is not unique to processes; jobs must also contend with it. Spoilage in jobs occurs (1) because of the overall production process or (2) because of a specific job.

Spoilage Resulting from Production Process

Spoilage often occurs as a result of the overall production process. For example, production equipment might break down periodically. Given this set of circumstances, spoilage cannot be attributed to any particular job, and it is inappropriate to charge spoilage costs to any one particular job. Thus, spoilage costs are spread evenly across all jobs rather than to the particular job under way at the time of the breakdown. Accountants spread these costs to other jobs by reducing Work in Process by the total cost of spoilage, increasing Overhead by the net cost of spoilage (cost of spoiled goods less disposal value), and increasing Spoiled Goods Inventory by the disposal value. Thus, spoilage costs are spread over all jobs when manufacturing overhead is applied.

Let's look at an example. Suppose that Mike's Upholstery Repair replaces upholstery and carpeting in automobiles and recreational vehicles. Occasionally, Mike's old machinery malfunctions and ruins a job as it did recently on Job X1 not long after the job was started. Costs assigned to the job at the point where it was ruined total $50; the fabric can be salvaged for $10.

To account for this spoilage, the disposal value of spoiled goods is recorded in the Spoiled Goods Inventory account ($10), Work in Process for the job is reduced by the cost assigned to the spoiled goods ($50), and Overhead is increased by the net cost of spoilage ($40). The journal entry follows:

Spoiled Goods Inventory	10	
Overhead	40	
Work in Process—Job X1		50

The $40 debited to overhead becomes part of Mike's overhead that is applied generally to jobs, like the rent on the building where the work is done. Later, Mike sells the spoiled goods for $10 cash, which accountants record as follows:

Cash	10	
Spoiled Goods Inventory		10

SELF-STUDY QUESTION

2. Valve Machine Shop produces intake and exhaust valves for custom automobiles and has some spoilage on jobs. This spoilage is part of the normal production process and should not be assigned entirely to just one job. Costs assigned to the product for Job A1 at the point of inspection total $20,000. The current disposal price of spoiled goods is $4,000 (sold for cash).

a. Prepare the journal entry to account for spoilage.

b. Prepare the journal entry to account for the sale of spoiled goods.

The solution to this question is at the end of this chapter on page 183.

Spoilage Resulting from Specific Job

If the spoilage described for Mike's Upholstery Repair results from a particular production process used for a specific job, spoilage costs should be assigned to that particular job. Accountants should identify the amount of spoilage as a part of job costs separately from materials, labor, and overhead. Then they should make a journal entry to transfer the disposal value of the spoiled goods out of Work in Process Job X1 into Spoiled Goods Inventory. Using these data, that entry follows:

Spoiled Goods Inventory 10
    Work in Process—Job X1 10

Note that only $10 is removed from the job unlike the example on page 170 in which $50 was removed, so the job still has $40 of spoilage assigned to it.

Later, the spoiled goods are sold for $10 cash, which accountants record as follows:

Cash 10
    Spoiled Goods Inventory 10

Here a young lawyer puts in a lot of time on a particular case. If the lawyer is new, then much of his time may be spent in learning how to do the work, which is like "spoilage" in manufacturing. Should that learning time be charged to this particular case? (See pages 170–171 for a discussion of the accounting treatment of these costs. Many law firms do not charge the client for the time that young lawyers spend learning how to be lawyers.) (© Dennis O'Clair/Tony Stone Images)

How Spoilage Ends Up in Employees' Lunch Buckets

Although we used a manufacturing example, spoilage of jobs also occurs in service organizations. Consulting firms, public accounting firms, advertising agencies, architectural firms, and other service organizations face the same issues: Should costs be associated with a particular job or with the underlying process of providing services? Public accounting firms face this problem when they hire new people who are inefficient at first. If you are just learning how to do auditing or tax work, should your first client bear the cost of your learning? Probably not.

It is important to maintain control over spoiled goods. As shown earlier, a separate account, Spoiled Goods Inventory, is established to track spoiled goods. Spoiled goods often have value, albeit less than good units produced, and should be treated as such. All too often, companies discard spoiled goods, creating an incentive for employees to take them. Even if disposal values are negligible, management should track spoiled goods (both in terms of cost and physical whereabouts) if not for their value, for management's use in assessing the efficiency of the production process.

MANAGING SPOILAGE AND LOST UNITS IN MERCHANDISING

The loss of goods through theft or spoilage in merchandising is a major cost for many companies. Perhaps the best example is the fresh vegetable and fruit area in a supermarket. Some supermarkets report losses as high as 20 percent of the total goods purchased due to spoilage. Some retail firms also report high losses due to theft.

First consider the case of spoilable goods, such as fruits, vegetables, and milk, and losses due to obsolescence such as seasonal products.

- Too much merchandise results in spoilage or obsolescence because the merchandise does not sell before its time is up.
- Too little merchandise means the loss of a sale and possibly the loss of a customer who goes elsewhere to get the product.

These situations require managers to figure out the correct amount of goods to stock to minimize losses due to spoilage or obsolescence versus losses due to lost sales. To make these decisions, accountants should track the costs of spoiled goods for each type of product.

The problem for managers of stores facing theft problems is similar. These managers must weigh the costs of increased security against the costs from theft. That's why stores selling electronic equipment or jewelry generally use elaborate security devices but small corner grocery stores do not. Security devices are more likely to be used where the probability of theft is high.

Managers who must make these trade-offs need to know the cost not just of stolen goods but also of each type of product stolen. That way, managers can focus on problem products in considering the cost and benefits of various security devices.

Accounting for these losses is straightforward, much like the cost of recording abnormal spoilage in manufacturing or service organizations. Assume that the loss due to spoilage of tomatoes in the fresh fruits and vegetables section of a Safeway supermarket for a week is $800. The accounting entry to record this loss is

Spoilage—Tomatoes	800	
Tomatoes Inventories		800

The amount of the loss can be determined simply by tracking the tomatoes spoiled by observation or comparing the physical inventory of tomatoes at the end of the week with the perpetual inventory. If the physical inventory showed $800 less inventory of tomatoes than the perpetual inventory, the accountants record this entry.

SELF-STUDY QUESTION

3. Interview a manager of a farmers' market, a grocery store, or some other retail store. Ask what percentage of a particular set of goods, such as fruit and vegetables in a grocery store, becomes spoiled, obsolete, or lost due to theft. Ask which products have the highest such losses.

The solution to this question is at the end of this chapter on page 183.

MANAGING THE COSTS OF REWORKING PRODUCTS

Reworked products are those that did not pass inspection and are subsequently reworked and sold. Many of us do a job, find that it is not acceptable, and **rework** it. The accounting issue is how to account for the additional costs of reworking the defective products.

If a job has gone through several stages of production before a defect is discovered, considerable costs have already been assigned to it. If the additional rework costs are added to that particular job's costs, the job's costs are higher (sometimes considerably) than the cost of similar jobs that did not have to go through rework.

Directly Assigning Costs to Specific Products

Two approaches can be used to account for the cost of rework. First, using the *product identification method,* the cost can be assigned to the particular job, batch, or unit that is being reworked. Assigning rework costs to the particular job has the advantage of sending a message to management that the company has a problem. If a particular job is considerably more costly than similar jobs or than estimated, management can take action to solve the problems that created the defects in the first place. By measuring and reporting the costs of rework, accountants can show man-

rework
Work performed on products that do not pass inspection and subsequently require additional work (including labor, materials, and/or overhead) before being sold.

agement the benefits from employee training, new machinery, better materials, and other quality improvement methods to avoid the problems.

Accounting for rework using the product identification approach is a simple concept, but it may be difficult to apply. In concept, if a job incurs $1,000 in costs from normal production plus $600 for additional rework, it costs $1,600. The total costs debited to WIP Inventory amounts to $1,600. Assume that the original materials costs were $600, the direct labor costs were $100, and the manufacturing overhead costs were $300 (these costs represent the $1,000 in costs from normal production). Further, the rework required $150 additional materials and $150 additional direct labor, and $300 additional manufacturing overhead was applied. The journal entry is as follows:

WIP Inventory	1,600	
Materials Inventory		600
Wages Payable		100
Manufacturing Overhead Applied		300
Materials Inventory—Rework		150
Wages Payable—Rework		150
Manufacturing Overhead Applied—Rework		300

The amount transferred from WIP Inventory to Finished Goods Inventory and ultimately to Cost of Goods Sold for that job is $1,600, with the $600 for rework accounted for separately in Finished Goods Inventory and Cost of Goods Sold. Note in this entry that we follow three accounts (Materials Inventory, Wages Payable, and Manufacturing Overhead Applied) with the term *rework* added for illustrative purposes only. The actual accounts used do not typically use the term *rework*.

Spreading the Costs across All Products

In practice, the product identification approach may be difficult to implement because it may be time consuming (and perhaps impossible) to tie the rework costs to a particular product. If the unit is a job, such as a building, accountants likely find it feasible to tie rework costs to it. In a process, however, the costs of rework are difficult to tie to particular units. Consequently, in practice, the costs of rework are often charged to manufacturing overhead. Using this method, which we call the *overhead method*, these rework costs are spread over all units produced, whether good or defective units. The journal entry to record the costs of rework using the overhead method with the same data as the preceding example follows.

First, to record the initial costs incurred in making the product:

Work in Process Inventory	1,000	
Materials Inventory		600
Wages Payable		100
Manufacturing Overhead Applied[2]		300

Second, to record the additional costs to rework these units:

Manufacturing Overhead	600	
Materials Inventory		150
Wages Payable		150
Manufacturing Overhead Applied		300

Applied manufacturing overhead rates are increased to include the costs of rework charged to Manufacturing Overhead (much like accounting for spoilage using a job cost system).[2] Thus, all products share in rework costs, whether they needed rework or not, because all products are charged with more overhead.

---

[2]Manufacturing Overhead Applied would typically be higher using this method as a result of higher overhead rates reflecting additional rework costs. To keep this example simple, however, we have not changed the amount applied to overhead. Instead, we focus on the different entries made for each approach.

ILLUSTRATION   6.3   The Value Chain

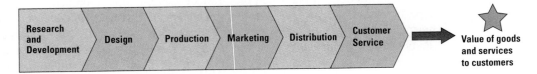

Without considering the costs of getting the information, the product identification method is better than the overhead method because it better informs managers. When considering the costs of getting the information, managers may decide that the product identification method is not worth the expense, however.

ADDING VALUE TO COMPANIES BY REDUCING SPOILAGE

L.O. 5: Add value to companies by identifying spoilage at the beginning of the value chain.

Identifying spoilage as far upstream in the value chain as possible can add considerable value to companies. In Illustration 6.3, identifying spoilage at the beginning (left side) of the value chain adds value because it eliminates nonvalue-added work on the right.

You may have experienced this phenomenon in your own schoolwork. Suppose you were given an assignment to write a paper on successful business ventures in Eastern Europe. Unfortunately, you thought the assignment was to write on successful business ventures in the Middle East. You start at the left side of the value chain and work toward the right, starting with your research, developing your ideas, designing the paper (for example, outlining topics), and producing a draft of the paper. This work is analogous to the first three functions in the value chain in Illustration 6.3.

Next you market and distribute the paper by rewriting it to meet the customer's specifications (your professor's requirements for typing, length, and so forth) and turn it in. Finally, customer service involves answering your professor's questions about your work and perhaps responding to criticisms.

Your product is "spoiled," however, and you have done all this work for nothing because your topic was wrong. If you had identified the spoilage at the early stages of the project, you could have saved all the subsequent work on the spoiled product. In general, the closer to the beginning of the value chain you can identify the spoilage, the better. The moral: Find out if the product is spoiled as far upstream in the value chain as possible.

SUMMARY

This chapter discusses accounting for and managing spoilage and rework costs. Although we differentiate between normal and abnormal spoilage, advocates of total quality management might consider all spoilage to be abnormal. Accounting practices that "bury" spoilage in the cost of products reduce information about an important cost and can deter management's efforts to identify and eliminate spoilage.

The following summarizes key ideas tied to the chapter's learning objectives.

LO1: Differentiate between "normal" and "abnormal" spoilage. Normal spoilage occurs under efficient operating conditions and is inherent to the production process. Abnormal spoilage is not expected to occur under efficient operating conditions.

LO2: Demonstrate how to account for abnormal spoilage. The costs of abnormal spoilage are tracked separately to provide management with useful cost information regarding spoilage costs.

LO3: Account for normal spoilage in process costing using the weighted-average method. The five-step process is used to allocate production costs to finished goods inventory, spoilage, and ending WIP inventory when the weighted-average approach is utilized.

LO4: Account for normal spoilage using a job costing system. Spoilage can be accounted for two ways when using a job costing system. First, spoilage resulting from the production process cannot easily be assigned to a specific job and is therefore allocated to all jobs through the manufacturing overhead applied account. Second, spoilage resulting from a specific job should remain with the job and is not allocated to all jobs.

LO5: Add value to companies by identifying spoilage at the beginning of the value chain. Identifying spoilage on the left side (upstream) of the value chain saves wasted work on the right side (downstream) of the value chain.

LO6: Account for spoilage in process costing using the FIFO method (appendix). The five-step process is also used to allocate production costs when the FIFO approach is utilized.

KEY TERMS

abnormal spoilage, 164	normal spoilage, 164
good output, 164	rework, 172
lost units, 164	spoilage, 163

APPENDIX

L.O. 6: Account for normal spoilage in process costing using FIFO method (appendix).

FIFO Process Costing

With the exception of adding spoilage, the FIFO method is the same as discussed in the previous chapter. Using the same data as in the weighted-average process costing example in the chapter (see page 168), we allocate costs using the FIFO method. The five-step approach is still applicable with a few modifications.

1. **Summarize the flow of physical units.**

Units to account for:	
Units in beginning WIP inventory	200
Units started this period	2,800
Total units to account for	3,000
Units accounted for:	
Units transferred out	
Good units from beginning WIP	200
Good units started and completed	1,900
Spoilage	500
Units in ending WIP inventory	400
Total units accounted for	3,000

2. **Compute the equivalent units produced.**

	Direct Materials	Conversion Costs
Good units transferred out		
From beginning inventory		
[200 × (100% − 100%)]	–0–	
[200 × (100% − 35%)]		130
Started and completed	1,900	1,900
Spoilage		
(500 × 100%)	500	
(500 × 30%)		150
Units in ending WIP inventory		
(400 × 100%)	400	
(400 × 20%)		80
Total equivalent units	2,800	2,260

3. **Summarize the total costs to be accounted for** (same as weighted-average approach).

	Total Costs	Direct Materials	Conversion Costs
Costs to be accounted for:			
Costs in beginning WIP inventory	$ 4,400	$ 2,000	$ 2,400
Current period costs	72,200	28,000	44,200
Total costs to be accounted for	$76,600	$30,000	$46,600

4. **Compute costs per equivalent unit.**

	Direct Materials	Conversion Costs
Current period costs (from step 3)	$28,000	$44,200
Equivalent units (from step 2)	2,800	2,260
Cost per equivalent unit	$10.000	$19.558*

Note: Although the cost per equivalent unit for direct materials using this method happens to be the same as the cost per equivalent unit using the weighted-average method, this holds true only if beginning inventory is 100 percent complete with respect to direct materials and material prices remain constant over time.

5. **Assign costs to goods transferred out (good and spoiled) and to ending inventory.**

Costs accounted for as follows:		
Transferred out to finished goods		
From beginning WIP inventory	$ 4,400	
Current costs added to complete beginning WIP inventory		
Direct materials (0 × $10)	–0–	
Conversion costs (130 × $19.558)	2,542*	
Started and completed		
Direct materials (1,900 × $10)	19,000	
Conversion costs (1,900 × $19.558)	37,160*	
Subtotal		63,102
Transferred out to spoilage		
Direct materials (500 × $10)	$ 5,000	
Conversion costs (150 × $19.558)	2,933*	
Subtotal		7,933
Total transferred out		$71,035
Work in process, December 31		
Direct materials (400 × $10)	$ 4,000	
Conversion costs (80 × $19.558)	1,565*	
Total in ending WIP inventory		$ 5,565
Total costs accounted for		$76,600

*Results may differ slightly from your answer due to rounding.

Comparison: Weighted-Average versus FIFO

A summary of the two approaches to allocating costs is shown here.

	Weighted Average	FIFO
Transferred to finished goods inventory (2,100 units)	$63,000	$63,102
Spoilage (500 units)	8,000	7,933
Ending WIP inventory (400 units)	5,600	5,565
Total costs	$76,600	$76,600

SELF-STUDY QUESTION

4. Assume that the company in Self-Study Question 1 in the chapter uses the FIFO costing method. Using the five-step process, allocate costs to the appropriate categories (finished goods inventory, spoilage, and ending WIP inventory).

The solution to this question is at the end of this chapter on page 184.

REVIEW QUESTIONS

6.1 What is the difference between normal spoilage and abnormal spoilage?

6.2 Suppose that a company had $5,000 in abnormal spoilage for the period. Give the journal entry to record this spoilage. Where does abnormal spoilage appear in the financial statements?

6.3 How is the five-step process used to account for normal spoilage in a process costing system?

6.4 What are the two approaches to recording spoilage in a job costing system? Describe them.

6.5 In a job costing system, why would the overhead rate be higher when spoilage results from the production process rather than from specific jobs?

6.6 What is *rework*? Describe the two methods of accounting for the cost of rework.

CRITICAL ANALYSIS AND DISCUSSION QUESTIONS

6.7 What are the advantages of moving the inspection point as far upstream on the value chain as possible? What are the disadvantages of doing this?

6.8 Why might advocates of total quality management prefer to see all spoilage considered abnormal spoilage?

6.9 The chapter discusses the cost of spoilage when spoilage is detected during the production. What costs might a company incur if spoilage is not detected during production and defective goods are sold to customers?

6.10 Interview the manager of grocery store. What is the cost of spoilage in the vegetable and fruit section as a percentage of the total costs of goods sold? Write your findings in a short report.

6.11 Interview the manager of a fast food restaurant such as McDonald's. What is the cost of spoilage as a percentage of the total costs of food purchased? Write your findings in a short report.

6.12 Interview the manager of grocery store. How does she or he decide on the correct amount of dairy products to avoid spoilage yet provide enough goods so customers won't find empty shelves? (See discussion on pages 171–72.) Write your findings in a short report.

EXERCISES

6.13 Normal Spoilage (L.O. 3)

Management of Sierra Company is concerned about the cost of spoilage. It provides the following facts:

	Units	Dollars
Beginning WIP inventory.	–0–	–0–
Units started	2,000	
Costs incurred for units started		$20,000
Good units of output produced	1,600	
Spoiled units	400	
Ending WIP inventory.	–0–	–0–

Required **a.** Using the five-step approach, calculate the cost of spoiled units, assuming that spoilage occurs at the end of the process. There is no need to include separate columns for direct materials and conversion costs since all units were transferred out of WIP inventory by the end of the period. (Since there is no beginning WIP inventory, it does not matter whether weighted average or FIFO is used.)

b. Show the flow of these costs through T-accounts from work in process to cost of goods sold.

6.14   Normal Spoilage (L.O. 3)   Management of Appalachian Enterprises is concerned about the cost of spoilage. It provides the following facts:

	Units	Dollars
Beginning WIP inventory	–0–	–0–
Units started	1,000	
Costs incurred for units started		$20,000
Good units of output produced	800	
Spoiled units	200	
Ending WIP inventory	–0–	–0–

Required Using the five-step approach, calculate the cost of spoiled units, assuming that spoilage occurs at the end of the process. There is no need to include separate columns for direct materials and conversion costs since all units were transferred out of WIP inventory by the end of the period. (Since there is no beginning WIP inventory, it does not matter whether weighted average or FIFO is used, however.)

6.15   Normal Spoilage (L.O. 3)   Refer to the facts for Exercise 6.13. Assume that spoilage occurred when the process was 50 percent complete and costs are added evenly throughout the process.

Required Using the five-step approach, calculate the cost of spoiled units and the cost of good units.

6.16   Spoilage Occurs during the Process (L.O. 3)   Refer to the facts for Exercise 6.14. Assume that spoilage occurred when the process was 40 percent complete and costs are added evenly throughout the process.

Required Using the five-step approach, calculate the cost of spoiled units and the cost of good units.

6.17   Normal Spoilage (L.O. 3)   Vail Company has the following facts regarding spoilage:

	Units	Dollars
Beginning WIP inventory	–0–	–0–
Units started	2,000	
Costs incurred for units started		$10,800
Good units of output produced	1,800	
Spoiled units	200	
Ending WIP inventory	–0–	–0–

Management is concerned about the cost of spoilage. Assume that 1,500 units were sold and 300 good units remained in ending finished goods inventory.

Required **a.** Using the five-step approach, calculate the cost of spoiled units assuming that spoilage occurs at the end of the process; there is no need to include separate columns for direct materials and conversion costs since all units were transferred out of WIP inventory by the end of the period. (Since there is no beginning WIP inventory, it does not matter whether weighted average or FIFO is used.)

b. Show the flow of these costs through T-accounts from work in process to cost of goods sold.

6.18   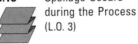 Spoilage Occurs during the Process (L.O. 3)   Refer to the facts for Exercise 6.17. Assume that spoilage occurred when the process was 60 percent complete, costs are added evenly throughout the process, and the ending inventory is 100 percent complete.

Required

Using the five-step approach, calculate the cost of spoiled units and the cost of good units.

6.19 Abnormal Spoilage (L.O. 2)

In manufacturing its products for the month of March, Park City Company incurred abnormal spoilage of $120,000 that occurred during work in process.

Required

What is the journal entry to record this abnormal spoilage?

6.20 Abnormal Spoilage (L.O. 2)

In cutting holiday trees during November, Tree Company incurred abnormal spoilage of $100,000 when an enthusiastic tree cutter trimmed all the branches on the trees.

Required

What is the journal entry to record this abnormal spoilage?

6.21 Normal versus Abnormal Spoilage—Multiple Choice (L.O. 1)

In its June production, Alta Co. incurred $15,000 normal spoilage and $20,000 abnormal spoilage.

Which of the following describes how Alta would account for spoilage costs?

(1) Period expense of $15,000 and inventoriable cost of $20,000.
(2) Inventoriable cost of $15,000 and period expense of $20,000.
(3) Inventoriable cost of $35,000.
(4) Period cost of $35,000.

6.22 Spoilage Occurs during the Process (L.O. 3)

Davis Company has no beginning WIP inventory and started 6,000 units. These units cost $72,000 ($27,000 for materials and $45,000 for conversion costs). Davis produced 5,000 good units but lost the remaining 1,000 units to spoilage. There is no ending WIP inventory. Spoilage is detected when the production process is 60 percent complete for direct materials and 30 percent complete with respect to conversion costs. (There is no need to distinguish between the weighted-average or FIFO methods because beginning WIP inventory balances are zero.)

Required

Using the five-step approach, calculate the cost of spoiled units and the cost of good units.

6.23 Moving the Inspection Point (L.O. 5)

Refer to the data in Exercise 6.22. Assume that the inspection point is moved back in the production process so that spoiled goods are 50 percent complete with respect to direct materials and 20 percent complete with respect to conversion costs. As a result of identifying spoilage earlier in the production process, Davis will save $7,000 in direct materials costs and $5,000 in conversion costs compared to the amounts spent in Exercise 6.22.

Required

Calculate the cost of spoiled units and good units (assume that the *number* of good units and spoiled units remains the same as in Exercise 6.22). Why is the cost per unit lower in Exercise 6.23 than in 6.22?

PROBLEMS

6.24 Spoilage Occurs during the Process

Woodland Company's management is concerned about the level of spoilage and has called you in to help. You have been asked to compute the amount of spoilage. If the amount exceeds 1 percent of the cost of good units transferred out, a special team of analysts will be called in to find the source of spoilage. Your work is particularly important because the company does not want to spend the money on the analysts unless spoilage really exceeds 1 percent.

Woodland has no beginning WIP inventory and started 20,000 units. These units cost $750,000 ($300,000 for materials and $450,000 for conversion costs). It produced 18,500 good units but lost the remaining 1,500 units to spoilage; there is no ending WIP inventory. Spoilage is detected when the production process is 35 percent complete for direct materials and 55 percent complete for conversion costs. Assume that direct materials and conversion costs are added evenly throughout the process. (There is no need to distinguish between the weighted-average or FIFO methods because beginning WIP inventory balances are zero.)

Required

a. Using the five-step approach, calculate the cost of spoiled units and the cost of good units.

b. Does the spoilage exceed the 1 percent threshold? Write a short report telling management about your findings and recommending whether to bring in the special team.

6.25 Spoilage Occurs during the Process— Weighted Average

The management of Orth & Kids is concerned about the level of spoilage and has called you in to help. You have been asked to compute the amount of spoilage. If the amount exceeds 2 percent of the cost of good units transferred out, a special team of analysts will be called in to find the source of spoilage. Your work is particularly important because the company does not want to spend the money on the analysts unless spoilage really exceeds 2 percent of the cost of good units transferred out.

Orth & Kids uses the weighted-average costing method. At the beginning of the period, it had 3,000 units in beginning inventory that were 75 percent complete with respect to materials and 65 percent complete with respect to conversion costs. All units in beginning inventory were good units. During the period, the company started 12,000 units. Of these 12,000 units, 1,750 units were lost to spoilage.

The production people detect spoiled goods at the point that 30 percent of conversion costs and 50 percent of materials costs had been applied. We learn that 11,000 units were transferred out to finished goods inventory. The remaining 2,250 units were in ending WIP inventory, 30 percent complete with respect to materials, and 20 percent complete with respect to conversion costs.

The accounting records show the following information for the activities in the WIP Inventory account:

	Beginning Inventory	Current Period Costs	Total
Materials	$5,000	$20,000	$25,000
Conversion costs	6,000	70,000	76,000

Required

a. Using the five-step process, allocate costs to the appropriate categories (finished goods inventory, spoilage, and ending WIP inventory).

b. Does the spoilage exceed the 2 percent threshold set by management? Write a short report telling management about your findings and recommending whether to bring in the analysts.

6.26 Spoilage Occurs during the Process—FIFO (Appendix)

Refer to the data in Problem 6.25. Assume that Orth & Kids uses the FIFO costing method.

a. Using the five-step process, allocate costs to the appropriate categories (finished goods inventory, spoilage, and ending WIP inventory).

b. Does the spoilage exceed the 2 percent threshold set by management? Write a short report telling management about your findings and recommending whether to bring in the analysts.

6.27 Spoilage

Mesa Verde Co. had the following production for the month of June:

Work in process at June 1	20,000 units
Started during June	80,000
Completed and transferred to finished goods	66,000
Normal spoilage incurred	4,000
Work in process at June 30	30,000

Materials are added at the beginning of the process. As to conversion costs, the beginning work in process was 70 percent complete and the ending work in process was 60 percent complete. Spoilage is detected at the end of the process.

Required

Using the weighted-average method, what were the equivalent units for June with respect to conversion costs?

(1) 84,000.
(2) 88,000.
(3) 90,000.
(4) 100,000.

(CPA adapted)

6.28 Spoilage—Rework

Orlando Co. makes Disney character toys to the exacting specifications of various customers. During April, Work Order 403 for the production of 1,100 Mickeys was completed at the following costs per unit:

Direct materials	. . . .	$ 5
Direct labor	. . . .	4
Applied factory overhead	. . . . . .	6
Total	. . . .	$15

Final inspection of Work Order 403 disclosed 50 defective units and 100 spoiled units. The defective Mickeys were reworked at an additional cost of $250, and the spoiled units were sold to a manufacturer of generic toys for $750.

Required

Write a report to management presenting the alternative ways to account for the cost of rework and spoiled Mickeys sold to the manufacturer of generic toys. State which you recommend and why.

6.29 Cost of Spoilage

Oregonian, Inc., uses weighted-average costing to compute product costs. At the beginning of the period, it had 200 units in beginning inventory that were complete 100 percent with respect to materials and 40 percent with respect to conversion costs. All units in beginning inventory were good units. During the period, the company started 4,800 units; it produced 4,000 good units but lost 1,000 to spoilage.

Oregonian's production people detect spoilage after the application of 20 percent of conversion costs and 100 percent of materials costs. Of the 4,000 good units, 3,600 were transferred out to Finished Goods Inventory. The remaining 400 units were in ending WIP inventory, complete 100 percent with respect to materials and 50 percent with respect to conversion costs. From the accounting records, we find the following costs:

	Beginning Inventory	Current Period Costs	Total
Materials	$10,000	$190,000	$200,000
Conversion costs	4,000	196,000	200,000

Required

Management is concerned that so many units were spoiled and has asked you to determine the cost of spoiled units. Compute the cost of spoiled units and write a report to management recommending whether further action should be taken to reduce spoilage, which management will take if the cost of spoilage exceeds 10 percent of the cost of good units transferred out.

6.30 Spoilage

Racquet Products, Inc., manufactures tennis racquets. The process requires two manufacturing departments; Frames and Strings. Racquets are formed in the Frames Department using aluminum tubing, handle materials, and frame decorations. The completed frames are sent to the Strings Department for stringing and packaging for shipment to sporting goods stores. Six thousand frames were transferred to the Strings Department this month.

Management is concerned about the cost of spoilage. The following information is available for manufacturing activities in the Strings Department during the past month. (Since there is no beginning inventory, it does not matter whether weighted average or FIFO is used.)

		Strings Department		
	Units	Prior Department Costs	Direct Materials	Conversion Costs
Physical flow (No beginning inventory)				
Transferred out	3,300			
Ending inventory	2,600	100% complete	80% complete	45% complete
Spoilage.	100			
Transferred in	6,000			
Current costs		$43,200	$2,500	$6,475

Spoilage occurred at the end of the stringing process when the frames were bent by tension. Spoilage amounted to 100 units, and, consequently, the number of good units in ending inventory is 2,600. The good units are complete 80 percent for materials and 45 percent for conversion costs.

Required

a. Compute the cost of spoiled units for management.

b. Prepare a journal entry that removes the spoiled units from WIP Inventory and debits two-thirds of their costs to Finished Goods Inventory and one-third to Cost of Goods Sold.

c. Prepare a journal entry that treats all spoilage as abnormal spoilage.

d. Write a short report to management summarizing your findings about the cost of spoilage and recommend whether spoilage should be treated as normal or abnormal.

6.31   Process Costing with Spoilage

Stateside Corporation makes a product called Aggregate in one department of the Westcoast Division. Direct materials are added at the beginning of the process. Labor and overhead are added continuously throughout the process. Spoilage occurs at the beginning of the process just after materials have been added but before any conversion costs have been incurred. In the Westcoast Division, all departmental overhead is charged to the departments, and divisional overhead is allocated to the departments on the basis of direct labor-hours. The divisional overhead rate is $2 per direct labor-hour.

The following information relates to production during November:

1. Work in process inventory, November 1 (4,000 pounds—75 percent complete):

Direct materials	$22,800
Direct labor at $5 per hour	24,650
Departmental overhead	12,000
Divisional overhead.	9,860

2. Direct materials:

Inventory, November 1—2,000 pounds.	$10,000
Purchases, November 3—10,000 pounds	51,000
Purchases, November 18—10,000 pounds	51,500
Sent to production during November—16,000 pounds	

3. Direct labor costs at $5 per hour, $103,350.

4. Departmental overhead costs, $52,000; divisional overhead to be computed.

5. Transferred out of work in process, 15,000 pounds.

6. Work in process inventory, November 30, 3,000 pounds, 33⅓ percent complete.

The FIFO method is used for materials inventory valuation, and the weighted-average method is used for WIP inventories.

Required

a. Prepare a production cost report for this department of the Westcoast Division for November. Be sure to show the costs assigned to spoiled units.

b. Write a short report to management indicating whether additional action should be taken to find the source of spoilage. Generally, management follows the following decision rule in deciding what action to take: (1) if spoilage is less than 1 percent of the cost of good units transferred out, ignore it; (2) if spoilage is at least 1 percent but less than 4 percent out, call in a special team to investigate and fix the problems; (3) if spoilage is 4 percent or more, stop production immediately and fix the problem. This last action is very costly.

(CMA adapted)

SOLUTIONS TO SELF-STUDY QUESTIONS

1.

Spoilage during the Process
Weighted-Average Method

	(Step 1) Physical Units	(Step 2) Equivalent Units Materials	Conversion Costs
Flow of Units			
Units to be accounted for			
Beginning WIP inventory....	1,000		
Units started this period	8,000		
Total units to account for	**9,000**		
Units accounted for			
Good units completed and transferred out ..	5,000	5,000	5,000
Spoiled units transferred out.....	1,500		
Materials (1500 × 55%)		825	
Conversion costs (1,500 × 40%)			600
Units in ending inventory....	2,500		
Materials (2,500 × 30%)		750	
Conversion costs (2,500 × 20%)			500
Total units accounted for	**9,000**	**6,575**	**6,100**

	Total	Direct Materials	Conversion Costs
Flow of Costs (step 3)			
Costs to be accounted for			
Costs in beginning WIP inventory....	$ 30,000	$10,000	$ 20,000
Current period costs	120,000	40,000	80,000
Total costs to be accounted for	**$150,000**	**$50,000**	**$100,000**

Cost per Equivalent Unit (step 4)
Materials ($50,000/ 6,575 units)...... $ 7.605
Conversion costs ($100,000/6,100) ... $16.393

	Total	Direct Materials	Conversion Costs
Costs Accounted for (step 5)			
Costs assigned to units transferred out ...	$119,990	$38,023	$81,967
Costs assigned to spoiled goods	16,110	6,274	9,836
Cost of ending WIP inventory....	13,900	5,703	8,197
Total costs accounted for	**$150,000**	**$50,000**	**$100,000**

2. a. To account for this spoilage, the disposal value of spoiled goods is recorded in the Spoiled Goods Inventory account ($200 per unit), Work in Process for Job A1 is reduced by the cost assigned to the spoiled goods ($1,000 per unit), and Overhead is increased by the net cost of spoilage ($800 per unit). The journal entry follows:

Spoiled Goods Inventory........	4,000	
Overhead	16,000	
Work in Process—Job A1 ...		20,000

b. Later, the sale of spoiled goods is recorded as follows:

Cash	4,000	
Spoiled Goods Inventory		4,000

3. Answers will vary. However, most store managers should be aware of the issue of spoilage and how it affects the store's profits.

4. Note: Your answers in Steps 4 and 5 may differ somewhat from ours because of rounding.

Spoilage during the Process
FIFO

| | | Equivalent Units | |
	Physical Units	Materials	Conversion Costs
Flow of Units			
Units to be accounted for			
Beginning WIP inventory....	1,000		
Units started this period......	8,000		
Total units to account for....	9,000		
Units accounted for			
Good units completed and transferred out			
From beginning WIP inventory....	1,000		
Materials 1,000 × (1 − 70%).....		300	
Conversion costs 1,000 × (1 − 60%).....			400
Started and completed currently.......	4,000	4,000	4,000
Spoiled units transferred out.....	1,500		
Materials (1,500 × 55%)....		825	
Conversion costs (1,500 × 40%)....			600
Units in ending WIP inventory	2,500		
Materials (2,500 × 30%)....		750	
Conversion costs (2,500 × 20%)....			500
Total units accounted for	9,000	5,875	5,500

	Total	Direct Materials	Conversion Costs
Flow of Costs			
Costs to be accounted for			
Costs in beginning WIP inventory....	$ 30,000	$10,000	$ 20,000
Current period costs.........	120,000	40,000	80,000

	Total	Direct Materials	Conversion Costs
Total costs to be accounted for	$150,000	$50,000	$100,000
Cost per equivalent unit			
Materials ($40,000/ 5,875 units)......		$ 6.809	
Conversion Costs ($80,000/ 5,500 units)......			$ 14.545
Costs accounted for			
Costs assigned to units transferred out			
Costs from beginning WIP inventory ..	$ 30,000	$10,000	$ 20,000
Current costs added to complete beginning WIP inventory ..	7,861		
Materials ($6.809 × 300 units)....		2,043	
Conversion costs ($14.545 × 400 units)..			5,818
Current costs of units started and completed	85,416		
Materials ($6.809 × 4,000 units) ..		27,234	
Conversion costs ($14.545 × 4,000 units)			58,182
Costs of spoilage ..	14,344		
Materials ($6.809 × 825 units) ...		5,617	
Conversion costs ($14.545 × 600 units)			8,727
Total costs transferred out ...	$137,621	$44,894	$ 92,727
Cost of ending WIP inventory....	$ 12,379		
Materials ($6.809 × 750 units) ...		$ 5,106	
Conversion costs ($14.545 × 500 units)			$ 7,273
Total costs accounted for	$150,000	$50,000	$100,000

Allocating Costs to Departments

LEARNING OBJECTIVES

After reading this chapter, you should be able to:

1. Explain why costs are allocated.

2. Explain issues in selecting allocation bases (or cost drivers).

3. Allocate service department costs using the direct method.

4. Allocate service department costs using the step method.

5. Allocate service department costs using the reciprocal method.

6. Analyze the effect of dual versus single allocation bases.

7. Explain multiple-factor cost allocation.

8. Understand incentive problems with cost allocation methods.

9. Use spreadsheets to solve reciprocal cost allocation problems (appendix).

This chapter discusses cost allocation. Here's the problem. Three students share a house. Having better things to do than clean house, they hire someone to come in and clean once each week. How should they share the costs of the housekeeper? One simple solution is to share the cost equally. Suppose, however, that one student's bedroom is twice as large as each of the other students' bedrooms. The second student has a small bedroom and uses the house only four days per week. The third student uses the house all week, has a small bedroom, and is generally acknowledged to be the cleanest of the three. Sharing the cost equally is simple, but is it fair? The answer to that question probably depends on each student's point of view.

For managers, cost allocation is largely about decision making. As you read the following conversation between a small business manager, Joe, and his efficiency expert who is not proficient in cost accounting, ask yourself how the cost allocation affects Joe's decisions.[1]

Expert: Joe, you said you put in these peanuts because some people ask for them, but do you realize what this rack of peanuts is costing you?

Joe: It's not going to cost! It's going to be a profit. Sure, I had to pay $100 for a fancy rack to hold the bags, but the peanuts cost 24 cents a bag, and I sell 'em for 40 cents. Suppose I sell 50 bags a week to start. It'll take 12½ weeks to cover the cost of the rack. After that I have a clear profit of 16 cents a bag. The more I sell, the more I make.

Expert: That is an antiquated and completely unrealistic approach, Joe. Fortunately, modern accounting procedures permit a more accurate picture, which reveals the complexities involved.

Joe: Huh?

Expert: To be precise, those peanuts must be integrated into your entire operation and be allocated their appropriate share of business overhead. They must share a proportion of your expenditures for rent, heat, light, equipment depreciation, decorating, salaries for your waitresses, cook . . .

Joe: The cook? What's he got to do with the peanuts? He doesn't even know I have them.

Expert: Look, Joe, the cook is in the kitchen, the kitchen prepares the food, the food is what brings people in here, and the people ask to buy peanuts. That's why you must charge a portion of the cook's wages, as well as a part of your own salary, to peanut sales. This sheet contains a carefully calculated cost analysis, which indicates that the peanut operation should pay exactly $2,278 per year toward these general overhead costs.

Joe: The peanuts? $2,278 a year for overhead? Nuts! The peanuts salesman said I'd make money—put 'em on the end of the counter, he said, and get 16 cents a bag profit.

Expert [with a sniff]: He's not an accountant. Do you actually know what the portion of the counter occupied by the peanut rack is worth to you?

Joe: Nothing. No stool there, just a dead spot at the end.

Expert: The modern cost picture permits no dead spots. Your counter contains 60 square feet, and your counter business grosses $60,000 a year. Consequently, the square foot of space occupied by the peanut rack is worth $1,000 per year. Since you have taken that area away from general counter use, you must charge the value of the space to the occupant.

Joe [eagerly]: Look! I have a better idea. Why don't I just throw the nuts out—put them in a trash can?

Expert: Can you afford it?

Joe: Sure. All I have is about 50 bags of peanuts—cost about 12 bucks—so I lose $100 on the rack, but I'm out of this nutsy business and no more grief.

Expert [shaking head]: Joe, it isn't quite that simple. You are in the peanut business! The minute you throw those peanuts out, you are adding $2,278 of annual overhead to the rest of your operation. Joe—be realistic—can you afford to do that?

---

[1]This piece appeared in a publication by Coopers & Lybrand as a reprint. The author is unknown to us.

Joe [completely crushed]: It's unbelievable! Last week I was making money. Now I'm in trouble—just because I believe 50 bags of peanuts a week is easy.

Expert [with raised eyebrow]: That is the object of modern cost studies, Joe—to dispel those false illusions.

What should Joe do?

Joe should fire his efficiency expert. Joe has made a business decision that likely has little or no effect on overhead, yet the expert wants to allocate overhead to the otherwise unused counter space. Note how the allocation affects Joe's incentives. Initially, he likes the idea of selling peanuts. Then he wants to get rid of them and get out of the "nutsy" peanut business. At the end, he is trapped; he loses no matter what he does. The cost allocation has dampened Joe's enthusiasm for getting into any other ventures.

During your career, you will have many encounters with people about cost allocation. Don't be misled by "experts" who are not really experts in modern costing methods. This expert is clearly not familiar with the three underlying themes critical to designing a cost system for managerial purposes.

- **Cost systems should have a decision focus.** Cost systems must meet the needs of the decision makers. Remember that the decision makers are the users of cost accounting information. The "expert" is not providing useful cost information to Joe.

- **Different cost information is used for different purposes.** What works for one purpose will not necessarily work for another purpose. Cost information must provide the appropriate data for its intended purpose.

- **Cost information for managerial purposes must meet the cost-benefit test.** Cost information can invariably be improved. The benefits of improvements (i.e., improved decision making), however, must outweigh the costs of making the improvements. The "expert" is providing Joe with cost information that does not meet the cost-benefit test: the benefits of improvements (if any!) do not outweigh the costs (of hiring the "expert").

Had the expert been trained in modern cost accounting methods and understood the themes underlying the design of costing systems, Joe would likely have reached a different conclusion regarding his new peanut stand.

WHAT IS COST ALLOCATION?

common costs
Costs of shared facilities, products, or services.

Cost allocation is a proportional assignment of an indirect cost to cost objects. A cost object is any end to which a cost is assigned. Each student in the example at the beginning of this chapter is a cost object; in companies they usually are departments.

A **common cost** is an example of an indirect cost. The cost of housecleaning in the opening example is a common cost because the housecleaning service is shared by the three students.

WHY ARE COSTS ALLOCATED?

L.O. 1: Explain why costs are allocated.

There are numerous cost allocation requirements in organizations. Tax regulations and external reporting under GAAP require allocating manufacturing overhead to units produced. Depreciation of long-term assets, which allocates the original cost of an asset over time periods, is required for external financial reporting under GAAP. Costs are allocated for regulatory purposes in public utilities.

Many organizations work on a cost-basis or cost-plus basis. Defense contractors are sometimes reimbursed by the federal government for work done on a cost plus a profit basis. Universities are reimbursed by government agencies, foundations, and private industry for research on a cost plus an overhead rate basis. Costs must be allocated to the research work or the defense contract job. Anyone being reimbursed for costs has incentives to allocate as much cost to the cost-reimbursed contract as possible. For example, universities have incentives to allocate as much cost to

A study of Australian companies concluded that companies allocated the costs of service departments externally for two reasons.

Divisions would have to incur the costs by acquiring the services provided by service departments. To evaluate the division's performance, these service department costs should be included in division costs.

• Cost allocations make the division managers aware that the central services cost money to provide.

Source: From G. W. Dean, M. P. Joye, and P. J. Blayney, *Overhead Cost Allocation and Performance Evaluation Practices of Australian Manufacturers* (Sidney, Australia: The Accounting and Finance Foundation, The University of Sidney, 1991).

cost-reimbursed research contracts as possible. Defense contractors that work on both cost-reimbursed jobs and jobs sold in the market at competitive prices have incentives to allocate as much cost to the cost-reimbursed contracts as possible.

For managerial purposes, costs are often allocated to influence behavior. In the example of the students and housecleaning, allocating costs based on the amount of time the housecleaner spent in each room would give the students incentives to keep their rooms clean. Allocating the cost of computer support to departments in a university gives department chairs an incentive to monitor the department's use of the computer support services.

Many organizations allocate headquarters' costs to divisions to give division managers incentives to make enough profits to cover them. For example, an executive of Kmart, a retail company with more than 2,000 stores, told us during an interview that "allocating corporate headquarters' costs to stores makes each store manager aware that these costs exist and must be covered by the individual stores for the company as a whole to be profitable."[2] A study of corporate cost allocation found that 84 percent of companies participating in the survey reported allocating common headquarters' costs to divisions.[3] The study indicated that the primary managerial reason for cost allocation was to give incentives to division managers to cover division profits for the company as a whole to be profitable. The Real World Application, "Why Do Companies Allocate Costs?" at the top of this page gives similar results in a study of Australian companies.

THE ARBITRARY NATURE OF COST ALLOCATION

By definition, costs that are common to two or more cost objects are likely to be allocated to those cost objects on a somewhat arbitrary basis. This arbitrariness has led critics of cost allocation to claim that arbitrary cost allocations may result in misleading information and poor decisions.

For example, suppose that headquarters' costs (e.g., president's salary, depreciation, utilities) are allocated to divisions based on total revenues for each division. An older division with relatively high revenues may be much more independent from the headquarters office than a newer, less profitable division that consumes much of the headquarters' time. If costs are allocated based on revenue, however, the older division will be allocated a higher share of headquarters' costs.

Although the allocation base (in this example, revenues for each division) may seem reasonable, a certain degree of arbitrariness associated with any method of

[2]Based on personal communication with the Kmart executive.
[3]See J. M. Fremgen and S. S. Liao, *The Allocation of Corporate Indirect Costs* (New York: National Association of Accountants [now the Institute of Management Accountants], 1981).

allocating costs always exists. Later in this chapter we will discuss the criteria most often used in selecting an allocation base.

COST ALLOCATION FROM SERVICE DEPARTMENTS TO USER DEPARTMENTS

This chapter focuses on allocating the costs of a service department to other departments that use the service.

Service departments provide services to other departments. For example, an information systems department is a service department that provides information to other departments, and a human resources department provides personnel hiring and training services to other departments. **User departments** use the services of service departments. For example, the production department probably uses the services provided by the information systems or human resources departments. (In the example of the students and housecleaning, assuming that both parties are in the same organization, the students are the users and the housekeeper is the service department.) User departments could be other service departments or production or marketing departments that produce or market the organization's products, as shown in Illustration 7.1.

Any cost center whose costs are charged to other departments in the organization is called an **intermediate cost center. Final cost centers,** on the other hand, are cost centers whose costs are not allocated to another cost center.

Illustration 7.2 shows examples of service departments and user departments in a hospital. In this case, the user departments are also production departments. Both the Emergency Room and the X Ray Departments are production departments that use the services of the two service departments, Information Services and Maintenance.

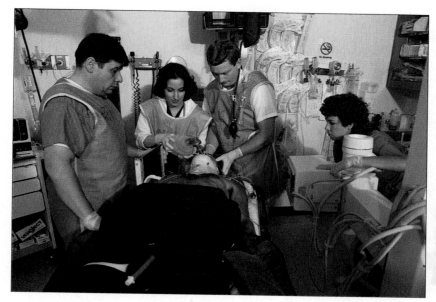

This patient in the emergency room is an example of a customer using the services of a production department—the Emergency Room—as discussed on this page. Maintenance, Information Services, Supplies and Security are examples of service departments that support the production department—the Emergency Room. (© Charles Gupton/Tony Stone Images)

service department
A department that provides service to other subunits in the organization.

user department
A department that uses the services of service departments.

intermediate cost center
A cost center whose costs are charged to other departments in the organization.

final cost center
A cost center, such as a production or marketing department, whose costs are not allocated to another cost center.

If you have ever been an emergency room patient, you used the hospital's products, which were the services provided by the Emergency Room and X Ray Departments. Maintenance cleaned up after you in those two departments, and Information Services helped the Emergency Room and X Ray Departments track your medical history and billing information. To the Emergency Room and X Ray departments, you were the customer. To Maintenance and Information Services, the customers were X Ray and the Emergency Room. Our task in this chapter is to determine how to allocate costs of service departments, such as Maintenance and Information Services, to the production departments, such as Emergency Room and X Ray. This cost allocation is done so the hospital can determine the cost of services performed for each patient.

Service organizations, merchandising organizations, and manufacturing organizations have production or marketing departments and service departments. These are examples of production or marketing and service departments in various organizations:

ILLUSTRATION   7.1   Service and User Departments

Service department

Service Department → Production or Marketing Department

Service Department provides service to the final user department.

Service departments   User department

Service Department A → Service Department B → Production or Marketing Department

Service Department A provides service to Service Department B, which provides
service to the final user department.

ILLUSTRATION   7.2   Examples of Service and User Departments

Hospital

Service Departments
— Information Services
— Maintenance

User Departments
— X Ray
— Emergency Room

Organization	Service Department	Production or Marketing Department
Packard Bell (computer manufacturer)	Maintenance	Assembly
Marshall Fields (retail department store)	Data Processing	Sportswear
Massachusetts General Hospital	Laundry	Emergency Room
City of Miami	Motor Pool	City Parks

CHOOSE ALLOCATION BASES

allocation base
A measure related to two or more cost objects that is used to allocate indirect or common costs to those cost objects.

Next we learn about one of the most challenging tasks in cost allocation: selecting the base(s) for allocating costs to user departments. If a factor drives or causes a cost, it is a cost driver. Ideally, accountants allocate costs using cost drivers. Sometimes common costs have indistinguishable cost drivers or cost drivers that are too hard to measure. Then accountants use some other **allocation base.** A cost driver is a good allocation base, but it may not always be feasible to find or measure cost drivers.

The following are four typical categories of common costs and related allocation bases.

ILLUSTRATION 7.3 | Typical Allocation Bases for Common Costs

	Common Cost	Typical Allocation Base
Labor Related	1. Supervision	Number of employees
		Payroll dollars or labor-hours
	2. Personnel services	Number of employees
Machine Related	3. Insurance on equipment	Value of equipment
	4. Taxes on equipment	Value of equipment
	5. Equipment depreciation	Machine-hours, equipment value
	6. Equipment maintenance	Number of machines, machine-hours
Occupancy Related	7. Building rental	Space occupied
	8. Building insurance	Space occupied
	9. Heat and air conditioning	Space occupied, volume occupied
	10. Concession rental	Space occupied and desirability of location
	11. Interior building maintenance	Space occupied
Service Related	12. Materials handling	Quantity or value of materials
	13. Laundry	Weight of laundry processed
	14. Billing and accounting	Number of documents
	15. Indirect materials	Value of direct materials
	16. Dietary	Number of meals

L.O. 2: Explain issues in selecting allocation bases (or cost drivers).

- *Labor-related common costs.* These costs are usually allocated on the basis of number of employees, labor hours, wages paid, or similar labor-related criteria. (See items 1 and 2 in Illustration 7.3.)
- *Machine-related common costs.* These costs are usually allocated on the basis of machine-hours, current value of machinery and equipment, number of machines, or similar machine-related criteria. (See items 3 through 6 in Illustration 7.3.)
- *Occupancy-related common costs.* These common costs are usually allocated on the basis of area or volume occupied or similar space-related criteria. (See items 7 through 11 in Illustration 7.3.)
- *Service-related common costs.* These costs may be allocated on the basis of quantity, value, time, and similar service-related criteria. (See items 12 through 16 in Illustration 7.3.)

One question about the typical categories of common costs and their related allocation bases must be asked: How do we select the best allocation base? The three common approaches to selecting an allocation base are outlined here.

- *Causal relation.* If possible, find a cause-and-effect relation between the cost object and the cost and use a cost driver that reflects that cause-and-effect relationship. For example, if maintenance on an aircraft is based on the number of flight hours, number of flight hours is a cost driver. Allocating maintenance costs to a particular flight based on that flight's hours is appropriate.
- *Benefits received.* If a causal relation cannot be found, it is appropriate to select an allocation base that reflects benefits received. For example, the cost of employee training to improve quality is not necessarily caused by a particular product, but the quality of the product might benefit if employees participate in a training program. In this case, the costs of employee training might be allocated based on the reduction in defective units produced.
- *Reasonableness.* If managers cannot come up with an allocation base that reflects causality or benefits received, they select an allocation base that represents a "reasonable" cost allocation. For example, it is reasonable to allocate space-related costs, such as housekeeping, on the basis of square feet cleaned.

REAL WORLD APPLICATION | **Inappropriate Cost Allocations**

A research and engineering organization developed a system of cost allocations to determine the cost of each research or engineering job performed.

Afterward, management noticed that its technical staff was spending a lot of time formatting and preparing graphics even though the company had a publishing department to do that work.

Upon further investigation, management learned that the publishing department was charging an excessive amount for its services to cover its costs. Building occupancy costs, which were allocated based on square feet in the department, were high because lab space was three times as expensive as the type of office space used for publishing (due to the sterile environment required in a lab), yet all space was allocated the same amount per square foot. The result was a substantial overcharge for building occupancy costs charged to the publishing group, which increased the costs it had to recover through its charges to technical staff.

Similar problems were found with library and travel support costs. Library and travel support costs were allocated based on number of employees in the department. Although some of the library and travel support costs were allocated to the publishing department, none of the publishing employees used library or travel support services. Again, these costs were passed through the publishing department in the form of higher charges to the technical staff.

The company changed its allocation system, and the publishing department charges fell to the point that technical staff found it more economical to work on research and engineering projects rather than to do graphics and formatting, and their use of the publishing department increased. By adjusting the cost allocation system, the company was able to improve its overall productivity.

Source: Based on the authors' research.

Incentive Issues in Allocating Costs

It is usually advisable to allocate costs on a cause-and-effect basis. By establishing a cause-and-effect relationship for allocating costs, service department managers can trace costs to their cause. Moreover, managers of user departments have an incentive to limit their use if the costs of the service center are allocated on a cause-and-effect basis. When the basis of cost allocation does not reflect cause-and-effect, cost control becomes difficult because departments tend to make excessive demands for underpriced services or underuse overpriced services, as in the Real World Application on this page.

METHODS OF ALLOCATING SERVICE DEPARTMENT COSTS

In this section, we describe three methods to allocate service department overhead costs: the direct method, the step method, and the reciprocal method. To make each method easier to understand, we use a comprehensive example.

Wetlands Engineering, Inc., designs and monitors wetlands for several clients. Assume that Wetlands has three service departments: Biology (S1), Building Occupancy (S2), and Project Supervision (S3). Costs are recorded in these departments and are allocated to two project departments and one marketing department: Wetlands Production (P1), Wetlands Monitoring (P2), and the Marketing Department (P3). All six departments share the same building.

Wetlands allocates costs to Wetlands Production and Wetlands Monitoring for two purposes: (1) to determine the cost to produce and market its services and (2) to encourage department managers to monitor each other's costs; that is, cross-department monitoring.

Each service department is an intermediate cost center whose costs are recorded as incurred and then distributed to other cost centers. At Wetlands, Biology (S1) costs are distributed on the basis of biology staff time required by the user department. Building Occupancy (S2) costs are distributed on the basis of area occupied

ILLUSTRATION	7.4	Bases for Service Department Cost Allocations

WETLANDS ENGINEERING, INC.
Biology (S1)

Allocation base: Biology labor hours worked in each user department.

User Department	Biology Labor Hours Used	Proportion of Total
Wetlands Production (P1)	14,000	0.20
Wetlands Monitoring (P2)	56,000	0.80
Marketing (P3)	–0–	–0–
Totals	70,000	1.00

Building Occupancy (S2)

Allocation base: Area (square footage) in each user department.

User Department	Square Footage	Proportion of Total
Wetlands Production (P1)	80,000	0.32
Wetlands Monitoring (P2)	60,000	0.24
Marketing (P3)	60,000	0.24
Biology (S1)	20,000	0.08
Project Supervision (S3)	30,000	0.12
Totals	250,000	1.00

Project Supervision (S3)

Allocation base: Annual payroll dollars of user departments.

User Department	Payroll Dollars	Proportion of Total
Wetlands Production (P1)	$360,000	0.45
Wetlands Monitoring (P2)	240,000	0.30
Marketing (P3)	–0–	–0–
Biology (S1)	120,000	0.15
Building Occupancy (S2)	80,000	0.10
Totals	$800,000	1.00

by the user department, and Project Supervision (S3) costs are distributed on the basis of the user department's payroll dollars.

Allocation Bases

Illustration 7.4 shows the cost drivers for each service department and the proportions of costs allocated to user departments. For example, Biology costs are allocated on the basis of labor hours worked for each user department. During the period, Biology worked 14,000 hours for Wetlands Production and 56,000 hours for Wetlands Monitoring. Thus, 20 percent of Biology costs are allocated to Wetlands Production (20 percent = 14,000 hours/[14,000 + 56,000 hours]) and 80 percent to Wetlands Monitoring (Marketing does not use the Biology Department; thus, no Biology costs are allocated to Marketing). Identical methods are used to derive the percentages for allocating building occupancy and project supervision costs. These percentages are shown in Illustration 7.4.

We use these percentages extensively in the examples that follow.

| ILLUSTRATION | 7.5 | Flow of Cost Allocations—Direct Method |

WETLANDS ENGINEERING, INC.

Service Departments

Biology Department (S1)

| Direct costs of Biology 36,000 | Allocated to: Wetlands Production Wetlands Monitoring |

Overhead—Wetlands Production (P1)

| Direct overhead costs of user department Allocated costs from service departments: Biology Building Occupancy Project Supervision | |

Building Occupancy Department (S2)

| Direct costs of Building Occupancy 84,000 | Allocated to: Wetlands Production Wetlands Monitoring Marketing |

Overhead—Wetlands Monitoring (P2)

| Direct overhead costs of user department Allocated costs from service departments: Biology Building Occupancy Project Supervision | |

Project Supervision Department (S3)

| Direct costs of Project Supervision 25,000 | Allocated to: Wetlands Production Wetlands Monitoring |

Marketing (P3)

| Direct costs of the Marketing Department Allocated costs from service departments: Building Occupancy | |

DIRECT METHOD

L.O. 3: Allocate service department costs using the direct method.

direct method
A cost allocation method that charges costs of service departments to user departments without making allocations between service departments.

The **direct method** allocates costs directly to the final user of a service, ignoring intermediate users. Illustration 7.5 shows the flow of costs and the allocations to be recognized for the departments when the direct method is used. The direct costs of service departments are first recorded in those service departments. These costs are shown on the debit side of the service department accounts. Then service department costs are allocated to the user departments.

The production departments also have direct costs such as the department manager's salary. These costs are indicated as the "direct overhead costs of user department" or "direct costs of the Marketing Department" in the T-accounts in Illustration 7.5. These costs do not have to be allocated to the user departments because they are debited to the department accounts when incurred.

Using the direct method, there are no allocations between service departments. Thus, the building occupancy costs and the project supervision costs attributable to the Biology Department are not allocated to Biology. Likewise, the project supervision costs that are related to the building occupancy function and the costs of the building space occupied by the project supervision activity are not allocated to their respective service departments.

The use of the direct method of cost allocation at Wetlands is discussed here and shown in Illustration 7.6. Assume that the accounting records show that costs of

---

ILLUSTRATION   7.6 | Cost Allocation Computations—Direct Method

Panel A: Proportions

| | | Proportion Chargeable to: | | |
Service Department	Department's Direct Costs	Wetlands Production (P1)	Wetlands Monitoring (P2)	Marketing (P3)
Biology (S1)	$36,000	0.2	0.8	–0–
Building Occupancy (S2) . . .	84,000	0.4	0.3	0.3
Project Supervision (S3) . . .	25,000	0.6	0.4	–0–

Panel B: Direct Method Cost Allocation

| From | | To | | |
Service Department	Amount	Wetlands Production (P1)	Wetlands Monitoring (P2)	Marketing (P3)
Biology (S1)	$ 36,000	$ 7,200	$28,800	–0–
Building Occupancy (S2) . . .	84,000	33,600	25,200	$25,200
Project Supervision (S3) . . .	25,000	15,000	10,000	–0–
Total allocated.	$145,000	$55,800	$64,000	$25,200

Panel C: Selected Additional Computations

	Amount Allocated	Proportions, from Panel A		Amount to Be Allocated
Biology	$ 7,200	=	0.2 ×	$36,000
Building Occupancy:	$33,600	=	0.4 ×	$84,000
	$25,200	=	0.3 ×	$84,000
Project Supervision	$15,000	=	0.6 ×	$25,000

$36,000, $84,000, and $25,000 are recorded in each service department, S1, S2, and S3, respectively. Costs are allocated directly to Wetlands Production (P1), Wetlands Monitoring (P2), and Marketing (P3)—hence, the name *direct method*.

Note that these are overhead costs only. Direct labor and direct materials (plants, planting materials, etc.) are charged directly to the job. Only overhead must be allocated.

Allocate Biology Department Costs

Biology Department costs of $36,000 are allocated to P1, P2, and P3 based on the biology labor hours used by P1, P2, and P3. According to the facts given in Illustration 7.4, P1 (Wetlands Production) used 20 percent and P2 (Wetlands Monitoring) used 80 percent of the total Biology labor-hours. The Marketing Department did not use any Biology labor hours. Hence, the allocation of Biology Department costs is simply

P1	20% × $36,000 =	$ 7,200
P2	80 × 36,000 =	28,800
Total	100%	$36,000

These proportions are used to allocate Biology costs, as shown in Illustration 7.6. (Read across the Biology [S1] row in Panel B.)

Allocate Building Occupancy Department Costs

Building Occupancy Department costs are distributed to P1, P2, and P3 in the same ratio as the proportions of the square footage occupied by those departments alone. That is, the square footage proportions for P1, P2, and P3, based on data given in Illustration 7.4, are

P1	0.32
P2	0.24
P3	0.24
Total	0.80

When these are scaled to 100 percent, we have

P1	40%	= 0.32/0.80
P2	30	= 0.24/0.80
P3	30	= 0.24/0.80
Total	100%	

These proportions are used to allocate Building Occupancy Department costs as shown in Illustration 7.6. (Read across the Building Occupancy [S2] row in Panel B.)

Allocate Project Supervision Department Costs

Similar calculations are made for Project Supervision Department costs that are allocated on the basis of payroll-dollars. The payroll-dollars proportions for P1, P2, and P3 follow (see Illustration 7.4):

P1	0.45
P2	0.30
P3	0.00
Total	0.75

When these are scaled to 100 percent, we have

P1	60%	= 0.45/0.75
P2	40	= 0.30/0.75
P3	0	= 0/0.75
Total	100%	

These proportions are used to allocate Project Supervision Department costs, as shown in Illustration 7.6. (Read across the Project Supervision [S3] row in Panel B.)

Once these proportions are computed, the direct costs for each service department are allocated to each user department as shown in Illustration 7.6. The Biology costs of $36,000 are allocated $7,200 (or 20 percent) to Wetlands Production and $28,800 (or 80 percent) to Wetlands Monitoring. The total allocated ($7,200 + $28,800) equals the total costs in the Biology user department ($36,000). (The step of scaling to 100 percent ensures this result.)

Panels B and C of Illustration 7.6 explain allocations for the three service centers. As a result of these allocations, the total service department costs charged are $55,800 to Wetlands Production, $64,000 to Wetlands Monitoring, and $25,200 to Marketing.

Limitations of the Direct Method

Some people have criticized the direct method because it ignores services provided by one service department to another. If one purpose of cost allocation is to encourage cross-department monitoring, the direct method falls short because it ignores the costs that service departments themselves incur when they use services from other departments. An attempt to remedy this problem has resulted in the step method of allocating service department costs, discussed in the next section.

SELF-STUDY QUESTION

1. T. Schurt & Company manufactures and sells T-shirts for advertising and promotional purposes. The company has two manufacturing operations, shirtmaking and printing. When an order for T-shirts is received, the Shirtmaking Department obtains the materials and colors requested and has the shirts made in the desired mix of sizes. The completed shirts are then sent to the Printing Department where the custom labels or designs are prepared and embossed on the shirts.

To support the manufacturing activity, the company has a building that houses the two manufacturing departments as well as the Sales Department, a payroll department, and a design and patterns staff. To aid in cost control, the company accumulates the costs of these support functions in separate service departments: (1) building occupancy, (2) payroll accounting, and (3) design and patterns.

During the current period, the direct costs incurred in each of the departments are as follows:

Shirtmaking (P1)	$210,000
Printing (P2)	140,000
Sales (P3)	80,000
Building Occupancy (S1)	45,000
Payroll Accounting (S2)	20,000
Design and Patterns (S3)	10,000

Building Occupancy costs are allocated on the basis of the number of square feet of each user department. Payroll Accounting costs are allocated on the basis of the number of employees. The Design and Pattern costs are charged to departments on the basis of the number of designs requested by each department. For the current period, the following table summarizes the usage of services by other service cost centers and other departments:

	S1	S2	S3	P1	P2	P3
Building Occupancy (S1) (square feet)	—	8,100	3,900	27,000	36,000	6,000
Payroll Accounting (S2) (employees)	3	—	6	30	15	6
Design and Patterns (S3) (designs)	—	—	—	15	40	5

Using the direct method for service cost allocations, what are the total costs in each of the three "producing" departments?

The solution to this question is at the end of this chapter on page 227.

STEP METHOD

L.O. 4: Allocate service department costs using the step method.

step method
The method of service department cost allocation that recognizes some services are provided by service departments to other service departments.

The **step method** recognizes some services are provided by one service department to others. Allocations usually begin from the service department that has provided the largest proportion of its total services to other service departments. Once an allocation is made from a service department, no further allocations are made back to that department. Hence, one service department that provides services to another and receives services from that department has only one of these two relationships recognized.

By choosing the allocation order suggested, we minimize the percentage of services ignored in the step allocation process. For example, when the step method is used at Wetlands Engineering, costs are allocated from the Project Supervision Department to the Building Occupancy Department but not vice versa.

An analysis of service usage among service departments of Wetlands Engineering indicates that Project Supervision supplies 25 percent of its services to other service departments; Building Occupancy supplies 20 percent of its services to other service departments. (See Illustration 7.4.) Biology provides no services to other service departments. Based on services provided to other service departments, the rank ordering for step allocation is as follows:

Order	Service Department
1	Project Supervision (S3)
2	Building Occupancy (S2)
3	Biology (S1)

Allocating Project Supervision Department Costs

Project Supervision costs are allocated to all service departments that used Project Supervision's services, whereas Building Occupancy's costs are allocated only to the service department that ranks below it in the allocation order. Recall that under the step method, once a service department's costs have been allocated to other departments, no costs can be allocated back to it. The computation of service department costs allocated to other service departments at Wetlands Engineering is shown in Illustration 7.7.

ILLUSTRATION 7.7 Cost Allocation Computations—Step Method

WETLANDS ENGINEERING, INC.

Panel A: Proportions

Service Department	Department's Direct Costs				Proportion Chargeable To			
		S3	S2	S1	P1	P2	P3
Project Supervision (S3) . . .	$ 25,000	–0–	0.10[a]	0.15[a]	0.45[a]	0.30[a]	–0–
Building Occupancy (S2) . . .	84,000	–0–	–0–	0.09[b]	0.37[b]	0.27[b]	0.27[b]
Biology (S1)	36,000	–0–	–0–	–0–	0.20[a]	0.80[a]	–0–
	$145,000						

Panel B: Step Method Allocation

From				Cost Allocation To		
	S3	S2	S1	P1	P2	P3
Direct service department costs	$ 25,000	$ 84,000	$ 36,000			
Project Supervision (S3)[c]	$(25,000)	2,500	3,750	$11,250	$ 7,500	–0–
Building Occupancy (S2)[d]		$(86,500)	7,785	32,005	23,355	$23,355
Biology (S1)[e]			$(47,535)	9,507	38,028	–0–
Total costs allocated				$52,762	$68,883	$23,355

---

[a]Percentages from Illustration 7.4.

[b]Allocation of building occupancy to departments on a square footage basis. Total square feet are 220,000, which equals 250,000 total minus 30,000 used by Project Supervision, according to Illustration 7.4:
 0.09 = 20,000 ÷ 220,000 square feet (rounded)
Similarly,
 0.37 = 80,000 ÷ 220,000 square feet (rounded)
and
 0.27 = 60,000 ÷ 220,000 square feet (rounded)

[c]Project Supervision (S3):
 $2,500 = 0.10 × $25,000; $3,750 = 0.15 × $25,000; etc.

[d]Building Occupancy (S2):
 $86,500 = $84,000 + $2,500 (allocated costs from S3)
 $ 7,785 = 0.09 × $86,500; $32,005 = 0.37 × $86,500; etc.

[e]Biology (S1):
 $47,535 = $36,000 + $3,750 (allocated from S3) + $7,785 (allocated costs from S2)
 $ 9,507 = 0.20 × $47,535; $38,028 = 0.80 × $47,535
Proof:
Costs to be allocated = Costs allocated
 $25,000 + $84,000 + $36,000 = $52,762 + $68,883 + $23,355

ILLUSTRATION 7.8 Flow of Cost Allocations—Step Method

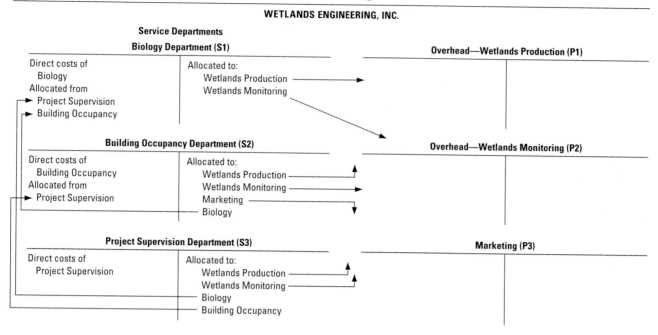

Project Supervision Department costs are charged to user departments based on the total labor-dollars recorded for each. The distribution results in 15 percent of the $25,000 in Project Supervision Department costs being charged to Biology, 10 percent to Building Occupancy, 45 percent to Wetlands Production, and the remaining 30 percent to Wetlands Monitoring (based on Illustration 7.4). (See the Project Supervision [S3] row in Panel A of Illustration 7.7.)

Allocating Building Occupancy Department Costs

In calculating the allocation of Building Occupancy Department costs (second in the allocation order), the step method ignores the area occupied by the Project Supervision Department because costs have already been allocated from that department. As a result, the portion of Building Occupancy Department costs to be allocated to Biology is determined by taking the 20,000 square feet used by Biology (as shown in Illustration 7.4) and dividing by the 220,000 square-foot basis (250,000 total square feet less the 30,000 occupied by Project Supervision). The result is approximately 9 percent.

The total cost to be allocated from Building Occupancy is $86,500, which equals the sum of the direct costs ($84,000) plus the allocated costs ($2,500 from Project Supervision). Therefore, the transfer to Biology is 9 percent of $86,500, which equals $7,785. Similar computations are made to allocate Building Occupancy's costs to the other departments as shown in Illustration 7.7.

Allocating Biology Costs

Biology was used 20 percent by Wetlands Production and 80 percent by Wetlands Monitoring, according to Illustration 7.4. These services are not used by any other service department, so they are allocated directly to the user departments (20 percent to P1 and 80 percent to P2).

The flow of costs under the step method is diagrammed in Illustration 7.8. Notice that Illustration 7.8 differs from Illustration 7.5, which showed cost flows using the direct method, because some costs flow from one service department to another. In addition, the costs allocated from service departments include not only the direct costs of the service departments but also costs allocated to the service departments.

Limitations of the Step Method

The step method may result in more reasonable allocations than the direct method because it recognizes that some service departments use other service departments. However, it does not recognize reciprocal services–for example, that Building Occupancy and Project Supervision both provide and use each other's services. The step method is not necessarily better than the direct method when both the costs and benefits of using cost allocation are considered. A company that already uses the direct method may find it uneconomical to switch methods.

SELF-STUDY QUESTION

2. Refer to the facts for Self-Study Question 1. Compute the cost allocations and total costs in each production department using the step method. Start with S2.

The solution to this question is at the end of this chapter on page 228.

THE RECIPROCAL METHOD

L.O. 5: Allocate service department costs using the reciprocal method.

reciprocal method
The method to allocate service department costs that recognizes all services provided by any service department, including services provided to other service departments.

The reciprocal method addresses a limitation of the step method by making a reciprocal cost allocation when service departments provide reciprocal services (that is, they provide services to each other). The **reciprocal method** recognizes all services provided by any department, including those provided to other service departments. This method is identical to the actual process by which services are exchanged among departments within the organization.

With the reciprocal method, the costs of each production, marketing, and service department are written in equation form:

$$\text{Total costs} = \frac{\text{Direct costs of}}{\text{the service department}} + \frac{\text{Costs to be allocated}}{\text{to the service department}}$$

The system of equations is then solved simultaneously using matrix algebra. By solving all of the equations simultaneously, we provide for all service department allocations, including services provided by service departments to each other. This method is called the *reciprocal method* because it accounts for cost flows in both directions among service departments that provide services to each other. It is also known as the *simultaneous solution method* because it solves a system of equations simultaneously. The key difference between the step and reciprocal methods can be seen by comparing Illustrations 7.8 and 7.9. Note that the reciprocal method accounts for the reciprocal services between the Building Occupancy and Project Supervision departments. The step method accounted for only one direction of services, from Project Supervision to Building Occupancy, but not vice versa.

Both the step method and the direct method might understate the cost of running service departments. These methods omit costs of certain services consumed by one service department that were provided by other service departments. For example, only the reciprocal method considered services provided by Building Occupancy to Project Supervision.

Reciprocal Method Using Matrix Algebra with Three or More Service Departments

The mathematical details of the reciprocal method when there are three (or more) service departments are presented in the appendix to this chapter. Generally, a computer is used to solve this allocation problem. Illustration 7.10 presents the costs allocated to the Production (Wetlands Production and Wetlands Monitoring) and Marketing Departments using each of the three methods for Wetlands Engineering so you can see the impact on the costs allocated to the user departments.

ILLUSTRATION   7.9   **Flow of Cost Allocations—Reciprocal Method**

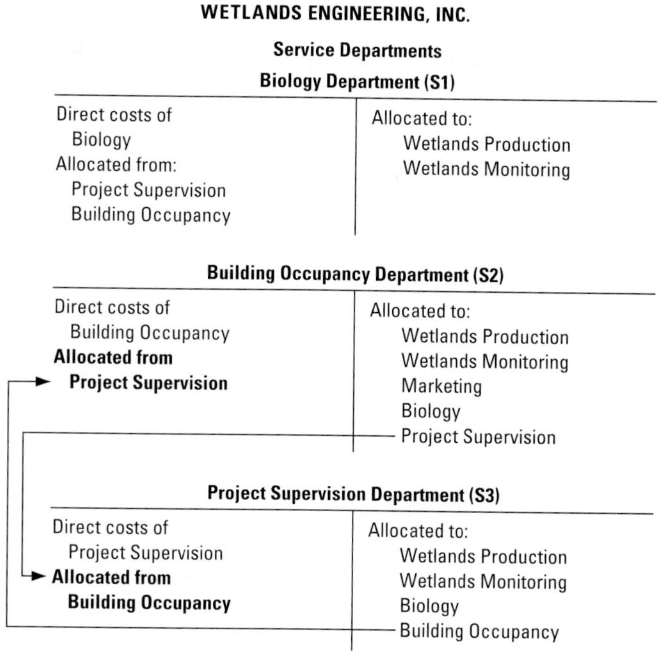

WETLANDS ENGINEERING, INC.

Service Departments

Biology Department (S1)

Direct costs of
  Biology
Allocated from:
  Project Supervision
  Building Occupancy
	Allocated to:
	  Wetlands Production
	  Wetlands Monitoring

Building Occupancy Department (S2)

Direct costs of
  Building Occupancy
Allocated from
  Project Supervision
	Allocated to:
	  Wetlands Production
	  Wetlands Monitoring
	  Marketing
	  Biology
	  Project Supervision

Project Supervision Department (S3)

Direct costs of
  Project Supervision
Allocated from
  Building Occupancy
	Allocated to:
	  Wetlands Production
	  Wetlands Monitoring
	  Biology
	  Building Occupancy

ILLUSTRATION 7.10 | **Comparison of Dollar Amounts Allocated under Each Cost Allocation Method**

WETLANDS ENGINEERING, INC.

	Allocated Service Costs		
Department	**Direct Method**	**Step Method**	**Reciprocal Method[a]**
Wetlands Production (P1)	$ 55,800	$ 52,762	$ 53,660
Wetlands Monitoring (P2)	64,000	68,883	70,328
Marketing (P3)	25,200	23,355	21,012
Totals	$145,000	$145,000	$145,000

[a]These costs are computed in the appendix to this chapter.

Reciprocal Method Using Linear Algebra with Only Two Service Departments

When there are only two service departments, simple algebra can be used to solve the allocation problem. To show how this works, we present a simpler example than the one previously used in this chapter.

Assume that a company has two service departments, S1 and S2, and three production departments, P1, P2, and P3, with the following direct costs and allocation percentages:

		Percent of Costs Allocated To				
Department	Direct Costs	S1	S2	P1	P2	P3
S1	$ 79,000	—	30%	30%	30%	10%
S2	26,000	10%	—	15	15	60
	$105,000					

The two service departments' costs may be expressed in equation form as follows:

$$\text{Total costs} = \begin{array}{c}\text{Direct costs of}\\ \text{the service}\\ \text{department}\end{array} + \begin{array}{c}\text{Costs to be allocated}\\ \text{to the service department}\end{array}$$

$$S1 = \$79{,}000 + 0.1\ S2$$
$$S2 = \$26{,}000 + 0.3\ S1$$

These yield two equations with two unknowns that can be solved by substitution. Substituting Equation (2) into Equation (1) gives

$$S1 = \$79{,}000 + 0.1(\$26{,}000 + 0.3\ S1)$$
$$S1 = \$79{,}000 + \$2{,}600 + 0.03\ S1$$

We collect terms and solve:

$$0.97\ S1 = \$81{,}600$$
$$S1 = \$81{,}600/0.97 = \$84{,}124$$

Substituting this value for S1 back into Equation (2) gives

$$S2 = \$26{,}000 + 0.3(\$84{,}124)$$
$$S2 = \$26{,}000 + \$25{,}237$$
$$S2 = \$51{,}237$$

Thus, costs are simultaneously allocated between the two service departments. The values for S1 ($84,124) and S2 ($51,237) are then used as the total costs of the service departments that are to be allocated to the production departments. The allocations are

		Allocated To					
		P1		**P2**		**P3**	
From	**Total Cost**	**Amount**	**%**	**Amount**	**%**	**Amount**	**%**
S1	$ 84,124	$25,237	30%	$25,237	30%	$ 8,412	10%
S2	51,237	7,686	15	7,686	15	30,742	60
Totals	$135,361	$32,923		$32,923		$39,154	

Computations follow:

	For P1 and P2	For P3
S1:	$25,237 = 0.3 × $84,124	$ 8,412 = 0.1 × $84,124
S2:	$ 7,686 = 0.15 × $51,237	$30,742 = 0.6 × $51,237

The total cost allocated to the production departments amounts to $105,000 (= $32,923 + $32,923 + $39,154), which equals the costs to be allocated from the service departments ($79,000 + $26,000 = $105,000).

SELF-STUDY QUESTION

3. Assume that a company has two service departments, S1 and S2, and three production departments, P1, P2, and P3, with the following direct costs and allocation percentages:

		Percent of Costs Allocated To				
Department	**Direct Costs**	**S1**	**S2**	**P1**	**P2**	**P3**
S1	$100,000	—	20%	30%	30%	20%
S2	200,000	10%	—	20	40	30
	$300,000					

What is the allocation of service department costs using the reciprocal method?

The solution to this question is at the end of this chapter on page 228.

COMPARING THE DIRECT, STEP, AND RECIPROCAL METHODS

These three service department allocation methods can be compared in two ways. The first is to examine how each allocates costs to departments receiving services. Returning to the Wetlands Engineering example, as shown in Illustration 7.11, only the reciprocal method allocates costs to all departments receiving services from other departments.

The second way to compare these three methods is to examine the costs each ultimately allocates to manufacturing and marketing departments, as shown in Illustration 7.10. Each method allocates the same total cost for Wetlands Engineering—$145,000. The difference is in the amounts allocated to particular production and marketing departments.

The major factor affecting these allocations is the distribution of building occupancy costs. Under the direct method, the use of the building by other service departments is ignored. This results in a higher cost allocation to the Marketing Department (and less cost allocated to production) because that department makes no use of the other service departments. As the utilization of the building by other service departments is recognized, the allocation to Marketing decreases.

If performance evaluations of these departments' managers are based on their abilities to keep costs down, which cost allocation method would they prefer? According to Illustration 7.10, Marketing would prefer the reciprocal method; Wetlands Production would prefer the step method; and Wetlands Monitoring would prefer the direct method!

As a general rule, when service departments provide services to each other, the amount of costs allocated to production and marketing departments differ under each method. However, if service departments do not provide services to each other, then all three methods give identical results.

ILLUSTRATION 7.11	Comparison of Services Provided with Departments Receiving Costs for Each Cost Allocation Method

WETLANDS ENGINEERING, INC.

Service Department	Services Provided to:	Departments Receiving Costs under Each Method		
		Direct Method	Step Method	Reciprocal Method[a]
Biology (S1)	P1	P1	P1	P1
	P2	P2	P2	P2
Building Occupancy (S2)	S1	None[b]	S1	S1
	S3	None[b]	None[b]	S3
	P1	P1	P1	P1
	P2	P2	P2	P2
	P3	P3	P3	P3
Project Supervision (S3)	S1	None[b]	S1	S1
	S2	None[b]	S2	S2
	P1	P1	P1	P1
	P2	P2	P2	P2

[a]Cost computations appear in the appendix to this chapter.
[b]These are user departments receiving services, but costs are not allocated to them under the indicated method.

USING MULTIPLE RATES

L.O. 6: Analyze the effect of dual versus single allocation bases.

dual rate method
A cost allocation method that separates a common cost into fixed and variable components and then allocates each component using a different allocation base.

Accountants often use the **dual rate method** when common costs have both a fixed and a variable component. For example, United Bank leased computer equipment based on projected demand for services. In addition to costs of leasing the computer, it incurs costs when the equipment is used, mostly supplies and labor costs for computer operators. Thus, two different relationships exist between the computer costs and the user departments: (1) capacity available to the user department and (2) current time usage.

Assume that the costs of renting the computer and other capacity costs are fixed and the costs incurred for time usage are variable. The following equation could be used to allocate costs:

$$\text{Rate per unit of time charged} = \text{Variable cost per unit of time} + \frac{\text{Fixed capacity costs}}{\text{Units of time}}$$

Hence, user departments are charged for an "average" use of both time and capacity. Further, departments that use a good deal of time but do not need much capacity subsidize departments that need more capacity but do not use as much time.

An alternative method is to divide the computer costs into two separate components:

* The fixed or capacity costs allocated on the basis of capacity demanded.
* The variable costs allocated on the basis of time used.

This bank employee uses computerized equipment to process transactions. What two types of costs are associated with the leasing of computerized equipment in a bank? (See discussion on this page for the answer.)

With this alternative, the costs assigned to individual departments reflect as closely as possible the relationship between the cost allocated and the factors that caused the company to incur the cost.

For example, United Bank leased a specialty computer for $55,000 per month. This fee is based on the equipment's capacity. The computer costs $250 per hour to operate. Department A requested that it have access to 500 units of capacity, and Department B requested that it have access to 300 units of capacity. During the past month, Department A used 200 hours of computer time, and Department B used 400 hours. Assuming that these are the only two departments using the computer, how should the computer costs be allocated?

The bank first considered allocating costs on the basis of time usage alone. The cost allocation on the basis of time usage was

Department A: $\dfrac{200 \text{ Department hours used}}{600 \text{ Total hours used}} \times \$205,000^a = \$\ 68,333$

Department B: $\dfrac{400 \text{ Department hours used}}{600 \text{ Total hours used}} \times \$205,000^a = \underline{\ 136,667}$

Total cost of the computer center $\qquad\qquad\qquad \underline{\underline{\$205,000^a}}$

^{a} $\$205,000 = \$55,000 + [(200 \text{ hours} + 400 \text{ hours}) \times \$250]$.

When this method was proposed, the manager of Department B argued, "My department is being charged for the monthly fixed rental fee on the basis of com-

ILLUSTRATION 7.12	Dual Rates for Cost Allocation

Department A: Capacity: $\frac{5}{8} \times \$55,000$ = $ 34,375

Time: 200 hours × \$250 per hour =   50,000

Total Department A $ 84,375

Department B: Capacity: $\frac{3}{8} \times \$55,000$ = $ 20,625

Time: 400 hours × \$250 per hour =   100,000

Total Department B $120,625

Total cost of the computer center $205,000

puter time used, but that monthly fee might have been lower if Department A had not demanded so much capacity!"

To deal with this argument, the firm then allocated solely on the basis of capacity demanded. The resulting allocation was

Department A: $\dfrac{500 \text{ Department units of capacity requested}}{800 \text{ Total units of capacity requested}} \times \$205,000 = \$128,125$

Department B: $\dfrac{300 \text{ Department units of capacity requested}}{800 \text{ Total units of capacity requested}} \times \$205,000 =$ 76,875

Total cost of the computer center $205,000

When this method was proposed, Department B manager was happy, but Department A manager argued, "My department is being penalized because of our demand for capacity. We believe more costs should be allocated to Department B because it used 400 hours of computer time while we only used 200 hours."

Instead of using either method alone, the firm used a dual rate based on both capacity demanded and time used. The resulting allocation is shown in Illustration 7.12.

SELF-STUDY QUESTION

4. Dual Division Corporation allocates common costs to its Uno and Duo Divisions. During the past month, the following common costs were incurred:

Computer services (80% fixed) $254,000
Building occupancy   615,000
Personnel.   104,000

The following information is available concerning various activity measures and service uses by each of the divisions:

	Uno	Duo
Area occupied.	15,000 sq. ft.	40,000 sq. ft.
Payroll.	$380,000	$170,000
Computer time	200 hrs.	140 hrs.
Computer storage	25 gbytes	35 gbytes
Equipment value	$175,000	$220,000
Operating profit, before allocations	$439,000	$522,000

a. Allocate the common costs to the two divisions using the most appropriate of these allocation bases. For computer services, use computer time only.

b. Allocate the common costs to the two divisions using dual rates for the computer services.

The solution to this question is at the end of this chapter on page 229.

ILLUSTRATION 7.13	Multiple-Factor Method	
Division	**Fraction**	**Allocated Cost**
New York	$\dfrac{65\% + 75\% + 40\%}{3} = 60\%$	60% × $300,000 = $180,000
California	$\dfrac{35\% + 25\% + 60\%}{3} = 40\%$	40% × $300,000 = 120,000
Total allocated costs		$300,000

MULTIPLE-FACTOR METHOD

L.O. 7: Explain multiple-factor cost allocation.

multiple-factor formula
An allocation formula that uses multiple bases for allocating costs.

The dual method can be extended to multiple factors. The multiple-factor method is often used when many relationships exist between common costs and cost objects.

Suppose, for example, that Far Flung Co. wants to allocate corporate headquarters' costs to each of its two divisions: New York and California. Some people might assert that headquarters' costs are related to the size of the payroll; others might argue that they are related to the volume of business. Still others might argue that they are related to investment in assets. Actually, all three suggested bases may be valid.

In such cases, a company may use a **multiple-factor formula** that uses multiple bases for allocating costs. For Far Flung, the percentage of the common cost to be allocated to a plant may be the arithmetic average of the following three percentages:

- Percentage of payroll dollars in each division to the total payroll dollars for all divisions.
- Percentage of sales volume in each division to the total sales volume in all divisions.
- Percentage of the average gross book value of tangible assets of each division to the total gross book value of tangible assets in all divisions.

Assume that the company has $300,000 in corporate headquarters' costs to apportion to the two divisions. An analysis of company records provides the following information:

Division	Payroll Dollars Amount	Payroll Dollars Percent	Sales Volume of Business Amount	Sales Volume of Business Percent	Gross Book Value of Tangible Assets Amount	Gross Book Value of Tangible Assets Percent
New York	$1,300	65%	$6,750	75%	$ 5,600	40%
California	700	35	2,250	25	8,400	60
Totals	$2,000	100%	$9,000	100%	$14,000	100%

The multiple-factor allocation to each division is computed as shown in Illustration 7.13.

In recent years, many state taxing authorities have used this "three-factor" formula approach to assign the income of a multistate business to the individual states for state income tax purposes. Illustration 7.14 shows a section of a typical state income tax return. (We have included handwritten amounts to make the form easier to follow.) The amount in line 5 is multiplied by total business taxable income to compute the amount of taxable income for the state.

States that use these factors assume that the measures of property or assets, sales, and payrolls reflect the income generated in the states where the company operates.

SELF-STUDY QUESTION

5. Merrill's Machine Tools Company has two plants and allocates the headquarters' costs to the plants based on a three-factor formula using plant payroll, plant volume, and gross book value of plant tangible assets. The allocation percentage is an arithmetic average of three percentages:

- Percentage of payroll dollars in each plant to the total payroll dollars for both plants.
- Percentage of volume, in dollars, in each plant to the total volume in both plants.
- Percentage of the average gross book value of tangible assets of each plant to the total book value of tangible assets for both plants.

The company has $480,000 in headquarters' costs to be allocated. The relevant factors for each plant are as follows:

	Payroll	Volume	Assets
Michigan plant	$120,000	$ 600,000	$ 400,000
Texas plant.	180,000	1,000,000	800,000
Total	$300,000	$1,600,000	$1,200,000

Determine the amount of headquarters' costs to be allocated to each plant using the multiple-factor allocation method.

The solution to this question is at the end of this chapter on page 229.

ILLUSTRATION   7.14   State Tax Form Use of Multiple-Factor Method

Business Income Apportionment Formula

			1 Total Everywhere	2 Inside Illinois	3 Column 2 ÷ Column 1	
1	Property factor	1	*1,000,000*	*100,000*	*.10*	
2	Payroll factor	2	*200,000*	*30,000*	*.15*	
3	Sales factor	3	*800,000*	*160,000*	*.20*	
4	Total—add lines 1 through 3			4	*.45*	
5	Average				5	*.15*

Determining how detailed and precise to make cost allocations is like other managerial decisions: on a cost-benefit basis. Cost allocation is, in itself, a costly procedure. If the benefits from increasing the detail of cost allocation are minimal, doing so is probably not wise.

INCENTIVE PROBLEMS WITH COST ALLOCATIONS

L.O. 8: Understand incentive problems with cost allocation methods.

Although the allocation of service department variable costs can be useful for charging user departments, the allocation of fixed costs can have unintended effects. For example, the top administrators of a famous university observed that faculty and staff were using the university's Wide Area Telephone Service (WATS) so much that the lines were seldom free during the day.[4] WATS allowed the university unlimited toll-free service within the United States. Its fixed cost was $10,000 per month; variable cost per call was zero.

Allocating Fixed Service Department Costs

University administrators learned that the average use on the WATS line was 50,000 minutes per month, so they initially allocated the $10,000 monthly charge to callers (that is, departments) at a rate of 20 cents per minute ($10,000 ÷ 50,000 minutes). Now that they were being charged for the use of WATS, department heads discouraged their faculty and staff from using it. Hence, the number of minutes used on

---

[4]This example is based on one given by Jerold L. Zimmerman, "The Costs and Benefits of Cost Allocations," *The Accounting Review* 54, no. 3, pp. 510–11.

WATS dropped to 25,000 per month, which increased the rate to 40 cents per minute ($10,000 ÷ 25,000). This continued until the internal cost allocation per minute exceeded the normal long-distance rates, and the use of WATS dropped almost to zero. The university's total telephone bill increased dramatically.[5]

University administrators subsequently compromised by charging a nominal fee of 10 cents per minute. According to the university's chief financial officer, "The 10 cents per minute charge made us aware that there was a cost to the WATS service, albeit a fixed cost. The charge was sufficiently low, however, so as not to discourage bona fide use of WATS."

Cost Allocations in Cost-Plus Contracts

Many organizations sell products on a "cost-plus" basis; the "plus" is a profit. Defense contractors, for example, traditionally have sold products to national governments on a cost-plus basis. Hospitals and nursing homes traditionally have provided medical services and are reimbursed on a cost-plus basis for their costs from government agencies for particular types of patients.

Cost-plus contracts give incentives to the supplier of the good or service to seek as much reimbursement as possible and therefore to allocate as much cost as possible to the product for which reimbursement is possible. For example, suppose that McBoheed Aircraft Co. is deciding how to allocate $120 million of overhead between two major contracts, commercial and governmental. This overhead is common to the two contracts and cannot be directly traced to either. Commercial products are sold at a price set in the market, but governmental products are sold for cost plus a fixed profit. Thus, every dollar of overhead that can be allocated to the governmental product line results in an additional dollar of revenue by way of cost reimbursement.

Suppose that McBoheed is choosing between labor-hours and machine-hours as the two possible allocation bases. The relative use of labor-hours and machine-hours follows:

	Lines of Business	
	Commercial	Governmental
Percentage of labor-hours used	30%	70%
Percentage of machine-hours used	60	40

Naturally, McBoheed prefers to allocate the $120 million using labor-hours because it could seek $84 million (70 percent × $120 million) reimbursement from the government using labor-hours, but only $48 million (40 percent × $120 million) from the government using machine-hours.

McBoheed would be $36 million ($84 million − $48 million) better off if it could use labor-hours as the allocation base. Of course, the government could argue for machine-hours. Since the allocable costs cannot, by definition, be directly attributed to a contract, allocation debates abound in cost-plus contracting.

In these cases, specifying in the contract precisely how costs will be defined and how allocations will be made is important. Facing numerous disputes over cost reimbursements, the U.S. government has established the Cost Accounting Standards Board to establish cost accounting standards to reduce disputes between defense contractors and government agencies.

---

[5]The solution to this problem is not necessarily zero. According to Zimmerman in "The Costs and Benefits . . ." the correct price to charge users is "the cost imposed by forcing others who want to use the WATS line to either wait or place a regular call . . . this cost varies between zero (if no one is delayed) to, at most, the cost of a regular toll call if a user cannot use the WATS line" (p. 510). The necessary procedure to implement such a pricing system is very difficult and costly. Zimmerman suggests that fixed allocations could be a simplified way to approximate the results of the more complicated, theoretically correct pricing systems.

Cost Accounting Standards Board

Contracts with the U.S. government must generally comply with the standards issued by the Cost Accounting Standards Board (CASB), which was established in 1970 as a result of systematic cost overruns incurred by contractors using cost-reimbursement contracts and of accusations that contractors were overstating costs. In 1980, Congress essentially disbanded CASB by failing to appropriate its funding. However, the Office of Federal Procurement Policy recreated CASB as an independent board in 1988.

Accounting standards issued by the CASB are incorporated into federal acquisition regulations (FARs). They are procurement regulations governing companies contracting with the U.S. government. In general, CASB standards cover issues related to the definition of cost items and consistency.

SIDE EFFECTS OF COST ALLOCATIONS

Cost allocations are common in all types of organizations. Costs are allocated for a variety of reasons: incentives, decision-making and regulatory purposes, and cost-based contracting, for example. Costs allocated for one purpose usually have unexpected side effects. Hence, cost allocations should be made much like doctors prescribe medicine, "with an eye on the side effects."

Most organizations have problems with cost allocations. The following are some helpful hints for dealing with two types of cost allocation problems.

Problem	Solution
Users overuse or underuse services of service departments. This usually occurs because the cost allocated for the service is too high or too low as in the university case with its WATS (p. 207) or the Real World Application with its publishing department (p. 192).	Change allocation rates or charges for services up or down to get the desired behavior by users. This may require some trial and error experimentation.
An allocation established for one purpose has undesirable side effects. For example, a company allocates its headquarters' costs to divisions so top management can evaluate how well each division would perform if it were a stand-alone company. This discourages division managers who are rewarded based on division performance because they have no control over headquarters' costs.	Do not try to use one method for all purposes. In this example, do not deduct the allocated headquarters' costs from divisional profits to evaluate the division managers' performance.

ETHICAL ISSUES

The inherent arbitrariness of cost allocation implies that often no clear-cut way to allocate costs exists. A lack of objective guidelines for allocating costs often leads to difficult ethical choices. An example mentioned above is the allocation of costs in cost-plus contracts. We have seen cases in which the contracts specified manufacturing cost plus a profit and the producer hid advertising, general administrative, and similar costs in manufacturing overhead. Many lawsuits involving contract and tax disputes arise because people have allocated costs in inappropriate ways.

SUMMARY

Cost allocation is the process of assigning common costs to two or more cost objects. Ideally, cost allocation reflects a cause-and-effect relation between costs and the objects to which they are allocated.

The following summarizes key ideas tied to the chapter's learning objectives.

LO1: Why costs are allocated. Costs are allocated to inform managers about the costs of running departments that use the services of other departments. Cost allocations are required for external financial reporting and tax purposes.

LO2: Selecting allocation bases. Allocation bases are factors that cause an activity's costs (for example, direct labor-hours or machine-hours). Allocation bases are selected based on three criteria: causal relationship, benefits received, and, if all else fails, reasonableness.

LO3: Allocating costs using the direct method. The direct method allocates service department costs to user departments and ignores any services used by other service departments.

LO4: Allocating costs using the step method. Based on an allocation order, the step method allocates service department costs to other service departments and then to production departments. Once an allocation is made from a service department, no further costs are allocated back to that department.

LO5: Allocating costs using the reciprocal method. The reciprocal method allows for the simultaneous allocation of service department costs to and from all other service departments.

LO6: Dual versus single allocation bases. When a single allocation base is used to allocate costs, we assume that the allocation base reflects the best causal relationship between the cost object and the cost. It might be more appropriate, however, to use two (or dual) allocation bases to allocate costs.

LO7: Multiple-factor cost allocation. Multiple bases are often used to allocate costs when more than one relationship exists between a common cost and a cost object.

LO8: Incentive problems with cost allocation methods. Recognize that allocations affect behavior. Think about the desired behavior when allocating costs and adjust the allocations to get the desired behavior.

LO9: Using spreadsheets to solve reciprocal cost allocation problems (appendix). Spreadsheets are used to solve complex reciprocal cost allocation problems.

KEY TERMS

allocation base, 190	multiple-factor formula, 205
common costs, 187	reciprocal method, 200
direct method, 193	service department, 189
dual rate method, 203	step method, 197
final cost center, 189	user department, 189
intermediate cost center, 189	

APPENDIX

L.O. 9: Use spreadsheets to solve reciprocal cost allocation problems (appendix).

The Reciprocal Method Using Computer Spreadsheets

The reciprocal method requires that cost relationships be written in equation form. The method then solves the equations for the total costs to be allocated to each department. The direct costs of each department are typically included in the solution. Thus, for any department, we can state the equation:

$$\text{Total costs} = \text{Direct costs} + \text{Allocated costs}$$

The total costs are the unknowns that we attempt to derive.

For example, let's assume that the direct overhead costs of the departments at Wetlands Engineering, Inc., are

Biology (S1)	$ 36,000
Building Occupancy (S2)	84,000
Project Supervision (S3)	25,000
Wetlands Production (P1)	500,000
Wetlands Monitoring (P2)	270,000
Marketing (P3)	185,000

(Note that the direct costs for each service department were given earlier in the chapter, and direct costs for each of the production departments are given for the first time here because they are required when using the reciprocal method to allocate costs.) Using the information in Illustration 7.4, the total costs of Wetlands Production (P1) may be expressed as follows:

$$\text{Total costs} = \text{Direct costs} + \text{Allocated costs}$$
$$P1 = \$500,000 + 20\% \text{ S1} + 32\% \text{ S2} + 45\% \text{ S3}$$

Similar equations are constructed for each of the other production departments:

$$P2 = \$270,000 + 80\% \text{ S1} + 24\% \text{ S2} + 30\% \text{ S3}$$
$$P3 = \$185,000 + 0 \text{ S1} + 24\% \text{ S2} + 0 \text{ S3}$$

And for the service departments, the equations are

$$S1 = \$36,000 + 8\% \text{ S2} + 15\% \text{ S3}$$
$$S2 = \$84,000 + \text{OS1} + 10\% \text{ S3}$$
$$S3 = \$25,000 + \text{OS1} + 12\% \text{ S2}$$

Now we have a set of equations that express the total cost of each department as a function of direct costs and allocated costs.

With the cost relationships written in equation form, the solution can now be easily found using the matrix invert function of a spreadsheet, such as Lotus 1-2-3® or Excel®. The matrix invert function uses inverse matrices, which are generally used to solve systems of mathematical equations involving several variables.

Setting the Equations in Matrix Form

When using matrix algebra to solve simultaneous equations, all coefficients need to be stated in the same terms. For instance,

$$\text{Total Costs P1} = \$500,000 + 20\% \text{ S1} + 32\% \text{ S2} + 45\% \text{ S3}$$

should be restated as

$$\text{Total Costs P1} = 100\% \text{ P1(direct costs)} + 20\% \text{ S1} + 32\% \text{ S2} + 45\% \text{ S3}$$

This allows the information to be entered into a matrix on a spreadsheet, such as the one described next.

The following is based on using Lotus 1-2-3 or Excel to solve reciprocal method cost allocations. The commands are shown in "quotes." At the end of the appendix, you will find a section on basic spreadsheet commands for those unfamiliar with the programs.

Step 1: Set Up the Parameter Section   The top section of Illustration 7.15 (on page 214), titled "Services," is the parameter section of the spreadsheet. This is the section on which the rest of the spreadsheet is calculated. It includes the matrix into which the percentage of services used and the amount of costs to be allocated will be entered.

Notice that all service and production departments are included in both the "performed by" and "used by" categories regardless of whether they perform services for other departments. This creates a matrix with an equal number of rows and columns (remember that a matrix must have an equal number of rows and columns). The percentage of each department's use of another department's services and the amount of costs to be allocated to the user department are entered in the corresponding position.

For example, using the equation $S1 = 100\% \text{ S1(direct costs)} + 8\% \text{ S2} + 15\% \text{ S3}$, we enter the amount of S2 services used by S1, 8%, in cell C8; the amount of S3 services used by S1, 15%, in cell D8; and -100% in cell B8 because none of S1 services were used by S1. Stated another way, none of the S1 direct costs were incurred for S1 use. We entered 0% in cells E8, F8, and G8 because S1 used none of production's services or did not cause production to incur any costs. Using the equation P1 = 100% P1(direct costs) + 20% S1 + 32% S2 + 45% S3, we enter 20% in cell B11, 32% in cell C11, 45% in cell D11, and 100% in cell E11 (because P1 used all of its own direct costs incurred), and 0% in F11 and G11.

The totals presented in row 14 represent the amount of costs remaining in each department after allocation. As you can see, the service departments retain none of their costs but allocate all costs to production departments when finished, and the production departments retain all of their costs. The costs to be allocated, entered in row 18, are entered under the department that incurred them.

Step 2: Set Up the Inverse Matrix   The middle section of Illustration 7.15, "Inverse Matrix," displays the output of the inverse matrix function of the spreadsheet. The output in this section is the same size as the parameter matrix and may be style formatted.

Procedure (Lotus 1-2-3)

1. Select "/DATA MATRIX INVERT".
2. Specify the matrix range you want to invert by highlighting it.
3. Specify the output range by highlighting it; you can specify the entire range or only the first cell in the range (top/left cell). Be careful because Lotus will overwrite the contents of any cells that are not blank.

Procedure (Excel)

1. Specify the area for inverse matrix output by highlighting it. Be sure to make it the same size as the parameter matrix because Excel will use only the area you specify, so if it is too small, information will be lost.
2. Enter "=MINVERSE(" and highlight parameter matrix. Then press CTRL SHIFT ENTER in unison.

Note: Not every matrix can be inverted. An error message is displayed if Lotus cannot create an inverse for the matrix you specified {#NUM} or if the rows and columns are unequal {#VALUE}.

The inverse matrix presents the percentage allocation of each department's costs to other departments. The negative percentages represent a service department's direct costs allocated to/from other service departments. They are negative because they will be reallocated to production departments.

You will notice that for departments S2 and S3, the total of the negative percentages is more than 100%. This is due to the reciprocal nature of the allocations. The service departments allocate costs to other service departments, which are allocated back to them, bringing service departments' total costs to more than their direct costs. Therefore, there will be allocations out of the service departments in excess of 100% of their direct costs.

Step 3: Set Up the Cost Allocation Table   The bottom section of Illustration 7.15, "Cost Allocation," presents the actual dollar amount of allocation to each department based on the inverse matrix and each department's direct costs. The amount calculated in each cell is the percentage in the corresponding inverse matrix cell multiplied by the direct cost in the same column. For instance, the cost allocated out of S1 ($36,000) equals the percentage allocated out of S1 represented in the inverse matrix −100% multiplied by S1 direct costs $36,000. Note that the percentages shown in the "Inverse Matrix" section are rounded for presentation purposes. However, unrounded numbers are used to calculate the cost allocations. Thus, when checking the math, notice that several amounts in the "Cost Allocation" section have rounding discrepancies.

ILLUSTRATION	7.15	**Reciprocal Method Computer Spreadsheet**

	A	B	C	D	E	F	G	H
1								
2				WETLANDS ENGINEERING, INC.				
3								
4	Services							
5		Performed by:						
6		S1	S2	S3	P1	P2	P3	
7	Used by:							
8	S1	−100.0%	8.0%	15.0%	0.0%	0.0%	0.0%	
9	S2	0.0%	−100.0%	10.0%	0.0%	0.0%	0.0%	
10	S3	0.0%	12.0%	−100.0%	0.0%	0.0%	0.0%	
11	P1	20.0%	32.0%	45.0%	100.0%	0.0%	0.0%	
12	P2	80.0%	24.0%	30.0%	0.0%	100.0%	0.0%	
13	P3	0.0%	24.0%	0.0%	0.0%	0.0%	100.0%	
14		0.0%	0.0%	0.0%	100.0%	100.0%	100.0%	
15								
16								
17	Costs to Be Allocated:							
18		$36,000	$84,000	$25,000	$0	$0	$0	
19								
20								
21								
22	Inverse Matrix							
23		S1	S2	S3	P1	P2	P3	
24	S1	−100.0%	−9.9%	−16.0%	0.0%	0.0%	0.0%	
25	S2	0.0%	−101.2%	−10.1%	0.0%	0.0%	0.0%	
26	S3	0.0%	−12.1%	−101.2%	0.0%	0.0%	0.0%	
27	P1	20.0%	39.8%	52.0%	100.0%	0.0%	0.0%	
28	P2	80.0%	35.9%	45.6%	0.0%	100.0%	0.0%	
29	P3	0.0%	24.3%	2.4%	0.0%	0.0%	100.0%	
30								
31	Cost Allocation							
32		From:						Total
33		S1	S2	S3	P1	P2	P3	Allocated to Production
34	To:							
35	S1	($36,000)	($8,332)	($3,998)	$0	$0	$0	
36	S2	$0	($85,020)	($2,530)	$0	$0	$0	
37	S3	$0	($10,202)	($25,304)	$0	$0	$0	
38	P1	$7,200	$33,464	$12,996	$0	$0	$0	$53,660
39	P2	$28,800	$30,131	$11,397	$0	$0	$0	$70,328
40	P3	$0	$20,405	$607	$0	$0	$0	$21,012
41								$145,000
42								

The totals on the right of the table show the total costs allocated to each department. Again, the totals for the service departments are negative because they do not remain in the department but are allocated out to the production departments. If you add these negative totals, you will find that they total more than the total service department costs because some amounts are included twice. For example, the total cost of S1 (the sum of all amounts shown on line 35) includes the allocated costs from S2 and S3 plus all of the S1 direct costs, even though some of the direct costs are allocated to S2 and S3.

Department P1 was allocated $7,200 from S1 plus $33,464 from S2 (which included some of S2's allocation to S1 and S3), plus $12,996 allocated from S3 (which included some of S3's allocation to S1 and S2), for a total allocation of $53,660 from service departments.

Some spreadsheet basics follow. (If Lotus and Excel commands differ, Lotus is shown in "quotes", and Excel is shown in {brackets}.)

* Labels that are longer than the cell width may be entered in any cell and will be fully displayed as long as the adjoining cell is empty.
* Labels may be centered in a cell by entering "^" {highlight, click on FORMAT, ALIGNMENT, CENTER} prior to the label (see cell B6).
* Cells may be filled with a character, such as = , by entering "\" prior to the character.
* Underlining may be done by highlighting cells and clicking on U icon.
* Sums may be calculated by entering "@SUM(highlight area of column or row)" {=SUM(highlight area of column or row)} in the cell where the sum is to appear.
* Individual cells or ranges may be formatted to present numbers in different formats by first highlighting cells to format and then clicking on "STYLE" {FORMAT} in the command line; when selections are presented, click on "Number Format" {CELLS} and then click on your choice, "Currency" or "Percentage." You will then be asked to specify the number of decimal places to be shown. (*Note:* It is not necessary for the spreadsheet to be formatted in this manner; it will not affect the outcome of calculations. Nor will the number of decimal places have any effect on the calculations because the program uses the full number, not just what appears on the screen.)
* Column width may be insufficient to display some numbers; ###### appearing in a cell indicates this. Column width may be increased by clicking on the right border of the column in the upper margin and dragging it to the right.
* Content of cells may be copied to other cells by highlighting and using the "EDIT/COPY," "EDIT/PASTE" commands or clicking on the icons. If the cell being copied contains a formula that addresses another cell, the address in the cell into which it is copied changes relative to position (see B14 and C14; C14 was copied from B14). Using a "$" before the column or row designation keeps that part of the address from changing when copied.

REVIEW QUESTIONS

7.1 What are some of the costs of cost allocation?

7.2 What are some of the benefits of cost allocation?

7.3 What principle is used to decide whether to allocate costs to cost objects?

7.4 What are some management uses of information based on allocated costs?

7.5 What are four broad categories of common costs and the usual basis for allocation of costs in each category?

7.6 What are the similarities and differences among the direct method, the step method, and the reciprocal method of allocating costs?

7.7 What criterion should be used to determine the order of allocation from service departments when the step method is used? Explain why.

CRITICAL ANALYSIS AND DISCUSSION QUESTIONS

7.8 If cost allocations are arbitrary and potentially misleading, should we assume that management is foolish for using information based on allocated costs?

7.9 One critic of cost allocation noted, "You can avoid the problem of arbitrary cost allocations by simply not allocating any common costs to other cost objects." What are your thoughts on this suggestion?

7.10 Refer to the Real World Application on page 192. What effect did the initial cost allocations have? Why were the allocated costs so high?

7.11 A cost such as company headquarters' cost does not fit into any one of the broad categories of common costs. Such costs may be a result of a number of different factors. Is there a way to allocate such a cost? If so, describe the approach.

7.12 Materials are considered direct with respect both to the manufacturing department using them and to the product. However, indirect materials cannot be associated directly with a specific job or product but may be related directly to the manufacturing department where the indirect materials are used. What are the concepts of direct and indirect costs in this setting?

7.13 What argument(s) could be given in support of the reciprocal method as the preferred method for distributing the costs of service departments?

7.14 Under what conditions are the results from using the direct method of allocations the same as those from using either other method? Why?

7.15 Consider a company with two producing departments and one service department. The service department distributes its costs to the producing departments on the basis of number of employees in each department. If the costs in the service department are fixed, what effect would the addition of employees in one department have on the costs allocated to the other department? Comment on the reasonableness of the situation.

7.16 The manager of an operating department just received a cost report and has made the following comment with respect to the costs allocated from one of the service departments: "This charge to my division does not seem right. The service center installed equipment with more capacity than our division requires. Most of the service department costs are fixed, but we seem to be allocated more costs in periods when other departments use less. We are paying for excess capacity of other departments when other departments cut their usage levels." How might this manager's problem be solved?

EXERCISES

7.17 Why Are Costs Allocated? (L.O. 1)

The Barfields and the McAllisters own two adjacent tracts of land. Each tract has a surface area of 4,000 acres. During a recent shoot-out, crude oil came bubbling to the surface where a bullet entered the ground. A petroleum geologist determined that an underground rock formation that extended under both tracts of land contained a substantial amount of oil. The formation was estimated at 800,000 acre feet of volume, of which 200,000 acre feet were under the McAllisters' tract of land.

The Barfields and the McAllisters received an offer to buy the mineral rights for $8.5 million provided that they can agree on how much of the purchase price should be allocated to each family.

Required

a. As a Barfield, what basis would you recommend for allocating the purchase price? What arguments would you use to support your claim?

b. As a McAllister, what basis would you recommend for allocating the purchase price? What arguments would you use to support your claim?

7.18 Alternative Allocation Bases (L.O. 2)

For each of the types of common costs in the first column, select the most appropriate allocation base from the second column:

Common Cost	Allocation Base
Building utilities	Value of inventories
Payroll accounting	Number of units produced
Property taxes on inventories	Number of employees
Equipment repair	Space occupied
Quality control inspection	Number of service calls

7.19 Alternative Allocation Bases— Service (L.O. 2)

Cytotech Company has a TV and a radio station that share the common costs of the company's AP wire service, which is $100,000 a year. You have the following information about the AP wire and the two stations:

Station	Wire Service Hours Used This Period	Hours of News Broadcasts
TV	450	100
Radio	300	460

Required

a. What is the AP wire service cost charged to each station if wire service hours are used as an allocation basis?

b. What is the AP wire service cost charged to each station using hours of news broadcast as a basis for allocation?

c. Which method allocates more costs to TV? Which method allocates more costs to radio?

7.20 Alternative Allocation Bases (L.O. 2)

WARP Enterprises operates a 120,000-square-foot supermarket. Each department in the store is charged with a share of the cost of the building. The following information is available concerning two of the departments in the store:

	Department	
	Meat	Dry Goods
Sales revenues.	$250,000	$300,000
Cost of goods sold	85,000	90,000
Salaries and other direct expenses	55,000	70,000
Allocated administrative expenses	25,000	27,500
Operating profit before building occupancy costs.	$ 85,000	$112,500
Area occupied (square feet).	10,000	30,000

Other departments use the other 80,000 square feet. The total building occupancy costs are $400,000 per year.

Required

a. If area occupied is the basis for allocating building occupancy costs, what is the operating profit or loss for each of these two departments?

b. Would you allocate based on something other than square feet if you learned that the Dry Goods Department is located in a back corner of the store? Explain.

7.21 Alternative Allocation Bases (L.O. 2)

Quality Jacket Company produces two styles of leather jackets, standard and deluxe. The difference between the two is in the amount of handcrafting. The deluxe jacket uses more skilled labor because additional cutting and trimming are done by hand. The relevant figures for the year just completed follow.

Allocation Base	Standard	Deluxe
Materials used	$300,000	$200,000
Direct labor-hours	100,000	150,000
Machine-hours	40,000	10,000
Output.	80,000	15,000

The company has $1,600,000 in manufacturing overhead costs to allocate to these two product lines.

Required

For each of the four potential allocation bases, determine the amount of manufacturing overhead to be allocated to each unit of output.

7.22 Alternative Allocation Bases (L.O. 2)

Required

Refer to your calculations for Exercise 7.21. Your supervisor wants to know how much it costs to make a standard jacket and a deluxe jacket, including the cost of materials, labor (which costs $8 per hour), and manufacturing overhead.

a. Give your supervisor four different answers for each type of jacket to the question: "How much does it cost to make?"

b. Explain to your supervisor why there are four different cost numbers for each product. Also indicate whether total manufacturing costs are the same for Quality Jacket Company regardless of the overhead allocation base used.

7.23 Cost Allocations— Direct Method (L.O. 3)

Acme Corporation has two producing departments P1 and P2, and two service departments, S1 and S2. Direct costs for each department and the proportion of service costs used by the various departments for the month of May are as follows:

Department	Direct Costs	Proportion of Services Used By			
		S1	S2	P1	P2
P1	$160,000				
P2	140,000				
S1	80,000	—	0.80	0.10	0.10
S2	100,000	0.20	—	0.50	0.30

Required

Compute the allocation of service department costs to producing departments using the direct method.

7.24 Allocating Service Department Costs First to Production Departments and Then to Jobs (L.O. 3)

Refer to the facts in Exercise 7.23. Assume that P1 and P2 each work on just two jobs during the month of May: 10 and 11. Costs are allocated to jobs based on labor-hours in P1 and machine-hours in P2. The labor- and machine-hours worked in each department are as follows:

	P1	P2
Job 10: Labor-hours	80	10
Machine-hours	10	20
Job 11: Labor-hours	10	10
Machine-hours	10	90

Required

How much of the service department costs allocated to P1 and P2 in the direct method should be allocated to Job 10? How much to Job 11?

7.25 Cost Allocations— Direct Method (L.O. 3)

Custom Tailors, Inc., has two service departments (Maintenance and General Factory Administration) and two operating departments (Cutting and Assembly). Management has decided to allocate maintenance costs on the basis of the area in each department and general factory administration costs on the basis of labor-hours worked by the employees in each of their respective departments.

The following data appear in the company records for the current period:

	General Factory Administration	Maintenance	Cutting	Assembly
Area occupied (square feet)	1,000	—	1,000	3,000
Labor-hours	—	100	100	400
Direct labor costs (operating departments only)			$3,000	$8,000
Service department direct costs.	$20,000	$48,000		

Required

Use the direct method to allocate these service department costs to the operating departments.

7.26 Cost Allocations—
Step Method
(L.O. 4)

Refer to the data for Acme Corporation (Exercise 7.23).
Use the step method to allocate the service costs, using

a. The order of allocation starting with S1.

b. The allocations made in the reverse order (starting with S2).

7.27 Cost Allocation—
Step Method
(L.O. 4)

Refer to the data for Custom Tailors, Inc., in Exercise 7.25.
Allocate the service department costs using the step method, starting with the Maintenance Department. What effect does using this method have on the allocation of costs?

7.28 Cost Allocations—
Reciprocal Method
(L.O. 5)

Refer to the data for Acme Corporation (Exercise 7.23).
Use the reciprocal method to allocate the service costs. (Matrix algebra is not required.)

7.29 Cost Allocations—
Reciprocal Method:
Two Service
Departments
(L.O. 5)

During the past month, the following costs were incurred in the three production departments and two service departments in the company:

P1	$120,000
P2	312,500
P3	390,000
S1	67,000
S2	59,500

Use of services by other departments follows:

Service Cost Center	User Department				
	S1	S2	P1	P2	P3
S1.	—	0.40	0.30	0.20	0.10
S2.	0.10	—	0.20	0.15	0.55

Required

Allocate service department costs to P1, P2, and P3 using the reciprocal method, and present the total costs of P1, P2, and P3 after this allocation.

7.30 Cost Allocation—
Reciprocal Method
(L.O. 5)

Refer to the data for Custom Tailors, Inc., in Exercise 7.25.

Required

Allocate the service department costs using the reciprocal method. (Matrix algebra is not required because there are only two service departments.)

7.31 Evaluate Cost
Allocation Methods
(L.O. 3, L.O. 4, L.O. 5)

Refer to Exercises 7.25, 7.27, and 7.30 (Custom Tailors, Inc.).
Which method do you think is best? How much would it be worth to the company to use the best method compared to the worst of the three methods? (Numbers not required in this answer.)

7.32 Single versus
Dual Rates
(L.O. 6)

Refer to data for the company in Exercise 7.19.
Determine the cost allocation if $52,000 of the wire service costs are fixed and allocated on the basis of hours of news broadcast; and the remaining costs, which are variable, are allocated on the basis of wire service hours used.

7.33 Single versus
Dual Rates
(L.O. 6)

A law firm has two departments, Bankruptcy and Personal Injury. Word processing is common to both departments. The cost of word processing is $200,000. The following information is given:

	Pages of Word Processing Used by Department	Department Payroll
Bankruptcy.	4,000	$1,000,000
Personal Injury	12,000	900,000

Required

a. What is the cost charged to each department if the allocation is based on pages of word processing?

b. What is the cost charged to each department if departmental payroll is the allocation basis?

7.34   Single versus Dual Rates (L.O. 6)

Using the data for the law firm in Exercise 7.33, what is the cost allocation if fixed word processing costs of $100,000 are allocated on the basis of department payroll and the remaining costs (all variable) are allocated on the basis of pages of word processing used by the department?

7.35   Multiple-Factor Allocations (L.O. 7)

Edee Bower Clothing operates four clothing stores and allocates headquarters' costs based on the arithmetical average of three factors:

- Percentage of payroll dollars in each store to the total payroll dollars for all stores.
- Percentage of sales dollars in each store to the total sales in all stores.
- Percentage of the average gross book value of tangible assets of each store to the total book value of tangible assets for all stores.

The company has headquarters' costs of $300,000. The relevant factors for the stores follow:

	Stores				
	Anchorage	Boise	Columbus	Detroit	Total
Payroll	$ 85,000	$ 35,000	$ 60,000	$ 70,000	$ 250,000
Sales	1,000,000	1,200,000	1,100,000	700,000	4,000,000
Assets	240,000	250,000	210,000	200,000	900,000

Required

Determine the amount of headquarters' costs allocated to each store.

7.36   Multiple-Factor Allocations (L.O. 7)

Multi-State, Inc., operates in three states: Missouri, Illinois, and California. The following information is available concerning the activities and taxing bases for each of the three states:

	Missouri	Illinois	California
Income tax rate	–0–	5%	7%
Basis for allocating income	—	Illinois sales, payroll, and property three-factor formula	California sales, payroll, and property three-factor formula
Company sales occurring by state . .	—	$2.4 million	$1.8 million
Company payrolls by state	$2.6 mil.	0.8	0.6
Company property by state	1.2	0.3	0.5

Company headquarters are located in Missouri. Total company profits were $400,000 before state taxes.

Required

What is the income tax liability due to each state using the multiple-factor formula?

PROBLEMS

7.37   Choosing an Appropriate Allocation Base in a High-Tech Environment

Chips Corp. manufactures two types of computer chips: the ROM-A chip is a commonly used chip for personal computer systems, and the RAM-B chip is used for specialized scientific applications. Direct materials costs for the ROM-A chip are 25 cents per unit and for the RAM-B are 28 cents per unit. The company's annual output is 32 million chips. At this level of output, manufacturing overhead amounts to $2.4 million, and direct labor costs total $625,000.

The company's assembly process is highly automated. As a result, the primary function for direct labor is to set up a production run and to check equipment settings on a periodic basis.

Yesterday the equipment was set up to run 1,600 RAM-B units. When that run was completed, equipment settings were changed, and 200,000 ROM-A units were produced. Part of the daily cost report follows:

	ROM-A	RAM-B
Units produced	200,000	1,600
Direct materials	$25,000	$224
Direct labor	$1,000	$600

Required

a. For yesterday's production run, what is the total manufacturing cost per unit for ROM-A and RAM-B if direct labor costs are used to allocate manufacturing overhead?

b. For yesterday's production run, what is the total manufacturing cost per unit for ROM-A and RAM-B if units produced is the basis used to allocate manufacturing overhead?

c. When you show the results of your work to managers in the company, they express concern about the fact that two methods of cost allocation give such big differences in unit costs for the two products. Write a short report to management explaining why the two methods give a different measure of costs. If you think one method is preferable, say so and support your answer.

7.38 Choosing an Appropriate Allocation Base in an Automated Environment

Fences Plus Corp. produces fence materials. One division manufactures fence rails and fence posts. As a general rule, more fence rails are produced than posts. For example, during the past week, 900 rails and 30 posts were manufactured. Direct materials costs are $6.20 per rail and $6.00 per post. Direct labor of $400 was attributed to the rail manufacturing operation, and $500 was attributed to posts during the past week. Most of the direct labor costs are incurred in setting up the automated equipment. In the manufacturing process, it takes about the same amount of time for the equipment to produce one rail as it does to produce one post.

This division has $550,000 in annual manufacturing overhead that is allocated based on direct labor costs. The annual direct labor costs are estimated at $88,000. The company produces 250,000 units per year.

Required

a. Prepare a schedule to show the cost assigned to each rail and each post using direct labor costs as the basis for allocating overhead.

b. Prepare a schedule computing the unit costs of rails and posts using units of production as a basis for allocating overhead costs.

c. Write a short report to management that indicates which method of overhead allocation appears more reasonable. Support your answer.

7.39 Step Method with Three Service Departments

Crash Test Corporation refinishes automobiles. It operates two production departments, Painting and Polishing, and has three service departments for its plant, Building Occupancy, Payroll Accounting, and Equipment Maintenance. The accumulated costs in the three service departments were $360,000, $500,000, and $264,000, respectively. Management is concerned that the costs of its service departments are getting too high. In particular, management would like to keep the costs of service departments under $500 per unit on average. You have been asked to allocate service department costs to the two production departments and compute the unit costs.

The company decided that Building Occupancy costs should be allocated on the basis of square footage used by each production and service department. Payroll Accounting costs are allocated on the basis of number of employees; Equipment Maintenance costs are allocated on the basis of the dollar value of the equipment in each department. The use of each basis by all departments during the current period follows:

	Used by				
Allocation Base	**Building Occupancy**	**Payroll Accounting**	**Equipment Maintenance**	**Painting**	**Polishing**
Building area	5,000	15,000	10,000	180,000	45,000
Employees	9	5	6	35	50
Equipment value (in thousands)	$12	$240	$35	$624	$324

Direct costs of the Painting Department included $475,000 in direct materials, $650,000 in direct labor, and $225,000 in overhead. In the Polishing Department, direct costs consisted of $820,000 in direct labor and $145,000 in overhead.

Required

a. Using the step method, determine the allocated costs and the total costs in each of the two producing departments. Ignore self-usage (for example, ignore work done by Building Occupancy for itself). Rank-order the allocation as follows: (1) Equipment Mainte-nance, (2) Payroll Accounting, and (3) Building Occupancy.

b. Assume that 1,000 units were processed through these two departments. What is the unit cost for the sum of direct materials, direct labor, and overhead (1) for Painting, (2) for Polishing, and (3) total?

c. Compute the cost per unit for the service department costs allocated to the production departments. Did the company meet management's standards of keeping service depart-ment costs below $500 per unit?

7.40	Solve for Unknowns

Pete's Delicious Foods has a commissary that supplies food and other products to its restau-rants. Its two service departments, Computer Services (S1) and Administration and Mainte-nance (S2), support two operating departments, Food Products (P1) and Supplies (P2). As an internal auditor, you are checking the company's procedures for cost allocation. You find the following cost allocation results for June:

Costs allocated to P1
$40,000 from S1
? from S2

Costs allocated to P2
$22,500 from S2
? from S1

Total costs for the two service departments $100,000

S2's services are provided as follows

20 percent to S1
50 percent to P1
30 percent to P2

The direct method of allocating costs is used.

Required

a. What are the total service department costs (S1 + S2) allocated to P2?

b. Complete the following:

	To	
From	**P1**	**P2**
S1........	$40,000	?
S2........	?	$22,500

c. What were the proportions of S1's costs allocated to P1 and P2?

7.41	Cost Allocation: Step Method with Analysis and Decision Making

Elektrik Corporation is reviewing its operations to see what additional energy-saving projects it might carry out. The company's Iowa plant has its own electric generating facilities pow-ered by the production of some natural gas wells that the company owns and that are located on the same property as the plant. A summary of the use of service departments by other service departments as well as by the two producing departments at the plant follows:

			Services Used By				
			Electric Generating			Production Department	
Service Department	**Production**	**Natural Gas**	**Fixed Costs**	**Variable Costs**	**Equipment Maintenance**	**No. 1**	**No. 2**
Natural gas production	—	—	0.40		—	0.10	0.50
Electric generating							
Fixed costs	0.10	—	—	0.10		0.30	0.50
Variable costs	0.10	—	—	0.05		0.55	0.30
Equipment maintenance	0.20	0.10		0.05	—	0.50	0.15

Direct costs (in thousands) in the various departments and the labels used to abbreviate the departments in the calculations are as follows:

Department	Direct Costs	Label
Natural Gas Production	$ 70	S1
Electric Generating		
Fixed costs	30	S2
Variable costs	80	S3
Equipment Maintenance	48	S4
Production Maintenance		
No. 1	600	P1
No. 2	440	P2

The company currently allocates costs of service departments to production departments using the step method. The local power company indicates that the power company would charge $160,000 per year for the electricity now being generated by the company internally. Management rejected switching to the public utility on the grounds that its rates would cost more than the $110,000 ($30,000 + $80,000) costs of the present company-owned system.

Required

a. What costs of electric service did management use to prepare the basis for its decision to continue generating power internally?

b. Prepare for management an analysis of the costs of the company's own electric generating operations. (Use the step method.) The rank order of allocation is (1) S1, (2) S4, (3) S2, and (4) S3.

c. Add a section to your report to management that you prepared for requirement (*b*) to indicate whether your answer there would change if the company could realize $58,000 per year from the sale of the natural gas now used for electric generating. (Assume no selling costs.)

7.42 (Appendix) Cost Allocations Reciprocal Method (computer required)

Using the reciprocal methods spreadsheet (shown in Illustration 7.15), show the costs allocated to production for Elektrik Corporation. Use the data in Problem 7.41.

7.43 Cost Allocation and Decision Making

Parker Company's Promotion Department is responsible for designing and developing all marketing campaign materials and related literature, pamphlets, and brochures. Management is reviewing the effectiveness of the Promotion Department to determine whether its services could be acquired more economically from an outside promotion agency. Management has received a summary of the Promotion Department's costs for the most recent year:

PROMOTION DEPARTMENT
Costs for the Year Ended November 30

Direct department costs.	$128,750
Charges from other departments	33,460
Allocated share of general administrative overhead	22,125
Total costs.	$184,335

Direct department costs can be traced directly to Promotion Department's activities such as staff and clerical salaries, including related employee benefits, supplies, and so on. Charges from other departments represent the costs of services that other departments of Parker provide at Promotion Department's request. The company has developed a system to charge for such interdepartmental uses of services. For instance, the in-house Printing Department charges the Promotion Department for the promotional literature printed. All services provided to the Promotion Department by other departments of Parker are included in the charges from other departments. General administrative overhead includes such costs as executive salaries and benefits, depreciation, heat, insurance, and property taxes. These costs are allocated to each department in proportion to the number of its employees.

Required

Prepare a report that discusses the usefulness of the cost figures as presented for the Promotion Department as a basis for comparison with a bid from an outside agency to provide the same type of activities that Parker's Promotion Department now provides.

(CMA adapted)

7.44 **Allocate Service Department Costs—Direct and Step Methods: Multiple Choice**

Doxolby Manufacturing Company has three service departments (General Factory Administration, Factory Maintenance, and Factory Cafeteria), and two production departments (Fabrication and Assembly). A summary of costs and other data for each department prior to allocation of service department costs for the year ended June 30 follows:

	General Factory Admin	Factory Maintenance	Factory Cafeteria	Fabrication	Assembly
Direct material	–0–	$ 65,000	$ 91,000	$3,130,000	$ 950,000
Direct labor	$ 90,000	82,100	87,000	1,950,000	2,050,000
Manufacturing overhead.	70,000	56,100	62,000	1,650,000	1,850,000
	$160,000	$203,200	$240,000	$6,730,000	$4,850,000
Direct labor-hours	31,000	27,000	42,000	562,500	437,500
Number of employees	12	8	20	280	200
Square footage occupied	1,750	2,000	4,800	88,000	72,000

The costs of the service departments are allocated on the following bases: General Factory Administration Department, direct labor-hours; Factory Maintenance Department, square footage occupied; and Factory Cafeteria, number of employees.

Required

Round all final calculations to the nearest dollar.

a. Assume that Doxolby elects to distribute service department costs directly to production departments using the direct method. The amount of Factory Maintenance Department costs allocated to the Fabrication Department is
  (1) $0.
  (2) $111,760.
  (3) $106,091.
  (4) $91,440.
  (5) None of the above.

b. Assume the same method of allocation as in requirement (*a*). The amount of General Factory Administration Department costs allocated to the Assembly Department is
  (1) $0.
  (2) $63,636.
  (3) $70,000.
  (4) $90,000.
  (5) None of the above.

c. Assuming that Doxolby elects to distribute service department costs to other departments using the step method (starting with Factory Cafeteria and then Factory Maintenance), the amount of Factory Cafeteria Department costs allocated to the Factory Maintenance Department is
  (1) $0.
  (2) $96,000.
  (3) $3,840.
  (4) $6,124.
  (5) None of the above.

d. Assume the same method of allocation as in requirement (*c*). The amount of Factory Maintenance Department costs allocated to Factory Cafeteria is
  (1) $0.
  (2) $5,787.
  (3) $5,856.
  (4) $148,910.
  (5) None of the above.

(CPA adapted)

7.45 **Cost Allocations: Comparison of Dual and Single Rates**

SkyBlue Airlines operates a centralized computer center for the data processing needs of its Reservation, Scheduling, Maintenance, and Accounting divisions. Costs associated with use of the computer are charged to the individual departments on the basis of time usage. Due to recent increased competition in the airline industry, the company has decided that it is necessary to more accurately allocate its costs to price its services competitively and profitably. During the current period, the use of data processing services and the storage capacity required for each of the divisions was as follows (in thousands of seconds for time usage and in gigabytes for storage capacity):

Division	Time Usage	Storage Capacity
Reservations	2,500	1,500
Scheduling.	1,700	600
Maintenance	6,300	210
Accounting	5,000	190

During this period, the cost of the computer center amounted to $7,050,000 for time usage and $5,000,000 for storage-related costs.

Required

Determine the allocation to each of the divisions using (you may round all decimals to three places):

a. A single rate based on time used.

b. Dual rates based on time used and capacity used.

c. Write a short report to management explaining whether a single rate or dual rates should be used and why.

7.46 **Cost Allocation for Rate-Making Purposes**

Worryfree Insurance Company asked the regulatory board for permission to increase the premiums of its insurance operations. Insurance premium rates in the jurisdiction in which Worryfree operates are designed to cover the operating costs and insurance claims. As a part of Worryfree's expenses, its agents earn commissions based on premium revenues. Premium revenues also are used to pay claims and to invest in securities. Administrative expenses include costs to manage the company's investments. All administrative costs are charged against premium revenue. Worryfree claims that its insurance operations "just broke even" last year and that a rate increase is necessary. The following income statement (in millions) was submitted to support Worryfree's request:

Insurance income	
Premium revenue	$200
Operating costs	
Claims	125
Administrative	35
Sales commissions	40
Total operating costs.	200
Insurance profit (loss)	–0–
Investment income	15
Profits after investment income	$ 15

Further investigation reveals that approximately 20 percent of the sales commissions may be considered related to investment activities. In addition, 10 percent of the administrative costs are incurred by the investment management division. The state insurance commission (which sets insurance rates) believes that Worryfree's insurance activities should earn about 5 percent on its premium revenues.

Required

a. If you were a consumer group, how would you present Worryfree's income statement? (For example, how would you allocate administrative costs and sales commissions between the insurance income and investment income categories?)

b. If you were Worryfree's management, what arguments would you present in support of the cost allocations included in this income statement?

7.47 **Cost Allocation for Travel Reimbursement**

Your company has a travel policy that reimburses employees for the "ordinary and necessary" costs of business travel. Employees often mix a business trip with pleasure either by extending the time at the destination or traveling from the business destination to a nearby resort or other personal destination. When this happens, an allocation must be made between the business and personal portions of the trip. However, the travel policy is unclear on the allocation method to follow.

Consider this example. An employee obtained a first-class excursion ticket for $2,640 and traveled the following itinerary:

From	To	Mileage	One-Way Regular Fare	Purpose
Washington, D.C.	Salt Lake City	1,839	$1,400	Business
Salt Lake City	Los Angeles	590	600	Personal
Los Angeles	Washington, D.C.	2,288	1,600	Return

Required

Compute the business portion of the airfare and state the basis for the indicated allocation that is appropriate according to each of the following independent scenarios:

a. Based on the maximum reimbursement for the employee.

b. Based on the minimum cost to the company.

c. Write a short report to management explaining the method that you think should be used and why. You do not have to restrict your recommendation to either of the methods in requirements (*a*) or (*b*).

7.48

Wecare Hospital—
Cost Allocation,
Step Method[6]

The annual costs of hospital care under the medicare program exceed $20 billion per year. In the medicare legislation, Congress mandated that reimbursement to hospitals be limited to the costs of treating medicare patients. Ideally, neither nonmedicare patients nor hospitals would bear the costs of medicare patients nor would the government bear costs of nonmedicare patients. Given the large sums involved, it is not surprising that cost reimbursement specialists, computer programs, publications, and other products and services have arisen to provide hospital administrators with the assistance needed to obtain an appropriate reimbursement for medicare patient services.

Hospital departments may be divided into two categories: (1) revenue producing and (2) nonrevenue producing. This classification is simple but useful. The traditional accounting concepts associated with "service department cost allocation," while appropriate to this context, lead to a great deal of confusion in terminology since all of the hospital's departments are considered to be rendering services.

Costs of revenue-producing departments are charged to medicare and nonmedicare patients on the basis of actual use of the departments. These costs are relatively simple to apportion. Costs of nonrevenue-producing departments are somewhat more difficult to apportion. The approach to finding the appropriate distribution of these costs begins with the establishment of a reasonable basis for allocating nonrevenue-producing department costs to revenue-producing departments. Statistical measures of the relationships between departments must be ascertained. The cost allocation bases listed in Illustration 7.16 were established as acceptable for cost reimbursement purposes. The regulated order of allocation must be used for medicare reimbursement.

A hospital may then use either the reciprocal method to the cost allocation problem or the step method. If the step method is used, the order of departments for allocation is the same order as that by which the departments are listed in Illustration 7.16. Thus, Buildings Depreciation and Maintenance is allocated before Depreciation—Movable Equipment. Cost centers must be established for each of these nonrevenue-producing costs that are relevant to a particular hospital's operations.

In the past year, Wecare Hospital reported the following departmental costs:

Nonrevenue producing

Laundry and Linen.	$ 250,000
Buildings Depreciation and Maintenance	830,000
Employee Health and Welfare	375,000
Maintenance of Personnel.	210,000
Central Supply	745,000

Revenue producing

Operating Room	1,450,000
Radiology	160,000
Laboratory.	125,000
Patient Rooms	2,800,000

[6]© 1993 by CIPT Co.

ILLUSTRATION   7.16 **Bases for Allocating Nonrevenue-Producing Department Costs to Revenue-Producing Departments**

Nonrevenue Cost Center	Basis for Allocation
Buildings Depreciation and Maintenance	Square feet in each department
Depreciation—Movable Equipment	Dollar value of equipment in each department
Employee Health and Welfare	Gross salaries in each department
Administrative and General	Accumulated costs by department
Maintenance and Repairs	Square feet in each department
Operation of Plant	Square feet in each department
Laundry and Linen	Pounds used in each department
Housekeeping	Hours of service to each department
Dietary	Meals served in each department
Maintenance of Personnel	Number of departmental employees
Nursing Administration	Hours of supervision in each department
Central Supply	Costs of requisitions processed
Pharmacy	Costs of drug orders processed
Medical Records	Hours worked for each department
Social Service	Hours worked for each department
Nursing School	Assigned time by department
Intern/Resident Service	Assigned time by department

Percentage usage of one department's services by another department were as follows:

From	Laundry and Linen	Buildings Depreciation and Maintenance	Employee Health and Welfare	Maintenance of Personnel	Central Supply
Laundry and Linen	—	0.05	0.10	—	—
Buildings Depreciation and Maintenance	0.10	—	—	0.10	—
Employee Health and Welfare	0.15	—	—	0.05	0.03
Maintenance of Personnel.	—	—	—	—	0.12
Central Supply	0.10	—	—	0.08	—

	Operating Rooms	Radiology	Laboratory	Patient Rooms
Laundry and Linen.	0.30	0.10	0.05	0.40
Buildings Depreciation and Maintenance . .	0.05	0.02	0.02	0.71
Employee Health and Welfare	0.25	0.05	0.04	0.43
Maintenance of Personnel.	0.36	0.10	0.08	0.34
Central Supply	0.09	0.04	0.03	0.66

The proportional use of revenue-producing department services by medicare and other patients follows:

	Medicare	Other
Operating Rooms	25%	75%
Radiology	20	80
Laboratory	28	72
Patient Rooms	36	64

Required   What is the amount of the reimbursement claim for medicare services, using the step method of allocation? Use the following order of allocation: (1) Buildings Depreciation and Maintenance, (2) Employee Health and Welfare, (3) Laundry and Linen, (4) Maintenance of Personnel, and (5) Central Supply.

SOLUTIONS TO SELF-STUDY QUESTIONS

1. To facilitate solving the problem, first express usage in percentage terms:

Service	Used By					
Center	S1	S2	S3	P1	P2	P3
S1	—	0.100[a]	0.049	0.333	0.444	0.074
S2	0.050	—	0.100	0.500	0.250	0.100
S3	—	—	—	0.250	0.667	0.083

[a]0.100 = 8,100 ÷ (8,100 + 3,900 + 27,000 + 36,000 + 6,000). Other computations use the same approach.

Direct method: Usage of services by producing departments only:

Service	Used By		
Center	P1	P2	S3
S1.	0.391[a]	0.522	0.087
S2.	0.588[b]	0.294	0.118
S3.	0.250	0.667	0.083

[a]0.391 = 0.333 ÷ (0.333 + 0.444 + 0.074); 0.522 = 0.444 ÷ (0.333 + 0.444 + 0.074); etc.

[b]0.588 = 0.500 ÷ (0.500 + 0.250 + 0.100); etc.

Allocation		To		
From	Amount	P1	P2	P3
S1.	$45,000	$ 17,595[a]	$ 23,490[a]	$ 3,915[a]
S2.	$20,000	11,760[b]	5,880[b]	2,360[b]
S3.	$10,000	2,500[c]	6,670[c]	830[c]
Allocated costs . .		31,855	36,040	7,105
Direct costs.		210,000	140,000	80,000
Total costs		$241,855	$176,040	$87,105

Note: Allocations are rounded. Unrounded answers will be slightly different.

[a]$17,595 = $45,000 × 0.391; $23,490 = $45,000 × 0.522; $3,915 = $45,000 × 0.087.

[b]$11,760 = $20,000 × 0.588; $5,880 = $20,000 × 0.294; $2,360 = $20,000 × 0.118.

[c]$2,500 = $10,000 × 0.25; $6,670 = $10,000 × 0.667; $830 = $10,000 × 0.083.

2. **Step Method:** Order of allocation: S2, S1, S3.

   Usage of services by producing departments and service cost centers excluding reciprocal allocations:

Service Center	Used By				
	S1	**S3**	**P1**	**P2**	**P3**
S2.	0.050	0.100	0.500	0.250	0.100
S1.	—	0.054[a]	0.370[a]	0.494[a]	0.082[a]
S3.	—	—	0.250	0.667	0.083

[a]We use the numbers from the first display in the solution to Self-Study Question 1.
$0.054 = 0.049 \div (0.049 + 0.333 + 0.444 + 0.074) = 0.049 \div 0.900$; $0.370 = 0.333 \div 0.900$; $0.494 = 0.444 \div 0.900$ (rounded); $0.082 = 0.074 \div 0.90$.

Allocation

From	To					
	S2	**S1**	**S3**	**P1**	**P2**	**P3**
Direct department costs.	$ 20,000	$ 45,000	$ 10,000			
S2	(20,000)	1,000[a]	2,000[a]	$ 10,000	$ 5,000	$ 2,000
S1		$(46,000)[b]	2,484[b]	17,020[b]	22,724	3,772
S3			$(14,484)[c]	3,621[c]	9,661	1,202
Total allocated costs				30,641	37,385	6,974
Direct costs of P1, P2, P3				210,000	140,000	80,000
Total costs				$240,641	$177,385	$86,974

[a]$1,000 = $20,000 \times 0.05$; $2,000 = $20,000 \times 0.10$; etc.

[b]$46,000 = $45,000 \text{ direct costs} + $1,000 \text{ allocated from S2}$; $2,484 = $46,000 \times 0.054$; $17,020 = $46,000 \times 0.37$; etc.

[c]$14,484 = $10,000 \text{ direct costs} + $4,484 \text{ allocated from S1 and S2}$; $3,621 = $14,484 \times 0.25$; etc.

3. **Reciprocal method:**

$$\frac{\text{Total}}{\text{costs}} = \frac{\text{Direct}}{\text{costs}} + \begin{array}{l}\text{Costs to be}\\ \text{allocated to the}\\ \text{service department}\end{array}$$

$$S1 = \$100,000 + 0.1\ S2$$
$$S2 = \$200,000 + 0.2\ S1$$

Substituting:

$$S1 = \$100,000 + 0.1(\$200,000 + 0.2\ S1)$$
$$S1 = \$120,000 + 0.02\ S1$$
$$0.98\ S1 = \$120,000$$
$$S1 = \frac{\$120,000}{0.98} = \$122,449$$
$$S2 = \$200,000 + 0.2(\$122,449)$$
$$S2 = \$224,490$$

Allocation

	To		
From	**P1**	**P2**	**P3**
S1........	0.3($122,449) = $36,735	0.3($122,449) = $36,735	0.2($122,449) = $24,490
S2........	0.2($224,490) = $44,898	0.4($224,490) = $89,796	0.3($224,490) = $67,347

Total costs allocated to P1 + P2 + P3 = $300,001 (difference due to rounding).

4. a.

Cost	Allocation Base	Allocated to Uno	Allocated to Duo
Computer services	Computer time	$\frac{200}{200 + 140} \times \$254,000$ $= \$149,412$	$\frac{140}{200 + 140} \times \$254,000$ $= \$104,588$
Building occupancy	Area occupied	$\frac{15,000}{15,000 + 40,000} \times \$615,000$ $= \$167,727$	$\frac{40,000}{15,000 + 40,000} \times \$615,000$ $= \$447,273$
Personnel	Payroll	$\frac{\$380,000}{\$380,000 + \$170,000} \times \$104,000$ $= \$\ 71,855$	$\frac{\$170,000}{\$380,000 + \$170,000} \times \$104,000$ $= \$\ 32,145$
Totals		$\$388,994$	$\$584,006$

Check: $254,000 + $615,000 + $104,000 = $388,994 + $584,006 = $973,000.

b.

Computer variable costs	Computer time	$\frac{200}{200 + 140} \times \$254,000 \times 20\%$ $= \$\ 29,882$	$\frac{140}{200 + 140} \times \$254,000 \times 20\%$ $= \$\ 20,918$
Computer fixed costs	Computer storage	$\frac{25}{25 + 35} \times \$254,000 \times 80\%$ $= \$\ 84,667$	$\frac{35}{25 + 35} \times \$254,000 \times 80\%$ $= \$118,533$
Building occupancy— per *(a)*		$\$167,727$	$\$447,273$
Personnel—per *(a)*		$\$\ 71,855$	$\$\ 32,145$
Totals		$\$354,131$	$\$618,869$

Check: $254,000 + $615,000 + $104,000 = $354,131 + $618,869 = $973,000.

5.

	Michigan Plant	**Texas Plant**	**Total**
Percentage factors			

Payroll $\dfrac{\$120,000}{\$300,000} = 40.0\%$ $\dfrac{\$180,000}{\$300,000} = 60.0\%$ 100%

Volume $\dfrac{\$600,000}{\$1,600,000} = 37.5\%$ $\dfrac{\$1,000,000}{\$1,600,000} = 62.5\%$ 100%

Assets $\dfrac{\$400,000}{\$1,200,000} = 33.3\%$ $\dfrac{\$800,000}{\$1,200,000} = 66.7\%$ 100%

Average

Michigan $\dfrac{(40.0\% + 37.5\% + 33.3\%)}{3} = 36.9\%$

Texas $\dfrac{(60.0\% + 62.5\% + 66.7\%)}{3} = 63.1\%$

Allocation of headquarters costs
  Michigan $\$480,000 \times 36.9\% = \$177,120$
  Texas $\$480,000 \times 63.1\% = \underline{\$302,880}$
                              $\underline{\underline{\$480,000}}$

Activity-Based Costing

LEARNING OBJECTIVES

After reading this chapter, you should be able to:

1. Describe the allocation of costs to products.

2. Compare and contrast plantwide and department allocation methods.

3. Explain the advantages and disadvantages of activity-based costing.

4. Compute product costs using activity-based costing.

5. Compare activity-based product costing to traditional department product-costing methods.

6. Demonstrate the flow of costs through accounts using activity-based costing.

7. Apply activity-based costing to marketing and administrative services.

8. Describe how activity-based costing adds value to companies.

Assume that the following discussion takes place in the offices of a company that makes denim clothes.

> *Pam* (president of the company) [clearly frustrated]: Ten years ago, we were a highly profitable industry leader. In the last few years, our profits have shrunk to almost nothing. We can't even meet the competition on the prices of our basic denim pants, which have been our most important and highest volume product. We need to turn this situation around fast!
>
> *Lynn* (vice president of marketing): I agree that we aren't meeting the competition on jeans, but our prices are just barely above costs now. Surely you don't expect me to price below cost! I don't think the problem is in marketing; I think the problem is in production where the costs are too high.
>
> *Martha* (vice president of production): I think we could reduce costs if we had a better cost system to tell us where to direct our efforts. To be frank, I don't trust the cost numbers we're getting now; I think they are way out of line with reality. Our overhead, which is about 50 percent of the cost of making the product, is allocated arbitrarily to our products. If you want us to reduce costs, we want a better cost system than the one we have now!
>
> *George* (controller) [disturbed]: I hadn't realized that the situation was quite this bad. This discussion prompts me to get started on a project that I've been planning for a long time. Could we meet tomorrow after I've had time to get some ideas together?
>
> *Pam:* Fine. We'll meet at this time tomorrow.

Discussions like this one are taking place in many companies as you read this book. The exchange between the controller and his fellow managers emphasizes the importance of having accurate cost numbers for marketing and production decisions. Yet cost numbers can differ considerably, depending on how overhead costs are allocated to products. Dealing with overhead allocations is one of the most difficult tasks accountants face in computing accurate cost numbers.

Numerous companies, such as Hewlett-Packard, Procter & Gamble, Boeing, Caterpillar, and IBM, have implemented new, more sophisticated cost methods to improve the way they allocate overhead costs. These new methods have revealed startling inaccuracies in the way that product costs had previously been computed. For example, after installing new cost allocation methods, Tektronix, Inc., found that one of its products, a printed circuit board, was generating negative margins of 46 percent.[1]

OVERVIEW OF COST METHODS

L.O. 1: Describe the allocation of costs to products.

cost pools
Groups of individual costs.

This chapter deals with allocating indirect costs to products. In this chapter, the cost object is a product. The product can be a good, such as an automobile, or a service, such as an X-ray examination in a hospital. Recall that indirect costs cannot be traced directly to a product.

Indirect costs can be the overhead costs incurred in manufacturing a good or providing a service, or they can be indirect costs incurred in marketing the product or in administration. Some marketing costs, such as sales commissions, are direct, but many are indirect. Unlike direct materials and direct labor, which can be traced directly to a product, indirect costs must be *allocated* to products.

Chapter 7 described how companies allocate costs to production departments. This chapter describes how companies allocate costs from cost pools to products. **Cost pools** are simply groups of individual costs. In Chapter 7, the cost pools were departments. In this chapter, we expand our discussion to allow cost pools to be (1) plants, which are entire factories or stores, (2) departments within plants, or (3) activities.

---

[1] "A Bean-Counter's Best Friend," *Business Week/Quality,* 1991, pp. 42–43.

We use predetermined overhead rates throughout this chapter. Recall from Chapter 4 that using predetermined rates normally results in over- or underapplied overhead. To keep the examples from becoming too complex, we will not use examples that involve over- or underapplied overhead in this chapter.

USING ONE ALLOCATION RATE FOR THE ENTIRE PLANT

L.O. 2: Compare and contrast plantwide and department allocation methods.

plantwide allocation method
An allocation method that uses one cost pool for the entire plant. It uses one overhead allocation rate, or one set of rates, for all of the departments in a plant.

We start with the simplest allocation method, which is known as *plantwide allocation*. In the **plantwide allocation method,** the cost pool is the entire plant. This method uses one overhead allocation rate, or one set of rates, to allocate overhead to products for *all* departments in a particular plant. We use the term *plant* to refer to an entire factory, store, hospital, or other multidepartment segment of a company. The key word in the definition is *all*; that is, a single rate or set of rates is used for every department. We note that a company might use more than one rate, such as the dual rate method discussed in Chapter 7.

Although it is called *plantwide* allocation, this allocation concept can be used in both manufacturing and nonmanufacturing organizations. In a bank, for example, overhead could be applied to different customer accounts, to different types of loans, and to other products using just one overhead rate for the entire bank. Although we refer to the costs that are being allocated as *overhead* costs, the concepts apply to *any* indirect cost allocation.

The top of Illustration 8.1 shows overhead allocation using plantwide allocation. Accounting for overhead is simple. All overhead costs are recorded in one cost pool in the Manufacturing Overhead (Actual) account for the plant without regard to the department or activity that caused them. A single overhead rate is used to apply overhead to products, crediting Manufacturing Overhead Applied. For example, if overhead is applied using a predetermined rate per machine-hour, the amount of the credit to the Manufacturing Overhead Applied account and the debit to Work in Process for overhead costs equal the rate per machine-hour times the total number of machine-hours worked.

For Domino's Pizza, using multiple overhead rates would probably not have much effect on the accuracy of determining the costs of making pizzas because different sizes and types of pizzas all have about the same effect on overhead costs. See discussion on this page.

Companies using a single plantwide rate generally use a volume-based allocation base, such as direct labor-hours, machine-hours, volume of activity, or materials costs. Later in this chapter, we discuss other types of allocation bases with which companies are experimenting.

A single plantwide rate might be justified in simple organizations having only a few departments and not much variety in products. At Domino's Pizza, for example, using multiple overhead rates versus only one overhead rate for all of the products probably would not make much difference in the estimated costs of the regular or the large pizzas. Suppose that Domino's becomes a more complex operation that includes extensive restaurant facilities as well as home delivery and food service for schools and hospitals. In this case, using different overhead rates for different departments is appropriate because overhead costs are likely to be caused by different activities in different departments.

ILLUSTRATION   8.1   Plantwide versus Department Allocation

Plantwide Allocation

Manufacturing Overhead (Actual)	Manufacturing Overhead Applied	Work in Process—Entire Plant
All overhead incurred in the plant	All overhead in the plant allocated to products	Direct Materials Direct Labor Manufacturing Overhead

Department Allocation

Manufacturing Overhead— Production Department L	Manufacturing Overhead Applied— Production Department L	Work in Process— Production Department L
Overhead in Department L	Overhead allocated to products worked on in Department L	Direct Materials Direct Labor Manufacturing Overhead

Allocating department costs to products

Manufacturing Overhead— Production Department M	Manufacturing Overhead Applied— Production Department M	Work in Process— Production Department M
Overhead in Department M	Overhead allocated to products worked on in Department M	Direct Materials Direct Labor Manufacturing Overhead

Allocating department costs to products

Overhead— Service Department 1
Overhead incurred in Service Department 1	Overhead allocated to production departments

Overhead— Service Department 2
Overhead incurred in Service Department 2	Overhead allocated to production departments

Note: Cost flows for direct materials and direct labor are omitted to simplify the presentation.

USING A DIFFERENT ALLOCATION RATE FOR EACH DEPARTMENT IN THE PLANT

department allocation method
Using this allocation method, companies have a separate cost pool for each department. Each department has its own overhead allocation rate or set of rates.

Using a separate department overhead application rate for the mortgage loan department instead of a single bankwide rate gives managers a better idea of the costs of each loan.

Using the **department allocation method,** a company has a separate cost pool for each department. The company establishes a separate overhead allocation rate for each department. (Multiple rates could be set for each department if the company uses dual or multiple-factor cost allocation, as discussed in Chapter 7.) Recall from Chapter 7 that service departments provide services to production departments, which produce goods and services. Each production department is a separate cost pool. In contrast, using the plantwide allocation method, the entire plant is one cost pool.

The middle and bottom of Illustration 8.1 show department allocation. Each department is a cost pool and has an allocation rate. The illustration has four overhead cost pools, one each for Service Departments 1 and 2, and one each for Production Departments L and M. As each production department works on a product, it applies overhead based on the allocation rate for that department. The more departments the company has, the more overhead cost pools it has, and the more allocation rates there are to compute.

Choice of Cost Allocation Methods: A Cost-Benefit Decision

The choice of a plantwide rate versus the more complex department rate versus the even more complex activity-based costing, discussed next, requires managers to make a cost-benefit decision. Selecting more complex allocation methods requires more time and skill to collect and process accounting information. Such incremental costs of additional information must be justified by an increase in benefits from improved decisions.

Note that companies using plantwide allocation, as shown in the top panel of Illustration 8.1, do not need to allocate service department costs to production departments. Although it is simpler, omitting the allocation of service department costs to production departments could have negative behavioral effects for the company. Allocating service department costs to production departments enables management to assign responsibility for service costs to the people in the production department who wanted the services.

A department rate provides more detailed cost measures and more accurate product cost numbers than a plantwide rate, particularly if the departments perform quite different activities. For example, if one department is labor intensive and another is machine intensive, it makes little sense to use a rate based on either machine-hours or labor-hours for both departments. Product costs are more accurate if labor-hours are used for the labor-intensive department and machine-hours for the machine-intensive department.

The following self-study question demonstrates the differences between plantwide and department rates when computing product costs.

SELF-STUDY QUESTION

1. Bank of Durango is considering either a bankwide overhead rate or a department rate. To get more information about these alternatives, management decided to test both rates for two departments: Commercial Loans and Mortgage Loans. The bankwide rate was based on a percentage of direct labor time and was computed to be 50 percent of labor. The direct labor costs for the two departments for the test period were as follows:

Commercial loans $100,000
Mortgage loans.   300,000

To develop department rates, the bank's accountants estimated overhead rates of 40 percent of direct labor for Mortgage Loans and a dual rate for Commercial Loans of 20 percent of direct labor plus $40 per loan. Commercial Loans made 900 loans during the test period.

Compute the cost of labor and overhead for these two departments using (1) the bankwide rate and (2) the department rates. What are the advantages and disadvantages of the department rate compared to the bankwide rate?

The solution to this question is at the end of this chapter on page 266.

ACTIVITY-BASED COSTING

L.O. 3: Explain the advantages and disadvantages of activity-based costing.

activity-based costing
A costing method that first assigns costs to activities and then assigns them to products based on the products' consumption of activities.

Activity-based costing is a costing method that assigns costs first to activities and then to the products based on each product's use of activities. An *activity* is any discrete task that an organization undertakes to make or deliver a product or service. Acivity-based costing is based on the concept that products consume activities and activities consume resources.

If managers want their products to be competitive, they must know (1) the activities that go into making the good or providing the service and (2) the cost of those activities. To reduce a product's costs, managers will likely have to change the activities consumed by the product. It is rarely sufficient for a manager to announce, "I want everyone to reduce costs by 10 percent" to effect a cost decrease. More likely, significant cost reduction requires managers, production and marketing people, accountants, engineers, and others to examine thoroughly the activities that a product consumes to determine how to rework those activities to make the product more efficiently.

For example, the Admissions Department of a university listed its activities: (1) receiving applications, (2) filing, (3) reviewing, checking, and completing files, (4) admitting students, and (5) notifying students. Management studied the activities of admitting students and found that certain activities could be made more efficient and others could be eliminated for certain categories of students. By focusing on activities, the university was able to reduce costs.

Some people argue that activity-based costing is simply an extension of department allocation. Just as department allocation is more detailed than plantwide allocation, activity-based costing is generally more detailed than department allocation.

Many proponents of activity-based costing argue, however, that it is not just an extension of traditional department allocation but is an entirely new way to manage by focusing on activities. People manage activities, not costs, these proponents argue. Activity-based costing focuses attention on the things that matter, namely, those activities that are costly and should be made more efficient or otherwise changed.

To demonstrate important issues about the difficulty with traditional plantwide and department cost allocation methods and the advantages of activity-based costing, we continue the discussion at the denim clothing manufacturer from the beginning of this chapter. Recall that the participants had expressed concerns about the company's ability to compete and the inadequate information provided by the company's cost accounting system. George, the controller, returned the next day with new ideas about activity-based costing.

George: I have been reading numerous articles about companies, such as Ford, Deere, and Hewlett-Packard, that have discovered major problems with their cost systems. Their symptoms appear similar to our experience; namely, they can't lower prices to be competitive on high-volume products, and their profits are shrinking.

Pam (president): That sounds like us. What are they doing about it?

George: First, they're putting in a new type of cost system known as activity-based costing, or ABC for short. This system provides more detailed and better estimates of product costs, which helps our friends in marketing set prices. We may find, for example, that activity-based costing reveals that the cost of shirts is lower than we thought, meaning that we could lower our prices.

Lynn (vice president of marketing): That would be good news, but I thought costs were pretty cut and dried. How can it be that a product costs less under one cost system than under another system?

George: Lynn, the product doesn't cost less under one system or another. The problem is that no cost system can measure costs perfectly. We're able to trace some costs directly to the product. For example, we're pretty accurate in measuring the cost of denim, which is a direct material, in each of our products—shirts, pants, jackets, and so forth.

Overhead costs are another matter. Overhead, which includes such costs as electricity to run machines and salaries of product designers, inspectors, and machine operators, is allocated to products using an allocation base such as the number of hours that machines are used in cutting and stitching. Products that require more machine-hours are allocated more overhead costs, even if the overhead isn't related to machine-hours. For example, the salaries of inspectors are related to the number of inspections, which is more related to how complicated the stitching is than to the number of machine-hours. If we change the allocation base, we change the product cost.

Pam: I understand that overhead allocation is somewhat arbitrary. How will activity-based costing help?

George: Activity-based costing provides more accurate information because we identify which activities cause costs, and we determine the costs of these activities. Activity-based costing more clearly identifies and measures costs of performing the activities that go into a product than traditional costing methods. For example, if a particular type of jacket requires 10 inspections for a production run of 1,000 jackets, we figure out the cost of those inspections and assign that cost to the production run for this particular jacket.

Martha (vice president of production): That makes sense to me. How would activity-based costing help us cut production costs?

George: By identifying activities that cause costs, we can eliminate or modify costly activities. For example, if we find that jackets require too many costly inspections, we could redesign the jacket to reduce the need for inspections. Our current cost system allocates all overhead costs, including inspection costs, to products based on machine-hours. We really don't know how much it costs to make an inspection and how much inspection cost is required by each product.

Pam: George, why haven't you used activity-based costing before?

George [somewhat defensive]: Activity-based costing provides more information, but it takes more time than traditional cost systems. New accounting methods sound great in theory, but there must be enough benefit from improved management decisions to justify the additional work required to provide numbers. Until now, I didn't think activity-based costing would pass a cost-benefit test.

Pam: I see many benefits to better costing methods: reducing costs of high-cost activities and possibly dropping some products if we learn that their costs are too high. Our long-term strategy calls for new product lines in new markets where we are low-cost, low-price producers. We need the best cost information we can get to succeed in those markets. George, what do you need to get started developing an activity-based costing system for us?

George: I need a lot of support. Installing a new cost system requires teamwork between management, accounting, marketing, engineering, production, purchasing, and many other areas. This is not something to be done in an ivory tower. You need to educate us accountants about the activities that cause costs.

The preceding discussion made the following important points about activity-based costing:

- Different cost allocation methods result in different estimates of how much it costs to make a product.
- Activity-based costing provides more detailed measures of costs than do plantwide or department allocation methods.
- Activity-based costing can help marketing people by providing more accurate product cost numbers for decisions about pricing and which products to eliminate.
- Production also benefits because activity-based costing provides better information about how much each activity costs. In fact, it helps identify cost drivers (that is, the activities that cause costs) that were previously unknown. To manage costs, production managers learn to manage the cost drivers.
- Activity-based costing provides more information about product costs but requires more recordkeeping. Managers must decide whether the benefits of improved decisions justify the additional cost of activity-based costing compared to department or plantwide allocation.
- Installing activity-based costing requires teamwork between accounting, production, marketing, management, and other nonaccounting people.

We next discuss the methods used for activity-based costing and then present an example.

Methods

Activity-based costing involves the following four steps:

1. Identify the activities—such as purchasing materials—that consume resources and assign costs to them.
2. Identify the cost driver(s) associated with each activity. A **cost driver** causes, or "drives," an activity's costs. For the purchasing materials activity, the cost driver could be number of orders.
3. Compute a cost rate per cost driver unit or transaction. The cost driver rate could be the cost per purchase order, for example. Each activity could have multiple cost drivers.
4. Assign costs to products by multiplying the cost driver rate times the volume of cost driver units consumed by the product. For example, the cost per purchase order times the number of orders required for product A for the month of December measures the cost of the purchasing activity for product A for December.

cost driver
A factor that causes, or "drives," an activity's costs.

Identifying Activities That Use Resources

Often the most interesting and challenging part of the exercise is identifying activities that use resources because it requires people to understand all of the activities required to make the product. Imagine the activities involved in making a simple product like a pizza—ordering, receiving, and inspecting materials; making the dough; putting on the ingredients; cooking; and so forth. Now imagine the number of activities involved in making a complex product like an automobile or computer.

Using common sense and the principle that the benefits of more detailed costs should exceed the costs of getting the information, companies identify only the most important activities. A Deere & Company plant identified six major activities required to produce its products, for example, and used one cost driver for each activity. Then it developed two cost rates for each cost driver, one for variable costs and one for fixed costs.[2]

---

[2]See "John Deere Component Works," Harvard Business School case 187-107.

Complexity as a Resource-Consuming Activity

One lesson of activity-based costing has been that costs are a function of both volume and complexity.[3] It might be obvious that a higher volume of production consumes resources, but assuming that the company has at least some variable costs, why does complexity consume resources?

To understand the answer to that question, imagine that you produce 100,000 gallons of vanilla ice cream per month and your friend produces 100,000 gallons of 39 different flavors of ice cream per month. Assume further that your ice cream is sold only in one-liter containers, but your friend sells ice cream in various container sizes. Although both of you produce the same total volume of ice cream, it is not hard to imagine that your friend's overhead costs are considerably higher. Your friend has more complicated ordering, storage, product testing (one of the more desirable jobs, nevertheless), and packing activities. Your friend has more machine setups, too. Presumably, you can set the machinery to one setting to obtain the desired product quality and taste; your friend has to set the machines each time a new flavor is produced.

In general, the number of activities that consumes resources is a function of the company's complexity. The number of cost drivers increases as companies become more highly automated and more complex. Cost systems based on a simple direct labor base are generally inadequate in all but the simplest production or selling enterprise.

When accountants use allocation rates based on volume, such as direct labor hours or machine hours, they naturally allocate costs to products proportional to volume. High-volume products are allocated a high proportion of overhead costs, and low-volume products are allocated a low proportion of overhead costs. After installing activity-based costing, managers have frequently found that the low-volume products should be allocated more overhead. Low-volume products may be more specialized, requiring, for example, more drawings, specifications, and inspections.

Low-volume products often require more machine setups for a given level of production output because they are produced in smaller batches. In the ice cream example, one batch of 1,000 gallons of the low-volume 39th flavor might require as much overhead cost for machine setups, quality inspection, and purchase orders as one batch of 100,000 gallons of the highest-volume flavor. In addition, the low-volume product adds complexity to the operation by disrupting the production flow of the high-volume items. You appreciate this fact every time you stand in line when someone ahead of you has a special and complex transaction.

When overhead is applied based on the volume of output, high-volume products are allocated relatively more overhead than are low-volume products. High-volume products "subsidize" low-volume products in this case. The cost effects of keeping a large number of low-volume products are hidden by volume-based allocation methods. This has led many companies to continue producing or selling products without realizing how costly they are.

Choosing Cost Drivers

Illustration 8.2 presents several examples of the types of cost drivers that companies use. Most are related either to the volume of production or to the complexity of the production or marketing process.

How do managers decide which cost driver to use? Chapter 7 discussed three criteria for selecting allocation bases. The first criterion involves identifying a cost driver; it makes the case that the cost driver should be used as an allocation base. It

---

[3]For example, see R. D. Banker, G. Potter and R. Schroeder, "An Empirical Study of Manufacturing Overhead Cost Drivers," *Journal of Accounting and Economics* 119, no. 1 (February 1995); R. D. Banker and H. H. Johnston, "An Empirical Study of Cost Drivers in the U.S. Airline Industry," *The Accounting Review* 68, no. 3 (July 1993); and E. Noreen and N. Soderstrom, "Are Overhead Costs Strictly Proportional to Activity? Evidence from Hospital Service Departments," *Journal of Accounting and Economics* 17 (January 1994).

ILLUSTRATION	8.2	**Examples of Cost Drivers**

Machine-hours	Computer time
Labor-hours or labor cost	Items produced or sold
Pounds of materials handled	Customers served
Pages typed	Flight hours
Machine setups	Number of surgeries
Purchase orders	Scrap/rework orders
Quality inspections	Hours of testing time
Number of parts in a product	Number of different customers
Miles driven	

is not always possible, however, to identify a cost driver. The other two criteria generally involve selecting an allocation base when a cost driver cannot be identified.

- *Causal relation.* Choose a cost driver that causes the cost. This is ideal.
- *Benefits received.* Choose a cost driver to assign costs in proportion to benefits received. For example, if the Physics Department in a university benefits more from the university's supercomputer than does the History Department, the university should select a cost driver that recognizes such differences in benefits (for example, the number of faculty and/or students in each department who use the computer).
- *Reasonableness.* Some costs cannot be linked to products based on causality or benefits received, so they are assigned on the basis of fairness or reasonableness. We noted earlier that Deere & Company selected six cost drivers for a certain product. The costs of a seventh activity, general and administrative overhead, was allocated to the product using the reasonableness approach; namely, they were allocated as a simple percentage of the costs of labor plus the other six activities that had been allocated to the product.

Computing a Cost Rate Per Cost Driver

In general, predetermined rates for allocating indirect costs to products are computed as follows:

$$\text{Predetermined rate} = \frac{\text{Estimated indirect cost}}{\text{Estimated volume of allocation base}}$$

This formula applies to any indirect cost, whether manufacturing overhead or administrative, distribution, selling, or any other indirect costs.

Companies using department rates compute the predetermined rate for each department. We first must consider the **activity center,** which is a unit of the organization that performs some activity. For example, the costs of setting up machines are assigned to the activity center that sets up machines. Instead of a department rate, using activity-based costing, we must compute a cost driver rate for each activity center. This means that each activity has an associated cost pool, as shown in Illustration 8.3. If the cost driver is the number of inspections, for example, the company must be able to estimate the inspection costs before the period and, ideally, track the actual cost of inspections as it is incurred during the period.

activity center
A unit of the organization that performs some activity.

Assigning Costs to Products

Workers and machines perform activities on each product as it is produced. Costs are allocated to a product by multiplying each activity's predetermined rate by the volume of activity used in making it.

Assume in Illustration 8.3 that the service department overhead costs have already been allocated to the production department's overhead accounts. Assume further that the illustration is for only one production department, Department L. This

ILLUSTRATION   8.3   Cost Pools and Activities

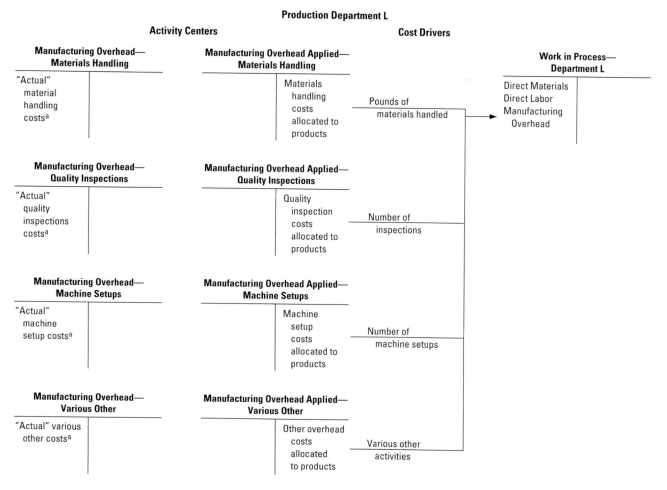

Production Department L

| Activity Centers | Cost Drivers |

**Manufacturing Overhead—
Materials Handling**

"Actual" material handling costs[a]

**Manufacturing Overhead Applied—
Materials Handling**

Materials handling costs allocated to products

Pounds of materials handled

**Work in Process—
Department L**

Direct Materials
Direct Labor
Manufacturing Overhead

**Manufacturing Overhead—
Quality Inspections**

"Actual" quality inspections costs[a]

**Manufacturing Overhead Applied—
Quality Inspections**

Quality inspection costs allocated to products

Number of inspections

**Manufacturing Overhead—
Machine Setups**

"Actual" machine setup costs[a]

**Manufacturing Overhead Applied—
Machine Setups**

Machine setup costs allocated to products

Number of machine setups

**Manufacturing Overhead—
Various Other**

"Actual" various other costs[a]

**Manufacturing Overhead Applied—
Various Other**

Other overhead costs allocated to products

Various other activities

[a]"Actual" costs refer both to overhead costs directly traceable to the activity and to service department costs allocated to the activity.

illustrates that companies identify numerous activities, or cost drivers, for each department.

As a product is worked on in Department L, materials are moved to the work area. Materials handling overhead, such as the wages paid to the materials movers, is allocated to the product by multiplying the overhead allocation rate for materials handling times the number of pounds of materials moved. For quality inspections, the overhead is allocated based on the rate for inspections times the number of inspections made on the product. The same procedure is followed for all other activities. The procedure is repeated for each product worked on in Department L.

Circuit Board Illustration

Next we present an example that shows how activity-based costing was developed for printed circuit boards in a Hewlett-Packard plant.[4] (We have simplified some of the activities and rounded some of the numbers for presentation purposes.) The activities required to make the product, from materials purchasing to quality testing, are described in the top panel of Illustration 8.4. Examples of the overhead costs

---

[4]Berlant, Browning, and Foster, "How Hewlett-Packard Gets Numbers It Can Trust," *Harvard Business Review,* January–February 1990, pp. 178–83.

ILLUSTRATION 8.4	**Activity-Based Costing of a Circuit Board**

Activities	Typical Overhead Costs
1. Purchasing materials	Costs of people involved in purchasing, inspecting, and storing materials.
2. Starting the product	Costs of people who prepare software for computer-driven machinery.
3. Inserting components	Costs of machines and people who insert components on the circuit boards.
4. Soldering	Cost of machines that solder components onto the board.
5. Quality testing	Costs of machines and people who check to see that components are properly inserted and the circuit board meets specifications.

(1) Activity	(2) Cost Driver Used to Allocate Overhead	(3) Rate per Cost Driver		(4) Number of Cost Driver Units in One Circuit Board		(5) Cost per Circuit Board for PC Board Type 67A
1. Purchasing materials	Number of parts in each circuit board	$.10 per part	×	90 parts	=	$ 9.00
2. Starting the product	Number of boards in the product	$1.00 per board	×	1 raw board	=	1.00
3. Inserting the components	Number of insertions per board	$.20 per insertion	×	80 insertions	=	16.00
4. Soldering	Number of boards soldered	$3.00 per board	×	1 board	=	3.00
5. Quality testing	Number of hours board is in testing	$70.00 per hour	×	.20 hours	=	14.00
Total overhead per printed-circuit board[a]						43.00
Cost of direct materials						75.00
Total cost of manufacturing the product						$118.00

[a]Direct labor is small and part of overhead in this plant.

Source: Adapted from Debbie Berlant, Reese Browning, and George Foster, "How Hewlett-Packard Gets Numbers It Can Trust," *Harvard Business Review,* January–February 1990, pp. 178–83.

associated with each activity are shown next to it. The company must keep a separate overhead account to record the cost of each activity.

In the bottom panel of the illustration, these activities are shown in the first column, and the related cost drivers used to apply the activities, such as the number of parts for materials purchasing overhead, are presented in the second column.

The next step is to compute indirect cost rates using the formula on page 240. These rates are shown in the third column of the bottom panel of Illustration 8.4. Managers have calculated the rates to be $.10 per part, $1.00 per board, and so forth. The fourth column shows the number of cost driver activities per circuit board required to make this particular product, PC Board Type 67A. Every other type of printed circuit board has different activities. The fifth column shows the overhead cost per circuit board of each activity required to make the product. When summed, the total overhead cost allocated to PC Board Type 67A is $43 per board.

We have just demonstrated how overhead is applied to the product. This particular Hewlett-Packard plant is sufficiently automated so that virtually no direct labor costs are traceable to a particular product. All labor cost is combined with overhead and is part of the indirect cost rates in Illustration 8.4. The cost of direct materials is traceable to the product and is added to the overhead cost of $43 per unit to derive the total cost of manufacturing the product.

Armed with this information, Hewlett-Packard managers can investigate ways to change the product or production methods to manage costs. For example, if a way could be found to reduce test time from .20 hours to .10 hours, only six minutes fewer, the company could save $7 per circuit board, assuming that these costs are variable. In fact, based on our interviews of managers and workers in this particular Hewlett-Packard plant, activity-based costing revealed surprising information about the cost of activities, which caused a change in product design and production methods. New cost accounting methods had a valuable impact on the company.

ACTIVITY-BASED COSTING ILLUSTRATED

L.O. 4: Compute product costs using activity-based costing.

The following example illustrates how unit costs are computed when companies use activity-based costing. We contrast the results using activity-based costing to those using a department-based rate.

Assume that SU Company makes two products, Standard and Unique. The Standard product line is a high-volume line, and the Unique line is a low-volume, specialized product. Assume that the overhead costs from service departments have already been allocated to Department A's Manufacturing Overhead account.

Department Allocation

Using department allocation, SU Company used the following procedure to allocate manufacturing overhead costs to the two products for January, Year 2.

* Late in Year 1, managers and accountants developed a predetermined overhead rate based on the following estimates for Year 2:

> Estimated annual overhead for
> Department A for Year 2 . . . . $2,000,000
> Estimated machine-hours to be worked
> during Year 2 in Department A . . . . 20,000 hours
> Department A overhead rate
> ($2,000,000/20,000 hours) . . . . $100 per machine-hour

* At the end of January, Year 2, the following information for the month of January was available:

> Actual machine-hours used in January, Year 2
>   Standard products 1,500
>   Unique products. 500
>   Total actual machine-hours in January 2,000

* Accountants then allocated overhead to the products worked on in January using the predetermined rate of $100 per hour times the actual machine-hours worked on each product in Department A:

> Overhead allocated to products worked on in January
>   Standard products ($100 × 1,500 hours) $150,000
>   Unique products ($100 × 500 hours). 50,000
>   Total overhead allocated to products $200,000

These calculations are summarized in Illustration 8.5.

Assigning Costs Using Activity-Based Costing

When SU Company began to use activity-based costing, it first identified four activities that were important cost drivers, which were used to allocate overhead. These activities were (1) purchasing materials, (2) setting up machines when a new product was started, (3) inspecting products, and (4) operating machines.

The amount of overhead and the volume of activity were estimated for each activity. For example, management estimated that the company would purchase 100,000 pounds of materials requiring overhead costs of $200,000 for the year. Examples of these overhead costs are the salaries of people who purchase, inspect, and

ILLUSTRATION   8.5   SU Company: Department Allocation

Department Allocation

Late in Year 1, managers and accountants estimated the following for Year 2

Annual overhead for the department $2,000,000

Machine-hours to be worked during the year in the department . . . . 20,000 hours

Department overhead rate ($2,000,000/20,000 hours) . . . . $100 per hour

At the end of January, Year 2, the following information is available

Actual machine-hours in January

Standard products   1,500

Unique products   500

Total actual machine-hours in January   2,000

Overhead is allocated to products worked on in January using
the predetermined rate of $100 per hour times the actual
machine-hours in January

Standard products ($100 × 1,500 hours) $150,000

Unique products ($100 × 500 hours)   50,000

Total overhead allocated to products $200,000

store materials. Consequently, each pound of materials used to make a product is assigned an overhead cost of $2 ($200,000/100,000 pounds).

These estimates made in Year 1 were to be used during all of Year 2. (In practice, companies frequently set rates for the entire year; sometimes they set rates for shorter periods, such as a quarter.) Illustration 8.6 shows the predetermined annual rates computed for the four activities. The estimated overhead cost in column (3) is divided by the cost driver volume in column (4) to get the rate in column (5).

The total overhead estimated for Year 2 using activity-based costing is $2,000,000, as it was using department allocation. The estimate of total overhead should be the same whether using plantwide allocation, department allocation, or activity-based costing. The primary difference between activity-based costing and department allocation is the number of cost pools and activities used to allocate overhead costs. Department allocation uses only one cost pool per department; activity-based costing uses four in this case. In practice, companies generally use more than four cost pools because more than four activities are important, but we keep the illustration as simple as possible.

By the end of January, Year 2, SU Company has collected the information about the actual cost driver volume for each of the two products for January shown below.

	Standard Product	Unique Product
1. Purchasing materials	6,000 pounds	4,000 pounds
2. Machine setups	10 setups	30 setups
3. Inspections	200 hours	200 hours
4. Running machines	1,500 hours	500 hours

Multiplying the actual activity events for each product times the predetermined rates computed resulted in the overhead allocated to the two products shown in Illustration 8.7.

Unit Costs Compared

Assume that SU Company produced 1,000 units of Standard and 200 units of Unique in January. In addition, the direct materials cost is $100 per unit for Standard and $200 per unit for Unique. Direct labor cost is $20 per unit for Standard and $30

ILLUSTRATION 8.6	Predetermined Annual Overhead Rates for Activity-Based Costing			
(1)	(2)	(3)	(4)	(5)
Activity	Cost Driver Used to Allocate Overhead	Estimated Overhead Cost for the Activity	Estimated Cost Driver Volume for Year 2	Rate Col. (3)/Col. (4)
1. Purchasing materials	Number of pounds of materials in each unit of product	$ 200,000	100,000 pounds	$2 per pound
2. Machine setups	Number of machine setups	800,000	400 setups	$2,000 per setup
3. Inspections	Hours of inspections	400,000	4,000 hours	$100 per hour
4. Running machines	Machine hours	600,000	20,000 hours	$30 per hour
Total estimated overhead		$2,000,000		

ILLUSTRATION 8.7	Overhead Costs Assigned to Products Using Activity-Based Costing				
		Standard Product		Unique Product	
Activity	Rate	Actual Cost Driver Units in January	Cost Allocated to Standard Product	Actual Cost Driver Units in January	Cost Allocated to Unique Product
1. Purchasing materials	$2 per pound	6,000 pounds	$12,000	4,000 pounds	$ 8,000
2. Machine setups	$2,000 per setup	10 setups	20,000	30 setups	60,000
3. Inspections	$100 per inspection hour	200 hours	20,000	200 hours	20,000
4. Running machines	$30 per hour	1,500 hours	45,000	500 hours	15,000
Total cost allocated to each product			$97,000		$103,000

L.O. 5: Compare activity-based product costing to traditional department product-costing methods.

per unit for Unique. Comparing the overhead allocations of the department allocation and the activity-based costing allocation methods reveals the differences in unit costs shown in Illustration 8.8.

Using activity-based costing more overhead is allocated per unit to the more specialized, lower-volume Unique product. Unique is allocated more overhead primarily because activity-based costing recognizes the need for more setups and for as many inspection hours of Unique as for the higher-volume Standard. By failing to assign costs to all of the activities, Standard was subsidizing Unique.

Many companies have found their situation to be similar to this example. For example, a Hewlett-Packard division in Boise, Idaho, found that many of its high-volume products had been overcosted by conventional costing compared to activity-based costing because conventional costing allocated costs proportional to volume.[5] Activity-based costing revealed that low-volume, specialized products were the cause of higher costs than managers had realized.

---

[5]C. M. Merz and A. Hardy, "ABC Puts Accountants on Design Team at HP," *Management Accounting*, September 1993.

ILLUSTRATION 8.8	Comparison of Product Costs Using Department Allocation and Activity-Based Costing			
	Department Allocation		Activity-Based Costing	
	Standard	Unique	Standard	Unique
Direct materials.	$100	$200	$100	$200
Direct labor.	20	30	20	30
Overhead	150[a]	250[b]	97[c]	515[d]
Total unit cost	$270	$480	$217	$745

[a]$150 = Overhead cost allocation to products using department allocation from Illustration 8.5 ÷ Units produced = $150,000/1,000 units.

[b]$250 = Overhead cost allocation to products using department allocation from Illustration 8.5 ÷ Units produced = $50,000/200 units.

[c]$97 = Overhead cost allocation to products using activity-based costing from Illustration 8.7 ÷ Units produced = $97,000/1,000 units.

[d]$515 = Overhead cost allocation to products using activity-based costing from Illustration 8.7 ÷ Units produced = $103,000/200 units.

COST FLOWS THROUGH ACCOUNTS

Illustration 8.9 shows the flow of costs through accounts using activity-based costing. The amounts for direct labor and direct materials are based on the preceding facts. The manufacturing overhead applied appeared in Illustration 8.7. We assume that all costs were transferred out of WIP Inventory–Department A to subsequent WIP departments.

L.O. 6: Demonstrate the flow of costs through accounts using activity-based costing.

SELF-STUDY QUESTION

2. Recall that SU Company's department overhead rate for Year 2 was $100 per machine-hour. At the end of December, Year 2, the following information is available for the month:

	Machine-Hours	Units
Standard products	2,000 hours	1,300 units
Unique products.	1,000 hours	400 units
Total	3,000 hours	

Activities	Standard Products	Unique Products
1. Purchasing materials	8,000 pounds	8,000 pounds
2. Machine setups.	15 setups	50 setups
3. Inspections.	220 hours	400 hours
4. Running machines	2,000 hours	1,000 hours

Compute the costs per unit for both the Standard and the Unique using both the department overhead rate and the activity-based costing rates. The actual activity levels for December are given in this self-study question. Use the rates presented in the text; do not assume that the total overhead assigned to products for December using activity-based costing equals the total overhead allocated using the department allocation rate. Assume that the direct materials costs are $100 and $200 per unit for Standard and Unique, respectively; direct labor costs are $20 and $30 per unit, respectively. Round unit costs to the nearest dollar.

The solution to this question is at the end of this chapter on page 266.

ILLUSTRATION   8.9   **Flow of Costs through Accounts Using Activity-Based Costing**

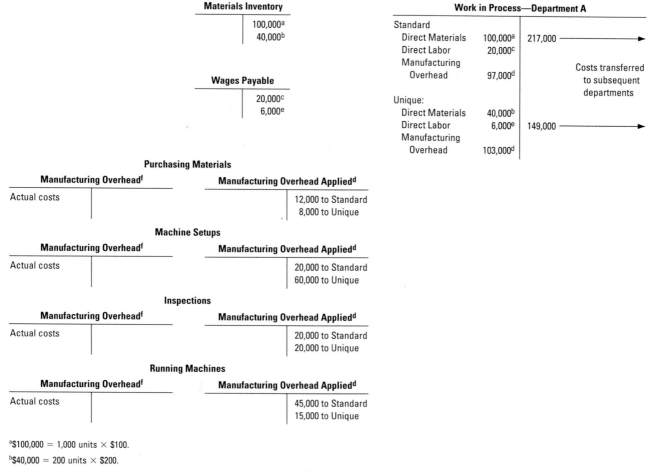

^{a}$100,000 = 1,000 units × $100.

^{b}$40,000 = 200 units × $200.

^{c}$20,000 = 1,000 units × $20.

^{d}Given as the overhead applied in Illustration 8.7.

^{e}$6,000 = 200 units × $30.

^{f}Actual manufacturing overhead for each activity center, or cost pool, in Department A is recorded here, including costs allocated to Department A.

CHOOSING ACTIVITY BASES IN MODERN PRODUCTION SETTINGS

When cost systems were first being developed in industry, companies were far more labor intensive than today. Much of the overhead cost was related to the support of labor, so it made sense to allocate overhead to products based on the amount of labor in the products. Labor is still a major product cost in many companies, especially service organizations like public accounting firms. In those cases, overhead is often allocated to products (which are called *jobs*) on the basis of the amount of labor in the product.

As companies have become more automated, including companies in the service sector such as banks, direct labor has become less appropriate as a basis for allocating overhead. As direct labor has dropped to less than 5 percent of product costs in many companies and overhead has increased, companies that stubbornly continue to allocate overhead to products based on direct labor are experiencing rate increases as high as 500 percent or more. (We have seen cases in which overhead rates are more than 1,000 percent of direct labor costs.)

When labor is such a small part of product costs, there is little, if any, relation between labor and overhead. In addition, small errors in assigning labor to products are magnified many times when overhead rates are several hundred percent or more of labor costs. Finally, allocating overhead on the basis of direct labor sends signals that direct labor is more expensive than it really is. This also creates tremendous incentives to reduce the labor content of products. This may be desirable in particular circumstances, but such decisions should be based on accurate cost numbers, not those that are heavily biased because of an arbitrary cost allocation method.

ACTIVITY-BASED COSTING IN MARKETING AND ADMINISTRATION

L.O. 7: Apply activity-based costing to marketing and administrative services.

Activity-based costing also can be applied to marketing or administrative activities. The principles and methods are the same as those discussed:

- Identify activities that consume resources.
- Identify cost drivers associated with each activity.
- Compute a cost rate for each cost driver.
- Assign costs to products by multiplying the cost driver rate by the volume of cost driver units consumed for the marketing or administration activity.

Instead of computing the cost of a product, however, accountants compute a cost of performing an administrative or marketing service. The following is an example.

Activity-Based Costing for a Service Activity

SU Company has an order-filling service. Customers can call an 800 number and order either the Standard or Unique product. Management is concerned about the cost for this service and is considering outsourcing it to another company. As a result, SU accepted bids from outside companies to perform the order-filling service, the lowest of which was $30 per unit. Managers wanted to know how much this service costs SU so they can decide whether to continue filling orders internally, and, if so, to identify ways to improve efficiency. The team appointed to the task proceeded as follows:

- Identified the activities that cause costs. The team identified order taking, order filling, shipping, and customer returns. These are listed in column (1) in Illustration 8.10.
- Identified cost drivers. These are listed in column (2) for each activity in Illustration 8.10.
- Computed cost driver rates. Column (3) in Illustration 8.10 presents the estimated monthly cost for each activity. Column (4) shows the estimated monthly cost driver volume, and column (5) shows the cost driver rate for each cost driver.

ILLUSTRATION 8.10	Activity-Based Costing for Selling–SU Company			
(1)	(2)	(3)	(4)	(5)
Activities	Cost Drivers	Estimated Monthly Cost	Estimated Monthly Cost Driver Volume	Cost Driver Rate
Order taking	Number of orders	$ 5,000	1,000	$ 5
Order filling	Number of orders	3,000	1,000	3
Shipping	1. Number of orders	1,000	1,000	1
	2. Number of units shipped	6,000	3,000	2
Customer returns	Number of units shipped	10,000	1,000	10
Total order filling costs				$21

Based on this analysis, management determined that order-filling costs total $21 per unit, much lower than the best outside bid of $30 per unit. Management decided to reject the idea of outsourcing this activity and took action to improve the efficiency of its order-filling service. Recognizing that customer returns were expensive ($10 per unit), management looked for ways to reduce them. They found that by improving their descriptions of the products in advertisements, the company was able to reduce the number of customer returns by nearly 50 percent.

ADDING VALUE USING ACTIVITY-BASED COSTING

L.O. 8: Describe how activity-based costing adds value to companies.

Activity-based costing offers many opportunities to add value to organizations. Many consulting firms have opened in the last decade to advise companies on activity-based costing systems, and many organizations have their own internal groups implementing activity-based costing. Surveys have indicated that hundreds and perhaps thousands of companies have implemented activity-based costing, including service, merchandising, and manufacturing companies.

Experience over the past 10 to 15 years indicates two key ways to add value to companies using activity-based costing.

- *Better information about product costs.* Activity-based costing uses more data than conventional costing and provides more informed estimates of product costs. Better product cost information helps managers make decisions about pricing and whether to keep or drop products. Although managers must respond to the market, they also consider their product costs in setting prices. Marketing managers, in particular, often strategically price these products below the market price to capture a larger share of the market. Or they may want to offer special prices to certain customers, such as the special discount fares offered by airlines or to open new markets in third world countries in which they must charge lower prices. Good product cost information can help them decide how far to drop these prices.

  Managers also use this information to decide whether to continue selling certain products. If a product's profit margins are too low, or if it loses money, managers will probably decide to stop selling it. Deciding to discontinue selling goods or services is difficult, and managers need the best possible information to make such decisions.

- *Better information about the cost of activities and processes.* As noted in the example about the cost of filling orders in the previous section, by using activity-based costing, managers realized how expensive one of the activities was and took steps to reduce its costs. By identifying the cost of various activities, managers gain useful information that the accounting system previously buried. The idea is analogous to lowering the water in a river to expose the rocks. Before lowering the water, you probably suspected or knew that the rocks were there. Until you lowered the water, however, you didn't know where the big ones were or how big they were. Sometimes managers find all sorts of interesting and helpful information about the cost of activities. Other times, implementing activity-based costing doesn't reveal anything new but confirms what managers already knew. Until you lower the water or implement activity-based costing, however, you don't know about the size of the rocks or the cost of the activities.

So far, the discussion has implied that implementing activity-based costing will add value to the organization. That is likely to be true in varying degrees. Companies that have complex production processes producing many different products and that operate in highly competitive markets probably stand to benefit the most. That's why companies such as Hewlett-Packard, Chrysler, and IBM have implemented activity-based costing. Companies such as Starbucks and Nike would probably benefit also but less than more complex companies.

In considering how much value activity-based costing adds to a company, remember that implementing activity-based costing is costly. These costs include the costs of the accountants and other people who develop and implement activity-based costing, additional recordkeeping costs, software costs, and, possibly, consulting costs. It also shakes up the organization by changing the accounting rules. This can be a good thing, but many companies also have found it to be painful.

SUMMARY

This chapter deals with the allocation of indirect costs to products. Product cost information helps managers make numerous decisions, including pricing, whether to keep or drop a product, estimating the cost to make a similar product, and determining how to reduce the costs of making products.

Activity-based costing is a costing method that assigns costs first to activities and then to the products based on each product's use of activities. Activity-based costing is based on the premise that products consume activities and activities consume resources. Activity-based costing involves the following four steps:

- Identify the activities that consume resources and assign costs to those activities. Purchasing materials is an activity, for example.
- Identify the cost driver(s) associated with each activity. As discussed, a cost driver is a factor that causes, or "drives," an activity's costs. For the purchasing materials activity, the cost driver could be number of orders.
- Compute a cost rate per cost driver unit or transaction. The cost driver rate could be the cost per purchase order, for example. Each activity could have multiple cost drivers.
- Assign costs to products by multiplying the cost driver rate times the volume of cost driver units consumed by the product. For example, the cost per purchase order times the number of orders required for product A for December measures the cost of the purchasing activity for December.

The chapter discussion made the following important points about activity-based costing:

- Different cost allocation methods result in different estimates of how much it costs to make a product.
- Activity-based costing provides more detailed measures of costs than do plantwide or department allocation methods.
- Activity-based costing can help marketing people by providing more accurate product cost numbers for decisions about pricing and the products to eliminate.
- Production also benefits because activity-based costing provides better information about how much activities cost. In fact, it helps identify cost drivers that were previously unknown. To manage costs, production managers learn to manage the cost drivers, that is, the activities that cause costs.
- Activity-based costing provides more information about product costs but requires more recordkeeping. Managers must decide whether the benefits of improved decisions justify the additional cost of activity-based costing.
- Installing activity-based costing requires teamwork between accounting, production, marketing, management, and other nonaccounting people.

The following summarizes key ideas tied to the chapter's learning objectives.

LO1: Cost allocation to products. Indirect costs (overhead) are allocated to products to provide management with product cost information. Management uses this information for decision making in areas such as pricing or cost reductions.

LO2: Plantwide versus department allocation methods. A single plantwide rate pools all overhead costs into one cost pool and allocates them based on one predetermined overhead rate. Using department allocation, each production department is a separate cost pool with overhead allocated based on individual predetermined overhead rates for each department.

LO3: Pros and cons of activity-based costing. Activity-based costing provides more detailed measures of costs than do plantwide or department allocation methods; however, its costing systems are more expensive to maintain.

LO4: Calculating product costs using activity-based costing. The SU Company illustration in this chapter shows how to calculate product costs using activity-based costing.

LO5: Comparison of activity-based costing to traditional methods. Activity-based costing tends to provide management with more detailed product cost information than does traditional costing methods. By identifying activities that cause costs (or consume resources), activity-based costing allows management to assess the efficiency of relatively costly activities.

LO6: Flow of costs through accounts. Illustration 8.9 outlines the flow of costs in an activity-based costing system.

LO7: Know how to apply activity-based costing to marketing and administration. Instead of computing the cost of the product, accountants compute the cost of performing an administrative or marketing service.

LO8: Describe how activity-based costing adds value to companies. Activity-based costing adds information about both the costs of products and the processes that add value to the company, and it is costly to implement. What is important is the net value added to the company after considering both its costs and benefits.

KEY TERMS

activity-based costing, 236

activity center, 240

cost driver, 238

cost pools, 232

department allocation method, 235

plantwide allocation method, 233

REVIEW QUESTIONS

8.1 What cost drivers do companies using a single plantwide rate usually select for allocating indirect costs?

8.2 What is the basic difference between plantwide and department allocation?

8.3 What is a cost driver? Give at least three examples.

8.4 A drawback to activity-based costing is that it requires more recordkeeping and extensive teamwork between all departments. What are the potential benefits of a more detailed product cost system?

8.5 What are the basic steps to computing costs using activity-based costing?

8.6 Allocating overhead based on the volume of output, such as direct labor-hours or machine-hours, seems fair and equitable. Why then do many people claim that high-volume products subsidize low-volume products?

8.7 How do managers decide which bases to use to allocate costs? Give three criteria for choosing cost drivers and allocation bases.

8.8 What technological change has occurred in many companies that has resulted in great potential for erroneous product cost figures?

CRITICAL ANALYSIS AND DISCUSSION QUESTIONS

8.9 "The problem of allocating direct costs to products is the primary subject of this chapter." Is this statement true, false, or uncertain? Explain.

8.10 "Activity-based costing is great for manufacturing plants, but it doesn't really address the needs of the service sector." Do you agree? Explain.

8.11 "A shortcut using department allocation is to ignore the allocation of service department costs to the production departments." Is this true, false, or uncertain? Explain.

8.12 Lynn, the vice president of marketing, wonders how products can cost less under one cost system than under another: "Aren't costs cut and dried?" How would you respond?

8.13 "Activity-based costing is the wave of the future. Everyone should drop existing cost systems and adopt it!" Do you agree? Explain.

8.14 "One of the lessons learned from activity-based costing is that all costs are really a function of volume of output." Is this true, false, or uncertain? Explain.

8.15 "Activity-based costing breaks down the indirect costs into several activities that cause costs (cost drivers). These should be the same for each department in an organization." Is this true, false, or uncertain? Explain.

8.16 "The total amount of estimated overhead used to determine allocation rates will differ depending on whether you use department allocation or activity-based costing." Do you agree? Explain.

8.17 If the allocation of overhead based on direct labor can yield erroneous results, why do highly automated plants continue this practice?

8.18 "Activity-based costing is for accountants and production managers. I plan to be a marketing specialist, so it won't help me." Do you agree with this statement? Explain.

EXERCISES

8.19 Plantwide versus Department Allocation (L.O. 2)

Comprehensive Publishers, Inc., publishes hardbacks, paperbacks, and other products. Department P produces the paperbacks and Department H produces the hardbacks. Comprehensive currently uses plantwide allocation to allocate its overhead to both types of books. The company uses machine-hours as its volume-based allocation base at a rate of $40 per machine-hour. Last year, revenue, materials, and direct labor were as follows:

	Paperbacks (P)	Hardbacks (H)
Revenue	$3,600,000	$2,500,000
Direct labor	600,000	400,000
Direct materials	1,600,000	800,000

Required

a. Compute the profit of each book type using plantwide allocation. Machine-hours totaled 10,000 for paperbacks and 15,000 for hardbacks.

b. Harry, the manager of Department H, was convinced that hardbacks were really more profitable than paperbacks. He asked his good friend in accounting to break down the overhead costs into the two departments. Harry discovered that had department rates been used, Department P would have had a rate of $36 per machine-hour and Department H would have had a rate of $50 per machine-hour.

Recompute the profits for each type of book using the department allocation rates for each department (use machine-hours as the allocation base).

c. How do you explain the discrepancy between the two methods used in requirements (*a*) and (*b*)?

8.20 Plantwide versus Department Allocation (L.O. 2)

Specialty Sweets, Inc., produces several different candy bars. The company currently uses a plantwide allocation method to allocate overhead based on direct labor-hours at a rate of $15 per labor-hour. Charlie Flem is department manager of Department C, which manufactures the Chocco Bar and the Chewynutta Bar. Monica Everhart is department manager of Department M, which manufactures the Marsh Bar. The product costs (per case of 1,000) follow:

	Chocco Bar	Chewynutta Bar	Marsh Bar
Direct labor (per case)	$100	$110	$150
Raw materials (per case)	50	80	60

Required

a. If the number of hours of labor per case is 10 for the Chocco Bar, 11 for the Chewy-nutta bar, and 15 for the Marsh Bar, compute the total cost of a case of each candy bar using plantwide allocation.

b. Monica's department uses older, outdated machines. She believes that her department is being allocated some of the overhead of Department C, which recently bought state-of-the-art machines.

   After requesting that overhead costs be broken down by department, the following information was discovered:

	Department C	Department M
Overhead	$17,640	$3,960
Machine-hours	2,520	3,600
Labor-hours	2,520	1,800

Using machine-hours as the department allocation base for Department C and labor-hours as the department allocation base for Department M, compute the allocation rate for each.

c. Compute the cost of a case of each type of candy bar using the department allocation rates computed in requirement (*b*) if a case of Chocco Bars requires 10 machine-hours, a case of Chewynutta 11 machine-hours, and a case of Marsh Bar 15 labor-hours.

d. Was Monica correct in her belief? What happened to the cost of a case of Marsh Bars when the department allocation was used? Which costing method provides more accurate product costs?

8.21 Activity-Based Costing (L.O. 4)

Assume that Bill Board, manager of the Engineering Department at Hewlett-Packard, has designed a new circuit board, the PC BB Special, which he believes can replace Type 67A described in the chapter. Bill is excited because he believes that this new circuit board will save Hewlett-Packard money. The PC BB Special has 100 parts but requires only 60 insertions since some of the components can be joined together easily without an extra insertion into the board. Furthermore, this new board will require only 0.15 hours of quality testing. There are still one raw board and one board for soldering. Despite the fact that the direct materials cost $85, Bill still believes that this board will be cheaper to produce than Type 67A.

Required

a. Refer to Illustration 8.4 and compute the total cost of manufacturing the PC BB Special using the facts stated.

b. Do you recommend that Hewlett-Packard start producing the PC BB Special?

8.22 Activity-Based Costing (L.O. 4)

Ned O. Williamson has just joined SU Company (text example) as its new production manager. He was pleased to see that SU uses activity-based costing. Ned believes that he can reduce production costs if he reduces the number of machine setups. He has spent the last month working with Purchasing and Sales to better coordinate raw material arrivals and the anticipated demand for the Standard and Unique products. Ned plans to produce 1,000 units of Standard and 200 units of Unique in March. He believes that with his efficient production scheduling, he can reduce the number of setups for both the Standard and Unique products by 50 percent.

Required

a. Refer to Illustration 8.7. Compute the amount of overhead allocated to the Standard and Unique products for March using activity-based costing. Assume that all events are the same in March as in January (the text example), except for the number of machine setups.

b. Assume that SU had used machine-hours and a department allocation method to allocate its overhead and that the setup rate for March is $2,000 per setup. Could Ned have made the cost reductions that he planned? What are the advantages and disadvantages of activity-based costing compared to the traditional volume-based allocation methods?

8.23 Activity-Based Costing in a Nonmanufacturing Environment (L.O. 4)

Jamie Nichols, the manager of River Rafting, Inc., uses activity-based costing to compute the costs of her raft trips. Each raft holds six paying customers and a guide. Jamie offers three-day float trips for beginners and three-day white-water trips for seasoned rafters. The breakdown of the costs follows:

Activities (and Cost Drivers)	Float Trip Costs	White-Water Trip Costs
Advertising (trips)	$430 per trip	$430 per trip
Permit to use the river (trips)	60 per trip	100 per trip
Equipment use (trips, people)	40 per trip plus 10 per person	80 per trip plus 16 per person
Insurance (trips)	150 per trip	254 per trip
Paying guides (trips, guides)	600 per trip per guide	800 per trip per guide
Food (people)	120 per person	120 per person

Note: Per trip costs do not vary with the number of rafts or customers.

Required

a. Compute the cost of a 28-person (including guides) float trip with four rafts and four guides.

b. Compute the cost of a 28-person (including guides) white-water trip with four rafts and four guides.

c. How much should Jamie charge each customer if she wants to cover her costs?

8.24 Activity-Based versus Traditional Costing (L.O. 4, L.O. 5)

Audio Corporation produces two types of audio cassettes, standard and high grade. The standard cassettes, used primarily in answering machines, are designed for durability rather than accurate sound reproduction. The company only recently began producing the higher-quality high-grade model to enter the lucrative music recording market. Since the introduction of the new product, profits have been steadily declining. Management believes that the accounting system may not be accurately allocating costs to products, particularly since sales of the new product have been increasing.

Management has asked you to investigate the cost allocation problem. You find that manufacturing overhead is currently assigned to products based on the direct labor costs in the products. For your investigation, you have data from last year. Last year's manufacturing overhead was $220,000 based on production of 320,000 standard cassettes and 100,000 high-grade cassettes. Direct labor and direct materials costs were as follows:

	Standard	High Grade	Total
Direct labor	$174,000	$ 66,000	$240,000
Materials.	125,000	114,000	239,000

Management determined that overhead costs are caused by three cost drivers. The cost drivers and their costs for last year were as follows:

		Activity Level		
Cost Driver	Costs Assigned	Standard	High Grade	Total
Number of production runs	$100,000	40	10	50
Quality tests performed	90,000	12	18	30
Shipping orders processed	30,000	100	50	150
Total overhead	$220,000			

Required

a. How much of the overhead will be assigned to each product if these three cost drivers are used to allocate overhead? What is the total cost per unit produced for each product?

b. How much of the overhead was assigned to each product if direct labor cost had been used to allocate overhead? What is the total cost per unit produced for each product?

c. How might the results from using activity-based costing in requirement (*a*) help management understand Audio's declining profits?

8.25 Activity-Based Costing in a Service Environment (L.O. 3, L.O. 4, L.O. 5)

Green Garden Care, Inc., is a lawn and garden care service. The company originally specialized in serving small residential clients but has recently started contracting for work on large apartment and office building grounds. Since Greta Greenthumb (owner) believes that commercial lawn care is more profitable, she is considering dropping residential services altogether.

Five field employees worked a total of 20,000 hours last year, 13,000 on residential jobs and 7,000 on commercial jobs. Wages amounted to $9 per hour for all work done. Direct materials used are included in overhead as supplies. All overhead is allocated on the basis of labor-hours worked, which is also the basis for customer charges. Because of increased competition for commercial accounts, Greta can charge $22 per hour for residential work but only $19 per hour for commercial work.

Required

a. If overhead for the year was $62,000, what were the profits of commercial and residential service using labor-hours as the allocation base?

b. Overhead consists of costs of transportation, equipment use, and supplies, which can be traced to the following activities:

Activity	Cost Driver	Cost	Activity Level	
			Commercial	Residential
Transportation	Number of clients serviced	$ 8,000	15	45
Equipment use	Equipment hours	18,000	3,500	2,100
Supplies	Area serviced in square yards	36,000	130,000	70,000
Total overhead		$62,000		

Recalculate profits for commercial and residential services based on these activity bases.

c. What recommendations do you have for management regarding the profitability of these two types of services?

8.26 Activity-Based Costing versus Traditional Costing (L.O. 3, L.O. 4, L.O. 5)

Travel Gadgets Corporation manufactures travel clocks and watches. Overhead costs are currently allocated using direct labor-hours, but the controller has recommended an activity-based costing system using the following data:

Activity	Cost Driver	Cost	Activity Level	
			Travel Clocks	Watches
Production setup	Number of setups	$50,000	10	15
Material handling and requisition	Number of parts	15,000	18	36
Packaging and shipping	Number of units shipped	30,000	45,000	75,000
Total overhead		$95,000		

Required

a. Compute the amount of overhead to be allocated to each of the products under activity-based costing.

b. Compute the amount of overhead to be allocated to each product using labor-hours as the allocation base. Assume that the number of labor-hours required to assemble each unit is 0.5 per travel clock and 1.0 per watch and that 45,000 travel clocks and 75,000 watches were produced.

c. Should the company follow the controller's recommendations?

8.27 Activity-Based Costing versus Traditional Costing (L.O. 3, L.O. 4, L.O. 5)

Jack Chapman & Associates provides consulting and tax preparation services to its clients. Jack charges a fee of $100.00 per hour for each service. His revenues and costs for the year are shown in the following income statement:

	Tax	Consulting	Total
Revenue.	$130,000	$270,000	$400,000
Expenses			
Secretarial support	_____	_____	80,000
Supplies	_____	_____	72,000
Computer costs, etc.	_____	_____	40,000
Profit.	_____	_____	$208,000

Being an accountant, Jack has kept good records of the following data for cost allocation purposes:

		Activity Level	
Overhead Cost	Cost Driver	Tax Preparation	Consulting
Secretarial support	Number of clients	72	48
Supplies	Transactions with clients	200	300
Computer costs	Computer hours	1,000	600

Required

a. Complete the income statement using activity-based costing and Jack's three cost drivers.

b. Recompute the income statement using direct labor-hours as the only allocation base (1,300 hours for tax; 2,700 hours for consulting).

c. How might Jack's decisions be altered if he were to allocate all overhead costs using direct labor-hours?

d. Under what circumstances would the labor-based allocation and activity-based costing (using Jack's three cost drivers) result in similar profit results?

8.28 Activity-Based Costing: Cost Flows through T-Accounts (L.O. 6)

Moss Manufacturing, Inc., recently switched to activity-based costing from the department allocation method. Department F's manager has estimated the following cost drivers and rates:

Activity Centers	Cost Drivers	Rate per Cost Driver Unit
Materials handling	Pounds of material handled	$12 per pound
Quality inspections	Number of inspections	$150 per inspection
Machine setups	Number of machine setups	$1,800 per setup
Running machines	Number of machine-hours	$15 per hour

Direct materials costs were $200,000, and direct labor costs were $100,000 during March, when Department F handled 2,500 pounds of materials, made 500 inspections, had 25 set-ups, and ran the machines for 10,000 hours.

Required

Use T-accounts to show the flow of materials, labor, and overhead costs from the four over-head activity centers through WIP Inventory and out to Finished Goods Inventory. Use the accounts Materials Inventory, Wages Payable, WIP Inventory, Finished Goods Inventory, and four Overhead Applied accounts.

8.29 Activity-Based Costing: Cost Flows through T-Accounts (L.O. 6)

Fleetfoot, Inc., a shoe manufacturer, recently switched to activity-based costing from the department allocation method. The manager of Department B, which manufactures the shoes, has identified the following cost drivers and rates:

Activity Centers	Cost Drivers	Rate per Cost Driver Unit
Materials handling	Yards of material handled	$0.50 per yard
Quality inspections	Number of inspections	$50 per inspection
Machine setups	Number of machine setups	$400 per setup
Running machines	Number of machine-hours	$5 per hour

Direct materials costs were $100,000, and direct labor costs were $50,000 during July. During July, Department B handled 20,000 yards of materials, made 400 inspections, had 50 setups, and ran the machines for 10,000 hours.

Required

Use T-accounts to show the flow of materials, labor, and overhead costs from the four overhead activity centers through WIP Inventory and out to Finished Goods Inventory. Use the following accounts: Materials Inventory, Wages Payable, Work in Process Inventory, Finished Goods Inventory, and four Overhead Applied accounts.

PROBLEMS

8.30   Comparative Income Statements and Management Analysis

Nykee, Inc., manufactures two types of shoes, B-Ball and Marathon. B-Ball has a complex design that uses gel-filled compartments to provide support. Marathon is simpler to manufacture and uses conventional foam padding. Last year, Nykee had the following revenues and costs:

NYKEE, INC.
Income Statement

	B-Ball	Marathon	Total
Revenue.	$195,000	$184,000	$379,000
Direct materials	55,000	50,000	105,000
Direct labor.	40,000	20,000	60,000
Indirect costs			
Administration	_____	_____	19,500
Production setup.	_____	_____	45,000
Quality control	_____	_____	30,000
Sales and marketing	_____	_____	60,000
Operating profit			$ 59,500

Nykee currently uses labor costs to allocate all overhead, but management is considering implementing an activity-based costing system. After interviewing the sales and production staff, management decides to allocate administrative costs on the basis of direct labor costs but to use the following bases to allocate the remaining costs:

		Activity Level	
Activity	**Cost Driver**	**B-Ball**	**Marathon**
Production setup	Number of production runs	10	20
Quality control	Number of inspections	40	40
Sales and marketing	Number of advertisements	12	48

Required

a. Complete the income statement using the preceding activity bases.

b. Write a brief report indicating how management could use activity-based costing to reduce costs.

c. Restate the income statement for Nykee using direct labor costs as the only overhead allocation base.

d. Write a report to management stating why product line profits differ using activity-based costing compared to the traditional approach. Indicate whether activity-based costing provides more accurate information and why (if you believe it does provide more accurate information). Indicate in your report how the use of labor-based overhead allocation could result in Nykee management making suboptimal decisions.

8.31

Comparative Income Statements and Management Analysis

Filmworks, Inc., offers two types of services, Deluxe and Standard portraits. Last year, Filmworks had the following costs and revenues:

FILMWORKS, INC.
Income Statement

	Deluxe	Standard	Total
Revenue.	$720,000	$800,000	$1,520,000
Direct materials	100,000	100,000	200,000
Direct labor.	360,000	240,000	600,000
Indirect costs			
Administration	*60,000*	*40,000*	100,000
Production setup.	*75,000*	*125,000*	200,000
Quality control	*60,000*	*40,000*	100,000
Sales and marketing	*48,000*	*32,000*	80,000
Operating profit	*17,000*	*223,000*	$ 240,000

Filmworks currently uses labor costs to allocate all overhead but is considering implementing an activity-based costing system. After interviewing the sales and production staff, management decides to allocate administrative costs on the basis of direct labor costs but to use the following bases to allocate the remaining overhead:

		Activity Level	
Overhead Cost	**Allocation Base**	**Deluxe**	**Standard**
Production setup	Number of photo sessions	150	250
Quality control	Number of customer inspections	300	200
Sales and marketing	Number of advertisements	60	40

Required

a. Complete the income statement using the preceding activity bases.

b. Write a report indicating how management might use activity-based costing to reduce costs.

c. Restate the income statement for Filmworks using direct labor costs as the only overhead allocation base.

d. Write a report to management stating why product line profits differ using activity-based costing compared to the traditional approach. Indicate whether activity-based costing provides more accurate information and why (if you believe it does provide more accurate information). Indicate in your report how the use of labor-based overhead allocation could result in Filmworks' management making suboptimal decisions.

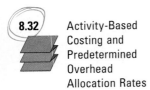

8.32

Activity-Based Costing and Predetermined Overhead Allocation Rates

Import Glass & Crystal Company manufactures three types of glassware, unleaded glass, low-lead crystal, and high-lead crystal. Glass quality increases with higher lead content, which allows for more detailed cutting and etching. Unleaded glass production is highly automated, but cutting and etching crystal products require a varying degree of labor, depending on the intricacy of the pattern. Import Glass & Crystal applies all indirect costs according to a predetermined rate based on direct labor-hours. A consultant recently suggested that the company switch to an activity-based costing system and prepared the following cost estimates for Year 5 for the recommended cost drivers.

Activity	Recommended Cost Driver	Estimated Costs	Estimated Cost Driver Units	
Order processing	Number of orders	$ 15,000	100 orders	*150*
Production setup	Number of production runs	60,000	50 runs	*1200*
Materials handling	Pounds of materials used	100,000	80,000 pounds	*1.25*
Machine depreciation and maintenance	Machine-hours	80,000	8,000 hours	*10*
Quality control	Number of inspections	20,000	30 inspections	*667*
Packing	Number of units	40,000	320,000 units	*.125*
Total estimated overhead		$315,000		

In addition, management estimated 5,000 direct labor-hours for Year 5.
Assume that the following activities occurred in January of Year 5:

	Unleaded Glass	Low-Lead Crystal	High-Lead Crystal
Number of units produced	20,000	8,000	3,000
Direct materials costs.	$13,000	$8,000	$5,000
Direct labor-hours	150	150	200
Number of orders	4	3	2
Number of production runs	1	1	2
Pounds of material.	5,000	2,000	1,000
Machine-hours	580	140	80
Number of inspections	1	1	1
Units shipped	20,000	8,000	3,000

Actual labor costs were $15 per hour. .

Required

a. Compute a predetermined overhead rate for Year 5 for each of the cost drivers using the estimated costs and estimated cost driver units prepared by the consultant. Also compute a predetermined rate for Year 5 using direct labor-hours as the allocation base.

b. Compute the production costs for each product for January using direct labor-hours as the allocation base and the predetermined rate computed in requirement (a).

c. Compute the production costs for each product for January using the cost drivers recommended by the consultant and the predetermined rates computed in requirement (a). (*Note:* Do not assume that total overhead applied to products in January will be the same for activity-based costing as it was for the labor-hour-based allocation.)

d. Management has seen your numbers and wants to know how you account for the discrepancy between the product costs using direct labor-hours as the allocation base and the product costs using activity-based costing. Write a brief response to management.

8.33 **Activity-Based Costing and Predetermined Overhead Rates**

Shades Company makes three types of sunglasses; Nerds, Stars, and Fashions. Shades presently applies overhead using a predetermined rate based on direct labor-hours. A group of company employees recommended that Shades switch to activity-based costing and identified the following activities, cost drivers, estimated costs, and estimated cost driver units for Year 2 for each activity center.

Activity	Recommended Cost Driver	Estimated Costs	Estimated Cost Driver Units
Production setup	Number of production runs	$ 60,000	100 runs
Order processing	Number of orders	100,000	200 orders
Materials handling	Pounds of materials	40,000	8,000 pounds
Equipment depreciation and maintenance	Machine-hours	120,000	10,000 hours
Quality management	Number of inspections	100,000	40 inspections
Packing and shipping	Units shipped	80,000	20,000 units
		$500,000	

In addition, management estimated 2,000 direct labor-hours for Year 2. Assume that the following activities occurred in February of Year 2:

	Nerds	Stars	Fashions
Number of units produced	1,000	500	400
Direct materials costs.	$4,000	$2,500	$2,000
Direct labor-hours	100	120	110
Number of orders	8	8	4
Number of production runs	2	4	8
Pounds of material.	400	200	200
Machine-hours	500	300	300
Number of inspections	2	2	2
Units shipped	1,000	500	300

Direct labor costs were $20 per hour.

Required

a. Compute a predetermined overhead rate for Year 2 for each cost driver recommended by the employees. Also compute a predetermined rate using direct labor-hours as the allocation base.

b. Compute the production costs for each product for February using direct labor-hours as the allocation base and the predetermined rate computed in requirement (*a*).

c. Compute the production costs for each product for February using the cost drivers recommended by the employees and the predetermined rates computed in requirement (*a*). (*Note:* Do not assume that total overhead applied to products in February will be the same for activity-based costing as it was for the labor-hour-based allocation.)

d. Management has seen your numbers and wants to know how you account for the discrepancy between the product costs using direct labor-hours as the allocation base and the product costs using activity-based costing. Write a brief response to management.

8.34 Choosing an Activity-Based Costing System

Cannonball Corporation manufactures three bicycle models, a racing bike, a mountain bike, and a children's model. The racing model called the Aerolight is made of a titanium-aluminum alloy. The mountain bike called the Summit is made of aluminum. The steel-framed children's bike is called the Spinner. Because of the different materials used, production processes differ significantly among models in terms of machine types and time requirements. Once parts are produced, however, assembly time per unit required for each type of bike is similar. For this reason, Cannonball allocates overhead on the basis of machine-hours. Last year, the company produced 1,000 Aerolights, 2,000 Summits, and 5,000 Spinners and had the following revenues and expenses:

CANNONBALL CORPORATION
Income Statement

	Aerolight	Summit	Spinner	Total
Sales.	$380,000	$560,000	$475,000	$1,415,000
Direct costs				
Direct materials.	150,000	240,000	200,000	590,000
Direct labor	14,400	24,000	54,000	92,400
Variable overhead				
Machine setup				26,000
Order processing.				64,000
Warehousing costs				93,000
Energy to run machines				42,000
Shipping				36,000
Contribution margin.				471,600
Fixed overhead				
Plant administration				88,000
Other fixed overhead				140,000
Gross profit				$ 243,600

The chief financial officer (CFO) of Cannonball hired a consultant to recommend cost allocation bases. The consultant recommended the following:

Activity	Cost Driver	Aerolight	Summit	Spinner
		Activity Level		
1. Machine setup	Number of production runs	22	34	44
2. Sales order processing	Number of sales orders received	400	600	600
3. Warehousing costs	Number of units held in inventory	200	200	400
4. Energy	Machine-hours	10,000	16,000	24,000
5. Shipping	Number of units shipped	1,000	4,000	10,000

The consultant found no basis for allocating the plant administration and other fixed overhead costs and recommended that these not be applied to products.

Required

a. Using machine-hours to allocate production overhead, complete the income statement for Cannonball Company. (See activity 4 for machine-hours.) Do not attempt to allocate plant administration or other fixed overhead.

b. Complete the income statement using the bases recommended by the consultant.

c. How might activity-based costing result in better decisions by Cannonball's management?

d. After hearing the consultant's recommendations, the CFO decided to adopt activity-based costing but expressed concern about not allocating some of the overhead to the products (plant administration and other fixed overhead). In the CFO's view, "Products have to bear a fair share of all overhead or we won't be covering all of our costs." How would you respond to this comment?

8.35 Benefits of Activity-Based Costing

Many companies recognize that their cost systems are inadequate for today's global market. Managers in companies selling multiple products are making important product decisions based on distorted cost information. Most systems of the past were designed to focus on inventory valuation.

Required

If management should decide to implement an activity-based costing system, what benefits should it expect?

(CMA adapted)

8.36 Benefits of Activity-Based Costing

Sparkle Manufacturing has just completed a major change in its method to inspect its product. Previously, 10 inspectors examined the product after each major process. The salaries of these inspectors were charged as direct labor to the operation or job. In an effort to improve efficiency, Sparkle's production manager recently bought a computerized quality control system consisting of a microcomputer, 15 video cameras, peripheral hardware, and software. The cameras are placed at key points in the production process, taking pictures of the product and comparing these pictures with a known "good" image supplied by a quality control engineer. This new system allows Sparkle to replace the 10 quality control inspectors with only two quality control engineers.

The president of the company is concerned. She was told that the production process was now more efficient, yet she notices a large increase in the factory overhead rate. The computation of the rate before and after automation is as follows:

	Before	After
Estimated overhead	$1,900,000	$2,100,000
Estimated direct labor	$1,000,000	$ 700,000
Predetermined overhead rate	190%	300%

Required

Prepare a report that states how an activity-based costing system might benefit Sparkle Manufacturing and clear up the president's confusion.

(CMA adapted)

8.37   Choosing an Activity-Based Costing System

Home Manufacturers, Inc. (HMI), makes three types of mobile homes: Basic, Homevalue, and Castle. In the past, HMI has allocated overhead to products using machine-hours. Last year, the company produced 2,000 units of Castle, 3,500 units of Homevalue, and 2,000 units of the Basic model and had the following revenues and costs:

HOME MANUFACTURERS, INC.
Income Statement

	Basic	Homevalue	Castle	Total
Sales.	$6,000,000	$10,000,000	$9,000,000	$25,000,000
Direct costs				
Direct materials.	2,000,000	3,000,000	2,200,000	7,200,000
Direct labor	400,000	600,000	1,200,000	2,200,000
Variable overhead				
Machine setup	320,000	640,000	640,000	1,600,000
Order processing.	270,000	600,000	330,000	1,200,000
Warehousing costs	400,000	800,000	400,000	1,600,000
Machine operation.	192,000	288,000	320,000	800,000
Shipping	160,000	280,000	160,000	600,000
Contribution margin.	2,258,000	3,792,000	3,750,000	9,800,000
Plant administration.				4,000,000
Gross profit				$ 5,800,000

HMI's controller had heard about activity-based costing and put together an employee team to recommend cost allocation bases. The employee team recommended the following:

			Activity Level	
Activity	**Cost Driver**	**Basic**	**Homevalue**	**Castle**
Machine setup	Number of production runs	10	20	20
Sales order processing	Number of sales orders received	180	400	220
Warehousing costs	Number of units held in inventory	100	200	100
Machine operation	Machine-hours	6,000	9,000	10,000
Shipping	Number of units shipped	2,000	3,500	2,000

The employee team recommended that plant administration costs not be allocated to products.

Required

a. Using machine-hours to allocate overhead, complete the income statement for HMI. Do not allocate plant administrative costs to products.

b. Complete the income statement using the activity-based costing method suggested by the employee team.

c. Write a brief report indicating how activity-based costing might result in better decisions by HMI.

d. After hearing the recommendations, the president expressed concern about failing to allocate plant administrative costs. If plant administrative costs were to be allocated to products, how would you allocate them?

INTEGRATIVE CASES

8.38

Plantwide versus
Departmental
Overhead
Allocation

Carryall Corporation manufactures a complete line of fiberglass attaché cases and suitcases. Carryall has three manufacturing departments, Molding, Component, and Assembly, and two service departments, Power and Maintenance.

The Molding Department manufactures the sides of the cases. The Component Department manufactures frames, hinges, locks, and so on; the Assembly Department completes the cases. Varying amounts of materials, time, and effort are required for each of the various cases. The Power Department and Maintenance Department provide services to the three manufacturing departments.

Carryall always has used a plantwide overhead rate. Direct labor-hours are used to assign the overhead to its product. The predetermined rate is calculated by dividing the company's total estimated overhead by the total estimated direct labor-hours to be worked in the three manufacturing departments.

Whit Portlock, manager of Cost Accounting, has recommended that Carryall use departmental overhead rates. He had developed the planned operating costs and expected levels of activity for the coming year, which are presented by department in the following schedules (figures are in thousands):

	Manufacturing Departments		
	Molding	**Component**	**Assembly**
Departmental activity measures			
Direct labor-hours.	500	2,000	1,500
Machine-hours.	875	125	–0–
Department costs			
Raw materials	$12,400	$30,000	$ 1,250
Direct labor	3,500	20,000	12,000
Variable overhead.	3,500	10,000	16,500
Fixed overhead.	17,500	6,200	6,100
Total departmental costs	$36,900	$66,200	$35,850
Use of service departments			
Maintenance			
Estimated usage in labor-hours for coming year	90	25	10
Power (in kilowatt-hours)			
Estimated usage for coming year	360	320	120
Long-term capacity	500	350	150

	Service Departments	
	Power	**Maintenance**
Departmental activity measures		
Maximum capacity.	1,000 kwhr.	Adjustable
Estimated usage in coming year	800 kwhr.	125 hours
Departmental costs		
Materials and supplies	$ 5,000	$1,500
Variable labor	1,400	2,250
Fixed overhead	12,000	250
Total service department costs.	$18,400	$4,000

Required

a. Calculate the plantwide overhead rate for Carryall Corporation for the coming year using the same method as used in the past.

b. Whit has been asked to develop departmental overhead rates for comparison with the plantwide rate. The following steps are to be followed in developing the departmental rates.

1. Using the direct method, the Maintenance Department should allocate its costs to the three manufacturing departments.
2. The Power Department costs should be allocated to the three manufacturing departments as follows: the fixed costs allocated according to long-term capacity and the variable costs according to planned usage.
3. Calculate departmental overhead rates for the three manufacturing departments using a machine-hour base for the Molding Department and a direct labor-hour base for the Component and Assembly departments.

c. Should Carryall Corporation use a plantwide rate or departmental rates to assign overhead to its products? Write a brief report explaining your answer.

(CMA adapted)

8.39

Distortions Caused by Inappropriate Overhead Allocation Base[6]

Chocolate Bars, Inc. (CBI), manufactures creamy deluxe chocolate candy bars. The firm has developed three distinct products, Almond Dream, Krispy Krackle, and Creamy Crunch.

CBI is profitable, but management is quite concerned about the profitability of each product and the product costing methods currently employed. In particular, management questions whether the overhead allocation base of direct labor-hours accurately reflects the costs incurred during the production process of each product.

In reviewing cost reports with the marketing manager, Steve Hoffman, the cost accountant, notices that Creamy Crunch appears exceptionally profitable while Almond Dream appears to be produced at a loss. This surprises both Steve and the manager, and after much discussion, they are convinced that the cost accounting system is at fault and that Almond Dream is performing very well at the current market price.

Steve decides to hire Jean Sharpe, a management consultant, to study the firm's cost system over the next month and present her findings and recommendations to senior management. Her objective is to identify and demonstrate how the cost accounting system might be distorting the firm's product costs.

Jean begins her study by gathering information and documenting the existing cost accounting system. It is rather simplistic, using a single overhead allocation base, direct labor-hours, to calculate and apply overhead rates to all products. The rate is calculated by summing variable and fixed overhead costs and then dividing the result by the number of direct labor-hours. The product cost is determined by multiplying the number of direct labor-hours required to manufacture the product by the overhead rate and adding this amount to the direct labor and direct material costs.

CBI engages in two distinct production processes for each product. Process 1 is labor intensive, using a high proportion of direct materials and labor. Process 2 uses special packing equipment that wraps each individual candy bar and then packs it into a box of 24 bars. The boxes are then packaged into cases of six boxes. Special packing equipment is used on all three products and has a monthly capacity of 3,000 boxes, each containing 144 candy bars.

To illustrate the source of the distortions to senior management, Jean collects the cost data for the three products, Almond Dream, Krispy Krackle, and Creamy Crunch (see Illustration 8.11).

CBI recently adopted a general policy of discontinuing all products whose gross profit margin ([Gross margin/Selling price] × 100) percentages were less than 10 percent. By comparing the selling prices to the firm's costs and then calculating the gross margin percentages, Jean could determine which products, under the current cost system, should be dropped. The current selling prices of Almond Dream, Krispy Krackle, and Creamy Crunch are $85, $55, and $35 per case, respectively.

Required

a. Complete Illustration 8.11 under the current cost system and determine which product(s), if any, should be dropped.

b. What characteristic of the product that should be dropped makes it appear relatively unprofitable?

c. Calculate the gross profit margin percentage for the remaining products. Assume that CBI can sell all products it manufactures and that it will use the excess capacity from

[6]Copyright © Michael W. Maher, 1996.

ILLUSTRATION 8.11

	Almond Dream	Krispy Krackle	Creamy Crunch
Product costs			
Labor-hours per unit.	7	3	1
Total units produced.	1,000	1,000	1,000
Material cost per unit.	$ 8.00	$ 2.00	$9.00
Direct labor cost per unit	$42.00	$18.00	$6.00
Labor-hours per product	7,000	3,000	1,000

Total overhead = $69,500
Total labor-hours = 11,000
Direct labor costs per hour = $6.00
Allocation rate per labor-hour = (a) $6.32

Costs of products			
Material cost per unit	$ 8.00	$ 2.00	$9.00
Direct labor cost per unit	42.00	18.00	6.00
Allocated overhead per unit (to be computed)	44.24 (b)	18.96 (c)	6.32 (d)
Product cost.	(e) 94.24	(f) 38.96	(g) 21.32

dropping a product to produce more of the most profitable product. If CBI maintains its current rule about dropping products, which additional products, if any, should CBI drop under the existing cost system? Overhead will remain $69,500 per month under all alternatives.

d. Recalculate the gross profit margin percentage for the remaining product(s) and ascertain whether any additional product(s) should be dropped.

e. Discuss the outcome and any recommendations you might make to management regarding the current cost system and decision policies.

8.40
Multiple Allocation Bases

Refer to Problem 8.39. Jean Sharpe decides to gather additional data to identify the cause of overhead costs and figure out which products are most profitable.

Jean notices that $30,000 of the overhead originated from the equipment used. She decides to incorporate machine-hours into the overhead allocation base to see its effect on product profitability. Almond Dream requires two hours of machine time, Krispy Krackle requires seven hours, and Creamy Crunch requires six hours. Additionally, Jean notices that the $15,000 per month spent to rent 10,000 square feet of factory space accounts for almost 22 percent of the overhead. Almond Dream is assigned 1,000 square feet, Krispy Krackle 4,000 square feet, and Creamy Crunch 5,000 square feet. Jean decides to incorporate this into the allocation base for the rental costs.

Since labor-hours are still an important cost driver for overhead, Jean decides that she should use labor-hours to allocate the remaining $24,500.

CBI still plans to produce 1,000 cases each of Almond Dream, Krispy Krackle, and Creamy Crunch. Assume that CBI can sell all the products it manufactures and that it will use excess capacity, if it drops any products, to produce additional units of the most profitable product. Overhead will remain $69,500 per month under all alternatives.

Required

a. Based on the additional data, determine the product cost and gross profit margin percentages of each product using the three allocation bases to determine the allocation assigned to each product.

b. Would management recommend dropping any of the products based on the criterion of dropping products with less than 10 percent gross profit margin?

c. Based on the recommendation you make in requirement (*b*), recalculate the allocations and profit margins to determine whether any of the remaining products should be dropped from the product line. If any additional products are dropped, substantiate the profitability of remaining products.

SOLUTIONS TO SELF-STUDY QUESTIONS

1. (1) Using the bankwide rate:

	Commercial Loan Department	Mortgage Loan Department
Labor.........	$100,000	$300,000
Overhead	50,000[a]	150,000[a]
Total	$150,000	$450,000

[a]Overhead = 50 percent of direct labor.

(2) Using department rates:

	Commercial Loan Department	Mortgage Loan Department
Labor.........	$100,000	$300,000
Overhead	56,000[a]	120,000[b]
Total	$156,000	$420,000

[a]$56,000 = ($40 × 900 loans) + (20% × $100,000).

[b]$120,000 = 40% × $300,000

The department rate is likely to be more informative, but it is also likely to be more time consuming and difficult to compute. Department rates provide better identification of the activities that cause costs in each separate department. Department rates generally provide better estimates of product costs both because different departments may have different activities that cause costs and because the allocation rate is likely to be different across departments. (Note that different allocation methods using predetermined rates do not necessarily allocate the same *total* overhead.)

2. Using department allocation, overhead is allocated to products worked on in December using the predetermined rate of $100 per hour times the actual machine-hours in December:

Standard products ($100 × 2,000 hours)	$200,000
Unique products ($100 × 1,000 hours)........	100,000
Total overhead allocated to products	$300,000

Assignment of overhead using activity-based costing:

		Standard Product		Unique Product	
Activity	Rate	Actual Cost Driver Units	Costs Allocated	Actual Cost Driver Units	Costs Allocated
1. Purchasing materials	$2 per pound	8,000 pounds	$ 16,000	8,000 pounds	$ 16,000
2. Machine setups	$2,000 per setup	15 setups	30,000	50 setups	100,000
3. Inspections	$100 per inspection hour	220 hours	22,000	400 hours	40,000
4. Running machines	$30 per hour	2,000 hours	60,000	1,000 hours	30,000
Total cost allocated to each product			$128,000		$186,000

Based on production of 1,300 units of Standard and 400 units of Unique, the per unit product costs (rounded to the nearest dollar) using the two costing methods are as follows:

	Department Allocation		Activity-Based Costing	
	Standard	Unique	Standard	Unique
Direct materials	$100	$200	$100	$200
Direct labor.......	20	30	20	30
Overhead	154[a]	250[b]	98[c]	465[d]
Total..........	$274	$480	$218	$695

[a]$154 = Allocation to products using department allocation ÷ Units produced = $200,000/1,300 units.

[b]$250 = Allocation to products using department allocation ÷ Units produced = $100,000/400 units.

[c]$98 = Allocation to products using activity-based costing ÷ Units produced = $128,000/1,300 units.

[d]$465 = Allocation to products using activity-based costing ÷ Units produced = $186,000/400 units.

Activity-Based Management

LEARNING OBJECTIVES

After reading this chapter, you should be able to:

1. Explain the concept of activity-based management.

2. Explain how activity-based costing is used for strategic purposes.

3. Use activity-based cost information to eliminate nonvalue-added activities.

4. Manage customer response time using activity-based costing information.

5. Use the hierarchy of costs to manage costs.

6. Distinguish between resources used and resources supplied.

7. Use your knowledge about cost hierarchies and the difference between resources used and resources supplied to create innovative management reports.

L.O. 1: Explain the concept of activity-based management.

Activity-based costing provides management with detailed costing information and allows management to make better-informed decisions. It is up to management, however, to decide how to establish activity-based costing. Activity-based costing is a flexible system designed to meet management's needs in a variety of different ways. Does management need more detailed cost information to make pricing decisions? Will product implementation decisions be based on product costs? Does management intend to provide employees with bonuses based on departmental profits computed using activity-based costing?

activity-based management
The use of activity analysis to help management make decisions.

This chapter focuses on the use of activity analysis to help management make decisions, referred to as **activity-based management.** Activity-based management does not focus on the detailed calculation of product costs using activity-based costing (already covered in Chapter 8) but explores management's uses of activity-based costing.

STRATEGIC USE OF ACTIVITY-BASED COSTING

L.O. 2: Explain how activity-based costing is used for strategic purposes.

Many experts view activity-based costing as offering companies strategic opportunities.[1] One key way that companies develop competitive advantages is to become a low-cost producer or seller. Companies such as Wal-Mart in retailing, United Parcel Service in delivery services, and Southwest Airlines in the airline industry have created a competitive advantage by reducing costs. M. E. Porter, among others, has pointed out that certain companies have learned to use the information gained from their cost systems to cut prices substantially to increase market share.[2]

Activity-based costing plays an important role in companies' strategies and long-range plans to develop a competitive cost advantage. *Activity-based costing* focuses attention on activities in allocating overhead costs to products. *Activity-based management*, on the other hand, focuses on managing activities to reduce costs. Cost reduction generally requires a change in activities. Top management can send notices to company employees to reduce costs, but the implementation requires a change in activities. If you have been in school during a period in which education costs have been cut, you know that achieving the cut required a change in activities such as canceled classes, larger class sizes, and reduced services. It is impossible to know the effect of a change in activities on costs without the type of cost information provided by activity-based costing.

ACTIVITY-BASED MANAGEMENT AND THE VALUE CHAIN

L.O. 3: Use activity-based cost information to eliminate nonvalue-added activities.

Activity analysis is an approach to operations control. As noted in Chapter 8, an *activity* is any discrete task that an organization undertakes to make or deliver a product or service. Specifically, activity analysis has four steps:

1. Identify the process objectives defined by what the customer wants or expects from the process.
2. Record by charting, from start to finish, the activities used to complete the product or service.
3. Classify all activities as value-added or nonvalue-added.
4. Continuously improve the efficiency of all value-added activities and develop plans to eliminate or reduce nonvalue-added activities.

Value-added activities make up the value chain. As shown in Illustration 9.1, the value chain is a linked set of value-creating activities leading from research and development to the end use of goods and services produced.

Managers should be constantly asking whether activities add value. As shown in Illustration 9.2, managers should analyze activities and classify them as value added

---

[1]See J. Shank and V. Govindarajan, *Strategic Cost Analysis* (Homewood, IL: Richard D. Irwin, 1989), for an extensive discussion of the strategic use of cost analysis.
[2]M. E. Porter, *Competitive Advantage* (New York: Free Press, 1985).

ILLUSTRATION   9.1   The Value Chain

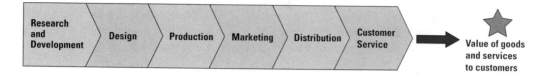

ILLUSTRATION   9.2   Are Activities Value Added?

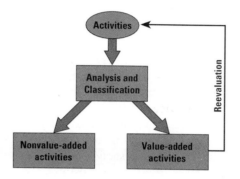

or nonvalue added. If they do not add value, attempts to eliminate or at least reduce them should be made. If they do add value, they should be reevaluated continually to ensure that they are in fact value added.

Activity analysis represents a systematic way for organizations to think about the processes that they use to provide products to their customers. Activity-based management can be used to identify and eliminate activities that add costs but not value to the product. Nonvalue-added costs are costs of activities that could be eliminated without reducing product quality, performance, or value. For example, storing bicycle frames until needed for production does not add to the finished bike's value. Suppose that management can find ways to eliminate storing the frames by using just-in-time purchasing. If so, the company could save money without reducing the finished product's quality.

The following types of activities are candidates for elimination because they do not add value to the product:

- *Storage.* Storage of materials, WIP, and finished goods inventories are obvious nonvalue-added activities. Many companies have applied the just-in-time philosophy to purchasing and production to reduce or even eliminate storage.

- *Moving items.* Moving parts, materials, and other items around the factory floor does not add value to the finished product. A steel mill in Michigan once had hundreds of miles of railroad tracks to move materials and partially finished products from one part of the factory to another. Eliminating 100 miles or so of track reduced both labor and overhead costs and even eliminated some spoilage because products were sometimes damaged by train accidents.

- *Waiting for work.* Idle time does not add value to products. Reducing the amount of time people wait to work on something reduces the cost of idle time.

- *Production process.* Managers should investigate the entire production process, from purchasing, to production, to inspection, to shipping; they should identify activities that do not add value to the finished product. Managers should ascertain whether the company needs as many setups, whether the cost of higher-quality materials and labor could be justified by a reduction in inspection time, whether the cost of ordering could be reduced, and so forth.

These are only a few examples of nonvalue-added costs. We are certain that if you observe activities at health care organizations, fast-food restaurants, construction sites, government agencies, and many other organizations, even universities, you will see numerous examples of nonvalue-added activities.

Activity-based costing helps measure the costs of nonvalue-added activities. For example, Deere & Company, which makes John Deere tractors, measured the variable cost of moving materials to be $293 per load (defined as a movement of materials around the factory). If the company could have eliminated 1,000 loads per year, it would have saved $293,000, all things being equal, without reducing the value of the finished product.

USING ACTIVITY-BASED COST INFORMATION TO MANAGE CUSTOMER RESPONSE TIME

L.O. 4: Manage customer response time using activity-based costing information.

Illustration 9.3 shows the chain of events from the placement of a customer order to customer delivery.[3] Reducing that time can increase output, customer satisfaction, and profits. For example, suppose that a loan officer at a mortgage company can process 30 loan applications per month. If the process can be improved so that the loan officer can process 30 loan applications in one-half month, several good things happen. Customers are pleased that their applications are processed faster, the cost per application goes down, and more applications per month can be processed.

Activity-based management helps to reduce customer response time by identifying activities that consume the most resources, both in dollars and time. For example, one of the holdups in mortgage loan applications is verifying credit, bank, employment, and other key information required. Using computer networks could substantially reduce that verification time. Further, many loan applicants can be easily rejected or approved with limited financial information. Many universities use this approach with telephone or in-person acceptance before receiving the detailed transcripts, letters of recommendation, and so forth.

Activity-based management also helps reduce customer response time by identifying nonvalue-added activities. For example, if you apply to graduate or law school, you will find that many schools want transcripts from all of the colleges attended, even if the applicant took only a few lower-division classes at a local college during the summer. Using activity-based management, admissions officers should consider whether obtaining these transcripts adds value to their universities. If not, why not eliminate this costly activity that slows down customer response time?

ILLUSTRATION   9.3   Elements of Customer Response Time

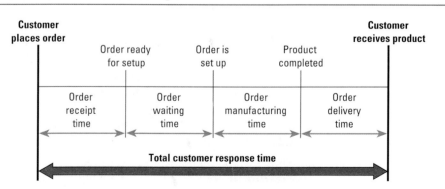

[3]For an example in a manufacturing setting, see R. Campbell, "Steeling Time with ABC or TOC," *Management Accounting,* January 1995.

Many people use customer response time as a measure of waste in the organization. Nonvalue-added costs can be reduced by eliminating the causes of long customer response times. Waiting, storing, moving, and inspecting products add to customer response time and cost money.

As we improve the efficiency of value-added activities or eliminate nonvalue-added activities, both customer response time and costs will fall. Of course, customers also value a quick response to their orders, which is another important benefit of short customer response time.

COST HIERARCHIES

L.O. 5: Use the hierarchy of costs to manage costs.

Some costs can be associated with units; others cannot. Consequently, allocating all costs (such as building leases) to units is misleading if some costs do not vary with the volume of units. As a result, management cannot effectively manage these costs by focusing on the volume of units. For example, the costs of machine setups are generally batch-related costs. A machine setup is required for each new batch of products whether the batch contains 1 unit or 1,000 units. The setup cost is not affected by the number of units but by the number of batches.

Management can establish a hierarchy of costs like that shown in Illustration 9.4.[4] Strictly variable costs, such as energy costs to run machines, are affected by the volume of units produced. These appear at the bottom of the illustration as unit-level costs. Naturally, any variable costs such as direct materials costs are unit-level costs.

At the other extreme (the top of the illustration) are capacity-related costs. These costs are essentially fixed by management's decisions to have a particular size of store, factory, hospital, or other facility. Although these costs are fixed with respect to volume, it would be misleading to give the impression that they cannot be changed. Managers can make decisions that affect capacity costs; such decisions just require a longer time horizon to implement than do decisions to reduce unit-level costs.

The two middle categories of costs are affected by the way the company manages its activities. A company that makes custom products will have more product/customer-level costs than a company that provides limited choices. A company that schedules its work to make one product on Monday, a second product on Tuesday, and so on through Friday has lower batch-related costs than if it produced all five products on Monday, all five again on Tuesday, and so on through the week. In prac-

ILLUSTRATION 9.4	Hierarchy of Product Costs
Cost Category	**Cost-Generating Activities**
1. Capacity-related costs	Plant management Building depreciation and rent Heating and lighting
2. Product- and customer-level costs	Customer records and files Product specifications Customer service
3. Batch-related costs	Machine setups Quality inspections
4. Unit-level costs	Energy to run machines Direct materials

Adapted from R. Cooper and R. S. Kaplan, "Profit Priorities from Activity-Based Costing," *Harvard Business Review,* May–June 1991, p. 132.

---

[4]R. Cooper and R. S. Kaplan, "Profit Priorities from Activity-Based Costing," *Harvard Business Review,* May–June 1991, pp. 130–35.

tice, many of the greatest opportunities for reducing costs through activity-based management are in these middle categories of product/customer-level and batch-related costs.

Using a hierarchy like this, if management makes decisions that affect units, but not batches, products, customers, or capacity, it would analyze category 4 costs of unit-level activities. If management makes decisions that affect capacity, however, all activities in categories 1 through 4 would probably be affected, and costs in all four categories would be analyzed.

SELF-STUDY QUESTION

1. Classify the following items as to whether they generate capacity-related costs, product- or customer-related costs, batch-related costs, or unit-level costs.

   a. Piecework labor.

   b. Long-term lease on a building.

   c. Energy to run machines.

   d. Engineering drawings for a product.

   e. Purchase order.

   f. Movement of materials for products in production.

   g. Change order to meet new customer specifications.

The solution to this question is at the end of this chapter on page 285.

DISTINGUISHING BETWEEN RESOURCES USED AND RESOURCES SUPPLIED

L.O. 6: Distinguish between resources used and resources supplied.

Many strawberry workers are paid a piece-rate which is an amount per crate filled. If so, then the rate per cost driver unit (that is, per crate of strawberries) equals the piece-rate. (In the example on this page, this rate is $1.50 per crate when workers are paid a piece-rate.) If workers are paid on an hourly basis, the amount paid to the workers might not equal the cost driver rate per crate times the number of crates filled.

In some situations, costs go up and down proportionately with the cost driver. Materials, energy, and piecework labor are excellent examples. Suppose that workers are paid $1.50 per crate to pick strawberries from a field. The cost driver is obviously crates of strawberries, and the cost driver rate is $1.50 per crate.

Now suppose that strawberry workers are hired for a month for $8 per hour. The cost driver might still be crates of strawberries. The cost driver rate is computed as follows: estimated wages of strawberry workers for the month divided by estimated number of crates of strawberries that workers can pick during the month. Assume that this calculation gives a rate of $2 per crate. In general, this cost driver rate could be higher, lower, or the same as the piecework rate. We assume that the rate is $2, just to help you recognize that a difference exists between the piecework rate and the cost driver rate when workers were paid by the hour.

The grower employs five workers who each work 8-hour days. These workers each have the capacity to pick four crates per hour, or a total of 160 crates per day. Assume, however, that on Tuesday, the workers picked 140 crates. That means there were 20 crates, or $40 ($2 cost driver rate × 20 crates), of unused capacity on Tuesday. The grower has costs of $320 computed either of two ways:

REAL WORLD APPLICATION | **Using Activity-Based Management to Control Health Care Costs While Improving Quality**

In the current era of managed competition, health maintenance organizations (HMOs) are looking for ways to reduce costs while improving the quality of care. Several health care organizations recently experimented with new anesthesia that enables patients to leave the recovery room sooner. Managers hoped that the new anesthesia would both reduce the costs of nurse staffing in the recovery room and increase customer satisfaction because patients would leave the surgery center earlier.

The managers faced the problem that resources used (patient minutes in the recovery room) did not equal resources supplied (the cost of nurses staffed to the recovery room). The new anesthesia reduced patient time in the recovery room and resources used in the recovery room by 33 percent. Were resources supplied also reduced by 33 percent?

Researchers found the answer to be no in this case. By simulating the staffing of the recovery room using the new anesthesia, researchers found that the resources supplied (that is, expenditures) would probably decrease by only 20 percent, despite the 33 percent decrease in patient use. This happened primarily because the outpatient surgery

center employed nurses in 4-hour shifts. Once nurses started duty, the managers would not send them home even if the patient census dropped in the recovery room.

In the end, managers realized that the new anesthesia would have three desirable effects:

- Patients would go home sooner.
- Costs would be lower; even a 20 percent reduction is better than no reduction.
- Patient care and nurse morale would be better. Reducing resource usage by 33 percent and resource supply by only 20 percent creates unused capacity. Nurses could use this unused capacity for many desirable purposes, including spending more time with each patient, taking more time on patient follow-up, and doing unscheduled training.

Incidentally, turnover in the hospital provided enough jobs for nurses who would no longer be needed in the outpatient surgery center recovery room.

Source: Based on research by M. L. Marais and M. W. Maher; see for example, "Process-Oriented Activity-Based Costing" (Davis, CA: Graduate School of Management, University of California, November 1996).

- $320 = 5$ Workers $\times$ \$8 per Hour $\times$ 8-Hour day.
- $320 = \$2$ per Crate $\times$ 160 Crate capacity.

The grower supplied resources of \$320 to the strawberry-picking activity. Only \$280 of strawberry-picking resources were used, however, leaving \$40 of unused capacity (\$280 = \$2 $\times$ 140 crates actually picked). The grower knows that the five workers could have picked more strawberries without increasing the resources supplied to the activity.

In general, activity-based costing estimates the cost of resources used. In activity-based costing, **resources used** for an activity are measured by the cost driver rate times the cost driver volume. In the strawberry example, resources used were \$280.

The **resources supplied** to an activity are the expenditures or the amounts spent on the activity. In the strawberry example, resources supplied were the \$320 paid to the strawberry pickers. Resources supplied is what appears on financial statements. The difference between resources used and resources supplied is **unused resource capacity.**

Activity-based management involves looking for ways to reduce unused resource capacity. For example, the strawberry grower may look for ways to reduce the \$40 (or 20 crates) of unused resource capacity. Suppose that the grower had not sufficiently trained the people to check each case for quantity and quality. Consequently, the checkers were slowing the picking process. The activity-based management information (provided by the activity-based costing system) signaled the existence of unused resource capacity, which helped the grower and workers improve the production flow.

Differences between resource usage and resource supply generally occur because managers commit to supply a certain level of resources before they are used. In the strawberry example, the grower committed to the \$8 per hour in advance of the actual picking of the strawberries.

resources used
The cost driver rate times the cost driver volume.

resources supplied
The expenditures or the amounts spent on the activity.

unused resource capacity
The difference between resources used and resources supplied.

In cases when resources are supplied as they are used, the resource supply generally equals the resource used, resulting in no unused capacity. Good examples are materials costs and piecework labor. If the grower had paid the piecework labor rate of $1.50 per crate, the resources supplied *and* the resources used would have been $1.50 per crate of strawberries picked. There would have been no unused resource capacity. The next section expands these ideas by suggesting a new reporting format that presents managers important information about resources used, resources supplied, and unused resource capacity.

SELF-STUDY QUESTION

2. Assume that a purchasing agent is paid $5,000 per month to process purchase orders. The purchasing agent has the capacity to process 500 orders per month.
   a. Compute the cost driver rate.
   b. Suppose that the number of purchase orders drops to 300 in March; calculate the unused resource capacity and resources used.

The solution to this question is at the end of this chapter on page 285.

ACTIVITY-BASED REPORTING OF UNUSED RESOURCES

L.O. 7: Use your knowledge about cost hierarchies and the difference between resources used and resources supplied to create innovative management reports.

We now discuss an important way to add value to managers and their companies. The previous sections have demonstrated the importance of two key concepts, the cost hierarchy and the difference between resources used and resources supplied. Conventional management reports do not make those distinctions. Typical reports show costs as line items as shown for Cooper Company in Illustration 9.5. It is impossible for managers to distinguish resources used from resources supplied in such reports.

This section presents a new type of report that shows managers a comparison of resources used with resources supplied and classifies costs into cost hierarchies. This type of reporting is important if managers are to manage resources wisely.

This new type of report appears in Illustration 9.6. Note first that it categorizes costs into the cost hierarchies discussed earlier in this chapter. Managers can look at the amount of costs in each hierarchy and find ways to manage those resources

---

ILLUSTRATION 9.5	Traditional (Detailed) Income Statement

COOPER CO.
January

Sales.		$180,000
Costs		
Materials	$30,000	
Energy	10,000	
Short-term labor	4,000	
Outside contracts	6,000	
Setups	20,000	
Quality inspection	10,000	
Parts management	7,000	
Marketing	15,000	
Customer service	4,000	
Engineering changes	6,000	
Long-term labor	7,000	
Depreciation (buildings)	20,000	
Administrative	13,000	
Total costs		152,000
Operating profit		$ 28,000

ILLUSTRATION 9.6	Activity-Based Management Income Statement[a]

COOPER CO.
January

Sales. $180,000

	Resources Used	Unused Resource Capacity	Resources Supplied
Costs			
Unit			
Materials	$ 30,000	$ 0	$ 30,000
Energy.	10,000	0	10,000
Short-term labor.	3,500	500	4,000
Outside contracts.	6,000	0	6,000
	$ 49,500	$ 500	$ 50,000
Batch			
Setups.	$ 14,000	$ 6,000	$ 20,000
Quality inspections.	8,500	1,500	10,000
	$ 22,500	$ 7,500	$ 30,000
Product and customer sustaining			
Parts management	$ 6,000	$ 1,000	$ 7,000
Marketing.	14,000	1,000	15,000
Customer service	2,000	2,000	4,000
Engineering changes	5,000	1,000	6,000
	$ 27,000	$ 5,000	$ 32,000
Capacity sustaining			
Long-term labor	$ 5,000	$ 2,000	$ 7,000
Depreciation (buildings)	12,000	8,000	20,000
Administrative	10,000	3,000	13,000
	$ 27,000	$13,000	$ 40,000
Total costs	$126,000	$26,000	$152,000

Operating profits. . . . . $ 28,000

[a]This income statement was inspired by R. Cooper and R. S. Kaplan, "Activity-Based Systems: Measuring the Costs of Resource Usage," *Accounting Horizons* 6, no. 3 (1992), pp. 1–13.

effectively. For example, managers see that $30,000 of resources are supplied to batch-related activities such as setups. They investigate how much of that $30,000 can be saved by changing the production process, for example, by cutting the number of setups in half.

Perhaps of more interest, the report shows managers how much of the resources for each type of cost are unused. Here's how it works. Assume that the cost driver for setup costs is hours of setup and the rate is $100 per hour. Based on the information in the income statement, Cooper spent $20,000 on setups. That represents 200 hours of setup capacity ($20,000/$100 per setup hour = 200 setup hours of available resource). However, only 140 hours were used during the month ($14,000 resources used ÷ $100 cost driver rate = 140 hours of setup used). The report shows managers that $6,000 (or 60 hours) of unused setup resources is available.

All other things being equal, perhaps as much as 60 additional hours of setup could have been done in January without increasing expenditures. In reality, managers know that some unused resources are a good thing. Having some unstructured time for ad hoc training, leisure, and thinking about ways to improve the work and work environment can be useful for morale and productivity.

Note that some costs have more unused resources than others. The items listed under unit-related costs at the top of the report show little or no unused resources. These costs vary proportionately with output and often have little or no unused resources. Short-term labor, for example, is the cost of piecework labor or temporary help that is employed on an as-needed basis. In a college, a part-time lecturer hired for only one class is an example of short-term labor. Many of us have worked as short-term laborers during the summer in resorts, on farms, in forests fighting fires, or in retail stores or providing delivery services during the holidays.

Capacity-related costs have unused resources unless the company is operating at full capacity. Long-term labor resources are the costs of employing people who are not laid off during temporary fluctuations in production. In colleges, permanent faculty and staff are examples of long-term labor.

SELF-STUDY QUESTION

3. Refer to Illustration 9.6.
   a. Assume that quality inspections cost $100 per inspection. How many additional inspections can Cooper do without increasing expenditures on these items?
   b. Assume that each engineering change costs $500. How many additional engineering changes can Cooper make without increasing expenditures on them?

The solution to this question is at the end of this chapter on page 285.

IMPLEMENTING ADVANCED COST MANAGEMENT SYSTEMS

Accountants cannot implement activity-based management without becoming familiar with a company's operations. In identifying activities, accountants become part of a team with management and people from production, engineering, marketing, and other parts of the company who work to identify the activities that drive the company's costs. This often creates discomfort at first as accountants are forced to deal with unfamiliar areas, but in the long run, their familiarity with the company's operating activities can improve their contribution to it. Nonaccounting personnel also feel a greater sense of ownership of the numbers that the accounting system reports as accounting improves its credibility among nonaccountants.

One of the problems encountered when implementing activity-based management is the failure of influential people in the organization to buy into the process. Accounting methods in companies are like rules in sports; people become accustomed to playing by them and oppose change to something unknown. In fact, two specialists in advising companies how to implement advanced cost-management systems, J. A. Ness and T. G. Cucuzza, believe that employee resistance is the single largest obstacle to implementing activity-based management.[5]

For example, two analysts at one company spent several months and hundreds of hours of computer time developing an activity-based costing system. Their analysis revealed several hundred products that were clearly unprofitable and should be eliminated. However, the key managers to make product elimination decisions agreed to eliminate only about 20 products. Why? The analysts had failed to talk to these managers early in the process. When presented with the final results, the managers raised numerous objections that the analysts had not anticipated. The moral is this: If you are involved in trying to make a change, involve all of the people who are important to that change early in the process.

---

[5] J. A. Ness and T. G. Cucuzza, "Tapping the Full Potential of ABC," *Harvard Business Review,* July–August 1995, pp. 130–38.

REAL WORLD APPLICATION | Implementing Activity-Based Management at Chrysler

Robert A. Lutz, president and chief operating officer at Chrysler, was determined to replace the company's old cost accounting system with a system that could report costs by process and separate value-added from nonvalue-added activities. After reading an article about activity-based costing (ABC), Lutz decided that this was the system for Chrysler.

As Chrysler introduced ABC, many employees at various levels resisted. The new system represented a threat by changing the existing power structure and revealing inefficient processes hidden by the old cost accounting system. Chrysler took several steps to mitigate the resistance of employees as follows:

- Critical employees were persuaded of the benefits associated with ABC.
- Employees at all levels were educated in the principles of ABC.
- One plant initially implemented ABC to serve as a visible success story to the rest of the company.
- The old cost accounting system was eliminated immediately after the introduction of ABC.

After convincing employees that ABC would empower management to make better-informed decisions through the use of activity-based management, Chrysler was able

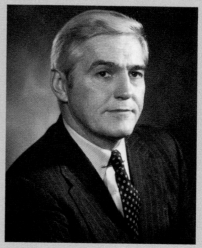

Robert Lutz

to implement ABC throughout the company. It estimates that since it began implementing ABC in 1991, it has saved hundreds of millions of dollars by simplifying product designs and eliminating inefficient practices. The benefits have been 10 to 20 times greater than the company's initial investment in the ABC system.

Source: J. A. Ness and T. G. Cucuzza, "Tapping the Full Potential of ABC," *Harvard Business Review*, July–August 1995, pp. 130–38.

SUMMARY

Management can utilize activity-based costing systems in a number of different ways:

- Making pricing decisions.
- Creating incentives for employees (for example, if overhead is applied based on direct labor-hours, the incentive is to reduce them).
- Identifying and reducing or eliminating costly activities that do not add value to the product.

The concept of using activity-based costing to be more effective as a manager is referred to as *activity-based management.*

In thinking about what affects costs, management will likely improve decisions by categorizing costs according to major categories of activities. Using the example in the text, management could categorize costs according to the following hierarchy of costs:

1. Capacity-related costs generated by activities such as building rent.
2. Product- and customer-level costs generated by activities such as product and customer records.

3. Batch-related costs generated by activities such as machine setups.

4. Unit-level costs generated by activities such as energy to run machines.

Using this hierarchy, if management makes decisions that affect units but not batches, products, customers, or capacity, it would analyze costs in category 4, costs of unit-level activities. If management makes decisions that affect capacity, however, all activities in categories 1 through 4 probably would be affected, and costs in all four categories would be analyzed.

The following summarizes key ideas tied to the chapter's learning objectives.

LO1: Activity-based management. Activity-based management explores the benefits of activity-based costing systems from a manager's perspective. The issue goes beyond how to calculate the cost of products using activity-based costing. Once a new costing system is in place, management needs to determine how the new, more detailed information is going to help it.

LO2: Strategic uses of activity-based costing. Many experts believe that activity-based costing offers a potential competitive advantage over companies that elect not to utilize it. Given more detailed cost data, management is better able to identify costly activities and manage them.

LO3: Eliminating nonvalue-added activities. Activity-based management can help management identify nonvalue-added activities (for example, storage and movement of inventory, idle workers, or inefficient production processes).

LO4: Manage customer response time using activity-based costing information. Activity-based management helps reduce customer response time by identifying activities that consume both dollar and time resources. Eliminating nonvalue-added activities usually reduces costs and customer response time and increases customer satisfaction.

LO5: Using the hierarchy of costs to manage costs. Establishing a hierarchy of costs can help management understand which production processes must be changed to affect certain costs. For example, cutting unit-level costs would not likely affect capacity-level costs, at least in the short run.

LO6: Difference between resources used and resources supplied. Companies must pay for activities supplied even if they are not fully utilized. For example, if assembly workers earn hourly wages but are idle for half of an 8-hour shift, the company must compensate them for 8 hours. Management must try to match activities supplied to activities used to be as efficient as possible.

LO7: Create innovative management reports that classify costs according to cost hierarchies and distinguish between resources used and resources supplied. See Illustration 9.6 for an example of such a report.

KEY TERMS

activity-based management, 268	resources used, 273
resources supplied, 273	unused resource capacity, 273

REVIEW QUESTIONS

9.1 How are activity-based costing and activity-based management similar? How do they differ?

9.2 Can activity-based management be implemented without an activity-based costing system?

9.3 What are the four steps used to analyze activities? Describe each.

9.4 Why is it important for managers to assess whether activities are value-added or nonvalue-added?

9.5 What are some common nonvalue-added activities found in many businesses?

9.6 What is customer response time? How does activity-based management help to reduce it?

9.7 What are the four cost hierarchies? Describe each.

9.8 What is the difference between a capacity-sustaining cost and a unit-level cost? How can managers use a hierarchy of overhead costs like the one presented in Illustration 9.4?

CRITICAL ANALYSIS AND DISCUSSION QUESTIONS

9.9 What are examples of two nonvalue-added activities that may be found in each of the following service organizations: (1) a university and (2) a restaurant?

9.10 What are examples of two nonvalue-added activities that may be found in each of the following service organizations: (1) a hospital and (2) a bicycle repair shop?

9.11 What are examples of two nonvalue-added activities that may be found in organizations that manufacture (1) automobiles and (2) computers?

9.12 What are examples of two nonvalue-added activities that may be found in organizations that manufacture (1) lumber and (2) furniture?

9.13 What are examples of two nonvalue-added activities that may be found in merchandising organizations: (1) a clothing retail store and (2) a record store?

9.14 Refer to the Real World Application "Using Activity-Based Management to Control Health Care Costs While Improving Quality." If the new anesthesia reduces the number of minutes a patient stays in the recovery room after surgery, why wouldn't nursing costs be reduced in proportion to the reduction in the number of minutes the patient stays in the recovery room?

9.15 Of the four categories of costs in the hierarchy, which would you expect to have the most unused resources? Why?

9.16 How are "resources used" measured?

9.17 How is unused resource capacity measured? What does it represent?

9.18 Describe the difference between conventional income statements and activity-based reports. How do activity-based reports help managers?

9.19 Refer to the Real World Application "Implementing Activity-Based Management at Chrysler." Write a short report to Robert Lutz explaining why you think the Chrysler employees opposed activity-based management. What steps would you recommend to mitigate the resistance of Chrysler employees?

EXERCISES

9.20

Resources Used versus Resources Supplied
(L.O. 6)

Information about resources on a saw used to cut marble for Great Lakes Corporation follow:

	Cost Driver Rate	Cost Driver Volume
Resources used		
Energy	$0.60	5,000 machine-hours
Repairs.	$1.00	5,000 machine-hours
Resources supplied		
Energy $3,300		
Repairs. 6,000		

Required

Compute unused resource capacity in energy and repairs for Great Lakes Corporation.

9.21

Resources Used
versus Resources
Supplied
(L.O. 6)

Information about resources for Steamboat Industries, Inc., follows:

	Cost Driver Rate	Cost Driver Volume
Resources used		
Setups	$175	50 runs
Clerical.	30	200 pages typed
Resources supplied		
Setups	$8,925	
Clerical.	6,300	

Required

Compute unused resource capacity in setups and clerical for Steamboat Industries.

9.22

Resources Used
versus Resources
Supplied
(L.O. 6)

Information about resources for Eagle Products Corporation follows:

	Cost Driver Rate	Cost Driver Volume
Resources used		
Materials.	$ 6	8,000 pounds
Energy	24	340 machine-hours
Setups	150	80 setups
Purchasing	120	80 purchase orders
Customer service	80	50 returns
Long-term labor	40	320 labor-hours
Administrative	30	420 labor-hours
Resources supplied		
Materials.	$48,000	
Energy	9,120	
Setups	12,600	
Purchasing	11,000	
Customer service	4,800	
Long-term labor	13,250	
Administrative	13,500	

In addition, sales for the period totaled $150,000.

Required

Compute unused resource capacity for each preceding item. Describe what the term *unused resource capacity* means.

9.23

Resources Used
versus Resources
Supplied
(L.O. 5, 6)

Required

Refer to Exercise 9.22.

a. Prepare a traditional income statement like the one shown in Illustration 9.5.

b. Prepare an activity-based income statement like the one shown in Illustration 9.6.

9.24

Resources Used
versus Resources
Supplied
(L.O. 5, 6)

Required

Refer to Exercises 9.22 and 9.23.

a. Describe the differences between a traditional income statement and an activity-based income statement.

b. Write a short report to management of Eagle Products explaining how the activity-based income statement can help them.

9.25 Resources Used versus Resources Supplied (L.O. 6)

Information about resources for Inntell Corporation follows:

	Cost Driver Rate	Cost Driver Volume
Resources used		
Materials...............	$22	750 tons
Energy................	15	255 machine-hours
Setups................	80	220 setups
Purchasing	75	160 purchases
Customer service	30	120 service calls
Long-term labor	30	1,250 labor-hours
Administrative	50	420 labor-hours
Resources supplied		
Materials............$16,500		
Energy............. 4,400		
Setups............. 18,750		
Purchasing 16,500		
Customer service 5,500		
Long-term labor 51,650		
Administrative 26,250		

In addition, sales for the period totaled $215,000.

Required

Compute unused resource capacity for each preceding item. Describe what the term *unused resource capacity* means.

9.26 Resources Used versus Resources Supplied (L.O. 5, 6)

Refer to Exercise 9.25.

a. Prepare a traditional income statement like the one shown in Illustration 9.5.

b. Prepare an activity-based income statement like the one shown in Illustration 9.6.

9.27 Resources Used versus Resources Supplied (L.O. 5, 6)

Refer to Exercises 9.25 and 9.26.

a. Describe the differences between a traditional income statement and an activity-based income statement.

b. Write a short report to Inntell Corporation's management explaining how the activity-based income statement can help them.

9.28 Resources Used versus Resources Supplied (L.O. 6)

Information about resources for Arther Consultants follows:

	Cost Driver Rate	Cost Driver Volume
Resources used		
Energy..................	$ 6	5,420 labor hours
Human resources	1,000	30 new employees
Customer service	20	275 client calls
Long-term labor	90	5,000 labor hours
Administrative	50	420 labor hours
Resources supplied		
Energy............. $ 35,500		
Human resources 40,000		
Customer service 9,800		
Long-term labor 560,000		
Administrative 22,750		

In addition, sales for the period totaled $825,000.

Required

Compute the unused resource capacity for each preceding item. Describe what the term *unused resource capacity* means.

9.29   Resources Used versus Resources Supplied (L.O. 5, 6)

Refer to Exercise 9.28.

Required

a. Prepare a traditional income statement like the one shown in Illustration 9.5.

b. Prepare an activity-based income statement like the one shown in Illustration 9.6.

9.30   Resources Used versus Resources Supplied (L.O. 5, 6)

Refer to Exercises 9.28 and 9.29.

Required

a. Describe the differences between a traditional income statement and an activity-based income statement.

b. Write a short report to management of Arther Consultants explaining how the activity-based income statement can help them.

PROBLEMS

9.31   Activity-Based Reporting: Manufacturing

Beam Corporation manufactures small airplane propellers. Sales for March totaled $85,000. Information regarding resources for the month follows:

	Resources Used	Resources Supplied
Parts management.	$ 3,000	$ 3,500
Energy	5,000	5,000
Quality inspections	4,500	5,000
Long-term labor	2,500	3,500
Short-term labor	2,000	2,400
Setups	7,000	10,000
Materials.	15,000	15,000
Depreciation.	6,000	10,000
Marketing	7,000	7,500
Customer service	1,000	2,000
Administrative	5,000	7,000

In addition, Beam spent $2,500 on 10 engineering changes with a cost driver rate of $250 and $3,000 on four outside contracts with a cost driver rate of $750.

Required

Management has requested that you

a. Prepare a traditional income statement.

b. Prepare an activity-based income statement.

c. Write a short report explaining why the activity-based income statement provides useful information to managers. Use the information from requirements (*a*) and (*b*) to develop examples for your report.

9.32   Activity-Based Reporting: Manufacturing

Almay Corporation manufactures oxygen tanks for deep sea divers. Sales for May totaled $375,000. Information regarding resources for the month follows:

	Resources Used	Resources Supplied
Marketing	$28,000	$30,000
Depreciation	24,000	40,000
Outside contracts	12,000	12,000
Materials	60,000	60,000
Setups	14,000	20,000
Energy	20,000	21,000
Parts management	15,000	16,000
Engineering changes	10,000	12,000
Short-term labor	7,000	7,000
Long-term labor	10,000	14,000
Administrative	20,000	26,000

In addition, Almay spent $22,000 on 800 quality inspections with a cost driver rate of $25 and $8,000 on 200 customer service cost driver units with a cost driver rate of $30.

Required

Management has requested that you:

a. Prepare a traditional income statement.

b. Prepare an activity-based income statement.

c. Write a short report to management explaining why the activity-based income statement provides useful information to managers. Use the information from requirements (*a*) and (*b*) to develop examples for your report.

9.33 Activity-Based Reporting: Manufacturing

Allbrite Corporation manufactures cleaning supplies for commercial use. Sales for February totaled $650,000. Information regarding resources for the month follows:

	Resources Used	Resources Supplied
Marketing	$ 56,000	$ 70,000
Depreciation	50,500	52,250
Materials	145,000	145,000
Setups	28,000	35,000
Energy	40,000	42,000
Parts management	15,000	16,000
Short-term labor	14,000	14,000
Long-term labor	80,000	88,000
Administrative	40,000	52,000

In addition, Allbrite spent $44,000 on 1,000 quality inspections with a cost driver rate of $40 and $10,000 on 150 customer service cost driver units with a cost driver rate of $55.

Required

Management has requested that you

a. Prepare a traditional income statement.

b. Prepare an activity-based income statement.

c. Write a short report to management explaining why the activity-based income statement provides useful information to managers. Use the information from requirements (*a*) and (*b*) to develop examples for your report.

9.34 Activity-Based Reporting: Service Organization

Freefall Engineering Corporation provides structural design work for skyscraper projects. Sales for November totaled $1,350,000. Information regarding resources for the month follows:

	Resources Used	Resources Supplied
Marketing.	$112,000	$120,000
Depreciation	87,000	89,500
Training personnel	45,000	54,000
Energy.	80,000	85,500
Short-term labor.	245,000	310,000
Long-term labor	415,000	425,000
Administrative	70,000	79,000

In addition, Freefall spent $42,000 on 250 quality inspections with a cost driver rate of $150.

Required Management has requested that you

a. Prepare a traditional income statement.

b. Prepare an activity-based income statement.

c. Write a short report to management explaining why the activity-based income statement provides useful information to managers. Use the information from requirements (*a*) and (*b*) to develop examples for your report.

9.35 Activity-Based Reporting: Service Organization

Investment Advisory Services, Inc., provides financial planning services to its clients. Sales for July totaled $345,000. Information regarding resources for the month follow:

	Resources Used	Resources Supplied
Marketing	$ 5,000	$ 5,000
Depreciation.	15,000	19,500
Training	25,000	28,000
Energy.	14,000	16,500
Short-term labor	32,000	36,000
Long-term labor.	94,000	107,000
Administrative.	19,000	22,000

In addition, the company spent $9,000 on 175 customer service cost driver units with a cost driver rate of $45.

Required Management has requested that you

a. Prepare a traditional income statement.

b. Prepare an activity-based income statement. p275

c. Write a short report to management explaining why the activity-based income statement provides useful information to managers. Use the information from requirements (*a*) and (*b*) to develop examples for your report.

9.36 Customer Response Time

Kurt Corporation, which manufactures custom-made bicycle racing equipment and parts, engages in the following activities (not in sequence):

1. Making phone sales to bicycle shops.

2. Processing mail in orders.

3. Queuing orders to be shipped.

4. Sending orders to the appropriate production department at the end of each day.

5. Taking call-in orders from on-site salespeople at the end of each day.

6. Shipping parts.

7. Performing quality inspection during production.

8. Taking catalog orders over the phone.

9. Placing production department orders for special materials for ordered parts.

10. Queuing orders in the production department.

11. Setting machinery up to produce parts according to specifications.

12. Producing parts.

13. Making on-site sales to bicycle shops.

14. Classifying orders according to process required for production.

15. Making quality inspection after production.

16. Sending parts to shipping department.

17. Staffing on-site booths to take orders at the races.

18. Holding parts until the completion of other parts in an order.

Required

a. Categorize these activities according to the elements of customer response time shown in Illustration 9.3.

b. Write a short report to management indicating how customer response time can be reduced.

SOLUTIONS TO SELF-STUDY QUESTIONS

1.

Item	Cost Category
a. Piecework labor	Unit level
b. Long-term lease on a building	Capacity related
c. Energy to run machines	Unit level
d. Engineering drawings for a product	Product related
e. Purchase order	Batch related
f. Movement of materials for products in production	Batch related
g. Change order to meet new customer specifications	Customer related

2. a. The cost driver rate is $10 per purchase order:

$$\$10 = \frac{\$5,000 \text{ Salary of purchasing agent}}{500 \text{ Purchase order processing capacity}}$$

b. Unused resource capacity totals $2,000:

$$\$2,000 = \$10 \text{ Cost driver rate} \\ \times 200 \text{ Unused capacity}$$

Resources used total $3,000:

$$\$3,000 = \$5,000 \\ - \$2,000 \text{ Unused resource capacity}$$

3. a. Cooper can perform 15 additional inspections:

$$15 = \frac{\$1,500 \text{ Unused resource capacity}}{\$100 \text{ per inspection}}$$

b. Cooper can make two additional engineering changes:

$$2 = \frac{\$1,000 \text{ Unused resource capacity}}{\$500 \text{ Cost per engineering change}}$$

Allocating Joint Costs

LEARNING OBJECTIVES

After reading this chapter, you should be able to:

1. Allocate joint costs using the net realizable value method.

2. Allocate joint costs using the physical quantities method.

3. Explain how cost data are used in the sell-or-process-further decision.

4. Account for by-products.

5. Understand the constant gross margin percentage method of allocating joint costs (appendix).

A **joint cost** is a cost of a manufacturing process with several different outputs. For example, logs can be the input to grade A lumber (high quality with few imperfections) and grade B lumber (low quality with knots and other imperfections). The cost of the logs is a joint cost of these two **joint products.** The problem in such cases is whether and how to allocate the joint cost of the input (for example the logs) to the joint products (for example, grade A and grade B lumber).

WHAT IS JOINT COSTING?

Illustration 10.1 is a diagram of the flow of costs incurred to process logs by Sacramento-Sierra Company. These costs include materials, labor, and manufacturing overhead. As the logs are processed, two products, grade A and grade B lumber, emerge. The stage of processing when the two products are separated is called the **split-off point.** Processing costs incurred prior to the split-off point are the *joint costs.* This chapter shows how to allocate those joint costs to products.

Managers are often interested in another issue. Should a product be sold at the split-off point or processed further? Rather than selling grade A lumber at the split-off point, should Sacramento-Sierra Company process it further to produce an even higher quality of lumber (grade AA used for finish work)? The higher-quality lumber requires additional processing costs, but the sales price for grade AA lumber is higher than for grade A lumber sold at the split-off point.

Relating Joint Costing to the Value Chain

The "production" business function of the value chain is our primary focus here. Remember that the value chain represents the sequence of business functions in which value is added to an organization's products. If we increase value by further processing grade A into grade AA and incremental value exceeds incremental costs, producing grade AA lumber adds value to the company. However, allocating joint costs to each grade of lumber is still an issue.

WHY ALLOCATE JOINT COSTS?

Joint costs are allocated for many reasons. Cost allocations are often used to determine departmental or division costs for measuring executive performance. Many companies compensate executives and other employees, at least partly, on the basis of departmental or division earnings for the year. When a single raw material is converted into products sold by two or more departments, the cost of the raw material must be allocated to the products concerned. For example, if one division at Sacramento-Sierra is responsible for selling grade A lumber and another is

ILLUSTRATION   10.1   Diagram of Joint Cost Flows

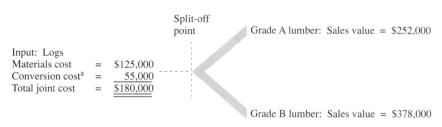

SACRAMENTO-SIERRA COMPANY

April

Input: Logs
Materials cost   = $125,000
Conversion cost[a]   =   55,000
Total joint cost   = $180,000

Split-off point

Grade A lumber: Sales value = $252,000

Grade B lumber: Sales value = $378,000

[a]Conversion costs are direct labor plus manufacturing overhead.

responsible for selling grade B lumber, the cost of processing logs may be allocated partly to the grade A lumber division and partly to the grade B lumber division.

Joint cost allocations are useful in valuing inventory for insurance purposes. Should a casualty loss occur, the insurance company and the insured party must agree on the value of the lost goods. For example, suppose that a portion of the grade A lumber at Sacramento-Sierra was destroyed in a fire. The cost of the lumber destroyed includes a portion of the costs of processing the logs.

Manufacturing companies must allocate joint costs to measure the value of the products that result from the joint process (for example, grade A and grade B lumber in the Sacramento-Sierra example). When companies are subject to rate regulation, the allocation of joint costs can be a significant factor in determining the regulated rates. Crude oil and natural gas are usually produced from a common well. In recent years, energy price policies and gas utility rates have been based in part on the allocation of the joint costs of crude oil and natural gas.

Each of these cases involves opposing interests. For example, neither the insurance company nor the insured party wishes to pay more or receive less than is fair. Executives and employees of one department object to a cost of goods sold figure that they believe is overstated but is understated for another department. Both buyers and sellers of regulated products or services are affected by pricing, and neither wishes to give the other an advantage. When the allocation of costs can impinge on the financial fortunes of opposing parties, both sides critically review the allocation method.

Any cost allocation method contains an element of arbitrariness. No allocation method is beyond dispute. Consequently, allocation methods must be clearly stated before they are implemented.

Why Joint Costs Are Good Business for Lawyers

The inherent arbitrariness of joint cost allocation makes good business for lawyers and litigation support consultants who know something about accounting. In many cases, people or companies are involved in disputes because they did not consider every possibility in written or oral contracts.

Disputes often arise over the application of the word *cost* in cost-sharing agreements. Suppose that two companies enter a joint venture to drill for oil and natural gas. Company O wants the oil from the well; Company G wants the natural gas. The costs of exploration, drilling, pumping, and separating oil from natural gas are the joint costs shared by the two companies. Neither company would find the venture profitable alone, but by sharing the costs, both companies find it profitable.

After 10 years without dispute, worldwide natural gas prices dropped substantially because of new discoveries and increased distribution of natural gas from Russia and other republics of the former USSR. Company G wants out of the joint venture because it is no longer profitable to sell natural gas from this venture. Company O wants Company G to continue sharing the costs of pumping and separating natural gas and oil, so it does not want Company G to back out. Company G ceases operations and stops paying the costs of the joint venture. Legal war breaks out!

Those of you who become lawyers or litigation consultants are likely to work on legal cases involving joint costs because of their inherent arbitrariness. As this book goes to print, legal cases involving oil and gas companies alone have hundreds of millions of dollars at stake. (See the Real World Application, "Legal Wrangling over Who Pays for Joint Costs" on page 289.) To minimize the incidence of such disputes, carefully word contracts to define the meaning of *costs* and anticipate as many future events as possible.

REAL WORLD APPLICATION

Legal Wrangling over Who Pays for Joint Costs

On its North Slope, the State of Alaska had a dispute with ARCO, British Petroleum and Exxon over the joint costs of gas-processing plants. The oil companies paid the State of Alaska royalties amounting to one-eighth of the value of oil pumped off the North Slope. However, the oil companies reduced the royalty payment for certain costs incurred by gas-processing plants, which took a joint product, fluid from the ground, and processed it into products A, B and C. Products B and C were then mostly pumped back into the ground.

Product A was added to the oil pumped from the North Slope, however. The oil companies paid royalties to the State of Alaska on Product A, but they reduced their royalty payment by a portion of the joint costs of the gas-processing plants that had separated the fluid from the ground into Products A, B, and C. This is the controversial issue. How much of the joint cost of the gas-processing plant should be allocated to Product A? The oil companies wanted to allocate as much as possible to it to reduce their royalty payment to the state. The state wanted to allocate as much to Products B and C as possible.

Crude oil is the source of many joint products, including oil, gasoline and kerosene. (© Chris Arend/Tony Stone Images)

After years of discussion and tens of millions of dollars of legal expense, the case was settled out of court just before going to trial. The resulting allocation was a compromise worked out by the parties to the lawsuit.
Source: Based on the author's research.

JOINT COST ALLOCATION METHODS

Net Realizable Value Method

L.O. 1: Allocate joint costs using the net realizable value method.

net realizable value method
Joint cost allocation based on the proportional values of the joint products at the split-off point.

estimated net realizable value
The sales price of a final product minus additional processing costs necessary to prepare a product for sale.

The two major methods of allocating joint costs are (1) the net realizable value method and (2) the physical quantities method. Another method—the gross margin method—is discussed in the appendix to the chapter.

The **net realizable value method** allocates joint costs based on the net realizable value of each product at the split-off point. The net realizable value is the estimated sales value of each product at the split-off point. If the joint products can be sold at the split-off point, the market value or sales price should be used for this allocation.

If the products require further processing before they are marketable, it may be necessary to estimate the net realizable value at the split-off point. This approach is called the **estimated net realizable value** method, sometimes referred to as the *net-back* or *workback method*. Normally, when a market value is available at the split-off point, it is preferable to use that value rather than the netback method. The *net realizable value* at the split-off point is estimated by taking the sales value after further processing and deducting those added processing costs. Joint costs are then allocated to the products in proportion to their net realizable values at the split-off point.

First we look at an example of the net realizable method. The section following the self-study question discusses the *estimated net realizable value* method in more detail.

From the previous example, we know that Sacramento-Sierra Company produces grade A and grade B lumber as shown in Illustration 10.2. In April, materials (that is, logs) cost $125,000, and conversion costs are $55,000, for a total of $180,000. Grade A and grade B lumber have a $630,000 total sales value at the split-off point.

ILLUSTRATION   10.2   Joint Products for Sacramento-Sierra Company

---

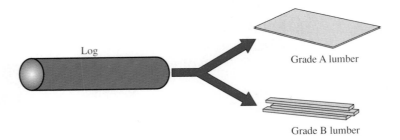

Log

Grade A lumber

Grade B lumber

Grade A has $252,000 sales value, or 40 percent of the total, and grade B's value is $378,000, or 60 percent of the total. We assume for the purpose of this example that no additional processing is required after the split-off point to make grade A and grade B lumber.

The cost allocation follows the proportional distribution of net realizable values:

	Grade A	Grade B	Total
Final sales value	$252,000	$378,000	$630,000
Less: Additional processing costs	–0–	–0–	–0–
Net realizable value at split-off point	$252,000	$378,000	$630,000
Proportionate share			
$252,000/$630,000	40%		
$378,000/$630,000		60%	
Allocated joint costs			
$180,000 × 40%	$ 72,000		
$180,000 × 60%		$108,000	

A condensed statement of gross margins at the split-off point is shown in Illustration 10.3.

Note that the gross margins as a percentage of sales are 71.43 percent for both products. This demonstrates an important concept of the net realizable value method, namely, that revenue dollars from any joint product are assumed to make the same percentage contribution at the split-off point as the revenue dollars from any other joint product. The net realizable value approach implies a matching of input costs with revenues generated by each output.

Now that we have determined how to allocate joint costs using the net realizable value method, let's look at the flow of these costs through T-accounts as shown in Illustration 10.4. Note that logs are materials held in materials inventory until they are allocated to WIP inventory.

SELF-STUDY QUESTION

1. Ferguson Confections Company purchases cocoa beans and processes them into cocoa butter, cocoa powder, and cocoa shells. The standard yield from each 100-pound sack of unprocessed cocoa beans is 20 pounds of butter, 45 pounds of powder, and 35 pounds of shells. The powder can be sold for $.90 per pound and the butter for $1.10 per pound at the split-off point. The shells are thrown away at no cost.

    The cost of the cocoa beans is $15 per hundred pounds. It costs $37 in labor and overhead to process each 100 pounds of beans up to the split-off point.

    Compute the joint cost allocated to butter and powder produced from 100 pounds of cocoa beans using the net realizable value method.

The solution to this question is at the end of this chapter on page 310.

ILLUSTRATION 10.3	Gross Margin Computations Using Net Realizable Value Method

SACRAMENTO-SIERRA COMPANY
April

	Grade A	Grade B	Total
Sales value.	$252,000	$378,000	$630,000
Less allocated joint costs	72,000	108,000	180,000
Gross margin	$180,000	$270,000	$450,000
Gross margin as a percent of sales	71.43[a]	71.43[a]	71.43[a]

[a]71.43 = $180,000 ÷ $252,000 = $270,000 ÷ $378,000 = $450,000 ÷ 630,000.

ILLUSTRATION   10.4   Flow of Costs Using Net Realizable Value Method

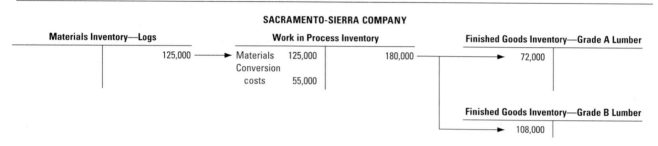

SACRAMENTO-SIERRA COMPANY

Estimating Net Realizable Value

In the previous example, we assumed that no further processing was required after the split-off point. Not all joint products can be sold at the split-off point, however. Further processing may be required before a product is marketable. When no sales values exist for the outputs at the split-off point, the *estimated net realizable values* should be determined by taking the sales value of each product at the first point at which it can be marketed and deducting the processing costs that must be incurred after the split-off point. The resulting estimated net realizable value is used for joint cost allocation in the same way as an actual market value at the split-off point.

Suppose that management of Sacramento-Sierra finds that there are excellent opportunities to sell a better product, grade AA lumber (used for finish work). Grade AA lumber requires additional processing, as shown in Illustration 10.5. This additional processing costs $98,000 for the grade AA lumber produced in April, after which the grade AA lumber could be sold for $260,000. The Grade B lumber could still be sold at the split-off point for $378,000. Illustration 10.6 is a diagram of the process.

Illustration 10.7 shows the allocation of the joint cost of $180,000 to grade AA lumber and grade B lumber using the estimated net realizable value method. First, we compute the estimated net realizable values at split-off for grade AA lumber and grade B lumber, which are $162,000 and $378,000, respectively. Next we multiply the ratio of each product's net realizable value to the total estimated net realizable value by the joint cost. To determine the portion of the joint cost allocated to grade B lumber, for example, the computations are $378,000/$540,000 times the joint cost of $180,000 (70% × $180,000 = $126,000, as shown in Illustration 10.7).

ILLUSTRATION   10.5   Sacramento-Sierra Processes Grade A Lumber beyond Split-Off Point

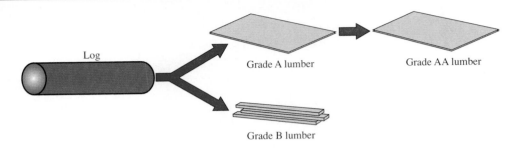

ILLUSTRATION   10.6   Flow of Costs—Further Processing beyond Split-Off Point

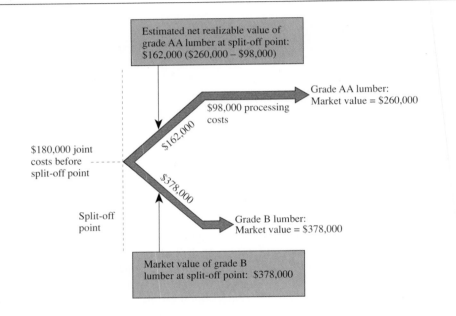

ILLUSTRATION 10.7	Estimated Net Realizable Value Method		
SACRAMENTO-SIERRA COMPANY April			
	Grade AA Lumber	Grade B Lumber	Total
Sales value	$260,000	$378,000	$638,000
Less additional processing costs to point of marketability	98,000	–0–	98,000
Estimated net realizable value at split-off point.	162,000	378,000	540,000
Allocation of joint costs			
$\left[\dfrac{\$162,000}{\$540,000}\right] \times \$180,000 = 30\% \times \$180,000 =$	54,000		180,000
$\left[\dfrac{\$378,000}{\$540,000}\right] \times \$180,000 = 70\% \times \$180,000 =$		126,000	
Gross margin	$108,000	$252,000	$360,000
Gross margin as a percent of estimated net realizable value at split-off	66.67	66.67	66.67

SELF-STUDY QUESTION

2. Refer to Self-Study Question 1. Assume that the cocoa butter cannot be sold at split-off but requires additional processing. The additional processing costs $.15 per pound, at which point the butter can be sold for $1.20 per pound. Allocate the joint costs to the two products using the estimated net realizable value method.

The solution to this question is at the end of this chapter on page 310.

Physical Quantities Method

L.O. 2: Allocate joint costs using the physical quantities method.

physical quantities method
Joint cost allocation based on measurement of the volume, weight, or other physical measure of the joint products at the split-off point.

The **physical quantities method** is often used when output product prices are highly volatile. This method is also used when significant processing occurs between the split-off point and the first point of marketability, or when product prices are not set by the market. The latter situation may arise when regulators set prices in regulated pricing situations or in cost-based contract situations, for example.

Using the physical quantities method, joint costs are assigned to products based on a physical measure. This might be volume, weight, or any other common measure of physical characteristics.

Many companies allocate joint costs incurred in producing oil and gas on the basis of energy equivalent (BTU content). They use this method because the products are typically measured in different physical units (gas by thousand cubic feet, oil by barrel), although oil and gas often are produced simultaneously from the same well. Moreover, the price of most gas is regulated so that relative market values are artificial.

Let's return to the Sacramento-Sierra Company example; the company produces grade A and grade B lumber. Assume that relative market values at the split-off point are not available and for every $180,000 of joint costs in processing logs, we obtain 1,400 units of grade A lumber and 1,960 units of grade B lumber (1 unit = 1 board-foot). The allocation of joint costs using these physical quantity measures is shown in Illustration 10.8. A total of 3,360 units is produced. Joint costs are allocated to grade A lumber by dividing grade A units (1,400) by the total units (3,360) and multiplying the result by total joint costs ($180,000). Thus, $75,000 in joint costs is allocated to grade A lumber.

Evaluation of Joint Cost Methods

The "jointness" of joint production processes makes it impossible to separate the portion of joint costs attributable to one product from another on a cause-and-effect basis. As a result, allocating joint costs is always somewhat arbitrary. If allocated joint costs are used for decision-making purposes, they should be used only with full recognition of their limitations.

Companies allocate joint costs in practice in a variety of ways as the results of a study of joint costing in the United Kingdom indicate. Illustration 10.9 shows

---

ILLUSTRATION 10.8 | **Physical Quantities Method**

SACRAMENTO-SIERRA COMPANY
April

	Grade A Lumber	Grade B Lumber	Total
Output quantities.	1,400 units	1,960 units	3,360 units
Joint allocation			
$\left[\dfrac{1,400}{3,360}\right] \times \$180,000$	$75,000		
$\left[\dfrac{1,960}{3,360}\right] \times \$180,000$		$105,000	$180,000

ILLUSTRATION 10.9	Joint Cost Allocations in Practice			
	No Allocations	Net Realizable Value Method	Physical Quantities	Other
Oil refining	7	–0–	–0–	2
Petrochemicals.	1	5	4	–0–
Coal chemicals.	–0–	1	6	4
Inorganic chemicals.	1	2	2	3
Other companies in the chemicals industry	–0–	3	8	3
Total	9	11	20	12

Source: K. Slater and C. Wooten, *A Study of Joint and By-Product Costing in the U.K.* (London, U.K.: The Chartered Institute of Management Accountants, 1988).

key findings. The results show considerable variety in methods used. This likely reflects the inherent arbitrary nature of joint cost allocation. Accountants and managers realize that no one allocation method is right for all situations.

The study shows that some companies did not allocate joint costs at all because of the difficulty in allocating joint cost and the arbitrariness of those allocations. Many companies used the net realizable value method, but even more companies used the physical quantities method because it seemed more objective and easily obtainable than did measures of sales at split-off points.

SELF-STUDY QUESTION

3. Refer to Self-Study Question 1. Use the physical quantities method to allocate joint costs.

The solution to this question is at the end of this chapter on page 310.

EFFECT OF ALTERNATIVE JOINT COST METHODS ON THE VALUE CHAIN

As different costing methods are considered, one question should come to mind. Which costing method is most effective in adding value to the company? All across the value chain, we should be looking for areas where value-added activities can be implemented and nonvalue-added activities can be eliminated.

The estimated net realizable value method allocates joint costs based on the final sales value less additional processing costs after the split-off point. This method encourages companies or divisions to consider where the most value can be added—that is, if additional processing is to occur after the split-off point, which final product will yield the highest gross margin? To maximize the gross margin, companies maximize the sales price by undertaking activities that add the highest incremental value to the product and reduce costs by eliminating nonvalue-added activities.

DECIDING WHETHER TO SELL GOODS NOW OR PROCESS THEM FURTHER

L.O. 3: Explain how cost data are used in the sell-or-process-further decision.

Many companies have opportunities to sell partly processed products at various production stages. Management must decide whether it is more profitable to sell the output at an intermediate stage or to process it further. In such a sell-or-process-further decision, the relevant data to be considered are (1) the additional revenue after further processing and (2) the additional costs of processing further.

Suppose that Sacramento-Sierra Company can sell grade B lumber for $378,000 at the split-off point or process it further to make a new product, grade BB lumber. The additional processing costs would be $20,000, and the revenue from grade BB lumber would be $416,000. Should the company sell grade B lumber or process it further?

ILLUSTRATION 10.10	Income Statements for Sell-or-Process-Further Decisions		
	Sell (Grade B)	Process Further (Grade BB)	Additional Revenue and Costs from Processing Further
Revenues			
From lumber	$378,000	$416,000	$38,000
Less separate processing of lumber.	–0–	20,000	20,000
Margin.	$378,000	$396,000	$18,000 net gain from processing further

As shown in Illustration 10.10 the profit will be $18,000 higher if grade B lumber is processed further into Grade BB lumber. It is important to note that the allocation of the $180,000 joint costs between grade A and grade B lumber is irrelevant. The $38,000 additional revenue from processing beyond the split-off point justified the expenditure of $20,000 for additional processing, regardless of the way joint costs are allocated. *The only costs and revenues relevant to the decision are those that result from it.* Total joint costs incurred prior to the split-off point are not affected by the decision to process further after the split-off point.

WHAT TO DO WITH BY-PRODUCTS

L.O. 4: Account for by-products.

by-products
Outputs of joint production processes that are relatively minor in quantity or value.

Sawdust and wood chips are by-products of lumber production. What distinguishes a by-product from a joint product? (© Matthew McVay/Tony Stone Images)

By-products are outputs from a joint production process that are relatively minor in quantity and/or value when compared to the main products. For example, sawdust and wood chips are by-products of lumber production, and kerosene is a by-product of gasoline production. You may have seen advertisements for carpet and cloth mill ends at bargain prices. These are often by-products of textile production.

By-product accounting attempts to reflect the economic relationship between the by-products and the main products with a minimum of recordkeeping for inventory valuation purposes. Two common methods of accounting for by-products are

Method 1: The net realizable value from sale of the by-products is deducted from the cost of the main product.

Method 2: The proceeds from sale of the by-product are treated as other revenue.

Assume that By-Product Company has a production process that yields output C as the main product and output D as the by-product, both of which are sold this period. Sales of C total $200,000, and the sales of D total $1,100. Processing costs

ILLUSTRATION 10.11	Accounting for By-Products	

BY-PRODUCT COMPANY

	Accounting Method[a]	
	(1)	**(2)**
Sales revenue from output C	$200,000	$200,000
Other revenue	–0–	800[b]
Total revenue	200,000	200,800
Cost of sales— Total production costs	80,000	80,000
Less by-product— Net realizable value	800[b]	–0–
Adjusted cost of sales	79,200	80,000
Gross margin	$120,800	$120,800

[a]Description of accounting methods:
1. The net realizable value of the by-product is deducted from the cost of the main product.
2. The net realizable value from the sale of the by-product is treated as other income.

[b]$800 is the net realizable value of the by-product ($1,100 selling price minus $300 separate costs to process the by-product).

up to the split-off point are $80,000, which are like joint costs, but they are not allocated between output C and output D; instead, they are all allocated to output C, the main product.

Also assume that output D requires $300 additional costs of processing to make it salable; hence, its net realizable value is $800 ($1,100 − $300). The two accounting methods for the by-product, output D, are shown in Illustration 10.11.

Column 1 of Illustration 10.11 shows the reduction in the cost of sales for the net realizable value of the by-product when method 1 is used. Illustration 10.12 shows the cost and revenue flows using this method. First, assume in entry 1 that the joint production costs amounting to $80,000 have been debited to WIP Inventory, as follows.

(1) WIP Inventory.	80,000	
Various Accounts (e.g., Direct Materials Inventory, Wages Payable)		80,000

Second, assume that the additional processing of by-products cost $100 in direct labor and $200 in manufacturing overhead. Entry 2 appears as follows:

(2) Additional By-Product Costs.	300	
Wages Payable.		100
Manufacturing Overhead		200

The debit part of entry 2 appears in the Additional By-Product Costs account in Illustration 10.12. Third, assume that the by-product is sold for cash, $1,100:

(3) Cash.	1,100	
By-Product Revenue		1,100

The credit portion of entry 3 appears in the By-Product Revenue account in Illustration 10.12.

The next step depends on whether the joint product has been sold or is still in inventory. If sold, Cost of Goods Sold is credited for $800. If the joint product is in Finished Goods Inventory, that account is credited for $800. Finally, as demonstrated by entry 4 in Illustration 10.12, if the joint product is still in WIP Inventory, the following entry is made:

ILLUSTRATION 10.12   **Accounting for By-Products**

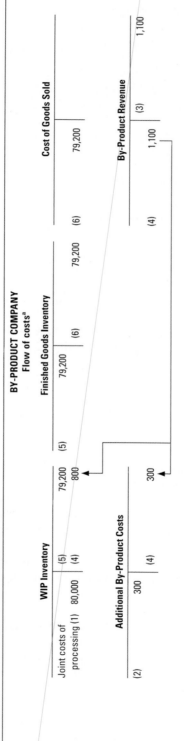

BY-PRODUCT COMPANY
Flow of costs[a]

WIP Inventory

		(5)	(4)
Joint costs of processing (1)	80,000	79,200	800

Additional By-Product Costs

		(4)
(2)	300	300

Finished Goods Inventory

		(6)
(5)	79,200	79,200

Cost of Goods Sold

(6)	79,200

By-Product Revenue

		(3)
(4)	1,100	1,100

[a]Cost flows are shown using method 1 in the text. According to it, the net realizable value of the by-product is deducted from the product costs of the main product.

(4) By-Product Revenue	1,100	
Additional By-Product Costs		300
WIP Inventory		800

Entries 5 and 6 in Illustration 10.12 show the transfer of the joint product, now at a cost of $79,200 instead of $80,000, through Finished Goods Inventory to Cost of Goods Sold.

Method 2, which appears in column 2 of Illustration 10.11, is generally simpler than method 1. Using method 2, the by-product's net realizable value is simply treated as other revenue at the point of sale. Assume that By-Product Company had set up the accounts shown in Illustration 10.12 and had recorded the $300 of additional by-product costs in the Additional By-Product Costs account. Now assume that the by-product is sold for $1,100 cash. The following entry records the transaction in accordance with method 2:

Cash	1,100	
Additional By-Product Costs		300
Other Revenue from Sale of By-Product		800

A complication can arise under both methods if the cost of processing by-products occurs in one period but they are not sold until the next period. In such a case, companies may find it necessary to keep an inventory of the by-product processing costs in the Additional By-Product Cost account until the by-products are sold.

In our experience, some companies make by-product accounting as easy as possible by simply expensing the by-products' costs in the period they are incurred and then recording the total revenue from by-products when they are sold. Using this method, the accountants do not have to bother keeping an inventory of by-product processing costs, nor do they have to compute their net realizable value. Although this simple approach technically violates the principle that revenues and expenses should be matched in the same accounting period, the amounts involved are often immaterial.

Although we have indicated two methods to account for by-products, many variations of these methods are used in practice. By-products are by definition relatively minor products; hence, alternative methods to account for them are not likely to have a material effect on the financial statements for either internal or external reporting.

What to Do with Scrap

Our discussion so far has assumed that the secondary or by-product output has a positive net realizable value; that is, its sales value exceeds the costs of processing and marketing it further. If an output's net realizable value is negative, it is usually considered scrap and is disposed of at minimum cost. The cost of scrapping an output is usually debited to manufacturing overhead and applied to products as part of the manufacturing overhead allocation process.

Once again, the value chain should be considered here. Is there a way to add value to scrap so that the net realizable value is positive? It might be possible to use scrap lumber to produce landscaping materials, such as tree stakes or ground cover. As long as incremental revenues exceed incremental costs, Sacramento-Sierra Company would likely prefer to add value to scrap lumber and avoid taking a loss (debiting manufacturing overhead).

SELF-STUDY QUESTION

4. Refer to Self-Study Question 1. Assume that the cocoa shells can be processed for $.10 per pound and sold for $.30 per pound to crafters who make them into jewelry. For this example, assume that the joint costs to process 100 pounds of cocoa beans total $52, as in Self-Study Question 1. The joint process produces 20 pounds of butter that can be sold for $1.10 per pound, 45 pounds of powder that can be sold for $.90 per pound, and 35 pounds of cocoa shells.

   a. Allocate the joint costs to the two main products using the net realizable value method in which the net realizable value of the by-product reduces the joint production costs.

   b. Prepare an income statement down to the gross margin in which the net realizable value of the by-product is treated as other revenue.

The solution to this question is at the end of this chapter on page 310.

SUMMARY

Joint cost allocations arise from the need to assign common costs to two or more products manufactured from a common input. The usual objective of joint cost allocation is to relate the economic sacrifice (costs) of the inputs to the economic benefits received. There is no direct way to do this for joint products, so approximations are necessary. The two methods of joint cost allocation distribute joint costs based on net realizable value (or *estimated* net realizable value) or the physical quantities method. These methods are acceptable for financial reporting purposes, but care must be exercised before attempting to use the data for decision-making purposes because of the inherent arbitrariness in joint cost allocations.

The following summarizes key ideas tied to the chapter's learning objectives.

LO1: Net realizable method of allocating joint costs. The net realizable value method allocates joint costs to products in proportion to their relative sales values. If additional processing is required beyond the split-off point before the product can be sold, an estimate of the net realizable value can be derived at the split-off point by subtracting the additional processing costs from the sales value that is known.

LO2: Physical quantities method of allocating joint costs. The physical quantities method allocates joint costs to products in proportion to a physical measure (for example, volume or weight).

LO3: Cost data used in sell-or-process-further decisions. Management must often decide whether to sell products at split-off points or process them further. Joint cost allocations are usually irrelevant for these decisions.

LO4: Accounting for by-products. By-products are relatively minor outputs from a joint production process. The two methods most commonly used to account for by-products are (1) to reduce the cost of the main product by the net realizable value (sales value minus by-product processing cost) of the by-product or (2) to treat the net realizable value of the by-product as other income.

LO5: Constant gross margin percentage method of allocating joint costs (appendix). The constant gross margin percentage method assumes that each product has the same gross margin and that joint costs should be allocated in a way that results in the same gross margin across all products. A three-step approach is used to achieve the correct allocation of joint costs using this method.

KEY TERMS

_____

*Term appears in the appendix.

_____

APPENDIX

L.O. 5: Understand the constant gross margin percentage method of allocating joint costs (appendix).

constant gross margin percentage method
A method of joint cost allocation that allocates joint costs to products in a way that the gross margins are the same for each product.

Constant Gross Margin Percentage Method

The **constant gross margin percentage method** allocates joint costs to all products in a way that results in the same gross margin for each product. Three steps are required to use this method:

1. Compute the total gross margin percentage.
2. Use the total gross margin percentage calculated in step 1 to calculate the gross margin for each product (total gross margin percentage × sales value).
3. Deduct the additional processing costs from the total costs to calculate joint costs allocated to each product.

Using the data from our previous example for Sacramento-Sierra Company, we can calculate the allocation of joint costs using the constant gross margin percentage method. Panel A of Illustration 10.13 shows the data provided and the calculation of the total gross margin (step 1). Panel A also indicates the amounts that remain to be calculated (denoted with a question mark). Panel B of Illustration 10.13 shows the calculation of the gross margin dollar amount for each product (step 2). Once the gross margin dollar amount has been calculated for each product, we can solve for the joint costs to be allocated to each product (step 3). This calculation also is shown in panel B of Illustration 10.13.

ILLUSTRATION 10.13	Joint Costs Allocated Using the Constant Gross Margin Percentage Method		
Panel A	**Grade AA Lumber**	**Grade B Lumber**	**Total**
Sales value.	$260,000	$378,000	$638,000
Joint costs (step 3).	?	?	180,000
Additional process costs	98,000	–0–	98,000
Gross margin (step 2)	?	?	$360,000
Gross margin percentage (step 1).	56.426	56.426	56.426
Panel B			
Sales value.	$260,000	$378,000	$638,000
Joint costs (step 3).	15,290	164,710	180,000
Additional process costs	98,000	–0–	98,000
Gross margin, rounded (step 2)	$146,710	$213,290	$360,000
Gross margin percentage (step 1).	56.426	56.426	56.426

Although the constant gross margin percentage method is relatively simple, it is important to understand the assumption involved. We are assuming that all products have the same ratio of costs to sales value, an assumption rarely seen in companies with multiple products.

SELF-STUDY QUESTION

5. Refer to Self-Study Question 2. Allocate the joint costs to the two products using the constant gross margin percentage method.

The solution to this question is at the end of this chapter on page 310.

REVIEW QUESTIONS

10.1 What is the objective of joint cost allocation?

10.2 Why would a number of accountants express a preference for the net realizable value method of joint cost allocation over the physical quantities method?

10.3 When would one prefer a physical quantities method for allocation?

10.4 What is the basic difference between the allocation of joint costs to joint products and to by-products?

10.5 What is the condition under which an item should be treated as a by-product rather than as a joint product?

10.6 What are the two principal methods of assigning joint costs to joint products? State circumstances under which each is appropriate.

10.7 Why are joint costs irrelevant in the sell-or-process-further decision?

10.8 What is the difference between joint products, by-products, and scrap?

CRITICAL ANALYSIS AND DISCUSSION QUESTIONS

10.9 The chapter indicated that joint costing is used for inventory valuation and regulatory purposes. Under what conditions might the method of joint cost allocation have an impact on other decisions?

10.10 How is joint cost allocation like service department cost allocation?

10.11 What are three industries that have joint products?

10.12 Refer to the chapter's Real World Application "How One Person's Scrap Becomes Someone Else's Raw Materials" on page 298. How does recycling wood scrap add value to a company?

EXERCISES

10.13 Net Realizable Value Method (L.O. 1)

A company processes Chemical DX-1 through a pressure treatment operation. The complete process has two outputs, L and T. The January costs to process DX-1 are $50,000 for materials and $100,000 for conversion costs. This processing results in two outputs, L and T, that sell for a total of $250,000. The sales revenue from L amounts to $200,000 of the total.

Required

Using the net realizable value method, assign costs to L and T for January.

10.14 Estimated Net Realizable Value Method (L.O. 1)

Durango Corporation operates an ore-processing plant. A typical batch of ore run through the plant yields three refined products: lead, copper, and manganese. At the split-off point, the intermediate products cannot be sold without further processing. The lead from a typical batch sells for $40,000 after incurring additional processing costs of $12,000. The copper is sold for $80,000 after additional processing costs of $10,000, and the manganese yield sells for $60,000 but requires additional processing costs of $18,000. The costs of processing the raw ore, including the cost of the ore, are $100,000 per batch.

Required   Use the estimated net realizable value method to allocate the joint processing costs.

10.15   Net Realizable Value Method to Solve for Unknowns (L.O. 1)

Green Products, Inc., manufactures leprechauns and shamrocks from a joint process using raw material called Green. For leprechauns, 4,000 units were produced having a sales value at the split-off point of $10,500. For shamrocks, 2,000 units were produced having a sales value at split-off of $7,000. Using the net realizable value method, the portion of the total joint product costs allocated to leprechauns was $6,000.

Required   Compute the total joint product costs before allocation.

(CPA adapted)

10.16   Net Realizable Value Method— Multiple Choice (L.O. 1)

a.   Net realizable value at split-off is used to
   (1)   Allocate separable costs.
   (2)   Determine relevant costs.
   (3)   Determine break-even in sales dollars.
   (4)   Allocate joint costs.

b.   Net realizable value at split-off is used to allocate

	Cost beyond Split-Off	Joint Costs
(1)	Yes	Yes
(2)	Yes	No
(3)	No	Yes
(4)	No	No

c.   For purposes of allocating joint costs to joint products, the estimated net realizable value at split-off is equal to
   (1)   Sales price less a normal profit margin at point of sale.
   (2)   Final sales price reduced by cost to complete after split-off.
   (3)   Total sales value less joint costs at point of split-off.
   (4)   Separable product cost plus a normal profit margin.

d.   The method of accounting for joint product costs that will produce the same gross margin as a percentage of sales for all products is
   (1)   The net realizable value method.
   (2)   The physical quantities method.
   (3)   Both methods.
   (4)   Neither method.

10.17   Net Realizable Value Method— Multiple Choice (L.O. 1)

Each of the three multiple-choice exercises should be considered independent of each other.

a.   The Barney Company manufactures products C and R from a joint process. The total joint costs are $120,000. The sales value at split-off was $140,000 for 8,000 units of product C and $60,000 for 2,000 units of product R. Assuming that total joint costs are allocated using the net realizable value at split-off approach, what were the joint costs allocated to product C?
   (1) $36,000.
   (2) $60,000.
   (3) $84,000.
   (4) $96,000.
   (5)   Some other answer.

b.   Crucible Company manufactures products A and B from a joint process, which also yields a by-product, X. Crucible accounts for the revenues from its by-product sales as other income. Additional information follows:

	A	B	X	Total
Units produced	15,000	9,000	6,000	30,000
Joint costs	?	?	?	$117,000
Sales value at split-off	$125,000	$100,000	$25,000	$250,000

Assuming that joint product costs are allocated using the net realizable value at split-off approach, what was the joint cost allocated to product B?

(1) $35,100.
(2) $46,800.
(3) $52,000.
(4) $58,500.
(5) Some other answer.

c. Superior Corp. manufactures products W, X, Y, and Z from a joint process. Additional information follows:

Product	Units Produced	Sales Value at Split-Off	If Processed Further Additional Costs	If Processed Further Sales Values
W.........	7,000	$ 70,000	$ 7,500	$ 90,000
X	5,000	60,000	6,000	70,000
Y	4,000	40,000	4,000	50,000
Z	4,000	30,000	2,500	30,000
	20,000	$200,000	$20,000	$240,000

Assuming that total joint costs of $80,000 were allocated using the sales value at split-off (net realizable value method), what joint costs were allocated to each product?

	W	X	Y	Z
(1)	$20,000	$20,000	$20,000	$20,000
(2)	$28,000	$20,000	$16,000	$16,000
(3)	$30,000	$23,334	$16,667	$10,000
(4)	$28,000	$24,000	$16,000	$12,000
(5)	Some other answer.			

(CPA adapted)

10.18 Physical Quantities Method (L.O. 2)

The following questions are based on Rote Company, which manufactures products X, Y, and Z from a joint process. Joint product costs were $63,000. Additional information is provided:

Product	Units Produced	Sales Value at Split-Off	If Processed Further Sales Values	If Processed Further Additional Costs
X	14,000	$80,000	$110,000	$18,000
Y	10,000	70,000	90,000	14,000
Z	4,000	50,000	60,000	10,000

a. Assuming that joint product costs are allocated using the physical quantities (units produced) method, what were the total costs of product X (including $18,000 if processed further)?

(1) $39,000.
(2) $40,500.
(3) $45,000.
(4) $49,500.
(5) Some other answer.

b. Assuming that joint product costs are allocated using the sales value at split-off (net realizable value method), what were the total costs of product Y (including the $14,000 if processed further)?

(1) $35,000.
(2) $36,050.
(3) $36,500.
(4) $39,200.
(5) Some other answer.

(CPA adapted)

10.19   Physical Quantities   Friendly Fertilizer Corporation uses organic materials to produce fertilizers for home gar-
            Method with   dens. Through its production processes, the company manufactures Nitro, a high nitrogen
            By-Product   fertilizer, and Phospho, a high phosphorus fertilizer. A by-product of the process is methane,
            (L.O. 4)   which is used to generate power for the company's operations. The fertilizers are sold either
                               in bulk to nurseries or in individual packages to home consumers. The company chooses to
                               allocate the costs on the basis of the physical quantities method.
                                   Last month, 250,000 units of input were processed at a total cost of $90,000. The output
                               of the process consisted of 50,000 units of Nitro, 75,000 units of Phospho, and 150,000 units
                               of methane. The by-product methane would have cost $2,000 had it been purchased from
                               the local gas utility. This is considered to be its net realizable value, which is deducted from
                               the processing costs of the main products.

            Required   What share of the joint costs should be assigned to each of the main products?

10.20   By-Products   Leather Products, Inc., engages in a manufacturing process that uses cowhide to produce
            (L.O. 4)   three outputs (leather, suede, dog chews). Leather and suede are considered main products,
                               and dog chews are a by-product. During a recent month, the following events occurred:

                               Produced and sold 200 units of leather and 100 units of suede. Produced 25 units of
                               dog chews.

                               Recorded $70,000 sales revenue from leather and suede. The cost of sales before
                               accounting for the by-product was $36,000.

                               Incurred $50 to process the 25 units of dog chews to completion. These costs are
                               charged as they are incurred against any by-product sales. (None of the by-product costs
                               are kept in inventory at the end of the period.)

                               Received $225 in revenue from the sale of the 25 units of dog chews.

            Required   Prepare a statement showing, in two columns (as in Illustration 10.11), the sales revenue,
                               other income, cost of goods sold, other relevant data, and gross margin that would be re-
                               ported for each of the two methods of by-product accounting described in the text.

10.21   By-Products—   The following questions are based on Seinfeld Corporation, which manufactures a product
            Multiple Choice   that gives rise to a by-product called Costanza. The only costs associated with Costanza are
            (L.O. 4)   additional processing costs of $1 for each unit. Seinfeld accounts for Costanza sales first by
                               deducting its separable costs from such sales and then by deducting this net amount from
                               the cost of sales of the major product. (This is method 1 discussed in the text. See Illustra-
                               tion 10.11, for example.) This year, 2,400 units of Costanza were produced. They were all
                               sold at $5 each.

            Required   a. Sales revenue and cost of goods sold from the main product were $400,000 and
                                   $200,000, respectively, for the year. What was the gross margin after considering the
                                   by-product sales and costs (that is, the "gross margin" in Illustration 10.11).
                                   (1) $195,200.
                                   (2) $200,000.
                                   (3) $209,600.
                                   (4) $204,800.
                                   (5) Some other answer.
                               b. If Seinfeld changes its method of accounting for Costanza sales by showing the net
                                   amount as other income, Seinfeld's *gross margin* would
                                   (1) Be unaffected.
                                   (2) Increase by $4,800.
                                   (3) Decrease by $4,800.
                                   (4) Decrease by $6,000.
                                   (5) Some other answer.
                               c. If Seinfeld changes its method of accounting as indicated in (*b*), what are the effects of
                                   the change on the company's profits?
                                   (1) No effect.
                                   (2) Increase by $4,800.
                                   (3) Decrease by $4,800.
                                   (4) Decrease by $6,000.
                                   (5) Some other answer.

                                                                                                    (CPA adapted)

10.22	Sell or Process Further (L.O. 3)	Yuba Sawmill, Inc., operates a sawmill facility. The company accounts for the bark chips that result from the primary sawing operation as a by-product. The chips are sold to another company at a price of $12 per hundred cubic feet. Normally, sales revenue from this bark is $900,000 per month. Processing bark chips incurs no direct cost.

As an alternative, the company can rent equipment that will process the chips and bag them for sale as horticultural bark. Approximately 30 percent of the bark will be graded "large" and will sell for $32 per hundred cubic feet. About 60 percent will be graded "medium" and will sell for $16 per hundred cubic feet. The remainder will be mulch and will sell for $4 per hundred cubic feet.

Costs of the equipment to process and bag the chips and the personnel to operate the equipment are $520,000 per month and are fixed regardless of the amount of bark processed.

Required — Assuming a typical month, should the company sell the bark for $12 per hundred cubic feet or process it further?

10.23 Constant Gross Margin Method (appendix) (L.O. 5) — Refer to Exercise 10.14. Allocate joint costs using the constant gross margin percentage method.

PROBLEMS

10.24 Net Realizable Value of Joint Products— Multiple Choice

Bryce Manufacturing Company buys zeon for $1.60 a gallon. At the end of distilling in Department 1, zeon splits off into three products: argon, xon, and neon. Argon is sold at the split-off point, with no further processing; xon and neon require further processing before they can be sold. Xon is fused in Department 2, and neon is solidified in Department 3. Following is a summary of costs and other related data for the year ended December 31.

	Department		
	(1) Distilling	**(2) Fusing**	**(3) Solidifying**
Cost of zeon.........	$192,000	—	—
Direct labor	48,000	$90,000	$130,000
Manufacturing overhead...........	40,000	42,000	108,000

	Products		
	Argon	**Xon**	**Neon**
Gallons sold.........	15,000	30,000	45,000
Gallons on hand at year-end	10,000	—	15,000
Sales in dollars.......	$60,000	$192,000	$283,500

There were no beginning inventories on hand at January 1, and there was no zeon on hand at the end of the year on December 31. All gallons on hand on December 31 were complete as to processing. Bryce uses the net realizable value method to allocate joint costs.

Required

a. For allocating joint costs, the net realizable value of argon for the year ended December 31 is
  (1) $60,000.
  (2) $50,000.
  (3) $100,000.
  (4) $40,000.
  (5) Some other answer.

b. The joint costs for the year ended December 31 to be allocated are
  (1) $650,000.
  (2) $280,000.
  (3) $232,000.
  (4) $192,000.
  (5) Some other answer.

c. The cost of xon sold for the year ended December 31 is
   (1) $188,000.
   (2) $132,000.
   (3) $177,714.
   (4) Some other answer.

d. The value of the ending inventory for argon is
   (1) $56,000.
   (2) $37,333.
   (3) $40,000.
   (4) Some other answer.

(CPA adapted)

10.25

Estimated Net Realizable Value and Effects of Processing Further

Miller Manufacturing Company produces three products by a joint production process. Raw materials are put into production in Department A, and at the end of processing in this department, three products appear. Product X is immediately sold at the split-off point, with no further processing. Products Y and Z require further processing before they are sold. Product Y is processed in Department B, and product Z is processed in Department C. The company uses the estimated net realizable value method of allocating joint production costs. Following is a summary of costs and other data for the quarter ended September 30.

No inventories were on hand at the beginning of the quarter or July 1. No raw material was on hand at September 30. All the units on hand at the end of the quarter were fully complete as to processing.

	Products		
	X	Y	Z
Pounds sold	40,000	118,000	140,000
Pounds on hand at September 30	100,000	–0–	80,000
Sales revenues	$30,000	$177,000	$245,000

	Departments		
	A	B	C
Raw material cost	$112,000	–0–	–0–
Direct labor cost	48,000	$80,900	$191,750
Manufacturing overhead	20,000	21,100	73,250

Required

a. Determine the following amounts for each product: (1) estimated net realizable value used for allocating joint costs, (2) joint costs allocated to each of the three products, (3) cost of goods sold, and (4) finished goods inventory costs, September 30.

b. Assume that the entire output of product X could be processed further at an additional cost of $2.00 per pound and then sold at a price of $4.30 per pound. What is the effect on operating profits if all the product X output for the quarter had been processed and sold, rather than all being sold at the split-off point?

c. Write a memo to management indicating whether the company should process product X further and why.

10.26

Finding Missing Data— Net Realizable Value

Air Extracts, Inc., manufactures nitrogen, oxygen, and hydrogen from a joint process. Each gas can be liquified and sold for more. Data on the process are as follows:

	Product			
	Nitrogen	Oxygen	Hydrogen	Total
Units produced.	8,000	4,000	2,000	14,000
Joint costs	$30,000[a]	(a)	(b)	$ 60,000
Sales value at split-off.	(c)	(d)	$15,000	100,000
Additional costs to liquify.	7,000	$ 5,000	3,000	15,000
Sales value if liquified	70,000	30,000	20,000	120,000

[a]This amount is the portion of the total joint cost of $60,000 that had been allocated to nitrogen.

Required

Determine the values for the lettered spaces.

(CPA adapted)

10.27 Joint Cost Allocations with By-Product

Exotic Aroma Company buys bulk flowers and processes them into perfumes in a two-stage process. Their highest-grade perfume, Seduction, and a residue that is processed into a medium-grade perfume, Romance, come from a certain mix of petals. In July, the company used 25,000 pounds of petals. The first stage is a joint process, reduction, that reduces the petals to Seduction and the residue. This first stage had the following costs:

- $400,000 direct materials.
- $220,000 direct labor.
- $180,000 overhead and other costs.

The additional costs of producing Romance in the second pressing stage were as follows:

- $44,000 direct materials.
- $100,000 direct labor.
- $80,000 overhead and other costs.

For July, total production equaled 10,000 ounces of Seduction and 42,000 ounces of Romance. There was no beginning inventory on July 1, nor were there uncompleted units.

Packaging costs incurred for each product as completed were $120,000 for Seduction and $308,000 for Romance. The sales price of Seduction is $180 an ounce; Romance sells for $63 per ounce.

Required

a. Allocate joint costs using the estimated net realizable value method. (Packaging and additional processing costs must be subtracted from revenue to compute net realizable values.)

b. Allocate the joint costs using the physical quantities method. Round all percentages to one decimal place.

c. Management is concerned about the large disparity in allocation amounts using the physical quantities method and has asked you to explain why this occurred. Write a memo to management explaining it.

d. Assume that Exotic Aroma can sell the squeezed petals from the reduction process to greenhouses for fertilizer. In July, 12,000 pounds of squeezed petals that were left over sold for $1.50 per pound. The squeezed petals are a by-product of reduction. Assume that the net realizable value of by-products reduces joint costs of main products. Answer parts (*a*) and (*b*) using this new information.

10.28 Cost Flows through T-Accounts

Refer to Problem 10.27. Show the flow of costs through T-accounts using the net realizable value method. Assume that the net realizable value of by-products in requirement (*d*) was credited to WIP Inventory and that the joint products were sold.

10.29 Joint Costing in a Process Costing Context— Estimated Net Realizable Value Method

Ninja Turtle Company produces three products: alpha, beta, and gamma. Alpha and gamma are main products; beta is a by-product of alpha. Information on the past month's production processes are as follows:

- In Department 1, 110,000 units of the raw material rho are processed at a total cost of $290,000. After processing in Department 1, 60 percent of the units are transferred to Department 2, and 40 percent of the units (now unprocessed gamma) are transferred to Department 3.

- In Department 2, the materials received from Department 1 are processed at an additional cost of $76,000. Seventy percent of the units become alpha and are transferred to Department 4. The remaining 30 percent emerge as beta and are sold at $4.20 per unit. The additional processing costs to make beta salable are $16,200.

- In Department 3, gamma is processed at an additional cost of $330,000. A normal loss of units of gamma occurs in this department. The loss equals 10 percent of the units of good output. The remaining good output is then sold for $24 per unit.

- In Department 4, alpha is processed at an additional cost of $32,960. After this processing, alpha can be sold for $10 per unit.

Required

Prepare a schedule showing the allocation of the $290,000 joint cost between alpha and gamma using the estimated net realizable value approach. Revenue from the sale of by-products should be credited to the manufacturing costs of the related main product (method 1 in the text).

(CPA adapted)

10.30   **Find Maximum Input Price— Estimated Net Realizable Value Method**

Harrison Corporation produces two joint products from its manufacturing operation. Product J sells for $41.50 per unit, and product M sells for $12 per unit at the split-off point. In a typical month, 38,000 units are processed; 30,000 units become Product M and 8,000 units become product J after an additional $56,250 of processing costs are incurred.

The joint process has only variable costs. In a typical month, the conversion costs of the joint products amount to $114,075. Materials prices are volatile, and if prices are too high, the company stops production.

Required

Management has asked you to determine the maximum price that the company should pay for the materials.

a. Calculate the maximum price that Harrison should pay for the materials.

b. Write a brief memo to management explaining how you arrived at your answer in requirement (*a*).

10.31   **Effect of By-Product versus Joint Cost Accounting**

Rambling Rose Corporation processes input Leonardo into three outputs: Michaelangelo, Raphael, and Donatello. Michaelangelo accounts for 60 percent of the net realizable value at the split-off point, Raphael accounts for 30 percent, and Donatello accounts for the balance. The joint costs total $365,500. If Donatello is accounted for as a by-product, its net realizable value at split-off of $37,600 is credited to the joint manufacturing costs using method 1 described in the text, which credits the by-product's net realizable value against the joint costs.

Required

a. What are the allocated joint costs for the three outputs
    (1) If Donatello is accounted for as a joint product?
    (2) If Donatello is accounted for as a by-product?

b. Management does not understand why no joint costs are allocated to Donatello when it is accounted for as a by-product. Write a brief memo explaining why this occurs.

10.32   **Joint Cost Allocation and Product Profitability**

Silicon Materials, Inc., processes silicon crystals into purified wafers and chips. Silicon crystals cost $60,000 per tank-car load. The process involves heating the crystals for 12 hours, producing 45,000 purified wafers with a market value of $20,000, and 15,000 chips with a market value of $140,000. The cost of the heat process is $25,600.

Required

a. If the crystal costs and the heat process costs are to be allocated on the basis of units of output, what cost would be assigned to each product?

b. If the crystal costs and the heat process costs are allocated on the basis of the net realizable value, what cost is assigned to each product?

c. How much profit or loss does the purified wafers product provide using the data in this problem and your analysis in requirement (*a*)? Is it really possible to determine which product is more profitable? Explain why or why not.

INTEGRATIVE CASE

10.33   **Effect of Cost Allocation on Pricing and Make versus Buy Decisions**

Ag-Coop is a large farm cooperative with a number of agriculture-related manufacturing and service divisions. As a cooperative, the company pays no federal income taxes. The company owns a fertilizer plant, which processes and mixes petrochemical compounds into three brands of agricultural fertilizer: Greenup, Maintane, and Winterizer. The three brands differ with respect to selling price and the proportional content of basic chemicals.

The Fertilizer Manufacturing Division transfers the completed product to the cooperative's Retail Sales Division at a price based on the cost of each type of fertilizer plus a markup.

The Manufacturing Division is completely automated so that the only costs incurred are the costs of the petrochemical feedstocks plus overhead that is all considered fixed. The primary feedstock costs $1.50 per pound. Each 100 pounds of feedstock can produce either of the following mixtures of fertilizer.

	Output Schedules (in pounds)	
	A	B
Greenup........	50	60
Maintane.......	30	10
Winterizer......	20	30

Production is limited to the 750,000 kilowatt-hours monthly capacity of the dehydrator. Due to different chemical makeup, each brand of fertilizer requires different dehydrator use. Dehydrator usage in kilowatt-hours per pound of product is

Product	Kilowatt-Hour Usage per Pound
Greenup........	32
Maintane.......	20
Winterizer......	40

Monthly fixed costs are $81,250. Now the company is producing according to output schedule A. Joint production costs including fixed overhead are allocated to each product on the basis of weight.

The fertilizer is packed into 100-pound bags for sale in the cooperative's retail stores. The Manufacturing Division charges the retail stores the cost plus a markup. The sales price for each product charged by the cooperative's Retail Sales Division is as follows:

	Sales Price per Pound
Greenup........	$10.50
Maintane.......	9.00
Winterizer......	10.40

Selling expenses are 20 percent of the sales price.

The manager of the Retail Sales Division has complained that the prices charged are excessive and that he would prefer to purchase from another supplier.

The Manufacturing Division manager argues that the processing mix was determined based on a careful analysis of the costs of each product compared to the prices charged by the Retail Sales Division.

Required

a. Assume that joint production costs including fixed overhead are allocated to each product on the basis of weight. What is the cost per pound of each product including fixed overhead and the feedstock cost of $1.50 per pound, given the current production schedule?

b. Assume that joint production costs including fixed overhead are allocated to each product on the basis of net realizable value if sold through the cooperative's Retail Sales Division. What is the allocated cost per pound of each product, given the current production schedule?

c. Assume that joint production costs including fixed overhead are allocated to each product on the basis of weight. Which of the two production schedules, A or B, produces the higher operating profit to the firm as a whole?

d. Would your answer to requirement (*c*) be different if joint production costs including fixed overhead are allocated to each product on the basis of net realizable value? If so, by how much?

SOLUTIONS TO SELF-STUDY QUESTIONS

1. The joint costs to be allocated amount to $52—the total of the $15 in direct materials costs and the $37 in conversion costs. The net realizable value for butter is $22, $1.10 per pound times 20 pounds. The net realizable value of the powder is $40.50, $.90 per pound times 45 pounds per hundred pounds of input. The allocation follows:

   To cocoa butter:

   $$\frac{\$22}{\$22 + \$40.50} \times \$52 = \$18.304$$

   To cocoa powder:

   $$\frac{\$40.50}{\$22 + \$40.50} \times \$52 = \$33.696$$

   This results in an allocation of the total cost of $52 (which is $18.304 + $33.696) to the two products.

2. Using the estimated net realizable value method, first compute the estimated net realizable value of cocoa butter of $21 ([$1.20 − $.15] × 20 pounds). Now the allocations are as follows:

   To cocoa butter:

   $$\frac{\$21}{\$21 + \$40.50} \times \$52 = \$17.756$$

   To cocoa powder:

   $$\frac{\$40.50}{\$21 + \$40.50} \times \$52 = \$34.244$$

   Compared to Self-Study Question 1, the allocation to cocoa butter has decreased and the allocation to cocoa powder has increased. Why did this happen? (Answer: The allocation of cocoa butter decreased because its estimated net realizable value also decreased.)

3. Since there is a total of 65 pounds of output of major products (20 pounds of butter and 45 pounds of powder) at the split-off point, the allocation is

   To cocoa butter:

   $$\frac{20}{20 + 45} \times \$52 = \$16.00$$

   To cocoa powder:

   $$\frac{45}{20 + 45} \times \$52 = \$36.00$$

   resulting in an allocation of the total $52 to the two products.

4. The by-product of 100 pounds of cocoa beans amounts to $7 [($.30 per pound selling price − $.10 per pound to process) × 35 pounds of cocoa shells produced].

   a. The joint costs are now reduced to $45 ($52 − $7 for the net realizable value of the by-product). The new joint cost allocations are:

   To cocoa butter:

   $$\frac{\$22}{\$22 + \$40.50} \times \$45 = \$15.84$$

   To cocoa powder:

   $$\frac{\$40.50}{\$22 + \$40.50} \times \$45 = \$29.16$$

   b.

   FERGUSON CONFECTIONS COMPANY
   Income Statement

Revenue from sale of cocoa butter and cocoa powder	$62.50
Other revenue from sale of shells	7.00
Total revenue	69.50
Joint production costs	52.00
Gross margin	$17.50

5.

	Cocoa Butter	Cocoa Powder	Total
Sales value	24.00	40.50	64.50
Joint costs	17.47	34.53	52.00
Additional process costs	3.00	0.00	3.00
Gross margin	3.53	5.97	9.50
Gross margin percentage	14.729%	14.729%	14.729%

Variable Costing

LEARNING OBJECTIVES

After reading this chapter, you should be able to:

1. Explain how variable costing supports managerial decisions.

2. See how additional information is provided on the income statement using the contribution margin format compared to the traditional format.

3. Compare and contrast product costs computed under variable costing to those computed using full-absorption costing.

4. Compare the effects of variable costing and full-absorption costing on the value chain.

5. Explain how normal costing with predetermined overhead rates is used in variable costing.

6. Understand the long-running debate over variable costing versus full-absorption costing.

7. Explain how variable costing and activity-based costing can be used concurrently.

8. Understand the ethics of increasing production to increase profits using full-absorption costing.

full-absorption costing
A system of accounting for costs in which both fixed and variable production costs are considered product costs.

variable costing (direct costing)
A system of cost accounting that assigns only the variable cost of production to products.

VARIABLE COSTING FOR DECISION MAKING

L.O. 1: Explain how variable costing supports managerial decisions.

Companies use various methods to report revenue, cost, and profit information. One method, called *full-absorption costing* (also called *absorption costing*) assumes that products fully absorb production costs. This chapter introduces an alternative method, *variable costing* (also called *direct costing*). Under **full-absorption costing,** all production costs, fixed and variable, are assigned to units produced. Under **variable costing,** only variable production costs are assigned to units produced. Fixed production costs are considered to be period expenses.[1]

This chapter compares full-absorption and variable costing. We examine the differences between the two methods that arise in cost flows, income statements, and decision making. We also discuss the uses for which the two methods are appropriate.

Have you ever wondered why airlines charge a fare from a few hundred to more than a thousand dollars for a seat on one flight? How can the same product (an airplane seat between two cities) vary by such a substantial amount? The answer lies in the cost structure of the airlines and the way they treat fixed and variable costs for pricing purposes.

Once an air carrier decides to offer a flight between two cities, more than 90 percent of the costs of that flight are fixed. Given a specific model of aircraft on the route, the flight costs the airline almost the same amount to operate whether the plane carries 5 or 300 passengers. Airlines can maximize revenues by setting a base fare that is high enough so that the revenues from travelers who need to take a specific flight cover the variable costs of carrying them plus the fixed costs of that flight.

Lower fares can be used to induce others to take additional seats on that particular flight. These lower fares need be only slightly in excess of the variable costs of the flight for the airline to increase profits. As a practical matter, the discount fares add substantially to airline operating profits.

For example, suppose that the costs of flying a 150-seat plane from Chicago to Boston are $20,000 fixed plus $15 per passenger variable. From past experience, an airline estimates that on the particular flight we are studying, approximately 80 passengers will take the flight regardless of ticket price. To cover the fixed and variable costs for those 80 passengers, the fare must amount to

$$\frac{\$20,000}{80} + \$15 = \$265$$

If the airline sets its full fare at $300, its operating profits from the flight are

Revenues ($300 × 80)	$24,000
Costs	
Fixed costs	20,000
Variable costs ($15 × 80)	1,200
Total costs	$21,200
Operating profits.	$ 2,800

However, there are 70 empty seats on that flight if only full-fare seats are sold. Suppose that the airline offers a discount fare of 60 percent off the regular fare to fill up some of the empty seats. This fare adds 40 more passengers to the flight. Operating profits are now

---

[1]Recall from Chapter 2 that total variable manufacturing costs vary with the volume of production while total fixed costs remain the same despite changes in production volume within a relevant range of activity. We explore the distinction between fixed and variable costs in more depth in Chapter 12.

REAL WORLD APPLICATION	Full versus Variable Costing in Banking

American National Bank in Chicago offers a check-processing service for small banks in the area. Small banks accumulate their day's checks and send them to American National, which presents them to the banks they are drawn on. The major variable costs of this service are for processing the checks and outside vendor charges, such as the use of the Federal Reserve clearinghouse for checks drawn on certain banks. In addition, fixed indirect costs are added to the variable costs of each product line. The sum of variable and fixed costs are full costs that cover all costs of running the bank, including general and administrative costs.

Several other financial institutions also offer this service. Although American National relies on its excellent reputation for quality service to justify charging a higher price than its competitors do, it nevertheless has dropped its prices in recent years to avoid losing customers. At one point, its prices were less than 80 percent of the unit costs charged to the product line. Although it appeared that the bank could not justify continuing to offer the service based on a comparison of prices and full costs, several executives were not convinced that the full cost numbers developed for monthly financial reporting purposes were appropriate for the decision about whether to drop this service. Consequently, these executives decided to analyze which costs and revenues would change from dropping the service.

Their analysis indicated that few, if any, of the indirect costs allocated to the product lines would be saved if this service were dropped. Further, some of the processing costs included depreciation and other costs that would not be a cash savings if the service were discontinued. Their analysis indicated that the bank could lose several million dollars in contribution margin if the service were dropped. Based on this analysis, the bank decided against dropping the service.

Source: Based on the authors' research.

Revenues	
Full fare ($300 × 80)	$24,000
Discount ($120 × 40)	4,800
Total revenues.	$28,800
Costs	
Fixed costs	20,000
Variable costs ($15 × 120)	1,800
Total costs	$21,800
Operating profits	$ 7,000

Profits from the flight have increased from $2,800 to $7,000 (250 percent) despite offering seats at a 60 percent discount.

Of course, this solution assumes that none of the full-fare passengers will buy discount tickets. It also assumes that a larger plane will not be needed to accommodate the added passenger load. To avoid losing full-fare passengers to discounting, airlines put restrictions on the discount tickets. The other issues involved in fare setting to maximize profits for varying cost structures are complex.

Major airlines have marketing departments that have been creative in setting fares. Marketing managers need to know all the costs of operating a flight, both fixed and variable, to set fares.

Decision Application

Most managers recognize the difference between variable costs and full-absorption costs in decision making. Managers need to know all the costs of operating a business, both fixed and variable, to set prices and estimate costs that change with output. Variable costing statements provide that information. The Real World Application on this page tells how managers in a Chicago bank wisely knew this difference.

ILLUSTRATION 11.1	**Income Statement Comparison: Traditional and Contribution Margin Format**

STONEWALL MANUFACTURING

Traditional Format	January–February Total	Contribution Margin Format	January–February Total
Sales revenue	$90,000	Sales revenue	$90,000
Cost of goods sold	52,000	Less	
Gross margin	38,000	Variable cost of goods sold	36,000
Marketing and		Variable marketing and administrative costs . . .	4,000
administrative costs	28,000	Contribution margin	50,000
Operating profit	$10,000	Less	
		Fixed manufacturing costs	16,000
		Fixed marketing and administrative costs	24,000
		Operating profit	$10,000

USING CONTRIBUTION MARGIN INCOME STATEMENTS

L.O. 2: See how additional information is provided on the income statement using the contribution margin format compared to the traditional format.

contribution margin format
The format of a financial statement that shows the contribution margin as an intermediate step in the computation of operating profits or income.

Traditional income statement formats do not lend themselves to variable costing because they do not separate fixed and variable costs. The format used with variable costing is known as the **contribution margin format.** The variable costing income statements in this chapter use the contribution margin format. For comparative purposes, the two formats are shown in Illustration 11.1. These two statements are based on the Stonewall Manufacturing example we will be presenting throughout this chapter.

If income statements are used to make decisions involving changes in volume, the contribution margin format can be very helpful. Managers can often better understand relationships between prices, costs, and volume with the contribution margin format than with the traditional approach. Further, the contribution margin format presents more information—namely, the breakdown of costs into fixed and variable portions.

Note the difference between the *contribution margin* and the *gross margin* in Illustration 11.1. The total contribution margin is $50,000 and represents the net revenue available to meet fixed costs and provide operating profits. The contribution margin ratio represents the fraction of each revenue dollar contributed toward fixed costs and profits. For the illustration, this amount is 55.6 percent, which is $50,000 ÷ $90,000.

On the other hand, the gross margin is the difference between revenues and production costs, regardless of whether those production costs are fixed or variable.

COMPARING VARIABLE COSTING WITH FULL-ABSORPTION COSTING

L.O. 3: Compare and contrast product costs computed under variable costing to those computed using full-absorption costing.

This section presents a numerical comparison of variable and full-absorption costing. Assume the facts for Stonewall Manufacturing for the months of January and February shown in the following chart.

	January	February
Units		
Beginning inventory	–0–	100
Production	1,000	1,000
Sales	900	1,100
Ending inventory (all units finished at the end of the period; no WIP inventory)	100	–0–

Costs	January	February
Variable production costs		
(per unit produced)		
Direct materials	$ 10	$ 10
Direct labor	5	5
Variable manufacturing overhead	3	3
Fixed production costs (per month)	8,000	8,000
Variable marketing costs (per unit sold) . . .	2	2
Fixed marketing and administrative		
costs (per month)	12,000	12,000
Price per unit sold	$ 45	$ 45

actual costing
A system of accounting that assigns overhead based on actual overhead costs incurred.

normal costing
A system of accounting that charges direct materials and direct labor to objects at actual costs and applies manufacturing overhead using a predetermined overhead rate.

Illustration 11.2 presents the flow of production costs through T-accounts in January for both full-absorption and variable costing. For now, we use **actual costing;** that is, actual direct materials, direct labor, and manufacturing overhead costs are debited to WIP Inventory. (Later in the chapter, we use **normal costing,** which is like actual costing except that manufacturing overhead is debited to WIP Inventory using a predetermined rate.)

Note that although total actual costs incurred are the same under both full-absorption and variable costing, fixed production costs are debited to WIP Inventory under full-absorption costing but not under variable costing. As a consequence, the amounts in WIP Inventory and Finished Goods Inventory are higher under full-absorption costing.

Under full-absorption costing, the inventory value is as follows:

Number of units × (Variable production cost per unit + Fixed production cost per unit)

$$= 100 \text{ units} \times \left(\$18 + \frac{\$8,000 \text{ fixed production costs}}{1,000 \text{ units}} \right)$$
$$= 100 \times (\$18 + \$8)$$
$$= \$2,600$$

Under variable costing, the inventory value is

Number of units × Variable production cost per unit
100 units × $18 = $1,800

product costs
Costs attributed to a product.

period costs
Costs attributed to time intervals.

Fixed production costs are treated as **product costs** and therefore are assigned to each unit under full-absorption costing. Under variable costing, they are treated as **period costs** and thus are expensed in the period incurred.

Note that all production costs must be either expensed or inventoried for both methods. The fundamental concept follows:

Cost incurred − Inventory increase + Inventory decrease = Cost expensed

Using full-absorption costing, increases and decreases in finished goods and WIP inventory are more than they are using variable costing because these inventories include fixed production costs. For example, note the relation between production costs incurred and those expensed under the two systems shown in Illustration 11.3.

Both methods treat variable production costs as product costs and marketing and administrative costs as period expenses. The source of the *difference* is the treatment of fixed production costs. *Fixed production costs are treated as product costs under full-absorption costing and as period expenses under variable costing.*

Effects on Profits

As shown in Illustration 11.4, the $800 higher profit in January under full-absorption costing is exactly the same as the difference in the amount of costs inventoried under the two methods. Full absorption inventories $800 of fixed production costs that are

**ILLUSTRATION   11.2   Variable and Full-Absorption Costing Comparison:
Flow of Production Costs**

STONEWALL MANUFACTURING
January

Full-Absorption Costing

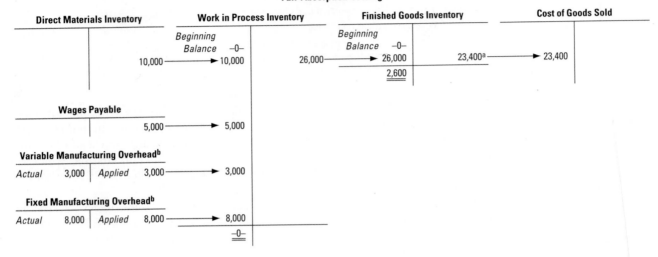

Variable Costing

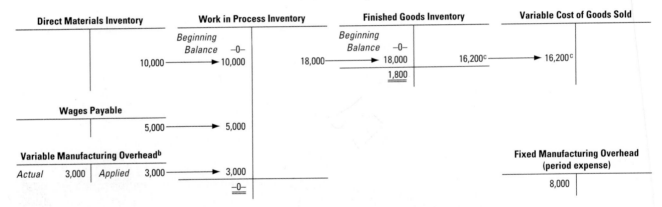

[a]$23,400 = 900 × ($8 + $18) = 900 × $26.

[b]We have placed actual and applied overhead in the same account with actual costs as debits and applied costs as credits for convenience in presentation. An alternative is to place actual overhead in one account and applied overhead in another account. Both methods are used in practice.

[c]Variable cost of goods sold = $18 per unit (direct materials, direct labor, and variable manufacturing overhead) × 900 units sold = $16,200.

ILLUSTRATION 11.3	Production Costs Incurred and Expensed when Production Volume Exceeds Sales Volume

STONEWALL MANUFACTURING
January

	Production Costs Incurred	Minus Increase in Inventory	Equals Production Costs Expensed
Full-Absorption Costing			
Variable manufacturing costs	$18,000	$1,800ª	$16,200ᵇ
Fixed manufacturing costs	8,000	800ᶜ	7,200ᵈ
Total	$26,000	$2,600	$23,400
Variable Costing			
Variable manufacturing costs	$18,000	$1,800ª	$16,200ᵇ
Fixed manufacturing costs	8,000	–0–	8,000
Total	$26,000	$1,800	$24,200

ª$1,800 = 100 units inventoried × $18 per unit.

ᵇ$16,200 = 900 units sold × $18 per unit.

ᶜ$800 = 100 units inventoried × $8 per unit.

ᵈ$7,200 = 900 units sold × $8 per unit.

ILLUSTRATION 11.4	Variable and Full-Absorption Costing Comparison: Income Statements

STONEWALL MANUFACTURING
January

Full-Absorption Costing

Sales revenue	$40,500ª
Cost of goods sold	23,400
Gross margin	17,100
Marketing and administrative costs	13,800ᵇ
Operating profit	$ 3,300

Variable Costing

Sales revenue	$40,500ª
Less	
Variable cost of goods sold	16,200
Variable marketing and administrative costs	1,800ᶜ
Contribution margin........................	22,500
Less	
Fixed manufacturing costs..................	8,000
Fixed marketing and administrative costs	12,000
Operating profit	$ 2,500

ª$45 × 900 units sold = $40,500.

ᵇFixed costs + Variable costs = $12,000 + ($2 × 900 units sold) = $13,800.

ᶜ$2 × 900 units sold = $1,800.

expensed under variable costing. Hence, under full-absorption, costs expensed are $800 lower and operating profits are $800 higher than under variable costing. Under full absorption, the expensing of $800 of fixed production costs is deferred until the period when the units are sold.

As a general rule, under full-absorption costing, *when units produced exceed units sold* in a period, a portion of the period's fixed production costs is inventoried rather than expensed in that period. Under variable costing, however, all of the period's fixed production costs are expensed. Thus, when production exceeds sales, fewer fixed production costs are expensed, and operating profits are higher under full-absorption than under variable costing.

On the other hand, if units sold exceed units produced, more fixed production costs are expensed under full-absorption costing, so operating profits are lower under full-absorption than under variable costing. We show this case in Illustration 11.5, which presents Stonewall Manufacturing's cost flows for February. The

ILLUSTRATION   11.5   Variable and Full-Absorption Costing Comparison: Flow of Production Costs

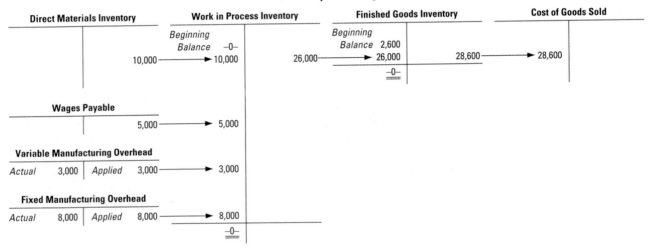

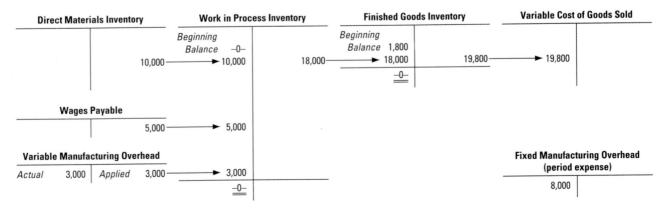

company produced 1,000 units and sold 1,100 units, including 100 units from inventory. In this case, full-absorption costing expenses more fixed production costs than does variable costing, because full absorption now expenses the fixed production costs that were deferred from January.

Our analysis of production costs in February is summarized in Illustration 11.6. Note that production costs expensed equal costs incurred plus the decrease in inventory. Note in Illustration 11.3 that in January, production costs expensed equaled costs incurred minus the increase in inventory.

Illustration 11.7 compares full-absorption costing (FAC) and variable costing (VC) at Stonewall Manufacturing for January and February. It presents some important results.

First, Illustration 11.7 shows that operating profit for the two-month period is the same—$10,000—under both methods. This occurs because the company had no units in inventory at either the beginning or end of the period in question. Operating profits were higher under full-absorption costing in January, however, because units produced exceeded units sold. The reverse was true in February.

Second, Illustration 11.7 shows that the difference in operating profits between the two costing methods (FAC is greater than VC by $800 in January, and VC is greater than FAC by $800 in February) equals the differences in the changes in the Finished Goods Inventory account. In January, FAC inventory increased by $2,600; VC inventory increased by $1,800. In February, FAC inventory decreased by $2,600; VC inventory decreased by $1,800.

Third, the difference in operating profits in each period equals the difference in fixed production costs expensed under the two systems.

In general, if no inventories exist, operating profits are the same under both methods. If production volume equals sales volume, the profit figures differ only if the fixed production costs per unit differ in beginning and ending inventory.

ILLUSTRATION 11.6	**Production Costs Incurred and Expensed when Sales Volume Exceeds Production Volume**		
	STONEWALL MANUFACTURING February		
	Production Costs Incurred	**Plus Decrease in Inventory**	**Equals Production Costs Expensed**
Full-absorption costing			
Variable manufacturing costs	$18,000	$1,800[a]	$19,800[b]
Fixed manufacturing costs	8,000	800[c]	8,800[d]
Total	$26,000	$2,600	$28,600
Variable costing			
Variable manufacturing costs	$18,000	$1,800[a]	$19,800[b]
Fixed manufacturing costs	8,000	–0–	8,000
Total	$26,000	$1,800	$27,800

[a]$1,800 = 100 units from inventory × $18 variable cost per unit.

[b]$19,800 = 1,100 units sold × $18 variable cost per unit.

[c]$800   = 100 units from inventory × $8 fixed cost per unit.

[d]$8,800 = 1,100 units sold × $8 fixed cost per unit.

ILLUSTRATION 11.7	Variable and Full-Absorption Costing Comparison: Comparative Income Statements

STONEWALL MANUFACTURING
January and February

Full-Absorption Costing

	January	February	Total
Sales revenue	$40,500	$49,500	$90,000
Cost of goods sold	23,400	28,600	52,000
Gross margin	17,100	20,900	38,000
Marketing and administrative costs	13,800[a]	14,200[b]	28,000
Operating profits.	$ 3,300	$ 6,700	$10,000
Change in finished goods inventory.	+$ 2,600[c]	−$ 2,600[d]	−0−

Variable Costing

	January	February	Total
Sales revenue	$40,500	$49,500	$90,000
Less			
Variable cost of goods sold	16,200	19,800	36,000
Variable marketing and administrative costs	1,800	2,200	4,000
Contribution margin.	22,500	27,500	50,000
Less			
Fixed manufacturing costs.	8,000	8,000	16,000
Fixed marketing and administrative costs	12,000	12,000	24,000
Operating profits.	$ 2,500	$ 7,500	$10,000
Change in finished goods inventory.	+$ 1,800[c]	−$ 1,800[d]	−0−

[a]$12,000 + ($2 × 900 units sold) = $13,800.

[b]$12,000 + ($2 × 1,100 units sold) = $14,200.

[c]From Illustration 11.2.

[d]From Illustration 11.5.

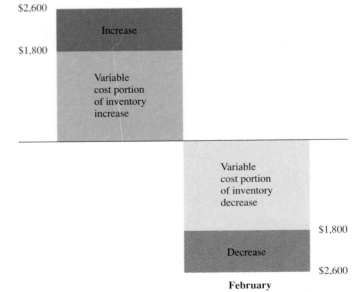

Important Observations

Four important observations should be noted before leaving this discussion. First, our example assumes that a portion of manufacturing overhead is the only fixed cost. In fact, some or all of direct labor might be fixed as well. This occurs when direct labor costs are neither reduced when production volume decreases nor increased when production volume increases. If direct labor is fixed, it is treated as a *product* cost under full-absorption costing and a *period* cost under variable costing, just like fixed manufacturing overhead in our example.

Second, although our example has assumed that finished goods are the only inventories, the results also hold for WIP inventory. That is, fixed production costs are part of WIP inventory under full-absorption costing, but they are not under variable costing.

Third, this entire discussion refers only to production costs, which are the only costs inventoried. It does *not* refer to marketing and administrative costs, which are not inventoried.

Fourth, we find that companies usually use FIFO for internal reporting purposes. External financial reports usually are based on an adjustment to FIFO data. All problems in this chapter assume FIFO to be consistent with practice.

SELF-STUDY QUESTION

1. Mario Enterprises produced 84,000 units last year and sold 76,000 units. Costs incurred that year follow:

Direct materials.	$462,000
Direct labor	315,000
Variable manufacturing overhead	105,000
Fixed manufacturing overhead	399,000
Variable marketing and administrative costs	50,400
Fixed marketing and administrative costs	200,600

a. Compute the product cost per unit (that is, the inventoriable amount per unit) using full-absorption and variable costing.
b. Prepare income statements. Assume that Mario had no beginning or ending inventories except for the 8,000 units in finished goods ending inventory. Mario sold its product for $20 per unit.
c. Explain why operating profits under full-absorption costing are higher (or lower) than under variable costing.

The solution to this question is at the end of this chapter on page 342.

EFFECTS ON THE VALUE CHAIN

L.O. 4: Compare the effects of variable costing and full-absorption costing on the value chain.

The effects of using full-absorption costing versus variable costing on the value chain depend on the section of the value chain being considered. We have addressed selected areas of the value chain:

Production: Full-absorption costing may create the incentive to produce more than is necessary to "hide" fixed costs in ending inventory. Excess inventory is the result of performing nonvalue-added activities to hide fixed costs.

Marketing: Prices set based on full-absorption costing may be overstated or understated as fixed costs are allocated to products based on some arbitrary cost driver. If the quality of data used for decision making can be improved (by using variable costing in this example), thus helping managers to make better decisions, value is added to the company.

Customer service: Management may decide to eliminate a product using variable costing because the price does not exceed variable costs. We may assume that this adds value to the company because an unprofitable product has been eliminated. However, other factors must also be considered. Marketing may need the product for strategic reasons. Customers who buy the unprofitable product (in relatively small quantities) also may buy other products with relatively large contribution margins in large quantities. These customers may demand a large and diverse product line. Thus, value-added activities are not always clear cut. Although eliminating an unprofitable product may seem prudent, the larger picture may show that the product actually adds value by enabling marketing to obtain customers who demand large and diverse product lines.

EFFECT OF PREDETERMINED OVERHEAD RATES

L.O. 5: Explain how normal costing with predetermined overhead rates is used in variable costing.

Normal costing uses predetermined overhead rates to apply manufacturing overhead to production; direct materials and direct labor are charged to objects at actual costs. In the previous example, we compared full-absorption costing with variable costing when there were no manufacturing overhead cost variances. When a manufacturing overhead cost variance exists, as under normal costing, the mechanics of comparison become a little more difficult. The essential effects of the different costing methods on calculated profits remain the same as previously discussed, however.

For example, assume that Stonewall Manufacturing decided to use predetermined manufacturing overhead rates of $1.75 per actual direct labor-hour for variable manufacturing overhead and $3.50 per direct labor-hour for fixed manufacturing overhead. In both January and February, each unit required an average of two direct labor-hours to make. You can also think of overhead as applied at the rate of $3.50 per unit produced for *variable* manufacturing overhead and $7 per unit produced for *fixed* manufacturing overhead. These rates were used for both January and February.

Illustration 11.8 shows the flow of production costs for January under both variable and full-absorption costing. (Recall that 1,000 units were produced and 900 were sold in January.) A comparison of Illustration 11.8 with Illustration 11.2 indicates that actual and applied manufacturing overhead are no longer equal; overapplied variable overhead is $500 and underapplied fixed overhead $1,000. We assume that the overhead variance is written off as a period cost, not prorated to inventories and cost of goods sold.

Illustration 11.9 compares full-absorption and variable costing when an overhead variance exists. Note the over- or underapplied overhead.

The use of predetermined overhead rates instead of actual costs in normal costing usually has little effect on the relationship between full-absorption and variable costing. For example, a comparison of Illustration 11.7 (no overhead variance) with Illustration 11.9 (with overhead variance) shows two key similarities:

- The conceptual difference between full-absorption and variable costing is the same whether or not an overhead variance exists. Differences in operating profits occur because fixed production costs are inventoried under full-absorption costing but not under variable costing.

- When all inventory is sold at the end of a period, total operating profits are the same under all methods. For example, in Illustrations 11.7 and 11.9, operating profits for the entire period, January and February, are $10,000, whether or not an overhead variance exists and whether full-absorption or variable costing is used.

ILLUSTRATION   11.8   **Variable and Full-Absorption Costing Comparison: Flow of Production Costs with Overhead Variances**

STONEWALL MANUFACTURING
January

Full-Absorption Costing

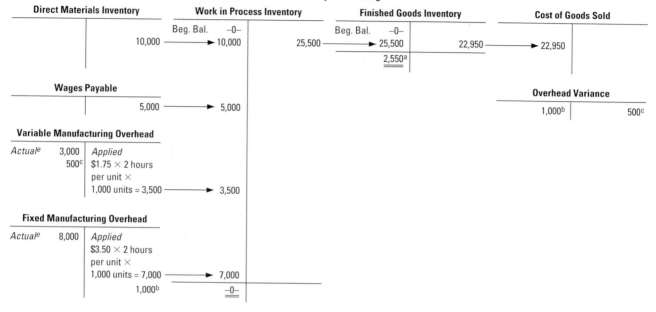

Variable Costing

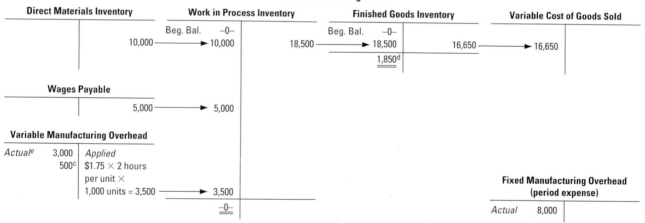

[a]$2,550 = 100 units left in inventory $\times \dfrac{\$25,500}{1,000 \text{ units produced}}$.

[b]This entry closes the Fixed Manufacturing Overhead account. Amount is included in the line below "Cost of goods sold" in Illustration 11.9.

[c]This entry closes the Variable Manufacturing Overhead account. Amount is included in the line below "Cost of goods sold" in Illustration 11.9.

[d]$1,850 = 100 units left in inventory $\times \dfrac{\$18,500}{1,000 \text{ units produced}}$.

[e]To simplify the presentation, we have combined the actual and applied overhead into one account. In practice, you may find actual and applied overhead combined in one account or separated into two accounts—one for actual and one for applied.

ILLUSTRATION 11.9	Variable and Full-Absorption Costing: Comparative Income Statements

STONEWALL MANUFACTURING
January and February

	January	February	Total
Full-Absorption Costing			
Sales revenue	$40,500	$49,500	$90,000
Less			
Cost of goods sold	22,950[a]	28,050[b]	51,000
Underapplied overhead	500[c]	500[d]	1,000
Gross margin	17,050	20,950	38,000
Less: Marketing and administrative costs	13,800	14,200	28,000
Operating profits	$ 3,250	$ 6,750	$10,000
Change in finished goods inventory	+$ 2,550	−$ 2,550	−0−
Variable costing			
Sales revenue	$40,500	$49,500	$90,000
Less: Variable cost of goods sold	16,650[e]	20,350[f]	37,000
Add: Overapplied variable overhead.	500[g]	500[g]	1,000
Less: Variable marketing and administrative costs	1,800	2,200	4,000
Contribution margin	22,550	27,450	50,000
Less			
Fixed manufacturing costs	8,000	8,000	16,000
Fixed marketing and administrative costs	12,000	12,000	24,000
Operating profits	$ 2,550	$ 7,450	$10,000
Change in finished goods inventory	+$ 1,850	−$ 1,850	−0−

[a]$22,950 = 900 units sold × $25.50 cost per unit.

[b]$28,050 = 1,100 units sold × $25.50 cost per unit. It also equals the cost of producing 1,000 units, or $25,500, plus the $2,550 cost of the 100 units sold from beginning finished goods inventory.

[c]The $500 underapplied overhead is the net result of $1,000 underapplied fixed manufacturing overhead and $500 overapplied variable manufacturing overhead. (See Illustration 11.8.)

[d]The underapplied overhead is the same in February as in January because all production quantities and costs are the same in February as in January.

[e]$16,650 = 900 units sold × $18.50 cost per unit.

[f]$20,350 = 1,100 units sold × $18.50 cost per unit. It also equals the variable cost of producing 1,000 units, or $18,500, plus the $1,850 cost of the 100 units sold from beginning finished goods inventory.

[g]See Illustration 11.8. Overapplied variable overhead is the same in February as in January because all production quantities and costs are the same in both months.

SELF-STUDY QUESTION

2. Refer to the data in Self-Study Question 1. Now assume Mario Enterprises uses normal costing and applies variable manufacturing overhead at the rate of 40 percent of direct labor costs and fixed manufacturing overhead at the rate of 125 percent of direct labor costs. Note that applied overhead equals these predetermined rates times the actual direct labor cost.
   a. Compute the product cost per unit (that is, the inventoriable amount per unit) using full-absorption costing and variable costing.
   b. Prepare income statements. Assume that Mario had no beginning or ending inventories except the 8,000 units in ending finished goods inventory. Mario sold its product for $20 per unit.

The solution to this question is at the end of this chapter on page 342.

THE LONG-RUNNING DEBATE OVER VARIABLE VERSUS FULL-ABSORPTION COSTING

L.O. 6: Understand the long-running debate over variable costing versus full-absorption costing.

The desirability of full-absorption costing versus variable costing has been debated for decades.[2] For the most part, differences of opinion stem from the search for a "conceptually superior" method to value inventory and measure income in external financial statements. Our perspective is much different. *We are not as concerned about selecting a "true" measure of inventory value or net income as we are with selecting the cost measure that is most appropriate for decision making, after considering the costs and benefits of alternative costing methods.*

The most appropriate cost measure is usually situation specific; it depends on the nature of the decision and costs, the preferences of decision makers, and many other factors. As the airline and other industries have learned, full costs may be appropriate for some decisions and variable costs for others. The accountant's objective is to provide the information that is most useful in a specific setting. The appropriate method depends on the decision at hand. The following discussions present advantages of each costing method—variable and full-absorption—for different uses by decision makers.

Advantages of Variable Costing; Disadvantages of Full-Absorption Costing

Variable Costing Breaks Down Production Costs into Fixed and Variable Components

Many managerial decisions require a breakdown of costs into variable and fixed components. The variable costing method is consistent with this breakdown, but the full-absorption costing method is not; it treats fixed production costs as if they were unit (that is, variable) costs. Note also that variable costing presents more data than does full-absorption costing in Illustration 11.7. Variable costing presents fixed and variable cost breakdowns and contribution margins.

Managers usually prefer to plan and control variable costs on a unit basis and fixed costs on a period basis. For example, managers plan and control the amount of direct materials and direct labor required to make a unit of output or the number of hours required to perform a job. Building rent, property taxes, and other fixed costs are planned and controlled per week, month, or year. It seldom makes much managerial sense to refer to rent costs as an amount per unit produced. Instead, rent is referred to as an amount per month.

Criticism of Unit Fixed Cost under Full-Absorption Costing

Treating fixed costs as unit costs can be misleading. A unit fixed cost is a function of both the amount of fixed costs and the volume of activity. Any given unit fixed cost is valid only when production equals the number of units used to calculate the fixed cost per unit.

For example, a plant manager observed that fixed maintenance costs had decreased from $12 per unit of output in May to $10 per unit in August. She was on her way to congratulate the Maintenance Department manager for the cost reduction when she stopped in the plant controller's office. There she learned that maintenance costs had *increased* from $12,000 in May to $18,000 in August. Meanwhile, volume had increased from 1,000 units in May to 1,800 units in August. This explained the decrease in unit costs from $12 ($12,000 ÷ 1,000 units) to $10 ($18,000 ÷ 1,800 units).

The plant manager knew that maintenance costs are supposed to be fixed; they should not have increased when volume increased. When she investigated further, she found that the Maintenance Department manager had hired several temporary employees to cover for a major absenteeism problem that occurred in August.

The moral of this story is that the conversion of fixed manufacturing costs to unit costs, which is done under full-absorption costing, can be misleading. Managers frequently find it necessary to convert the "unitized" fixed manufacturing cost (that

---

[2]For example, see C. Horngren and G. Sorter, "Direct Costing for External Reporting," *The Accounting Review,* January 1961; and J. Fremgen, "The Direct Costing Controversy—An Identification of Issues," *The Accounting Review,* January 1964.

is, the $12 and $10 per unit in the previous example) back to the original total for performance evaluation and decision-making purposes.

Variable Costing Removes the Effects of Inventory Changes from Income Measurement

Another advantage to variable costing is that it removes the effects of inventory changes from income measurement. For example, under full-absorption costing, a company could increase its reported profits by building up inventory or decrease them by reducing inventory.

For example, Full Products, Inc., uses full-absorption costing to value inventory. After seeing the period 1 financial statements shown in the bottom part of Illustration 11.10, the board of directors fired the president and hired a new one, stating, "Whatever else you do, increase profits in period 2."

The new president promptly stepped up production from 100,000 units to 200,000 units, as shown in column 2 of Illustration 11.10. Operating profits increased from $0 in period 1 to $200,000 in period 2, and the new president collected a generous bonus.

Was Full Products, Inc., more profitable in period 2? No; in fact, the company had 100,000 additional units in inventory to carry and sell. The apparent increase in profits is due solely to the deferral of fixed manufacturing costs under full-absorption costing by increasing ending inventory. Variable costing would expense the entire $400,000 of fixed production costs in period 2 despite the increase in inventory. Thus, the period 2 operating profits would have been zero under variable costing—the same as in period 1.

In short, variable costing tends to fit managerial decision models better than full-absorption costing does. In subsequent chapters in this book, when we discuss uses of accounting information for managerial decision making, planning, and perfor-

---

ILLUSTRATION 11.10 | **Profit Improvement Program**

FULL PRODUCTS, INC.

Facts

	(1) Period 1	(2) Period 2
Sales units	100,000	100,000
Production units	100,000	200,000
Selling price per unit	$ 10	$ 10
Variable manufacturing cost per unit	5	5
Fixed manufacturing costs per period	400,000	400,000
Fixed manufacturing costs per unit produced	4	2
Marketing and administrative costs per period	100,000	100,000

Income Statements
(Full-Absorption Costing Methods)

Sales	$1,000,000	$1,000,000
Cost of goods sold.	900,000[a]	700,000[b]
Gross margin	100,000	300,000
Marketing and administrative costs.	100,000	100,000
Operating profits	–0–	$ 200,000

---

[a]$900,000 = 100,000 units sold × ($5 + $4) manufacturing costs per unit.

[b]$700,000 = 100,000 units sold × ($5 + $2) manufacturing costs per unit.

mance evaluation, we assume that the company uses variable costing for internal purposes unless otherwise stated.

Advantages of Full-Absorption Costing; Disadvantages of Variable Costing

Neither the Financial Accounting Standards Board (FASB) nor the Internal Revenue Service (IRS) has recognized variable costing as *generally acceptable* in valuing inventory for external reports and tax purposes. The IRS defines inventory cost to include (1) direct materials and supplies entering into or consumed in connection with the product, (2) expenditures for direct labor, and (3) indirect expenses incident to and necessary for the production of the particular item. Indirect expenses necessary for production would include fixed production costs. Thus, the most obvious advantage of full-absorption costing is that it complies with FASB pronouncements and tax laws.

Proponents of full-absorption costing contend that this method recognizes the importance of fixed production costs. They hold that all production costs are costs of the product. Further, they argue, companies that build up inventories in anticipation of additional increases in sales are penalized under variable costing: They should be allowed to defer fixed production costs until the goods are sold, just as they defer variable production costs.

In practice, companies may prepare *both* variable and full-absorption costing income statements, depending on how such information is used. Variable costing reports can be used for internal purposes; full-absorption reports are prepared for external use. Preparation of many kinds of reports based on alternative accounting methods is possible at rapid speed and low cost with appropriately programmed computer equipment.

Another advantage of full-absorption costing is that it may be less costly to implement since it does not require a breakdown of production costs into fixed and variable components. Although some production costs may fall neatly into fixed or variable categories, others do not. Supervision, indirect labor, and utilities, for example, are seldom either entirely fixed or entirely variable. Hence, variable costing may be more costly to implement than full-absorption costing. Like other accounting system choices, the costs and benefits of each method should dictate the best course of action in specific situations.

SOURCE OF INFORMATION: ACTIVITY-BASED COSTING

L.0. 7: Explain how variable costing and activity-based costing can be used concurrently.

The costs used for variable costing often come from an activity-based costing system. Remember that activity-based costing assigns indirect costs first to activities and then to products based on each product's use of activities. Costs are categorized using the cost hierarchy as follows:

1. *Capacity-related costs* generated by activities such as building rent.
2. *Product- and customer-level costs* generated by activities such as product and customer records.
3. *Batch-related costs* generated by activities such as machine setups.
4. *Unit-level costs* generated by activities such as energy to run machines.

Management decisions affecting category 1 would likely affect all four categories. Management decisions affecting category 4 would likely have a minimal impact on categories 1 through 3, thus the term *hierarchy of costs.*

By categorizing costs in one of the four categories in the cost hierarchy, we are better able to identify fixed and variable costs. Category 1 costs are clearly fixed; category 4 costs are typically variable. Categories 2 and 3 depend on the nature of the activity. For example, product- and customer-level costs that include marketing staff salaries might be considered fixed costs while product order-processing costs are likely variable. Most batch-level costs are typically variable because they are driven by the number of batches (for example, machine setups).

Let's look at an example of how data for a variable costing income statement could come from an activity-based costing system. Zoom Trucking Company transports furniture and auto parts. To keep the example simple, we introduce only one or two costs for each cost hierarchy category. In reality, many more costs would be incurred to run a trucking company. The following costs and related activities (cost drivers) have been identified:

1. *Capacity-related cost:* Garage rent of $50,000 per year is a fixed cost.
2. *Product- and customer-level cost:* Order processing ($100 per order) is a variable cost because temporary employees handle this process. Salaried customer support ($30,000 per year) is a fixed cost.
3. *Batch-related cost:* Truck setup ($500 per truck load for auto parts and $750 per truck load for furniture). These are fixed costs at $62,500 per year because salaried employees are responsible for truck setups.
4. *Unit-level cost:* Truck operating cost is based on miles driven ($1.00 per mile), a strictly variable cost.

Assume that Zoom made 60 furniture deliveries (or orders) and 35 deliveries (or orders) of auto parts during the year. A total of 15,000 miles were driven during the year. Sales revenue totals $150,000 for the year. How would variable costing be applied to this scenario?

Using the variable costing approach, all fixed costs are period expenses and all variable manufacturing costs are product costs. Thus, the result of our example is as follows:

Sales revenue	$150,000
Less	
Variable cost of services (15,000 miles × $1.00)	15,000
Variable marketing and administrative costs	
(95 orders × $100)	9,500
Contribution margin	$125,500
Less	
Fixed capacity costs (garage rent)	50,000
Fixed truck setup costs	62,500
Fixed marketing and administrative costs	
(customer support)	30,000
Operating profit	$ (17,000)

Activity-based costing provides detailed data with which management can more accurately classify costs into fixed and variable categories. This in turn enhances management's decision-making ability.

SELF-STUDY QUESTION

3. Barton Chemicals produces a line of extra-strength paint remover. The company produced 8,000 barrels and sold 7,500 barrels at $60 per barrel. The costs incurred were as follows:

Direct materials (unit level costs)	$ 24,000
Direct labor (unit level costs)	80,000
Manufacturing overhead (unit level costs)	19,200
Marketing and administrative costs (unit level costs)	24,800
Manufacturing overhead (capacity level costs)	120,000
Marketing and administrative costs (capacity level costs)	110,000

There were no beginning inventories.

a. Using T-accounts, trace the manufacturing cost flows under variable costing.

b. Using T-accounts, trace the manufacturing cost flows under full-absorption costing.

c. Prepare an income statement for this period using the contribution margin format.

d. Prepare an income statement for this period using the traditional format.

The solution to this problem is at the end of this chapter on page 343.

IS INCREASING PRODUCTION TO INCREASE PROFITS ETHICAL?

L.O. 8: Understand the ethics of increasing production to increase profits using full-absorption costing.

Few nonaccountants understand that, using full-absorption costing, companies can increase profits just by increasing production. Consequently, nonaccountants can be misled by people who understand that fixed costs can be inventoried instead of expensed when full-absorption costing is used.

We encountered a large Fortune 100 company that had a division manager who decided to increase production so some of his division's fixed production costs would be inventoried instead of expensed. He knew the fixed production costs would be expensed in the future when the inventory was sold, but that would be someone else's problem because he expected to be transferred the following year. Furthermore, if his division's current year profits were high enough, he would be promoted to a better position in the company.

Increasing production to defer recognizing fixed production costs as expenses did not conflict with the company's accounting policies. Nor did it conflict with generally accepted accounting principles. Nevertheless, this manager's actions were intended to deceive his superiors. Was his action ethical?

We believe that this manager's action was unethical because he intended to deceive his superiors and did not fully disclose how profits were increased. Although his superiors *could* have discovered that the increase in profit was correlated with an increase in ending inventory, it is unlikely that they would have made that connection unless they had accounting expertise or advice.

SUMMARY

This chapter compares full-absorption costing with variable costing. Manufacturing companies use full-absorption costing for external reporting to comply with generally accepted accounting principles and income tax laws, both of which require that product costs include fixed and variable production costs.

With variable costing, only variable production costs are inventoriable; fixed production costs are treated as period costs. Many manufacturing companies use variable costing for internal reporting because it is consistent with the cost-behavior assumptions used in managerial decision making.

In the remaining chapters in this book, we focus on cost analysis for decision making. Hence, we assume that variable costing is used for internal managerial purposes, and that full-absorption costing is used for external financial reporting.

The following summarizes key ideas tied to the chapter's learning objectives.

LO1: Variable costing supports managerial decisions. Most managers recognize the difference between variable costs and full-absorption costs in decision making.

LO2: Contribution margin income statement. The contribution margin income statement separates fixed and variable costs. This allows management to understand relationships between prices, costs, and volume. The contribution margin is different from the gross margin (see Illustration 11.1).

ILLUSTRATION   11.11   Summary Comparison of Full-Absorption Costing (FAC) and Variable Costing (VC)

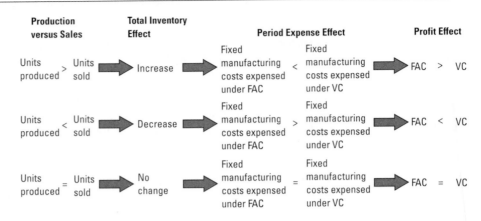

FAC refers to full-absorption costing.

VC refers to variable costing.

Note: These relationships assume that the unit costs of inventory do not change from period to period.

LO3: Product costs: Variable costing versus full-absorption costing. The key difference between the two methods is the treatment of fixed production costs: Full-absorption costing "unitizes" them and treats them as product costs; variable costing treats them as period costs. Operating profits differ under each method if units produced and sold are not the same. Using variable costing, fixed production costs are treated as product costs (expensed during the period). Full-absorption costing treats fixed production costs as product costs (costs that are assigned to inventory and expensed when the inventory is sold). Illustration 11.11 shows the profit effect using each method.

LO4: Variable costing, full-absorption costing, and the value chain. The effect of using full-absorption versus variable costing on the value chain depends on the section of the value chain being considered. If the quality of data used for decision making can be improved, thus helping managers to make better decisions, value is added to the company.

LO5: Variable costing and predetermined overhead rates. The use of predetermined manufacturing overhead rates (that is, normal costing) may give a different unit cost to inventory than does actual costing. But the conceptual differences between full-absorption costing and variable costing are the same regardless of the form of overhead rate; namely, fixed production costs are inventoried under full-absorption costing but not under variable costing. Illustration 11.12 reviews the conceptual differences among the four methods: (1) actual, variable costing; (2) normal, variable costing; (3) actual, full-absorption costing; and (4) normal, full-absorption costing.

LO6: Debate over variable versus full-absorption costing. In practice, companies may prepare *both* variable and full-absorption costing income statements, depending on how they use the information. Variable costing reports can be used for internal purposes; full-absorption reports are prepared for external use.

LO7: Activity-based costing and variable costing. These two methods can be utilized at the same time. Activity-based costing simply provides more detailed cost data, allowing management to make more informed decisions.

LO8: The ethics of increasing production to increase profits. Increasing production to increase profits under full-absorption costing may be unethical.

ILLUSTRATION 11.12 **How Costs Are Measured: Treatment of Overhead by Four Costing Methods—Full-Absorption, Variable, Actual, and Normal**

	Actual Costing	**Normal Costing**
Variable Costing	Uses actual costs. Treats actual fixed manufacturing costs as period costs.	Uses predetermined overhead rates for variable overhead. Treats actual fixed manufacturing costs as period costs.
Full-Absorption Costing	Uses actual costs. Treats actual fixed manufacturing costs as product costs.	Uses predetermined overhead rates for both fixed and variable overhead. Treats fixed manufacturing costs (using predetermined rates) as product costs.

KEY TERMS

actual costing, 315

contribution margin format, 314

full-absorption costing (absorption costing), 312

normal costing, 315

period costs, 315

product costs, 315

variable costing (direct costing), 312

REVIEW QUESTIONS

11.1 What are the key differences between full-absorption costing and variable costing?

11.2 How are marketing and administrative costs treated under variable costing? Under full-absorption costing?

11.3 Under what circumstances do you find that operating profits under variable costing equal full-absorption costing profits? When are variable costing profits smaller? When are they larger?

11.4 What are the advantages of variable costing? What are some of the criticisms of it?

11.5 How can a company using full-absorption costing manipulate profits without changing sales volume?

11.6 The following multiple choice questions assume that direct materials and direct labor are variable costs.
    a. The basic assumption made in a variable costing system with respect to fixed manufacturing costs is that fixed manufacturing costs are which of the following?
        (1) A sunk cost.
        (2) A product cost.
        (3) A part of inventory.
        (4) A period cost.
    b. Which costs are included in inventory under variable costing?
        (1) Only prime costs.
        (2) Only variable manufacturing costs.
        (3) All variable costs.
        (4) All variable and fixed manufacturing costs.

(CPA adapted)

11.7 Multiple choice:
    a. Inventory under the variable costing method includes which of the following?
        (1) Direct materials cost and direct labor cost but not factory overhead cost.

(2)   Direct materials cost, direct labor cost, and variable factory overhead cost.

(3)   Prime cost but not conversion cost.

(4)   Prime cost and total conversion cost.

b.   Which of the following must be known about a production process to institute a variable costing system?

(1)   The variable and fixed components of all costs related to production.

(2)   The controllable and noncontrollable components of all costs related to production.

(3)   Standard production rates and times for all elements of production.

(4)   Contribution margin and break-even point for all goods in production.

(CPA adapted)

CRITICAL ANALYSIS AND DISCUSSION QUESTIONS

11.8   What are the comparative inventory changes under both variable costing and full-absorption costing when

a.   Sales volume exceeds production volume?

b.   Production volume exceeds sales volume?

11.9   Refer to the section of the chapter, "Is Increasing Production to Increase Profits Ethical?" on page 329. What is your view of the division manager's actions? How could increasing ending inventory hurt the company? How might increasing ending inventory help the company?

11.10   Refer again to the section of the chapter, "Is Increasing Production to Increase Profits Ethical?" Is full-absorption costing a less ethical accounting method than variable costing?

11.11   Refer to the Real World Application, "Full versus Variable Costing in Banking," on page 313. Why did American National Bank decide not to drop the check-processing service from its product line even though the service appeared to be unprofitable?

EXERCISES

11.12   Variable and Full-Absorption Costing: Comparison of Operating Profit (L.O. 2, L.O. 3)

Jarrard, Inc., produces a single product that sells for $21.50. Jarrard produced 120,000 units and sold 104,000 units last year. There were no beginning inventories or ending WIP inventories last year.

Manufacturing costs and marketing and administrative costs for last year follow:

Materials (unit level)	$780,000
Labor (unit level).	450,000
Manufacturing overhead (unit level)	180,000
Manufacturing overhead (capacity)	180,000
Marketing and administrative (unit level)	140,000
Marketing and administrative (capacity)	120,000

Required

a.   Compute the unit product (manufacturing) cost using variable costing.

b.   Compute Jarrard's operating profit using variable costing.

c.   Compute operating profit using full-absorption costing.

11.13   Comparison of Variable and Full-Absorption Costing: Multiple Choice (L.O. 2, L.O. 3)

The following questions are based on Larue Corporation, which produces a single product it sells for $12 per unit. Of the 100,000 units produced, 80,000 were sold during year 1; all ending inventory was in finished goods inventory. Larue had no inventory at the beginning of the year.

Direct materials (unit-level cost)	$240,000
Direct labor (unit-level cost)	160,000
Factory overhead (unit-level cost)	80,000
Factory overhead (capacity cost)	240,000
Marketing and administrative (unit-level cost)	80,000
Marketing and administrative (capacity cost)	128,000

Required

a. In presenting inventory on the balance sheet at December 31, what is the unit cost under full-absorption?
   (1) $7.20.
   (2) $5.60.
   (3) $4.80.
   (4) $4.00.

b. In presenting inventory on a variable costing balance sheet, what is the unit cost?
   (1) $7.20.
   (2) $5.60.
   (3) $4.80.
   (4) $4.00.

c. What is the operating profit using variable costing?
   (1) $208,000.
   (2) $192,000.
   (3) $144,000.
   (4) $80,000.
   (5) Some other answer.

d. What is the operating profit using full-absorption costing?
   (1) $208,000.
   (2) $192,000.
   (3) $144,000.
   (4) $80,000.
   (5) Some other answer.

e. What is the ending inventory using full-absorption costing?
   (1) $148,000.
   (2) $144,000.
   (3) $112,000.
   (4) $96,000.

f. What is the ending inventory under variable costing?
   (1) $148,000.
   (2) $144,000.
   (3) $112,000.
   (4) $96,000.

(CPA adapted)

11.14   Comparison of Variable and Full-Absorption Costing: Analyzing Profit Performance (L.O. 2, L.O. 3)

Tammari Enterprises released the following figures from its records for year 1 and year 2:

	Year 1	Year 2
Sales units	250,000	250,000
Production units	250,000	344,000
Selling price per unit	$40	$40
Variable manufacturing cost per unit	$24	$24
Annual fixed manufacturing cost	$860,000	$860,000
Variable marketing and administrative costs per unit sold	$2.40	$2.40
Fixed marketing and administrative costs	$840,000	$840,000
Beginning inventory	$0	?

Required

a. Prepare income statements for both years using the traditional method with full-absorption costing.

b. Prepare income statements for both years using the contribution margin method with variable costing.

c. Comment on the different operating profit figures. Write a brief report explaining why the operating profits are different, if they are.

11.15

Comparison of Cost Flows under Full-Absorption and Variable Costing

(L.O. 3)

H2O Company incurred the following costs for its line of diving tanks:

	Variable	Fixed
Direct materials	$300,000	—
Labor.	262,500	—
Supplies (manufacturing)	40,000	—
Depreciation (manufacturing)	—	$85,000
Repairs and maintenance (manufacturing)	20,000	60,000
Other manufacturing	15,000	20,000
Marketing and administrative costs	20,000	55,000

Of the 100,000 units produced, 80,000 units were sold. There were no beginning inventories.

Required

a. Using T-accounts, trace the manufacturing cost flows under variable costing.

b. Using T-accounts, trace the manufacturing cost flows under full-absorption costing.

11.16

Comparison of Full-Absorption and Variable Cost Flows Using Normal Costing

(L.O. 5)

Jumpin' Jimminy manufactures pogo sticks. Variable manufacturing overhead is applied at the rate of $3.20 per labor-hour and fixed manufacturing overhead at a rate of $4.00 per labor-hour. Actual costs follow:

Direct materials.	$100,000
Direct labor (at $8.40 per hour)	252,000
Actual variable manufacturing overhead.	104,000
Variable marketing and administrative costs	90,000
Actual fixed manufacturing overhead	116,000
Fixed marketing and administrative costs	56,000

During the period, 50,000 units were produced, and 47,600 units were sold at a selling price of $20 each. There were no beginning inventories.

Required

a. Use T-accounts to trace the cost flows using variable costing.

b. Use T-accounts to trace the cost flows using full-absorption costing.

11.17

Comparison of Full-Absorption and Variable Costing Income Statements Using Normal Costing

(L.O. 5)

Required

Refer to Exercise 11.16 and assume that Jumpin' Jimminy debits or credits under- or over-applied overhead to Cost of Goods Sold.

a. Prepare an income statement for the period using variable costing.

b. Prepare an income statement for the period using full-absorption costing.

11.18

Comparison of Full-Absorption and Variable Costing—Income Statement Formats

(L.O. 3)

Consider the following facts:

	Year 1	Year 2
Sales volume	25,000 units	75,000 units
Production volume.	50,000 units	50,000 units
Selling price.	$6 per unit	$6 per unit
Variable manufacturing costs.	$4.50 per unit	$4.50 per unit
Fixed manufacturing costs	$50,000	$50,000
Nonmanufacturing costs (all fixed)	$25,000	$25,000

Prepare comparative income statements using the contribution margin format for variable costing and the traditional format for full-absorption costing. Show the total results for years 1 and 2 combined in addition to the results for each year individually. There were no beginning inventories at the beginning of year 1.

11.19 Compare Income Statement Amounts Using Actual Costing (L.O. 3)

Barrett, Inc., uses the following unit costs for one of the products it manufactures:

Direct materials.	$164.00
Direct labor	70.80
Manufacturing overhead (based on 5,000 units)	
Variable	31.20
Fixed	28.00
Marketing and administrative costs (based on 6,500 units)	
Variable	20.80
Fixed	14.00

This year, 1,500 units were in beginning finished goods inventory, 5,000 units were produced, and 6,500 units were sold at $400 per unit. The beginning inventory was valued at $266 per unit using variable costing and at $294 per unit using full-absorption costing. There was no beginning or ending WIP inventory.

Required

a. Prepare an income statement for the year using the contribution margin format.

b. Would reported operating profits be more, less, or the same if full-absorption costing were used? Support your conclusions with an income statement using full-absorption costing and the traditional format.

PROBLEMS

11.20 Conversion of Variable to Full-Absorption Costing

Hathaway Company uses variable costing for internal management purposes and full-absorption costing for external reporting purposes. Thus, at the end of each year, financial information must be converted from variable costing to full-absorption costing for external reports.

At the end of last year, management anticipated that sales would rise 20 percent this year. Therefore, production was increased from 20,000 units to 24,000 units. However, economic conditions kept sales volume at 20,000 units for both years.

The following data pertain to the two years:

	Last Year	This Year
Selling price per unit	$ 60	$ 60
Sales (units).	20,000	20,000
Beginning inventory (units)	2,000	2,000
Production (units)	20,000	24,000
Ending inventory (units).	2,000	6,000
Underapplied variable overhead	$10,000	$ 8,000

Variable cost per unit for both years was composed of the following:

Labor	$15
Materials	9
Variable overhead	6
	$30

Estimated and actual fixed costs for each year follow:

Production	$180,000
Selling and administrative	200,000
	$380,000

The overhead rate under full-absorption costing is based on estimated volume of 30,000 units per year. Under- or overapplied overhead is debited or credited to Cost of Goods Sold.

Required

Use the preceding data to complete the following:

a. Present the income statement based on variable costing for this year.

b. Present the income statement based on full-absorption costing for this year.

c. Write a short report to management that explains the difference, if any, in the operating profit figures.

(CMA adapted)

11.21 **Variable Costing Operating Profit and Reconciliation with Full-Absorption Costing**

Assume that Emerson Corporation employs a full-absorption costing system for its external reporting as well as for internal management purposes. The latest annual income statement follows:

Sales revenue		$415,000
Cost of goods sold		
Beginning finished goods inventory	$ 22,000[a]	
Cost of goods manufactured.	315,000	
Ending finished goods inventory	(86,000)[b]	
Cost of goods sold		251,000
Gross margin.		$164,000
Marketing costs.		83,000
Administrative costs.		49,800
Operating profit before taxes		$ 31,200

[a]Includes $9,900 variable costs.

[b]Includes $60,200 variable costs.

Management is somewhat concerned that although Emerson is showing adequate income, it is short of cash to meet operating costs. The following information has been provided to assist management with its evaluation of the situation:

Statement of Cost of Goods Manufactured

Direct materials		
Beginning inventory	$16,000	
Purchases	62,000	
Ending inventory	(22,000)	$ 56,000
Direct labor		125,100
Manufacturing overhead		
Variable		39,400
Fixed (including depreciation of $30,000)		94,500
Cost of goods manufactured		$315,000

There are no WIP inventories. Management reports that it is pleased that this year's manufacturing costs are 70 percent variable compared to last year's costs, when they were only 45 percent variable. Although 80 percent of the marketing costs are variable, only 40 percent of the administrative costs are considered variable. The company uses FIFO.

Required

a. Prepare a variable costing income statement for the year.

b. Write a short report to management that explains (1) the difference between the full-absorption costing operating profit given in requirement (a) and (2) why the company may be experiencing a cash flow shortage despite the adequate income shown in its full-absorption income statement.

11.22 **Variable Costing Operating Profit and Reconciliation with Full-Absorption Costing**

You have been given the following information concerning Korona Company:

- *Sales:* 10,000 units per year at a price of $46 per unit.
- *Production:* 15,000 units in year 1; 5,000 units in year 2.
- *Beginning inventory:* None in year 1.
- *Annual production batch costs:* All fixed and equal $100,000 per year.
- *Capacity-level production costs for the year:* $125,000.
- *Ending finished goods inventory in year 1:* One-third of that year's current production.
- *Annual marketing and administrative capacity costs:* $140,000 each year.

Required

a. Prepare full-absorption costing income statements for year 1, year 2, and the two years taken together.

b. Prepare variable costing income statements for year 1, year 2, and the two years taken together.

c. Write a short report to management that reconciles full-absorption operating profit to variable costing operating profit for year 1 and year 2.

11.23

Effect of Changes in Production and Costing Method on Operating Profit ("I Enjoy Challenges")

(This classic problem is based on an actual company's experience.) Brassinni Company uses an actual cost system to apply all production costs to units produced. The plant has a maximum production capacity of 40 million units, but only 10 million units were produced and sold during year 1. There were no beginning or ending inventories.

Brassinni Company's income statement for year 1 follows:

BRASSINNI COMPANY
Income Statement
For the Year Ending December 31, Year 1

Sales (10,000,000 units at $6)...........		$ 60,000,000
Cost of goods sold		
Variable (10,000,000 at $2)...........	$20,000,000	
Fixed	48,000,000	68,000,000
Gross margin...................		$ (8,000,000)
Marketing and administrative costs		10,000,000
Operating profit (loss)		$(18,000,000)

The board of directors is concerned about the $18 million loss. A consultant approached the board with the following offer: "I agree to become president for no fixed salary. But I insist on a year-end bonus of 10 percent of operating profit (before considering the bonus)." The board of directors agreed to these terms and hired the consultant.

The new president promptly stepped up production to an annual rate of 30 million units. Sales for year 2 remained at 10 million units.

The resulting Brassinni Company full-absorption costing income statement for year 2 follows:

BRASSINNI COMPANY
Income Statement
For the Year Ending December 31, Year 2

Sales (10,000,000 units at $6)...........		$60,000,000
Cost of goods sold		
Cost of goods manufactured		
Variable (30,000,000 at $2)	$ 60,000,000	
Fixed......................	48,000,000	
Total cost of goods manufactured......	$108,000,000	
Less ending inventory		
Variable (20,000,000 at $2)	$ 40,000,000	
Fixed (20/30 × $48,000,000).........	32,000,000	
Total inventory	$ 72,000,000	
Cost of goods sold		36,000,000
Gross margin...................		$24,000,000
Marketing and administrative costs		10,000,000
Operating profit before bonus		$14,000,000
Bonus		1,400,000
Operating profit after bonus		$12,600,000

The day after the statement was verified, the president took his check for $1,400,000 and resigned to take a job with another corporation. He remarked, "I enjoy challenges. Now that Brassinni Company is in the black, I'd prefer tackling another challenging situation." (His contract with his new employer is similar to the one he had with Brassinni Company.)

Required

a. Write a report to Brassinni's management evaluating the year 2 performance.

b.   Using variable costing, what would operating profit be for year 1? For year 2? What are the inventory values? (Assume that all marketing and administrative costs are fixed.) Compare those results with the preceding full-absorption statements.

11.24   "I Enjoy Challenges"— Normal Costing

Refer to the facts for problem 11.23. What would year 2's operating profit (loss) be if Brassinni used full-absorption normal costing with a fixed manufacturing overhead rate of

$$\$4.80 = \left(\frac{\$48,000,000 \text{ fixed manufacturing costs}}{10,000,000 \text{ estimated unit sales}} \right)?$$

Required

Prepare an income statement and a T-account diagram of cost flows.

11.25   Comparison of Full-Absorption and Variable Normal Costing in a Process Operation

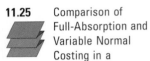

After a dispute with the company president, the controller of Devonelli Company resigned. At that time, his office was converting the internal reporting system from full-absorption to variable costing. You have been called in to prepare financial reports for last year. A considerable amount of data is missing, but you piece together the following information.

1.   The company manufactures valves, which pass through one department. All materials are added at the beginning of production, and processing is applied evenly throughout the department. There is no spoilage. FIFO costing is used.

2.   From the Marketing Department, you learn that 90,000 units were sold for $20 each during last year.

3.   From various sources, you determine that actual variable manufacturing overhead was $330,000 and fixed manufacturing overhead was $210,000 for last year. Nonmanufacturing costs (all fixed) were $580,000.

4.   In one of the former controller's desk drawers, you discover the draft of a report with the following information:

   a.   The present accounting system uses the normal costing approach for both internal and external reporting. We write off over- or underapplied overhead as part of cost of goods sold rather than allocate it to inventories.

   b.   Equivalent unit costs during the year and in beginning inventories were $4 per unit for materials costs and $2 per unit for direct labor. Variable overhead is applied at $3 per unit and fixed overhead at $2 per unit.

   c.   110,000 units were transferred from WIP inventory to finished goods inventory. 120,000 units of materials were purchased, and 115,000 units were requisitioned to work in process inventory.

   d.   Inventory summary (in units):

	Beginning Inventories, January 1	Ending Inventories, December 31
Work in process inventory	10,000 (40% complete)	15,000 (20% complete)
Finished goods inventory	No records	30,000
Direct materials	No records	10,000

Required

a.   Show the flow of whole units, including units started in WIP inventory, transferred to finished goods, and sold. Be sure to include both beginning and ending inventories.

b.   Show the flow of manufacturing costs during the year, including beginning and ending inventories, using full-absorption normal costing.

c.   Prepare income statements using:
   (1)   Full-absorption normal costing.
   (2)   Variable normal costing.

11.26   Incomplete Records

On December 31 of last year, a fire destroyed the bulk of the accounting records of Solano Company, a small, one-product manufacturing firm. In addition, the chief accountant mysteriously disappeared. You have the task to reconstruct last year's records. The general manager has said that the accountant had been experimenting with both full-absorption costing and variable costing on an actual costing basis.

The records are a mess, but you have gathered the following data for last year:

Sales.	$450,000
Actual fixed manufacturing costs incurred.	66,000
Actual variable manufacturing costs per unit for last year and for units in beginning finished goods inventory on January 1 of last year	3
Operating profit, full-absorption costing basis.	60,000
Notes receivable from chief accountant	14,000
Contribution margin	180,000
Direct material purchases	175,000
Actual marketing and administrative costs (all fixed)	21,000
Gross margin.	81,000

The company had no beginning or ending WIP inventories. You also learn that full-absorption costs per unit in last year's beginning finished goods inventory is the same as the full-absorption cost per unit for units produced during the year.

Required

a. Prepare a comparative income statement on a full-absorption and variable costing basis.

b. At a meeting with the board of directors, the following questions were raised:
(1) How many units did we sell last year?
(2) How many units did we produce last year?
(3) What were the unit production costs last year under both full-absorption and variable costing?

Write a short report responding to these questions.

c. Reconcile the operating profit under variable costing with that under full-absorption costing, showing the exact source of the difference.

11.27 Comparative Income Statements with Fixed Overhead Adjustment

Management of Tenna Company uses the following unit costs for the one product it manufactures:

	Cost per Unit
Direct material (all variable).	$30.00
Direct labor (all variable).	19.00
Manufacturing overhead	
Variable cost	6.00
Fixed cost (based on 10,000 estimated units per month)	5.00
Nonmanufacturing	
Variable cost	4.00
Fixed cost (based on 10,000 estimated units per month)	2.80

The projected selling price is $80 per unit. The fixed costs remain fixed within the range of 4,000 to 16,000 units of production.

Management has also projected the following data for June:

	Units
Beginning inventory	–0–
Production	9,000
Available	9,000
Sales.	7,500
Ending inventory	1,500

Required

Prepare a projected income statement for June for management purposes under each of the following product cost methods.

a. Full-absorption costing. Under- or overapplied fixed overhead should be debited or credited to Cost of Goods Sold. There is no under- or overapplied variable overhead.

b. Variable costing.

(CPA adapted)

11.28 Evaluate Full-
Absorption and
Variable Costing;
Normal Costing

Lockard Company's vice president for sales received the following income statement for November. The statement has been prepared using variable costing, which the firm has just adopted for internal reporting purposes.

LOCKARD COMPANY
Income Statement
For the Month of November
(in thousands)

Sales revenue	$2,400
Less variable cost of goods sold.	1,200
Contribution margin.	$1,200
Less fixed manufacturing costs	600
Gross margin	$ 600
Less fixed nonmanufacturing costs	400
Operating profits before taxes	$ 200

The controller attached the following notes to the statements.

- The unit sales price for November averaged $24.
- The unit manufacturing costs for the month follow:

Variable costs	$12
Fixed cost	4
Total cost	$16

The unit rate for fixed manufacturing costs is a predetermined rate based on a normal monthly production of 150,000 units. Both actual and estimated fixed overhead was $600,000.

- Production for November was 45,000 units in excess of sales.
- The inventory at November 30 consisted of 45,000 units.

Required

a. The vice president for sales is not comfortable with the variable cost basis and wonders what the operating profit would have been under the full-absorption cost basis applying fixed overhead using a predetermined rate.
   (1) Present the November income statement on a full-absorption cost basis.
   (2) Reconcile and explain the difference between the variable costing and the full-absorption costing operating profit figures.

b. Explain the features associated with the variable costing approach to profit measurement that should be attractive to the vice president for sales.

(CMA adapted)

INTEGRATIVE CASES

11.29 Comprehensive
Problem on
Process Costing,
Variable Costing,
and Full-Absorption
Costing

(This problem requires knowing how to compute equivalent units.) Assume that Sega Corporation manufactures Vedral, which is sold for $20 per unit. Lynch (a direct material) is added before processing starts, and labor and overhead are added evenly during the manufacturing process. Actual costs per unit of Vedral this year follow:

Lynch, 2 pounds	$3.00
Labor	6.00
Variable manufacturing overhead	1.00
Fixed manufacturing overhead	1.10

These costs have remained the same for several periods. Inventory data for this year follow:

	Units	
	Beginning: January 1	**Ending: December 31**
Lynch (pounds).	50,000	40,000
WIP inventory	10,000 (½ processed)	15,000 (⅓ processed)
Finished goods inventory	17,000	12,000

During the year, 220,000 pounds of Lynch were purchased, and 230,000 pounds were transferred to WIP inventory. Also, 110,000 units of Vedral were transferred to finished goods inventory. Actual fixed manufacturing overhead during the year was $121,000. FIFO is used for inventory flows. Marketing and administrative costs were $145,000 for the year.

Required

a. Determine the number of equivalent units produced for both materials (Lynch) and conversion costs.

b. Determine the WIP and finished goods inventories (in dollars) under (1) full-absorption costing and (2) variable costing on January 1 and December 31.

c. Prepare comparative income statements for the year using full-absorption and variable costing.

d. Reconcile full-absorption to variable costing comparing the fixed manufacturing costs deducted from revenue (that is, expensed) under each method.

(CPA adapted)

11.30 Full-Absorption and Variable Costing Importing Decisions

Cotierre imports designer clothing that subcontractors in Mexico manufacture. Clothing is a seasonal product. The goods must be ready for sale prior to the start of the season. Any goods left over at the end of the season must usually be sold at steep discounts. The company prepares a dress design and selects fabrics approximately six months before a given season. It receives these goods and distributes them at the start of the season. Based on past experience, the company estimates that 60 percent of a particular lot of dresses will be unsold at the end of the season and are marked down to one-half of the initial retail price. Even with the markdown, a substantial number of dresses remain unsold. They are returned to Cotierre and destroyed. Even though a large number of dresses must be discounted or destroyed, the company needs to place a minimum order of 1,000 dresses to have a sufficient selection of styles and sizes to market the design.

Recently, the company placed an order for 1,000 dresses of a particular design for $25,000 plus import duties of $5,000 and a $7 commission for each dress sold at retail, regardless of the price. Return mailing and disposing of each unsold dress cost $3 after the end of the markdown period.

Required

a. Use full-absorption costing to compute the inventoriable cost of each dress in this lot of dresses.

b. Suppose that the company sells 30 percent of the dresses in this lot for $75 each during the first accounting period. Using full-absorption costing, what is the value of the ending inventory? What is the operating profit or loss for the period, assuming no other transactions and that the season has not ended, so that the number of dresses subject to markdown or to be returned is unknown?

c. During the second period, 10 percent of the 1,000 dresses were sold at full price and 30 percent were sold at the half-price markdown. The remaining dresses were returned and disposed of. Using full-absorption costing, what is the operating profit or loss for the period, assuming no other transactions?

d. Suggest a method of accounting for these dresses that would more closely relate revenues and costs.

SOLUTIONS TO SELF-STUDY QUESTIONS

1. a. *Product costs* are the actual costs given in the question divided by the 84,000 units produced (not the units sold).

	Full-Absorption Costing	Variable Costing
Direct materials	$ 5.50	$ 5.50
Direct labor.	3.75	3.75
Variable manufacturing overhead	1.25	1.25
Fixed manufacturing overhead	4.75	–0–
Total	$15.25	$10.50

b. *Income statements.* Note that the cost of goods sold (full-absorption costing) and variable cost of goods sold (variable costing) are based on the 76,000 units sold, not the 84,000 units produced.

	Full-Absorption Costing
Sales revenue	$1,520,000[a]
Cost of goods sold.	1,159,000[b]
Gross margin	$ 361,000
Marketing and administrative.	251,000[c]
Operating profits	$ 110,000

	Variable Costing
Sales revenue	$1,520,000[a]
Variable cost of goods sold	798,000[d]
Variable marketing and administrative	50,400
Contribution margin	671,600
Fixed manufacturing overhead	399,000
Fixed marketing and administrative	200,600
Operating profits	$ 72,000

[a]$1,520,000 = $20 × 76,000 units sold.

[b]$1,159,000 = $15.25 × 76,000 units sold.

[c]$251,000 = Sum of variable and fixed marketing and administrative costs. Fixed and variable marketing and administrative costs could be reported separately or combined as shown here.

[d]$798,000 = $10.50 × 76,000 units sold.

c. *Explanation.* Operating profits are $38,000 higher under full-absorption costing. The difference in operating profits occurs solely because of the treatment of fixed manufacturing costs. Under variable costing, all fixed manufacturing costs are expensed on the income statement in the period in which they occurred. If production exceeds sales, a portion of fixed manufacturing costs are not expensed in the current period under full-absorption costing. In this case, 8,000 units remain in ending inventory. Under full-absorption costing, $38,000 of the fixed manufacturing cost (8,000 units × $4.75 fixed manufacturing cost per unit) remains in ending inventory. If the total number of units sold had exceeded the total number of units produced, full-absorption costing would show lower operating profits than would variable costing.

2. a. Product costs are the actual costs given in the question divided by the 84,000 units for materials and labor, but normal costs are used for overhead.

	Full-Absorption Costing	Variable Costing
Direct materials	$ 5.50	$ 5.50
Direct labor.	3.75	3.75
Variable manufacturing overhead	1.50[a]	1.50[a]
Fixed manufacturing overhead	4.6875[b]	–0–
Total	$15.4375	$10.75

[a]$1.50 = 40% of direct labor.

[b]$4.6875 = 125% of direct labor.

b. *Income statements.* Note that the cost of goods sold (full-absorption costing) and variable cost of goods sold (variable costing) are based on the 76,000 units sold, not the 84,000 units produced. To compute the over- or underapplied overhead, first compute the applied amounts based on the predetermined rates times the actual direct labor cost shown in Self-Study Question 1 for the 84,000 units produced:

$$\text{Variable overhead applied} = 40\% \times \$315,000$$
$$= \$126,000$$
$$\text{Fixed overhead applied} = 125\% \times \$315,000$$
$$= \$393,750$$

Now find the difference between actual and applied:

	Actual Overhead per Self-Study Question 1	Applied Overhead	Difference	
Variable manufacturing overhead.	$105,000	$126,000	$21,000	overapplied
Fixed manufacturing overhead.	399,000	393,750	5,250	underapplied
Net overapplied manufacturing overhead			$15,750	

	Full-Absorption Costing			Variable Costing
Sales revenue	$1,520,000[a]	Sales revenue		$1,520,000[a]
Cost of goods sold	1,173,250[b]	Variable cost of goods sold		817,000[d]
Overapplied overhead	15,750	Overapplied variable overhead		21,000
Gross margin	$ 362,500	Variable marketing and administrative costs		50,400
Marketing and administrative costs	251,000[c]	Contribution margin		$ 673,600
Operating profits	$ 111,500	Fixed manufacturing overhead		399,000
		Fixed marketing and administrative costs		200,600
		Operating profits		$ 74,000

[a]$1,520,000 = $20 \times 76,000$ units sold.

[b]$1,173,250 = $15.4375 \times 76,000$ units sold.

[c]$251,000 = Sum of variable and fixed marketing and administrative costs. Fixed marketing and administrative costs could be separated from variable marketing and administrative costs, or they could be combined as shown here.

[d]$817,000 = $10.75 \times 76,000$ units sold.

3. a.

BARTON CHEMICALS
Variable Costing

Direct Materials Inventory	Work in Process Inventory	Finished Goods Inventory	Cost of Goods Sold
24,000 ──→	24,000		
		–0–	
		123,200 ──→ 123,200 115,500[a] ──→	115,500
		7,700	

Wages Payable	
	80,000 ──→ 80,000

Variable Manufacturing Overhead	
19,200	19,200 ──→ 19,200

Fixed Manufacturing Overhead	
120,000	

b.   **Full-Absorption Costing**

Direct Materials Inventory	Work in Process Inventory	Finished Goods Inventory	Cost of Goods Sold
24,000 ──→	24,000		
		–0–	
		243,200 ──→ 243,200 228,000[a] ──→	228,000
		15,200	

Wages Payable	
	80,000 ──→ 80,000

Variable Manufacturing Overhead	
19,200	19,200 ──→ 19,200

Fixed Manufacturing Overhead	
120,000	120,000 ──→ 120,000
	–0–

[a]$115,500 = \left(\frac{7,500}{8,000}\right) \times 123,200$; $228,000 = \left(\frac{7,500}{8,000}\right) \times $243,200$.

c.

Contribution Margin Approach	
Sales revenue	$450,000
Less	
Variable cost of goods sold	115,500
Variable marketing and administrative costs	24,800
Contribution margin	309,700
Less	
Fixed manufacturing overhead	120,000
Fixed marketing and administrative costs	110,000
Operating profit	$ 79,700

d.

Traditional Approach	
Sales revenue	$450,000
Cost of goods sold	228,000
Gross margin	222,000
Less	
Variable marketing and administrative costs	24,800
Fixed marketing and administrative costs	110,000
Operating profit	$ 87,200

Cost Estimation

LEARNING OBJECTIVES

After reading this chapter, you should be able to:

1. Understand the reasons for estimating fixed and variable costs.

2. Understand the effect of cost estimates on the value chain.

3. Estimate costs using engineering estimates.

4. Estimate costs using account analysis.

5. Interpret cost data presented in scattergraphs and the results of high-low cost estimates.

6. Estimate costs using regression analysis.

7. Interpret the results of regression output.

8. Identify potential problems with regression data.

9. Evaluate the advantages and disadvantages of alternative cost estimation methods.

10. Explain the effect of learning curves on costs.

11. Construct confidence intervals for regression estimates (appendix).

WHY ESTIMATE COSTS?

In deciding among alternative actions, management needs to know the costs that each alternative is likely to incur. These are examples of frequently asked questions that require cost estimates:

> University of Illinois administrators ask: "What will happen to total costs if we increase enrollment by 10 percent over the present level?"
>
> Managers at Andersen Consulting ask: "What bid should we enter on this systems job?"
>
> Managers of Tower Records ask: "What profit can we expect if we sell the projected number of CDs this period?"

This chapter discusses methods to estimate costs to answer such questions.

EFFECT OF COST ESTIMATES ON VALUE

In making cost estimates, managers frequently ask, "How will my cost estimates affect the value of the company?" Accurate estimates improve decision making; inaccurate ones result in inefficiencies and increase nonvalue-added decisions. The university administrators mentioned above might find that the increase in costs will exceed that of revenues if enrollment is increased 10 percent, leading to an overall decrease in the monetary value of the university. With this information, the administrator can make the decision that is in accordance with the University's goals. The more accurate the estimate, the more value added is the decision.

Andersen Consulting may find that the only way to retain the systems job is to bid lower than its total expected cost for strategic purposes, realizing that more lucrative contracts will be available in the future. Thus, in the short run, Andersen is taking what appears to be a nonprofitable job. In the long run, however, significant value will be added to the company as it secures more profitable contracts with the same client. Some companies bid as low as possible, just covering variable costs, to obtain a client. Once they have proven themselves on the job, they can raise the bid on future jobs.

Clearly, cost estimates can be an important element in helping managers make decisions that add value to the company.

BASIC COST BEHAVIOR PATTERNS

L.O. 1: Understand the reasons for estimating fixed and variable costs.

The basic idea in cost estimation is to estimate the relation between costs and the variables affecting costs. In this chapter, we focus on the relation between costs and one important variable that affects them: activity levels. Activities can be measured by volume (for example, units of output, machine-hours, pages typed, miles driven), by complexity (for example, number of setups, number of different types of products), or by any other cost driver.

You are already familiar with the term *variable costs,* and you know that they change proportionately with activity levels. The formula that we use to estimate costs is the familiar cost equation:

$$TC = F + VX$$

where TC refers to total costs, F refers to fixed costs that do not vary with activity levels, V refers to variable costs per unit of activity, and X refers to the volume of activity.

In practice, we usually have data about the total costs incurred at each of various activity levels, but we do not have a breakdown of costs into fixed and variable components. Knowing which costs are fixed and how costs change as the volume of activity changes is important, however, for most decisions made in companies.

METHODS TO ESTIMATE COSTS

L.O. 2: Understand the effect of cost estimates on the value chain.

This chapter discusses four methods to estimate the relation between cost behavior and activity levels that are commonly used in practice:

- Engineering estimates.
- Account analysis.
- Scattergraph and high-low estimates.
- Statistical methods (usually employing regression analysis).

Results are likely to differ from method to method. Consequently, more than one approach is often applied so that results can be compared. Because line managers bear ultimate responsibility for all cost estimates, they frequently apply their own best judgment as a final step in the estimation process, modifying the estimate submitted by the controller's staff. These methods, therefore, should be seen as ways to help management to arrive at the best estimates possible. Their weaknesses as well as their strengths require attention.

The discussion of regression methods centers on practical applications rather than underlying statistical theory. A brief overview of the theory and some important considerations for its application are discussed in the appendix to this chapter.

ENGINEERING METHOD

L.O. 3: Estimate costs using engineering estimates.

engineering estimates
Cost estimates based on measurement and pricing of the work involved in a task.

Engineering estimates of costs are usually made by measuring the work involved in a task. A detailed step-by-step analysis of each phase of each manufacturing process, together with the kinds of work performed and the costs involved, is prepared. (This is sometimes part of a time and motion study.) The time it should take to perform each step is then estimated. These times are often available from widely published manuals and trade association documents.

The times required for each step in the process are summed to obtain an estimate of the total time involved, including an allowance for unproductive time. This serves as a basis for estimating direct labor costs. Engineering estimates of the materials required for each unit of production are usually obtained from drawings and specification sheets.

Other costs are estimated similarly; for example, the size and cost of a building needed to house the manufacturing operation can be estimated based on area construction costs and space requirements. The necessary number of supervisors and support personnel can be estimated based on a direct labor time estimate.

One advantage to the engineering approach is that it can detail each step required to perform an operation. This permits comparison with other settings in which similar operations are performed and enables a company to review its manufacturing productivity and identify specific strengths and weaknesses. Another advantage to this approach is that it does not require data from prior activities in the organization. Hence, it can be used to estimate costs for totally new activities.

A company that uses engineering estimates often can identify where "slack" exists in its operations. For example, if an engineering estimate indicates that 80,000 square feet of floor area are required for an assembly process but the company has been using 125,000 square feet, the company may find it beneficial to rearrange the plant to make floor space available for other uses.

A difficulty with the engineering approach is that it can be quite expensive to use because it analyzes each activity. Another consideration is that engineering estimates are often based on optimal conditions. Therefore, when evaluating performance, bidding on a contract, planning expected costs, or estimating costs for any other purpose, it is wise to consider that the actual work conditions will be less than optimal.

ACCOUNT ANALYSIS METHOD

L.O. 4: Estimate costs using account analysis.

account analysis
The cost estimation method that calls for a review of each account making up the total cost being analyzed.

Accountants often use the **account analysis** approach to estimate costs. This method calls for a review of each cost account used to record the costs of interest, identifying each as fixed or variable, depending on the relationship between the cost and some activity.

The relationship between the activity and the cost is extremely important. For example, in estimating the production costs for a specified number of units within the range of present manufacturing capacity, direct materials and direct labor costs are considered variable, and building occupancy costs are considered fixed.

Housekeeping services in a hotel like this are usually mixed costs because they include some fixed and some variable components. The fixed costs exist because some housekeeping is necessary to keep hallways and lobby clean even if the hotel has few guests. As the number of guests increases, the amount of housekeeping costs increases. (© David Austen/Tony Stone Images)

Illustration 12.1 shows a typical schedule of estimated overhead costs per week prepared for a particular activity level by Escondido, Inc. The production process is assumed to produce 40 units per machine-hour. Management has initially considered producing 4,600 units per week. To attain this level, 115 machine-hours (4,600 units/40 units per hour) are required. The variable overhead may be expressed as a cost per machine-hour or as a cost per unit, depending on management's preference.

Following this approach, each major class of overhead costs is itemized and then is divided into its estimated variable and fixed components. Management considers building occupancy costs, for example, to be entirely fixed and classifies the costs of quality inspections as entirely variable. The other costs are mixed, having some fixed and some variable elements. The fixed and variable components of each cost item may be determined on the basis of the experience and judgment of accounting or other personnel. Additionally, other cost estimation methods discussed later in this chapter might be used to divide mixed costs into fixed and variable components.

The total costs for the coming period are the sum of the estimated total variable and total fixed costs. For Escondido, Inc., assume that accounting personnel have relied on the judgment of a number of people in the company and have estimated fixed costs at $1,205 and the total variable costs at $1,426 for 115 machine-hours, as shown in Illustration 12.1.

Since the variable costs are directly related to the expected activity, we may state the variable overhead per unit as $0.31($1,426/4,600 units) and the general cost equation as

$$TC = F + VX$$

Overhead costs = $1,205 per period + ($0.31 per unit × Number of units)

For 4,600 units

$$\text{Overhead costs} = \$1,205 + (\$0.31 \times 4{,}600 \text{ units})$$
$$= \$1,205 + \$1,426$$
$$= \underline{\underline{\$2,631}}$$

If management wants to estimate the costs at a production level of 4,800 units, it substitutes that figure for the 4,600 units in the previous equation, resulting in

| ILLUSTRATION 12.1 | Cost Estimation Using Account Analysis, Escondido, Inc. | | |

| | Costs at 4,600 Units of Output (115 machine-hours) | | |
Account	Total	Variable Cost	Fixed Cost
Indirect labor	$ 321	$ 103	$ 218
Indirect materials	422	307	115
Building occupancy	615	—	615
Property taxes and insurance	51	40	11
Power	589	535	54
Equipment repairs and maintenance	218	119	99
Data processing	113	88	25
Quality inspections	187	187	—
Personnel services	115	47	68
Totals.	$2,631	$1,426	$1,205

$$\text{Overhead costs} = \$1,205 + (\$0.31 \times 4,800 \text{ units})$$
$$= \$1,205 + \$1,488$$
$$= \underline{\underline{\$2,693}}$$

This is simpler than reestimating all of the overhead cost elements listed in Illustration 12.1 for the different activity levels that management might wish to consider. Moreover, management's attention is drawn to the variable cost amount as the cost that changes with each change in occupancy volume.

The variable costs also could be expressed in terms of costs per machine-hour. Assume that producing 4,600 units (at 40 units per hour) requires 115 machine-hours; the variable cost per machine-hour is

$$\$1,426 \div 115 \text{ hours} = \$12.40 \text{ per hour}$$

Account analysis is a useful way to estimate costs. It uses the experience and judgment of managers and accountants who are familiar with company operations and the way costs react to changes in activity levels. Account analysis relies heavily on personal judgment, however; this may be an advantage or disadvantage, depending on the bias of the person making the estimate. Decisions based on cost estimates often have major economic consequences for the people making them. Thus, these individuals may not be entirely objective. More objective methods are often used in conjunction with account analysis to obtain the advantages of multiple methods.

SELF-STUDY QUESTION

1. Propylon, the wonder fabric of the 21st century, is the primary product of Propylon Textiles. By the end of its second year of operations, Propylon Textiles had enough data for Natalie Martin, the company's chief financial officer, to do a detailed analysis of its overhead cost behavior. Natalie summarized monthly data as two-year totals:

Indirect materials	$503,000
Indirect labor	630,000
Lease.	288,000
Utilities (heat, light, etc.)	206,000
Power to run machines	104,000
Insurance	24,000
Maintenance	200,000

Depreciation	72,000
Research and development.	171,000
Total overhead	$2,198,000

Direct labor-hours	815,800
Direct labor costs	$4,997,400
Machine-hours	1,022,700
Units produced	202,500

Natalie has asked you to prepare three analyses that, using the account analysis method, calculate the monthly average fixed costs and the variable cost rate per (1) direct labor-hour, (2) machine-hour, and (3) unit of output.

You discuss operations with production managers, who inform you that three costs—indirect labor, indirect materials, and power to run machines—are variable. All other costs are fixed.

The solution to this question is at the end of this chapter on page 380.

SCATTERGRAPH AND HIGH-LOW ESTIMATES

L.O. 5: Interpret cost data presented in scattergraphs and the results of high-low cost estimates.

If a company's operations have followed a particular pattern in the past and that pattern is expected to continue in the future, using the relationship between past costs and activity to estimate future costs may be possible. Of course, if the relationship changes, it may be necessary to adjust the estimated costs accordingly.

Analysts must be careful when predicting future costs from past data. In many cases, the cost-activity relationship changes. Technological innovation, increased use of robots, more mechanized processes, and the like have made the past cost-activity relationships inappropriate for prediction purposes in many organizations.

In other cases, the costs themselves change so dramatically that old cost data are almost worthless predictors of future costs. Because of the high variation in costs, companies using precious metals and companies relying on labor in Third World countries have found that past cost data are not very helpful in predicting future costs. Although accountants may adjust the data, the resulting cost estimates tend to lose their objectivity as the number of adjustments increases.

Preparing a Scattergraph

scattergraph
A graph that plots costs against past activity levels.

Plotting past costs against past activity levels is often a useful way to visually depict cost-activity relationships. Such a plot, called a **scattergraph,** also indicates any significant change in the relationship between costs and activity at different activity levels.

To prepare such a plot, we first obtain the relevant data. For example, if estimates of manufacturing overhead costs are to be based on direct labor-hours, we must obtain information about past manufacturing overhead costs and related direct labor-hours.

Number of Observations

The number of observations to include depends on the availability of the data, the variability within the data, and the relative costs and benefits of obtaining reliable data. A rule of thumb is to use three years of monthly data if the physical processes have not changed significantly within that time. If the company's operations have recently changed significantly, however, data that predate the change may not be useful. If cost and activity levels are highly stable, a relatively short period (12 months or so) may be adequate.

Data for the past 15 months were collected for Escondido, Inc., to estimate variable and fixed manufacturing overhead. These data are presented and plotted on the scattergraph in Illustration 12.2. Once all the data points were plotted, a line was drawn to fit them as closely as possible and was extended to the vertical axis on the scattergraph.

The slope of the line represents the estimated variable costs, and the intercept with the vertical axis represents an estimate of fixed costs. The slope is referred to

ILLUSTRATION   12.2   Data and Scattergraph for Cost Estimation, Escondido, Inc.

Time Period	Overhead Costs	Machine-Hours (MH)
1.	$2,107	62
2.	2,040	62
3.	2,916	120
4.	2,322	71
5.	1,896	50
6.	2,471	95
7.	3,105	142
8.	2,316	86
9.	2,555	112
10.	2,780	136
11.	2,061	85
12.	2,910	103
13.	2,835	96
14.	2,715	101
15.	1,986	53

as the *variable cost per unit* because it represents the change in costs that occurs as a result of changes in activity. The intercept is referred to as the *fixed cost* because it represents the costs incurred at a zero activity level given existing capacity if the relationship plotted is valid from the data points back to the origin. Note that there are no observations of cost behavior around the zero activity level in this example, so the data do not indicate the costs that would occur when the activity level was zero. Rather, they provide an estimating equation useful within the relevant range. The slope and intercept may be measured using a ruler.

Preparing an estimate on this basis is subject to a high level of error, especially if the points are scattered widely. Determining the best fit is often a matter of "eyeball judgment." Consequently, scattergraphs are usually not used as the sole basis for cost estimates but are used to illustrate the relationships between costs and activity levels and to point out any past data items that might be significantly out of line.

High-Low Cost Estimation

If the cost relationships can be described by a straight line, any two points on a scattergraph may be used to prepare a cost-estimating equation. Typically, the highest and the lowest activity points are chosen, hence the name **high-low cost**

high-low cost estimation
A method to estimate costs
based on two cost observations,
usually at the highest activity
level and at the lowest
activity level.

estimation. Activity may be defined in terms of units of production, hours of work, or any other measure that makes sense for the problem at hand.

The slope of the total cost line, which estimates the increase of variable costs associated with an increase of one unit of activity, may be estimated using the following equation:

$$\text{Variable cost per unit } (V) = \frac{\text{Cost at highest activity} - \text{Cost at lowest activity}}{\text{Highest activity} - \text{Lowest activity}}$$

The intercept is estimated by taking the total cost at either activity level and subtracting its estimated variable cost.

$$\text{Fixed cost} = \text{Total cost at highest activity} - (\text{Variable cost} \times \text{Highest activity})$$

or

$$\text{Fixed cost} = \text{Total cost at lowest activity} - (\text{Variable cost} \times \text{Lowest activity})$$

Based on the data for Escondido, Inc., in Illustration 12.2, the highest activity level is 142 machine-hours (MH). At this activity level, total overhead costs are $3,105. The lowest activity level is 50 hours, with overhead costs of $1,896. Substituting these data in the equation for variable cost yields the following:

$$\begin{aligned}
\text{Variable cost per MH} &= \frac{\$3,105 - \$1,896}{142 \text{ MH} - 50 \text{ MH}} \\
&= \frac{\$1,209}{92 \text{ MH}} \\
&= \$13.141 \text{ per MH}
\end{aligned}$$

To obtain the fixed cost estimate, either the highest or lowest activity level and costs may be used. Assuming that the highest activity level is used:

$$\begin{aligned}
\text{Fixed cost} &= \$3,105 - (\$13.141 \times 142 \text{ MH}) \\
&= \$3,105 - \$1,866 \\
&= \$1,239
\end{aligned}$$

An estimate for the costs at any given activity level can be computed using this equation:

$$TC = F + VX$$
$$\text{Total cost} = \$1,239 + (\$13.141 \times \text{specified MH})$$

For the 115 hours required for 4,600 units, the total cost is

$$\begin{aligned}
\text{Total cost} &= \$1,239 + (\$13.141 \times 115 \text{ MH}) \\
&= \$1,239 + \$1,511 \\
&= \$2,750
\end{aligned}$$

Although the high-low method is easy to apply, care must be taken to ensure that the two points used to prepare the estimates represent cost and activity relationships over the range of activity for which the prediction is made. The highest and lowest points, however, could represent unusual circumstances. When this happens, one should choose the highest and lowest points within the normal range of activity.

The scattergraph can be used graphically to illustrate cost-activity relationships based on past experience. When costs and activity levels can be plotted in two-dimensional space, the scattergraph is a useful visual display. We recommend using it in conjunction with other cost estimation methods.

RELEVANT RANGE OF ACTIVITY

When attempting to extrapolate from past observations, one must consider the relevance of past activity levels to anticipated future activity levels. Extrapolations beyond the upper and lower bounds of past observations are highly subjective. Suppose, for example, that the highest activity level observed in the past resulted in

5,000 units per month and we wish to predict the cost of occupancy for 6,000 units per month. An estimate may be highly inaccurate because the past data do not reflect cost behavior with output over 5,000 units.

relevant range
The limits within which a cost projection may be valid.

The limits within which a cost projection may be valid is the **relevant range** for that estimate. The relevant range should include only those activity levels for which the assumed cost relationships used in the estimate are considered to hold. Thus, when past data are used, the relevant range for the projection is usually between the upper and lower limits of the past activity levels for which data are available.

Although the use of past data for future cost estimation has limitations, in many cases it works quite well. In many estimates, past data, even if outside the relevant range, are adequate representations of future cost relationships. Moreover, reliance on past data is relatively inexpensive; it may be the only readily available, cost-effective basis for estimating costs.

Past data do show the relationships that held in prior periods and at least may be a meaningful starting point for estimating costs as long as their limitations are recognized. A common statistical method used for estimating costs is regression analysis.

STATISTICAL COST ESTIMATION USING REGRESSION ANALYSIS

L.O. 6: Estimate costs using regression analysis.

regression
Statistical procedure to determine the relationship between variables.

Regression techniques are designed to generate a line that best fits a set of data points. Because the regression procedure uses all data points, the resulting estimates have a broader base than those based only on a few select points. In addition, regression techniques generate information that helps a manager to determine how well the estimated regression equation describes the relationship between costs and activities. The regression process also permits the inclusion of more than one predictor, a feature that may be useful when more than one activity affects costs. For example, variable overhead may be a function of both direct labor-hours and the amounts of direct materials processed.

Many moderately priced hand-held calculators have regression capabilities. Computer spreadsheets such as Microsoft's Excel® and Lotus 1-2-3® have regression programs. We leave descriptions of the computational details to statistics and computer courses. Instead, we deal with regression from the standpoint of accountants and managers who must interpret and use regression estimates. (The appendix to this chapter discusses some of the more technical considerations that may interest users of such programs.)

Obtaining Regression Estimates

L.O. 7: Interpret the results of regression output.

independent variables
The X terms, or predictors, on the right-hand side of a regression equation.

dependent variable
The Y term or the left-hand side of a regression equation.

The most important step in obtaining regression estimates for cost estimation is to establish the existence of a logical relationship between activities and the cost to be estimated. These activities are referred to as predictors, X terms, **independent variables,** or the *right-hand side (RHS)* of a regression equation. The cost to be estimated may be called the **dependent variable,** the Y term, or the *left-hand side (LHS)* of the regression equation.

Although regression programs accept any data for the Y and X terms, entering numbers that have no logical relationship may result in misleading estimates. The accountant has the important responsibility to ensure that the activities are logically related to costs.

Assume, for example, that a logical relationship exists between machine-hours and overhead costs for Escondido, Inc. Assume that a logical relationship also exists between direct materials costs and overhead costs. This latter assumption is reasonable if the service process employs a substantial amount of materials and overhead costs that include materials handling and storage. The data on overhead costs, direct labor-hours, and direct materials costs for this process are presented in Illustration 12.3.

| | **ILLUSTRATION 12.3** | **Data for Regression Estimation, Escondido, Inc.** |

Overhead Costs	Machine- Hours	Direct Materials Costs
$2,107	62	$1,964
2,040	62	1,851
2,916	120	3,615
2,322	71	2,902
1,896	50	1,136
2,471	95	2,315
3,105	142	5,013
2,316	86	2,751
2,555	112	2,816
2,780	136	3,461
2,061	85	1,702
2,910	103	3,819
2,835	96	3,940
2,715	101	3,613
1,986	53	1,741

Escondido, Inc., starts by estimating the parameters (machine-hours) to use in a simple regression—only one independent variable—to predict manufacturing overhead costs. It chooses machine-hours, so past data on machine-hours are entered as the X, or independent, variable. Past data on overhead costs are entered as the Y, or dependent, variable. The computer output giving the estimated relationship between machine-hours and overhead for this situation follows:

Regression output
Intercept   1,334
X coefficient (or b)   12.373

which is interpreted as follows:

Total overhead = $1,334 + ($12.373 per MH × Number of MHs)

For cost estimation purposes, when reading the output of a regression program, understand that the intercept term, $1,334, is an estimate of fixed costs. Of course, it should be used with caution because the intercept at zero activity is outside the relevant range of observations. The coefficient of the X term (in this example, $12.373 per machine-hour) is an estimate of the variable cost per machine-hour. This is the slope of the cost line. The coefficients are often labeled b on the program output. Thus, the cost estimation equation based on this regression result is

Total costs = Intercept + (b × MH)

Substituting 115 MH into the equation yields

Total costs = $1,334 + ($12.373 × 115 MH)
= $1,334 + $1,423
= $2,757

This estimate of cost behavior is shown graphically in Illustration 12.4.

ILLUSTRATION   12.4   Scattergraph with Regression-Estimated Cost Line, Escondido, Inc.

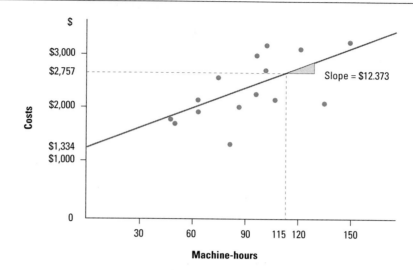

Correlation Coefficients

correlation coefficient
A measure of the linear relationship between two or more variables, such as cost and some activity measure.

In addition to the cost-estimating equation, the regression program provides other useful statistics. The **correlation coefficient** (R) is a measure of the proximity of the data points to the regression line. The closer R is to 1.0, the closer the data points are to the regression line. Conversely, the closer R is to zero, the poorer the fit of the regression line.

The square of R is called R-square (R^2) or the *coefficient of determination*. R^2 is interpreted as the proportion of the variation in Y explained by the right-hand side of the regression equation, that is, by the X predictors.

For Escondido, Inc., the correlation coefficient, R^2, and adjusted R^2 are the following:

Correlation coefficient (R)	.896
R^2	.802

Since the R^2 is .802, it can be said that 80.2 percent of the changes in overhead costs can be explained by changes in machine-hours. For data drawn from accounting records, an R^2 of .802 is considered a good fit of the regression equation to the data.

The most commonly used regression technique is called *ordinary least squares regression*. With this technique, the regression line is computed so that the sum of the squares of the vertical distances from each point to the regression line is minimized. Thus, as a practical consideration, it is important to beware of including data points that vary significantly from the usual. Because the regression program seeks to minimize squared differences, the inclusion of these extreme outliers may significantly affect the results. Consequently, organizations often exclude data for periods of such unusual occurrences as strikes, extreme weather conditions, and shutdowns for equipment retooling. Plotting data on a graph often reveals such outliers so they can be easily identified and omitted.

SELF-STUDY QUESTION

2. The following computer output presents the results of two simple regressions for Propylon Textiles, using (1) machine-hours and (2) units of output as the independent variables. Each regression has 24 data points, one data point per month for two years. Which activity base, units of output or machine-hours, do you believe best explains variation in overhead costs?

OUTPUT NO. 1
Dependent variable: Overhead
Independent variable: Machine-hours
$R^2 = .863$
24 observations

Variable	Estimated Coefficient
Machine-hours	4.9015
Intercept	−117.28

OUTPUT NO. 2
Dependent variable: Overhead
Independent variable: Units produced
$R^2 = .870$
24 observations

Variable	Estimated Coefficient
Units produced	23.799
Intercept	−109.22

The solution to this question is at the end of this chapter on page 380.

Multiple Regression

Although the prediction of overhead costs in the previous example, with its R^2 of .802, was considered good, management may wish to see whether a better estimate might be obtained using additional predictor variables. In such a case, they examine the nature of the operation to determine which additional predictors might be useful in deriving a cost estimation equation.

Assume that Escondido, Inc., has determined that direct materials costs may also affect overhead. The results of using both machine-hours (X_1) and direct materials costs (X_2) as *predictors* of overhead (Y) were obtained using a computer program. The computer output from the program using machine-hours and direct materials costs yields the prediction equation:

$$\text{Overhead costs} = \text{Intercept} + b_1X_1 + b_2X_2$$
$$= \$1,334 + \$4.359X_1 + .258X_2$$

where X_1 refers to machine-hours and X_2 refers to direct materials costs. (The intercepts in the simple and multiple regressions round to the same whole number by coincidence.) The statistics supplied with the output are

Correlation coefficient (multiple R)	.976
R^2	.952
Adjusted R^2	.944

adjusted R-square (R^2)
The correlation coefficient squared and adjusted for the number of independent variables used to make the estimate.

The **adjusted R-square** is the correlation coefficient squared and adjusted for the number of independent variables used to make the estimate. This adjustment to R^2 recognizes that as the number of independent variables increases, R^2 (unadjusted) increases. Statisticians believe that adjusted R^2 is a better measure of the association between X and Y than the unadjusted R^2 value when more than one X predictor exists.

The correlation coefficient (now expressed as multiple R because it is related to more than one predictor variable) for this regression is .976, and the adjusted multiple R^2 is .944. This is an improvement over the results obtained when the regression equation included only direct machine-hours. Improved results may be expected because some overhead costs may be related to direct materials costs (for example, indirect materials) but not to machine-hours.

Preparing a cost estimate using this multiple regression equation requires not only the estimated machine-hours for the coming period but also the direct materials costs. The additional data requirements for multiple regression models may limit their usefulness in many applications. Of course, in planning for the next period's production activity, companies usually have already estimated direct materials costs and machine-hours, and in such a situation the added costs of obtaining data may be quite low.

Practical Implementation Problems

L.O. 8: Identify potential problems with regression data.

Advances in easy-to-use computer software and hand-held calculators have greatly simplified regression analysis and made it available to more people. Consequently, regression has been increasingly used (and potentially misused). In particular, people may be tempted to enter many variables into a regression model without careful thought to their validity. The results can be disastrous.

Some of the more common problems with using regression estimates include (1) attempting to fit a linear equation to nonlinear data, (2) failing to exclude outliers, and (3) including predictors with apparent but spurious relationships.

Effect of Nonlinear Relationships

The effect of attempting to fit a linear model to nonlinear data is likely to occur when a company is operating close to capacity limits. Close to maximum capacity, costs increase more rapidly than activity due to overtime premiums paid to employees, increased maintenance and repair costs for equipment, and similar factors. The linear cost estimate understates the slope of the cost line in the ranges close to capacity. This situation is shown in Illustration 12.5.

One way to overcome the problem is to define a relevant range of activity up to, say, 80 percent capacity and use the range for one set of cost-estimating regression equations. Another equation could be derived for the 81 percent to 100 percent capacity levels. Another approach is to use nonlinear regression techniques to estimate the curve directly. However, nonlinear regression does not provide a constant variable cost estimate; the estimate is different at each level.

Effect of Outliers

Because regression seeks to minimize the sum of the squared deviations from the regression line, observations that lie a significant distance away from the line may

---

ILLUSTRATION   12.5   Effect of Fitting a Linear Model to Nonlinear Data

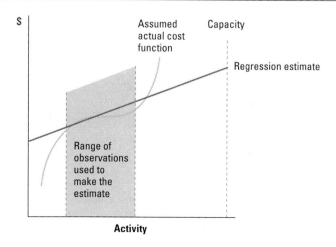

ILLUSTRATION   12.6   Effect of Failure to Exclude Outliers

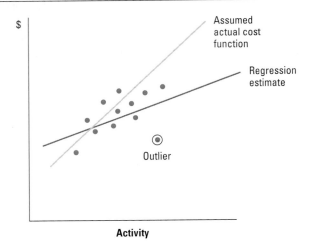

have an overwhelming effect on the regression estimates. Illustration 12.6 shows a case in which most of the data points lie close to a straight line, but due to the effect of one significant outlier, the computed regression line is a significant distance from most of the points.

This type of problem can easily arise in accounting settings. Suppose that a year's worth of supplies was purchased and expensed entirely in one month or a large adjustment was made for underaccruing payroll taxes. The accounting records in such cases are clearly abnormal with respect to the activity measure. An inspection of a plot of the data can sometimes reveal this problem.

When an extreme outlier appears in the data set, scrutiny of the output from the regression equation will rarely identify it. Instead, a plot of the regression line on the data points is usually needed. If multiple predictors are used, an outlier will be even more difficult to find. The best way to avoid this problem is to examine the data in advance and eliminate highly unusual observations before running the regression.

Spurious Relationships

It is sometimes tempting to feed the computer many data and let the regression program "find" relationships among variables. This can lead, however, to spurious relationships. For example, a relationship between variable 1 and variable 2 may appear to exist, when, in fact, variable 3, which was left out of the equation, explains the situation. Early medical studies that found an apparent relationship between cholesterol and heart disease were criticized because the relationship may have been spurious. Numerous other variables that may have been correlated with

Hurricane Andrew created outlier problems by reducing activity and increasing overhead costs in many companies. See discussion of outliers on page 357. (© Peter Le Gand/Tony Stone Images)

both cholesterol and heart disease, such as age and diet, were left out. Moreover, later studies found there were two types of cholesterol, each with an opposite effect on heart disease.

It is important to have a good model for constructing regression equations. A cause-and-effect relation should exist between the predictor variable and the dependent variable. If such a relation does not exist, it is still possible to obtain a good fit and a regression estimate that, on the surface, appears significant. However, there is no assurance that the relation will continue into the future.

For example, a good statistical relation may exist between indirect labor costs and energy costs. One might create a regression equation using such a relation and find that the regression explains much of the change in indirect labor costs. However, there is no logical relation between the two costs. Both indirect labor and energy costs may, in part, be driven by inflationary factors, but there is no cause-and-effect relationship between them.

Data Problems

No matter what method is used to estimate costs, the results are only as good as the data used. Collecting appropriate data is complicated by the following problems:

- *Missing data.* Misplaced source documents or failure to record a transaction can result in missing data.
- *Outliers.* Extreme observations of cost-activity relations may unduly affect cost estimates. For example, a hurricane affected operations in a Florida company in August, resulting in high overhead due to one-time costs.
- *Allocated and discretionary costs.* Fixed costs are often allocated on a volume basis, resulting in costs that may appear to be variable. Discretionary costs also may be budgeted so that they appear variable (e.g., advertising expense budgeted as a percentage of revenue).
- *Inflation.* During periods of inflation, historical cost data do not accurately reflect future cost estimates.
- *Mismatched time periods.* The time period for the dependent and independent variables may not match (e.g., running a machine in February and receiving [recording] the energy bill in March).

Managers should be aware of problems in the data. No substitute exists for knowing how costs and activities are related based on experience.

Regression Must Be Used with Caution

A regression estimate is only an estimate. Computerized statistical techniques sometimes have an aura of truth about them. In fact, a regression estimate may be little better than an eyeball estimate based on plotted data. Regression has advantages, however. It is objective, it provides a number of statistics not available from other methods, and it may be the only feasible method when more than one predictor is used.

We recommend that users of regression (1) fully understand the methodology and its limitations, (2) specify the model, that is, the hypothesized relationship between costs and cost predictors, (3) know the characteristics of the data being used, and (4) examine a plot of the data.

CHOOSING AN ESTIMATION METHOD

L.O. 9: Evaluate the advantages and disadvantages of alternative cost estimation methods.

Each of the methods discussed has advantages and disadvantages. Probably the most informative estimate of cost behavior results from using several methods discussed because each has the potential to provide information that the others do not.

We have discussed a variety of cost estimation methods ranging from the simple account analysis approach to sophisticated techniques involving regression analysis. Which of these methods is best? In general, the more sophisticated methods yield more accurate cost estimates than the simpler methods. However, even a sophisticated method yields only an imperfect estimate of an unknown cost behavior pattern.

ILLUSTRATION 12.7	Summary of Cost Estimates, Escondido, Inc.		
Method	Total Estimated Costs[a]	Estimated Fixed Costs	Estimated Variable Cost
Account analysis...........	$2,631	$1,205	$12.40 per hour
High-low................	2,750	1,239	13.141 per hour
Simple regression (MH)......	2,757	1,334	12.373 per hour
Multiple regression (MH) + DMC[b]............	2,784	1,334	4.359 per hour + .258 per DMC

[a]Estimated for activity levels of 115 machine-hours (and for $3,680 direct materials for multiple regression).

[b]DMC = Direct material costs.

Analysts often simplify all cost estimation methods. The two most common simplifications follow:

- Assuming that cost behavior depends on just one cost driver. (Multiple regression is an exception.) In reality, however, costs may be affected by a host of factors including the weather and the mood of the employees.
- Assuming that cost behavior patterns are linear within the relevant range. We know that cost actually follows curvilinear, step, semivariable, and other patterns.

You must consider on a case-by-case basis whether these assumptions are reasonable. You also must decide when it is important to use a more sophisticated, and more costly, cost estimation method and when it is acceptable to use a simpler approach. Like the rest of managerial accounting, you must evaluate the costs and benefits of various cost estimation techniques.

Each cost estimation method may yield a different estimate of the costs that are likely to result from a particular management decision. This underscores the advantages to using two or more methods to arrive at a final estimate. The different manufacturing overhead estimates that resulted from the use of four different estimation methods for Escondido, Inc., are summarized in Illustration 12.7.

The numbers in Illustration 12.7 are close, but there are differences. It is impossible to state which method is best, so management may find that having all four alternatives gives the best indication of the likely range within which actual costs will fall. Moreover, by observing the range of cost estimates, management may be better able to determine whether more data need to be gathered. If decisions are the same for all four cost estimates, management may conclude that additional information gathering is not warranted.

USING REGRESSION ANALYSIS IN ACTIVITY-BASED COSTING

Regression can be particularly helpful in activity-based costing because of the need to identify which of numerous possible cost drivers is related to overhead costs.[1] The use of activity-based costing requires increasing the number of cost drivers beyond the simple one or two independent variables discussed so far. For instance, a company estimating the cost of the purchasing activity may find that the number of purchase orders made and the number of vendors used are reflected in the activity cost. The equation reflecting this is

---

[1]See A. M. Novin, "Applying Overhead: How to Find the Right Bases and Rates," *Management Accounting*, March 1992, for a discussion of the use of the Lotus 1-2-3 regression function to find cost drivers and overhead rates.

Based on a study of 31 manufacturing plants in three industries—electronics, automobile components, and machinery—researchers at the University of Minnesota used regression analysis to identify manufacturing overhead cost drivers. Their approach treated manufacturing overhead cost as the dependent variable and various possible cost drivers as independent variables. Each plant was a separate data point, so there were 31 observations in total. The researchers' model appeared to fit the data well, with an adjusted R^2 of .779.

As we discussed in previous chapters, many accountants and managers believe that simple volume-based overhead cost drivers, like machine-hours and labor-hours, do not fully capture the causes of overhead costs. They argue that other factors, such as the complexity of the production process, also cause overhead costs and that activity-based costing is superior to traditional volume-based overhead allocation methods. Others disagree about the need to identify additional cost drivers, claiming that more complicated accounting systems will not solve most business problems.

Despite often intense arguments for and against ex-

panding the set of cost drivers, little empirical work has been performed to provide guidance to managers and accountants. A previous study, using regression analysis, found a statistically significant relation between overhead costs and volume-based cost drivers but only a limited association between overhead costs and cost drivers based on the complexity of the production process. The University of Minnesota researchers, however, found a strong relation between overhead costs and both complexity-based and volume-based cost drivers.

The researchers also found that plants implementing new manufacturing methods, namely, just-in-time production, total quality management, and the use of work teams for problem solving on the shop floor had lower overhead costs than those that had not implemented these new manufacturing methods, all other things being equal. This result is particularly important as to whether improved quality increases or decreases costs.

Sources: Based on R. J. Banker, G. Potter, and R. G. Schroeder, "An Empirical Analysis of Manufacturing Overhead Cost Drivers," *Journal of Accounting and Economics* 19, no. 1; and G. Foster and M. Gupta, "Manufacturing Overhead Cost Driver Analysis," *Journal of Accounting and Economics* 12, no. 1.

$$\text{Cost} = a + b_1 X_1 + b_2 X_2$$

where b_1 is the cost per purchase order (X_1) and b_2 is the cost per vendor (X_2).

The basic concepts for using regression analysis are the same, nevertheless, whether two independent variables (that is, cost drivers) or many independent variables exist.

University researchers and industry analysts use regression analysis to identify which cost drivers to use in activity-based costing. (See the Real World Application, "Using Regression Analysis to Estimate the Effect of Quality on Costs," for an example of the work being done.) When you graduate with an understanding of regression analysis and cost accounting and are able to use computer spreadsheets with regression functions, you will have ample opportunities to help organizations better understand their costs. Of course, it is important to remember that statistical analysis merely aids our understanding of the relation between costs and causes of costs; it does not substitute for experience, good sense, and managerial judgment.

Where does one start to identify possible cost drivers? Research to date has found overhead costs to be associated with cost drivers reflecting (1) the complexity of operations (for example, number of setups or different products), (2) volume, and (3) capacity (for example, the value of buildings and equipment). But for the best source of cost driver information: start with people who are familiar with the company's day-to-day operations, such as supervisors and department heads.

HOW DO LEARNING CURVES AFFECT COST ESTIMATES?

L.O. 10: Explain the effect of learning curves on costs.

learning phenomenon
A systematic relationship between the amount of experience in performing a task and the time required to perform it.

learning curve
The mathematical or graphic representation of the learning phenomenon.

Companies have found a systematic nonlinear cost function when employees gain experience performing a particular task. As their experience increases, their productivity improves and costs per unit decrease. Experience, or learning, obviously affects direct labor costs, and it affects costs related to direct labor, such as supervision.

The **learning phenomenon** often occurs when new production methods are introduced, when new products (either goods or services) are made, and when new employees are hired. For example, the effect of learning on the cost of aircraft manufacturing is well known. Manufacturers of products for the aerospace industry, such as Martin Marietta and Grumman, write contracts that recognize the effect of learning by establishing a lower cost for the second item of an order than for the first, a lower cost for the third than for the second, and so forth.

For example, Foothill Commercial Bank provides home improvement loans to qualifying customers. The direct labor to process the loan applications is subject to an 80 percent cumulative **learning curve.** This means that the average unit time required to process two applications is 80 percent of the time required for one; the unit average time for four applications is 80 percent of the average time required per unit for two applications, and so forth.

The first loan application, one unit, processed by an employee is estimated to require 1.25 direct labor-hours. If the 80 percent cumulative learning curve is used, the average for two loans is estimated to be 1.00 hour (.80 × 1.25 hours), a total of 2.0 hours for both units. Four units take an average of .80 hours each (.80 × 1.00 hours), or a total of 3.20 hours. This means that a total of 1.20 hours (3.20 − 2.00) must be expended to produce the third and fourth units. As the labor-hours change, so do the costs affected by labor-hours.

Mathematically, the learning curve effect can be expressed as

$$Y = aX^b$$

where

Y = Average number of labor-hours required for the first X units
a = Number of labor-hours required for the first unit
X = Cumulative number of units produced
b = Index of learning equal to the log of the learning rate divided by the log of 2; for the example with an 80 percent cumulative learning rate, $b = -.322$

Thus, the number of labor-hours for the Foothill Commercial Bank example could be derived as follows:

Number of Labor-Hours

X	Average[a] (Y)	Total	Marginal
1	1.25	1.25	1.25
2	1.00 (80% × 1.25)	2.00[b]	0.75[c]
3	0.878	2.634[b]	0.634[c]
4	0.80 (80% × 1.00)	3.20	0.566
⋮		⋮	⋮
8	0.64 (80% × .80)	5.12	1.92

[a]Computations for Y using formula with logarithm:
$Y = 1.25 \times (2^{-.322}) = 1.00$
$Y = 1.25 \times (3^{-.322}) = 0.878$
$Y = 1.25 \times (4^{-.322}) = 0.80$
$Y = 1.25 \times (8^{-.322}) = 0.64$

[b]2.00 = 2 units × 1.00 hour, 2.634 = 3 units × 0.878 hour, and so on.

[c]0.75 = 2.00 hours − 1.25 hours, 0.634 = 2.634 hours − 2.00 hours, and so on.

Illustration 12.8 presents the total and average labor-hours required for loan processing per employee at Foothill Commercial Bank. The curvilinear nature of the

ILLUSTRATION   12.8   Labor-Hours and Volume Graphs, Foothill Commercial Bank

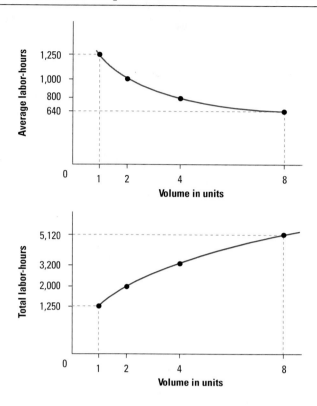

relationship between activity volume and labor-hours shows large initial learning effects that become increasingly smaller as employees learn more about how to process the loans.

The function

$$Y = aX^b$$

is curvilinear, as shown in Illustration 12.8. The function is linear when expressed in logs because

$$\log Y = \log a + b \log X$$

The function is linear when plotted on log-log paper as shown in Illustration 12.9. A good approximation of the average labor-hours required for *X* units can be obtained from a plot on log-log paper.

Applications to Accounting

The learning phenomenon applies to time; thus, it could affect any costs that are a function of time. It affects hourly labor costs per unit but not straight piecework pay per unit. Any overhead costs affected by labor time also are affected. For example, if indirect labor is a variable cost, reductions in worker time could result in a reduction in indirect labor.

When costs are estimated, the potential impact of learning should be considered. The learning phenomenon can affect costs used in inventory valuation, in decision making, and in performance evaluation. However, learning curves usually apply only to the early phases of production. After the steady state is achieved, costs tend to stabilize. Failing to recognize learning effects can have some unexpected consequences, as shown in the following examples.

ILLUSTRATION   12.9   Labor-Hours and Volume—Log-Log Relationship

---

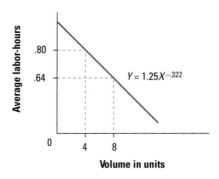

Decision Making   AAA Company is considering the production of a new product that would not affect fixed costs. The per unit variable costs to make and sell the first unit are $40, and $38, respectively. At first glance, the product appears unprofitable because it doesn't even cover variable costs. However, because of learning, the variable cost will drop from $40 to $20 by the end of the first year of production, making it much more profitable.

Performance Evaluation   Elite University has developed labor time and cost standards for some of its clerical activities that are subject to the learning curve phenomenon. Management observed that time spent on these activities systematically exceeded the standard. Upon investigating the problem, management found high personnel turnover, which meant that the activities were performed by inexperienced people. After changes in personnel policy, turnover was reduced and the jobs were staffed with more experienced people. The time spent on clerical activities no longer exceeded standards.

SELF-STUDY QUESTION

3. A company recently recorded the following costs that are subject to a 75 percent cumulative learning effect.

Cumulative Number of Units Produced	Average Manufacturing Cost per Unit	Total Manufacturing Costs
1	$1,333	$1,333
2	?	?
4	?	?
8	?	?
16	?	?

Complete the chart by filling in the cost amounts for volumes of 2, 4, 8, and 16 units.

The solution to this question is at the end of the chapter on page 380.

SUMMARY

Accurate cost estimation is important to most companies for decision-making purposes. Although no estimation method is completely accurate, some are better than others. The usefulness of a cost estimation method depends highly on the user's knowledge of the business and the costs being analyzed.

The following summarizes the key ideas tied to the chapter's learning objectives.

LO1: Reasons for estimating costs. Accurate cost estimation helps management to make informed decisions concerning the incurrence of future costs and how they may vary if conditions change.

LO2: Cost estimation and value. To add value to the company, projects generally should be profitable. Managers know whether projects add value only after estimating the revenues and costs involved. Thus, cost estimation techniques can play a pivotal role in projecting whether a project will add value to the company.

LO3: Using engineering estimates. Engineering estimates involve careful measurement of the actual cost-causing process. Engineers break the process into steps and estimate the cost of each step. The advantage of the engineering approach is that it can detail each step required to perform an operation. This provides a useful way to review a company's total manufacturing process. Disadvantages are that the engineering approach often is quite expensive and that engineering estimates often are based on particular past conditions that may not occur in the future.

LO4: Using account analysis. Account analysis calls for judgmental determination of whether a cost is fixed or variable. The method's advantages are its relative ease of application and its use of managerial experience and judgment. The disadvantage is that heavy reliance on judgmental decisions may cause estimates to be biased toward the decision makers' personal biases or perceptions.

LO5: Using scattergraphs and high-low estimates. Scattergraphs and high-low estimates show past cost behaviors and their relation to some activity measure to estimate future costs given a specific activity level. This approach (and any other approach that uses past data) is limited to future estimates made within the relevant range of past activity levels.

LO6: Using regression analysis. Regression analysis forms a mathematically determined line of best fits (minimal variation). We must be careful to find any unrepresentative outliers and to restrict cost estimates to the relevant range.

LO7: Interpreting regression output. The correlation coefficient (R) and the adjusted R^2 help to indicate the amount of the cost variation that is explained by the predictors (independent variables). Simple regression uses only one predictor, and multiple regression uses more than one predictor to help explain a particular cost.

LO8: Potential problems with regression data. Regression is so accessible that it can be used indiscriminately with unfortunate results. To avoid pitfalls, users must (1) fully understand the methodology and its limitations, (2) specify the model, that is, the hypothesized relationship between costs and cost predictors, (3) know the characteristics of the data being used, and (4) examine a plot of the data.

LO9: Pros and cons of alternative cost estimation methods. The engineering approach details each step required to perform an operation that enables the company to review its manufacturing productivity. This approach does not require historical data and, thus, can be used for new activities. Account analysis relies heavily on the experience and judgment of managers and accountants who are familiar with company operations. This can be an advantage if the person estimating the costs is objective. Regression analysis assumes that historical data accurately reflects what will happen in the future—an assumption that may or may not be true. To effectively use this approach, accountants and managers must fully understand the regression output (for example, R^2, adjusted R^2).

LO10: The effect of learning curves on costs. The systematic relation between labor time and experience is a common nonlinear relationship between costs and activity. This learning curve phenomenon implies that unit costs decrease as more and more units are made (up to a point) because labor time per unit decreases. The potential impact of the phenomenon should be considered any time that costs are estimated.

L011: Confidence intervals for regression estimates (appendix). A prediction interval represents a range within which the actual cost is expected to fall a specified percentage of the time. Thus, a 95 percent prediction interval represents a range within which the actual costs are expected to fall 95 percent of the time. The boundaries of a prediction interval equal the predicted Y value plus or minus the standard error of the estimate of Y times the t-statistic for the specified prediction level.

KEY TERMS

account analysis, 348

adjusted R-square (R^2), 356

correlation coefficient, 355

dependent variable, 353

engineering estimates, 347

high-low cost estimation, 352

independent variables, 353

learning curve, 362

learning phenomenon, 362

multicollinearity (appendix), 368

regression, 353

relevant range, 353

scattergraph, 350

t-statistic (appendix), 366

APPENDIX

L.O. 11: Construct confidence intervals for regression estimates (appendix).

t-statistic

t is the value of b, the coefficient, divided by its standard error.

Technical Notes on Regression

This appendix discusses technical issues that often arise when regression analysis is used.

Confidence in the Coefficients

In many cases, it may be desirable to determine whether the bs (that is, the coefficients of the independent variables) are significantly different from zero. The **t-statistic** is used to test for the significance of bs.

This t is simply the value of b divided by its standard error (SE_b). For the data used in the simple regression for Escondido, Inc., the t-statistic for the coefficient is

$$t = b/SE_b$$
$$= \frac{12.373}{1.703}$$
$$= 7.265$$

where both the b of 12.373 and the SE_b of 1.703 are given by the computer output of the regression. As a rule of thumb, a t of 2.0 or better is usually considered statistically significant. With $t > 2$, analysts generally reject the hypothesis that the regression results are due to chance and reject the hypothesis that the true value of b is zero.

To construct a 95 percent confidence interval around b, we add or subtract to b the appropriate t value for the 95 percent confidence interval times the standard error of b, as follows:

$$b \pm t \times SE_b$$

Recall that for this example, $SE_b = 1.703$. The value of t for a 95 percent confidence interval may be obtained from a table of t values in a statistics book. From this table, we find:

$$t = 2.160$$

Hence, the confidence intervals are

$$b \pm 2.160 \times 1.703 = b \pm 3.678$$

With b equal to $12.373, the upper limit is

$$\$16.051 \text{ (that is, } \$12.373 + \$3.678)$$

and the lower confidence limit is

$$\$8.695 \text{ (that is, } \$12.373 - \$3.678)$$

We would be 95 percent confident that the variable cost coefficient is between $8.695 and $16.051.

Confidence Intervals for Cost Estimates

When predicting future costs, it is almost impossible to develop an estimate that will exactly equal the costs that are finally incurred. Although it is not possible to eliminate all estimation errors, it is possible to place bounds on an estimate so that a decision maker can know the range of likely costs. These bounds are usually expressed in the form of a prediction interval, sometimes called a *confidence interval*.

A *prediction interval* represents a range within which the actual cost is expected to fall a specified percentage of the time. Thus, a 95 percent prediction interval represents a range within which the actual costs are expected to fall 95 percent of the time. The boundaries of a prediction interval are based on the assumption that the residuals from a regression are normally distributed. If this assumption holds, the boundaries equal the predicted Y value plus or minus the standard error of the estimate of Y times the t-statistic for the specified prediction level. This may be expressed mathematically as

$$Y \pm t \times SE_Y$$

For example, assume that management of Escondido, Inc., had estimated the overhead costs for 115 machine-hours (MH) as follows:

$$
\begin{aligned}
Y &= \$1,334 + \$12.373 \text{ per MH} \\
&= \$1,334 + (\$12.373 \times 115 \text{ MH}) \\
&= \$2,757
\end{aligned}
$$

The computer provides the information necessary to construct the prediction interval and, in many cases, computes the interval itself. In this example, we obtain the following output from the computer to compute the 95% confidence interval for

Standard error of estimate SE_Y (for 115 machine-hours): $192
t-statistic for 95% confidence interval: 2.160

We compute the prediction interval as

$$\$2,757 \pm (\$192 \times 2.160) = \$2,757 \pm \$415$$

The upper limit of the prediction interval is

$$\$3,172 = \$2,757 + \$415$$

and the lower limit is

$$\$2,342 = \$2,757 - \$415$$

which means that we are 95 percent confident that the overhead will be between $2,342 and $3,172 when an activity level of 115 machine-hours is attained.

Assumptions about the Residuals   The differences between the estimated Y values (found on the regression line) and the actual Ys are called *residuals*. If a residual is random, its expected value is zero for any observation. The three important assumptions about the residuals are that (1) they are independent of each other,

(2) their variance is constant over the range of independent variables, and (3) they are normally distributed. Violation of these assumptions makes certain inferences about confidence intervals and the significance levels of *b* estimates questionable.

If the residuals are not normally distributed, the residual for any observation may be statistically related to that for another observation. The expected value for the residual is not zero. One such condition in which residuals are related to each other, because observations are related to each other over time, is known as *serial correlation* or *autocorrelation*. When the residuals are related to each other, the correlation coefficients and the presence of autocorrelation may be tested by the Durbin-Watson statistic, which is provided on the regression computer output.

The variance in cost data may not be constant over all levels of costs, a condition known as *heteroscedasticity*. To determine whether heteroscedasticity is present, a plot of the residuals over different values of *Y* is needed. If the scatter of residuals is not constant over these *Y* values, the assumption of constant variance may be rejected. The problem may be cured by transforming the variables (*X*s and *Y*s) to their logarithms or square roots or by constructing a regression with a new set of variables.

We mention these assumptions because they are often violated in cost data. Consequently, we should be careful about the inferences that we draw from regressions. You should consult statistics books for more information about how to deal with violations of these assumptions.

Using the *b*s as Variable Cost Estimates

When using a simple linear regression, the intercept is often considered analogous to fixed costs and the slope to variable cost. Indeed, in many companies, regression estimates are used to estimate the fixed and variable components of manufacturing overhead for overhead application and analysis. Care should be exercised when doing this, however. For example, it is possible to have negative intercepts in empirical estimates, but it is highly unlikely that a company would have negative fixed costs.

If more than one predictor variable is used, as in Escondido, Inc.'s multiple regression, the interpretation of the *b*s as variable costs is somewhat more hazardous. For the multiple regression of Escondido, Inc., the following correlation matrix was part of the computer output. It shows that the machine-hours and direct material dollars are highly correlated with one another (that is, a correlation of 0.832).

Variable	*b*
Machine-hours (MH)	4.359
Direct materials cost (DMC)	0.258

Correlation Matrix

	MH	**DMC**
MH	1.00	0.832
DMC	0.832	1.00

multicollinearity
Correlation between two or more independent variables in a multiple regression equation.

This means that there is overlapping explanatory power among the two predictors. This problem is referred to as **multicollinearity.** It does not affect the *Y* estimate, but it does affect the interpretation of the contribution that each of the *X*s (that is, direct material dollars and machine-hours) is making to the prediction of *Y*.

SELF-STUDY QUESTION

4. The data from Self-Study Question 1 yield the following computer output: a multiple linear regression with overhead as the dependent variable and direct labor-hours, direct labor costs, machine-hours, and units of output as independent variables. Explain the paradox between the high adjusted R^2 value and low *t*-statistics.

Dependent variable = Overhead

Independent variables: DL-hrs., DL cost, Mach.-hrs., units produced

$R^2 = .894$ Adjusted $R^2 = .871$

24 observations

Variable Name	No.	Estimated Coefficient	Standard Error	t-Statistic
Direct labor-hours	1	3.1337	2.7705	1.1311
DL cost	2	0.30600	0.32961	0.92839
Machine-hours	3	0.79964	2.0756	0.38526
Units produced	4	−0.09679	12.539	0.00772
Intercept		−111.91	17.246	−6.4892

Correlation Matrix of Coefficients

Variable

1	1.000			
2	0.970	1.000		
3	0.973	0.962	1.000	
4	0.982	0.970	0.980	1.000
	1 DL-hours	2 DL cost	3 Mach.-hours	4 units produced

The solution to this question is at the end of this chapter on page 380.

REVIEW QUESTIONS

12.1 Which method of cost estimation is not usually based on company records?

12.2 What is the connection between the relevant range and the range of observations included in a data set for cost estimation purposes?

12.3 Under what conditions is the engineering estimates technique preferred to other estimation techniques?

12.4 If one simply wishes to prepare a cost estimate using regression analysis and enters data into a program to compute regression estimates, what problems might be encountered?

12.5 When using cost estimation methods based on past data, what are the trade-offs between gathering more data and gathering less?

12.6 What needs to be known to construct a confidence interval for a specific cost estimate (Y) (appendix)?

12.7 How do cost estimates affect a company's value?

CRITICAL ANALYSIS AND DISCUSSION QUESTIONS

12.8 The following costs are labeled fixed or variable according to a typical designation in accounting. Under which circumstances would any of these costs behave in a manner opposite to that listed?
a. Direct labor—variable.
b. Equipment depreciation—fixed.
c. Utilities (with a minimum charge)—variable.
d. Supervisory salaries—fixed.
e. Indirect materials purchased in given sizes that become spoiled within a few days—variable.

12.9 Why might a long-time executive prefer account analysis to statistical cost estimation methods?

12.10 When preparing cost estimates for account analysis purposes, should the costs be extracted from the historical accounting records?

12.11 How can one compensate for the effects of price instability when preparing cost estimates using high-low or regression techniques?

12.12 Some people claim that the scattergraph and the regression methods go hand in hand. Why?

12.13 What problems might arise when multiple independent variables are used?

12.14 When using past data to predict a cost that has fixed and variable components, it is possible to have an equation with a negative intercept. Does this mean that at a zero production level the company will make money on its fixed costs? Explain.

12.15 A decision maker is interested in obtaining a cost estimate based on a regression equation. There are no problems with changes in prices, costs, technology, or relationships between activity and cost. Only one variable is to be used. What caveats might be in order if a regression is prepared for this purpose (appendix)?

EXERCISES

12.16 Methods of Estimating Costs— Account Analysis (L.O. 4)

The accounting records of a company report the following manufacturing costs for the past year:

Direct materials	$420,000
Direct labor	350,000
Manufacturing overhead	788,000

Production was 70,000 units. Fixed manufacturing overhead was $480,000.

For the coming year, the direct materials costs are expected to increase by 20 percent, excluding any effects of volume changes. Direct labor rates are scheduled to increase by 4 percent. Fixed manufacturing overhead is expected to increase 7.5 percent, and variable manufacturing overhead per unit is expected to remain the same.

Required

a. Prepare a cost estimate for an activity level of 80,000 units of product this year.

b. Determine the costs per unit for last year and for this year.

12.17 Methods of Estimating Costs— Account Analysis (L.O. 4)

The accounting records of a company indicate that the following manufacturing costs were incurred in year 1:

Direct materials	$307,500
Direct labor	239,500
Manufacturing overhead	380,000

These costs were incurred to produce 50,000 units of product. Fixed manufacturing overhead amounts to $237,500.

For year 2, direct materials costs are expected to increase by 10 percent per unit. Direct labor costs are due to increase by 15 percent per unit. Variable manufacturing costs are expected to remain constant per unit, but fixed manufacturing overhead is expected to increase by 5 percent.

Required

a. Year 2 production is estimated to be 65,000 units. What are the estimated direct materials, direct labor, variable overhead, and fixed overhead costs for year 2?

b. Determine the total manufacturing costs per unit for years 1 and 2.

12.18 Methods of Estimating Costs— High-Low (L.O. 5)

Continental Company provides the following cost data for maintenance work on its fleet of limousines:

Miles per Year	Maintenance Cost ($ millions)
20,800	$1.2
27,200	1.4
33,600	1.6

Required

a. Use the high-low method to estimate the fixed cost per month and the variable cost per hour.

    b. What would be Continental's estimated costs if it drove 32,000 miles this year? 40,000 miles?

12.19 Methods of Estimating Costs— High-Low (L.O. 5)

Nate Corporation manufactures golf carts. Management wants to estimate overhead costs to plan their operations. A recent trade publication revealed that overhead costs tend to vary with machine-hours and/or materials costs. To check this, they collected the following data for the past 12 months:

Month Number	Machine-Hours	Materials Cost	Overhead Costs
1	350	$4,750	$4,500
2	340	4,600	4,225
3	320	4,200	3,780
4	380	5,900	5,250
5	350	4,600	4,800
6	400	5,250	5,100
7	320	4,350	4,450
8	300	4,350	4,200
9	420	6,000	5,475
10	390	4,950	4,760
11	340	4,450	4,325
12	290	3,800	3,975

Required

    a. Use the high-low method to estimate the fixed and variable portions of overhead costs based on machine-hours.

    b. If the plant is planning to operate at a level of 380 machine-hours next period, what are the estimated overhead costs? (Assume no inflation.)

12.20 Methods of Estimating Costs— Scattergraph (L.O. 5)

Prepare a scattergraph based on the overhead and direct machine-hour data in Exercise 12.19.

12.21 Methods of Estimating Costs— Scattergraph (L.O. 5)

Prepare a scattergraph based on the overhead and materials cost data in Exercise 12.19.

12.22 Estimating Costs— Simple Regression (L.O. 6, L.O. 7)

Simple regression results from the data of Nate Company (Exercise 12.19) are as follows:

Equation

Overhead = $348.17 + ($12.149 × Machine-hours)

Statistical data
Correlation coefficient 904
R^2 .818

Required

Estimate overhead if the company expects to use 380 machine-hours for the next period and costs are stable.

12.23 Estimating Costs— Simple Regression (L.O. 6, L.O. 7)

Ginfee, Inc., has developed a regression equation to analyze the behavior of its maintenance costs (Q) as a function of machine-hours (Z). The following equation was developed using 30 monthly observations:

$$Q = \$6,000 + \$5.25Z$$

Required

If 1,000 machine-hours are worked in one month, the estimate of total maintenance costs is

    a. $ 4,725.

    b. $ 5,250.

    c. $10,125.

    d. $11,250.

(CPA adapted)

12.24 **Estimating Costs—Multiple Regression** (L.O. 6, L.O. 7)

Multiple regression results from the data of Nate Company (Exercise 12.19) follow:

Equation

Overhead = $694.24 + ($4.5920 × Machine-hours) + (.2392 × Materials cost)

Statistical data
Correlation coefficient 935
R^2 874

Assume that management predicts $5,000 materials cost and 380 machine-hours for the coming period.

Required   Use the multiple regression results to estimate overhead costs for the coming period.

12.25 **Interpreting Regression Results—Multiple Choice** (L.O. 7)

Pentag Company is planning to introduce a new product that will sell for $12 a unit. The following manufacturing cost estimates have been made on 100,000 units to be produced the first year:

Direct materials $100,000
Direct labor . . . .   80,000 (the labor rate is $8 an hour × 10,000 hours)

Manufacturing overhead costs have not yet been estimated for the new product, but monthly data on total production and overhead costs for the past 24 months have been analyzed using simple linear regression. The following results were derived from the simple regression and provide the basis for overhead cost estimates for the new product.

Simple Regression Analysis Results

Dependent variable—Factory overhead costs
Independent variable—Direct labor-hours
Computed values
  Intercept $110,000
  Coefficient of independent variable . . . . $ 6.40
  Coefficient of correlation 0.953
  R^2. . . . .   0.908

Required
a. What percentage of the variation in overhead costs is explained by the independent variable?
   (1) 90.8.
   (2) 42.
   (3) 48.8.
   (4) 95.3.
   (5) Some other amount.

b. The total overhead cost for an estimated activity level of 20,000 direct labor-hours is
   (1) $110,000.
   (2) $128,000.
   (3) $164,000.
   (4) $238,000.
   (5) Some other amount.

c. What is the expected contribution margin per unit to be earned during the first year on 100,000 units of the new product? (Assume that all marketing and administrative costs are fixed.)
   (1) $9.56.
   (2) $9.78.
   (3) $8.18.
   (4) $10.20.
   (5) Some other amount.

d. How much is the variable manufacturing cost per unit, using the variable overhead estimated by the regression (assuming that direct materials and direct labor are variable costs)?
   (1) $1.80.
   (2) $2.22.
   (3) $2.44.

(4) $6.

(5) Some other amount.

e. What is the manufacturing cost equation implied by these results, where x refers to units produced?

(1) $TC = \$80,000 + \$2.22x$.

(2) $TC = \$110,000 + \$2.44x$.

(3) $TC = \$290,000 + \$6.40x$.

(4) Some other equation.

(CMA adapted)

12.26 Interpreting Regression Results (L.O. 7)

The advertising manager of Leonine Company wants to know whether the company's advertising program is successful. The manager used a pocket calculator to estimate the relation between advertising expenditures (the independent variable) and sales dollars. Monthly data for the past two years were entered into the calculator. The regression results indicated the following equation:

$$\text{Sales dollars} = \$845,000 - (\$520 \times \text{Advertising})$$
$$\text{Correlation coefficient} = -.902$$

These results might imply that the advertising was reducing sales. The manager was about to conclude that statistical methods were so much nonsense when you walked into the room.

Required

Help the manager. What might cause the negative relationship between advertising expenditures and sales?

12.27 Interpreting Regression Results—Simple Regression (L.O. 7)

A fast-food restaurant, Ben's Big Burgers, is estimating overhead based on food cost. Data were gathered for the past 24 months and entered into a regression program. The following output was obtained:

Equation

Intercept	$37,650
Slope	1.150

Statistical data

Correlation coefficient	.872
R^2	.760

The company is planning to operate at a level of $25,000 of food costs per month for the coming year.

Required

a. Use the regression output to write the overhead cost equation.

b. Based on the cost equation, compute the estimated overhead cost per month for the coming year.

12.28 Interpreting Regression Data (L.O. 7, L.O. 11—appendix)

Comador Commercial Bank needs to forecast its Personnel Department costs. The following output was obtained from a regression program used to estimate the department's costs as a function of the number of employees:

Equation

$$\text{Personnel costs} = \$8,420 + (\$492 \times \text{Employees})$$

Statistical data

Correlation coefficient	.923
R^2	.852
Adjusted R^2	.834
Standard error of slope	34.250
t-statistic for slope	11.912

Monthly data for the past two years were used to construct these estimates. Cost relationships are expected to be the same for the coming period.

Required

a. What are the estimated personnel costs for 4,200 employees?

b. Construct a 95 percent confidence interval for the slope coefficient (appendix). (Use $t = 2.074$.)

12.29 Learning Curves (L.O. 10)

Paradigm Stainless Steel Company manufactures high-technology instruments for spacecraft. The company recorded the following costs subject to a 75 percent cumulative learning effect.

Cumulative Number of Units Produced, X	Average Manufacturing Costs per Unit	Total Manufacturing Costs
1	$4,000	$4,000
2	3,000	6,000
4	?	?
8	?	?
16	?	?

Required   Complete the chart by filling in the cost amounts for volumes of 4, 8, and 16 units.

12.30   Learning Curves (L.O. 10)   Dianetics Manufacturing estimates the variable cost of producing each unit of a product as follows:

Materials	$750 per unit
Direct labor	15 per hour
Variable overhead	100 per unit plus 75% of direct labor costs

The first unit requires 100 hours to make. Labor time is subject to an 80 percent cumulative learning curve; therefore, $Y = aX^{-.322}$.

Required   Compute the variable costs to make two units and four units.

PROBLEMS

12.31   Methods of Estimating Costs— High-Low, Scattergraph, and Regression

The Lincoln plant of Nilsine Company manufactures electrical components. Plant management has experienced fluctuating monthly overhead costs and wants to be able to estimate overhead costs accurately to plan its operations and its financial needs. A trade association publication reports that for companies manufacturing electrical components, overhead tends to vary with machine-hours.

A member of the controller's staff proposed that the behavior pattern of these overhead costs be determined to improve cost estimation.

Another staff member suggested that a good starting place for determining cost behavior patterns is to analyze historical data.

Following this suggestion, monthly data were gathered on machine-hours and overhead costs for the past two years. There were no major changes in operations over this period of time. The raw data follow:

Month Number	Machine-Hours	Overhead Costs
1	20,000	$84,000
2	25,000	99,000
3	22,000	89,500
4	23,000	90,000
5	20,000	81,500
6	19,000	75,500
7	14,000	70,500
8	10,000	64,500
9	12,000	69,000
10	17,000	75,000
11	16,000	71,500
12	19,000	78,000
13	21,000	86,000
14	24,000	93,000
15	23,000	93,000
16	22,000	87,000
17	20,000	80,000
18	18,000	76,500
19	12,000	67,500
20	13,000	71,000
21	15,000	73,500
22	17,000	72,500
23	15,000	71,000
24	18,000	75,000

These data were entered into a computer regression program. The following output was obtained:

Coefficient of correlation	.9544
R^2	.9109
Coefficients of the equation	
Intercept	39,859.000
Independent variable (slope)	2.1549

Required

a. Use the high-low method to estimate Lincoln plant's overhead costs.

b. Prepare a scattergraph showing the overhead costs plotted against machine-hours.

c. Use the results of the regression analysis to prepare the cost estimation equation and a cost estimate for 22,500 machine-hours.

(CMA adapted)

12.32 Methods of Cost Estimation— Account Analysis, Simple and Multiple Regression

Dellila Undersea Gear Corporation has prepared a schedule of estimated overhead costs for the coming year on the assumption that production will equal 80,000 units. Costs have been classified as fixed or variable, according to the controller's judgment.

The following overhead items and the classification as fixed or variable form the basis for the overhead cost schedule:

Item	Total Cost
Indirect materials	$ 37,500 (all variable)
Indirect labor	194,200 ($171,000 fixed)
Building occupancy	236,420 (all fixed)
Power.	27,210 (all variable)
Equipment depreciation	181,000 (all fixed)
Equipment maintenance	24,330 ($8,500 fixed)
Personal property taxes	14,100 ($6,350 fixed)
Data processing	11,220 ($9,470 fixed)
Technical support	16,940 (all fixed)
Total estimated overhead	$742,920

In the past, the overhead costs have been related to production levels. Price instability has led management to suggest, however, that explicit consideration be given to including an appropriate price index in the cost equation. Management realizes that to estimate future costs using a regression model that includes both production and a price index as independent variables requires predicting a future value not only for production but also for the price index, but at least some recognition will be given to the dramatic price changes that have been experienced in the past few years. For cost estimation purposes, the next value of the index is assumed to be the same as the last period value of the index (that is, 113).

Following management instructions, data were gathered on past costs, production levels, and an appropriate price index. These data follow:

Overhead Costs	Production (Units)	Price Index
$718,480	62,800	89
735,110	72,800	90
768,310	93,400	93
717,670	56,900	95
715,960	58,800	98
726,880	69,000	100
753,420	87,000	101
777,640	98,000	103
720,410	59,200	103
718,100	62,600	106
736,800	73,100	108
714,220	60,400	113

No significant changes in operations occurred during the period covered by these data and none are expected in the coming period.

When these data were entered into a regression program using only the production level as the independent variable, the following results were obtained:

Equation

Overhead = $626,547 + ($1.504 × Production units)

Statistical data
Correlation coefficient	.988
R^2	.976
Adjusted R^2	.974

When both predictors were entered in the regression program, the following results were obtained:

Multiple Regression Results

Equation

Overhead = $632,640 + ($1.501 × Production) − ($59.067 × Index)

Statistical data
Correlation coefficient (multiple R)	.988
R^2	.976
Adjusted R^2	.972

Correlation matrix

	Production	Index
Production	1.00	−0.087
Index	−0.087	1.00

Required

a. Prepare a cost estimation equation using the account analysis approach.

b. Use the high-low method to prepare a cost estimate for the 80,000 units of activity expected in the coming period.

c. Prepare a cost estimate for 80,000 units using simple linear regression.

d. Use the multiple regression results to estimate overhead costs for 80,000 units for the coming period.

e. Comment on the method that you think is more appropriate under the circumstances.

12.33 Interpreting Regression Results—Simple Regression

Your company is preparing an estimate of its production costs for the coming period. The controller estimates that direct materials costs are $7.35 per unit and that direct labor costs are $15.40 per hour. Estimating overhead, which is applied on the basis of direct labor costs, is difficult.

The controller's office estimated overhead costs at $300 for fixed costs and $12 per unit for variable costs. Your nemesis on the staff, Gearld Lukcas, suggested that the company use the regression approach. Gearld has already done the analysis on a home computer and reports the "correct" cost equation as

Overhead = $883 + $10.70 per unit

Gearld also reports that the correlation coefficient for the regression is .82 and says, "With 82 percent of the variation in overhead explained by the equation, it certainly should be adopted as the best basis for estimating costs."

When asked for the data used to generate the regression, Gearld produces the following list:

Month	Overhead	Unit Production
1	$4,762	381
2	5,063	406
3	6,420	522
4	4,701	375
5	6,783	426
6	6,021	491
7	5,321	417
8	6,133	502
9	6,481	515
10	5,004	399
11	5,136	421
12	6,160	510
13	6,104	486

The company controller is somewhat surprised that the cost estimates are so different. You have therefore been assigned to check Gearld's equation.

Required

Analyze Gearld's results and state your reasons for supporting or rejecting his cost equation.

12.34 Interpreting Regression Results— Multiple Choice

Lerner, Inc., is accumulating data to prepare its annual profit plan for the coming year. The behavior pattern of the maintenance costs must be determined. The accounting staff has suggested that regression be employed to derive an equation in the form of $y = a + bx$ for maintenance costs. Data regarding maintenance-hours and costs for the preceding year and the results of the regression analysis follow:

	Hours of Activity	Maintenance Costs
January	480	$ 4,200
February	320	3,000
March	400	3,600
April	300	2,820
May	500	4,350
June	310	2,960
July	320	3,030
August	520	4,470
September	490	4,260
October	470	4,050
November	350	3,300
December	340	3,160
Sum	4,800	43,200
Average	400	3,600

Average cost per hour ($43,200 ÷ 4,800) =	$9.00
Intercept	$684.65
b coefficient	$7.2884
Standard error of the intercept	$49.515
Standard error of the *b* coefficient	$.12126
R^2	.99724
t-value; intercept	13.827
t-value; *b*	60.105

Required

a. In the standard regression equation $y = a + bx$, the letter b is best described as the
(1) Independent variable.
(2) Dependent variable.
(3) Constant coefficient.
(4) Variable cost coefficient.
(5) Correlation.

b. The letter y in the standard regression equation is best described as the
(1) Independent variable.

    (2) Dependent variable.

    (3) Constant coefficient.

    (4) Variable coefficient.

    (5) Correlation.

c. The letter x in the standard regression equation is best described as the

    (1) Independent variable.

    (2) Dependent variable.

    (3) Constant coefficient.

    (4) Variable coefficient.

    (5) Correlation.

d. If Lerner Company uses the high-low method of analysis, the equation for the relationship between hours of activity and maintenance cost is

    (1) $y = 400 + 9.0x$.

    (2) $y = 570 + 7.5x$.

    (3) $y = 3,600 + 400x$.

    (4) $y = 570 + 9.0x$.

    (5) Some other equation.

e. Based on the data derived from the regression analysis, 420 maintenance-hours in a month means budgeting maintenance at

    (1) $3,780.

    (2) $3,461.

    (3) $3,797.

    (4) $3,746.

    (5) Some other amount.

f. The correlation coefficient for the regression equation for the maintenance activities is

    (1) 34.469/49.515.

    (2) $\overline{99724.}$

    (3) $\sqrt{0.99724}$.

    (4) $(.99724)^2$.

    (5) Some other amount.

g. The percent of the total variance that can be explained by the regression equation is

    (1) 99.724.

    (2) 69.613.

    (3) 80.982.

    (4) 99.862.

    (5) Some other amount.

(CMA adapted)

12.35   Learning Curves   Jammin' Corporation plans to manufacture Inexcess, a product that requires a substantial amount of direct labor on each unit. Based on the company's experience with other products that required similar amounts of direct labor, management believes that a learning factor exists in the production process used to manufacture Inexcess.

Each unit of Inexcess requires 50 square feet of direct material at a cost of $30 per square foot, for a total material cost of $1,500. The standard direct labor rate is $25 per direct labor-hour. Variable manufacturing overhead is assigned to products at a rate of $40 per direct labor-hour. In determining an initial bid price for all products, the company marks up variable manufacturing costs 30 percent.

Data on the production of the first two lots (16 units) of Inexcess follow:

1. The first lot of eight units required a total of 3,200 direct labor-hours.

2. The second lot of eight units required a total of 2,240 direct labor-hours.

Based on prior production experience, Jammin' anticipates that production time will show no significant improvement after the first 32 units. Therefore, a standard for direct labor-hours will be established on the average hours per unit for units 17–32.

Required

a. What is the basic premise of the learning curve?

b. Based on the data presented for the first 16 units, what learning rate appears to be applicable to the direct labor required to produce Inexcess? Support your answer with appropriate calculations.

c. Calculate the standard for direct labor-hours that Jammin' should establish for each unit of Inexcess.

d. After the first 32 units have been manufactured, Jammin' was asked to submit a bid on an additional 96 units. What price should Jammin' bid on this order of 96 units? Explain your answer.

e. Knowledge of the learning curve phenomenon can be a valuable management tool. Explain how management can apply this tool in planning and controlling business operations.

(CMA adapted)

12.36   Learning Curves

Krylon Company has purchased 80,000 pressure gauges annually from CO2, Inc. The price has increased each year, reaching $68 per unit last year. Because the purchase price has increased significantly, Krylon management has asked for a cost estimate of manufacturing gauges in its own facilities. Krylon's products consist of stampings and castings. The company has little experience with products requiring assembly.

The engineering, manufacturing, and accounting departments have prepared a report for management that included the following estimate for an assembly run of 10,000 units. Additional production employees will be hired to manufacture the subassembly. However, no additional equipment, space, or supervision is needed.

The report states that total costs for 10,000 units are estimated at $957,000, or $95.70 a unit. The current purchase price is $68 a unit, so the report recommends a continued purchase of the product.

Components (outside purchases).	$120,000
Assembly labor[a]	300,000
Factory overhead[b]	450,000
General and administrative overhead[c]	87,000
Total costs.	$957,000

Fixed overhead	50% of direct labor-dollars
Variable overhead	100% of direct labor-dollars
Factory overhead rate	150% of direct labor-dollars

[a]Assembly labor consists of hourly production workers.

[b]Factory overhead is applied to products on a direct labor-dollar basis. Variable overhead costs vary closely with direct labor-dollars.

[c]General and administrative overhead is applied at 10 percent of the total cost of materials (or components), assembly labor, and factory overhead.

Required

a. Were the analysis prepared by Krylon's Engineering, Manufacturing, and Accounting Departments and the recommendation to continue purchasing the gauges, which followed from the analysis, correct? Explain your answer and include any supportive calculations you consider necessary.

b. Assume that Krylon could experience labor cost improvements on the gauge assembly consistent with an 80 percent learning curve. An assembly run of 10,000 units represents the initial lot or batch for measurement purposes. Should Krylon produce the 80,000 gauges in this situation? Explain your answer.

(CMA adapted)

SOLUTIONS TO SELF-STUDY QUESTIONS

1.

Indirect materials.	$ 503,000
Indirect labor	630,000
Power.	104,000
Total variable costs	$1,237,000
Lease	$288,000
Utilities	206,000
Insurance.	24,000
Maintenance.	200,000
Depreciation.	72,000
Research and development	171,000
Total fixed costs	$961,000

$$\text{Average monthly fixed costs} = \frac{\$961,000}{24} = \underline{\$40,042}$$

$$\text{Variable cost per DLH} = \frac{\$1,237,000}{815,800} = \underline{\$1.516}$$

$$\text{Variable cost per machine-hour} = \frac{\$1,237,000}{1,022,700} = \underline{\$1.210}$$

$$\text{Variable cost per unit produced} = \frac{\$1,237,000}{202,500} = \underline{6.109}$$

2. Selecting either choice appears appropriate on a purely statistical basis, considering the high adjusted R^2 values. The choice of an activity base should not be based purely on statistical results, in any case, but should be determined by common sense and good judgment. Statistical results can help, but they do not substitute for good sense.

3.

Cumulative Number of Units Produced	Average Manufacturing Cost per Unit	Total Manufacturing Costs
1.	$1,333	$1,333
2.	1,000 ($1,333 × 75%)	2,000
4.	750 ($1,000 × 75%)	3,000
8.	562.50 ($750 × 75%)	4,500
16.	421.88 ($562.50 × 75%)	6,750

4. The independent variables are correlated to each other, causing the problem of multicollinearity and the large standard errors resulting in low t-statistics. Nevertheless, most of the variance in the dependent variable is explained by the regression, and, hence, the high adjusted R^2.

Cost-Volume-Profit
Analysis

HOW COST-VOLUME-PROFIT HELPS MANAGERS

L.O. 1: Understand how costs, volume, and profit are related.

Cellular telephone companies generally offer multiple cost levels for service, ranging from a high fixed cost per month with a low variable cost per minute to a low fixed cost per month with a high variable cost per minute. Cost-volume-profit analysis helps you decide which is the best cost level depending on the number of minutes you use per month. (© Bill Bachmann/ Tony Stone Images)

cost-volume-profit (CVP) analysis
The study of the interrelationships between costs and volume and the way that they impact profit.

The local cellular telephone company is advertising two levels of service: level 1 for $50 per month plus $.40 per minute for air time and level 2 for $20 per month plus $.70 per minute for air time. How many minutes of air time justifies moving from level 2 to level 1? (The answer is in the solution to Self-Study Question 1, part (*g*), on page 415 at the end of this chapter.)

A student organization wants to show movies on campus. It can rent a particular movie for one weekend for $1,000. Rent for an auditorium, salaries to the ticket takers and other personnel, and other fixed costs are $800 for the weekend. The organization would sell tickets for $4 per person. In addition, profits from the sale of soft drinks, popcorn, and candy are estimated to be $1 per ticket holder. How many people would have to buy tickets to justify renting the movie? (The answer is in the solution to Self-Study Question 1, part [*g*]).

During one of the many recent crises in the U.S. automobile industry, automobile executives announced a price increase. Several business news reporters expressed surprise that the executives would increase prices in the face of declining sales volume. The executives believed that the price increase would increase profits. Does this make sense?

The solution to the preceding problems requires an understanding of the relationship among costs, volume, and profit. This chapter discusses the use of **cost-volume-profit (CVP) analysis** for managerial decision making. Managers must understand the interrelationship of cost, volume, and profit for planning and decision making. They rely on their cost accounting departments to supply the information and analyses that help them anticipate and make sound decisions involving any of these three items.

Regarding the automobile industry example, the executives needed to understand relationships among selling prices, revenues, volume, and costs. They also needed to understand which costs vary with changes in volume and which stay the same. Without this kind of analysis, they could not accurately estimate the effect of price, volume, or cost changes on the company's operating profits.

The automobile executives' decision to raise prices in the face of decreasing demand struck some people as odd. However, these executives believed that the increase in price, coupled with an expected decrease in volume, would have little impact on total revenue, but since lower volume would reduce variable costs, operating profits would increase.

CVP analysis helps to define the relationships of costs used in budgeting. Managers also use the analysis in determining how the expansion of facilities and the related changes in costs would impact profits. They may even find that more volume doesn't mean more profits, depending on how the expansion changes fixed costs.

CVP AND THE VALUE CHAIN

value chain
The sequence of activities that creates the good or service.

In the production of a good or service, an organization undertakes a sequence of activities resulting in output that is delivered to the customer. Remember that the sequence of activities that creates the good or service is called a **value chain,** because each stage in the chain should add something that the customer values to the product. CVP analysis can be utilized in various stages of the value chain.

For instance, increasing quality may cause higher fixed and variable costs, increasing fixed costs due to better equipment and variable costs for higher-quality raw materials or labor. Increasing quality also may have a positive effect on sales due to increased market share and customer loyalty; the costs of rework, scrap, and returns should decrease. This combination may result in increased profits, which CVP analysis would show.

In the research and development of a product, CVP analysis can be used to evaluate the impact of the various fixed and variable cost combinations available for production of the product on profit, given the expected level of demand. This allows management to determine the design and production manner that meet the customer's needs of quality and price while still creating profit for the company.

THE PROFIT EQUATION

profit equation
Operating profit equals total revenue less total costs.

Every organization's financial operations can be stated as a simple relation among total revenues (TR), total costs (TC), and operating profit π:

$$\text{Operating profit} = \text{Total revenues} - \text{Total costs}$$
$$\pi = TR - TC$$

(If the organization is not for profit, $\pi = 0$.) Both total revenues and total costs are likely to be affected by changes in the amount of output.[1] A statement of the **profit equation** that considers amount of output adds useful information for examining the effects of revenue, costs, and volume on operating profits. Total revenue (TR) equals average selling price per unit (P) times the units of output (X):

$$\text{Total revenue} = \text{Price} \times \text{Units of output produced and sold}$$
$$TR = PX$$

Total costs (TC) may be divided into a fixed component that does not vary with changes in output levels and a variable component that does vary. The fixed component is made up of total fixed costs (F) per period; the variable component is the product of the average variable cost per unit (V) times the quantity of output (X). Therefore, the cost function is

$$\text{Total costs} = (\text{Variable costs per unit} \times \text{Units of output}) + \text{Fixed costs}$$
$$TC = VX + F$$

Substituting the expanded expressions in the profit equation yields a more useful form, as follows:

$$\text{Operating profit} = \text{Total revenue} - \text{Total costs}$$
$$\pi = TR - TC$$
$$TC = VX + F$$

Therefore

$$\pi = PX - (VX + F)$$

---

[1]Unless otherwise stated, we adopt the simplifying assumption that production volume equals sales volume so that changes in inventories may be ignored.

Collecting terms gives

$$\text{Profit} = [(\text{Price} - \text{Variable costs}) \times \text{Units of output}] - \text{Fixed costs}$$
$$\pi = (P - V)X - F$$

contribution margin
The difference between revenues and variable costs.

The **contribution margin** (Price − Variable costs) × Units of output, $(P - V)X$, is the amount that units sold contribute toward (1) covering fixed costs and (2) providing operating profits. Sometimes we use the contribution margin, in total, as in the preceding equation. Other times, we use the contribution margin per unit, which is

$$\text{Price} - \text{Variable costs}$$
$$P - V$$

Note that V is the sum of variable manufacturing costs per unit and variable marketing and administrative costs per unit; F is the sum of total fixed manufacturing costs, fixed marketing costs, and fixed administrative costs for the period; and X refers to the number of units produced and sold during the period.

Example

Assume that Sport Autos is an automobile dealership that carries one line of sports cars. During February, Sport Autos purchased 30 cars and sold each at an average price of $30,000. The average variable cost of each car was $22,000, computed as follows:

Cost of each automobile to Sport Autos	$21,000
Dealer preparation costs and sales commission	1,000
Average variable cost per car	$22,000

The fixed costs to operate the dealership for a typical month are $200,000.

Using the profit equation, the results for February are

$$\text{Operating profit} = \text{Contribution margin} - \text{Fixed costs}$$
$$\pi = (P - V)X - F$$
$$= (\$30,000 - \$22,000)\, 30 \text{ cars} - \$200,000$$
$$= \$40,000$$

Although the $40,000 operating profit was derived algebraically, it also could be determined from the company's income statement for the month, as shown in Illustration 13.1.

The profit equation is useful for managers to determine how much volume is required to obtain desired profit levels. Assume, for example, that Sport Autos' manager is hoping for sales to improve in April, when many people's thoughts turn to the joys of driving a sports car. Given the data, price (P) = $30,000, variable cost per unit (V) = $22,000 (therefore contribution margin per unit = $8,000), and fixed costs (F) for April are estimated to be $200,000, the manager asks two questions: What volume is required to break even? What volume is required to make a $120,000 operating profit?

The following formulas enable us to answer these questions. We start with the answer to the last question, which we call *finding a target volume for the target profit*. Managers may want to know the volume for a target profit expressed either in units or in sales dollars. If the company makes many products, it is often much easier to think of volume in terms of sales dollars; if we are dealing with only one product, it's easier to work with units as the measure of volume.

L.O. 2: Use cost-volume-profit (CVP) analysis as a planning and decision-making aid.

Finding Target Volumes

Target Volume in Units   The formula to find a volume expressed in units for a target profit is:

ILLUSTRATION 13.1	Income Statement

SPORT AUTOS
Income Statement
February

Sales (30 cars at $30,000)	$900,000
Less	
Variable cost of goods sold (30 × $21,000)	630,000
Variable selling costs (30 × $1,000)	30,000
Contribution margin	240,000
Less: Fixed costs	200,000
Operating profit	$ 40,000

$$\text{Target volume (units)} = \frac{\text{Fixed costs} + \text{Target profit}}{\text{Contribution margin per unit}}$$

Using the data from Sport Autos, we find the volume that provides an operating profit of $120,000 as follows:

$$\begin{aligned}\text{Target volume} &= \frac{\text{Fixed costs} + \text{Target profit}}{\text{Contribution margin per unit}} \\ &= \frac{\$200,000 + \$120,000}{\$8,000} \\ &= 40 \text{ cars}\end{aligned}$$

Proof: If Sport Autos sells 40 cars, its operating profit is

$$\begin{aligned}\pi &= (P - V)X - F \\ &= (\$8,000 \times 40 \text{ cars}) - \$200,000 \\ &= \$120,000\end{aligned}$$

Also

$$\begin{aligned}\pi &= TR - TC \\ &= PX - VX - F \\ &= (\$30,000 \times 40 \text{ cars}) - (\$22,000 \times 40 \text{ cars}) - \$200,000 \\ &= \$120,000\end{aligned}$$

contribution margin ratio
Contribution margin as a percentage of sales revenue.

Target Volume in Sales Dollars To use the formula to find a target volume expressed in sales dollars, we must first define a new term, **contribution margin ratio.** The contribution margin ratio is the contribution margin as a percentage of sales revenue. For example, for Sport Autos, the contribution margin ratio equals

$$\begin{aligned}\frac{\text{Contribution margin per unit}}{\text{Sales price per unit}} &= \frac{\$8,000}{\$30,000} \\ &= .267 \text{ (rounded)}\end{aligned}$$

We also can compute the contribution margin ratio for a total volume of activity. Pick, say, 30 units for Sport Autos. Now we compute the contribution margin ratio as follows:

$$\begin{aligned}\frac{\text{Contribution margin}}{\text{Sales revenue}} &= \frac{\$240,000}{\$900,000} = \frac{\$8,000 \times 30 \text{ units}}{\$30,000 \times 30 \text{ units}} \\ &= .267 \text{ (rounded)}\end{aligned}$$

Note that the contribution margin ratio is the same whether it is computed per unit or in total.

Using the contribution margin ratio, the formula to find the target volume for a target profit follows:

$$\text{Target sales dollars}^2 = \frac{\text{Fixed costs} + \text{Target profit}}{\text{Contribution margin ratio}}$$

For Sport Autos, the target volume expressed in sales dollars is

$$\text{Target sales dollars} = \frac{\$200,000 + \$120,000}{.267 \text{ (rounded)}}$$
$$= \$1,200,000$$

Note that $1,200,000 of sales dollars translates into 40 automobiles at a price of $30,000 each. We get the same result whether expressed in units (40 cars) or dollars (sales of 40 cars generates revenue of $1,200,000).

Finding Target Volume for a Target Profit Percent   Suppose that instead of a target dollar profit, Sport Autos' manager wants to find the number of sales dollars that would provide a sales profit margin of 20 percent. We use the same concept, but express the target operating profit as a percentage of sales instead of a target dollar amount, as follows:

$$\text{Target volume (sales dollars)} = \frac{\text{Fixed costs} + \text{Target profit}}{\text{Contribution margin ratio}}$$
$$\text{Target } PX = \frac{\$200,000 + (20\% \times \text{Sales dollars})}{.267}$$
$$\text{Target } PX = \frac{\$200,000 + .2PX}{.267}$$
$$\text{Target } PX = \frac{\$200,000}{.267} + \frac{.2PX}{.267}$$
$$\text{Target } PX = \$750,000 + .75PX$$
$$\text{Target } PX - .75PX = \$750,000$$
$$.25PX = \$750,000$$
$$\text{Target } PX = \$3,000,000$$

That is, Sport Autos must generate sales of $3,000,000 to provide a profit of 20 percent of sales.

Proof: The total contribution margin equals the contribution margin ratio times total revenue. When total revenue equals $3,000,000, the total contribution margin equals .267 (rounded) $\times$ $3,000,000 = $800,000. If fixed costs are $200,000, operating profit equals $600,000 ($800,000 contribution margin $-$ $200,000 fixed costs). Profit of $600,000 equals 20 percent of sales revenue, as required.

---

[2]We can derive the target volume for sales dollars from the original formula for units:

$$X = \frac{F + \pi}{P - V}$$

The modified formula for dollars multiplies both sides of the equation by P:

$$PX = \frac{(F + \pi)P}{P - V}$$

Since dividing the denominator by P is the same as multiplying the entire term by P, we obtain

$$PX = \frac{F + \pi}{(P - V)/P}$$

The term $(P - V)/P$ is the contribution margin ratio.

Finding the Break-Even Point

break-even point
The volume level at which profits equal zero.

The **break-even point** is the volume level where profits equal zero. Thus, to find the break-even point, we use the target volume formulas, but set profits equal to zero ($p = 0$).

Break-Even Point in Units   The formula to find the break-even point in units is

$$\text{Break-even volume (units)} = \frac{\text{Fixed costs}}{\text{Contribution margin per unit}}$$

Using the data from Sport Autos, we find the volume that provides an operating profit of zero as follows:

$$\text{Break-even volume} = \frac{\text{Fixed costs}}{\text{Contribution margin per unit}}$$
$$= \frac{\$200,000}{\$8,000}$$
$$= 25 \text{ automobiles}$$

Sport Autos must sell 25 cars per month to break even. Each additional car sold increases operating profits by $8,000.

Break-Even Point in Sales Dollars   To find the break-even point in sales dollars, we use the contribution margin ratio instead of the contribution margin per unit. The formula to find the break-even volume is

$$\text{Break-even volume (sales dollars)} = \frac{\text{Fixed costs}}{\text{Contribution margin ratio}}$$

For Sport Autos, the break-even volume expressed in sales dollars is

$$\text{Break-even volume (sales dollars)} = \frac{\$200,000}{.267 \text{ (rounded)}}$$
$$= \$750,000$$

Note that sales dollars of $750,000 translates into 25 automobiles at $30,000 each. We get the same break-even point whether expressed in units (25 cars) or dollars (sales of 25 cars generates revenue of $750,000).

Illustration 13.2 summarizes the four formulas for finding target and break-even volumes.

Graphic Presentation

Illustration 13.3 graphically presents the cost-volume-profit (CVP) relationships for Sport Autos. Such a graph is a helpful aid in presenting cost-volume-profit relationships. We may want to project the profits that could be earned from a product or a division or a company using a graph like the one in Illustration 13.3, for example. Or we may want to show various versions of the graph that result if the product's prices, variable costs per unit, and/or fixed costs per time period change. Next, we discuss specific features of the graph.

The vertical axis represents dollars (for example, revenue dollars, cost dollars). The horizontal axis represents the volume of activity for a time period (for example, number of cars sold per month or sales dollars).

The total revenue (TR) line relates total revenue to volume (for example, if Sport Autos sells 40 cars in a month, its total revenue would be $1,200,000, according to the graph). The slope of TR is the price per unit, P (for example, $30,000 per car for Sport Autos).

The total cost (TC) line shows the total cost for each volume (for example, the total cost for a volume of 40 cars is $1,080,000 = [40 \times \$22,000] + \$200,000$). The intercept of the total cost line is the fixed cost for the period, F (for example, $200,000 for the month), and the slope is the variable cost per unit, V (for example, $22,000 per car).

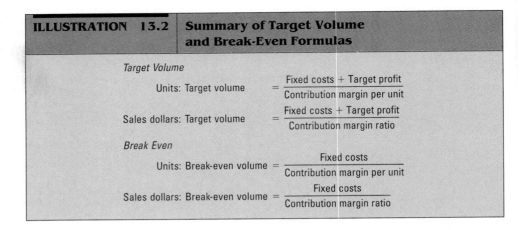

ILLUSTRATION 13.2   Summary of Target Volume and Break-Even Formulas

Target Volume

Units: Target volume $= \dfrac{\text{Fixed costs} + \text{Target profit}}{\text{Contribution margin per unit}}$

Sales dollars: Target volume $= \dfrac{\text{Fixed costs} + \text{Target profit}}{\text{Contribution margin ratio}}$

Break Even

Units: Break-even volume $= \dfrac{\text{Fixed costs}}{\text{Contribution margin per unit}}$

Sales dollars: Break-even volume $= \dfrac{\text{Fixed costs}}{\text{Contribution margin ratio}}$

ILLUSTRATION   13.3   CVP Graph, Sport Autos

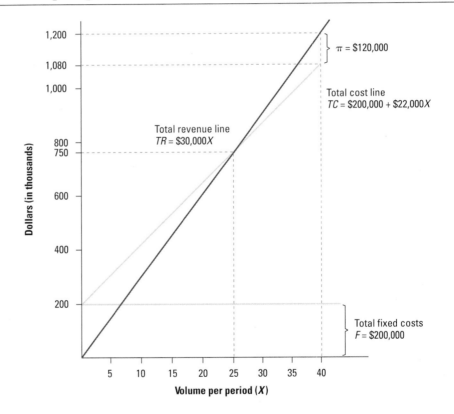

The break-even point is the volume at which $TR = TC$ (that is, the TR and TC lines intersect). Volumes lower than break even result in an operating loss because $TR > TC$; volumes higher than break even result in an operating profit because $TR > TC$. For Sport Autos, the break-even volume is 25 cars.

The amount of operating profit or loss can be read from the graph by measuring the vertical distance between TR and TC. For example, the vertical distance between TR and TC when $X = 40$ indicates $\pi = \$120,000$.

SELF-STUDY QUESTION

1. The following information for Marge and Sara's Ice Cream Company is given for April:

Sales	$180,000
Fixed manufacturing costs	22,000
Fixed marketing and administrative costs	14,000
Total fixed costs	36,000
Total variable costs	120,000
Unit price	$9
Unit variable manufacturing cost	5
Unit variable marketing cost	1

Compute the following:

a. Operating profit when sales are $180,000 (as above).

b. Break-even number in units.

c. Number of units sold that would produce an operating profit of $30,000.

d. Sales dollars required to generate an operating profit of $20,000.

e. Number of units sold in April.

f. Number of units sold that would produce an operating profit of 20 percent of sales dollars.

g. Answer the two questions—cellular phone example and student organization example—posed at the beginning of this chapter.

The solution to this question is at the end of this chapter on page 415.

PROFIT-VOLUME MODEL

profit-volume analysis
A version of CVP analysis using a single profit line.

The summary version of CVP analysis is called **profit-volume analysis.** For convenience, the cost and revenue lines are often collapsed into a single profit line.

A graphic comparison of profit-volume and CVP relationships is shown in Illustration 13.4. Note that the slope of the profit-volume line equals the average unit contribution margin. The intercept equals the loss at zero volume, which equals fixed costs. The vertical axis shows the amount of operating profit or loss.

USING CVP TO ANALYZE THE EFFECT OF DIFFERENT COST STRUCTURES

L.O. 3: Identify the effects of cost structure and operating leverage on the sensitivity of profit to changes in volume.

cost structure
The proportion of fixed and variable costs to total costs of an organization.

operating leverage
The extent to which an organization's cost structure is made up of fixed costs.

An organization's **cost structure** is the proportion of fixed and variable costs to total costs. Cost structures differ widely among industries and among firms within an industry. Manufacturers using computer-integrated manufacturing systems have a large investment in plant and equipment, which results in a cost structure with high fixed costs. In contrast, a home builder has a cost structure with a higher proportion of variable costs. The highly automated manufacturing firm is capital intensive; the builder is labor intensive.

An organization's cost structure has a significant effect on the sensitivity of its profits to changes in volume. The extent to which an organization's cost structure is made up of fixed costs is called **operating leverage.** It is high in firms with a high proportion of fixed costs and a low proportion of variable costs and results in a high contribution margin per unit. The higher the firm's fixed costs, the higher the break-even point. Once the break-even point is reached, profit increases at a high rate. Illustration 13.5 demonstrates the primary differences between two companies, Variable Company (with relatively high variable costs) and Fixed Company (with relatively high fixed costs).

Note that although these firms have the same sales revenue and operating profit, they have different cost structures. Variable Company's cost structure is dominated by variable costs with a lower contribution margin ratio of .25. Every dollar of sales contributes 25 cents toward fixed costs and profit. Fixed Company's cost structure is dominated by fixed costs with a higher contribution margin of .75. Every dollar of sales contributes 75 cents toward fixed costs and profit.

ILLUSTRATION   13.4   Comparison of CVP and Profit-Volume Graphs, Sport Autos

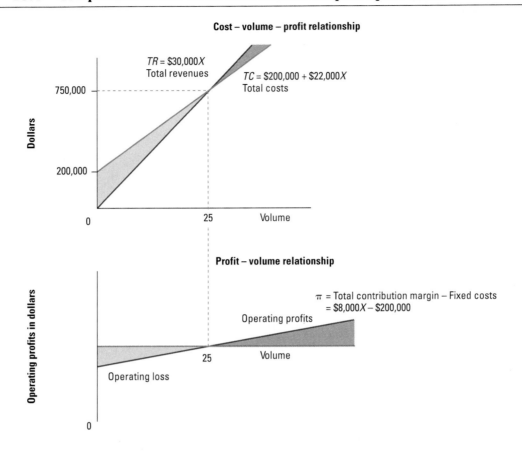

Cost – volume – profit relationship

$TR = \$30,000X$
Total revenues

$TC = \$200,000 + \$22,000X$
Total costs

Profit – volume relationship

π = Total contribution margin – Fixed costs
= $\$8,000X - \$200,000$

Operating profits

Operating loss

ILLUSTRATION 13.5	Comparison of Cost Structures			
	Variable Company (1,000,000 units)		Fixed Company (1,000,000 units)	
	Amount	Percentage	Amount	Percentage
Sales	$1,000,000	100	$1,000,000	100
Variable costs	750,000	75	250,000	25
Contribution margin	$ 250,000	25	$ 750,000	75
Fixed costs	50,000	5	550,000	55
Operating profit	$ 200,000	20	$ 200,000	20
Break-even point	200,000 units		733,334 units	
Contribution margin per unit	$0.25		$0.75	

Suppose that both companies experience a 10 percent increase in sales. Variable Company's profit increases by $25,000 (.25 × $100,000), and Fixed Company's profit increases by $75,000 (.75 × $100,000).

In general, companies with lower fixed costs have the ability to be more flexible to changes in market demands than do companies with higher fixed costs and are better able to survive tough times. The Real World Application in this chapter points to the problems the Big Three automakers encountered in the 1980s and their desire

REAL WORLD APPLICATION | **When Breaking Even Is Something to Shoot For**

For some companies, the break-even point is a target to achieve for survival. At various times during the 1980s and first half of the 1990s, Chrysler, Ford, and General Motors found themselves striving to reach the break-even point.

Chrysler was the first of the Big Three automobile companies to reach the brink of disaster when, in the early 1980s, it substantially reduced fixed costs to cut its break-even point from 2.2 million units in 1979 to 1.2 million units in 1982. In the mid-1980s, Ford found that its most successful cars still cost thousands of dollars more to manufacture than did comparable cars made by Japanese companies. During the 1980s and early 1990s, Ford suffered losses but retooled its manufacturing facilities; came out with new, popular designs; improved quality; and developed efficiencies that substantially cut costs.

General Motors was the last of the Big Three to see losses, possibly because its huge size enabled it to make profits despite its problems. After a top-management shake-up in 1992 that brought in more outside talent, the company increased its focus on improving production methods, improving quality, and reducing costs.

Perhaps because these three companies were so large, all three were among the top 10 companies in the United States at one time, their management became complacent about the need to improve quality, provide cars that appealed to younger customers, and reduce costs. Now that the Japanese automobile industry has become a competitive force in the United States, the Big Three had to become more competitive.

Source: Based on the authors' research.

ILLUSTRATION 13.6 | **Computer Spreadsheet Output**

	A	B	C	D	E
	Price	Volume	Variable Cost per Unit	Fixed Costs	Operating Profit
	$30,000	40	$22,000	$200,000	$120,000
	31,000	38	22,000	200,000	142,000
	29,000	42	22,000	200,000	94,000
	30,000	40	22,000	180,000	140,000
	31,000	38	22,000	180,000	162,000
	29,000	42	22,000	180,000	114,000
	30,000	40	22,000	220,000	100,000
	31,000	38	22,000	220,000	122,000
	29,000	42	22,000	220,000	74,000

to reduce fixed costs and thereby reduce the break-even point. Management realized that increased flexibility (and, therefore, higher potential for profits) could be attained by reducing fixed costs.

USING SPREADSHEETS IN COST-VOLUME-PROFIT ANALYSIS

Computer spreadsheets, like Lotus 1-2-3® and Excel®, provide considerable additional power in analyzing costs, volume, and profits. For example, Illustration 13.6 presents a what-if analysis prepared using a computer spreadsheet based on data for Sport Autos. Column A shows three different price scenarios, and column B shows three different volume scenarios. To keep the presentation simple, we did not change the variable cost per unit (column C). Column D shows three different fixed cost scenarios. Column E shows the operating profit computed by the spreadsheet program for each of nine different scenarios.

Once you have set up the basic CVP formula, you can see how easy it is to determine the effect if you change the value of prices, costs, and volume. CVP spreadsheet applications are particularly helpful in answering what-if questions for planning and decision making. Computer spreadsheets also make CVP analysis more fun!

USING CVP AS A TOOL TO FIND MISSING INFORMATION

A major application of the CVP model is solving for unknowns. For example, suppose that after examining the figures just presented, Sport Autos' manager pointed out, "We can't obtain 40 cars from the manufacturer to sell in April. If we can get only 30 cars to sell, can we still make $120,000 in April?" An answer can be obtained by holding outputs at 30 units and operating profits at $120,000 and then solving for each of the other terms in the following profit equation:

$$\$120,000 = (P - V)30 \text{ cars} - F$$

Solving for the Contribution Margin

Find the average contribution margin per unit required to cover Sport Autos' $200,000 fixed costs and provide target operating profits of $120,000:

$$\$120,000 = (P - V)\,30 - \$200,000$$
$$\$320,000 = (P - V)30$$
$$(P - V) = \frac{\$320,000}{30}$$
$$= \$10,667$$

Thus, the average contribution margin per car must be increased from $8,000 to $10,667 if Sport Autos is to make $120,000. The increase in the contribution margin must come from a price increase, a decrease in variable costs per unit, or a combination of the two.

Solving for Fixed Costs

Next, we try holding the contribution margin per unit constant at $8,000 to find the decrease in fixed costs that provides operating profits of $120,000 if 30 cars are sold:

$$\$120,000 = (\$8,000 \times 30 \text{ cars}) - F$$
$$\$120,000 = \$240,000 - F$$
$$F = \$120,000$$

For Sport Autos to sell 30 cars while holding the unit contribution margin at $8,000 and to make operating profits of $120,000, a reduction in fixed costs from $200,000 to $120,000 is required.

Managers thus can use CVP analysis to determine how to achieve profit goals by changing particular variables in the CVP equation, as noted in the discussion of computerized spreadsheet analysis.

CVP analysis provides a valuable tool for determining the impact of prices, costs, and volume on operating profits. An important part of management's job is to manage each variable that affects operating profits to improve profitability.

MARGIN OF SAFETY

margin of safety
The excess of projected or actual sales over the break-even volume.

The **margin of safety** is the excess of projected (or actual) sales over the break-even sales level. This tells managers the margin between current sales and the break-even point. In a sense, margin of safety indicates the risk of losing money that a company faces; that is, the amount by which sales can fall before the company is in the loss area. The margin of safety formula is

Sales volume − Break-even sales volume = Margin of safety

If Sport Autos sells 30 cars and its break-even volume is 25 cars, then its margin of safety is

$$\text{Sales} - \text{Break-even} = 30 - 25$$
$$= 5 \text{ cars}$$

ILLUSTRATION   13.7   Margin of Safety

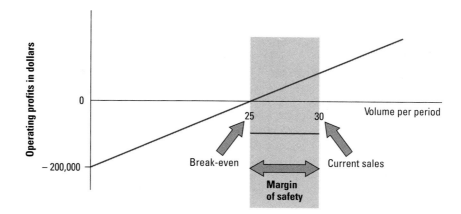

Sales volume could drop by five cars per month before it incurs a loss, all other things held constant, as shown in Illustration 13.7. In practice, the margin of safety also may be expressed in sales dollars or as a percent of current sales.

USEFUL EXTENSIONS OF THE BASIC MODEL

Cash Flow Analysis

L.O. 4: Apply extensions of the basic CVP model.

Sometimes decision makers may be more interested in the impact of the volume of activity on cash or working capital than on accrual profits. They often want to know whether it is possible to operate at a loss and still generate positive cash flows. This type of analysis may be particularly relevant in adverse economic times or when a company is phasing out part of its operations. So long as there are sufficient cash flows, it may be optimal (profit maximizing or loss minimizing) to continue the operation, even though it represents an accounting loss.

Both revenues and costs include noncash items, but the most significant noncash item tends to be depreciation, which is usually included in fixed costs. This classification is common because depreciation generally represents the allocation of the acquisition cost of plant and equipment (capacity) over time based on an estimate of their useful lives.

To see how noncash items can affect CVP analysis, suppose that the fixed costs of Sport Autos include $40,000 per month of depreciation of equipment and other assets and that this is the only noncash revenue or expense.

Illustration 13.8 compares cash flow and accrual profit-volume relationships. By substituting appropriate numbers into the profit equation, you can demonstrate that if Sport Autos operates at an accrual profit break-even volume each month, it will generate monthly net cash flows of $40,000. This is a short-run phenomenon only, of course. When the time comes to replace the depreciable assets, the need for a large cash outflow must be faced.

Depreciation also may be included in variable costs if it is based on the units of production of some asset and thus is related to volume. A common example is the depreciation of a machine based on its usage. Oil companies such as Exxon and Louisiana Land and Exploration deplete the costs of oil or gas wells over the number of units of oil or gas produced since the economic life depends on the number of units of the resource rather than the age of the well.

Income Taxes

Assuming that operating profits before taxes and taxable income are the same, income taxes may be incorporated into the basic model as follows:

$$\text{After-tax operating profits} = [(P - V)X - F](1 - t)$$

where t is the tax rate.

ILLUSTRATION   13.8   Comparison of Short-Run Cash and Accrual Profit-Volume Relationships for Sport Autos

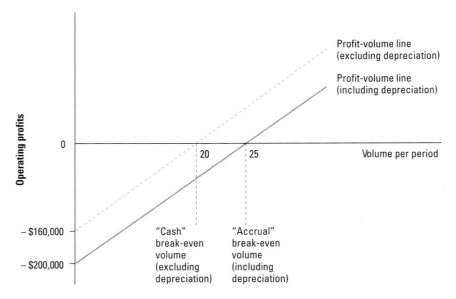

Note: The cash break-even point is found as follows:

$$X = \frac{\text{Fixed cash costs}}{\text{Cash contributon margin per unit}}$$
$$= \frac{\$200,000 - \$40,000 \text{ depreciation}}{\$8,000} = \frac{\$160,000}{\$8,000} = 20 \text{ cars}$$

Suppose that the manager of Sport Autos wants to find the number of units required to generate after-tax operating profits of $60,000. Recall that $P = \$30,000$, $V = \$22,000$, the contribution margin per unit = \$8,000, and $F = \$200,000$. We assume the tax rate $t = .4$; that is, Sport Autos has a 40 percent tax rate.

To find the target volume, we modify the original target volume formula to after-tax amounts, as follows:

$$\text{Target volume} = \frac{\text{After-tax fixed costs} + \text{Target after-tax profits}}{\text{After-tax contribution margin}}$$

Fixed costs are tax deductible. With a 40 percent tax rate, the $200,000 fixed costs save $80,000 in taxes. Thus, the after-tax fixed costs are $120,000 ($200,000 − $80,000). In general, to compute the after-tax fixed costs, we multiply before-tax fixed costs by $1 -$ tax rate. In the case of Sport Autos, using this formula gives the following

$$\begin{aligned}\text{After-tax fixed costs} &= \$200,000 \times (1 - .4) \\ &= \$200,000 \times .6 \\ &= \$120,000\end{aligned}$$

Using the same reasoning, we determine that the contribution margin per unit adds to taxable income. To compute the after-tax contribution margin per unit, multiply the contribution margin by $1 -$ tax rate. Recall that for Sport Autos, the before-tax contribution margin per unit was $8,000. Therefore

$$\begin{aligned}\text{After-tax contribution margin} &= \$8,000 \times (1 - .4) \\ &= \$8,000 \times .6 \\ &= \$4,800\end{aligned}$$

Having found the after-tax fixed costs and contribution margin, we compute the target volume to provide after-tax operating profits of $120,000 as follows:

$$\text{Target volume} = \frac{\text{After-tax fixed costs} + \text{Target after-tax profits}}{\text{After-tax contribution margin}}$$
$$= \frac{\$120,000 + \$60,000}{\$4,800}$$
$$= 37.5 \text{ cars}$$

We assume that the company cannot sell fractional cars (at least, we hope not), so we arbitrarily choose to round the number of cars up to 38, which provides somewhat more than the required $60,000 after-tax profits.[3]

What if you want to find the target volume expressed in sales dollars? Simply convert the contribution margin ratio to an after-tax ratio as follows:

$$\text{After-tax contribution margin ratio} = \text{Before-tax ratio} \times (1 - t)$$

For Sport Autos, the before-tax contribution ratio was .267 (rounded), so

$$\text{After-tax contribution margin ratio} = .267 \times (1 - .4)$$
$$= .267 \times .6$$
$$= .16$$

To find the target volume

$$\text{Target volume (sales dollars)} = \frac{\text{After-tax fixed costs} + \text{Target after-tax profits}}{\text{After-tax contribution margin ratio}}$$
$$= \frac{\$120,000 + \$60,000}{.16}$$
$$= \$1,125,000$$

which is 37.5 cars at $30,000 each.

Step (Semifixed) Costs

step cost
A cost that increases with volume in steps. Also called a semifixed cost.

It is common for fixed costs to behave in a step fashion as shown in Illustration 13.9.

Suppose that the managers of a company are considering adding an evening shift. Assume that the prices, volumes, and costs would be as follows:

Monthly Production and Sales	Total Fixed Costs	Variable Cost	Price
Regular shift: 0–10,000 units	$200,000	$15 per unit	$40 per unit
Evening shift: 10,001–18,000 units	300,000	15 per unit	40 per unit

The CVP lines are shown in Illustration 13.10. The slope of the total cost (V) is $15, but the line "steps up" at 10,000 units.

As the graph shows, if the company operates only one shift, its capacity is limited to 10,000 units. Adding the second shift increases the capacity to 18,000 units. Profits will increase if enough additional units can be sold.

The company would have two break-even points, one within each level of activity:

$$X = \frac{F}{P - V}$$
$$\text{Break-even volume (regular shift)} = \frac{\$200,000}{\$40 - \$15}$$
$$= 8,000 \text{ units}$$
$$\text{Break-even volume (regular and evening shifts)} = \frac{\$300,000}{\$40 - \$15}$$
$$= 12,000 \text{ units}$$

---

[3]Don't be too concerned about rounding fractional products in practice. Simply report the results, fully disclose whether you are rounding up or down, and, if necessary, indicate how much above or below the target profit the company will earn if it sells at the volume you report.

ILLUSTRATION   13.9   Step (Semifixed) Costs

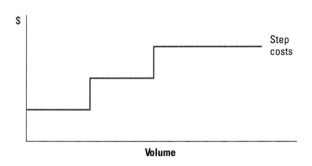

ILLUSTRATION   13.10   CVP Analysis with Semifixed Costs

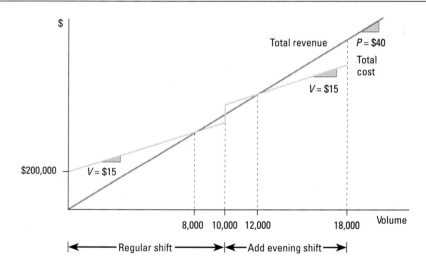

Should the company operate a second shift, assuming that all other things are the same except for the increase in each period's fixed costs and in volume shown? From the following calculations, and assuming that the company can sell everything it makes, it is more profitable to operate with two shifts than with one.

	Regular Shift Only	Two Shifts
Volume in units	10,000	18,000
Sales revenue	$400,000 ($40 × 10,000)	$720,000 ($40 × 18,000)
Variable costs	150,000 ($15 × 10,000)	270,000 ($15 × 18,000)
Total contribution	250,000	450,000
Fixed costs	200,000	300,000
Operating profit	$ 50,000	$150,000

SELF-STUDY QUESTION

2. Refer to the data for Self-Study Question 1. The following two questions are independent of each other.

   a. Holding everything else constant, what contribution margin per unit is required for the company to make an operating profit of $30,000 if the sales volume is 20,000 units?

   b. Assume a tax rate of 30 percent of before-tax operating profit. What sales volume in dollars is required for the company to earn an after-tax profit of $40,000?

The solution to this question is at the end of this chapter on page 416.

MULTIPRODUCT CVP ANALYSIS

L.O. 5: Apply CVP analysis in multiproduct situations.

We assumed that Sport Autos buys and sells only one line of sports cars. Many companies, of course, produce and/or sell many products from the same asset base.

Dual Autos sells two car models, Sport and Deluxe. The prices and costs of the two follow:

	Sport	Deluxe
Average sales price	$25,000	$35,000
Less average variable costs	20,000	25,000
Average contribution margin per car	$ 5,000	$10,000

Average monthly fixed costs are $300,000.

The profit equation presented earlier now must be expanded to consider each product's contribution

Operating profit = (Contribution margin per unit for Sports × Volume of Sports)
+ (Contribution margin per unit for Deluxes × Volume of Deluxes)
− Fixed costs

Let the subscript s designate the Sport model and subscript d designate the Deluxe model. Thus, the company's profit equation is

$$\pi = (\$5,000X_s) + (\$10,000X_d) - \$300,000$$

The manager of Dual Autos has been following a debate between two of the sales personnel about the company's break-even point. According to one, Dual must have to sell 60 cars a month to break even. But the other claims that 30 cars a month would be sufficient. Who is right? The claim that 60 cars must be sold to break even is correct if only the Sport model is sold; the claim that 30 cars need to be sold to break even is correct if only the Deluxe model is sold. In fact, there are many break-even points. This is evident from Dual Auto's profit equation, which has two unknown variables. Alternative break-even points for Dual Autos are listed in Illustration 13.11.

Illustration 13.12 is a graphic presentation of the possible break-even volumes for Dual Autos. Operating profits are zero for any combination of volumes at any point on that line. (We present a solid line with no breaks, although each car actually represents a point on the line.)

The dashed line parallel to the break-even line shows the various combinations of volumes that would provide $10,000 in operating profits. Note in Illustration 13.12 that any combination of products to the right of the break-even line provides profits and any combination to the left results in losses.

In general, the multiproduct CVP equation for n different products is

$$\pi = (P_1 - V_1)X_1 + (P_2 - V_2)X_2 + \cdots + (P_n - V_n)X_n - F$$

ILLUSTRATION 13.11		Combinations of Break-Even Volumes for Dual Autos		
Sport Model		**Deluxe Model**		
Quantity	Total Contribution	Quantity	Total Contribution	Total Contribution for Both Models
60	$300,000	0	–0–	$300,000
58	290,000	1	$ 10,000	300,000
56	280,000	2	20,000	300,000
. . . .	.	.	.	.
. . . .	.	.	.	.
. . . .	.	.	.	.
4	20,000	28	280,000	300,000
2	10,000	29	290,000	300,000
0	–0–	30	300,000	300,000

ILLUSTRATION   13.12   Possible Break-Even Volumes for Dual Autos

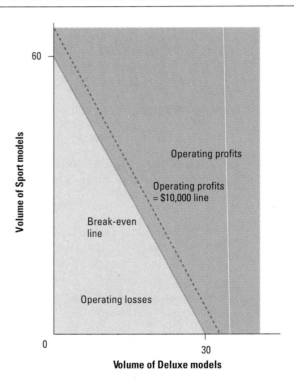

CVP analysis of multiple products is much more complex than is the analysis of a single product. As the Dual Autos example indicates, even for a two-product company, the number of possible solutions is large because many combinations of product volumes will yield a given profit. You can imagine the complications when hundreds of products are involved.

Simplifying Multiproduct CVP

To simplify matters, managers often assume a particular product mix and compute break-even or target volumes using either of two methods, *fixed product mix* or *weighted-average contribution margin*.

Fixed Product Mix

Using the fixed product mix method, managers define a "package" of products in the typical product mix and then compute the break-even or target volume for the package. For example, suppose that the manager of Dual Autos is willing to assume that the Sport and Deluxe models will sell in a 3:1 ratio; that is, of every four cars sold, three will be Sport models and one will be a Deluxe model. Defining X as a package of three Sports and one Deluxe, the contribution margin from this package is

Sport (3 × $5,000)	$15,000
Deluxe (1 × $10,000)	$10,000
Contribution margin	$25,000

Now the break-even point is computed as follows

$$X = \frac{\text{Fixed costs}}{\text{Contribution margin}}$$
$$= \frac{\$300,000}{\$25,000}$$
$$= 12 \text{ packages}$$

where X refers to the break-even number of packages. This means that the sale of 12 packages of three Sports and one Deluxe per package, totaling 36 Sports and 12 Deluxes, is required to break even.

Weighted-Average Contribution Margin

The weighted-average contribution margin also requires an assumed product mix, which we continue to assume is 75 percent Sports and 25 percent Deluxes. The problem can be solved by using a weighted-average contribution margin per unit. When a company assumes a constant product mix, the contribution margin is the **weighted-average contribution margin** of all of its products.

weighted-average contribution margin
The contribution margin of more than one product when a constant product mix is assumed.

For Dual Autos, the weighted-average contribution margin per unit can be computed by multiplying each product's proportion by its contribution margin per unit

$$(.75 \times \$5,000) + (.25 \times \$10,000) = \$6,250$$

The multiple-product break-even for Dual Autos can be determined from the break-even formula:

$$X = \frac{\$300,000}{\$6,250}$$
$$= 48 \text{ cars}$$

where X refers to the break-even number. The product mix assumption means that Dual Autos must sell 36 (.75 × 48) Sport models and 12 (.25 × 48) Deluxe models to break even.

How to Deal with Fixed Costs Common to Multiple Products

Suppose that Dual Autos' total fixed costs of $300,000 can be attributed to the two products as follows:

Direct fixed costs	
Sport model	$ 80,000
Deluxe model	100,000
Common fixed costs	120,000
Total fixed costs	$300,000

What is the break-even number for each product and for the company as a whole? We compute the break-even volume for the Sport model

$$X_s = \frac{F}{P - V}$$
$$= \frac{\$80,000}{\$5,000}$$
$$= \underline{\underline{16 \text{ cars}}}$$

and break-even volume for the Deluxe model

$$X_d = \frac{F}{P - V}$$
$$= \frac{\$100,000}{\$10,000}$$
$$= \underline{\underline{10 \text{ cars}}}$$

If each product line just breaks even, the operating loss for the company as a whole is

$$\pi = (\$5,000 \times 16) + (\$10,000 \times 10) - \$300,000$$
$$= \underline{\underline{-\$120,000}}$$

Although the sale of 16 Sport models and 10 Deluxe models appears to make each product break even, the company would lose $120,000.

This demonstrates a common problem in applying CVP analysis. The volume required for a specific product to break even will not cover unassigned common costs.

One way to address the problem is to allocate the common costs to the products. This permits a CVP analysis for each product. Of course, the results depend on the allocation method. In such cases, it is wise to perform sensitivity analysis with various allocation methods to discover any that might affect management decisions.

For example, Illustration 13.13 presents profit-volume graphs for Dual Autos. Allocation Method A assumes that the $120,000 in common fixed costs is allocated evenly to the two products. Allocation Method B allocates two-thirds of the common fixed costs to the Deluxe model and one-third to the Sport model. As you can see, changing the allocation of fixed costs changes the product mix required to break even or to achieve a target level of operating profits for the company as a whole.

The break-even volumes shown in Illustration 13.13 are only two of many possible combinations. Allocating common fixed costs to products does not dispense with the product mix problem. Nonetheless, it makes product-line CVP analysis possible, and it ensures that common fixed costs are not ignored. Because the allocation of common fixed costs is often arbitrary, we recommend performing sensitivity analysis on the allocation method before using the information for decision making.

SELF-STUDY QUESTION

3. Multiproduct Company produces three products with the following characteristics:

	Product I	Product II	Product III
Price per unit	$5	$6	$7
Variable cost per unit	3	2	4
Expected sales (units)	100,000	150,000	250,000

Total fixed costs for the company are $1,240,000. Assuming that the product mix is the same at the break-even point, compute the break-even point in units.

The solution to this question is at the end of this chapter on page 416.

ILLUSTRATION 13.13 **Impact of Common Cost Allocation Methods on Break-Even Volume, Dual Autos**

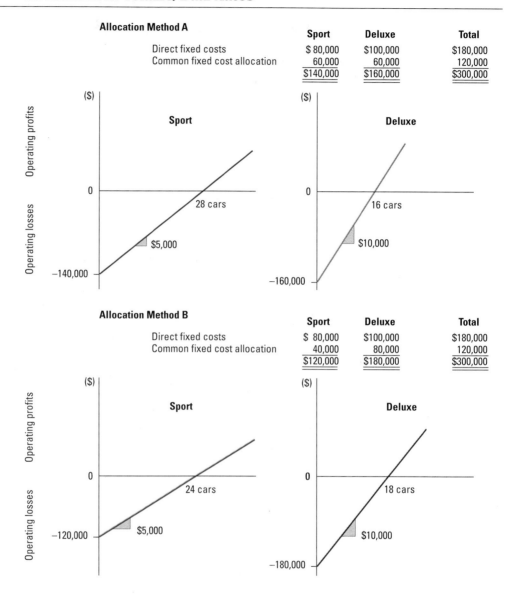

Allocation Method A

	Sport	Deluxe	Total
Direct fixed costs	$ 80,000	$100,000	$180,000
Common fixed cost allocation	60,000	60,000	120,000
	$140,000	$160,000	$300,000

Allocation Method B

	Sport	Deluxe	Total
Direct fixed costs	$ 80,000	$100,000	$180,000
Common fixed cost allocation	40,000	80,000	120,000
	$120,000	$180,000	$300,000

THE ACCOUNTANT'S VIEW OF CVP VERSUS THE ECONOMIST'S VIEW

The classical economist's profit maximization model provides the foundation for CVP analysis. It assumes that management's goal is to maximize profit, with profits being the difference between total revenues and total costs. Management's job is to determine the most profitable actions possible and to take them.

In general, accountants accept the classical economist's model, but they make two simplifying assumptions:

* In economics, total revenue and total cost curves are usually assumed to be nonlinear. The accountant's linearity simplifications are usually considered valid within some appropriate range of volume, termed the *relevant range*.

* The opportunity cost of invested equity capital is usually excluded in the accountant's cost measures, but it is included in the economist's model. Thus, in economic terms, the accountant's measurement of total costs is understated.

REAL WORLD APPLICATION	**Even Colleges Use CVP**

The dean of the Graduate School of Management at the University of California at Davis was considering whether to offer a particular seminar for executives. The tuition would be $650 per person. Variable costs, including meals, parking, and materials, would be $80 per person. Certain costs of offering the seminar, including advertising, instructors' fees, room rent, and audiovisual equipment rent, would not be affected by the number of people attending (within a "relevant range"). Such costs, which could be thought of as step costs, amounted to $8,000 for the seminar.

In addition to these costs, a number of staff, including the dean, would work on the program. Although the salaries paid to these staff were not affected by offering the seminar, working on it took these people away from other duties, thus creating an opportunity cost, estimated to be $7,000 for this seminar.

Given this information, the school estimated the break-even point to be ($8,000 + $7,000)/($650 − $80) = 26.3 students. If the school wanted at least to break even on this program, it should offer the program only if it expected at least 27 students to attend.

Source: Based on the authors' research.

ILLUSTRATION   13.14   Comparison of Economists' and Accountants' Assumed Cost and Revenue Behavior

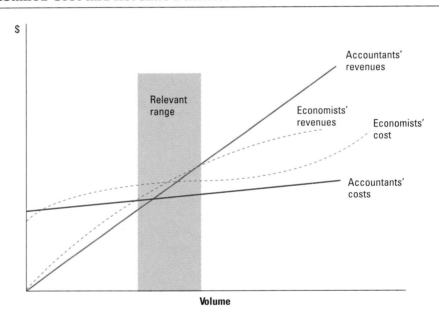

A comparison of accountants' and economists' assumptions about the behavior of costs and revenue is shown in Illustration 13.14. The solid lines represent accountants' assumptions about cost and revenue behavior; the dashed lines designate economists' assumptions. Note the difference in assumptions about linearity as well as the systematically higher economists' costs because accounting costs do not include the opportunity cost of capital.

Simplifying Assumptions about Cost and Revenue Behavior

Strictly speaking, neither model is "correct" because both economists and accountants have made simplifying assumptions about cost and revenue behavior. The actual curves would be disjointed and would consider inconsistencies such as sales discounts for certain customers, costs that are neither strictly fixed nor strictly variable, and so forth. However, a cost-benefit analysis of more "accurate" data about cost and revenue behavior may yield little additional benefit to decision makers.

WATCH OUT FOR LIMITATIONS AND ASSUMPTIONS

L.O. 6: Critically evaluate CVP analysis in view of the assumptions underlying CVP.

Like any other tool, the limitations of CVP analysis make it more applicable to some decisions than to others. A discussion of some of these limitations and the impact they can have on the results of CVP analysis follows. As with any management information, the information-gathering system is judged in terms of a cost-benefit test. Overcoming some of the listed limitations may not be cost justified.

Assumed and Actual Cost Behavior

A linear CVP analysis assumes that

* Revenues change proportionately with volume.
* Total variable costs change proportionately with volume.
* Fixed costs do not change with volume.

Any estimate of this company's cost behavior should explicitly assume whether the company's volume of activity justifies operating the furnace in this picture. If the volume is sufficiently low, the company may stop operating this blast furnace and continue operating others. In that case, certain "fixed" costs would probably not exist (for example, wages paid to repair and operating personnel). An example of how costs seldom behave in a neat linear pattern is discussed in the limitations of linear CVP analysis on page 401. (© Dawson Jones/Tony Stone Images)

One useful CVP analysis feature is its simplicity in showing the impact of sales prices, costs, and volume on operating profits (or cash flows). But the cost of this simplicity is often the lack of realism. Some costs cannot be easily classified, and costs seldom behave in a neat linear fashion. CVP analysis is based on the assumption that within a specific range of activity, the linear expression approximates reality closely enough that the results will not be badly distorted.

Assumed linear relationships are more likely to be valid for short time periods (one year or less) and small changes in volume than for long periods and large changes in volume. Most fixed costs are fixed only in the short run. Over time, management may make decisions that change fixed costs. For example, during a recent downturn in the economy, a steel company announced the closing of two of the four blast furnaces in one of its plants. Many costs that were fixed while all four blast furnaces were operating (for example, supervisory salaries, product inspection costs, some maintenance and utilities costs) were temporarily eliminated.

Many nonvolume factors that also affect prices and costs (for example, limited capacity, technological changes, and input factor prices) are more likely to be constant over short time periods.

Constant Product Mix

As we saw earlier in the chapter, with multiple products, a change in product mix can affect operating profits. Holding the product mix constant allows the analyst to focus on the impact of prices, costs, and volume on operating profits. Product mix usually changes constantly in the real world; thus, spreadsheets that show many alternative product mixes are quite helpful.

ABC's Effects on CVP

Activity-based costing shows that categorizing costs as strictly fixed or variable may be misleading. The incurrence of costs may be related to unit, batch, product, customer, or capacity level activities. This and the type of activities involved should be considered when defining fixed and variable costs in constructing a CVP analysis, and in interpreting the results.

SUMMARY

CVP analysis is both a management tool for determining the impact of selling prices, costs, and volume on profits and a conceptual tool, or way of thinking, about managing a company. It helps management focus on the objective of obtaining the best possible combination of prices, volume, variable costs, and fixed costs.

The following summarizes key ideas tied to the chapter's learning objectives.

LO1: The relationship of costs, volume, and profit. CVP analysis examines the impact of prices, costs, and volume on operating profits, as summarized in the profit equation

$$\pi = (P - V)X - F$$

where

π = Operating profits
P = Average unit selling price
V = Average unit variable costs
X = Quantity of output
F = Total fixed costs

LO2: CVP for planning and decision making. Management can use CVP analysis to plan future projects and to help in determining a project's feasibility. By altering different variables within the equation (e.g., selling price or amount of output), managers are able to perform a what-if analysis (often referred to as a *sensitivity analysis*).

LO3: Effect of cost structure an operating leverage. An organization's cost structure is the proportion of fixed and variable costs to total costs. Operating leverage is high in firms with a high proportion of fixed costs, small proportion of variable costs, and the resulting high contribution margin per unit. The higher the firm's leverage, the higher the degree of profits' sensitivity to volume.

LO4: Extensions of the CVP analysis. CVP analysis can be used for a variety of purposes beyond the simple break-even point analysis or target profit analysis. The following are additional uses for the CVP model:

- Cash flow analysis
- CVP analysis with income taxes
- Factoring in semifixed costs

LO5: CVP analysis with multiple products. CVP analysis also can be used in multiproduct situations; however, a constant product mix must be assumed or common costs must be allocated.

LO6: Pros and cons of CVP analysis. An advantage of CVP analysis is its simplicity. However, the price of such simplicity is a set of limiting assumptions that result in some loss of realism. When assumptions are made, it is advisable to perform sensitivity analysis to determine whether (and how) the assumption affects decisions.

KEY TERMS

break-even point, 387

contribution margin, 384

contribution margin ratio, 385

cost structure, 389

cost-volume-profit (CVP) analysis, 382

margin of safety, 392

operating leverage, 389

profit equation, 383

profit-volume analysis, 389

step (semifixed) costs, 395

value chain, 383

weighted-average contribution margin, 399

REVIEW QUESTIONS

13.1 What does the term *profit equation* mean?

13.2 What are the components of total costs in the profit equation?

13.3 What does the term *contribution margin* mean?

13.4 How does the total contribution margin differ from the gross margin that is often shown on companies' financial statements?

13.5 Compare cost-volume-profit (CVP) analysis with profit-volume analysis. How do they differ?

13.6 How is the profit equation expanded when multiproduct CVP analysis is used?

13.7 Why is a constant product mix often assumed in multiproduct CVP analysis?

13.8 What does *contribution margin* mean when a constant product mix is assumed in multiproduct CVP analyses?

13.9 What is the difference between economic "profit" and accounting "net income" or "operating profit"?

13.10 What are three common assumptions of linear CVP analysis?

13.11 Fixed costs are often defined as "fixed over the short run." Does this mean that they are not fixed over the long run? Why or why not?

13.12 Refer to the Real World Application "Even Colleges Use CVP" on page 402. What costs were "step" costs? Why are they called step costs?

CRITICAL ANALYSIS AND DISCUSSION QUESTIONS

13.13 Is a company really breaking even if it produces and sells at the break-even point? What costs might not be covered?

13.14 What is usually the difference between CVP analysis on a cash basis and on an accounting accrual basis? For a company having depreciable assets, would you expect the accrual break-even point to be higher, lower, or the same as the cash break-even point?

13.15 Is it possible to have many break-even points and many alternative ways to achieve a target operating profit when a company has multiple products?

13.16 When would the sum of the break-even amounts for each of a company's products not be the break-even point for the company as a whole?

13.17 How can CVP analysis be used for planning and performance evaluation?

13.18 Why might the operating profit calculated by CVP analysis differ from the net income reported in financial statements for external reporting?

13.19 Why does the accountant use a linear representation of cost and revenue behavior in CVP analysis? How is this justified?

13.20   The following graph implies that profits increase continually as volume increases:

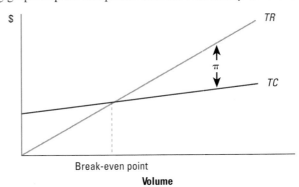

Break-even point

Volume

What are some of the factors that might prevent the increasing profits that are indicated when linear CVP analysis is employed?

13.21   Why would fixed costs tend not to be relevant for a typical CVP analysis? Under what circumstances might the fixed costs be relevant in CVP analyses?

13.22   "CVP analysis is an oversimplification of the real world environment. For this reason, it has little to offer a decision maker." Comment.

13.23   Refer to the Real World Application on page 391. If the auto companies cannot raise prices, what must they do to break even?

EXERCISES

13.24   Profit Equation
Components
(L.O. 1)

Identify each of the following profit equation components on the graph that follows:

a.   The total cost line.

b.   The total revenue line.

c.   The total variable costs area.

d.   Variable cost per unit.

e.   The fixed costs area.

f.   The break-even point.

g.   The profit area (or volume).

h.   The loss area (or volume).

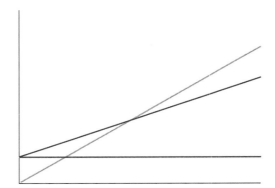

13.25   Profit Equation
Components
(L.O. 1)

Identify the profit equation components on the graph that follows (indicated by the letters):

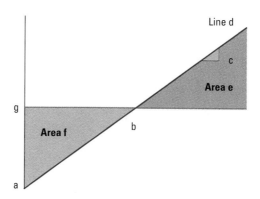

13.26 CVP Analysis—
Planning and
Decision Making
(L.O. 2)

Galaxy Cinema has the following costs and revenues for movie ticket sales for the year:

Total revenues.	$3,600,000
Total fixed costs	750,000
Total variable costs	2,400,000
Total tickets sold	800,000

Required

a. What is the average selling price per unit?

b. What is the average variable cost per unit?

c. What is the average contribution margin per unit?

d. What is the break-even point?

e. What number of movie tickets must be sold for Galaxy Cinema to make a $2 million operating profit for the year on ticket sales?

13.27 CVP Analysis—
Planning and
Decision Making
(L.O. 2)

Choose the *best* answer for each of the following:

a. If a firm has a negative contribution margin, to reach break-even it must
   (1) Increase unit selling price.
   (2) Increase sales volume.
   (3) Decrease sales volume.
   (4) Decrease fixed cost.
   (5) Increase fixed cost.

b. If total contribution margin is decreased by a given amount, operating profit
   (1) Remains unchanged.
   (2) Decreases by the same amount.
   (3) Decreases by more than the given amount.
   (4) Increases by the same amount.
   (5) Does none of the above.

c. The break-even point is increased by
   (1) A decrease in variable costs.
   (2) A decrease in fixed costs.
   (3) An increase in contribution margin ratio.
   (4) An increase in variable costs.
   (5) None of the above.

(CPA adapted)

13.28 CVP Analysis—
Planning and
Decision Making
(L.O. 2)

Airpower Corporation sells and installs wind-powered generator systems. The company's marketing consultants estimate that at a selling price of $8,000 per unit, the company should be able to sell 10,000 units per year. However, the company's financial advisor believes that sales will be only 7,000 units per year at that price.

The company's controller estimates that annual fixed costs will be $24 million regardless of volume and that the variable cost on each unit will be $4,800.

Required

a. Determine the profit or loss at the 7,000-unit and 10,000-unit activity levels.

b. What is the break-even point?

13.29 CVP Analysis— Planning and Decision Making (L.O. 2)

Esmark, Inc., is considering the introduction of a new water ski with the following price and cost characteristics:

Sales price	$	100 each
Variable costs		60 each
Fixed costs		150,000 per year

Required

a. What number must Esmark sell to break even?

b. What number must Esmark sell to make an operating profit of $100,000 for the year?

13.30 CVP Analysis— Planning and Decision Making (L.O. 2)

Refer to the data for Esmark, Inc., in Exercise 13.29. Assume that the projected number for the year is 8,000 units. Consider requirements (*b*), (*c*), and (*d*) independent of each other.

Required

a. What will the operating profit be?

b. What is the impact on operating profit if the sales price decreases by 10 percent? Increases by 20 percent?

c. What is the impact on operating profit if variable costs per unit decrease by 10 percent? Increase by 20 percent?

d. Suppose that fixed costs for the year are 10 percent lower than projected, and variable costs per unit are 10 percent higher than projected. What impact will these cost changes have on operating profit for the year? Will profit go up? Down? By how much?

13.31 CVP Analysis— Planning and Decision Making (L.O. 2)

a. Given the following formulas, which one represents the break-even sales level in units? P = Selling price per unit; F = Total fixed costs; V = Variable cost per unit.

(1) $\dfrac{P}{F - V}$

(2) $\dfrac{F}{P - V}$

(3) $\dfrac{P}{F/V}$

(4) $\dfrac{F}{V/F}$

(5) $\dfrac{V}{P - F}$

b. Which of the following assumptions is not made in break-even analysis?
(1) The sales mix is maintained as volume changes.
(2) Volume is the only factor affecting cost.
(3) No change occurs between beginning and ending inventory.
(4) All of these are assumptions sometimes required in break-even analysis.

c. A company increased the selling price for its products from $1.00 to $1.10 a unit when total fixed cost increased from $400,000 to $480,000 and variable cost per unit remained the same. How would these changes affect the break-even point?
(1) In units it remains unchanged.
(2) In units it increases.
(3) In units it decreases.
(4) The effect cannot be determined from the given information.

(CPA adapted)

13.32 Extensions of the Basic Model— Semifixed (Step) Costs (L.O. 4)

Luress Company manufactures and sells one product. The sales price of $15 and the variable cost of $9 per unit remain constant regardless of volume. The company can choose to operate at one of the following three levels of monthly operations:

	Volume Range (Production and Sales)	Total Fixed Costs
Level 1	0–16,000	$ 84,000
Level 2	16,001–28,000	123,000
Level 3	28,001–38,000	162,000

Required

a. Calculate the break-even point(s).

b. If the company can sell everything it makes, should it operate at level 1, level 2, or level 3? Support your answer.

13.33 Extensions of the Basic Model—Taxes (L.O. 4)

Melborne Surfboard Shop is considering adding a type of wetsuit to its merchandise products. This wetsuit has the following prices and costs:

Selling price per wetsuit	$ 80.00
Variable cost per wetsuit	47.20
Fixed costs per year associated with these wetsuits	984,000.00
Income tax rate	40%

Required

a. Melborne's break-even point in units is
   (1) 18,000.
   (2) 90,000.
   (3) 30,000.
   (4) 72,000.
   (5) Some other amount.

b. How many units must Melborne sell to earn $492,000 after taxes?
   (1) 6,150 units.
   (2) 25,000 units.
   (3) 45,000 units.
   (4) 55,000 units.
   (5) Some other amount.

13.34 Extensions of the Basic Model—Taxes (L.O. 4)

Luxurious Hair Products is contemplating introducing a new line of home perm kits that would sell for $8 each. The variable costs associated with each kit amount to $2. If the kits are to be introduced nationwide, the company must obtain acceptable profits on a test-market basis. The fixed costs associated with test marketing amount to $216,000 per year.

Required

a. Compute the break-even point in units for test-market sales.

b. If the desired profit level is $60,000 before tax, compute the sales level in units required to attain that profit level.

c. Assuming that the tax rate is 40 percent and the desired profit level is $60,000 after tax, compute the required unit sales level.

13.35 Using CVP Analysis to Measure Volume (L.O. 2)

Hose's Herbal Remedies estimates its fixed costs to be $56,000 per month.

Required

a. Determine the break-even point in sales dollars if the contribution margin ratio is 1/3.

b. Determine the break-even point in sales dollars if fixed costs remained at $56,000 per month but the contribution margin ratio was 4/10.

13.36 CVP Analysis—Multiple Products (L.O. 5)

Lorocette's Sandwich Shop produces two products, 6-inch and 12-inch sandwiches with the following characteristics:

	6-Inch Sandwich	12-Inch Sandwich
Selling price per unit.	$4	$6
Variable cost per unit	$2	$3.50
Expected sales (units)	10,000	15,000

The total fixed costs for the company are $34,500.

Required

a. What is the anticipated level of profits for the expected sales volumes?

b. Assuming that the product mix is the same at the break-even point, compute the break-even point.

c. If the product sales mix were to change to four 6-inch sandwiches for each 12-inch sandwich, what would be the new break-even volume for each of the products?

13.37 CVP Analysis—Multiple Products (L.O. 5)

Assume that Almay sells three products with the following prices and costs:

	Selling Price per Sandwich	Variable Cost per Sandwich	Fixed Cost per Month
Product 1	$ 6	$ 4	—
Product 2	10	6	—
Product 3	16	10	—
Entire company	—	—	$80,000

The sales mix is 50 percent product 1, 33.33 percent product 2, and 16.66 percent product 3.

Required

a.   At what sales revenue does the company break even?

b.   Draw a cost-volume-profit graph for the company.

13.38   Analysis of Cost Structure (L.O. 3)

Maribell Company's cost structure is dominated by variable costs with a contribution margin ratio of .30 and fixed costs of $60,000. Every dollar of sales contributes 30 cents toward fixed costs and profit. The cost structure of a competitor, Forshiem Company, is dominated by fixed costs with a higher contribution margin of .80 and fixed costs of $560,000. Every dollar of sales contributes 80 cents toward fixed costs and profit.
Both companies have sales of $1,000,000.

Required

a.   Compare the two companies' cost structures using the format shown in Illustration 13.5.

b.   Suppose that both companies experience a 10 percent increase in sales. By how much would each company's profits increase?

13.39   Analysis of Cost Structure (L.O. 3)

The following facts pertain to Thyme Corporation:

Sales.	$2,000,000
Variable costs	1,200,000
Contribution margin	800,000
Fixed costs	200,000
Operating profit	$ 600,000
Units produced and sold	500,000

Required

a.   Calculate the contribution margin ratio.

b.   Calculate the contribution margin per unit.

PROBLEMS

13.40   CVP and Decisions

Schill Education Corporation is currently offering a line of executive education courses for $90 per course. The company's annual fixed costs for the office facilities are $800,000 and for the publishing operations are $720,000. The variable costs of each course unit include $15 for promotion, $6 for administration, and $12 for the published materials. At the present time, the company distributes 25,000 course units per year. Management is dissatisfied with the profitability of current operations and wishes to investigate the profit effects of several alternatives. Members of management have raised the following questions in an attempt to evaluate the alternatives, each of which should be considered independently.

Required

a.   What is the break-even level in terms of unit sales?

b.   The company can hire an educational representative to sell the course materials independently of current sales activity. Current sales would remain the same, but the representative should be able to sell an additional 10,000 units at the $90 price. Promotion costs would amount to $20 per unit, and the representative would receive a commission of 25 percent of the sales price of each course unit. All other costs would remain unchanged. What is the profit effect of hiring the representative?

c.   A publishing company has offered to produce the course materials for $40 per course unit regardless of the number of course units. If this alternative is chosen, the fixed and variable costs of the current publishing operation would be eliminated. What is the profit effect of this alternative if sales remain at 25,000 units? If sales increase to 40,000 units?

13.41 CVP Analysis and Price Changes

Knoll's Manufacturing is concerned about the possible effects of inflation on its operations. Presently, the company sells 200,000 units for $15 each unit. The variable production costs are $8, and fixed costs amount to $1,120,000. The present profit level is $280,000. Production engineers have advised management that they expect unit labor costs to rise by 10 percent and unit materials costs to rise by 15 percent in the coming year. Of the $8 variable costs, 25 percent are from labor and 50 percent are from materials. Variable overhead costs are expected to increase by 5 percent. Sales prices cannot increase more than 8 percent. It is also expected that fixed costs will rise by 2 percent as a result of increased taxes and other miscellaneous fixed charges.

The company wishes to maintain the same level of profit in real dollar terms. It is expected that to accomplish this objective, profits must increase by 6 percent during the year.

Required

a. Compute the volume in units and the dollar sales level necessary to maintain the present profit level of $280,000, assuming that the maximum price increase is implemented.

b. Compute the volume of sales and the dollar sales level necessary to provide the 6 percent increase in profits, assuming that the maximum price increase is implemented.

c. If the volume of sales were to remain at 200,000 units, what price increase would be required to attain the 6 percent increase in profits?

13.42 CVP Analysis

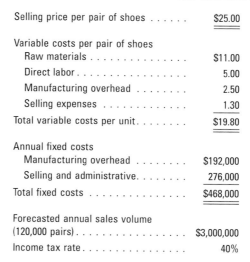

Softcush Company manufactures and sells shoes. Price and cost data are as follows:

Selling price per pair of shoes	$25.00
Variable costs per pair of shoes	
Raw materials	$11.00
Direct labor	5.00
Manufacturing overhead	2.50
Selling expenses	1.30
Total variable costs per unit.	$19.80
Annual fixed costs	
Manufacturing overhead	$192,000
Selling and administrative.	276,000
Total fixed costs	$468,000
Forecasted annual sales volume	
(120,000 pairs)	$3,000,000
Income tax rate	40%

Required

a. Softcush Company estimates that its direct labor costs will increase 8 percent next year. How many units must it sell next year to reach break even?
 (1) 97,500 units.
 (2) 101,740 units.
 (3) 83,572 units.
 (4) 86,250 units.
 (5) Some other amount.

b. If Softcush's direct labor costs do increase 8 percent, what selling price per unit of product must it charge to maintain the same contribution margin ratio?
 (1) $25.51.
 (2) $27.00.
 (3) $25.40.
 (4) $26.64.
 (5) Some other amount.

13.43 CVP Analysis with Changes in Cost Structure

Pallamar Prefab manufactures prefabricated fence sections that sell for $6 per unit. The present facilities use an older model of semiautomated equipment. Variable costs are $4.50 per unit, and fixed costs total $300,000 per year.

A newer semiautomated fence machine can be rented, which would increase fixed costs to $550,000 per year, but variable costs would be reduced to $3.25 per unit.

Another fence machine supplier offers a fully automatic machine that would result in annual fixed costs of $800,000. However, this machine would reduce the variable costs to $2 per unit.

No other costs or cash flows are affected by the choice among these three alternatives.

Management is concerned about the break-even point for operations using each machine. Moreover, the sales volume for fence sections is quite erratic. Management is interested in the profit or losses that would occur with each type of equipment if the sales volume were either 175,000 or 250,000 units.

Required

Prepare a schedule showing the break-even point and the profit or loss obtainable for each equipment alternative at sales volumes of 175,000 and 250,000 units.

13.44 CVP Analysis with Semifixed Costs: Le Muir Preschool[4]

Abigail Le Muir, director and owner of the Le Muir Preschool, has a master's degree in elementary education. In the seven years she has been running the school, her salary has ranged from nothing to $10,000 per year. "The second year," she says, "I made 62 cents an hour." Her salary is what's left over after all other expenses are met.

Could she run a more profitable school? She thinks perhaps she could if she increased the student-teacher ratio, which is currently five students to one teacher. (Government standards for such a center set a maximum of 10 students per teacher.) However, she refuses to increase the ratio to more than six to one. "If you increase the ratio to more than six to one, the children don't get enough attention. In addition, the demands on the teacher are far too great." She does not hire part-time teachers.

Abigail rents the space for her center in the basement of a church for $1,000 per month, including utilities. She estimates that supplies, snacks, and other nonpersonnel costs are $100 per student per month; tuition is $400 per month per student. Teachers are paid $1,200 per month, including fringe benefits. There are no other operating costs. At present, the school has 30 students and six teachers in addition to Abigail, who is not considered a teacher for this analysis.

Required

a. What is the present operating profit per month of the school before Abigail's salary?

b. What is (are) the break-even point(s), assuming a student-teacher ratio of 6:1?

c. What is (are) the break-even point(s) if the student-teacher ratio were allowed to increase to 10:1?

d. Abigail has an opportunity to increase the student body by six students. She must take all six or none. Should she accept the six students if she wants to maintain a maximum student-teacher ratio of six to one?

e. (Continuation of requirement [d].) Suppose that Abigail accepts the six children. Now she has the opportunity to accept one more. What would happen to profit if she did, assuming that she has to hire one more teacher?

13.45 Profit Targets: Maus & Company

Maus & Company, maker of quality handmade pipes, has experienced a steady growth in sales for the past five years. However, increased competition has led Michael Maus, the president, to believe that an aggressive advertising campaign will be necessary next year to maintain the company's present growth.

To prepare for next year's advertising campaign, the company's accountant has prepared and presented the president with the following data for this year (year 1):

---
[4]Michael W. Maher, 1993.

Cost Schedule

Variable cost per pipe:

Direct labor	$ 8.00
Direct materials	3.25
Variable overhead	2.50
Total variable costs	$13.75

Fixed costs:

Manufacturing	$ 25,000
Selling	40,000
Administrative	70,000
Total fixed costs	$135,000

Selling price per pipe	$25.00
Expected sales this year (year 1) (20,000 units)	$500,000
Tax rate: 40%	

Michael has set the sales target for year 2 at the level of $550,000 (or 22,000 pipes).

Required
a. What is the projected after-tax operating profit for year 1?

b. What is the break-even point in units for year 1?

c. Michael believes that an additional expense of $11,250 for advertising in year 2, with all other costs remaining constant, will be necessary to attain the sales target. What will be the after-tax net income for year 2 if the additional $11,250 is spent?

d. What will be the break-even point in dollar sales for year 2 if the additional $11,250 is spent for advertising?

e. If the additional $11,250 is spent for advertising in year 2, what is the required sales level in dollars to equal year 1 after-tax operating profit?

f. At a sales level of 22,000 units, what is the maximum amount that can be spent on advertising in year 2 if an after-tax operating profit of $60,000 is desired?

(CMA adapted)

13.46 **CVP Analysis with Step Costs and Changing Unit Variable Costs**

Theloneous & Company manufactures and sells one product. The sales price, $50 per unit, remains constant regardless of volume. Last year's sales were 12,000 units, and operating profits were −$20,000 (i.e., a loss). "Fixed" costs depended on production levels, as shown here. Variable costs per unit are 20 percent higher in level 2 (night shift) than in level 1 (day shift) because of additional labor costs due primarily to higher wages required to employ workers for the night shift.

	Annual Production Range (in units)	Annual Total Fixed Costs
Level 1 (day shift)	0–15,000	$200,000
Level 2 (night shift)	15,001–25,000	264,000

Last year's cost structure and selling price are not expected to change this year. Maximum plant capacity is 25,000 units. The company sells everything it produces.

Required
a. Compute the contribution margin per unit for last year for each of the two production levels.

b. Compute the break-even points for last year for each of the two production levels.

c. Compute the volume in units that will maximize operating profits. Defend your choice.

INTEGRATIVE CASE

13.47 Converting Full-Absorption Costing Income Statements to CVP Analysis

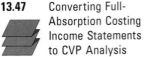

Crandell Products is a regional firm that has three major product lines, cereals, breakfast bars, and dog food. The income statement for the year ended April 30, year 4, follows; the statement was prepared by product line using full-absorption costing.

CRANDELL PRODUCTS COMPANY
Income Statement
For the Year Ended April 30, Year 4
(in thousands)

	Cereals	Breakfast Bars	Dog Food	Total
Sales in pounds....................	2,000	500	500	3,000
Revenue from sales	$1,000	$400	$200	$1,600
Cost of sales				
Direct materials	330	160	100	590
Direct labor.....................	90	40	20	150
Factory overhead	108	48	24	180
Total cost of sales	528	248	144	920
Gross margin.....................	472	152	56	680
Operating costs				
Selling costs				
Advertising	50	30	20	100
Commissions	50	40	20	110
Salaries and related benefits	30	20	10	60
Total selling expenses	130	90	50	270
General and administrative costs				
Licenses	50	20	15	85
Salaries and related benefits	60	25	15	100
Total general and administrative costs.....	110	45	30	185
Total operating costs	240	135	80	455
Operating profit before taxes	$ 232	$ 17	$ (24)	$ 225

Other Data

1. *Costs of sales.* The company's inventories of direct materials and finished products do not vary significantly from year to year. The inventories at April 30, year 4, were essentially identical to those at April 30, year 3.

   Factory overhead was applied to products at 120 percent of direct labor-dollars. The factory overhead costs for the year 4 fiscal year follow:

Variable indirect labor and supplies	$ 15,000
Variable employee benefits on factory labor.....................	30,000
Supervisory salaries and related benefits	35,000
Plant occupancy costs...............	100,000
	$180,000

   There was no overapplied or underapplied overhead at year-end.

2. *Advertising.* The company has been unable to determine any direct causal relationship between the level of sales volume and the level of advertising expenditures. However, because management believes that advertising is necessary, an annual advertising program is implemented for each product line, which is advertised independent of the others.

3. *Commissions.* Sales commissions are paid to the sales force at the rates of 5 percent on the cereals and 10 percent on the breakfast bars and dog food.

4. *Licenses.* Various licenses required for each product line are renewed annually.

5. *Salaries and related benefits.* Sales and general administrative personnel devote time and effort to all product lines. Their salaries and wages are allocated on the basis of management's estimates of time spent on each product line.

Required

a. Crandell's controller has recommended that the company perform a CVP analysis of its operations. As a first step, the controller has requested that you prepare a revised income statement for Crandell that employs a product contribution margin format that will be useful in CVP analysis. The statement should show the profit contribution for each product line and the operating profit before taxes for the company as a whole.

b. Crandell's controller is preparing a report, which he will present to the other members of top management, explaining CVP analysis. Expand on the following points for the report:
   (1) The advantages that CVP analysis can provide to a company.
   (2) The difficulties that Crandell could experience in the calculations involved in CVP analysis.
   (3) The dangers that Crandell should consider in using the information derived from the CVP analysis.

(CMA adapted)

SOLUTIONS TO SELF-STUDY QUESTIONS

1. a. Operating profit

$$\pi = PX - VX - F$$
$$= \$180,000 - \$120,000 - \$36,000$$
$$= \$24,000$$

b. Break-even point

$$X = \frac{F}{P - V}$$
$$= \frac{\$36,000}{\$9 - \$6}$$
$$= 12,000 \text{ units}$$

c. Target volume

$$X = \frac{F + \text{Target } p}{P - V}$$
$$= \frac{\$36,000 + \$30,000}{\$3}$$
$$= 22,000 \text{ units}$$

d. Target volume in sales dollars

$$\text{Contribution margin ratio} = \frac{\$3}{\$9} = .333 \text{ (rounded)}$$
$$\text{Target volume} = \frac{\$36,000 + \$20,000}{.333}$$
$$= \$168,000$$

e. Units sold in April

$$X = \frac{\$180,000}{\$9}$$
$$= 20,000 \text{ units}$$

f. $\dfrac{\text{Target volume}}{\text{(sales dollars)}} = \dfrac{\text{Fixed costs} + \text{Target profit}}{\text{Contribution margin ratio}}$

$$\text{Target } PX = \frac{\$36,000 + .2PX}{.333} = \frac{\$36,000}{.333} + \frac{.2PX}{.333}$$
$$\text{Target } PX = \$108,000 + .6PX$$
$$.4PX = \$108,000$$
$$PX = \$270,000$$
$$X = \frac{\$270,000}{\$9 \text{ per unit}} = 30,000 \text{ units}$$

g. *Solution to cellular phone problem:*

Let X = Minutes of air activity. Set equations for the two levels of service equal to each other to find the indifference point.

Level 1		Level 2
$\$50 + \$.40X$	=	$\$20 + \$.70X$
$\$30$	=	$\$.30X$
$X = \dfrac{\$30}{\$.30}$	=	100 minutes

Level 1 is cheaper if you use more than 100 minutes per month; level 2 is cheaper if you use fewer than 100 minutes per month.

Solution to student organization problem:

$$\text{Break-even volume} = \frac{\$1{,}000 + \$800}{\$4 + \$1}$$

$$= 360 \text{ ticket holders}$$

2. **a.** To find the required contribution margin per unit

$$\$30{,}000 = (P - V)20{,}000 \text{ units} - \$36{,}000$$
$$\$66{,}000 = (P - V)20{,}000 \text{ units}$$
$$\frac{\$66{,}000}{20{,}000} = (P - V) = \$3.30$$

The contribution margin per unit must be $3.30.

b. To find the target volume expressed in sales dollars

$$\text{Target volume} = \frac{\dfrac{\text{After-tax}}{\text{fixed costs}} + \dfrac{\text{Target after-tax}}{\text{profits}}}{\text{After-tax contribution margin ratio}}$$

$$= \frac{(\$36{,}000 \times (1 - .3)) + \$40{,}000}{.333 \times (1 - .3)}$$

$$= \frac{\$25{,}200 + \$40{,}000}{.233 \text{ (rounded)}}$$

$$= \$279{,}828^*$$

---

*Your answer may differ slightly due to rounding.

3. Compute the weighted-average contribution margin:

	I	II	III	Total
Units	100,000	150,000	250,000	500,000
Product mix	20%	30%	50%	100%

Weighted-average contribution margin

$$.20(\$2) + .30(\$4) + .50(\$3) = \$3.10 \text{ per unit}$$

Or

$$\frac{\begin{array}{ccc}(100{,}000 & (150{,}000 & (250{,}000 \\ \text{units}) + & \text{units}) + & \text{units}) \\ (\$2) & (\$4) & (\$3)\end{array}}{500{,}000} = \$3.10$$

$$X = \frac{\$1{,}240{,}000}{\$3.10} = \frac{400{,}000}{\text{units}}$$

Differential Cost and Revenue Analysis

In this chapter, we discuss the use of cost and revenue analysis in making marketing decisions such as pricing, accepting special orders, and determining customer profitability. Each decision requires comparing one or more proposed alternatives with the status quo. The task is to determine how costs in particular and profits in general will be affected if one alternative is chosen over another. This process is called *differential analysis*. Although decision makers are usually interested in all differences between alternatives, including financial and nonfinancial ones, we focus on financial decisions involving costs and revenues.

We start this chapter by developing an approach to differential cost analysis for decision making. Then we apply the differential cost analysis model to a variety of situations and discuss the effect of differential analysis on pricing decisions.

DIFFERENTIAL COST ANALYSIS: A VALUABLE MANAGERIAL TOOL

L.O. 1: Understand how to use differential analysis for decision making.

differential analysis
The process of estimating revenues and costs of alternative actions available to decision makers and of comparing these estimates to the status quo.

short run
The period of time over which capacity will be unchanged, usually one year.

differential costs
Costs that change in response to a particular course of action.

Differential analysis is the process of estimating revenues and costs of alternative actions available to decision makers and of comparing these estimates to the status quo. Differential analysis is used for both short-run decisions, such as the ones we discuss in this chapter and the next, and for long-run decisions, such as those discussed in Chapter 23. Generally, when the term **short run** is applied to decision horizons over which capacity will be unchanged, one year is usually used for convenience.

There is an important distinction between short-run and long-run decisions. Short-run decisions affect cash flow for such a short period of time that the time value of money is immaterial and hence ignored. Thus, the amount of cash flows is important for short-run analysis, but the timing of the flows is assumed to be unimportant. If an action affects cash flows over a longer period of time (usually more than one year), the time value of money is considered, as discussed in Chapter 23.

Decisions by colleges concerning whether to drop their football programs and decisions by professional sports teams to sign draft picks involve long-run differential analysis. Decisions by airlines to drop prices, such as USAir's decision to cut fares in the Northeast United States, are generally short run but have long-run implications.

Differential costs change in response to alternative courses of action. Both variable costs and fixed costs may be differential costs. Variable costs are differential when a decision involves possible changes in volume. For example, a decision to close a plant usually reduces variable costs and some fixed costs. All of the affected costs are termed *differential*. On the other hand, if a machine replacement does not affect either the volume of output or the variable cost per unit, variable costs are not differential.

As the illustrations in this chapter are presented, you will find that differential analysis requires examining the facts for each option relevant to the decision to determine which costs will be affected. Differential and variable costs have independent meanings and applications and should not be considered interchangable.

Are Historical Costs Relevant for Decision Making?

sunk cost
An expenditure made in the past that cannot be changed by present or future decisions.

You have probably seen retailers advertise their products for sale at prices below invoice cost, and you may have wondered how they could stay in business if they sell their products below cost. Of course, they could not stay in business if they consistently sold below cost. Retailers recognize, however, that the original cost of their merchandise is a **sunk cost**, a cost that has already been incurred and is *not differential* when it comes to holding versus selling merchandise.[1]

---

[1]Many of the concepts presented in this chapter were developed by J. M. Clark in his classic work, *Studies in the Economics of Overhead Costs* (Chicago: University of Chicago Press, 1923). Clark developed the notion that costs that are relevant for one purpose are not necessarily relevant for another. If the term *sacrifice* is used to summarize the various meanings of cost, it becomes clear that the sacrifices (costs) for one set of actions are not necessarily the same as those for another set of actions.

Should this tennis player continue to play in pain after suffering an injury to "get his money's worth" from his membership in the tennis club? (© Henley and Savage/Tony Stone Images)

For example, suppose that a clothing shop has 15 pairs of slacks that each cost the retailer $20. The retailer has sold no slacks at the $39.95 established price and believes that they can be sold only at a reduced price. In repricing, the retailer should disregard the original $20 per pair cost. A number of marketing and inventory control issues might be considered, but the historical cost is irrelevant.

Of course, if the slacks are sold for less than $20 per pair, the retailer's financial statement would show a loss. If the slacks are sold for $18 per pair, for example, the statement is as follows:

Sale of slacks (15 pairs at $18)	$270
Cost of goods sold (15 pairs at $20)	300
Loss on sale	$ (30)

Decision makers are sometimes tempted to hold merchandise rather than sell it below cost to avoid showing a loss on their financial statements. In doing so, they may make a bad decision. If they do not sell the merchandise immediately at a loss, they may sell it at a larger loss later or may have to write it off entirely if it cannot be sold at all. Under the circumstances, unless a higher price is possible later, the decision to sell now is the best.

An item's historical cost is not always irrelevant, however. The decision to purchase an item for resale requires information about both its cost and probable selling price. Nonetheless, once the merchandise *has been purchased*, the cash outlay (or promise to pay) has already occurred and is a *sunk cost*, and although it is relevant to income determination, it is irrelevant to subsequent decisions.

SELF-STUDY QUESTION

1. The following is a true story. An executive joined a tennis club and paid a $1,000 yearly membership fee. After two weeks of playing, the executive developed "tennis elbow" but continued to play (in pain), saying, "I don't want to waste the $1,000!" Comment.

The solution to this question is at the end of this chapter on page 440.

DIFFERENTIAL COSTS: THE BIG PICTURE

Differential Costs versus Total Costs

Although we have focused on differential costs, the information presented to management can show the detailed costs that were included for making a decision, or it can show just the differences between alternatives, as shown here in the right-hand column (in thousands).

	Status Quo	Alternative	Difference
Sales revenue	$750	$900	$150
Variable Costs	(250)	(300)	(50)
Contribution margin	500	600	100
Fixed costs	(350)	(350)	–0–
Operating profit	$150	$250	$100

The first two columns show the total operating profit under the status quo and the alternative. This part of the presentation is referred to as the *total format*. The third column shows only the differences; this presentation is called the *differential format*.

Some managers prefer the total format because it enables them to see what their total revenues, costs, and profits will be under each alternative. Others prefer the differential format because it highlights the costs and revenues affected by the decision and enables them to focus on those items alone. We have found that, in practice, managers ask for both total and differential costs; they tell us that the costs to present both formats is relatively low. In addition, in complex organizations, decisions often must be approved by more than one person. By including both formats with a recommendation, one need not worry whether every person that must sign off on the report is going to want a total cost or a differential cost format.

The Full-Cost Fallacy in Setting Prices

full cost
The sum of the fixed and variable costs of manufacturing and selling a unit.

The terms **full cost** or *full product cost* describe a product's cost that includes both (1) the variable costs of producing and selling the product and (2) a share of the organization's fixed costs. Sometimes decision makers use these full costs, mistakenly thinking that they are variable costs.

For example, a printing company employee claims that accepting a special order from a customer for 8 cents a copy is a mistake. "Since our variable costs are $.06 per copy and our fixed costs are $2,500 per week, our total costs for the week without the special order are $8,500 for 100,000 copies. That is 8 and one-half cents per copy ($8,500/100,000), which is more than the 8 cents per copy offered by the customer. We'd be losing half a cent per copy!"

By considering fixed costs in the analysis, the employee may be including irrelevant information. If the fixed costs will be incurred whether the special order is accepted or rejected, these costs should not bear on the decision. Instead, the employee should focus on the variable costs of 6 cents a copy in deciding whether to accept the special order from the customer.

This is a common mistake in short-run decisions. Although all costs must be covered in the long run or the company will fail; in the short run, it will be profitable to accept the order because the price of 8 cents per copy exceeds variable costs of 6 cents a copy. Full product costs serve a wide variety of important purposes; they are generally not relevant to the type of short-run operating decision described in this example.

Can Fixed Costs Be Differential?

In many short-run operating decisions, fixed costs usually remain unchanged because they are the costs to provide production capacity, and capacity does not change in the short run. When short-run operating decisions do not involve a change in capacity, fixed costs remain unchanged and therefore are not differential. The example in the previous section assumes that the printing company has the capacity to accept the special order without having to increase its fixed costs. Thus, fixed costs are not differential costs.

In long-run decisions, however, fixed costs may be differential costs. For example, if the printing company must purchase additional equipment and lease additional space to accept the special order, which is expected to last for several years, then the decision includes differential fixed costs in addition to differential variable costs. Therefore, like variable costs, fixed costs must be examined carefully to determine whether they are differential.

MAJOR INFLUENCES ON PRICING

L.O. 2: Describe the major influences on pricing.

Not only is differential cost and revenue analysis useful for making special order decisions, but many managers also use it to help in making pricing decisions. Cost information is only one factor influencing pricing decisions. As companies have become customer driven, focusing on delivering quality products at competitive prices, their pricing decisions also are influenced by factors other than cost. The three major influences on pricing decisions are *customers, competitors,* and *costs.*

Customers

Managers examine pricing problems through the eyes of their customers. Increasing prices may cause the loss of customers to a competitor, or it may cause customers to choose a less expensive substitute product.

Competitors

Competitors' reactions also influence pricing decisions. A competitor's aggressive pricing may force a business to lower its prices. On the other hand, a business without a competitor has some discretion and can set high prices. A business that knows its competitors' technology, plant capacity, and operating policies is able to estimate the competitors' costs, which is valuable in making pricing decisions.

In many cases, competition crosses international borders. Firms with overcapacity in their domestic markets (i.e., supply exceeds demand domestically) may price aggressively in their export markets. For instance, a software development company like Microsoft with high development costs and low variable costs may look for foreign markets. In a foreign market, it can exploit the high development costs that it has already incurred while it charges lower prices than do local competitors who must incur high development costs to compete. Increasingly, managers consider both their domestic and international competition in making pricing decisions.

Costs

Lower cost means the company can lower its prices and still be profitable. Continuous improvement and activity-based management are the keys to cutting costs.

In making pricing decisions, companies weigh customers, competitors, and costs differently. Companies selling homogeneous products in highly competitive markets must accept the market price. On the other hand, managers have some discretion in setting prices in markets with little competition. The pricing decision considers the value that customers place on the product, the pricing strategies of competitors, and the costs of the product.

Before we begin using differential cost and revenue analysis for making pricing decisions, we must first understand the differences between short-run and long-run decisions.

SHORT-RUN VERSUS LONG-RUN DECISIONS

L.O. 3: Differentiate between short-run and long-run pricing decisions.

The time horizon of the decision is critical in computing the relevant costs in a pricing decision. The two ends of the time-horizon spectrum are:

	Short-Run Pricing Decisions	Long-Run Pricing Decisions
Years	0 ———→ 1	———→ Longer than 1

Short-run decisions include (1) pricing for a one-time-only special order with no long-term implications and (2) adjusting product mix and volume in a competitive market. The time horizon is typically one year or less. Long-run decisions include pricing a main product in a large market in which price setting has considerable leeway. Managers often use a time horizon of longer than a year for these long-run decisions.

For example, an athletic team's special order for shoes involves a short-run pricing decision by Nike. Introducing a new type of running shoe to the market, however, is a long-run decision.

ILLUSTRATION   14.1   Framework for Decision Making

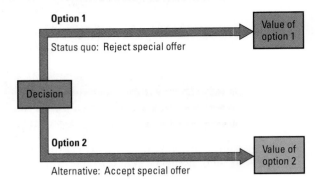

SHORT-RUN PRICING DECISIONS: SPECIAL ORDERS

special order
An order that will not affect other sales and is usually a short-run occurrence.

The differential approach particularly helps in making special-order decisions. Determining which costs are relevant depends on the decision being considered. A framework for decision making, based on a company that receives a **special order,** is diagrammed in Illustration 14.1. Each alternative is stated as a branch of a decision tree and then the value of each alternative is determined. Finally, the alternative with the highest value is chosen.

For example, Quick-Print uses a modern copy machine to make copies for walk-in customers. The machine is usually idle about two hours each day. On October 15, B. Onst, who is running for political office, asks Quick-Print to produce 10,000 copies of letters, speeches, memoranda, and other campaign materials to be ready on October 22. Quick-Print has idle capacity adequate for this job, which will not affect other sales. The candidate wants to pay only 8 cents per copy, even though the regular price is 10 cents.

In deciding whether to accept the special order, Quick-Print's owner estimates the following operating data for the week in question:

Sales (100,000 copies at 10¢).	$10,000
Variable costs, including paper, maintenance, and usage payment to machine owner (100,000 copies at 6¢).	6,000
Total contribution margin	4,000
Fixed costs (operators, plus allocated costs of the print shop)	2,500
Operating profit	$ 1,500

To make the decision, the owner identifies the alternatives, determines the value of each alternative to the company, and selects the alternative with the highest value to the company.

The values of the alternatives are shown in Illustration 14.2. The best economic decision is to accept the order because the company will gain $200 from it. Fixed costs are not affected by the decision because they are not differential in this situation. Therefore, they are not relevant.

The differential approach to pricing works well for special orders, but some criticize its use for pricing a firm's regular products. Critics suggest that following the differential approach in the short run leads to underpricing in the long run because the contribution to covering fixed costs and generating profits will be inadequate.

Others respond to this criticism in two ways.

First, the differential approach does lead to correct short-run pricing decisions. Once the firm has set plant capacity and incurred fixed costs, the fixed costs become

ILLUSTRATION 14.2	Analysis of Special Order, Quick-Print		
	Status Quo: Reject Special Order	Alternative: Accept Special Order	Difference
Comparison of Totals			
Sales revenue.	$10,000	$10,800	$800
Variable costs.	(6,000)	(6,600)	(600)
Total contribution	4,000	4,200	200
Fixed costs.	(2,500)	(2,500)	–0–
Operating profit.	$ 1,500	$ 1,700	$200
Alternative Presentation: Differential Analysis			
Differential sales, 10,000 at 8¢.	$800		
Less differential costs, 10,000 at 6¢	600		
Differential operating profit (before taxes)	$200		

irrelevant to the short-run pricing decision. Clearly, airlines understand this with their discount fares. The firm must attempt to set a price that at least equals the differential, or variable, costs.

Second, in both the short and long run, the differential approach indicates only the minimum acceptable price. The firm always can charge a higher amount, depending on its customers and competitors.

SELF-STUDY QUESTION

2. Vista Enterprises, Inc., has an annual plant capacity to produce 2,500 units. Its predicted operations for the year follow:

Sales revenue (2,000 units at $40 each)	$80,000
Manufacturing costs	
Variable	$24 per unit
Fixed	$17,000
Selling and administrative costs	
Variable (commissions on sales)	$2.50 per unit
Fixed	$2,500

Should the company accept a special order for 400 units at a selling price of $32 each, which is subject to half the usual sales commission rate per unit? Assume no effect on regular sales at regular prices. What is the effect of the decision on the company's operating profit?

The solution to this question is at the end of this chapter on page 440.

DIFFERENTIAL APPROACH TO PRICING

The differential approach to pricing is useful for both short-run and long-run decisions. It presumes that the price must at least equal the differential cost to produce and sell the product. In the short run, this practice results in a positive contribution to covering fixed costs and generating profit. In the long run, it requires covering all costs because both fixed and variable costs become differential costs in the long run.

Consider the data for Quick-Print. The minimum acceptable price in the short run equals the differential cost of $0.06 per unit. In the long run, the minimum acceptable price is $0.085 per unit because the firm must cover both variable and fixed costs. A more desirable long-run price is the current price, $0.10, which includes a profit. Between the $0.06 short-run minimum price and the $0.085 long-run desired price lies the firm's range of price flexibility. The firm may set a price slightly higher than the variable cost for a special order as long as excess capacity exists and doing so will not affect its regular market.

Suppose that Quick-Print wants to price aggressively. It can set a price slightly higher than the $0.06 minimum. Managers hope to underprice competitors and to capture a larger share of the market.

If the firm is the only supplier of this product, it can charge a price higher than $0.085. If it sets the price too high, however, it may earn high profits that entice other firms into the market.

LONG-RUN PRICING DECISIONS

Most firms rely on full cost information reports when setting prices as discussed in the Real World Application on this page, "Differences in Pricing Practices in Various Countries." Full cost is the total cost to produce and sell a unit; it includes all of the costs incurred by the activities that make up the value chain, as shown in Illustration 14.3.

Typically, the accounting department provides cost reports to the marketing department, which then adds appropriate markups to determine benchmark or target prices for all products the firm normally sells.

Using full costs for pricing decisions can be justified in three circumstances:

- When a firm enters into a long-term contractual relationship to supply a product, most activity costs depend on the production decisions under the long-term contract. Therefore, full costs are relevant for the long-term pricing decision.
- Many contracts for developing and producing customized products and with governmental agencies specify prices as full costs plus a markup. Prices set in regulated industries such as electric utilities also are based on full costs.
- Firms initially can set prices based on full costs and then make short-term adjustments to reflect market conditions. Accordingly, they adjust the prices of the product downward to acquire additional business.

ILLUSTRATION   14.3   The Value Chain

Begin value chain → Research and development → Design → Production → Marketing → Distribution → Customer service → Value of goods and services to customers

Conversely, when demand for their products is high, firms recognize the greater likelihood that the existing capacity of activity resources is inadequate to satisfy all of the demand. Accordingly, they adjust the prices upward based on the higher incremental costs when capacity is fully utilized.

Long-Run versus Short-Run Pricing: Is There a Difference?

When used in pricing decisions, the differential costs required to sell and/or produce a product provide a floor. In the short run, differential costs may be very low, as when selling one additional seat on an already scheduled airline flight or allowing one more student into an already scheduled college course.

In the long run, however, differential costs are much higher than in the short run. Returning to the airline example, long-run differential costs include the costs to buy and maintain the aircraft and to pay crew salaries, landing fees, and so forth. In the long run, these costs must be covered. To simplify this type of analysis, the *full product costs* to make and/or sell a product are often used to estimate long-run differential costs. Hence, a common saying in business is, "I can drop my prices to just cover variable costs in the short run, but in the long run, my prices have to cover full product costs."

COST ANALYSIS FOR PRICING

L.O. 5: Understand several approaches to establishing prices based on costs (primarily for long-run pricing decisions).

To this point, we have discussed differential analysis and its usefulness for short-run and long-run pricing decisions. Several other approaches are used, however, to establish prices based on costs. Three approaches—life-cycle product costing and pricing, cost-plus pricing, and target costing for target pricing—are discussed here. In general, these approaches are especially useful in making long-run pricing decisions.

Life-Cycle Product Costing and Pricing

product life cycle
The time from initial research and development to the time that support to the customer ends.

The **product life cycle** covers the time from initial research and development to the time at which support to the customer is withdrawn. For motor vehicles, such as the Jeep Grand Cherokee, this time span may range from 5 to 10 years. For toys or fashion clothing products, it may be less than one year.

Managers estimate the revenues and costs for each product from its initial research and development to its final customer support. Life-cycle costing tracks costs attributable to each product from start to finish. The term *cradle-to-grave costing* conveys the sense of capturing all life-cycle costs associated with a product.

Life-cycle costs provide important information for pricing. For some products, particularly electronics, the development period is relatively long, and many costs are incurred prior to manufacturing.

A product life-cycle budget highlights to managers the importance of setting prices that will cover costs in *all* the value-chain categories (as shown in Illustration 14.3), not just in the production through customer service categories. To be profitable, companies must generate enough revenue to cover costs incurred in all six categories.

Cost-Plus Pricing

Some products are so unique, or the market price is so difficult to determine, that costs plus a specified allowance for profits provides a pricing basis. For construction jobs, defense contracts, most custom orders, and many new products, the cost of the product plays a significant role in determining its price.

An estimate of specific job costs is also an important guide for bidding on a job. If a bid price is too low compared to costs, the contract may be obtained, but it will

REAL WORLD APPLICATION | **A Target Costing Challenge in Forest Products**

A forest products company was losing money on a particular product. Management wondered whether the loss per ton was a price problem rather than a cost problem.

Sales management saw pricing as given, based on market competition, and did not consider the loss its problem. Manufacturing saw cost as given, based on well-established production processes and materials requirements, and did not consider the loss its problem.

Study of a competitor revealed that it was producing the product at a much lower cost. After accepting the fact that the product cost was too high, management decided to "value engineer" the manufacturing process for that product.

Once the mill management team really accepted the challenge to cut the cost by more than 60 percent, its attention focused on three areas:

- Fiber mix (use of recycled paper to reduce the raw materials cost).
- Paper machine yields (getting "on grade" faster).
- Conversion cost ("make" versus "buy").

The result of this project was a dramatic turnaround. The project started with a cost of $2,900 per ton versus a target cost of $1,075. After about 18 months of price-based costing initiatives, mill management could see the possibility of an achievable cost of $1,162. The mill management team had no idea when the target cost project started that the results could be so dramatic.

Source: J. Shank, "Strategic Cost Management: A Target Costing Field Study," The Amos Tuck School of Business Administration, Dartmouth College, 1995.

result in a loss. If a bid is considerably higher than costs, the contract probably will be lost.

Target Costing from Target Pricing

target price
The price based on customers' perceived value for the product and the price competitors charge.

target cost
Equals the target price minus desired profit margin.

value engineering
A systematic evaluation of all aspects of research and development, design of products and processes, production, marketing, distribution, and customer service to reduce costs and satisfy customer needs.

Simply stated, target costing is the concept of "price-based costing" instead of "cost-based pricing." A **target price** is the estimated price for a product or service that potential customers will be willing to pay. A target cost is the estimated long-run cost of a product or service whose sale enables the company to achieve targeted profit. **Target cost** is derived by subtracting the target profit from the target price. For instance, assume Reebok can sell a particular shoe style for $33 a pair and wants profits of $6 per pair; this leaves a $27 limit on costs per pair. Target costing is widely used by companies including Mercedes Benz and Toyota in the automobile industry, Panasonic and Sharp in the electronics industry, and Apple and Toshiba in the personal computer industry.

Developing target prices and target costs requires the following four steps:

Step 1: Develop a product that satisfies the needs of potential customers.

Step 2: Choose a target price based on consumers' perceived value of the product and the prices competitors charge.

Step 3: Derive a target cost by subtracting the desired profit margin from target price.

Step 4: Perform value engineering to achieve target costs. **Value engineering** is a systematic evaluation of all aspects of research and development, design of products and processes, production, marketing, distribution, and customer service to reduce costs and satisfy customer needs. Value engineering can result in improvements in product designs, changes in materials specifications, or modifications in process methods.

Value engineering starts with an analysis of the value-chain activities. An example of value-chain analysis in conjunction with target costing is presented in the Real World Application, "A Target Costing Challenge in Forest Products."

ACTIVITY-BASED COSTING AND DIFFERENTIAL COST ANALYSIS: A NATURAL FIT

L.O. 6: Understand how activity-based costing and differential cost analysis can be used together.

As discussed on this page, activity-based costing can be used to compute the differential costs of a decision to start a training program to reduce setup time for surgeries in this hospital.
(© David Joel/Tony Stone Images)

Activity-based costing helps managers perform differential cost analysis, which attempts to estimate the cost effects of a decision. Activity-based costing provides information about the costs of activities affected by a decision. Remember that activity-based costing is a costing method that assigns costs first to activities and then to products based on each product's use of the activities. Four steps are involved:

1. Identify the activities that consume resources and assign costs to those activities.
2. Identify the cost driver(s) associated with each activity.
3. Compute a cost rate per cost driver unit or transaction.
4. Assign costs to products by multiplying the cost driver rate times the volume of cost driver units consumed by the product.

Activity-based costing provides more detailed cost data that might lead to more informed decision making. As a result, activity-based costing is a natural fit with differential cost analysis.

For example, suppose that a health care manager is considering a training program that will reduce the time required to setup an operating room for surgery. Assume that the setup can be reduced from 40 minutes to 30 minutes per surgery. Assume also that activity-based costing indicates that the cost driver rate is $2 per minute of setup time for costs affected by the decision to reduce setup time. With this information, the manager can figure the cost savings per surgery setup to be $20 ($2 × 10 minutes saved).

USING ACTIVITY-BASED COSTING AND PRICING

Activity-based costing also helps managers to make pricing decisions when prices and costs are interrelated. Recent surveys of companies indicate that many companies use activity-based costing for product pricing. In many situations, as when companies bid on jobs, prices are based at least in part on costs. For example, when bidding to build a hospital or office building, a building contractor estimates the cost of the job to help determine the amount to bid. Generally, the firm prefers not to bid a price below its costs; therefore, it needs to estimate costs before bidding.

Activity-based costing helps managers prepare bids by providing a realistic estimate of costs. Using activity-based costing, managers can estimate the activities required to perform the work and then multiply the cost driver rates by the volume of activities required to do it. The product of this multiplication is the cost estimate for the job.

Activity-based costing has taught managers that their cost estimates have been too low on some jobs, especially complicated ones, and too high on others, usually simple ones, because the managers used conventional costing methods that relied on volume-based cost drivers such as labor and machine-hours to allocate costs to jobs. Switching to activity-based costing has revealed many additional cost drivers, such as the number of hours of set-up and quality inspection.

To demonstrate this point, assume that a building contractor bids on two jobs, both requiring the same number of labor-hours, which are the building contractor's basis of allocating overhead costs under conventional costing. Using conventional costing, the two jobs would have equal estimated overhead. But assume that job A requires the use of several foreign vendors because the materials are exotic and highly specialized. Job B, on the other hand, requires only local vendors. Because of the shipping costs, language differences, time zone differences, and other complications, dealing with the foreign vendors will cost the building contractor more than with the domestic vendors; therefore, job A will likely have higher overhead costs than job B.

Activity-based costing highlights this difference between the overhead costs of jobs A and B if the building contractor identifies the use of foreign vendors as an activity that drives costs. In general, activity-based costing has helped companies that bid on jobs improve their cost estimates because, unlike conventional costing, activity-based costing recognizes that more complex jobs cost more than less complex jobs, all other things being equal.

USE OF COSTS TO DETERMINE THE LEGALITY OF PRICING PRACTICES

L.O. 7: Recognize legal issues in price setting.

price discrimination
Sale of product or service at different prices that do not reflect differences in marginal costs.

We observe theaters charging lower prices for matinee performances and airlines charging lower prices for certain kinds of passengers. These are examples of price discrimination to sell a product. **Price discrimination** exists when a product or service is sold at two or more prices that do not reflect proportional differences in marginal costs. If a seat would otherwise go unsold, airlines and theaters should be willing to sell it at a lower price, as long as the price exceeds the variable cost of filling the seat and does not decrease normal sales.

The Clayton and Sherman Antitrust acts, the Robinson-Patman Act, and many state and local laws forbid certain pricing practices unless they are cost justified. For example, predatory pricing (below differential cost) to prevent or eliminate competition is illegal. Certain kinds of price discrimination among customers are also illegal unless the discrimination is justified by actual differences in the costs of serving different customers. This is only a brief overview of the highly complex legal issues involved, but it is a reminder of the necessity to maintain cost records to justify pricing practices.

CUSTOMER PROFITABILITY AND DIFFERENTIAL ANALYSIS

L.O. 8: Understand how to use differential analysis to determine customer profitability.

You know that companies choose products and customers based on profitability. Differential costing is useful for deciding which customers they should keep and which they should stop servicing.

Assume that Harrison and Associates, an advertising firm, performs ongoing services for three clients, Sonora Hospital, Beairds Department Store, and Servinties Resort. Illustration 14.4 presents Harrison's revenues and costs by customer, which is typical for the last few years.

Illustration 14.4 shows a loss of $18,000 on services to Servinties. Should Harrison discontinue that account?

The key issue concerns the differential revenues and costs for this client. You learn the following information:

- Dropping the Servinties account will save the cost of services incurred on that account.
- Dropping the Servinties account will have no effect on salaries, rent, or general administration costs.

Illustration 14.5 presents the computations. Harrison's operating profits will be $20,000 higher if it keeps the Servinties account. The last column in Illustration 14.5 shows that the cost savings from dropping the Servinties account, $330,000, is not enough to offset the loss of $350,000 in revenue. The key reason is that salaries, rent, and general administration costs will not decrease if the Servinties account is dropped.

ILLUSTRATION 14.4	Customer Profitability Analysis at Harrison and Associates (in thousands)			
	Sonora Hospital	Beairds Department Store	Servinties Resort	Total
Revenues (fees charged)	$450	$270	$350	$1,070
Operating costs				
Cost of services (variable)	370	220	330	920
Salaries, rent, and general administration (fixed)	44	26	38	108
Total operating costs	414	246	368	1,028
Operating profits	$ 36	$ 24	$ (18)	$ 42

ILLUSTRATION 14.5	Computations for Decision Whether to Drop the Servinties Account		
	Status Quo (total for company)	Drop Servinties (total minus Servinties)	Difference
Revenues	$1,070	$720	$350
Operating costs			
Cost of goods sold (variable)	920	590	330
Salaries, rent, and general administration	108	108	–0–
Total operating costs	1,028	698	330
Operating profits	$ 42	$ 22	$ 20

The conclusion would be different if, after dropping the Servinties account, Harrison could utilize the extra capacity to generate profits greater than $20,000 per year from another client. Before coming to a final decision, however, Harrison must consider both the possibility of changing Servinties into a profitable customer and qualitative factors, such as the effect the decision might have on Harrison's reputation for developing stable, long-run relationships.

SELF-STUDY QUESTION

3. McKlintoff and Associates, an accounting firm, performs ongoing services for two clients, Jamoca Joe's and Levinon Industries. The following is information about McKlintoff's revenues and costs (in thousands) by customer, which is typical over the last few years.

	Jamoca Joe's	Levinon Industries	Total
Revenues (fees charged)	$460	$700	$1,160
Operating costs			
Cost of services (variable)	425	610	1,035
Salaries, rent, and general administration (fixed)	40	60	100
Total operating costs	465	670	1,135
Operating profits	$ (5)	$ 30	$ 25

This shows a $5,000 loss on services to Jamoca Joe's. Use differential analysis to determine whether McKlintoff should discontinue Jamoca Joe's account.

The solution to this question is at the end of this chapter on page 440.

SUMMARY

This chapter discusses *differential analysis,* which determines *what* would differ and by *how much* if alternative actions are taken. Differential analysis is performed by comparing alternatives to the *status quo,* using the following model:

Status Quo	Alternative	Difference
Revenue	Revenue	Change in revenue
less	less	less
Variable costs	Variable costs	Change in variable costs
equals	equals	equals
Total contribution	Total contribution	Change in total contribution
less	less	less
Fixed costs	Fixed costs	Change in fixed costs
equals	equals	equals
Status quo's profit	Alternative's profit	Change in profits

The following summarizes key ideas tied to the chapter's learning objectives.

LO1: Using differential analysis for decision making. Differential analysis, which compares alternative actions with the status quo, is used by decision makers to select a specific course of action given several different alternatives.

LO2: Influences on pricing. The three major influences on pricing are customers, competition, and costs. All three should be considered when making pricing decisions.

LO3: Short-run and long-run pricing decisions. Short-run decisions are applied to time horizons over which capacity will be unchanged, typically one year or less. Long-run decisions apply to time horizons longer than a year. Relevant costs in making a decision will change, depending on whether the decision is over the short run or the long run.

LO4: Using differential analysis to make short-run pricing decisions. Differential analysis is particularly helpful in making short-run pricing decisions, an example of which is a special order. Once each alternative is presented with related revenues and costs, the alternative with the highest value is chosen.

LO5: Establishing prices based on costs. Three approaches for establishing prices based on costs are described in this chapter: life-cycle product costing and pricing, cost-plus costing, and target costing and pricing. In general, these approaches are best for long-run pricing decisions.

LO6: Using activity-based costing and differential analysis. Activity-based costing provides more detailed cost data that managers can use when performing a differential analysis. Some people argue that differential analysis is much more effective when used with activity-based costing.

LO7: Legal issues in setting prices. The Clayton and Sherman Antitrust Acts and the Robinson-Patman Act forbid certain pricing practices unless they are cost justified.

LO8: Using differential analysis to determine customer profitability. Many companies are interested in identifying the most profitable customers. Differential cost analysis is useful in deciding whether to keep or drop customers.

KEY TERMS

differential analysis, 418	special order, 422
differential costs, 418	sunk cost, 418
full cost, 420	target cost, 426
price discrimination, 428	target price, 426
product life cycle, 425	value engineering, 426
short run, 418	

REVIEW QUESTIONS

14.1 When, if ever, are fixed costs differential?

14.2 What is the difference between a sunk cost and a differential cost?

14.3 Are sunk costs ever differential costs?

14.4 Which of the following *best* completes the statement or answers the question?
  a. Production of a special order increases operating profit when the additional revenue from the special order is more than
   (1) The conversion costs incurred.
   (2) The direct material costs.
   (3) The fixed costs.
   (4) The indirect costs.
   (5) The differential costs.
  b. In considering a special-order situation that will enable a company to use presently idle capacity, which costs are probably not differential?
   (1) Materials.
   (2) Depreciation of buildings.
   (3) Direct labor.
   (4) Variable overhead.

(CPA adapted)

14.5 What is the difference between short-run and long-run decisions? Give one example of each.

14.6 What costs are included in the full cost of a product? Is a product's full cost always the appropriate cost for decision makers to use?

14.7 What are the three major influences on pricing? Why isn't cost the only factor to consider when setting prices?

14.8 What are life-cycle product costing and pricing?

14.9 When is cost-plus pricing most likely to be used?

14.10 What do the terms *target cost* and *target price* mean? Explain how they are developed.

CRITICAL ANALYSIS AND DISCUSSION QUESTIONS

14.11 One of your acquaintances notes, "This whole subject of differential costing is easy; variable costs are the only costs that are relevant." How would you respond?

14.12 A manager in your organization just received a special order at a price that is "below cost." The manager points to the document and says, "These are the kinds of orders that will get you in trouble. Every sale must bear its share of the full costs of running the business. If we sell below our full cost, we'll be out of business in no time." What do you think of this remark?

14.13 If you are considering driving to a weekend resort for a quick break from school, what are the differential costs of operating your car for that drive?

14.14 If you are considering buying a second car, what are the differential costs of that decision? Are they the same as in Question 14.13? Why or why not?

14.15 Assume that your company uses activity-based costing. You must set the price for a custom order and suggest that your boss use a cost-plus pricing approach. Your boss states, "We can't possibly use cost-plus pricing given the activity-based costing system we recently implemented!" Respond to your boss's comment. What recommendation would you make as to how to price a custom order?

14.16 You work for a company that has 15 primary customers. Your supervisor has asked you to prepare a profitability report for each of them. What difficulties do you think you will encounter in preparing this report?

14.17 Refer to Question 14.16. Assume that you have overcome the difficulties identified in that question and have identified four customers who appear not to be profitable. Your supervisor has asked you to submit a report recommending what to do with each of them. What issues should you consider in making your recommendations?

EXERCISES

Note: Income taxes should be ignored unless explicitly required in the exercise, problem, or case.

14.18 **Using Differential Analysis** (L.O. 1)

Peterson Publishing Machinery has a batch of obsolete binding machines, which it carries in inventory at a $10,000 cost. If the machines are retooled for $2,500, Peterson could sell them for $4,500. If they are scrapped, they could be sold for $1,500.

Required

What is the optimal alternative?

(CPA adapted)

14.19 **Special Orders** (L.O. 1, 4)

Torous Company makes paper shredders for government officials. Data from the forecasted income statement for the year before any special orders are as follows:

	Amount	Per Unit
Sales revenue.	$8,000,000	$20.00
Manufacturing costs	6,400,000	16.00
Gross profit	1,600,000	4.00
Marketing costs	600,000	1.50
Operating profit.	$1,000,000	$ 2.50

Fixed costs included in this forecasted income statement are $2,800,000 in manufacturing costs and $200,000 in marketing costs. These costs are not affected by a special order offering to buy 50,000 shredders for $13 each. Torous has enough idle capacity to process this order.

Required

What impact would accepting the special order have on operating profit?

(CPA adapted)

14.20 **Special Orders** (L.O. 1, 4)

Pralina Products Company is presently operating at 50 percent of practical capacity and producing about 100,000 units of a patented electronic component annually. Pralina recently received an offer from a company in Yokohama, Japan, to purchase 60,000 components at $6 per unit. No other orders are foreseen from the Japanese company. Pralina has not previously sold components in Japan. Budgeted production costs for 100,000 and 160,000 units of output follow:

Units	100,000	160,000
Costs		
Direct materials	$150,000	$240,000
Direct labor	150,000	240,000
Factory overhead	400,000	496,000
Total costs	$700,000	$976,000
Cost per unit	$7.00	$6.10

The sales manager believes that the order should be accepted, even if it results in a loss, because the sales may build future markets. The production manager does not wish to have the order accepted, primarily because it would show a loss of $.10 per unit when computed on the new average unit cost.

Required   **a.** Explain what caused the drop in cost from $7 per unit to $6.10 per unit when budgeted production increased from 100,000 to 160,000 units. Show supporting computations.

b. Should the order from the company in Yokohama be accepted?

(CPA adapted)

14.21   Pricing Decisions   The following data relate to a year's budgeted activity (100,000 units) for Lucky Locks, a
(L.O. 1, 4)   single-product company:

	Per Unit
Selling price	$5.00
Variable manufacturing costs	1.00
Variable market costs	2.00
Fixed manufacturing costs (based on 100,000 units)	.25
Fixed marketing costs (based on 100,000 units)	.65

Total fixed costs remain unchanged between 25,000 units and total capacity of 160,000 units.

Lucky received an order for 20,000 units to be used in an unrelated market. The sale requires production of 20,000 extra units.

Required   What price per unit should Lucky charge on the special order to increase its operating profit by $30,000?

(CPA adapted)

14.22   Pricing Decisions   Assume that Ben & Jerry's sells ice cream for $3 per quart. The cost of each quart follows:
(L.O. 1, 4)

Materials	$1.00
Labor.	.50
Variable overhead.	.25
Fixed overhead ($20,000 per month, 20,000 quarts per month)	1.00
Total cost per quart	$2.75

One of Ben & Jerry's regular customers asked the company to fill a special order of 400 quarts at a selling price of $2.25 per quart for a special picnic. It could be filled with Ben & Jerry's capacity without affecting total fixed costs for the month.

Ben & Jerry's general manager was concerned about selling the ice cream below the cost of $2.75 per quart and has asked for your advice.

Required   **a.** Prepare a schedule to show the impact of providing 400 quarts of ice cream on Ben & Jerry's profits in addition to the regular production and sales of 20,000 quarts per month.

b. Based solely on the data given, what is the lowest price per quart at which the ice cream in the special order could be sold without reducing Ben & Jerry's profits?

14.23   Cost Analysis for   Easton, Inc., has manufactured violin cases since they became popular with gangsters in the
Pricing Decisions   1920s. The regular price of a violin case is $50 each. Easton's controller has prepared cost
(L.O. 1, 4)   data on these cases based on a normal selling volume of 20,000 per year:

Direct materials	$ 7.50
Direct labor	10.00
Overhead	8.00 (75% fixed)
Marketing and administrative	4.00 (all fixed)
Total cost	$29.50

This week, Ness Corporation moved into Easton's market area. Ness instituted a media campaign designed to lure Easton's customers. Indeed, Ness offered violin cases at one-half of Easton's selling price.

Easton estimates that if it meets Ness's price, its volume will increase to 50,000 cases because people who previously were buying elsewhere would be induced to buy locally. However, if it does not meet Ness's price, Easton's volume will fall to 10,000 cases per year.

Required

a. Prepare a schedule that compares the status quo (price = $50; quantity = 10,000) with the alternative (price = $25; quantity = 50,000).

b. What should Easton do?

14.24 **Differential Customer Analysis (L.O. 8)**

Hillson & Brady, a commercial laundry service, has two clients, Super 6 Motel and Seaside Inn. The following is information about H&B's revenues and costs (in thousands) by customer for the previous year:

	Super 6 Motel	Seaside Inn	Total
Revenues (fees charged)	$230	$350	$580
Operating costs			
Cost of services (variable).	212	305	517
Salaries, rent, and general administration (fixed).	20	30	50
Total operating costs	232	335	567
Operating profits	$ (2)	$ 15	$ 13

The analysis shows that Super 6 Motel is not profitable for H&B.

Required

Use differential analysis to determine whether H&B should discontinue the Super 6 account.

14.25 **Differential Customer Analysis (L.O. 8)**

How Clean, a janitorial service, has two clients, Greeley Hospital and Greeley Junior High School. The following is information about How Clean's revenues and costs (in thousands) by customer for the previous year:

	Greeley Hospital	Greeley Junior High	Total
Revenues (fees charged)	$920	$1,400	$2,320
Operating costs			
Cost of services (variable).	848	1,220	2,068
Salaries, rent, and general administration (fixed).	80	120	200
Total operating costs	928	1,340	2,268
Operating profits	$ (8)	$ 60	$ 52

This analysis shows that Greeley Hospital is not profitable for How Clean.

Required

Use differential analysis to determine whether How Clean should discontinue the hospital account.

14.26 **Differential Customer Analysis (L.O. 8)**

Wee One's, a diaper service, has two clients, Madison Children's Hospital and Little Bits Day Care Centers. The following is information about Wee One's revenues and costs by customer for the previous year (in thousands):

	Madison Hospital	Little Bits	Total
Revenues (fees charged)	$105	$185	$290
Operating costs			
Cost of services (variable).	106	153	259
Salaries, rent, and general administration (fixed).	12	13	25
Total operating costs	118	166	284
Operating profits	$ (13)	$ 19	$ 6

This analysis shows that Madison Children's Hospital is not profitable for Wee One's.

Required

Use differential analysis to determine whether Wee One's should discontinue the hospital account.

14.27 Special Order (L.O. 1, 3, 4)

Sam's Sport Shop makes jerseys for athletic teams. The Diggers baseball club has offered to buy 80 jerseys for its team for $18 per jersey. The normal price for such jerseys is $20. Sam's purchases the plain jerseys for $12 each and then adds a name and number to each jersey at a variable cost of $3 per jersey. Sam's makes about 2,000 jerseys per year and has a capacity limit of 4,000 jerseys. The annual fixed cost of equipment used in the embroidery process is $5,000 and other fixed costs allocated to jerseys is $2,000, bringing the total costs allocated to each jersey to $3.50. Sam's management is concerned that it will lose money on the deal with Diggers.

Required

Compute the amount by which the operating profit of Sam's would change if the special order from Diggers were accepted. Should Sam's accept the special order?

14.28 Target Costing and Pricing (L.O. 5)

Brown's Wheels makes wheels for a variety of toys and sport equipment. It sells the wheels to manufacturers that assemble and sell the toy or equipment. The company's market research department has discovered a market for in-line skate wheels, which it presently does not produce. The market research department has indicated that a set of four wheels for in-line skates would likely sell for $6.

Assume that Brown's desires an operating profit of 20 percent.

Required

What is the highest acceptable manufacturing cost for which Brown's would be willing to produce the sets of wheels?

14.29 Target Costing and Pricing (L.O. 5)

Durham Industries makes high-pressure lines for a variety of heavy road improvement equipment. It sells the lines to companies that manufacture and sell the equipment. The company's market research department has discovered a market for high-pressure lines used in automated manufacturing equipment, which Durham presently does not produce. The market research department has indicated that these lines will likely sell for $11 a foot.

Required

Assume that Durham desires a 10 percent operating profit. What is the highest acceptable manufacturing cost for which Durham would be willing to produce the lines?

PROBLEMS

14.30 Special Order

Gilbert Company, the maker of a variety of rubber products, is in the midst of a business downturn and has many idle facilities. Nationwide Tire Company has approached Gilbert to produce 300,000 oversized tire tubes for $2.40 each.

Gilbert predicts that its variable costs will be $2.60 each. Its fixed costs, which had been averaging $2 per unit on a variety of products, will now be spread over twice as much volume, however. The president commented, "Sure, we'll lose $0.20 each on the variable costs, but we'll gain $1 per unit by spreading our fixed costs over more units. Therefore, we should take the offer because it would gain us $0.80 per unit."

Gilbert currently has a volume of 300,000 units, sales of $1,200,000, variable costs of $780,000, and fixed costs of $600,000.

Required

a. Compute the impact on operating profit if the special order is accepted.

b. Do you agree with the president? Write a short report explaining why or why not.

14.31 Target Costing and Pricing

Marklee Industries makes electric motors for a variety of small appliances. It sells the motors to manufacturers that assemble and sell the appliances. The company's market research department has discovered a market for electric motors used for trolling in small fishing boats, which Marklee presently does not produce.

The market research department has indicated that motors likely would sell for $46 each. A similar motor currently being produced has the following manufacturing costs:

Direct materials	$24
Direct labor	10
Overhead	8
Total	$42

Assume that Marklee desires an operating profit margin of 10 percent.

Required   **a.** Suppose that Marklee uses cost-plus pricing, setting the price 10 percent above the manufacturing cost. What price should it charge for the motor?

b. Suppose that Marklee uses target costing. What price should it charge for a trolling motor? What is the highest acceptable manufacturing cost for which Marklee would be willing to produce the motor?

c. Would you produce such a motor if you were a manager at Marklee? Explain.

14.32   Special Order   Marshall's Electronics, Inc., sells high-quality oversized printers for making blueprints. It manufactures two printers, the BP041 and the XBP400, for which the following information is available:

Costs per Unit	BP041	XBP400
Direct materials	$ 450	$ 550
Direct labor	600	750
Variable overhead	750	900
Fixed overhead	600	750
Total cost per unit	$2,400	$2,950
Price	$3,000	$3,900
Units sold	400	200

The average wage rate is $20 per hour. The plant has a capacity of 21,000 direct labor-hours, but current production uses only 19,500 direct labor-hours.

Required   **a.** A new customer has offered to buy 40 units of XBP400 if the price is lowered to $3,000 per unit. How many direct labor-hours are required to produce 40 units of XBP400? How much will the profit increase (or decrease) if Marshall's accepts this proposal? All other prices will remain the same.

b. Suppose that the customer has offered instead to buy 60 units of XBP400 at $3,000 per unit. How much will the profits change if the order is accepted? Assume that the company cannot increase its production capacity to meet the extra demand.

c. Answer the question in requirement (*b*), assuming instead that the plant can work overtime. Direct labor costs for the overtime production increase to $30 per hour. Variable overhead costs for overtime production are 50 percent more than for normal production.

14.33   Special Order   Golden Company, which manufactures robes, has enough idle capacity available to accept a special order of 10,000 robes at $16 each. A predicted income statement for the year without this special order follows:

	Per Unit	Total
Sales revenue	$25.00	$2,500,000
Manufacturing costs		
Variable	12.50	1,250,000
Fixed	3.50	350,000
Total manufacturing costs	16.00	1,600,000
Gross profit	9.00	900,000
Marketing costs		
Variable	3.60	360,000
Fixed	2.90	290,000
Total marketing costs	6.50	650,000
Operating profit	$ 2.50	$ 250,000

If the order is accepted, variable marketing costs on the special order would be reduced by 25 percent because all of the robes would be packed and shipped in one lot. However, if the offer is accepted, management estimates that it will lose the sale of 2,000 robes at regular prices.

Required   **a.** What is the net gain or loss from the special order?

b. Write a brief memo to management explaining why you think the company should or should not take the special order.

(CPA adapted)

14.34   Pricing Based
on Costs—
Multiple Choice

Cruizers Unlimited builds custom-made pleasure boats selling for $10,000 to $250,000. For the past 30 years, Cruizers has determined the selling price of each boat by estimating the costs of material, labor, and a prorated portion of overhead and adding 20 percent to these estimated costs.

For example, a recent price quotation for boat A was determined as follows:

Direct materials	$5,000
Direct labor	8,000
Overhead	2,000
	$15,000
Plus 20 percent.	3,000
Selling price.	$18,000

(handwritten: 5000 / 8000 / 800 *)*

The overhead amount was determined by estimating total overhead costs for the year and allocating them at 25 percent of direct labor costs.

If a customer rejects the price and business is slack, Cruizers is often willing to reduce markup to as little as 5 percent over estimated costs. Thus, average markup for the year is estimated at 15 percent.

The son of Cruizers Unlimited's manager has just completed a course on pricing and believes that the firm could use some of the techniques discussed in the course, which emphasized the contribution margin approach to pricing. The manager believes that such an approach would be helpful in determining the selling prices of the custom-made boats.

Total manufacturing overhead for the year has been estimated at $150,000, of which $90,000 is fixed and the remainder varies in direct proportion to direct labor.

Required

a.   What is the proportion of variable overhead to total overhead used by Cruizers?
   (1)   60 percent.
   (2)   40 percent.
   (3)   25 percent.
   (4)   30 percent.

b.   What is the variable overhead rate as a percentage of direct labor-dollars?
   (1)   25 percent.
   (2)   30 percent.
   (3)   10 percent.
   (4)   15 percent.

c.   If Cruizers accepts a customer's offer of $15,000 for boat A, what is the effect on profit (loss)?   *cm*
   (1)   ($8,000).
   (2)   ($1,500).
   (3) $800.
   (4) $1,200.   *with assumptions*

d.   What is the minimum price that Cruizers should accept for boat A, assuming no markup over cost?
   (1) $13,800.
   (2) $15,000.
   (3) $15,750.
   (4) $18,000.

(CMA adapted)

14.35   Special Order

R.A. Ro operates a small machine shop. He manufactures one standard product, which is available from many other similar businesses in addition to custom-made products. His accountant prepared the following annual income statement:

	Custom Sales	Standard Sales	Total
Sales revenue	$50,000	$25,000	$75,000
Materials	10,000	8,000 √	18,000
Labor	20,000	9,000 √	29,000
Depreciation	6,300	3,600	9,900
Power	700	400	1,100
Rent	6,000	1,000	7,000
Heat and light	600	100	700
Other	400	900 √	1,300
Total costs	$44,000	$23,000	$67,000
Operating profit	$ 6,000	$ 2,000	$ 8,000

The depreciation charges are for machines (based on time) used in the respective product lines. The power charge is apportioned based on the estimate of power consumed. The rent is for the building space, which has been leased for 10 years at $7,000 per year. The rent, heat, and electricity are apportioned to the product lines based on the amount of floor space occupied. All other costs are current expenses identified with the product line causing them.

A valued custom parts customer has asked R.A. to manufacture 10,000 special units. R.A. is working at capacity and would have to give up some other business to take this business. He can't renege on custom orders already agreed to, but he can reduce the output of his standard product by about one-half for one year while producing the custom part. The customer is willing to pay $7 for each unit. Materials will cost about $2 per unit and the labor $3.60 per unit. R.A. will have to spend $2,000 for a special device, which will be discarded when the job is done.

Required   Should R.A. take the order? Explain your answer.

                                                                (CMA adapted)

14.36   Special Order—   Aggie Enterprises, Inc., has plant capacity to produce 10,000 units annually. Its predicted
            Multiple Choice   operations for the year follow:

Sales (8,000 units at $10 each)	$80,000
Manufacturing costs	
Variable	$4 per unit
Fixed	$10,000
Marketing and administrative costs	
Variable	$2 per unit
Fixed	$8,000

Aggie is considering a special order of 1,000 units from a prospective customer willing to pay $8 per unit. Assume this order will have no effect on regular sales at regular prices, on total fixed costs, or on variable costs per unit.

Required   **a.** The effect of the special order on sales will be an increase of
    (1) $10,000.
    (2) $72,000.
    (3) $80,000.
    (4) $8,000.
    (5)   Some other amount.

   b. The effect of the special order on total variable costs will be an increase of
    (1) $8,000.
    (2) $6,000.
    (3) $5,000.
    (4) $4,000.
    (5)   Some other amount.

   c. The effect of the special order on total fixed costs will be an increase of
    (1) $0.
    (2) $2,250.
    (3) $8,000.
    (4) $1,250.
    (5)   Some other amount.

d. The effect of the special order on fixed costs per unit will be
   (1) Zero.
   (2) An increase of $2.25.
   (3) A decrease of $2.25.
   (4) A decrease of some other amount.
   (5) An increase of some other amount.

e. How will the special order affect operating profit?
   (1) Increase it.
   (2) Decrease it.
   (3) Have no effect.

14.37 Comprehensive Differential Costing Problem

Garden Bay, Inc., produces hydraulic hoists that hospitals use to move bedridden patients. The costs to manufacture and market the hydraulic hoists at the company's normal volume of 3,000 units per month are shown in Illustration 14.6.

Unless otherwise stated, assume that no connection exists between the situations described in the questions; each is independent. Unless otherwise stated, assume a regular selling price of $740 per unit. Ignore income taxes and other costs that are not mentioned in Illustration 14.6 or in the question itself.

Required

a. Market research estimates that volume could be increased to 3,500 units, which is well within production capacity limitations if the price were cut from $740 to $650 per unit. Assuming that the cost behavior patterns implied by the data in Illustration 14.6 are correct, would you recommend taking this action? What would be the impact on monthly sales, costs, and income?

b. On March 1, the federal government offers Garden Bay a contract to supply 500 units to Veterans Administration hospitals for a March 31 delivery. Because of an unusually large number of rush orders from its regular customers, Garden Bay plans to produce 4,000 units during March, which will use all available capacity. If it accepts the government order, it would lose 500 units normally sold to regular customers to a competitor. The government contract would reimburse its "share of March manufacturing costs" plus pay a $50,000 fixed fee (profit). (No variable marketing costs would be incurred on the government's units.) What impact would accepting the government contract have on March income? (Part of your problem is to figure out the meaning of "share of March manufacturing costs.")

c. Garden Bay has an opportunity to enter a foreign market in which price competition is keen. An attraction of the foreign market is that its demand is greatest when the domestic market's demand is quite low; thus, idle production facilities could be used without affecting domestic business.

An order for 1,000 units is being sought at a below-normal price to enter this market. For this order, shipping costs will total $75 per unit; total (marketing) costs to obtain the contract will be $4,000. No other variable marketing costs would be required on this order, and it would not affect domestic business. What is the minimum unit price that Garden Bay should consider for this order of 1,000 units?

ILLUSTRATION 14.6

Unit manufacturing costs		
Variable materials	$100	
Variable labor	150	
Variable overhead	50	
Fixed overhead	120	
Total unit manufacturing costs		$420
Unit marketing costs		
Variable	50	
Fixed	140	
Total unit marketing costs		190
Total unit costs		$610

d. An inventory of 230 units of an obsolete model of the hoist remains in the stockroom. These must be sold through regular channels (thus incurring variable marketing costs) at reduced prices or the inventory will soon be valueless. What is the minimum acceptable selling price for these units?

SOLUTIONS TO SELF-STUDY QUESTIONS

1. The $1,000 is a sunk cost and should be irrelevant to the executive, who should consider only the advantages and disadvantages of playing henceforth, including the pain, but should ignore the $1,000. (The executive later quit playing until the tennis elbow healed.)

2. The special order should be accepted, as the following two alternative analyses show:

	Status Quo	Alternative	Difference
Sales revenues	$80,000	$92,800	$12,800
Variable costs	(53,000)	(63,100)	(10,100)
Contribution	27,000	29,700	2,700
Fixed costs	(19,500)	(19,500)	–0–
Operating profit	$ 7,500	$10,200	$ 2,700

    Alternative Approach

Special-order sales		
(400 × $32)		$12,800
Less variable costs		
Manufacturing (400 × $24)	$9,600	
Sales commission (400 × $1.25)	500	10,100
Addition to company profit		$ 2,700

3. Computations for decision whether to drop Jamoca Joe's account (in thousands):

	Status Quo	Drop Jamoca Joe's	Difference
Revenues (fees charged)	$1,160	$700	$460
Operating costs			
Cost of services (variable)	1,035	610	425
Salaries, rent, and general administration (fixed)	100	100	–0–
Total operating costs	1,135	710	425
Operating profit/(loss)	$ 25	$ (10)	$ 35

    McKlintoff should not drop Jamoca Joe's in the short run because profits would drop by $35,000.

Using Differential Analysis for Production Decisions

LEARNING OBJECTIVES

After reading this chapter, you should be able to:

1. Understand the factors of make-or-buy decisions.

2. Use differential analysis to determine when to add or drop parts of operations.

3. Apply differential analysis to product choice decisions.

4. Understand the theory of constraints.

5. Use linear programming to optimize the use of scarce resources (appendix).

This chapter continues the discussion of differential analysis by explaining how differential costing is used to make production and operating decisions. The following are typical production and operating questions that managers often ask:

- Should we make the product internally or buy it from an outside source (called *outsourcing*)?
- Should we add to or drop parts of our operations?
- Which products should we continue to produce and which should we drop?

This chapter provides several approaches to addressing these questions. As you go through each, ask yourself what costs and revenues will differ as a result of the choices made and which course of action would be the most profitable for the company.

MAKE IT OR BUY IT?

L.O. 1: Understand the factors of make-or-buy decisions.

make-or-buy decision
A decision concerning whether to make needed goods internally or purchase them from outside sources.

A **make-or-buy decision** is any decision by a company to acquire goods or services internally or externally. A restaurant that uses its own ingredients in preparing meals "makes"; one that serves meals from frozen entrees "buys." A steel company that mines its own iron ore and processes it into pig iron makes; one that purchases it for further processing buys.

The make-or-buy decision is often part of a company's long-run strategy. Some companies choose to integrate vertically to control the activities that lead to the final product; others prefer to rely on outsiders for some inputs and specialize in only certain steps of the total manufacturing process.

Whether to rely on outsiders for a substantial amount of materials depends on both differential cost comparisons and other factors that are not easily quantified, such as suppliers' dependability and quality control. Although make-or-buy decisions sometimes appear to be simple one-time choices, frequently they are part of a more strategic analysis in which top management makes a policy decision to move the company toward more or less vertical integration.

For example, Better Homes Construction Company currently does its own site preparation and foundation work on the houses it builds. This work costs Better Homes $15,000 per house for labor, materials, and variable overhead. Should it consider buying site preparation and foundation work from an outside supplier? If satisfactory quality work could be subcontracted at anything below $15,000, Better Homes could save some of the money it now spends. The decision to buy provides a differential cost saving.

Make-or-Buy Decisions Involving Differential Fixed Costs

Net Minder Manufacturing produces tennis rackets. It currently makes a cover for each racket at the following cost:

	Per Unit	10,000 Units
Costs that can be directly assigned to the product:		
Direct materials	$2.00	$20,000
Direct labor	1.00	10,000
Variable manufacturing overhead	.75	7,500
Fixed manufacturing overhead		2,500
Common costs allocated to this product line		15,000
		$55,000

This year's expected production is 10,000 units, so the full product cost is $5.50 ($55,000/10,000 units).

Net Minder has received an offer from an outside supplier to supply any desired volume of covers for $4.10 each. The accounting department prepared this differential cost analysis for management:

ILLUSTRATION 15.1	Make-or-Buy Analysis, Net Minder Manufacturing		

	Status Quo: Make Product	Alternative: Buy Product	Difference
10,000 Units			
Direct costs			
Direct materials	$20,000	$41,000[a]	$21,000 higher
Labor	10,000	–0–	10,000 lower
Variable overhead	7,500	–0–	7,500 lower
Fixed overhead	2,500	–0–	2,500 lower
Common costs.	15,000[b]	15,000[b]	–0–
Total costs	$55,000	$56,000	$ 1,000 higher

Differential costs *increase* by $1,000, so *reject* alternative to *buy.*

	Status Quo: Make Product	Alternative: Buy Product	Difference
5,000 Units			
Direct costs			
Direct materials	$10,000[c]	$20,500[d]	$10,500 higher
Labor	5,000[c]	–0–	5,000 lower
Variable overhead	3,750[c]	–0–	3,750 lower
Fixed overhead	2,500	–0–	2,500 lower
Common costs.	15,000[b]	15,000[b]	–0–
Total costs	$36,250	$35,500	$ 750 lower

Differential costs *decrease* by $750, so *accept* alternative to *buy.*

[a]10,000 units purchased at $4.10 = $41,000.

[b]These common costs remain unchanged for these volumes. Since they do not change, they could be omitted from the analysis.

[c]Total variable costs reduced by half because volume was reduced by half.

[d]5,000 units purchased at $4.10 = $20,500.

- Differential costs are materials, labor, and variable overhead and definitely will be saved by buying the covers.
- The direct fixed manufacturing overhead is the cost of leasing the machine to produce the covers. Although the machine cost is fixed for levels of production ranging from 1 to 20,000 units, we can eliminate it if we stop producing covers. Thus, although the machine cost is a fixed cost of producing covers, it is a *differential cost* if we eliminate the product.
- No other costs are affected.

The accounting department also prepared cost analyses at volume levels of 5,000 and 10,000 units per year (see Illustration 15.1). At the 10,000 unit volume, it is less costly for Net Minder to make the racket covers, but if the volume drops to 5,000, Net Minder would save money by buying the racket covers.

This decision is sensitive to volume. To see why, consider only the costs affected by the make-or-buy decision: direct materials, direct labor, variable overhead, and fixed overhead. By setting the costs to make equal to the costs to buy, we find that a unique volume exists at which Net Minder is indifferent (in terms of costs):

Make		Buy
Direct Fixed Manufacturing Overhead	Variable Manufacturing Costs	Costs to Purchase Covers
$2,500	+ $3.75X	= $4.10X

where *X* equals the number of racket covers.

ILLUSTRATION   15.2   Graphical Illustration of Make-or-Buy Analysis

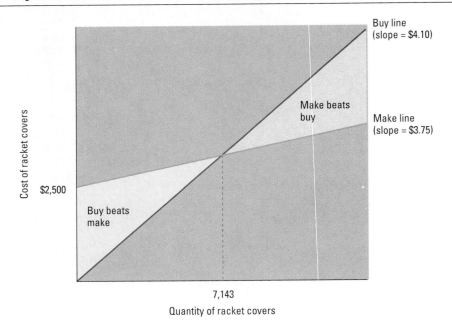

Solving for X

$$\$2,500 + \$3.75X = \$4.10X$$
$$\$2,500 = \$.35X$$
$$\$2,500/\$.35 = X$$
$$X = 7,143$$

Illustration 15.2 shows the result graphically. At a volume higher than 7,143, the preferred alternative is to make; less than 7,143, the preferred alternative is to buy.

Note the importance of separating fixed and variable costs for this analysis. Although determining differential costs usually requires a special analysis, the work can be made simpler if the accounting system routinely separates costs into fixed and variable components. The previous analysis would not have been possible for Net Minder had overhead costs not been separated into fixed and variable components.

Opportunity Costs of Making

Suppose that Net Minder's volume is projected to be 10,000 covers. If it is expected to be more than 7,143 covers, the preceding analysis indicates that Net Minder should continue to produce the covers. However, that analysis has not considered the opportunity cost of using the facilities to make racket covers. Recall that *opportunity costs* are the forgone returns from not employing a resource in its best alternative use. Theoretically, determining opportunity cost requires considering every possible use of the resource in question. If Net Minder has no alternative beneficial use for its facilities, the opportunity cost is zero, in which case the previous analysis would stand.

But suppose that the facilities to make covers could be used to assemble a cheaper version of the racket that Net Minder presently produces. This cheaper version would provide a $4,000 differential contribution. If making rackets is the best alternative use of the facility, the opportunity cost of using the facility to make covers is $4,000. In that case, Net Minder would be better off buying the covers and using the facilities to make rackets, as shown by the two alternative analyses of the problem in Illustration 15.3.

ILLUSTRATION 15.3	Make-or-Buy Analysis with Opportunity Cost of Facilities, Net Minder Manufacturing		

	Status Quo: Make Product	Alternative: Buy Product	Difference
Method 1			
Total costs of 10,000 covers from Illustration 15.1.	$55,000	$56,000	$1,000 higher[a]
Opportunity cost of using facilities to make covers.	4,000	–0–	4,000 lower[a]
Total costs, including opportunity cost.	$59,000	$56,000	$3,000 lower[a]

Differential costs *decrease* by $3,000, so *accept* alternative to *buy*.

	Status Quo: Make Product	Alternative: Buy Product, Use Facility to Make Rackets	Difference
Method 2			
Total costs of 10,000 covers from Illustration 15.1.	$55,000	$56,000	$1,000 higher[a]
Less margin from use of facilities for making rackets	–0–	–4,000	4,000 lower[a]
Net cost	$55,000	$52,000	$3,000 lower[a]

Although the presentation is different, the result is still a $3,000 cost *decrease* if the alternative is accepted.

[a]These indicate whether the alternative is higher or lower than the status quo.

Almost without exception, determining opportunity cost is very difficult and involves considerable subjectivity. Opportunity costs are not routinely reported with other accounting cost data because they are not the result of completed transactions. They are possibilities only and must be estimated for each individual decision.

Some opportunity costs, such as the possible wages from the best job forgone, may be estimated in monetary terms; others, like the status that accompanies certain occupations, may not be so readily quantified. Furthermore, if a benefit is forgone—and therefore never concretely existed—it is difficult to attach a realistic value to it.

Because they are so nebulous, opportunity costs are often omitted from decision-making analysis. It is easy to neglect them because they are not paid for and recorded in the accounts. Consequently, it is an accountant's responsibility to assist decision makers by reminding them that such costs exist. In general, opportunity costs occur when a scarce resource has multiple uses. Plants, equipment, money, time, and managerial talent usually have opportunity costs. When a resource is not scarce or when a scarce resource can be used only in one way, opportunity costs are zero. Whether such costs should be measured precisely or only approximately depends on the costs and benefits of the resulting information.

SELF-STUDY QUESTION

1. Electronics, Inc., produces an electronic part that is used in guidance and navigation systems. Major customers are aircraft manufacturers.

The costs of the electronic part at the company's normal volume of 4,000 units per month are shown below.

Unit manufacturing costs		
Variable materials	$200	
Variable labor	150	
Variable overhead	50	
Fixed overhead	120	
Total unit manufacturing costs		$520
Unit nonmanufacturing costs		
Variable	150	
Fixed	140	
Total unit nonmanufacturing costs		290
Total unit costs		$810

A proposal is received from an outside contractor who will make and ship 1,000 units per month directly to Electronics, Inc.'s customers as orders are received from Electronics, Inc.'s sales force. Electronics, Inc.'s fixed nonmanufacturing costs would be unaffected, but its variable manufacturing costs would be cut by 20 percent for those 1,000 units produced by the contractor. Electronics, Inc.'s plant would operate at three-fourths of its normal level, and total fixed manufacturing costs per month would be cut by 10 percent. Should the proposal be accepted for a payment to the contractor of $400 per unit? (Revenue information is not needed to answer this question.)

The solution to this question is at the end of this chapter on page 482.

Identifying Activities of Making a Product

Using differential analysis to evaluate alternatives requires full knowledge of the costs involved for each. In the make-or-buy decision for a product that a company does not presently produce, management must determine the costs by identifying the activities involved in making it.

The value chain model presents a format for such an investigation. (See Illustration 14.3 in the previous chapter if you need to refresh your memory about the value chain.) By following the chain from research and design to after-sale service, the activities—or resource requirements—for each phase can be determined. Then an engineering estimate or historical cost estimate of similar activities can be utilized to determine the costs of the activities required to make the product.

How Buying Can Eliminate Nonvalue-Added Activities

Lawyers such as this often subcontract to firms that specialize in research and to ligitation support firms. (© David R. Frazier/ Tony Stone Images)

The full cost of a product or service often includes the cost of activities that are necessary to run the company but that do not add value directly to the product or service. Often these costs can be eliminated by buying components or subcontracting activities.

As an example, consider the law firm of Hanson & Weigh, which provides legal services for medical and legal malpractice suits. Kyra Hanson and Lee Weigh are litigators who spend 60 percent of their time in court and 40 percent with clients and preparing cases. The nature of their services requires in-depth research for each case; however, they have no in-house research staff. The medical research amounts to one researcher working three-quarters time and the legal research amounts to one researcher working one-half time. Because these are specialized areas, in-house research requires that the litigators hire two full-time researchers, leaving much of their paid time unproductive. By subcontracting the researchers on a per case basis, however, the firm avoids the expense of maintaining more staff time than the cases require.

You probably have heard of the trend in government to "privatize." Privatization means that an activity formerly performed by government is performed by the private sector. The federal government is currently encouraging government entities to contract activities that can be performed more efficiently and less expensively to outside contractors. A common example is trash pickup in cities. The city bills residents but contracts the service to a private business. Sometimes the city allows the business to bill customers directly.

Some economists and political activists support privatizing the public school system, prisons, and even the Social Security system. Throughout history, countries have hired even their armies (called *mercenaries*).

These are examples of choosing the buy alternative in what we have called the *make-or-buy decision.* Because businesses often operate more efficiently and with a higher-quality service, governments find that the buy alternative provides better quality service at lower cost. In addition, by buying the services, governments create a competitive market in which businesses compete to obtain and keep their contracts with the governmental units. If a business-operated trash pickup service does not provide high-quality service at low cost, the business will lose its contract to another business that can perform the service better. If the city operates the trash pickup service with poor quality and high cost, the residents may be out of luck. The news of a government service going private may imply that the government did not perform it well.

Trash pickup is a common example of a make or buy decision by cities. (© David Young Wolff/Tony Stone Images)

ADD OR DROP A PRODUCT LINE OR CLOSE A BUSINESS UNIT?

L.O. 2: Use differential analysis to determine when to add or drop parts of operations.

Managers often must decide whether to add or drop a product line or close a business unit. Product lines that were formerly profitable may be losing market share to newer products. Existing business units (for example, typewriter production) may be having difficulty competing with new computer technology. As a result, companies are forced to rethink their approach to the market.

Campus Bookstore hired a new general manager, a recent business school graduate, to improve its profit performance. As could be expected, the new manager asked to see the store's financial statements for the past year. They were prepared by product line for each of the store's three product categories: books, supplies, and general merchandise.

The statement that the manager received showed that the general merchandise department lost money during the third quarter (see Illustration 15.4). "We could have increased operating profits from $6,000 to $13,000 for the quarter if we had dropped general merchandise," claimed the supplies department manager. "That department sold $120,000 worth of merchandise but cost us $127,000 to operate."

Although the economics of dropping the general merchandise line appeared favorable, the new manager asked an accountant to investigate which costs were differential (that is, avoidable in this case) if that product line were dropped. The accountant reported the following:

- All variable costs of goods sold for that line could be avoided.
- All salaries presently charged to general merchandise, $14,000, could be avoided.
- None of the rent could be avoided.
- Marketing and administrative costs of $6,000 could be saved.

ILLUSTRATION 15.4

CAMPUS BOOKSTORE
Third-Quarter Product-Line Financial Statement
(in thousands)

	Total	Books	Supplies	General Merchandise
Sales revenue.	$400	$200	$80	$120
Cost of goods sold (all variable)	300	160	45	95
Contribution margin	100	40	35	25
Less fixed costs				
Rent	18	6	6	6
Salaries	40	16	10	14
Marketing and administrative	36	12	12	12
Operating profit (loss)	$ 6	$ 6	$ 7	$ (7)

ILLUSTRATION 15.5

CAMPUS BOOKSTORE
Differential Analysis
(in thousands)

	Status Quo: Keep General Merchandise	Alternative: Drop General Merchandise	Differential: Increase (or Decrease) in Operating Profits
Sales revenue	$400	$280	$120 decrease
Cost of goods sold (all variable).	300	205	95 decrease
Contribution margin	100	75	25 decrease
Less fixed costs			
Rent.	18	18	–0–
Salaries	40	26	14 decrease
Marketing and administrative	36	30	6 decrease
Operating profits	$ 6	$ 1	$ 5 decrease

The accountant prepared the differential cost and revenue analysis shown in Illustration 15.5 and observed the following:

- Assuming that the sales of the other product lines would be unaffected, sales would decrease by $120,000 from dropping the general merchandise line.
- Variable cost of goods sold of $95,000 would be saved by dropping the product line.
- Fixed costs of $20,000 ($14,000 in salaries and $6,000 in marketing and administrative expenses) would be saved.
- In total, the lost revenue of $120,000 exceeds the total differential cost saving by $5,000. Thus, Campus Bookstore's net income for the third quarter would have been $5,000 lower if general merchandise had been dropped.

The discrepancy between the claim of the supplies department's manager that operating profits would have *increased* by $7,000 and the accountant's finding that operating profits would have decreased by $5,000 stems from their basic assumptions. The supplies manager assumed that the entire $32,000 in fixed costs allocated to general merchandise was differential and would be saved if the product line were dropped. The accountant's closer examination revealed that only $20,000 of the fixed costs would be saved, thus the $12,000 discrepancy.

This example demonstrates the fallacy of assuming that all costs presented on financial statements are differential. The financial statement presented in Illustration 15.4 was designed to calculate department profits, not to identify the differential costs for this decision. Thus, using operating profit calculated after all cost allocations, including some that were not differential to this decision, incorrectly indicated that the product line should be dropped. Financial statements prepared in accordance with generally accepted accounting principles do not routinely provide differential cost information. Differential cost estimates depend on unique information that usually requires separate analysis.

The bookstore statement, which was prepared on a contribution margin basis, clearly reveals the revenues and variable costs that are differential to this decision. A separate analysis was required, however, to determine which fixed costs were differential. It is possible, of course, to prepare reports that reflect each division's contribution to companywide costs and profits. This *segment margin* would include division revenues less all direct costs of the division and would exclude allocated costs.

Opportunity Cost of Keeping Product Lines

Keeping the general merchandise department may have an opportunity cost that we have not yet considered. Assume that the shelf space currently occupied by general merchandise could be used to increase the number of books for sale. The opportunity cost of retaining general merchandise is then measured by the probable forgone differential profits from the increased book sales. The accountant estimated the following figures to describe the substitution of books for general merchandise:

Drop general merchandise (from Illustration 15.5)	
Lost revenue	$120,000
Cost savings	115,000
Differential lost profit	$ 5,000
Add additional book sales	
Additional book sales	$155,000
Less additional cost of books sold (all variable)	120,000
Contribution margin	35,000
Less additional fixed costs	
Salaries	14,000
Marketing and administrative	4,000
Profit gained from additional book sales	$17,000

The analysis presented in Illustration 15.5 indicates that Campus Bookstore would lose $5,000 by eliminating general merchandise. Given this additional information, however, an opportunity loss of $17,000 is incurred if the bookstore retains general merchandise and forgoes the opportunity to increase book sales. Based on these facts, Campus Bookstore is $12,000 ($17,000 gained from additional book sales—$5,000 lost from dropping general merchandise) better off to drop the general merchandise department and increase book sales. Illustration 15.6 is a summary analysis of all three options: status quo, eliminate general merchandise, and eliminate general merchandise and increase book sales.

It is important to understand that we are basing this illustration on the assumption that dropping the general merchandise department would not affect sales in other departments. In reality, however, other factors must be considered. For example, customers may prefer to shop at stores that offer a full range of products. If the general merchandise department is closed, Campus Bookstore might lose customers

ILLUSTRATION 15.6

CAMPUS BOOKSTORE
Comparison of Three Alternatives
(in thousands)

	Status Quo: Keep General Merchandise[a]	Alternative 1: Drop General Merchandise[a]	Alternative 2: Drop General Merchandise, Increase Book Sales
Sales revenue	$400	$280	$435 ($280 + $155[b])
Cost of goods sold (all variable)	300	205	325 ($205 + $120[b])
Contribution margin	100	75	110
Less fixed costs			
Rent	18	18	18
Salaries	40	26	40 ($26 + $14[b])
Marketing and administrative	36	30	34 ($30 + $4[b])
Operating profit	$ 6	$ 1	$ 18
		Worst	Best

[a]These columns are taken directly from Illustration 15.5.

[b]These amounts are the increase in revenue and costs taken from the discussion in the text.

to competing stores that provide a wider range of products. Thus, for any product line decision, we must consider the adverse side effects of dropping a product line along with the potential benefits.

Nonfinancial Considerations of Closing a Business Unit

Estimating the cost savings and lost revenues from closing a business unit is only part of the story. Employees' personal lives are affected, morale of employees who are still employed is affected, and the community suffers a loss. These nonfinancial considerations are often so important that they outweigh the financial issues. For example, a clothing company in South Carolina decided not to close an old, relatively inefficient plant. Why? Closing it would have had a large impact on the local community and many loyal employees would have lost their jobs. This plant had been the first in the company, and the company president did not want to close it for sentimental reasons.

Considering Competing Interests in Closing a Business Unit

Closing a business unit creates difficult decisions for managers. It may be the right thing to do for the shareholders but may have a negative effect on the community and, of course, on the employees who lose their jobs. Not closing a unit may help the employees and the community in the short run but drain the company of needed resources in the long run. Sometimes it is better to make a hard decision that hurts in the short run but is better for the long-run good of the company, its shareholders, and the employees who remain with the company.

PRODUCT CHOICE DECISIONS

L.O. 3: Apply differential analysis to product choice decisions.

Choosing which products to manufacture and sell is a common managerial decision. The products chosen to be produced directly affect costs. Most companies are capable of producing a large variety of goods and services but may be limited in the short run by available capacity. For instance, Campus Bookstore had to decide whether to use its limited space to sell general merchandise or to increase book sales. Due to a personnel shortage, a small CPA firm may have to choose between working for client A or client B. Students have to choose how to allocate their study time among their courses. Chrysler Corporation's Grand Cherokee plant will have to choose among producing the Laredo and other models.

ILLUSTRATION 15.7	Revenue and Cost Information, Glover Manufacturing	
	Hardballs	**Softballs**
Sales revenue per unit.	$10.00	$9.00
Less variable costs per unit		
Materials.	4.00	2.50
Labor	1.50	2.00
Variable overhead	.50	.50
Contribution margin per unit	$ 4.00	$4.00

Fixed manufacturing costs: $800,000 per month.
Marketing and administrative costs (all fixed): $200,000 per month.

ILLUSTRATION   15.8   Profit-Volume Relationship Assuming that Hardballs and Softballs Use Equal Scarce Resources, Glover Manufacturing

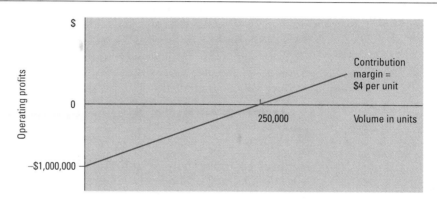

We usually think of product choices as short-run decisions because we have adopted the definition that in the short run, capacity is fixed, but in the long run, it can be changed. Thus, McDonnell-Douglas and Boeing may be able to produce both jumbo and narrow-body models in the *long run* by increasing capacity, and the CPA firm may be able to serve both client A and client B in the *long run* by hiring more professional staff. Nonetheless, in the short run, capacity limitations require choices.

For example, Glover Manufacturing makes two kinds of baseballs, hardballs and softballs. For now, assume that the company can sell all the baseballs it produces. Its cost and revenue information is presented in Illustration 15.7.

The profit-volume relationship for Glover's products is shown in Illustration 15.8. For instance, Glover can sell 250,000 hardballs or 250,000 softballs or any combination totaling 250,000 to break even. The contribution margin of each product is the same, so the profit-volume relationship is the same regardless of the mix of products produced and sold.

USING ACTIVITY-BASED COSTING TO DETERMINE THE BEST PRODUCT MIX

One advantage of activity-based costing is that it provides a good understanding of the cost of making a product. Managers are able to make informed product mix decisions using information from an activity-based costing system.

For example, activity-based costing should reveal the costs of quality inspection, an activity that drives costs. Suppose that an ice cream maker makes chocolate and strawberry ice cream. The two flavors have exactly the same costs and revenues except that strawberry requires twice as much quality inspection work as chocolate because of high variation in the strawberry flavoring. Activity-based costing would reveal that strawberry costs more to make than chocolate, but conventional costing would not because the quality inspection costs are buried in overhead and allocated based on a volume measure such as machine-hours, gallons of ice cream made, or labor-hours.

When the manager makes product choice decisions, knowing that strawberry ice cream costs more to make than chocolate is helpful. If the selling price were the same for both, and if chocolate and strawberry were substitutes, the ice cream maker would prefer to sell chocolate and perhaps encourage its purchase by offering coupons that discount it.

PRODUCT MIX DECISIONS

Recall that Glover Manufacturing can sell all of the baseballs it can produce. Its objective is to maximize the contribution from its sales of hardballs and softballs, but which should it produce? Without knowing either Glover's maximum production capacity or the amount of that capacity used to produce one product or the other, we might say that it doesn't matter because both products are equally profitable. But because capacity is limited, that answer is incorrect if Glover uses its capacity at a different rate for each product.

Suppose that Glover's capacity is limited to 7,200 machine-hours per month. This limitation is known as a **constraint.** (We are introducing a simple example of linear programming here. The appendix to this chapter offers a more comprehensive example of it and its complexities.) Further assume that machines may be used to produce either 30 hardballs or 50 softballs per machine-hour.

constraints
Activities, resources, or policies that limit or bound the attainment of an objective.

With a constrained resource, the important measure of profitability is the **contribution margin per unit of scarce resource** used, *not* contribution margin per unit of product. In this case, softballs are more profitable than hardballs because softballs contribute $200 per machine-hour ($4 per softball $\times$ 50 softballs per hour), but hardballs contribute only $120 per machine-hour ($4 per hardball $\times$ 30 hardballs per machine-hour). The hours required to produce one ball times the contribution per hour equals the contribution per ball.

contribution margin per unit of scarce resource
Contribution margin per unit of a particular input with limited availability.

For the month, Glover could produce 360,000 softballs (50 per hour $\times$ 7,200 hours) or 216,000 hardballs (30 per hour $\times$ 7,200 hours). If it produces only softballs, Glover's operating *profit* would be $440,000 (360,000 softballs times a contribution of $4 each minus fixed costs of $1 million). If only hardballs are produced, Glover's net *loss* would be $136,000 (216,000 hardballs times a contribution margin of $4 each minus $1 million). By concentrating on the product that yields the higher contribution per unit of scarce resource, Glover can maximize its profit.

Mathematical Representation of the Problem

The relationship between the use of machine-hours to produce hardballs (H) and softballs (S) may be expressed as

$$(1/30)H + (1/50)S \leq 7,200 \text{ machine-hours}$$

(To be precise, two more constraints prevent negative production of either product. These are $H \geq 0$ and $S \geq 0$ but are ignored in our discussion because negative production is not possible.)

The first term in the production expression reflects the fact that a hardball uses 1/30 hour of machine time. The second term indicates that each softball uses 1/50 hour of machine time. The third term, or right-hand side, constrains production time to 7,200 hours or fewer. Although it is possible to use fewer than 7,200 hours, that would indicate idle capacity. Hence, Glover is better off to use as many hours as possible. This point may also be shown mathematically, but we leave that to operations researchers.

ILLUSTRATION 15.9 **Relationship between Production and Scarce Resources**

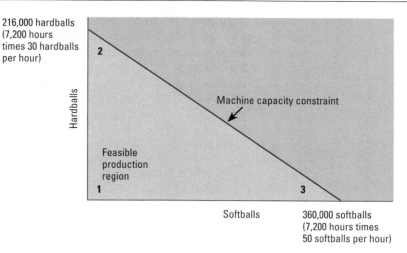

216,000 hardballs
(7,200 hours
times 30 hardballs
per hour)

360,000 softballs
(7,200 hours times
50 softballs per hour)

In short, the relationship between the product contribution margins and the constraints for Glover is written as follows:

Objective function:
Maximize: $\$4H + \$4S$
Constraints:
Subject to: $(1/30)H + (1/50)S \leq 7,200$ hours

The objective function states that the objective is to select the product mix that maximizes total contribution, given that the unit contribution of hardballs is $4 and of softballs is $4. The constraint states that each hardball uses 1/30 of a machine-hour, each softball uses 1/50 of a machine-hour, and in total, no more than 7,200 hours are available.

Graphic Solution

feasible production region
The area in a graph of production opportunities bounded by the limits on production.

corner point
A corner of the feasible production region in linear programming.

Illustration 15.9 shows that relationship between production of each product and the amount of the scarce resources available. Glover can produce at any point along the machine capacity constraint line or at any interior point in the **feasible production region,** which is the area in the graph bounded by the constraints on operating activities. In this case, production is bounded by zero on the low side and by 7,200 machine-hours on the high side.

Because Glover can sell all that it produces at a positive contribution margin for each product, it would prefer to produce as much as possible, which is some point on the machine capacity line. Analysis of each **corner point** (that is, each corner of the feasible region) shows that it is optimal for Glover to produce and sell 360,000 softballs and no hardballs at corner point 3. At corner point 3, Glover's profit would be $440,000 [= (360,000 softballs × $4 contribution margin per softball) − $1 million fixed costs].

Why Will the Optimal Solution Always Be at a Corner Point?

If point 3 is better than point 2, it must also be better than any place on the straight line between points 2 and 3.[1] Knowing that no solution can be better than the one at the optimal corner enables us to limit our search for the maximum profit

---

[1] Of course, if two corner points have the same total contribution, any point on a straight line between those two corners would have the same total contribution as either corner point.

combination to the corner points in the feasible region. The following example shows what happens if we move from corner point 3.

Glover's total contribution (and, therefore, total operating profit) is reduced if it moves toward corner point 2 from corner point 3. For example, the total contribution with production of 360,000 softballs is $1,440,000. Moving from corner point 3 toward corner point 2 by producing one hardball requires giving up 5/3 softballs, calculated as follows:

1. Start with the following constraint:

$$(1/30)H + (1/50)S \leq 7{,}200 \text{ machine-hours}$$

2. The choice requires no change in total machine-hours; 7,200 machine-hours are still used. There is only a substitution of hardballs for softballs, so set $1/30H + 1/50S = 0$.

3. Now find the number of softballs given up for each hardball produced (Δ refers to change):

$$(1/50)\Delta S = -(1/30)\Delta H$$

$$\Delta S = -\frac{\left(\dfrac{1}{30}\right)}{\left(\dfrac{1}{50}\right)}\Delta H = -\frac{.03333}{.02000}\Delta H$$

$$\Delta S = -(5/3)\Delta H$$

4. If you substitute 1 for ΔH, then $\Delta S = -5/3$. Thus, every hardball produced requires giving up 5/3 softballs.

5. The net effect on total contribution is

Contribution gained (1 hardball × $4)	$4.00
Contribution lost (5/3 softballs × $4).	6.67
Net contribution lost per hardball produced	$2.67

This loss occurs as we move from corner point 3 toward corner point 2.

What Is Really Sold?

In working with production constraints, it is often useful to think in terms of selling the service of the productive resources rather than selling units of product. For example, we can think of Glover as selling machine-hours, with each machine-hour contributing $200 if used to make softballs ($200 = $4 × 50 softballs per hour), $120 if used to make hardballs ($120 = $4 × 30 hardballs per hour), and $0 if not used at all.

Contribution Margin versus Gross Margin

Notice that Glover Manufacturing's costs were divided into fixed and variable portions. By definition, the variable costs are differential with volume changes. In some companies, variable costs are not separated from fixed costs, which can lead to serious product mix errors if fixed costs allocated to each unit of product are included when comparing the profitability of products. This error would result from treating fixed costs as differential costs.

For example, suppose that before any attempt was made to determine the optimal product mix for Glover, the accounting department had prepared the report in Illustration 15.10, which does not separate fixed and variable overhead costs. By applying overhead at 200 percent of labor, overhead *appears to vary with labor,* whereas we know that a substantial amount of it is fixed. Based on this presentation, hardballs

ILLUSTRATION 15.10	Full Costs of the Product, Glover Manufacturing		
		Hardballs	Softballs
Sales revenue per unit.		$10.00	$9.00
Less full-absorption costs per unit			
Materials.		4.00	2.50
Labor		1.50	2.00
Overhead (applied at a rate of 200% of labor)[a]		3.00	4.00
Gross margin per unit		$ 1.50	$ .50
Marketing and administrative costs (all fixed): $200,000 per month.			

[a] Any under- or overapplied overhead is written off as an expense of the period.

ILLUSTRATION 15.11	Comparison of Product Mix Analyses, Glover Manufacturing	
	Gross Margin Method, Wrong Decision: Produce All Hardballs	Contribution Margin Method, Right Decision: Produce All Softballs
Sales revenue		
Hardballs (216,000 × $10)	$2,160,000	
Softballs (360,000 × $9)		$3,240,00
Less variable manufacturing costs		
Hardballs (216,000 × $6).	1,296,000	
Softballs (360,000 × $5)		1,800,000
Total contribution margin	864,000	1,440,000
Less fixed costs		
Manufacturing	800,000	800,000
Marketing and administrative.	200,000	200,000
Operating profit (loss)	$ (136,000)	$ 440,000

appear to be more profitable per unit of scarce resource than softballs, but, in fact, the opposite is true.

Accounting information is sometimes sent to personnel in operations and engineering who are unaware of the important but subtle distinction between *gross margin* and *contribution margin* that we have emphasized in this book. For example, suppose that the gross margin per unit from Illustration 15.10 is used instead of the contribution margin per unit from Illustration 15.7.

Illustration 15.9 shows two extreme production possibilities; 216,000 hardballs or 360,000 softballs. Using the gross margins from Illustration 15.10, we determine that production of 216,000 hardballs at $1.50 (total gross margin = $324,000) appears economically superior to production of 360,000 softballs at $.50 (total gross margin = $180,000).

Of course, we know that is wrong. As Illustration 15.11 shows, producing 216,000 hardballs and no softballs results in a net loss of $136,000; the correct product mix of 360,000 softballs and no hardballs provides operating profit of $440,000.

Thus, a common mistake in product mix decisions stems from the failure to recognize which costs are differential. Fixed costs for different product mixes often do not differ in the short run. For purposes of valuing inventory for external reporting, however, fixed manufacturing overhead is assigned to units produced, thereby making fixed costs appear variable to the unsophisticated user of cost information. As in the other differential cost problems we have seen, it is important to determine which costs are *really differential* for decision making.

This is another example of a common problem in accounting. Costs that were assigned to units for one purpose (inventory valuation) could be inappropriately used for another purpose (product mix decisions).

Opportunity Cost of Resources

In the multiproduct setting, machine capacity or any other constraint may have an opportunity cost. Computing the opportunity cost is facilitated with the type of analysis presented in this chapter. For example, what is the opportunity cost to Glover Manufacturing of not having one more hour of machine capacity? First, assume that the increase in machine time would change neither fixed manufacturing nor fixed selling costs. With one more hour of machine-time, Glover could produce 50 more softballs, as follows.

Before: $1/30H + 1/50S \leq 7,200$ machine-hours. If only softballs are produced

$$(1/50)S = 7,200$$
$$S = \frac{7,200}{(1/50)}$$
$$= 360,000 \text{ softballs}$$

With one additional machine-hour and producing only softballs

$$(1/50)S = 7,201$$
$$S = \frac{7,201}{(1/50)}$$
$$= 360,050 \text{ softballs}$$

With a $4 unit contribution margin, production of 50 more softballs would add $200 to profits. Thus, the opportunity cost of one hour of machine time is $200. This opportunity cost is also known as a **shadow price.**

shadow price
Opportunity cost (that is, forgone profits) of not being able to produce an additional unit.

With this information, Glover's management can decide whether it is worthwhile to add machine time. If additional machine-time can be leased for any amount less than $200 per hour, for example, doing so would increase operating profits.

Multiple Constraints

With one constraint, it is easy to see that Glover could maximize contribution by producing only softballs. But the situation becomes more complex when multiple constraints exist. Suppose that the sale of softballs is temporarily restricted so that only 200,000 can be sold during the next production period. Suppose also that Glover cannot hold baseballs in inventory, so everything produced must be sold in the same period. Now the constraints are

$$(1/30)H + (1/50)S \leq 7,200 \text{ machine-hours}$$
$$S \leq 200,000$$

These relationships are shown graphically in Illustration 15.12. Now, to determine the optimal product mix, we find the monthly operating profit at each of the four corner points labeled. The solution for corner point 3 is found by simultaneously solving for the machine and sales constraints. The calculations are as follows

$$(1/30)H + (1/50)S = 7,200 \text{ machine-hours}$$
$$S = \underline{\underline{200,000}}$$

ILLUSTRATION 15.12 Product Choice with Multiple Constraints, Glover Manufacturing

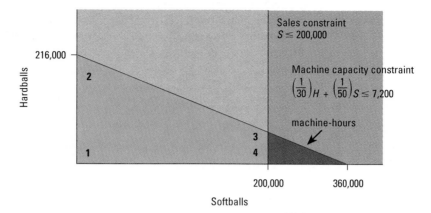

Corner Point	Produce and Sell		Total Contribution Margin	Fixed Costs	Operating Profit (Loss)
	Hardballs	Softballs			
1	–0–	–0–	–0–	$1,000,000	$(1,000,000)
2	216,000	–0–	216,000 × $4 = $864,000	1,000,000	(136,000)
3	96,000	200,000	(96,000 × $4) + (200,000 × $4) = $1,184,000	1,000,000	184,000
4	–0–	200,000	200,000 × $4 = $800,000	1,000,000	(200,000)

so

$$(1/30)H + (1/50)(200,000) = 7,200$$
$$(1/30)H + 4,000 = 7,200$$
$$(1/30)H = 3,200$$
$$H = \underline{96,000}$$

The optimal solution is to produce as many softballs as can be sold, 200,000, and use the remaining capacity to produce 96,000 hardballs.

As more constraints and products are added, solving for product mixes becomes more complex. Although it is possible to solve these problems by hand, they are typically solved by computer). Nevertheless, a simple graph can be quite an effective means to present your results.

SELF-STUDY QUESTION

2. Pacperson, Inc., manufactures two series of computer hardware: Twopack and Threepack. Data concerning selling prices and costs for each unit follow:

	Twopack	Threepack
Selling price	$1,000	$1,700
Materials	350	370
Direct labor	210	230
Overhead (80% fixed)	150	200
Gross margin	290	900
Marketing costs (variable)	80	240
Administrative costs (fixed)	60	80
Profit.	$ 150	$ 580

Management decided that at least 500 units of Twopack and at least 150 units of Threepack must be manufactured and sold each month.

The company's production facilities are limited by machine capacity in the assembly control section. Each Twopack model and each Threepack model require one-fourth and three-fourths hour in the assembly control section, respectively. A total of 250 hours is available per month in the assembly control section; there are no other relevant constraints on production.

a. What is the appropriate objective function for these two products if management's objective is to maximize profits?

b. What equations represent the constraints?

c. Given the information in the problem, which product would management prefer to produce to maximize profits?

d. What is the optimal production schedule? What is the total contribution margin for that schedule?

The solution to this question is at the end of this chapter on page 482.

THEORY OF CONSTRAINTS AND THROUGHPUT CONTRIBUTION ANALYSIS

L.O. 4: Understand the theory of constraints.

theory of constraints (TOC)
Focuses on revenue and cost management when faced with bottlenecks.

bottleneck
Operation where the work required limits production.

throughput contribution
Sales dollars minus direct materials costs and variables such as energy and piecework labor.

Organizations often have constraints, or limits, on what they can accomplish. The **theory of constraints (TOC)** is a newly developing management method for dealing with constraints.

The theory of constraints focuses on increasing the excess of differential revenue over differential costs when faced with bottlenecks. A **bottleneck** is an operation where the work required to be performed limits production. With multiple parts of a production process, each operation depends on the preceding operations. One operation cannot be started until the previous one has completed its work.

For example, assume that Pete's Pizza suddenly has orders at 7 PM for pizza to be delivered to 20 locations. Pete's has one delivery car that can deliver to five locations per trip. Pete's guarantees delivery in 30 minutes and has decided not to accept orders that it cannot deliver within 30 minutes. As a result of the delivery constraint, a bottleneck exists in the delivery process.

The theory of constraints focuses on such bottlenecks. It encourages managers to find ways to increase profits by relaxing constraints and increasing throughput. At Pete's Pizza, this means finding ways to deliver pizzas when demand is high.

The theory of constraints focuses on three factors:

- The rate of *throughput contribution:* **Throughput contribution** equals sales dollars minus direct materials costs and other variable costs such as energy and piecework labor.

- Minimizing *investments:* Investments are inventories, equipment, buildings, and other assets used to generate throughput contribution.

- Minimizing *other operating costs:* Other operating costs are all operating costs other than direct materials and other variable costs. Other operating costs are incurred to earn throughput contribution; they include most salaries and wages, rent, utilities, and depreciation.

The objective of the theory of constraints is to maximize throughput contribution while minimizing investments and operating costs. The theory of constraints assumes a short-run time horizon. Managing bottleneck resources involves five key steps:

1. Recognize that the bottleneck resource determines throughput contribution of the plant as a whole. For example, Pete's Pizza cannot deliver all the pizzas on time, resulting in lower profit.

2. Search and find the bottleneck resource by identifying resources with large amounts of inventory waiting to be worked on (lots of pizzas waiting more than 30 minutes to be delivered).

3. Subordinate all nonbottleneck resources to the bottleneck resource. The needs of the bottleneck resource determine the production schedule of nonbottleneck

resources. (A nonbottleneck process at Pete's is the preparation area, where the dough is made and appropriate toppings are put on prior to cooking. The delivery rate should set the preparation rate of pizzas for delivery.)

4. Increase bottleneck efficiency and capacity. The intent is to increase throughput contribution minus the differential costs of taking such actions (such as leasing another car and hiring another driver).

5. Repeat steps 1 through 4 for new bottleneck.

Let's look at an example of how to manage constraints. Pete's Pizza makes pizzas in three operations: preparing, cooking, and delivering. Pete's managers find that the delivery bottleneck occurs for two hours each night. Pertinent production information for those 60 hours (30 days × 2 hours) per month follows:

	Preparation	Cooking	Delivery
Hourly capacity	40 units	24 units	10 units
Monthly capacity (60 hours)	2,400	1,440	600
Monthly production	600	600	600

The demand for pizzas during those 60 hours per month is 800 units. The average pizza sells for $15 and has variable costs of $6. The variable costs include ingredients and packaging, energy to cook pizzas, and mileage costs of the delivery car. (Pete's has no piecework labor.) Pete's output is constrained by the 600 units per month on-time delivery capacity. Several options that can relieve the bottleneck at the delivery operation exist. It is necessary to consider differential costs associated with each option:

1. Eliminate the idle time on the bottleneck operation. Pete's can increase bottleneck output by hiring one employee to organize the preparation and cooking to ensure that pizzas are ready for delivery to five locations immediately upon arrival of the delivery car and to schedule delivery so that the most efficient route is taken to those five locations. The cost for the employee is $1,200 per month and on-time delivery capacity is increased by 100 units per month. Thus, the throughput contribution increases by $900 (100 units × [$15 selling price − $6 variable costs]), which is less than the additional cost of $1,200 per month.

2. Increase the capacity of the bottleneck process. Pete's could hire another car and driver for the two hours a night, increasing the delivery capacity by 600 units, costing an additional $1,300 per month. However, the additional demand is for 200 more units per month, so adding the car and driver would increase throughput contribution by $1,800 (200 units × [$15 selling price − $6 variable costs]), which is more than the additional costs of $1,300 per month.

Pete's should go with option 2 to increase capacity at the bottleneck constraint.

Theory of Constraints and Cost Assumptions

The theory of constraints assumes that few costs are variable—generally only materials, purchased parts, piecework labor, and energy to run machines. Most direct labor and overhead costs are assumed to be fixed. This is consistent with the ideas that the shorter the time period, the more costs are fixed and that the theory of constraints focuses on the short run. Generally, this assumption about cost behavior seems reasonable.

Theory of Constraints, Total Quality, and Just in Time

The theory of constraints identifies bottlenecks and possible disruptions that threaten throughput. For example, when disruptions are hard to pinpoint or eliminate, quality control techniques from total quality management (TQM) may be utilized. TQM stabilizes and improves processes to decrease variation and is well suited to removing disruptions in the process. A manager interviewed in the book *The Theory of*

Constraints and Its Implications for Managerial Accounting stated the relations among recent management techniques well: "Essentially, JIT [just in time] improves lead times and due date performance, TQM [total quality management] improves people, and TOC [theory of constraints] provides focus for the entire improvement process."[2]

SUMMARY

This chapter presents the use of differential costing and linear programming models in making production and operating decisions.

The following summarizes key ideas tied to the chapter's learning objectives.

LO1: Using differential analysis with make-or-buy decisions. Make-or-buy decisions are based on differential analysis in conjunction with nonquantitative factors such as dependability of suppliers and the quality of purchased materials. Companies often reduce the size of their operations by outsourcing their products (that is, by having an outside contractor produce the product).

LO2: Using differential analysis to decide whether to add or drop parts of operations. In the short run, if the differential revenue from the sale of a product exceeds the differential costs required to provide it, the product generates profits and the firm should continue production.

LO3: Using differential analysis to make product mix decisions. A problem arises when limited amounts of resources are being fully utilized and must be assigned to multiple products. The objective of product mix decisions is to maximize the contribution margin per unit of scarce resource used. For example, if the scarce resource is the limited number of hours a machine can operate per month and the machine can make either of two products, the objective is to maximize the contribution per hour (or other unit of time) that each of the two products makes and then produce the product with the higher contribution margin per hour of machine-time used.

LO4: Using the theory of constraints. The theory of constraints focuses on revenue and cost management when dealing with bottlenecks. The objective is to increase throughput contribution—sales dollars minus variable costs—finding ways to increase production at bottlenecks.

LO5: Using linear programming to optimize the use of scarce resources (appendix). Computerized linear programming models are widely used to determine the optimal product mix. Data are input into these models using objective functions that specify the contribution margin of each product and constraints that indicate the amount of scarce resource each product uses. The linear programming model then computes the contribution margin per unit of scarce resource for all products and all constraints. Linear programming maximizes the total contribution margin given these constraints.

KEY TERMS

bottleneck, 458

constraints, 452

contribution margin per unit of scarce resource, 452

corner point, 453

feasible production region, 453

graphic method,* 461

make-or-buy decision, 442

shadow price, 456

simplex method,* 461

theory of constraints (TOC), 458

throughput contribution, 458

---

*Term appears in the appendix.
[2]E. Noreen, D. Smith, and J. Mackey, *The Theory of Constraints and Its Implications for Managerial Accounting* (Great Barrington, MA: North River Press, 1995), p. 42.

APPENDIX

Linear Programming

The product choice problem is often much more complex than the two-product, two-constraint problems presented for Glover Manufacturing earlier in the chapter. Companies often have many constraints and many choices. The method we used to find the optimal product mix for Glover Manufacturing is called the **graphic method.** The graphic method is a useful way to see how linear programming works, but it is impractical for complex problems with many choices and constraints.

A mathematical technique, known as the **simplex method,** has been developed for solving complex product mix problems. This technique solves for corner solutions much as we did earlier in this chapter using graphs. Many computer software packages use the simplex method, or a variation of it, for solving product mix problems.

For this Appendix, we assume that product mix decisions are solved on the computer. Our focus is on setting up the problems so they can be entered into the computer and on interpreting the output, not on the mathematical procedures used to derive the solutions.[3]

Comprehensive Linear Programming Example

This section presents a linear programming problem solved by using the computer. We discuss how to set up the problem, how to enter it into the computer, and how to interpret the results.

Assume that Hixon Company manufactures and sells three wood products, armchairs (A), bookshelves (B), and cabinets (C). Each product must be processed through two departments (cutting, and assembly and finishing) before it is sold.

Illustration 15.13 presents data about product selling prices, costs, and the rate at which each product uses scarce resources. In addition to the information provided in Illustration 15.13, we learn that only 2,000 board-feet of direct material can be obtained per week. The cutting department has 180 hours of labor available each week, and the assembly and finishing department has 240 hours of labor available each week. No overtime is allowed.

Hixon's contract commitments require it to make at least 100 armchairs per week. Also, due to keen competition, no more than 100 bookshelves can be sold each week.

Estimated fixed manufacturing overhead costs of $1,500 per week are arbitrarily allocated to each unit at the rate of $5 per unit. Fixed manufacturing costs are unaffected by the product mix. Nonmanufacturing costs of $1,000 per week are fixed and unaffected by the product mix decision.

Problem Formulation Hixon's product mix decision problem can be solved using linear programming. The constrained optimization problem is formulated as follows:

(a) Maximize total contribution margin

$$\$5.68A + \$7.40B + \$8.24C$$

(b) Subject to the following constraints

$4A + 7B + 10C \le 2{,}000$ board-feet	Direct material
$.30A + .30B + .40C \le 180$ labor-hours	Cutting
$.20A + .30B + .50C \le 240$ labor-hours	Assembly and finishing
$A \ge 100$ units sold	Product A's sales
$B \le 100$ units sold	Product B's sales

---

[3]More details on the mathematics of linear programming are available from books on operations research and quantitative methods. See, for example, H. Bierman, C. Bonini, and W. Hausman, *Quantitative Analysis for Business Decisions,* 8th ed. (Burr Ridge, IL: Richard D. Irwin, 1991).

ILLUSTRATION 15.13	Hixon Company Facts		
	Armchairs per Unit	Bookshelves per Unit	Cabinets per Unit
Selling price	$14.00	$18.00	$24.00
Direct labor cost	6.00	7.20	10.80
Direct material cost.	.80	1.40	2.00
Variable overhead	1.52	2.00	2.96
Contribution margins	5.68	7.40	8.24
Fixed manufacturing overhead	5.00	5.00	5.00
Gross margins.	$ .68	$ 2.40	$ 3.24
Material requirements in board-feet per unit of output . .	4	7	10
Labor requirements in hours per unit of output			
Cutting Department.	.30	.30	.40
Assembly and Finishing Department	.20	.30	.50

ILLUSTRATION 15.14	Linear Programming Input,[a] Hixon Company

```
                    :
    (a & b)         MAX $5.68A + $7.40B + $8.24C
                    ?
                    SUBJECT TO
                    ?
                    (DIRECT MATERIAL) 4A + 7B + 10C < 2000
                    ?
                    (CUTTING) .3A + .3B + .4C < 180
                    ?
                    (ASSEMBLY AND FINISHING) .2A + .3B + .5C < 240
                    ?
                    (PROD A SALES) A > 100
                    ?
                    (PROD B SALES) B < 100
                    ?
                    END

                    A = Armchairs
                    B = Bookshelves
                    C = Cabinets
```

Note: Circled letters cross-reference to the problem formulation in the text.

[a]Based on the linear programming package called LINDO.

Using a linear programming computer package, we can obtain a solution for this model. Illustration 15.14 is the printout of the linear program problem formulation using a particular software package. The circled letters are there to help you trace the steps in the computer input back to the preceding formulation. Illustration 15.15 shows the output, which is shown as most software packages present it.

Solution   The Summary of Problem in Illustration 15.15 lists the linear programming solution to the optimization problem. The total contribution margin is maximized if Hixon produces 500 armchairs and no bookshelves or cabinets. The maximum total contribution obtainable under the present resource constraints is approximately $2,840 (see (c)). Hence, the operating profit realized from this production mix is $340 ($2,840 − $1,500 fixed manufacturing costs − $1,000 fixed nonmanufacturing costs).

ILLUSTRATION 15.15	Linear Programming Output, Hixon Company

Summary of Problem

OBJECTIVE FUNCTION VALUE $2,840 ⓒ

VARIABLE	VALUE	REDUCED VALUE
Armchairs	500.00	0.0
Bookshelves	0.0	2.54
Cabinets	0.0	5.96

CONSTRAINTS	TYPE	VALUE	SHADOW PRICE
Direct material	Slack	0.0	ⓓ $1.42
Cutting	Slack	30.00	0.0
Assembly and finishing	Slack	140.00	0.0
Armchair sales	Surplus	400.00	0.0
Bookshelf sales	Slack	100.00	0.0

Objective Function Coefficient Ranges

VARIABLE	CURRENT COEFFICIENT	ALLOWABLE INCREASE	ALLOWABLE DECREASE
Armchairs	5.68	Infinity	1.45
Bookshelves	7.40	2.54	Infinity
Cabinets	8.24	5.96	Infinity

Right-Hand-Side Ranges

CONSTRAINTS	CURRENT RIGHT-HAND SIDE	ALLOWABLE INCREASE	ALLOWABLE DECREASE
Direct material	2000.00	400.00	1600.00
Cutting	180.00	Infinity	30.00
Assembly and finishing	240.00	Infinity	140.00
Armchair sales	100.00	400.00	Infinity
Bookshelf sales	100.00	Infinity	100.00

Opportunity Costs   Of the five constraints, only the direct material constraint has an opportunity cost attached to it. This opportunity cost figure, which is reflected on the output as a shadow price, shows us how total contribution margin changes as a result of a per unit change in the constraint. Thus, if we increase the direct material constraint from 2,000 board-feet to 2,001 board-feet, Hixon's contribution margin increases by approximately $1.42 (see ⓓ in Illustration 15.15).

Effects of Forcing Nonsolution Products into the Solution   The optimal solution *excludes* bookshelves and cabinets. What happens if we *force* one bookshelf or cabinet into the solution? That is, we require producing one unit that the optimal solution would not produce. You would predict that the value of the optimal solution (the $2,840 in Illustration 15.15) would go down—but by how much?

The Reduced Value column in Illustration 15.15 answers the following question: How much will the value of the solution (that is, Hixon's contribution margin) go down if it produces one unit of a product that is not produced in the optimal solution? Bookshelves and cabinets have values of $2.54 and $5.96, respectively, as shown in Illustration 15.15. This means that if we force Hixon to produce one bookshelf, for example, total contribution margin to the firm will be reduced by $2.54. This happens because some production of the more profitable armchairs will have to be given up to produce a bookshelf. Similarly, the production of an additional cabinet would lower the contribution margin by $5.96.

Nonbinding Constraints   Four constraints have a nonzero value, meaning that they are not binding. The amounts shown under the Value column in Illustration

15.15 are for scarce resources, or constraints, still available. For example, 30 labor-hours are still available in the cutting department; only 150 hours of the available 180 labor-hours were used. This unused scarce resource is sometimes known as *slack*. In the assembly and finishing department, 140 labor-hours are still available. For bookshelf *sales,* an additional 100 units could be produced and sold before the market constraint becomes binding. (Recall that no more than 100 bookshelves could be sold per week. The optimal solution is to sell no bookshelves.) Finally, for armchairs, the solution value shows that optimal production of armchairs exceeds the specified minimum by 400 units; that is, there is a "surplus" over the specified minimum.

Binding constraints have an opportunity cost (for example, $1.42 per unit for direct materials), but no shadow price, or opportunity cost, is shown in the solution for the constraints that are not binding. For example, there is no shadow price for labor-hours in the cutting department because there is neither value for having one additional hour nor a loss for having one fewer hour.

Sensitivity Analysis   The parameters specified in this linear programming (LP) model are subject to some degree of estimation error. Decision makers need to know how much error can be tolerated before making a difference in the decision.

The Objective Function Coefficient Ranges panel of Illustration 15.15 gives the ranges within which each product's contribution margin can change without changing the optimal mix of products, all other things being equal. For example, an armchair's contribution margin is $5.68 and could increase by an infinite amount without changing the fact that the optimal product mix includes 500 armchairs.

Bookshelves presently have a zero value in the optimal solution. If their contribution margin were increased (by raising the selling price, for example) by more than $2.54 from the present level of $7.40, bookshelves would become part of the optimal solution with a value higher than zero. In general, the optimal solution for Hixon is to produce 500 armchairs and none of the other two products within the objective function ranges shown, all other things being equal.

The Right-Hand-Side Ranges panel in Illustration 15.15 gives the allowable increase or decrease for values of the constraints before a binding constraint becomes nonbinding or a nonbinding constraint becomes binding, all other things being equal.

For example, the direct material constraint, which is presently a binding constraint, could increase by 400 or decrease by 1,600 board-feet before it would become nonbinding, all other things being held constant. Suppose that the number of board-feet dropped by more than 1,600 to fewer than 400 available (that is, current level of 2,000 minus 1,600 leaves 400 board-feet). Then the company could not satisfy its constraint to make at least 100 armchairs because each requires 4 board-feet.

Labor-hours in the cutting department are not binding in the solution in Illustration 15.15. In fact, there are 30 available hours for this constraint. The Right-Hand-Side Ranges panel indicates that this constraint could decrease as much as 30 hours before it becomes binding.

Misspecifying the Objective Function   Suppose that Hixon Company incorrectly specified its objective function using gross margins instead of contribution margins. Based on the gross margins given in Illustration 15.13, this would result in the following formulation of the problem:

Maximize total gross margin:

$$\$.68A + \$2.40B + \$3.24C$$

Subject to the following constraints:

ILLUSTRATION 15.16	Linear Programming Output Incorrectly Using Gross Margins instead of Contribution Margins, Hixon Company

Linear Programming Input

MAX $0.68 A + $2.4 B + $3.24 C

SUBJECT TO

Direct material	$4 A + 7 B + 10 C \leq 2000$
Cutting	$0.3 A + 0.3 B + 0.4 C \leq 180$
Assembly and finishing	$0.2 A + 0.3 B + 0.5 C \leq 240$
Armchair sales	$A \geq 100$
Bookshelf sales	$B \leq 100$

Summary of Problem

OBJECTIVE FUNCTION VALUE $599.60[a]

VARIABLE	VALUE	REDUCED VALUE
Armchairs	100.00	0.0
Bookshelves	100.00	0.0
Cabinets	90.00	0.0

CONSTRAINT	TYPE	VALUE	SHADOW PRICE
Direct material	Slack	0.0	0.32
Cutting	Slack	84.00	0.0
Assembly and finishing	Slack	145.00	0.0
Armchair sales	Surplus	−0.0	−0.62
Bookshelf sales	Slack	0.0	0.13

[a]This is not the correct contribution because of the data errors noted in the text.

Material	$4A + 7B + 10C \leq 2,000$ board-feet
Cutting	$.30A + .30B + .40C \leq 180$ hours
Assembly and finishing	$.20A + .30B + .50C \leq 240$ hours
Armchairs	$A \geq 100$ units
Bookshelves	$B \leq 100$ units

The constraints are the same as those previously formulated.

The computer solution to this LP problem is given in Illustration 15.16. Note that as a result of misspecifying the values of the objective function, Hixon will make a suboptimal production decision to manufacture 100 armchairs, 100 bookshelves, and 90 cabinets. Compare this solution with the prior optimal solution in which contribution margins were used in the objective function.

The optimal value of the solution reported in the output of Illustration 15.16, $599.60, is an incorrect number because the analysis incorrectly treats fixed manufacturing costs as variable costs. Comparing the solution in Illustration 15.16 with the correct solution in Illustration 15.15 identifies numerous errors in Illustration 15.16. This demonstrates the importance of using contribution margins, not gross margins, in LP problems.

Removing a Binding Constraint   Suppose that Hixon Company has access to an unlimited supply of direct material. The optimal production mix for Hixon can be found using the LP formulation in Illustration 15.17. Without a materials constraint, the solution to the production decision problem is to produce 100 armchairs, 100 bookshelves, and 300 cabinets. Armchairs, which use the least amount of

ILLUSTRATION 15.17	Removal of a Binding Constraint, Problem Formulation, Hixon Company

Linear Programming Input

MAX $5.68A + $7.40B + $8.24C
SUBJECT TO

Cutting	.30A + .30B + .40C ≤ 180
Assembly and finishing	.20A + .30B + .50C ≤ 240
Armchair sales	A ≥ 100
Bookshelf sales	B ≤ 100

Summary of Problem

OBJECTIVE FUNCTION VALUE $3,780

VARIABLE	VALUE	REDUCED VALUE	
Armchairs	100.00	0.0	
Bookshelves	100.00	0.0	
Cabinets	300.00	0.0	

CONSTRAINT	TYPE	VALUE	SHADOW PRICE
Cutting	Slack	0.0	$20.60
Assembly and finishing	Slack	40.00	0.0
Armchair sales	Surplus	0.0	1.22
Bookshelf sales	Slack	0.0	0.50

material, are not as attractive as they were before because the supply of material is no longer a binding constraint.

This new optimum production point has a total contribution margin of $3,780. This is $940 ($3,780 − $2,840) higher than the optimum obtained in Illustration 15.15 where availability of direct material was a binding constraint. The current constraints are the availability of labor in the cutting department, the size of the market for bookshelves, and the minimum required sales for armchairs.

Note that the opportunity costs associated with the binding constraints on this new optimum differ from those in Illustration 15.15. The cutting department, which had an excess of 30 labor-hours before, now has an opportunity cost of $20.60 per unit of the scarce resource, labor-hours.

Introducing an Additional Constraint   Now, suppose that Hixon's contract commitments require it also to produce a minimum of 100 cabinets each week. Assume also that Hixon once again faces a limited availability of direct material. The effect of an additional constraint on Hixon's optimal production decision can be seen in Illustration 15.18.

The Summary of Problem panel shows that Hixon's optimal product decision is to produce 250 armchairs and 100 cabinets. The total contribution margin now drops from $2,840 to $2,244.

One of the benefits of linear programming is the opportunity to examine the effects of introducing additional constraints. Is the optimal solution affected? Does the solution value change when additional constraints are added? Managers frequently do not know the answers to these questions without using linear programming. For example, managers frequently ask what-if questions such as these: What if at least 40 percent of the material in our hot dogs is beef (or chicken or turkey)? What if class enrollments are limited to 50 students per class? Linear programming often can be used to help answer similar questions, making it a useful short-run planning tool.

ILLUSTRATION 15.18	Introducing an Additional Constraint, Problem Formulation, Hixon Company

Linear Programming Input

MAX $5.68A + $7.40B + $8.24C
SUBJECT TO

Direct material	4 A + 7 B + 10 C ≤ 2000
Cutting	0.3 A + 0.3 B + 0.4 C ≤ 180
Assembly and finishing	0.2 A + 0.3 B + 0.5 C ≤ 240
Armchair sales	A ≥ 100
Bookshelf sales	B ≤ 100
Cabinet sales	C ≥ 100

Summary of Problem

OBJECTIVE FUNCTION VALUE $2,244

VARIABLE	VALUE	REDUCED VALUE
Armchairs	250.00	0.0
Bookshelves	0.0	$2.54
Cabinets	100.00	0.0

CONSTRAINTS	TYPE	VALUE	SHADOW PRICE
Direct material	Slack	0.0	$1.42
Cutting	Slack	65.00	0.0
Assembly and finishing	Slack	140.00	0.0
Armchair sales	Surplus	150.00	0.0
Bookshelf sales	Slack	100.0	0.0
Cabinet sales	Slack	0.0	5.96

REVIEW QUESTIONS		

15.1 If we want to maximize profit, why do we use unit contribution margins in our analysis instead of unit gross margins?

15.2 A company has learned that a particular input product required for its production is in limited supply. What approach should management take to maximize profits in the presence of this constraint?

15.3 What is the *feasible production region*?

15.4 Why are corner points on the feasible production region important for profitability analysis?

15.5 What does the *opportunity cost of a constraint* mean?

15.6 What are the three main factors focused on by the theory of constraints?

CRITICAL ANALYSIS AND DISCUSSION QUESTIONS

15.7 Management notes that the contribution from one product is higher than the contribution from a second product. Hence, it concludes that the company should concentrate on production of the first product. Under what, if any, conditions will this approach result in maximum profits?

15.8 Under what circumstances would fixed costs be relevant when management is making decisions in a multiproduct setting?

15.9 In the theory of constraints, what are ways to improve performance at the bottleneck?

15.10 According to the theory of constraints, what are the ways to increase profits?

EXERCISES

15.11   Make-or-Buy Decisions (L.0. 1)

Dabelles Company makes bicycles. For years it has made the rear wheel assembly for its bicycles. Recently, Trice Company offered to sell these rear wheel assemblies to Dabelles. If Dabelles makes the assembly, its cost per rear wheel assembly is as follows:

Direct materials........	$3.50
Direct labor..........	15.00
Variable overhead	6.00
Fixed overhead	8.00
Total	$32.50

These costs are based on annual production of 20,000 units.

Trice offered to sell the assembly to Dabelles for $30 each. The total order would amount to 20,000 rear wheel assemblies per year, which Dabelles' management will buy instead of making if the company can save at least $12,500 per year. Accepting Trice's offer would eliminate annual fixed overhead of $100,000.

Required   Should Dabelles make rear wheel assemblies or buy them from Trice? Prepare a schedule that shows the differential costs per rear wheel assembly.

15.12   Make-or-Buy Decisions (L.0. 1)

Collins, Inc., has been manufacturing 5,000 units of part 10541 per month, which is used in manufacturing one of its products. At this level of production, the per unit cost to manufacture part 10541 follows:

Direct materials........	$6
Direct labor..........	22
Variable overhead	8
Fixed overhead	12
Total	$48

Thatcher Company has offered to sell Collins 5,000 units of part 10541 for $44 a unit. Collins has determined that it could use the facilities presently used to manufacture part 10541 to manufacture product RAC, which would generate an additional contribution margin per month of $30,000. Collins also has determined that one-third of the fixed overhead will be saved even if it purchases part 10541 from Thatcher and makes product RAC.

Required   Prepare a schedule to show the effect of purchasing part 10541 from Thatcher at $44 a unit. Assume that Collins would take the opportunity to make product RAC.

(CPA adapted)

15.13   Make-or-Buy Decisions (L.0. 1)

Assume that Casio Company needs 20,000 units of a certain part in its production cycle. It estimates the costs to make the part as follows:

Direct materials........	$3.00
Direct labor..........	10.50
Variable overhead	4.00
Fixed overhead	5.00
Total	$22.50

It can buy the part from Lincs Company for $21. Sixty percent of the fixed overhead costs will continue regardless of what decision is made.

Required   What are the differential costs of the make-or-buy decision?

(CPA adapted)

15.14 Make-or-Buy Decisions (L.O. 1)

Columbus Company purchases sails that it uses in the 1,500 sailboats it produces a year, operating at 70 percent of capacity. Columbus purchases the sails for $560 each but is considering making them instead. Columbus can manufacture each sail for $180 for materials, $160 for direct labor, and $260 for overhead without increasing its capacity.

Sam Christopher, the president of Columbus, has come to you for advice. "It would cost me $600 to make the sails," he said, "but only $560 to buy. Should I continue buying them?" He added, "Materials and labor are variable costs, but variable overhead would be only $120 per sail." (Columbus uses one sail per boat.)

Required

What should Sam do? Prepare a schedule to show the differential costs.

15.15 Make or Buy with Opportunity Costs (L.O. 1)

Refer to the facts in Exercise 15.14. If Sam suddenly finds an opportunity to rent out the unused capacity of his factory for $160,000 per year, would your answer in Exercise 15.14 change? Why or why not?

15.16 Dropping Product Lines (L.O. 2)

Refer to the data for Campus Bookstore that appear in Illustration 15.6. Assume that all facts are the same except the following:

- Salaries listed under fixed costs are $40,000 under all three alternatives (that is, there is no reduction in fixed costs salaries under alternative 1).
- Under alternative 2, rent increases to $32,000.

Required

Prepare a new comparison of the three choices; namely, status quo, alternative 1, and alternative 2.

15.17 Dropping Product Lines (L.O. 2)

Sierra Ski Company is presently operating at 75 percent of capacity. Worried about the company's performance, the president is considering dropping its line of cross-country skis. If they are dropped, the revenue associated with them would be lost and the related variable costs saved. In addition, the company's fixed costs would be reduced by 15 percent of the total fixed costs.

Segmented income statements appear as follows:

	Downhill Racing	Cross-Country	Regular Downhill
Sales	$65,200	$85,600	$102,400
Variable costs	44,000	77,200	80,200
Contribution margin	21,200	8,400	22,200
Fixed costs allocated to each product line	9,400	12,000	14,200
Operating profit (loss)	$11,800	$ (3,600)	$ 8,000

Required

Prepare a differential cost schedule like the one in Illustration 15.5 to indicate whether Sierra should drop the cross-country ski product line.

15.18 Dropping Product Lines (L.O. 2)

Cliff & Bassman is a public accounting firm that offers audit, tax, and consulting services. The firm is concerned about the profitability of its consulting business and is considering dropping it. If it does so, it could do more tax work. It would lose all consulting revenues but would save all variable costs and 50 percent of the fixed costs associated with consulting. Tax revenues are expected to increase by 45 percent, but the fixed costs associated with auditing would not be affected.

Segmented income statements for these three product lines follow:

	Consulting	Tax	Auditing
Sales	$300,000	$500,000	$600,000
Variable costs	250,000	300,000	350,000
Contribution margin	50,000	200,000	250,000
Fixed costs allocated to each product line	50,000	60,000	80,000
Operating profit (loss)	$ –0–	$140,000	$170,000

Required

Prepare a differential cost schedule like the one in Illustration 15.6 to indicate whether Cliff & Bassman should (1) drop the consulting line without increasing tax work or (2) drop consulting and increase tax work.

15.19 Product Choice Decisions (L.O. 3)

Burnett, Inc., manufactures three products labeled A, B, and C. Data concerning the three products are as follows:

	A	B	C
Selling price.	$15	$20	$25
Manufacturing costs			
Materials	2.50	3	3.50
Direct labor.	3.50	3.50	5.50
Overhead			
Variable	1.50	1.50	3
Fixed	1	1	2

Variable marketing costs equal 15 percent of the sales price of each product. Variable administrative costs are estimated at $0.50 per unit of product. Fixed administrative costs are allocated to each unit produced as follows: product A, $1.50; product B, $2; and product C, $2.50.

Required

What is the equation representing the objective function for the product mix decision?

15.20 Product Choice Decisions (L.O. 3)

Quicksilver Corporation's management has been reviewing the company's profitability and is attempting to improve performance through better planning. The company manufactures three products—necklaces, bracelets, and rings—in its jewelry line. Selected data on these items follow:

	Necklaces	Bracelets	Rings
Selling price	$50	$37.50	$25
Contribution margin	$20	$15	$10
Machining time required	.5 hour	.25 hour	.30 hour

The machining time is limited to 120 hours per month. Demand for each product far exceeds the company's ability to meet the demand. There are no other relevant production constraints.

At the present time, management produces an equal number of each product. The production vice president has urged the company to concentrate on necklace production because that has the greatest margin. No bracelets or rings would be produced if this recommendation were followed.

Required

a. If fixed costs are $2,500 per month, what profit will be obtained by following the production vice president's recommendation?

b. What is the maximum profit obtainable and what product or product combination must be sold to obtain that maximum?

15.21 Theory of Constraints (L.O. 4)

Racketeer, Inc., makes tennis rackets in two departments: Department A makes the frame and Department B adds the grip and paints the racket. Monthly capacities and production levels are as follows:

	Department A	Department B
Monthly capacity	800 rackets	1,000 rackets
Monthly production	800 rackets	800 rackets

The company can sell 1,000 rackets per month. Department B produces only 800 rackets because Department A is a bottleneck. The rackets sell for $100 each and have a variable cost of $40 each.

Required

a. Racketeer's production supervisors state they could increase Department A capacity by 200 rackets per month by producing rackets on the weekend. Producing on the weekend would not affect the sales price or variable cost per unit, but would increase fixed costs by $10,000 per month. Should Racketeer produce rackets on the weekend?

b. Independent of the situation in requirement (*a*), Racketeer could add additional equipment and workers to Department A, which would increase Department A capacity by 200 rackets per month. This would not affect sales price or variable cost per unit, but would increase fixed costs by $20,000 per month. Should Racketeer add the additional equipment and workers to Department A?

15.22   Theory of Constraints (L.O. 4)

Bud's Bakery makes cakes in three activity centers: (1) Preparation mixes ingredients and prepares the dough for baking, (2) Baking bakes the cakes, and (3) Frosting prepares the frosting, frosts the cake, decorates the cake, and puts the cake in a container. Daily capacities and production levels are as follows:

	Preparation	Baking	Frosting
Daily capacity	40 cakes	30 cakes	50 cakes
Daily production	30 cakes	30 cakes	30 cakes

The cakes sell for $9 each and have a variable cost of $4 each. Bud's Bakery could sell 50 cakes per day for $9 each, but does not because of production limitations.

Required

a. Bud's production supervisors state they could increase Baking capacity by 10 cakes per day by working overtime. Working overtime would not affect the sales price or variable cost per unit, but would increase fixed costs by $100 per day. Should Bud's Bakery work overtime to increase output by 10 cakes per day?

b. Independent of the situation in requirement (*a*), Bud's could add an additional oven to Baking that would increase Baking output by 10 cakes per day. This would not affect sales price or variable cost per unit, but would increase fixed costs by $40 per day. Should Bud's add the additional oven to Baking?

15.23   (Appendix) Linear Programming (L.O. 5)

Classic Corporation manufactures two models, small and large. Each model is processed as follows:

	Machining	Polishing
Small (S)	1 hour	2 hours
Large (L)	4 hours	3 hours

The weekly time available for processing the two models is 100 hours in machining and 90 hours in polishing. The contribution margin is $3 for the small model and $4 for the large model.

Required

Formulate the equations necessary to solve this product mix problem.

(CPA adapted)

15.24   (Appendix) Linear Programming (L.O. 5)

Snead Company manufactures two products, Zeta and Beta, each of which passes through two processing operations. All materials are introduced at the start of process 1. No work in process inventories exist. Snead may produce either one product exclusively or various combinations of both products subject to the following constraints:

	Process Number 1	Process Number 2	Contribution Margin per Unit
Hours required to produce one unit of			
Zeta	2	1	$4.00
Beta	1	3	5.25
Total capacity in hours per day	1,000	1,275	

A shortage of technical labor has limited Beta production to 400 units per day. There are no constraints on the production of Zeta other than the hour constraints in the preceding schedule. Assume that all relationships between capacity and production are linear.

Required

a. Given the objective to maximize total contribution margin, what is the production constraint for process 1?
(1)   Zeta + Beta $\geq$ 1,000.
(2)   Zeta + Beta $\leq$ 1,000.
(3)   2 Zeta + Beta $\geq$ 1,000.
(4)   2 Zeta + Beta $\leq$ 1,000.
(5)   Some other answer.

b. Given the objective to maximize total contribution margin, what is the labor constraint for production of Beta?
   (1) Beta ≤ 425.
   (2) Beta ≥ 400.
   (3) Beta ≤ 400.
   (4) Beta ≥ 425.
   (5) Some other answer.

c. What is the objective function of the data presented? Maximum is
   (1) 2 Zeta + 1 Beta.
   (2) $4.00 Zeta + $5.25 Beta.
   (3) $4.00 Zeta + 3($5.25) Beta.
   (4) 2($4.00) Zeta + 3($5.25) Beta.
   (5) Some other answer.

(CPA adapted)

15.25 Cost Data Sensitivity (L.O. 3)

Servo Company produces two types of gloves, G1 and G2. The cost and production data concerning these two products follow:

	G1	G2
Selling price	$11.00	$13.00
Manufacturing costs		
Materials	4.00	1.50
Labor	3.00	6.00
Fixed overhead	2.50	5.00
Gross margin per unit	$ 1.50	$ 0.50
Required production time/unit	2 hours	2 hours

Total production time available is 2,500 hours per month. Since production time is limited and G1's gross margin per unit is higher than that for Servo's G2, management decided to produce and sell G1 exclusively.

Required   Did Servo management make the correct decision?

PROBLEMS

15.26 Decision Whether to Add or Drop

Justa Corporation produces and sells three products. The three products, A, B, and C, are sold in a local market and in a regional market. At the end of the first quarter of the current year, the following income statement has been prepared:

	Total	Local	Regional
Sales revenue	$1,300,000	$1,000,000	$300,000
Cost of goods sold	1,010,000	775,000	235,000
Gross margin	290,000	225,000	65,000
Marketing costs	105,000	60,000	45,000
Administrative costs	52,000	40,000	12,000
Total marketing and administrative	157,000	100,000	57,000
Operating profits	$ 133,000	$ 125,000	$ 8,000

Management has expressed special concern with the regional market because of the extremely poor return on sales. This market was entered a year ago because of excess capacity. It was originally believed that the return on sales would improve with time, but after a year, no noticeable improvement can be seen from the results as reported in the above quarterly statement.

In attempting to decide whether to eliminate the regional market, the following information has been gathered:

	Products		
	A	B	C
Sales revenue	$500,000	$400,000	$400,000
Variable manufacturing costs as a percentage of sales revenue	60%	70%	60%
Variable marketing costs as a percentage of sales revenue	3	2	2

	Sales by Markets	
Product	Local	Regional
A	$400,000	$100,000
B	300,000	100,000
C	300,000	100,000

All administrative costs and fixed manufacturing costs are common to the three products and the two markets and are fixed for the period. Remaining marketing costs are fixed for the period and separable by market. All fixed costs have been arbitrarily allocated to markets.

Required

a. Assuming there are no alternative uses for the Justa Corporation's present capacity, would you recommend dropping the regional market? Why or why not?

b. Prepare the quarterly income statement showing contribution margins by products. Do not allocate fixed costs to products.

c. It is believed that a new product can be ready for sale next year if the Justa Corporation decides to go ahead with continued research. The new product can be produced by simply converting equipment presently used in producing product C. This conversion will increase fixed costs by $10,000 per quarter. What must be the minimum contribution margin per quarter for the new product to make the changeover financially feasible?

(CMA adapted)

15.27 Make or Buy

Hospital Supply, Inc., produces hydraulic hoists that are used by hospitals to move bedridden patients. The costs of manufacturing and marketing hydraulic hoists at the company's normal volume of 3,000 units per month are shown below. A regular selling price of $740 per unit should be assumed.

Costs per Unit for Hydraulic Hoists
Unit manufacturing costs
Variable materials	$100	
Variable labor.	150	
Variable overhead	50	
Fixed overhead.	120	
Total unit manufacturing costs		$420
Unit marketing costs		
Variable	50	
Fixed	140	
Total unit marketing costs		190
Total unit costs		$610

Required

a. A proposal is received from an outside contractor who will make and ship 1,000 hydraulic hoist units per month directly to Hospital Supply's customers as orders are received from Hospital Supply's sales force. Hospital Supply's fixed marketing costs would be unaffected, but its variable marketing costs would be cut by 20 percent for these 1,000 units produced by the contractor. Hospital Supply's plant would operate at two-thirds of its normal level, and total fixed manufacturing costs would be cut by 30 percent. What in-house unit cost should be used to compare with the quotation received from the supplier? Should the proposal be accepted for a price (that is, payment to the contractor) of $425 per unit?

b. Assume the same facts as above in requirement (*b*) except that the idle facilities would be used to produce 800 modified hydraulic hoists per month for use in hospital operating rooms. These modified hoists could be sold for $900 each, while the costs of production would be $550 per unit variable manufacturing expense. Variable marketing costs would be $100 per unit. Fixed marketing and manufacturing costs would be unchanged whether the original 3,000 regular hoists were manufactured or the mix of 2,000 regular hoists plus 800 modified hoists were produced. What is the maximum purchase price per unit that Hospital Supply should be willing to pay the outside contractor? Should the proposal be accepted for a price of $425 per unit to the contractor?

15.28   Ocean Company manufactures and sells three different products: Ex, Why, and Zee. Projected income statements by product line for the year are presented below:

	Ex	Why	Zee	Total
Unit sales	10,000	500,000	125,000	635,000
Sales revenue	$925,000	$1,000,000	$575,000	$2,500,000
Variable cost of units sold	285,000	350,000	150,000	785,000
Fixed cost of units sold	304,200	289,000	166,800	760,000
Gross margin	335,800	361,000	258,200	955,000
Variable nonmanufacturing costs	270,000	200,000	80,000	550,000
Fixed nonmanufacturing costs	125,800	136,000	78,200	340,000
Operating profit	$ (60,000)	$ 25,000	$100,000	$ 65,000

Fixed nonmanufacturing costs are allocated to products in proportion to revenues. The fixed cost of units sold is allocated to products by various allocation bases, such as square feet for factory rent, machine-hours for repairs, and so forth.

Ocean management is concerned about the loss on product Ex and is considering an alternative course of corrective action.

Alternative. Ocean would discontinue the manufacture of product Ex. Selling prices of products Why and Zee would remain constant. Management expects that product Zee production and revenues would increase by 50 percent. The machinery devoted to product Ex could be sold at scrap value that equals its removal costs. Removal of this machinery would reduce fixed costs allocated to product Ex by $30,000 per year. The remaining fixed costs allocated to product Ex include $155,000 of rent expense per year. The space previously used for product Ex can be rented to an outside organization for $157,500 per year.

Required   Prepare a schedule analyzing the effect of this alternative on projected total operating profit.

(CPA adapted)

15.29   Closing a Plant   You have been asked to assist the management of Arcadia Corporation in arriving at certain decisions. Arcadia has its home office in Ohio and leases factory buildings in Texas, Montana, and Maine, all of which produce the same product. The management of Arcadia provided you with a projection of operations for next year as follows:

	Total	Texas	Montana	Maine
Sales revenue	$4,400,000	$2,200,000	$1,400,000	$800,000
Fixed costs				
Factory	1,100,000	560,000	280,000	260,000
Administration	350,000	210,000	110,000	30,000
Variable costs	1,450,000	665,000	425,000	360,000
Allocated home office costs	500,000	225,000	175,000	100,000
Total	3,400,000	1,660,000	990,000	750,000
Operating profit	$1,000,000	$ 540,000	$ 410,000	$ 50,000

The sales price per unit is $25.

Due to the marginal results of operations of the factory in Maine, Arcadia has decided to cease operations and sell that factory's machinery and equipment by the end of this year. Arcadia expects that the proceeds from the sale of these assets would be greater than their book value and would cover all termination costs.

Arcadia, however, would like to continue serving its customers in that area if it is economically feasible and is considering one of the following three alternatives:

1. Expand the operations of the Montana factory by using space presently idle. This move would result in the following changes in that factory's operations:

	Increase over Factory's Current Operations
Sales revenue	50%
Fixed costs	
Factory	20
Administration	10

Under this proposal, variable costs would be $8 per unit sold.

2. Enter into a long-term contract with a competitor who will serve that area's customers. This competitor would pay Arcadia a royalty of $4 per unit based on an estimate of 30,000 units being sold.

3. Close the Maine factory and not expand the operations of the Montana factory.

Total home office costs of $500,000 will remain the same under each situation.

Required

To assist the management of Arcadia Corporation, prepare a schedule computing Arcadia's estimated operating profit from each of the following options:

a. Expansion of the Montana factory.

b. Negotiation of long-term contract on a royalty basis

c. Shutdown of Maine operations with no expansion at other locations.

(CPA adapted)

15.30 Product Mix— Graphic Analysis

The following graph shows the constraints (all ≤) of a chair manufacturing company. Each kitchen chair contributes $8; each office chair contributes $5. Only 3,000 kitchen chairs can be produced.

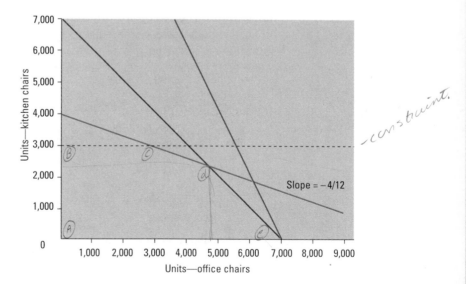

Required

What mix of chairs maximizes profits?

✗ 15.31   Optimum Product Mix

Jackson Enterprises makes and sells three types of stuffed toys. Management is trying to determine the most profitable mix. Sales prices, demand, and use of manufacturing inputs follow:

	Bears	Cows	Dogs
Sales price	$15	$32	$95
Annual demand (units)	20,000	10,000	30,000
Input requirement per unit			
Direct material	.5 yards	.3 yards	.6 yards
Direct labor	.7 hours	2 hours	7 hours
Costs			
Variable costs			
Materials	$10 per yard		
Direct labor	8 per hour		
Factory overhead	2 per direct labor-hour		
Marketing	10% of sales price		
Annual fixed costs[a]			
Manufacturing	$18,000		
Marketing	4,000		
Administration	15,000		

[a]Fixed costs are allocated using direct labor-hours.

The company faces two limits: (1) the volume of stuffed toys that it can sell and (2) 30,000 direct labor-hours per year caused by the plant layout.

Required

Show supporting data in good form.

a. How much operating profit could the company earn if it were able to satisfy the annual demand?

b. Which of the three product lines makes the most profitable use of the constrained resource, direct labor?

c. Given the information in the problem so far, what product mix do you recommend?

d. How much operating profit should your recommended product mix generate?

e. Suppose that the company could expand its labor capacity by running an extra shift that could provide up to 10,000 more hours. The cost would increase from $8 to $9.50 per hour. What additional product(s) should Jackson manufacture and what additional profit would be expected with the use of the added shift?

15.32   Theory of Constraints

University Hospital has an outpatient surgery center that treats patients in three activity centers: (1) Surgery, which does surgery on the patients, (2) Phase I recovery, where patients recover from surgery while still asleep, and (3) Phase II surgery, where the patients continue recovering after they awake. At the end of Phase II surgery, patients go home. Daily capacities and production levels are as follows:

	Surgery	Phase I Recovery	Phase II Recovery
Daily capacity	40 surgeries	30 surgeries	60 surgeries
Daily production	30 surgeries	30 surgeries	30 surgeries

The hospital receives an average of $1,000 per surgery. (The surgeon's fee and anesthesiologist's fee are billed separately.) The variable cost per surgery is $300. There is sufficient demand for surgeries that the hospital could perform 60 per day. Surgeries not performed by the outpatient surgery center are sent to the hospital's regular surgery rooms in the hospital. The variable cost per surgery for the regular surgery rooms is $700, while the hospital still receives $1,000 per surgery.

Here are some alternatives that management is considering.

a. Continue performing 30 surgeries per day in the outpatient surgery center and send 30 patients to the hospital's regular surgery rooms for the other 30 patients.

b. Rebuild the recovery rooms so that some of the Phase II space could be used for Phase I recovery. This would cost $2,000 per day and would enable the outpatient surgery center to perform 40 surgeries per day and send 20 patients to the hospital's regular operating rooms.

c. Expand the facilities of the outpatient surgery center at a differential cost of $15,000 per day so it could perform 60 surgeries per day, service 60 patients per day in Phase I recovery, and continue to service 60 patients per day in Phase II recovery.

Required

Write a report to the management of University Hospital recommending which of the above alternatives it should take and why.

15.33   Interpreting Computer Output— One Constraint (appendix)

Computer output is as follows:

Summary of Problem

| OBJECTIVE FUNCTION VALUE | | $30,000 |

VARIABLE	VALUE	REDUCED VALUE
Product X	600.00	0.0
Product Y	0.0	$1.67
Product Z	0.0	0.0

CONSTRAINT	TYPE	VALUE	SHADOW PRICE
Machining time	Slack	0.0	$166.67

Objective Function Coefficient Ranges

VARIABLE	CURRENT COEFFICIENT	ALLOWABLE INCREASE	ALLOWABLE DECREASE
Product X	$50.00	Infinity	$0.0
Product Y	40.00	$1.67	Infinity
Product Z	25.00	0.0	Infinity

Right-Hand-Side Ranges

	CURRENT RHS	ALLOWABLE INCREASE	ALLOWABLE DECREASE
Machining time	180.00	Infinity	180.00

Required

Interpret the computer output for this problem by answering the following questions:

a. What is the objective function for this problem?

b. What is the optimal production level of product X?

c. What is the total contribution at the optimal production level? How was it computed?

d. How much would the company be willing to pay for an additional hour of machining capacity?

e. Product Y shows a reduced value of $1.67. What does this value mean?

f. Suppose that an error was made in figuring out the contribution margin for product Y. Its contribution margin is supposed to be $41 instead of $40. What is the optimal production level for Y?

15.34   Interpreting Computer Output— Multiple Constraints (appendix)

Computer output for this problem follows:

Linear Programming Input

MAX   41.5 P1 + 35.5 P2

SUBJECT TO

Machining	2 P1 + 1.5 P2 ≤ 2000
Assembly	3 P1 + 3 P2 ≤ 3000
Demand for P2	P2 ≥ 500

Summary of Problem

OBJECTIVE FUNCTION VALUE $38,500

VARIABLE	VALUE	REDUCED VALUE
P1	500.00	0.0
P2	500.00	0.0

CONSTRAINT	TYPE	VALUE	SHADOW PRICE
Machining	Slack	250.0	0.0
Assembly	Slack	0.0	13.83
Demand for P2	Surplus	0.0	−6.00

Required

Answer the following questions using the computer output.

a. What is the optimal production level for P1? For P2?

b. What is the total contribution margin obtained at the optimal production level and how was it computed?

c. How much of the machine-hours resource is unused? How much of the assembly-hours resource is unused?

d. How much would the company be willing to pay for an additional hour of machining time? For an additional hour of assembly time?

15.35   Product Mix Choice

Rupee Corporation manufactures and sells two kinds of containers, paperboard and plastic. It produced and sold 100,000 paperboard containers and 75,000 plastic containers during April. It used 4,000 and 6,000 direct labor-hours in producing the paperboard and plastic containers, respectively.

The company has not been able to maintain an inventory of either product due to the high demand; this situation is expected to continue in the future. Workers can be shifted from the production of paperboard to plastic containers and vice versa, but additional labor is not available in the community. In addition, a shortage of plastic material used in the manufacture of the plastic container is expected in the coming months due to a labor strike at a key supplier's facilities. Management has estimated that it has enough direct material to produce only 60,000 plastic containers during June.

Rupee's income statement for April follows. The costs presented represent prior periods and are expected to continue at the same rates or levels in the future.

RUPEE CORPORATION
Income Statement
For the Month Ended April 30

	Paperboard Containers	Plastic Containers
Sales revenue	$220,800	$222,900
Less		
Returns and allowances	6,360	7,200
Discounts	2,440	3,450
Total	8,800	10,650
Net sales	212,000	212,250
Cost of sales		
Direct material cost	123,000	120,750
Direct labor	26,000	28,500
Indirect labor (variable with direct labor-hours)	4,000	4,500
Depreciation—machinery	14,000	12,250
Depreciation—building	10,000	10,000
Cost of sales	177,000	176,000
Gross profit	35,000	36,250
Nonmanufacturing expenses		
Variable	8,000	7,500
Fixed	1,000	1,000
Commissions—variable	11,000	15,750
Total operating expenses	20,000	24,250
Income before tax	15,000	12,000
Income taxes (40%)	6,000	4,800
Net income	$ 9,000	$ 7,200

Required   **a.** What is the optimal product mix, given the constraints in the problem?

b. Write a brief memo to management explaining how you arrived at the optimal product mix described in requirement (*a*).

(CMA adapted)

15.36 Multiple Choice

A company markets two products, Alpha and Gamma. The contribution margins per gallon are $5 for Alpha and $4 for Gamma. Both products consist of two ingredients, D and K. Alpha contains 80 percent D and 20 percent K; the proportions in Gamma are 40 percent and 60 percent, respectively. The current inventory is 16,000 gallons of D and 6,000 gallons of K. The only company producing D and K is on strike and will neither deliver nor produce them in the foreseeable future. The company wishes to know the numbers of gallons of Alpha and Gamma that it should produce with its present stock of raw materials to maximize its total profit. Let X_1 refer to Alpha and X_2 refer to Gamma.

Required   **a.** The objective function for this problem could be expressed as
   (1)   Max $0X_1 + 0X_2$.
   (2)   Min $5X_1 + 4X_2$.
   (3)   Max $5X_1 + 4X_2$.
   (4)   Max $X_1 + X_2$.
   (5)   Max $4X_1 + 5X_2$.
   (6)   Some other answer.

b. The constraint imposed by the amount of D on hand could be expressed as
  (1) $X_1 + X_2 \geq 16{,}000.$
  (2) $X_1 + X_2 \leq 16{,}000.$
  (3) $.4X_1 + .6X_2 \leq 16{,}000.$
  (4) $.8X_1 + .4X_2 \geq 16{,}000.$
  (5) $.8X_1 + .4X_2 \leq 16{,}000.$
  (6) Some other answer.

c. The constraint imposed by the amount of K on hand could be expressed as
  (1) $X_1 + X_2 \geq 6{,}000.$
  (2) $X_1 + X_2 \leq 6{,}000.$
  (3) $.8X_1 + .2X_2 \leq 6{,}000.$
  (4) $.8X_1 + .2X_2 \geq 6{,}000.$
  (5) $.2X_1 + .6X_2 \leq 6{,}000.$
  (6) Some other answer.

d. To maximize total profit, the company should produce and market
  (1) 106,000 gallons of Alpha only.
  (2) 90,000 gallons of Alpha and 16,000 gallons of Gamma.
  (3) 16,000 gallons of Alpha and 90,000 gallons of Gamma.
  (4) 18,000 gallons of Alpha and 4,000 gallons of Gamma.
  (5) 4,000 gallons of Alpha and 18,000 gallons of Gamma.
  (6) Some other answer.

e. Assuming that the marginal contributions per gallon are $7 for Alpha and $9 for Gamma, the company should produce and market
  (1) 106,000 gallons of Alpha only.
  (2) 90,000 gallons of Alpha and 16,000 gallons of Gamma.
  (3) 16,000 gallons of Alpha and 90,000 gallons of Gamma.
  (4) 18,000 gallons of Alpha and 4,000 gallons of Gamma.
  (5) 4,000 gallons of Alpha and 18,000 gallons of Gamma.
  (6) Some other answer.

(CPA adapted)

15.37 Analyze Alternative Actions with Multiple Products

Essen Corporation manufactures two models: average and deluxe. The following data are derived from company accounting records for the two products for the past month:

	Average	Deluxe
Sales volume	1,000 units	800 units
Sales revenue	$135,000	$160,000
Manufacturing costs		
Variable	25,000	40,000
Fixed	45,000	50,000
Marketing costs (all variable)	27,000	32,000
Administrative costs (all fixed)	20,000	25,000
Total costs	117,000	147,000
Division profit	$ 18,000	$ 13,000

Production is constrained by the availability of certain materials. Each average model takes 10 kg of these materials; each deluxe model uses 15 kg. Each month 22,000 kg of materials are available and marketing constraints limit the number of Average models to 1,800 per month. Deluxe models also are limited to 1,200 per month.

The fixed manufacturing costs for each product would be eliminated if the product were no longer manufactured. However, administrative costs will not change with the elimination of either product.

Required

What are the optimal product mix and the profit at that product mix? Show computations.

15.38 Analyze Alternative Products with Differential Fixed Costs

Edmonton Company recently expanded its manufacturing capacity, allowing it to produce up to 15,000 pairs of cross-country skis of the Mountaineering model or the Touring model. The sales department assures management that it can sell between 9,000 and 13,000 of either product this year. Because the models are very similar, Edmonton will produce only one of the two models. The accounting department compiled the following information:

	Model	
	Mountaineering	**Touring**
Selling price per unit	$88.00	$80.00
Variable costs per unit	52.80	52.80

Fixed costs will total $369,600 if the Mountaineering model is produced but only $316,800 if the Touring model is produced.

Required
a. If Edmonton could be assured of selling 12,000 of either model, which model should it sell? How much operating profit would it earn with sales of that product?
b. At what sales level, in units, would Edmonton be indifferent regardless of the model it chooses to produce?
c. If Edmonton faces a limitation on labor so that a maximum of 6,000 Mountaineering models or a maximum of 12,000 Touring models or some combination of the two that would fall along that constraint can be produced, what is the optimal production schedule?

(CMA adapted)

15.39 Formulate and Solve Linear Program

Baxter, Inc., manufactures two industrial products, X-10, which sells for $90 a unit, and Y-12, which sells for $85 a unit. Each product is processed through both of the company's manufacturing departments. The limited availability of labor, material, and equipment capacity has restricted the firm's ability to meet the demand for its products. The production department believes that linear programming can be used to routinize the production schedule for the two products. It has the following weekly data:

	Amount Required per Unit Weekly	
	X-10	**Y-12**
Direct material: Supply limited to 1,800 pounds at $12 per pound	4 pounds	2 pounds
Direct labor		
Department 1: Supply limited to 10 people at 40 hours each at an hourly cost of $6	⅔ hour	1 hour
Department 2: Supply limited to 15 people at 40 hours each at an hourly rate of $8	1¼ hours	1 hour
Machine time		
Department 1: Capacity limited to 250 hours	½ hour	½ hour
Department 2: Capacity limited to 300 hours	0 hours	1 hour

Baxter's overhead costs are accumulated on a plantwide basis and are assigned to products on the basis of the number of direct labor-hours required to manufacture the product. This base is appropriate for overhead assignment because most of the variable overhead costs vary as a function of labor time. The estimated overhead cost per direct labor-hour follows:

Variable overhead cost	$ 6
Fixed overhead cost	6
Total overhead cost per direct labor-hour	$12

The production department formulated the following equations for the linear programming statement of the problem:

A = Number of units of X-10 to be produced.
B = Number of units of Y-12 to be produced.

Objective function to minimize costs:

$$\text{Minimize } 85A + 62B$$

Constraints:

Material

$$4A + 2B \leq 1{,}800 \text{ pounds}$$

Department 1 labor

$$\tfrac{2}{3}A + 1B \leq 400 \text{ hours}$$

Department 2 labor

$$1\tfrac{1}{4}A + 1B \leq 600 \text{ hours}$$

Other

$$A \geq 0,\ B \geq 0$$

Required

a. The formulation of the linear programming equations prepared by Baxter's production department is incorrect. Write a brief memo to management explaining what errors were made in its formulation.

b. Formulate and label the proper equations for the linear programming statement of Baxter's production problem.

c. (Computer required). Solve the linear program and determine the increase in the price of direct materials required to change the product mix from that obtained in the optimal solution.

(CMA adapted)

SOLUTIONS TO SELF-STUDY QUESTIONS

1. Using the outside contractor at a cost of $400 per unit would increase profits by $78,000 (= $478,000 increase in profit shown below − $400,000 paid to contractor).

	Status Quo	Alternative	Difference
Variable cost ignoring payment to contractor.	$2,200,000	$1,770,000[a]	$430,000 lower
Fixed costs	1,040,000	992,000[b]	48,000 lower
Costs	$3,240,000	$2,762,000	$478,000 lower

[a]$1,770,000 = (1,000 units × $120) + (3,000 units × $550).

[b]$992,000 = $560,000 nonmanufacturing costs
    + (.90 × $480,000) manufacturing costs
  = $560,000 + 432,000.

2. a. Determine the contributions for each product:

	Twopack	Threepack
Selling price	$1,000	$1,700
Variable costs		
Materials.	350	370
Direct labor	210	230
Variable overhead (20%)	30	40
Variable marketing.	80	240
Total variable costs.	670	880
Contribution margin.	$ 330	$ 820

Maximize profit = $330 (Twopack) + $820 (Threepack)

b. Constraints:

$$\text{Twopack} \geq 500$$
$$\text{Threepack} \geq 150$$
$$\tfrac{1}{4}\,(\text{Twopack}) + \tfrac{3}{4}\,(\text{Threepack}) \leq 250$$

c. Contribution per assembly control-hour:

$$\text{Twopack } \$330/.25 = \$1{,}320$$
$$\text{Threepack } \$820/.75 = \$1{,}093$$

The Twopack is preferred because it provides a higher contribution per assembly control-hour.

d.

Produce and Sell		Total Contribution
Twopacks	**Threepacks**	**Margin**
500	150	$330(500) + $820(150) = $288,000
500	167[a]	$330(500) + $820(167) = $301,940
550[b]	150	$330(550) + $820(150) = $304,500

[a] $\tfrac{1}{4}(500) + \tfrac{3}{4}$ Threepack $= 250$, from assembly control constraint

$$\text{Threepack} = \frac{250 - \tfrac{1}{4}(500)}{\tfrac{3}{4}}$$
$$= 167$$

[b] $\tfrac{1}{4}$ Twopack $+ \tfrac{3}{4}(150) = 250$, from assembly control constraint

$$\text{Twopack} = \frac{250 - \tfrac{3}{4}(150)}{\tfrac{1}{4}}$$
$$= 550$$

Optimal schedule is 550 Twopacks and 150 Threepacks.

Managing
Quality and Time

LEARNING OBJECTIVES

After reading this chapter, you should be able to:

1. Identify the differences between the traditional view of quality and the new quality-based view.

2. Know how just-in-time relates to total quality management.

3. Identify the changes to the managerial accounting system that must be implemented for effective total quality management.

4. Define quality according to the customer.

5. Compare the costs of quality control to the costs of failing to control quality.

6. Know why trade-offs in quality control and failure costs are made.

7. Compare and contrast the *cost of quality* and *quality is free* concepts.

8. Know what tools are used to identify quality control problems.

9. Know why time is important in a competitive environment.

WHY IS QUALITY IMPORTANT?

L.O. 1: Identify the differences between the traditional view of quality and the new quality-based view.

You undoubtedly have experienced poor-quality service or defective merchandise. As a result, you may have decided never to deal with that particular company again. It lost you as a customer, which is the reason that managers are concerned about providing quality products.

A recent survey asked chief financial officers to select the three most important changes in their company's strategy in recent years. The most frequently cited change was to improve customer satisfaction and product quality. In today's globally competitive environment, improving quality is clearly a high priority for multinational companies.

Several prestigious, internationally renowned awards are given to companies for quality. For example, the Baldrige Quality Award, created by Congress in 1987, recognizes U.S. firms with outstanding records of quality improvement and quality management. The Deming Prize, created in Japan long before the Baldrige Quality Award, also is awarded to companies that focus on quality improvement.

Improving quality has become one of the most important strategic factors affecting most companies. In fact, the International Organization for Standardization developed international standards for quality management called *ISO 9000*. The ISO standards are guidelines for the design, development, production, final inspection and testing, installation, and servicing of products, processes, and services. To register, a company must document its quality systems and go through a third-party audit of its manufacturing and customer service processes. The creation of ISO 9000 provides clear evidence of a global movement toward quality improvement.

Illustration 16.1 compares the traditional view of managing quality with the new quality-based view. In general, the traditional view assumes a trade-off between the cost of improving quality and maintaining the status quo. Although quality is important, it may be cheaper to produce lower-quality goods and have a minimum level of defective goods. The quality-based view assumes that quality can and should always be improved. Rather than waiting for inspections of finished products or reworking defective goods, the quality-based view establishes quality at the beginning of the process with zero defects being the goal.

ILLUSTRATION 16.1	Traditional versus Quality-Based View
Traditional View	**Quality-Based View**
Quality is expensive to produce: Producing quality products may involve high costs.	*Quality lowers costs:* Reworking poor-quality parts and warranty repairs can be costly.
Inspection is necessary: Product inspections are the only way to ensure quality.	*Defect-free goods do not need to be inspected:* Quality must be established prior to inspections.
Workers cause defects: Defects must result from worker errors.	*The system causes defects:* Defects must result from production process deficiencies.
Standards, quotas, and goals are set: Companies must constantly strive to meet standards.	*Standards, quotas, and goals should be eliminated:* The production process can always be improved.
Buy from lowest cost supplier: The cost of production materials must be minimized.	*Buy on the basis of the lowest total cost, including inspection, rework, and poor customer relations costs:* Consider the consequences of purchasing poor-quality production materials (reworking, scrap, etc.).
High revenues less low costs equal high profits: Maximize revenues and minimize expenses at all costs, even if result is poor quality.	*Loyal customers equal higher profits:* High quality leads to loyal, repeat customers. This maximizes long-run profits.

**HOW THE
JUST-IN-TIME
PHILOSOPHY
AND TOTAL
QUALITY
MANAGEMENT
REINFORCE
EACH OTHER**

L.O. 2: Know how just-in-time relates to total quality management.

just-in-time
A system designed to produce or purchase goods or services just in time for the next step of the production process or for sale.

The **just-in-time** (JIT) philosophy is closely linked to total quality management. Its objective is to purchase and/or produce goods and services just when needed. Companies that apply JIT find that it not only reduces, or potentially eliminates, inventory carrying costs but also requires high-quality standards. Processes or people making defective units must be corrected immediately because there is no inventory to which defective units can be sent to await reworking or scrapping. Manufacturing managers find that JIT can prevent production problems from being hidden, but it also requires a smooth production flow without downtime to correct problems.

Think of JIT and quality requirements for a course project. Suppose that you schedule your time so you have just enough to complete a project before class. If all goes as planned, you will finish typing the report just before class and hand it in on time. Fine—if all goes well.

Suppose, however, that your personal computer crashes while you are typing the report. This presents a major problem for you because of the combination of your JIT philosophy and the defective machine in your production process. JIT forces you to think through all the things that could go wrong and to correct them in advance of your project. If you use JIT for course projects, you need to be sure that everything involved is reliable: your machine (or a backup), your transportation to deliver the product (your report), and your access to other resources, such as the library or the Internet. In short, you need total quality management!

Companies using JIT find that the following factors are essential for JIT to work.

Total quality. All employees must be involved in the quality process.

Smooth production flow. Fluctuations in production lead to delays. Delays require inventory.

Purchasing quality materials. Suppliers must be reliable, providing on-time deliveries of high-quality materials.

Well-trained flexible workforce. Workers must be well-trained and cross-trained to use various machines and work on various parts of the production process. (If your personal computer crashes, you must know how to use another personal computer, perhaps with a different platform, than the one you normally use.)

Short customer response cycles. Keeping the customer response cycle short enables companies to respond quickly to customer needs. Suppose that you are considering purchasing either a new Camaro or Mustang but the particular cars you want are not in stock because both the Ford and Chevrolet dealerships use JIT. Suppose that either the Mustang or the Camaro can be delivered in three months. What would you do? Probably buy a car from a different dealership. If the customer response cycle were sufficiently short that you could receive the car of your dreams within five days, however, you might not care that it wasn't already in stock.

Backlog of orders. A company needs to have a backlog of orders to keep the production line moving with a JIT system. With no backlog, production stops when an order has been filled and remains idle until a new one is received, possibly creating chaos in the factory. Continuing production in the plant without a backlog of orders creates chaos for distributors and dealers. Several Japanese motorcycle companies that were using JIT in their production plants in Japan had trouble with the lack of order backlog from U.S. motorcycle dealers. Rather than disrupt production in the plants, the motorcycle manufacturers continued to supply their U.S. distributors. The plants continued their efficient production flows, but inventory piled up for the dealers and distributors—up to a one year's supply of inventory for some distributors and dealers.

REAL WORLD APPLICATION | **The International Effects of Labor Strife and JIT**

A labor strike at General Motors' Dayton, Ohio, plant, which produces brake parts, demonstrated the far-reaching effects of just-in-time when companies face plant shutdowns. When the United Auto Workers (UAW) struck the Dayton plant, they forced 30,000 non–UAW workers off their jobs. As General Motors has moved toward just-in-time production methods, its inventories of brakes and other parts have decreased. Because of the strike at the Dayton plant, U.S. and

Canadian plants using the brakes shut down quickly. Mexican plants were slower to shut down because inventory in transit kept the Mexican plants going for about a week longer than their U.S. and Canadian counterparts.

Sources: G. Burkins and F.R. Bleakley, "UAW Strike Hit GM Just in Time' to Cripple Firm," *The Wall Street Journal*, March 14, 1996, p. A3; and N. Templin, "GM Walkout Hits Production at Mexican Sites," *The Wall Street Journal*, March 20, 1996, p. A3.

Many manufacturing companies have found that JIT can be used to varying degrees. If replacement goods could be obtained rapidly from reliable suppliers, inventory levels of one week's supply or less could be optimal. On the other hand, if replacement materials were difficult to obtain (for example, goods imported from overseas), companies required substantially higher inventory levels.

Why Implement a Just-in-Time System?

As with most unique production or merchandising systems, JIT has its pros and cons. First, several financial benefits can result from implementing it. By decreasing inventory levels, companies no longer need to tie up cash in inventory or in warehouse space to store inventory. The emphasis on eliminating nonvalue-added activities (such as storing inventory) and improving the production process results in reduced production costs. Also, the risk of producing inventory that becomes obsolete—a major concern in the computer industry—is eliminated.

Implementing JIT systems can present problems for companies not prepared for the complexities inherent in such a system. Implementing JIT systems requires the highly efficient coordination of purchasing and production processes. Companies that have consistent problems in either of these areas should not implement JIT until they have resolved the problems.

The Real World Application presented above, "The International Effects of Labor Strife and JIT," shows how much companies that use JIT must rely on their suppliers. Since suppliers ship parts needed in the production process just prior to their use, any problem with the supply of parts can lead to a costly disruption of the production process.

HOW TRADITIONAL MANAGERIAL ACCOUNTING SYSTEMS CAN LIMIT THE IMPACT OF TOTAL QUALITY MANAGEMENT

Companies that implement total quality management (TQM) are likely to find that it has little economic benefit unless the company's management accounting system supports it. In many companies, managers respond to the management accounting system instead of the TQM initiatives. For example, suppose that TQM requires expenditures to train employees to improve quality but increases short-run costs. Suppose also that the company records and reports cost increases but not quality improvements. Given a choice between a recorded cost increase and an unrecorded quality improvement, the manager may choose not to increase cost to improve quality.

Effective implementation of TQM requires five changes to traditional managerial accounting systems.[1]

L.O. 3: Identify the changes to the managerial accounting system that must be implemented for effective total quality management.

[1]See C. Ittner and D. Larcker, "Total Quality Management and the Choice of Information and Reward Systems," *Journal of Accounting Research*, Supplement to vol. 33.

1. The information should include problem-solving information like that coming from quality control charts, not just financial reports. Financial reports would indicate a decline in revenues, for example, but not its causes. Control charts, however, could show an increase in customer complaints as the cause of the revenue decline. To carry this a step further, other charts could indicate the cause of increased customer complaints. (We describe these charts later in the chapter.)

2. The workers themselves should collect the information and use it to get feedback and solve problems. The information should be bottom up in the organization, not just top down. Traditional managerial accounting reports are based on data collected and aggregated by accountants, who present reports to managers, who then typically send some of the information down to the workers. These reports are likely to be meaningful to accountants and managers but not necessarily to workers unfamiliar with accounting concepts.

3. The information should be available quickly (for example, daily) so workers can get quick feedback. Frequent information accelerates identifying and correcting problems. Traditional managerial accounting systems often report weekly or monthly, which does not facilitate a quick response to problems.

4. Information should be more detailed than that found in traditional managerial accounting systems. Instead of reporting just the cost of defects, for example, the information system should also report the types and causes of defects.

5. Rewards should be based more on quality and customer satisfaction measures of performance to obtain quality. This is the idea that "you get what you reward."

QUALITY ACCORDING TO THE CUSTOMER

Many organizations develop performance measures to assess performance on their *critical success factors,* which are the elements of performance required for success. The three critical success factors that relate to meeting customer requirements are service, quality, and cost.

L.O. 4: Define quality according to the customer.

Service

service
Includes the product's tangible features ("service of the product" including performance and functionality) and intangible features ("service of the company" such as courtesy of sales people and on-time deliveries).

Service refers to both a product's tangible and intangible features. *Tangible features* are those such as performance, taste, and functionality. *Intangible features* include how people are treated by salespeople and delivery time to the customer after the product is ordered. In short, service is everything about the product that the customer values. Service relates to the customer's expectations about all the aspects of a product's purchase and use. Organizations can develop a profile of the type of service that customers expect by asking them.

Some elements of service are difficult to measure directly because they reflect the customer's personal valuation of the package of product attributes. In these cases, performance is often measured indirectly using criteria such as sales volume, a measure of revealed customer valuation. However, performance on other features can be measured directly. Developing measures of service performance is a major role of management accounting.

Quality

quality
Providing the service (including tangible and intangible features) expected by the customer.

Quality is related to the organization's ability to deliver on its service commitments and means different things to different people. It is interpreted relative to service, which is everything that the customer expects from the product and the company that provides it. We define *quality* as meeting or exceeding customer expectations; it is measured by how well the product conforms to specifications.

Although some people associate a product's quality with its performance, attributes, or features, *quality* is defined by the extent to which the customer is satisfied. For a customer expecting and getting a product life of three years, the quality is as high for that product as for another product purchased by a customer expecting and getting a product life of five years.

Customers expect to get what they have paid for; therefore, quality is important. The promised attributes are what you pay for and determine your expectations; quality is judged relative to your expectations. *High quality* means that the customer is rarely disappointed. As organizations get better at meeting or exceeding customer expectations, quality improves.

Quality is not limited to meeting customer expectations. The quest for quality often leads to improved efficiency by improving production processes and reducing nonvalue-added activities. A process that produces high-quality products usually has high efficiency ratings. When quality is poor, products have to either be reworked or destroyed (a nonvalue-added activity), increasing the cost per unit of good output. As quality increases, the production process becomes more efficient, scrap and rework fall, and so do costs. Although quality typically leads to improved efficiency, the reverse is not necessarily true. It is possible to refine the production process to allow for a higher rate of production of low-quality products. Thus, the goal should be improving quality; the result will be improved quality and a more efficient production process.

Cost

Cost is a function of the organization's ability to efficiently use resources to obtain its objectives. Accomplishing the same things using fewer resources and, therefore, lower costs, means that the organization is increasing efficiency.

Cost is important because of the relationship between product cost and price. In the long run, a product's price must cover its costs or the organization will go out of the business of making it. Since customers buy the product from the company with the lowest price, all other things being equal, keeping costs low is a priority for organizations in maintaining a strong competitive advantage.

In choosing among all the products that provide them with the quality and services they want, customers will buy the product that provides them with the preferred mix of quality, services, and price. If two products provide the same quality and services, the customer will choose the product with the lower price.

The stockholders' expectations of returns require that the difference between the revenue produced by the organization's products and the products' costs (the organization's profit) must be ample enough to meet the owners' return requirements. To keep prices low and to meet the return requirements of stockholders, organizations must maintain efficiency to keep their costs low.

Customers value service, quality, and cost (price) performance; therefore, the organization must measure these attributes to manage the performance of its activities. Illustration 16.2 presents some basic examples of performance measures. For example, companies routinely measure service and product quality with customer satisfaction surveys. Managers also consider the ratio of materials in the final product to material purchased, to measure cost performance. For example, if a company purchases $100,000 in materials for June and uses $90,000 of these materials in the final products produced for the month (all other materials purchased were scrapped and had no value), the ratio of materials in the final product to material purchased would

ILLUSTRATION 16.2	Customer Satisfaction Measures
Factor	**Examples of Performance Measures**
Service	Number of customers
	Amount of purchases per customer
	Customer satisfaction surveys
Quality	Number of customer complaints per 1,000 orders filled
	Customer satisfaction surveys
Cost	Ratio of material in final product to material purchased
	Ratio of labor allowed for work done to total labor

be 0.9 ($90,000/$100,000). If the industry standard is 0.85, this company likely has an efficient production process with respect to the use of materials.

QUALITY CONTROL

L.O. 5: Compare the costs of quality control to the costs of failing to control quality.

prevention costs
Costs incurred to prevent defects in the products or services being produced.

Most—if not all—managers would agree that quality is important. As the previous section indicated, customers look at service, quality, and cost (price) as a guide in determining their satisfaction with the product. As a result, managers often ask two questions: "What can we do to improve quality?" "How much will it cost?" We start to answer these questions by introducing two costs of *controlling quality* and two costs of *failing to control quality*.

The two costs of controlling quality are prevention costs and appraisal costs.

1. **Prevention costs** are incurred to prevent defects in the products or services being produced, including the following:
   * *Materials inspection.* Inspecting production materials upon delivery.
   * *Processing control (process inspection).* Inspecting the production process.
   * *Process control (equipment inspection).* Equipment used to track the production process.
   * *Quality training.* Training employees to improve quality.
   * *Machine inspection.* Ensuring that machines are operating properly within specifications.

appraisal costs (also called *detection costs*)
Costs incurred to detect individual units of products that do not conform to specifications.

2. **Appraisal costs** (also called *detection costs*) are incurred to detect individual units of products that do not conform to specifications, including these:
   * *End-of-process sampling.* Inspecting a sample of finished goods to ensure quality.
   * *Field testing.* Testing products in use at customer sites.

Suppose that you are the manager at Pete's Pizza, a pizza delivery restaurant. What quality costs might you incur? You may decide to have all tomato paste, cheese, and other ingredients inspected before accepting delivery to ensure that they meet specifications (prevention cost). You could test sample pizzas for taste (appraisal cost).

FAILURE TO CONTROL QUALITY

internal failure costs
Costs incurred when nonconforming products and services are detected before being delivered to customers.

external failure costs
Costs incurred when nonconforming products and services are detected after being delivered to customers.

The two costs of failing to control quality are internal failure costs and external failure costs.

1. **Internal failure costs** are incurred when nonconforming products and services are detected before being delivered to customers. These include
   * *Scrap.* Materials wasted in the production process.
   * *Rework.* Correcting product defects before the product is sold.
   * *Reinspection/Retesting.* Quality control testing after rework is performed.
2. **External failure costs** are incurred when nonconforming products and services are detected after being delivered to customers. These include
   * *Warranty repairs.* Repairing defective products.
   * *Product liability.* Liability to company resulting from product failure.
   * *Marketing costs.* Marketing necessary to improve the company's image tarnished from poor product quality.
   * *Lost sales.* Decrease in sales resulting from poor-quality products (customers will go to competitors).

TRADING-OFF QUALITY CONTROL AND FAILURE COSTS

L.O. 6: Know why trade-offs in quality control and failure costs are made.

If flaws are detected before these pastries are cooked, then the uncooked dough can usually be converted into raw materials for the next batch of pastries. If the flaws are not detected until after cooking, then the pastry might be sold at a discount or become scrap. Clearly, it is better to find the flaw as early in the production process as possible. (You might disagree with that statement if you are the person who consumes the scrap.)
(© Mark Williams/Tony Stone Images)

As a manager at Pete's, you would probably throw away any prepared pizzas that do not meet the strict quality standards established by Pete (internal failure cost) or feed them to the employees. You might be concerned about lost customer loyalty (and thus, lost future sales) as a result of selling pizzas that taste bad or have the wrong toppings (external failure cost).

The ultimate goal in implementing a quality improvement program is to achieve zero defects while incurring minimal costs of quality. Managers must make trade-offs between the four cost categories, and total costs of quality must be reduced over time.

How would Pete's estimate the cost of quality? One employee performs the materials inspections as part of her daily duties. Assume that the cost of materials inspections (prevention cost) is $5,580 per year. Pete's must decide how much to spend on material inspections versus finished product (cooked pizza) inspections. It may be cheaper to inspect cooked pizzas for the quality of ingredients rather than inspecting all the ingredients when delivered.

Costs of quality are often expressed as a percentage of sales. An example of a cost of quality report prepared for Pete's is shown in Illustration 16.3. This report indicates that Pete's spent $11,580 on quality training and materials inspections (prevention costs), which represents 2.3 percent of sales. This is the smallest amount spent on quality for any of the four categories. Pete's spent most of its money on appraisal costs ($18,000, or 3.6 percent of sales). Scrap costs totaled $14,400 (2.9 percent of sales), and the cost of dealing with customer complaints totaled $12,000 (2.4 percent of sales).

Managers of Pete's Pizza use the information to see how they can reduce the overall cost of quality. For example, suppose that "scrap" occurs because pizzas are not made to meet customer orders. Adding an additional check to ensure that each order is correct could reduce scrap costs. "Customer complaints" is the cost of dealing with customers, including managerial time and reimbursement to irate customers. Perhaps this cost could be reduced by finding the source of customer complaints and dealing with the problem before it becomes a customer complaint.

The goal for Pete's Pizza is to reduce the total cost of quality ($55,980) as a percentage of sales (11.2 percent) while maximizing the value of each dollar spent on quality. Thus, Pete's may find that spending an additional $3,000 on prevention costs will reduce the cost of scrap by $2,000 and the cost of customer complaints by $2,500, for a total of $4,500 saved for an additional cost of $3,000. This gives a net reduction in the cost of quality of $1,500. As a result, the total cost of quality would be reduced to $54,480, or 10.90 percent of sales.

Note that accounting measures of external failure costs do not explicitly represent the cost of lost business. That is generally true of accounting-based cost of quality reports. Such reports often show the results of transactions but not the opportunity cost of lost business. To obtain qualitative measures of lost business, organizations often use customer satisfaction surveys and measures of repeat business.

ILLUSTRATION 16.3

PETE'S PIZZA
Cost of Quality Report
For the Year Ended December 31

			Percent of Sales (Sales = $500,000)
Costs of quality			
Prevention costs			
Quality training	$6,000		
Materials inspection	5,580	$11,580	2.3%
Appraisal costs			
End of process sampling		18,000	3.6
Internal failure costs			
Scrap		14,400	2.9
External failure costs			
Customer complaints		12,000	2.4
Total costs of quality		$55,980	11.2%

SELF-STUDY QUESTION

1. **Costs of quality.** Merideth Industries manufactures zippers. The following presents its financial information for one year.

	Year 1
Sales	$450,000
Costs	
Materials inspection	6,500
Scrap	8,500
Employee training	13,000
Returned goods	3,000
Finished goods inspection	15,000
Customer complaints	8,000

   a. Classify these items into prevention, appraisal, internal failure, or external failure costs.

   b. Create a cost of quality report for year 1.

   The solution to this question is at the end of this chapter on page 504.

IS QUALITY WORTH THE INVESTMENT?

Differential analysis determines what revenues and costs would differ and by how much if alternative actions are taken. Costs that differ under alternative actions are relevant costs. Costs that do not differ are not relevant to the analysis.

A problem at Pete's Pizza involves the length of time each pizza is cooked. As a result, the restaurant incurs $2,000 per month in scrap and loss of business costs. Two potential solutions have been identified. Pete's can hire an additional cook to check every pizza for proper cooking time at a cost of $2,200 per month. Alternatively, the restaurant can lease new and improved equipment that can substantially decrease the number of defects (overcooked pizza) costing the restaurant $1,500 per month. Given this information, which approach should Pete's take? (Answer: Lease the equipment for $1,500 per month to save $2,000 per month in scrap and lost business costs.)

THE QUALITY IS FREE CONCEPT

L.O. 7: Compare and contrast the *cost of quality* and *quality is free* concepts.

As you already may have figured out, measuring the cost of quality has a major disadvantage. It is difficult to measure increased customer satisfaction (reflected in sales) resulting from additional spending on prevention costs (or any of the four categories), and it is difficult to measure decreased customer satisfaction resulting from a reduction in prevention costs. For example, if prevention costs are *reduced,* how do we measure lost sales as a result of this reduction? Conversely, how do we measure the increase in sales directly associated with an *increase* in prevention costs? It is difficult to accurately measure the change in sales specifically resulting from either scenario.

A current theme in business today is that "quality is free." The belief is that if quality is built into the product, the resulting benefits in customer satisfaction, reduced rework and warranty costs, and other important factors far outweigh the costs of improving quality. Cost-benefit analyses are no longer the primary focus in improving quality. Instead, the emphasis is on improving quality with the understanding that quality is free in the long run.

Those who subscribe to the quality is free concept believe that zero defects is the only acceptable goal. The production process should be continuously improved by eliminating as many nonvalue-added activities as possible and improving the process for all value-added activities. The result? Quality will improve, customers will be increasingly satisfied, and the cost of improving quality will pay for itself through increased sales and lower costs (providing for increased profit margins).

Although both cost of quality and quality is free concepts strive for improved quality, the cost of quality approach assumes a cost-benefit trade-off when spending money on quality improvement. The quality is free approach assumes that the long-run benefits will always outweigh the costs of improving quality. One thing is for certain: quality is important to the success of any company!

IDENTIFYING QUALITY PROBLEMS

L.O. 8: Know what tools are used to identify quality control problems.

warning signal
The signal that a problem needs to be investigated

diagnostic signal
A signal identifying the problem and perhaps how to correct it.

control chart
A chart that shows the results of a statistical process control measure—for a sample, batch, or some other unit of measure—designed to provide warning signals that something is wrong.

How does a company know whether quality is a problem? Managers use several tools to identify quality problems. The following tools—control charts, cause-and-effect analysis, and Pareto charts—are basic components of quality control.

A signal is information provided to a decision maker. Tools used to identify quality control problems provide two types of signals. The first type is a **warning signal** that something is wrong in the same way that an increase in your body temperature signals a problem. The warning signal triggers an investigation to determine the cause in order to correct the problem. The second type is a **diagnostic signal** and suggests what the problem is and perhaps a way to solve it.

Managers need both warning and diagnostic information about activities to identify problems that require attention. However, most diagnostic information is expensive to collect, so managers use warning information to trigger collection of diagnostic information.

Control charts help managers distinguish between random or routine variations in quality and variations that should be investigated. They show the results of a statistical process control measure for a sample, batch, or some other unit of measure. Control charts provide warning signals that something may be wrong.

Control charts are used to study variation in a process and to analyze the variation over time. A specified level of variation may be acceptable, but deviation beyond it is unacceptable. Illustration 16.4 is a control chart for Pete's that shows how many pizzas were undercooked or overcooked. When the cooking is done properly, Pete's management believes less than 2 percent of the pizzas should fall outside the upper (overcooked) limit and less than 2 percent should fall outside the lower (undercooked) control limit.

The control chart in Illustration 16.4 shows that more than 2 percent of pizzas were overcooked on Day 1, indicating a problem with the cooking process. On Days 2–4, 1 or 2 percent were undercooked, but management considers this to be within acceptable quality limits.

ILLUSTRATION   16.4   Control Chart for Pete's Pizza
(Percent of Pizzas Overcooked or Undercooked)

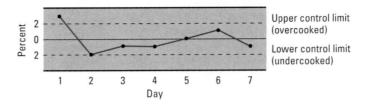

ILLUSTRATION   16.5   Pareto Chart for Pete's Pizza (One-week Period)

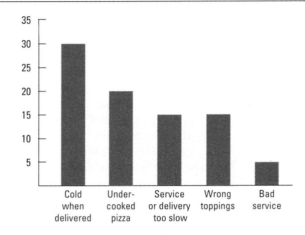

cause-and-effect analysis
An analysis that provides diagnostic signals identifying potential causes of defects.

Cause-and-effect analysis provides diagnostic signals that identify potential causes of defects. It first defines the effect (for example, overcooked pizza) and then the events (causes) that may contribute to the problem. The potential causes of these problems can be: human (for example, people are not trained in proper cooking methods), machine related (for example, oven temperature is not precise), and other causes. As the prevailing causes are identified, corrective measures are developed and implemented.

Pareto chart
A chart used to display the number of problems or defects in a product over time.

Pareto charts also provide diagnostic signals. They are used to display the number of problems or defects in a product over time. Pareto charts are fairly simple to construct, displaying the results as bars of varying length. Illustration 16.5 is a Pareto chart for Pete's.

As companies increase their focus on quality in the intensely competitive global marketplace, quality control has become an essential element in competing effectively. Managers use the tools discussed here to identify quality problems and find solutions.

THE IMPORTANCE OF TIME IN A COMPETITIVE ENVIRONMENT

L.O. 9: Know why time is important in a competitive environment.

Success in competitive markets increasingly demands ever shorter new product development time and more rapid response to customers. Indeed, fast response itself is often a major quality attribute. Rapid response to customers can occur when work processes are designed to meet both quality and response goals. Accordingly, response time improvement should be included as a major focus within all quality improvement processes of work units. This requires that all designs, objectives, and work unit activities include measurement of cycle time and responsiveness. Major improvements in response time may require simplifying and shortening the work processes and paths. Response time improvements often drive simultaneous improvements in quality and productivity. Hence, it is highly beneficial to consider response time, quality, and customer satisfaction objectives together.

It is easiest to think of customer response time in two categories: (1) new product development time and (2) operational measures of time.

New Product Development Time

new product development time
The period between the first consideration of a product and its sale to the customer.

break-even time (BET)
The length of time it takes to recover the investment made in new product development.

New product development time is the period between the first consideration of a product and its sale to the customer. Firms that respond quickly to customer needs for new products may develop an advantage over competitors. For example, Honda identified U.S. consumers' need for fuel-efficient cars, and its early development of them gave Honda a competitive advantage for several years.

Management is interested not only in improving new product development time, but also in how quickly a company can recover its investment in a new product. **Break-even time (BET)** is the length of time it takes to recover the investment made in new product development.

It is important to identify the relevant cash flows in break-even time analysis. The relevant cash flows are the differential future cash inflows and outflows that change as a result of introducing the new product. Overhead costs are irrelevant if adding a new product changes only the way overhead is allocated, not the total cash outflow for overhead costs. Break-even time analysis also should include both positive and negative cash flow effects that the new product may have on sales of existing products.

Break-even time works as follows.

1. It starts counting time when management approves a project rather than when cash outflows first occur.
2. It considers the time value of money by discounting all cash flows.[2]

Although Hewlett-Packard and other successful companies utilize break-even time in assessing new product development, this approach has several limitations.

- Break-even time ignores all cash flows after it has been identified. Thus, projects with high profit potential in later years may be rejected in favor of less profitable projects with higher cash inflows in the early years. As a result, managers may pursue short-term projects with lower profits rather than long-term innovative projects that may contribute more to the company's long-run viability.

- Break-even time does not consider strategic and nonfinancial reasons for product development. The focus is strictly on cash flows.

- Break-even time varies greatly from one business to the next, depending on product life cycles and investment requirements. For example, an acceptable break-even time for the automobile industry may be five years, but the computer industry might demand a break-even time of two or fewer years.

Let's look at an example. Pete's Pizza just approved adding salad to its menu, requiring an expansion of its walk-in refrigerator for $3,000. Pete calculated the discounted cash flows per year as $11,600 revenues and $10,100 for materials, labor, and increased energy consumption starting in six months when the expansion is complete. The break-even time is calculated as

---

[2]Because the time horizon for many projects can extend over many years, the *time value of money* is often a significant factor. The basic premise is that cash received earlier is worth more than cash received later. As a result, the future cash flows associated with a project are adjusted to their present value using a predetermined discount rate. This is referred to as *discounted cash flows,* and it is presented in detail in Chapter 23.

$$\frac{\text{Investment}}{\text{Annual net discounted cash flow}} + \begin{array}{l}\text{Time period from} \\ \text{approval to} \\ \text{providing product}\end{array}$$

$$\frac{\$3,000}{(\$11,600 - \$10,100)} + .5 \text{ years} = 2.5 \text{ years}$$

The break-even time for the salad product line is 2.5 years.

SELF-STUDY QUESTION

2. **Break-even time.** Jammin' Company manufactures skate boards and roller blades and has just approved production of a new line of roller blades scheduled to begin sales in nine months. The roller blades production will require a $150,000 investment for new machinery and an additional building. The manager has determined that expected production and sales of 200,000 units per year will generate $1,100,000 discounted cash flow in revenues and $800,000 discounted cash flow in expenses. Calculate the break-even time for the roller blade line.

(© Gary Bettnacher/Tony Stone Images)

The solution to this question is at the end of this chapter on page 504.

Operational Measures of Time

operational measures of time
Measures that indicate the speed and reliability with which organizations supply products and services to customers.

customer response time
The amount of time between a customer's placing an order for a product or requesting service and the delivery of the product or service to the customer.

on-time performance
Situations in which the product or service is delivered when it is scheduled to be delivered.

Operational measures of time indicate the speed and reliability with which organizations supply products and services to customers. Companies generally use two operational measures of time, customer response time and on-time performance.

Customer response time is the amount of time between a customer's placing an order for a product or requesting service and the delivery of the product or service to the customer. The shorter the response time, the more competitive the company. Several components of customer response time appear in Illustration 16.6. Order receipt time and order delivery time are typically minimal. Thus, improvement may be made within order waiting time and order manufacturing time.

For example, Pete's order receipt time is minimal; an employee answers the phone and takes the order. The time the order waits between being taken at the phone and being passed to the preparation area varies. During rush times, the order taker cannot always transfer the order immediately as other calls are coming in. This time could be decreased by moving the phone closer to the preparation area. Order preparation time might be decreased by arranging the ingredients in a more efficient manner and premeasuring toppings. Order delivery time is a function of distance to the client, which Pete's is not able to decrease.

On-time performance refers to situations in which the product or service is actually delivered when it is scheduled to be delivered. For example, Pete's keeps records of when orders are taken, the stated delivery time, and the actual delivery time. The company then measures performance as the ratio of on-time deliveries to total deliveries.

ILLUSTRATION   16.6   Customer Response Time

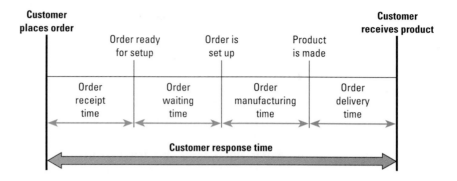

SUMMARY

This chapter defines quality and presents two views regarding the costs associated with improving quality: *cost of quality* and *quality is free.* Several tools are used to identify quality problems including control charts, cause-and-effect analysis, and Pareto charts.

The following summarizes key ideas tied to the chapter's learning objectives.

LO1: Identify the differences between the traditional view of quality and the quality-based view. Improving quality has become one of the most important strategic factors affecting most companies. Significant differences exist between the traditional view of quality versus the emerging quality-based view that relate to quality production, inspections, causes of defects, standards, purchasing, and customer focus.

LO2: Know how just-in-time (JIT) relates to total quality management. Companies that apply JIT find that it not only reduces inventory carrying costs but also requires high-quality standards and a smooth production flow without downtime to correct problems.

LO3: Identify the changes to the managerial accounting system that must be implemented for effective total quality management. First, information should include problem-solving information, not just financial information. Second, the workers themselves should collect the information and use it to get feedback and solve problems. Third, the information should be available quickly so workers can get quick feedback. Fourth, information should be more detailed than that found in traditional managerial accounting systems. Fifth, rewards should be based more on quality and customer satisfaction measures of performance.

LO4: Define quality according to the customer. The three critical success factors that relate to meeting customer requirements are service, quality, and cost. Service relates to the expectations the customer has about all the aspects, tangible and intangible, of the product's purchase and use. Quality is meeting or exceeding customer expectations; it is the extent to which the customer is satisfied. Cost is important because of the relationship between product cost and price. In the long run, the price of a product must cover its costs or the organization will go out of the business of making that product.

LO5: Compare the costs of quality control to the costs of failing to control quality. The two costs of controlling quality are prevention costs—costs incurred to prevent defects in the products or services being produced—and appraisal costs—costs incurred to detect individual units of products that do not conform to specifications. The two costs of failing to control quality are internal failure costs—costs incurred when nonconforming products and services are detected before being delivered to customers—and external failure costs—costs incurred when nonconforming products and services are detected after being delivered to customers.

LO6: Know why trade-offs in quality control and failure costs are made. Trade-offs must be made in and among the four cost categories, and total costs of quality must be reduced over time. An optimal level of defective units (often defined as zero) is identified, and the company works to achieve this level.

LO7: Compare and contrast the *costs of quality* and *quality is free* concepts. Although both concepts strive for improved quality, the cost of quality approach assumes a cost-benefit trade-off when spending money on quality improvement. The quality is free approach assumes that the long-run benefits will always outweigh the costs of improving quality.

LO8: Know what tools are used to identify quality control problems. Control charts, cause-and-effect diagrams, and Pareto charts are tools used to identify quality problems. Control charts show the results of statistical process control measures for a sample, batch, or some other unit over time. The cause-and-effect diagram defines the effect and lists events (causes) that may contribute to the problem. Pareto charts are used to display the number of problems or defects in a product over time as bars of varying length.

LO9: Know why time is important in a competitive environment. Success in competitive markets increasingly demands ever shorter new product development time and more rapid customer response time. Fast response itself is often a major quality attribute. Response time improvements often drive simultaneous improvements in quality and productivity.

KEY TERMS

appraisal costs (also called *detection costs*), 490

break-even time (BET), 495

cause-and-effect analysis, 494

control chart, 493

customer response time, 496

diagnostic signal, 493

external failure costs, 490

internal failure costs, 490

just-in-time, 486

new product development time, 495

on-time performance, 496

operational measures of time, 496

Pareto chart, 494

prevention costs, 490

quality, 488

service, 488

warning signal, 493

REVIEW QUESTIONS

16.1 What is the meaning of the terms and concepts listed in Key Terms?

16.2 What are the three factors that relate to meeting customer requirements? Describe each.

16.3 How does the quality-based view differ from the traditional management of inspections?

16.4 Why does quality-based management expect to earn higher profits?

16.5 How do "service" and "quality" differ?

16.6 What are the two costs of controlling quality?

16.7 What are the two costs of failing to control quality?

CRITICAL ANALYSIS AND DISCUSSION QUESTIONS

16.8 How does service relate to customers' expectations?

16.9 Can you think of any products for which one or several of the elements of service, quality, and cost are not important to the customer? If so, explain why.

16.10 How might a manufacturing system differ under a quality-based view versus the traditional view of managing quality?

16.11 Based on the Real World Application, "The International Effects of Labor Strife and JIT," what are some possible shortcomings of implementing JIT?

16.12 What are examples of a warning signal and a diagnostic signal?

16.13 How can control charts be used? Give four different examples.

16.14 How are JIT and TQM conducive to each other?

16.15 Why is time important in a competitive environment?

16.16 Why would improvements in response time drive improvements in quality and productivity? Use a specific example.

16.17 Southwest Airlines has emphasized the importance of on-time flight arrivals. Why?

16.18 Allegiance Insurance Company sends a questionnaire to policyholders who have filed a claim. The questionnaire asks them whether they are satisfied with the way the claim has been handled. Why does Allegiance Insurance do this?

16.19 Why were course evaluations by students introduced to the classrooms? Why were they introduced during the 1960s?

16.20 What are two examples of managers responding to the accounting system instead of TQM initiatives?

EXERCISES

16.21 Quality According to the Customer (L.O. 4)

What are the three most important elements of service for each of the following products?
(a) Tuxedo for a bridegroom.
(b) Microwave oven.
(c) Accounting course at an university.
(d) Cruise on a Princess ship.
(e) Frozen dinner.

16.22 Quality According to the Customer (L.O. 4)

What are the three most important elements of service for each of the following products?
(a) Cowboy boots.
(b) Televisions.
(c) Meals in a fine restaurant.
(d) Student study guides for managerial accounting.
(e) Dishwashers.

16.23 Quality According to the Customer (L.O. 4)

What are the three most important elements of service for each of the following products?
(a) Personal computer keyboards.
(b) Portable compact disc players.
(c) Checking accounts.
(d) Taxi rides through New York.
(e) Sewing machines.

16.24 Costs of Quality (L.O. 5)

Vedral Industries manufactures computer printers. The following represents its financial information for two years:

	Year 1	Year 2
Sales	$2,450,000	$2,200,000
Costs		
Process inspection	16,500	18,800
Scrap	18,500	19,300
Quality training	198,000	130,000
Warranty repairs	43,000	48,000
Testing equipment	70,000	70,000
Customer complaints	28,000	34,000
Rework	170,000	185,000
Preventive maintenance	135,000	95,000
Materials inspection	65,000	48,000
Field testing	94,000	124,000

Required

a. Classify these items into prevention, appraisal, internal failure, or external failure costs.

b. Calculate the ratio of the prevention, appraisal, internal failure, and external failure costs to sales for year 1 and year 2.

16.25 Costs of Quality (L.O. 5)

Owenborrogh Corporation manufactures air conditioners. The following represents its financial information for two years.

	Year 1	Year 2
Sales	$1,960,000	$1,760,000
Costs		
Process inspection	13,200	15,000
Scrap	14,800	15,500
Quality training	158,000	105,000
Warranty repairs	34,000	38,000
Testing equipment	56,000	56,000
Customer complaints	22,500	27,200
Rework	136,000	148,000
Preventive maintenance	108,000	76,000
Materials inspection	52,000	38,000
Field testing	75,000	99,000

Required

a. Classify these items into prevention, appraisal, internal failure, or external failure costs.

b. Calculate the ratio of the prevention, appraisal, internal failure, and external failure costs to sales for year 1 and year 2.

16.26 Costs of Quality (L.O. 5)

Ramirez Corporation manufactures refrigerators. The following represents its financial information for two years.

	Year 1	Year 2
Sales	$3,920,000	$3,520,000
Costs		
Process inspection	26,400	30,000
Scrap	28,800	30,100
Quality training	305,000	220,000
Warranty repairs	70,000	75,000
Testing equipment	115,000	115,000
Customer complaints	44,500	54,200
Rework	272,000	195,000
Preventive maintenance	220,000	152,000
Materials inspection	105,000	75,000
Field testing	150,000	200,000

Required

a. Classify these items into prevention, appraisal, internal failure, or external failure costs.

b. Calculate the ratio of the prevention, appraisal, internal failure, and external failure costs to sales for year 1 and year 2.

16.27	Trading-Off Costs of Quality (L.O. 6)	Using the costs calculated in Exercise 16.24, construct a cost of quality report for year 1 and year 2.
16.28	Trading-Off Costs of Quality (L.O. 6)	Using the costs calculated in Exercise 16.25, construct a cost of quality report for year 1 and year 2.
16.29	Trading-Off Costs of Quality (L.O. 6)	Using the costs calculated in Exercise 16.26, construct a cost of quality report for year 1 and year 2.

16.30 Quality versus Costs (L.O. 6)

Canadian Seltzers has discovered a problem involving its mix of flavor to seltzer water that costs the company $3,000 in waste and $2,500 in lost business per period. There are two alternative solutions. The first is to lease a new mix regulator at a cost of $4,000 per period, which would save $2,000 in waste and $2,000 in lost business. The second alternative is to hire an additional employee to manually monitor the existing regulator at a cost of $2,500 per period, saving $1,500 in waste and $1,800 in lost business per period.

Required   Prepare a differential analysis of the two alternatives. Which alternative should Canadian choose?

16.31 Quality versus Costs (L.O. 6)

Hillman Industries has discovered a problem involving the mix of lye to the dry concrete mix that costs the company $5,000 in waste and $3,500 in lost business per period. There are two alternative solutions. The first is to lease a new mix regulator at a cost of $3,500 per period, which would save $3,500 in waste and $2,000 in lost business. The second alternative is to hire an additional employee to manually monitor the existing regulator at a cost of $3,000 per period, saving $2,500 in waste and $2,000 in lost business per period.

Required   Prepare a differential analysis of the two alternatives. Which alternative should Hillman choose?

16.32 Quality versus Costs (L.O. 6)

Carlson Corporation has discovered a problem involving welding its bicycle frames that costs the company $3,000 in waste and $1,500 in lost business per period. There are two alternative solutions. The first is to lease a new automated welder at a cost of $3,500 per period, which would save $1,500 in waste and $1,000 in lost business. The second alternative is to hire an additional employee to manually weld the frames at a cost of $3,000 per period, which would save $2,500 in waste and $1,000 in lost business per period.

Required   Prepare a differential analysis of the two alternatives. Which alternative should Carlson choose?

16.33 Break-Even Time (L.O. 9)

Dallas Oil Company's research and development department is presenting a proposal for new product research. The new product will require research, development, and design investments of $300 million (discounted cash flow). Sales will begin after three years and will generate an annual discounted net cash flow of $125 million starting in year four.

Required   Calculate the break-even time for the new product.

16.34 Break-Even Time (L.O. 9)

Nugget Company's research and development department is presenting a proposal for new product research. The new product will require research, development, and design investments of $500,000 (discounted cash flow). Sales will begin after two years and will generate an annual discounted net cash flow of $200,000 starting in year three.

Required   Calculate the break-even time for the new product.

16.35 Break-Even Time (L.O. 9)

Peugeot Corporation's research and development department is presenting a proposal for new product research. The new product will require research, development, and design investments of $8 million (discounted cash flow). Sales will begin after two years and will generate an annual discounted net cash flow of $1.5 million starting in year three.

Required   Calculate the break-even time for the new product.

PROBLEMS

16.36   Just-in-Time   Individually or as a group with your classmates, interview the manager of a retail (or whole-sale) store such as a music store, an automobile parts store, or the parts department of an appliance dealership. Ask the manager how items are ordered to replace those sold. For example, does he or she order based on observing inventory levels or place an order each time a customer buys an item? Does he or she appear to use just-in-time inventory? Write a report to your instructor summarizing the results of your interview.

16.37   Total Quality Management   Individually or as a group with your classmates, interview the manager of a fast-food restaurant. Ask the manager how quality of service is measured and used to evaluate his or her performance. Write a report to your instructor summarizing the results of your interview.

16.38   Identifying Quality Control Problems   Individually or as a group with your classmates, observe an organization of your choice—wholesale, retail, or service. Give examples of warning and diagnostic signals the organization uses. How could it use control charts, Pareto charts, and cause-and-effect analysis?

16.39   Break-Even Time   Refer to Exercise 16.33. What steps can Dallas Oil Company take to reduce break-even time on the project?

16.40   Break-Even Time   Refer to Exercise 16.34. What steps can Nugget Company take to reduce break-even time on the project?

16.41   Quality Control   Norsk Ferries operates daily round-trip voyages between Seattle and Vancouver using a fleet of three ferries, the *Sea Quill,* the *Neptune,* and the *Orcas.*

   The budgeted amount of fuel for each round-trip is the average fuel usage, which over the last 12 months has been 150 gallons. Norsk has set the upper control limit at 180 gallons and the lower control limit at 130 gallons. The operations manager received the following report for round-trip fuel usage by the three ferries for the period:

| | **Number of Gallons per Round-Trip** | | |
Trip	Sea Quill	Neptune	Orcas
1	156	155	146
2	141	141	156
3	146	144	167
4	152	161	156
5	156	138	183
6	161	170	177
7	167	149	189
8	186	159	171
9	173	152	176
10	179	140	185

Required

a.   Create quality control charts for round-trip fuel usage for each of the three ferries for the period. What inferences can you draw from them?

b.   Some managers propose that Norsk present its quality control charts in monetary terms rather than in physical amount (gallons) terms. What are the advantages and disadvantages of using monetary fuel costs rather than gallons in the quality control charts?

16.42 Break-Even Time, Working Backward

Tiju Instruments is considering manufacturing the M-Board, a new mother board for personal computers. The new product development committee will not approve a new product proposal if it has a break-even time of more than four years. If the project is approved, the investments to make the M-Board will begin on January 1, Year 1. The projected sales for the M-Board are $5 million each year for years 1 through 4. The costs of manufacturing, distribution, marketing, and customer service are expected to be $3 million each year.

Assume that all cash flows are discounted.

Required

a. What is the maximum cash investment that the new product development committee will agree to fund for the M-Board project?

b. Why might Tiju specify a policy not to fund new product proposals with an estimated breakeven of more than four years?

16.43 Quality Improvement

Billington Corporation makes bicycle frames in two processes, tubing and welding. The tubing and welding processes have a capacity of 100,000 and 150,000 units per year, respectively. Costs of quality information follow:

Design of product and process costs	$220,000
Inspection and testing costs	85,000
Scrap costs (all in the tubing department)	50,000

The demand is very strong. Billington can sell all of the output it can produce at $50 per frame.

Billington can begin producing only 100,000 units in the tubing department because of capacity constraints on the tubing machines; any defective units it produces are scrapped. Of the 100,000 units started at the tubing department, 10,000 units (10 percent) are scrapped. (Scrap is detected at the end of the tubing operation.) Scrap costs, based on total (fixed and variable) manufacturing costs incurred through the tubing operation, equal $35 per unit:

Direct materials (variable)	$18
Direct manufacturing, setup, and materials handling labor (variable)	7
Equipment, rent, and other overhead (fixed)	10
	$35

The good units from the tubing department are sent to the welding department. Variable manufacturing costs at the welding department are $3.50 per unit; it has no scrap. Therefore, Billington's total sales amount equals the tubing department's output.

Billington's designers have determined that adding a different type of material to the existing direct materials would reduce scrap to zero, but it would increase the variable costs per unit in the tubing department by $2. Recall that only 100,000 units can be started each year.

Required

a. What is the additional direct materials cost of implementing the new method?

b. What is the additional benefit to Billington from using the new material and improving quality?

c. Should Billington use the new materials?

d. What other nonfinancial and qualitative factors should Billington consider in making the decision?

SOLUTIONS TO SELF-STUDY QUESTIONS

1. **a.** and **b.**

MERIDETH INDUSTRIES
Cost of Quality Report
For the Year Ended December 31

	Amounts		Percentage of Sales (Sales = $450,000)
Costs of quality			
Prevention costs			
Employee training	$13,000		
Materials inspection	6,500	$19,500	4.3%
Appraisal costs			
Finished goods inspection		15,000	3.3
Internal failure costs			
Scrap		8,500	1.9
External failure costs			
Returned goods	$ 3,000		
Customer complaints	8,000	11,000	2.4
Total costs of quality		$54,000	12.0%*

*Slight difference due to rounding.

2. The break-even time is calculated as

$$\frac{\text{Investment}}{\text{Annual net discounted cash flow}} + \begin{array}{l}\text{Time period from}\\\text{approval to}\\\text{providing product}\end{array}$$

$$\frac{\$150,000}{(\$1,100,000 - \$800,000)} + .75 \text{ years} = 1.25 \text{ years}$$

The break-even time for the roller blade line is 1.25 years.

Planning and Budgeting

LEARNING OBJECTIVES

After reading this chapter, you should be able to:

1. Understand the role of budgets in overall organization plans.

2. Understand the importance of people in the budgeting process.

3. Estimate sales.

4. Develop production and cost budgets.

5. Estimate cash flows.

6. Develop budgeted financial statements.

7. Explain budgeting in service, retail and wholesale, and nonprofit organizations.

8. Explain why ethical issues arise in budgeting.

The use of budgeting in organizations was well stated by a company's controller who explained,

> At our company, we view our master **budget** as a blueprint for operations, much like an architect's blueprint for the construction of a building. Like the architect's blueprint, our master budget helps us plan and coordinate activities, determine the means for achieving our goals, and establish some norms against which we can measure our performance. We consider our budget to be a comprehensive plan through which all levels of management formally indicate what they expect the future to hold. It expresses, in dollars, our plans for achieving company goals.[1]

This chapter shows how a master budget is developed and how it fits into the overall plan for achieving organization goals. Before we investigate the details of developing a master budget, we discuss the way that strategic planning can increase competitiveness and affect global operations.

HOW STRATEGIC PLANNING INCREASES COMPETITIVENESS

During the strategic planning process, companies often outline their **critical success factors,** their strengths that are responsible for making them successful. Critical success factors enable a company to outperform its competitors. By identifying these factors and ensuring that they are incorporated into the strategic plan, companies are able to maintain an edge over competitors. In addition, important critical success factors can be exploited to improve the company's overall competitiveness.

For example, Southwest Airlines has relied on several factors to maintain its competitive edge. It keeps its prices consistently low and routes in the short to medium range and uses only one type of plane (keeping costs to a minimum). The company knows that these are among its critical success factors and has continued to increase its competitiveness by building these factors into its strategic planning process.

STRATEGIC ADVANTAGES IN A GLOBAL ECONOMY

McDonald's has successfully used its name recognition and its reputation for consistency and value to succeed internationally. McDonald's international success is just one benefit of its long-term commitment to value, quality, and consistency.

It is not always enough simply to identify critical success factors and build them into the strategic planning process. Large companies also must consider expanding their businesses overseas in what is increasingly becoming a global economy. The idea is to exploit the company's strategic advantages in the international marketplace.

For example, McDonald's has developed expertise in the fast-food business over many years, which it has used to establish a solid presence in the United

States. As McDonald's began strategic planning for the future, it realized that its expertise and worldwide reputation could be used to successfully operate in other countries. As a result, McDonald's has expanded throughout the world and continues to use its strategic advantages (e.g., name recognition, value, quality, and consistency) to succeed in areas outside the United States.

---

[1]Source: Interview with the company's controller.

THE OVERALL PLAN

A **master budget** is part of an overall organization plan for the next year made up of three components: (1) organization goals, (2) the strategic long-range profit plan, and (3) the master budget (tactical short-range profit plan).

Organization Goals

organization goals
A company's broad objectives established by management that employees work to achieve.

Organization goals are the broad objectives established by management that company employees work to achieve. For example, the following quote is taken from internal documents of a manufacturing company in the paper industry:

> Our organizational goal is to increase earnings steadily while maintaining our current share of market sales and maintain profitability within the top one-third of our industry. We plan to achieve this goal while providing our customers with high-quality products and meeting our social responsibilities to our employees and the communities in which they live.[2]

Such broad goals provide a philosophical statement that the company is expected to follow in its operations. Many companies include their goal statements in published codes of conduct and annual reports to stockholders.

Strategic Long-Range Profit Plan

strategic long-range plan
A statement detailing steps to take to achieve a company's organization goals.

Although a statement of goals is necessary to guide an organization, it is important to detail the specific steps required to achieve them.[3] These steps are expressed in a **strategic long-range plan.** Because the long-range plans look into the intermediate and distant future, they are usually stated in rather broad terms. Strategic plans discuss the major capital investments required to maintain present facilities, increase capacity, diversify products and/or processes, and develop particular markets. For example, the previously mentioned paper company's strategies, as stated in its policy manual, included the following:

1. *Cost control.* Optimize contribution from existing product lines by holding product cost increases to less than the general rate of inflation. This will involve acquiring new machinery proposed in the capital budget as well as replacing our five least efficient plants over the next five years.
2. *Market share.* Maintain our market share by providing a level of service and quality comparable to our top competitors. This requires improving our quality control so that customer complaints and returned merchandise are reduced from a current level of 4 percent to 1 percent within two years.[4]

Each strategy statement was supported by projected activity levels (sales volumes, aggregate costs, and cash flow projections) for each of the next five years. At this stage, the plans were not stated in much detail, but they were well thought out. Hence, the plans provided a general framework for guiding management's operating decisions.

The Master Budget (Tactical Short-Range Profit Plan): Tying the Strategic Plan to the Operating Plan

Long-range plans are achieved in year-by-year steps. The guidance is more specific for the coming year than it is for more distant years. The plan for the coming year is called the *master budget.* The master budget is also known as the *static budget,* the *budget plan,* or the *planning budget.* The income statement portion of the master budget is often called the **profit plan.** The master budget indicates the sales levels, production and cost levels, income, and cash flows anticipated for the coming

---

[2]Taken from the company's internal documents.
[3]A classic discussion of organization goal setting is provided by J. March and H. Simon, *Organizations* (New York: John Wiley & Sons, 1958).
[4]Taken from the company's internal documents.

ILLUSTRATION   17.1   **Organizational and Individual Interaction in Developing the Master Budget**

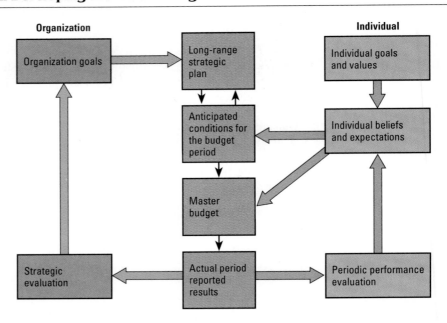

Organization

Individual

profit plan
The income statement portion of the master budget.

year. In addition, these budget data are used to construct a budgeted statement of financial position (balance sheet).

Budgeting is a dynamic process that ties together goals, plans, decision making, and employee performance evaluation. The master budget and its relationship to other plans, accounting reports, and management decision-making processes is diagrammed in Illustration 17.1. On the left side are the organizational goals, strategies, and objectives that set the company's long-term plan. The master budget is derived from the long-range plan in consideration of conditions expected during the coming period. Such plans are subject to change as the events of the year unfold. Recently, the long-range plan for a U.S. automobile manufacturer called for developing several new product lines but unfavorable short-run economic conditions required their postponement.

benchmarking
The continuous process of measuring products, services, or activities against competitors' performance.

The conditions anticipated for the coming year are based in part on managers' near-term projections. Companies may gather this information from production managers, purchasing agents (materials prices), the accounting department, and employee relations (wage agreements), among others. As part of a **benchmarking** activity, some companies gather information through "competitive intelligence," speaking to their competitors, customers, and suppliers.

THE HUMAN ELEMENT IN BUDGETING

L.O. 2: Understand the importance of people in the budgeting process.

A number of factors, including their personal goals and values, affect managers' beliefs about the coming period. Although budgets are often viewed in purely quantitative, technical terms, the importance of this human factor cannot be overemphasized. The individual's relationship to the budget is diagrammed on the right side of Illustration 17.1.

Budget preparation rests on human estimates of an unknown future. People's forecasts are likely to be greatly influenced by their experiences with various segments of the company. For example, district sales managers are in an excellent position to

---

REAL WORLD APPLICATION | **Different Cultures Use Different Approaches to Budgeting**

   Recent surveys indicate that master budgets are used around the world in countries such as Australia, the United Kingdom, and Japan. In fact, more than 90 percent of all companies surveyed in these countries utilize a master budget. Differences arise however, with respect to budget planning participants and budget goals.

Of Japanese firms, 67 percent request division managers' participation compared to 78 percent in the United States. Return on investment is the most important budget goal in the United States; the Japanese focus on sales revenue. (Both countries consider operating income to be the second most important budget goal.)

Although different cultures focus on different elements of the budget, master budgets are a common business practice from one country to the next.

Source: Working Paper by T. Asada, J. Bailes, and M. Amano, "An Empirical Study of Japanese and American Budget Planning and Control Systems," Tsu Kuba University and Oregon State University, 1989.

---

project customer orders over the next several months, but market researchers are usually better able to identify long-run market trends and make macro forecasts of sales. One challenge of budgeting is to identify who in the organization is best able to provide the most accurate information about particular topics.

The Value of Employee Participation

participative budgeting
The use of input from lower- and middle-management employees; also called *grass roots budgeting.*

The use of input from lower- and middle-management employees is often called **participative budgeting** or *grass roots budgeting.* The use of lower and middle managers in budgeting has an obvious cost; it is time-consuming. It also has some benefits; it enhances employee motivation and acceptance of goals and provides information that enables employees to associate rewards and penalties with performance. Participative budgeting can yield information that employees know but managers do not.

A number of studies have shown that employees often provide inaccurate data when asked to give budget estimates. They may request more money than they need because they expect their request to be cut. Employees who believe that the budget will be used as a norm for evaluating their performance may provide an estimate that will not be too hard to achieve.

Thus, managers usually view the technical steps required to construct a comprehensive tactical budget plan in the context of the effect that people have on the budget and the effect that the budget will have on them. Ideally, the budget will motivate people and facilitate their activities so that organization goals can be achieved.

DEVELOPING THE MASTER BUDGET

Although each organization is unique in the way it puts together its budget, all budgeting processes share some common elements. After organizational goals, strategies, and long-range plans have been developed, work begins on the master budget, a detailed budget for the coming fiscal year with some less-detailed figures for subsequent years. Although budgeting is an ongoing process in most companies, the bulk of the work is usually done in the six months immediately preceding the beginning of the coming fiscal year. Final budget approvals by the chief executive and board of directors are made a month to six weeks before the beginning of the fiscal year.

To envision the master budgeting process, picture the financial statements most commonly prepared by companies: the income statement, the balance sheet, and the cash flow statement. Then imagine preparing these statements before the fiscal period.

WHERE TO START? WITH YOUR CUSTOMERS (FORECASTING SALES)

L.O. 3: Estimate sales.

Forecasting sales is perhaps the most difficult aspect of budgeting because it involves considerable subjectivity. To reduce subjectivity and gather as much information as possible, management often uses a number of different methods to obtain forecasts from a number of different sources. We begin with a forecast of revenues for the budget period.

Sales Staff

Salespeople are in the unique position of being close to the customers, and they may possess the best information in the company about customers' immediate and near-term needs. As previously indicated, however, they may be tempted to bias their sales forecasts if such forecasts are used as the norm for performance evaluation.

For example, Peter Jones is a district sales manager for Shasta Design, Inc., which manufactures tents for backpacking. The company purchases fabric, makes tents, and sells them to companies that add frames. For the coming budget year, he expects his district's sales to be $1 million, although they could drop as low as $800,000 or run as high as $1.2 million. His bonus at the end of next year will be 1 percent of the excess of actual sales over the sales budget. So if the budget is $1 million and actual sales are also $1 million, he will receive no bonus.

If Peter provides a sales forecast that is too low, however, he will not be able to justify retaining his current number of employees. If his sales forecasts are consistently much below the actual sales results or below what management thinks his district should be doing, he will lose credibility. Thus, Peter decides on a conservative but reasonable sales forecast of $900,000, which, he believes, will give him a high probability of getting a bonus and a low risk of losing his other objectives.

Of course, if Peter's performance were compared against a different set of norms, he would have a different incentive. If, for instance, his bonus were a fixed percentage of sales, he would have incentive to maximize sales. Then he would be motivated to make an optimistic sales forecast to justify obtaining a larger sales staff. The high sales forecast also would be used to estimate the amount of production capacity needed, thus ensuring that adequate inventory would be available to satisfy any and all customer needs. Of course, the managers and staff who receive forecasts usually recognize the subjectivity of the situation. As Peter's superior put it, "We've received sales forecasts from him for several years, and they're always a bit conservative. We don't ask him to revise his estimates. We simply take his conservatism into account when we put together the overall sales forecast."

Market Researchers

To provide a check on forecasts from local sales personnel, management often turns to market researchers. This group probably does not have the same incentives that sales personnel have to bias the budget. Furthermore, researchers have a different perspective on the market. They may know little about customers' immediate needs, but they can predict long-term trends in attitudes and the effects of social and economic changes on the company's sales, potential markets, and products.

The Delphi Technique

Delphi technique
Forecasting method in which individual forecasts of group members are submitted anonymously and evaluated by the group as a whole.

The **Delphi technique** is another method used to enhance forecasting and reduce bias in estimates. With this method, members of the forecasting group prepare individual forecasts and submit them anonymously. Each group member obtains a copy of all forecasts but is unaware of their sources. The group then discusses the results. In this way, differences among individual forecasts can be addressed and reconciled without involving the personality or position of individual forecasters. After the differences are discussed, each group member prepares a new forecast and distributes it anonymously to the others. These forecasts are then discussed in the same manner as before. The process is repeated until the forecasts converge on a single best estimate of the coming year's sales level.

Trend Analysis

Trend analysis, which can range from a simple visual extrapolation of points on a graph to a highly sophisticated computerized time series analysis, also may be helpful in preparing sales forecasts.

Time series techniques use only past observations of the data series to be forecasted. No other data are included. This methodology is justified on the grounds that since all factors that affect the data series are reflected in the actual past observations, the past data are the best reflection of available information. This approach also is relatively economical because only a list of past sales figures is needed, no other data are gathered.

Forecasting techniques based on trend analysis often require long series of past data to derive a suitable solution. Generally, when these models are used in accounting applications, monthly data are required to obtain an adequate number of observations.

Econometric Models

Another forecasting approach is to enter past sales data into a regression model to obtain a statistical estimate of factors affecting sales. For example, the predicted sales for the coming period may be related to such factors as economic indicators, consumer-confidence indexes, back-order volume, and other internal and external factors that the company deems relevant.

Advocates of these **econometric models** contend that they can include many relevant predictors and manipulating the assumed values of the predictors makes it possible to examine a variety of hypothetical conditions and relate them to the sales forecast. This is particularly useful for performing sensitivity analysis, which we discuss later in this chapter.

Sophisticated analytical models for forecasting are now widely available. Most companies' computers have software packages that allow economical use of these models. Nonetheless, it is important to remember that no model removes the uncertainty surrounding sales forecasts. Management often has found that the intuition of local sales personnel is a better predictor than sophisticated analysis and models. As in any management decision, cost-benefit tests should be used to determine which methods are most appropriate.

Comprehensive Illustration

To make our discussion of the budgeting process more concrete, we'll develop the budget for Shasta Design, Inc., using a manufacturing example because it is the most comprehensive. The methods we discuss are also applicable to nonmanufacturing organizations.

Assume that Shasta Design's management went through the steps discussed here and arrived at the following sales budget for the next budget year:

	Units	Price per Unit	Total Sales Revenues
Estimated sales	6,400	$800	$5,120,000

The **production budget** plans the resources needed to meet current sales demand and ensure that inventory levels are sufficient for expected activity levels. It is necessary, therefore, to determine the required inventory level for the beginning and end of the budget period. The production level may be computed from the basic cost flow equation (also known as the *basic inventory formula*)

$$\text{Beginning balance} + \text{Transfers in} - \text{Transfers out} = \text{Ending balance}$$
$$BB \quad + \quad TI \quad - \quad TO \quad = \quad EB$$

---

trend analysis
Forcasting method that ranges from simple visual extrapolation of points on a graph to highly sophisticated computerized time series analysis.

econometric models
Statistical method of forecasting economic data using regression models.

FORECASTING PRODUCTION

L.O. 4: Develop production and cost budgets.

ILLUSTRATION 17.2

SHASTA DESIGN, INC.
Production Budget
For the Budget Year Ended December 31
(in units)

Expected sales...................	6,400 units
Add: Desired ending inventory of finished goods..................	1,000
Total needs....................	7,400
Less: Beginning inventory of finished goods..................	900
Units to be produced.............	6,500

production budget
Production plan of resources needed to meet current sales demand and ensure that inventory levels are sufficient for future sales.

Adapting that equation to inventories, production, and sales, we have

$$\begin{array}{ccccc} \text{Units in} & & \text{Required} & \text{Budgeted} & & \text{Units in} \\ \text{beginning} & + & \text{production} & - \text{ sales units} & = & \text{ending} \\ \text{inventory} & & \text{units} & \text{for the period} & & \text{inventory} \end{array}$$

Rearranging terms to solve for required production

$$\begin{array}{ccccc} \text{Units} & & \text{Budgeted} & \text{Units in} & \text{Units in} \\ \text{required in} & = & \text{sales units} & + \text{ ending} & - \text{ beginning} \\ \text{production} & & \text{for the period} & \text{inventory} & \text{inventory} \end{array}$$

This equation states that production equals the sales demand plus or minus an inventory adjustment. Production and inventory are assumed to be stated in equivalent finished units.

Shasta Design's sales budget projects sales of 6,400 units. Management estimates that 900 units will be in the beginning inventory of finished goods. Based on management's analysis, the required ending inventory is estimated to be 1,000 units. We assume for simplicity that there is no beginning or ending work in process inventory. With this information, the budgeted level of production is computed:

$$\begin{array}{l} \text{Required} \\ \text{production} \end{array} = \begin{array}{c} 6{,}400 \text{ units} \\ \text{(sales)} \end{array} + \begin{array}{c} 1{,}000 \text{ units} \\ \text{(ending inventory)} \end{array} - \begin{array}{c} 900 \text{ units} \\ \text{(beginning inventory)} \end{array}$$

$$= \underline{\underline{6{,}500 \text{ units}}}$$

Illustration 17.2 presents the production budget for Shasta Design. Management of the production facilities reviews the production budget to ascertain whether the budgeted level of production can be reached with the capacity available. If not, management may revise the sales forecast or consider ways to increase capacity. If it appears that production capacity will exceed requirements, management may want to consider other opportunities for using the capacity.

One benefit of the budgeting process is that it facilitates the coordination of activities. It is far better to learn about discrepancies between the sales forecast and production capacity in advance so that remedial action can be taken. Lost sales opportunities due to inadequate production capacity or unnecessary idle capacity can thus be avoided.

FORECASTING PRODUCTION COSTS

Once the sales and production budgets have been developed and the efforts of the sales and production groups are coordinated, the budgeted cost of goods sold (production costs) can be prepared. The primary job is to estimate costs of direct materials, direct labor, and manufacturing overhead at budgeted levels of production.

ILLUSTRATION   17.3

SHASTA DESIGN, INC.
Direct Materials Budget
For the Budget Year Ended December 31
(in units)

Units to be produced (from the production
budget in Illustration 17.2).   6,500

	Material R	Material S
Direct materials needed per unit.	3 yards	5 yards
Total production needs (amount per unit times 6,500 units)	19,500	32,500
Add: Desired ending inventory	1,300	4,600
Total direct materials needs	20,800	37,100
Less: Beginning inventory of materials.	2,200	4,000
Direct materials to be purchased	18,600 yards	33,100 yards
Cost of materials, per yard	$10	$30
Total cost of direct materials to be purchased	$186,000	$ 993,000
Sum of materials R and S to be purchased ($186,000 + $993,000).		$1,179,000

Direct Materials

Direct materials purchases needed for the budget period are derived from this equation:

$$\begin{matrix}\text{Required} \\ \text{materials} \\ \text{purchases}\end{matrix} = \begin{matrix}\text{Materials to} \\ \text{be used in} \\ \text{production}\end{matrix} + \begin{matrix}\text{Estimated} \\ \text{ending} \\ \text{materials} \\ \text{inventory}\end{matrix} - \begin{matrix}\text{Estimated} \\ \text{beginning} \\ \text{materials} \\ \text{inventory}\end{matrix}$$

The beginning and ending levels of materials inventory for the budget period are estimated, often with the help of an inventory control model; the materials to be used in production are based on production requirements.

Production at Shasta Design for the coming period will require two kinds of materials, R and S, as follows:

	Estimated Production Material Data	
	R	**S**
Material per unit of output	3 yards	5 yards
Beginning materials inventory	2,200 yards	4,000 yards
Ending inventory	1,300 yards	4,600 yards
Cost per yard	$10	$30

The cost per yard is expected to remain constant during the coming budget period. Required production for the production budget is 6,500 units.

Computation of the required materials purchases in units of each material follows:

$$R = (6,500 \times 3) + 1,300 - 2,200$$
$$= 18,600 \text{ yards}$$

$$S = (6,500 \times 5) + 4,600 - 4,000$$
$$= 33,100 \text{ yards}$$

In dollar terms, this amounts to estimated purchases of $186,000 for R (18,600 × $10) and $993,000 for S (33,100 × $30).

The direct materials budget, Illustration 17.3, shows the materials required for production.

ILLUSTRATION   17.4

SHASTA DESIGN, INC.
Direct Labor Budget
For the Budget Year Ended December 31

Units to be produced (from Illustration 17.2)	6,500
Direct labor time per unit (in hours).	7.3
Total direct labor-hours needed	47,450
Direct labor cost per hour.	$20
Total direct labor cost	$949,000

Direct Labor

Estimates of direct labor costs often are obtained from engineering and production management. For Shasta Design, the direct labor costs are estimated at 7.3 hours per unit at $20 per hour (or $146 per output unit produced). Thus, for the budget year, the budgeted direct labor cost of production of 6,500 units is $949,000, as computed and shown in Illustration 17.4.

Overhead

Unlike direct materials and direct labor, which often can be determined from an engineer's specifications for a product, overhead is composed of many different types of costs with varying cost behaviors. Some overhead costs vary in direct proportion to production (variable overhead); some costs vary with production but in a step fashion (for example, supervisory labor); and other costs are fixed and remain the same unless capacity or long-range policies are changed. Other costs (e.g., some maintenance costs) do not necessarily vary with production but may be changed at management's discretion.

Budgeting overhead requires an estimate based on production levels, management discretion, long-range capacity and other corporate policies, and external factors such as increases in property taxes. Due to the complexity and diversity of overhead costs, several cost estimation methods are frequently used. To simplify the budgeting process, costs usually are divided into fixed and variable components, with discretionary and semifixed costs treated as fixed costs within the relevant range.

Shasta Design's schedule of budgeted manufacturing overhead is presented in Illustration 17.5. For convenience, after consultation with department management, the budget staff has divided all overhead into fixed and variable costs. Shasta Design now can determine the budgeted total manufacturing costs by adding the three components, materials, labor, and overhead. This total is $3,250,000, as shown in Illustration 17.6.

Completing the Budgeted Cost of Goods Sold

We need only to include the estimated beginning and ending work in process and finished goods inventories to determine the required number of units produced—6,500. As previously indicated, no work in process inventories exist.[5] Finished goods inventories are as follows, assuming that the cost per unit is estimated to be $500 in both beginning and ending inventory:

	Units	Dollars
Beginning finished goods inventory	900	$450,000
Ending finished goods inventory	1,000	500,000

---

[5]If the company has beginning and ending work in process inventories, units are usually expressed as equivalent finished units and treated the way we have treated finished goods inventories. In most companies, estimates of work in process inventories are omitted from the budget because they have a minimal impact on the budget.

ILLUSTRATION 17.5

SHASTA DESIGN, INC.
Schedule of Budgeted Manufacturing Overhead
For the Budget Year Ended December 31

Variable overhead needed to produce 6,500 units		
Indirect materials and supplies..................	$ 38,000	
Materials handing........................	59,000	
Other indirect labor......................	33,000	$ 130,000
Fixed manufacturing overhead		
Supervisory labor.........................	175,000	
Maintenance and repairs	85,000	
Plant administration	173,000	
Utilities	87,000	
Depreciation	280,000	
Insurance	43,000	
Property taxes...........................	117,000	
Other...................................	41,000	1,001,000
Total manufacturing overhead...................		$1,131,000

ILLUSTRATION 17.6

SHASTA DESIGN, INC.
Budgeted Statement of Cost of Goods Sold
For the Budget Year Ended December 31

Beginning work in process inventory...................			–0–
Manufacturing costs			
Direct materials:			
Beginning inventory (2,200 R @ $10 + 4,000 S @ $30).....	$ 142,000		
Purchases (from Illustration 17.3)..................	1,179,000		
Materials available for manufacturing...............	1,321,000		
Less: Ending inventory (1,300 R @ $10 + 4,600 S @ 30)....	(151,000)		
Total direct materials costs		$1,170,000	
Direct labor (from Illustration 17.4)..................		949,000	
Manufacturing overhead (from Illustration 17.5)		1,131,000	
Total manufacturing costs........................			$3,250,000
Deduct: Ending work in process inventory			–0–
Cost of goods manufactured			3,250,000
Add: Beginning finished goods inventory (900 units)[a].........			450,000
Deduct: Ending finished goods inventory (1,000 units)[a]........			(500,000)
Cost of goods sold			$3,200,000

[a]Finished goods are valued at $500 per unit ($3,250,000/6,500 units produced) assuming FIFO. Hence, beginning finished goods inventory is estimated to be $450,000 (900 units × $500), and ending finished goods inventory is estimated to be $500,000 (1,000 units × $500).

Adding the estimated beginning finished goods inventory to the estimated cost of goods manufactured and then deducting the ending finished goods inventory yields a cost of goods sold of $3,200,000, as shown in Illustration 17.6.

This completes the second major step in the budgeting process: determining budgeted production requirements and the cost of goods sold. Obviously, this part of the budgeting effort can be extremely complex for manufacturing companies. It can be very difficult to coordinate production schedules among numerous plants, some using other plants' products as their direct materials. It also is difficult to coordinate production schedules with sales forecasts. New estimates of material availability, labor shortages, strikes, availability of energy, and production capacity often require reworking the entire budget.

Revising the Initial Budget

At this point in the budget cycle, a first-draft budget has been prepared. It usually undergoes a good deal of coordinating and revising before it is considered final. For example, projected production figures may call for revised estimates of direct materials purchases and direct labor costs. Bottlenecks may be discovered in production that will hamper the company's ability to deliver a particular product and thus affect the sales forecast. The revision process may be repeated several times until a coordinated, feasible master budget evolves. No part of the budget is really formally adopted until the board of directors finally approves the master budget.

SELF-STUDY QUESTION

1. The self-study questions in this chapter provide a comprehensive budgeting problem based on data from the example in the chapter.

   Refer to the problem for Shasta Design, Inc., in the chapter example. Assume that the sales forecast was increased to 7,000 units with no change in price. The new target ending inventories are

Finished goods	1,200 units
Material R	1,500 yards
Material S	4,900 yards

   Expected production = 7,300 units.
   Prepare a budgeted cost of goods sold statement and budgeted overhead statement with these new data.

The solution to this question is at the end of this chapter on page 545.

MARKETING AND ADMINISTRATIVE BUDGET

Marketing and administrative costs are difficult to budget and control because management has considerable discretion about how much money is spent. Many companies keep their private airplanes, such as this one, even though they might save money by having executives take commercial flights. The executives point out that the company planes are convenient and that they get more work done when they don't have to deal with crowded airports and inconvenient flight schedules.

Budgeting marketing and administrative costs is very difficult because managers have discretion about how much money is spent and the timing of expenditures. For example, a company hired a new marketing executive who was famous for cost-cutting skills. The executive ordered an immediate 50 percent cut in the company's advertising budget, a freeze on hiring, and a 50 percent cut in the travel budget. As a result, costs fell but with little immediate impact on sales. A year later, looking for new challenges, the executive moved to another company. Soon afterward, the executive's former employers noticed that sales were down because the company had lost market share to some aggressive competitors. Were the marketing executive's cost-cutting actions really in the best interests of the company? To this day, nobody can give a documented answer to that question because it is difficult to prove a causal link between the cost cutting and the subsequent decrease in sales.

In another case, a company's president

ILLUSTRATION 17.7

SHASTA DESIGN, INC.
Schedule of Budgeted Marketing and Administrative Costs
For the Budget Year Ended December 31

Variable marketing costs		
Sales commissions.	$260,000	
Other marketing.	104,000	
Total variable marketing costs		$ 364,000
Fixed marketing costs		
Sales salaries	100,000	
Advertising.	193,000	
Other	78,000	
Total fixed marketing costs		371,000
Total marketing costs.		735,000
Administrative costs (all fixed)		
Administrative salaries	254,000	
Legal and accounting staff.	141,000	
Data processing services.	103,000	
Outside professional services.	39,000	
Depreciation—building, furniture, and equipment	94,000	
Other, including interest.	26,000	
Taxes—other than income	160,000	
Total administrative costs		817,000
Total budgeted marketing and administrative costs.		$1,552,000

was the only one who used the corporate jet, and he used it only rarely. So the internal audit staff recommended selling it. The company president rejected the idea, saying, "One of the reasons I put up with the pressures and responsibilities of this job is because I enjoy some of its perquisites, including the corporate jet." Some costs that appear unnecessary, especially perquisites, are really part of the total compensation package and may therefore be necessary costs.

The budgeting objective here is to estimate the amount of marketing and administrative costs required to operate the company at its projected level of sales and production and to achieve long-term company goals. For example, the budgeted sales figures may be based on a new product promotion campaign. If production and sales are projected to increase, it is likely that an increase in support services—data processing, accounting, personnel, and so forth—will be needed to operate the company at the higher projected levels.

An easy way to deal with the problem is to start with a previous period's actual or budgeted amounts and make adjustments for inflation, changes in operations, and similar changes between periods. This method has been criticized and may be viewed as being very simplistic, but it does have one advantage: it is relatively easy and inexpensive. As always, the benefits of improving budgeting methods must justify their increased costs.

At Shasta Design, each management level submits a budget request for marketing and administrative costs to the next higher level, which reviews it and approves it, usually after some adjustments. The budget is passed up through the ranks until it reaches top management. As shown in Illustration 17.7, the schedule of marketing and administrative costs is divided into variable and fixed components. In this case, variable marketing costs are those that vary with sales (not production). Fixed marketing costs are usually those that can be changed at management's discretion, for example, advertising.

ILLUSTRATION   17.8

SHASTA DESIGN, INC.
Budgeted Income Statement
For the Budget Year Ended December 31

Budgeted revenues		
Sales (6,400 units at $800)		$5,120,000
Costs		
Cost of goods sold		
(from Illustration 17.6)	$3,200,000	
Marketing and administrative costs		
(from Illustration 17.7)	1,552,000	
Total budgeted costs		4,752,000
Operating profit.		368,000
Federal and other income taxes[a]		128,000
Operating profit after taxes		$ 240,000

[a]Computed by the company's tax staff.

PULLING IT TOGETHER INTO THE INCOME STATEMENT

According to the controller at Shasta Design,

> At this point, we're able to put together the entire budgeted income statement for the period (Illustration 17.8), so we can determine our projected operating profits. By making whatever adjustments are required to satisfy generally accepted accounting principles for external reporting, we can project net income after income taxes and earnings per share. If we don't like the results, we go back to the budgeted income statement and, starting at the top, go through each step to see if we can increase sales revenues or cut costs. We usually find some plant overhead, marketing, or administrative costs that can be cut or postponed without doing too much damage to the company's operations.

Shasta Design's board of directors approved the sales, production, and marketing and administrative budgets and budgeted income statements as submitted. Note that the budgeted income statement also includes estimated federal and other income taxes, which the tax staff provided. We will not detail the tax estimation process because it is a highly technical area separate from cost accounting.

SELF-STUDY QUESTION

2. Refer to Self-Study Question 1. Recall that Shasta Design, Inc., has a sales forecast of 7,000 units and new target ending inventories as follows:

Finished goods	1,200 units
Material R	1,500 yards
Material S	4,900 yards

In addition, you learn that income tax expense is $214,547. Variable marketing costs increase proportionately with volume (that is, the amount now is 7,000/6,400 times the amount in the text example).

Prepare a budgeted schedule of marketing and administrative costs and a budgeted income statement.

The solution to this question is at the end of this chapter on page 547.

KEY RELATIONSHIPS: THE SALES CYCLE

Assembling the master budget demonstrates some key relations among sales, accounts receivable, and cash flows in the sales cycle. Advantages of understanding these relations include the ability to solve for unknown amounts and to audit the master budget to ensure that the basic accounting equation has been correctly applied.

At Shasta Design, for example, the relations among budgeted sales, accounts receivable, and cash receipts were as follows:

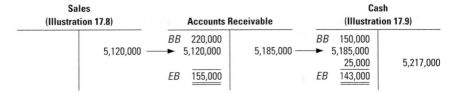

Note: *BB* and *EB* refer to beginning and ending balances. These balances for accounts receivable appear in later illustrations. We present them here to help you see how cash, sales, and accounts receivable are interrelated.

Sales are assumed to be on account.

If an amount in the sales cycle is unknown, the basic accounting equation can be used to find the unknown amount. For example, suppose that all of the amounts in the preceding diagram are known except ending cash balance and sales. Using the basic cost flow equation,

$$BB + TI - TO = EB$$

find sales from the Accounts Receivable account:

$$\$220,000 + TI \text{ (sales)} - \$5,185,000 = \$155,000$$
$$TI = \$155,000 - \$220,000 + \$5,185,000$$
$$TI = \underline{\underline{\$5,120,000}}$$

find ending cash balance from the Cash account:

$$\$150,000 + (\$5,185,000 + \$25,000) - \$5,217,000 = EB$$
$$EB = \underline{\underline{\$143,000}}$$

USING CASH FLOW BUDGETS TO ESTIMATE CASH NEEDS

L.O. 5: Estimate cash flows.

cash budget
A statement of cash on hand at the start of the budget period, expected cash receipts, expected cash disbursements, and the resulting cash balance at the end of the budget period.

Although the budgeted income statement is an important tool for planning operations, a company also requires cash to operate. Cash budgeting is important to ensure company solvency, maximize interest earned on cash balances, and determine whether the company is generating enough cash for present and future operations.

Preparing a **cash budget** requires that all revenues, costs, and other transactions be examined in terms of their effects on cash. The budgeted cash receipts are computed from the collections from accounts receivable, cash sales, sale of assets, borrowing, issuing stock, and other cash-generating activities. Disbursements are computed by counting the cash required to pay for materials purchases, manufacturing and other operations, federal income taxes, and stockholder dividends. In addition, the cash disbursements necessary to repay debt and acquire new assets also must be incorporated into the cash budget.

Shasta Design's cash budget is shown in Illustration 17.9. The source of each item is indicated.

MULTIPERIOD CASH FLOWS

Cash flows often are analyzed in more detail than shown in the Shasta Design example. For example, assume that Near-Cash Wholesale Co. has the following information available about its monthly collection experience for sales or credit:

ILLUSTRATION 17.9

SHASTA DESIGN, INC.
Cash Budget
For the Budget Year Ended December 31

Cash balance beginning of period[a]		$ 150,000
Receipts		
Collections on accounts[a]	$5,185,000	
Sales of assets[a]	25,000	
Total receipts		5,210,000
Less disbursements		
Payments for accounts payable[a]	1,164,000	
Direct labor (from Illustration 17.4)	949,000	
Manufacturing overhead requiring cash less noncash depreciation charges (from Illustration 17.5)	851,000	
Marketing and administrative costs less noncash charges (from Illustration 17.7)	1,458,000	
Payments for federal income taxes (per discussion with the tax staff)	252,000	
Dividends[a]	140,000	
Reduction in long-term debts[a]	83,000	
Acquisition of new assets[b]	320,000	
Total disbursements		5,217,000
Budgeted ending cash balance (ties to Illustration 17.12)		$ 143,000

[a]Estimated by the treasurer's office.

[b]Estimated by the treasurer's office, per the capital budget.

Cash collected from current month's sales	50%
Cash collected from last month's sales	45
Cash discounts taken (percentage of gross sales)	2
Written off as a bad debt	3
	100%

This means that if July's credit sales are $200,000, expected collections are $100,000 in July and $90,000 in August; $4,000 is not expected to be collected because the customers paid early enough to get a discount; and $6,000 is not expected to be collected because these accounts will be written off as bad debts.

Illustration 17.10 shows a multiperiod schedule of cash collections for the three months of the quarter ending September 30 for Near-Cash Wholesale. Assume that the beginning accounts receivable balance on July 1 is expected to be $100,000, all of which is expected to be collected during July. The expected sales for the three months follow:

July sales	$200,000
August sales	300,000
September sales	200,000

The same approach is used for cash disbursements. Illustration 17.11 shows the cash disbursements for Near-Cash Wholesale, which pays for 70 percent of its purchases in the month of purchase and 28 percent in the following month, and takes a 2 percent discount for paying on time. Following is a list of purchases for the three months July through September:

ILLUSTRATION 17.10

NEAR-CASH WHOLESALE CO.
Multiperiod Schedule of Cash Collections
For the Quarter Ended September 30

	Month			Total for
	July	August	September	Quarter
Beginning accounts receivable, July 1, $100,000	$100,000			$100,000
July sales, $200,000[a]	100,000	$ 90,000		190,000
August sales, $300,000[b]		150,000	$135,000	285,000
September sales, $200,000			100,000	100,000
Total cash collections	$200,000	$240,000	$235,000	$675,000

Note: Assumptions for the budget: 50 percent of a month's sales are collected in cash during the month: 45 percent are collected in the next month; 2 percent are taken as a cash discount for early payments; and 3 percent will not be collected because they are written off as bad debts.

[a]50 percent collected in July, 45 percent collected in August, and 5 percent not collected according to the preceding assumption.

[b]50 percent collected in August, 45 percent collected in September, and 5 percent not collected according to the preceding assumption.

ILLUSTRATION 17.11

NEAR-CASH WHOLESALE CO.
Multiperiod Schedule of Cash Disbursements
For the Quarter Ended September 30

	Month			Total for
	July	August	September	Quarter
Beginning accounts payable, July 1, $40,000	$ 40,000			$ 40,000
July purchases. $100,000[a]	70,000	$ 28,000		98,000
August purchases, $150,000[b]		105,000	$ 42,000	147,000
September purchases, $80,000			56,000	56,000
Additional cash payments	70,000	70,000	70,000	210,000
Total cash disbursements	$180,000	$203,000	$168,000	$551,000

Note: Assumptions for the budget: 70 percent of a month's purchases are paid in cash during the month; 28 percent are paid in the next month; and 2 percent are taken as a cash discount for early payments and not paid.

[a]70 percent paid in July, 28 percent paid in August, and 2 percent not paid according to the preceding assumption.

[b]70 percent paid in August, 28 percent paid in September, and 2 percent not paid according to the preceding assumption.

July	$100,000
August	150,000
September	80,000

In addition, all other cash payments are expected to be $70,000 per month. Near-Cash had accounts payable of $40,000 on July 1, all of which it paid in July.

SELF-STUDY QUESTION

3. This question is based on the previous Self-Study Questions in this chapter and on the Shasta Design example in the text. Prepare a cash budget given the revised figures for Shasta Design provided in the previous two Self-Study Questions. Compared to the text example, assume that cash collections will increase proportionately to the increase in sales except that the ending accounts receivable level will increase by another $40,000. Additional payments for purchases of materials will be required, but ending accounts payable also will increase by $2,000. Payments for income taxes will increase to $282,390.

The solution to this question is at the end of this chapter on page 548.

PLANNING FOR THE ASSETS AND LIABILITIES ON THE BUDGETED BALANCE SHEETS

L.O. 6: Develop budgeted financial statements.

budgeted balance sheets
Statements of budgeted financial position.

Budgeted balance sheets, or statements of financial position, combine an estimate of financial position at the beginning of the budget period with the estimated results of operations for the period (from the income statements) and estimated changes in assets and liabilities. The latter result from management's decisions about optimal levels of capital investment in long-term assets (the capital budget), investment in working capital, and financing decisions. Decision making in these areas is, for the most part, the treasurer's function. We assume that these decisions have been made and incorporate their results in the budgeted balance sheets. Illustration 17.12 presents Shasta Design's budgeted balance sheets at the beginning and end of the budget year.

THE BIG PICTURE: HOW IT ALL FITS TOGETHER

We have completed the development of a comprehensive budget for Shasta Design. A model of the budgeting process is presented in Illustration 17.13. Although we have simplified the presentation, you can still see that assembling a master budget is a complex process requiring careful coordination of many different organization segments.

BUDGETING IN SERVICE ORGANIZATIONS

L.O. 7: Explain budgeting in service, retail and wholesale, and nonprofit organizations.

Although a manufacturing operation provides a good comprehensive example, budgeting is used extensively in other environments as well, as discussed in this and the following sections.

A key difference in the master budget of a service enterprise is the absence of product or material inventories. Consequently, neither a production budget (prepared in manufacturing firm budgets) nor a merchandise purchases budget (prepared in merchandising firm budgets) is needed. Instead, service businesses need to carefully coordinate sales (that is, services rendered) with the necessary labor. Managers must ensure that personnel with the right skills are available at the right times.

The budget for David & Sons Company, a regional accounting firm, is developed around the three major services offered: audit, tax, and consulting. Revenue projections are based on estimates of the number and types of clients the firm would service in the budget year and the amount of services requested. The forecasts stem primarily from services provided in previous years with adjustments for new clients, new services to existing clients, loss of clients, and changes in the rates charged for services.

Once the amount of services (expressed in labor-hours) is forecast, the firm develops its budget for personnel. Staffing to meet client needs is a very important part of the budgeting process. As a partner of the firm put it, "If we overestimate the

ILLUSTRATION 17.12

SHASTA DESIGN, INC.
Budgeted Balance Sheets
For the Budget Year Ended December 31
(in thousands)

	Balance (January 1)	Budget Year Additions	Budget Year Subtractions	Balance (December 31)
Assets				
Current assets				
Cash	$ 150[a]	$ 5,210[a]	$ 5.217[a]	$ 143[a]
Accounts receivable	220[b]	5,120[c]	5,185[a]	155[b]
Inventories	592[d]	3,259[e]	3,200[f]	651[g]
Other current assets	23[b]	100[b]	100[b]	23[b]
Total current assets	985	13,689	13,702	972
Long-term assets				
Property, plant, and equipment	2,475[b]	320[a]	300[b]	2,495[b]
Less: Accumulated depreciation	(850)[b]	(374)[h]	(275)[b]	(949)[b]
Total assets	$2,610	$13,635	$13,727	$2,518
Liabilities and Shareholders' Equity				
Current liabilities				
Accounts payable	$ 140[b]	$ 1,179[i]	$ 1,164[a]	$ 155[b]
Taxes payable	156[b]	128[b]	252[a]	32[b]
Current portion of long-term debt	83[b]	–0– [b]	83[a]	–0– [b]
Total current liabilities	379	1,307	1,499	187
Long-term liabilities	576[b]	–0– [b]	–0– [b]	576[b]
Total liabilities	955	1,307	1,499	763
Shareholders' equity				
Common stock	350[b]	–0– [b]	–0– [b]	350[b]
Retained earnings	1,305[b]	240[i]	140[a]	1,405[b]
Total shareholders equity	1,655	240	140	1,755
Total liabilities and shareholders equity	$2,610	$ 1,547	$ 1,639	$2,518

[a]From cash budget (Illustration 17.9).

[b]Estimated by personnel in the company's accounting department

[c]From budgeted income statement (Illustration 17.8). Assumes that all sales are on account.

[d]From budgeted statement of cost of goods sold (Illustration 17.6), sum of beginning direct materials, work in process, and finished goods inventories ($142 + 0 + $450 = $592).

[e]From budgeted statement of costs of goods sold (Illustration 17.6), sum of materials purchases, direct labor, and manufacturing overhead ($1,179 + $949 + $1,131 = $3,259).

[f]From budgeted statement of cost of goods sold (Illustration 17.6).

[g]From budgeted statement of cost of goods sold (Illustration 17.6), sum of ending direct materials, work in process, and finished goods inventories ($151 + $500 = $651).

[h]Depreciation of $280 from schedule of budgeted manufacturing overhead (Illustration 17.5) plus depreciation of $94 from the schedule of budgeted marketing and administrative costs (Illustration 17.7) equals $374 increase in accumulated depreciation.

[i]From budgeted statement of cost of goods sold (Illustration 17.6). Accounts payable increases are assumed to be for materials purchases only.

[i]From budgeted income statement (Illustration 17.8), operating profit after taxes.

amount of services we'll provide, we may lose money because we have overstaffed. Our labor costs will be too high compared to our revenues. If we underestimate, we may lose business because we can't provide the services our clients need."

REAL WORLD APPLICATION	**New Approaches to Budgeting**

 HON Company is the largest maker of mid-priced office furniture in the United States and Canada. HON determined that the budget is an important control device for achieving two strategic objectives: ongoing new product development and rapid continuous improvement. In linking its strategy with the budget, the company discovered that its budget would have to be revised more often than annually.

HON decided to prepare an annual budget every quarter. This requires updating the budget for the next three quarters (prepared in the previous budget) and creating the fourth quarter budget. The five-step process works as follows:

1. Develop the sales budget by product line.

2. Convert the sales budget to a plant production and shipping schedule.
3. Prepare cost/expense budgets for production and distribution and for sales and general administration.
4. Consolidate department and plant budgets and compare budget results with the strategic plan.
5. Prepare a complete budget package for the parent company.

Management and employees at HON believe that by planning in quarterly periods, they can make a fair assessment of their work improvements and thus can set realistic targets.

Source: Drtina, Hoeger, and Schaub, "*Management Accounting,* January" 1996, p. 20.

ILLUSTRATION 17.13 **Assembling the Master Budget: Manufacturing Organization**

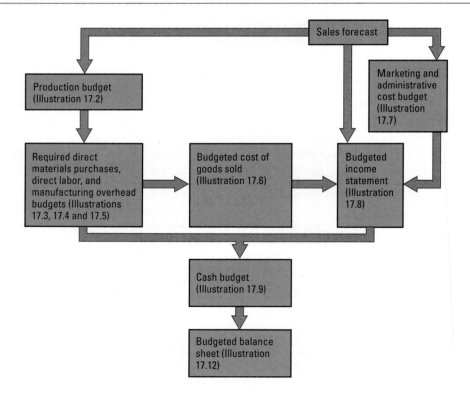

BUDGETING IN RETAIL AND WHOLESALE ORGANIZATIONS

As in manufacturing, the sales budget in retail and wholesale (often called *merchandising*) drives the rest of the budgeted income statement. A merchandiser has no production budget but a merchandise purchases budget, which is much like the direct materials purchases budget in manufacturing. For example, managers at Fashions, Inc., prepared the following purchases budget for a line of women's suits:

ILLUSTRATION 17.14

FASHIONS, INC.
Merchandise Purchases Budget
For the Year Ended December 31
(in units)

Estimated sales	100 units
Add: Estimated ending inventory	10
Total merchandise needs	110
Less: Beginning inventory	15
Merchandise to be purchased	95 units
Estimated cost per unit	$ 200
Total estimated cost of merchandise	$19,000

Estimated sales	100 units
Estimated ending inventory	10
Estimated beginning inventory	15
Estimated cost per unit	$200

Illustration 17.14 presents the merchandise purchases budget for Fashions.

As you can see, this budget requires extensive coordination between the managers responsible for sales and those in charge of buying. Because of the critical importance of timing and seasonality in merchandising, special attention is usually given to short-term budgets (for example, spring, summer, Christmas season budgets). The budget helps formalize an ongoing process of coordinating buying and selling. This coordination is critical to the success of merchandising enterprises.

BUDGETING IN NONPROFIT ORGANIZATIONS

The master budget has added importance in nonprofit organizations because it is used to authorize the expenditure of funds. In many governmental units, the approved budget is a legal authorization for expenditure, and the penalties for exceeding the expenditures authorized in the budget could be severe. This partially explains why a balanced budget takes on added importance in nonprofit organizations.

The Budget Is the Law in Government

State, provincial, and local governments generally are required to have a balanced budget, that is, a budget in which expenditures do not exceed revenues. During its recent budget crisis, the State of California installed an 800 hot line for citizens to call with suggestions to help balance the budget. (Many suggestions were implemented; one idea that was not adopted was to abolish the legislature.)[6]

ETHICAL PROBLEMS IN BUDGETING

L.O. 8: Explain why ethical issues arise in budgeting.

Budgeting creates serious ethical issues for many people. Managers and employees provide much of the information for the budget; their performance then is compared with the budget they helped develop. For example, as a manager, suppose that you believed that although it is possible to achieve a 10 percent increase in your department's sales, a 2 percent increase is almost certain. If you tell upper management that a 10 percent increase is an appropriate budget but you fall short of it, you will lose opportunities for merit pay increases and a promotion. Management may

---

[6]For further discussion of budgeting in government and other nonprofit organizations, see K. Ramanathan, *Management Control in Nonprofit Organizations* (New York: John Wiley, 1982); and R. Anthony and D. Young, *Management Control in Nonprofit Organizations,* 5th ed. (Burr Ridge, IL: Richard D. Irwin, 1993).

REAL WORLD APPLICATION **How Companies Deal with Ethical Dilemmas**

Accroding to an instruction manual at General Electric (GE), "If confronted with apparent conflicts between the demands of their jobs and the highest standards of ethical conduct, employees should be guided by their sense of honor until the inconsistency has been resolved." GE now has one of the most elaborate programs in the country to promote ethical conduct. According to one report, "The effort GE makes is remarkable. Besides seminars and videos for employees, the company goes so far as to spring pop quizzes on workers in hallways, asking, for instance, 'What are the three ways to report wrongdoing?' Correct answers win a coffee mug."

A GE attorney who is vice president of the company's aerospace division stated that pressure in the company is increasing to send a message to employees to achieve their performance numbers but also to comply with the company's standards for ethical and legal behavior.

Source: The Wall Street Journal, July 22, 1992, pp. A1–A4.

assume that you fell short of 10 percent not because of market circumstances beyond your control but because you did not perform well in making sales. On the other hand, if you report that only a 2 percent increase is possible, the company will not provide enough production capacity to fill the sales orders if the 10 percent increase comes through. Should you do what is in your best interest or give your best estimate of reality?

People in companies face these dilemmas all the time. We hope that companies provide incentives for people to report truthfully, which means that the company must reward both for honest estimates and good performance. In reality, however, many companies put considerable pressure on employees to achieve increasingly difficult targets. Fraudulent financial reporting at the division level occurs because managers could not meet difficult targets. The Real World Application at the top of this page describes General Electric's attempts to instruct employees on ways to deal with conflicts between high standards of ethical conduct and the demands of their jobs.

BUDGETING UNDER UNCERTAINTY

Any projection of the future is uncertain. Recognizing this, managers often perform sensitivity analysis on their projections. This analysis is based on hypothetical questions such as these: What if labor costs are 10 percent higher (or lower) than projected? What if new health and safety regulations that increase our costs of operations are passed? What if our major supplier of direct materials goes bankrupt? By asking and answering such questions during the planning phase, management can determine the risk of various phases of its operations and can develop contingency plans.

As part of the budget plan at Shasta Design, for example, local managers were asked to provide three forecasts: their best estimate, an optimistic estimate (defined as "an estimate so high that there is only a 10 percent or less chance that conditions will be better than the optimistic estimate"), and a pessimistic estimate (defined as "an estimate so low that there is only a 10 percent or less chance that conditions will be worse then the pessimistic estimate"). The optimistic and pessimistic forecasts were not as detailed as the best estimates, but they did highlight some potential problems and risks. From this analysis, top management learned that a major supplier to a distant plant was on the verge of bankruptcy. As a result, management developed relationships with other suppliers, increased the stockpiles of direct materials in the plant, and worked with the supplier to improve its financial position.

Shasta Design's top management also learned that if all costs were as expected and the pessimistic forecast of sales actually occurred, the company would suffer an operating loss. The primary reason for this would be decreasing demand for the company's products due to a worsening of general economic conditions. This was important information to consider in making financial analyses. Further, manage-

ILLUSTRATION 17.15	**Sensitivity Analysis and Contingency Planning**

Sensitivity analysis "What if?"	Contingency planning "If, then"
Optimistic (Economic conditions and sales better than expected)	• Status quo • Increase discretionary cost • Increase production
Expected sales	• Status quo
Pessimistic (Economic conditions and sales worse than expected)	• Status quo • Reduce discretionary costs • Curtail production

ment put an "early warning" system in place by which it carefully monitored such key economic variables as unemployment, consumer spending, gross national product, and the like. If these indicators signaled a downturn in the economy, management's contingency plan was to reduce production gradually to prevent a buildup of excess inventories and to reduce discretionary spending on overhead, marketing, and administrative costs.

Illustration 17.15 provides a diagram of sensitivity analysis and contingency planning. For each hypothesis in the sensitivity analysis, a choice of steps can be taken. The procedure can be as simple as a diagram and a few notes on a piece of paper or as complex as a mathematical model incorporated into computerized formal planning models. Of course, decisions about the degree of sophistication of these models should be subjected to cost-benefit analysis.

The incorporation of uncertainty into budget estimates can be quite useful. A major benefit of formal planning models is to explore many alternatives and options in the planning process. Although it is beyond the scope of this book to go into details of formal corporate planning models, we believe that you can see how to integrate the budget plan with formal planning models that set forth mathematical relationships among an organization's operating and financial activities. The use of computer-based simulation models facilitates asking numerous what-if questions, which become too difficult to deal with by hand as they increase.

BUDGETING AND SPREADSHEETS

Spreadsheets are extremely helpful in preparing budgets, which requires considerable what-if thinking. Spreadsheets help link the various what-if scenarios to changes in financial variables and to financial consequences.

For example, the simple spreadsheet in Illustration 17.16 shows three scenarios of estimated sales prices and sales quantities. Each scenario is associated with estimated changes in cost of goods sold and in marketing and administrative costs. (Row 4 presents the budget used in the text; assume that the other scenarios were worked out by management and presented to us.) Note that operating profits before tax varies considerably between the worst scenario in row 6 and the best scenario shown in row 5. This analysis alerts management that Shasta Designs will incur losses under the scenario shown in row 6 unless management finds ways to cut costs or takes other actions.

These are only a few of the numerous scenarios that management could develop. Further, managers could develop alternative scenarios for any of the budgets that we have discussed. Large companies usually develop complex financial models to deal with the numerous interactions of the budget.

For example, a decision support system model has been developed to help managers assess the trade-offs of different business approaches. Most budgeting

| ILLUSTRATION 17.16 | Spreadsheet Analysis of Alternative Budgets, Shasta Designs, Inc. |

	A Sales Price	B Sales Quantity	C Cost of Goods Sold	D Marketing and Administrative Costs	E Operating Profits before Tax
1 2					
3					
4	$800	6,400	$3,200,000	$1,552,000	$ 368,000
5	$900	6,000	$3,000,000	$1,400,000	$1,000,000
6	$700	6,750	$3,350,000	$1,650,000	($ 275,000)
7	$850	6,300	$3,170,000	$1,515,000	$ 670,000
8	$750	6,620	$3,290,000	$1,590,000	$ 85,000
9	$800	6,400	$3,300,000	$1,560,000	$ 260,000
10	$800	6,400	$3,100,000	$1,540,000	$ 480,000

activities involve decisions having more than one strategic objective. For example, a company may have two objectives, maximize income and minimize labor overtime. As the number of objectives increases and they begin to conflict, the decision-making process becomes more complex. The interactive, multiple-objective, linear programming model allows managers to deal with often conflicting objectives by using a straightforward set of equations and constraints. The result is a solution that maximizes each objective.[7]

ZERO-BASE BUDGETING: LESSONS FROM THE PAST

zero-base budgeting
A system of establishing financial plans beginning with the assumption that no activity is necessary and justifying each program or activity level budgeted.

Many organizations have attempted to manage discretionary costs through a budgeting method called **zero-base budgeting.** Numerous companies (including Texas Instruments, Xerox, and Control Data) and governmental units (including some agencies of the federal government) have implemented zero-base budgeting at one time or another. One reason that the approach has attracted considerable popularity in public sector organizations is that it is seen as a way to manage expenditures in a setting in which the benefits of the expenditures cannot be traced to the costs as easily as they can in manufacturing.

The novel part of zero-base budgeting is the requirement that the budgeting process start at zero, with all expenditures to be completely justified. This contrasts with the usual approach, in which a certain level of expenditures is allowed as a starting point and the budgeting process focuses on requests for incremental expenditures. A strict zero-base approach has been found to be generally impracticable, however, because of the massive amount of time required to implement it. Thus, many organizations that use zero-base budgeting in fact allow a floor that does not have to be justified in as much detail as the pure process requires. In many organizations, this has been set at around 80 percent of the current level of expenditures. This floor represents the lowest amount of funding that would enable a responsibility center to continue its operations at a minimal level. Proposed increments of activity above this level are evaluated one by one in terms of costs and benefits.

[7]For further information see Godfrey, Leitch, and Steuer, "Budgeting for Multiple Objectives," *Management Accounting,* January 1996, pp. 38–41; and Y. Ijiri, F. K. Levy, and R. C. Lyon, "A Linear Programming Model for Budgeting and Financial Planning," *Journal of Accounting Research,* Autumn 1963.

SUMMARY

This chapter has discussed and illustrated the budget process. The budget is part of the overall plan for achieving an organization's objectives. The master budget is usually a one-year plan that encompasses budgeted sales and production, budgeted income statement, balance sheet, and cash flow statement, as well as supporting schedules.

The following summarizes key ideas tied to the chapter's learning objectives.

LO1: The role of budgets. Budgets, which are used as a blueprint for operations, help companies determine the means for achieving their goals by outlining projected sales, production costs, and marketing and administrative costs.

LO2: The importance of people in the budgeting process. Budgets are based on people's estimates, which are affected by their own goals, values, and abilities. Managers should consider these "soft" factors when collecting information for budgets.

LO3: Estimating sales. The key to the budget is a good sales forecast because so many other parts of the budget depend on the sales forecast. The sales forecast usually is derived from multiple sources of data, including data provided by sales personnel, market researchers, and statistical analyses.

LO4: Production and cost budgets. Once sales forecasts have been developed, the number of units to be produced is estimated. The cost of goods sold is derived in this process. An estimate of marketing and administrative costs also is made based on the previous period's actual and budgeted amounts adjusted for several factors including inflation and changes in operations.

LO5: Estimating cash flows. Preparing a cash budget requires that all revenues, costs, and other transactions be examined in terms of their effects on cash.

LO6: Developing budgeted financial statements. Budgeted sales, production costs, and marketing and administrative costs are combined to form the budgeted income statement. To complete the budgeted financial statements, projected cash flows and a balance sheet are prepared.

LO7: Budgeting in service, retail and wholesale, and nonprofit organizations. Retail and wholesale organization budgets are similar to manufacturing budgets except that they have no production budget. Service organizations are similar except that they have no inventories. The budget is not only a planning tool but also a legal authorization for expenditure in governmental (nonprofit) units.

LO8: Ethical issues in budgeting. Conflicts of interest often arise when employees are asked for input to help establish a budget. Incentive exists for employees to provide targets that are relatively easy to achieve. Conversely, companies typically hope to establish challenging goals and reward employees for meeting the challenge. As a result, employees do not always provide accurate information for the budgeting process. In addition, if budget targets are difficult to meet, employees may turn to fraudulent financial reporting.

KEY TERMS

benchmarking, 508	organization goals, 507
budget, 506	participative budgeting, 509
budgeted balance sheets, 522	production budget, 512
cash budget, 519	profit plan, 507
critical success factors, 506	strategic long-range plan, 507
Delphi technique, 510	trend analysis, 511
econometric models, 511	zero-base budgeting, 528
master budget, 507	

REVIEW QUESTIONS	**17.1** Why would more detail be included in a budget for the coming period than in a longer-range forecast?
	17.2 If a company prepares budgeted income statements and balance sheets, why is there a need to prepare a cash budget?
	17.3 What are four methods used to estimate sales for budgeting purposes?
	17.4 What are the relationships between organization goals, strategic plans, and a master budget for the coming period?
	17.5 What is the danger of relying entirely on middle management estimates of sales, costs, and other data used in budget planning?
	17.6 How can budgeting aid in coordinating corporate activities?
	17.7 What is zero-base budgeting, and how does it differ from other budgeting practices?

CRITICAL ANALYSIS AND DISCUSSION QUESTIONS	**17.8** What is the difference between strategic plans and the budget plan?
	17.9 The chief executive officer of Rigid Plastics Corporation remarked to a colleague, "I don't understand why other companies waste so much time in the budgeting process. I set our company goals, and everyone strives to meet them. What's wrong with that approach?" Comment on the executive's remarks.
	17.10 How would the use of a just-in-time inventory system affect a company's budget plans?
	17.11 For governmental agencies, a budget is also a legal limitation on expenditures. If governmental employees are asked about their agencies' needs for the coming fiscal period, what types of biases are they likely to incorporate in their estimates? Why?
	17.12 Multigoal Corporation has established a bonus plan for its employees. An employee receives a bonus if his or her subunit meets the cost levels specified in the annual budget plan. If the subunit's costs exceed the budget, its employees earn no bonus. What problems might arise with this bonus plan?
	17.13 Surveying the accounts payable records, a clerk in the controller's office noted that expenses appeared to rise significantly within a month of the close of the budget period. The organization did not have a seasonal product or service to explain this behavior. Can you suggest an explanation?
	17.14 Which of the following budgets is most important from management's perspective, the budgeted balance sheet or the budgeted income statement? Why?

EXERCISES

17.15 Estimate Sales Revenues (L.O. 3)

Orcutt & Daughter is a large securities dealer. Last year, the company made 60,000 trades with an average commission of $220. Smaller investors are abandoning the market, whose volume is expected to decline by 15 percent for the coming year. Orcutt's volume generally changes with the market. However, in addition to market factors, Orcutt expects an additional 10 percent decline in the number of trades due to unfavorable publicity.

Offsetting these factors is the observation that the average commission per trade is likely to increase by 20 percent because trades are expected to be large in the coming year.

Required

Estimate Orcutt's commission revenues for the coming year.

17.16 Estimate Sales Revenues (L.O. 3)

Jackson City Bank (JCB) has $20 million in commercial loans with an average interest rate of 11.5 percent. The bank also has $16 million in consumer loans with an average interest rate of 16 percent. Finally, the bank owns $3 million in government securities with an average rate of 9 percent.

JCB estimates that next year its commercial loan portfolio will fall to $19 million, and the interest rate will fall to 11 percent. Its consumer loans will expand to $17 million with an average interest rate of 16 percent, and its government securities portfolio will increase to $5 million with an average rate of 8 percent.

Required   Estimate JCB's revenues for the coming year.

17.17 Estimate Sales Revenues (L.O. 3)

Reiser Company manufactures ballpoint pens. Last year, it sold 225,000 type A pens for $2 per unit. The company estimates that this volume represents a 20 percent share of the current type A pen market. The market is expected to increase by 5 percent. Marketing specialists have determined that as a result of a new advertising campaign and packaging, the company will increase its share of this larger market to 24 percent. Due to changes in prices, the new price for the type A pens will be $2.10 per unit. This new price is expected to be in line with the competition and have no effect on the volume estimates.

Required   Estimate Reiser's sales revenues for the coming year.

17.18 Estimate Production Levels (L.O. 4)

Cordelias Corporation has just made its sales forecasts for the coming period. Its marketing department estimates that the company will sell 960,000 units during the coming year. In the past, management has maintained inventories of finished goods at approximately two months' sales. The inventory at the start of the budget period is 52,000 units. Sales occur evenly throughout the year.

Required   Estimate the production level required for the coming year to meet these objectives.

17.19 Estimate Production and Materials Requirements (L.O. 4)

Visions, Inc., makes a special line of graphic tubing items. During each of the next two years, it expects to sell 320,000 units. The beginning finished goods inventory is 80,000 units. However, the target ending finished goods inventory for each year is 40,000 units.

Each unit requires 5 feet of plastic tubing. At the beginning of the year, 200,000 feet of plastic tubing are in inventory. Management has set a target to have tubing materials on hand equal to three months' production requirements. Sales and production take place evenly throughout the year.

Required   Compute the total targeted production of the finished product for the coming year. Compute the required purchases of tubing materials for the coming year. (Note that production in the following year should be 320,000 units of the finished product.)

17.20 Estimate Purchases and Cash Disbursements (L.O. 4, L.O. 5)

Lazarus Company buys plain mylar balloons and prints different designs on them for various occasions. It imports the balloons from Taiwan, so it keeps on hand at all times a stock equal to the balloons needed for two months' sales. The balloons cost $.70 each and must be paid for in cash. The company has 14,000 balloons in stock. Sales estimates, based on contracts received, are as follows for the next six months:

June	6,200
July	8,900
August	6,600
September	7,100
October	4,800
November	3,600

Required   **a.** Estimate purchases (in units) for June, July, and August.

b. Estimate cash required to make purchases in June, July, and August.

17.21 Estimate Purchases and Cash Disbursements (L.O. 4, L.O. 5)

Oleander Products wishes to purchase goods in one month for sale in the next. On January 31, the company has 8,000 digital tape players in stock, although sales for the next month (February) are estimated to total 8,600 players. Sales for March are expected to equal 7,000 players, and April sales are expected to total 7,400 players.

Tape players are purchased at a wholesale price of $290. The supplier has a financing arrangement by which Oleander pays 60 percent of the purchase price in the month when the players are delivered and 40 percent in the following month. Ten thousand players were purchased in December.

Required   **a.** Estimate purchases (in units) for January and February.

b. Estimate the cash required to make purchases in February and March.

17.22 Estimate Cash Disbursements (L.O. 5)

Walsh Company is preparing its cash budget for May. The following information is available concerning its inventories:

Inventories at beginning of May	$ 45,000
Estimated purchases for May.	220,000
Estimated cost of goods sold for May	225,000
Estimated payments in May for purchases in April	55,000
Estimated payments in May for purchases prior to April	10,000
Estimated payments in May for purchases in May	70%

Required   What are the estimated cash disbursements in May?

17.23   Estimate Cash
Collections
(L.O. 5)

47th Street Company is preparing its cash budget for July. The following information is available concerning its accounts receivable:

Estimated credit sales for July	$400,000
Actual credit sales for June	300,000
Estimated collections in July for credit sales in July	25%
Estimated collections in July for credit sales in June	70%
Estimated collections in July for credit sales prior to June.	$32,000
Estimated write-offs in July for uncollectible credit sales.	16,000
Estimated provision for bad debts in July for credit sales in July	14,000

Required   What are the estimated cash receipts from accounts receivable collections in July?
(1) $312,000.
(2) $326,000.
(3) $328,000.
(4) $342,000.
(5)   Some other answer.

(CPA adapted)

17.24   Estimate Cash
Collections
(L.O. 5)

Kingstons Products is preparing a cash budget for September. The following information on accounts receivable collections is available from past collection experience:

Percent of current month's sales collected this month	28%
Percent of prior month's sales collected this month.	60
Percent of sales two months prior to current month collected this month.	6
Percent of sales three months prior to current month collected this month.	3

The remaining 3 percent is not collected and is written off as bad debts.
    Credit sales to date follow:

September—estimated	$100,000
August.	90,000
July.	80,000
June	95,000

Required   What are the estimated cash receipts from accounts receivable collections in September?
(1) $100,000.
(2) $92,450.
(3) $89,650.
(4) $83,000.
(5)   Some other answer.

(CPA adapted)

17.25   Estimate
Cash Receipts
(L.O. 5)

Bride To Be specializes in custom wedding attire. The average price of each of Bride's wedding ensembles is $3,200. For each wedding, Bride's receives a 20 percent deposit two months before the wedding, 50 percent the month before, and the remainder on the day the goods are delivered. Based on information at hand, Bride's expects to prepare outfits for the following number of weddings during the coming months:

January	5
February	3
March	2
April	4
May	5
June	11

Required

a. What are the expected revenues for Bride's for each month, January through June? Revenues are recorded in the month of the wedding.

b. What are the expected cash receipts for each month, January through April?

17.26 Estimate Cash Receipts (L.O. 5)

Water Works manages neighborhood pools in Oceanside. The company attempts to make service calls at least once a month to all homes that subscribe to its service. More frequent calls are made during the summer. The number of subscribers also varies with the season. The number of subscribers and the average number of calls to each subscriber for the months of interest follow:

	Subscribers	Service Calls
March	100	0.5
April	120	1.0
May	260	1.8
June	300	2.2
July	300	2.0
August	280	1.7

The average price charged for a service call is $50. Of the service calls, 20 percent are paid in the month the service is rendered, 60 percent in the month after the service is rendered, and 18 percent in the second month after. The remaining 2 percent is uncollectible.

Required

What are Water Works' expected cash receipts for May, June, July, and August?

17.27 Prepare Budgeted Financial Statements (L.O. 6)

Refer to the data in Exercise 17.26.

Water Works estimates that the number of subscribers in September should fall 10 percent below August levels, and the number of service calls should decrease by an estimated 20 percent. The following information is available for costs incurred in August. All costs except depreciation are paid in cash.

Service costs	
Variable costs	$ 4,720
Maintenance and repair	4,200
Depreciation (fixed)	2,200
Total	11,120
Marketing and administrative costs	
Marketing (variable)	2,500
Administrative (fixed)	2,300
Total	4,800
Total costs	$15,920

Variable cash and marketing costs change with volume. Fixed depreciation will remain the same, but fixed administrative costs will increase by 5 percent beginning September 1. Maintenance and repair are provided by contract, which calls for a 1 percent increase in September.

Required

Prepare a budgeted income statement for September.

17.28 Prepare Budgeted Financial Statements (L.O. 6)

Hampton, Inc., is a fast-growing start-up firm that manufactures surfboards. The following income statement is available for year 1:

Revenues (100 units @ $250/unit)		$25,000
Less		
Manufacturing costs		
Variable	3,640	
Depreciation (fixed)	1,325	
Marketing and administrative		
Fixed costs (cash)	4,390	
Depreciation (fixed)	675	
Total costs		10,030
Operating profits		$ 1,595

Sales volume is expected to increase by 20 percent in year 2, but the sales price is expected to fall 10 percent. Variable manufacturing costs are expected to increase by 3 percent per unit in year 2. In addition to these cost changes, variable manufacturing costs also will change with sales volume. Marketing and administrative cash costs are expected to increase by 10 percent.

Hampton operates on a cash basis and maintains no inventories. Depreciation is fixed and should remain unchanged over the next three years.

Required Prepare a budgeted income statement for year 2.

17.29 Ethics and Budgeting (L.O. 8)   El Dorado Company manufactures infant furniture and carriages. The accounting staff is currently preparing next year's budget. Michelle Jackson is new to the firm and is interested in learning how this process occurs. She has lunch with Maria Bradley, the sales manager, and Barry Popov, the production manager, to discuss the planning process. Over the course of lunch, Michelle discovers that Maria lowers sales projections 5 to 10 percent before submitting her figures and that Barry increases cost estimates by 10 percent before submitting his figures. When Michelle asks why they do this the response is simply that everyone around here does it.

Required

a. What do Maria and Barry hope to accomplish by their methods?

b. How might this backfire and work against them?

c. Are Maria's and Barry's actions unethical?

(CMA adapted)

PROBLEMS

17.30 Prepare Budgeted Financial Statements   The following information is available for year 1 for Parker Products:

Revenues (100,000 units)		$725,000
Manufacturing costs		
Materials.	42,000	
Variable cash costs	35,600	
Fixed cash costs	81,900	
Depreciation (fixed)	249,750	
Marketing and administrative costs		
Marketing (variable, cash)	105,600	
Marketing depreciation.	37,400	
Administrative (fixed, cash)	127,300	
Administrative depreciation	18,700	
Total costs		698,250
Operating profits		$ 26,750

All depreciation charges are fixed and are expected to remain the same for year 2. Sales volume is expected to increase by 18 percent, but prices are expected to fall by 5 percent. Materials costs are expected to decrease by 8 percent. Variable manufacturing costs are expected to decrease by 2 percent per unit. Fixed manufacturing costs are expected to increase by 5 percent.

Variable marketing costs change with volume. Administrative cash costs are expected to increase by 10 percent. Inventories are kept at zero.

Required

Prepare a budgeted income statement for year 2.

17.31 Estimate Cash Receipts

Refer to the data in Problem 17.30. Estimate the cash from operations expected in year 2.

17.32 Prepare Budgeted Financial Statements

Quinn Electronics has the following data from year 1 operations, which are to be used for developing year 2 budget estimates:

Revenues (100,000)	$746,000
Manufacturing costs	
Materials.	133,000
Variable cash costs	180,900
Fixed cash costs	72,000
Depreciation (fixed)	89,000
Marketing and administrative costs	
Marketing (variable, cash).	95,000
Marketing depreciation.	22,600
Administrative (fixed, cash)	90,110
Administrative depreciation	8,400
Total costs	691,010
Operating profits	$ 54,990

All depreciation charges are fixed. Old manufacturing equipment with an annual depreciation charge of $9,700 will be replaced in year 2 with new equipment that will incur an annual depreciation charge of $14,000. Sales volume and prices are expected to increase by 12 percent and 6 percent, respectively. On a per unit basis, expectations are that materials costs will increase by 10 percent and variable manufacturing costs will decrease by 4 percent. Fixed manufacturing costs are expected to decrease by 7 percent.

Variable marketing costs will change with volume. Administrative cash costs are expected to increase by 8 percent. Inventories are kept at close to zero.

Required

Prepare a budgeted income statement for year 2.

17.33 Estimate Cash Receipts

Refer to the data in Problem 17.32. Estimate the cash from operations expected in year 2.

17.34 Prepare a Production Budget

Sevi, Inc., manufactures floral containers. The controller is preparing a budget for the coming year and asks for your assistance. The following costs and other data apply to container production:

Direct materials per container	
1 pound Z-A styrene at $.40 per pound	
2 pounds Vasa finish at $.80 per pound	
Direct labor per container	
¼ hour at $8.60 per hour	
Overhead per container	
Indirect labor	$.12
Indirect materials	.03
Power	.07
Equipment costs.	.36
Building occupancy.	.19
Total overhead per unit.	$.77

You learn that equipment costs and building occupancy are fixed and are based on a normal production of 20,000 units per year. Other overhead costs are variable. Plant capacity is sufficient to produce 25,000 units per year.

Labor costs per hour are not expected to change during the year. However, the Vasa finish supplier has informed Sevi that it will impose a 10 percent price increase at the start of the coming budget period. No other costs are expected to change.

During the coming budget period, Sevi expects to sell 18,000 units. Finished goods inventory is targeted to increase from 4,000 units to 7,000 units to prepare for an expected sales increase the year after next. Production will occur evenly throughout the year. Inventory levels for Vasa finish and Z-A styrene are expected to remain unchanged throughout the year. There is no work in process inventory.

Required   Prepare a production budget and estimate the materials, labor, and overhead costs for the coming year.

17.35 Sales Expense Budget

Gemini Corporation has just received its sales expense report for January, which follows.

Item	Amount
Sales commissions	$135,000
Sales staff salaries.	32,000
Telephone and mailing	16,200
Building lease payment	20,000
Heat, light, and water	4,100
Packaging and delivery	27,400
Depreciation	12,500
Marketing consultants.	19,700

You have been asked to develop budgeted costs for the coming year. Since this month is typical, you decide to prepare an estimated budget for a typical month in the coming year and you uncover the following additional data:

- Sales volume is expected to increase by 5 percent.
- Sales prices are expected to increase by 10 percent.
- Commissions are based on a percentage of selling price.
- Sales staff salaries will increase 4 percent next year regardless of sales volume.
- Building rent is based on a five-year lease that expires in three years.
- Telephone and mailing expenses are scheduled to increase by 8 percent even with no change in sales volume. However, these costs are variable with the number of units sold, as are packaging and delivery costs.
- Heat, light, and water are scheduled to increase by 12 percent regardless of sales volume.
- Depreciation includes furniture and fixtures used by the sales staff. The company has just acquired an additional $19,000 in furniture that will be received at the start of next year and will be depreciated over a 10-year life using the straight-line method.
- Marketing consultant expenses were for a special advertising campaign that runs from time to time. During the coming year, the costs are expected to average $35,000 per month.

Required   Prepare a budget for sales expenses for a typical month in the coming year.

17.36 Budgeted Purchases and Cash Flows— Multiple Choice

Warner Corporation seeks your assistance in developing cash and other budget information for May, June, and July. At April 30, the company had cash of $5,500, accounts receivable of $437,000, inventories of $309,400, and accounts payable of $133,055. The budget is to be based on the following assumptions.

Sales

Each month's sales are billed on the last day of the month.

Customers are allowed a 3 percent discount if payment is made within 10 days after the billing date. Receivables are recorded in the accounts at their gross amounts (not net of discounts).

The billings are collected as follows: 60 percent within the discount period, 25 percent by the end of the month, 9 percent by the end of the second month, and 6 percent are uncollectible.

Purchases

Of all purchases of merchandise and selling, general, and administrative expenses, 54 percent is paid in the month purchased and the remainder in the following month.

The number of units in each month's ending inventory equals 130 percent of the next month's units of sales.

The cost of each unit of inventory is $20.

Selling, general, and administrative expenses, of which $2,000 is depreciation, equal 15 percent of the current month's sales.

Actual and projected sales follow:

	Dollars	Units
March.......	$354,000	11,800
April........	363,000	12,100
May	357,000	11,900
June........	342,000	11,400
July	360,000	12,000
August	366,000	12,200

Required

Choose the best answer or indicate none of the above.

a. Budgeted purchases in dollars for May are
   (1) $357,000.
   (2) $238,000.
   (3) $225,000.
   (4) $244,800.
   (5) None of the above.

b. Budgeted purchases in dollars for June are
   (1) $292,000.
   (2) $243,600.
   (3) $242,000.
   (4) $228,000.
   (5) None of the above.

c. Budgeted cash collections during May are
   (1) $355,656.
   (2) $355,116.
   (3) $340,410.
   (4) $333,876.
   (5) None of the above.

d. Budgeted cash disbursements during June are
   (1) $285,379.
   (2) $287,379.
   (3) $292,900.
   (4) $294,900.
   (5) None of the above.

e. The budgeted number of units of inventory to be purchased during July is
   (1) 15,860.
   (2) 15,600.
   (3) 12,260.
   (4) 12,000.
   (5) None of the above.

(CPA adapted)

17.37 Comprehensive Budget Plan

Tipless, Inc., a manufacturer of coffee cups, decided in October 19X0 that it needed cash to continue operations. It began negotiating for a one-month bank loan of $100,000 starting November 1, 19X0. The bank would charge interest at the rate of 1 percent per month and require the company to repay interest and principal on November 30, 19X0. In considering the loan, the bank requested a projected income statement and cash budget for November.

The following information is available:

• The company budgeted sales at 120,000 units per month in October 19X0, December 19X0, and January 19X1, and at 90,000 units in November 19X0. The selling price is $2 per unit.

- The inventory of finished goods on October 1 was 24,000 units. The finished goods inventory at the end of each month equals 20 percent of sales anticipated for the following month. There is no work in process.
- The inventory of raw materials on October 1 was 22,800 pounds. At the end of each month, the raw materials inventory equals no less than 40 percent of production requirements for the following month. The company purchases materials as needed in minimum quantities of 25,000 pounds per shipment.
- Selling expenses are 10 percent of gross sales. Administrative expenses, which include depreciation of $500 per month on office furniture and fixtures, total $33,000 per month.
- The manufacturing budget for coffee cups, based on normal production of 100,000 units per month, follows:

Materials (½ pound per cup, 50,000 pounds, $2.00 per pound)	$ 50,000
Labor	40,000
Variable overhead	20,000
Fixed overhead (includes depreciation of $4,000)	10,000
Total	$120,000

Required

a. Prepare schedules computing inventory budgets by months for
  (1) Production in units for October, November, and December.
  (2) Raw material purchases in pounds for October and November.

b. Prepare a projected income statement for November. Cost of goods sold should equal the variable manufacturing cost per unit times the number of units sold plus the total fixed manufacturing cost budgeted for the period.

(CPA adapted)

17.38   Comprehensive Budget Plan

Eagle Corporation appeared to be experiencing a good year. Sales in the first quarter were one-third ahead of last year, and the sales department predicted that this rate would continue throughout the entire year. Ruth Keenan, assistant controller, was asked to prepare a new forecast for the year and to analyze the differences from last year's results. She based the forecast on actual results obtained in the first quarter plus the expected costs of programs to be carried out in the remainder of the year. She worked with various department heads (production, sales, and so on) to get the necessary information. The results of these efforts follow:

EAGLE CORPORATION
Expected Account Balances for December 31, This Year
(in thousands)

Cash	$ 1,200	
Accounts receivable	80,000	
Inventory (January 1, next year)	48,000	
Plant and equipment	130,000	
Accumulated depreciation		$ 41,000
Accounts payable		45,000
Notes payable (due within one year)		50,000
Accrued payables		23,250
Common stock		70,000
Retained earnings		108,200
Sales		600,000
Other income		9,000
Manufacturing costs		
Materials	213,000	
Direct labor	218,000	
Variable overhead	130,000	
Depreciation	5,000	
Other fixed overhead	7,750	

Marketing

Commissions	20,000
Salaries	16,000
Promotion and advertising	45,000

Administrative

Salaries	16,000
Travel	2,500
Office costs	9,000
Income taxes	—
Dividends	5,000
	$946,450 $946,450

Adjustments for the change in inventory and for income taxes have not been made. The schedules production for this year is 450 million units, and planned sales volume is 400 million units. Sales and production volume was 300 million units last year. The company uses a full-absorption costing, FIFO inventory system and is subject to a 40 percent income tax rate. The actual income statement for last year follows:

EAGLE CORPORATION
Statement of Income and Retained Earnings
For the Budget Year Ended December 31, Last Year
(in thousands)

Revenues			
Sales		$450,000	
Other income		15,000	$465,000
Expenses			
Cost of goods sold			
Materials	$132,000		
Direct labor	135,000		
Variable overhead	81,000		
Fixed overhead	12,000		
	360,000		
Beginning inventory	48,000		
	408,000		
Ending inventory	48,000	360,000	
Selling			
Salaries	13,500		
Commissions	15,000		
Promotion and advertising	31,500	60,000	
General and administrative			
Salaries	14,000		
Travel	2,000		
Office costs	8,000	24,000	
Income taxes		8,400	452,400
Operating profit			12,600
Beginning retained earnings			100,600
Subtotal			113,200
Less: Dividends			5,000
Ending retained earnings			$108,200

Required   Prepared a budgeted income statement and balance sheet.

(CMA adapted)

INTEGRATIVE CASES

17.39   Prepare Cash Budget for Service Organization

Triple-F Health Club (Family, Fitness, and Fun) is a nonprofit health club. Its board of directors is developing plans to acquire more equipment and expand club facilities. The board plans to purchase about $25,000 of new equipment each year and wants to begin a fund to purchase an adjoining property in four or five years when the expansion will need the space. The adjoining property has a market value of about $300,000.

The club manager is concerned that the board has unrealistic goals in light of its recent financial performance. She sought the help of a club member with an accounting background to assist her in preparing the club's records, including the cash basis income statements that follow. The review and discussions with the manager disclosed the additional information that follows the statement.

TRIPLE-F HEALTH CLUB
Statement of Income (Cash Basis)
For the Year Ended October 31
(in thousands)

	19X7	19X6
Cash revenues		
Annual membership fees	$355.0	$300.0
Lesson and class fees	234.0	180.0
Miscellaneous	2.0	1.5
Total cash received	591.0	481.5
Cash costs		
Manager's salary and benefits	36.0	36.0
Regular employees' wages and benefits	190.0	190.0
Lesson and class employee wages and benefits	195.0	150.0
Towels and supplies	16.0	15.5
Utilities (heat and light)	22.0	15.0
Mortgage interest	35.1	37.8
Miscellaneous	2.0	1.5
Total cash costs	496.1	445.8
Cash income	$ 94.9	$ 35.7

Additional Information

1. Other financial information as of October 31, 19X7:
   a. Cash in checking account, $7,000.
   b. Petty cash, $300.
   c. Outstanding mortgage balance, $360,000.
   d. Accounts payable for supplies and utilities unpaid as of October 31, 19X7, and due in November 19X7, $2,500.

2. The club purchased $25,000 worth of exercise equipment during the current fiscal year. Cash of $10,000 was paid on delivery, with the balance due on October 1, which had not been paid as of October 31, 19X7.

3. The club began operations in 19X1 in rental quarters. In October 19X3, it purchased its current property (land and building) for $600,000, paying $120,000 down and agreeing to pay $30,000 plus 9 percent interest annually on the unpaid loan balance each November 1, starting November 1, 19X4.

ILLUSTRATION 17.17A

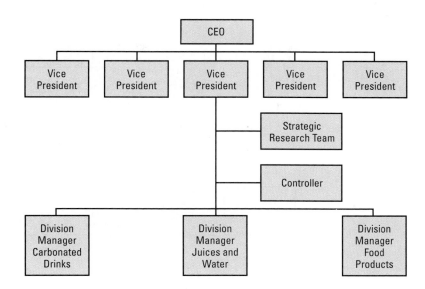

4. Membership rose 3 percent during 19X7, approximately the same annual rate of increase the club has experienced since it opened and that is expected to continue in the future.

5. Membership fees were increased by 15 percent in 19X7. The board has tentative plans to increase them by 10 percent in 19X8.

6. Lesson and class fees have not been increased for three years. The number of classes and lessons has grown significantly each year the percentage growth experienced in 19X7 is expected to be repeated in 19X8.

7. Miscellaneous revenues are expected to grow in 19X8 (over 19X7) at the same percentage as experienced in 19X7 (over 19X6).

8. Lesson and class employees' wages and benefits will increase to $291,525. The wages and benefits of regular employees and the manager will increase 15 percent. Towels and supplies, utilities, and miscellaneous expenses are expected to increase 25 percent.

Required

a. Construct a cash budget for 19X8 for the Triple-F Health Club.

b. Identify any operating problem(s) that this budget discloses for the Triple-F Health Club. Explain your answer.

c. Is the manager's concern that the board's goals are unrealistic justified? Explain your answer.

(CMA adapted)

17.40   River Beverages Case: Budget Preparation

Overview

River Beverages is a food and soft drink company with worldwide operations. The company is organized into five regional divisions with each vice president reporting directly to the CEO, Cindy Wilkins. Each vice president has an R&D department, controller, and three divisions; Carbonated Drinks, Noncarbonated Drinks, and Food Products (see Illustration 17.17A). Management believes that the structure works well for River because different regions have different tastes and the division's products complement each other.

ILLUSTRATION 17.17B

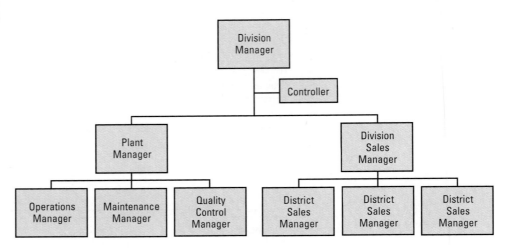

Industry

The U.S. beverage industry has become mature with growth in stride with population growth. Consumers drank about 50 billion gallons of fluids in 1995. Most of the industry growth has come from the nonalcoholic beverage market which is growing by about 1.1 percent annually. In the nonalcoholic arena, soft drinks are the largest segment accounting for 53.4 percent of the beverages consumed. Americans consume about 26 billion gallons of soft drinks ringing up retail sales of $50 billion every year. Water (bottled and tap) is the next largest segment representing 23.7 percent of the market. Juices represent about 12 percent of the beverages consumed. The smallest but fastest growing segment is ready-to-drink teas which is growing by more than 91 percent in volume, but accounts for less than 1 percent of the beverages consumed.

Sales Budgets

Susan Johnson, plant manager at River Beverages' Noncarbonated Drink plant in St. Louis (see Illustration 17.17B), recently completed the annual budgeting process. According to Johnson, division managers have decision making authority in their business units except for capital financing activities. Budgets keep the division managers focused on corporate goals.

At the beginning of December, division managers submit a report to the vice president for the region summarizing capital, sales, and income forecasts for the upcoming fiscal year beginning July 1. Although the initial report is not prepared with much detail, it is prepared with care because it is used in the strategic planning process.

Next, the strategic research team begins a formal assessment of each market segment in its region. The team develops sales forecasts for each division and compiles them into a company forecast. The team considers economic conditions and current market share in each region. Management believes the strategic research team is effective because it is able to integrate division products and more accurately forecast demand for complementary products. In addition, the team ensures continuity of assumptions and achievable sales goals.

Once the corporate forecast is completed, the district sales managers estimate sales for the upcoming budget year. The district sales managers are ultimately responsible for the forecasts they prepare. The district sales forecasts are then compiled and returned to the division manager. The division manager reviews the forecast but cannot make any revisions without discussing the changes with the district sales managers. Next, the district sales forecasts are reviewed by the strategic research team and the division controller. Finally, top management reviews each division's competitive position including plans to increase market share, capital spending, and quality improvement plans.

Plant Budgets

After the sales budget is approved by top management, it is separated into a sales budget for each plant. Plant location is determined by product type and where the product needs to be distributed. The budget is broken down further by price, volume, and product type. Plant managers budget contribution margins, fixed costs, and pretax income using information from the plant sales budget.

Budgeted profit is determined by subtracting budgeted variable costs and budgeted fixed costs from the sales forecast. If actual sales fall below forecasts, the plant manager is still responsible for achieving the budgeted profit. One of the most important aspects of the plant budgeting process is that plant managers break the plant budget down into various plant departments.

Operations and maintenance managers work together to develop cost standards and cost reduction targets for all departments. Budgeted cost reductions from productivity improvements, unfavorable variances, and fixed costs are developed for each department, operation, and cost center in the plant.

Before plant managers submit their budgets, a member of the strategy team and the regional controller visit the plant to keep Corporate in touch with what is happening at the plant level and to help Corporate understand how plant managers determine their budgets. The visits also allow corporate to provide budget preparation guidance if necessary. The visits are especially important because they force plant management to keep in touch with corporate level managers.

The final budgets are submitted and consolidated by April 1. The vice president reviews them to ensure they are in line with corporate objectives. After all changes have been made by the vice presidents and the Chief Executive Officer (CEO), the budgets are submitted to the board of directors for approval. The board votes on the final budget in early June.

Performance Measurement

Variance reports are generated monthly at the corporate office. River has a sophisticated information system that automatically generates reports based on input that is downloaded daily from each plant. The reports can also be generated manually by managers in the organization. Most managers generate variance reports several times during the month allowing them to solve problems before things get out of control.

Corporate reviews the variance reports, looking closely at over-budget variance problems. Plant managers are only questioned about over-budget items. Management feels that this ensures the plant managers are staying on top of problem areas and that this keeps the plant operating as efficiently as possible. One week after the variance reports are generated, plant managers are required to submit a response outlining the causes of any variances and how they plan to prevent the problems in the future. If a plant manager has repeated problems, corporate may send a specialist to the plant to work with the plant manager to solve the problems.

Sales and Manufacturing Relations

"We are expected to meet our approved budget," remarked Kevin Greely, a division controller at River. Greely continues, "A couple years ago one of our major restaurant customers switched to another brand. Even though the restaurant sold over one million cases of our product annually, we were not allowed to make revisions to our budget."

Budgets are rarely adjusted after approval. However, if there is a decline in sales early in the year, plant managers may file an appeal to revise the budgeted profit for the year. If sales decline late in the year, management usually does not revise the budgeted amounts. Rather, plant managers are asked to cut costs wherever possible and delay any unnecessary expenditures until the following year. It is important to remember that River sets budgets so it is able to see where to make cuts or where it can find any operating inefficiencies. Plant managers are not forced to meet their goals, but they are encouraged to cut costs below budget.

The sales department is primarily responsible for product price, sales volume, and delivery timing while plant managers are responsible for plant operations. As you might imagine, problems occur between plant and regional sales managers from time to time. For example, rush orders may cause production costs to be higher than normal for some production runs. Another problem may occur when a sales manager runs a promotional campaign that causes margins to shrink. In both instances, a plant manager's profit budget will be affected negatively while a sales manager's forecasted sales budget will be affected positively. Such situations are often passed up to the division level for resolution; however, it is important to remember that the customer is always the primary concern.

Incentives

River Beverages' management has devised what it thinks is an effective system to motivate plant managers. First, plant managers are only promoted when they have displayed outstanding performance in their current position. Next, River has monetary incentives in place that reward plant managers for reaching profit goals. Finally, charts are produced each month that display budgeted items versus actual results. Although not required to do so, most plant managers publicize the charts and use them as a motivational tool. The charts allow department supervisors and staff to compare activities in their department to similar activities in other plants around the world.

CEO's Message

Cindy Wilkins, CEO of River Beverages' looks to the future and comments, "Planning is an important aspect of budget preparation for every level of our organization. I would like to decrease the time spent on preparing the budget, but I feel that it keeps people thinking about the future. The negative aspect of the budgeting process is that sometimes it over controls our managers. We need to stay nimble enough to react to customer demands, while staying structured enough to achieve corporate objectives. For the most part, our budget process keeps our managers aware of sales goals and alerts them when sales or expenses are off track."

Required

a. Discuss each step in the budgeting process at River Beverages. Begin with the division manager's initial reports and end with the board of directors' approval. Discuss why each step is necessary.

b. Should plant managers be held responsible for costs or profits?

c. Write a report to River Beverages' management stating the advantages and disadvantages of the company's budgeting process. Start your report by stating your assumption(s) about what River Beverages' management wants the budgeting process to accomplish.

(CMA adapted)

SOLUTIONS TO SELF-STUDY QUESTIONS

1.

EXHIBIT A	

SHASTA DESIGN, INC.
Schedule of Budgeted Manufacturing Overhead
For the Budget Year Ended December 31
(compare to Illustration 17.5)

Variable (based on production of 7,300 units)[a]		
Indirect materials and supplies	$	42,677.00
Materials handling		66,261.50
Other indirect labor.		37,061.50
	$	146,000.00
Fixed (same as for production of 6,500 units)		
Supervisory labor.		175,000
Maintenance and repairs		85,000
Plant administration		173,000
Utilities		87,000
Depreciation		280,000
Insurance		43,000
Property taxes.		117,000
Other.		41,000
		1,001,000
Total manufacturing overhead	$	1,147,000

[a]Additional computations:

$$\text{Indirect materials: } \$38,000 \times \frac{7,300}{6,500} = \$42,677.00$$

$$\text{Materials handling: } \$59,000 \times \frac{7,300}{6,500} = \$66,261.50$$

$$\text{Other indirect labor: } \$33,000 \times \frac{7,300}{6,500} = \$37,061.50$$

1. (concluded)

EXHIBIT B	

SHASTA DESIGN, INC.
Budgeted Statement of Cost of Goods Sold
For the Budget Year Ended December 31
(compare to Illustration 17.6)

Beginning work in process inventory		–0–
Manufacturing costs		
Direct materials		
Beginning inventory (Illustration 17.6)	$ 142,000	
Purchases[a] (21,200 R @ $10 + 37,400 S @ $30)	1,334,000	
Materials available for manufacturing	1,476,000	
Less: Ending inventory (1,500 R @ $10 + 4,900 S @ $30)	(162,000)	
Total direct materials costs.		$1,314,000
Direct labor $\left(\$949,000 \times \dfrac{7,300}{6,500} \right)$		1,065,800
Manufacturing overhead (Exhibit A)		1,147,000
Total manufacturing costs		$3,526,800
Deduct: Ending work in process inventory		–0–
Cost of goods manufactured.		3,526,800
Add: Beginning finished goods inventory.		450,000
Deduct: Ending finished goods inventory[a]		(579,748)
Cost of goods sold		$3,397,052

[a]Additional computations:

Required production:
$$\text{Beginning Balance } (BB) + \text{Production} = \text{Sales} + \text{Ending Balance } (EB)$$
$$900 + P = 7,000 + 1,200$$
$$P = \underline{\underline{7,300}}$$

Materials requirements:
R: BB + Purchases = Production + EB
$$2,200 + P = (7,300 \times 3) + 1,500$$
$$P = \underline{\underline{21,200}}$$

S: BB + Purchases = Production + EB
$$4,000 + P = (7,300 \times 5) + 4,900$$
$$P = \underline{\underline{37,400}}$$

Ending finished goods inventory (assuming FIFO):

$$\frac{\text{Ending units}}{\text{Units produced}} \times \text{Cost of goods manufactured} = \frac{1,200}{7,300} \times \$3,526,800$$
$$= \underline{\underline{\$579,748}}$$

2.

EXHIBIT C	

SHASTA DESIGN, INC.
Schedule of Budgeted Marketing and Administrative Costs
For the Budget Year Ended December 31
(compare to Illustration 17.7)

Variable marketing costs[a]		
Sales commissions.	$284,375	
Other marketing.	113,750	
Total variable marketing costs		$ 398,125
Fixed marketing costs		
Sales salaries.	100,000	
Advertising.	193,000	
Other	78,000	
Total fixed marketing costs		371,000
Total marketing costs.		769,125
Administrative costs (all fixed)		
Administrative salaries	254,000	
Legal and accounting staff.	141,000	
Data processing services.	103,000	
Outside professional services.	39,000	
Depreciation—building, furniture, and equipment	94,000	
Insurance.	26,000	
Taxes—other than income	160,000	
Total administrative costs		817,000
Total budgeted marketing and administrative costs.		$1,586,125

[a]Additional computations:

$$\text{Sales commissions: } \$284,375 = \$260,000 \times \frac{7,000 \text{ units}}{6,400 \text{ units}}$$

$$\text{Other marketing:} \quad \$113,750 = \$104,000 \times \frac{7,000 \text{ units}}{6,400 \text{ units}}$$

2.

EXHIBIT D

SHASTA DESIGN, INC.
Budgeted Income Statement
For the Budget Year Ended December 31
(compare to Illustration 17.8)

Budgeted revenues		
Sales (7,000 units at $800)		$5,600,000
Budgeted expenses		
Cost of goods sold (see solution to Self-Study		
Question 1, Exhibit B)	$3,397,052	
Marketing and administrative costs (Exhibit C)	1,586,125	
Total budgeted costs		4,983,177
Budgeted operating profits.		616,823
Federal and other income taxes (given in question)		214,547
Budgeted operating profits after taxes		$ 402,276

3.

EXHIBIT E

SHASTA DESIGN, INC.
Cash Budget
For the Budget Year Ended December 31
(compare to Illustration 17.9)

Cash balance beginning of period		$ 150,000
Receipts		
Collections on accounts[a]	$5,625,000	
Sales of assets (per management)	25,000	
Total receipts		5,650,000
Less disbursements		
Payments for accounts payable[b]	1,317,000	
Direct labor[c]	1,065,800	
Manufacturing overhead requiring cash less noncash		
depreciation charges[c]	867,000	
Marketing and administrative costs less noncash		
charges[d]	1,492,125	
Required payments for federal income taxes (given).	282,390	
Dividends and other distributions to shareholders	140,000	
Reduction in long-term debt	83,000	
Acquisition of new assets	320,000	
Total disbursements		5,567,315
Budgeted ending cash balance		$ 232,685

[a]Collections on account per Illustration 17.9	$5,185,000
Additional sales ($5,600,000 − $5,120,000)	
(from Exhibit D and Illustration 17.8)	480,000
Less increase in receivables.	(40,000)
	$5,625,000

[b]Payments on account per Illustration 17.9	$1,164,000
Additional materials purchases—per Exhibit B	
and Illustration 17.6 ($1,334,000 − $1,179,000)	155,000
Less increase in payables	(2,000)
	$1,317,000

[c]See solution to Self-Study Question 1.

[d]See solution to Self-Study Question 2.

Flexible Budgeting and Performance Evaluation

LEARNING OBJECTIVES

After reading this chapter, you should be able to:

1. Use budgets for performance evaluation.

2. Develop and use flexible budgets.

3. Compute and interpret the sales activity variance.

4. Prepare and use a profit variance analysis.

5. Compare and contrast target costing, *kaizen* budgeting, and standard costing.

6. Explain responsibility centers' use of budgeting.

7. Identify the ethical problems that arise when budgets are used for performance evaluation.

USING BUDGETS FOR PERFORMANCE EVALUATION

L.O. 1: Use budgets for performance evaluation.

operating budgets
The budgeted income statement, the production budget, the budgeted cost of goods sold, and supporting budgets.

financial budgets
Budgets of financial resources; for example, the cash budget and the budgeted balance sheet.

variances
Differences between planned results and actual outcomes.

In Chapter 17, we described the development of the master budget as a first step in the budgetary planning and control cycle. This chapter carries the process a step further to use the budget as a tool for performance evaluation and control. The master budget can be thought of as a blueprint for achieving the company's goals. The control process ensures that the blueprint is followed or, if changes are required, that the best alternative is chosen.

The master budget includes **operating budgets** (for example, the budgeted income statement, the production budget, the budgeted cost of goods sold) and **financial budgets** (for example, the cash budget, the budgeted balance sheet). When management uses the master budget for control purposes, it focuses on the key items that must be controlled to ensure the company's success. Most of these items are in the operating budgets, although some also appear in the financial budgets. In this chapter, we focus on the income statement because it is the most important financial statement that managers use to control operations.

When reported income statements are compared to budgeted income statements, there are nearly always **variances,** or differences, between the budgeted and reported amounts. Managers spend considerable time and effort understanding causes of these variances, interpreting them, and taking corrective action. Subsequent chapters discuss these variances in detail; this chapter presents the "big-picture" comparison of budgeted to reported profits. Understanding this big picture will help you understand how the details discussed in later chapters fit.

HOW BUDGETING FITS INTO THE VALUE CHAIN

Budgeting impacts all areas of the value chain, from research and development to customer service. Since the goal is to maximize value-added activities and minimize nonvalue-added activities, budgets should serve as an incentive for employees to focus on this goal. For example, in the marketing section of the value chain, management may decide to increase the budget for costs associated with direct customer contact (for example, travel, lodging)—an activity that presumes to add value to the company—and reduce the budget for mass mailing advertising—an activity that may be less likely to add value to the company.

Budgeting is an essential element in steering the company in the right direction all along the value chain; it helps to convey management's ideas on maximizing value-added activities and minimizing nonvalue-added activities.

BUDGETING WITH STANDARD COSTING SYSTEMS

standard cost
The anticipated cost of producing and/or selling a unit of output.

A *standard* is a benchmark or norm. There are, for example, standards for admission to school, passing a course, and product safety. In accounting, *standard* is used in a similar fashion. A **standard cost** is the anticipated cost of producing and/or selling a unit of output; it is a predetermined cost assigned to goods produced.

Some Clarifications

Standards versus Budgets

A standard cost is a *predetermined unit cost*; a budget is a *financial plan*. Standard costs often are used to make up the financial plan. In practice these terms are sometimes used interchangeably, but *standards* usually refer to *per unit amounts* while *budgets* usually refer to *total amounts.*

Many companies develop standards, like budgets, and maintain them "off the books." That is, they are not part of the formal accounting system. So when we discuss standard costs, we are referring to standards developed to facilitate control of personnel and operations. Whether they are entered into the records to value inventory is another issue.

Sources of Standard Costs

The following description of setting standard costs is based on an interview with the controller of a manufacturing company. It represents the standard-setting process in most companies.

Production Costs

Materials   A standard cost for every direct material used is computed by (1) examining current purchase prices and adjusting them for expected changes and (2) estimating the amount of each direct material required to make each final product. The purchasing department helps estimate how material prices will change. Operations managers and industrial engineers help determine the amounts of materials needed to make the product.

Labor   Industrial engineers and operating managers often estimate the number of direct labor-hours (or fractions thereof) required for each production step by timing employees while they perform their duties. Employees themselves set standards in many cases. Accountants cost these hours based on expected wage rates and fringe benefits during the period.

Variable Overhead   Variable overhead includes energy to run machines, indirect materials, supplies and so on. Several years ago the company began using regression analysis to estimate variable overhead rates. The company ran actual variable overhead as the dependent variable and actual machine-hours as the independent variable or cost driver for each production department. Each year the unit variable overhead rate is adjusted based on feedback from production managers and accountants about changes in cost. In the future, the company expects to use activity-based costing and increase the number of cost drivers.

Budgeted Fixed Overhead   Production department managers and the accountants estimate the amount of fixed overhead that each production department will incur, including service department costs (for example, maintenance) that have been allocated to the production department.

Review   The accounting staff and internal auditors review all of these estimates on a sample basis for reasonableness. They are adjusted once a year to reflect changes.

Approvals   All standards are approved once a year by top management.

Despite the use of statistical techniques and industrial engineering methods for cost estimation, setting cost standards is more an art than a science. In Chapter 19, we will provide an illustration of how Evergreen Company sets standards.

FLEXIBLE BUDGETING

L.O. 2: Develop and use flexible budgets.

static budget
A budget for a single activity level; usually the master budget.

A master budget presents a comprehensive view of anticipated operations. Such a budget is typically a **static budget;** that is, it is developed in detail for one level of anticipated activity. A **flexible budget,** by contrast, indicates budgeted revenues, costs, and profits for virtually all feasible levels of activities. Since variable costs and revenues change with changes in activity levels, these amounts are budgeted to be different at each activity level in the flexible budget.

For example, studies of past behavior of labor costs of the surgical nurses in the operating rooms of Sierra Memorial Outpatient Center indicate that the surgical nursing department expects to incur fixed costs of $500,000 per year and variable costs of $50 per operating room–hour. This cost function is graphed in Illustration 18.1. This is the same type of cost line used for cost-volume-profit (CVP) analysis. The expected activity level for the period is budgeted at 100,000 hours. From the

flexible budget
A budget that indicates revenues, costs, and profits for different levels of activity.

flexible budget line
The expected monthly costs at different output levels.

flexible budget line in Illustration 18.1, we find the budgeted costs at a planned activity of 100,000 operating room–hours to be $5.5 million [$500,000 + ($50 × 100,000 hours)].

Suppose that actual costs are only $5 million. At first glance, it might appear that the department had done a good job of cost control because costs were $500,000 lower than the budget plan. In fact, only 80,000 operating room–hours were actually incurred instead of the 100,000 hours originally planned. According to the flexible budget concept, the master budget must be adjusted for this change in activity. The adjusted budgeted costs for control and performance evaluation purposes would be the flexible budget that matches actual activity, $4.5 million ($500,000 + [$50 × 80,000 hours]). Now it is clear that although costs are lower than planned, they are $500,000 higher than they should be after considering the level of the department's activity.

The estimated cost-volume line in Illustration 18.1 is known as the *flexible budget line* because it shows the budgeted costs allowed for each level of activity. For example, if activity increased to 120,000 operating room-hours, budgeted costs would be $6.5 million ($500,000 + [$50 × 120,000 hours]). If activity drops to 50,000 operating room-hours, budgeted costs would drop to $3 million ($500,000 + [$50 × 50,000 operating room-hours]). The level of activity that occurred during the period is entered into the flexible budget equation:

$$TC = F + VX$$

where

TC = Total budgeted costs for the period
F = Fixed costs for the period
V = Variable costs per unit
X = Activity expressed as number of units

For Sierra Memorial's surgical nursing department,

$$TC = \$500,000 + \$50X$$

ILLUSTRATION   18.1   Comparison of Master and Flexible Budget, Surgical Nursing Department, Sierra Memorial Outpatient Center

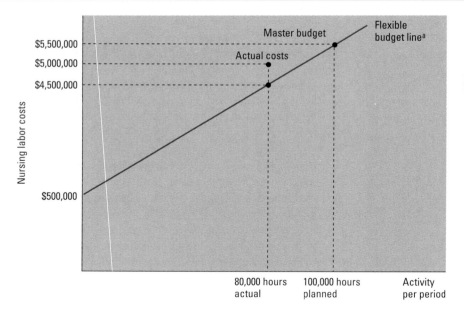

[a]This is the cost line from cost-volume-profit analysis.

You can compare the master budget with the flexible budget by thinking of the master budget as an ex ante (before-the-fact) prediction of *X* (activity); the flexible budget is based on ex post (after-the-fact) knowledge of the actual *X*.

COMPARING BUDGETS AND RESULTS

A comparison of the master budget with the flexible budget and with actual results forms the basis for analyzing differences between plans and actual performance. The following example is used in this and the next chapter to illustrate the comparison of plans with actual performance.

Evergreen Company makes wooden crates for shipping fruits. Its master budget income statement is presented in Illustration 18.2. The format is consistent with variable costing, not full-absorption costing. We use this variable costing format to analyze differences between actual and planned results because it separates fixed and variable costs. This separation is important for managerial estimates of cost behavior and profits.

The flexible budget, presented in Illustration 18.3, is based on *actual* activity. In May, Evergreen actually produced and sold 10,000 crates. The difference between operating profits in the master budget and operating profits in the flexible budget is called an **activity variance.** The $22,000 variance is due to the 2,000-unit difference between actual sales and planned sales. This difference also can be seen on the flexible budget profit-volume line in Illustration 18.4.

activity variance
Effect of changes in sales or production activity on profits.

Interpreting Variances

Note the use of F for favorable and U for unfavorable beside each variance in Illustration 18.3. These terms describe the impact of the variance on the budgeted operating profits. A *favorable variance increases operating profits*, holding all other things constant. An *unfavorable variance decreases operating profits*, holding all

ILLUSTRATION 18.2 | Master Budget, Evergreen Company

	Master Budget (based on 8,000 units planned)
Sales revenue (8,000 units at $20)	$160,000
Less	
Variable manufacturing costs	64,000[a]
Variable marketing and administrative costs	8,000[b]
Contribution margin	88,000
Less	
Fixed manufacturing costs	36,000
Fixed marketing and administrative costs	40,000
Operating profit	$ 12,000
Evergreen Company uses the following estimates to prepare the master budget	
Sales price	$20 per crate
Sales volume	8,000 crates
Production volume	8,000 crates
Variable manufacturing costs	$8 per crate
Variable marketing and administrative costs	$1 per crate
Fixed manufacturing costs	$36,000 per period
Fixed marketing and administrative costs	$40,000 per period

[a]8,000 budgeted units at $8 per unit.
[b]8,000 budgeted units at $1 per unit.

ILLUSTRATION 18.3	Flexible and Master Budget, Evergreen Company (May)		
	Flexible Budget[a] (based on actual activity of 10,000 units)	Sales Activity Variance (based on variance in sales volume)	Master Budget (based on 8,000 units planned)
Sales revenue.	$200,000	$40,000 F	$160,000
Less			
Variable manufacturing costs[b] (at $8 per unit).	80,000	16,000 U	64,000
Variable marketing and administrative costs (at $1 per unit).	10,000	2,000 U	8,000
Contribution margin	110,000	22,000 F	88,000
Less			
Fixed manufacturing costs	36,000	—	36,000
Fixed marketing and administrative costs.	40,000	—	40,000
Operating profits	$ 34,000	$22,000 F	$ 12,000

[a]Calculations for flexible budget:

$200,000 = 10,000/8,000 × $160,000.

$ 80,000 = 10,000/8,000 × $64,000.

$ 10,000 = 10,000/8,000 × $8,000.

Fixed costs are not expected to change between 8,000 and 10,000 units.

[b]This can be thought of as variable cost of goods sold.

U = Unfavorable variance.

F = Favorable variance.

favorable variance
Variance that, taken alone, results in an addition to operating profit.

unfavorable variance
Variance that, taken alone, reduces operating profit.

other things constant. These terms are not intended to be used in a normative sense; thus, a **favorable variance** is *not necessarily good*, and an **unfavorable variance** is *not necessarily bad*.

An excellent case in point is the sales activity or volume variance in Illustration 18.3. Holding everything else constant, the 2,000-unit increase in sales creates a favorable variance. Is this really good? Perhaps not. Economic conditions may have been better than planned, increasing the volume demanded by the market. Hence, perhaps, the 2,000-unit increase in sales volume should have been even greater, taking everything into account.

Note that both variable cost variances are labeled *unfavorable*, but this doesn't mean that they are bad for the company. Variable costs are expected to increase when volume is higher than planned.

Sales Activity Variance

L.O. 3: Compute and interpret the sales activity variance.

The information in Illustration 18.3 provides a lot of useful information. First, it isolates the increase in operating profits caused by the increase in activity from the master budget. Further, the resulting flexible budget shows budgeted sales, costs, and operating profits *after* considering the activity increase but *before* considering differences in *unit* selling prices, variable costs, and fixed costs from the master budget. As noted, we refer to this change from the master budget plan as the **sales activity variance,** also known as *sales volume variance*.

ILLUSTRATION   18.4   Flexible Budget Line, Evergreen Company

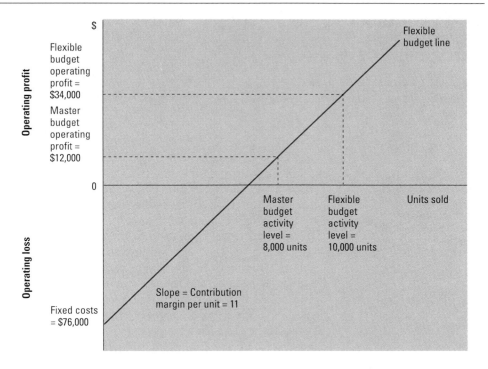

sales activity variance
Difference between operating
profit in the master budget and
operating profit in flexible budget
that arises because the actual
number of units sold is different
from the budgeted number; also
known as *sales volume variance.*

Some writers suggest that variance analysis is unnecessary when differences be-tween planned and actual activity levels exist. They suggest instead that tabulating the difference in volume alone is sufficient. For example, rather than point out that Evergreen had a favorable sales activity variance of $22,000, they would report that it sold 2,000 more units than planned. In practice, managers prefer variance data because it provides information about the impact of differences between plans and actual results on profit amounts.

Note the makeup of the $22,000 sales activity variance in Illustration 18.3. First, the difference between the master budget sales of $160,000 and the flexible budget sales of $200,000, which is the estimated $20 unit sales price times the 10,000 units actually sold, is $40,000. This is based on the 2,000-unit increase in sales volume times the estimated $20 unit sales price. We use the *estimated* unit sales price instead of the *actual* price because we want to isolate the impact of the activity increase from changes in the sales price. We want to focus on the effects of volume alone. Thus, the sales amount in the flexible budget is *not the actual revenue* (actual price times actual volume) but the *estimated unit sales price times the actual number of units sold.* Second, variable costs are *expected* to increase by $18,000, giving a favorable contribution margin of $22,000 ($40,000 − $18,000), which is the favor-able sales activity variance.

SELF-STUDY QUESTION

1. Prepare a flexible budget for Evergreen Company for May with the same master budget as in Illustration 18.3 but assuming that 7,000 units were actually sold.

The solution to this question is at the end of this chapter on page 578.

THE PROFIT VARIANCE ANALYSIS AS A KEY TOOL FOR MANAGERS

L.O. 4: Prepare and use a profit variance analysis.

Assume that the Evergreen Company's actual results for May are shown in the following table.

	Actual
Sales price	$21 per crate
Sales volume	10,000 crates
Variable production costs	$85,440
Variable marketing and administrative costs	11,000
Fixed production costs	37,000 for May
Fixed marketing and administrative costs	44,000 for May

profit variance analysis
Analysis of the causes of differences between budgeted profits and the actual profits earned.

The **profit variance analysis** shows the cause of differences between the budgeted profits and the actual profits earned. The actual results can be compared with both the flexible budget and the master budget in a profit variance analysis, as shown in Illustration 18.5. Columns 5, 6, and 7 are carried forward from Illustration 18.3.

Column 1 is the reported income statement based on the facts presented. Column 2 summarizes production variances, which are discussed in more detail in Chapter 19, and column 3 shows marketing and administrative variances. Costs have been divided into fixed and variable portions here and would be presented in more detail to the managers of centers having responsibility for them.

Cost variances result from deviations in costs and efficiencies in operating the company. They are important for measuring productivity and helping to control costs.

Sales Price Variance

The sales price variance, column 4, is derived from the *difference between the actual and budgeted selling price times the actual number of units sold* [$10,000 = ($21 − $20) × 10,000 units].

Variable Production Cost Variances

Be careful to distinguish the variable cost variances in columns 2 and 3 of Illustration 18.5, which are input variances, from the variable cost variances in column 6, which are part of the sales activity variance. Management expects the costs in the flexible budget to be higher, creating a sales activity variance, in this case because the sales volume is higher than planned.

As indicated in column 5, variable production costs *should have been* $80,000 for a production and sales volume of 10,000 units, not $64,000 as expressed in the master budget in column 7. Column 1 indicates that the actual variable production costs *were* $85,440, $21,440 higher than the master budget but only $5,440 higher than the flexible budget. Which number should be used to evaluate production cost control, the $21,440 variance from the master budget or the $5,440 variance from the flexible budget?

The number to use to evaluate production performance is the $5,440 variance from the flexible budget. This points out a benefit of flexible budgeting. A superficial comparison of the master budget plan with the actual results would have indicated the variance to be $21,440, but, in fact, production is responsible for only $5,440, which is caused by deviation from production norms. We discuss the source of this $5,440 in more detail in Chapter 19.

Fixed Production Cost Variance

The fixed production cost variance is simply the difference between actual and budgeted costs. Fixed costs are treated as period costs; they are not expected to be affected by activity levels within a relevant range. Hence, the flexible budget's fixed costs equal the master budget's fixed costs.

ILLUSTRATION 18.5 Profit Variance Analysis, Evergreen Company (May)

	(1) Actual (based on actual activity of 10,000 units sold)	(2) Manufacturing Variances	(3) Marketing and Administrative Variances	(4) Sales Price Variance	(5) Flexible Budget (based on actual activity of 10,000 units sold)	(6) Sales Activity Variance	(7) Master Budget (based on 8,000 units planned)
Sales revenue	$210,000	—	—	$10,000 F	$200,000	$40,000 F	$160,000
Less							
Variable manufacturing costs	85,440	$5,440 U [a]	—		80,000	16,000 U	64,000
Variable marketing and administrative costs	11,000	—	$1,000 U	—	10,000	2,000 U	8,000
Contribution margin	113,560	5,440 U	1,000 U	10,000 F	110,000	22,000 F	88,000
Less							
Fixed manufacturing costs	37,000	1,000 U	—	—	36,000	—	36,000
Fixed marketing and administrative costs	44,000	—	4,000 U	—	40,000	—	40,000
Operating profits	$ 32,560	$6,440 U	$5,000 U	$10,000 F	$ 34,000	$22,000 F	$ 12,000

Total variance from flexible budget = $1,440 U

Total variance from master budget = $20,560 F

[a]Highlighted to make this amount easier for reference throughout this chapter and in Chapter 19.

Marketing and Administrative Variances

Marketing and administrative costs are treated like production costs. Variable costs are expected to change as activity changes; hence, variable costs were expected to increase by $2,000 between the flexible and master budgets, as shown in Illustration 18.5, because volume increased by 2,000 units. Comparing actual with the flexible budget reveals $1,000 U variance for marketing and administrative costs. Fixed marketing and administrative costs do not change as volume changes; hence, the flexible and master budget amounts are the same.

SELF-STUDY QUESTION

2. In August, Containers, Inc., produced and sold 50,000 notebook computer cases for $10 each. Budgeted sales were 45,000 units at $10.15.

Budget	
Standard variable costs per unit (that is, per case)	$ 4.00
Fixed production overhead cost Monthly budget	80,000
Marketing and administrative	
Variable	1.00 per case
Fixed	100,000
Actual	
Actual production costs	
Variable costs per unit	4.88
Fixed overhead	83,000
Actual marketing and administrative	
Variable (50,000 @ $1.04)	52,000
Fixed	96,000

Using variable costing, prepare a profit variance analysis comparing actual results with the flexible and master budgets for August. Include variances.

The solution to this question is at the end of this chapter on page 579.

PROFIT VARIANCE ANALYSIS WHEN UNITS PRODUCED DO NOT EQUAL UNITS SOLD

In the previous example, production volume and sales volume were equal, but the analysis becomes more complicated when the units sold do not equal the units produced.

Suppose that Evergreen produced 12,000 units in May but sold only 10,000 units. Also assume that there was no beginning inventory. This has no effect on the sales activity variance because the master budget and flexible budget are based on *sales volume*. Thus, columns 5, 6, and 7 of Illustration 18.5 remain unchanged. In addition, the sales price variance is based on units sold, so column 4 remains the same. Generally, marketing and administrative costs are not affected by *producing* 12,000 instead of 10,000 units, so we assume that they do not change. This allows us to focus on columns 1 and 2, which do change.

Assume that actual production manufacturing costs are $8.544 *per unit* and fixed production costs are $37,000 *for the period*. This leaves the fixed production cost variance of $1,000 U unchanged. However, the variable production cost variance changes. In the month that units are produced, the following variable production cost variances are computed:

Units produced $\times$ (Actual variable cost $-$ Estimated variable cost) = Variance

The previous example for *10,000 units produced* (Illustration 18.5) is computed:

$$10,000 \times (\$8.544 - \$8.00) = \$5,440 \text{ U}$$

The present example for *12,000 units produced* (Illustration 18.6) is computed:

$$12,000 \times (\$8.544 - \$8.00) = \$6,528 \text{ U}$$

ILLUSTRATION 18.6 Profit Variance Analysis When Units Produced Do Not Equal Units Sold, Evergreen Company (May)

	(1) Actual (based on 10,000 units)[a]	(2) Manufacturing Variances	(3) Marketing and Administrative Variances	(4) Sales Price Variance	(5) Flexible Budget (based on 10,000 units)	(6) Sales Activity (volume) Variance	(7) Master Budget (based on 8,000 units planned)
Sales revenue	$210,000	—	—	$10,000 F	$200,000	$40,000 F	$160,000
Less							
Variable manufacturing costs	86,528	$6,528 U	—	—	80,000	16,000 U	64,000
Variable marketing and administrative costs	11,000	—	$1,000 U	—	10,000	2,000 U	8,000
Contribution margin	$112,472	$6,528 U	$1,000 U	$10,000 F	$110,000	$22,000 F	$ 88,000
Less							
Fixed manufacturing costs	37,000	1,000 U	—	—	36,000	—	36,000
Fixed marketing and administrative costs	44,000	—	4,000 U	—	40,000	—	40,000
Operating profits	$ 31,472	$7,528 U	$5,000 U	$10,000 F	$ 34,000	$22,000 F	$ 12,000

Total variance from flexible budget = $2,528 U

Total variance from master budget = $19,472 F

[a] Based on 10,000 units sold and 12,000 units produced.

The entire variable production cost variance for units *produced* in May is $6,528. This amount may be treated as a period cost and expensed in May, or it may be prorated to units sold and to units still in inventory. If prorated, $\frac{2}{12} \times \$6,528$ is charged to inventory in this case because 2,000 of the 12,000 units produced in May are still in inventory at the end of May. In most companies, the $6,528 variance due to May's production is written off as a period expense. The $6,528 appears as a variance, as shown in Illustration 18.6.

Note that the actual variable production costs of $86,528 in Illustration 18.6 are really a hybrid: $80,000 in flexible budget costs (based on 10,000 units sold this period times $8 estimated cost per unit) plus the $6,528 variable production cost variance from the 12,000 units produced this period.

RECONCILING VARIABLE BUDGETS AND FULL-ABSORPTION INCOME STATEMENTS

Assume that Evergreen Company produced 12,000 units and sold 10,000 units in May. There was no beginning inventory on May 1, so the ending inventory on May 31 was 2,000 units. Using variable costing, the entire *fixed production* cost of $37,000 is expensed, as shown in Illustrations 18.3 through 18.6. Such would not be the case, however, when full-absorption costing is used and production and sales volume are not the same.

Using full-absorption costing, a portion of the fixed production costs is allocated to the 2,000 units in ending inventory:

$$\frac{2,000 \text{ units}}{12,000 \text{ units}} \times \$37,000 = \$6,167$$

Or

$$\frac{\$37,000}{12,000 \text{ units}} = \$3.08\frac{1}{3} \text{ fixed manufacturing cost per unit}$$

Two thousand units are in ending inventory from current period production, so $6,167 (2,000 units $\times$ $3.08⅓) fixed production costs are allocated to ending inventory.

Thus, only $30,833 ($37,000 − $6,167) of the actual fixed production costs are expensed in May using full-absorption costing. In this case, full-absorption operating profit would be $37,639 in May, or $6,167 higher than variable costing operating profit.[1] This $6,167 difference in profits is due to the accounting system, not to managerial efficiencies. Care should be taken to identify the cause of such profit differences so those due to accounting method are not misinterpreted as being caused by operating activities.

The budget planning and control methods presented in this book are based on the variable costing approach to product costing unless otherwise stated. Illustration 18.7 shows how the reported income statement under full-absorption is reconciled with that using variable costing. The comparison of budgeted to actual results presented in Illustration 18.6 is still used; however, additional columns (1a and 1b) are added to reconcile actual results using variable costing to those using full-absorption costing.

---

[1] Of course, if the number of units sold exceed the number of units produced, we expect the reverse to be true; that is, full-absorption operating profit is lower than variable costing operating profit.

ILLUSTRATION 18.7	Reconciling Actual Income Using Full-Absorption Costing and Variable Costing		
	(1a)	(1b) (Inventory Adjustment) Fixed Manufacturing Costs Going into Inventory Using Full Absorption	(1c)
	Actual Using Full Absorption		Actual Using Variable Costing
Sales revenue	$210,000		$210,000
Less			
Variable manufacturing costs	86,528		86,528
Variable marketing and administrative costs	11,000		11,000
Contribution margin.	$112,472		$112,472
Less			
Fixed manufacturing costs.	30,833	$6,167[a]	37,000
Fixed marketing and administrative costs	44,000		44,000
Operating profits.	$ 37,639	$6,167	$ 31,472

[a]2,000 units put into inventory times $3.083 $\left(= \dfrac{\$37,000}{12,000 \text{ units}} \right)$ fixed manufacturing cost per unit.

USING THE PROFIT VARIANCE ANALYSIS IN SERVICE AND MERCHANDISE ORGANIZATIONS

The comparison of the master budget, the flexible budget, and actual results also can be used in service and merchandising organizations. The basic framework in Illustration 18.5 is retained. Output is usually defined as sales units in merchandising, but service organizations use other measures, for example:

Organization	Units of Activity
Public accounting, legal, and consulting firms	Professional staff hours
Laundry	Weight or pieces of clothing
Hospital	Patient-days

Merchandising and service organizations focus on marketing and administrative costs to measure efficiency and control costs. The key items to control are labor costs, particularly for service organizations, and occupancy costs per sales-dollar, particularly for merchandising organizations.

USING ACTIVITY-BASED COSTING IN BUDGETING

A flexible budget often is prepared using activity-based costing. Companies that use activity-based costing divide variable production costs among multiple activity bases, or cost drivers, one for each activity center. For example, Evergreen Company might have three activity centers and related cost drivers as follows:

Activity Center	Cost Driver
Indirect materials	Number of board-feet
Energy	Machine-minutes
Quality testing and repair	Number of minutes in testing

A standard cost per cost driver is established (for example, $.05 per board-foot) and is used in preparing the master budget (based on planned activity) and the flexible budget (based on actual activity). The profit variance analysis looks much like the analysis shown in Illustration 18.5 except that Evergreen has the ability to identify the cause of variable production cost variances with more precision. We discuss the variance analysis process using activity-based costing in more detail in Chapter 19.

COMPARING STANDARD COSTING, TARGET COSTING, AND *KAIZEN* COSTING

L.O. 5: Compare and contrast target costing, *kaizen* budgeting, and standard costing.

We have described how standard costs are established in a standard costing system. One question remains unanswered, however: How are standard costs established in target costing and *kaizen* costing systems?

Target Costing

target costing
A market-driven method of establishing target costs by starting with a target sales price and deducting the target margin.

Target costing is a systematic approach to establishing product cost goals based on market-driven factors. This approach is quite different from standard costing in that target costing begins by identifying customers' needs and calculating an acceptable sales price for the product. Working backward from the sales price, companies establish an acceptable target margin and calculate the target cost (target sales price − target margin = target cost).

Since target costing is used primarily for new products, no historical data are available for establishing standard costs. Target costing emphasizes reducing costs in the research, development, design, and production phases of the process. Target costs serve as goals for research and development, designers, and production personnel (the first three areas in the value chain). If the target cost cannot be achieved, management looks closely at the viability of making the proposed product.

Target costs are determined by market-driven factors (i.e., a target sales price as determined by the market), whereas standard costs typically are determined by design-driven standards with less emphasis on what the market will pay (i.e., design costs + the desired markup = desired sales price).

Kaizen Costing

kaizen costing
A costing system that emphasizes continuous improvement in small activities by seeking to reduce production costs continually.

In contrast to the target costing approach that supports the cost reduction process in the development and design phases of *new* products, **kaizen costing (or budgeting)** supports the cost reduction process in the manufacturing phase of *existing* products. *Kaizen* is a Japanese term referring to continuous improvement in relatively small steps to reduce production costs.

The goal of *kaizen* costing is to reduce actual costs to manufacture a product below previous cost levels. Standard cost systems generally focus on meeting the cost standard set by management. *Kaizen* costing systems are more concerned with continually reducing actual costs below previous levels. Under *kaizen* costing, employees are expected to continually reduce production costs and increase efficiency. This approach is used by Citizen Watch, a well known Japanese watch maker. When setting goals, the company seeks to reduce past costs by 3 percent each year.

Culp, Inc., Institutes Target Costing

Culp, Inc., a textile manufacturer for the home furnishings industry, recently implemented target costing after deciding that cost management was one of Culp's most strategically imperative issues. Culp combined the efforts of marketing, operations, and accounting while recognizing that target costing depends on a relationship with and working knowledge of each to be successful.

Culp undertook the target costing program to help decrease the cost of products at the design stage and to build profits. This team approach to cost management brings together the diverse interests in the company—engineering, operations, finance, and accounting.

Culp views target costing as a change in the way it uses the costing information already available, not as a costing issue. It has achieved the changes by integrating cost management with the firm's other activities. The results have exceeded the firm's expectations.

Source: J. M. Brausch, "Beyond ABC: Target Costing," *Management Accounting* 76, no. 5 (November 1994), pp. 45–49.

BUDGETING BY RESPONSIBILITY CENTER

L.O. 6: Explain responsibility centers' use of budgeting.

responsibility centers
Organization units for which someone has responsibility.

Budgets for performance evaluation and cost control are typically organized into **responsibility centers,** which are organization units for which someone has responsibility. For example, a business school within a university is often a responsibility center. The dean of the business school has a budgeted level of resources to work with and is responsible to university officials for the way those resources are used to achieve the university's goals. The following are other examples:

Responsibility Center	Person in Charge	Responsible For
Company	Chief executive officer	All assets, equities, revenues, and costs of the company
Division	Division vice president	Divisional assets, equities, revenues, and costs
Plant	Plant manager	Plant production and costs
Department store	Store manager	Store's revenues and costs
Secretarial pool	Secretarial pool supervisor	Costs and secretarial production

For example, the assignment of responsibilities for Electronics, Inc., is shown in Illustration 18.8. Each of the three vice presidents—administrative, production, and marketing—is responsible for part of the organization.

The administrative responsibility center is subdivided into departments (data processing, accounting, personnel). The production responsibility center is further divided among plant managers, who assign responsibility to department heads (assembly, processing, quality control, warehousing). The marketing vice president assigns marketing responsibility to the district sales managers.

Profit and Cost Centers

cost center
Organizational unit responsible for costs.

profit center
Organizational unit responsible for revenues and costs.

Organizations use two basic types of responsibility centers with a profit variance analysis. The first is a **cost center,** in which managers of organizational units are responsible for costs. Of course, managers are also responsible for the quality and the amount of output, employee morale, and other things. Managers of cost centers are not responsible for revenues, however. For example, the department heads of the production plants are probably in charge of cost centers.

Profit center managers are responsible for both revenue and costs. The manager of the bank where you keep your accounts, the manager of the service station or auto repair shop where you have your car repaired, and the manager of your favorite restaurant are likely to be profit center managers. Profit center managers use a profit variance analysis to plan and control their operations. Cost center managers use the

---

ILLUSTRATION   18.8   Responsibility Centers, Electronics, Inc.

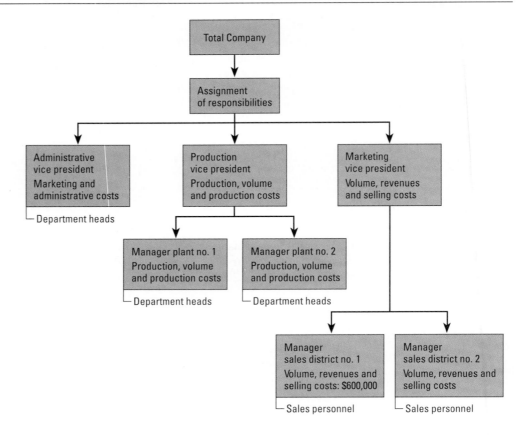

cost portion of a profit variance analysis to manage activities. Both profit and cost center managers require more detailed information about expected and actual costs than that presented in a profit variance analysis. Chapter 19 discusses additional cost variance analyses for managers to use.

BEHAVIORAL ISSUES IN BUDGETING

"You should hold employees responsible for those things they can control" sometimes is considered an important behavioral factor in designing accounting systems. This appeals to a sense of fairness that, for example, the manager of the assembly department should not be charged with inefficiencies caused by the cutting department. Perhaps of more significance, in an economic sense, is the idea that holding employees responsible for the things they can control focuses managers' attention on the things they can influence and reduces their risk. Flexible budgets can reduce risk to people, as the following example demonstrates.

Assume that the manager of the repairs department had a $100,000 budget for December. Machine time turned out to be low in December, and repairs were scheduled easily without overtime. As a result, the manager spent only $90,000 of the budget. Suppose, however, that production increased during January, and department personnel worked overtime to make the necessary repairs. The repairs department's expenditures were $110,000 in January.

The manager of the repairs department believes that performance is evaluated according to the budget and that his bonus, raises, promotions, and job could depend on meeting the budget. A risk-averse manager prefers a system that adjusts the budget down to $90,000 in December and up to $110,000 in January to reflect the changing levels of production, even though the average results for the two months are the same.

The idea that employees should be held accountable for what they control does not mean that factors outside of their control should be ignored in evaluating performance. For example, information from an employee's peers may be useful in evaluating how well the employee is performing. This is analogous to grading on the curve, where knowing how well a specific student did relative to the rest of the class is usually more informative about student exam performance than just knowing that student's exam score. Few employers ignore information about factors outside an employee's control that nevertheless affect his or her performance.

How Hard Should It Be to Achieve Goals?

According to research, budgets that are very difficult or very easy to achieve may not lead to the best employee performance. Motivating employees is similar to motivating students. For example, if it is virtually impossible to improve your grade by studying hard for a test, you may not be as motivated to study as hard as you would if you believed that studying might well improve your grade. On the other hand, if you believe that you will get a good grade with minimal studying, you may not be inclined to study beyond that minimal level.

In general, the budget levels that seem to motivate best are moderately tight but are perceived by employees as reasonable and attainable. This generalization may vary from situation to situation, of course.

MEETING THE BUDGET: POSSIBLE ETHICAL CONFLICTS

L.O. 7: Identify the ethical problems that arise when budgets are used for performance evaluation.

The pressure to meet budgeted levels can be considerable, so much so that sometimes people play games with revenue recognition. For example, how would you deal with the following situation? You made a large sale on December 31, the last day of your company's fiscal year. The paperwork cannot be processed until January 2 of next year, meaning that the sale will be recorded next year. Your department's sales performance has not been good this year, so you face the prospect of being fired. Recording the sale this year would considerably help your prospects for keeping the job. You learn from a friend in accounting that you could backdate the paperwork from January 2 to December 31, as long as no other sales have been recorded for next year. What would you do?

Employees constantly face such situations. Most companies have a policy allowing employees a reasonable period of time to prepare necessary paperwork. In addition, by explaining the circumstances to your supervisors, you would probably be given some credit for the sale even if it were not recorded until next year. Nevertheless, many people in organizations face considerable pressure to recognize revenue early, which means that they record the sale before it has been finalized.

For example, Comserv Corporation was a computer software company that installed specialized software for manufacturing companies. It recorded a portion of the revenue from a contract when it was signed and recorded the remaining revenue when the software was installed. (A similar case involved MiniScribe Corporation, described in the Real World Application on page 566.) Comserv's management felt the pressure to report substantial profits so the company could keep up with its competitors in the computer software industry. Salespeople backdated contracts and wrote contracts based only on oral confirmation from customers.

Employees at a plant in Ronson Corporation's Aerospace Division claimed that they had completed and sold large jobs when in fact the uncompleted jobs were hidden from the auditors in buildings the auditors did not inspect. In both the Comserv and Ronson cases, the Securities and Exchange Commission (SEC) filed formal charges against corporate employees alleging they had committed financial fraud.

No matter what your career choice, whether in a large business or in a one-person operation, whether public accounting, private industry, or the public sector, you will face pressure to perform that could compromise your ethical standards. We hope that you will recognize these situations. A key signal is the "tone at the top."

REAL WORLD APPLICATION | **When Is a Sale Not Really a Sale?**

MiniScribe Corporation, a manufacturer of computer disk drives, reported record earnings for several quarters. Its stock had increased fivefold over an 18-month period, but fabricated financial results lay behind the company's reported excellent financial performance. A subsequent court suit revealed that $16 million of sales made on the day after the fiscal year-end were backdated to the previous year. The company had shipped disk drives to customers who had not ordered them and had booked revenue for 432 disk drives that it shipped to its own warehouse instead of to customers. Two years after the fraud, the company restated its originally reported profits of $22.7 million to $12.2 million.

Based on Lee Berton, "How MiniScribe Got Its Auditor's Blessing on Questionable Sales," *The Wall Street Journal,* May 14, 1992, pp. A1 and A5.

Top managers who emphasize results at all costs create an environment in which performing well professionally while maintaining high ethical standards may be difficult. Watch also for situations in which people are desperate to perform well, perhaps because of financial difficulties.

SUMMARY

This chapter discussed and illustrated the use of the budgeted income statement for performance evaluation and control. The master budget income statement was compared with actual results. Differences, or variances, between actual results and the master budget were analyzed to determine why budgeted results did not occur.

The following summarizes key ideas tied to the chapter's learning objectives.

LO1: Using budgets for performance evaluation. *Budgets* provide a view of anticipated operations and enable management to measure the performance of employees in various areas of the production and sales processes.

LO2: Developing and using flexible budgets. The *master budget* is typically static; that is, it is developed in detail for one level of activity. A *flexible budget* recognizes that variable costs and revenues are expected to differ from the budget if the actual activity (for example, actual sales volume) differs from what was budgeted. A flexible budget can be thought of as the costs and revenues that would have been budgeted if the activity level had been correctly estimated in the master budget. The general relationship between the actual results, the flexible budget, and the master budget follows:

Actual	Flexible Budget	Master Budget
Actual costs and revenues based on actual activity	Cost and revenues that would have been budgeted if actual activity had been budgeted	Budgeted costs and revenues based on budgeted activity

LO3: Computing the sales activity variance. The sales activity variance is simply the difference in the operating profit from the master budget to the flexible budget. This difference (or variance) arises because the actual number of units sold is different from the number budgeted in the master budget.

LO4: Preparing and using the profit variance analysis. The *profit variance analysis* outlines the causes of differences between budgeted profits and the actual profits earned. Variances are separated into four categories: production, marketing and administrative, sales price, and sales activity.

LO5: Target costing, *kaizen* budgeting, and standard costing. Target costing is a market-driven approach to establishing standard costs for new products (target sales price − target margin = target cost). *Kaizen* budgeting supports the cost reduction process in the production phase of existing products by implementing the concept of continuous improvement in all activities. Standard costing systems set predetermined costs and assign them to goods produced. Continuous improvement is not necessarily a goal of standard costing systems unless implemented with *kaizen* budgeting.

LO6: Responsibility centers. Budgets for performance evaluation and cost control are typically organized into *responsibility centers*. Two responsibility centers—cost centers and profit centers—are outlined in this chapter. Cost centers are organization units responsible only for costs (for example, a production department). Profit center managers are responsible for both revenue and costs (for example, the manager at a restaurant).

LO7: Ethical problems in budgeting. Evaluating employees based on a profit variance analysis often can provide an incentive for employees to manipulate revenues and/or costs to improve their departmental results. The SEC recently has scrutinized several large companies for committing financial fraud. Employees manipulated the books as a result of heavy pressure from the top to improve financial performance.

KEY TERMS

activity variance, 553	profit variance analysis, 556
cost center, 563	responsibility centers, 563
favorable variance, 554	sales activity variance, 555
financial budgets, 550	standard cost, 550
flexible budget, 551	static budget, 551
flexible budget line, 552	target costing, 562
kaizen costing, 562	unfavorable variance, 554
operating budgets, 550	variances, 550
profit center, 563	

REVIEW QUESTIONS

18.1 What is a responsibility center?

18.2 Could some responsibility centers differ as to the type of budget items for which they are accountable? That is, might some responsibility centers be responsible only for costs, some only for revenues, and some for both? Give examples.

18.3 Why is a contribution margin format based on variable costing more useful for performance evaluation purposes than the traditional format based on full-absorption costing?

18.4 "All costs 'flex' with activity." Is this true or false? Why or why not?

18.5 What is the difference between standard costing and target costing?

18.6 The basic difference between a master budget and a flexible budget is that
- **a.** A flexible budget considers only variable costs; a master budget considers all costs.
- **b.** A flexible budget allows management latitude in meeting goals; a master budget is based on a fixed standard.
- **c.** A master budget is for an entire production facility; a flexible budget is applicable only to individual departments.
- **d.** A master budget is based on a predicted level of activity; a flexible budget is based on the actual level of activity.

(CPA adapted)

18.7 A flexible budget is
   a. Appropriate for control of factory overhead but not for control of direct materials and direct labor.
   b. Appropriate for control of direct materials and direct labor but not for control of factory overhead.
   c. Not appropriate when costs and expenses are affected by fluctuations in volume.
   d. Appropriate for any level of activity.

(CPA adapted)

CRITICAL ANALYSIS AND DISCUSSION QUESTIONS

18.8 Does a line worker avoid responsibility because he or she is not included formally in the responsibility reporting system? How can management control the line worker's activities in the absence of formal budget control?

18.9 Budgets for government units are usually prepared one year in advance of the budget period. Expenditures are limited to the budgeted amount. At the end of the period, performance is evaluated by comparing budget authorizations with actual receipts and outlays. What management control problems are likely to arise from such a system?

18.10 "I don't understand why you accountants want to prepare a budget for a period that is already over. We know the actual results by then—all that flexible budgeting does is increase the controller's staff and add to our overhead." Comment on this remark.

18.11 How will a company's performance measurement system differ under the LIFO inventory system compared to the FIFO system?

18.12 Refer to the Real World Application, "When Is a Sale Not Really a Sale?" on page 566. Why did MiniScribe managers ship disk drives to customers who had not ordered them and backdate invoices to the previous fiscal year?

18.13 How does the concept of flexible budgeting reinforce the notion that employees should be held responsible only for what they can control?

EXERCISES

18.14 Flexible Budgeting (L.O. 2)

Davidson, Inc., prepared a budget last period that called for sales of 18,000 units at $12 each. The costs were estimated to be $5 variable per unit and $54,000 fixed. During the period, actual production and actual sales were 18,400 units. The selling price was $12.15 per unit. Variable costs were $5.90 per unit. Actual fixed costs were $54,000.

Required

Prepare a flexible budget for Davidson.

18.15 Sales Activity Variance (L.O. 3)

Refer to the data in Exercise 18.14. Prepare a sales activity variance analysis like the one in Illustration 18.3.

18.16 Profit Variance Analysis (L.O. 4)

Refer to the data in Exercises 18.14 and 18.15. Prepare a profit variance analysis like the one in Illustration 18.5.

18.17 Flexible Budgeting, Service Organization (L.O. 2)

Wright & Allen is a CPA firm that obtains a large portion of its revenue from tax services. Last year, Wright & Allen is billed more tax hours than expected; but as the following data show, profits from the tax department were lower than anticipated.

	Reported Income Statement	Master Budget
Billable hours[a]	23,000	20,000
Revenue	$1,650,000	$1,500,000
Professional salaries (all variable)	925,000	750,000
Other variable costs (e.g., supplies, computer services)	212,500	200,000
Fixed costs.	290,000	300,000
Tax department profit	$222,500	$250,000

[a]These are hours billed to clients. They are fewer than the number of hours worked because there is nonbillable time (e.g., slack periods, time in training sessions) and because some time worked for clients is not charged to them.

Required

Prepare a flexible budget for Wright & Allen. Use billable hours as the measure of output (that is, units produced).

18.18   Sales Activity Variance, Service Organization (L.O. 3)

Refer to the data in Exercise 18.17. Prepare a sales activity variance analysis like the one in Illustration 18.3.

18.19   Profit Variance Analysis, Service Organization (L.O. 4)

Refer to the data in Exercise in 18.17. Prepare a profit variance analysis for Wright & Allen like the one in Illustration 18.5.

18.20   Flexible Budget (L.O. 2)

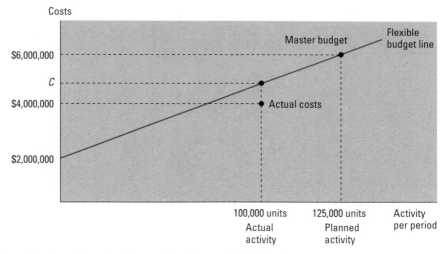

Required

Given the data shown in the graph, what are the following:

a.   Budgeted fixed cost per period?

b.   Budgeted variable cost per unit?

c.   Value of *C* (that is, the flexible budget for an activity level of 100,000 units)?

d.   Flexible budget cost amount if the actual activity had been 200,000 units?

18.21   Fill in Amounts on Flexible Budget Graph (L.O. 2)

Fill in the missing amounts for (a) and (b) in the following graph.

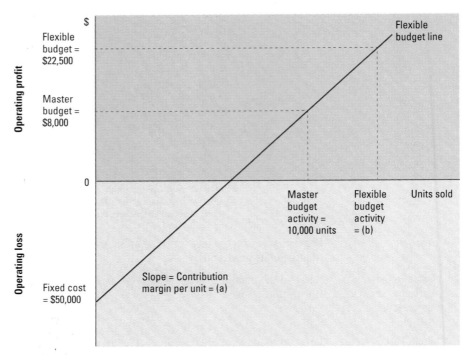

| **18.22** | Flexible Budget
(L.O. 2) | Label (a) and (b) in the graph and give the number of units sold for each. |

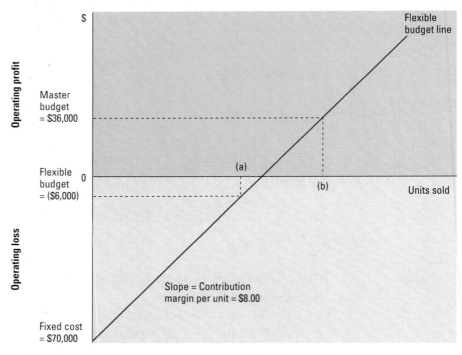

| **18.23** | Prepare
Flexible Budget
(L.O. 2) | Graphix, Inc., manufactures and sells compact discs for a variety of New Age groups. The company produces only when it receives orders and, therefore, has no inventories. The following information is available for the current month: |

	Actual (based on actual of 850,000 units)	Master Budget (based on budgeted 800,000 units)
Sales revenue	$3,860,000	$4,000,000
Less		
Variable costs		
Blank discs	$1,200,000	$1,200,000
Direct labor	330,000	280,000
Variable overhead	478,000	520,000
Variable marketing and administrative	410,000	400,000
Total variable costs	2,418,000	2,400,000
Contribution margin	$1,442,000	$1,600,000
Less		
Fixed costs		
Manufacturing overhead	776,000	800,000
Marketing	240,000	240,000
Administrative	130,000	150,000
Total fixed costs	$1,146,000	$1,190,000
Operating profits	$ 296,000	$ 410,000

Required Prepare a flexible budget for Graphix.

18.24 **Sales Activity Variance** (L.O. 3) Refer to the data in Exercise 18.23. Prepare a sales activity variance analysis for Graphix like the one in Illustration 18.3.

18.25 **Profit Variance Analysis** (L.O. 4) Use the information from Exercise 18.23 to prepare a profit variance analysis for Graphix like the one in Illustration 18.5.

18.26 **Assigning Responsibility** (L.O. 6) Berg & Jordan public accountants perform both audit and tax work for clients. The tax department relies on the audit department's work to prepare tax returns. On a recent job, the audit team goofed. Consequently, the tax department prepared the tax return improperly.

Now the Internal Revenue Service is auditing the client. The audit requires a great deal of time and effort by the tax department with no compensation from the client. The tax department manager argues that the audit department should bear some of the cost of the tax audit. The audit department manager says that the tax department should have checked the numbers before using them.

Required As the manager of the accounting firm, how would you assign responsibility?

18.27 **Assigning Responsibility** (L.O. 6) The manager of the soldering area of a company that manufactures computer circuit boards asked the manager of the start station to stop production for a few hours to perform emergency maintenance on the soldering machines. The start station manager refused, saying, "My job requires me to keep the production line going." Consequently, the production line kept running, and the quality reject rate for products coming out of the soldering operation increased from virtually zero to nearly 50 percent.

Management learned about the quality problem and ordered the production line to be stopped. The product rejects cost the company about $50,000.

Required As top management, to whom would you assign the responsibility for the $50,000 of product rejects?

PROBLEMS

18.28   **Solve for Master Budget Given Actual Results**

Kentron Enterprises lost the only copy of this period's master budget. Management wants to evaluate performance for this period but needs the master budget to do so. Actual results for the period follow:

Sales volume	120,000 units
Sales revenue.	$672,000
Variable costs	
Manufacturing.	147,200
Marketing and administrative	61,400
Contribution margin.	$463,400
Fixed costs	
Manufacturing.	205,000
Marketing and administrative	113,200
Operating profit.	$145,200

The company planned to produce and sell 108,000 units for $5 each. At that volume, the contribution margin would have been $380,000. Variable marketing and administrative costs are budgeted at 10 percent of sales revenue. Manufacturing fixed costs are estimated at $2 per unit at the normal volume of 108,000 units. Management notes, "We budget an operating profit of $1 per unit at the normal volume."

Required

a.   Construct the master budget for the period.

b.   Prepare a profit variance analysis like the one in Illustration 18.5.

18.29   **Find Missing Data for Profit Variance Analysis**

	Reported Income Statement (750 units)	Manu-facturing Variance	Marketing and Administrative Variance	Sales Price variance	Flexible Budget (a)	Sales Activity Variance	Master Budget (800 units)
Sales revenue	$1,950			(b)	$2,025	(c)	(d)
Variable manu-facturing costs	(e)	$60 F			(f)	$38 F	(g)
Variable marketing and administrative costs	(h)		(i)		(j)	(k)	$240
Contribution margin . . .	$1,240	(l)	(m)	(n)	(o)	(p)	(q)

Required

Find the values of the missing items (*a*) through (*q*). Assume that the actual sales volume equals actual production volume. (There are no inventory level changes.)

18.30   **Find Data for Profit Variance Analysis**

Refer to Illustration 18.9. Find the values of the missing items (*a*) through (*x*). Assume that actual sales volume equals actual production volume. (There are no inventory level changes.)

18.31   **Ethical Issues in Managing Reported Profits**

Herald Company manufactures lighting fixtures and electronic timers. Midyear, the CEO suffered a heart attack and retired. The new CEO did some reorganization, including discontinuing the lighting fixtures division's mid-range product line. The new CEO, relying on market research, wanted to focus production on the remaining two product lines produced by the lighting fixtures division. (The electronic timers division was unaffected by the change in top management.)

Market studies proved correct, and, by the end of the year, the lighting fixtures division had exceeded budgeted profits by 15 percent. The controller, Mary Chan, knew that her annual bonus depended on exceeding budgeted profit and that her bonus would plateau at 10 percent above budgeted profit. Mary expected that next year's profit plan would be similar but that next year's budget would consider the changes in the product lines. Mary discovered that she could accrue some of next year's expenses and defer some of this year's revenue while still exceeding budgeted profit by 10 percent.

Required

Why would Mary Chan, Herald Company's controller, want to defer revenue but accrue expenses? Is this ethical?

(CMA adapted)

ILLUSTRATION   18.9

	Reported Income Statement (based on actual sales volume)	Manufacturing Variance	Marketing and Administrative Variance	Sales Price Variances	Flexible Budget (based on actual sales volume)	Sales Activity Variance	Master Budget (based on budgeted sales volume)
Units..................	(a)				(b)	2,000 F	10,000
Sales revenue............	(g)			$18,000 F	(h)	(i)	$150,000
Less							
Variable manufacturing costs................	(n)	(o)			$96,000	(j)	80,000
Variable marketing and administrative costs......	$21,600		(p)		24,000	$4,000 U	(c)
Contribution margin........	(q)	$9,000 U	(s)	(x)	60,000	(k)	50,000
Less							
Fixed manufacturing costs ..	(r)	2,000 F			(m)		(d)
Fixed marketing and administrative costs......	18,000		(v)		15,000		(e)
Operating profits..........	(t)	(u)	(w)	$18,000 F	$20,000	(l)	(f)

18.32

Prepare
Flexible Budget

The following information is provided concerning the operations of Ishima Corporation for the current period:

	Actual (based on actual of 90 units)	Master Budget (based on budgeted 100 units)
Sales revenue	$9,200	$10,000
Less		
Manufacturing costs		
Direct labor...........	1,420	1,500
Materials	1,200	1,400
Variable overhead	820	1,000
Marketing	530	600
Administrative	500	500
Total variable costs........	$4,470	$ 5,000
Contribution margin........	$4,730	$ 5,000
Less		
Fixed costs		
Manufacturing.........	485	500
Marketing............	1,040	1,000
Administrative.........	995	1,000
Total fixed costs..........	2,520	2,500
Operating profits..........	$2,210	$ 2,500

There are no inventories.

Required   Prepare a flexible budget for Ishima Corporation.

18.33 Sales Activity Variance

Refer to the data in Problem 18.32. Prepare a sales activity variance analysis for Ishima Corporation like the one in Illustration 18.3.

18.34 Profit Variance Analysis

Use the information for Ishima Corporation in Problem 18.32 to prepare a profit variance analysis like the one in Illustration 18.5.

18.35 Derive Amounts for Profit Variance Analysis

Checker Cab Company operates a limousine and taxicab service. It wants to compare this month's results with last month's, which management believed to be a typical "base period." Assume that the following information is provided:

	Last Month	This Month
Number of trips	14,000	16,100
Revenues	$151,000	$152,000
Variable costs	38,200	43,500
Contribution margin	$112,800	$108,500

Required

Compute the flexible budget and sales activity variance and prepare a profit variance analysis (like the one in Illustration 18.5) in as much detail as possible. (*Hint*: Use last month as the master budget and this month as the "actual.") What impact did the changes in number of trips and average revenues (i.e., sales price) have on Checker Cab's contribution margin?

18.36 Flexible Budget— Multiple Choice

The City of Dixon operates a motor pool with 20 vehicles. The motor pool furnishes gasoline, oil, and other supplies for the cars and hires one mechanic who does routine maintenance and minor repairs. Major repairs are done at a nearby commercial garage. A supervisor manages the operations.

Each year, the supervisor prepares a master budget for the motor pool. Depreciation on the automobiles is recorded in the budget to determine the costs per mile.

The schedule below presents the master budget for the year and for the month of March.

DIXON MOTOR POOL
Budget Report for March

	Annual Master Budget	One-Month Master Budget	March Actual	Over- or (Under) Budget
Gasoline.	$ 36,000	$3,000	$3,800	$800
Oil, minor repairs, parts, and supplies	3,600	300	380	80
Outside repairs	2,700	225	50	(175)
Insurance.	6,000	500	525	25
Salaries and benefits	30,000	2,500	2,500	—
Depreciation	26,400	2,200	2,310	110
	$104,700	$8,725	$9,565	$840
Total miles	600,000	50,000	63,000	
Cost per mile	$0.1745	$0.1745	$0.1518	
Number of automobiles	20	20	21	

The annual budget was based on the following assumptions:

1. Automobiles in the pool—20.
2. Miles per year per automobile—30,000.
3. Miles per gallon per automobile—20.
4. Gas per gallon—$1.20.
5. Oil, minor repairs, parts, and supplies per mile—$0.006.
6. Outside repairs per automobile per year—$135.

The supervisor is unhappy with the monthly report, claiming that it unfairly presents his performance for March. His previous employer used flexible budgeting to compare actual costs to budgeted amounts.

Required

a. What is the gasoline monthly flexible budget and the resulting over or under budget? (Use miles as the activity base.)

	Flexible Budget	Over (Under) Budget
(1).	$3,000	$800
(2).	3,520	280
(3).	3,800	–0–
(4).	3,780	20
(5) Some other answer.		

b. What is the monthly flexible budget for the oil, minor repairs, parts, and supplies and the amount over or under budget? (Use miles as the activity base.)

	Flexible Budget	Over (Under) Budget
(1).	$400	$(20)
(2).	300	80
(3).	378	2
(4).	300	–0–
(5) Some other answer.		

c. What is the monthly flexible budget for salaries and benefits and the resulting over or under budget?

	Flexible Budget	Over (Under) Budget
(1).	$2,625	$125
(2).	2,500	(125)
(3).	2,625	–0–
(4).	2,500	–0–
(5) Some other answer.		

d. What is the major reason for the cost per mile to decrease from $0.1745 budgeted to $0.1518 actual?
  (1) Decreased unit fixed costs.
  (2) Decreased unit variable costs.
  (3) Increased unit fixed cost and decreased unit variable cost.
  (4) Neither variable nor fixed unit costs decreased.

(CMA adapted)

18.37

Analyze Performance for a Restaurant

Arbuckles is planning to expand operations and, hence, is concerned that its reporting system may need improvement. The master budget income statement for the Chicago Arbuckles, which contains a delicatessen and restaurant operation, follows (in thousands):

	Delicatessen	Restaurant	Total
Gross sales.	$1,000	$2,500	$3,500
Purchases.	600	1,000	1,600
Hourly wages	50	875	925
Franchise fee.	30	75	105
Advertising	100	200	300
Utilities	70	125	195
Depreciation	50	75	125
Lease cost	30	50	80
Salaries	30	50	80
Total costs	$ 960	$2,450	$3,410
Operating profit	$ 40	$ 50	$ 90

The company uses the following performance report for management evaluation:

ARBUCKLES
Chicago, Illinois
Net Income for the Year
(in thousands)

	Actual Results				Over (Under) Budget
	Delicatessen	Restaurant	Total	Budget	
Gross sales	$1,200	$2,000	$3,200	$3,500	$(300)[a]
Purchases[b]	780	800	1,580	1,600	(20)
Hourly wages[b]	60	700	760	925	(165)
Franchise fee[b]	36	60	96	105	(9)
Advertising	100	200	300	300	—
Utilities[b]	76	100	176	195	(19)
Depreciation	50	75	125	125	—
Lease cost	30	50	80	80	—
Salaries	30	50	80	80	—
Total costs	$1,162	$2,035	$3,197	$3,410	$(213)
Operating profit	$ 38	$ (35)	$ 3	$ 90	$ (87)

[a]There is no sales price variance.

[b]Variable costs; all other costs are fixed.

Required   Prepare a profit variance analysis for the delicatessen segment. (*Hint:* Use gross sales as your measure of volume.)

(CMA adapted)

INTEGRATIVE CASES

18.38 Analyze the Budget Planning Process: Behavioral Issues

RV Industries manufactures and sells recreation vehicles. The company has eight divisions strategically located near major markets each with a sales force and two to four manufacturing plants. These divisions operate as autonomous profit centers responsible for purchasing, operations, and sales.

The corporate controller, T. Collins, describes the divisional performance measurement system as follows:

> We allow the divisions to control the entire operation from the purchase of direct materials to the sale of the product. We at corporate headquarters get involved only in strategic decisions such as developing new product lines. Each division is responsible for meeting its market needs by providing the right products at a low cost on a timely basis. Frankly, the divisions need to focus on cost control, delivery, and services to customers to become more profitable. However, being as close as they are to their markets, they are best qualified to determine how to do this.
>
> We give the divisions considerable autonomy, but we watch their monthly income statements very closely. Each month's actual performance is compared with the budget in considerable detail. If the actual sales or contribution margin is more than 4 or 5 percent below budget, we demand an immediate report from the division people. I might add that we don't have much trouble getting their attention. All of the management people at the plant and division level can add appreciably to their annual salaries with bonuses if actual net income is considerably higher than budget.

The budgeting process begins in August when division sales managers consult their sales personnel to estimate sales for the next calendar year. These estimates are sent to plant managers, who use them to prepare production estimates. At the plants, production statistics, including direct material amounts, labor-hours, production schedules, and output quantities, are developed by operating personnel. Using the statistics prepared by the operating personnel, the plant accounting staff determines costs and estimates the plant's budgeted variable cost of goods sold and other plant expenses for each month of the coming calendar year.

In October, each division's accounting staff combines plant budgets with sales estimates and adds additional division expenses. "After the divisional management is satisfied with the budget," says Collins, "I visit each division to review its budget and make sure it is in line with corporate strategy and projections. I really emphasize sales forecasts because of the volatility in the demand for our product. For many years, we lost sales to our competitors because we projected production and sales too low and couldn't meet market demand. More recently, we were caught with large excess inventory when the bottom dropped out of the market for recreational vehicles.

"I generally visit all eight divisions during the first two weeks in November. After that my staff combines and reconciles the division budgets which are ready for approval by the board of directors in early December. The board seldom questions the budget.

"One complaint we've had from plant and division management is that they are penalized for circumstances beyond their control. For example, they failed to predict the recent sales decline. As a result, they didn't make their budget targets and, of course, they received no bonuses. However, I point out that they are well rewarded when they exceed their budget. Furthermore, they provide most of the information for the budget, so it's their own fault if the budget is too optimistic. Indeed, they should have been the first to see the coming sales decline."

Required

a. Identify and explain the biases the corporate management of RV Industries should expect in the communication of budget estimates by its division and plant personnel.

b. What sources of information can RV Industries' top management use to monitor the budget estimates prepared by its divisions and plants?

c. What services could RV Industries' top management offer the divisions to help them develop their budget without appearing to interfere with the division budget decisions?

d. RV Industries' top management is attempting to decide whether it should get more involved in the budget process. Identify and explain what management needs to consider in reaching its decision.

(CMA adapted)

18.39 Adapt Budget Control Concepts to Research Organization

Argo Company has a well-organized research program. Each project is separated into phases, with completion times and the cost of each phase estimated. Project description and related estimates are used to develop the annual research department budget.

The following schedule presents the costs for the research activities budgeted for last year. Actual costs incurred by projects or overhead category are compared to estimates for each activity, and the variances are noted on this same schedule.

ARGO COMPANY
Profit Variance Analysis of Research Costs
(in thousands)

	Approved Activity for the Year	Actual Costs for the Year	(Over) Under Budget
Total research costs			
Projects in progress			
4-1	$ 23.2	$ 46.8	$(23.6)
5-3	464.0	514.8	(50.8)
New projects			
8-1	348.0	351.0	(3.0)
8-2	232.0	257.4	(25.4)
8-3	92.8	—	92.8
Total research costs, including the indirect costs listed below	$1,160.0	$1,170.0	$(10.0)
Indirect research costs (allocated to projects in proportion to their direct costs)			
Administration	50.0	52.0	(2.0)
Laboratory facilities.	110.0	118.0	(8.0)
Total	$ 160.0	$ 170.0	$(10.0)

The director of research prepared the following narrative statement of research performance for the year to accompany the schedule.

"The year has been most successful. The two projects, 4-1 and 8-1, scheduled for completion in this year were finished. Project 8-2 is progressing satisfactorily and should be completed next year as scheduled. The fourth phase of project 5-3, with estimated direct research costs of $100,000, and the first phase of project 8-3, both included in the approved activity for the year, could not be started because the principal researcher left our employment. They were resubmitted for approval in next year's activity plan."

Required   From the information given, prepare an alternative schedule that will provide Argo management with better information to evaluate research cost performance for the year.

(CMA adapted)

18.40 Analyze Activity Variances—FIFO Process Costing   Fellite, Inc., manufactures foam padding for medical uses in a continuous process. Fellite uses the FIFO process costing system for internal recordkeeping purposes. Materials and conversion costs are added evenly throughout the process, so it is not necessary to maintain separate accounts of materials and conversion costs for equivalent unit computations.

The master budget and actual results for the current period are as follows:

	Actual	Master Budget
Physical count of units		
Beginning work in process inventory.	1,000 units	1,000 units
	(80% complete)	(50% complete)
Transferred to next department.	2,500 units	3,200 units
Ending inventory	800 units	600 units
	(⅝ complete)	(⅔ complete)
Current period costs		
Direct materials	$30,000	$32,500
Direct labor.	24,600	27,000
Manufacturing overhead		
Variable	16,200	14,500
Fixed	24,100	26,000

Required   **a.** Compute the equivalent units of production this period. (*Note*: Equivalent unit computations are discussed in Chapter 5.)

b. Prepare a profit variance analysis like the one in Illustration 18.5.

SOLUTIONS TO SELF-STUDY QUESTIONS

1. Flexible budget for Evergreen Company based on actual sales of 7,000 units:

Sales.	$140,000
Variable manufacturing costs	56,000
Variable marketing and administrative.	7,000
Contribution margin	$ 77,000
Fixed manufacturing costs	36,000
Fixed marketing and administrative	40,000
Operating profits	$ 1,000

Note: Sales and variable costs are 7/8 (7,000 units/8,000 units) of the amounts in the master budget. Fixed costs are unchanged from the master budget.

2.

EXHIBIT A | Profit Variance Analysis, Containers, Inc. (August)

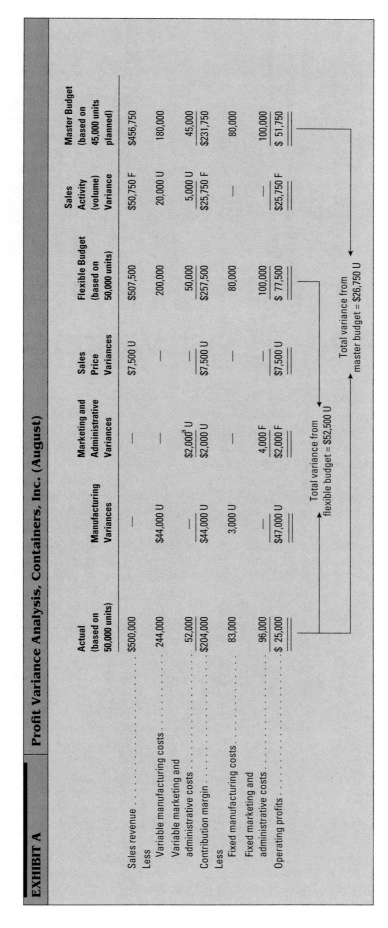

	Actual (based on 50,000 units)	Manufacturing Variances	Marketing and Administrative Variances	Sales Price Variances	Flexible Budget (based on 50,000 units)	Sales Activity (volume) Variance	Master Budget (based on 45,000 units planned)
Sales revenue	$500,000	—	—	$7,500 U	$507,500	$50,750 F	$456,750
Less Variable manufacturing costs	244,000	$44,000 U	—		200,000	20,000 U	180,000
Variable marketing and administrative costs	52,000		$2,000ᵃ U		50,000	5,000 U	45,000
Contribution margin	$204,000	$44,000 U	$2,000 U	$7,500 U	$257,500	$25,750 F	$231,750
Less Fixed manufacturing costs	83,000	3,000 U	—	—	80,000	—	80,000
Fixed marketing and administrative costs	96,000	—	4,000 F	—	100,000	—	100,000
Operating profits	$ 25,000	$47,000 U	$2,000 F	$7,500 U	$ 77,500	$25,750 F	$ 51,750

Total variance from flexible budget = $52,500 U

Total variance from master budget = $26,750 U

ᵃ$2,000 = $.04 × 50,000 = ($1.04 − $1.00) × 50,000 units.

579

Performance Evaluation:
Cost Variances

LEARNING OBJECTIVES

After reading this chapter, you should be able to:

1. Compute and use variable cost variances.

2. Compute and use variances from activity-based costs.

3. Compute and use fixed cost variances.

4. Develop the comprehensive cost variance analysis.

5. Apply the variance analysis model to nonmanufacturing costs.

6. Determine which variances to investigate.

7. Demonstrate how standard costs flow through accounts (Appendix A).

8. Explain how to prorate variances to inventories and cost of goods sold (Appendix A).

9. Compare standard costing in a just-in-time environment to standard costing in a traditional environment (Appendix A).

10. Compare the two-way, three-way, and four-way analyses of overhead variances (Appendix B).

L.O. 1: Compute and use variable cost variances.

In management accounting, any deviation from a predetermined amount is a *variance*. In Chapter 17, we developed the master budget and, in Chapter 18, the flexible budget. We saw that the difference between the flexible budget and the master budget creates an activity variance and that differences between actual results and the flexible budget create a number of other variances. In this chapter, we examine in detail how a specific group of variances—cost variances—are developed, interpreted, and used.

Although we use a manufacturing company example in this chapter because it is the most comprehensive application, the variances that we describe also are used in nonmanufacturing organizations. Service organizations in particular can use the labor and overhead variances to assess efficiency and control costs. Many financial institutions, such as banks, use labor standards and variances to assess transaction and check-processing efficiency. Fast-food restaurants use labor standards to assess efficiency in preparing and serving food.

SETTING STANDARDS: AN ILLUSTRATION

At the end of Chapter 18, we discussed how standards are set for a typical standard costing system. We now take the discussion a step further by illustrating the development of standard costs for Evergreen Company. The standard variable production cost, which we called the *estimated cost*, was $8 per crate.

Direct Materials

Evergreen Company determines the standard price of the lumber it uses to make crates as follows. The standard price reflects the price of the product delivered to Evergreen, net of purchase discounts.

Direct Materials: Standard Price (per board-foot)

Purchase price of lumber	$.23
Shipping costs	.04
Less purchase discounts	(.02)
Standard price per board-foot	$.25

Note: A board-foot is 12 inches by 12 inches and 1 inch thick.

Direct materials are purchased by the board-foot, so the purchase price standard is expressed per *foot*, not per *crate*.

The quantity standards for direct materials are based on the amount of direct material that should be used to make one unit under normal operating conditions. Each crate requires 9 board-feet of lumber; 1 additional board-foot is allowed for waste in cutting the lumber to the proper size and constructing the crate.

Direct Materials: Standard Quantity (board-feet)

Requirements per crate	9
Allowance for waste	1
Standard quantity per crate	10

The standard direct material cost per crate is then computed:

$.25 per board-foot $\times$ 10 board-feet per crate = $2.50 per crate

Direct Labor

Direct labor standards are based on a standard labor rate for the work performed and the standard number of labor-hours required. The standard labor rate includes wages earned as well as fringe benefits, such as medical insurance and pension plan contributions, and paid employer-taxes (for example, unemployment taxes and the employer's share of an employee's social security taxes).

Direct Labor: Standard Rate (price per hour)

Wage rate	$ 8.00
Employer's payroll taxes and fringe benefits	2.00
Standard rate	$10.00

Most companies develop one standard for each labor category. We assume that Evergreen Company has only one category of labor.

Standard direct labor time is based on an estimate of the time required to perform each operation. For example, at Evergreen, the time required to make each crate—to cut the lumber to size, assemble the crate, and finish and inspect it—is estimated by timing each step and adding some time for personal needs and breaks. Sometimes a crate is assembled but rejected when it is inspected, so an allowance is made for time spent on crates that will be rejected. These estimates for each crate are as follows:

Direct Labor: Standard Time (hours)

Cutting Department	
Cutting	.04
Personal time	.01
Allowance for rejects	.01
Total cutting department	.06
Assembly Department	
Assembly	.18
Personal time	.02
Total assembly department	.20
Finishing and Inspection Department	
Finishing and inspection	.03
Personal time	.01
Total finishing and inspection department	.04
Standard time per good crate completed	.30

The standard labor cost for each good crate completed is:

$10 per hour $\times$ .30 hours per crate = $3 per crate

Variable Production Overhead

The first step in setting variable overhead standards is to find an activity measure that relates the cost to the product, that is, to determine x in the formula

$$Y = a + bx$$

where

Y = Estimated total overhead (the dependent variable)
a = Estimated fixed overhead
b = Estimated variable overhead rate per unit
x = Independent variable (a cost driver)

For example, Evergreen could develop a variable overhead rate per crate using crates as an activity measure and apply that rate to each crate produced. Companies that use activity-based costing will have multiple bs and xs.

Selecting Activity Measures for Applying Overhead

Output Measures versus Input Measures of Activity

Output measures of activity (for example, number of crates produced at Evergreen or number of automobiles produced in an automobile factory) sometimes work well as a basis for applying overhead, especially when a single product is completely produced in a single work operation. However, it becomes difficult to measure departmental activity in terms of output when the department works on multiple products and only a portion of the product is completed in each department. Hence, most companies find input measures, such as direct labor-hours or machine-hours, more practical.

If an input measure is used, a company should consider the following issues in its selection:

- *Causal relationship between the activity measure and variable overhead costs.* An increase in the activity measure should result in an increase in variable overhead costs. If an operation is labor intensive, labor-hours probably would be related causally to variable overhead, which is made up of support staff, supervisors, and other indirect labor. On the other hand, for a capital-intensive operation, machine-hours could be the cause of variable overhead. As a product moves through several departments in a manufacturing operation, different activity bases may be used, as shown in the following diagram (the arrows refer to the movement of the product through various departments until it is finished):

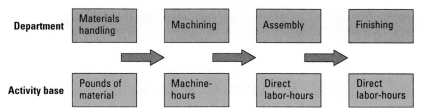

Variable overhead usually has more than one cause, but to simplify matters, one independent variable is usually selected for a particular production department or work station.

- *Physical units versus dollars.* Physical units often are used for the activity base instead of dollars. If labor-dollars are used, a contract settlement or other wage change could affect labor costs, but that does not necessarily mean that variable overhead costs would change.

- *Cost-benefit constraints.* A model that specifies the relationship between variable overhead costs and their causes in so much detail that measures are precise could be quite costly. The benefits of such a complete model rarely justify its costs. Thus, a simplified model is usually preferred. For example, a simple regression model with one independent variable often is used instead of a multiple regression model, although multiple regression may explain more variation in variable overhead. When examining variances between actual and standard costs, managers recognize that some variance occurs because establishing perfect standards is not feasible.

Evergreen uses a simple variable overhead basis, direct labor-hours, to determine its variable overhead standards. Management reviewed prior period activities and costs, estimated how costs will change in the future, and performed a regression analysis in which overhead cost was the dependent variable and labor-hours the independent variable. After analyzing these estimates, the accountants decided to use $8.333 per standard labor-hour as the variable production overhead rate for each department because variable overhead averaged about $8.333 per standard direct labor-hour.

In practice, different departments may have different rates. Activity-based costing acknowledges that each activity center will have a different rate. At times, different departments will have different rates, and multiple bases are used.

ILLUSTRATION 19.1	Summary of Costs, Evergreen Company		
	Standard Costs		
	(1) **Standard Input Quantity**	(2) **Standard Input Price or Rate**	(1) × (2) **Standard Cost per Crate**
Direct materials (all charged to cutting department).	10 feet	$ .25 per foot	$2.50
Direct labor	.30 hour	10.00 per hour	3.00
Variable manufacturing overhead	.30 hour	8.33⅓ per hour	2.50
Total standard variable cost per crate . . .			$8.00
	Actual Costs		
	(1) **Actual Input Quantity**	(2) **Actual Input Price or Rate**	(1) × (2) **Actual Cost per crate**
Direct materials (all charged to cutting department).	11 feet	$ .264 per foot	$2.904
Direct labor	.32 hour	9.35 per hour	2.992
Variable manufacturing overhead	.32 hour	8.275 per hour	2.648
Total actual variable cost per crate			$8.544

Variable production cost standards are summarized in a standard cost computer record or file. Illustration 19.1 presents the contents of such a file for Evergreen Company.

VARIABLE COST VARIANCE ANALYSIS

Standard costs are used to evaluate a company's performance. Comparing the budget (prepared using standard costs) to actual results identifies production cost variances. We now review production cost variances in detail.

General Model

cost variance analysis
Comparison of actual input amounts and prices with standard input amounts and prices.

price variance
Difference between actual costs and budgeted costs arising from changes in the cost of inputs to a production process or other activity.

efficiency variance
Difference between budgeted and actual results arising from differences between the inputs that were budgeted per unit of output and the inputs actually used.

The conceptual **cost variance analysis** model compares actual input quantities and prices with standard input quantities and prices. *Both the actual and standard input quantities are for the actual output attained.* As shown in Illustration 19.2, a **price variance** and an **efficiency variance** can be computed for each variable manufacturing input. The actual costs incurred (column 1) for the time period are compared with the standard allowed per unit times the number of good units of output produced (column 3). This comparison provides the **total variance** for the cost or input.

Some companies compute only the total variance. Others make a more detailed breakdown into price and efficiency variances.

Managers who are responsible for price variances may not be responsible for efficiency variances and vice versa. For example, purchasing department managers are usually held responsible for direct materials price variances, and manufacturing department managers are usually held responsible for using the direct materials efficiently.

This breakdown of the total variance into price and efficiency components is facilitated by the middle term, column 2, in Illustration 19.2. In going from column 1 to column 2, we go from *actual prices (AP)* times *actual quantity (AQ)* of input to *standard price (SP)* times *actual quantity (AQ)* of input. Thus, the variance is calculated as

$$\text{Price variance} = (AP \times AQ) - (SP \times AQ)$$
$$= (AP - SP)AQ$$

REAL WORLD APPLICATION **How Workers Develop Their Own Standards at the Toyota-GM Joint Venture**

The Toyota–General Motors joint venture in Fremont, California, known as New United Motor Manufacturing, Inc. (NUMMI), allows employees to set their own work standards. The NUMMI plant had been a General Motors plant that was notorious for poor quality, low productivity, and morale problems.

At the old Fremont GM plant, industrial engineers who had little, if any, work experience making cars would shut themselves in a room and ponder how to set standards, ignoring the workers, who in turn ignored the standards. Now, at NUMMI, workers themselves hold the stopwatches and set the standards. Worker team members time each other, looking for the most efficient and safest way to do the work.

The workers standardize each task so that everyone in the team will do it the same way. They compare the standards across shifts and for different tasks and prepare detailed written specifications for each task. The workers are more informed about how to do the work right than industrial engineers are and are more motivated to meet the standards they set than those set by industrial engineers working in an ivory tower.

Involving the workers has had benefits in addition to

This Toyota-General Motors plant in Fremont, California, succeeded in letting employees set their own standards.

improved motivation and standards. These include improved safety, higher quality, easier job rotation because tasks are standardized, and more flexibility because workers are both assembly line workers and industrial engineers.

Source: P. Adler, "Time-and-Motion Regained," *Harvard Business Review*, January–February 1993, pp. 97–108.

ILLUSTRATION 19.2 **General Model for Cost Variance Analysis**

Actual	Actual Inputs at Standard Price	Flexible Production Budget
Actual input price (*AP*) times *actual* quantity (*AQ*) of input	*Standard* input price (*SP*) times *actual* quantity (*AQ*) of input	*Standard* input price (*SP*) times *standard* quantity (*SQ*) of input allowed for actual good output
(1) $(AP \times AQ)$	**(2)** $(SP \times AQ)$	**(3)** $(SP \times SQ)$

Price variance[a]
(1) minus (2)

Efficiency variance[a]
(2) minus (3)

Total variance
(1) minus (3)

[a]The terms *price* and *efficiency* variances are general categories. Terminology varies from company to company, but the following specific variance titles are frequently used:

Input	Price Variance Category	Efficiency Category
Direct materials	Price (or purchase price) variance	Usage or quantity variance
Direct labor	Rate variance	Efficiency variance
Variable overhead	Spending variance	Efficiency variance

We shall avoid unnecessary complications by simply referring to these variances as either a *price* or *efficiency* variance.

total variance
Difference between total actual costs for the time period and the standard allowed per unit times the number of good units produced.

The efficiency variance is derived by comparing column 2, standard price times actual quantity of input, with column 3, standard price times standard quantity of input. Thus, the efficiency variance is calculated as

$$\text{Efficiency variance} = (SP \times AQ) - (SP \times SQ)$$
$$= SP(AQ - SQ)$$

This general model may seem rather abstract at this point, but as we work examples, it will become more concrete and intuitive to you.

As the general model outlined in Illustration 19.2 is applied to each variable and fixed cost incurred, a more comprehensive cost variance analysis results. The general model of the comprehensive cost variance analysis will be applied to Evergreen Company's production costs. The comprehensive cost variance analysis will ultimately explain, in detail, the unfavorable variable production variance of $5,440 that we showed in Chapter 18, column 2 of Illustration 18.5.

As we proceed through the variance analysis for each production cost input—direct materials, direct labor, variable production overhead, and fixed production costs—you will notice some minor modifications from the general model presented in Illustration 19.2. It is important to recognize that these are modifications of one general approach rather than a number of independent approaches to variance analysis. In variance analysis, a few basic methods can be applied with minor modifications to numerous business and nonbusiness situations.

Direct Materials

Information about Evergreen Company's use of direct materials for May follows:

Standard costs
    10 board-feet per crate @ $.25 per board-foot = $2.50 per crate
Crates produced in May
    10,000
Actual materials purchased and used
    110,000 board-feet @ .264 per board-foot = $29,040

These relationships are shown graphically as follows:

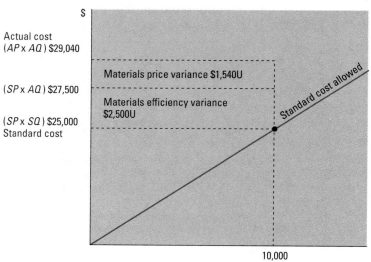

Based on these data, the direct materials price and efficiency variances were calculated as shown in Illustration 19.3. Note that with a standard of 10 board-feet per crate and 10,000 crates actually produced in May, Evergreen expects to use 100,000 board-feet to produce the 10,000 crates. Since each board-foot has a standard cost of $.25, the standard materials cost allowed to make 10,000 crates is:

ILLUSTRATION 19.3	**Direct Materials Variances, Evergreen Company (May) (10,000 crates)**

(1) Actual	(2) Actual Inputs at Standard Price	(3) Flexible Production Budget
Actual materials price (AP = $.264) times *actual* quantity (AQ = 110,000 feet) of direct materials	*Standard* materials price (SP = $.25) times *actual* quantity (AQ = 110,000 feet) of direct materials	*Standard* materials price (SP = $.25) times *standard* quantity (SQ = 10,000 crates × 10 feet) of direct materials allowed for actual good output
(AP × AQ)	**(SP × AQ)**	**(SP × SQ)**
$.264 × 110,000 feet = $29,040	$.25 × 110,000 feet = $27,500	$.25 × (10,000 crates × 10 feet) = $.25 × 100,000 feet = $25,000

Price variance.[a]
$29,040 − $27,500
= $1,540 U

Efficiency variance.[a]
$27,500 − $25,000
= $2,500 U

[a]Shortcut formulas:

$(AP \times AQ) - (SP \times AQ)$
$= (AP - SP) \times AQ$
$= (\$.264 - \$.25) \times 110,000$
$= \$1,540 \text{ U}$

$(SP \times AQ) - (SP \times SQ)$
$= SP \times (AQ - SQ)$
$= \$.25 \times (110,000 - 100,000)$
$= \$2,500 \text{ U}$

Total variance
= $4,040 U

$$\text{Standard cost allowed to produce 10,000 crates} = SP \times SQ$$
$$= \$.25 \times (10 \text{ board-feet} \times 10,000 \text{ crates})$$
$$= \$25,000$$

flexible production budget
Standard input price times standard quantity of input allowed for actual good output.

Note that column 3 of Illustration 19.3 is called the **flexible production budget.** The flexible budget concept can be applied to production as well as to sales. The flexible budget in Chapter 18 was based on actual sales volume (that is, crates *sold*). The flexible budget in Illustration 19.3 is based on actual production volume (that is, crates *produced*).

Responsibility for Direct Materials Variances

The direct materials price variance shows that in May, the prices paid for direct materials exceeded the standards allowed, thus creating an unfavorable variance of $1,540. Responsibility for this variance is usually assigned to the purchasing department. Reports to management include an explanation of the variance, for example, failure to take purchase discounts, higher transportation costs than expected, different grade of direct material purchased, or changes in the market price of direct materials.

The explanation for Evergreen's variance was that home construction in the economy has increased significantly, driving the price of lumber higher than expected. In addition, prices were expected to continue rising during the year. Based on this information, management began market research to determine whether Evergreen should increase sales prices for its crates.

Direct materials efficiency variances are typically the responsibility of production departments. In setting standards, an allowance is usually made for defects in direct

ILLUSTRATION 19.4	Direct Labor Variances, Evergreen Company (May)	

(1) Actual	(2) Actual Inputs at Standard Price	(3) Flexible Production Budget
Actual labor price (*AP* = $9.35) times *actual* quantity (*AQ* = 3,200 hours) of direct labor-hours used	*Standard* labor price (*SP* = $10) times *actual* quantity (*AQ* = 3,200 hours) of direct labor-hours used	*Standard* labor price (*SP* = $10) times *standard* quantity *SQ* = (10,000 crates × .3 hour) of direct labor-hours allowed for actual good output
(*AP* × *AQ*)	(*SP* × *AQ*)	(*SP* × *SQ*)
$9.35 × 3,200 hours = $29,920	$10 × 3,200 hours = $32,000	$10 × (10,000 crates × .3 hour) = $10 × 3,000 hours = $30,000

Price variance:
$29,920 − $32,000
= $2,080 F

Efficiency variance:
$32,000 − $30,000
= $2,000 U

Total variance
= $80 F

materials, inexperienced workers, poor supervision, and the like. If actual materials usage is less than these standards, a favorable variance occurs. If usage is in excess of standards, an unfavorable variance occurs.

At Evergreen, the unfavorable materials efficiency variance was attributed to the recent hiring of some inexperienced laborers who, in an effort to keep up with the production schedule, improperly measured and cut lumber in the wrong lengths. The cutting department manager claimed that this was a one-time occurrence and foresaw no similar problems in the future.

Direct Labor

To illustrate the computations of direct labor variances, assume the following for Evergreen Company:

Standard costs: .30 hour per crate @ $10 per hour = $3 per crate

Number of crates produced in May: 10,000

Actual direct labor costs: Actual hours worked—3,200; total actual labor cost— $29,920. Hence, the average cost per hour was $9.35 ($29,920/3,200 hours).

The computation of the direct labor price and efficiency variances is shown in Illustration 19.4.

Direct Labor Price Variance

The direct labor price variance is caused by the difference between actual and standard labor costs per hour. Evergreen direct labor costs were less than the standard allowed, creating a favorable labor price variance of $2,080. The explanation given for this favorable labor price variance is that Evergreen hired many inexperienced workers in May; they were paid a lower than standard wage, thus reducing the *average* wage rate for all workers to $9.35.

Wage rates for many companies are set by union contract. If the wage rates used in setting standards are the same as those in the union contract, labor price variances will not occur.

Labor Efficiency Variance

The labor efficiency variance is a measure of labor productivity. It is one of the most closely watched variances because production managers usually can control it. A financial vice president of a manufacturing company told us:

> Direct materials are 57 percent of our product cost, while direct labor is only 22 percent. We give direct materials price variances only a passing glance. But we carry out the labor efficiency variance to the penny; and we break it down by product line, by department, and sometimes by specific operation. Why? Because there's not much we can do about materials price changes, but there's a lot we can do to keep our labor efficiency in line.[1]

Unfavorable labor efficiency variances have many causes, including the workers themselves. Poorly motivated or poorly trained workers are less productive; highly motivated and well-trained workers are more likely to generate favorable efficiency variances. Sometimes poor materials or faulty equipment can cause productivity problems. Poor supervision and scheduling can lead to unnecessary idle time.

Production department managers are usually responsible for direct labor efficiency variances. Scheduling problems may stem from other production departments that have delayed production. The personnel department may be responsible if the variance occurs because they provided the wrong kind of worker. The $2,000 unfavorable direct labor efficiency variance at Evergreen was attributed to the inexperienced workers previously mentioned. Note that one event, such as hiring inexperienced workers, can affect more than one variance.

Variable Production Overhead

To illustrate the computation of variable production overhead variances, assume the following for Evergreen:

Standard costs: .30 direct labor-hour per crate @ $8.33⅓ per hour (variable production overhead rate) = $2.50 per crate

Crates produced in May: 10,000

Actual variable overhead costs in May: $26,480

The computation of the variable production overhead price and efficiency variances is shown in Illustration 19.5.

Variable Production Overhead Price Variances

The variable overhead standard rate was derived from a two-stage estimation (1) of costs at various levels of activity and (2) of the relationship between those estimated costs and the basis, which is direct labor-hours at Evergreen. The price variance could have occurred because (1) actual costs—for example, machine power, materials handling, supplies, some direct labor—were different from those expected and, (2) the relationship between variable production overhead costs and direct labor-hours is not perfect.

The variable overhead price variance actually contains some efficiency items as well as price items. For example, suppose that utilities costs are higher than expected. The reason could be that utility rates are higher than expected or that kilowatt-hours (kwh) per labor-hour are higher than expected (for example, if workers do not turn off power switches when machines are not being used). Both are part of the price variance because together they cause utility costs to be higher than expected. Some companies separate these components of the variable overhead price variance; this commonly is done for energy costs in heavy manufacturing companies, for example.

---

[1]Personal interview.

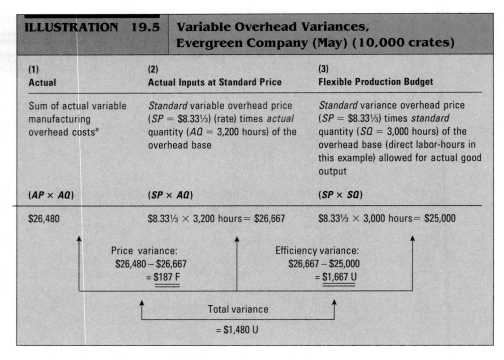

ILLUSTRATION 19.5   **Variable Overhead Variances, Evergreen Company (May) (10,000 crates)**

(1) Actual	(2) Actual Inputs at Standard Price	(3) Flexible Production Budget
Sum of actual variable manufacturing overhead costs[a]	*Standard* variable overhead price (SP = \$8.33⅓) (rate) times *actual* quantity (AQ = 3,200 hours) of the overhead base	*Standard* variance overhead price (SP = \$8.33⅓) times *standard* quantity (SQ = 3,000 hours) of the overhead base (direct labor-hours in this example) allowed for actual good output
($AP \times AQ$)	**($SP \times AQ$)**	**($SP \times SQ$)**
\$26,480	\$8.33⅓ × 3,200 hours = \$26,667	\$8.33⅓ × 3,000 hours = \$25,000

Price variance:
\$26,480 − \$26,667
= \$187 F

Efficiency variance:
\$26,667 − \$25,000
= \$1,667 U

Total variance
= \$1,480 U

[a]Total actual variable overhead costs also can be thought of as actual price (AP) times actual quantity (AQ). Divide the total actual variable overhead costs by the actual quantity of the variable overhead base:

AP = \$26,480 ÷ AQ
= \$26,480 ÷ 3,200 direct labor-hours
= \$8.275

At Evergreen, the unfavorable price variance for May was attributed to waste in using supplies and recent increases in rates charged for power to run the saws in the cutting department.

Variable Overhead Efficiency Variance

The variable overhead efficiency variance must be interpreted carefully. It is related to efficiency in using the base on which variable overhead is applied.

For example, Evergreen applies variable overhead on the basis of direct labor-hours. Thus, if there is an unfavorable direct labor efficiency variance because actual direct labor-hours were higher than the standard allowed, there will be a corresponding unfavorable variable overhead efficiency variance. Evergreen used 200 direct labor-hours more than the standard allowed, resulting in the direct labor and variable overhead efficiency variances shown below.

Direct labor efficiency (Illustration 19.4):

$$\$10 \times 200 \text{ hours} = \$2,000 \text{ U}$$

Variable overhead efficiency (Illustration 19.5):

$$\$8.33⅓ \times 200 \text{ hours} = \underline{1,667 \text{ U}}$$

Total direct labor and variable overhead efficiency variances:

$$\$18.33⅓ \times 200 \text{ hours} = \underline{\$3,667 \text{ U}}$$

Variable overhead is assumed to vary directly with direct labor-hours, which is the base on which variable overhead is applied.

Thus, inefficiency in using the base (for example, direct labor-hours, machine-hours, units of output) is assumed to cause an increase in variable overhead. This emphasizes the importance of selecting the proper base for applying variable overhead. Managers who are responsible for controlling the base will probably be held responsible for the variable overhead efficiency variance as well. Whoever is respon-

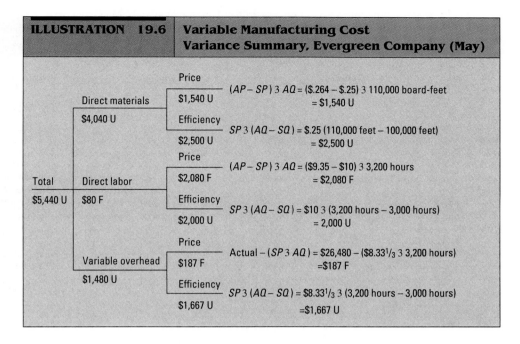

ILLUSTRATION 19.6 — Variable Manufacturing Cost Variance Summary, Evergreen Company (May)

		Price	$(AP - SP) \times AQ = (\$.264 - \$.25) \times 110,000$ board-feet
	Direct materials	$1,540 U	$= \$1,540$ U
	$4,040 U	Efficiency	$SP \times (AQ - SQ) = \$.25 (110,000 \text{ feet} - 100,000 \text{ feet})$
		$2,500 U	$= \$2,500$ U
		Price	$(AP - SP) \times AQ = (\$9.35 - \$10) \times 3,200$ hours
Total	Direct labor	$2,080 F	$= \$2,080$ F
$5,440 U	$80 F	Efficiency	$SP \times (AQ - SQ) = \$10 \times (3,200 \text{ hours} - 3,000 \text{ hours})$
		$2,000 U	$= 2,000$ U
		Price	$\text{Actual} - (SP \times AQ) = \$26,480 - (\$8.33^1/_3 \times 3,200 \text{ hours})$
	Variable overhead	$187 F	$= \$187$ F
	$1,480 U	Efficiency	$SP \times (AQ - SQ) = \$8.33^1/_3 \times (3,200 \text{ hours} - 3,000 \text{ hours})$
		$1,667 U	$= \$1,667$ U

sible for the $2,000 unfavorable direct labor efficiency variance at Evergreen also will probably be held responsible for the unfavorable variable overhead efficiency variance.

Variable Cost Variances Summarized in Graphic Form

The variable production cost variances are summarized in Illustration 19.6. Note that the total variable production cost variance is the same as that derived in Chapter 18. The analysis of cost variances in this chapter is a more detailed analysis of the variable production cost variance derived in Chapter 18.

A summary of this nature is useful for reporting variances to high-level managers. It provides both an overview of variances and their sources. When used for reporting, the computations shown at the right of Illustration 19.6 usually are replaced with a brief explanation of the cause of the variance.

Management may want more detailed information about some of the variances. This can be provided by extending each variance branch in Illustration 19.6 to show variances by product line, department, or other categories.

USING ACTIVITY-BASED COSTING: STANDARDS AND VARIANCES

Setting Standards

L.O. 2: Compute and use variances from activity-based costs.

Activity-based costing commonly is used with standard costing. Hewlett-Packard, a pioneer in the development of activity-based costing, used it to develop standard costs. A company using activity-based costing has multiple activity bases, or cost drivers, one for each activity center. Each activity center has an overhead cost pool charged to the center's activities and then to the product based on the activities required to make the product.

For example, assume that Evergreen used activity-based costing to set standard costs for its variable costs. Assume that the company has the three activity centers shown in the top panel of Illustration 19.7. (In practice, companies typically have more than three activity centers, but we want to keep the example simple while demonstrating how to use activity-based costing.) Managers and accountants determine a cost driver for each activity center and a rate per cost driver unit.

As shown in Illustration 19.7, the cost driver for activity center 2 is machine-minutes because the more machine-minutes, the more energy is required to run the machines. The rate per cost driver unit is $.02 per machine-minute. This rate could be determined by relating energy costs to machine time from the records or by getting input from energy experts. The rate could be determined by running a

ILLUSTRATION 19.7	Using Activity-Based Costing to Develop Standard Costs	

Activity Center	Cost Driver	Standard Rate per Cost Driver
1. Indirect materials	Number of board-feet	$.05 board-foot
2. Energy	Machine-minutes	.02 per machine-minute
3. Quality testing and repair	Number of minutes in testing	.50 per minute in testing

	Standard Rate per Cost Driver (from top panel)	Standard Number of Cost Driver Units Required to Make One Crate	Standard Cost per Crate
1. Indirect materials.	$.05 per board-foot	10 board-feet	$ .50 per crate
2. Energy.	.02 per machine-minute	25 minutes	.50 per crate
3. Quality testing and repair . . .	.50 per test minute	3 minutes	1.50 per crate
Total variable overhead.			$2.50 per crate

regression of machine time on overhead costs from data for past periods and using the coefficient, b, from the regression equation. In fact, all of the rates for the cost drivers could be derived from a multiple regression in which the cost drivers are independent variables. However derived, whether by simple common sense or sophisticated analyses, management must determine the standard rate per cost driver unit, which appears in the top panel of Illustration 19.7.

Next we compute the standard cost per crate produced based on the number of cost driver units required to make one crate. These calculations appear in the bottom panel of Illustration 19.7. Determining the standard cost driver units per crate—for example, the number of minutes of machine time required to make a crate—requires information from engineering and production. (Developing good standards requires much teamwork between production, engineering, accounting, and management.)

Note that the total variable cost per crate, $2.50, is assumed to be the same as that calculated earlier in this chapter using the simple traditional approach for Evergreen. In the real world, however, different costing methods usually give different product costs.

Variance Analysis

We use the same approach to variance analysis for activity-based costing as for traditional costing. The price variance is the difference between standard prices and actual prices for the actual quantity of input used for each cost driver. The efficiency variance measures the difference between the actual amount of input, or cost driver units used, and the standard allowed to make the output, with this difference multiplied by the standard price per cost driver unit.

To make this idea concrete, assume the following data for Evergreen for the three activities in Illustration 19.7:

	Standard Price per Unit (from Illustration 19.7)	Standard Quantity per Crate (from Illustration 19.7)	Actual Cost	Actual Quantity of Input Used
Indirect materials	$.05 per board-foot	10 board-feet	$ 5,180	110,000 board-feet
Energy	$.02 per machine-minute	25 minutes	5,300	240,000 machine-minutes
Quality testing and repair	$.50 per test minute	3 minutes	16,000	34,000 test minutes

ILLUSTRATION 19.8	**Activity-Based Costing Variances**

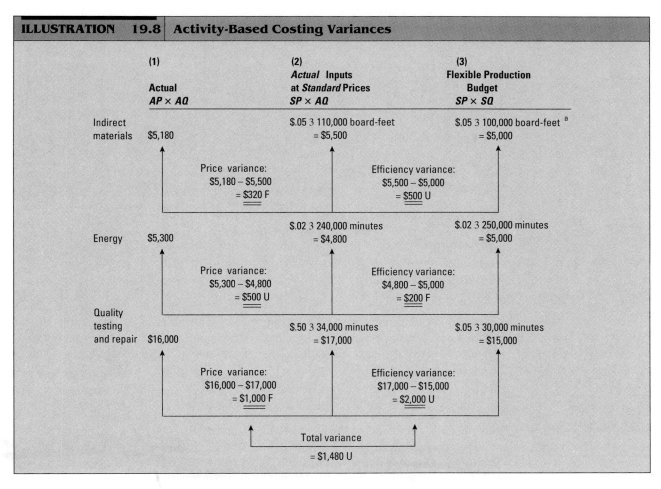

ᵃ10,000 crates at 10 board-feet per crate = 100,000 board-feet.

Recall that the company produced 10,000 crates, so the total standard quantity of input allowed is 10,000 times the standard quantity per crate. Related to the quality testing and repair, for example, the standard per crate is 3 minutes in testing and repair, so the total allowed for 10,000 crates is 30,000 minutes. Using the same reasoning, the total allowed for standard board-feet is 100,000 and the total allowed for machine-minutes is 250,000 minutes.

Illustration 19.8 shows the results of the variance analysis. In effect, we have taken the principle underlying variance computations shown throughout this chapter and applied it to a situation having three activity centers. If a company had 50 activity centers, the computations would be similar to those in Illustration 19.8 but with 50 computations of price and efficiency variances instead of only 3.

Even with only three activity drivers, we believe that you can see the potential for managers to get much more information from activity-based costing than from the traditional costing approach. Compare Illustration 19.8 with Illustration 19.5. Illustration 19.5 contains almost no information about the causes of variable overhead cost variances except that the total variance equals $1,480 unfavorable. We have purposely constructed the example so that the total variance is still $1,480 unfavorable using activity-based costing, but note that in Illustration 19.8, the manager has more information about the cause of the variance.[2] For example, quality testing and

---

[2]We have not constructed the example to make the total price (or efficiency) variance in Illustration 19.8 equal the price (or efficiency) variance in Illustration 19.5 because the input used to break the total variance into price and efficiency components in Illustration 19.5 is unrelated to the input used in Illustration 19.8.

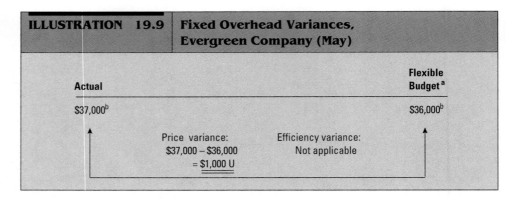

ILLUSTRATION   19.9   Fixed Overhead Variances, Evergreen Company (May)

	Actual		Flexible Budget[a]
	$37,000[b]		$36,000[b]

Price variance:
$37,000 – $36,000
= $1,000 U

Efficiency variance:
Not applicable

[a]For fixed costs, there is no difference between the flexible and master (or static) budget within the relevant range.

[b]These amounts tie to Illustration 18.5, which presents an overview of the use of budgets for performance evaluation at Evergreen Company.

repair required 34,000 minutes instead of the 30,000 minutes allowed. Does this "inefficiency" reflect poorer quality materials or production than expected? Does it represent extra concern about putting out a quality product? Is the standard of 3 minutes per crate too low? In short, Illustration 19.8 raises numerous specific questions that managers can address to improve quality and productivity.

FIXED COST VARIANCES

L.O. 3: Compute and use fixed cost variances.

spending (or budget) variance
A price variance for fixed overhead.

Variance analysis treats fixed production costs and variable production costs differently. For illustrative purposes, we assume that these fixed production costs are all overhead. Other manufacturing costs also may be fixed; if so, they can be treated the same way that we treat fixed production overhead. It is usually assumed that fixed costs are unchanged when volume changes, so the amount budgeted for fixed overhead is the same in both the master and flexible budgets. This is consistent with the variable costing method of product costing.

Fixed overhead has no input-output relationships, and thus, no efficiency variance. The difference between the flexible budget and the actual fixed overhead is entirely due to changes in the costs that make up fixed overhead (for example, insurance premiums on the factory are higher than expected). Hence, the variance falls under the category of a price variance (also called a **spending** or a **budget variance**).

The fixed production overhead in both the flexible and master budgets in Chapter 18 was $36,000. Assume that the actual cost is $37,000. The variance analysis is shown in Illustration 19.9. Note that there is no calculation of the efficiency with which inputs are used.

COMPARISON OF ACTUAL TO FLEXIBLE PRODUCTION BUDGET TO MASTER PRODUCTION BUDGET

L.O. 4: Develop the comprehensive cost variance analysis.

A comparison of actual results with the flexible and master budget was presented in Chapter 18 for sales volume. A similar comparison can be made for production volume, as shown in Illustration 19.10. This difference between the master production budget and the flexible production budget is the production **activity variance.**

Now that the actual production costs, flexible budget amounts, and variances have been presented (see columns 1, 2, 3, and 4 of Illustration 19.10), we can make the final comparison of budget to actual results. The master budget shown in column 6 is based on a projected or budgeted production of 8,000 crates, based on the information given in Chapter 18. The flexible production budget (column 4) tells us the standard variable costs allowed when the actual production output is 10,000 crates (total = $80,000). The actual costs (column 1) tell us the actual amounts spent for each cost.

Comparing Illustration 19.10 with Illustration 18.5 in Chapter 18 will help you to relate these detailed price and efficiency variances with the big-picture overview pre-

ILLUSTRATION 19.10	Cost Variance Analysis, Evergreen Company					
	(1) Actual (based on production of 10,000 crates)	(2) Price Variance	(3) Efficiency Variance	(4) Flexible Budget (based on actual production of 10,000 crates)	(5) Production Activity Variance	(6) Master Budget (based on estimated production of 8,000 crates)
Variable manufacturing costs						
Direct materials	$29,040	$1,540 U	$2,500 U	$25,000	$ 5,000 U	$20,000
Direct labor.	29,920	2,080 F	2,000 U	30,000	6,000 U	24,000
Variable overhead	26,480	187 F	1,667 U	25,000	5,000 U	20,000
Subtotal	$85,440[a]	$ 727 F	$6,167 U	$80,000[a]	$16,000 U	$64,000

Total
= 5,440 U[a]

[a]Numbers tie to Illustration 18.5, Chapter 18.

activity variance
Difference between the master production budget and the flexible production budget resulting from changes in volume of sales or production.

sented in Chapter 18. What we have done here is to break down the variable cost variances from Chapter 18 into more detail. Note that the $5,440 unfavorable variable cost variance from column 2 of Illustration 18.5 has been explained in more detail because of our analysis in this chapter.

This completes the basic variance analysis process. We next consider two extensions.

EXTENSIONS

Materials Purchases Do Not Equal Materials Used

So far we have assumed that the amount of materials used equals the amount of materials purchased. Now we show how to calculate variances when the quantities purchased and used are not the same.

Recall the following facts from the Evergreen Company example:

Standard costs: 10 board-feet per crate @ $.25 per board-foot = $2.50 per crate

Crates produced in May: 10,000

Actual materials used: 110,000 board-feet @ $.264 per board-foot = $29,040

purchase price variance
The price variance based on the quantity of materials purchased.

Now let's assume that 250,000 board-feet were purchased in May at $.264 per board-foot, 110,000 board-feet were used, and there was no inventory on May 1.

The variance calculations are shown in Illustration 19.11. Note that the **purchase price variance** differs from the earlier example in the chapter because it is based on the materials purchased. The efficiency variance is the same as in the previous example because it is based on materials used, which has not changed.

SELF-STUDY QUESTION

1. Last month, the following events took place at Containers, Inc.:

   • Produced 50,000 plastic "notebook computer" cases.
   • Standard variable costs per unit (that is, per case):

Direct materials: 2 pounds at $1	$2.00
Direct labor: .10 labor-hour at $15	1.50
Variable production overhead: .10 labor-hour at $5	.50
Total per case	$4.00

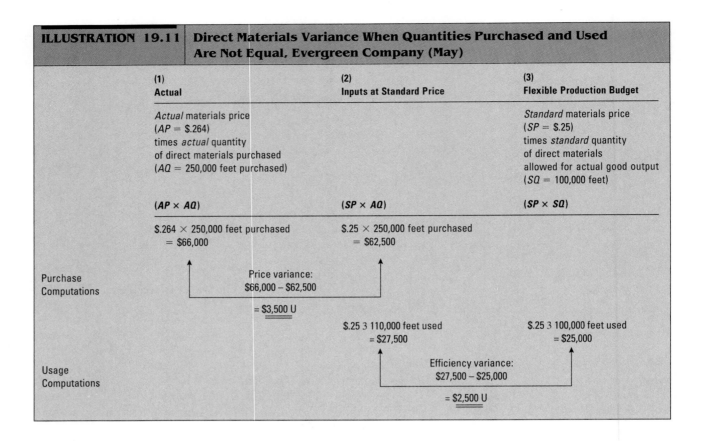

ILLUSTRATION 19.11	Direct Materials Variance When Quantities Purchased and Used Are Not Equal, Evergreen Company (May)		
	(1) Actual	**(2)** Inputs at Standard Price	**(3)** Flexible Production Budget
	Actual materials price (AP = $.264) times *actual* quantity of direct materials purchased (AQ = 250,000 feet purchased)		*Standard* materials price (SP = $.25) times *standard* quantity of direct materials allowed for actual good output (SQ = 100,000 feet)
	(AP × AQ)	**(SP × AQ)**	**(SP × SQ)**
	$.264 × 250,000 feet purchased = $66,000	$.25 × 250,000 feet purchased = $62,500	
Purchase Computations		Price variance: $66,000 − $62,500	
	= $3,500 U		
		$.25 3 110,000 feet used = $27,500	$.25 3 100,000 feet used = $25,000
Usage Computations		Efficiency variance: $27,500 − $25,000	
		= $2,500 U	

- Actual production costs:

Direct materials purchased: 200,000 pounds at $1.20	$240,000
Direct materials used: 110,000 pounds at $1.20	132,000
Direct labor: 6,000 labor-hours at $14	84,000
Variable overhead	28,000

Compute the direct materials, labor, and variable production overhead price and efficiency variances.

The solution to this question is at the end of this chapter on page 630.

The Production Volume Variance

So far, we have assumed that fixed production costs are treated as period costs, which is consistent with variable costing. If fixed production costs are unitized and treated as product costs, another variance is computed. *This occurs when companies use full-absorption, standard costing.*

Developing the Standard Unit Cost for Fixed Production Costs

Like other standard costs, the fixed production standard cost is determined before the start of the production period. Unlike standard variable production costs, fixed costs are period costs by nature. To convert them to product costs requires an estimation of both the period cost and the production volume for the period. The formula is

$$\text{Standard (or predetermined) fixed production overhead cost} = \frac{\text{Budgeted fixed production cost}}{\text{Budgeted activity level}}$$

Assume that the estimated annual fixed production overhead at Evergreen Company was $432,000 and the estimated annual production volume was estimated to be

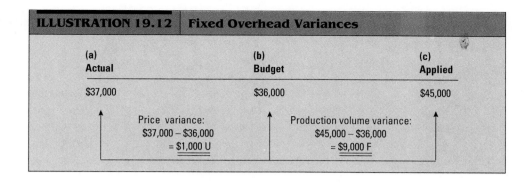

ILLUSTRATION 19.12 | **Fixed Overhead Variances**

(a) Actual	(b) Budget	(c) Applied
$37,000	$36,000	$45,000

Price variance:
$37,000 − $36,000
= $1,000 U

Production volume variance:
$45,000 − $36,000
= $9,000 F

96,000 crates (or 28,800 direct labor-hours at .30 hour per crate). Thus, Evergreen determines its standard fixed production cost per crate as follows:

$$\text{Standard cost per crate} = \frac{\$432,000 \text{ (budgeted fixed production cost)}}{96,000 \text{ crates (budgeted activity level for the year)}} = \underline{\$4.50 \text{ per crate}}$$

Or the rate could be computed per direct labor-hour, as follows:

$$\text{Standard rate per direct labor-hour} = \frac{\$432,000}{28,800 \text{ hours}} = \underline{\$15 \text{ per direct labor-hour}}$$

Each crate is expected to require .3 direct labor-hour (28,800 hours/96,000 crates), so the standard cost per crate is still $4.50 ($15 per hour × .3 hour per crate).

If 10,000 units are actually produced during the month, $45,000 of fixed overhead costs is applied to these units produced.

production volume variance
A variance that arises because the amount used to apply fixed overhead differs from the estimated amount used to estimate fixed costs per unit.

The **production volume variance** is the difference between the $45,000 applied fixed overhead and the $36,000 budgeted fixed overhead as shown in Illustration 19.12. Hence, in this situation a $9,000 favorable production volume variance exists. It is favorable because more overhead was applied than was budgeted—production was higher than the average monthly estimate. This variance is a result of the full-absorption costing system; it does not occur in variable costing.

This $45,000 applied equals $4.50 per crate times 10,000 units actually produced. (See Illustration 19.13.) If the $15 rate per direct labor-hour had been used, the amount applied to the 10,000 units produced would still be $45,000, computed as follows: $15 per hour times .3 standard direct labor-hour per crate times 10,000 crates actually produced ($15 × .3 × 10,000 = $45,000).

A variance arises if the number of units actually produced differs from the number of units used to estimate the fixed cost per unit. As previsouly stated, this variance is commonly referred to as a *production volume variance* (also called a *capacity variance*, an *idle capacity variance*, or a *denominator variance*).

Our example has a production volume variance because the 10,000 crates actually produced during the month do not equal the 8,000 (96,000/12 months) estimated for the month. Consequently, production is charged with $45,000 (point A in Illustration 19.13) instead of $36,000 (point B in Illustration 19.13). The $9,000 difference is the production volume variance because it is caused by a deviation in production volume level (number of crates produced) from that estimated to arrive at the standard cost.

If Evergreen had estimated 10,000 crates per month instead of 8,000 crates, the standard cost would have been $3.60 per crate ($36,000/10,000 crates). Thus, $36,000 ($3.60 × 10,000 crates) would have been applied to units produced, and there would have been no production volume variance.

The production volume variance applies only to fixed costs; it emerges because we are allocating a fixed period cost to units on a predetermined basis. It does not represent resources spent or saved. It is unique to full-absorption costing. The benefits of calculating the variance for control purposes are questionable. Although the

---

ILLUSTRATION 19.13   Fixed Overhead Variances: Graphic Presentation

---

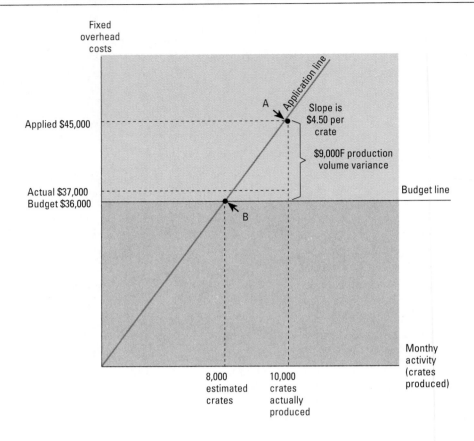

production volume variance signals a difference between expected and actual production levels, so does a simple production report of actual versus expected production quantities.

Compare with the Fixed Production Cost Price Variance

The fixed production cost price variance is the difference between actual and budgeted fixed production costs. Unlike the production volume variance, the price variance commonly is used for control purposes because it is a measure of differences between actual and budgeted period costs.

Illustrations 19.12 and 19.13 should help you see the relationship between actual, budgeted, and applied fixed production costs and to summarize the computation of the fixed production price (spending) and production volume variances.

SUMMARY OF OVERHEAD VARIANCES

The method of computing overhead variances described in this chapter is known as the *four-way analysis of overhead variances* because it computes the following four variances: price and efficiency variances for variable overhead, and price and production volume variances for fixed overhead. Illustration 19.14 summarizes the four-way analysis of variable and fixed overhead variances based on facts given in the

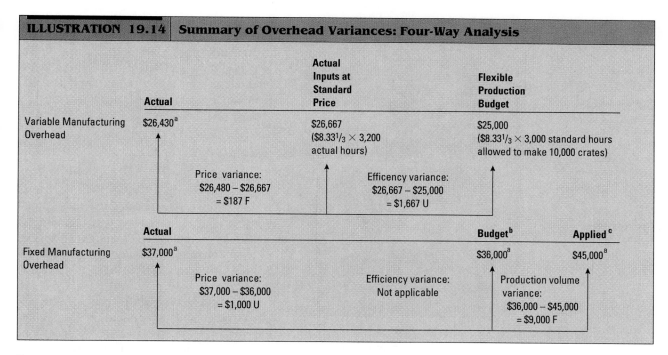

ILLUSTRATION 19.14	Summary of Overhead Variances: Four-Way Analysis

	Actual		Actual Inputs at Standard Price		Flexible Production Budget
Variable Manufacturing Overhead	$26,430[a]		$26,667 ($8.33⅓ × 3,200 actual hours)		$25,000 ($8.33⅓ × 3,000 standard hours allowed to make 10,000 crates)
		Price variance: $26,480 − $26,667 = $187 F		Effiency variance: $26,667 − $25,000 = $1,667 U	

	Actual				Budget[b]	Applied[c]
Fixed Manufacturing Overhead	$37,000[a]				$36,000[a]	$45,000[a]
		Price variance: $37,000 − $36,000 = $1,000 U		Efficiency variance: Not applicable	Production volume variance: $36,000 − $45,000 = $9,000 F	

[a]Amount given in chapter.

[b]This amount appears in both the master budget and the flexible budget.

[c]This is the amount of fixed manufacturing overhead applied to units produced under full-absorption costing.

chapter. Appendix B to this chapter shows alternative overhead variance computations known as the two-way and three-way methods.

Key Points

Several key points regarding overhead variances are important.

- The variable overhead efficiency variance measures the efficiency in using the base (for example, direct labor-hours).
- The production volume variance occurs only when fixed production cost is unitized (for example, when using full-absorption costing). Further, the budgeted fixed overhead is not the amount applied to units produced.
- There is no efficiency variance for fixed production costs. (Do not confuse production volume variance with an efficiency variance.)

SELF-STUDY QUESTION

2. This question follows up Self-Study Question 1. Assume that the fixed production cost budget was $80,000 for the month, and actual fixed production overhead costs were $83,000. The estimated monthly production was 40,000 cases (or 4,000 standard labor-hours).

   Compute the fixed production overhead price variance and the fixed production overhead production volume variance.

The solution to this question is at the end of this chapter on page 630.

VARIANCE ANALYSIS IN NON-MANUFACTURING SETTINGS

L.O. 5: Apply the variance analysis model to nonmanufacturing costs.

Efficiency Measures

Standards in shipping departments such as this are often based on the number of packages mailed. For example, the department is expected to spend no more than a particular amount of labor time on each package. These standards are adjusted for fragile or unusually shaped packages that require extra time.
© Paul Damien/Tony Stone Images

The need for analysis of price and efficiency variances in nonmanufacturing settings for nonmanufacturing costs is increasing. Banks, fast-food outlets, hospitals, consulting firms, retail stores, and many others apply the variance analysis techniques discussed in this chapter to their labor and overhead costs.

In some cases, an efficiency variance can be used to analyze variable nonmanufacturing costs; its computation requires a reliable measure of output activity. Ideally, this requires some quantitative input that can be linked to output.

For example, the personnel in the accounts receivable department of a retail merchandiser are expected to contact 10 delinquent customers per hour. The standard labor cost is $12 per hour including benefits. During July, personnel worked 7,000 hours, made 65,000 contacts, and had an average wage rate of $13 per hour. For 65,000 contacts, the standard labor-hours allowed were 6,500 (65,000 contacts/10 contacts per hour). Unfavorable price and efficiency variances were computed as shown in Illustration 19.15. The calculations shown in the illustration are similar to the ones used for labor variances in manufacturing.

Computing nonmanufacturing efficiency variances requires some assumed relationship between input and output activity. Some examples follow:

Department	Input	Output
Mailing	Labor-hours worked	Number of pieces mailed
Personnel	Labor-hours worked	Number of personnel changes processed
Food service	Labor-hours worked	Number of meals served
Consulting	Billable hours worked	Customer revenues
Nursing	Labor-hours worked	Patients (of a particular care level) served
Check processing	Computer-hours worked	Checks processed

In general, jobs with routine tasks lend themselves to efficiency measures, and jobs with nonroutine tasks—like most administrative positions—do not.

Attempts to measure efficiency sometimes lead to employee resentment. In other cases, the measurement results in better performance and morale. Often employee participation in the measurement process helps improve morale, but a top-down imposed measurement system provokes employee resentment.

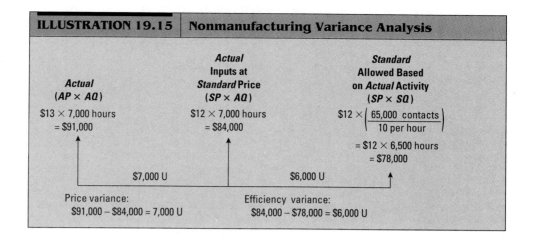

ILLUSTRATION 19.15	Nonmanufacturing Variance Analysis

We noted at the beginning of this chapter that every organization has its own approach to variance analysis, although virtually all are based on the fundamental model presented here. Because of the unique circumstances in each organization, we cannot generalize very much about which variances should be calculated. Managers and accountants in each organization should perform their own cost-benefit analysis to ascertain which calculations are justified.

In deciding how many variances to calculate, it is important to note the **impact** and **controllability** of each variance. When considering *impact*, we ask: "Does this variance matter? Is it so small that the best efforts to improve efficiency or control costs would have very little impact even if the efforts were successful?" If so, it's probably not worth the trouble to calculate and analyze. Hence, detailed variance calculations for small overhead items may not be worthwhile.

When considering the *controllability* of a variance, we ask: "Can we do something about it?" No matter how great its impact, if nothing can be done about the variance, justifying spending resources to compute and analyze it is difficult. For example, materials purchase price variances are often high-impact items. They are hard to control, however, because materials prices fluctuate due to market conditions that are outside the control of managers.

In general, high-impact, highly controllable variances should get the most attention, and low-impact, uncontrollable variances should get the least attention, as shown here:

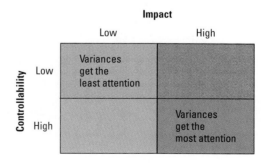

Labor and materials efficiency variances often are highly controllable. With sufficient attention to scheduling, quality of employees, motivation, and incentives, these variances often can be dealt with effectively. An example of a high-impact but hard-to-control item for many companies has been the cost of energy. Many organizations, from airlines to taxicab companies to steel mills, have been able to do little about rising energy costs in the short run. Over time, of course, they can take actions to

---

KEEPING AN EYE ON VARIANCES AND STANDARDS

How Many Variances to Calculate

L.O. 6: Determine which variances to investigate.

impact
The likely monetary effect from an activity (such as a variance).

controllability
The extent to which an item can be managed.

ILLUSTRATION 19.16 **Variance Investigation Meeting**

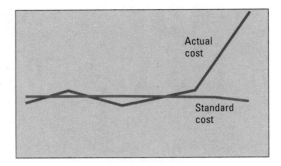

reduce energy usage through acquisition of energy-efficient equipment. In general, the longer the time interval, the greater the ability to control an item.

When to Investigate Variances

management by exception
An approach to management requiring that reports emphasize the deviation from an accepted base point, such as a standard, a budget, an industry average, or a prior period experience.

After computing variances, managers and accountants must decide which ones to investigate. Illustration 19.16 shows one such investigation for which a manager's (Joe's) efficiency idea apparently has not worked out very well.

Because their time is a scarce resource, managers must set some priorities. This can be done by using cost-benefit analysis. Only the variances for which the benefits of correction exceed the costs of follow-up should be pursued. In general, this is consistent with the **management by exception** philosophy, which says, in effect, "Don't worry about what is going according to plan; worry about the exceptions."

This is easier said than done, however. It may be almost impossible to predict either the costs or benefits of investigating variances. So, although the principle is straightforward, the application is difficult. In this section, we identify some characteristics that are important in determining which variances to investigate.

Some problems are easily corrected as soon as they are discovered. When a machine is improperly set or a worker needs minor instruction, the investigation cost is low and the benefits are very likely to exceed costs. This is often a usage or efficiency variance and is reported frequently, often daily, so that immediate corrective action can be taken.

Some variances are not controllable in the short run. Labor price variances due to changes in union contracts and overhead spending variances due to unplanned utility and property tax rate changes may require little or no follow-up in the short run. Such variances sometimes prompt long-run action, such as moving a plant to a locale with lower wage rates and lower utility and property tax rates. In such cases, the short-run benefits of variance investigation are low, but the long-run benefits may be higher.

Many variances occur because of errors in recording, bookkeeping adjust-

An unexpected series of snowstorms or other bad weather conditions can create inefficiencies. Materials prices may be higher because materials are destroyed; labor efficiency may be lower because workers have to clear snow or debris from work areas; and power outages may reduce output.

ments, or timing problems. A variance reporting system (and the accounting department) can lose credibility if it makes bookkeeping errors and adjustments. For this reason, the accounting staff must carefully check variance reports before sending them to operating managers.

Updating Standards

planned variance
A variance that is expected to arise if certain conditions affect operations.

Standards are estimates. As such, they may not reflect conditions that actually occur, especially when standards are not updated and revised to reflect current conditions. If prices and operating methods are changed frequently, standards may be constantly out of date.

Many companies revise standards once a year. Thus, variances occur because conditions change during the year but the standards don't. When conditions change but are known to be temporary, some companies develop a **planned variance.** For example, an unexpected series of snowstorms curtailed activities to much below normal in a steel plant in the Midwest. This affected the workers' productivity and created large unfavorable labor efficiency variances. In response, the accounting staff developed planned variances for a number of costs based on expected differences between actual costs and standard costs due to the snowstorms. For example, the January labor report for a particular department was as follows:

Item	Total Efficiency Variance	Planned Efficiency Variance	Unplanned Efficiency Variance
Direct labor: Department xx	$11,242 U	$9,100 U	$2,142 U

The department manager was not held responsible for the entire $11,242 U variance, but only for the $2,142 U unplanned efficiency variance.

SUMMARY

This chapter discusses the computation and analysis of production cost variances. A *variance* is the difference between a predetermined standard and an actual result.

The following summarizes key ideas tied to the chapter's learning objectives.

LO1: Computing variable cost variances. The model used for calculating variable production cost variances is based on the following diagram, which divides the total variance between actual and standard into *price* and *efficiency* components:

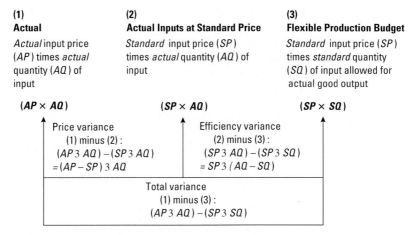

(1) Actual	(2) Actual Inputs at Standard Price	(3) Flexible Production Budget
Actual input price (*AP*) times *actual* quantity (*AQ*) of input	*Standard* input price (*SP*) times *actual* quantity (*AQ*) of input	*Standard* input price (*SP*) times *standard* quantity (*SQ*) of input allowed for actual good output
$(AP \times AQ)$	$(SP \times AQ)$	$(SP \times SQ)$

Price variance
(1) minus (2):
$(AP \times AQ) - (SP \times AQ)$
$= (AP - SP) \times AQ$

Efficiency variance
(2) minus (3):
$(SP \times AQ) - (SP \times SQ)$
$= SP \times (AQ - SQ)$

Total variance
(1) minus (3):
$(AP \times AQ) - (SP \times SQ)$

LO2: Computing variances using activity-based costs. We use the same approach to variance analysis for activity-based costing as for traditional costing (shown in the preceding diagram). However, activity-based costing breaks variable production overhead into many more categories (or activity centers). Price and efficiency variances are then computed for each activity center.

LO3: Computing fixed cost variances. Fixed production costs have no efficiency variance. The price variance is the difference between actual fixed costs and the fixed costs in the flexible budget. If fixed costs are unitized and assigned to units produced, a production volume variance also can arise. The production volume variance is the difference between the budgeted fixed costs and the amount applied to production.

LO4: Developing a comprehensive cost variance analysis. A comprehensive cost variance analysis includes fixed overhead variances as shown in Illustration 19.9 and variable production cost variances as shown in Illustration 19.10. Variable cost variances are calculated for direct materials, direct labor, and variable overhead.

LO5: Nonmanufacturing cost variance analysis. An efficiency variance can be used to analyze variable nonmanufacturing costs. This efficiency computation requires a reliable measure of output activity. Ideally, this requires some quantitative input that can be linked to output. In general, jobs with routine tasks lend themselves to efficiency measures, and jobs with nonroutine tasks—like most administrative positions—do not.

LO6: Determining which variances to investigate. Setting priorities for investigating variances requires performing a cost-benefit analysis. Only the variances for which the benefits of correction exceed the costs of follow-up should be pursued.

LO7: How standard costs flow through accounts (Appendix A). In standard cost systems, the standard costs are part of the accounting system; they replace actual costs in recording transactions between Work in Process Inventory and Finished Goods Inventory. The basic idea is that costs are accumulated at actual cost in Accounts Payable, Accrued Payroll, and similar accounts. Costs are debited to Work in Process Inventory at standard cost. Standard costs are used to reflect the transfer of units between work in process departments, from Work in Process Inventory to Finished Goods Inventory, and from Finished Goods Inventory to Cost of Goods Sold.

LO8: Prorating variances to inventories and cost of goods sold (Appendix A). Manufacturing cost variances for a period are sometimes prorated among inventories and Cost of Goods Sold. This has the effect of restating Cost of Goods Sold and ending inventories to actual cost.

LO9: Standard costing in a just-in-time environment compared to standard costing in a traditional environment (Appendix A). The accounting system in a just-in-time environment is simplified because all costs are charged directly to Cost of Goods Sold. If inventories exist at the end of the period, a portion of the current period costs originally charged to Cost of Goods Sold is credited to Cost of Goods Sold and debited to the respective inventory account as an end-of-period adjustment. This method of accounting is known as *backflush costing.*

LO10: Compare the two-way, three-way, and four-way analyses of overhead variances (Appendix B). The two-way analysis of overhead variances has just two variances: a production volume variance, computed like the production volume variance in the four-way analysis, and a spending, or budget variance, which is the difference between the actual and budgeted overhead. Think of the spending variance as including all three of the overhead variances computed in the four-way analysis in addition to the production volume variance.

The three-way analysis is like the four-way analysis except the two fixed and variable price variances are combined into one overhead price variance. Companies that do not separate costs into fixed and variable components use the three-way analysis.

KEY TERMS

*Term appears in Appendix.

APPENDIX A

L.O. 7: Demonstrate how standard costs flow through accounts (Appendix A).

standard costing
An accounting method that assigns costs to cost objects at predetermined amounts.

Standard Costing System

Standard Cost Flows

When using **standard costing,** costs are transferred through the production process at their standard costs. This means that the entry debiting Work in Process Inventory at standard cost could be made before actual costs are known. In process costing, units transferred between departments are valued at standard cost; in job costing, standard costs are used to charge the job for its components. Actual costs are accumulated in accounts such as Accounts Payable and Factory Payroll and are compared with the standard costs allowed for the output produced. The difference between the actual costs assigned to a department and the standard cost of the work done is the *variance* for the department.

The following sections discuss the flow of costs in a standard cost system, compare the actual and standard costs of work, and demonstrate how the variances are isolated in the accounting system. The variances are based on the calculations introduced in the chapter. Standard cost systems vary somewhat from company to company, so in reality, the method presented here may be modified a bit to meet a company's particular needs.

The example in this appendix continues the Evergreen Company example started in Chapter 18 and carried through this chapter. The variances shown in the following journal entries were computed earlier in this chapter. (We use the example from this chapter in which direct materials purchases do not equal usage.)

Direct Materials   Direct materials are purchased at their actual cost, but in a standard cost system they are often carried in direct materials inventory at the standard price per unit.[3] We assume that 250,000 feet are purchased and that 110,000 feet are used, as shown in Illustration 19.11. We assume that the price variance is recorded at the time materials are purchased. Therefore, materials inventory will be carried at standard prices. The purchasing entry follows:

Direct Materials Inventory	62,500	
Materials Price Variance	3,500	
Accounts Payable		66,000

To record the purchase of 250,000 board-feet at the actual cost of 26.4 cents per foot, the transfer to Direct Materials Inventory at the standard cost per foot of 25 cents, and the materials purchase price variance for the difference.

We refer to the cost of direct materials inventory as a standard cost because 25 cents per foot is the standard allowed per unit of input (board-feet), not the standard cost per unit of output (crates).

---

[3]An alternative treatment carries materials at actual cost and then charges materials to production at a standard price per unit.

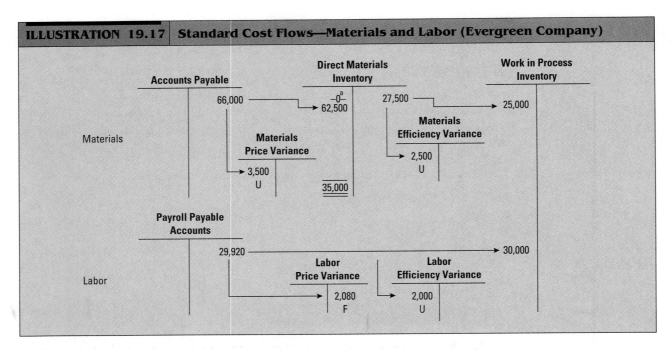

ILLUSTRATION 19.17 | **Standard Cost Flows—Materials and Labor (Evergreen Company)**

ªAssume no beginning materials inventory balance.

When materials are placed in production, Work in Process Inventory is debited for the standard amount of input used at the standard cost per unit. The cutting department is allowed a standard of 100,000 board-feet of lumber to make 10,000 crates at 25 cents per foot, but it actually used 110,000 board-feet. The entry charging production for the standard cost of direct materials follows:

Work in Process Inventory	25,000	
Materials Efficiency Variance	2,500	
Direct Materials Inventory		27,500

To record the requisition of 110,000 actual board-feet at the standard cost per foot of 25 cents, the charge to Work in Process Inventory at $2.50 per crate times 10,000 crates (or 25 cents per foot times 100,000 board-feet allowed for 10,000 crates), and the materials efficiency variance for the difference.

The materials price variance is usually the responsibility of the purchasing department, whereas the efficiency variance is usually the responsibility of the production departments.

Direct Labor   Direct labor is credited to payroll liability accounts, such as Accrued Payroll or Payroll Payable, for the actual cost (including accruals for fringe benefits and payroll taxes) and charged to Work in Process Inventory at standard. The following entry is based on the facts about the standard costs allowed for Evergreen Company as described in the chapter and in Illustration 19.10:

Work in Process Inventory	30,000	
Labor Efficiency Variance	2,000	
Labor Price Variance		2,080
Payroll Payable Accounts		29,920

To charge the production departments for the standard cost of direct labor at $10 per hour times 3,000 hours (10,000 crates times .30 hour allowed), to record the actual cost of $29,920, and to record the labor efficiency variance and the labor price variance.

This completes the presentation of standard cost journal entries for materials and labor. These journal entries are summarized in Illustration 19.17.

Variable Manufacturing Overhead   Standard overhead costs are charged to production based on standard direct labor-hours per unit of output produced at Evergreen. Overhead costs often are charged to production before the actual costs are known. This is demonstrated by the following sequence of entries:

1. Standard overhead costs are charged to production during the period. The credit entry is to an overhead applied account.

2. Actual costs are recorded in various accounts and transferred to an overhead summary account. This accounting procedure is completed after the end of the period.

3. Variances are computed as the difference between the standard costs charged to production (overhead applied) and the actual costs.

This approach is similar to that used to charge overhead to production using predetermined rates in normal costing.

Based on the data from the chapter and Illustration 19.14, variable overhead is charged to production as follows:

Work in Process Inventory	25,000	
Variable Overhead Applied		25,000

Note that overhead is applied to Work in Process Inventory on the basis of standard labor-hours allowed. As we shall see shortly, over- or underapplied overhead represents a combination of the variable overhead price and efficiency variances.

Actual variable overhead costs are recorded in various accounts and transferred to each department's variable manufacturing overhead account as follows:

Variable Overhead (Actual)	26,480	
Supplies Inventory		
Accrued Payroll—Indirect Labor		
Accounts Payable—Power.		26,480
Maintenance Department.		
Etc. (other accounts and service departments)		

Variable overhead variances were computed in the chapter: price, $187 F, and efficiency, $1,667 U. These variable overhead variances are recorded by closing the applied and actual accounts as follows:

Variable Overhead Applied	25,000	
Variable Overhead Efficiency Variance	1,667	
Variable Overhead Price Variance		187
Variable Overhead (Actual)		26,480

These entries are shown in T-accounts in Illustration 19.18.

Fixed Manufacturing Overhead   For the purposes of this example, we assume that Evergreen uses full-absorption costing because the amounts recorded ultimately will be used to prepare statements for external financial reporting. Fixed manufacturing costs are charged to units at $4.50 per crate ($15 per standard direct labor-hour) using full-absorption costing. The company produced 10,000 crates in May, for which 3,000 standard direct labor-hours are allowed at the rate of .3 hour per crate. Hence, the total fixed manufacturing overhead costs applied to production (that is, debited to Work in Process Inventory) amounted to $45,000 ($4.50 × 10,000 crates or $15 × 3,000 hours), as shown in the following entry:

Work in Process Inventory	45,000	
Fixed Overhead Applied.		45,000

ILLUSTRATION 19.18 | Standard Cost Flows—Overhead (Evergreen Company)

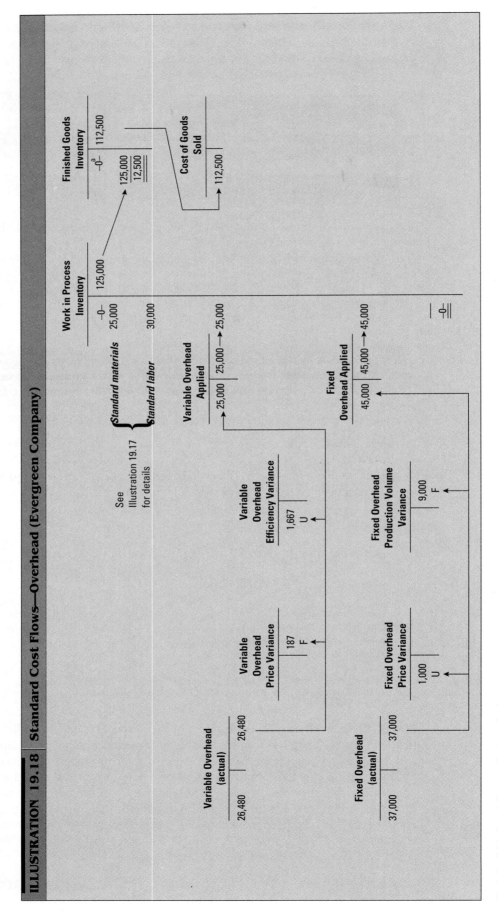

[a]Beginning finished goods inventory is assumed to be zero.

Actual fixed overhead costs are recorded in various accounts and transferred to each department's fixed overhead account as follows:

Fixed Overhead (Actual).	37,000	
Accumulated Depreciation—Building		
Accrued Payroll—Indirect Labor		
Accounts Payable—Heat.		37,000
Plant Administration		
Etc. (other accounts and allocations from service departments).		

Recall that the price variance ($1,000 U) is the difference between actual ($37,000) and budgeted ($36,000) fixed manufacturing costs. The production volume variance ($9,000 F) is the difference between budgeted ($36,000) and applied ($45,000) fixed manufacturing costs. Fixed overhead variances are recorded by closing the applied overhead and actual overhead accounts as follows:

Fixed Overhead Applied.	45,000	
Fixed Overhead Price Variance	1,000	
Fixed Overhead Production Volume Variance		9,000
Fixed Overhead (Actual)		37,000

This entry shows a favorable fixed overhead production volume variance that occurred because Evergreen produced 10,000 crates when it had estimated only 8,000. Recall from the chapter that this production volume variance results from attempting to compute unit costs under full-absorption costing. It has no meaning for planning and control purposes.

These entries are summarized in Illustration 19.18.

Transfer to Finished Goods Inventory and to Cost of Goods Sold

When all production work has been completed, units are transferred to Finished Goods Inventory and to Cost of Goods Sold at standard cost.

Finished Goods Inventory This month 10,000 crates were finished and transferred to Finished Goods Inventory. After they have been finished and inspected, they are transferred to a finished goods storage area and recorded by the following entry (full-absorption, standard costing):

Finished Goods Inventory	125,000	
Work in Process Inventory		125,000
To record the transfer of 10,000 completed crates at $12.50 per unit		
($8.00 variable plus $4.50 fixed) times 10,000 crates.		

Cost of Goods Sold For this example, assume that the company sold 9,000 of the crates it produced for $21 per crate. This was recorded by the following entries:

Accounts Receivable	189,000	
Sales Revenue		189,000
Cost of Goods Sold	112,500	
Finished Goods Inventory		112,500
To record the sale of 9,000 crates at a price of $21 and a standard cost of		
$12.50 per crate.		

SELF-STUDY QUESTION

3. (This is a continuation of the Containers, Inc., Self-Study Questions 1 and 2 from the chapter.)

- Containers, Inc., produced 50,000 plastic notebook computer cases and sold 40,000 of them at $10 each. Budgeted sales were 45,000 units at $10.15 each.

- Standard variable costs per unit (that is, per case):

Direct materials: 2 pounds at $1	$2.00
Direct labor: .10 hour at $15	1.50
Variable manufacturing overhead:	
.10 hour at $5	.50
	$4.00 per case

- Fixed manufacturing overhead:

Monthly budget.	$80,000
Estimated monthly production	40,000 cases or 4,000 hours
Fixed overhead application rate	?

- Actual production costs:

Direct materials purchased: 200,000 pounds at $1.20	$240,000
Direct materials used: 110,000 pounds at $1.20	132,000
Direct labor: 6,000 hours at $14	84,000
Variable overhead	28,000
Fixed overhead	83,000

Use a full-absorption, standard costing system to
  a. Record the transactions using journal entries.
  b. Show the flow of transactions through T-accounts.

The solution to this question is at the end of this chapter on page 630.

Prorating Standard Cost Variances

L.O. 8: Explain how to prorate variances to inventories and cost of goods sold (Appendix A).

prorating variances
Assigning portions of variances to the inventory and Cost of Goods Sold accounts to which the variances are related.

Inventory values are often adjusted to actual costs for contract settlements, taxes, and financial reporting purposes. This usually requires **prorating variances** to each account that has been debited or credited with the standard cost that is now being adjusted to actual. When proration is complete, the balances in the inventory accounts closely approximate actual costs, and the variance accounts have no balances.

To illustrate the proration of variances, we use the Evergreen Company example to prorate one variance: materials price variance.

Materials Price Variance   The materials price variance is prorated *to all accounts that contain standard materials costs purchased in the current period;* namely, Direct Materials Inventory, Materials Efficiency Variance, Work in Process Inventory, Finished Goods Inventory, and Cost of Goods Sold. Standard direct materials costs are 20 percent ($25,000 direct materials debit to Work in Process ÷ $125,000 total debit to Work in Process) of the total standard cost per crate. The amounts for direct materials at standard prices in each of these accounts are:

Ending Direct Materials Inventory (from Illustration 19.17)		Materials Efficiency Variance (from Illustration 19.17)		Ending Work in Process Inventory (see Illustration 19.18)		Ending Finished Goods Inventory (20% × $12,500 finished goods ending inventory is direct materials cost)		Cost of Goods Sold (20% of the $112,500 Cost of Goods Sold is direct materials cost)		Total Materials Purchased This Period, at Standard Prices (see debit to Materials Inventory in Illustration 19.17)
$35,000	+	$2,500	+	$0	+	$2,500	+	$22,500	=	$62,500

These balances add up to the total materials costs purchased at standard prices. The materials price variance of $3,500 U is prorated to each account in proportion to the

	(1)	(2)	
Account	**Materials at Standard Price in the Account**	**Amount as a Percent of Total Materials Costs at Standard Price**	**Variance to Be Prorated (column 2 × $3,500)**
Materials Inventory.	$35,000	56%ᵃ	$1,960
Efficiency Variance.	2,500	4	140
Work in Process Inventory	–0–	–0–	–0–
Finished Goods Inventory.	2,500	4	140
Cost of Goods Sold.	22,500	36	1,260
Total	$62,500	100%	$3,500

ILLUSTRATION 19.19 | Prorating Materials Price Variance

ᵃ56% = $35,000 ÷ $62,500, etc.

account balance's percentage of the total materials costs at standard prices. The proration of the $3,500 U appears in Illustration 19.19.

The journal entry to assign the prorated variance to accounts follows (amounts are from Illustration 19.19):

Direct Materials Inventory.	1,960	
Materials Efficiency Variance.	140	
Finished Goods Inventory	140	
Cost of Goods Sold	1,260	
Materials Price Variance		3,500

The variance account is closed when this journal entry is made.

Standard Costing in a Just-in-Time Environment

L.O. 9: Compare standard costing in a just-in-time environment to standard costing in a traditional environment (Appendix A).

In just-in-time manufacturing settings with demand-pull of products through manufacturing inventories are minimized. As a result, the accounting system is simplified because all costs are charged directly to Cost of Goods Sold. If inventories exist at the end of the period, a portion of the current period costs originally charged to Cost of Goods Sold is credited to Cost of Goods Sold and debited to the respective inventory account as an end-of-period adjustment. This method of accounting is known as *backflush costing.*

Using backflush standard costing, costs are charged to Cost of Goods Sold at standard. Variances are charged to a separate account. If there are no inventories at the end of the period, the variance account is expensed or combined with Cost of Goods Sold at standard. The latter result is Cost of Goods Sold at actual.

If inventories exist at the end of the period and if the difference between the standard cost of inventories and actual cost is immaterial, the inventories may be stated at standard cost. In this situation, variances need not be prorated.

If prorating variances makes a material difference in the financial statements or is required by contract, the variance is prorated from the variance account to the respective inventory accounts based on the proportions of the current period costs in each of the inventory and Cost of Goods Sold accounts, as described in the preceding discussion on variance proration. The results should be the same as if one had accounted for the variances in the traditional manner discussed earlier in this chapter.

For example, if a company were using demand-pull accounting, assume that the Cost of Goods Sold and related variance account appear as follows before adjustment:

Cost of Goods Sold (Standard Costs)

Materials	60,000
Labor	30,000
Overhead	70,000

Cost Variances

Materials price	3,500		
Materials efficiency	2,500		
		Labor and overhead	6,600

Debits to Cost of Goods Sold are standard price (SP) × standard quantity of input per unit of output (SQ) × actual units produced. If inventories were minimal, the balance in the variance account would be expensed.

If the company has substantial ending inventories, the costs in Cost of Goods Sold are transferred to the inventory accounts. Assume that no beginning inventories exist and that $42,000 of the $60,000 standard cost of materials is traced to the inventory accounts:

Materials Inventory	$35,000
Work in Process	5,000
Finished Goods	2,000
Total	$42,000

The total amount is credited to Cost of Goods Sold with debits to each inventory account, as shown in Illustration 19.20.

A similar adjustment is made for labor and overhead. Assume that 20 percent of the labor and overhead amounts are still in Work in Process and 8 percent are in Finished Goods. The dollar amounts to be transferred from Cost of Goods Sold to the inventory accounts are as follows:

	Labor	Overhead
Work in Process	$6,000	$14,000
Finished Goods	2,400	5,600
Total	$8,400	$19,600

The resulting inventory and Cost of Goods Sold accounts appear in Illustration 19.20 after adjustments.

ILLUSTRATION 19.20 Backflush Standard Costing

Materials Inventory

-0-	
35,000	

Work in Process

-0-		
Materials	5,000	
Labor	6,000	
Overhead	14,000	
	25,000	
Balance		

Finished Goods

-0-		
Materials	2,000	
Labor	2,400	
Overhead	5,600	
	10,000	
Balance		

Cost of Goods Sold (Standard Costs)

Materials	60,000	42,000
Labor	30,000	8,400
Overhead	70,000	19,600

Variances

Materials price	3,500	Labor and overhead	6,600
Materials efficiency	2,500		

APPENDIX B

L.O. 10: Compare the two-way, three-way, and four-way analyses of overhead variances (Appendix B).

Two-Way and Three-Way Analysis of Overhead Variance

The method of computing overhead variances described in this chapter is known as the *four-way analysis of overhead variances* because it computes the following four variances:

	Price	Efficiency	Production Volume
Variable Costs	$ 187 F	$1,667 U	Not applicable
Fixed Costs	1,000 U	Not applicable	$9,000 F

Companies also prepare alternative two-way or three-way analyses of production overhead variances.

Two-Way Analysis

The two-way analysis of overhead variances has just two variances: a production volume variance, computed like the production volume variance in the four-way analysis, and a spending, or budget variance, which is the difference between the actual and budgeted overhead. Think of the spending variance as including all three of the overhead variances computed in the four-way analysis in addition to the production volume variance. The spending variance is useful for management control purposes, but the production volume variance is not.

If Evergreen does not break down its variances into fixed and variable components, the actual overhead costs are $63,480 ($26,480 variable plus $37,000 fixed, as shown in Illustration 19.14), and the budgeted overhead totals $61,000 ($25,000 variable plus $36,000 fixed, as shown in Illustration 19.14).

The following diagram shows how to compute the two overhead variances.

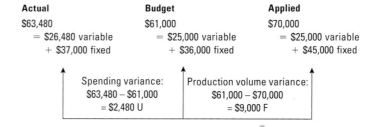

Actual	Budget	Applied
$63,480	$61,000	$70,000
= $26,480 variable	= $25,000 variable	= $25,000 variable
+ $37,000 fixed	+ $36,000 fixed	+ $45,000 fixed

Spending variance:
$63,480 − $61,000
= $2,480 U

Production volume variance:
$61,000 − $70,000
= $9,000 F

The amount of variable overhead applied to units produced ($25,000) is the standard allowed for the flexible production budget, so "applied equals budget" for variable overhead. This is not true for fixed overhead if a production volume variance exists.

Three-Way Analysis

The three-way analysis is like the four-way analysis except the two fixed and variable price variances are combined into one overhead price variance. Companies that do not separate costs into fixed and variable components use the three-way analysis.

The three variances computed in the three-way analysis are (1) the overhead price variance, (2) the variable overhead efficiency variance, and (3) the fixed overhead production volume variance. These are computed for Evergreen as follows (page 615).

The budget (column 3) and applied overhead (column 4) for the three-way analysis are the same as for the two-way analysis.

In deciding whether to use two-way analysis or three-way analysis, managers should weigh the costs of computing and interpreting the variable overhead efficiency variance against the benefits of obtaining the data from that variance.

ILLUSTRATION 19.21   Alternative Ways of Computing Overhead Variances

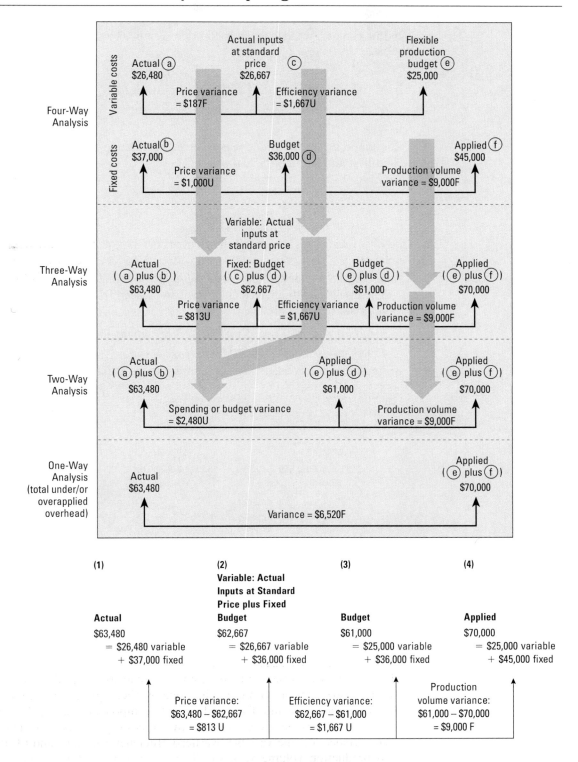

Illustration 19.21 summarizes the two-way, three-way, and four-way analyses of overhead variance. We start with the four-way analysis at the top and show how the numbers in the two-way and three-way analyses fit into the four-way analysis. Note that there also could be a one-way analysis, which is the total under or overapplied overhead; that is, the $6,520 F difference between actual overhead ($63,480 in this example) and the amount applied to production ($70,000 in this example).

APPENDIX C   ### An Alternative Way to Divide Variances into Price and Efficiency Components

In this chapter, we calculated each price variance based on actual quantity. That is,

But suppose that the order was reversed so that the efficiency variance was calculated first and based on actual prices:

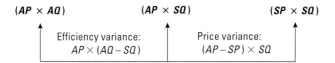

Note that the two endpoints are the same, but the middle point is different.

The effect on variance calculations can be seen from the following if Evergreen's direct materials data are used:

Standard costs: 10 board-feet @ $.25 per board-foot = $2.50 per crate

Crates produced in May: 10,000

Actual materials used: 110,000 board-feet @ $.264 per board-foot = $29,040

For this example, assume that the quantity of board-feet purchased equals the quantity used.

The calculation in the chapter was as follows:

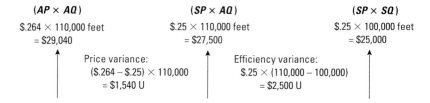

The alternative calculation is as follows:

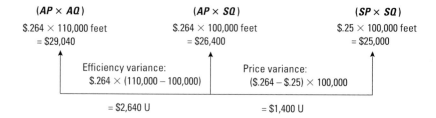

Note that the *total* variance is the same in both cases: $4,040 U. However, the partition into price and efficiency (quantity) variances is different. There are really three variances: a pure price variance ($1,400 in this case), a pure efficiency variance ($2,500), and a joint variance ($140 in this case). The joint variance is part of the price variance in the first calculation and part of the efficiency variance in the second. The graph in Illustration 19.22 shows these relationships.

By isolating the joint variance, we may be able to resolve disputes between purchasing people and production people. Purchasing argues that it should not be ac-

ILLUSTRATION   19.22   Graphic Analysis of Variance, Direct Materials, Evergreen Company

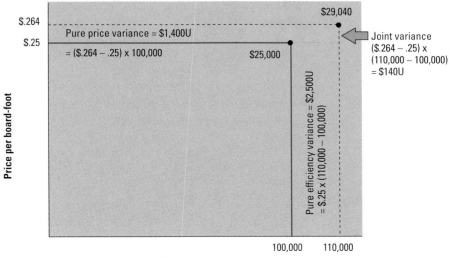

Note: The area inside the solid line represents the total standard costs allowed to make 10,000 crates. The area inside the dashed line represents the total actual costs incurred.

countable for the joint variance because production controls quantities. Production people say they manage quantities, not prices. Illustration 19.22 shows that a piece of the variance is, in fact, a joint responsibility.

REVIEW QUESTIONS

19.1   What is the difference between a standard and a budget?

19.2   One of the principles espoused by management is that one should manage by exception. How can responsibility reporting systems and/or analysis of variances assist in that process?

19.3   What are the three primary sources of variances for variable costs?

19.4   Why are the variances for fixed costs different from the variances computed for variable costs?

19.5   In a service environment with no inventories, would variance analysis be useful? Why or why not?

19.6   **(Appendix A)** How do you distinguish between a standard cost and an actual cost?

19.7   **(Appendix A)** How should variances be disposed of at the end of the year?

19.8   **(Appendix A)** Why is it difficult to relate fixed costs to outputs from a production process?

CRITICAL ANALYSIS AND DISCUSSION QUESTIONS

19.9   Why should management want to divide production cost variances into price and efficiency variances?

19.10   What is the difference between a flexible budget and inputs priced at standard?

19.11   The production department manager has just received a responsibility report showing a substantial unfavorable variance for overtime premium. The manager objects to the inclusion of this variance because the overtime was due to the acceptance of a large rush order by the sales department. To whom should this variance be charged?

19.12 Many companies set wage rates through negotiations with unions. Under these circumstances, how would a labor price variance arise that would be the responsibility of a line manager?

19.13 Would the production volume variance represent a difference in the cash outflows for the company when compared to budgeted cash outflows?

19.14 Why might management decision making be enhanced if materials price variances are recognized at the time of purchase rather than at the time of use?

19.15 (**Appendix A**) What is the difference in the way that labor and material costs are accounted for versus the way overhead costs are accounted for in a standard costing system?

19.16 (**Appendix A**) "Just like price and efficiency variances, the production volume variance indicates whether a company has spent more or less than called for in the budget." Comment on this quote.

EXERCISES

19.17	Variable Cost Variances (L.O. 1)	The standard direct labor cost per reservation for Eagle Air Charters is $0.65 ($6.50 per hour divided by 10 reservations per hour). Actual direct labor costs during the period totaled $44,500, 6,800 labor-hours were worked during the period, and 72,000 reservations were made.
	Required	Compute the direct labor price and efficiency variances for the period. (Refer to Illustration 19.4 for format.)
19.18	Variable Cost Variances (L.O. 1)	The standard direct labor cost per unit for a company was $10 ($5 per hour times 2 hours per unit). Actual direct labor costs during the period amounted to $18,800, 3,900 labor-hours were worked during the period, and 1,900 units were produced.
	Required	Compute the direct labor price and efficiency variances for the period. (Refer to Illustration 19.4 for format.)
19.19	Variable Cost Variances (L.O. 1)	The following data reflect the current month's activity for Nugget, Inc.:

Actual total direct labor.	$88,400
Actual hours worked	14,000
Standard labor-hours allowed for actual output (flexible budget).	15,000
Direct labor price variance.	$ 1,600 U
Actual variable overhead.	$44,200
Standard variable overhead rate per standard direct labor-hour	$3.40

Variable overhead is applied based on standard direct labor-hours allowed.

	Required	Compute the labor and variable overhead price and efficiency variances.
19.20	Variable Cost Variances (L.O. 1)	Information on Almay Corporation's direct materials costs follows:

Actual quantities of direct materials used.	30,000
Actual costs of direct materials used.	$131,400
Standard price per unit of direct materials	$4.20
Flexible budget for direct materials	$119,700

Almay Corporation has no materials inventories.

	Required	Prepare a short report for management showing Almay Corporation's direct materials price and efficiency variances.

19.21 Variances from Activity-Based Costs (L.O. 2)

Analysis of the variable overhead costs for Crucible Company reveals three cost drivers with the following standard and actual amounts:

Activity Center	Cost Driver	Standard Rate per Cost Driver Unit	Standard Input per Unit of Output	Actual Costs	Actual Number of Inputs Used
Quality testing	Test minutes	$1.00	2 test minutes	$10,000	10,000 test minutes
Energy	Machine-hours	2.00	2 machine-hours	20,000	10,500 machine-hours
Indirect labor	Direct labor-hours	1.00	3 hours	14,200	14,000 hours

Assume that 5,000 units of output were actually produced.

Required Prepare an analysis of variances in these three activity centers.

19.22 Variable Cost Variances (L.O. 1)

Information on Blarney Chemical's direct materials costs follows:

Quantities of palladium purchased and used	1,200 ounces
Actual cost of palladium used.	$103,000
Standard price per unit of palladium.	$90
Standard quantity of palladium allowed.	1,100 ounces

Required What were Blarney's direct materials price and efficiency variances?

19.23 Variable Cost Variances: Materials Purchased and Materials Used Are Not Equal (L.O. 4)

Durango Company reported the following information concerning its direct materials:

Direct materials purchased (actual)	$58,158
Standard cost of materials purchased	57,510
Standard price times actual amount of materials used.	38,340
Actual production.	28,000 units
Standard direct materials costs per unit produced.	$1.31

Required Compute the direct materials cost variances. Prepare an analysis for management like the one in Illustration 19.11.

19.24 Fixed Cost Variances (L.O. 3)

Information on Cramden Company's fixed overhead costs follows:

Overhead applied	$240,000
Actual overhead	257,000
Budgeted overhead	246,000

Required What are the fixed overhead price and production volume variances? (Refer to Illustration 19.12 for format.)

19.25 Fixed Cost Variances (L.O. 3)

Mahalo Corporation applies overhead at the rate of $2.20 per unit. Budgeted fixed overhead was $33,930. This month 16,000 units were produced, and actual overhead was $32,555.

Required What are the fixed overhead price and production volume variances for Mahalo?

19.26 Comprehensive Cost Variance Analysis (L.O. 4)

Miller, Inc., manufactures construction equipment and farm machinery tires. The following information is available for June, year 1.

- Miller produced and sold 2,300 tires for $1,000 each. Budgeted production was 2,500 tires.
- Standard variable costs per tire follows:

Direct materials: 100 pounds at $2.	$200
Direct labor: 20 hours at $9	180
Variable production overhead: 4.5 machine-hours at $10 per hour	45
Total variable costs	$425

• Fixed production overhead costs:

Monthly budget $950,000

• Fixed overhead is applied at the rate of $380 per tire.
• Actual production costs:

Direct materials purchased and used: 240,000 pounds at $1.80 . . . . . . $432,000
Direct labor: 44,000 hours at $9.20 404,800
Variable overhead: 10,800 machine-hours at $10.20 per hour 110,160
Fixed overhead 1,000,000

• Machine-hours: 10,800.

Required

a. Prepare a cost variance analysis for each variable cost for Miller.

b. Prepare a fixed overhead cost variance analysis.

19.27 Graphical Presentation (L.O. 4)

Refer to the data in Exercise 19.24. Management would like to see results reported graphically. Prepare a graph like that shown in Illustration 19.13.

19.28 Comprehensive Cost Variance Analysis (L.O. 4)

Bryce, Inc., is a fast-growing chain of operations that specializes in optical care and contact lenses. The following data are available for last year's eye care exam services:

• Bryce performed 100,000 eye exams last year. Budgeted exams were 90,000 exams, averaging 40 minutes each.
• Standard variable costs per exam were as follows:

Direct optometrist services: 40 minutes at $36 per hour. $24.00
Variable support staff and overhead: 1.1 labor-hours at $15 per hour 16.50

• Fixed overhead costs:

Annual budget $360,000

• Fixed overhead is applied at the rate of $4 per exam.
• Actual eye exam costs:

Direct optometrist services: 100,000 exams averaging 45 minutes at $39 . . . . $2,925,000
Variable support staff and overhead: 1.2 labor-hours at $14 per hour × 100,000 exams 1,680,000
Fixed overhead 374,000

Required

a. Prepare a cost variance analysis for each variable cost for last year.

b. Prepare a fixed overhead cost variance analysis like the one in Illustration 19.12.

19.29 Variances from Activity-Based Costs (L.O. 2)

Klien's offers optical care. Management has asked you to analyze its variable overhead. Analysis of the variable overhead costs reveals three cost drivers with the following standard and actual amounts:

Activity Center	Cost Driver	Standard Rate per Cost Driver Unit	Standard Input per Unit of Output (exam)	Actual Costs	Actual Number of Inputs Used
Purchasing	Number of purchases	$2 per purchase	1 purchase per exam	$100,000	46,000 purchases
Support staff labor	Number of fittings	10 per fitting	1.2 fittings per exam	550,000	52,000 fittings
Special contact lenses	Pairs of contacts sold	5 per pair	0.6 pairs per exam	145,000	31,000 pairs of contact lenses

Last year, the number of units of output, that is, exams, was 50,000.

Required

Prepare a cost variance analysis.

19.30 Two-Way and Three-Way Overhead Variances (Appendix B) (L.O. 10)

Using the data in Exercise 19.28, compute the following (assume that full-absorption costing is used to apply overhead to units produced):

a. Total over- or underapplied overhead.

b. Two-way analysis of overhead variances.

c. Three-way analysis of overhead variances.

19.31 Overhead Variances (L.O. 1, L.O. 3)

Jasper Corporation shows the following overhead information for the current period:

Actual overhead incurred	$26,600, ($7,600 fixed and $19,000 variable)
Budgeted fixed overhead	$7,800 (3,000 direct labor-hours budgeted)
Standard variable overhead rate per direct labor-hour	$6
Standard hours allowed for actual production	3,500 hours
Actual labor-hours used	3,300 hours

Required

What are the variable overhead price and efficiency variances and the fixed overhead price variance?

19.32 Two-Way and Three-Way Overhead Variances (Appendix B) (L.O. 10)

Using the data in Exercise 19.31, compute the following (assume that full-absorption costing is used to apply overhead to units produced).

a. Total over- or underapplied overhead.

b. Two-way analysis of overhead variances.

c. Three-way analysis of overhead variances.

19.33 Two-Way and Three-Way Overhead Variances (Appendix B) (L.O. 10)

Indio Company incurred total overhead costs of $89,180 during the month when 2,050 hours were worked. The normal workload for the company is 2,000 hours. The flexible budget for the output attained this period indicates that 2,150 hours were allowed.

Standard costs per hour are as follows:	
Variable overhead	$13.75
Fixed overhead	27.70

Fixed overhead cost $4,217 more than budgeted.

Required

Compute the following:

a. Total over- or underapplied overhead, assuming that full-absorption costing is used.

b. Two-way analysis of overhead variances.

c. Three-way analysis of overhead variances.

19.34 Standard Materials Costs (Appendix A) (L.O. 7)

Armadillo Corporation acquired 50,000 units of direct materials for $70,000 last year. The standard price paid for the materials was $1.30 per unit. During last year, 45,000 units of materials were used in the production process. Materials are entered into production at the beginning of the process. The standard allowed was 48,000 units for the amount of output that was actually produced. Eighty percent of the units that used these materials were completed and transferred to Finished Goods Inventory. Sixty percent of these units that had been transferred to Finished Goods Inventory were sold this period. There were no beginning inventories.

Required

Prepare journal entries and show the flow of costs through T-accounts.

19.35 Prorate Materials Variances (Appendix A) (L.O. 8)

Refer to the variances calculated for Exercise 19.34. Prorate the Materials Price Variance to the Materials Efficiency Variance, Ending Inventories, and Cost of Goods Sold.

19.36 Standard Costing in a Just-in-Time Environment (Appendix A) (L.O. 9)

During the current period, Otter Co. paid $38,000 for 30,000 units of material, all of which were immediately put into process. During the period, 14,800 units of output were produced, and 14,500 units were sold. Three hundred units remain in Finished Goods Inventory. Each unit of output requires two units of material, which has a standard cost of $1.35 per unit of material. Standard variable overhead is $69,600 for 15,000 units of production. The variable overhead efficiency variance was $1,800 U, and actual variable overhead was $69,341.

Fixed overhead, which includes all labor costs, is budgeted at $146,000. Actual fixed overhead for the period was $143,200. Fixed overhead is applied to production at $10 per unit of output. All variances are expensed.

Required	**a.** Show the flow of these costs if the company initially charges all manufacturing costs to Cost of Goods Sold at standard (that is, using backflush standard costing).
	b. Show the adjustment that would be made to reflect the ending inventory balances.
19.37 Standard Costing in a Just-in-Time Environment (Appendix A) (L.O. 9)	Refer to the data for Armadillo Corporation, Exercise 19.34. If Armadillo were operating in a just-in-time environment and charging its standard costs directly to Standard Cost of Goods Sold, show the flow of costs through T-accounts that would be required to adjust the Standard Cost of Goods Sold account to reflect end-of-period inventories. Variances are expensed.

PROBLEMS

19.38 Nonmanufacturing Cost Variances	Seattle Financial originates mortgage loans for residential housing. The company charges a service fee for processing loan applications. This fee is set twice a year based on the cost of processing a loan application. For the first half of this year, Seattle Financial estimated that it would process 75 loans. Correspondence, credit reports, supplies, and other materials that vary with each loan are estimated to cost $45 per loan. The company hires a loan processor at an estimated cost of $27,000 per year and an assistant at an estimated cost of $20,000 per year. The cost to lease office space and pay utilities and other related costs are estimated at $58,000 per year.
	During the first six months of this year, Seattle Financial processed 79 loans. Cost of materials, credit reports, and other items related to loan processing were 8 percent higher than expected for the volume of loans processed.
	The loan processor and her assistant cost $23,800 for the six months. Leasing and related office costs were $28,100.
Required	Prepare an analysis of the variances for Seattle Financial. (*Hint:* Loans are the output.)
19.39 Direct Materials	Information about Stanley Company's direct materials cost follows:

Standard price per materials ounce	$345
Actual quantity used.	420 ounces
Standard quantity allowed for production	435 ounces
Price variance.	$2,950 F

Required	What was the actual purchase price per ounce, rounded to the nearest cent?
19.40 Solve for Direct Labor-Hours	Harrison Company reports the following direct labor information for product HAV for October:

Standard rate	$7.00 per hour
Actual rate paid	$7.20 per hour
Standard hours allowed for actual production	1,400 hours
Labor efficiency variance	$500 U

Required	Based on these data, what were the actual hours worked and what was the labor price variance?
19.41 Overhead Variances	Cyclaris, Inc., shows the following overhead information for the current period:

Actual overhead incurred.	$14,700, of which $9,800 is variable
Budgeted fixed overhead	$4,320
Standard variable overhead rate per direct labor-hour	$3
Standard hours allowed for actual production.	3,500 hours
Actual labor-hours used.	3,300 hours

Required	What are the variable overhead price and efficiency variances and fixed overhead price variance?
19.42 Manufacturing Variances	Adiamo Company prepares its budgets on the basis of standard costs. A responsibility report is prepared monthly showing the differences between master budget and actual. Variances are analyzed and reported separately. Materials price variances are computed at the time of purchase.

The following information relates to the current period:

Standard costs (per unit of output)

Direct materials, 1 kilogram @ $1 per kilogram	$ 1
Direct labor, 2 hours @ $4 per hour.	8
Factory overhead	
Variable (25% of direct labor cost).	2
Total standard cost per unit	$11

Actual costs for the month follow:

Materials purchased	3,000 kilograms at $.90 per kilogram
Output	1,900 units using 2,100 kilograms of materials
Actual labor costs.	3,200 hours at $5 per hour
Actual variable overhead	$4,500

Required

Prepare a cost variance analysis for the variable costs.

19.43   Alternative Variance Calculations (Appendix C)

Refer to the labor and variable overhead data given in Problem 19.42. Compute the labor variances using the method set forth in Appendix C.

19.44   Overhead Cost and Variance Relationships

Sparkle Company reported a $50 unfavorable price variance for variable overhead and a $500 unfavorable price variance for fixed overhead. The flexible budget had $32,100 variable overhead based on 10,700 direct labor-hours; only 10,600 hours were worked. Total actual overhead was $54,350. Estimated hours for computing the fixed overhead application rate were 11,000 hours.

Required

a. Prepare a variable overhead analysis like the one in Illustration 19.5.

b. Prepare a fixed overhead analysis like the one in Illustration 19.12.

19.45   Analysis of Cost Reports

Eric is the production manager of the Cifloxo Plant, a division of the larger corporation, Plantimum, Inc. He has complained several times to the corporate office that the cost reports used to evaluate his plant are misleading. Eric states, "I know how to get good quality product out. Over a number of years, I've even cut raw materials used to do it. The cost reports don't show any of this; they're always negative, no matter what I do. There's no way I can win with accounting or the people at headquarters who use these reports."

A copy of the latest report is shown below.

CIFLOXO PLANT
Cost Report
Month of November 1992
(in thousands)

	Master Budget	Actual Cost	Excess Cost
Raw material	$ 400	$ 437	$37
Direct labor	560	540	(20)
Overhead.	100	134	34
Total.	$1,060	$1,111	$51

Required

Identify and explain at least three changes to the report that would make the cost information more meaningful and less threatening to the production managers.

(CMA adapted)

19.46   Change of Policy to Improve Productivity

Bichlor Bike Company has been experiencing declining profit margins and has been looking for ways to increase operating income. It cannot raise selling prices for fear of losing business to its competitors. It must either cut costs or improve productivity.

Bichlor uses a standard cost system to evaluate the performance of the assembly department. It investigates all negative variances at the end of the month. The assembly department rarely completes the operations in less time than the standard allows (which would result in a positive variance). Most months the variance is zero or slightly unfavorable. Reasoning that the application of lower standard costs to the products manufactured will result in improved profit margins, the production manager has recommended that all standard times for assembly operations be drastically reduced. The production manager has informed the assembly personnel that she expects the assembly department to meet these new standards.

Required Will the lowering of the standard costs (by reducing the time of the assembly operations) result in improved profit margins and increased productivity?

(CMA adapted)

19.47 **Behavioral Impact of Implementing Standard Cost System**

Lavoy, Inc., a manufacturer of custom-designed home health care equipment, has been in business for 15 years. Last year, to better control the costs of their products, the controller implemented a standard cost system. Reports are issued monthly for tracking performance and any negative variances are further investigated.

The production manager complained that the standards are unrealistic, stifle motivation by concentrating only on negative variances, and are out of date too quickly. He noted that his recent switch to titanium for the wheelchairs has resulted in higher materials costs but decreased labor-hours. The net result was no increase in the total cost of producing the wheelchair. The monthly reports continue to show a negative materials variance and a positive labor variance, despite indications that the workers are slowing down.

A standard cost system can have a strong impact on both costs and employees.

Required
a. Describe several ways that a standard cost system strengthens management cost control.

b. Give at least two reasons that a standard cost system may negatively impact the motivation of production employees.

(CMA adapted)

19.48 **Ethics and Standard Costs**

Jamestown Joe's is a producer of items made from local farm products that it distributes to supermarkets. Because over the years price competition has become increasingly important, Abby Tiler, the company's controller, is planning to implement a standard cost system for Joe's. She asked her cost accountant, Larry Madison, to gather cost information on the production of strawberry jam (Jamestown Joe's most popular product). Larry reported that strawberries cost $.80 per quart, the price he intends to pay to his good friend who has been operating a strawberry farm in the red for the last few years. Due to an oversupply in the market, the prices for strawberries have dropped to $.50 per quart. Larry is sure that the $.80 price will be enough to pull his friend's strawberry farm out of the red and into the black.

Required Is Larry's behavior regarding the cost information he provided to Abby unethical? Explain your answer.

(CMA adapted)

19.49 **Comprehensive Variance Problem**

Soundex Manufacturing Company manufactures one product, with a standard cost detailed as follows:

Direct materials, 20 meters at $.90 per meter	$18
Direct labor, 4 hours at $6 per hour.	24
Factory overhead applied at five-sixths of direct labor (Variable costs = $15; Fixed costs = $5).	20
Variable selling and administrative	12
Fixed selling and administrative	7
Total unit costs	$81

Standards have been computed based on a master budget activity level of 2,400 direct labor-hours per month.

Actual activity for the past month was as follows:

Materials purchased.	18,000 meters at $.92 per meter
Materials used	9,500 meters
Direct labor	2,100 hours at $6.10 per hour
Total factory overhead	$11,100
Production	500 units

Required   Prepare variance analyses for the variable and fixed costs. Indicate which variances cannot be computed.

(CPA adapted)

19.50 Find Actual and Budget Amounts from Variances   Assume that Nintendo manufactures a new electronic game. The current standard costs per game follows:

Direct materials, 6 kilograms at $1 per kilogram	$ 6 per game
Direct labor, 1 hour at $4 per hour	4 per game
Overhead................................	3 per game
Total costs	$13 per game

Assume that the following data appeared in Nintendo's records at the end of the past month:

Actual production	4,000 units
Actual sales.................	2,500 units
Purchases (26,000 kilograms)	$27,300
Materials price variance...........	1,300 U
Materials efficiency variance........	1,000 U
Direct labor price variance	760 U
Direct labor efficiency variance	800 F
Underapplied overhead (total)........	500 U

The materials price variance is computed at the time of purchase.

Required   **a.** Prepare a variance analysis for direct materials and direct labor.

b. Assume that all production overhead is fixed and that the $500 underapplied is the only overhead variance that can be computed. What are the actual and applied overhead amounts?

(CPA adapted)

19.51 Variance Computations with Missing Data   The following information is provided to assist you in evaluating the performance of the production operations of Paramount Company:

Units produced (actual)	21,000
Master production budget	
Direct materials	$165,000
Direct labor	140,000
Overhead	199,000
Standard costs per unit	
Direct materials	$1.65 × 5 pounds per unit of output
Direct labor	$14 per hour × ½ hour per unit
Variable overhead..........	$11.90 per direct labor-hour
Actual costs	
Direct materials purchased and used	$188,700 (102,000 pounds)
Direct labor.......................	140,000 (10,700 hours)
Overhead	204,000 (61% is variable)

Variable overhead is applied on the basis of direct labor-hours.

Required   Prepare a report that shows all variable production cost price and efficiency variances and fixed production cost price and production volume variances.

19.52 Comprehensive Variance Problem   Flintco Company manufactures two products, Florimene and Glyoxide, used in the plastics industry. The company prepares its master budget on the basis of standard costs. The following data are for August:

	Florimene	Glyoxide
Standards		
Direct materials.	3 kilograms at $1 per kilogram	4 kilograms at $1.10 per kilogram
Direct labor	5 hours at $4 per hour	6 hours at $5 per hour
Variable overhead (per direct labor-hour)	$3.20	$3.50
Fixed overhead (per month)	$22,356	$26,520
Expected activity (direct labor-hours)	5,750	7,800
Actual data		
Direct material	3,100 kilograms at $.90 per kilogram	4,700 kilograms at $1.15 per kilogram
Direct labor	4,900 hours at $4.05 per hour	7,400 hours at $5.10 per hour
Variable overhead	$16,170	$25,234
Fixed overhead	$20,930	$26,400
Units produced (actual)	1,000 units	1,200 units

Required

a. Prepare a variance analysis for each variable cost for each product.

b. Prepare a fixed overhead variance analysis for each product like the one in Illustration 19.12.

19.53 Two-Way, Three-Way, and Four-Way Overhead Variances (Appendix B)

Refer to the data in Problem 19.52. Assume that the fixed overhead costs are applied to units produced using the following standard rate per labor-hour:

$$\text{Florimene: } \$3.888 \text{ per hour} = \frac{\$22,356}{5,750 \text{ expected labor-hours}}$$

$$\text{Glyoxide: } \$3.40 \text{ per hour} = \frac{\$26,520}{7,800 \text{ expected labor-hours}}$$

Required

Prepare two-way, three-way, and four-way analyses of overhead variances for each product.

19.54 Performance Evaluation in Service Industries

Safe-City Insurance Company estimates that its overhead costs for policy administration should be $72 for each new policy obtained and $2 per year for each $1,000 face amount of insurance outstanding. The company set a budget of selling 5,000 new policies during the coming period. In addition, it estimated that the total face amount of insurance outstanding for the period would equal $10,800,000.

During the period, actual costs related to new policies amounted to $358,400. A total of 4,800 new policies were sold.

The cost of maintaining existing policies was $23,200. Had these costs been incurred at the same prices as were in effect when the budget was prepared, the costs would have been $22,900; however, some costs changed. Also, there was $12,100,000 in policies outstanding during the period.

Required

Prepare a schedule to show the differences between master budget and actual costs for this question.

INTEGRATIVE CASES

19.55 Process Costing Variances; Equivalent Units

Cornwell, Inc., produces Honeysuckle, a single product. Cornwell uses the FIFO process costing method.

To analyze production performance, actual results are compared to the flexible budget, and any variances are computed. The standard costs that form the basis for the budget follow:

Direct materials . . . . 1 kilogram at $10 per kilogram
Direct labor . . . . 2 hours at $4 per hour
Variable overhead . . . . . . 2 hours at $1.25 per hour

Data for the month follow:

- Beginning inventory consisted of 2,500 units that were 100 percent complete with respect to direct materials and 40 percent complete with respect to conversion costs.
- Ten thousand units were started during the month.
- Ending inventory consisted of 2,000 units that were 100 percent complete with respect to direct materials and 40 percent complete with respect to conversion costs.
- Costs applicable to the current period production follow:

	Actual Costs	Flexible Budget
Direct materials (11,000 kilograms)	$123,750	$100,000
Direct labor (25,000 hours)	105,575	82,400
Variable overhead	30,350	25,750

Required

Compute variances. Materials are added at the beginning of the process; conversion costs are added evenly throughout.

19.56

Racketeer, Inc.*
(Comprehensive
Overview of
Budgets and
Variance)

"I just don't understand these financial statements at all!" exclaimed Mr. Elmo Knapp. Mr. Knapp explained that he had turned over management of Racketeer, Inc., a division of American Recreation Equipment, Inc., to his son, Otto, the previous month. Racketeer, Inc., manufactures tennis rackets.

"I was really proud of Otto," he beamed. "He was showing us all the tricks he learned in business school, and if I say so myself, I think he was doing a rather good job for us. For example, he put together this budget for Racketeer, which makes it very easy to see how much profit we'll make at any sales volume (Illustration 19.23A). As best as I can figure it, in March we expected to have a volume of 8,000 units and a profit of $14,500 on our rackets. But we did much better than that! We sold 10,000 rackets, so we should have made almost $21,000 on them."

"Another one of Otto's innovations is this standard cost system," said Mr. Knapp proudly. "He sat down with our production people and came up with a standard production cost per unit (see Illustration 19.23B). He tells me this will let us know how well our production people are performing. Also, he claims it will cut down on our clerical work."

Mr. Knapp continued, "But one thing puzzles me. My calculations show that we should have earned profit of nearly $21,000 in March. However, our accountants came up with less than $19,000 in the monthly income statement (Illustration 19.23C). This bothers me a great deal. Now, I'm sure our accountants are doing their job properly. But still, it appears to me that they're about $2,200 short."

"As you can probably guess," Mr. Knapp concluded, "we are one big happy family around here. I just wish I knew what those accountants are up to . . . coming in with a low net income like that."

Required

Prepare a report for Mr. Elmo Knapp and Mr. Otto Knapp that reconciles the profit graph with the actual results for March (see Illustration 19.23D). Show the source of each variance from the original plan (8,000 rackets) in as much detail as you can and evaluate Racketeer's performance in March. Recommend improvements in Racketeer's profit planning and control methods.

*© Michael W. Maher, 1996.

ILLUSTRATION 19.23A   Profit Graph, Racketeer, Inc.

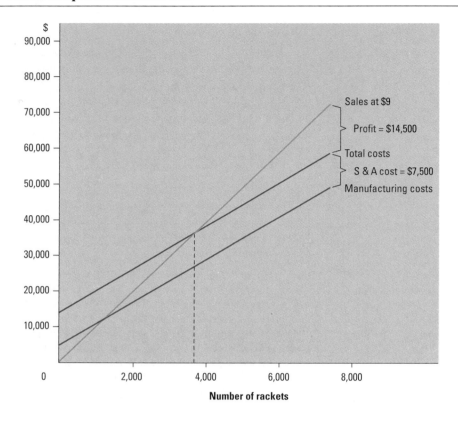

ILLUSTRATION 19.23B	Standard Costs,[a] Racketeer, Inc.	
		Per Racket
Raw material		
Frame (one frame per racket).............		$3.15
Stringing materials: 20 feet at 3¢ per foot		.60
Direct labor		
Skilled: ⅛ hour at $9.60 per hour...........		1.20
Unskilled: ⅛ hour at $5.60 per hour..........		.70
Plant overhead		
Indirect labor		.10
Power.............................		.03
Supervision		.12[b]
Depreciation.........................		.20[b]
Other		.15[b]
Total standard cost per frame		$6.25

[a]Standard costs are calculated for an estimated production volume of 8,000 units each month.

[b]Fixed costs.

ILLUSTRATION 19.23C

RACKETEER, INC.
Income Statement for March
Actual

Sales		
10,000 rackets at $9		$90,000
Standard cost of goods sold		
10,000 rackets at $6.25		62,500
Gross profit after standard costs		27,500
Variances		
Materials variance	(490)	
Labor variance	(392)	
Overhead variance	(660)	
Gross profit		25,958
Selling and administrative expense		7,200
Operating profit		$18,758

ILLUSTRATION 19.23D   **Actual Production Data for March, Racketeer, Inc.**

Direct materials purchased and used		
Stringing materials		175,000 feet at 2.5¢ per foot
Frames (note: some frames were ruined during production)		7,100 at $3.15 per frame
Labor		
Skilled ($9.80 per hour)		900 hours
Unskilled ($5.80 per hour)		840 hours
Overhead		
Indirect labor	$ 800	
Power	250	
Depreciation	1,600	
Supervision	960	
Other	1,250	
Production	7,000 rackets	

SOLUTIONS TO SELF-STUDY QUESTIONS

1. Variable cost variances:

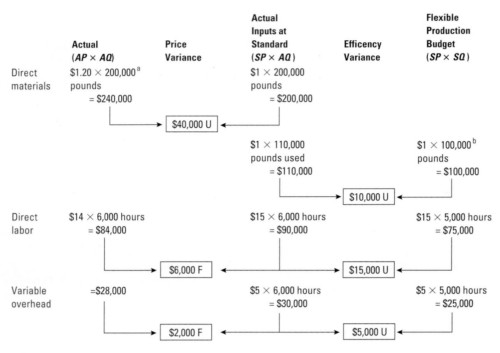

	Actual (AP × AQ)	Price Variance	Actual Inputs at Standard (SP × AQ)	Efficiency Variance	Flexible Production Budget (SP × SQ)
Direct materials	$1.20 × 200,000[a] pounds = $240,000		$1 × 200,000 pounds = $200,000		
		$40,000 U			
			$1 × 110,000 pounds used = $110,000		$1 × 100,000[b] pounds = $100,000
				$10,000 U	
Direct labor	$14 × 6,000 hours = $84,000		$15 × 6,000 hours = $90,000		$15 × 5,000 hours = $75,000
		$6,000 F		$15,000 U	
Variable overhead	=$28,000		$5 × 6,000 hours = $30,000		$5 × 5,000 hours = $25,000
		$2,000 F		$5,000 U	

[a]Direct materials pounds purchased.

[b]Standard direct materials pounds used in production per unit times units produced (2 pounds × 50,000 units).

2. Fixed overhead variances:

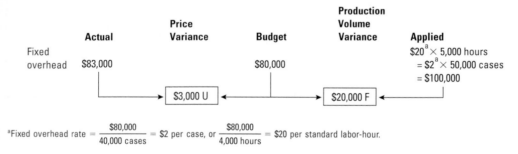

	Actual	Price Variance	Budget	Production Volume Variance	Applied
Fixed overhead	$83,000		$80,000		$20[a] × 5,000 hours = $2[a] × 50,000 cases = $100,000
		$3,000 U		$20,000 F	

[a]Fixed overhead rate = $\dfrac{\$80,000}{40,000 \text{ cases}}$ = $2 per case, or $\dfrac{\$80,000}{4,000 \text{ hours}}$ = $20 per standard labor-hour.

3. a. Journal entries:

(1) Direct Materials Inventory 200,000
Materials Price Variance 40,000
    Accounts Payable   240,000
To record the purchase of 200,000
pounds of materials at an actual
cost of $1.20 per pound and to
record the transfer to Direct
Materials Inventory at the
standard cost of $1 per pound.

(2) Work in Process Inventory 100,000
Materials Efficiency Variance 10,000
    Direct Materials Inventory . . .   110,000

To record the requisition of
110,000 pounds of materials at the
standard cost of $1 per pound
and to charge Work in Process
Inventory with the standard
usage of 100,000 pounds of
materials at the standard price.

(3) Work In Process Inventory 75,000
Labor Efficiency Variance. 15,000
    Labor Price Variance   6,000
    Accrued Payroll.   84,000

To charge Work in Process
Inventory for the standard cost of
direct labor at $15 per hour times
5,000 standard hours allowed and
to record the actual cost of $14
per hour times the 6,000 hours
actually worked.

(4) Work in Process Inventory   25,000
    Variable Overhead Applied. . .   25,000
To apply overhead to production
at $5 per standard direct labor-
hour times the 5,000 hours
allowed.

(5) Variable Overhead (Actual).   28,000
    Miscellaneous accounts (Cash,
    Accounts Payable, etc.).   28,000
To record actual variable
overhead.

(6) Variable Overhead Applied   25,000
    Variable Overhead
    Efficiency Variance.   5,000
    Variable Overhead
    Price Variance.   2,000
    Variable Overhead (Actual) . .   28,000
To record variable overhead
variances and to close the
Variable Overhead Applied and
Variable Overhead (Actual)
accounts.

(7) Work in Process Inventory   100,000
    Fixed Overhead Applied.   100,000

To record fixed overhead at a
standard cost of $20 per direct
labor-hour times 5,000 standard
hours

$$\left(\frac{\$80,000}{4,000 \text{ hours}} = \$20 \text{ per hour} \right).$$

(8) Fixed Overhead (Actual).   83,000
    Miscellaneous accounts (Cash,
    Accounts Payable, etc.).   83,000
To record actual fixed overhead.

(9) Fixed Overhead Applied.   100,000
    Fixed Overhead Price Variance . . .   3,000
    Fixed Overhead Production
    Volume Variance   20,000
    Fixed Overhead (Actual)   83,000
To record fixed overhead
variances and to close the
Fixed Overhead accounts.

(10) Finished Goods Inventory.   300,000
    Work in Process Inventory. . .   300,000
To record the transfer of 50,000
units of finished goods at the
standard cost of $6 per unit.

(11) Cost of Goods Sold.   240,000
    Finished Goods Inventory . . .   240,000
To record the sale of 40,000 units
at a standard cost of $6 per unit.

b. Cost flows through T-accounts:

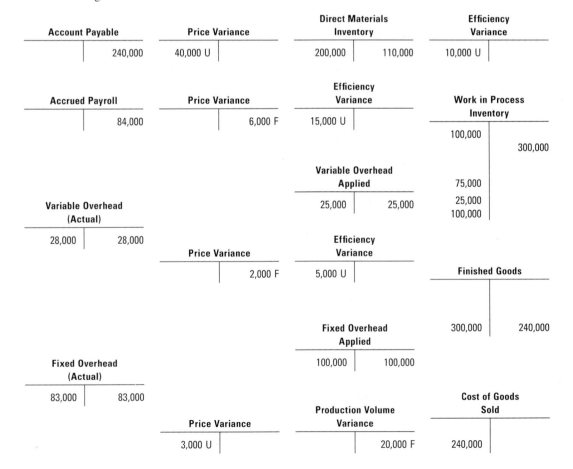

Performance Evaluation in Decentralized Organizations

LEARNING OBJECTIVES

After reading this chapter, you should be able to:

1. Explain the role of accounting in measuring performance in decentralized organizations.

2. Identify the advantages and disadvantages of decentralization.

3. Explain the relation between organization structure and responsibility centers.

4. Interpret and use return on investment (ROI), residual income (RI), and economic value added (EVA).

5. Explain how historical cost and net book value-based accounting measures can be misleading in evaluating performance.

6. Understand how managers evaluate performance.

7. Understand the use of incentive compensation plans (Appendix).

L.O. 1: Explain the role of accounting in measuring performance in decentralized organizations.

responsibility accounting
A system of reporting tailored to an organizational structure so that costs and revenues are reported at the level having the related responsibility within the organization.

The manager's task is increasingly difficult as an organization becomes large and complex. A common rule of thumb is that one supervisor usually can manage about 10 subordinates. Consequently, all but very small organizations delegate managerial duties.

Accounting plays an important role in evaluating the performance of those who have been delegated responsibility. The use of accounting for performance evaluation is often called **responsibility accounting.**

Budgeting and variance analysis, as discussed in Chapters 17 through 19, are part of the responsibility accounting process. In this and the following chapter, we discuss the costs and benefits of decentralization, the structure of organizational units, and the accounting measures used to evaluate the performance of organizational units and their managers.

DECENTRALIZED ORGANIZATIONS

principal-agent relationship
The relationship between a superior referred to as the *principal*, and a subordinate, called the *agent*.

When authority is decentralized, a superior, whom we call a *principal*, delegates duties to a subordinate, whom we call an *agent*. We find **principal-agent relationships** in many settings, including these:

Principals	Agents
General Motors (GM) stockholders	Top GM management
Corporate (top) GM managers	Divisional managers of the Oldsmobile Division, Saturn Division, etc.
Yellow Cab company manager	Taxicab drivers
Macy's retail store manager	Department managers of the children's clothing department, women's shoes, etc.

Many aspects of both financial and managerial accounting have been developed to measure agents' (that is, subordinates') performance. For example, accounting information can be used in setting conditions of employment contracts, and employee compensation often is based on accounting performance measures.

Goal Congruence and Performance Measurement

goal congruence
When all members of a group hold a common set of objectives.

Military units such as this work to develop goal congruence and a strong team spirit. © Jim Pickerell/Tony Stone Images

Total **goal congruence** exists when all members of an organization have incentives to perform in the common interest. This occurs when the group acts as a team in pursuit of a mutually agreed upon objective. Individual goal congruence occurs when an individual's personal goals are congruent with organizational goals.

While total congruence is rare, in some cases a strong team spirit suppresses individual desires to act differently. Examples include some military units and some athletic teams. Many companies attempt to achieve this esprit de corps. Japanese companies have worked particularly hard to create a strong team orientation among workers that has resulted in considerable goal congruence.

behavioral congruence
When individuals behave in the best interest of the organization regardless of their own goals.

In most business settings, however, personal goals and organization goals differ. Performance evaluation and incentive systems are designed to encourage employees to behave as if their goals were congruent with organization goals. This results in **behavioral congruence;** that is, an individual behaves in the best interests of the organization, regardless of his or her own goals.

You have experienced behavioral congruence in your education. Examinations, homework, and the entire grading process are parts of a performance evaluation and incentive system that encourages students to behave in a certain manner. Sometimes the system appears to encourage the wrong kind of behavior, however. For example, if the goal of education is to encourage students to learn, they might be better off taking very difficult courses. But if students' grades suffer when they take difficult courses, they may have an incentive to take easier courses. As a result, some students take difficult courses and learn more while others take easier courses in an attempt to maximize their grade point averages.

Problems like this occur in all organizations. Consider the case of a plant manager who believes that she will receive a promotion and bonus if the plant has high operating profits. If she closes the production line for much-needed maintenance short-run profits will be lower, but the company may be better off in the long run. The manager must decide between doing what makes her look good in the short run and doing what is in the best interest of the company.

Although such conflicts cannot be totally removed, they can be minimized if they are recognized. To deal with the problem just described, some companies budget maintenance separately. Others encourage employees to take a long-run interest in the company through stock option and pension plans tied to long-run performance. Still others retain employees in a position long enough that any short-term counter-productive actions catch up with them.

The Two Basic Questions

Managers must address two basic questions when thinking about their performance evaluation systems:

- What behavior does the system motivate?
- What behavior should the system motivate?

As we go about daily life, we see many instances in which the performance evaluation system does not create the right incentives because managers have not satisfactorily addressed these two questions. We also see many cases in which people work hard and make the right decisions despite the lack of explicit rewards. Ideally, organization managers will design performance evaluation systems to reward people when they do the right thing. At least, managers should design systems so people are not punished when they do the right thing.

WHY DECENTRALIZE THE ORGANIZATION?

L.O. 2: Identify the advantages and disadvantages of decentralization.

centralized
Describes those organizations in which decisions are made by a relatively few individuals in the high ranks of the organization.

decentralized
Describes those organizations in which decisions are spread among relatively many divisional and departmental managers.

Some organizations are very **centralized;** decisions are handed down from the top and subordinates carry them out. The military is a good example of centralized authority. At the other extreme are highly **decentralized** companies in which decisions are made at divisional and departmental levels. In many conglomerates, operating decisions are made in the field; corporate headquarters is, in effect, a holding company.

The majority of companies fall between these two extremes. At General Motors, for example, operating units are decentralized, and the research and development and finance functions are centralized.

Many companies begin with a centralized structure but become more and more decentralized as they grow. Consider the following example of a fast-food franchise that started with one hamburger stand.

We had a counter and 10 stools when we started. When winter came, we had to take out two stools to put in a heating furnace and almost went broke from the loss of revenue! But during the following year, I obtained the statewide franchise for a nationally known barbecue chain, and I expanded my menu.

At first, I did a little of everything—cooking, serving, bookkeeping, and advertising. I hired one full-time employee. There was little need for any formal management control system—I made all important decisions, and they were carried out. Soon we had eight outlets. I was still trying to manage everything personally. Decisions were delayed. A particular outlet would receive food shipments, but no one was authorized to accept delivery. If an outlet ran out of supplies or change, its employees had to wait until I arrived to authorize whatever needed to be done. With only one outlet, I was able to spend a reasonable amount of time on what I call high-level decision making—planning for expansion, arranging financing, developing new marketing strategies, and so forth. But with eight outlets, all of my time was consumed with day-to-day operating decisions.

Finally, I realized that the company had grown too big for me to manage alone. So I decentralized, setting up each outlet just like it was an independent operation. Now each outlet manager takes care of day-to-day operating decisions. This has not only freed my time for more high-level decision making but also provides a better opportunity for the managers to learn about management, and it gives me a chance to evaluate their performance for promotion to higher management positions, which I intend to create soon.[1]

Advantages of Decentralization

The larger and more complex an organization is, the more advantages decentralization offers. Some advantages of decentralization follow:

- *Faster response.* As the owner-manager of the fast-food chain described, local managers can react to a changing environment more quickly than top management can. With centralized decision making, delays occur while information is transmitted to decision makers, and further delays occur while instructions are communicated to local managers.

- *Wiser use of management's time.* The owner-manager of the fast-food chain complained that there was too little time for high-level decision making. Top management usually has a comparative advantage over middle management in this area. If their time is consumed by day-to-day operating decisions, they will be forced to ignore important strategic decisions. Furthermore, local managers may be able to make better operating decisions because of their technical expertise and knowledge about local conditions.

- *Reduction of problems to manageable size.* The complexity of problems that humans can solve has limits. Even with the aid of computers, some problems are too complex to be solved by central management. By dividing large problems into smaller, more manageable parts, decentralization reduces the complexity of problems.

- *Training, evaluation, and motivation of local managers.* Decentralization allows managers to receive on-the-job training in decision making. Top management can observe the outcome of local managers' decisions and evaluate their potential for advancement. By practicing with small decisions, managers learn how to make big decisions. Finally, ambitious managers are likely to be frustrated if they only implement the decisions of others and never have the satisfaction of making their own decisions and carrying them out. This satisfaction can be an important motivational reward for managers.

Disadvantages of Decentralization

Decentralization has many advantages, as well as disadvantages. The major disadvantage is that local managers may make decisions that are not congruent with the preferences of top management and constituents of the organization (such as stockholders). Thus, decentralized companies incur the cost of monitoring and controlling the activities of local managers. They incur the costs that result when local managers make decisions and take actions that are not in the best interest of the organization.

A company must weigh the costs and benefits of decentralization and decide on an economically optimal level. One can assume that the disadvantages of

---

[1]This example is based on the actual experience of a small company.

decentralization for highly centralized organizations outweigh the advantages while the reverse is true for decentralized companies.

TYPES OF RESPONSIBILITY CENTERS

L.O. 3: Explain the relation between organization structure and responsibility centers.

The five basic kinds of decentralized units are cost centers, discretionary cost centers, revenue centers, profit centers, and investment centers. (A *center* is a responsibility unit in an organization, such as a department in a store or a division in a company.)

Cost Centers

cost centers
Organization subunits responsible only for costs.

standard cost center
An organization subunit whose managers are held responsible for costs and in which the relationship between costs and output is well defined.

In **cost centers,** managers are responsible for the cost of an activity for which a well-defined relationship exists between inputs and outputs. Cost centers often are found in manufacturing operations where inputs, such as direct materials and direct labor, can be specified for each output. The production departments of manufacturing plants are examples of cost centers. The concept has been applied in nonmanufacturing settings as well. In banks, for example, standards can be established for check processing, so check-processing departments might be cost centers. In hospitals, food service departments, laundries, and laboratories often are set up as cost centers.

Managers of cost centers are held responsible for the costs and volumes of inputs used to produce an output. Often these costs and volumes are determined by someone other than the cost center manager, such as the marketplace, top management, or the marketing department. A plant manager often is given a production schedule to meet as efficiently as possible. If the plant is operated as a cost center, manufacturing cost variances, like those discussed in Chapter 19, typically are used to help measure performance. (Illustration 20.1 shows how the cost center typically appears on the organization chart.)

If the relationship between costs and outputs can be specified, the unit is called a **standard cost center.**

Discretionary Cost Centers

discretionary cost center
An organization subunit whose managers are held responsible for costs where the relationship between costs and outputs is not well established.

This advertising department is an example of a discretionary cost center because the relationship between advertising expenditures and sales is not well specified. © Robert E. Daemmrich/Tony Stone Images

The cost centers just described require a well-specified relationship between inputs and outputs for performance evaluation. When managers are held responsible for costs, but the input-output relationship is not well specified, a **discretionary cost center** is established. Legal, accounting, research and development, advertising, and many other administrative and marketing departments are usually discretionary cost centers (for example, see Illustration 20.1). Discretionary cost centers also are common in government and other nonprofit organizations whose budgets are used as a ceiling on expenditures. Managers are usually evaluated on bases other than costs. However, there are usually penalties for exceeding the budget ceiling.

ILLUSTRATION   20.1   Organization Structure and Responsibility Centers

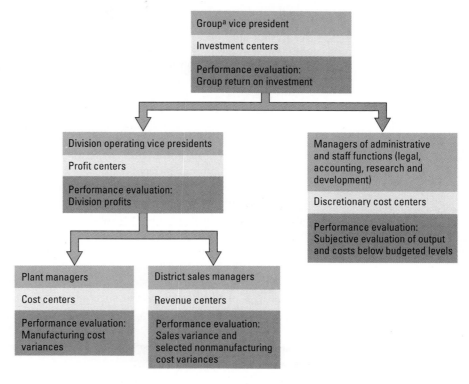

```
Group^a vice president
Investment centers
Performance evaluation:
Group return on investment
```

```
Division operating vice presidents
Profit centers
Performance evaluation:
Division profits
```

```
Managers of administrative
and staff functions (legal,
accounting, research and
development)
Discretionary cost centers
Performance evaluation:
Subjective evaluation of output
and costs below budgeted levels
```

```
Plant managers
Cost centers
Performance evaluation:
Manufacturing cost
variances
```

```
District sales managers
Revenue centers
Performance evaluation:
Sales variance and
selected nonmanufacturing
cost variances
```

^a *Group* refers to a group of divisions.

Revenue Centers

revenue center
An organization subunit
responsible for revenues and,
typically, for marketing costs.

Profit Centers

profit center
An organization subunit
responsible for profits; thus
responsible for revenues, costs,
production, and sales volumes.

By operating this KFC restaurant as a profit center, its managers are given incentives both to increase revenues and to decrease costs. © Nicholas Communications

Managers of **revenue centers** typically are responsible for marketing a product. Consequently, the manager is held responsible for sales price or sales activity variances (see Chapter 18 for discussions of these variances). An example of a revenue center is the sportswear department of a large department store in which the manager is held responsible for merchandise sales.

Managers of **profit centers** are held accountable for profits. They manage both revenues and costs (as shown in Illustration 20.1). For example, a Kentucky Fried Chicken franchise may operate its warehouses as cost centers but its restaurants as profit centers. Managers of profit centers have more autonomy than do managers of cost or revenue centers; thus, they sometimes have more status.

Investment Centers

investment center
Organization subunit responsible for profits and for investment in assets.

Managers of **investment centers** have responsibility for profits and investment in assets. These managers have relatively large amounts of money with which to make capital budgeting decisions. For instance, in one company, the manager of a cost center cannot acquire assets that cost more than $5,000 without a superior's approval, but an investment center manager can make acquisitions costing up to $500,000 without higher approval. Investment centers are evaluated using some measure of profits related to the invested assets in the center.

Responsibility Centers and Organization Structure

As Illustration 20.1 shows, the type of responsibility center is closely related to its position in the organization structure. For the company shown, plant managers run cost centers, and district sales managers operate revenue centers. Moving up the organization chart, we find that division managers in charge of both plant managers and district sales managers have responsibility for profits.

Of course, every company is organized uniquely (in some highly decentralized companies, manufacturing plants are profit centers, for example). However, it is generally true that a broader scope of authority and responsibility, hence profit or investment centers, is found at higher levels in an organization.

PERFORMANCE MEASUREMENT

We discussed the use of variances for evaluating performance in Chapters 18 and 19. Here we look at additional performance measures in discretionary cost centers, profit centers, and investment centers.

Discretionary Cost Centers

Discretionary costs, which may include those for research and development and accounting systems, are difficult to manage because it is hard to tie costs to output. For the same reason, it is difficult to evaluate the performance of a discretionary cost center manager. Companies have tried numerous methods of determining appropriate relationships between discretionary costs and activity levels and comparison with other firms. But relating costs to activity levels remains primarily a matter of management judgment or discretion. Consequently, managers of discretionary cost centers are typically given a budget and instructed not to exceed it without higher-level authorization. In most governmental units, it is against the law to exceed the budget without obtaining authorization from a legislative body (Congress, the state legislature, the city council).

Such situations can invite suboptimal behavior. Managers have incentives to spend all of their budgets, even if some savings could be achieved, to support their request for the same or higher budgets in the following year. Furthermore, often no well-specified relationship exists between the quality of services and their costs. (Would the quality of research and development decrease 10 percent with a 10 percent cut in funds? Would crime increase 10 percent if police department funds were cut 10 percent?)

Ideally, performance should be measured in a well-specified way, as actual inputs are compared to standard inputs in a cost center. But it is very difficult and costly to measure the performance of the manager and workers in a discretionary cost center. Thus, it also is hard to provide incentives for employees to perform at the levels that best achieve organization goals. We discuss nonfinancial performance measures in Chapter 22.

Profit Centers

Decentralized organizations depend heavily on profit measures to evaluate the performance of decentralized units and their managers. Due to the difficulties of measuring profits, many companies have tried to use multiple performance measures. In the early 1950s, General Electric proposed an extensive and innovative performance measurement system that evaluated market position, productivity, product leadership, personnel development, employee attitudes, public responsibility, and balance between short-range and long-range goals in addition to profitability. But even when a company uses a broad range of performance measures, accounting results continue to play an important role in performance evaluation. A commonly heard adage is that "hard" measures of performance tend to drive out "soft" measures. Nevertheless, no accounting measure can fully measure the performance of an organizational unit or its manager.

In profit centers, we encounter the usual problems related to measuring profits for the company as a whole plus an important additional one: How are the company's revenues and costs allocated to each profit center? A profit center that is totally separate from all other parts of the company operates like an autonomous company. The profits of that type of center can be uniquely identified with it.

A completely independent profit center is a highly unusual case, however. Most profit centers have costs (and perhaps revenues) in common with other units. The profit center may share facilities with other units or use headquarters' staff services, for example. If so, the company faces a cost allocation problem (see Chapter 7).

A related problem involves the transfer of goods between a profit center and other parts of the organization. Such goods must be priced so that the profit center manager has incentives to trade with other units when it is in the organization's best interests. Chapter 21 discusses this transfer pricing problem in more detail.

No easy ways to determine how to measure performance in a profit center exist. Much is left to managerial judgment. No matter what process is chosen, its objectives should be straightforward: Measure employees' performance in ways that motivate them to work in the best interest of their employers and compare that performance to standards or budget plans.

Investment Centers

L.O. 4: Interpret and use return on investment (ROI), residual income (RI), and economic value added (EVA).

return on investment (ROI)
The ratio of profits to investment in the asset that generates those profits.

Managers of investment centers are responsible for profits and investment in assets. They are evaluated on their ability to generate a sufficiently high **return on investment (ROI)** to justify the investment in the division.

The ROI is computed as follows:

$$ROI = \frac{\text{Operating profits}}{\text{Investment center assets}}$$

It often is divided into profit margin and asset turnover parts, as follows:

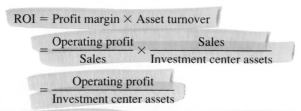

$$ROI = \text{Profit margin} \times \text{Asset turnover}$$

$$= \frac{\text{Operating profit}}{\text{Sales}} \times \frac{\text{Sales}}{\text{Investment center assets}}$$

$$= \frac{\text{Operating profit}}{\text{Investment center assets}}$$

The profit margin is a measure of the investment center's ability to control its costs for a given level of revenues. The lower the costs required to generate a dollar of revenue, the higher the profit margin.

The asset turnover ratio is a measure of the investment center's ability to generate sales for each dollar of assets invested in the center.

Relating profits to capital investment is an intuitively appealing concept. Capital is a scarce resource. If one unit of a company shows a low return, the capital may be better employed in another unit where the return is higher, invested elsewhere, or paid to stockholders.

Relating profits to investment also provides a scale for measuring performance. For example, investment A generated $200,000 in operating profits while investment B generated $2 million. But investment A required a capital investment of $500,000 while investment B required an investment of $20 million. As you can see from the following calculation, ROI provides a different picture from operating profits.

	Investment	
	A	**B**
1. Operating profits	$200,000	$ 2,000,000
2. Investment	500,000	20,000,000
3. Return on investment (1)/(2)	40%	10%

Although ROI is a commonly used performance measure, it has its limitations. The many difficulties of measuring profits affect the numerator, and problems in measuring the investment base affect the denominator. Consequently, it is difficult to make precise comparisons among investment centers.

Measuring Investment Center Assets and Profits

Each company is likely to measure an investment center's operating profits and assets in somewhat different ways. For example, Reece and Cool found that 40 percent of the companies that had investment centers defined investment center profits consistently with the way net income is calculated for shareholder reporting.[2] However, many companies did not assess income taxes, allocate corporate administrative costs, or allocate interest on corporate debt to investment centers.

Companies also differ as to the assets that they assign to an investment center. Reece and Cool asked which assets were included in the calculation of an investment center's asset base and found that the following assets were included by the indicated percentage of companies.

Asset	Percentage Included
Cash	63%
Receivables	94
Inventories	95
Land and buildings used solely by the investment center	94
Allocated share of corporate headquarters' assets	16

Most companies define an asset base that is easily understandable and approximates the assets for which the investment center manager is accountable. Including assets in the base encourages managers to manage those assets.

ROI VERSUS RESIDUAL INCOME

ROI evaluation is widely used in companies. However, the method has some drawbacks; some contend that if managers are encouraged to maximize ROI, they may turn down investment opportunities that are above the minimum acceptable rate for the corporation but below the rate their center is currently earning. For example, suppose that a corporation has a 15 percent cost of capital. A division has an opportunity to make an additional investment that will return $400,000 per year for a $2 million investment. The ROI for this project is 20 percent ($400,000/$2,000,000), so the project qualified at the corporate level in meeting ROI targets. Assuming that the project meets all other corporate requirements, it should be accepted. However, the manager of the division in which the investment would take place may reject it if the division's ROI is higher than 20 percent. For example, suppose that the center currently earns the following:

$$\text{ROI} = \frac{\$1,000,000}{\$4,000,000} = 25 \text{ percent}$$

---

[2] J. Reece and W. Cool, "Measuring Investment Center Performance," *Harvard Business Review*, May–June 1978, p. 28.

With the new investment, ROI is

$$ROI = \frac{\$1,000,000 + \$400,000}{\$4,000,000 + \$2,000,000} = 23.3 \text{ percent}$$

Because a comparison of the old and new returns implies that performance had worsened, the center's manager might hesitate to make such an investment, even though the investment would have a positive benefit for the company as a whole.

An alternative is to measure **residual income (RI).** Residual income is defined as follows:

$$\text{Investment center operating profits} - (\text{Capital charge} \times \text{Investment center assets})$$

where the capital charge is the minimum acceptable rate of return.

Using the numbers from the previous example, we can see the impact of the investment in additional capacity on residual income. Before the investment,

$$
\begin{aligned}
RI &= \$1,000,000 - (.15 \times \$4,000,000) \\
&= \$1,000,000 - \$600,000 \\
&= \$400,000
\end{aligned}
$$

The residual income from the additional investment in plant capacity is

$$
\begin{aligned}
RI &= \$400,000 - (.15 \times \$2,000,000) \\
&= \$400,000 - \$300,000 \\
&= \$100,000
\end{aligned}
$$

Hence, after the additional investment, the residual income of the division will increase to

$$
\begin{aligned}
RI &= (\$1,000,000 + \$400,000) - [.15 \times (\$4,000,000 + \$2,000,000)] \\
&= \$1,400,000 - (.15 \times \$6,000,000) \\
&= \$1,400,000 - \$900,000 \\
&= \$500,000
\end{aligned}
$$

The additional investment in plant capacity increases residual income, appropriately improving the measure of performance.

Most managers recognize the weakness of ROI and consider it when ROI is lowered by a new investment. This may partially explain why residual income does not dominate ROI as a performance measure. Moreover, residual income is not the net income reported to shareholders. Thus, it may be a less familiar concept for managers than operating profits or divisional net income. In addition, ROI is expressed as a percentage that can be compared with related percentages, such as the cost of capital, the prime interest rate, and the Treasury bill rate. In practice, few companies use residual income as the only performance measure, but many companies use both ROI and RI. We use ROI for illustrative purposes, but the issues we discuss apply equally to ROI and RI.

residual income (RI)
The excess of actual profit over the profit targeted for an organization subunit.

economic value added (EVA)
Annual after-tax operating profit minus the total annual cost of capital.

Economic Value Added: Is the Company Earning More Than Its Cost of Capital?

cost of capital
The weighted average cost of debt and equity used to finance a project or an operation (e.g., product or product line).

Economic value added (EVA) is based on the premise that all capital—debt or equity—has a cost. The cost of debt is relatively straightforward and is represented by the interest payments made on the debt. The cost of equity is more difficult to calculate. In general, this cost is what a company's shareholders could be getting in price appreciation and dividends if they invested in a portfolio of companies about as risky as that company. The weighted average combination of the cost of debt and equity is referred to as the **cost of capital.** The capital is the cash used to purchase items such as equipment, land, buildings, computers, and other assets necessary to run an operation. *EVA* is defined as annual after-tax operating profit minus the total annual cost of capital.

What does an EVA analysis tell us? EVA indicates how much shareholder wealth is being created, as Roberto Goizueta, Coca-Cola CEO, explained: "We raise capital to make concentrate and sell it at an operating profit. Then we pay the cost of that capital. Shareholders pocket the difference (EVA amount)."

If a project's EVA is negative, shareholder wealth is being reduced and management should consider how to improve EVA. Improving EVA is not complicated; it can be done three ways:

- Increase profit without using more capital (cost cutting is the current trend).
- Use less capital (e.g., less expensive equipment).
- Invest capital in high-return projects (high growth is typically an important factor).

Let's look at a relatively simple example of calculating EVA. Assume the following facts for a project implemented within a large company:

Capital employed	
Equipment	$1,000,000
Land	750,000
Building	2,000,000
Total capital employed	3,750,000
Cost of capital	
Debt ($1,750,000 at 10%)	175,000
Equity ($2,000,000 at 15%)	300,000
Total cost of capital	475,000
After-tax operating profit	600,000
EVA ($600,000 − $475,000)	$ 125,000

The EVA calculation here identifies a $125,000 increase in shareholders' wealth. Thus, value is clearly added to the company by undertaking this project.

1. Mars Division of Hyperspace Company has assets of $1.4 billion, operating profits of $.35 billion, and a cost of capital of 30 percent. Compute ROI and residual income.

    The solution to this question is at the end of this chapter on page 658.

MEASURING THE INVESTMENT BASE

L.O. 5: Explain how historical cost and net book value-based accounting measures can be misleading in evaluating performance.

Three issues are frequently raised in measuring investment bases: (1) Should *gross* book value be used? (2) Should investment in assets be valued at historical cost or current value? (3) Should investment be measured at the beginning or at the end of the year? Although no method is inherently right or wrong, some may have advantages over others. Further, it is important to understand how the measure of the investment base will affect ROI.

Gross Book Value versus Net Book Value

Suppose that a company uses straight-line depreciation for a physical asset with a 10-year life and no salvage value.

The cost of the asset does not change; it is the same in year 3 as in year 1. Illustration 20.2 compares ROI under net book value and gross book value for the first three years. For simplicity, all operating profits before depreciation in the computation are assumed to take place at the end of the year, and ROI is based on year-end value of the investment.

ILLUSTRATION 20.2	The Impact of Net Book Value versus Gross Book Value Methods on ROI (in thousands)

Facts: Operating profits before depreciation (all in cash flows at end of year):
  Year 1, $100; Year 2, $100; and Year 3, $100.
  Asset cost at *beginning* of year 1, $500. The only asset is depreciable, with a 10-year life and no salvage value. Straight-line depreciation is used. The straight-line rate is 10% per year. The denominator in the ROI calculations is based on *end-of-year* asset values.

Year	Net Book Value	Gross Book Value
1	$ROI = \dfrac{\$100^a - (.1 \times \$500)^b}{\$500^c - (.1 \times \$500)^d}$	$ROI = \dfrac{\$50^e}{\$500}$
	$= \dfrac{\$50}{\$450} = 11.1\%$	$= 10\%$
2	$ROI = \dfrac{\$100 - (.1 \times \$500)}{\$450 - (.1 \times \$500)}$	$ROI = \dfrac{\$50}{\$500}$
	$= \dfrac{\$50}{\$400} = 12.5\%$	$= 10\%$
3	$ROI = \dfrac{\$100 - (.1 \times \$500)}{\$400 - (.1 \times \$500)}$	$ROI = \dfrac{\$50}{\$500}$
	$= \dfrac{\$50}{\$350} = 14.3\%$	$= 10\%$

[a]The first term in the numerator is the annual cash operating profit.

[b]The second term in the numerator is depreciation for the year.

[c]The first term in the denominator is the beginning-of-the-year value of the assets used in the investment base.

[d]The second term in the denominator reduces the beginning-of-year value of the asset by the amount of current year's depreciation.

[e]Net income = $50 = $100 − ($500 × .1). Companies sometimes use only cash flows in the numerator.

Note that the ROI increases each year under the net book value method even though no operating changes take place. This occurs because the numerator remains constant while the denominator decreases each year as depreciation accumulates.

Critics contend that if these ROI numbers are used naively, investment center managers have incentives to postpone replacing assets longer than economically wise because their ROI will go down upon replacement. In addition, the net book value method makes a center with old assets look better than a comparable center with new assets. As one manager told us, "The secret is to get into a center just after assets have been bought and run until it's time to replace them. ROI is at a peak then because there is very little investment base. Then transfer to another center that has new assets. Of course, the poor fellow that follows you has to replace assets and watch ROI plummet." Although such a strategy may work, we suspect that the opportunities for such game playing are relatively few. Moreover, if top management is observant, a manager playing such a strategy should be detected after relatively few moves.

Historical Cost versus Current Cost

current cost
Cost to replace or rebuild an existing asset.

The previous example assumed no inflation. Working with the same facts, assume that the current replacement cost of the asset increases about 20 percent per year, as do operating cash flows. Illustration 20.3 compares ROI under historical cost and **current cost.**

Note that ROI increases each year under the historical cost methods even though no operating changes take place. This occurs because the numerator is measured in current dollars to reflect current cash transactions while the denominator and

ILLUSTRATION 20.3	Historical Cost versus Current Cost Methods on ROI (in thousands)

Facts: Operating profits before depreciation (all in cash flows at end of year):
   Year 1, $100; Year 2, $120; and Year 3, $144.
   Annual rate of price changes is 20 percent.
   Asset cost at *beginning* of year 1 is $500. At the *end* of year 1 the asset would cost $600; at the end of year 2 it would cost $720; and at the end of year 3 it would cost $864. The only asset is depreciable with a 10-year life and no salvage value.
   Straight-line depreciation is used; the straight-line rate is 10 percent per year. The denominator in the ROI computation is based on *end-of-year* asset value for this illustration.

Year	(1) Historical Cost Net Book Value	(2) Current Cost Net Book Value
1	$\text{ROI} = \dfrac{\$100^a - (.1 \times \$500)^b}{\$500^c - (.1^d \times \$500)}$	$\text{ROI} = \dfrac{\$100 - (.1 \times \$600)}{\$600 - (.1^d \times \$600)}$
	$= \dfrac{\$50}{\$450} = 11.1\%$	$= \dfrac{\$100 - \$60}{\$600 - \$60} = \dfrac{\$40}{\$540} = 7.4\%$
2	$\text{ROI} = \dfrac{\$120 - (.1 \times \$500)}{\$500 - (.2^d \times \$500)}$	$\text{ROI} = \dfrac{\$120 - (.1 \times \$720)}{\$720 - (.2^d \times \$720)}$
	$= \dfrac{\$70}{\$400} = 17.5\%$	$= \dfrac{\$120 - \$72}{\$720 - \$144} = \dfrac{\$48}{\$576} = 8.3\%$
3	$\text{ROI} = \dfrac{\$144 - (.1 \times \$500)}{\$500 - (.3^d \times \$500)}$	$\text{ROI} = \dfrac{\$144 - (.1 \times \$864)}{\$864 - (.3^d \times \$864)}$
	$= \dfrac{\$94}{\$350} = 26.9\%$	$= \dfrac{\$144 - \$86.4}{\$864 - \$259.2} = \dfrac{\$57.6}{\$604.8} = 9.5\%$

Year	(3) Historical Cost Gross Book Value	(4) Current Cost Gross Book Value
1	$\text{ROI} = \dfrac{\$100 - \$50}{\$500}$	$\text{ROI} = \dfrac{\$100 - \$60}{\$600}$
	$= \dfrac{\$50}{\$500} = 10\%$	$= \dfrac{\$40}{\$600} = 6.7\%$
2	$\text{ROI} = \dfrac{\$120 - \$50}{\$500}$	$\text{ROI} = \dfrac{\$120 - \$72}{\$720}$
	$= \dfrac{\$70}{\$500} = 14\%$	$= \dfrac{\$48}{\$720} = 6.7\%$
3	$\text{ROI} = \dfrac{\$144 - \$50}{\$500}$	$\text{ROI} = \dfrac{\$144 - \$86.4}{\$864}$
	$= \dfrac{\$94}{\$500} = 18.8\%$	$= \dfrac{\$57.6}{\$864} = 6.7\%$

[a] The first term in the numerator is the annual operating profit before depreciation.

[b] The second term in the numerator is depreciation for the year.

[c] The first term in the denominator is the beginning-of-the-first-year value of the assets used in the investment base.

[d] The second term in the denominator reduces the beginning-of-year value of the asset by the amount of accumulated depreciation: By 10 percent for accumulated depreciation at the end of year 1, by 20 percent at the end of year 2, and by 30 percent at the end of year 3.

depreciation charges are based on historical cost. The current cost methods reduce the effect by adjusting both the depreciation in the numerator and the investment base in the denominator to reflect price changes. Measuring current costs can be a difficult and expensive task, however, so there is a trade-off in the choice of performance measures.

We derived a level ROI in the current cost, gross book value method because the asset and all other prices increased at the same rate. If inflation affecting cash flows in the numerator increases faster than the current cost of the asset in the denominator, ROI will increase over the years until asset replacement, under the current cost method. Of course, ROI will decrease over the years until asset replacement if the denominator increases faster than the numerator.

Although current cost may seem to be a superior measure of ROI, recall that there is no single right or wrong measure. Surveys of corporate practice show that the vast majority of companies with investment centers used historical cost net book value. In many cases, many assets in the denominator are current assets that are not subject to distortions from changes in prices.

In general, how a performance measure is used is more important than how it is calculated. All of the measures we have presented can offer useful information. As long as the measurement method is understood, it can enhance performance evaluation.

Beginning, Ending, or Average Balance

An additional problem arises in measuring the investment base for performance evaluation. Should the base be the beginning, ending, or average balance? Using the beginning balance may encourage asset acquisitions early in the year to increase income for the entire year. Asset dispositions would be encouraged at the end of the year to reduce the investment base for next year. If end-of-year balances are used, similar incentives exist to manipulate purchases and dispositions. Average investments would tend to minimize this problem, although it may be more difficult to compute. In choosing an investment base, management must balance the costs of the additional computations required for average investment against the potential negative consequences of using the beginning or ending balances.

SELF-STUDY QUESTION

2. E. Division of E. T. Enterprises acquired depreciable assets costing $2 million. The cash flows from these assets for three years were as follows:

Year	Cash Flow
1	$500,000
2	600,000
3	710,000

Depreciation of these assets was 10 percent per year; the assets have no salvage value after 10 years. The denominator in the ROI calculation is based on end-of-year asset values. If replaced with identical new assets, these assets would cost $2,500,000 at the end of year 1, $3,125,000 at the end of year 2, and $3,900,000 at the end of year 3.

Compute the ROI for each year under each of the following methods:

a. Historical cost, net book value.

b. Historical cost, gross book value.

c. Current cost, net book value.

d. Current cost, gross book value.

The solution to this question is at the end of this chapter on page 658.

REAL WORLD APPLICATION | How to Avoid Stifling Good Ideas

 To encourage innovation and long-term growth, 3M Company requires that at least 25 percent of each division's sales come from products developed within the past five years. This encourages managers to invest in longer-term projects and take risks to invest in projects that may have an adverse impact on short-term performance indicators but will enable the company to stay competitive in the long run.

3M also provides incentives for innovation including allowing all employees to spend 15 percent of their time on innovative projects, encouraging employee feedback on any aspect of company performance, sharing technology across divisions, and providing "seed" grants for employees to develop new products.

3M's program and corporate culture result in the company having a worldwide reputation for innovation. Many other companies are studying 3M's approach and implementing similar programs.

EVALUATING PERFORMANCE

Relative Performance versus Absolute Performance Standards

L.O. 6: Understand how managers evaluate performance.

A company often is tempted to compare the performance of its investment centers and even to encourage competition among them. The problems inherent in ROI measurement complicate such comparisons. In addition, investment centers may be in very different businesses. It is very difficult to compare the performance of a manufacturing center with the performance of a center that provides consulting service and has a relatively small investment base. Differences in the riskiness of investment centers also should be considered. We recommend that when comparing the performance of investment centers, these systematic differences should be considered.

When diverse investment centers exist, management frequently establishes target ROIs for the individual investment centers. The investment center is evaluated by comparing the actual ROI with the target ROI. Such a comparison procedure is similar to the budget versus actual comparisons that are made for cost centers, revenue centers, and profit centers. It sometimes makes more sense to compare the ROI of an investment center with that of a company in the same industry than to compare it with that of other investment centers in its company.

Evaluating Managers' Performance versus Economic Performance of the Responsibility Center

controllability concept
The idea that managers should be held responsible for costs or profits over which they have decision-making authority.

The evaluation of a manager is not necessarily identical to the evaluation of the cost, profit, or investment center. As a general rule, managers are evaluated based on a comparison of actual results to targets. A manager who is asked to take over a marginal operation and turn it around may be given a minimal ROI target, consistent with the past performance of the division. A manager who meets or exceeds that target would be rewarded. However, it may be that even with the best management, a division cannot be turned around. Thus, it is entirely possible that the center would be disbanded even though the manager had received a highly positive evaluation. In addition, top management would like to reward the manager that performs well in an adverse situation but, conversely, should be willing to bail out of a bad operation if a better use can be made of company resources. Today, the **controllability concept** is widely used as a basis for managerial performance evaluation.

An interesting problem arises in implementing this concept in an ongoing division. How does one evaluate the performance of a manager who takes over an existing division whose assets, operating structure, and markets are established prior to the manager's arrival at the helm? The new manager cannot control the fact that certain assets are on hand or the markets in which the division operates at the time the manager takes over. However, in time, the new manager can change all of these factors.

As a general rule, evaluating the manager on the basis of performance targets, as suggested earlier in this chapter, overcomes this problem. The new manager establishes a plan for operating the division and works with top management to set targets

REAL WORLD APPLICATION

Implementing Relative Performance Evaluations at Honeywell

Although it does not explicitly use RPE in managerial incentive contracts, Honeywell uses it for strategic purposes and to initiate change in the company. Honeywell has almost 100 divisions organized into the following four businesses: (1) Aerospace and Defense (A&D); (2) Control Products; (3) Control Systems; and (4) Information Systems. Honeywell is a technology-oriented company, particularly in the Aerospace and Defense segment of the company.

Historically, the company has not been "run by the financial numbers" exclusively. In A&D, given a choice between one project that is very profitable but not technically challenging and another that is less profitable but has greater technical interest, the company usually chooses the latter. However, Honeywell recently began focusing on financial measures of performance. A&D, in particular, has developed a "peer company analysis" to reassess the status quo. Twenty competitors in aerospace and defense with publicly available information on A&D operations were identified. When compared to peer group five-year averages for return on assets, operating profit margin, and revenue growth, A&D ranked near the bottom of the third quartile.

Honeywell used this information to develop strategies for moving into new product lines and to emphasize the importance of return on investment and cost control.

Source: Based on the author's research.

for the future. Those targets are compared to actual results as the plan is enacted, and the manager is evaluated based on those results. In short, the longer the manager is at the division, the more responsibility the manager takes for its success.

Relative Performance Evaluations in Organizations

relative performance evaluation (RPE)
A managerial evaluation method that compares divisional performance with that of peer group divisions (i.e., divisions operating in similar product markets).

A major issue in evaluating divisional performance is the separation of performance results that are controllable by division managers from the effect of environmental factors outside of their control. As outlined in the previous section, division managers are generally held accountable for meeting or exceeding targets established for that particular division. However, these targets are often independent of the manager's performance as compared to those of peers (e.g., other divisions operating in similar product markets). **Relative performance evaluations (RPE)** address this issue by comparing managers of one division to their peers. A division earning a 10 percent profit margin is evaluated more favorably if the peers averaged 5 percent than 20 percent.

The purpose of RPE is to go beyond setting internal targets (e.g., divisional return on investment) and compare managers or divisions to other comparable divisions. It is possible for a division to meet or exceed its internal targets yet to perform well below its peer group. The only way to identify such a problem is to compare the division with its peers.

SUMMARY

The following summarizes key ideas tied to the chapter's learning objectives.

LO1: Measuring performance in decentralized organizations. Managers must address two basic questions when developing performance evaluation systems: (1) What behavior does the system motivate? (2) What behavior should the system motivate? Managers should design performance evaluation systems to reward people for doing the right thing.

LO2: Advantages and disadvantages of decentralization. The advantages of decentralization include faster response time; wiser use of management's time; reduction of problems to manageable size; and training, evaluation, and motivation of local managers. The disadvantage of such an organization is the potential for local managers to make wrong or bad decisions.

LO3: Relationship between organization structure and responsibility centers. Cost centers, revenue centers, and profit centers are usually evaluated based on a comparison of actual performance with budgeted goals. Investment centers are evaluated on the basis of the efficiency with which the assets employed in the center are used to generate profits. The usual form of measurement for investment centers is return on investment.

LO4: Return on investment (ROI), residual income (RI) and economic value added (EVA). ROI is the ratio of profits to investment in the asset that generates those profits. RI is the excess of actual profit over the profit targeted for an organization subunit. Economic value added is the after-tax operating profit minus the cost of capital. This amount represents the increase in shareholders' wealth.

LO5: Using historical cost and net book value in calculating ROI. Both of these measures can be misleading in evaluating performance. Investment center managers have an incentive to postpone replacing old assets using this approach.

LO6: Evaluating performance. Relative performance evaluation compares the performance of similar types of responsibility centers. Managers often distinguish between evaluating performance of the people from that of the responsibility center.

LO7: Understand how incentive compensation plans are used (appendix). Management often uses incentive compensation plans to improve labor productivity. In general, these plans offer additional compensation for meeting or exceeding predetermined goals. It is important that workers fully understand how to calculate incentive plan payments to provide the desired impact of encouraging increased productivity. When productivity relies on a group of individuals, a team or group incentive plan is appropriate.

KEY TERMS

behavioral congruence, 633

centralized, 634

controllability concept, 646

cost centers, 636

cost of capital, 641

current cost, 643

decentralized, 634

discretionary cost center, 636

economic value added, 641

goal congruence, 633

investment center, 638

principal-agent relationship, 633

profit center, 637

relative performance evaluation (RPE), 647

residual income (RI), 641

responsibility accounting, 633

return on investment (ROI), 639

revenue center, 637

standard cost center, 636

APPENDIX

L.O. 7: Understand the use of incentive compensation plans (appendix).

Incentive Plans To Improve Labor Productivity

Management often uses incentive compensation plans to improve labor productivity. In general, these plans offer additional compensation for meeting or exceeding predetermined goals. In a production environment, the goal is to increase units produced while decreasing conversion costs (direct labor + overhead) per unit.

For example, assume that Piecemeal Company pays its workers $10 per hour plus $0.10 for each unit completed over 500 units (within an 8-hour workday). Total daily overhead is \$350 and 550 units were produced in one day. The reduction in unit conversion costs is as follows, assuming that production efficiency increased from 500 units per day to 550 units:

	Units Produced	Direct Labor	Total Overhead	Conversion Cost	Cost per Unit
Before incentive plan	500	\$80	\$350	\$430	\$0.86
After incentive plan	550	85	350	435	0.79

This is a very simple example of how an individual incentive plan might increase efficiency and decrease costs on a per unit basis. Such a simple plan has many variations. However, it is important that workers fully understand how to calculate incentive plan payments to provide the desired impact of encouraging increased productivity.

The preceding example assumes that workers' productivity is independent of all other workers. In today's team-oriented production environment, this type of compensation plan would not create the proper individual incentive. Instead, when productivity relies on a group of individuals, a team or group incentive plan would be more appropriate.

For example, each worker in a group might receive \$0.10 for each unit that the group produces above the standard. Bonuses would then rely on the group's production efficiency rather than on any one individual. Thus, a strong incentive exists for the group to work effectively as a team and to push slower workers.

Group incentive plans can create problems if the group's goals conflict with the company's goals. For example, the group may be able to improve quality by slowing production. Even though the company might be emphasizing the need to improve quality, the group may not take the necessary steps (i.e., slow production and improve quality) for fear that each worker will lose the bonus. This comes back to the important notion that incentive systems must be established to create the desired behavior.

REVIEW QUESTIONS

20.1 Accounting is supposed to be a neutral, relevant, and objective measure of performance. Why would problems arise when applying accounting measures to performance evaluation contexts?

20.2 Is top management ever an agent in a principal-agent relationship as discussed in the chapter?

20.3 Is middle management ever a principal in a principal-agent relationship as discussed in the chapter?

20.4 What are the advantages of using an ROI-type measure rather than the absolute value of division profits as a performance evaluation technique?

20.5 Under what conditions would the use of ROI measures inhibit goal-congruent decision making by a division manager?

20.6 What impact does the use of gross book value or net book value in the investment base have on the computation of ROI?

20.7 You overhear the comment, "This whole problem of measuring performance for segment managers using accounting numbers is so much hogwash. We pay our managers a good salary and expect them to do the best possible job. At least with our system there is no incentive to play with the accounting data." Does the comment make sense?

CRITICAL ANALYSIS AND DISCUSSION QUESTIONS

20.8 A company prepares the master budget by taking each division manager's estimate of revenues and costs for the coming period and entering the data into the budget without adjustment. At the end of the year, division managers are given a bonus if their division profit is greater than the budget. Do you see any problems with this system?

20.9 Sales managers in a company were paid on an incentive system based on the number of units sold to ultimate buyers (that is, the units were not likely to be returned except if defective). How might that incentive system lead to dysfunctional consequences?

20.10 XYZ Division of Multitudenous Enterprises, Inc., produces and sells blank video disks. The division is evaluated based on income targets. The company uses the same measure of income for division performance evaluation as for external reporting. What problems, if any, can you envision in this performance evaluation system?

20.11 The chapter suggested there might be some problems in the use of residual income. Can you suggest what some of those problems might be?

20.12 Central management of Holdum, Inc., evaluated divisional performance using residual income measures. The division managers were ranked according to the residual income in each division. A bonus was paid to all division managers with residual income in the upper half of the ranking. The bonus amount was in proportion to the residual income amount. No bonus was paid to managers in the lower half of the ranking. What biases might arise in this system?

20.13 How would you respond to the following comment? "Residual income and economic value added are identical."

20.14 Parsed Phrases Corporation entered into a loan agreement requiring it to make additional interest payments if its net income should fall below a certain dollar amount. Immediately after the agreement was signed, the FASB instituted a new accounting requirement that caused Parsed's income to fall below the requirements. Absent the accounting change, Parsed would have met the income requirement.

a. Should the prechange or postchange income number be used to determine whether Parsed should pay the additional interest charge? Why or why not?

b. Would your answer in (a) change if Parsed had entered into a management contract that provided that the new manager would be paid a bonus based on achieving certain income levels (but, after the new manager was hired, the accounting rules changed so that the manager could never achieve those agreed-upon income levels)?

20.15 Management of Division A is evaluated based on residual income measures. The division can either rent or buy a certain asset. Might the performance evaluation technique have an impact on the rent-or-buy decision? Why or why not?

20.16 "Every one of our company's divisions has a return on investment in excess of our cost of capital. Our company must be a blockbuster." Comment on this statement.

20.17 Bleak Prospects, Inc., found that its market share was slipping. Division managers were encouraged to maximize ROI and made decisions consistent with that goal. Nonetheless, there were frequent customer complaints, with resulting loss of business. Moreover, Bleak depended on an established product line and was unable to find new products for expansion while its competitors seemed to be able to generate new products almost yearly. What would you suggest Bleak Products' management do to improve its situation?

EXERCISES

20.18 Compute RI and ROI (L.O. 4)

Plainsfield Division of Ullrich Corporation has assets of $2.4 million. During the past year, the division had profits of $600,000. Ullrich has a cost of capital of 14 percent.

Required

a. Compute the division ROI.

b. Compute the division RI.

20.19 ROI versus RI
(L.O. 4)

A division is considering the acquisition of a new asset that will cost $360,000 and have a cash flow of $140,000 per year for each of the five years of its life. Depreciation is computed on a straight-line basis with no salvage value.

Required

a. What is the ROI for each year of the asset's life if the division uses beginning-of-year asset balances and net book value for the computation?

b. What is the residual income each year if the cost of capital is 25 percent?

20.20 Compare Alternative Measures of Division Performance
(L.O. 4)

The following data are available for two divisions in your company:

	East Division	West Division
Division operating profit	$ 35,000	$195,000
Division investment	100,000	750,000

The cost of capital for the company is 20 percent.

Required

a. Which division had the better performance? Why?

b. Would your evaluation change if the company's cost of capital were 25 percent?

20.21 Impact of New Project on Performance Measures
(L.O. 4)

A division manager is considering the acquisition of a new asset that will add to profit. The division already earns $390,000 on assets of $1.3 million. The company's cost of capital is 20 percent. The new investment has a cost of $225,000 and will have a yearly cash flow of $84,000. The asset will be depreciated using the straight-line method over a six-year life and is expected to have no salvage value. Division performance is measured using ROI with beginning-of-year net book values in the denominator.

Required

a. What is the division ROI before acquisition of the new asset?

b. What is the division ROI in the first year after acquisition of the new asset?

20.22 Impact of Leasing on Performance Measures
(L.O. 4)

The division manager in Exercise 20.21 has the option to lease the asset on a year-to-year lease for $74,000 per year. All depreciation and other tax benefits would accrue to the lessor. What is the division ROI if it leases the asset?

20.23 Residual Income Measures and New Project Consideration
(L.O. 4)

Consider the investment project detailed in Exercises 20.21 and 20.22.

a. What is the division's residual income before considering the project?

b. What is the division's residual income if the asset is purchased?

c. What is the division's residual income if the asset is leased?

20.24 Compare Historical Cost, Net Book Value to Gross Book Value
(L.O. 4, 5)

Oracle Division of Monroe Corporation just started operations. It purchased depreciable assets costing $2 million and having an expected life of four years, after which the assets can be salvaged for $400,000. In addition, the division has $2 million in assets that are not depreciable. After four years, the division will have $2 million available from these non-depreciable assets. In short, the division has invested $4 million in assets that will last four years, after which it will salvage $2.4 million, so annual depreciation is $400,000. Annual cash operating flows are $1,000,000. In computing ROI, this division uses end-of-year asset values in the denominator. Depreciation is computed on a straight-line basis, recognizing the salvage values noted.

Required

a. Compute ROI, using net book value for each year.

b. Compute ROI, using gross book value for each year.

20.25 Compare ROI Using Net Book and Gross Book Values
(L.O. 4, 5)

Assume the same data as in Exercise 20.24 except the division uses beginning-of-year asset values in the denominator for computing ROI.

Required

a. Compute ROI, using net book value.

b. Compute ROI, using gross book value.

c. If you worked Exercise 20.24, compare those results with those in this exercise. How different is the ROI computed using end-of-year asset values, as in Exercise 20.24, from the ROI using beginning-of-year values in this exercise?

20.26   Compare
Current Cost to
Historical Cost
(L.O. 5)

Assume the same data as in Exercise 20.24 except that all cash flows increase 10 percent at the end of the year. This has the following effect on the assets' replacement cost and annual cash flows:

End of Year	Replacement Cost	Annual Cash Flow
1.	$4,000,000 × 1.1 = $4,400,000	$1,000,000 × 1.1 = $1,100,000
2.	$4,400,000 × 1.1 = $4,840,000	$1,100,000 × 1.1 = $1,210,000
:	Etc.	Etc.

Depreciation is as follows:

	For the Year	"Accumulated"	
1	$440,000	$ 440,000 (= 10% × $4,400,000)	
2	484,000	968,000 (= 20% × 4,840,000)	
3	532,400	1,597,200	etc.
4	585,600	2,342,560	

Note that "accumulated" depreciation is 10 percent of the gross book value of depreciable assets after one year, 20 percent after two years, and so forth.

Required

a. Compute ROI using historical cost, gross book value.

b. Compute ROI, using historical cost, net book value.

c. Compute ROI, using current cost, gross book value.

d. Compute ROI, using current cost, net book value.

20.27   Effects of
Current Cost on
Performance
Measurements
(L.O. 4, 5)

Otter Division of Armadillo Company acquired an asset with a cost of $100,000 and a life of four years. The cash flows from the asset, considering the effects of inflation, were scheduled as follows:

Year	Cash Flow
1	$30,000
2	34,000
3	38,000
4	40,000

The cost of the asset is expected to increase at a rate of 10 percent per year, compounded each year. Performance measures are based on beginning-of-year gross book values for the investment base.

Required

a. What is the ROI for each year of the asset's life, using a historical cost approach?

b. What is the ROI for each year of the asset's life if both the investment base and depreciation are based on the current cost of the asset at the start of each year?

PROBLEMS

20.28   Equipment
Replacement and
Performance
Measures

You have been appointed manager of an operating division of Juneau, Inc., a manufacturer of products using the latest microprocessor technology. Your division has $800,000 in assets and manufactures a special chip assembly. On January 2 of the current year, you invested $1 million in automated equipment for chip assembly. At that time, your expected income statement was as follows:

Sales revenue.	$3,200,000
Operating costs	
Variable	400,000
Fixed (all cash).	1,500,000
Depreciation	
New equipment	300,000
Other	250,000
Division operating profit	$750,000

On October 25 a sales representative from Klondike Machine Company approached you. Klondike offers for $1.3 million a new assembly machine that offers significant improvements over the equipment you bought on January 2. The new equipment would expand department output by 10 percent while reducing cash fixed costs by 5 percent. The new equipment would be depreciated for accounting purposes over a three-year life. Depreciation would be net of the $100,000 salvage value of the new machine. The new equipment meets your company's 20 percent cost of capital criterion. If you purchase the new machine, it must be installed prior to the end of the year. For practical purposes, though, you can ignore depreciation on the new machine because it will not go into operation until the start of the next year.

The old machine, which has no salvage value, must be disposed of to make room for the new machine.

Your company has a performance evaluation and bonus plan based on ROI. The return includes any losses on disposals of equipment. Investment is computed based on the end-of-year balance of assets, net book value.

Required
a. What is your division's ROI if it does not acquire the new machine?
b. What is your division's ROI this year if it does acquire the new machine?
c. If the new machine is acquired and operates according to specifications, what ROI is expected for next year?

20.29 Evaluate Trade-Offs in Return Measurement

As a division manager of Juneau, Inc. (Problem 20.28), you are still assessing the problem of whether to acquire Klondike Machine Company's machine. You learn that the new machine could be acquired next year. However, if you wait until next year, it will cost 15 percent more. The salvage value would still be $100,000. Other costs or revenue estimates would be apportioned on a month-by-month basis for the time each machine is in use. Fractions of months may be ignored.

Required
a. When would you want to purchase the new machine if you wait until next year?
b. What are the costs that must be considered in making this decision?

20.30 Analyze Performance Report for Decentralized Organization

Ashwood Products manufactures antique reproduction furniture. The need for a widely based manufacturing and distribution system has led to a highly decentralized management structure. Each division manager is responsible for producing and distributing corporate products in one of eight geographical areas of the country.

Residual income is used to evaluate division managers. The residual income for each division equals each division's contribution to corporate profits before taxes less a 20 percent investment charge on a division's investment base. The investment base of each division is the sum of its year-end balances of accounts receivable, inventories, and net plant fixed assets (cost less accumulated depreciation). Corporate policies dictate that divisions minimize their investments in receivables and inventories. Investments in plant fixed assets are a joint division/corporate decision based on proposals made by division plant managers, available corporate funds, and general corporate policy.

Patric Anderson, division manager for the southeastern sector, prepared the year 2 and preliminary year 3 budgets for his division late in year 1. Final approval of the year 3 budget took place in late year 2, after adjustments for trends and other information developed during year 2. Preliminary work on the year 4 budget also took place at that time. In early October of year 3, Anderson asked the division controller to prepare a report that presents performance for the first nine months of year 3. The report is reproduced in Illustration 20.4.

Required
a. Evaluate the performance of Patric Anderson for the nine months ending September Year 3. Support your evaluation with pertinent facts from the problem.

ILLUSTRATION 20.4

ASHWOOD PRODUCTS—SOUTHEASTERN SECTOR
(in thousands)

	Year 3			Year 2	
	Annual Budget	Nine-Month Budget[a]	Nine-Month Actual	Annual Budget	Actual Results
Sales	$2,800	$2,100	$2,200	$2,500	$2,430
Divisional costs and expenses					
Direct materials and labor	1,064	798	995	900	890
Supplies	44	33	35	35	43
Maintenance and repairs	200	150	60	175	160
Plant depreciation	120	90	90	110	110
Administration	120	90	90	90	100
Total divisional costs and expenses	1,548	1,161	1,270	1,310	1,303
Divisional margin	1,252	939	930	1,190	1,127
Allocated corporate fixed costs	360	270	240	340	320
Divisional profits	$ 892	$ 669	$ 690	$ 850	$ 807

	Budgeted Balance 12/31/Year 3	Budgeted Balance 9/30/Year 3	Actual Balance 9/30/Year 3	Budgeted Balance 12/31/Year 2	Actual Balance 12/31/Year 2
Divisional investment					
Accounts receivable	$ 280	$ 290	$ 250	$ 250	$ 250
Inventories	500	500	650	450	475
Plant fixed assets (net)	1,320	1,350	1,100	1,150	1,100
Total	$2,100	$2,140	$2,000	$1,850	$1,825

[a]Ashwood's sales occur uniformly throughout the year.

b. Identify the features of Ashwood's division performance measurement reporting and evaluation system that need to be revised if it is to effectively reflect the responsibilities of the divisional managers.

(CMA adapted)

20.31 ROI and Management Behavior

Thain Corporation is a highly diversified and decentralized company. Each division is responsible for its own sales, pricing, production, costs of operations, and management of accounts receivable, inventories, accounts payable, and use of existing facilities. Corporate headquarters manages cash.

Division executives present investment proposals to corporate management, which analyze and document them. The final decision to commit funds for investment purposes rests with corporate management.

The corporation evaluates division executive performance by the ROI measure. The asset base is composed of fixed assets employed plus working capital, exclusive of cash. The ROI performance of a division executive is the most important appraisal factor for salary changes. In addition, each executive's annual performance bonus is based on ROI results, with increases in ROI having a significant impact on the amount of the bonus.

Thain adopted the ROI performance measure and related compensation procedures about 10 years ago and seems to have benefited from the program. The ROI for the corporation as a whole increased during the first years of the program. Although the ROI continued to grow in each division, corporate ROI has declined in recent years. The corporation has accumulated a sizable amount of short-term marketable securities in the past three years.

Corporate management is concerned about the increase in the short-term marketable securities. A recent article in a financial publication suggested that some companies overemphasized the use of ROI, with results similar to those experienced by Thain.

Required

a. Describe the specific actions that division managers might have taken to cause the ROI to increase in each division but decrease for the corporation. Illustrate your explanation with appropriate examples.

b. Explain, using the concepts of goal congruence and motivation of division executives, how Thain Corporation's overemphasis on the use of the ROI measure might result in the recent decline in the corporation's ROI and the increase in cash and short-term marketable securities.

c. What changes could be made in Thain Corporation's compensation policy to avoid this problem? Explain your answer.

(CMA adapted)

20.32 Impact of Decisions to Capitalize or Expense on Performance Measurement

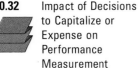

Oil and gas companies inevitably incur costs on unsuccessful exploration ventures. These ventures are called *dry holes*. A debate continues over whether those costs should be written off as period expense, or capitalized as part of the full cost of finding profitable oil and gas ventures. Lewison Drilling Company has been writing these costs off to expense as incurred. However, this year a new management team was hired to improve the profit picture of Lewison's Oil and Gas Exploration Division. The new management team was hired with the provision that it would receive a bonus equal to 10 percent of any profits in excess of base-year profits of the division. However, no bonus would be paid if profits were less than 20 percent of end-of-year investment. The following information was included in the performance report for the division:

	This Year	Base Year	Increase over Base Year
Sales revenues.	$4,100,000	$4,000,000	
Costs incurred			
Dry holes	–0–	800,000	
Depreciation and other amortization	780,000	750,000	
Other costs.	1,600,000	1,550,000	
Division profit.	$1,720,000	$ 900,000	$820,000
End-of-year investment.	$8,100,000[a]	$6,900,000	

[a]Includes other investments not at issue here.

During the year, the new team spent $1 million on exploratory activities, of which $900,000 was for unsuccessful ventures. The new management team has included the $900,000 in the current end-of-year investment base because, it states, "You can't find the good ones without hitting a few bad ones."

Required

a. What is the ROI for the base year and the current year?

b. What is the amount of the bonus that the new management team is likely to claim?

c. If you were on Lewison's board of directors, how would you respond to the new management's claim for the bonus?

20.33 Evaluate Performance Evaluation System: Behavioral Issues

Drawem Company purchased Bildem Company three years ago. Prior to the acquisition, Bildem manufactured and sold electronic products to third-party customers. Since becoming a division of Drawem, Bildem now manufactures electronic components only for products made by Drawem's Macon Division.

Drawem's corporate management gives the Bildem Division management considerable latitude in running the division's operations. However, corporate management retains authority for decisions regarding capital investments, product pricing, and production quantities.

Drawem has a formal performance evaluation program for all division managements. The evaluation program relies substantially on each division's ROI. Bildem Division's income statement provides the basis for the evaluation of Bildem's divisional management. (See the following income statement.)

The corporate accounting staff prepares the division financial statements. Corporate general services costs are allocated on the basis of sales dollars, and the computer department's actual costs are apportioned among the divisions on the basis of use. The net division investment includes division fixed assets at net book value (cost less depreciation), division inventory, and corporate working capital apportioned to the divisions on the basis of sales dollars.

DRAWEM COMPANY
Bildem Division
Income Statement
For the Year Ended October 31
(in thousands)

Sales revenue.		$4,000
Costs and expenses		
Product costs:		
Direct materials.	$ 500	
Direct labor	1,100	
Factory overhead	1,300	
Total	$2,900	
Less: Increase in inventory	350	2,550
Engineering and research		120
Shipping and receiving.		240
Division administration:		
Manager's office	$ 210	
Cost accounting	40	
Personnel	82	332
Corporate cost:		
General services	$ 230	
Computer.	48	278
Total costs and expenses.		$3,520
Divisional operating profit		$ 480
Net plant investment.		$1,600
Return on investment		30%

Required

a. Discuss Drawem Company's financial reporting and performance evaluation program as it relates to the responsibilities of Bildem Division.

b. Based on your response to requirement (*a*), recommend appropriate revisions of the financial information and reports used to evaluate the performance of Bildem's divisional management. If revisions are not necessary, explain why.

(CMA adapted)

20.34 Divisional Performance Measurement: Behavioral Issues

Division managers of Lenco Incorporated have been expressing growing dissatisfaction with the methods Lenco uses to measure division performance. Division operations are evaluated every quarter by comparison with the master budget prepared during the prior year. Division managers claim that many factors are completely out of their control but are included in this comparison. This results in an unfair and misleading performance evaluation.

The managers have been particularly critical of the process used to establish standards and budgets. The annual budget, stated by quarters, is prepared six months prior to the beginning of the operating year. Pressure by top management to reflect increased earnings has often caused divisional managers to overstate revenues and/or understate expenses. In addition, once the budget is established, divisions must "live with the budget." Frequently, external factors such as the state of the economy, changes in consumer preferences, and actions of competitors have not been recognized in the budgets that top management supplied to the divisions. The credibility of the performance review is curtailed when the budget cannot be adjusted to incorporate these changes.

Top management, recognizing these problems, agreed to establish a committee to review the situation and to make recommendations for a new performance evaluation system. The committee consists of each division manager, the corporate controller, and the executive vice president. At the first meeting, one division manager outlined an achievement of objectives system (AOS). In this performance evaluation system, division managers are evaluated according to three criteria:

- Doing better than last year. Various measures are compared to the same measures of the prior year.
- Planning realistically. Actual performance for the current year is compared to realistic plans and/or goals.
- Managing current assets. Various measures are used to evaluate division management's achievements and reactions to changing business and economic conditions.

One division manager believed that this system would overcome many of the inconsistencies of the current system because divisions could be evaluated from three different viewpoints. In addition, managers would have the opportunity to show how they would react and account for changes in uncontrollable external factors.

Another manager cautioned that the success of a new performance evaluation system would be limited unless it had the complete support of top management.

Required

a. Explain whether the proposed AOS would be an improvement over the evaluation of division performance now used by Lenco Incorporated.

b. Develop specific performance measures for each of the three criteria in the proposed AOS that could be used to evaluate division managers.

c. Discuss the motivational and behavioral aspects of the proposed performance system. Also recommend specific programs that could be instituted to promote morale and give incentives to divisional management.

(CMA adapted)

20.35 ROI, RI, and Different Asset Bases

The manager of the Woodside Products Store in Evanston is evaluated using ROI. Woodside headquarters requires an ROI of 10 percent of assets. For the coming year, the manager estimates revenues will be $163,000, and operating expenses for this level of sales will be $26,000. Investment in the store assets throughout the year is $187,500 before considering the following proposal.

A representative of Timber Trading Company approached the manager about carrying Timber's line of furniture. This line is expected to generate $75,000 in sales in the coming year at the Woodside store with a merchandise cost of $57,000. Annual operating expenses for this additional merchandise line are $8,500. To carry the line of goods, an inventory investment of $55,000 throughout the year is required. Timber is willing to floor plan the merchandise so that the Woodside store will not have to invest in any inventory. The cost of floor planning would be $6,750 per year. Woodside's marginal cost of capital is 10 percent.

Required

a. What is the Evanston Woodside store's expected ROI for the coming year if Timber's furniture is not carried in the store?

b. What is the store's expected ROI if the manager invests in the Timber inventory and carries the furniture line?

c. What would the store's expected ROI be if the manager elected to take the floor plan option?

d. Would the manager prefer (*a*), (*b*), or (*c*)? Why?

SOLUTIONS TO SELF-STUDY QUESTIONS

1. $\text{ROI} = \dfrac{\$.35 \text{ billion}}{\$1.4 \text{ billion}} = 25\%$

    $\text{RI} = \$.35 \text{ billion} - (.30 \times \$1.4 \text{ billion})$
    $\quad\;\, = \$.35 \text{ billion} - \$.42 \text{ billion}$
    $\quad\;\, = -\$.07 \text{ billion (that is, a residual ''loss'' of \$70 million)}$

2. (**a.**) and (**b.**) historical cost:

Year	Net Book Value[a]	Gross Book Value[b]
1	$\text{ROI} = \dfrac{\$500,000 - (.10 \times \$2,000,000)}{\$2,000,000 - (.10^c \times \$2,000,000)}$	$\text{ROI} = \dfrac{\$300,000}{\$2,000,000}$
	$\quad\;\, = \dfrac{\$300,000}{\$1,800,000} = 16.7\%$	$\quad\;\, = 15\%$
2	$\text{ROI} = \dfrac{\$600,000 - (.10 \times \$2,000,000)}{\$2,000,000 - (.20^c \times \$2,000,000)}$	$\text{ROI} = \dfrac{\$400,000}{\$2,000,000}$
	$\quad\;\, = \dfrac{\$400,000}{\$1,600,000} = 25\%$	$\quad\;\, = 20\%$
3	$\text{ROI} = \dfrac{\$710,000 - (.10 \times \$2,000,000)}{\$2,000,000 - (.30^c \times \$2,000,000)}$	$\text{ROI} = \dfrac{\$510,000}{\$2,000,000}$
	$\quad\;\, = \dfrac{\$510,000}{\$1,400,000} = 36.4\%$	$\quad\;\, = 25.5\%$

[a]The first term in the numerator is the annual cash flow. The second term is the annual depreciation. The first term in the denominator is the gross book value of the assets before accumulated depreciation. The second term is the accumulated depreciation.

[b]The numerator is the annual net income. The denominator is the gross book value of the assets.

[c]This amount is the percent accumulated depreciation: 10 percent of the gross book value after one year, 20 percent after two years, and 30 percent after three years.

(**c.**) and (**d.**) current cost:

Year	Net Book Value[a]	Gross Brook Value[b]

1 . . . . $\text{ROI} = \dfrac{\$500,000 - (.10 \times \$2,500,000)}{\$2,500,000 - (.10^c \times \$2,500,000)}$ $\text{ROI} = \dfrac{\$250,000}{\$2,500,000}$

$= \dfrac{\$500,000 - \$250,000}{\$2,500,000 - \$250,000} = \underline{\underline{11.1\%}}$ $= \underline{\underline{10\%}}$

2 . . . . $\text{ROI} = \dfrac{\$600,000 - (.10 \times \$3,125,000)}{\$3,125,000 - (.20^c \times \$3,125,000)}$ $\text{ROI} = \dfrac{\$287,500}{\$3,125,000}$

$= \dfrac{\$600,000 - \$312,500}{\$3,125,000 - \$625,000} = \underline{\underline{11.5\%}}$ $= \underline{\underline{9.2\%}}$

3 . . . . $\text{ROI} = \dfrac{\$710,000 - (.10 \times \$3,900,000)}{\$3,900,000 - (.30^c \times \$3,900,000)}$ $\text{ROI} = \dfrac{\$320,000}{\$3,900,000}$

$= \dfrac{\$710,000 - \$390,000}{\$3,900,000 - \$1,170,000}$ $= \underline{\underline{8.2\%}}$

$= \dfrac{\$320,000}{\$2,730,000} = \underline{\underline{11.7\%}}$

[a]The first term in the numerator is the annual cash flow. The second term is the annual depreciation. The first term in the denominator is the gross book value of the assets before accumulated depreciation. The second term is the accumulated depreciation.

[b]The numerator is the annual net income. The denominator is the gross book value of the assets.

[c]This amount is the percent accumulated depreciation: 10 percent of the gross book value after one year, 20 percent after two years, and 30 percent after three years.

Transfer Pricing

LEARNING OBJECTIVES

After reading this chapter, you should be able to:

1. Explain the basic issues involved with transfer pricing.

2. Explain the general transfer pricing rules and understand the underlying basis for these rules.

3. Identify the behavioral issues and incentive effects of negotiated transfer prices, cost-based transfer prices, and market-based transfer prices.

4. Explain the economic consequences of multinational transfer prices.

5. Describe the role of transfer prices in segment reporting.

WHAT IS TRANSFER PRICING?

L.O. 1: Explain the basic issues involved with transfer pricing.

When goods or services are transferred from one unit of an organization to another, the transaction is recorded in the accounting records. The value assigned to the transaction is called the **transfer price.** Considerable discretion can be used in putting a value on the transaction because this exchange takes place inside the organization. Transfer prices are widely used for decision making, product costing, and performance evaluation; hence, it is important to consider alternative transfer pricing methods and their advantages and disadvantages.

HOW TRANSFER PRICING AFFECTS PERFORMANCE MEASUREMENT

transfer price
The value assigned to the transaction when goods or services are transferred from one unit of an organization to another.

Responsibility centers in decentralized organizations often exchange products. At General Motors, for example, it is common for one division to buy direct materials from a number of suppliers, including other GM divisions. In effect, responsibility centers buy/sell from/to each other. Companies such as Sega of America and Nintendo, which buy video games from their Japanese parents, and Honda, which buys motorcycles from its Japanese parent, are companies that make international transfers. The transfer price becomes a cost to the buying division and revenue to the selling division.

If the divisions are evaluated using some profitability measure, such as return on investment (ROI), the transfer price can affect the performance of each division. For example, the higher the transfer price, the more profitable the selling division (from higher revenues) and the less profitable the buying division (from higher costs), all other things being equal.

SETTING TRANSFER PRICES

The value placed on transfer goods and services is used *to make it possible to transfer goods and services between divisions while allowing them to retain their autonomy.*[1] The transfer price can be a device to motivate managers to act in the best interest of the company.

To help you understand the issues involved with transfer pricing, we have established four transfer pricing examples as follows: (1) no outside suppliers are available, (2) outside suppliers are available but the selling division is below capacity, (3) outside suppliers are available and the selling division is at capacity, and (4) outside suppliers are available, the selling division is below capacity, and alternative facility uses exist. Each example is essentially a differential revenue/cost analysis.

Case I: Simple Case: No Outside Suppliers

Although the transfer price may be important to each division manager (who might be evaluated on division profit measures), the company as a whole will receive the same operating profit regardless of the transfer price, assuming that the part cannot be purchased from another company (externally).

For example, assume that E-Z Computing has two decentralized divisions, Hardware and Computers. Computers has always purchased certain units, from Hardware at $50 per unit, but Hardware is considering raising the price to $70 per unit (the current market price). Hardware's costs are as follows: variable costs per unit, $50, and annual fixed costs, $10,000. Computers bundles the units with other products and sells them for $100 each. Computers incurs no additional variable costs, and annual fixed costs total $5,000. Computers produces 1,500 units per year. Given this information, which transfer price will provide E-Z Computing with the

---

[1] The transfer pricing issue usually occurs at the division level, so we frequently refer to divisions or division managers instead of the larger responsibility centers or responsibility center managers.

highest operating profit? As shown next, the transfer price will not impact overall company operating profit.

Transfer Price of $50 per Unit

	Hardware	Computers
Sales		
$50 × 1,500	$ 75,000	
$100 × 1,500		$150,000
Variable costs		
$50 × 1,500	75,000	
$50 × 1,500		75,000
Fixed costs	10,000	5,000
Operating profit	$(10,000)	$ 70,000
Total company operating profit	$60,000	

Transfer Price of $70 per Unit

	Hardware	Computers
Sales		
$70 × 1,500	$105,000	
$100 × 1,500		$150,000
Variable costs		
$50 × 1,500	75,000	
$70 × 1,500		105,000
Fixed costs	10,000	5,000
Operating profit	$ 20,000	$ 40,000
Total company operating profit	$60,000	

Clearly, a change in transfer price does not change the total company operating profit, but does impact division performance. Hardware division would likely prefer the higher transfer price because its operating profit increases from a loss of $10,000 to a profit of $20,000, especially if management is evaluated based on division operating profit. However, Computers division would prefer the lower transfer price.

Case II: Transfer Pricing When Outside Suppliers Are Available (Selling Division *below* Capacity)

Using the same data as in Case I for E-Z Computing, let's add an additional option for Computers: purchasing units from an outside supplier for $60 (the outside supplier is offering a good deal to get Computers' business). *If Computers buys from an outside supplier, the facilities Hardware uses to manufacture these units would remain idle.* Which option yields the highest total company operating profit for E-Z Computing (transfer from Hardware or purchase from outside supplier)?

Transfer Price of $50 per unit (from Case I)

	Hardware	Computers
Sales		
$50 × 1,500	$ 75,000	
$100 × 1,500		$150,000
Variable costs		
$50 × 1,500	75,000	
$50 × 1,500		75,000
Fixed costs	10,000	5,000
Operating profit	$(10,000)	$ 70,000
Total company operating profit	$60,000	

Purchase Externally for $60 per Unit

	Hardware	Computers
Sales		
$70 × 0	$ –0–	
$100 × 1,500		$150,000
Variable costs		
$50 × 0	–0–	
$60 × 1,500		90,000
Fixed costs	10,000	5,000
Operating profit	$(10,000)	$ 55,000
Total company operating profit	$45,000	

The result of purchasing units from an outside supplier is a loss in companywide operating profit of $15,000, the additional cost to the company of purchasing the units externally for $60 versus purchasing the units internally for $50 ($15,000 = [$60 − $50] × 1,500 units).

General Economic Transfer Pricing Rule (When the Seller Is Operating Below Capacity)

The general economic transfer pricing rule *when the seller is operating below capacity* (with idle capacity) is that the seller should transfer at the variable cost per unit (or the differential cost of production). Thus, in this example, the seller should set the transfer price at its variable cost ($50 per unit) to maximize overall company operating profits and to send the correct signal from the Hardware Division to the Computer Division that the variable cost of producing the item is $50.

Case III: Transfer Pricing When Outside Suppliers Are Available (Selling Division *at Capacity*)

Using the same data as in Case II for E-Z Computing, let's make one change in our assumptions. Assume that Hardware does not have idle capacity if Computers buys from an outside supplier. Instead, *if Computers buys from an outside supplier, Hardware can sell all of its units to the outside at the market price of $70 (i.e., Hardware is operating at capacity)*. Which option yields the highest total company operating profit for E-Z Computing (transfer from Hardware or purchase from outside supplier)?

Transfer Price of $70 per Unit

	Hardware	Computers
Sales		
$70 × 1,500	$105,000	
$100 × 1,500		$150,000
Variable costs		
$50 × 1,500	75,000	
$70 × 1,500		105,000
Fixed costs	10,000	5,000
Operating profit	$ 20,000	$ 40,000
Total company operating profit	$60,000	

Purchase Externally for $60 per Unit

	Hardware	Computers
Sales		
$70 × 1,500	$105,000	
$100 × 1,500		$150,000
Variable costs		
$50 × 1,500	75,000	
$60 × 1,500		90,000
Fixed costs	10,000	5,000
Operating profit	$ 20,000	$ 55,000
Total company operating profit	$75,000	

The result of purchasing units from an outside supplier is a gain in companywide operating profit of $15,000, the savings for Computers of purchasing the units externally for $60 versus purchasing the units internally for $70 ([$70 − $60] × 1,500 units = $15,000).

General Economic Transfer Pricing Rule (When the Seller Is Operating at Capacity)

The general economic transfer pricing rule *when the seller is operating at capacity* is that the seller should transfer at the market price. Thus, with this example, the seller should set the transfer price at its market price ($70 per unit) to maximize overall company operating profits.

Case IV: Transfer Pricing When Outside Suppliers Are Available (Selling Division *below* Capacity with Alternative Facility Utilization)

Using the same data as in Case I for E-Z Computing, let's make additional changes in our assumptions. Assume that Hardware does have idle capacity if Computers buys from an outside supplier for $60 per unit. However, *if Computers buys from an outside supplier, the firm can use the Hardware idle capacity for other purposes, resulting in cash operating savings of $35,000.* Which option yields the highest total company operating profit for E-Z Computing (transfer from Hardware or purchase from outside supplier)?

Transfer Price of $50 per Unit (from Case I)

	Hardware	Computers
Sales		
$50 × 1,500	$ 75,000	
$100 × 1,500		$150,000
Variable costs		
$50 × 1,500	75,000	
$50 × 1,500		75,000
Fixed costs	10,000	5,000
Operating profit	$(10,000)	$ 70,000
Total company operating profit	$60,000	

Purchase Externally for $60 per Unit

	Hardware	Computers
Sales		
$70 × 0	$ –0–	
$100 × 1,500		$150,000
Variable costs		
$50 × 0	–0–	
$60 × 1,500		90,000
Fixed costs	10,000	5,000
Operating savings	35,000	–0–
Operating profit	$25,000	$ 55,000
Total company operating profit	$80,000	

The result of purchasing units from an outside supplier is a gain in companywide operating profit of $20,000, the operating savings ($35,000) less the additional cost of purchasing the units externally ([$60 − $50] × 1,500 units = $15,000).

SUMMARY OF GENERAL TRANSFER PRICING RULES

L.O. 2: Explain the general transfer pricing rules and understand the underlying basis for these rules.

As outlined in the preceding examples, two rules exist when establishing a transfer price:

- If the selling division *is operating at capacity*, the transfer price should be the market price.
- If the selling division *has idle capacity*, and the idle facilities cannot be used for other purposes, the transfer price should be at least the variable costs incurred to produce the goods.

HOW TO HELP MANAGERS ACHIEVE THEIR GOALS WHILE ACHIEVING THE ORGANIZATION'S GOALS

L.O. 3: Identify the behavioral issues and incentive effects of negotiated transfer prices, cost-based transfer prices, and market-based transfer prices.

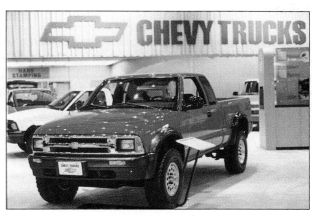

The Chevrolet Division may buy parts from other General Motors divisions or from outsiders to make its trucks. It may be easier to ensure quality control and reliable delivery by buying from another General Motors division rather than from outsiders. (See discussion on pages 666 and 667.) (Courtesy of GM Media Services)

As might be expected, a conflict can arise between the company's interests and an individual manager's interests when transfer price-based performance measures are used. The following example demonstrates such a conflict.

Ace Electronics Company's Production Division was operating below capacity. Its Assembly Division received a contract to assemble 10,000 units of a final product, XX-1. Each unit of XX-1 required one part, A-16, which Production Division makes. Both divisions are decentralized, autonomous investment centers and are evaluated based on operating profits and ROI.

The vice president of Assembly Division called the vice president of Production Division and made a proposal:

Meg (Assembly VP): Look, Joe, I know you're running below capacity out there in your department. I'd like to buy 10,000 units of A-16 at $30 per unit. That will enable you to keep your production lines busy.

Joe (Production VP): Are you kidding, Meg? I happen to know that it would cost you a lot more if you had to buy A-16s from an outside supplier. We refuse to accept less than $40 per unit, which gives us our usual markup and covers our costs.

Meg: Joe, we both know that your variable costs per unit are only $22. I realize I'd be getting a good deal at $30, but so would you. You should treat this as a special order. Anything over your differential costs on the order is pure profit. Look, Joe, if you can't do better than $40, I'll have to go elsewhere. I have to keep my costs down, too, you know.

Joe: The $40 per unit is firm. Take it or leave it!

Assembly Division subsequently sought bids on the part and was able to obtain its requirements from an outside supplier for $40 per unit. Production Division continued to operate below capacity. The actions of the two divisions cost the company $180,000. This amount is the difference between the price paid for the part from the outside supplier ($40) and the differential costs of producing in the Assembly Division ($22) times the 10,000 units in the order.

How can a decentralized organization avoid this type of cost? Although there is no easy solution to this type of problem, there are three general approaches to the problem:

- Direct intervention by top management.
- Centrally established transfer price policies.
- Negotiated transfer prices.

Each of these approaches has advantages and disadvantages and may be appropriate under different circumstances. We discuss these alternatives in the next sections.

TOP MANAGEMENT INTERVENTION IN TRANSFER PRICING

Ace Electronics' top management could have directly intervened in this pricing dispute and ordered Production Division to produce the A-16s and transfer them to Assembly Division at a management-specified transfer price. If this were an extraordinarily large order or if internal product transfers were rare, direct intervention might be the best solution to the problem.

The disadvantage of direct intervention is that top management may become swamped with pricing disputes, and individual division managers will lose the flexibility and other advantages of autonomous decision making. Thus, direct intervention promotes short-run profits by minimizing the type of uneconomic behavior demonstrated in the Ace Electronics case but reduces the benefits from decentralization.

As long as the transfer pricing problems are infrequent, the benefits of direct intervention may outweigh the costs. However, if transfer transactions are common, direct intervention can be costly by requiring substantial top-management involvement in decisions that should be made at the divisional level.

Imperfect Markets

Transfer pricing can be quite complex when selling and buying divisions cannot sell and buy all they want in perfectly competitive markets. In some cases, there may be no outside market at all. Companies often find that not all transactions between divisions occur as top management prefers. In extreme cases, the transfer pricing problem is so complex that top management reorganizes the company so that buying and selling divisions report to one manager who oversees the transfers.

CENTRALLY ESTABLISHED TRANSFER PRICE POLICIES

A transfer pricing policy should allow divisional autonomy yet encourage managers to pursue corporate goals consistent with their own personal goals. Additionally, the use of transfer prices to determine the selling division's revenue and the buying division's cost should be compatible with the company's performance evaluation system. The two economic bases on which to establish transfer price policies are market prices and cost.

Establishing a Market Price Policy

Externally based market prices are generally considered the best basis for transfer pricing when a competitive market exists for the product and market prices are readily available. An advantage of market prices is that both the buying and selling divisions can buy and sell as many units as they want at the market price. Managers of both buying and selling divisions are indifferent as to trading with each other or with outsiders. From the company's perspective, this is fine as long as the supplying unit is operating at capacity.

Situations are rare in which such markets exist, however. Usually there are differences between products produced internally and those that can be purchased from outsiders, such as costs, quality, or product characteristics. The very existence of two divisions that trade with each other in one company tends to indicate that there may be advantages to dealing internally instead of with outside markets.

For example, when Chevrolet Division of General Motors buys parts from other General Motors divisions, it may be easier to ensure quality control and reliable delivery. Furthermore, costs of negotiating transactions can be reduced or eliminated when dealing internally.

When such advantages exist, it is in the company's interest to create incentives for internal transfer. Top management may establish policies that direct two responsibility centers to trade internally unless they can show good reason why external trades are more advantageous. A common variation on this approach is to establish a policy that provides the buying division a discount for items purchased internally.

To encourage transfers that are in the interest of the company, management may set a transfer pricing policy based on market prices for the intermediate product, such as part A-16. As a general rule, a **market price–based transfer pricing** policy contains the following guidelines:

market price–based transfer pricing
Transfer pricing policy that sets the transfer price at the market price or at a small discount from the market price.

* The transfer price is usually set at a discount from the cost to acquire the item on the open market.
* The selling division may elect to transfer or to continue to sell to the outside.

Establishing a Cost Basis Policy

A cost-based transfer pricing policy should follow the following rule:

> Transfer at the differential outlay cost to the selling division (typically variable costs) plus the opportunity cost to the company of making the internal transfers ($0 if the seller has idle capacity; selling price minus variable costs if the seller is operating at capacity).

Using the Ace Electronics example to demonstrate, recall that the seller (Production Division) could sell in outside markets for $40 and had a variable cost of $22, which we shall assume is its differential cost.

Now consider two cases. In case 1, the seller (Production Division) operates below capacity, in which case there is probably no opportunity cost of the internal transfer because no outside sale is forgone. In case 2, the seller operates at capacity and would have to give up one unit of outside sales for every unit transferred internally.

In case 2, the opportunity cost of transferring the product to a division inside the company is the forgone contribution of selling the unit in an outside market. Consequently, the optimal transfer price for Ace Electronics is $22 for the below-capacity case or $40 for the at-capacity case, as shown in Illustration 21.1.

A seller operating at capacity is indifferent between selling in the outside market for $40 or transferring internally at $40. Note that this is the same solution as the market price rule for competitive markets (ignoring the wholesaler's markup) because sellers can sell everything they produce at the market price. Consequently, as a rule of thumb, the economic transfer pricing rule can be implemented as follows:

* A seller operating below capacity should transfer at the differential cost of production (variable cost).
* A seller operating at capacity should transfer at market price.

A seller operating below capacity is indifferent between providing the product and receiving a transfer price equal to the seller's differential outlay cost or not providing the product at all. For example, if Production Division received $22 for the product, it would be indifferent between selling it or not. In both the below-capacity and at-capacity cases, the selling division is no worse off if the internal transfer is made.

ILLUSTRATION 21.1	Application of General Transfer Pricing Rule— Ace Electronics		
	Differential + Outlay Cost	Opportunity Cost of Transferring Internally	= Transfer Price
If the seller (that is, Production Division) has idle capacity	$22	+ –0– (probably)	= $22
If the seller has no idle capacity	22	+ $18 ($40 selling price – $22 variable cost)	= 40

The selling division does not earn a contribution on the transaction in the below-capacity case, however. It earns only the same contribution for the internal transfer as it would for a sale to the outside market in the at-capacity case. The general rule as stated is optimal for the company but does not benefit the selling division for an internal transfer. (For practical purposes, we assume that the selling division will transfer internally if it is indifferent between an internal transfer and an external sale.)

Alternative Cost Measures

Full-Absorption Cost-Based Transfers   Although the transfer rule, differential outlay cost to the selling division plus the opportunity cost to the company of making the internal transfer, assumes that the company has a measure of differential or variable cost, this is not always the case. Consequently, manufacturing firms sometimes use full-absorption.

If measures of market prices are not available, it is impossible to compute the opportunity cost required by the general rule. Consequently, companies frequently use full-absorption costs, which are higher than variable costs but probably less than the market price.

The use of full-absorption costs does not necessarily lead to the profit-maximizing solution for the company; however, it has some advantages. First, these costs are available in the company's records. Second, they provide the selling division with a contribution equal to the excess of full-absorption costs over variable costs, which gives the selling division an incentive to transfer internally. Third, the full-absorption cost may sometimes be a better measure of the differential costs of transferring internally than the variable costs. For example, the transferred product may require engineering and design work that is buried in fixed overhead. In these cases, the full-absorption cost may be a reasonable measure of the differential costs, including the unknown engineering and design costs.

Activity-Based Costing   Many companies are implementing activity-based costing to improve the accuracy of costs in cost-based transfer pricing. One of the primary motives for Deere and Co. to develop activity-based costing, for example, was to improve the accuracy of cost numbers in its internal transfers of parts.

cost-plus transfer pricing
Transfer pricing policy based on full costing or variable costing and actual cost or standard cost plus an allowance for profit.

Cost-Plus Transfers   We also find companies using **cost-plus transfer pricing** based on either variable costs or full-absorption costs. These methods generally apply a normal markup to costs as a surrogate for market prices when intermediate market prices are not available.

Standard Costs or Actual Costs   If actual costs are used as a basis for the transfer, any variances or inefficiencies in the selling division are passed to the buying division. The problems of isolating the variances that have been transferred to subsequent buyer divisions becomes extremely complex. To promote responsibility in the selling division and to isolate variances within divisions, standard costs are usually used as a basis for transfer pricing in cost-based systems.

For example, suppose that Ace Electronics makes transfers based on variable costs for part A-16. The standard variable cost of producing the part is $22, but the actual cost is $29 because of inefficiencies in the Production Division. Should this inefficiency be passed on to the buying division? The answer is usually no, to give Production Division incentives to be efficient. In these cases, companies use standard costs for the transfer price. If standards are out of date or otherwise do not reflect reasonable estimates of costs, the actual cost may be a better measure to use in the transfer price.

Remedying Motivational Problems of Transfer Pricing Policies

When the transfer pricing policy does not give the supplier a profit on the transaction, motivational problems can arise. For example, if transfers are made at differential cost, the supplier earns no contribution toward profits on the transferred goods. Then the transfer price policy does not motivate the supplier to transfer internally because there is no likely profit from internal transfers. This situation can be remedied in several ways.

A supplier whose transfers are almost all internal is usually organized as a cost center. The center manager is normally held responsible for costs, not for revenues. Hence, the transfer price does not affect the manager's performance measures. In companies in which such a supplier is a profit center, the artificial nature of the transfer price should be considered when evaluating the results of that center's operations.

A supplying center that does business with both internal and external customers could be set up as a profit center for external business when the manager has price-setting power and as a cost center for internal transfers when the manager does not have such power. Performance on external business could be measured as if the center were a profit center; performance on internal business could be measured as if the center were a cost center.

Dual Transfer Prices

dual transfer pricing
Transfer pricing system that charges the buying division with costs only and credits the selling division with cost plus some profit allowance.

A **dual transfer pricing** system could be installed to provide the selling division with a profit but charge the buying division with costs only. That is, the buyer could be charged the cost of the unit, however cost might be determined, and the selling division could be credited with cost plus some profit allowance. The difference could be accounted for in a special centralized account. This system would preserve cost data for subsequent buyer divisions and would encourage internal transfers by providing a profit on such transfers for the selling divisions.

Some companies use dual transfer prices to encourage internal transfers; however, there are other ways to encourage internal transfers. For example, many companies recognize internal transfers and incorporate them explicitly in their reward systems. Other companies base part of a supplying manager's bonus on the purchasing center's profits.

NEGOTIATING THE TRANSFER PRICE

negotiated transfer pricing
System that arrives at transfer prices through negotiation between managers of buying and selling divisions.

An alternative to a centrally administered transfer pricing policy is to permit managers to negotiate the price for internally transferred goods and services. Under this system, the managers involved act in much the same way as the managers of independent companies. The major advantage to **negotiated transfer pricing** is that it preserves the autonomy of the division managers. However, the two primary disadvantages are that a great deal of management effort may be consumed in the negotiating process and the final price and its implications for performance measurement may depend more on the manager's ability to negotiate than on what is best for the company.

In the Ace Electronics case, the two managers have room to negotiate the price between $22 and $40. They may choose to "split the difference" or develop some other negotiating strategy.

SELF-STUDY QUESTION

1. Nykee Shoe Company has two divisions, Production and Marketing. Production manufactures Nykee shoes, which it sells to both the Marketing Division and to other retailers (the latter under a different brand name). Marketing operates several small shoe stores in shopping centers that sell both Nykee and other brands.

   Relevant facts for Production, which is operating far below its capacity, follow:

Sales price to outsiders	$	28.50 per pair
Variable cost to produce		18.00 per pair
Fixed costs	100,000	per month

   The following data pertain to the sale of Nykee shoes by Marketing, which is operating far below its capacity:

Sales price	$40 per pair
Variable marketing costs	1 per pair

   The company's variable manufacturing and marketing costs are differential to this decision, but fixed manufacturing and marketing costs are not.

   a. What is the minimum price that the Marketing Division can charge for the shoes and still cover the company's differential manufacturing and marketing costs?

   b. What is the appropriate transfer price for this decision?

   c. What effect would a transfer price set at $28.50 have on the minimum price set by the Marketing manager?

   d. How would your answer to (*b*) change if the Production Division were operating at full capacity?

   The solution to this question is at the end of this chapter on page 683.

GLOBAL PRACTICES

L.O. 4: Explain the economic consequences of multinational transfer prices.

The authors of surveys of corporate practices summarized in Illustration 21.2 reported that nearly half of the U.S. companies surveyed used a cost-based transfer pricing system. Thirty-three percent used a market price–based system, and 22 percent used a negotiated system. Similar results have been found for companies in Canada and Japan.

Generally, we find that when negotiated prices are used, the prices negotiated are between the market price at the upper limit and some measure of cost at the lower limit.[2]

---

[2]See R. Benke and J. Edwards, *Transfer Pricing: Techniques and Uses* (New York: National Association of Accountants, 1980).

ILLUSTRATION 21.2	Transfer Pricing Practices		
Method Used	United States[a]	Canada[b]	Japan[c]
Cost based	45%	47%	47%
Market based.	33	35	34
Negotiated transfer prices	22	18	19
Total	100%	100%	100%

Note: Companies using other methods were omitted from this illustration. These companies were 2 percent or less of the total.

[a]Source: S. Borkowski, "Environmental and Organizational Factors Affecting Transfer Pricing: A Survey," *Journal of Management Accounting Research,* Fall 1990.

[b]Source: R. Tang, "Canadian Transfer Pricing Practices," *CA Magazine,* March 1980.

[c]Source: R. Tang, C. Walter, and R. Raymond, "Transfer Pricing—Japanese vs. American Style," *Management Accounting,* January 1979.

No optimal transfer pricing policy dominates all others. An established policy most likely will be imperfect in the sense that it will not always work to induce the economically optimal outcome. As with other management decisions, however, the cost of any system must be weighed against its benefits. Improving a transfer pricing policy beyond some point (for example, to obtain better measures of variable costs and market prices) will result in the costs of the system exceeding its benefits. As a result, management tends to settle for a system that seems to work reasonably well rather than devise a "textbook" perfect system.

MULTINATIONAL TRANSFER PRICING

In international transactions, transfer prices may affect tax liabilities, royalties, and other payments because of different laws in different countries (or states). Because tax rates vary among countries, companies have incentives to set transfer prices that will increase revenues (and profits) in low-tax countries and increase costs (thereby reducing profits) in high-tax countries.

Tax avoidance by foreign companies using inflated transfer prices has been a major issue in recent U.S. presidential campaigns. Foreign companies that sell goods to their U.S. subsidiaries at inflated transfer prices artificially reduce the profit of the U.S. subsidiaries. According to certain presidential candidates, the United States could collect billions per year in additional taxes if transfer pricing was calculated according to U.S. tax laws. (Many foreign companies dispute this claim.)

To understand the effects of transfer pricing on taxes, consider the case of Nehru Jacket Corp. Its facility in Country N imports materials from the company's Country I facility. The tax rate in Country N is 70 percent, but in Country I it is 40 percent.

During the current year, Nehru incurred production costs of $2 million in Country I. Costs incurred in Country N, aside from the cost of the jackets, amounted to $6 million. (We call these "third-party" costs.) Sales revenues in Country N were $24 million. Similar goods imported by other companies in Country N would have cost an equivalent of $3 million. However, Nehru points out that because of its special control over its operations in Country I and the special approach it uses to manufacture its goods, the appropriate transfer price is $10 million. What would

| REAL WORLD APPLICATION | Just-in-Time Production in Japan and the Internal Revenue Service in the United States |

A Japanese motorcycle manufacturer uses just-in-time production for its manufacturing facility in Japan. Its U.S. subsidiary is a distribution company that sells to dealers in the United States. Both the Japanese manufacturing facility and the U.S. distribution subsidiary were profitable as long as demand for the product in the United States remained high.

Demand in the United States for motorcycles has dropped. The U.S. subsidiary found itself with lots of inventory, so much that it had more than a year's supply of the product on hand. Meanwhile, the Japanese manufacturing plant was reluctant to reduce production below its efficient operating level, and, because it followed the just-in-time philosophy, did not stockpile finished goods inventory in Japan.

As inventories increased at the U.S. subsidiary, so did expenses to store and sell them. The U.S. subsidiary showed declining profits and eventually incurred losses. The U.S. Internal Revenue Service claimed the low profits and losses were the result of the transfer price set by the Japanese manufacturer (which was based on full-absorption manufacturing costs) and the fact that the Japanese manufacturer continued to ship products that the U.S. subsidiary had difficulty selling. Consequently, according to the IRS, the Japanese manufacturer should bear some of the costs of the U.S. subsidiary's high inventory levels.

Source: Based on the authors' research.

Nehru's total tax liability in both jurisdictions be if it used the $3 million transfer price? What would the liability be if it used the $10 million transfer price?

Assuming the $3 million transfer price, the tax liabilities are computed as follows:

	Country I	Country N
Revenues	$3,000,000	$24,000,000
Third-party costs	2,000,000	6,000,000
Transferred goods costs		3,000,000
Taxable income	1,000,000	15,000,000
Tax rate	40%	70%
Tax liability	$ 400,000	$10,500,000
Total tax liability	$10,900,000	

Assuming the $10 million transfer price, the liabilities are computed as follows:

	Country I	Country N
Revenues	$10,000,000	$24,000,000
Third-party costs	2,000,000	6,000,000
Transferred goods costs		10,000,000
Taxable income	$ 8,000,000	$ 8,000,000
Tax rate	40%	70%
Tax liability	$ 3,200,000	$ 5,600,000
Total tax liability	$ 8,800,000	

Nehru Jacket Corp. can save $2,100,000 in taxes simply by changing its transfer price!

To say the least, international taxing authorities look closely at transfer prices when examining the tax returns of companies engaged in related-party transactions that cross national boundaries. Companies frequently must have adequate support for the use of the transfer price that they have chosen for such a situation, as discussed in this chapter's Real World Application above. Transfer pricing disputes also occur at the state and province level because of different tax rates.

SELF-STUDY QUESTION

2. Refer to the information on Nehru Jacket Corp. in the text. Assume that the tax rate for both countries is 40 percent. What would the tax liability be for Nehru if the transfer were set at $3 million? At $10 million?

The solution to this question is at the end of this chapter on page 684.

SEGMENT REPORTING

L.O. 5: Describe the role of transfer prices in segment reporting.

The FASB requires companies engaged in different lines of business to report certain information about segments that meet the FASB's technical requirements.[3] This reporting requirement is intended to provide a measure of the performance of those segments of a business that are significant to the company as a whole.

The following are the principal items that must be disclosed about each segment:

- Segment revenue.
- Segment operating profits or loss.
- Identifiable segment assets.
- Depreciation and amortization.
- Capital expenditures.
- Certain specialized items.

In addition, if a company has significant foreign operations, it must disclose revenues, operating profits or losses, and identifiable assets by geographic region.

Negotiated transfer prices, which may be useful for internal purposes, are not generally acceptable for external segment reporting. In general, the accounting profession has indicated a preference for market-based transfer prices.[4] This preference arises because the purpose of the segment disclosure is to enable an investor to evaluate a company's divisions as though they were free-standing enterprises. Presumably, sales would be based on market transactions, not on the ability of managers to negotiate prices.

Although the conceptual basis for market-based transfer prices is sound in this setting, the practical application may be difficult. Frequently, the segments are really interdependent, so market prices may not really reflect the same risk in an intracompany sale that they do in third-party sales.

In addition, in many situations, market prices are either not readily available or may exist for only some products. When these problems arise, management usually attempts to estimate the market by obtaining market prices for similar goods and adjusting the price to reflect the characteristics of the goods transferred within the company. An alternative is to take the cost of the item transferred and add an allowance to represent the normal profit for the item.

SUMMARY

The following summarizes key ideas tied to the chapter's learning objectives.

L01: Basic issues of transfer pricing. When companies transfer goods or services between divisions, a price is assigned to that transaction. This transfer price becomes a part of the recorded revenues and costs in the divisions involved in the transfer. As a result, the dollar value assigned to the transfer can have significant

---

[3]The requirements, which are too detailed to cover here, are specified in FASB, *Statement of Financial Accounting Standards No. 14,* "Financial Reporting for Segments of a Business Enterprise" (Stamford, CT: FASB, 1976).

[4]See, for example, FASB, *Statement of Financial Accounting Standards No. 69,* which specifies the use of market-based transfer prices when calculating the results of operations for an oil and gas exploration and production operation.

implications in measuring divisional performance. Establishing transfer prices can be a difficult task and depends on individual circumstances. The chapter outlined four common scenarios.

LO2: Transfer pricing rules. Two general rules exist when establishing a transfer price: (1) if the selling division *is operating at capacity,* the transfer price should be the market price and (2) if the selling division *has idle capacity* that cannot be used for other purposes, the transfer price should be at least the variable costs incurred to produce the goods.

LO3: Behavioral issues of transfer pricing. Transfer pricing systems may be based on direct intervention, market prices, costs, or negotiation among the division managers. The appropriate method depends on the markets in which the company operates and management's goals. Top management usually tries to choose the appropriate method to promote corporate goals without destroying the autonomy of division managers. Different approaches to transfer pricing create different motivations for behavior. In creating a basis for establishing transfer prices (e.g., negotiated, cost based, or market based), management must consider the behavior such a plan motivates.

LO4: Multinational transfer prices. Because tax rates vary in different countries, companies have incentives to set transfer prices to increase revenues (and profits) in low-tax countries and increase costs (thereby reducing profits) in high-tax countries.

LO5: Transfer pricing and segment reporting. Companies with significant segments are required to report on those segments separately in the financial statements. The accounting profession has indicated a preference for market-based transfer prices when reporting on a segment of a business.

KEY TERMS

cost-plus transfer pricing, 668	negotiated transfer pricing, 670
dual transfer pricing, 669	transfer price, 661
market price–based transfer pricing, 667	

REVIEW QUESTIONS

21.1 What are some of the bases for establishing a transfer price?

21.2 Why do transfer prices exist even in highly centralized organizations?

21.3 Why are market-based transfer prices considered optimal under many circumstances?

21.4 What are the limitations to market-based transfer prices?

21.5 What are the advantages of direct intervention? What are the disadvantages of such a practice?

21.6 Why do companies often use prices other than market prices for interdivisional transfers?

21.7 What is the basis for choosing between actual and standard costs for cost-based transfer pricing?

21.8 Some have suggested that managers should negotiate transfer prices. What are the disadvantages of a negotiated transfer price system?

21.9 What are the general transfer pricing rules?

CRITICAL ANALYSIS AND DISCUSSION QUESTIONS	

21.10 What are some goals of a transfer pricing system in a decentralized organization?

21.11 Division A has no external markets. It produces monofilament that is used by Division B, which cannot purchase this particular type of monofilament from any other source. What transfer pricing system would you recommend for the interdivisional sale of monofilament? Why?

21.12 How does the choice of a transfer price affect the operating profits of both segments involved in an intracompany transfer?

21.13 Refer to this chapter's Real World Application on page 672. Why did the Internal Revenue Service dispute the U.S. subsidiary's reported profits and losses?

21.14 When setting a transfer price for goods that are sold across international boundaries, what factors should management consider?

EXERCISES

21.15
Apply Transfer Pricing Rules
(L.O. 2)

Beamer & Associates is a real estate company. Its Leasing Division rents and manages properties for others and its Maintenance Division performs services such as carpentry, painting, plumbing, and electrical work. Maintenance Division, which has an estimated variable cost of $36 per labor-hour, works for both Beamer and other companies. It could spend 100 percent of its time working for outsiders. Maintenance Division charges $70 per hour for labor performed for outsiders, the same rate charged by other maintenance companies. Leasing Division complained that it could hire its own maintenance staff at an estimated variable cost of $40 per hour.

Required

a. What is the minimum transfer price that Maintenance Division should obtain for its services, assuming that it is operating at capacity?

b. What is the maximum price that Leasing Division should pay?

c. Would your answers in (*a*) or (*b*) change if Maintenance Division had idle capacity? If so, which answer would change, and what would the new amount be?

21.16
Evaluate Transfer Pricing System
(L.O. 2, 3)

Paridym, Inc., has two decentralized divisions, X and Y. Division X always has purchased certain units from Division Y at $150 per unit. Because Division Y plans to raise the price to $200 per unit, Division X desires to purchase these units from outside suppliers for $150 per unit. Division Y's costs follow:

Variable costs per unit.	$ 140
Annual fixed costs	30,000
Annual production of these units for X	1,000 units

Required

If Division X buys from an outside supplier, the facilities Division Y uses to manufacture these units would remain idle. What would be the result if Paridym enforces a transfer price of $200 per unit between Divisions X and Y?

(CPA adapted)

21.17
Evaluate Transfer Pricing System
(L.O. 2, L.O. 3)

A company permits its decentralized units to "lease" space to one another. Division X has leased some idle warehouse space to Division Y for $1.50 per square foot per month. Recently, Division X obtained a new five-year contract, which will increase its production sufficiently so that the warehouse space is more valuable to it. Division X has notified Division Y that it will increase the rental price to $5.25 per square foot per month. Division Y can lease space at $3 per square foot in another warehouse from an outside company but prefers to stay in the shared facilities. Division Y's management states that it would prefer not to move. If Division X cannot use the space now being leased to Division Y, it will have to rent other space for $4.50 per square foot per month. (The difference in rental prices occurs because Division X requires a more substantial warehouse building than Division Y.)

Required

Recommend a transfer price and explain your reasons for choosing that price.

21.18 Evaluate Transfer Pricing System (L.O. 3)

Selling Division offers its product to outside markets for $150. Selling incurs variable costs of $55 per unit and fixed costs of $37,500 per month based on monthly production of 1,000 units.

Buying Division can acquire the product from an alternate supplier for $157.50 per unit or from Selling Division for $150 plus $10 per unit in transportation costs in addition to the transfer price charged by Selling Division.

Required

a. What are the costs and benefits of the alternatives available to Selling and Buying Divisions with respect to the transfer of the Selling Division's product? Assume that Selling can market all that it can produce.

b. How would your answer change if Selling had idle capacity sufficient to cover all of Buying's needs?

21.19 Evaluate Transfer Pricing System (L.O. 3)

Seattle Transit, Ltd., operates a local mass transit system. The transit authority is a governmental agency related to the state government. It has an agreement with the state government to provide rides to senior citizens for 10 cents per trip. The government will reimburse Seattle Transit for the "cost" of each trip taken by a senior citizen.

The regular fare is $.80 per trip. After analyzing its costs, Seattle Transit figured that with its operating deficit, the full cost of each ride on the transit system is $2.00. Routes, capacity, and operating costs are unaffected by the number of senior citizens on any route.

Required

a. What are the alternative prices that could be used to determine the governmental reimbursement to Seattle Transit?

b. Which price would Seattle Transit prefer? Why?

c. Which price would the provincial government prefer? Why?

d. If Seattle Transit provides an average of 200,000 trips for senior citizens in a given month, what is the monthly value of the difference between the prices in (*b*) and (*c*)?

21.20 Evaluate Transfer Pricing System (L.O. 3)

Oracle Greenery, owned 60 percent by Mr. Peterson and 40 percent by Ms. Jefferies, grows specimen plants for landscape contractors. The wholesale price of each plant is $15. During the past year, Oracle sold 5,000 specimen plants.

Of the plants sold last year, 1,000 were sold to Lively Landscape Co. Mr. Peterson has a 20 percent interest in Lively Landscape Co., and Ms. Jefferies has a 60 percent interest in Lively Landscape Co. At the end of the year, Ms. Jefferies noted that Lively was the largest buyer of Oracle plants. She suggested that the plant company give Lively Landscape a 10 percent reduction in prices for the coming year in recognition of its position as a preferred customer.

Required

Assuming that Lively Landscape purchases the same number of plants at the same prices in the coming year, what effect would the price reduction have on the operating profits that accrue to Mr. Peterson and to Ms. Jefferies for the coming year?

21.21 International Transfer Prices (L.O. 4)

Pyramid Corp. has two operating divisions. At its logging operation in Canada, logs are milled and shipped to the United States where the company's Building Supplies Division uses them. Operating expenses amount to $2 million in Canada and $6 million in the United States exclusive of the costs of any goods transferred from Canada. Revenues in the United States are $15 million.

If the lumber were purchased from one of the company's U.S. lumber divisions, the costs would be $3 million. However, if the lumber had been purchased from an independent Canadian supplier, the cost would be $4 million. The marginal income tax rate is 60 percent in Canada and 40 percent in the United States.

Required

What is the company's total tax liability to both jurisdictions for each of the two alternative transfer pricing scenarios ($3 million or $4 million)?

21.22 Segment Reporting (L.O. 5)

Lincoln Homes, Inc., has two divisions, Building and Financing. Building Division oversees construction of single-family homes in "economically efficient" subdivisions. Financing Division takes loan applications and packages mortgages into pools and sells them in the loan markets. It also services the mortgages. Both divisions meet the requirements for segment disclosures under accounting rules.

Building Division had $68 million in sales last year. Costs, other than those charged by Finance Division, totaled $52 million. Financing Division obtained revenues of $16 million from servicing mortgages and incurred outside costs of $14 million. In addition, Financing Division charged Building Division $8 million for loan-related fees. Building Division's manager complained to Lincoln's CEO that Financing Division was charging twice the commercial rate for loan-related fees and that Building Division would be better off sending its buyers to an outside lender.

Financing Division's manager stated that although commercial rates might be lower, it was more difficult to service Lincoln mortgages, and therefore, the higher fees were justified.

Required

a. What are the reported segment operating profits for each division, ignoring income taxes and using the $8 million transfer price for the loan-related fees?

b. What are the reported segment operating profits for each division, ignoring income taxes and using a $4 million commercial rate as the transfer price for the loan-related fees?

21.23 Segment Reporting (L.O. 5)

Aussey Corporation has two operating divisions, an amusement park and a hotel. The two divisions meet the requirements for segment disclosures. Before transactions between the two divisions are considered, revenues and costs were as follows (dollars in thousands):

	Amusement Park	Hotel
Revenues	$11,200	$7,400
Costs	6,200	5,000

The amusement park and the hotel had a joint marketing arrangement by which the hotel gave free passes to the amusement park and the amusement park gave discount coupons good for stays at the hotel. The value of the free passes to the amusement park redeemed during the past year totaled $1,600,000. The discount coupons redeemed at the hotel resulted in a decrease in hotel revenues of $600,000. As of the end of the year, all of the coupons for the current year have expired.

Required

What are the operating profits for each division considering the effects of the costs arising from the joint marketing agreement?

PROBLEMS

21.24 Transfer Pricing with Imperfect Markets: ROI Evaluation, Normal Costing

Division S of Lazareth, Inc., has an investment base of $600,000. Division S produces and sells 90,000 units of a product at a market price of $10 per unit. Its variable costs total $3 per unit. The division also charges each unit with a share of fixed costs. The fixed cost is computed as $5 per unit.

Division T wants to purchase 20,000 units from Division S. However, it is willing to pay only $6.20 per unit because it has an opportunity to accept a special order at a reduced price. The order is economically justifiable only if Division T can acquire the Division S output at a reduced price.

Required

a. What is the ROI for Division S without the transfer to Division T?

b. What is Division S's ROI if it transfers 20,000 units to Division T at $6.20 each?

c. What is the minimum transfer price for the 20,000-unit order that Division S would accept if Division S were willing to maintain the same ROI with the transfer as it would accept by selling its 90,000 units to the outside market?

21.25 Evaluate Profit Impact of Alternative Transfer Decisions

Stickney Products Co. manufactures a line of men's colognes. The manufacturing process entails mixing and the addition of aromatic and coloring ingredients; the finished product is packaged in a company-produced glass bottle and packed in cases containing six bottles each.

Because sales volume is heavily influenced by the appearance of the bottle, the company developed unique bottle production processes.

All bottle production is used by the cologne manufacturing plant. Each division is considered a separate profit center and evaluated as such. As the new corporate controller, you are responsible for determining the proper transfer price to use for the bottles produced for Cologne Division.

At your request, Bottle Division's general manager asked other bottle manufacturers to quote a price for the number and sizes demanded by the Cologne Division. These competitive prices follow:

Volume	Total Price	Price per Case
2,000,000 equivalent cases[a]	$4,000,000	$2.00
4,000,000	7,000,000	1.75
6,000,000	10,000,000	1.67

[a]An equivalent case represents six bottles.

Bottle Division's cost analysis indicates that they can produce bottles at these costs:

Volume	Total Cost	Cost per Case
2,000,000 equivalent cases	$3,200,000	$1.60
4,000,000	5,200,000	1.30
6,000,000	7,200,000	1.20

These costs include fixed costs of $1.2 million and variable costs of $1 per equivalent case. These data have caused considerable corporate discussion as to the proper price to use in the transfer of bottles to Cologne Division. This interest is heightened because a significant portion of a division manager's income is an incentive bonus based on profit center results.

Cologne Division has the following costs in addition to the bottle costs:

Volume	Total Cost	Cost per Case
2,000,000 cases	$16,400,000	$8.20
4,000,000	32,400,000	8.10
6,000,000	48,400,000	8.07

Marketing Department furnished the following price-demand relationship for the finished product:

Sales Volume (in cases)	Total Sales Revenue	Sales Price per Case
2,000,000	$25,000,000	$12.50
4,000,000	45,600,000	11.40
6,000,000	63,900,000	10.65

Required

a. Stickney Products Co. has used market price transfer prices in the past. Using the current market prices and costs and assuming a volume of 6 million cases, calculate operating profits for:
   (1) Bottle Division.
   (2) Cologne Division.
   (3) The corporation.

b. Is this production and sales level the most profitable volume for
   (1) Bottle Division?
   (2) Cologne Division?
   (3) The corporation?

Explain your answers.

(CMA adapted)

21.26

International Transfer Prices

Tilden Merchants Co-op (TMC) operates a fleet of container ships in international trade between Great Britain and Thailand. All of the shipping income (that is, that related to TMC's ships) is deemed as earned in Great Britain. TMC also owns a dock facility in Thailand that services TMC's fleet. Income from the dock facility is deemed earned in Thailand, however. TMC's income deemed attributable to Great Britain is taxed at a 75 percent rate. Its income attributable to Thailand is taxed at a 20 percent rate. Last year, the dock facility had operating revenues of $4 million, excluding services performed for TMC's ships. TMC's shipping revenues for last year were $26 million.

Operating costs of the dock facility were $5 million last year and operating costs for the shipping operation, before deduction of dock facility costs, were $17 million. No similar dock facilities in Thailand are available to TMC.

However, there is a facility in Malaysia that would have charged TMC an estimated $3 million for the services that TMC's Thailand dock provided to its ships. TMC management noted that if the services had been provided in Great Britain, the costs for the year would have totaled $8 million. TMC argued to the British tax officials that the appropriate transfer price is the price that would have been charged in Great Britain. British tax officials suggest that the Malaysian price is the appropriate one.

Required

What is the difference in tax costs to TMC between the alternate transfer prices for dock services, that is, its price in Great Britain versus that in Malaysia?

21.27 Analyze Transfer Pricing Data

Notewon, Inc., is a decentralized organization that evaluates division management based on measures of division contribution margin. Divisions L and N operate in similar product markets. Division L produces a solid-state electronic assembly that it can sell to the outside market for $16 per unit. The outside market can absorb up to 140,000 units per year. These units require 2 direct labor-hours each.

If L modifies the units with an additional one-half hour of labor time, they can be sold to Division N for $18 per unit. Division N will accept up to 120,000 of these units per year.

If Division N does not obtain 120,000 units from L, it purchases them for $18.50 each from the outside. Division N incurs $8 of additional labor and other out-of-pocket costs to convert the assemblies into a home digital electronic radio, calculator, telephone monitor, and clock unit. The units can be sold to the outside market for $45 each.

Division L estimates that its total costs are $925,000 for fixed costs and $6 per direct labor-hour. Capacity in Division L is limited to 400,000 direct labor-hours per year.

Required

Determine the following:

a. Total contribution margin to L if it sells 140,000 units to the outside.

b. Total contribution margin to L if it sells 120,000 units to N.

c. The costs to be considered in determining the optimal company policy for sales by Division L.

d. The annual contributions and costs for Divisions L and N under the optimal policy.

21.28 Transfer Pricing— Performance Evaluation Issues

Delaware Division of Lillard Corporation, operating at capacity, has been asked by Jaydee Division to supply it with electrical fitting no. 1726. Delaware sells this part to its regular customers for $7.50 each. Jaydee, which is operating at 50 percent capacity, is willing to pay $5 each for the fitting. Jaydee will put the fitting into a brake unit that it is manufacturing on a cost-plus basis for a commercial airplane manufacturer.

Delaware has a $4.25 variable cost of producing fitting no. 1726. The cost of the brake unit as built by Jaydee follows:

Purchased parts—outside vendors	$22.50
Delaware fitting—1726	5.00
Other variable costs	14.00
Fixed overhead and administration	8.00
	$49.50

Jaydee believes that the price concession is necessary to get the job.

The company uses ROI and dollar profits in measuring division and division manager performance.

Required

a. If you were Delaware's division controller, would you recommend that it supply fitting 1726 to Jaydee? (Ignore any income tax issues.) Why or why not?

b. Would it be to the short-run economic advantage of Lillard Corporation for Delaware Division to supply Jaydee Division with fitting 1726 at $5 each? (Ignore any income tax issues.) Explain your answer.

c. Discuss the organizational and managerial behavior difficulties, if any, inherent in this situation. As Lillard's controller, what would you advise the corporation's president to do in this situation?

(CMA adapted)

21.29 Evaluate Transfer Price System

Tri-City, Inc., consists of three divisions—Boston Corporation, Raleigh Company, and Memphis Company—that operate as if they were independent companies. Each division has its own sales force and production facilities. Each division management is responsible for sales, cost of operations, acquisition and financing of divisional assets, and working capital management. Tri-City corporate management evaluates the performance of the divisions and division managements on the basis of ROI.

Memphis Company has just been awarded a contract for a product that uses a component manufactured by outside suppliers as well as by Raleigh Company, which is operating well below capacity. Memphis used a cost figure of $3.80 for the component in preparing its bid for the new product. Raleigh supplied this cost figure in response to Memphis's request for the average variable cost of the component; it represents the standard variable manufacturing cost and variable marketing costs.

Raleigh's regular selling price for the component that Memphis needs is $6.50. Raleigh management indicated that it could supply Memphis with the required quantities of the component at the regular selling price less variable selling and distribution expenses. Memphis management responded by offering to pay standard variable manufacturing cost plus 20 percent.

The two divisions have been unable to agree on a transfer price. Corporate management has never established a transfer price policy. The corporate vice president of finance suggested a price equal to the standard full manufacturing cost (that is, no selling and distribution expenses) plus a 15 percent markup. The two division managers rejected this price because each considered it grossly unfair.

The unit cost structure for the Raleigh component and the suggested prices follow.

Costs
Standard variable manufacturing cost	$3.20
Standard fixed manufacturing cost	1.20
Variable selling and distribution expenses	.60
	$5.00

Prices
Regular selling price	$6.50
Regular selling price less variable selling and distribution expenses ($6.50 − .60)	$5.90
Variable manufacturing plus 20% ($3.20 × 1.20)	$3.84
Standard full manufacturing cost plus 15% ($4.40 × 1.15)	$5.06

Required

a. Discuss the effect that each of the proposed prices might have on the attitude of Raleigh's management toward intracompany business.

b. Is the negotiation of a price between Memphis and Raleigh divisions a satisfactory method to solve the transfer price problem? Explain your answer.

c. Should Tri-City's corporate management become involved in this transfer price controversy? Explain your answer.

(CMA adapted)

21.30 Transfer Prices and Tax Regulations

Hellena, Inc., has two operating divisions in a semiautonomous organization structure. Division X is located in the United States. It produces part XZ-1, which is an input to Division Y, located in the south of France. Division X uses idle capacity to produce XZ-1, which has a domestic market price of $60. Its variable costs are $25 per unit. The company's U.S. tax rate is 40 percent of income.

In addition to the transfer price for each XZ-1 received from Division X, Division Y pays a shipping fee of $15 per unit. Part XZ-1 becomes a part of Division Y's output product. The output product costs an additional $10 to produce and sells for an equivalent $115. Division Y could purchase part XZ-1 from a Paris supplier for $50 per unit. The company's French tax rate is 70 percent of income. Assume that French tax laws permit transferring at either variable cost or market price.

Required

What transfer price is economically optimal for Hellena, Inc.? Show computations.

21.31 Segment Reporting

Tyejon Corp. has four operating divisions: Airline, Hotel, Auto Rental, and Travel Services. Each division is a separate segment for financial reporting purposes. Revenues and costs related to outside transactions were as follows for the past year (dollars in millions):

	Airline	Hotel	Auto Rental	Travel Services
Revenues	$245	$106	$89	$32
Costs	157	71	66	30

The airline participated in a frequent stayer program with the hotel chain. During the past year, the airline reported that it traded hotel award coupons for travel that had a retail value of $26 million, assuming that the travel was redeemed at full airline fares. Auto Rental Division offered 20 percent discounts to Tyejon's airline passengers and hotel guests. These discounts to airline passengers were estimated to have a retail value of $7 million. Tyejon hotel guests redeemed $3 million in auto rental discount coupons. Tyejon hotels also provided rooms for flight crews of the airline division. The value of the rooms for the year was $13 million.

Travel Services Division booked flights on Tyejon's airline valued at $4 million for the year. This service for intracompany hotel bookings was valued at $2 million and for intracompany auto rentals at $1 million.

While preparing all of these data for financial statement presentation, Hotel Division's controller stated that the value of the airline coupons should be based on the differential and opportunity costs of the travel awards, not on the full fare for the tickets issued. This argument was supported because a travel award is usually allocated to seats that would otherwise be empty or that is restricted similar to those on discount tickets. If the differential and opportunity costs were used for this transfer price, the value would be $5 million instead of $26 million. The airline controller made a similar argument concerning the auto rental discount coupons. If the differential cost basis were used for the auto rental coupons, the transfer price would be $1 million instead of the $7 million.

Tyejon reports assets in each segment as follows:

Airline	$955 million
Hotel	385 million
Car Rental	321 million
Travel Services	65 million

Required

a. Using the retail values for transfer pricing for segment reporting purposes, what are the operating profits for each Tyejon division?

b. What are the operating profits for each Tyejon division using the differential cost basis for pricing transfers?

c. Rank each division by ROI using the transfer pricing method in (*a*), as well as using the transfer pricing method in (*b*). What difference does the transfer pricing system have on the rankings?

INTEGRATIVE CASES

21.32 Custom Freight Systems (A): Transfer Pricing

"We can't drop our prices below $210 per hundred pounds," exclaimed Greg Berman, manager of Forwarders, a division of Custom Freight Systems. "Our margins are already razor thin. Our costs just won't allow us to go any lower. Corporate rewards our division based on our profitability and I won't lower my prices below $210."

Custom Freight Systems is organized into three divisions: Air Cargo provides air cargo services; Logistics Services operates distribution centers and provides truck cargo services; and Forwarders provides international freight forwarding services (see Exhibit 21.32A). Freight forwarders typically buy space on planes from international air cargo companies. This is analogous to a charter company that books seats on passenger planes and resells them to passengers. In many cases freight forwarders will hire trucking companies to transport the cargo from the plane to the domestic destination.

Management believes that the three divisions integrate together well and are able to provide customers with one-stop transportation services. For example, a Forwarders branch in

ILLUSTRATION 21.3A   Custom Freight Systems Operations

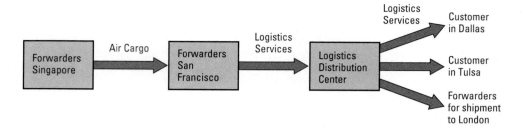

ILLUSTRATION 21.3B   Custom Freight Systems Organization Chart

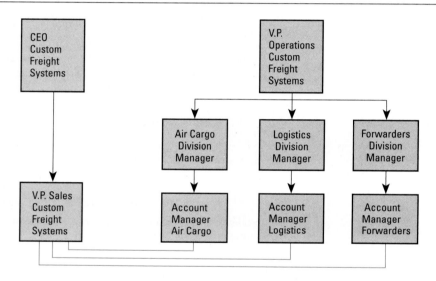

Singapore would receive cargo from a shipper, prepare the necessary documentation, and then ship the cargo on Air Cargo to a domestic Forwarders station. The domestic Forwarders station would ensure the cargo passes through customs and ship it to the final destination with Logistics Services as shown in Illustration 21.3A.

Management evaluates each division separately and rewards division managers based on profit and return on investment (ROI). Responsibility and decision making authority are decentralized. Similarly, each division has a sales and marketing organization. Division sales people report to the Vice President of Sales for Custom Freight Systems as well as a division sales manager. See Illustration 21.3B. Custom Freight Systems feels that it has been successful motivating division managers by paying bonuses for high division profits.

Recently, the Logistics division was completing a bid for a customer. The customer had freight to import from an overseas supplier and wanted Logistics to submit a bid for a distribution package that included air freight from the supplier, receiving the freight and providing customs clearance services at the airport, warehousing, and distributing to customers.

Because this was a contract for international shipping, Logistics needed to contact different freight forwarders for shipping quotes. Logistics requested quotes from the Forwarders division and United Systems, a competing freight forwarder. Divisions of Custom Freight Systems are free to use the most appropriate and cost effective suppliers.

Logistics received bids of $210 per hundred pounds from Forwarders and $185 per hundred pounds from United Systems. Forwarders specified in its bid that it will use Air Cargo, a division of Custom Freight Systems. Forwarder's variable costs were $175 per hundred pounds which included the cost of subcontracting air transportation. Air Cargo, which was experiencing a period of excess capacity, quoted Forwarders the market rate of $155. Typically, Air's variable costs are 60% of the market rate.

The price difference between the two different bids alarmed Susan Burns, a contract manager at Logistics. Burns knows this is a competitive business and is concerned because the difference between the high and low bids was at least $1,000,000 (current projections for the contract estimated 4,160,000 pounds during the first year). Burns contacted Greg Berman, the manager of Forwarders and discussed the quote. "Don't you think full markup is unwarranted due to the fact that you and the airlines have so much excess capacity?" Burns complained.

Burns soon realized that Berman was not going to drop the price quote. "You know how small margins are in this business. Why should I cut my margins even smaller just to make you look good?" Berman asked.

Burns went to Bennie Espinosa, vice president of Custom Freight Systems and chairperson for the corporate strategy committee. "That does sound strange," said Espinosa, "I need to examine the overall cost structure and talk to Berman. I'll get back to you by noon Monday."

Required

a. Which bid should the Logistics division accept: the internal bid from the Forwarders division or the external bid from United Systems.

b. What should the transfer price be on this transaction?

c. What should Bennie Espinosa do?

d. Do the reward systems for the division managers support the best interests of the Forwarders division and the best interests of Custom Freight Systems? Give examples that support your conclusion.

21.33   Custom Freight Systems (B): Transfer Pricing

Assume all of the information is the same as in Custom Freight Systems (A) in Problem 21.32, but instead of receiving one outside bid Logistics receives two. The new bid is from World Services for $195 per hundred pounds. World offered to use Air Cargo for air cargo. Air Cargo will charge World $155 per hundred pounds. The bids from Forwarders and United Systems remain the same as in part (A), $210 and $185, respectively.

Required

Which bid should the Logistics Division take? Why?

Prepared by Thomas B. Rumzie under the direction of Michael W. Maher. © Copyright Michael W. Maher 1996.

SOLUTIONS TO SELF-STUDY QUESTIONS

1. **a.** From a company's perspective, the minimum price would be the variable cost of producing and marketing the goods, $19. If the company were centralized, we would expect this information would be conveyed to the marketing manager, who would be instructed not to set a price below $19.

  b. The transfer price that correctly informs the marketing manager about the differential costs of manufacturing is $18.

  c. If the production manager set the price at $28.50, the marketing manager would set the minimum price at $29.50 ($28.50 + $1.00). So, the marketing manager sets the price in excess of $29.50 per pair. In fact, prices of $28, $25, or anything higher than

$19 would have generated a positive contribution margin from the production and sale of shoes.

  d. If the Production Division had been operating at capacity, an implicit opportunity cost to the company of internal transfers is lost contribution margin ($28.50 − $19 = $9.50) from not selling in the wholesale market.

The transfer price should have been as follows:

$$\text{Differential cost of production} + \begin{array}{l}\text{Implicit opportunity cost}\\\text{to company if goods}\\\text{are transferred internally}\end{array}$$
$$= \$19 + \$9.50$$
$$= \$28.50$$

Marketing would have appropriately treated the $28.50 as part of its differential cost of buying and selling the shoes.

2. For the $3 million transfer, the total tax is (40% $\times$ $1,000,000) + (40% $\times$ $15,000,000) = $6,400,000.

For $10 million, the total tax is (40% $\times$ $8,000,000) + (40% $\times$ $8,000,000) = $6,400,000. With equal tax rates, there is no advantage to inflating the transfer price.

Nonfinancial Performance Measures

LEARNING OBJECTIVES

After reading this chapter, you should be able to:

1. Know how organizations recognize and communicate their responsibilities.

2. Know why performance measures differ across levels of the organization.

3. Understand how the balanced scorecard helps organizations recognize and deal with opposing responsibilities.

4. Know methods to implement an effective performance measurement system.

5. Identify examples of nonfinancial performance measures and discuss the potential for improved performance resulting from improved activity management.

6. Explain why employee involvement is important in an effective performance measurement system.

BEYOND THE ACCOUNTING NUMBERS

Companies have traditionally relied heavily on financial performance measures to evaluate employee performance because they are easily quantifiable and motivate employees to improve the company's accounting profits. In recent years, more and more companies have begun using nonfinancial measures such as customer satisfaction and product quality measures. A primary reason is that nonfinancial performance measures direct employees' attention to those things that they can control.

For example, consider the case of a food server in a restaurant. The food server can have a big effect on customer satisfaction. Measuring his or her performance in terms of customer satisfaction should be meaningful. On the other hand, it would be difficult to measure the effect of the food server's performance in pleasing customers on the restaurant's profits because profits are affected by many factors outside the server's control. Furthermore, the food server might not even understand how profits are earned or calculated. Therefore, it makes sense to reward the food server directly for creating customer satisfaction rather than for his or her effect on profits.

This chapter discusses innovative ways to evaluate performance "beyond the numbers." Performance evaluation starts with an understanding of the organization's objectives and strategy. For example, does the firm want to be a low-cost producer or to be an innovator? In what markets will it compete? The organization evaluates performance by first defining what it wants to accomplish. Then it develops measures that help it evaluate its performance in achieving those accomplishments.

RESPONSIBILITIES BY LEVEL OF ORGANIZATION

L.O. 1: Know how organizations recognize and communicate their responsibilities.

L.O. 2: Know why performance measures differ across levels of the organization.

Performance measurement is based on two concepts. First, it focuses all organization members on the organization's objectives and reflects how individuals or units contribute to them. Second, it is designed to reflect each organization level's ability to affect results or what is controllable at that level.

Performance measurement emphasizes different things at different levels of the organization. At the lower levels in the organization, such as the sportswear department at Macy's department store or the painting center at a Honda automobile assembly plant, nonfinancial performance measures focus on customer satisfaction and product quality and reflect what these employees control. The performance measures emphasize customer satisfaction if employees deal directly with customers as they do at Macy's, Burger King, and Citibank, for example. The performance measures for employees in production, such as those at the Honda assembly plant, or those at Upjohn, emphasize product quality.

At middle levels in organizations, nonfinancial performance measurement focuses on how well the operating systems work together and how effective these systems are compared to those of competitors. At this organization level, coordination and improvement of ongoing activities take place in addition to redesigning products and processes. For example, poor customer service at Macy's because sales personnel are poorly trained is the responsibility of middle managers. The following are some of the nonfinancial performance measures that organizations use to evaluate middle managers' performance:

- Amount of unwanted employee turnover.
- Frequency of meeting customer delivery requirements.
- Employee development performance, such as quality and amount of training.
- Performance in dealing with business partners, such as quality of supplier relations and frequency that orders are miscommunicated to suppliers.

stakeholders
Groups or individuals, such as employees, suppliers, customers, shareholders, and the community, who have a stake in what the organization does.

At the top levels of the organization, performance measurement focuses on determining whether the organization is on track in meeting its responsibilities from the perspectives of its stakeholders. An organization's **stakeholders** are groups or individuals who have a stake in what the organization does. Stakeholders include

mission
An organization's purpose.

mission statement
Description of an organization's values, definition of its responsibilities to stakeholders, and identification of its major strategies.

business-level strategy
An organization's plan to compete in each of its businesses.

shareholders, customers, employees, the community in which the organization does business, and, in some cases, society as a whole. For example, employees depend on an organization for their employment. Shareholders depend on an organization to generate a return on their investment. Performance at this level requires delicately balancing trade-offs.

People at different levels in the organization have different responsibilities. Consequently, the performance measurement system measures different things at different levels in the organization. In general, performance measures should relate to what people at different levels control.

Values of the Organization

An organization states its **mission** in a **mission statement** describing its values, defining responsibilities to stakeholders, and identifying the major **business-level strategies** the organization plans to use to meet its commitments.

Mission statements should answer the following questions:

• Who are the organization's stakeholders? Who matters to the organization?

• How will the organization add value to each stakeholder group? This identifies the *critical success factors*, the factors important for the organization's success.

Ethical Behavior

As noted, the organization's mission statement communicates its guiding principles, beliefs, and values. It helps people in the organization identify what is important and guides employees as they make decisions that help the organization achieve its objectives.

For example, Johnson & Johnson's code of conduct sets forth the company's values in order of priority, stating its responsibilities to customers, employees, the community, and stockholders. Communicating what the organization stands for and what it needs to do to be successful is the foundation of organization performance.

SELF-STUDY QUESTION

1. Who are the stakeholders of a university recreation center?
   The solution to this question is at the end of this chapter on page 697.

BALANCED SCORECARD

L.O. 3: Understand how the balanced scorecard helps organizations recognize and deal with opposing responsibilities.

balanced scorecard
A set of performance targets and results that show an organization's performance in meeting its responsibilities to various stakeholders.

Ben and Jerry's measures its social performance along with its financial performance in its annual report. (Courtesy of Ben & Jerry's)

The **balanced scorecard** is a set of performance targets and results that show an organization's performance in meeting its objectives relating to its stakeholders. It is a management tool that recognizes organizational responsibility to different stakeholder groups, such as employees, suppliers, customers, business partners, the community, and shareholders. Often different stakeholders have different needs or desires that the managers of the organization must balance. The concept of a balanced scorecard is to measure how well the organization is doing in view of those competing stakeholder concerns.

An example of a balanced scorecard is shown in Illustration 22.1. As you can see, the focus is to balance the efforts of the organization between the financial,

ILLUSTRATION   22.1   Balanced Scorecard

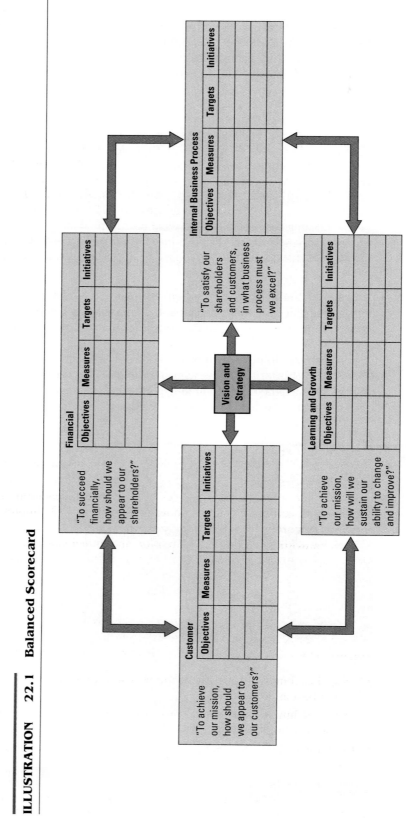

Source: R. S. Kaplan and D. P. Norton, "Using the Balanced Scorecard as a Strategic Management System," *Harvard Business Review*, January–February, 1996.

customer, process, and innovative responsibilities. Traditionally, business organizations have focused on financial results, which mainly have reflected the shareholders' interests. In recent years, organizations have shifted attention to customer issues, such as quality and service, to employees, and to the community. For example, Ben & Jerry's Ice Cream measures its social performance along with financial performance and presents a social audit in its annual report next to its financial audit. As previously noted, Johnson & Johnson's code of conduct makes it clear that the company has a responsibility to several competing stakeholders.

The balanced scorecard has been developed and used in many companies. It primarily has been used at the top management level to support the organization's development of strategies. For example, Kaplan and Norton describe the development of the balanced scorecard at an insurance company as follows:[1]

Step 1: Ten of the company's top executives formed a team to clarify the company's strategy and objectives to meet responsibilities.

Step 2: The top three layers of the company's management (100 people) were brought together to discuss the new strategy and to develop performance measures for each part of the company. These performance measures became the scorecards for each part of the business and reflected the company's desired balance in satisfying different stakeholders.

Step 3: Managers began eliminating programs that were not contributing to the company's objectives.

Step 4: Top management reviewed the scorecards for each part of the organization.

Step 5: Based on its reviews in step 4, top management went back to step 1 to refine and further clarify the company's strategy and objectives.

Organizations using the balanced scorecard generally have found it to be helpful for top and middle management to shape and clarify organization goals and strategy in the face of competing stakeholder wants.

IMPROVING PERFORMANCE MEASUREMENT

Continuous Improvement and Benchmarking

L.O. 4: Know methods to implement an effective performance measurement system.

continuous improvement
The continuous reevaluation and improvement of the efficiency of activities.

benchmarking
Identifying an activity that needs to be improved, finding an organization that is the most efficient at it, studying its process, and then utilizing that process.

Continuous improvement is a philosophy many organizations are utilizing to meet responsibilities and evaluate performance. It means continuously reevaluating and improving the efficiency of activities. It is the search to (1) improve the activities in which the organization engages through documentation and understanding, (2) eliminate activities that are nonvalue added, and (3) improve the efficiency of activities that are value added.

Benchmarking involves the search for, and implementation of, the best way to do something as practiced in other organizations or in other parts of one's own organization. Using benchmarking, managers identify an activity that needs to be improved, find who is the most efficient at that activity (sometimes in one's own organization), carefully study the process of the one who is most efficient, and then adopt (and adapt) that efficient process to their own organization.

Benchmarks are used to measure the performance of an activity, operation, or organization relative to others. Following are some important guidelines:

- Don't benchmark everything at the best-in-the-business level. No company can be the best at everything.

- Only benchmark best-in-class processes and activities that are of the most importance strategically.

- Look for internal, regional, or industry benchmarks for less important support activities.

---

[1]Based on R. S. Kaplan and D. P. Norton, "Using the Balanced Scorecard as a Strategic Management System," *Harvard Business Review*, January–February 1996.

ILLUSTRATION 22.2	Common Benchmark Questions

Product Performance
How well do our products perform compared to those of our competitors? (Many U.S. automobile, steel, camera, and television companies found that, much to their dismay, they were not performing well in the 1980s compared to their Japanese competitors.)

Employee Performance
How well do our employees perform compared to our competitors' employees? Are our employees as efficient as our competitors' employees? Are our employees as well trained as our competitors' employees?

New Product/Service Development
Are we as innovative as our competitors in developing new products and services?

Cost Performance
Are our costs as low as those of our competitors?

Illustration 22.2 presents some common questions raised in the benchmarking process.

PERFORMANCE MEASUREMENT: THE MEASURES

L.O. 5: Identify examples of nonfinancial performance measures and discuss the potential for improved performance resulting from improved activity management.

Performance measures must be based on the organization's responsibilities, goals, and strategies, which are likely to be different for each organization. The following are examples of performance measures that you are likely to use, or see used, in organizations. We give examples of customer satisfaction measures, which are clearly important to the success of any organization, and functional measures of how well the organization's internal processes are functioning. Our objective is to give you a sense of the types of nonfinancial measures that organizations use, not a comprehensive cookbook of the measures available. (A comprehensive cookbook of nonfinancial performance measures would be larger than this textbook.)

Customer Satisfaction Performance Measures

Customer satisfaction measures reflect the performance of the organization on several internal factors, including quality control and delivery performance.

Quality Control
The objective is to increase customer satisfaction with the product, reduce the costs of dealing with customer complaints, and reduce the costs of repairing products or providing a new service. (Measures may include number of customer complaints, number of service calls, and number of returns.)

Delivery Performance
The objective is to deliver goods and services when promised. (Measures may include the percentage of on-time deliveries and percentage of deliveries damaged.)

Functional Performance Measures

As well as an external customer focus, an organization must maintain internal functional performance evaluation. Many activities are performed throughout the product life cycle. The level of efficiency of processing activities affects the overall performance of the organization in meeting its responsibilities to other stakeholders, such as stockholders and employees. Illustration 22.3 presents several internal functional performance measures used by organizations.

As you can see, many internal performance measures relate to customer performance, as well. For instance, quality assurance relates *directly* to customer

ILLUSTRATION 22.3	Functional Measures of Performance

Accounting Quality
Percentage of late reports
Percentage of errors in reports
Percentage of errors in budget predictions
Manager satisfaction with accounting reports

Clerical Quality
Errors per typed page
Number of times messages are not delivered

Product/Development Engineering Quality Measurements
Percentage of errors in cost estimates
How well product meets customer expectations

Forecasting Quality
Percentage of error in sales forecasts
Number of forecasting assumption errors
Usefulness of forecasts to decision makers

Procurement/Purchasing Quality
Percentage of supplies delivered on schedule
Average time to fill emergency orders

Production Control Quality
Time required to incorporate engineering changes
Time that assembly line is down due to materials shortage

Quality Assurance Quality
Time to answer customer complaints

Source: Most of these measures are drawn from much longer lists in G. Fellers, *The Deming Vision: SPC/TQM for Administrators* (Milwaukee, WI: ASQC Quality Press, 1992); and D. Talley, *Total Quality Management* (Milwaukee, WI: ASQC Quality Press, 1991). Some of these measures were developed by the author.

performance while production control and product development relate *indirectly* to customer satisfaction.

Manufacturing Cycle Time

manufacturing cycle time
The time involved in processing, moving, storing, and inspecting products and materials.

The total time it takes to produce a good or service is called **manufacturing cycle time.** The cycle time includes processing, moving, storing, and inspecting. It is commonly believed that a product's service, quality, and cost are all related to cycle time. As cycle time increases, so do the costs of processing, inspecting, moving, and storing while service and quality go down.

Manufacturing Cycle Efficiency

manufacturing cycle efficiency
Measure of the efficiency of the total manufacturing cycle. Equals processing time divided by the manufacturing cycle time.

Manufacturing cycle efficiency measures the efficiency of the total manufacturing cycle. Manufacturing cycle efficiency for one unit is calculated as follows:

$$\text{Manufacturing cycle efficiency} = \frac{\text{Processing time}}{\text{Processing time} + \text{Moving time} + \text{Storing time} + \text{Inspection time}}$$

This formula calculates a percentage representing the time actually spent processing the unit. The higher the percentage, the less the time (and costs) spent on nonvalue-added activities such as moving and storage. Higher-quality control of the process and inputs results in less time spent on inspections.

REAL WORLD APPLICATION	Does Effective Total Quality Management Require Nontraditional Performance Measures?

Critics of management accounting contend that innovative management methods such as total quality management (TQM) require new approaches to management accounting and control. According to these critics, traditional financial performance measures are obstacles to effective implementation of innovative management methods.

Two professors at the Wharton School of Business, Chris Ittner and David Larcker, investigated this idea in a study of companies in the automotive and computer industries. They found that, in general, companies that adopted TQM also used nontraditional management performance measures. Examples of nontraditional performance

measures included the use of quality and other nonfinancial measures, such as the importance of customers in the identification of new products and processes, and the use of employee suggestion programs. Ittner and Larcker also noted the importance of teamwork as opposed to individual performance.

The results imply that companies that are innovative in using management methods like TQM are also innovative in management evaluation.

Source: C. Ittner and D. Larcker, "Total Quality Management and the Choice of Information and Reward Systems," *Journal of Accounting Research* 33 (Supplement 1995), pp. 1–40.

Nonfinancial Performance and Activity-Based Management

Many experts argue that organizations should manage by using activity data rather than cost data. Knowing the amount of time it takes to produce and deliver a product (e.g., materials handling, storage space used, and rework) could lead to improvement. The activity data could be used to identify problems, suggest an approach to solve problems, and prioritize improvement efforts.

Organizations also may find value in knowing the amount of time it takes to complete a sequence of activities. Many believe that by eliminating long cycle times, the costs of nonproduction personnel, equipment, and supplies could be reduced. Customers also value a prompt response and a short order processing time.

As discussed previously, many believe that a product's service, quality, and cost are all related to cycle time: As cycle time goes up, cost is thought to go up and service and quality are thought to go down. So, as the efficiency of value-added activities is improved or as nonvalue-added activities are eliminated, the process cycle time and cost will fall.

SELF-STUDY QUESTION

2. A manufacturing company has the following average times (in hours):

Product transportation	5
Product manufacturing	10
Inspection	3
Inventory storage	7

Calculate the manufacturing cycle efficiency.

The solution to this question is at the end of this chapter on page 697.

WORKER INVOLVEMENT

L.O. 6: Explain why employee involvement is important in an effective performance measurement system.

Many organizations involve workers in creating ideas for improving performance on critical success factors, as discussed in this chapter's Real World Application. In some Japanese companies that we have studied, every worker is expected to submit an idea for improvement at least once a week. Competent managers know that workers have good ideas for improving the operations of a company. After all, the workers are much closer to those operations than managers.

Worker involvement is important for three reasons:

- Many managers believe that when workers take on real decision-making authority, their commitment to the organization and its objectives increases.

- When decision-making responsibility lies with workers closer to the customer, workers are more responsive and make informed decisions.

- Giving decision-making responsibility to workers uses their skills and knowledge and provides them with motivation to further develop them in an effort to improve the organization's performance.

ILLUSTRATION 22.4	Worker Involvement and Commitment Measures

- Worker Development: Percentage of workers in mentor programs
- Worker Empowerment: Percentage of workers authorized to issue credit
- Worker Recognition: Percentage of workers recognized by awards
- Worker Recruitment: Percentage of employment offers accepted
- Worker Promotion: Percentage of positions filled from within the company
- Worker Succession Planning: Percentage of eligible positions filled through succession planning

How do companies evaluate their own performance in getting workers involved and committed? Illustration 22.4 lists performance measures that organizations can use to assess how well they are doing in terms of worker involvement and commitment. Increasing the percentages on these performance measures demonstrates the organization's attempt to increase worker involvement and commitment to the organization. For example, managers may attempt to increase worker commitment by providing mentors for them. (See top item in Illustration 22.4.) The more workers who are in mentor programs, the more workers who are committed to the organization.

Effective worker involvement presents three challenges for management. First, management must create a system that conveys the organization's objectives and critical success factors to all members. Information and training sessions and the performance indicators themselves determine the extent to which employees understand what behavior is desired of them.

Second, the measures the organization uses to judge individual performance determine the success of the system in promoting goal congruence. Management must analyze the performance measures chosen by each organization unit to make sure that they (1) promote the desired behavior, (2) are comprehensive, (3) support the achievement of organization objectives, and (4) reflect the unit's role in the organization.

Finally, management must ensure that the performance measures are applied consistently and accurately. The measures used to evaluate performance reflect each unit's understanding of its contribution to the organization.

SUMMARY

This chapter discusses innovative ways to evaluate performance "beyond the numbers." The following summarizes key ideas tied to the chapter's learning objectives.

L01: Know how organizations recognize and communicate their responsibilities. Mission statements describe the organization's values, recognize responsibilities to stakeholders, and identify the business-level strategies the organization plans to use to meet its commitments.

L02: Know why the performance measures differ across levels of the organization. At lower levels in the organization, control and performance measurement focus on how people carry out the daily activities that create the organization's products. At the middle level, performance measurement focuses on the organization's ability to meet its responsibilities to various stakeholder groups, how well the operating systems work together to meet these needs, and how effective these systems are compared to those of competitors. At the upper level of the organization, performance measurement focuses on whether the organization is on track with meeting its responsibilities and performance from the stakeholders' perspective.

L03: Understand how the balanced scorecard helps organizations recognize and deal with opposing responsibilities. The balanced scorecard concept recognizes that organizations are responsible to different stakeholder groups and must perform

Using nonfinancial measures of their performance in reducing water pollution, companies have improved the water quality in rivers such as this. Many companies attempt to measure their environmental impact and provide incentives for good performance.
(© Raymond Barnes/Tony Stone Images)

well on several dimensions for success. The balanced scorecard is a set of performance targets and results that show the organization's performance in meeting its objectives relating to financial, customer, process, and innovation factors.

LO4: Know methods of implementing an effective performance measurement system. Continuous improvement is the search to eliminate nonvalue-added activities and improve the efficiency of activities that add value. Continuous improvement uses a tool called *competitive benchmarking,* the search for, and implementation of, the best methods as practiced in other organizations.

LO5: Identify examples of nonfinancial performance measures and discuss the potential for improved performance resulting from improved activity management. Customer satisfaction performance measures are directed at service, quality, and cost. The efficiency of just-in-time production is measured by manufacturing cycle time and manufacturing cycle efficiency, the goal being a measurement of 1.

LO6: Explain why employee involvement is important in an effective performance measurement system. Worker involvement is important for three reasons: (1) it increases commitment to the organization and its goals, (2) it leads to more responsive and informed decision making, and (3) it utilizes worker skills and knowledge. Management must create a system that conveys the organization's goals and critical success factors to the workers.

KEY TERMS

balanced scorecard, 687

benchmarking, 689

business-level strategies, 687

continuous improvement, 689

manufacturing cycle time, 691

manufacturing cycle efficiency, 691

mission, 687

mission statement, 687

stakeholders, 686

REVIEW QUESTIONS

22.1   What is a balanced scorecard?

22.2   Who are the stakeholders of an organization?

22.3   Why are companies using nonfinancial measures such as customer satisfaction and product quality?

22.4   What is a critical success factor?

22.5 Why do performance measurement systems measure different things at different levels in the organization?

22.6 What is competitive benchmarking?

22.7 How is competitive benchmarking used?

22.8 What does an organization's mission statement communicate?

22.9 What performance factors do customer satisfaction measures attempt to evaluate?

22.10 Why is manufacturing cycle efficiency important to most organizations?

22.11 Why measure delivery performance?

22.12 Why is worker involvement important to an organization's success?

22.13 How do companies evaluate their own performance in getting workers involved and committed?

CRITICAL ANALYSIS AND DISCUSSION QUESTIONS

22.14 Consider your campus bookstore. Who do you think are the stakeholders? What do you think are the critical success factors?

22.15 What are three specific measures of quality control and delivery performance for Maytag washing machines?

22.16 Refer to the Real World Application "Does Effective Total Quality Management Require Nontraditional Performance Measures?" on page 692. Why do critics of management accounting contend that new approaches to management accounting and control are required?

22.17 Refer to Illustration 22.4 on page 693. How does percentage of positions filled from within the company measure worker involvement and commitment?

22.18 Refer to Illustration 22.4 on page 693. How does percentage of workers recognized by awards measure worker involvement and commitment?

EXERCISES

22.19 Balanced Scorecard (L.O. 3)

Write a report to the manager of a manufacturing company indicating why you believe that the use of a balanced scorecard for production level employees will not work.

22.20 Benchmarks (L.O. 4)

Match each of the following specific measurements with its benchmark category.

a. On-time delivery of materials	**1.** Employee performance
b. Percentage defective units	**2.** Product performance
c. Employee turnover	**3.** Supplier performance
d. Time to generate reports	**4.** Support performance

22.21 Benchmarks (L.O. 4)

Match each of the following specific measurements to its benchmark category.

a. On-time delivery to customer	**1.** Employee performance
b. Percentage defective raw materials	**2.** Product performance
c. Number of employee sick days	**3.** Supplier performance
d. Maintenance response time	**4.** Support performance

22.22 Performance Measures (L.O. 5)

Observe the operations of a retail clothing or sporting goods store. What is an important nonfinancial performance measure for it?

22.23 Manufacturing Cycle Time and Efficiency (L.O. 5)

A manufacturing company has the following average times (in hours):

Product transportation	2
Product production	6
Inspection	1
Inventory	24

Required		Calculate the manufacturing cycle efficiency.
22.24	Functional Measures (L.O. 5)	For each category of functional measures listed in Illustration 22.3, add one additional specific measurement that is not already listed.
22.25	Worker Involvement (L.O. 6)	List three measures of worker involvement and commitment in addition to those in Illustration 22.4. How would you use the information provided by the measures to improve worker involvement?
22.26	Manufacturing Cycle Time and Efficiency (L.O. 5)	A manufacturing company has the following average times (in days):

Product transportation	.5
Product production	2
Inspection	.25
Inventory	5

Required   Calculate the manufacturing cycle efficiency.

PROBLEMS

22.27	Benchmarks	Write a report to the CEO recommending specific benchmark measurements for General Motors' Saturn Division, which makes the Saturn automobile. Include specific competitors against which to measure.
22.28	Mission Statement	Write a report to the manager of a hospital indicating the factors that you believe should be included in its mission statement.
22.29	Performance Measures	Individually or in groups, interview the manager of any organization that has employees. Does the manager use nonfinancial performance measures to measure employee efficiency? If so, why did the manager choose those particular performance measures? If not, why did the manager choose not to use nonfinancial performance measures to measure employee efficiency?
22.30	Functional Measures	Write a report to the president of a bank recommending the use of functional measures of performance. Include specific examples of how they can be used to improve performance.
22.31	Performance Measures	Individually or in groups, interview the manager of a local retail store, for example one that sells sporting goods or clothing. Ask the manager what nonfinancial performance measures (such as measures of customer satisfaction) are used for the store? How is the measurement process done? By questionnaire? By measuring repeat business? By tracking complaints? Write a report to your instructor summarizing the results of your interview.
22.32	Operational Performance Measures	Seattle Co. manufactures a range of coffee makers. The controller prepares a weekly production efficiency report that is sent to corporate headquarters. The data compiled in these reports for a recent six-week period follow:

SEATTLE CO.
Production Efficiency Report
Week

	1	2	3	4	5	6
Percentage of manufacturing cycle efficiency	85	84	86	90	89	90
Percentage of on-time deliveries	94	95	99	100	96	99
Number of customer complaints	40	41	37	20	12	11

Required   **a.** Write a memo to the company president evaluating the plant's performance.

b. If you identify any areas of concern in your memo, indicate an appropriate action for management to take. Indicate any additional information you would like to have to make your evaluation.

| 22.33 | Operational Performance Measures | Kenston Corporation manufactures a range of wrought iron railings. Each month the controller prepares a production efficiency report, which is sent to corporate headquarters. The data compiled in these reports, for the first six months of the year, follow. |

KENSTON CORPORATION
Production Efficiency Report
January through June

	January	February	March	April	May	June
Percentage of orders filled and delivered on time	100	100	98	96	95	91
Number of defective units, in process	5	15	17	20	30	30
Number of customer complaints	–0–	1	–0–	3	5	8

Required

a. Write a memo to the company president evaluating the plant's performance.

b. If you identify any areas of concern in your memo, indicate an appropriate action for management to take. Indicate any additional information you would like to have to make your evaluation.

SOLUTIONS TO SELF-STUDY QUESTIONS

1. Stakeholders of a university's recreation center are groups or individuals who have a stake in what the recreation center does. This includes students, athletic teams, coaches, employees, special events committees, and the community as a whole.

2. Manufacturing cycle efficiency $= \dfrac{\text{Processing time}}{\text{Processing time + Moving time +}}$
$\text{Storing time + Inspection time}$

$= \dfrac{10}{10 + 5 + 7 + 3} = \underline{\underline{40\%}}$

CHAPTER

23

Capital Investment Decisions

LEARNING OBJECTIVES

After reading this chapter, you should be able to:

1. Recognize the strategic benefits of capital investments.

2. Explain the present value concept.

3. Compute the present value of cash flows.

4. Categorize cash flows and conduct net present value analysis.

5. Recognize the effects of inflation on cash flows and discount rate.

6. Conduct sensitivity analyses of capital investment decisions using spreadsheets.

7. Understand and compute a project's internal rate of return.

8. Understand difficulties in justifying investment in advanced production systems.

9. Know why audits are an important step in the capital investment process.

10. Conduct net present value analysis in nonprofit organizations.

11. Be sensitive to behavioral issues involved in capital budgeting.

12. Rank alternative projects with positive net present values (Appendix A).

13. Use alternative models to evaluate projects (Appendix A).

Capital investment decisions are very important because they commit companies to a particular course of action for years, sometimes for decades. General Motors' decision to invest in Saturn Company committed the company to the technology and concepts involved in making the Saturn for the foreseeable future. By deciding to expand outside of its home base in Arkansas, Wal-Mart made the commitment to change from a small, regional company to become a large, national company. When United Airlines purchased Hertz, it committed itself to be in the travelers' services business, not just the airline business. By investing in the Skoda automobile in the Czech Republic, Volkswagen AG made the commitment to become a major player in the eastern European automobile industry.

Capital investments often involve large sums of money and considerable risk. Specific investments over a certain dollar amount, often in the $100,000 to $500,000 range (or less for small companies), require approval by the board of directors in many companies. The investment should be both wise, economical, and consistent with the company's strategic plan. The investment by each of the companies listed in the previous paragraph was consistent with its long-term strategy for success.

Although the final decision about asset acquisition is the responsibility of management, accountants, economists, and other financial experts have developed capital investment models to help managers make those decisions. Accountants have the particularly important role of estimating the amount and timing of the cash flows used in capital investment decision models.

STRATEGIC CONSIDERATIONS

L.O. 1: Recognize the strategic benefits of capital investments.

The profits from or the expected cost savings offered by a capital asset are the most common benefits associated with acquiring capital assets, but the strategic benefits of capital assets are of increasing importance. Including the strategic benefits in capital budgeting is very controversial because they are as risky to include as they are difficult to estimate. However, strategic benefits are not likely to be any more difficult to estimate than the expected profits or cost savings.

Strategic benefits reflect the increased profit potential derived from some attribute of a capital asset. The following are some common strategic benefits that a capital asset may provide:

- Reducing the potential to make mistakes, thus improving the quality of the product (for instance, improving machine tolerances or reducing reliance on manual techniques).
- Making goods or delivering a service that competitors can't (for instance, developing a patented process to make a product that competitors can't replicate).
- Reducing the cycle time to make the product (for instance, making a custom designed product on the spot).

time value of money
The concept that cash received earlier is worth more than cash received later.

ANALYZING CASH FLOWS FOR PRESENT VALUE ANALYSIS

L.O. 2: Explain the present value concept.

net present value
The economic value of a project at a point in time.

Capital investment models are based on the future cash flows expected from a particular asset investment opportunity. The amount and timing of the cash flows from a capital investment project determine its economic value. The timing of those flows is important because cash received earlier in time has greater economic value than cash received later. As soon as cash is received, it can be reinvested in an alternative profit-making opportunity. Thus, any particular investment project has an opportunity cost for cash committed to it. Because the horizon of capital investment decisions extends over many years, the **time value of money** is often a significant decision factor for managers.

To recognize the time value of money, the future cash flows associated with a project are adjusted to their present value using a predetermined discount rate. Summing the discounted values of the future cash flows and subtracting the initial investment yields a project's **net present value (NPV),** which represents the economic value of the project to the company at a given point in time.

discount rate
An interest rate used to compute net present values.

The decision models used for capital investments attempt to optimize the economic value to the firm by maximizing the net present value of future cash flows. If the net present value of a project is positive, the project will earn a rate of return higher than its discount rate. The **discount rate** is the rate used to compute net present value.

Distinguishing between Revenues, Costs, and Cash Flows

A *timing difference* often exists between revenue recognition and cash inflow on the one hand and the incurrence of a cost and the related cash outflow on the other hand. When this occurs, it is important to *distinguish cash flows from revenues and costs.* Note that capital investment analysis often uses *cash flows, not revenues and costs.* For example, revenue from a sale often is recognized on one date but not collected until later. In such cases, the cash is not available for other investment or consumption purposes until it is collected.

NET PRESENT VALUE

present value
The amounts of future cash flows discounted to their equivalent worth today.

The **present value** of cash flows is the amount of future cash flows discounted to their equivalent worth today. The *net present value* of a project can be computed by using the equation:

$$NPV = \sum_{n=0}^{N} C_n \times (1 + d)^{-n}$$

where

C_n = Cash to be received or disbursed at the end of time period n
d = Appropriate discount rate for the future cash flows
n = Time period when the cash flow occurs
N = Life of the investment, in years

Use of the equation with a calculator or computer spreadsheet is the most efficient approach to computing net present values. Tables of present value factors are in Appendix C to this chapter and also may be used to find present values. We use the equation in many chapter illustrations, computations, and discussions, and we round all printed factors to three decimals. Therefore, if we want to discount $20,000, to be received in two years, at 10 percent, we find the value of $(1.10)^{-2}$ by a power function in the calculator. In the calculator, the result of this computation is .826446281, which, multiplied by $20,000, yields the present value of $16,529. We show such computations as follows:

$$\$20,000 \times (1 + .10)^{-2} = \$20,000 \times .826$$
$$= \underline{\underline{\$16,529}}$$

We abbreviate the present value factor because it is simply an intermediate result. If you use the abbreviated factor or the factors from the present value tables, your answer will differ due to rounding. This should not cause alarm. Capital investment decisions are yes or no decisions that are rarely (if ever) affected by rounding.

If you use the tables in Appendix C, on pages 731 and 732, simply look up the factor by referring to the appropriate year and discount rate. For a discount rate of 10 percent and a cash flow at the end of two years, Illustration 23.16 in Appendix C shows the present value factor to be .826.

Applying Present Value Analysis

L.O. 3: Compute the present value of cash flows.

Now let's look at how present value analysis is used for capital investment decisions. As an example, consider two projects. Each project requires an immediate cash outlay of $10,000. Project 1 will return $14,000 at the end of two years; Project 2 will return $14,000 at the end of three years. If the appropriate discount rate is 15 percent then the net present value of each project can be computed as follows:

ILLUSTRATION 23.1	Example of Net Present Value Calculations

Period	Net Cash Inflow or (Outflow)	PV Factor $(1 + d)^{-n}$ $d = 20$ Percent	Present Value[a]
0	$(80,000)	1.000	$(80,000)
1	(9,000)	.833	(7,500)
2	31,200	.694	21,667
3	14,800	.579	8,565
4	(42,100)	.482	(20,303)
5	76,800	.402	30,864
6	79,600	.335	26,658
7	74,500	.279	20,792
8	61,100	.233	14,210
9	43,600	.194	8,450
10	(39,700)	.162	(6,412)
Net present value			$ 16,991

[a]Cash flow times factor does not equal present value because factor is rounded to three places.

Project 1

Cash inflow	$14,000 \times (1 + .15)^{-2}$	
	= $14,000 \times .756	= $ 10,586
Cash outflow		= −10,000
Net present value		$ 586

Project 2

Cash inflow	$14,000 \times (1 + .15)^{-3}$	
	= $14,000 \times .658	= $ 9,205
Cash outflow		= −10,000
Net present value		$ (795)

The starting time for capital investment projects is assumed to be time 0. Therefore, any cash outlays required at the start of the project are not discounted. We enter them at their full amount.

At a discount rate of 15 percent, Project 1 is acceptable, but Project 2 is not. Project 1 will earn more than the required 15 percent return; while Project 2 will earn less.

You should check for yourself to see that at a 20 percent discount rate, the present value of both projects is negative. Therefore, if our required rate were 20 percent, neither project would meet the investment criterion. Alternatively, at 10 percent, both projects have positive net present values and would be acceptable.

Of course, the cash flows in most business investment opportunities are considerably more complex than our simplified examples, but the method for computing net present values remains the same.

Consider, for example, the cash flow pattern in Illustration 23.1. The cash flows can be either positive or negative in any year. This cash flow pattern is characteristic of a project that will begin with a pilot operation. If the pilot operation proves successful, full-scale facilities will be installed in year 4. Operations will continue until year 10, at which time costs will be incurred to dismantle the operation. Once the cash flows are determined, computation of the net present value is a mechanical operation. The critical problem for the accountant, however, is to estimate the amount and timing of the expected future cash flows.

CATEGORIES OF PROJECT CASH FLOWS

L.O. 4: Categorize cash flows and conduct net present value analysis.

This section of the chapter outlines a method for estimating cash flows for investment projects. This is an important part of the accountant's job in making investment decisions. We start by setting four major categories of cash flows for a project:

- Investment cash flows.
- Periodic operating cash flows.
- Cash flows from the depreciation tax shield.
- Disinvestment cash flows.

Each category of cash flows requires a separate treatment.

Investment Flows

There are three types of investment flows:

1. Asset acquisition, which includes
   a. New equipment costs, including installation (outflow).
   b. Proceeds of existing assets sold, net of taxes (inflow).
   c. Tax effects arising from a loss or gain (inflow or outflow).
2. Working capital commitments.
3. Investment tax credit.

Asset Acquisition

asset acquisition
Costs involved in purchasing and installing an asset may involve the disposal of old assets, resulting in a gain or a loss.

The company purchasing this asset should consider both the purchase price and the cost of installation in its asset acquisition cash flows. (© Tom McCarthy/Unicorn Stock Photos)

Asset acquisition involves both the cost of purchasing and installing new assets and the cash inflows that may result from the proceeds, net of taxes, of selling replaced equipment. Additionally, there may be a loss or gain to consider, arising from the difference between the sale proceeds and the tax basis of the equipment being replaced.

The primary outflow for most capital investments is the acquisition cost of the asset. Acquisition costs may be incurred in time 0 and in later years. In some cases, they are incurred over periods of 10 to 20 years. All acquisition costs are listed as cash outflows in the years in which they occur. Installation costs are also considered a cash outflow.

If the depreciation tax basis of the replaced equipment is not equal to the proceeds received from the sale of the replaced equipment, a gain or loss will occur and will affect the tax payment. The tax effect will be considered a cash inflow (for a loss) or a cash outflow (with a gain).

For example, Kwik Press, a publishing company, commissioned a team of business students to conduct a customer satisfaction survey. The results of the survey showed that the number one complaint by customers was the time it took Kwik Press to complete desktop publishing jobs. Kwik Press was working at capacity and losing customers to the local competition. Management decided to consider replacing slower machines with fast, state-of-the-art machines.

The new machines would cost $280,000 in two payments: $130,000 immediately (time 0) and $150,000 in year 1. The depreciation allowed for tax purposes would be $80,000 in years 1 and 2, and $40,000 in years 3 through 5. A 40 percent tax rate is used.

ILLUSTRATION 23.2	Projected Investment Flows, Kwik Press	
	Time 0	**Year 1**
Investment cash flows		
New equipment and installation	($130,000)	($150,000)
Proceeds, existing equipment	45,000	
Tax benefit from loss on equipment	3,000	
Working capital	(50,000)	
Total cash flows	($132,000)	($150,000)

Tax benefit from loss on existing equipment:
($52,500 tax basis − $45,000 salvage value) × 40% tax rate
= $7,500 loss for tax purposes × 40% tax rate
= $3,000 tax benefit from loss

The existing machines had been purchased several years ago. Their tax basis is $52,500, and they would have been depreciated for tax purposes at the rate of $26,250 in year 1 and $26,250 in year 2. The estimated current salvage value is $45,000, the estimated cash inflow from the sale of the existing machines. The difference between the tax basis of $52,500 and the salvage value of $45,000 results in a tax loss of $7,500. These cash flows for asset acquisition appear in Illustration 23.2.

Working Capital Commitments

working capital
Cash, accounts receivable, and other short-term assets required to maintain an activity.

In addition to the cash for purchase of long-term assets, many projects require additional funds for **working capital** needs; for example, a retail establishment needs to have cash available in a bank account because future cash payments often precede cash receipts. The working capital committed to the project normally remains constant over the life of the project, although it is sometimes increased because of inflation. Kwik Press plans to commit an additional $50,000 in working capital at time 0 to maintain a cash balance in a bank account to cover future cash transactions.

Outlays for working capital items are shown when those outflows occur. The projected investment cash flows of Kwik Press are summarized in Illustration 23.2.

investment tax credit
A reduction in federal income taxes arising from the purchase of certain assets.

Investment Tax Credit The **investment tax credit (ITC)** allows a credit against the federal income tax liability based on the cost of an acquired asset. This credit effectively reduces the cost of making investments by giving companies a credit against their corporate income taxes equal to, say, 10 percent of the purchase price. The investment tax credit has been in effect at various times since the early 1960s. Our examples in the text and in the exercises and problems will tell you whether to consider an investment tax credit.

For example, we assume that Kwik Press would not receive an investment tax credit under current tax laws. If they were to change to allow a 10 percent ITC, Kwik Press would receive a tax credit of $13,000 (.10 × $130,000) in year 1 and $15,000 (.10 × $150,000) in year 2. These amounts would be considered cash inflows in the present value analysis in each of years 1 and 2.

Periodic Operating Flows

The primary reason for acquiring long-term assets is usually to generate positive *periodic operating cash flows*. These positive flows may result from such *revenue-generating* activities as new products, or they may stem from *cost-saving* programs. In either case, actual cash inflows and outflows from operating the asset are usually determinable in a straightforward manner. The most important task is to identify and measure the cash flows that will differ because of the investment. *If the revenues and costs are differential cash items, they are relevant for the capital investment decision.*

ILLUSTRATION 23.3	Schedule of Project Revenues and Costs (Years 1–5), Kwik Press		

Differential Flows	Amount	Differential Cash Flow	Remarks
(1) Project revenues	$210,285	$210,285	All cash
(2) Direct materials and direct labor	(62,342)	(62,342)	All cash
Manufacturing overhead (3) through (7)			
(3) Indirect labor	(1,800)	(1,800)	All cash
(4) Supplies	(6,500)	(6,500)	All cash
(5) Allocated service department costs	(3,500)	(1,500)	2,000 is an allocation of costs that would not change with this decision
(6) Accounting depreciation	(70,000)	–0–	Depreciation is not a cash flow
(7) Other overhead	(6,076)	(6,076)	All cash
(8) Selling commissions	(1,985)	(1,985)	All cash
Administration (9) through (11)			
(9) Direct	(3,700)	(3,700)	All cash
(10) Indirect	(2,500)	–0–	Allocation of fixed costs
(11) Tax and insurance on equipment and inventory	(18,200)	(18,200)	All cash
Subtotals	$ 33,682	108,182	
(12) Income tax on differential cash flows		43,273	Based on analysis of tax regulations
Net operating cash flows for years 1–5		$64,909	

Periodic operating flows include the following:

- Period cash inflows (+) and outflows (−) before taxes.
- Income tax effects of inflows (−) and outflows (+).

Kwik Press has determined that the revenues and costs will differ because of the investment and should therefore be included as differential cash flow items. The differential revenues, net of taxes, would be cash inflows. The differential costs, net of taxes, would be considered cash outflows. The projected differential costs and revenues are presented in Illustration 23.3 and explained here.

The schedule in Illustration 23.3 has been divided into two columns to separate all accounting costs that will arise due to the project from the differential cash flows that would be considered for purposes of the present value analysis. The left column shows all costs that would be allocated to the project if the investment were made, including depreciation for financial accounting purposes and other costs, such as reallocated fixed costs that would be allocated to the new project. We show the two separate columns to emphasize that all periodic costs allocated to a project are not necessarily differential cash flows that would be considered in the analysis.

The operating revenues and costs that represent differential cash flows are included in the differential cash flow column. Costs that do not involve cash (depreciation, depletion, and amortization) are excluded from the differential cash flow column. (For example, see line [6] in Illustration 23.3.)

If cash costs in other departments change as a result of the project, those other department costs should be included in the differential cash flow schedule. For this reason, $1,500 of allocated service department costs are included in the differential cash flow column. For example, assume that $3,500 of service department costs (repairs and maintenance) would be allocated to this project if the investment is made; however, only $1,500 of that amount would actually increase *because* of the project. (That is, only $1,500 is a differential cost.) The remaining $2,000 ($3,500 − $1,500) is merely reallocated from other parts of the company. In this case, only the $1,500 would be shown as a *differential cash cost*. (See line [5] in Illustration 23.3.) Just because costs are allocated to a project does not mean that they are necessarily differential costs.

For another example of allocated costs that are not differential, note that indirect administrative costs of $2,500 have been allocated to the project but are not differential (line [10]). *Total indirect administrative costs* for the company are not affected in this example; they would just be allocated differently if the investment were made.

Financing costs such as interest costs on loans, principal repayments, and payments under financing leases are typically excluded under the assumption that the financing decision is separate from the asset-acquisition decision. Under this assumption, the decision to acquire the asset is made first. If the asset-acquisition decision is favorable, a decision will be made to select the best financing.

For analysis purposes, asset acquisitions typically are recorded in the full amount when the cash purchase payments are made, regardless of how that cash was acquired.

Tax Effects of Periodic Cash Flows

The income tax effects of the periodic cash flows from the project are also computed and considered in the present value analysis. (For this example, we assume that the marginal tax rate to be applied to these cash flows is 40 percent.) Note that for purposes of calculating the net present value, only the tax effects related to differential project cash flows are considered. We include in the present value analysis the *differential effect on our tax liability.*

The *income tax effect* of depreciation is different than the depreciation used for financial or internal reporting purposes, which is not considered a differential cash flow. Therefore, any reductions in tax payments arising from depreciation of these assets are considered differential cash flows and are treated separately.

The steps to compute the net operating cash flows for the project are repeated for each year in the project life. In some cases, the computations can be simplified by using an annuity factor if the project is expected to yield identical cash flows for more than one year.

Depreciation Tax Shield

tax shield
The reduction in tax payment because of depreciation deducted for tax purposes.

To measure the income of an organization or one of its subunits, depreciation is used to allocate the cost of long-term assets over their useful lives. These depreciation charges are not cash costs and thus do not directly affect the net present values of capital investments. However, tax regulations permit depreciation write-offs that reduce the required tax payment. The reduction in the tax payment is referred to as a **tax shield.** *The depreciation deduction computed for this tax shield is not necessarily the same amount as the depreciation computed for financial reporting purposes.* The predominant depreciation method for financial reporting has been the *straight-line method.* With this method, the cost of the asset, less any salvage value, is allocated equally to each year of the expected life of the asset. Income tax regulations allow faster depreciation write-offs.

The tax allowance for depreciation is one of the primary incentives used by tax policy makers to promote investment in long-term assets. The faster an asset's cost can be written off for tax purposes, the sooner the tax reductions are realized and, hence, the greater the net present value of the tax shield. In recent years, tax depreciation has been accelerated to allow write-offs over very short time periods regardless of an asset's expected life. To maximize present value, it is usually best to claim depreciation as rapidly as possible.

The depreciation tax shield has two effects:

* Depreciation tax shield on acquired assets.
* Forgone depreciation tax shield on disposed assets.

Consider the tax depreciation schedule of the new machines that Kwik Press is considering. They have a depreciation tax basis of $280,000 over five years. The annual depreciation tax shield and the present value of the tax shield are computed in columns 2–5 in Illustration 23.4 using the 40 percent tax rate and a 15 percent discount rate. (All amounts given in this text are for illustrative purposes only. They do not necessarily reflect the amount of depreciation allowed by the tax regulations, which varies by type of asset and often changes as Congress passes new "tax reforms.") Salvage value has been assumed to be zero for depreciation purposes. Present value factors appear in Appendix C.

Kwik Press also forgoes depreciation of $26,250 in each of years 1 and 2. Why? Because by buying new assets it will dispose of old assets having a depreciable tax base. The forgone depreciation and the forgone tax shield of $10,500 each year, assuming a 40 percent tax rate, appear in Illustration 23.5. The amounts in column 3 of Illustration 23.4 and column 3 of Illustration 23.5 then are transferred to the cash flow schedule, as shown later in Illustration 23.6.

To review the basic relationships, a portion of the $280,000 is deducted each year on the tax return as shown in column 2 of Illustration 23.4. The tax shield in column 3 is the tax rate times the depreciation deduction. This is the cash flow resulting from a reduction in the annual tax liability, which the tax shield generates.

Disinvestment Flows

The end of a project's life usually results in some or all of the following cash flows:

* Cash freed from working capital commitments (now as cash inflow).
* Salvage of the long-term assets (usually a cash inflow unless there are disposal costs).
* Tax consequences for differences between salvage proceeds and the remaining depreciation tax basis of the asset.
* Other cash flows, such as employee severance payments and restoration costs.

disinvestment flows
Cash flows that take place at the termination of a capital project.

The cash flows at the end of the life of the project are referred to as **disinvestment flows.**

Return of Working Capital

When a project ends, some inventory, cash, and other working capital items that were used to support operations are usually left over. These working capital items are then freed for use elsewhere or are liquidated for cash. Therefore, at the end of a project's life, the return of these working capital items is shown as a cash inflow. In the Kwik Press example, it will have $50,000 in working capital available for other uses, which is the money it put in the bank to facilitate cash transactions.

It is important not to double count these items. Suppose that cash collected from a customer was already recorded as a cash inflow to the company, but it was left in the project's bank account until the end of the project's life. It should not be counted again as a cash inflow at the project's end.

The return of working capital is recorded as an inflow when it is freed for use in other organizational activities. If that does not occur until the end of the project's life, the cash inflow is included as part of disinvestment flows.

Salvage of Long-Term Assets

Ending a project usually requires the disposal of its assets. These are usually sold in secondhand markets. In some cases, more money is spent in disassembling the assets and disposing of them than is gained from their sale. Any net outflows from disposal

ILLUSTRATION 23.4		Present Value of Depreciation Tax Shield—Kwik Press		

Tax rate: 40%		Depreciation basis: $280,000		
(1)	(2)	(3)	(4)	(5)
Year	Depreciation Deducted on the Tax Return	Tax Shield (40% × Depreciation Deduction)	PV Factor (15%)[a]	Present Value (Tax Shield × PV Factor)[a]
1	$ 80,000	$ 32,000	.870	$27,826
2	80,000	32,000	.756	24,197
3	40,000	16,000	.658	10,520
4	40,000	16,000	.572	9,148
5	40,000	16,000	.497	7,955
Totals	$280,000	$112,000		$79,646

[a]PV factor is rounded to three places. The present value amounts in column (5) are derived from unrounded PV computations.

ILLUSTRATION 23.5		Forgone Depreciation Tax Shield—Kwik Press

Tax rate: 40%	Depreciation basis: $52,500	
(1)	(2)	(3)
Year	Forgone Depreciation	Forgone Tax Shield (40% × Column 2)
1	$26,250	$10,500
2	26,250	10,500
Totals	$52,500	$21,000

tax basis
Remaining tax-depreciable "book value" of an asset for tax purposes.

of a project's assets become tax deductions in the year of disposal. The *net salvage value* (sometimes negative) of an asset is listed as a cash inflow or outflow at the time it is expected to be realized (or incurred), regardless of its book value or **tax basis.** The difference between the book value (tax basis) and the net salvage value may result in a taxable gain or loss.

For an asset replacement decision, the forgone salvage value (and related tax effects) from the old asset must also be considered. For example, assume "asset new" replaced "asset old" for the next five years. Asset old could be sold for $2,000 at the end of five years; asset new could be sold for $10,000 at the end of five years. If asset new replaces asset old, the $8,000 incremental salvage should be the disinvestment cash flow for the analysis. Any additional taxes paid (or tax payments reduced), because we are salvaging asset new instead of asset old, should be included in the analysis.

Tax Consequences of Disposal

Any difference between the tax basis of a project's assets (generally, the undepreciated balance) and the amount realized from project disposal results in a tax gain or loss. Therefore, a company's tax liability is affected in the year of disposal. Tax laws on asset dispositions are complex, so tax advice should be sought well in advance of the proposed disposal date. In this chapter, we assume that any gains or losses on disposal are treated as ordinary taxable income or losses.

Suppose that an asset is carried in the financial accounting records at a net book value of $80,000 and is salvaged for $30,000 cash. The tax basis of the asset is

$10,000, and the tax rate is 40 percent. What are the cash flows from disposal of this asset?

First, the company receives the $30,000 as a cash inflow. Second, it reports a $20,000 taxable gain, which is the difference between the $30,000 cash inflow and the $10,000 tax basis. This $20,000 gain is taxed at 40 percent, resulting in an $8,000 cash outflow. The net-of-tax cash inflow on disposal is $22,000, the net of the $30,000 inflow and the $8,000 cash outflow, as shown:

Cash inflow	$30,000
Tax payment	
($30,000 cash inflow − $10,000 tax basis)	
× 40% tax rate	(8,000)
Net-of-tax cash inflow	$22,000

Consider the tax consequences of Kwik Press's new machines upon disposal in year 5. They will have a remaining net book value in the accounting records of $70,000, which is irrelevant for the present value analysis. The assets will have been fully depreciated for tax purposes and are salvaged for $105,000 cash. (Assume that the old assets would have no salvage value in year 5, so all of the salvage value of the new machines is incremental.) The tax rate is 40 percent. What are the cash flows from disposal of this asset?

First, the company receives the $105,000 as a cash inflow. They report a taxable gain of $105,000 because the asset is fully depreciated for tax purposes. This $105,000 gain is taxed at 40 percent, resulting in a cash outflow of $42,000, which is Kwik Press's additional tax liability arising from the gain. The net cash inflow on disposal of the machines is $63,000, which equals $105,000 from the sale minus 40 percent times the $105,000 gain, or $105,000 − $42,000.

Other Disinvestment Flows

The end of project operations may result in a number of costs not directly related to the sale of assets. It may be necessary to make severance payments to employees. Sometimes payments are required to restore the project area to its original condition. Some projects may incur regulatory costs when they are closed down. A cost analyst must inquire about the consequences of disposal to determine the costs that should be included in the disinvestment flows for a project.

PREPARING THE NET PRESENT VALUE ANALYSIS

Once the cash flow data have been gathered, they are assembled into a schedule that shows the cash flows for each year of the project's life. These flows may be classified into the four categories we just discussed:

- Investment flows.
- Periodic operating flows.
- Depreciation tax shield.
- Disinvestment flows.

A summary schedule that shows the total of the annual cash flows and the net present value of the project is prepared. This summary may be supported by as much detail as management deems necessary for making the investment decision.

For example, consider the data collected thus far and summarized in Illustration 23.6 for the investment proposal for Kwik Press. The project is expected to earn more than the 15 percent used to discount the cash flows because the net present value of the project is higher than zero. (If the net present value of the project had been less than zero, the project would have been expected to earn less than the 15 percent used to discount the cash flows.)

Depreciation is deducted for tax purposes as follows: year 1, $80,000; year 2, $80,000; and $40,000 per year in each of years 3 through 5. Project costs include

| ILLUSTRATION 23.6 | Cash Flow Schedule with Present Value Computations, Kwik Press | | | | | |

| | Time | Year | | | | |
	0	1	2	3	4	5
Investment flows						
Equipment cost and installation.........	($130,000)	($150,000)				
Proceeds of assets sold, net of tax	45,000					
Tax benefit on loss[a]	3,000					
Working capital..................	(50,000)					
Periodic operating flows, net of tax[b]		64,909	$64,909	$64,909	$64,909	$ 64,909
Depreciation tax shield						
Tax shield from depreciation[c]..........		32,000	32,000	16,000	16,000	16,000
Forgone tax shield[d]		(10,500)	(10,500)			
Disinvestment flows						
Return of working capital						50,000
Proceeds on disposal						105,000
Tax on gain[e]						(42,000)
Total cash flows	($132,000)	($ 63,591)	$86,409	$80,909	$80,909	$193,909
PV factor at 15%	1.000	.870	.756	.658	.572	.497
Present values[f].................	($132,000)	($ 55,296)	$65,338	$53,199	$46,260	$ 96,407
Net present value of project	$ 73,908					

Computations:

[a]$3,000 = ($52,500 − $45,000) × 40%.

[b]Net operating cash flow (after tax)

Revenues.....................		$210,285
Differential cash outflows		
Direct materials and direct labor	($62,342)	
Taxes and insurance on equipment and inventory	(18,200)	
Manufacturing overhead	(15,876)	
Selling commission	(1,985)	
Direct administrative costs	(3,700)	(102,103)
Revenues net of differential cash costs (before tax)		108,182
Income taxes on differential net cash flows (40%)		43,273
Differential cash flows (after taxes)		$ 64,909

[c]Depreciation computations:

Year	Depreciation	Tax Shield (at 40%)
1	$ 80,000	$ 32,000
2	80,000	32,000
3	40,000	16,000
4	40,000	16,000
5	40,000	16,000
Totals	$280,000	$112,000

[d]Forgone depreciation:

Year	Forgone Depreciation	Forgone Tax Shield
1	$26,250	$10,500
2	26,250	10,500

[e]Gain is equal to salvage since the asset is fully depreciated for tax purposes. The tax is 40 percent of the gain, or 40% × $105,000 = $42,000.

[f]PV factor shown is rounded to three places. Present values are derived from unrounded PV computations. Present value factors are shown in Appendix C of this chapter.

the equipment outlays in time 0 and year 1. The working capital requirements are shown as outflows in time 0.

Annual cash flows are computed using the schedule of revenues and costs shown under computations in Illustration 23.6 and adjusted for the costs that are not differential (allocated service department costs and allocated administrative costs) or that are not cash costs (depreciation). The annual before-tax net cash inflow of $108,182 then is reduced by the tax liability expected to arise from taxing this inflow at the 40 percent marginal tax rate. The after-tax cash inflow of $64,909 is shown for each year of the project's life.

In the last year of the project, the disinvestment flows are given. These include the return of working capital and the proceeds from disposal of the asset. In addition, the tax consequences from selling the equipment for more than the zero tax basis are considered, and the related $42,000 tax liability is included in the cash flow computations.

The net present value of the project is computed as the sum of the present values of each year's cash flow. The positive net present value of $73,908 indicates that the project is expected to earn more than the 15 percent used to discount the cash flows.

The schedule in Illustration 23.6 indicates the net cash flows in each year, thus assisting management in preparing its cash budgets for the life of the project. The net present value of each year's cash flow is presented for computational purposes; it may not be required for management.

SELF-STUDY QUESTION

1. Melwood Corporation is considering the purchase of a new computer to further automate its accounting system. Management has been considering several alternative systems including a model P-25. The P-25's supplier has submitted a quote to the company of $7,500 for the equipment plus $8,400 for software. Assume that the equipment can be depreciated for tax purposes over three years as follows: year 1, $2,500; year 2, $2,500; year 3, $2,500. The software may be written off immediately for tax purposes. The company expects to use the new machine for four years and to use straight-line depreciation for financial reporting purposes. The market for used computer systems is such that Melwood would realize $1,000 for the equipment at the end of four years. The software would have no salvage value at that time.

Melwood management believes that introduction of the computer system will enable the company to dispose of its existing accounting equipment. The existing equipment is fully depreciated for tax purposes. It can be sold for an estimated $100 but would have no salvage value in four years. If Melwood does not buy the new computer system, it would continue to use the old accounting equipment for four years.

Management believes that it will realize improvements in operations and benefits from the computer system worth $8,000 per year before taxes.

Melwood uses a 15 percent discount rate for this investment and has a marginal income tax rate of 45 percent after considering both state and federal taxes.

a. Prepare a schedule showing the relevant cash flows for the project.

b. Indicate whether the equipment purchase meets Melwood's discount rate.

The solution to this question is at the end of this chapter on page 741.

---

nominal dollars
Actual numerical count of money exchanged.

RECOGNIZING THE EFFECTS OF INFLATION ON CAPITAL INVESTMENT DECISIONS

When prices and costs are expected to change significantly over a project's life, it is important to consider the effects of those changes on project cash flows. In many cases, the cash flows will not change uniformly over the life of the project. Therefore, a careful analysis of each cost item may be necessary. Cash flows that will be received in the future will have a different real value from dollars received today due to changes in the purchasing power of those dollars. The actual dollars to be received are called **nominal dollars.**

The schedule of project cash flows can be adjusted to consider the nominal cash flows. The resulting nominal net cash flows are then discounted at a rate that recognizes inflation, the **nominal discount rate.** These adjustments compensate the company for the effects of inflation as well as for a return on capital.

L.O. 5: Recognize the effects of inflation on cash flows and discount rate.

nominal discount rate
A rate of interest that includes compensation for inflation.

Adjusting the Discount Rate

It is commonly accepted that the interest rate that the market demands includes elements of a return on capital as well as an adjustment for the effects of inflation. The discounting equation can be expanded to include the inflation element as a specific component:

$$[(1 + r)(1 + i)]^{-n}$$

where

r = Real return on capital required from now to period n
i = Expected inflation rate between now and period n
n = Number of the period in the future when the cash is to be received

The **real return** is the return on capital after adjustment for the effects of inflation. This equation may be used with a constant value of i, or the value of i may be changed from one period to the next. In general, though, a constant inflation rate is assumed.

The terms within the brackets may be multiplied before the exponentation operation. Subtracting 1 from the result of this multiplication gives the nominal discount rate for the project:

$$\text{Nominal rate} = (1 + r)(1 + i) - 1$$

In practice, the nominal discount rate implicitly considers the need to compensate for inflation.

For example, a company has concluded that its projects should earn a real return of 15 percent and that the expected inflation rate over the project's life will be 6 percent per year. To find the nominal discount rate, d, for present value, the following calculation is performed:

$$(1 + r)(1 + i) - 1 = (1.15)(1.06) - 1$$
$$= .219, \text{ or } 21.9\%$$

Management will discount the future cash flows using a 21.9 percent rate in the discounting equation:

$$(1 + d)^{-n} = (1.219)^{-n}$$

Adjusting Future Cash Flows

The effects of inflation may be considered in the same four categories as the cash flows for capital investment projects. When considering inflation, the future cash flows also are adjusted for inflation by the factor $(1 + i)^n$.

Investment Outflows

Cash requirements for the initial investment may need to be adjusted if costs are likely to change over the investment period. This is particularly common with projects that require several years to construct.

Working capital requirements often increase with the increased volume of nominal dollars. That is, more dollars are required to support the same level of activity. The investment in inventory generally will not change. The initial costs were incurred to procure a given amount of inventory. Inventory may cost more to replace, but the replacement costs are included in period cash outflows.

For initial investment outlays, then, the inflation adjustment simply requires revising any outlays expected to change as a result of increasing costs. Any increases in working capital levels (other than inventory) are scheduled when they are required.

For example, consider the cash flows for Kwik Press in Illustration 23.6 which ignore the effects of inflation. Now let's consider the impact of inflation on these flows. Suppose that the equipment costs that were originally $130,000 in time 0 and $150,000 in year 1 are not expected to increase with inflation. The $50,000 in working capital requirements must increase with the rate of inflation. How will an inflation rate of 6 percent per year affect the investment cash outflows? The answer is determined as follows:

1. Equipment cost: The time 0 cost of $130,000 is unaffected. The year 1 cost of $150,000 is not changed in this example but could increase with inflation in other cases.
2. The initial cash outflow for working capital remains $50,000 in time 0. However, in year 1, working capital must be increased to $53,000 to keep up with the effects of inflation on nominal dollars ($50,000 $\times$ 1.06). Therefore, in year 1 there will be an additional $3,000 cash outflow to working capital to account for inflation.

In year 2, an additional $3,180 will be added to working capital to bring the balance to $56,180 (= $53,000 $\times$ 1.06). In year 3, working capital will need to be increased by an additional $3,371; and in year 4, the increase will be $3,573, for a total balance of $63,124. There is no increase in year 5 because that is the end of the project's life, and the working capital for noninventory items is returned at that time.

Periodic Operating Flows

The operating cash flows for each year are adjusted by multiplying the original amounts by $(1 + i)^N$. This restates the original cash inflow to the nominal dollar amount to be received in year n. In this case, the adjusted amounts are $64,909 $\times$ 1.06 = $68,804 for year 1; $64,909 $\times$ $(1.06)^2$ = $72,932 for year 2, and so forth. (We assume that year 1 operating flows increase by 6 percent over time 0.)

These net nominal cash flows are entered into the appropriate columns of the cash flow schedule in Illustration 23.7 in place of the original unadjusted cash flows.

Tax Shield

Depreciation is based on an asset's original cost. Hence, the tax shield from depreciation changes only if the original investment costs change. Under inflation, the real value of the tax shield from depreciation declines relative to the other cash flows from the project. Note that the discount rate recognizes inflation, but the tax shield does not increase with inflation. Consequently, the higher the inflation rate, the lower the net present value of the depreciation tax shield.

Disinvestment Flows

Under conditions of inflation, disinvestment flows become more complex. The return of working capital includes all nominal cash and accounts receivable committed to the project. Therefore, the periodic cash outflows for working capital are summed and the total listed as a recovery at the end of the project's life.

| ILLUSTRATION 23.7 | Cash Flow Schedule Adjusted for Inflation with Present Value Computations | | | | | |

| | Time | Year | | | | |
	0	1	2	3	4	5
Investment outflows						
Equipment cost........................	($130,000)	($150,000)				
Proceeds of assets sold, net of tax	45,000					
Tax benefit on loss.....................	3,000					
Working capital......................	(50,000)	(3,000)	($ 3,180)	($ 3,371)	($ 3,573)	
Periodic operating flows, net of tax[a]		68,804	72,932	77,308	81,946	$ 86,863
Depreciation tax shield						
Tax shield from depreciation		32,000	32,000	16,000	16,000	16,000
Forgone tax shield....................		(10,500)	(10,500)			
Disinvestment flows						
Return of working capital[b]................						63,124
Proceeds on disposal..................						147,268
Tax on gain						(58,907)
Total cash flows........................	($132,000)	($ 62,696)	$91,252	$89,937	$94,373	$254,348
PV factor at 21.9%	1.000	.820	.673	.552	.453	.372
Present values[c]	($132,000)	($ 51,432)	$61,409	$49,651	$42,740	$ 94,495
Net present value of project	$ 64,863					

Nominal rate = $1.15 \times 1.06 - 1 = .219 = 21.9\%$

[a]Operating cash flows = $64,909 (1.06)^n$. $n = 1, \ldots, 5$.

[b]$63,124 = Sum of cash released from working capital requirements = $50,000 + $3,000 + $3,180 + $3,371 + $3,573.

[c]Cash flow times PV factor does not equal present values because PV factors are rounded.

The working capital returned in year 5 includes the $50,000 initial outlay plus the outlays in years 1 through 4 for a total return of $63,124 ($50,000 + $3,000 + $3,180 + $3,371 + $3,573).

The proceeds from disposal of the long-term assets and their tax impact also are included in the disinvestment computation. Any difference between the proceeds on disposal as adjusted for inflation and the tax basis of the property is taxed.

For Kwik Press, we assume that the market for used equipment similar to that used in the project is increasing at the rate of 7 percent per year. As a result, the proceeds from disposal are estimated as follows:

$$\$105,000 \times (1.07)^5 = \underline{\$147,268}$$

Because the asset has been fully depreciated for tax purposes, this entire amount is a gain, taxable at ordinary rates. The tax liability from the gain is

$$40\% \times \$147,268 = \underline{\$58,907}$$

This amount is shown as an outflow in year 5.

Summarizing the Cash Flows

The adjusted cash flows for Kwik Press under inflation are summarized in the cash flow schedule in Illustration 23.7, as they were in Illustration 23.6 with no inflation considered. That is, all cash flows are scheduled and summed for each year of the project's life. In this case, however, yearly cash flows represent the amounts expected to be realized under certain inflation conditions.

The cash flows for the project are discounted using the 21.9 percent rate computed earlier, and the present values are shown for each year of the project's life. The net present value of the project is then computed. For this project, the net present value is $64,863.

SENSITIVITY OF NET PRESENT VALUE TO ESTIMATES

The calculation of the net present value of a proposed project requires three types of projections or estimates:

- The amount of future cash flows.
- The timing of future cash flows.
- The discount rate.

Some error in the amount predicted or estimated for each of these three items is likely. The net present value model exhibits different degrees of sensitivity to such errors. Errors in predicting the amounts of future cash flows will likely have the largest impact of the three items.

The degree of sensitivity of the net present value model to shifts in the pattern of cash flows, but not in the total amount, depends on the extent of the shifting. However, the shifts tend not to be as serious as errors in predicting the amount of cash flows.

The difficulty in estimating returns to alternative uses of capital causes uncertainty in the discount rate used to determine net present value. Financial economists have not yet developed foolproof techniques for empirically verifying a firm's estimate of its cost of capital rate. Small errors in estimating the cost of capital generally will not change the outcome of accepting or rejecting a project based on its net present value.

SELF-STUDY QUESTION

2. Refer to the data in Self-Study Question 1. Inflation has affected cash flows as follows: Operating cash flows are the same as for time 0 and year 1. Operating cash flows increase 10 percent in year 2 over the year 1 level, and another 10 percent in year 3 over the year 2 level, and another 10 percent in year 4. The salvage value of the new equipment increases to $1,330 at the end of year 4. All other facts about cash flows and taxes remain the same. Assume a discount rate of 26.5 percent for this question.

   a. Prepare a schedule showing the relevant cash flows for the project.

   b. Indicate whether the equipment purchase meets Melwood's discount rate.

The solution to this question is at the end of this chapter on page 742.

USING SPREADSHEETS FOR SENSITIVITY ANALYSIS

L.O. 6: Conduct sensitivity analyses of capital investment decisions using spreadsheets.

sensitivity analysis
The study of the effect of changes in assumptions on the results of a decision model.

Personal computer spreadsheet programs, such as Lotus 1-2-3® and Microsoft Excel®, have become the preferred tool for analysts carrying out discounted cash flow (DCF) computations. A useful feature of the spreadsheet programs is that they help the user see the effect on the net present value of changes in assumptions and estimates. Thoughtful design of a computer spreadsheet enables the user to change assumptions (such as for growth rates in sales, tax rates, discount rates) with a few key strokes. The net present value changes in only a few seconds as the assumptions change. This method is the best way to study the sensitivity of DCF analyses to assumptions.

For instance, Illustration 23.8 presents a sensitivity analysis spreadsheet in Lotus 1-2-3® for a basic example of an asset acquisition. Royal Realty is considering leasing a building for five years that it will sublet to small professional businesses, such as architects, lawyers, and therapists. Panel A presents the *basic case* on which we will perform a **sensitivity analysis.**

Panel B shows the *cell formulas* to set up the spreadsheet. Row labels are shown in column A. Column B shows the discount rate and year 0 data including the asset

ILLUSTRATION 23.8	Royal Realty Sensitivity Analysis

Panel A—Basic Case
Discount Rate: 20%

Year #	0	1	2	3	4	5
Asset Acquisition	($125,000)					
Rents		$120,000	$80,000	$60,000	$50,000	$40,000
Expenditures		(70,000)	(40,000)	(30,000)	(25,000)	(25,000)
Net Cash Inflow (Outflow)	($125,000)	$50,000	$40,000	$30,000	$25,000	$15,000
Net Present Value	($ 20,110)					

Panel B—Cell Formulas

	A	B	C	
1				
2	Discount Rate	20%		
3				
4	Year	0	1	
5				
6	Asset Acquisition	−125000		
7	Rents		120000	
8	Expenditures		−70000	
9				
10	Net cash			
11	Inflow (Outflow)	@SUM(B6 . . B8)	@SUM(C6 . . C8)	
12				
13	Net Present Value	@NPV(B2,C11 . . G11) + B11		
14				

Panel C—Change in Amounts of Cash Flows
Discount Rate: 20%

Year #	0	1	2	3	4	5
Asset Acquisition	($125,000)					
Rents		$118,000	$79,000	$59,000	$49,000	$39,000
Expenditures		(70,000)	(40,000)	(30,000)	(25,000)	(25,000)
Net Cash Inflow (Outflow)	($125,000)	$48,000	$39,000	$29,000	$24,000	$14,000
Net Present Value	($ 23,934)					

(continued)

acquisition for $125,000 (cell B6) and a summation of cash flows for the year (cell B11). Column B also shows the net present value of cash flows for all five years (cell B13). The formula in cell B13 uses the discount rate entered in cell B2 to discount the future cash flows of periods 1 through 5 to the present value period zero and then adds the present value of the period zero cash flow. Column C shows the data for year 1.

We do not show columns D through G, corresponding to years 2 through 5, to save space. However, the formulas in columns D through G are the same as for Column C. It is also important to note that the lines appearing in rows 5, 9, and 14 are used to separate data from the headings and calculations (and to show totals), and are not essential for the analysis.

ILLUSTRATION 23.8 *(concluded)*	Royal Realty Sensitivity Analysis					

Panel D—Change in Timing of Cash Flows
Discount Rate: 20%

Year #	0	1	2	3	4	5
Asset Acquisition	($125,000)					
Rents		$115,000	$75,000	$63,000	$55,000	$42,000
Expenditures		(70,000)	(40,000)	(30,000)	(25,000)	(25,000)
Net Cash Inflow (Outflow)	($125,000)	$45,000	$35,000	$33,000	$30,000	$17,000
Net Present Value	($ 22,798)					

Panel E—Change in Discount Rate
Discount Rate: 21%

Year #	0	1	2	3	4	5
Asset Acquisition	($125,000)					
Rents		$120,000	$80,000	$60,000	$50,000	$40,000
Expenditures		(70,000)	(40,000)	(30,000)	(25,000)	(25,000)
Net Cash Inflow (Outflow)	($125,000)	$50,000	$40,000	$30,000	$25,000	$15,000
Net Present Value	($ 21,977)					

Sensitivity to Amount of Cash Flows

Panel C shows the impact of changing the *amount* of cash flows. Forecasting cash flows accurately is critical in a cash flow analysis because the net present value is very sensitive to the amount of cash flows, as shown in Panel C. Lowering the cash flows by a total $6,000 over periods 1 through 5 lowers the net present value by $3,824 (= $20,110 − $23,934).

Sensitivity to Timing of Cash Flows

Panel D shows the impact of changing the *timing* of cash flows. The total net cash flow is the same, $35,000 in both cases, but moving cash inflows to later periods reduces the net present value of the project. The net present value drops by $2,688 ($20,110 − $22,798) simply because the cash inflows come later in the project.

Sensitivity to Change in Discount Rate

Panel E presents the impact of changing the *discount rate*. Assume that a manager at Royal Realty thinks a slightly higher discount rate would be appropriate. Raising the discount rate by 1 percent lowers the net present value only by $1,867 (= $20,110 − $21,977).

INTERNAL RATE OF RETURN

L.O. 7: Understand and compute a project's internal rate of return.

internal rate of return (IRR)
The interest rate that equates the present value of inflows and outflows from an investment project.

The **internal rate of return (IRR)** is the rate of interest that a project is expected to earn over its life. If the internal rate of return (also known as the *time-adjusted rate of return*) were used as the cost of capital for discounting project cash flows, the net present value of the project would equal zero. Thus, the IRR is that rate that makes the present value of project cash outflows equal to the present value of project cash inflows. This contrasts with the net present value method, which employs a predetermined discount rate.

The calculation of the internal rate of return can be done with many calculators or with the use of a spreadsheet. Illustration 23.9 presents the calculation using a spreadsheet in Lotus 1-2-3® for the Royal Realty example. The procedure is to insert cash flows and to use the IRR function. The footnote of Illustration 23.9 gives the formula for the calculation whose starting point at .10 is a "best guess" for the computer to search for the right answer. The internal rate of return for the example

ILLUSTRATION 23.9	Royal Realty: Internal Rate of Return						
	A	**B**	**C**	**D**	**E**	**F**	**G**
1							
2	Year #	0	1	2	3	4	5
3	Asset Acquisition	($125,000)					
4	Rents		$120,000	$80,000	$60,000	$50,000	$40,000
5	Expenditures		(70,000)	(40,000)	(30,000)	(25,000)	(25,000)
6							
7	Net Cash						
8	Inflow (Outflow)	($125,000)	$50,000	$40,000	$30,000	$25,000	$15,000
9							
10	Internal Rate						
11	of Return[a]	10.93%					

[a]Internal Rate of Return   @IRR(0.10,B8..G8)

is 10.93 percent, or at a discount rate of 10.93 percent, the net present value equals zero.

Internal Rate of Return with Constant Cash Flows

When the cash flows from a project are constant, it is possible to use the tables for present value of an annuity (Appendix C, page 732) to find the approximate rate of return. Dividing the required investment by the annual net cash flow gives the factor for a project with a life equal to that of the project and an interest rate equal to the internal rate of return. All we need do is look across the row for number of periods until we come to the factor closest to our computed factor. The interest rate for the column of the table related to that factor is the approximate internal rate of return.

For a project requiring a cash outflow of $170,000 in time 0 and receiving cash inflows of $60,000 in years 1 through 7, the factor follows:

$$\frac{\text{Annual net cash flow}}{\text{Required investment}} = \frac{\$170,000}{\$60,000} = 2.83$$

which, for a seven-year project, is closest to the factor 2.802 in the column headed by an interest rate of 30 percent. Therefore, we estimate the IRR on this project to be 30 percent.

Some Questions about IRR

Although the internal rate of return is widely used for project evaluations, it is sometimes considered inferior to net present value. Its primary disadvantage is its built-in assumption that net cash inflows are reinvested at the project's internal rate of return. By contrast, the net present value method assumes that the net cash inflows are invested at the cost of capital rate. If funds are reinvested at the cost of capital, the IRR method makes a project whose rate of return is higher than the cost of capital appear more attractive than a similar project using the net present value approach.

In some cases, the differences between the assumptions in the IRR method and the present value method result in differences in the rankings of projects using each method. The present value index ranking may differ from the IRR ranking. The choice that management makes in such a situation depends on management's objectives and evaluation of the assumptions underlying the two methods.

JUSTIFICATION OF INVESTMENTS IN ADVANCED PRODUCTION SYSTEMS

L.O. 8: Understand difficulties in justifying investment in advanced production systems.

Although many investments project a negative net present value in discounted cash flow analyses, managers often believe that such an investment is justified. The conflict between managerial judgment and the discounted cash flow model occurs because of the difficulties of applying discounted cash flow analysis to investments in advanced manufacturing systems. Some of these difficulties are as follows:

1. *Discount rate is too high.* Sometimes managers set discount rates that are too high in an advanced technology investment analysis. The appropriate discount rate for any investment decision is the cost of capital adjusted for risk. Because of uncertainty about advanced manufacturing methods, managers may overstate this risk and, therefore, the discount rate. In particular, uncertainty about cash flows because of the complexity of the machinery and inexperience with such advanced technology.

2. *Time horizons that are too short.* The acquisition cost of an advanced technology system can be enormous, and the benefits can be realized over a lengthy period of time. If the discounted cash flow analysis doesn't include the benefits in later years, it is incomplete and may lead to an incorrect rejection decision.

3. *Bias toward incremental projects.* Many firms require large investments to be authorized by managers at higher levels than are required for smaller investments. One result is an incentive for lower-level managers to request smaller, incremental projects to improve the manufacturing process rather than a large, comprehensive project. For example, if the investment limit for a plant manager is $50,000, the manager may institute a series of $45,000 improvements instead of requesting one investment in a million dollar advanced technology manufacturing system. A series of small incremental improvements may not have the same improving effect that could be gained with a full commitment to advanced manufacturing technology.

4. *Exclusion of benefits that are difficult to quantify.* Many significant benefits are difficult to quantify. Some of these benefits are the following:

- *Greater flexibility in the production process.* Flexible manufacturing can produce batches of several distinct products in the same day. Engineering changes can be made more easily as products are adapted to changing customer preferences.
- *Shorter cycle times and reduced lead times.*
- *Reduction of nonvalue-added costs.* These systems encourage employees to seek out activities that can be made more efficient or eliminated.

Because these benefits are difficult to quantify, they often are excluded from the discounted cash flow analysis. Excluding them from a discounted cash flow analysis means that they are being valued at zero. It is better to make some estimate of these benefits, no matter how rough an estimate it is, than to exclude them. If it is impossible to make such an estimate, the investment criteria should include these intangible benefits along with a proposal's net present value. For example, if the net present value of a project is ($45,000), management can then decide whether the nonquantifiable factors are worth more than $45,000. If they are, the investment is justified.

Because the estimation of cash flows from these projects is difficult, some people have suggested that companies make these decisions without considering the usual capital investment criteria such as NPV. In practice, though, companies do consider potential cash flows and net present values from such projects. Sensitivity analysis is usually performed to examine the effect of the widely different possible outcomes from the investment. Management then can consider not just one net present value but a range of present values when making an investment decision. Management then decides whether to invest in a given project based on a combination of the expected net present value and other performance measures as well as the range of the performance measures and the impact of the project on the future of the company.

For example, the project in Illustration 23.10 offers high cash returns late in the life of the investment. It is quite difficult to predict cash flows very far in the future.

ILLUSTRATION 23.10	Alternative NPV and IRR Scenarios (in thousands)		
	Cash Flows		
Year	**Best Case**	**Expected**	**Worst Case**
0	($ 80)	($ 80)	($80)
1	0	0	0
2	0	0	0
3	0	0	0
4	0	0	0
5	0	0	0
6	400	200	50
7	300	100	25
Net present value @ 15%	$206	$ 44	($49)
Internal rate of return	40%	23%	(1%)

Management might therefore analyze the alternative possibilities for this project to obtain some idea of its risk. Let's assume that there is a chance that the project will return only 25 percent of the estimated cash flows in years 6 and 7 but that there also is the possibility that the cash flows could be $400,000 in year 6 and $300,000 in year 7. These are the worst-case and best-case scenarios. Net present value and IRR analyses would be conducted under all three outcomes. A summary of the alternatives could be presented to management for its evaluation.

CAPITAL BUDGETING IN NONPROFIT ORGANIZATIONS

Not-for-profit organizations, including government agencies, are subject to limitations on the availability of capital for investment purposes. They also use capital investment analysis to allocate cash efficiently. Because not-for-profit organizations are exempt from income taxation, there are no tax effects on the operating cash flows or on disinvestment flows. Likewise, there is no tax shield from depreciation. These features result in a somewhat simplified analysis.

ILLUSTRATION 23.11	Capital Budgeting in Nonprofit Organizations					
	Time	**Year**				
Item	**0**	**1**	**2**	**3**	**4**	**5**
Investment flows						
New equipment	($600,000)					
Other investment costs	(8,000)					
Annual operating flows		$160,000[a]	$160,000	$160,000	$160,000	$160,000
Disinvestment flows						
Salvage value						10,000
Total cash flows	($608,000)	$160,000	$160,000	$160,000	$160,000	$170,000
Discount factor (10%)	1.000	0.909	0.826	0.751	0.683	0.621
Present value	($608,000)	$145,455	$132,231	$120,210	$109,282	$105,557
Net present value	$ 4,735					

[a]$160,000 = $40,000 + ($30,000 × 4).

L.O. 9: Know why audits are an important step in the capital investment process.

For example, assume that the U.S. Postal Service is considering the purchase of advanced automated sorting equipment for its Urbana station. The equipment will cost $600,000 and has a useful life of five years. Salvage value is estimated at $10,000. Installation of the equipment will cost $8,000. The old equipment can be shipped to a post office using semiautomated equipment. It is assumed that the costs to dismantle and ship the old equipment will exactly offset the benefits received at the other post office.

Using the new equipment, one operator will be able to handle the volume of letters that five operators handled in the past. The average pay for each operator is $30,000, including fringe benefits. Other cash flow savings equal $40,000 per year. The postal service uses a discount rate of 10 percent. What are the cash flows from the project and the net present value?

The results are shown in Illustration 23.11. As you may note, this is very similar to data in Illustration 23.6, which was used for a taxable organization.

AUDITS AND CAPITAL BUDGETING

L.O. 10: Conduct net present value analysis in nonprofit organizations.

The accuracy of a capital budgeting model relies heavily on the estimates it uses, particularly on the project's cash flows and its life span. These estimates come from past experience, judgment, or the experience of others, such as competitors.

Comparing the estimates made in the capital budgeting process with the actual results provides several advantages. Among the advantages are:

- Audits identify what estimates were wrong so planners can incorporate that knowledge in future estimates to avoid making similar mistakes.
- Audits can be used to identify and reward those planners who are good at making capital budgeting decisions. They also provide information to decision makers so they can consider the skill of the planner in making the capital investment decision.
- Audits create an environment in which planners will not be tempted to inflate their estimates of the benefits associated with the project to get it approved.

Some projects may improve reported accounting profits in the short run but result in suboptimal net present values. When this occurs, it is necessary to identify the reasons for choosing a project that improves accounting profits rather than net present value. There may be rational explanations for such decisions, but management should critically evaluate them.

Audits provide an important discipline to a subjective judgmental process and provide many valuable insights for decision makers.

BEHAVIORAL ISSUES

L.O. 11: Be sensitive to behavioral issues involved in capital budgeting.

Recognizing the behavioral implications that lie behind the estimates is important in capital budgeting. Planners cannot help but be influenced by their environment. Factors such as the desire to implement a project and performance evaluation measures may influence their objectivity in making estimates. Therefore, it is important that organizational policies, procedures, and performance measures support accurate estimations and that the effect they have on planners are considered when evaluating capital investment projects.

As an example of how personal desire might influence a planner, a production manager who is anxious to have the latest equipment might be overly optimistic in forecasting the benefits offered by the machine in terms of cost reduction, quality improvement, and cycle time reduction to promote its purchase. A standard procedure of comparing the results to the claims that were made in support of equipment acquisition after it has been acquired will help to curb this type of over optimistic behavior.

A potential conflict exists between the criteria for evaluating individual projects and the criteria used to evaluate an organization's overall performance or the performance of a unit. An example of the way that performance measures influence a planner follows.

Suppose that a manager at Desert Industries, a producer of microwaves, is considering the acquisition of machinery to produce another line of kitchen aids. The estimates of cash flows over the life of the equipment indicate that the acquisition should be undertaken. However, although the later years provide large positive cash flows, the first two years have negative cash flows due to low revenues. This creates a potential problem because the manager's performance evaluation is based in part on the annual operating profits based on financial (accrual) accounting, which the acquisition will lower during the first two years. Thus, a conflict exists between the capital budgeting model and financial accounting performance measures.

The possible result of this conflict is that a capital investment that would have a positive effect on the organization in the long run might be rejected because of its effect on a short-run performance measure.

ETHICAL ISSUES IN CAPITAL INVESTMENT DECISIONS

The people who request additional capital investment for a project often have a strong interest in ensuring that the project's net present value is positive. In a company that we studied, a group of engineers wanted the company to purchase new equipment with the latest technology. Because they were so interested in getting the new equipment, they omitted some of the costs to install the equipment in the data they submitted with the project proposal. By omitting them, the engineers reduced the initial investment outflow in the discounted cash flow analysis, which increased the chance that the net present value of the project would be positive.

If the company's top managers had known about the installation costs, they would have rejected the proposal. Based on the false data, the company subsequently purchased the equipment. The company's total investment in the equipment was considerably higher than originally projected because the costs of installing the equipment had been omitted from the discounted cash flow analysis.

During your career, you may be pressured to omit certain data from capital investment proposals or to make inaccurate projections. Don't. In the case just described, the engineers got their equipment, but they paid a price. Top management learned about the omitted installation costs after reviewing monthly divisional income statements. Some of the engineers were dismissed. The credibility of the remaining engineers was substantially undermined.

SUMMARY

The following summarizes key ideas tied to the chapter's learning objectives.

LO1: Recognize the strategic benefits of capital investments. Strategic benefits reflect the increased profit potential derived from some attribute of a capital asset. Some common strategic benefits that may be provided by a capital asset are reducing the potential to make mistakes, making goods or delivering a service that competitors can't, and reducing the cycle time to make the product.

LO2: Explain the present value concept. Because the horizon of capital investment decisions extends over many years, the time value of money often is a significant factor. To recognize the time value of money, the future cash flows associated with a project are adjusted to their present value using a predetermined discount rate. Summing the discounted values of the future cash flows and subtracting the initial investment yields a project's *net present value*, which represents the economic value of the project to the company at a given point in time.

LO3: Compute the present value of cash flows. A project's net present value is computed using the following equation:

$$NPV = \sum_{n=0}^{N} C_n \times (1 + d)^{-n}$$

where

C_n = Cash flows at the end of time period n
d = Discount rate
n = Time period when the cash flow occurs
N = Total number of time periods in the project's life

LO4: Categorize cash flows and conduct net present value analysis. The accountant's primary task is to estimate cash flows used in the net present value equation. These cash flows and their effects follow ("−" signifies cash outflow and "+" signifies cash inflow):

a. Investment:
   (1) Acquisition cost (−).
   (2) Investment tax credit (+).
   (3) Working capital commitments (−).
   (4) Proceeds of assets sold (+).
   (5) Tax effects from a loss or gain on sale of old assets (+/−).
b. Periodic operating flows, including
   (1) Period cash inflows (+) and outflows (−) before taxes.
   (2) Income tax effects of inflows (−) and outflows (+).
c. Depreciation tax shield:
   (1) Tax shield benefits (+).
   (2) Forgone tax shield benefits (−).
d. Disinvestment flows:
   (1) Cash freed from working capital commitments (+).
   (2) Incremental salvage value of long-term assets (usually + unless there are disposal costs).
   (3) Tax consequences of gain or loss on disposal (− or +, respectively).
   (4) Other cash flows, such as severance or relocation payments to employees, restoration costs, and similar costs (usually −).

LO5: Recognize the effects of inflation on cash flows and discount rate. Under conditions of inflation, the discount rate is usually adjusted to compensate for changes in price levels. When nominal cash flows are analyzed, a nominal discount rate is used.

LO6: Conduct sensitivity analyses of capital investment decisions using spreadsheets. Some error is likely in the amount predicted or estimated for the amount or timing of cash flows or the discount rate. Errors in predicting the amounts of future cash flows will likely have the largest impact of the three items. In general, if a project appears marginally desirable for a given discount rate, it will ordinarily not be grossly undesirable for slightly higher rates. A useful feature of spreadsheet programs is that they help the user see the effect on the net present value of changes in assumptions and estimates.

LO7: Understand and compute a project's internal rate of return. The internal rate of return (IRR) of a series of cash flows is the discount rate that equates the net present value of the series to zero. IRR can be calculated with many available calculators or with the use of a spreadsheet.

LO8: Understand difficulties in justifying investment in advanced production systems. Discounted cash flow analysis is the appropriate method to analyze investments in advanced manufacturing systems, but implementing the analysis presents a challenge. Managers should strive to make the best possible estimates of costs and benefits and ultimately make a judgment that recognizes the nonquantifiable benefits as well.

LO9: Conduct net present value analysis in nonprofit organizations. Nonprofit organizations also use net present value analyses to allocate cash efficiently. However, nonprofit organizations do not pay income taxes, and thus exclude tax effects from their net present value analysis.

LO10: Know why audits are an important step in the capital investment process. Comparing the estimates made in the capital budgeting process with the actual results provides several advantages. Audits identify what estimates were wrong, can be used to identify and reward good planners, and create an environment in which planners will not be tempted to inflate their estimates of the benefits associated with the project to get it approved.

LO11: Be sensitive to behavioral issues involved in capital budgeting. Planners cannot avoid being influenced by their environment. Factors such as the desire to implement a project and performance evaluation measures may influence their objectivity in making estimates. Therefore, it is important that organizational policies, procedures, and performance measures support accurate estimations and that the effect they have on planners are considered when evaluating capital investment projects.

LO12: Rank alternative projects with positive net present values (Appendix A). When capital investment opportunities with positive net present values exceed capital budget constraints, the net present value index may be used to rank the projects. This index is calculated as follows:

$$\text{Net present value index} = \frac{\text{Project net present value}}{\text{Investment in the project}}$$

LO13: Use alternative models to evaluate projects (Appendix A). The two most common alternatives to net present value and IRR are payback and accounting rate of return.

KEY TERMS

accounting rate of return,* 728
asset acquisition, 702
discount rate, 700
discounted payback method,* 727
disinvestment flows, 706
internal rate of return (IRR), 716

investment tax credit, 703
mutually exclusive,* 726
net present value, 699
net present value index,* 724
nominal discount rate, 711
nominal dollars, 711

KEY TERMS
Continued

payback,* 726

payback period,* 726

payback reciprocal,* 727

present value, 700

real return, 711

sensitivity analysis, 714

tax basis, 707

tax shield, 705

time value of money, 699

working capital, 703

*Terms appear in Appendix A.

APPENDIX A

L.O. 12: Rank alternative projects with positive net present values (Appendix A).

Effect of Constraints on Capital Investment Decisions

Let's consider a set of five investment projects with net cash flows as indicated in Illustration 23.12. Using a 15 percent discount rate, each project has a positive net present value. Therefore, if funds were available and if investment in one project did not exclude the possibility of investing in another project, all five projects would be chosen. However, there often are constraints on management's choice of projects.

For example, suppose that management wanted to invest no more than $450,000 in these projects because of a shortage of managers to supervise them. Which projects, if any, should it select? Or suppose that if Project B is selected, Project C cannot be selected. Which project should then be chosen?

When the amount to be invested in capital investment projects is limited, management usually considers the total net present values of all selected investments rather than the net present value of each investment alone. Although all of these projects have positive net present values, they must be ranked to decide which is more desirable.

Net Present Value Index Method

net present value index
Ratio of the net present value of a project to the funds invested in the project.

The **net present value index** is often used to rank projects. It relates the net present value of a project to the dollars invested in it. The index is computed by dividing the net present value of a project by the initial investment:

ILLUSTRATION 23.12 — **Cash Flow Schedules for Alternative Projects (in thousands)**

Year	A	B	C	D	E
			Project		
0	$(425)	$(135)	$ (80)	$(170)	$ (90)
1	25	0	0	60	10
2	50	90	0	60	20
3	75	80	0	60	40
4	100	70	0	60	40
5	150	50	0	60	40
6	300	20	200	60	30
7	380	10	100	60	20
Totals	$ 655	$ 185	$ 220	$ 250	$ 110
Net present value (at 15%)[a]	$ 88	$ 63	$ 44	$ 80	$ 23

[a]$88 = -$425 + ($25 \times 1.15^{-1}) + ($50 \times 1.15^{-2}) + ($75 \times 1.15^{-3}) + ($100 \times 1.15^{-4}) + ($150 \times 1.15^{-5}) + ($300 \times 1.15^{-6}) + ($380 \times 1.15^{-7}); $63 = -$135 + ($90 \times 1.15^{-2}) + ($80 \times 1.15^{-3}) + ($70 \times 1.15^{-4}) + ($50 \times 1.15^{-5}) + ($20 \times 1.15^{-6}) + ($10 \times 1.15^{-7}); and so forth.

$$\text{Net present value index} = \frac{\text{Project net present value}}{\text{Investment in the project}}$$

For Project A in Illustration 23.12, the net present value index is

$$\frac{\$88}{\$425} = \underline{\underline{.21}}$$

The net present value indexes for the other projects follow:

Project B: .47 = $63 ÷ $135
Project C: .55 = $44 ÷ $80
Project D: .47 = $80 ÷ $170
Project E: .26 = $23 ÷ $90

For investment choice purposes, projects are ranked by the amount of their net present value index. The higher the index, the more desirable the investment. Thus, Project C is the most desirable according to the net present value index method.

The net present value index is useful for ranking investments of different sizes. Net present value analysis tends to favor large projects over small ones if we rank projects in order of the size of their net present values. The net present value index is a means to correct this bias that favors large projects.

Partial Projects If it is possible to fund each project in part rather than in its entirety, such as through partnership or joint venture arrangements, then by taking the projects in rank order, the maximum net present value could be obtained. Partial investments are common in real estate and natural resource projects but are less common in manufacturing or other projects. Hence, the possibility of a partial investment may depend on the project's nature.

In the example, the $450,000 is apportioned first to Project C, which costs $80,000 and has the highest net present value index. Next selected are Project D, costing $170,000, and Project B, costing $135,000.

After making these three investments, $65,000 (= $450,000 − $80,000 − $135,000 − $170,000) is left for other projects. If we can fund a partial investment, we will invest the remaining $65,000 in Project E and obtain a 72.22 percent (= $65,000/$90,000) share in that project.

With this investment strategy, the net present value of the $450,000 investment is $203,611, the sum of the present values on Projects B through D plus 72.22 percent of the present value of Project E. No alternative strategy yields a higher net present value.

Indivisible Investments Of course, it may not be possible to acquire a partial interest in Project E. If the projects cannot be subdivided, their appropriate ranking becomes more complex. It may not be possible to invest the full $450,000. Any funds not invested in these projects would be expected to earn the cost of capital rate and, hence, have no positive net present value. The optimal solution to the project rank ordering could no longer be based entirely on the net present value index. Rather, we would have to consider the total present value of all selected projects, however chosen.

For the data in Illustration 23.12, the optimal ranking is to select Projects B, C, and D, which cost a total of $385,000 (total of $135,000 + $80,000 + $170,000). These three projects provide a combined net present value of $187,000 (= $63,000 + $44,000 + $80,000). The $65,000 uninvested funds (= $450,000 − $385,000) will earn a net present value of zero because they are presumed to earn the cost of capital and no more. No other combination of projects costing an aggregate of $450,000 or less will provide a higher net present value for the company when partial investment in projects is not possible. In this example, the ranking is identical to the net present value index ranking, but this is not always the case.

mutually exclusive
A situation where selection
of one project precludes
the selection of another.

In many cases, projects are **mutually exclusive.** That is, selecting one project precludes selecting another project. You can use an IBM personal computer or a MacIntosh, but you may not need both, for example.

When investment funds are limited, net present value cannot be the sole basis of choice because selection of one project reduces the capital available for investment in other projects. The opportunity cost of the mutually exclusive project is, in part, the return that could be earned on the excluded project rather than the cost of capital for the company as a whole.

For example, if Projects B and C from Illustration 23.12 are mutually exclusive and if investment funds are not limited, then the company prefers Project B. Investing in Project B results in a net present value of $63,000, whereas Project C yields a net present value of only $44,000. The critical assumption here is that the company has no better alternatives for the differential funds required for Project B. A comparison of differential investment and differential net present values shows the following:

	Project C	Project B	Differential
Initial cost	$80,000	$135,000	$55,000
Net present value	$44,000	$ 63,000	$19,000

The investment in Project B yields a differential net present value of $19,000. If the differential $55,000 could be invested in another project (for example, a new Project F) with a net present value higher than $19,000, the company would be better off selecting both Project C and the new Project F.

For example, if Project F costs $55,000 and has a net present value of $22,000, by investing in Projects C and F, the company obtains a net present value of $66,000 (which is the $44,000 from Project C plus $22,000 from Project F). This net present value is higher than the $63,000 from Project B. The increased present value is obtained with the same $135,000 investment.

Thus, when a company has limited capital and is unable to fund partial projects, the optimal set of projects is determined by considering the total net present value of all projects selected rather than the individual project net present values.

Alternate Capital Investment Models

L.O. 13: Use alternative models
to evaluate projects.

Due to the complexity of the capital investment decision, one model of analysis is sometimes considered insufficient for evaluating investment proposals.[1] Surveys show that companies use a variety of investment models. The two most common alternatives to NPV and IRR are *payback* and *accounting rate of return*. We will discuss each of these alternative models in turn. Each has its own advantages and may be encountered in certain decision settings. In a complex capital investment decision, it is likely that management will employ several alternative measures.

payback
A method to assess capital
investment projects using
the rationale that a positive
relationship exists between
the speed of payback and the
rate of return.

Payback   It is generally assumed that the longer a company's funds are tied up in an investment, the higher the risk to the company. In addition, a relationship exists between the speed of **payback** and the rate of return on a typical investment. For these reasons, companies often consider the length of time it takes to obtain a return of the investment in the project as a measure for project evaluation. The **payback period** is the number of years that will elapse before the original investment is repaid. As with most other capital investment models, cash flow data are used for this computation. With level annual cash flows, the payback formula is

payback period
The time required to recoup an
investment from the cash
flows from the project.

$$\text{Payback period} = \frac{\text{Investment}}{\text{Annual cash flow}}$$

---

[1]See T. Klammer, B. Koch, and N. Wilner, "Capital Budgeting Practices—A Survey of Corporate Use," *Journal of Management Accounting Research* 3, pp. 113–30, for a survey of practices.

ILLUSTRATION 23.13	Payback Method, Project B	
Year	Net Cash Flow	Cash Flow Balance
0	$(135,000)	$(135,000)
1	–0–	(135,000)
2	90,000	(45,000)
3	80,000	35,000

With different annual cash flows, the analysis is more complex. For example, using the data from Illustration 23.12, the payback period for Project B appears in Illustration 23.13. A running balance of the net cash flow for the investment is maintained until the balance turns positive; for this project, it is during the third year. The fraction of that third year that was required before the investment achieved payback is usually estimated by dividing the absolute value of the last negative balance in the balance column by the total cash flow in the payback year:

$$\frac{\text{Balance, end of year 2}}{\text{Net cash flow, year 3}}$$

or

$$\frac{\$45,000}{\$80,000} = .5625$$

Project payback is then stated as 2.5625 years, or approximately 2 years and 7 months. The fraction of a year computation is based on the assumption that the cash flows are received evenly throughout the payback year.

Shortcut Payback Computation   If a project has level cash flows throughout its life, the payback computation is simplified. The payback period may be computed in this case by dividing the project cost by the annual cash flow. For Project D from Illustration 23.12, the payback period is

$$\frac{\$170,000}{\$60,000} = 2.83 \text{ years}$$

payback reciprocal
One divided by the payback period in years.

Payback Reciprocal   When a project's life is at least twice the payback period and the annual cash flows are approximately equal, the **payback reciprocal** may be used to estimate the rate of return for the project.

Thus, for Project D from Illustration 23.12, the payback reciprocal is

$$\frac{1}{2.83} = .35, \text{ or } 35\%$$

Programmed functions in calculators and computers generally are used to compute the rate of return directly. Therefore, the use of the payback reciprocal approach is simply a rough, first-cut approximation.

discounted payback method
A method of assessing investment projects that recognizes the time value of money in a payback context.

Discounted Payback   A method that recognizes the time value of money in a payback context is the **discounted payback method.** This method is used to compute the payback in terms of discounted cash flows received in the future. That is, the periodic cash flows are discounted using an appropriate cost of capital rate. The payback period is computed using the discounted cash flow values rather than the actual cash flows. If the discounted payback method were used for Project D from Illustration 23.12 and a 15 percent cost of capital rate were employed, the discounted payback period would be as shown in Illustration 23.14, which is a discounted payback period of four years.

ILLUSTRATION 23.14	Discounted Payback Method, Project D (dollars in thousands)			
Year	Cash Flow	Discount Factor[a]	Discounted Cash Flow	Balance
0	$(170)	—	$(170)	$(170)
1	60	.870	52	(118)
2	60	.756	45	(73)
3	60	.658	39	(34)
4	60	.572	34	–0–

[a]Discount factors rounded to three places.

ILLUSTRATION 23.15	Comparison of Net Present Value and Payback Periods	
	Project 1	Project 2
Investment cost	$100,000	$100,000
Annual cash flows:		
Year 1	$100,000	$ 50,000
Year 2	–0–	50,000
Year 3	–0–	50,000
Years 4 and after	–0–	–0–
Payback	1 year[a]	2 years[b]
Net present value at 15%	$(13,043)[c]	$ 14,161[d]

Additional computations:
[a]One year = $100,000 investment/$100,000 annual cash flow.

[b]Two years = $100,000 investment/$50,000 annual cash flow.

[c]$ − 13,043 = $ − 100,000 + ($100,000 × 1.15^{-1}).

[d]$14,161 = $ − 100,000 + ($50,000 × 1.15^{-1}) + ($50,000 × 1.15^{-2}) + ($50,000 × 1.15^{-3}).

Evaluation of Payback Methods   Payback approaches are generally easy to compute and, to the extent that long payback implies high risk, give some measure of a company's risk exposure from a project. However, the payback period tells nothing about profitability. Thus, a project that returns the entire investment in year 1 but results in no further cash flows appears better using the payback criterion than does a project that returns 50 percent of the investment cost per year for three years. With a $100,000 investment and a 15 percent cost of capital, a comparison of the net present value and payback period for these two projects is shown in Illustration 23.15. Clearly, Project 2 is the better choice when discounting all cash flows. The payback method gives a misleading signal about the relative desirability of the two projects.

Thus, when using payback, it is important to consider what will happen when the payback period is over. Managers often use payback as a screening device because it is easy (and therefore inexpensive) to use. The choice of the investment analysis model should be based on its costs and benefits compared to the alternative models. If decisions are sensitive to the decision model, more care and expense are warranted than when decisions are the same regardless of the model used.

accounting rate of return
A measure of project returns using accounting concepts of income.

Accounting Rate of Return   The **accounting rate of return** measures a project's rate of return in terms of accounting income, however defined by management, rather than in terms of cash flows. It relates the average accounting income from a project to the investment in the project and is computed using the following equation:

$$\text{Accounting rate of return} = \frac{\text{Average accounting income}}{\text{Investment}}$$

The accounting income for this computation is approximately equal to the sum of the average incremental cash flow from the project less the average book depreciation. Investment may be based either on the *initial investment* or on the *average investment*. Average investment is usually assumed to equal one-half of the sum of initial investment and salvage value. Incremental cash flows are usually approximated using revenues minus costs other than depreciation.

For example, consider Project D in Illustration 23.12. The project has an annual cash flow of $60,000, an initial cost of $170,000, and no salvage value. Assume that $154,000 of the investment cost is depreciable using a straight-line rate over the seven-year project life. This basis was determined by management's internal accounting procedures. Book depreciation is $22,000 per year (computed as $154,000/7 years). Average investment in the project is $85,000, which is one-half of the original investment cost of $170,000.

$$R = \frac{C - D}{\frac{1}{2} \times I}$$

or

$$\frac{\$60,000 - \$22,000}{\$85,000} = 44.7\%$$

where

C = Average annual cash flow from the investment
D = Accounting depreciation
I = Initial investment

The accounting rate of return also may be computed using the initial investment rather than the average investment. This estimate of the accounting rate of return is

$$R = \frac{C - D}{I}$$

or

$$\frac{\$60,000 - \$22,000}{\$170,000} = 22.4\%$$

The accounting rate of return averages the cash flows to be received from a project as well as the depreciation. It also ignores the time value of money. Thus, the accounting rate of return method is rarely suitable for investment decision-making purposes.

Sometimes management will constrain the investment decision to include only those projects that exceed a particular accounting rate of return to maintain particular financial accounting ratios. However, such managers will not be maximizing the long-run wealth of the organization.

Comments on Alternative Methods

Capital investment decisions are among the most important decisions made by managers because they are long-run commitments. Consequently, managers typically use as much information as possible in making decisions. Although the net present value method discussed in the chapter is the most theoretically defensible model, managers often use the alternative models discussed in this appendix as ways to get a different picture of the project. If the information has already been collected to do a net present value analysis, the additional cost of using these additional models to the company is typically low.

SELF-STUDY QUESTION

3. Refer to the information in Self-Study Question 1. Compute the following:
   a. The payback period (use annual cash flows for years 1 through 3).
   b. Discounted payback, using the 15 percent cost of capital rate.

The solution to this question is at the end of this chapter on page 742.

APPENDIX B

Computing Net Present Values for Annuities

When periodic cash flows are expected to be equal over a period of time, a shortcut method may be used to compute the net present value of those cash flows. A series of level periodic payments is referred to as an *annuity*. The present value of an annuity may be obtained using this equation:

$$\text{Present value} = C \times \frac{1 - (1 + d)^{-n}}{d}$$

where

$d = \text{Discount rate}$
$n = \text{Number of periods over which the periodic payment } (C) \text{ will be received}$

For example, the present value of a series of six payments of \$40,000 each at a discount rate of 25 percent is

$$\text{PV} = \$40,000 \times \frac{1 - (1 + .25)^{-6}}{.25}$$
$$= \$40,000 \times 2.951424$$
$$= \$118,057$$

This amount also can be computed the long way by taking the present value of each year's cash flow as follows:

Year	Cash Flow	PV Factor	Present Value
1	$40,000	.800	$ 32,000
2	40,000	.640	25,600
3	40,000	.512	20,480
4	40,000	.410	16,384
5	40,000	.328	13,107
6	40,000	.262	10,486
		2.952	$118,057

The sum of the present value factors for the six periods is the same with rounding as the computed factor for the six-year annuity. The present values computed under either method are the same. As with other present value calculations, the use of a calculator is more efficient and gives more accurate answers than does use of the tables. A set of tables is given in Appendix C to this chapter.

APPENDIX C

Present Value Tables

The present value of \$1 shown in Illustration 23.16 gives the present value of an amount received *n* periods in the future. It is computed using the equation $(1 + d)^{-n}$ as discussed in the chapter.

ILLUSTRATION 23.16		Present Value of $1								
Year	**8%**	**10%**	**12%**	**14%**	**15%**	**16%**	**18%**	**20%**	**22%**	**24%**
1	.926	.909	.893	.877	.870	.862	.847	.833	.820	.806
2	.857	.826	.797	.769	.756	.743	.718	.694	.672	.650
3	.794	.751	.712	.675	.658	.641	.609	.579	.551	.524
4	.735	.683	.636	.592	.572	.552	.516	.482	.451	.423
5	.681	.621	.567	.519	.497	.476	.437	.402	.370	.341
6	.630	.564	.507	.456	.432	.410	.370	.335	.303	.275
7	.583	.513	.452	.400	.376	.354	.314	.279	.249	.222
8	.540	.467	.404	.351	.327	.305	.266	.233	.204	.179
9	.500	.424	.361	.308	.284	.263	.225	.194	.167	.144
10	.463	.386	.322	.270	.247	.227	.191	.162	.137	.116
11	.429	.350	.287	.237	.215	.195	.162	.135	.112	.094
12	.397	.319	.257	.208	.187	.168	.137	.112	.092	.076
13	.368	.290	.229	.182	.163	.145	.116	.093	.075	.061
14	.340	.263	.205	.160	.141	.125	.099	.078	.062	.049
15	.315	.239	.182	.140	.123	.108	.084	.065	.051	.040

Year	**25%**	**26%**	**28%**	**30%**	**32%**	**34%**	**35%**	**36%**	**38%**	**40%**
1	.800	.794	.781	.769	.758	.746	.741	.735	.725	.714
2	.640	.630	.610	.592	.574	.557	.549	.541	.525	.510
3	.512	.500	.477	.455	.435	.416	.406	.398	.381	.364
4	.410	.397	.373	.350	.329	.310	.301	.292	.276	.260
5	.328	.315	.291	.269	.250	.231	.223	.215	.200	.186
6	.262	.250	.227	.207	.189	.173	.165	.158	.145	.133
7	.210	.198	.178	.159	.143	.129	.122	.116	.105	.095
8	.168	.157	.139	.123	.108	.096	.091	.085	.076	.068
9	.134	.125	.108	.094	.082	.072	.067	.063	.055	.048
10	.107	.099	.085	.073	.062	.054	.050	.046	.040	.035
11	.086	.079	.066	.056	.047	.040	.037	.034	.029	.025
12	.069	.062	.052	.043	.036	.030	.027	.025	.021	.018
13	.055	.050	.040	.033	.027	.022	.020	.018	.015	.013
14	.044	.039	.032	.025	.021	.017	.015	.014	.011	.009
15	.035	.031	.025	.020	.016	.012	.011	.010	.008	.007

For example, to find the present value of $20,000 received 11 years from now at a discount of 16 percent, look over the 11-year row to the 16 percent column and find the relevant factor, .195. Multiply the $20,000 by this factor to obtain the present value of $3,900.

If you perform this same computation with a calculator, you will obtain the somewhat more precise answer of $3,908. The difference is due to rounding.

The present value of an annuity is the value of a series of equal periodic payments discounted at a stated rate. Illustration 23.17 gives a set of factors for present values of an annuity.

For example, to find the present value of a series of nine annual payments of $5,000 each at a discount rate of 18 percent, look across the 9-year row to the 18 percent column and find the factor, 4.303. Multiply the $5,000 by the 4.303 to obtain the present value of those future payments, $21,515.

Illustration 23.18 provides the net present values for the text problems based on the recognition of inflation in the cash flow analysis.

ILLUSTRATION 23.17		Present Value of an Annuity							

Year	8%	10%	12%	14%	15%	16%	18%	20%	22%	24%
1	.926	.909	.893	.877	.870	.862	.847	.833	.820	.806
2	1.783	1.736	1.690	1.647	1.626	1.605	1.566	1.528	1.492	1.457
3	2.577	2.487	2.402	2.322	2.283	2.246	2.174	2.106	2.042	1.981
4	3.312	3.170	3.037	2.914	2.855	2.798	2.690	2.589	2.494	2.404
5	3.993	3.791	3.605	3.433	3.352	3.274	3.127	2.991	2.864	2.745
6	4.623	4.355	4.111	3.889	3.784	3.685	3.498	3.326	3.167	3.020
7	5.206	4.868	4.564	4.288	4.160	4.039	3.812	3.605	3.416	3.242
8	5.747	5.335	4.968	4.639	4.487	4.344	4.078	3.837	3.619	3.421
9	6.247	5.759	5.328	4.946	4.772	4.607	4.303	4.031	3.786	3.566
10	6.710	6.145	5.650	5.216	5.019	4.833	4.494	4.192	3.923	3.682
11	7.139	6.495	5.938	5.453	5.234	5.029	4.656	4.327	4.035	3.776
12	7.536	6.814	6.194	5.660	5.421	5.197	4.793	4.439	4.127	3.851
13	7.904	7.103	6.424	5.842	5.583	5.342	4.910	4.533	4.203	3.912
14	8.244	7.367	6.628	6.002	5.724	5.468	5.008	4.611	4.265	3.962
15	8.559	7.606	6.811	6.142	5.847	5.575	5.092	4.675	4.315	4.001

Year	25%	26%	28%	30%	32%	34%	35%	36%	38%	40%
1	.800	.794	.781	.769	.758	.746	.741	.735	.725	.714
2	1.440	1.424	1.392	1.361	1.331	1.303	1.289	1.276	1.250	1.224
3	1.952	1.923	1.868	1.816	1.766	1.719	1.696	1.673	1.630	1.589
4	2.362	2.320	2.241	2.166	2.096	2.029	1.997	1.966	1.906	1.849
5	2.689	2.635	2.532	2.436	2.345	2.260	2.220	2.181	2.106	2.035
6	2.951	2.885	2.759	2.643	2.534	2.433	2.385	2.339	2.251	2.168
7	3.161	3.083	2.937	2.802	2.677	2.562	2.508	2.455	2.355	2.263
8	3.329	3.241	3.076	2.925	2.786	2.658	2.598	2.540	2.432	2.331
9	3.463	3.366	3.184	3.019	2.868	2.730	2.665	2.603	2.487	2.379
10	3.571	3.465	3.269	3.092	2.930	2.784	2.715	2.649	2.527	2.414
11	3.656	3.543	3.335	3.147	2.978	2.824	2.752	2.683	2.555	2.438
12	3.725	3.606	3.387	3.190	3.013	2.853	2.779	2.708	2.576	2.456
13	3.780	3.656	3.427	3.223	3.040	2.876	2.799	2.727	2.592	2.469
14	3.824	3.695	3.459	3.249	3.061	2.892	2.814	2.740	2.603	2.478
15	3.859	3.726	3.483	3.268	3.076	2.905	2.825	2.750	2.611	2.484

ILLUSTRATION 23.18		Present Value Table for Inflation Problems						

Year	18.80%	20.96%	21.90%	23.20%	26.50%	28.80%	31.76%	39.08%
1	.842	.827	.820	.812	.791	.776	.759	.719
2	.709	.683	.673	.659	.625	.603	.576	.517
3	.596	.565	.552	.535	.494	.468	.437	.372
4	.502	.467	.453	.434	.391	.363	.332	.267
5	.423	.386	.372	.352	.309	.282	.252	.192
6	.356	.319	.305	.286	.244	.219	.191	.138
7	.299	.264	.250	.232	.193	.170	.145	.099
8	.252	.218	.205	.188	.153	.132	.110	.071
9	.212	.180	.168	.153	.121	.103	.084	.051
10	.179	.149	.138	.124	.095	.080	.063	.037
11	.150	.123	.113	.101	.075	.062	.048	.027
12	.127	.102	.093	.082	.060	.048	.037	.019
13	.107	.084	.076	.066	.047	.037	.028	.014
14	.090	.070	.062	.054	.037	.029	.021	.010
15	.075	.058	.051	.044	.029	.022	.016	.008

REVIEW QUESTIONS

23.1 What are the two most important factors the accountant must estimate in the capital investment decision?

23.2 What does the time value of money mean?

23.3 How do tax policies provide an incentive for capital investment?

23.4 How can we express the relationship of the desired real return to capital (r) and the inflation rate (i) used to discount nominal project cash flows under conditions of inflation?

23.5 Why might inflation be a disincentive to investment? What impact might inflation have on the present value of future cash flows and the future tax shield from the original investment?

CRITICAL ANALYSIS AND DISCUSSION QUESTIONS

23.6 Given two projects with equal cash flows but different timing, how can we determine which (if either) project should be selected for investment?

23.7 What are the four types of cash flows related to a capital investment and why do we consider them separately?

23.8 How can a postaudit help a manager construct better cash flow analyses?

23.9 Fatigue Corporation has a division operating at a $200,000 cash loss per year. The company cannot dispose of it due to certain contractual arrangements that require the division's continued operation. However, Fatigue has just received a proposal to invest in some new equipment with an estimated operating life of 10 years for the division at a cost of $150,000. If the equipment is purchased, the division will operate at a $40,000 cash loss per year. Should Fatigue consider acquisition of the equipment? Why or why not?

23.10 Is depreciation included in the computation of net present value? Explain.

23.11 "Every project should bear its fair share of all of the costs of the company. To do otherwise would make present operations subsidize new projects." Comment.

23.12 "The total tax deduction for depreciation is the same over the life of the project regardless of depreciation method. Why then would one be concerned about the depreciation method for capital investment analysis?" Comment.

23.13 Why could the investment in working capital increase over a project's life under conditions of inflation while inventory values (under LIFO) would not?

EXERCISES

23.14 Present Value of Cash Flows* (L.O. 4)

A city government is considering investing in street reconstruction that will require outlays as follows:

Year	Item	Amount
0	Engineering studies	$ 100,000
1	Project initiation	400,000
2	Project construction	1,800,000

Required

Compute the net present value of these cash outlays if the appropriate discount rate is 10 percent.

23.15 Present Value of Cash Flows (L.O. 4)

Tribure City is considering investment in an addition to the community center that is expected to return the following cash flows:

---

*Refer to Appendix C of this chapter for present value tables.

Year	Net Cash Flow
1	$ 20,000
2	50,000
3	80,000
4	80,000
5	100,000

This schedule includes all cash inflows from the project, which will also require an immediate $200,000 cash outlay. The city is tax exempt; therefore, taxes need not be considered.

Required

a. What is the net present value of the project if the appropriate discount rate is 20 percent?

b. What is the net present value of the project if the appropriate discount rate is 12 percent?

23.16 Effects of Inflation
(L.O. 5)

Refer to the data in Exercise 23.15.

a. What is the net present value of the project if the inflation rate is 10 percent and the discount rate under no inflation is 12 percent? (*Hint:* Inflation affects both cash flows and the nominal rate of interest; the cash flows for year 1 are $22,000, 10 percent higher than in exercise 23.15.)

b. Compare your answer in (*a*) to the result you got in part (*b*) of Exercise 23.15. Explain why these two answers are the same (or different).

23.17 Present Value
of Cash Flows
(L.O. 4)

Titanic Entertainment is considering investment in a new show expected to return the following cash flows from syndication:

Year	Net Cash Flow (in thousands)
1	$ 750
2	850
3	1,200
4	1,000
5	600

This schedule includes all cash inflows from the project, which will also require an immediate cash outlay of $2.5 million at time 0. Titanic is tax exempt.

Required

a. Compute the net present value of the project if the appropriate discount rate is 20 percent. Refer to Illustration 23.6 for format.

b. Compute the net present value for the project if the appropriate discount rate is 15 percent.

23.18 Effects of Inflation
on Cash Flows
(L.O. 5)

Refer to the cash flow data in Exercise 23.17. Compute the net present value of the project if the inflation rate is 6 percent and the no-inflation discount rate is 15 percent. (*Hint:* Inflation affects both cash flows and the nominal rate of interest. Year 1 cash flows are $795, 6 percent higher than in Exercise 23.17.)

23.19 Effects of Inflation
on Cash Flows
(L.O. 5)

Refer to Exercise 23.18. Would your answer be different if you had used real (no-inflation) cash flows and discount rate instead of the nominal amounts in 23.18?

23.20 Compute Present
Value of Tax Shield
(L.O. 4)

Limbo Corporation plans to acquire production equipment for $600,000 that will be depreciated for tax purposes as follows: year 1, $120,000; year 2, $210,000; and $90,000 per year in each of years 3 through 5. An 18 percent discount rate is appropriate for this asset, and the company's tax rate is 40 percent.

Required

a. Compute the present value of the tax shield resulting from depreciation.

b. Compute the present value of the tax shield from depreciation assuming straight-line depreciation ($120,000 per year).

23.21 Present Value of Depreciation Tax Shield under Inflation (L.O. 4, L.O. 5)

Refer to the data in Exercise 23.20.

Required

a. Using the accelerated tax depreciation deductions in Exercise 23.20, what is the present value of the tax shield if the inflation rate is 8 percent and the no-inflation discount rate is 22 percent?

b. What is the present value of the tax shield if the inflation rate is 14 percent and the no-inflation discount rate is 22 percent?

c. What happens to the net present value of the tax shield as the inflation rate increases?

23.22 Present Value of Tax Shield (L.O. 4)

C.L. Corporation plans to acquire an asset for $400,000 that will be depreciated for tax purposes as follows: year 1, $115,000; year 2, $150,000; and $45,000 per year in each of years 3 through 5. A 15 percent discount rate is appropriate for this asset, and the company's tax rate is 35 percent.

Required

Compute the present value of the tax shield.

23.23 Present Value of Tax Shield (L.O. 4)

Refer to the data in Exercise 23.22. Compute the present value of the tax shield from depreciation, assuming that the asset qualifies for straight-line depreciation ($80,000 per year).

23.24 Present Value of Tax Shield under Inflation (L.O. 4, L.O. 5)

Refer to the data in Exercise 23.22. The no-inflation discount rate is 15 percent. Using the tax depreciation deductions in Exercise 23.22, what is the present value of the tax shield if the inflation rate is 6 percent?

23.25 Present Value of Cash Flows under Inflation (L.O. 4, L.O. 5)

Kentron Products has concluded that its cost of capital is 8 percent in real terms. The company is considering an investment in a project having annual cash flows (before taxes and inflation) of $72,000 per year for five years. At disinvestment, the costs of disposal will equal any liquidation value of the project. No additional working capital is required for the project. The project costs $240,000 and will be depreciated for tax purposes over five years as follows: year 1, 15 percent of the cost; year 2, 22 percent; and 21 percent per year in each of years 3 through 5. The company's marginal tax rate is 40 percent.

Required

a. Assuming no inflation, compute the net present value of this project. Refer to Illustration 23.6 for format.

b. If inflation is expected to be 12 percent, what is the present value of the project? Refer to the present value table under inflation in Illustration 23.18. (*Hint:* Inflation affects both cash flows and the nominal rate of interest.)

23.26 Present Value Analysis in Nonprofit Organizations (L.O. 4)

The Goldberg Research Organization, a nonprofit organization that does not pay taxes, is considering buying laboratory equipment with an estimated life of seven years so it will not have to use outsiders' laboratories for certain types of work. The following are all of the cash flows affected by the decision:

Investment outflows at time 0.	$4,000,000
Periodic operating flows:	
Annual cash savings because outside laboratories are not used	1,400,000
Additional cash outflow for people and supplies to operate the equipment	200,000
Disinvestment flows:	
Salvage value after seven years, which is the estimated life of this project.	400,000
Discount rate	12%

Required

Calculate the net present value of this decision. Refer to Illustration 23.6 for format. Should the organization buy the equipment?

23.27 Impact of Inflation on Net Present Value in Nonprofit Organizations (L.O. 5, L.O. 9)

Refer to the data in Exercise 23.26. Calculate the net present value if the real interest rate is 12 percent and inflation is expected to be 8 percent per year. Refer to Illustration 23.18 for present value table under inflation. (*Hint:* Inflation affects both the nominal rate of interest and cash flows, and the cash flows for year 1 will be 8 percent higher than the amounts indicated in Exercise 23.26.)

23.28 Sensitivity Analysis in Capital Investment Decisions (L.O. 6, L.O. 7)

Hearld Manufacturing is considering investing in a robotics manufacturing line. Installation of the line will cost an estimated $3 million. This amount must be paid immediately even though construction will take three years to complete (years 0, 1, and 2). Year 3 will be spent testing the production line and, hence, will not yield any positive cash flows. If the operation is very successful, the company expects after-tax cash savings of $2 million per year in each of years 4 through 7. After reviewing the use of these systems with managements of other companies, Hearld's controller concluded that the operation will most probably result in annual savings of $1,400,000 per year for each of years 4 through 7. Further, it is entirely possible that the savings could be as low as $600,000 per year for each of years 4 through 7.

Required

Compute the IRR and NPV under the three scenarios (use 16 percent for the NPV calculation). Refer to Illustration 23.10 for format.

23.29 Net Present Value Index (Appendix A) (L.O. 12)

A company with limited investment funds and a 20 percent cost of capital must choose from among three competing capital investment projects with the following cash flow patterns (in thousands):

			Year		
Project	0	1	2	3	4
A	$(200)	$50	$ 90	$100	$100
B	(350)	80	190	250	120
C	(300)	70	125	170	200

The company has $600,000 available for investment.

Required

How can the company optimally invest its $600,000 among the three projects, assuming that no other constraints on investment and partial investments in projects can be made?

23.30 Net Present Value Index (Appendix A) (L.O. 12)

Morris and Associates, a medical partnership, has $1.5 million available for investment in venture capital projects. The cost of capital is 15 percent. As a partnership, Morris pays no income taxes. The following opportunity ventures are available. Each has an estimated seven-year life. All of the money would be invested today.

1. Software Designs, an innovative software development company, has requested $900,000 for investment in software. The firm estimates no returns until year 5. Years 5 through 7 should return $1 million per year.

2. Sunset Mall, a new shopping center development, will cost Morris $550,000. The project will return $65,000 per year for each of years 1 through 3 and $250,000 per year in years 4 through 7.

3. Nutri-care, a health food chain, requires an investment of $650,000 to open a new store. This project will return $260,000 in each of years 1 through 3 and $60,000 per year in years 4 through 7.

4. Marvin Gardens, a housing development, would require $850,000 and return $250,000 in each of years 1 through 7.

Required

a. Calculate the net present value index for each investment.

b. Determine how the company can optimally invest its venture capital funds. Assume no other constraints on investment.

23.31 Alternative Project Evaluation Measures (Appendix A) (L.O. 13)

Farm Fresh Corporation is considering whether to invest in a pasteurizing machine that costs $300,000 and will return $80,000 after tax for each of the next seven years. After that, the asset will have no value.

Required

Compute the payback period for this project.

23.32 Alternative Project Evaluation Measures, No Discounting (Appendix A) (L.O. 13)

Quintana Company plans to replace an old piece of equipment that has no book value for tax purposes and no salvage value. The replacement equipment will provide annual cash savings of $8,000 before income taxes. The equipment costs $20,000 and will have no salvage value at the end of its five-year life. Quintana uses straight-line depreciation for both book and tax purposes. The company incurs a 40 percent marginal tax rate, and its after-tax cost of capital is 14 percent.

Required

Compute the following performance measures for Quintana's proposed investment:

a. Payback period.

b. Payback reciprocal.

c. Accounting rate of return on average investment.

(CMA adapted)

PROBLEMS

23.33

Assess Capital
Investment Project
with Alternative
Measures
(Appendix A)

Baxter Company manufactures toys and other short-lived products. Its research and development department developed a product that would be a good promotional gift for office equipment dealers. Efforts by Baxter's sales personnel resulted in commitments for this product for the next three years. It is expected that the product's value will be exhausted by that time.

To produce the amount demanded, Baxter will need to buy additional machinery and rent about 25,000 square feet of additional space; 12,500 square feet of presently unused space is available for the next three years. Baxter's present lease with 10 years to run costs $3 a foot, including the 12,500 feet of unused space. Baxter can rent another 12,500 square feet adjoining its facility for three years at $4 per square foot per year if it decides to make this product.

The equipment will be purchased for about $900,000 and will have a salvage value of about $180,000 at the end of the third year.

The following estimates of revenues and costs for this product for the three years have been developed:

	Year		
	1	2	3
Sales	$1,000,000	$1,600,000	$800,000
Material, labor, and variable overhead	400,000	750,000	350,000
Allocated fixed general overhead[a]	40,000	75,000	35,000
Rent	87,500	87,500	87,500
Depreciation.	300,000	300,000	300,000
	$ 827,500	$1,212,500	$772,500
Income before tax	172,500	387,500	27,500
Income tax (40%).	69,000	155,000	11,000
	$ 103,500	$ 232,500	$ 16,500

[a]Total fixed overhead will not be affected by this product. Each product is allocated some general overhead, however.

Required

a. Prepare a schedule to show the differential after-tax cash flows for this project. Assume that equipment must be depreciated on a three-year, straight-line basis, assuming no salvage value, for tax purposes.

b. If the company requires a two-year payback period for its investment, would it undertake this project?

c. Calculate the after-tax accounting rate of return for the project (based on the average investment).

d. If the company sets a required discount rate of 20 percent after taxes, will this project be accepted?

(CMA adapted)

23.34

New Machine
Decision

Assume that TCY, Inc., is considering the purchase of a newer, more efficient yogurt-making machine. If purchased, it would acquire the new machine on January 2, Year 1. TCY expects to sell 600,000 gallons of yogurt in each of the next five years at a $2 per gallon selling price.

TCY has two options: (1) continue to operate the old machine purchased four years ago or (2) sell it and purchase the new machine. The following information has been prepared to help decide which option is more desirable:

	Old Machine	New Machine
Original cost of machine at acquisition	$1,600,000	$2,000,000
Useful life from date of acquisition.	7 years	5 years
Expected annual cash operating expenses		
Variable cost per gallon	$1.20	$1.00
Total fixed cash costs.	$400,000	$160,000

Depreciation is as follows:

Age of Equipment (Years)	Tax Depreciation (Percent)
1	15%
2	25
3	20
4	20
5	20

Estimated cash value of machines follows:

	Old Machine	New Machine
January 2, Year 1	$400,000	$2,000,000
December 31, Year 3	$200,000	$1,000,000

TCY is subject to a 40 percent income tax rate on all income. Assume that tax depreciation is calculated without regard to salvage value. Use a three-year time horizon for the analysis.

Required

Use the net present value method to determine whether TCY should retain the old machine or acquire the new one. Assume that there is no inflation. Use an after-tax discount rate of 10 percent.

23.35 Ethical Issues

Ishima Corporation is considering expanding its manufacturing operations. It can either convert a warehouse it currently owns in the suburbs or it can expand its current manufacturing plant downtown. After the board of directors approved the expansion, George Watson, the controller, set about to determine which proposal had the higher net present value. He assigned this task to Helen Dodge, the assistant controller. She completed her task and discovered that the warehouse proposal had a negative net present value but the downtown expansion proposal was slightly positive. George was displeased with Helen's report on the warehouse proposal. He returned it to her stating that, "You must have made an error. This proposal should look better." She suspected that George wanted the warehouse proposal to succeed so that he could avoid his daily commute to the city. She checked her figures and found nothing wrong. She made some slight revisions to her report, however, changing her estimates from those that were probable to those that were remotely possible.

George was quite angry and demanded a second revision. He told her to start with a positive net present value of $100,000 and work backward to compute supporting estimates and projections. Helen is quite upset and unsure what she should do!

Required

a. Was Helen Dodge's first revision on the proposal for the warehouse conversion unethical?

b. Was George Watson's conduct unethical when he gave Helen specific instructions on preparing the second revision?

c. How should Helen Dodge attempt to resolve this issue? Should she discuss this issue with those outside the organization?

(CMA adapted)

23.36 Compute Net Present Value

Wright Corporation is evaluating a proposal to purchase a new drill press to replace a less efficient machine presently in use. The cost of the new equipment in time 0, including delivery and installation, is $200,000. If it is purchased, Wright will incur costs of $5,000 to remove the present equipment and revamp its facilities. This $5,000 is tax deductible at time 0.

Depreciation for tax purposes will be allowed as follows: year 1, $40,000; year 2, $70,000; and $30,000 per year in each of years 3 through 5. The existing equipment has a book and tax value of $100,000 and a remaining useful life of 10 years. However, the existing equipment could be sold for only $40,000 and is being depreciated for book and tax purposes using the straight-line method over its actual life.

Management has provided you with the following comparative manufacturing cost data:

	Present Equipment	New Equipment
Annual capacity	400,000 units	400,000 units
Annual costs		
Labor.	$30,000	$25,000
Depreciation	10,000	14,000
Other (all cash)	48,000	20,000
Total annual costs	$88,000	$59,000

The existing equipment is expected to have salvage value equal to its removal costs at the end of 10 years. The new equipment is expected to have a salvage value of $60,000 at the end of 10 years, which will be taxable, and no removal costs. No changes in working capital are required with the purchase of the new equipment. The sales force does not expect any changes in volume of sales over the next 10 years. The company's cost of capital is 15 percent, and its tax rate is 45 percent.

Required

a. Calculate the equipment removal costs net of tax effects.

b. Compute the depreciation tax shield.

c. Compute the forgone tax benefits of the old equipment.

d. Calculate the cash inflow, net of taxes, from the sale of new equipment in year 10.

e. Calculate the tax benefit arising from the loss on the old equipment.

f. Compute the annual differential cash flows arising from the investment in years 1 through 10.

g. Compute the net present value of the project. Refer to Illustration 23.6 for format.

23.37 Impact of Inflation on Net Present Value

Management of Wright Corporation (Problem 23.36) received your report on the estimated net present value of the new equipment. (All numbers in Problem 23.36 assumed no inflation.) However, management is disturbed about its economist's report, which indicates an expected inflation rate of 6 percent over the next 10 years.

Required

a. Calculate the new nominal interest rate.

b. Prepare a schedule showing how inflation would affect annual operating flows, assuming that year 1 operating flows are 6 percent higher than the annual savings computed in Problem 23.36.

c. Prepare a report indicating how this expectation would affect your computed net present values. Assume that the new equipment could be sold for $100,000 after 10 years. Show supporting computations in good form.

23.38 Assess Net Present Value of Training Costs

Zigfield, Inc., operates a diversified company with several operating divisions. Division C has consistently shown losses. Management is considering a proposal to offer Division C employees training designed to reduce labor and other operating costs.

The latest division income statement appears as follows (all dollar amounts in this problem are in thousands):

Revenues		$4,500
Costs		
Direct materials	$1,250	
Direct labor	1,400	
Factory overhead		
Indirect materials	200	
Indirect labor	350	
Utilities, taxes, etc.	600	
Depreciation	890	
Miscellaneous	120	
Division selling costs	450	
Division administrative costs	380	
Total costs		5,640
Division contribution		$(1,140)

The costs are expected to continue in the future unless the training is obtained.

With the training, direct labor is expected to be reduced by 55 percent, and other costs are expected to be reduced by $275 per year. These cost savings will continue for 10 years. The training will cost $5,000 and can be deducted for tax purposes in the year it is obtained.

Required

If the company's cost of capital is 12 percent and its marginal tax rate is 40 percent, determine whether the new training should be purchased. Show supporting computations.

23.39   Sensitivity Analysis in Capital Investment Decisions

Octagon Corporation is a large marketing company. Management is considering whether to expand operations by opening a new chain of specialty stores. If the company embarks on this program, cash outlays for inventories, lease rentals, working capital, and other costs are expected to amount to $3.5 million in year 0. The company expects break-even cash flows in each of years 1 and 2. Cash flows are expected to increase to $1 million in each of years 3 and 4, $2 million in year 5, and $3 million in each of years 6 and 7.

Management is aware that this is a risky venture because the economy can change over the next few years, as could consumer tastes. For these reasons, data were obtained on worst-case and best-case scenarios. In the worst case, cash flows in each of years 1 and 2 will be a negative $500,000. In each of years 3 through 7, cash flows may equal only $1 million. By contrast, the best case scenario projects positive cash flows of $500,000 in each of years 1 and 2, $1.5 million in each of years 3 and 4, and $3 million in each of years 5 through 7.

The company's after-tax cost of capital is 20 percent. All cash flows are net of tax.

Required

Compute the net present values and internal rates of return for this venture for the expected, worst-case, and best-case scenarios. Refer to Illustration 23.10 for format.

23.40   Capital Investment Analysis under Inflation with Investment Tax Credit

Each division of Norton Company has the authority to make capital expenditures up to $200,000 without approval of the corporate headquarters. The corporate controller has determined that Norton's cost of capital is 12 percent. This rate does not include an allowance for inflation, which is expected to occur at an average rate of 8 percent each year. Norton pays income taxes at the rate of 40 percent.

Norton's electronic division is considering purchasing automated machinery to manufacture its printed circuit boards. The division controller estimates that purchase of the machine will eliminate two positions, yielding a cost savings for wages and employee benefits. However, the machine would require additional supplies and more power. The cost savings and additional costs in beginning-of-year-1 prices follow:

Wages and employee benefits of the two positions eliminated ($25,000 each)	$50,000
Cost of additional supplies	3,000
Cost of additional power	10,000

The new machine would be purchased and installed at the beginning of year 1 at a net cost of $80,000. If purchased, it would be depreciated for tax purposes as follows: year 1, $16,000; year 2, $28,000; years 3 through 5, $12,000 each year. It would qualify for an investment tax credit of $8,000 in year 1. The machine will become technologically obsolete in eight years and will have no salvage value at that time.

The electronics division compensates for inflation in capital expenditure analyses by adjusting these cash flows for inflation, starting with end-of-year-1 cash flows. The adjusted after-tax cash flows are then discounted using the appropriate discount rate. No changes are expected in working capital.

Required

Prepare a schedule showing the expected future cash flows in nominal dollars. Also show the net present value of the project. (See Illustration 23.18 for present value factors under inflation.)

(CMA adapted)

SOLUTIONS TO SELF-STUDY QUESTIONS

1. a.

MELWOOD CORPORATION

	Time 0	Year 1	Year 2	Year 3	Year 4
Investment					
Equipment.	$ (7,500)				
Software ($8,400 × 55%)ᵃ	(4,620)				
Old equipment ($100 × 55%)	55				
Annual operating flows: ($8,000 × 55%)		$4,400	$4,400	$4,400	$4,400
Tax shieldᵇ		1,125	1,125	1,125	
Disinvestment ($1,000 × 55%).					550
Cash flows	$(12,065)	$5,525	$5,525	$5,525	$4,950
Discount factors at 15%.	1.0	.870	.756	.658	.572
Present values	$(12,065)	$4,808	$4,177	$3,635	$2,831
Net present value	$ 3,386				

Additional computations:
ᵃ55% = 1 − 45% tax rate, which converts before-tax cash flows to after-tax cash flows.

ᵇTax shield:

Year	Depreciation	Tax Shield
1	$2,500	$1,125
2	2,500	1,125
3	2,500	1,125
	$7,500	$3,375

b. With a positive net present value cash flow of $3,386, the equipment meets the discount rate. The cost savings justify purchase of the equipment.

2. a.

MELWOOD CORPORATION
With Inflation

	Time 0	Year 1	Year 2	Year 3	Year 4
Investment					
Equipment	$ (7,500)				
Software ($8,400 × 55%)	(4,620)				
Old equipment ($100 × 55%)	55				
Annual operating flows		$4,400	$4,840[a]	$5,324[b]	$5,856[c]
Tax shield		1,125	1,125	1,125	
Disinvestment ($1,330 × 55%)					732
Cash flows	$(12,065)	$5,525	$5,965	$6,449	$6,588
Discount factors at 26.5%	1.0	.791	.625	.494	.391
Present values.	$(12,065)	$4,370	$3,728	$3,186	$2,576
Net present value	$ 1,795				

Additional computations:
[a] $8,000 × 1.10 = $8,800 × .55 = $4,840.
[b] $8,800 × 1.10 = $9,680 × .55 = $5,324.
[c] $9,680 × 1.10 = $10,648 × .55 = $5,856.

b. With a positive net present value of $1,795, the
project meets the discount rate. The cost savings
justify purchase of the equipment.

3. a. Payback:

Year	Cash Flow
0	$(12,065)
1	5,525
2	5,525
3	5,525

$$\text{Payback} = \frac{\$12,065}{\$5,525} = \underline{\underline{2.18 \text{ years}}}$$

b. Discounted payback:

Year	Cash Flow	Balance
0	$(12,065)	$(12,065)
1	4,808	(7,257)
2	4,177	(3,080)
3	3,635	—

$$2 + \frac{\$3,080}{\$3,635} \text{ years} = \underline{\underline{2.85 \text{ years}}}$$

Note: Answers to self-study questions may vary slightly due to rounding.

Inventory Management

LEARNING OBJECTIVES

After reading this chapter, you should be able to:

1. Derive the economic order quantity (EOQ) for purchasing and production.

2. Apply the EOQ model to cases having order size restrictions or quantity discounts.

3. Find the optimal safety stock of inventory.

4. Identify the differential costs of a particular inventory policy.

In this chapter we discuss how cost data are used in inventory management. Inventory management costs should be distinguished from the cost of producing inventory. The cost of manufacturing products is made up of the materials, labor, and manufacturing overhead required to make the product. The inventory management costs discussed in this chapter are costs of keeping products in inventory.

Inventory management techniques are applicable in all types of organizations that have inventories, even those in which the only inventory is office supplies. Merchandise organizations, such as Macy's, Blockbuster Video, Toys "Я" Us, Nordstrom's, and Wal-Mart, are particularly concerned about inventory management. Too much inventory results in unnecessary costs of carrying inventory. Too little inventory results in lost sales if customers buy the product elsewhere.

Most companies use complex computer models to manage their inventories, but these models are all based on the fundamental models we introduce here. We present the classical economic order quantity (EOQ) model and the costs it should include. We examine the problem of stockouts and how to use cost data to determine the optimal safety-stock policy. Finally, we discuss recent innovations, such as just-in-time inventory models and flexible manufacturing, which are having an exciting impact on inventory management.

INVENTORY MANAGEMENT

Inventory management activities can range from ensuring that an adequate selection of clothing is available in a retail store to stocking necessary replacement parts for commercial aircraft. The underlying principles are similar in both situations. The primary objective is to minimize the total costs of maintaining inventory.

Inventory-related costs include the costs of carrying inventory, the costs of replenishing goods that have been sold or used, and the costs of running out of inventory. As we shall see, inventory management involves finding the minimum annual total of these three kinds of costs.

The cost of carrying inventory is a major reason why stores mark down their merchandise for sale. (© Dick Young/Unicorn Stock Photos)

Inventory control models have been in use for some time. Operations research techniques and the advancement of computer systems resulted in the development of highly sophisticated inventory models. These models can monitor demand, forecast usage, calculate the most economic quantity to order, indicate when to order, and determine the optimal levels of inventory to keep on hand.[1]

Engineers and operations research specialists depend on accountants for information about the costs that are relevant for use in these models. In cost accounting, we discuss issues in formulating the cost data necessary to use these techniques.

---

[1]These models and their mathematical derivation are presented in operations research texts such as T. E. Vollman, W. Barry, and D. C. Whybark, *Manufacturing, Planning and Control*, 2d ed. (Burr Ridge, IL: Richard D. Irwin, 1988).

ILLUSTRATION 24.1 Inventory Costs

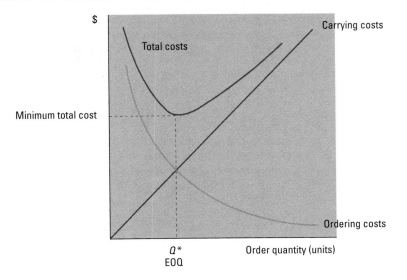

Q^* = optimal Q.

INVENTORY MANAGEMENT COSTS

L.0. 1: Derive the economic order quantity (EOQ) for purchasing and production.

carrying costs
Costs that increase with the number of units of inventory.

ordering costs
Costs that increase with the number of orders placed for inventory.

The goal in controlling inventory costs is to minimize total costs while maintaining the amount of inventories needed for smooth operation. Some costs increase with the amount of inventory on hand, while other costs decrease.

Carrying costs increase with the amount of inventory on hand. The two classes of carrying costs are (1) out-of-pocket costs and (2) cost of capital. Out-of-pocket costs include the cost of such items as insurance on the value of the inventory, inventory taxes, annual inspections, and obsolescence. The cost of capital is the opportunity cost of having funds in inventory rather than in other earning assets.

Ordering costs increase with the number of orders and decrease with the amount of inventory on hand. Ordering costs include people's time to place the order and costs of telephoning or placing an order by fax machine.

Given a constant usage rate, the more inventory on hand, the less frequently one must order, thus, the lower the ordering costs. An optimal inventory policy minimizes the sum of carrying costs and ordering costs.

Inventory costs can be represented graphically as in Illustration 24.1.

THE ECONOMIC ORDER QUANTITY (EOQ) MODEL

For analytical purposes, we divide inventory into two categories: (1) working inventory, which represents the units used in the normal course of operations, and (2) safety stock, the units kept on hand to protect against running out of inventory due to late deliveries, a speed-up in production rates, and other similar factors.

The cost-management problems for inventory are determining the optimal amount to order and deciding when to place an order. These two decisions should be based on the carrying cost of the inventory and the cost to place an order. The inventory manager wants to know the point at which the total of these costs is minimized. We will see next how these costs are represented in the basic inventory models.

Carrying Costs and Ordering Costs

Carrying costs are usually expressed in terms of the average number of units in the inventory. That is, in a given year, one would expect to incur carrying costs of

$$Q/2 \times S$$

where S is the cost to carry one unit in the inventory for one year and is composed of out-of-pocket costs as well as cost of capital. The average inventory is presumed to be the average of the Q units that arrive at the start of the inventory cycle and the zero units that are left at the end. That is, $(Q + 0)/2 = Q/2$.

Ordering costs are expressed as the product of the number of orders placed in a year times the cost to place one order. This function is

$$A/Q \times P$$

where A is the annual usage of the inventory item and P is the cost of placing one order. The term A/Q is the number of orders placed per year. As the amount per order increases, the number of orders required per year decreases. Thus, the ordering cost function decreases as Q increases, as shown in Illustration 24.1.

The total inventory carrying and ordering cost (TC) is

$$TC = QS/2 + AP/Q$$

Note from the graph in Illustration 24.1 that the minimum total cost occurs at the point where the two cost functions are equal. This coincidence occurs in the most basic EOQ problem but may not be generalized to more complex problems. For this problem, the optimal Q (labeled $Q*$) is referred to as the **economic order quantity (EOQ).** It may be found by the equation

economic order quantity (EOQ)
The order size that minimizes the total of carrying and ordering costs.

$$Q* = \sqrt{2AP/S}$$

If $Q*$ units are ordered each time and inventory usage and costs continue as planned, the inventory carrying and ordering costs will be at a minimum. Note how carrying costs increase with the amount of inventory on hand while ordering costs decrease with the amount on hand. Inventory management seeks to minimize total costs and to identify the point $Q*$. The total cost to maintain a given inventory level decreases in the range of zero to $Q*$ and then increases from $Q*$ to the maximum possible inventory level. To find $Q*$, it is necessary both to construct the mathematical relationship for the cost functions and to identify the elements of cost that should be included in each function. The first task is handled by operations research specialists; the second is the responsibility of cost accountants.

For example, Tri-Ply Company uses 25,000 units of material Z per year in manufacturing a specialty line of plywood laminates. Out-of-pocket costs for carrying material Z are $2.50 per unit. Each unit costs $80, and the company's cost of capital is 25 percent. Thus, carrying costs are $22.50 per unit ($2.50 + [$80 \times 25\%$]). The cost to place an order for material Z is $648. What is the optimal order size?

In this example, $A = 25,000$ units; $P = \$648$; and $S = \$2.50 + (\$80 \times 25\%) = \$22.50$. The optimal order size is

$$Q* = \sqrt{\frac{2 \times 25,000 \times \$648}{\$22.50}}$$

$$= \sqrt{1,440,000}$$

$$= 1,200 \text{ units}$$

Now, if Tri-Ply management follows the policy and orders 1,200 units each time, the annual costs of the inventory policy will be as follows:

Carrying Costs

$$QS/2 = \frac{1,200 \times \$22.50}{2} = \underline{\underline{\$13,500}}$$

Ordering Costs

$$AP/Q = \frac{25,000 \times \$648}{1,200} = \underline{\underline{\$13,500}}$$

so that costs amount to $27,000 (that is, the $13,500 carrying costs plus $13,500 ordering costs). This is the minimum cost. In this case, the total carrying costs equal total ordering costs, which is consistent with Illustration 24.1.

Applications

The EOQ model also can be used to compute the optimal (least-cost) length of a production run. The costs to set up a production run are analogous to the ordering costs in the basic EOQ model. Carrying costs are the same as for a basic model.

For example, if the differential cost of setting up a production line to produce a specific type of item is $2,500, the demand for the item is 720,000 per year, and the cost to carry each item in inventory is $1, then the economic production run size is

$$Q* = \sqrt{\frac{2 \times 720,000 \times \$2,500}{\$1}}$$

which equals 60,000 units.

Although the EOQ model discussed here sets forth the principles for inventory management models, actual applications are usually much more complex. Quite often the demand (or usage) variable changes from one order period to the next. In addition, rarely does a company order only one product from a given supplier. When multiple products are procured from one supplier, it may be possible to obtain ordering cost savings by ordering several items at one time. Inventory management models are so complex that they are almost always computerized. A computer model can simultaneously consider the various products ordered from a vendor and estimate the optimal time to place an order for one or more of them.

Although more complex models will be encountered, the basic model contains the elements that a cost accountant must consider in developing an optimal inventory policy.

EXTENSIONS OF THE BASIC EOQ MODEL

Orders in Round Lots

L.O. 2: Apply the EOQ model to cases having order size restrictions or quantity discounts.

The classical EOQ model may be extended to include other costs and considerations. The following examples show how inventory management costs may be incorporated in some more complex settings.

Many companies will accept orders only for round lots such as even dozens, hundreds, tons, and the like. These restrictions are often related to assembly line or packaging requirements. When there are restrictions on order size, computation of $Q*$ using the basic EOQ model will not necessarily provide an acceptable order quantity. If $Q*$ is not equal to one of the allowed order quantities, it is necessary to determine the total annual cost of ordering the two allowed quantities on either side of $Q*$. In such cases, the optimal order size will be either $Q*$, if allowed, or the allowed quantity closest to $Q*$, whether greater than or less than. Drawing lines on a cost graph to show order size restrictions as shown in Illustration 24.2 demonstrates why the optimal alternative is limited to the choices mentioned.

For example, suppose that the supplier of material Z accepts orders only in round lots of 500 units. An order for 1,200 units would not be acceptable, but Tri-Ply could order 500, 1,000, or 1,500 units. The two order sizes, 1,000 units and 1,500 units, compose the set from which the optimal order size is obtained. To determine which order size is optimal, the total annual costs for each alternative are examined.

ILLUSTRATION 24.2 EOQ with Order Size Restrictions

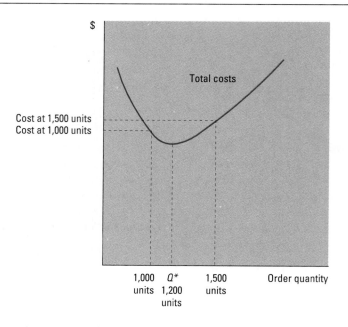

If 1,000 units are ordered, the annual inventory costs are $27,450. This is the sum of the carrying costs, computed as

$$QS/2 = \frac{1,000 \times \$22.50}{2} = \$11,250$$

and the ordering costs

$$AP/Q = \frac{25,000 \times \$648}{1,000} = \underline{\$16,200}$$

Total costs $\quad\quad\quad\quad\underline{\underline{\$27,450}}$

If 1,500 units are ordered at a time, the annual costs are $27,675, which is the sum of the carrying costs:

$$QS/2 = \frac{1,500 \times \$22.50}{2} = \$16,875$$

and the ordering costs

$$AP/Q = \frac{25,000 \times \$648}{1,500} = \underline{\$10,800}$$

Total $\quad\quad\quad\quad\quad\underline{\underline{\$27,675}}$

Therefore, the optimal policy, given the restrictions on order size, is to order 1,000 units each time.

Note that the difference in total costs between the two order sizes is relatively small ($225). If the actual order quantity is significantly different, however, the cost changes can be substantial. For example, at an order size of 500 units, the total costs increase to $38,025. (Carrying costs of $22.50 per unit times 250 units = $5,625, and ordering costs for 50 orders [25,000/500] at $648 = $32,400.) This computation highlights how the total costs change at different activity levels. Typically, they change very little for values close to Q^*; but as order size decreases, the total inventory management costs increase rather rapidly. However, we highlight the point that the optimal inventory quantity will be at one of the two feasible order quantities adjacent to the initial Q^*.

ILLUSTRATION   24.3   EOQ with Order Size Constraints

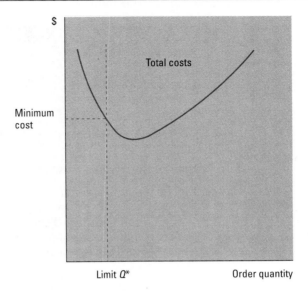

Order Size Constraints

In today's just-in-time business environment, inventory levels are kept deliberately low. Management sets maximum order sizes to avoid obsolescence or to keep carrying costs low.

If there are order size constraints on the maximum number of units that may be stored and the computed value of Q^* is more than the constraint, the appropriate order size is the value of the constraint. This may be confirmed by inspecting the cost function graph in Illustration 24.1 and drawing a constraint line anywhere between zero and Q^*. The minimum total cost is at the constraint. This may be seen from Illustration 24.3, which shows the constraint imposed on the inventory cost function.

When storage constraints exist, management may ask whether it is economically justifiable to relax the constraint. Suppose that Tri-Ply has a capacity constraint of 750 units. It could obtain additional warehouse space for $6,000 per year, enabling it to store the additional 450 units indicated by the economic lot size model. Should the company obtain the additional space?

To decide, management must look at the differential cost of the alternatives. If it ordered 750 units at a time (this is the best that can be done with the constraint), the costs are as follows:

Carrying Costs

$$QS/2 = \frac{750 \times \$22.50}{2} = \$8,437.50$$

Ordering Costs

$$AP/Q = \frac{25,000 \times \$648}{750} = \underline{\$21,600.00}$$

Total $\underline{\underline{\$30,037.50}}$

From the initial example, we know that the optimal inventory costs without the constraint are $27,000. The expected savings from the additional warehouse space are $3,037.50 (the difference between $30,037.50 and $27,000). Because the rental cost exceeds the expected savings, it is better to forgo the rental and order in lots of 750 units.

This also may be formulated in the same manner as other differential cost problems. A comparison of the costs for the alternatives to maintain present storage or rent space appears as follows:

Cost Item	Maintain Present Storage	Rent Space	Differential Costs
Carrying costs (excluding space rentals)	$ 8,437.50	$13,500.00	$5,062.50 higher
Ordering costs	21,600.00	13,500.00	8,100.00 lower
Space rental	–0–	6,000.00	6,000.00 higher
Total costs	$30,037.50	$33,000.00	$2,962.50 higher

This analysis yields the same results, that the differential costs of renting exceed the savings.

Quantity Discounts

quantity discounts
Price reductions offered for bulk purchases.

Suppliers often offer **quantity discounts** on purchases of materials or lower shipping charges for bulk shipments. In such situations, the savings from ordering in large lots may more than offset the incremental carrying costs. As a general rule, when quantity discounts are available, the minimum EOQ is the amount determined by the computation of Q^* without regard to price-break considerations. It may be less costly, however, to order a large quantity to obtain the discount.

Assume that material Z's supplier offers the following price breaks:

Number Ordered	Per Unit Discount
0–999	None
1,000–1,999	$1.00
2,000–4,999	1.50
5,000–9,999	1.75
10,000 and more	1.80

The optimal order quantity for Tri-Ply is either 1,200 units, the optimal quantity ignoring the price breaks, or 2,000, 5,000, or 10,000 units. No other quantity is more economic.

Tri-Ply management can determine which of the four quantities is least costly if the price breaks are considered as opportunity costs. Forgoing the maximum available discount results in an opportunity cost equal to the difference between that maximum and the discount that Tri-Ply could obtain with its selected order policy. For example, if Tri-Ply orders in lots of 1,200 units, it obtains a discount of $1 per unit but forgoes the opportunity to obtain a $1.80 discount. If it orders 1,200 units at a time, a discount cost of $.80 on each unit ordered is forgone. Over the year, Tri-Ply loses discounts of $20,000, based on the 25,000 units ordered per year times the $.80 in lost discounts per unit.

In addition, the dollar cost of capital per unit of inventory is reduced if Tri-Ply obtains a discount. The higher the discount, the greater the reduction. The reduction in cost equals the percentage cost of capital times the dollar amount of discount. For example, if Tri-Ply orders 1,200 units, the discount is $1.00 per unit. If its cost of capital is 25 percent, the reduction in cost of capital per unit is $.25 (25 percent × $1.00).

One way to analyze the EOQ when price breaks are available is to consider the total carrying cost, ordering cost, and forgone discount for the initial Q^* and the minimum quantities required to earn each additional price break. Such an analysis for Tri-Ply's purchases of material Z is presented in Illustration 24.4.

The optimal order quantity, then, is the one with the lowest total cost, 2,000 units in this case. Note the behavior of the carrying costs and ordering costs with changes in quantities, and compare them to the patterns in Illustration 24.1.

ILLUSTRATION 24.4	Optimal Order Quantity with Price Breaks			

Panel A

Order Size	Carrying Costs	Ordering Costs	Forgone Discount	Total Costs
1,200	$ 13,500[a]	$13,500[b]	$20,000[c]	$ 47,000
2,000	22,375[d]	8,100[e]	7,500[f]	37,975 (optimal)
5,000	55,781[g]	3,240[h]	1,250[i]	60,271
10,000	111,500[j]	1,620[k]	–0–	113,120

Panel B
Computations:

[a]$13,500 = $\dfrac{1,200 \times (\$2.50 + [25\% \times \$80.00])}{2}$, assuming the $80 price is net of the discount at this level. (Recall that $2.50 equals out-of-pocket carrying costs and 25% is the cost of capital expressed as a percentage.)

[b]$13,500 = $\dfrac{25,000}{1,200} \times \$648$. (Recall that the annual quantity ordered equals 25,000 and the cost to place an order is $648.)

[c]$20,000 = 25,000 \times (\$1.80 - \$1.00)$, where $1.80 is the maximum price break available.

[d]$22,375 = $\dfrac{2,000 \times (\$2.50 + [25\% \times \$79.50])}{2}$, where $79.50 is $80 less the incremental $.50 discount.

[e]$8,100 = $\dfrac{25,000}{2,000} \times \$648$.

[f]$7,500 = 25,000 \times (\$1.80 - \$1.50)$.

[g]$55,781$ (rounded) $= \dfrac{5,000 \times (\$2.50 + [25\% \times \$79.25])}{2}$, where $79.25 = $80.00 less the $.75 incremental discount.

[h]$3,240 = \dfrac{25,000}{5,000} \times \$648$.

[i]$1,250 = 25,000 \times (\$1.80 - \$1.75)$.

[j]$111,500 = \dfrac{10,000 \times (\$2.50 + [25\% \times \$79.20])}{2}$, where $79.20 is $80 less the $.80 incremental discount.

[k]$1,620 = \dfrac{25,000}{10,000} \times \$648$.

INVENTORY MANAGEMENT UNDER UNCERTAIN CONDITIONS

L.O. 3: Find the optimal safety stock of inventory.

lead time
The time between placing an order and its arrival.

stockout
Running out of inventory.

So far we have considered only working inventory in our cost analyses. Knowing usage rates and **lead time** (the time between placing an order and its arrival) simplifies inventory management. Usage rates may vary due to unforeseen circumstances, and lead times may vary due to events beyond management's control. If an inventory item is used more rapidly than anticipated or if lead time is longer than expected, a **stockout** may occur.

The use of just-in-time methods that expect inventory replenishment immediately as needed for production or sale, anticipates stockouts. Analyzing these costs may help minimize the costs of a just-in-time system.

Two reasons for stockouts are diagrammed in Illustration 24.5. In case A, an order was placed at time T, but the rate of use increased. As a result, the inventory on hand was used before the new shipment arrived. In case B, the usage rate remained constant, but the new shipment did not arrive on time.

Stockouts Can Be Costly

Depending on the nature of the product, a stockout may require a special trip to pick up extra materials or shutting down operations until new materials can be obtained, resulting in lost sales and customer ill will. Obtaining an optimal amount of safety stock can minimize such added costs. Had the company in the previous example maintained sufficient safety stock, no stockout would have occurred.

ILLUSTRATION   24.5   Inventory Flows under Uncertainty

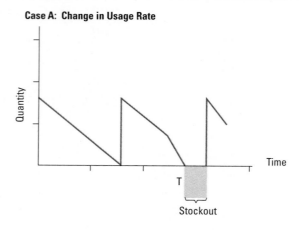

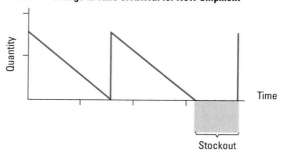

Restaurants often risk stock outs because the cost of carrying a perishable safety stock.
(© Jeff Greenberg/Unicorn Stock Photos)

In contrast, the costs to carry additional inventory may be so high that incurring stockouts is economical. The situations from Illustration 24.5 are reproduced in Illustration 24.6 with the addition of safety stock. Now, in case A, the increased usage is satisfied from the safety stock, and the new order replenishes both the safety stock and the working inventory. In case B, the safety stock is used while awaiting the delayed arrival of the inventory order. Safety stock is replenished with subsequent orders.

Cost Considerations for Safety Stock

Two costs must be considered in establishing an optimal safety-stock policy: the cost to carry it and the cost of a stockout.

The cost of carrying safety stock is the same as the cost of carrying working inventory. The full quantity of safety stock is the same as the average inventory of safety stock. Because the safety stock on hand at the start of the period should equal the safety stock on hand at the end of the period, the average of these two numbers is the full quantity of safety stock. Although safety stock may decrease from time to time as events require its use, these decreases are usually ignored.

Stockout costs require separate consideration. In the first place, the cost of one stockout is usually expressed in terms of the costs of alternative sources of supply

ILLUSTRATION   24.6   Inventory Flows with Safety Stock

Case A: Change in Usage Rate

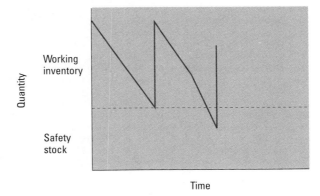

Case B: Change in Time of Arrival for New Shipment

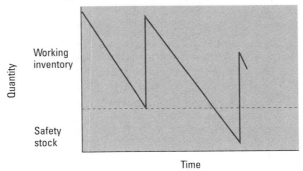

or shutting down operations over the stockout period. Stockouts also cause customer ill will, as you know if you have placed an order with Lands' End, Eddie Bauer, or any other company only to be told the item is out of stock. Second, the number of stockouts is an expected value. The expected annual stockout cost is the product of the cost of one stockout times the number of orders placed per year times the probability of a stockout on any one order.

Returning to the original example for Tri-Ply Company's inventory of material Z, let us consider that the company has a choice of alternative safety stock levels, each of which yields a different probability of a stockout. The staff determined that a .5 probability of a stockout exists if no safety stock is maintained. A safety stock of 100 units reduces the stockout probability to .3. If the safety stock is maintained at 250 units of material Z, a .05 probability of a stockout exists. Finally, a .01 probability of a stockout would be expected if the safety stock level were 500 units. If the costs of one stockout are estimated at $3,200, the best choice of these four safety stock levels is 250 units, as shown by the analysis in Illustration 24.7. (Recall that annual usage is 25,000 and optimal order size is 1,200.)

Even with the optimal safety stock level, the probability of a stockout is .05. Given that the company orders about 21 times a year ($25,000/1,200 \cong 20.8$), Tri-Ply can expect one stockout a year for material Z ($21 \times .05 \cong 1$). It is more economical to

ILLUSTRATION 24.7	Cost Analysis of Safety-Stock Policies		
Safety Stock	Carrying Costs	Expected Stockout Costs	Total Costs
0	$0 \times \$22.50$ $= \$0$	$\dfrac{25,000^a}{1,200} \times .5 \times \$3,200$ $= \$33,333$	$\$33,333$
100	$100 \times \$22.50$ $= \$2,250$	$\dfrac{25,000}{1,200} \times .3 \times \$3,200$ $= \$20,000$	$22,250$
250	$250 \times \$22.50$ $= \$5,625$	$\dfrac{25,000}{1,200} \times .05 \times \$3,200$ $= \$3,333$	$8,958$ (optimal)
500	$500 \times \$22.50$ $= \$11,250$	$\dfrac{25,000}{1,200} \times .01 \times \$3,200$ $= \$667$	$11,917$

[a]The ratio 25,000/1,200 is the number of orders per year and, therefore, the number of possible stockouts.

incur this stockout cost, however, than to maintain the additional safety stock. Inventory management seeks to find the least cost policy with respect to safety stock levels and stockouts.

Similar cost analyses can be prepared if, for example, different stockout costs exist depending on the size of the stockout. The shortage of a few items that can be obtained by alternative transportation may result in incurring only the cost of the incremental transport charges, but one that involves several hundred large items may not be so easily, or inexpensively, resolved.

Stockout Costs as Ordering Costs

Expected annual stockout costs vary directly with the number of orders placed in a year, so stockout costs are an ordering cost. The problem in including these costs in the EOQ and safety stock models is that the two models are interdependent. The cost per order used in the EOQ model depends on the optimal stockout probability. Discussion of some of the more complex problems in inventory management, such as the joint solution to this problem, is beyond the scope of this text. Our intention is to familiarize you with the nature of the problem and its implications for cost accounting.

Reorder Point

Goods should be reordered when the inventory on hand has fallen to the sum of the usage over the lead time plus the safety stock. If an order is placed when the inventory has reached that level, the new shipment is expected to arrive when the total number of units on hand equals the safety stock; that is, the working inventory has fallen to zero.

For example, a safety stock of 250 has been chosen for material Z. The lead time is six working days, and the annual usage is 25,000 units. Assuming 220 working days per year, the reorder point for material Z is 932 units, computed as follows:

$$([25,000/220 \text{ days}] \times 6) + 250 = (113.64 \times 6) + 250$$
$$= 682 + 250 = 932$$

When inventory falls to 932 units, an order should be placed for the optimal number of units (Q^* in the unconstrained problem or other cost-effective Q values in the presence of constraints). During the six days between placing an order and its arrival, units are used at the rate of 113.64 per day. After six days, if all goes as planned,

ILLUSTRATION   24.8   Reorder Point

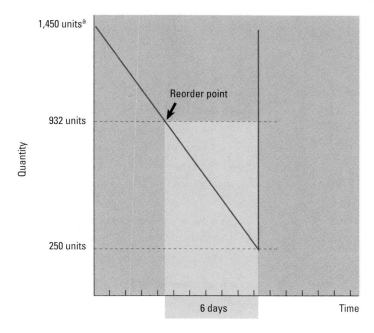

ᵃ1,450 units = Q^* + Safety stock = 1,200 units + 250 units.

approximately 250 units will be in inventory (the 932 units at reorder time less the [6 × 113.64] used during the lead time) when the new shipment of Q units arrives. This is diagrammed in Illustration 24.8. If an order is placed at that point in time, 682 units will be used between the reorder time and the time of arrival of the new order.

DIFFERENTIAL COSTS OF INVENTORY POLICY

L.O. 4: Identify the differential costs of a particular inventory policy.

Selecting the costs relevant to the EOQ is an application of differential costing. When preparing cost data for inventory models, we look at each cost and ask whether it will change with the number of (1) units carried in inventory, (2) units purchased, or (3) orders placed in a year.

For example, let's consider the costs obtained from Tri-Ply Company's records on a different inventory item. These costs are related to a specific inventory item:

Purchase price	$ 6.50 per unit
Transportation-in per unit	.50
Telephone call for order	11.00
Cost to unload a shipment	25.00 + $.15 per unit
Inventory taxes	.60 per unit per year
Costs to arrange to ship the material to the company	125.00
Receiving dock supervisor's salary (per month)	1,800.00
Insurance on inventory	.10 per unit per year
Warehouse rental	12,000.00 per month
Average spoilage costs	1.30 per unit per year
Cost of capital	20% per year
Orders handled per month	600

Which of these items should be included in the EOQ computation? Using the three cost categories mentioned earlier, let's classify each item.

1. Costs that vary with the average number of units carried in inventory:

Inventory taxes	$ .60 per unit
Insurance on inventory	.10
Average spoilage costs	1.30
Total	$2.00

2. Costs that vary with the number of units purchased:

Purchase price	$6.50 per unit
Transportation-in	.50
Costs to unload	.15
Total	$7.15

Total annual carrying cost per unit is the sum of the carrying costs from category 1 plus the cost of capital rate times the investment cost in category 2:

$$\$.60 + \$.10 + \$1.30 + (20\% \times \$7.15) = \$2.00 + (20\% \times \$7.15) = \$3.43$$

3. Costs to place an order:

Costs of placing the order	$ 11.00 per order
Unloading the shipment	25.00
Arranging for the shipment	125.00
Total	$161.00

The total ordering cost is $161 per order.

The other costs (warehouse rental and supervisor's salary) usually do not vary with the number of units in inventory, the number of units purchased, or the number of orders during the inventory planning horizon. Those costs are therefore irrelevant for this decision (although they may be important for long-range decision making).

SELF-STUDY QUESTION

Main Mart Discount Electronics is a customer of your bank. The company president was in your office earlier in the day to apply for an additional line of credit. Trying to help your client, you note that a substantial sum of money is tied up in inventory. When you pointed this out, the company president's response was, "We can't afford to run out of stock. Therefore, our policy is to order as infrequently as possible and to keep as much safety stock on hand as can be stored in our warehouse."

As part of your analysis of the company's loan requirements, you call the controller of the company for some further information. The conversation indicates that the company has a substantial amount of one particular product in its warehouse. The controller relates the following information on this product:

Invoice cost	$ 120.00
Shipping charges	2.50 per unit
Arranging for the shipment	175.00 per order
Inventory insurance	1.00 per unit per year
Annual costs to audit and inspect inventory	2.60 per unit
Warehouse utilities	980.00 per month
Warehouse rental	1,500.00 per month
Unloading costs for units received (paid to shipper)	.80 per unit
Receiving supervisor salary	1,760.00 per month
Processing invoices and other purchase documents	16.00 per order
Allowable order quantity: 250 or multiples thereof	

Company policy is to keep a safety stock of 3,000 units and to order 5,000 units at a time. Annual demand for the product is 45,000 units. The lead time for an order is 10 working days, and there are 250 working days per year for the purposes of purchasing this product. The controller indicated that if there is a stockout, it would be necessary to obtain the products by special air courier at an additional cost of $8,100 per stockout. The probabilities of a stockout with various safety stock levels are as follows:

Safety Stock	Probability of Stockout
500	.25
1,000	.08
1,500	.02
2,000	.01

You estimated that the company's cost of capital is approximately 30 percent. You also know that the state has an inventory tax equal to 1 percent of the cost of items in inventory, which the state defines as the sum of the invoice price, shipping cost per unit, and the unloading costs. You assume for analysis purposes that a stockout probability of .02 is reasonable for order cost determination in an optimal inventory policy.

a. What is the annual cost of the company's present inventory policy? Assume that 5,000 units are ordered each time an order is placed.

b. How many units should the company order at a time? (Note that the allowable order quantity is in multiples of 250 units.)

c. What is the optimal safety stock level?

d. What is the annual cost of the optimal inventory policy identified in *(b)* and *(c)* (including expected stockout costs)?

e. What is the reorder point?

The solution to this question is at the end of this chapter on page 766.

JUST-IN-TIME PRODUCTION

just-in-time
A system designed to obtain goods just in time for production (in manufacturing) or sale (in merchandising).

Recent innovations in inventory management and manufacturing methods have the potential to revolutionize both inventory management and accounting in manufacturing companies. One of these is the **just-in-time** philosophy. The objective of the just-in-time (JIT) philosophy is to obtain materials just in time for production and to provide finished goods just in time for sale and other inventory items just when needed. This reduces, or potentially eliminates, inventory carrying costs.

Just-in-time production also requires that processes or people making defective units be corrected immediately because there is no inventory where defective units can be sent to wait reworking or scrapping. Manufacturing managers find that eliminating inventories can prevent production problems from being hidden.

In theory, a JIT system eliminates the need for inventories because no production takes place until it is known that the item will be sold. As a practical matter, companies using this system normally have a backlog of orders so they can keep their production operations going. The benefits of the JIT system are lost if a company has to shut down its operations for lengthy periods of time awaiting the receipt of a new order.

Users of this system claim that it minimizes the need to carry inventories. Moreover, by producing only enough to fill orders, better control is maintained over goods lost or spoiled in production because the entire production line is set up to produce just enough units to fill the order received. If there are spoiled or lost units, a supplemental order that serves to notify management of the spoilage or lost goods is required.

REDUCING SETUP TIME

Companies that make several types of a product in a single operation are experimenting with flexible manufacturing methods to reduce both inventory levels and the cost of setups. Ford Motor Co., for example, used to make fenders for several models of cars using one manufacturing operation. When it was time to make left-side fenders instead of right-side fenders, or when it was time to stop making fenders for car model A and start making them for car model B, the production line was stopped while workers changed the machines to make the new fenders. It traditionally took from 4 to 16 hours to make this changeover and start producing new fenders without defects.

Companies are finding ways to reduce the length of these changeovers. This reduces the costs of setups because workers are not spending as much time making these changeovers and the company has less idle production time. Flexible manufacturing techniques allow companies to make quick changeovers using automated equipment and sophisticated computer software, allowing companies to make products just in time for use because of the flexibility in changing from making one product to another. Using flexible manufacturing, companies can maintain low inventories as well as have low setup costs.

These methods provide an opportunity for exciting advances in the way products are made and for reducing inventory management costs. These methods are still at an experimental stage in many companies, however, so their advantages and disadvantages remain to be learned. It is important for accountants to be involved in developing these production methods because their development affects an important cost, that of managing inventory. Future cost accountants may spend relatively little time determining inventory costs and more time helping managers plan and control production activities.

SUMMARY

Adopting an inventory management policy can be a source of significant cost savings to many organizations.

The following summarizes key ideas tied to the chapter's learning objectives.

LO1: Deriving the EOQ for purchasing and production. The equations for determining ordering costs and carrying costs are derived in the chapter. These are the two primary inventory costs.

LO2: EOQ and cases having order size restrictions or quantity discounts. The company's available storage space may restrict the amount of inventory ordered. Also, companies are often offered quantity discounts from suppliers. The EOQ model can be used for both these scenarios.

LO3: Finding the optimal safety stock of inventory. In a decision concerning safety stock levels, the differential costs include the costs to carry the safety stock and the stockout costs.

LO4: Identifying differential costs of a particular inventory policy. When preparing cost data for inventory models, we look at each cost and ask whether it will change with the number of (a) units carried in inventory, (b) units purchased, and (c) orders placed in a year. Only differential costs are pertinent to the inventory decision.

KEY TERMS

carrying costs, 745

economic order quantity (EOQ), 746

just-in-time, 757

lead time, 751

ordering costs, 745

quantity discounts, 750

stockout, 751

REVIEW QUESTIONS

24.1 If the operations research specialists develop and maintain inventory models, why does the accountant become concerned with inventory policy decisions?

24.2 Why is the cost of capital included as a carrying cost of inventory?

24.3 In determining economic order quantities, the carrying cost per unit is divided by 2. Why?

24.4 For each of the following costs, indicate whether the cost is an out-of-pocket carrying cost (C), a cost of placing an order (P), or a cost that does not qualify for either of these categories (N). Assume that wages vary with the level of work while salaries are fixed for a monthly or longer time period.
  a. Hourly fee for inventory audit.
  b. Salary of purchasing supervisor.
  c. Costs to audit purchase orders and invoices on a per order basis.
  d. Taxes on inventory.
  e. Stockout costs.
  f. Storage costs charged per unit in inventory.
  g. Fire insurance on inventory.
  h. Fire insurance on warehouse.
  i. Obsolescence costs on inventory.
  j. Shipping costs per shipment.

24.5 When constraints appear in an inventory problem, why is the optimal decision either Q^* or one of the alternatives adjacent to it?

24.6 The following is a diagram of the quantities of an inventory item on hand over a recent time period. Supply labels for the lettered items in the diagram.

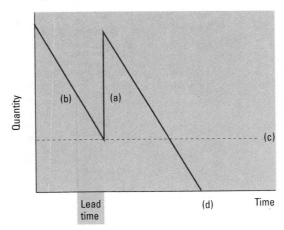

CRITICAL ANALYSIS AND DISCUSSION QUESTIONS

24.7   A staff accountant for Percolators, Inc., noted that the annual carrying cost for a specific inventory item is estimated at $28,500, and the annual order cost is estimated at $14,150. Does this information tell you anything about the relationship of the actual order quantity to the optimal order quantity? Explain.

24.8   In terms of the specifics of the costs associated with inventory policy, how does the concept of differential costs apply to the problem of inventory policy?

24.9   A company estimates that the lead time for a particular material is five days but that the demand over lead time is uncertain. The distribution of demand over lead time is best approximated by the normal distribution (that is, a symmetric, bell-shaped curve). If there is a great number of possible values for the demand over lead time and if no safety stock is maintained, how frequently would a stockout be expected?

24.10   "Our company orders 5,000 units at a time just to make sure we don't experience a stockout." Comment on this statement.

24.11   Phenerome Corporation, a diversified company that has acquired a number of subsidiaries through mergers, is instituting an inventory control system that would incorporate economic inventory policy considerations. One of the company officers has noted that some subsidiaries use last-in, first-out (LIFO) for financial reporting and others use first-in, first-out (FIFO). The officer asks you, "These different inventory methods make it very difficult for us to prepare the corporate financials and our tax return. How will they affect operation of an inventory system since the inventory costs will be different for the same item in a different subsidiary?"

24.12   How does a just-in-time philosophy result in better control over goods spoiled or lost in production?

24.13   How does flexible manufacturing work to support the just-in-time philosophy?

24.14   What problems might be encountered with companies that use just-in-time production?

EXERCISES

24.15   Compute EOQ (L.O. 1)

One of the inventory items at a company has a purchase price of $80. The annual demand for the item is 40,000 units. It costs $4,800 to place an order for the material, and out-of-pocket storage costs amount to $9.60 per unit. The company cost of capital is 18 percent.

Required   Determine the EOQ.

24.16   Compute EOQ (L.O. 1)

Sonoma Technology, Inc., uses 310,000 cartons of computer disks each year. Order costs amount to $620 each time an order is placed. Carrying costs are $125 per carton.

Required   Compute the EOQ.

24.17   Find Missing Data for EOQ (L.O. 1)

Errantos Corporation manufactures Olivas, a consumer product, in optimal production runs of 3,500 units 20 times per year. It is estimated that the setup costs (including nonproductive labor) amount to $306.25 for each batch. The company's cost of capital is 20 percent, and the out-of-pocket cost to store an Olivas for one year is $0.80.

Required   Solve the unknown inventory cost of an Olivas.

24.18   EOQ— Multiple Choice (L.O. 1)

a.   The following information relates to Coloma Industries:

Units required per year	240,000
Cost of placing an order	$300
Unit carrying cost per year	$400

Assuming that the units will be required evenly throughout the year, what is the EOQ?

(1)   400
(2)   600
(3)   800
(4)   1,000
(5)   Some other answer.

b. Fong Incorporated has to manufacture 48,000 blades for its electric lawn mower division. The blades will be used evenly throughout the year. The setup cost every time a production run is made is $100, and the cost to carry a blade in inventory for the year is $.60. Fong's objective is to produce the blades at the lowest cost possible. Assuming that each production run will be for the same number of blades, how many production runs should Fong make?

    (1) 12
    (2) 10
    (3) 8
    (4) 4
    (5) Some other answer.

c. Pierce Company requires 160,000 units of product Q for the year. The units will be required evenly throughout the year. It costs $54 to place an order and $12 to carry a unit in inventory for the year. What is the EOQ?

    (1) 400
    (2) 800
    (3) 1,200
    (4) 3,200
    (5) Some other answer.

(CPA adapted)

24.19   **Orders in Round Lots** (L.O. 2)

Loggins Corporation uses a direct material, Zelda, in its production processes. The company uses 172,000 units of Zelda a year. The carrying costs of Zelda amount to $25 per unit, and order costs are $325 per order. Zelda's manufacturer will accept orders only in lots of even thousands.

Required

What is the optimal order quantity and the annual inventory costs, given the restriction on order sizes?

24.20   **Impact of Quantity Discounts on Order Quantity** (L.O. 2)

Folsom Company uses 810 tankloads a year of a specific input material. The tankloads are delivered by rail to a siding on the company property. The supplier is offering a special discount for buyers of large quantities. The schedule is as follows:

Quantity Ordered (tankloads)	Percentage Discount
1–19	–0–
20–79	2
80–149	5
150 and more	6

Ordering costs amount to $500, and carrying costs are $450 per tankload and are not affected by the discounts. Each tankload costs $1,500.

Required

Compute the optimal order quantity. (Round to the nearest whole number.)

24.21   **Impact of Constraints on Optimal Order** (L.O. 2)

Considering the situation in Exercise 24.20, suppose that the maximum storage capacity for the company is 50 tankloads. What would the optimal order be? Demonstrate why.

24.22   **Evaluate Safety Stock Policy** (L.O. 3)

Rollins Corporation manufactures commercial fertilizer. The manufacturing process requires several inputs including a nitrogen fixer, NFX. The company uses 39,000 units of NFX per year and makes 15 orders per year in economic lot sizes of 2,600 units. The cost to carry a unit of NFX is $32. If there is a stockout, a carload of NFX must be purchased at retail from a local supplier. The retail price is $3,300 per order more than the price from the regular supplier.

Looking at the past order records, it appears that certain safety stock levels would result in stockouts according to the following schedule:

Safety-Stock Quantity	Probability of Stockout
–0–	.60
100	.20
175	.08
250	.04

Required

What level of safety stock would result in the lowest cost to the company?

24.23   Safety Stock—
Multiple Choice
(L.O. 3)

a.   Eaton Company wishes to determine the amount of safety stock to maintain for product No. 135 that will result in the lowest cost. Each stockout will cost $300, and the carrying cost of each unit of safety stock will be $1. Product No. 135 will be ordered five times a year. Which of the following will produce the lowest cost?
   (1)   A safety stock of 10 units that is associated with a 40 percent probability of running out of stock during an order period.
   (2)   A safety stock of 20 units that is associated with a 20 percent probability of running out of stock during an order period.
   (3)   A safety stock of 40 units that is associated with a 10 percent probability of running out of stock during an order period.
   (4)   A safety stock of 80 units that is associated with a 5 percent probability of running out of stock during an order period.

b.   McNeely Company wishes to determine the amount of safety stock to maintain for product D that will result in the lowest costs. The following information is available:

Stockout cost	$120 per occurrence
Carrying cost of safety stock	$8 per unit
Number of purchase orders	5 per year

The options available to McNeely are as follows:

Units of Safety Stock	Probability of Running Out of Safety Stock
10	50%
20	40
30	30
40	20
50	10
55	5

Which of the following number of units of safety stock will result in the lowest cost?
   (1)   10.
   (2)   30.
   (3)   40.
   (4)   55.

(CPA adapted)

24.24   Differential Costs
of Inventory Policy
(L.O. 4)

A review of the inventories of Sounds, Inc., indicates the following cost data for speaker cabinets:

Invoice price	$195.00 per unit
Cost to arrange for the shipment	$55.20 per order
Permit fees for shipping	$403.30 per truckload
Inventory tax	2% of the invoice price
Insurance on shipments	$3.00 per unit
Insurance on inventory	$5.60 per unit
Warehouse rental	$1,970 per month
Stockout costs	$244.00 per order
Cost of capital	25%
Unloading, per order	$160.40 per order

Required

Show the differential costs that would be included in an EOQ model.

24.25 Differential Costs of Inventory Policy (L.O. 4)

A company uses 5,400 units of Zeron per year. Each unit has an invoice cost of $317, including shipping costs. Because of the volatile nature of Zeron, it costs $860 for liability insurance on each shipment. The costs of carrying the inventory amount to $75 per unit per year exclusive of a 20 percent cost of capital. Other order costs amount to $18 per order.

At present, the company orders 500 units at a time.

Required

a. What is the annual cost of the company's current order policy?

b. What is the annual cost of the optimal economic order policy?

PROBLEMS

24.26 Determine Optimal Safety Stock Levels

Estatic Products, Inc., has expressed concern over the erratic delivery times for a critical product, Westovers. The company orders 1,500 at a time and has maintained a safety stock of 100 Westovers but has been experiencing frequent stockouts and production delays. The plant operates 270 days per year. The company estimates that the lead time for Westovers is five days, over which time 250 units will be used in production. The cost of storing a unit is $22 per year, including capital costs. A stockout is estimated to cost $4,200 for each day that the company must wait for shipment. Any time a stockout occurs, the company must wait until its sole supplier delivers these units.

Over the past several years, the lead times have been as follows:

Lead Time (days)	Probability Lead Time
9	.05
8	.15
6	.20
5	.40
4	.20

Other lead times have not occurred and may be ignored.

Required

Determine the most economic safety stock level.

24.27 Inventory Policy Cost Evaluation

Wilson, Inc., is a wholesaler of Protoxid for industrial clients. Demand for Protoxid is stable at 350,000 units per year. Wilson orders the product from its supplier four times a year. An order is placed when the total Protoxid on hand amounts to 25,000 units. This represents a nine-day working supply plus safety stock. The company works 300 days per year. Recently, Wilson management has expressed concern over the costs of carrying inventory and is seeking to evaluate the present inventory order and safety stock policies.

As a part of the study, the following costs were identified with respect to Protoxid:

Invoice price	$ 32.92
Weight per unit	1.5 kg
Shipping charges	$ 1.05 per unit + $640 per truck + $.40 per kg
Tax on each unit.	1.80
Special packaging per unit	3.65 ($1 is refunded on return of the shipping container)
Insurance on shipment.	1.76 per unit—casualty insurance
	415.00 per shipment—liability bond
Processing order documents	183.00
Unloading operations.	.82 per unit + $1,800 per week
Inspect and count for annual inventory	2.63 per unit
Rental of unloading equipment (1-day minimum rental—200,000-unit daily capacity).	222.00 per day
Estimated obsolescence costs	1.35 per unit
Inventory record maintenance	.92 per unit + $2,200 per week
Inventory tax	3% of invoice price
Inventory insurance.	15% of invoice price + $4,100 per month

The company estimates its cost of capital is 22 percent. In addition, it conducted a study on the costs of a stockout. The average stockout costs $5,400 due to the need to request special shipments from alternate suppliers. With various safety stock levels, the probabilities of a stockout decrease as follows:

Safety Stock	Probability of Stockout
–0–	.5
7,000	.1
14,000	.02
21,000	.01

To determine order quantity, assume a stockout probability per order of .02. Order sizes are restricted to round lots of 5,000. The company has the capacity to store 90,000 units.

Required

a. What are the differential costs for inventory policy making?

b. What are the annual costs under the present order and safety stock system?

c. What are the annual costs under the optimal order and safety stock system?

d. What is the reorder point under the optimal order and safety stock system?

24.28 Sensitivity of EOQ Computations to Changes in Cost Estimates

Wildridge, Inc., is instituting an economic order policy for its inventory. The following data are presented for one item in the inventory:

Annual usage	80,000 units
Storage costs	$7 per unit (out of pocket)
Cost of capital	30% of $275 purchase price per unit
Order costs	$808

Required

a. What is the EOQ, given these data?

b. What is the annual cost of following the order policy in requirement *(a)* if the cost of capital were 15 percent?

c. What are the EOQ and total annual costs if the cost of capital were 20 percent?

24.29 Inventory Cycle Analysis— Multiple Choice

Retem & Company began producing pacemakers last year. At that time, the company forecasted the annual need for 10,000 integrated circuits. During the first year, the company placed orders when the inventory dropped to 600 units so that it would have enough to produce pacemakers continuously during a three-week lead time. Unfortunately, the company ran out of this component on several occasions, causing costly production delays. Careful study of last year's experience resulted in the following expectations for the coming year:

Weekly Usage	Related Probability of Usage	Lead Time	Related Probability of Lead Time
280 units	.2	3 weeks	.1
180 units	.8	2 weeks	.9
	1.0		1.0

The study also suggested that usage during a given week was statistically independent of usage during any other week, and usage was also statistically independent of lead time.

a. The expected average usage during a regular production week is
   (1) 180 units.
   (2) 200 units.
   (3) 280 units.
   (4) 460 units.
   (5) Some usage other than those given.

b. The expected usage during lead time is
   (1) 840 units.
   (2) 400 units.
   (3) 360 units.
   (4) 420 units.
   (5) Some usage other than those given.

(CMA adapted)

24.30   Alternative Order Policy Costs

Save the Whales (SW) is planning a fund-raising benefit. To publicize its cause and to raise money, the committee plans to sell T-shirts with the SW logo and a design commemorating the benefit event. However, since the committee has never held one of these benefits previously, it has no experience about the number of T-shirts to order.

You've been asked to volunteer your knowledge of cost accounting and provide the committee with some information on the cost of alternatives. The committee expects to sell at least 500 shirts but will probably sell five times that amount. However, these numbers are very "soft." Since the committee is operating with limited funds, it wants to avoid undue risk in this T-shirt adventure.

After contacting several T-shirt manufacturers, you conclude that the best price structure is as follows:

Design logo and shirt	$150.00
Setup each production run	100.00
Cost per shirt	
Order of 1–99	10.00
100–499	6.00
500–749	5.00
750–999	4.50
1,000–1,999	4.00
2,000–2,999	3.80
3,000 and over	3.60

The shirts are expected to sell for $10 each. There are no costs to store the shirts because one of the committee members has volunteered storage space. However, unsold shirts are valueless.

Required

Analyze the costs of alternative T-shirt order policies for the committee. Because the sales volume is unknown, your report will have to focus on possible volumes. Use those suggested by the committee. Indicate to the committee the costs of each alternative and the differential or opportunity cost of selecting a less risky order size.

INTEGRATIVE CASE

24.31   Overhead Application and Inventory Management Costs

Commercial Furniture, Inc., manufactures and sells several brands of office furniture. The manufacturing operation is organized by the item produced rather than by the furniture line. Thus, the desks for all brands are manufactured on the same production line in batches. For example, 10 high-quality desks might be manufactured during the first two weeks in October and 50 units of a lower-quality desk during the last two weeks. Because each model has its own unique manufacturing requirement, the change from one model to another requires the factory's equipment to be adjusted.

Company management wants to determine the most economical production run for each item in its product lines. One of the costs that must be estimated is the setup cost incurred to change to a different furniture model. The accounting department has been asked to determine the setup cost for the desk model JE 40 as an example.

The equipment maintenance department is responsible for all changeover adjustments on production lines in addition to the preventive and regular maintenance of all the production equipment. The equipment maintenance staff has a 40-hour workweek; the size of the staff changes only if a change in the workload is expected to persist for an extended period of time. The equipment maintenance department had 10 employees last year, each of whom averaged 2,000 hours for the year. They are paid $10.80 an hour. The other departmental costs, including items such as supervision, depreciation, and insurance, total $50,000 per year.

Two workers from the equipment maintenance department spend an estimated five hours in setting up the equipment to make the change on the desk line for model JE 40. The desk production line on which model JE 40 is manufactured is operated by five workers. During the changeover, these workers assist the maintenance workers when needed and operate the line during the one-hour test run. However, they are idle for approximately 40 percent of the time required for the changeover.

The production workers are paid a basic wage rate of $7.50 an hour. Two overhead bases are used to apply the overhead costs of this production line because some of the costs vary in proportion to direct labor-hours while others vary with machine-hours. The overhead rates applicable for the current year are as follows:

	Based on Direct Labor-Hours	Based on Machine-Hours
Variable	$2.75	$ 5.00
Fixed	2.25	15.00
	$5.00	$20.00

These department overhead rates are based on an expected activity of 10,000 direct labor-hours and 1,500 machine-hours for the current year. This department is not scheduled to operate at full capacity because production capability currently exceeds sales potential.

The estimated cost of the direct materials used in the test run totals $200. Salvage material from the test run should total $50. Commercial Furniture's cost of capital is 20 percent.

Required
a. Estimate Commercial Furniture Company's setup cost for desk model JE 40 for use in the economic production run model. For each cost item identified in the problem, justify the amount and the reason for including that cost item in your estimate. Explain the reason for excluding any cost item from your estimate.

b. Identify the cost items that would be included in an estimate of Commercial Furniture Company's cost of carrying the desks in inventory.

(CMA adapted)

SOLUTION TO SELF-STUDY QUESTION

a. Investment costs:

Invoice cost.	$120.00
Shipping cost.	2.50
Unloading	.80
Total investment costs	$123.30

Carrying costs:

Cost of capital	$ 36.99 ($123.30 × 30%)
Insurance	1.00
Inventory tax.	1.23 (1% × $123.30)
Audit and inspection	2.60
Total carrying costs	$ 41.82

Carrying costs per year:

Working inventory	5,000 units × ½ × $41.82 =	$104,550
Safety stock	3,000 units × $41.82 =	125,460
Total carrying costs		$230,010

Order costs:

Arranging for the shipment	$175
Record processing.	16
Total	$191

Annual order costs:

$$\frac{45,000}{5,000 \text{ per order}} \times \$191 = \underline{\underline{\$1,719}}$$

Total annual costs of the present inventory policy:
$231,729, which is $230,010 + $1,719

b. Economic order quantity (EOQ):
First determine Q^*, ignoring the order size restrictions:
Carrying costs (S), $41.82 [per requirement ($a$)]. Order costs ($P$), $353.00 ($191 + [.02 \times $8,100]).

$$Q^* = \sqrt{\frac{2 \times 45,000 \times \$353}{\$41.82}}$$
$$= \sqrt{759,684.36}$$
$$= \underline{\underline{872 \text{ units}}}$$

Next, determine the annual costs at the next higher and lower allowable order quantity:

Quantity	Carrying Costs	Order Costs	Total Costs
750	$\frac{750}{2} \times \$41.82$	$\frac{45,000}{750} \times \$353.00$	
	$= \$15,682.50$	$= \$21,180.00$	$\$36,862.50$
1,000	$\frac{1,000}{2} \times \$41.82$	$\frac{45,000}{1,000} \times \$353.00$	
	$= \$20,910.00$	$= \$15,885.00$	$\$36,795.00$

The optimal order quantity given the restrictions on order size is 1,000 units.

c. Optimal safety stock level:
Prepare a schedule showing the expected annual costs of each alternative safety stock quantity:

Safety Stock Quantity	Carrying Costs	Expected Stockout Costs	Total Costs
500	$500 \times \$41.82$	$\frac{45,000}{1,000} \times \$8,100 \times .25$	
	$= \$20,910$	$= \$91,125$	$\$112,035$
1,000	$1,000 \times \$41.82$	$\frac{45,000}{1,000} \times \$8,100 \times .08$	
	$= \$41,820$	$= \$29,160$	$\$ 70,980$
1,500	$1,500 \times \$41.82$	$\frac{45,000}{1,000} \times \$8,100 \times .02$	
	$= \$62,730$	$= \$7,290$	$\$ 70,020$ (optimal)
2,000	$2,000 \times \$41.82$	$\frac{45,000}{1,000} \times \$8,100 \times .01$	
	$= \$83,640$	$= \$3,645$	$\$87,285$

Therefore, the most economic safety stock level would be 1,500 units with a total expected stockout and carrying cost of $70,020.

d. The total annual cost of the optimal inventory policy is computed as follows:

Costs of working inventory [per requirement (b)]. . . . . $ 36,795
Costs of safety stock 70,020
$106,815

e. The reorder point is:

$$\text{Usage over lead time + Safety stock} = \left(\frac{45,000}{250} \times 10\right) + 1,500$$
$$= 1,800 + 1,500$$
$$= \underline{\underline{3,300 \text{ units}}}$$

Management Ethics and Financial Fraud

LEARNING OBJECTIVES

After reading this chapter, you should be able to:

1. Explain the nature of fraudulent financial reporting.

2. Describe common types of fraudulent financial reporting, such as early revenue recognition and overstating inventory, and explain how they affect reported profits.

3. Recognize motives and opportunities that create conditions conducive to financial fraud.

4. Explain why the "tone at the top" of companies is important in preventing fraudulent financial reporting.

5. Explain how controls help prevent fraudulent financial reporting.

6. Describe actual case studies of fraudulent financial reporting.

7. Explain how the combination of autonomy and pressure to achieve short-term financial results is conducive to fraudulent financial reporting.

This chapter deals with ethical issues in financial reporting. We focus on motives and opportunities for committing fraud by managers and employees in companies.

We have added this chapter to the book because an increasing number of former students have stressed to us the importance of discussing real ethical dilemmas that people face on the job. This discussion should take place in a variety of classes, they say, but should not be limited to classes on ethics. We agree. Although we have included discussions on ethical issues in numerous chapters in this book, we believe that an entire chapter should be devoted to the problems associated with fraudulent financial reporting.

Former students and our own research indicate that many managers and other employees are often placed under enormous pressure to meet high performance standards. Performance is often measured by short-term financial results, such as profits and return on investment. Because of this pressure to meet short-term financial targets, managers and other employees may be tempted to "cook the books" by carrying obsolete inventory on the books, overstating revenues, understating costs, or using other methods.

Many of you will find yourselves in situations in which there is a great deal of pressure to fudge the numbers. Some of you will help companies design control systems to prevent unethical behavior. Still others will be auditors or examiners who will attempt to detect fraudulent reporting. Some of you will work in the growing field of forensic accounting in which you might assist attorneys in litigation, often as expert witnesses or as consultants. Forensic accountants also are involved in computing damages due to lost profits, finding problems in auditing procedures, and finding fraud in business records.

The purpose of this chapter is to help you recognize conditions that are conducive to fraudulent financial reporting. After discussing these conditions, we present three actual cases of fraudulent divisional financial reports: Doughtie's Foods, Ronson Corporation, and PepsiCo. These are not cases in which "bad people" committed criminal acts. These are not like certain highly publicized cases involving grand schemes designed to obtain funds illegally through insider trading or by establishing fictitious companies. Instead, these are cases in which managers and accountants in companies found themselves under a great deal of pressure to perform well, and they succumbed to the pressure. These people did not go to prison, but the consequences of their actions were serious. They all lost their jobs and, in some cases, were involved in lengthy litigation.

Before continuing, we want to emphasize that, in our view, the vast majority of people in business organizations behave ethically. However, even people who behave ethically find that they or people they know are sometimes in situations pressuring them to behave unethically.

fraudulent financial reporting
Intentional or reckless conduct that results in materially misleading financial statements.

FRAUDULENT FINANCIAL REPORTING

L.O. 1: Explain the nature of fraudulent financial reporting.

materiality
Magnitude of financial misstatement that is likely to affect the judgment of a reasonable person relying on the information.

Fraudulent financial reporting is conduct intended to produce materially misleading financial statements. Not writing off obsolete inventory and recognizing revenue before making the sale are common examples of fraudulent financial reporting. Embezzlement or theft of assets and unintentional errors in preparing financial statements do not constitute fraud.

The two key elements in the definition of fraudulent financial reporting are (1) intentional or reckless conduct and (2) misstatement that is material to the financial statements. **Materiality,** in this setting, refers to the magnitude of the misstatement. To be *material,* the magnitude of the misstatement must be large enough that it would likely affect the judgment of a reasonable person relying on the information. Simply stated, the misstatement must be important.

Intent to commit fraud or reckless conduct is difficult to prove in financial fraud cases. Consequently, when the Securities and Exchange Commission (SEC) charges someone with fraud under the provisions of the securities laws, the accused often signs a document consenting to certain restrictions without admitting to or denying

Barry Minkow, a well known fraudster who spent several years in prison, now has a talk show called "fraud talk."
(© AP/Wide World)

Who Commits Fraud?

the charges. In some cases, such as the one involving Barry Minkow and his company ZZZZ Best, the fraud is so extensive that criminal charges are brought.[1] The cases we discuss are the more common variety in which people reported inaccurate financial numbers, but authorities would find it difficult or even impossible to prove fraud. When we refer to cases of financial fraud, keep in mind that financial fraud has generally not been proven; therefore, the cases we discuss actually represent alleged fraud cases.

Employees at all levels in the organization, from top management to low-level employees, could be involved in fraudulent financial reporting. A company's external auditors also may be held responsible for their client's fraudulent financial reporting.

Department and division managers may commit fraud in financial reports to their superiors. For example, managers at certain PepsiCo bottling plants misled their superiors at corporate headquarters in Purchase, New York, by failing to write off obsolete or unusable bottle inventories. Fraudulent reporting inside a company misleads top management and the board of directors, as well as stockholders and other outsiders who rely on the company's financial information. In a recent fraud case involving the women's apparel manufacturer Leslie Fay, the chief executive expressed disappointment in the actions of the controller and other employees who had covered up financial problems by making false financial entries in the company's records. The chief executive said, "Had the false entries not been made and the senior management been furnished with accurate financial information during the year, we could have taken steps to improve the situation."[2]

Top managers may be involved in attempts to mislead outsiders. Most cases that are reported by the media involve top management. Many cases that occur inside the company are either too small to be considered material to the numbers in the external financial statements, or the frauds are detected and the numbers corrected before the frauds would have affected published annual reports and filings with the SEC. In many cases, people started out bending the rules a little, only to find themselves in deep trouble after bending the rules a little for a long time.

SELF-STUDY QUESTION

1. An accounting clerk leaves work early on December 31, year 1, to attend a New Year's Eve party. The clerk calls in sick every day for the first week of year 2, so management hires a temporary clerk.

   The temporary clerk records revenues from a stack of sales documents left on the sick clerk's desk. The sales documents were not dated, but since they had been left on the desk from December 31, year 1, the temporary clerk assumed that they represented year 1 sales. In fact, the sales documents actually related to year 2 sales that took place on January 2; the documents had been left undated because the sale had not taken place as of December 31. The temporary clerk recorded these sales in year 1. The error was never found.

   Is this an example of fraudulent financial reporting? Would your answer change if you knew that the amount of the sales was material?

   The solution to this question is at the end of this chapter on page 791.

---

[1] "Do You Know Me? I Stole Millions and Here's How," *The Wall Street Journal*, April 1, 1991, pp. A1, A6.

[2] "Leslie Fay Now Expects to Post '92 Loss of $13.7 Million, Will Restate '91 Results," *The Wall Street Journal*, March 1, 1993, p. A5.

TYPES OF FRAUD

L.O. 2: Describe common types of fraudulent financial reporting, such as early revenue recognition and overstating inventory, and explain how they affect reported profits.

The different types of financial fraud are too numerous to list. These include omitting liabilities from financial statements, overstating assets on the balance sheet, and preparing false appraisals and other documents to support loans, as was done by many of the savings and loan companies that failed in the 1980s. Many cases of fraud directly affect the income statement by understating costs, such as capitalizing items that should be expensed, or overstating revenues. In our research, we have found that the two most common types of fraud involve improper revenue recognition and overstating inventory.

Improper Revenue Recognition

Improper revenue recognition often results from backdating sales to report revenue on December 30, year 1, when the sales legitimately should have been reported in January of year 2. Thus, the company shows both the revenue and the cost of goods sold in year 1 instead of year 2. Assuming that revenue equals $100 and cost of goods sold equals $60, the journal entry recorded in year 1 would be as follows:

Accounts Receivable	100	
Sales		100
Cost of Goods Sold.	60	
Inventory.		60

Of course, this entry should be made in year 2, not in year 1. Therefore, the timing change overstates Accounts Receivable at the end of year 1 by $100 and understates Inventory at the end of year 1 by $60. After the sale is properly made in year 2, the Accounts Receivable and Inventory accounts are correct, but until then, the two asset accounts are incorrect. Recording the sale in year 1 overstates operating profits in year 1 by $40 and understates operating profits in year 2 by $40, assuming that no other expenses were affected by the fraudulent entry. Computing the effect on the corporate "bottom line" net income requires taking the effect of taxes into account. This entry also increases the taxes paid in year 1 and decreases them in year 2.

We can find plenty of examples of early revenue recognition. In the case of MiniScribe, a Denver-based computer disk drive manufacturer, invoices for sales made on the first day of the year were backdated to the last day of the previous year.[3] Among other activities, the company had shipped bricks to distributors and booked them as sales of disk drives. In other cases, companies have shipped products to company-owned warehouses but claimed the shipments were sales to customers.

Early revenue recognition, resulting from backdating invoices or prematurely recording a sale, has only a temporary effect on reported revenues and profits. Pulling a sale out of period 2 and reporting it in period 1 improves profits for period 1 but results in the loss of a legitimate sale in period 2. Now period 2 does not look as good as it should legitimately, so perhaps a sale from period 3 will be moved back to period 2 to cover for the sale previously moved from period 2 to period 1.

Overstating Inventory

An example of overstating inventory occurs when managers or accountants fail to write down obsolete inventory. Department or division managers may not want to "take a hit" on the financial reports now, postponing the write-off until a later period. In other cases, people falsify the ending inventory numbers during physical inventory counts or on audit papers. For example, investigators of the MiniScribe case said that senior company officials "apparently broke into locked trunks containing the auditors' workpapers" during the audit and inflated inventory values by

---

[3] "How MiniScribe Got Its Auditor's Blessing on Questionable Sales," *The Wall Street Journal*, May 14, 1992, p. A5.

ILLUSTRATION 25.1	The Effects of Overstating Ending Inventory

Panel A: Period 1

	(1) Correct	(2) Fraudulent
Sales.	$1,500	$1,500[a]
Beginning inventory.	100	100[a]
Add purchases.	900	900[a]
Subtract ending inventory.	100	200
Equals cost of goods sold.	900	800
Administrative and marketing expenses	450	450[a]
Operating profits.	$ 150	$ 250

Panel B: Period 2

	(1) Correct	(2) Fraudulent	(3) Fraudulent
Sales	$1,500	$1,500[a]	$1,500[a]
Beginning inventory	100[b]	200[b]	200[b]
Add purchases	900	900[a]	900[a]
Subtract ending inventory	100	200	300
Equals cost of goods sold	900	900	800
Administrative and marketing expenses	450	450[a]	450[a]
Operating profits	$ 150	$ 150	$ 250

[a]Correct amount, not a fraudulent number.

[b]From period 1 ending inventory.

approximately $1 million. In addition, employees created a computer program called Cook Book to inflate inventory figures.[4]

Overstating ending inventory increases reported profits in the period of overstatement, but it has the opposite effect in the following period. For example, the top panel of Illustration 25.1 shows both correct and fraudulent numbers for period 1. Sales are $1,500 and administrative and marketing expenses are $450 in both period 1 and period 2, for both the correct and fraudulent cases.

As column 2 of panel A shows, the operating profit is $100 higher because ending inventory was fraudulently overstated by $100. In the next period, the $200 beginning inventory, which should have been only $100, works in the opposite direction. As shown in column 2 of panel B, one must continue to overstate ending inventory to $200 just to stay even with the correct bottom line shown in column 1. As column 3 shows, if the perpetrators of the fraud want to appear as successful in period 2 as they did when they committed fraud in period 1, then they must overstate ending inventory to $300. In short, to continue to appear successful, the perpetrators of the fraud must continually overstate ending inventory, sometimes in increasing amounts.

Effect on Taxes

If fraudulent financial reporting also overstates taxable income, the present value of a company's tax payments are likely to increase. Overstating taxable income in one period is often offset by understating taxable income in some subsequent period. Thus, the fraud might not affect the total tax paid but would affect the timing of tax payments and therefore the present value of tax payments.

---

[4]"Coopers & Lybrand Agrees to Payment of $95 Million in the MiniScribe Case," *The Wall Street Journal*, October 30, 1992, p. A2.

SELF-STUDY QUESTION

2. Refer to the facts in Illustration 25.1. Assume that the perpetrator of the fraud decides to "come clean" at the end of period 2 and report the correct ending inventory numbers. What would be the profit for period 2, in this case?

The solution to this case is at the end of this chapter on page 791.

HOW SMALL "EARNINGS MANAGEMENT" LEADS TO BIG-TIME FRAUD

Most fraud that leads to big trouble starts small. For example, suppose that you take an exciting job as the financial analyst in a department of a well-known, highly successful company. After a few years of continually improving performance, your boss, the department manager, becomes worried that the department will not live up to top management's expectations that year. Because of his concern that the department will not achieve its profit target for year 1, your boss requests that you backdate some sales from January of year 2 to December of year 1. These are real sales, but they are not made until January of year 2. Your boss asks that you simply date the invoices that will be sent to the customers with a December date instead of the January date, when the sales are actually made. You are uncomfortable with this practice, but your boss points out that as a team player, you should cooperate. "Besides," your boss says, "what we are doing is just a little 'earnings management.'"

In the real world, some people call this practice *managing earnings,* but others call it *fraud.*

Early in year 2, top management gives your boss a good bonus based on meeting the department's profit target for year 1 and indicates he is in line for a promotion. Recognizing how well your department appeared to perform in year 1, top management increases the profit target for year 2. Now your boss really has a problem. Year 2 has already lost legitimate sales to year 1, but top management expects continually improved performance. At the end of year 2, your boss wants to backdate even more sales from year 3 to year 2 (to make up for the sales backdated from year 2 to year 1), and additional sales backdated to meet the higher profit targets! If this situation continues, what started as a small timing adjustment to manage earnings compounds into massive fraud.

Now we assume that, as the financial analyst, you did not "blow the whistle" on your boss or otherwise prevent the fraud because you wanted to keep your job and you consider yourself to be a team player. After a few years of managing earnings, you find that you are involved in a major fraud. If the fraud comes to light, your boss may even blame you for "cooking the books" because you are the financial expert. In the real world, you might hear your boss say something like, "Sure, I wanted the department to perform well, but I never wanted anyone to do anything unethical! My job is to manage the department; I leave the numbers to [insert your name here]. If there is a problem with the books, you should talk to [insert your name here]."

Consider a different scenario. Your boss gets promoted to division vice president at the beginning of year 4, and you are promoted to department head. Now you have a difficult choice. If you stop backdating sales, year 4 will look bad because its legitimate sales have been moved back to year 3. How do you explain the department's poor performance in year 4, just after you took over? If you report the fraud, you are obviously implicated because you were involved in years 1, 2, and 3. If you continue the fraud, you will get in deeper and deeper. If you resign, your successor will reveal the fraud and implicate you.

Our point is that small earnings management often ends in big trouble with no easy way out. Difficult as it may be to refuse to participate in a fraud or blow the whistle at the early stages, it is far better to do so than to face the consequences of extricating yourself from the problem at a later time.

If you find yourself involved in a possible fraud, you should tell someone. If your superior is involved, you should go to someone higher in the organization, if possible. Boards of directors, particularly the audit committee, internal auditors, and external auditors are groups outside the normal hierarchy that you can inform. Many companies have an ombudsperson whose job is to deal with unethical behavior. The Institute of Management Accountants offers an 800-number service for its members to call and discuss ethical dilemmas.

At minimum, put your concerns in writing and send them to people who can investigate the situation. If necessary, be prepared to resign. Otherwise, you may find yourself in the middle of a messy situation at work and may even get involved as a defendant in legal actions.

The next sections in the chapter focus on situations that are likely to lead to fraud.

CAUSES OF FINANCIAL FRAUD

Short-Term Orientation

L.O. 3: Recognize motives and opportunities that create conditions conducive to financial fraud.

Returning to the example of your boss who wanted you to backdate sales, why would managers inside companies report fraudulent numbers? The primary reason is to make themselves look good. Accounting numbers are often managers' "grades." Bonuses, merit pay increases, and promotions often depend on how well the numbers turn out.

You may ask why a manager would have incentives to backdate sales from one year to an earlier year. This practice merely shifts profits; it does not create them. Managers may want to manage earnings this way for several reasons. Managers may have a short-run perspective. In some companies, top management makes it clear to department and division managers that they may not be in their jobs next year if they do not meet the company's profit or return on investment (ROI) targets this year. Department and division managers may believe they have an opportunity to be promoted to a new position or transferred to another part of the company if they perform well in the current year. If this is the case, they have strong incentives to look good in their current jobs in the current year.

In some companies, rewards are based on achieving a performance threshold. Managers who achieve the threshold receive substantially greater rewards than if they do not. For example, a company may offer a bonus of 50 percent of salary if the manager's division achieves its target ROI, 25 percent of the manager's salary if the division achieves 90 percent of the target ROI, and no bonus if the division's ROI is less than 90 percent of the target. A manager who scores just below the threshold, say just under 90 percent of the target ROI, has a tremendous incentive to make the 90 percent level. The manager may believe that the benefit this year of moving some sales back from next year will outweigh the negative consequences of such action on next year's sales.

Do Performance Evaluation Systems Create Incentives to Commit Fraud?

Management should address two fundamental questions in evaluating how well the company's performance evaluation system works:

* What behavior *does* the system motivate?
* What behavior *should* the system motivate?

Management may find that their employees are highly motivated by high-pressure performance evaluation systems. In that case, management must also realize that pressuring people to perform well is also an incentive to commit fraud. The pressure to perform is not limited to middle managers and employees. Top executives in a company often feel considerable pressure to perform because of the demands of stockholders, the expectations of financial analysts, or, simply, their own egos.

In 1987, the Treadway Commission reported the results of its study of financial fraud involving top management and fraudulent reporting to stockholders. The commission concluded that fraudulent financial reporting occurred because of a combination of pressures, incentives, opportunities, and environment. According to the commission, the forces that seemed to give rise to financial fraud "are present to some degree in all companies. If the right combustible mixture of forces and opportunities is present, fraudulent financial reporting may occur."[5]

The commission went on to say that a frequent incentive for fraud in financial reporting was the desire to improve a company's financial appearance to obtain a higher stock price or escape penalty for poor performance. The commission listed examples of pressures that may lead to financial fraud, including these:

- Unrealistic budget pressures, particularly for short-term results. These pressures occur when headquarters arbitrarily determines profit objectives and budgets without considering actual conditions.
- Financial pressure resulting from bonus plans that depend on short-term economic performance. This pressure is particularly acute when the bonus is a significant component of the individual's total compensation.[6]

It is particularly important to note the Treadway Commission's reference to companies' emphasis on short-term performance. As we noted earlier, most cases of financial fraud involve a timing adjustment. Management is willing to take a chance on the future to make the current period look good. Why? Because companies emphasize short-term results for top managers and everyone else in the organization. One department manager told us, "Of course I'm more concerned about the short run than the long run. If I don't look good now, I won't be around in the long run!"

The Treadway Commission also noted that unrealistic profit objectives in budgets have been a cause of financial fraud. It is difficult for top management in large and widely dispersed companies to know what is realistic to expect in their far-flung divisions. One of the fraud cases that we discuss later involved the Mexican and Philippine operations of PepsiCo, which is headquartered in Purchase, New York. It would be surprising if top management at corporate headquarters knew enough about every local operation to set profit targets that are both realistic and challenging each and every year for every division. The fact that companies decentralize their operations reflects the reality that top management of large companies with dispersed divisions cannot be involved in the details of local operations. Consequently, top management may mistakenly expect unrealistically good performance.

Companies can mitigate the problem of unrealistic performance targets by using participative budgeting. Using participative budgeting, lower-level managers and employees provide input into the budgeting process that provides top management with information about local conditions. Participative budgeting should help top management understand local conditions and, therefore, set more realistic performance targets.

The MiniScribe case provides a clear example of extreme pressure to perform. According to investigators of the fraud at MiniScribe, its chief executive's "unrealistic sales targets and abusive management style created a pressure cooker that drove managers to cook the books or perish. And cook they did—booking shipments as sales, manipulating reserves, and simply fabricating figures—to maintain the illusion of unbounded growth even after the industry was hit by a severe slump."[7] The chief executive's style included inviting employees to an intensive retreat at which he would berate authors of business plans and budgets, showering the group with ripped-up copies of the reports he didn't like. At one meeting, the chief executive asked two controllers to stand and then fired them, saying, "That's just to show everyone that I'm in control of the company."[8]

---

[5]Treadway Commission, *Report of the National Commission on Fraudulent Financial Reporting* (Washington, D.C.: National Commission on Fraudulent Financial Reporting, 1987), p. 23.

[6]Ibid., p. 24.

[7]"How Pressure to Raise Sales Led MiniScribe to Falsify Numbers," *The Wall Street Journal*, September 11, 1989, p. A1.

[8]Ibid.

TONE AT THE TOP

L.O. 4: Explain why the "tone at the top" of companies is important in preventing fraudulent financial reporting.

Perhaps the most important factor in fraudulent financial reporting is known as the tone at the top. The tone at the top refers to the tone that top management sets in dealing with ethical issues. No matter how extensive the list of rules, no matter whether employees are expected to read and sign a code of conduct, top management sends a signal about how things are really done through its behavior. Just looking the other way when subordinates act unethically can set a tone that encourages fraudulent reporting.

During the 1970s, many companies operating in foreign countries paid bribes to top government officials to get business. Lockheed Aircraft Corporation, for example, bribed Japanese prime minister Tanaka in order to sell airplanes to the government-owned Japanese Airlines. The prime minister subsequently resigned. Grumman Corporation, Textron's Bell Helicopter division, and Rockwell International paid bribes to top Iranian government officials to sell aircraft to Iran.[9]

Many top executives of the companies paying bribes to foreign government officials claimed that they knew nothing of the bribes, which had been paid without their authorization. In many cases, however, top management expected employees to get the business by doing whatever was required. Since the local custom in many of these countries was to pay bribes to government officials (for example, in the form of political contributions), the employees of the U.S. companies felt that they had to pay bribes to compete. From the employees' viewpoint, top management had said, in effect, "Do whatever you have to do to get the business; we don't want to know about any bribes."

Because of both the bribery and the tone at the top in many companies that had paid bribes, Congress passed a two-part law entitled the Foreign Corrupt Practices Act of 1977. The first part of this law made it illegal to bribe foreign government officials. The second part required companies to maintain adequate internal controls and keep accurate accounting records so that, as Senator Proxmire stated, top management will know if a bribe is paid by someone in the company.[10]

During your careers, you will almost certainly get a sense of the tone at the top in companies that you work with or for. If top management exhibits a "look the other way" attitude toward unethical behavior, the chances are greater that people will commit financial fraud than if top managers set firm guidelines and follow those guidelines themselves.

CONTROLS TO PREVENT FRAUD

L.O. 5: Explain how controls help prevent fraudulent financial reporting.

internal controls
Policies and procedures designed to provide top management with reasonable assurances that organizational goals will be met.

collusion
The cooperative effort of employees to commit fraud or another unethical act against a company.

In general, it is almost impossible to prevent fraud if enough clever people work together to commit it. Companies have established internal controls to help prevent fraud, however. **Internal controls** are policies and procedures designed to provide top management with reasonable assurances that organizational goals will be met. Internal controls help assure top management that the data it relies on for decision making have not resulted from fraudulent reports by lower-level managers and employees. However, internal controls do not necessarily assure stockholders and other readers of companies' financial statements that top management is reporting accurately because it can override internal controls.

An example of an internal control to prevent fraud is the separation of duties. For example, separation of duties in a department store requires the duties of the person who makes a sale in the store to be separate from the accountant who records the sale in the financial records. For the sale to be fraudulently reported, the accountant and the salesperson would have to work together, or collude. **Collusion** is the cooperative effort of employees to commit fraud or another unethical act against a company.

---

[9]M. Clinard et al., *Illegal Corporate Behavior* (Washington, D.C.: Department of Justice, National Institute of Law Enforcement and Criminal Justice, 1979), pp. 196–98.

[10]M. Maher, "The Impact of Regulation on Controls: Firms' Response to the Foreign Corrupt Practices Act," *The Accounting Review* 56, no. 4, p. 754.

Internal controls that separate duties make it difficult for people to commit fraud unless there is collusion. If enough people are willing to collude to commit a fraud, however, fraudulent financial reporting is almost impossible to prevent. Where there is separation of duties, fraud can be committed only if there is collusion between people, perhaps among several people. As the number of people involved increases, so does the chance of whistle blowing to higher authorities, auditors, the SEC, the media, or others.

Internal Auditing

Internal auditors are employed to audit on behalf of management and/or the board of directors. They often report to the audit committee of a company's board of directors. Internal auditors can both deter and detect fraud.

They can deter fraud by reviewing and testing internal controls and ensuring that controls are in place and working well. For example, in a large insurance company in Connecticut that we studied, internal auditors spent weeks trying to break the secret codes set up by the information systems department to protect computer files.

Internal auditors check to see whether duties that are supposed to be separated really are. Internal auditors also deter fraud simply by their presence. The fact that the auditors make periodic visits, often unannounced, may deter fraud. In some companies, internal auditors are the people you turn to if you think fraud is occurring or if you feel pressured by others to commit fraud.

Internal auditors also detect fraud. Many companies now have specialized fraud examiners or investigators whose job is to identify fraud and build a case against its perpetrators. Fraud examiners sometimes work with law enforcement officials to bring legal action against people who commit fraud.

Independent Auditors

The primary purpose of independent audits by outside audit firms is to express an opinion on published financial statements, not to detect or deter fraud. Nevertheless, the presence of the independent auditors (also called *external auditors*) and their role in reviewing a company's internal controls may help prevent fraud and sometimes detect it. The board of directors, management, or stockholders can also hire independent auditors to do special examinations for fraud. Many people, including managers, mistakenly believe that no fraud exists if the independent auditors have issued an unqualified audit report on a company. That is simply not true. Independent auditors will not necessarily uncover fraud in performing a routine audit designed to express an opinion on whether the published financial statements comply with generally accepted accounting principles.

Public accounting firms are increasingly held accountable for fraudulent financial reports, nonetheless. In some cases, people who relied on financial statements, such as stockholders or bondholders, see the public accounting firms as one of the few entities from which they can collect damages, particularly if the auditee went bankrupt. For example, after MiniScribe Corp. sought protection in bankruptcy court, its bondholders filed a large lawsuit against MiniScribe's investment banking firm and its auditors; the lawsuit was settled before going to trial.

All of the large public accounting firms in the United States have been sued by people who claimed to rely in making investment decisions on financial statements that the firms had audited. Some of these cases are filed not because the independent auditors have failed to follow appropriate auditing procedures but because the auditing firm is a potential source of funds. In other cases, the auditors have allegedly failed to follow generally accepted auditing standards, which are the general professional guidelines that aid auditors in fulfilling their professional responsibilities in auditing financial statements. According to the Treadway Commission's study of fraud cases, auditors who were charged by the SEC with failure to follow generally accepted auditing standards had generally failed to recognize or investigate possible problems with weak internal controls. "In many cases, although indications of possible improprieties, or 'red flags' existed, independent public accountants failed to recognize or pursue them with skepticism."[11]

SELF-STUDY QUESTION

3. Your Uncle Harry recently inherited $300,000 that he wants to invest. He has a modest but steady retirement income that covers his living costs, so he claims that he does not really need the income from the $300,000. He tells you that he wants to invest it wisely because he would feel bad if he were to lose the money (and he points out that you may come in for a share of whatever amount he can accumulate with the $300,000). Uncle Harry is considering investing in a chain of coffee shops in your college community. He has no reason to suspect the integrity of the coffee shop's managers, but after reading the coffee shop's financial statements, he asks you how he can be sure that the numbers are right. He asks for your advice, saying, "Suppose I ask the coffee shop managers to have their books audited. Then can I rest assured that the financial numbers are correct? The company's stock isn't publicly traded, and the books haven't been audited before, but the managers have assured me they would be willing to have the books audited by an independent public accounting firm."

Remarking how clever Uncle Harry is to think about the audit, and pondering the future of the $300,000, you tell him you'll get back to him with some good advice.

Can Uncle Harry rest assured that the financial numbers are correct if the financial statements are audited?

The solution to this question is at the end of this chapter on page 791.

THREE CASES OF FINANCIAL FRAUD

L.O. 6: Describe actual case studies of fraudulent financial reporting.

The next three sections describe three financial fraud cases. As you read these cases, keep the following questions in mind:

- What were the incentives to commit fraud?
- What was the tone at the top of the organization?
- What controls or audit steps to prevent fraud were lacking?

Our objective in describing these cases is to provide you with a sense of conditions conducive to fraudulent financial reporting inside companies in the real world. These are real cases involving real people caught up in the daily rush of doing their jobs. These people did not have a record of criminal activities.

DOUGHTIE'S AND THE FICTITIOUS FROZEN FOODS

Doughtie's Foods was a food processor and distributor that operated in the south-eastern United States.[12] The fraud occurred in a food distribution division of the company that supplied food to schools and government agencies. Illustration 25.2 shows the company's organization chart.

During the years of the fraud, the company had been experiencing lower profit margins than others in the industry—less than 2 percent of sales compared to an industry average of approximately 7 percent. Other than low profit margins, the company's financial statements did not show signs of financial distress.

Mark Hanley had advanced rapidly through the ranks of Doughtie's Foods, starting as a salesperson and rising to manager of a large food distribution division.[13] After several years as division manager, top management began singling him out for criticism at corporate planning meetings because his division was not performing

---

[11]Treadway Commission, *Report of the National Commission on Fraudulent Financial Reporting,* p. 26.

[12]The description of this case is based on the following documents: Doughtie's Foods Form 8-K filed with the Securities and Exchange Commission, October 12, 1982; Securities and Exchange Commission, Docket 27, no. 11 (March 28, 1983), pp. 716–17; Securities and Exchange Commission, Docket 30, no. 11 (May 21, 1984), pp. 711–14; and *The Wall Street Journal,* June 2, 1983, pp. 1, 19.

[13]We have changed the name of the division manager to protect his privacy.

ILLUSTRATION   25.2   Doughtie's Foods: Organization Chart

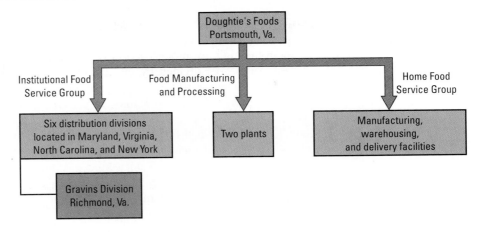

Note: The green box is the site of the alleged financial fraud.

well. After one particularly unpleasant session, another division manager gave Hanley the idea that he could boost his division's reported profits by overstating end-of-period inventory.

If Hanley could find a way to overstate ending inventory, he could understate cost of goods sold. (Recall from the basic cost flow model that cost of goods sold = beginning inventory + purchases − ending inventory.) By understating the cost of goods sold, Hanley could increase gross margin and profits.

According to Hanley, his associate said, "Man, if a guy's calling you from 200 miles away and asking what your [inventory] number is, you're a fool if you [give numbers showing you] lose money." Hanley said that he tried reporting honestly, but one day his superiors came up with some ridiculous figure showing poor results for his division. "I thought they were hosing me," he said.[14]

Although overstating ending inventories would increase the profits of Hanley's division, it would work against him in the next period, as previously discussed in this chapter. Hanley testified during the subsequent SEC investigation that he thought his division would eventually make enough profits to justify the false numbers. The economy went into a recession, however, and the anticipated profit recovery did not happen.

Description of the Fraudulent Activities

At month-end, Hanley and his employees would count the inventory. He would compile the data and report the figures to corporate headquarters. Headquarters required no documentation for monthly inventories, so he simply added a fictitious number to the inventory on hand. One method he used was to change the unit of measure when compiling inventory. For example, he changed one entry from "13 boxes of crab cakes" to "13 cases of crab cakes."

Year-end amounts were more difficult to fudge because the independent auditors performed a physical observation of the inventories. Hanley noted that the auditors did not like to spend much time in the freezers, so he was able to add fictitious items to frozen foods that the auditors did not question. One year, after the auditors had finished their inventory observation and left, Hanley sent three fictitious inventory count sheets to the auditors, claiming that they had overlooked the sheets and left them behind. The auditors were satisfied with Hanley's explanations and added the

---

[14]*The Wall Street Journal*, June 2, 1983, p. 19.

amounts from the fictitious count sheets to ending inventory. The inventory on these three count sheets totaled $140,000, which was 18.4 percent of the division's reported ending inventory for that year.

Discovering the Fraud

The fraud was discovered after an executive at corporate headquarters became curious about the high inventory levels at Hanley's division. Inventory turnover, defined as cost of goods sold divided by inventory, was lower at Hanley's division than at comparable divisions in the company, implying unusually high levels of inventory. The curious executive went to Hanley to get an explanation for the high inventory levels.

Recall that Hanley had felt considerable pressure when he started overstating the numbers, so you can imagine how much stress he felt when the executive from corporate headquarters showed up asking questions. Hanley immediately told the executive what he had been doing, handed over a notebook in which he had kept track of the inventory overstatements, and resigned.

Epilog

Realizing that the fraudulent numbers from Hanley's division had been included in the company's external financial statements, corporate officials at Doughtie's Foods informed the SEC. After an investigation by the company and Price Waterhouse, the company's new independent auditor firm that replaced the original one, the SEC filed a formal complaint against Hanley for violating securities laws.

The SEC also filed charges against two members of the audit firm, charging that the independent auditors had violated generally accepted auditing standards in conducting the audit. According to the SEC, the audit firm took inadequate steps in view of the importance of inventory as an asset and the weak internal controls. For example, there was no separation of duties in accounting for inventory. Hanley had sole control over the entire process from counting the inventory, to compiling the data, to reporting the numbers. The auditors did not check Hanley's excuses when they found irregularities, according to the SEC investigation. On one occasion, the auditors could not tie 22 of 99 count sheets to other data, so they wrote to Hanley to ask for an explanation. He did not reply, and the auditors did not pursue the discrepancy.

RONSON CORPORATION AND THE DISAPPEARING JOBS

Ronson Corporation is perhaps best known for such consumer products as lighters and butane gas appliances. Fraudulent financial reporting occurred in Ronson's aerospace division, however, at a plant in Duarte, California.[15] See Illustration 25.3 for the company's organization chart.

Although not on the verge of bankruptcy, Ronson faced serious financial difficulties at the time of the fraud. Ronson was continually renegotiating with its creditors to restructure debt and extend dates when principal payments were due. The aerospace division in which the fraud occurred appeared to be successful, however. Ronson pointed with pride to the success of its aerospace division in annual reports while putting pressure on it to perform well. The Duarte plant had pretax profit margin requirements of 9 to 12 percent of sales, although the company as a whole was barely breaking even in the best of years and showed more losses than profits in the years surrounding the fraud.

Nature of the Fraud

The Duarte plant management would meet shortly before year-end to determine which jobs were near completion and would presumably be shipped within a few weeks after the start of the year. Those jobs were recognized as sales in the current

---

[15]The description of this case is based on the following documents: Ronson Corporation Form 8-K filed with the Securities and Exchange Commission, November 2, 1982; Securities and Exchange Commission Docket, Release no. 19212, vol. 26, no. 10 (November 4, 1982), pp. 735–40; and Ronson Corporation Form 10-K filed with the Securities and Exchange Commission, December 31, 1981.

ILLUSTRATION   25.3   Ronson Corporation: Organization Chart

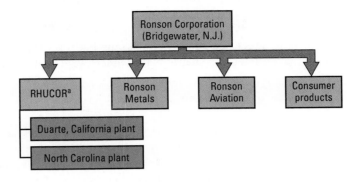

Note: The green box is where the alleged financial fraud occurred.

[a]Ronson Hydraulic Units Corp. (wholly owned subsidiary of Ronson).

year and removed from inventory with an entry similar to the following (XX refers to the amount of the sale and YY refers to the cost of the product):

Accounts Receivable	XX
Sales	XX
Cost of Goods Sold	YY
Inventory	YY

Although these jobs were recognized as sales in the financial records, they were physically unfinished and still in the production work area at the end of the year. This presented a dilemma. If the jobs were not removed from the production area, during their year-end inventory observation, the independent auditors would notice a discrepancy between the financial records and the physical inventory. Some of the jobs that were sold according to the books were actually still being produced. To hide these jobs from the independent auditors, plant personnel moved them from the production area to buildings that were not inspected by the auditors.

Meanwhile, plant personnel prepared false shipping documents so it would appear the jobs had been shipped to customers. These false shipping documents included invoices that were dated earlier than the date of the actual shipment. Now the plant was literally keeping two sets of books. According to the subsequent SEC investigation, "A clerk was assigned to keep a file of all invoices relating to products recognized as sales but not shipped. The accounting manager was assigned to review the file on a weekly basis and accumulate the 'value of unshipped goods.' The aged accounts receivable ledger was also reviewed weekly and annotated with a series of legend tickmarks to indicate the status of the receivables."[16]

At one point, the jobs recorded as sales but not yet shipped exceeded $3 million on division sales of $28 million, and the value of unshipped inventory was approximately 20 to 25 percent of the plant's total year-end inventory.

Epilog

As you can imagine, it became increasingly difficult to keep the fraud a secret, and after a few years, Ronson's top management learned of it. At that point, the company's independent auditors, Touche Ross & Co. (now part of Deloitte and Touche), Ronson's audit committee of its board of directors, senior management, and the SEC investigated the fraud. During their investigation, the independent auditors withdrew their certification of the previously published financial statements, at which point the New York Stock Exchange temporarily halted trading in Ronson common stock.

---

[16]Securities and Exchange Commission, Docket 26, no. 10 (November 4, 1982), p. 738.

In view of the extensive activities to commit the fraud and cover it up, numerous people at the plant may have colluded. However, the SEC charged only the plant manager, plant controller, and a clerk; it did not file a complaint against the independent auditors.

Meanwhile, Ronson announced that no funds were missing and that using incorrect accounting procedures had resulted in no substantial adverse effects. A year later, the Duarte plant's assets were sold to the Boeing Company at a substantial gain.

PEPSICO AND OLD BOTTLES

The PepsiCo case is particularly interesting because the company's management style was so attractive to aggressive, highly motivated management-level employees. Yet the very factors that made PepsiCo an attractive place to work contributed, in part, to the fraud. During the period in which the fraud was committed, PepsiCo portrayed itself as an aggressive, high-performance company.[17] Its annual report stated, "It is widely recognized that PepsiCo is a highly results-oriented company. This characteristic of our operating environment is frequently commented on by the press, and is supported by all our management programs and processes."[18] The annual report went on to say that the company rewarded outstanding results with high pay.

PepsiCo was known for giving its division managers a great deal of autonomy in their operations and supporting a wide range of management styles. According to its annual report, "Developing key managers is a top priority for us; whenever possible, we fill managerial vacancies by promoting from within. Besides ensuring a continuity of management, this is one of the ways we live up to our commitment to foster a climate of personal growth. . . . We value entrepreneurship, so we encourage risk-taking in strategy, programs, and people decisions."[19]

Nature of the Fraud

PepsiCo had five main groups of divisions: food products, including Frito-Lay, Inc.; transportation, including North American Van Lines, Inc.; sporting goods, including Wilson Sporting Goods Co.; food service, including Pizza Hut, Inc., and Taco Bell; and its primary business, beverages. (See Illustration 25.4 for the company's organization chart.) The beverage group included United Beverages International (UBI), a company that bottled soft drinks in 11 foreign countries.

The fraud was committed by employees in the UBI subsidiary in two countries: Mexico and the Philippines. These employees used numerous techniques to falsify income, including keeping inventories of broken or unusable bottles on the books, failing to write off uncollectible accounts receivable, writing up the value of bottle inventory above cost, and falsifying expense accounts. According to a company statement, these activities required extensive collusion. In the Philippines, employees kept more than $45 million of obsolete bottles on the books to satisfy the country's debt-to-equity requirements. (Writing off the bottle inventory would have reduced both assets and equity, thus creating a problem with the country's debt-to-equity requirements.)

PepsiCo's net income was overstated by a total of approximately $92 million over a five-year period from these fraudulent activities. At its highest, the overstatement was $36 million, which was 12 percent of PepsiCo's net income from all five of its main groups.

---

[17]The description of this case is based on the following documents: PepsiCo annual reports for the years ending 1979, 1980, 1981, and 1982; PepsiCo 8-K Form filed with the Securities and Exchange Commission; Securities and Exchange Commission, Docket, Release no. 10807, July 1, 1985, pp. 1005–7.
[18]PepsiCo 1980 Annual Report, p. 4.
[19]Ibid., p. 5.

ILLUSTRATION   25.4   PepsiCo: Organization Chart

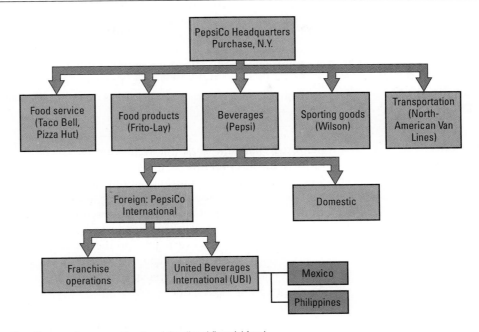

Note: The green boxes were the sites of the alleged financial fraud.

Internal Auditing

Consistent with its management style of granting considerable autonomy to division managers, PepsiCo's Internal Audit Department acted less like watchdogs and more like management consultants. For example, at PepsiCo, the Internal Audit Department did not conduct surprise audits but notified division managers in advance of its visit to ensure that key employees were present. Many companies use internal auditors as consultants because internal auditors gain broad experience with many parts of the company. Using their experience, internal auditors can assist managers all over the company. Using internal auditors as consultants has the advantage of improving operations and of making the Internal Audit Department an excellent place to develop managers.

In general, if companies use internal auditors more as consultants than as watchdogs, they are less likely to deter or detect financial fraud. Despite their role as consultants, PepsiCo's internal auditors uncovered the fraudulent activities at PepsiCo's Mexico and Philippines operations. After discovering the fraud, the Internal Audit Department at PepsiCo became less consulting oriented and started conducting surprise audits. Some people in the company believe that the reorientation of internal audit away from consulting was a major negative repercussion of the fraud.

Epilog

Prior to the fraud, PepsiCo prided itself on its morale and sense of community in the company. PepsiCo's management style and structure, which included giving autonomy to division managers and using internal auditors more as consultants than as watchdogs, and its decentralization policy supported the notion that the company had aggressive, hard-working, and trustworthy employees. After the fraud was discovered, the distressed PepsiCo chairman referred to the fraud perpetrators as a "conspiracy of trusted employees."[20]

---

[20]*The Wall Street Journal*, July 29, 1983, pp. 1, 12.

In all, the SEC filed formal complaints against 12 employees in the two countries. PepsiCo terminated the people involved, as well as the U.S.–based manager of the bottling unit of UBI. The SEC did not file a complaint against PepsiCo's independent auditors, Arthur Young & Co. (now part of Ernst & Young).

WHY WAS THE FRAUD COMMITTED?

We have described these three cases to provide you with some insights into conditions conducive to fraud. All three cases involved considerable pressure to perform, autonomy from corporate headquarters, and either a failure to perform proper audit practices or extensive collusion.

Pressure to Perform

All three companies had put significant pressure on the division managers to perform well. At Doughtie's Foods, the division manager felt considerable personal pressure from the top. Further, he felt singled out for criticism. Ronson was suffering from financial problems and looked to the aerospace division to bail out the rest of the company. PepsiCo's well-intentioned method of rewarding outstanding results, promoting aggressiveness, and encouraging risk taking created an environment in which some managers overreacted to these incentives.

We should note that all managers in these companies very likely felt pressure to meet demanding standards, yet only a few committed fraud. Although many companies place a great deal of pressure on employees, to our knowledge, the vast majority do not commit fraud. Nevertheless, fraud cases often can be traced to intensive pressure to achieve short-term financial results.

Autonomy

The PepsiCo and Ronson division managers had considerable autonomy. PepsiCo's corporate structure and culture encouraged autonomy. In addition, the geographical distance and language differences among corporate headquarters in Purchase, New York, and the divisions in Mexico and the Philippines made it difficult for top managers to know what was happening at these divisions. At Ronson, the California plant where the fraud occurred was geographically distant from corporate headquarters in New Jersey and produced a product that was not in the company's mainstream product line. Divisional autonomy was not as evident at Doughtie's Foods, but here too, the division manager had sole control over inventory.

Granting autonomy to a manager does not mean the manager is likely to commit fraud. Most managers operate with considerable autonomy, yet reported cases of fraud are rare. Granting autonomy does increase the risk of fraud, because autonomy creates an opportunity to commit it. Thus, most fraud cases inside organizations are committed by autonomous managers, but granting managers autonomy by no means implies that they will commit fraud.

Controls, Auditing, and Collusion

Earlier in this chapter, we noted that effective internal controls such as separation of duties make it difficult to commit fraud unless people collude. The fraud at PepsiCo and Ronson required the involvement of several people who colluded to commit the fraud. Doughtie's Foods is a case in which the lack of separation of duties in inventory counting, compiling, and reporting made it possible for the division manager to report fraudulent inventory numbers. Because the division manager had sole control, he was able to falsify the numbers without collusion. In view of the weak internal controls in Hanley's division, Doughtie's Foods' independent auditors should have performed additional audit steps.

Collusion often occurs because of an attitude that those in the field are fighting together against corporate headquarters. Integrative Case 25.35 (page 790) describes such an "us versus them" situation that developed at H. J. Heinz.

In general, it is very difficult for independent auditors to discover a fraud if management or a group of employees really wants to hide it. At Ronson, for example, the employees physically hid the jobs that they claimed had been shipped.

Compensating Factors

We noted earlier that financial fraud is usually the result of a combustible mixture of motives and opportunities. No one factor leads to fraud, but the right combination of factors creates conditions conducive to fraud. A company that has an incentive system that pressures employees to achieve short-term financial results should offset this motive to commit fraud by reducing opportunities to do so. The company could ensure that internal controls and internal auditing are effective, for example, and it could exhibit an ethical tone at the top.

If a company wants to give managers considerable autonomy, as PepsiCo does, it might compensate for this high opportunity to commit fraud in the following ways:

- Having a high degree of the watchdog variety of auditing, thus reducing the opportunity to commit fraud.
- Reducing pressure on division managers to achieve short-run financial results, thus reducing the motive to commit fraud.
- Having top management encourage excellence in ethics.

The ethical tone at the top reduces the motive to commit fraud because it reduces the tolerance for unethical behavior. It also decreases the opportunity for fraud because it signals support for antifraud devices such as strong internal controls. Also, it encourages people who are inclined to behave ethically to stay with the company and discourages people who are otherwise inclined.

Characteristics of People Who Commit Fraud

We have noted before that the combination of pressure to achieve short-term financial results, weak internal controls and auditing, an opportunity to commit fraud through autonomy, and a tone at the top that looks the other way at unethical employee behavior is a combustible mixture of forces conducive to fraud. One might liken this mixture of motives and opportunities to a mixture of dry fuel and oxygen on a hot summer afternoon in a forest. Just as a forest will not burn without a spark, fraud will not occur without a person committing the act. (A famous fraud examiner calls these people *fraudsters*.)

Many top executives in companies have observed that fraud is the work of a few "bad apples." If top management or the boards of directors knew who these bad apples were, they could eliminate fraud.

We have focused on management and organizational issues rather than on the personality characteristics of people who commit fraud, but we acknowledge that certain people may be more inclined to commit fraud than others. Although little is known about the personality types of these people, we may learn from the advice of a perpetrator of one of the biggest frauds in recent years. Barry Minkow, who formerly ran the ZZZZ Best carpet cleaning company and a fictitious restoration company, was sentenced to prison for several years for committing fraud (and released in 1995). According to Minkow, we should "watch out for that guy with the big ego. . . . Watch that guy that has no respect for anyone but himself."[21]

SUMMARY

The objective of this chapter is to help you understand conditions conducive to fraudulent financial reporting. There generally must be a motive and an opportunity for financial fraud to occur.

The following summarizes key ideas tied to the chapter's learning objectives.

LO1: Fraudulent financial reporting. Fraudulent financial reporting is intentional conduct that results in materially misleading financial statements. The two key

---

[21]"Do You Know Me? I Stole Millions—And Here's How," *The Wall Street Journal*, April 1, 1991, p. A6.

elements in the definition of fraudulent financial reporting are (1) intentional or reckless conduct and (2) misrepresentation that is material to the financial statements.

LO2: Common types of fraudulent financial reporting. Common examples of fraudulent financial reporting are the failure to write down obsolete inventory and the recognition of revenue before a sale has been made.

LO3: Motives and opportunities creating conditions conducive to financial fraud. Motives include pressure to achieve short-run financial targets. Opportunities include autonomy, weak internal controls, and the lack of "watchdog" auditing.

LO4: The importance of the tone at the top in preventing fraudulent financial reporting. A tone at the top of the company that promotes ethical behavior is particularly important to eliminate tolerance for unethical behavior. It also reduces the opportunity for fraud by signaling support for antifraud devices such as strong internal controls.

LO5: Controls help to prevent fraudulent financial reporting. Separating duties for important accounting functions can prevent fraud (for example, employees counting inventory should not be the ones recording inventory on the books). Effective internal controls, such as separation of duties, make it difficult to commit fraud unless people collude.

LO6: Actual case studies of fraudulent financial reporting. This chapter provides three real cases of fraudulent financial reporting that occurred at three companies, Doughtie's Foods, Ronson Corporation, and PepsiCo.

LO7: Combining autonomy and pressure to achieve short-term financial results can result in fraudulent financial reporting. The three cases discussed in the chapter had one common element: managers had autonomy and were pressured to achieve short-term financial results. Financial fraud often results from this combination.

KEY TERMS

collusion, 776

fraudulent financial reporting, 769

internal controls, 776

materiality, 769

REVIEW QUESTIONS

25.1   What is fraudulent financial reporting? What are the two key elements in the definition of fraudulent financial reporting?

25.2   What is materiality? Why is materiality difficult to define in practice?

25.3   What are common types of fraudulent financial reporting?

25.4   What does *the tone at the top* mean? Why is the tone at the top an important factor in preventing financial fraud?

25.5   The title of the Foreign Corrupt Practices Act implies that it deals with foreign corrupt practices. The law not only prohibits bribing foreign government officials but also regulates companies' internal controls. Why were the internal control regulations included in this law?

25.6   How does the separation of duties help prevent financial fraud?

25.7   How do internal auditors deter or detect financial fraud?

25.8   Why are public accounting firms increasingly held accountable for their clients' fraudulent financial reporting?

25.9   An employee has been stealing some of the company's parts and selling them. Is this behavior financial fraud?

25.10   Suppose that the employee in Question 25.9 covers up the theft by accounting for it as spoilage. Is accounting for the stolen items as spoilage financial fraud?

25.11   Suppose that an accounting clerk who knows nothing about the theft in Question 25.9 erroneously records the "lost" parts as spoilage. Is that fraudulent financial reporting?

25.12   Suppose that an accounting clerk fails to write off $5 million of obsolete inventory at a large department store, a material amount. Suppose that the SEC files a charge against the clerk, alleging financial fraud. Do you believe that the clerk's failure to write off the inventory, which resulted in misstated financial statements, could be considered unintentional? Explain your answer.

25.13   Why are the three cases discussed in the chapter—Doughtie's Foods, Ronson, and PepsiCo—actually cases of *alleged* financial fraud?

25.14   An automobile dealership sells an automobile on January 2, year 2, but records it as being sold on December 31, year 1. Accounts Receivable is credited for the amount of the sale on January 2, year 2, when the customer pays for the car in cash. The sales commission payable to the salesperson was recorded on January 2, year 2. What items on the dealership's financial statements are in error for year 1, including the balance sheet at December 31, year 1? What accounts are in error for year 2, including the balance sheet at December 31, year 2?

25.15   A friend says, "I don't see what's the big deal about early revenue recognition. It's just a matter of recording sales in the right time period. It's not like making up a fictitious sale. And after a few years everything is correct again." How would you respond?

25.16   In both the Doughtie's Foods and Ronson Corporation cases, people kept track of the amount of the fraud in separate records. In effect, they were keeping two sets of books. Why keep both sets of records? Why not simply keep the fraudulent records?

25.17   A friend was hired by a large company. She confides in you about a problem with her boss, who is asking customers to sign a sales agreement just before the end of the year that indicates a sale has been made. Her boss then tells these customers that he will give them 30 days, which is well into next year, to change their minds. If they do not change their minds, he sends them the merchandise. If they change their minds, her boss agrees to cancel the orders, take back the merchandise, and cancel the invoices. Her boss gives the sales agreements to the accounting department, which prepares an invoice and records the sale. One of the accounting people keeps the invoices and shipping documents for these customers in a desk drawer until the customers either change their minds, in which case the sale is canceled, or until the merchandise is sent at the end of the 30-day waiting period.

Your friend likes the company very much, and she wants to keep her job. What would you advise her to do?

25.18   Why does small earnings management often result in major fraud over time?

25.19   A manager says, "We avoid financial fraud by just paying workers a cost-of-living increase each year and promoting them based on the number of years they have been in their position. That way we avoid putting pressure on people and we avoid the problems of financial fraud." Comment on this incentive approach. What behavior will it motivate?

25.20   The Treadway Commission commented that the forces leading to financial fraud were present in all companies to some extent, but fraudulent financial reporting resulted from the right combustible mixture of forces and opportunities to commit fraud. Give examples of the combustible mixture the Treadway Commission mentioned.

25.21   The Treadway Commission commented that a factor giving rise to fraud is the existence of pressures on division managers to achieve unrealistic profit objectives. Why might top management set unrealistic profit targets?

25.22 The Treadway Commission indicated that bonus plans based on achieving short-run financial results have been a factor in financial frauds, particularly when the bonus is a large component of an individual's compensation. Why is this so?

25.23 International Telephone and Telegraph (ITT) historically put a great deal of pressure on its employees to achieve short-term profit targets and provided its division managers a lot of autonomy. What compensating factors should be present to reduce the likelihood of fraudulent financial reporting?

25.24 How was MiniScribe's top management behavior, as described in the chapter, potentially a factor in its fraud?

25.25 According to Barry Minkow, who was the perpetrator of a major fraud, "Watch out for the guy with the big ego." What do you think he meant by this?

PROBLEMS[22]

25.26	Early Revenue Recognition	You have been asked to advise a manufacturing company how to detect fraudulent financial reporting. Management does not understand how recognizing early revenue by backdating invoices from next year to this year affects financial statements. Further, management wants to know which accounts could be audited to detect evidence of fraud in the case of early revenue recognition.

Required

a. Using your own numbers, make up an example to show management the effect of early revenue recognition.

b. Prepare a short report to management explaining what accounts would be affected by early revenue recognition. Suggest some ways management could find errors in those accounts.

25.27 Inventory Overstatement

You have been asked to advise a merchandising company how to detect fraudulent financial reporting. Management wants your help in detecting inventory overstatement.

Required

a. Using your own numbers, make up an example to show management the effect of overstating inventory. Show how inventory overstatement at the end of Year 1 carries through to Year 2 beginning inventory overstatement.

b. Prepare a short report to management explaining how inventory might be overstated, including examples, and discuss how to detect it. To prepare your examples, it might be helpful to review the Doughtie's Foods and PepsiCo cases, as well as the other examples discussed in the chapter.

25.28 Causes of Fraudulent Financial Reporting: Doughtie's Foods

Refer to the Doughtie's Foods case described in the chapter, starting on page 778.

a. What were the incentives to commit fraud?

b. What was the tone at the top of the organization?

c. What controls to prevent fraud were lacking?

d. How did the independent auditors contribute to the fraud?

25.29 Causes of Fraudulent Financial Reporting: Ronson Corporation

Refer to the Ronson Corporation case described in the chapter, starting on page 780.

a. What were the incentives to commit fraud?

b. Could the fraud have been committed without collusion?

---

[22]We have not included exercises in this chapter because of the nature of the material.

  c. What controls to prevent fraud were lacking?

  d. Did the independent auditors have responsibility for the fraud? Why or why not?

25.30 Causes of Fraudulent Financial Reporting: PepsiCo

Refer to the PepsiCo case described in the chapter, starting on page 782.

  a. What were the incentives to commit fraud?

  b. What was the tone at the top of the organization?

  c. What controls to prevent fraud were lacking?

  d. How might the role of internal auditors as consultants be a factor in financial fraud in companies as in the PepsiCo case?

25.31 Effect of Bonus Plan on Financial Fraud

An article in *The Wall Street Journal* indicated that dressmaker Leslie Fay backdated invoices to record the revenue in the quarter before sales were actually made. "As long as sales remained strong, the practice could go undetected. But as the recession hit retailers in 1991, revenue sagged and it became more difficult to cover one quarter's shortfall with anticipated revenue from the next."[23]

Leslie Fay's compensation plan offered the chief operating officer and the chief financial officer bonuses if the company's net income reached $16 million (approximately 2 percent of sales). The company reported a net income of $23 million, and the two executives received bonuses.

The fraud occurred away from corporate headquarters in New York at the company's Wilkes-Barre, Pennsylvania, office where the company's financial affairs are handled. Leslie Fay's chief financial officer "was establishing something of an autocratic rule in Wilkes-Barre. What the growing operation lacked in organization, he evidently tried to make up through frenzied effort. Employees say they were sometimes pushed to work 16-hour days, including many weekends and holidays, and were sometimes reprimanded for arriving as little as two minutes late to work."[24]

The chairman and chief executive officer of the company, who was paid $3.6 million, mostly in the form of a bonus, "says he is bewildered by the accounting scandal. 'We just don't know why they would do it,' he says of the midlevel employees whose scheme concealed Leslie Fay's sliding fortunes."[25]

Required

  a. Describe how the invoice backdating could have affected reported profits. Would those profits have been overstated permanently or just for a period?

  b. What effect might the bonus plan for the chief operating officer and chief financial officer have had on the fraud, if any?

  c. How might the location of financial operations in Wilkes-Barre, Pennsylvania, instead of at corporate headquarters in New York, have made it easier for someone to commit fraud?

25.32 Top-Management Awareness of Fraud

The chief executive of Leslie Fay, the dressmaking company charged with committing financial fraud, was dismayed that the controller and other employees had committed fraud, saying the company could have taken steps to improve the situation if senior management had been informed of poor financial results. Financial analysts who follow the company had noted, however, that the company had marked down its clothing line in sales to retail stores such as May and Federated department stores.

After the company cut prices 20 percent across the board, retail executives who were customers of Leslie Fay wondered how it could continue to be profitable. "'When you cut 20 percent out, you must get dramatically large orders to make up for it,' says one. 'We were wondering how they could continue to make a profit.'"[26]

One analyst wondered how top management could not have known about the company's financial difficulties in view of the 20 percent markdown.

[23]"Loose Threads: Dressmaker Leslie Fay Is an Old-Style Firm That's in a Modern Fix," *The Wall Street Journal*, February 23, 1993, p. A20.
[24]Ibid.
[25]Ibid., p. A1.
[26]Ibid., p. A20.

For your information, top management is located in New York City, and the fraud occurred at the financial offices in Wilkes-Barre, Pennsylvania. The line of reporting was as follows: The controller reported to the chief financial officer, and the chief financial officer reported to the chief executive of the company. Both the controller and the chief financial officer worked in Wilkes-Barre. The chief financial officer reportedly had considerable autonomy.

Required

Write a short report indicating whether you think that top management of the company is responsible for the fraud and why (or why not).

25.33 Top Management's Responsibility for Fraud

In a *Dateline* news story, NBC employees allegedly rigged a General Motors truck to explode on impact to demonstrate that GM had improperly placed the trucks' gas tanks. Although this case does not involve fraudulent financial reporting, it involves a different type of fraud that is similar in many respects to fraudulent financial reporting. Of particular interest is the response of the NBC News chief executive, who resigned after NBC News issued an apology to General Motors.

The executive "was apparently enough out of touch with his troops that he didn't know all of GM's complaints until he saw them broadcast—along with thousands of other people—at a live GM news conference."[27]

Meanwhile, the NBC News executive's superior, the president of NBC, "told employees that the problem with the 'Dateline' incident wasn't so much that it happened, but that NBC got caught."[28]

Required

Comment on the apparent tone at the top at NBC. Should the NBC News executive have resigned? Why (or why not)?

25.34 Taking Action in the Face of Fraud

Refer to the example in the text (pages 773–774) in which we put you in the position of the financial analyst for a department manager who wanted you to backdate sales. Assume that your close friend is the financial analyst in the example. It is now Year 4, your friend's boss has been promoted, and your friend has been offered the job of department head.

Your friend comes to you for advice. Recall that your friend has been involved in the fraud for three years.

Required

What would you tell your friend to do?

INTEGRATIVE CASE

25.35 Motives and Opportunities for Fraud

A report on "income transferal" activities at the H. J. Heinz Company made the following statements.[29] First, decentralized authority is the central principle of the company's operations. Second, the company expected its divisions to generate an annual growth in profits of approximately 10 to 12 percent per year. Third, it was not unusual or undesirable for management to put pressure on the division managers and employees to produce improved results.

The report noted that pressuring the divisions to produce improved results coupled with the company's philosophy of autonomy, which it extended to financial and accounting controls, provided both an incentive and an opportunity for division managers to misstate financial results. The report further stated, "The autonomous nature of the [divisions] combined with the relatively small World Headquarters financial staff permitted the conception of what at best can be described as a communications gap. . . . In its simplest form, there seems to have been a tendency to issue an order or set a standard with respect to achieving a financial result without regard to whether complete attainment was possible."[30] It continued, "In the managements of certain of the [divisions], there was a feeling of 'us versus them' towards World Headquarters."[31]

---

[27]"NBC News President, Burned by Staged Fire and GM, Will Resign," *The Wall Street Journal,* March 2, 1993, p. A1.

[28]Ibid., p. A8.

[29]This case is based on the "Report of Audit Committee to the Board of Directors, Income Transferal and Other Practices," H. J. Heinz Company, May 6, 1980.

[30]Ibid., p. 9.

[31]Ibid., p. 14.

The report indicated an effort in certain divisions to transfer income from one fiscal period to another to provide a "financial cushion" for achieving the goal for the succeeding year. For example, divisions would overpay expenses to get a credit or refund in a subsequent year. Or they would pay an expense such as insurance or advertising early, but instead of charging the amount to a prepaid expense account, they would charge it to expense. In good years, this practice would keep profits down and provide a cushion to meet the company's target for constantly increasing profits.

Required

a. Using your own numbers, make up an example to demonstrate the income transferal that was done at H. J. Heinz.

b. What was the motive to transfer income from one period to the other? What were the opportunities to transfer income?

c. Comment on how the communications gap and the us-versus-them attitude contributed to the fraud.

d. Refer to requirement (*c*). Have you seen communications gaps in organizations that have resulted in an us-versus-them attitude on the part of employees? If so, briefly describe the circumstances and the cause of this attitude. Discuss in your example what could have been done (or be done) to change it.

SOLUTIONS TO SELF-STUDY QUESTIONS

1. It is unlikely that the temporary clerk either committed a reckless act or intended to commit fraud. The clerk's supervisor could be faulted for failing to provide adequate instructions, however. If the amounts are immaterial, this example would probably fall into the category of accounting errors. If the amounts are material, failure to supervise and instruct the temporary clerk could fall under the category of reckless conduct.

2. The "coming clean" results would be only $50 profit, computed as follows:

Sales	$1,500
Beginning inventory	200[a]
Add purchases	900
Subtract ending inventory	100[b]
Equals cost of goods sold	1,000
Administrative and marketing expenses	450
Operating profits	$ 50

[a]From Period 1 ending inventory.

[b]Correct amount, not a fraudulent number.

Moral: It's painful to come clean after one has committed a fraud.

3. An external audit will indicate whether the financial statements comply with generally accepted accounting principles, but it's no guarantee that the numbers are "right." It would be possible for the managers to mislead the auditors. If this is a small business, as it appears, it is difficult to have sufficient separation of duties to ensure that internal controls are adequate. Uncle Harry could get additional assurance by requesting a regular audit for compliance with generally accepted accounting principles and a special examination for fraud. A fraud examination implies suspicion of fraud and may sour the relationship between Uncle Harry and the managers of the coffee shops, however. The final word is that Uncle Harry will take some risk if he makes the investment; he has to decide whether the expected return on the investment justifies that risk.

Revenue, Mix, and Yield Variances

LEARNING OBJECTIVES

After reading this chapter, you should be able to:

1. Understand how to compute and use gross margin and contribution margin variances.

2. Use market share variances to evaluate marketing performance.

3. Use sales mix variances to evaluate marketing performance.

4. Evaluate production performance using production mix and yield variances.

In this supplemental chapter, we discuss variances for revenues and nonmanufacturing costs and the way that managers use these variances to evaluate marketing and administrative performance. The basic principles are the same as those presented in Chapters 18 and 19.

A *variance* is the difference between a predetermined norm and the actual results for a period. To illustrate the development of revenue and nonmanufacturing cost variances, we continue the Evergreen Company example discussed in Chapters 18 and 19. The basic facts about the Evergreen Company example are reviewed in Illustration 26.1.

REPORTING ON MARKETING PERFORMANCE

Like manufacturing managers, marketing managers usually are evaluated on the basis of planned results versus actual outcomes. Marketing performance analysis looks at how well the company has done in terms of revenues and marketing costs compared to the plans that are reflected in the master budget.

L.O. 1: Understand how to compute and use gross margin and contribution margin variances.

Using Sales Price and Activity Variances to Evaluate Marketing Performance

sales price variance
Variance arising from changes in the price of goods sold.

sales activity variance
Variance due to changes in volume of sales. (Also known as the *sales volume variance*.)

The **sales price** and **sales activity variances** are often used to evaluate marketing performance. Sales price and activity variances are computed as follows:

Price variance = (Actual sales price − Budgeted sales price) × Actual sales volume

For Evergreen Company, the price variance is

$$\left(\begin{array}{cc}\text{Actual} & \text{Budgeted}\\ \text{price} & \text{price}\end{array}\right) \times \text{Actual sales volume}$$
$$(\$21 - \$20) \times 10{,}000 \text{ units} = \underline{\$10{,}000 \text{ F}}$$

Sales activity variance = Budgeted contribution margin × (Actual sales volume − Master budget sales volume)

Evergreen Company's sales activity variance is:

$$\begin{array}{c}\text{Budgeted}\\ \text{contribution} \times\\ \text{margin}\end{array}\left(\begin{array}{ccc}\text{Actual} & & \text{Master}\\ \text{sales} & - & \text{budget}\\ \text{volume} & & \text{sales}\\ & & \text{volume}\end{array}\right)$$
$$(\$20 - \$9) \times (10{,}000 - 8{,}000)$$
$$\$11 \times 2{,}000 \text{ crates} \qquad = \underline{\$22{,}000 \text{ F}}$$

ILLUSTRATION 26.1	Evergreen Company	
	Actual	**Master Budget**
Sales price	$21 per crate	$20 per crate
Sales volume	10,000 crates	8,000 crates
Variable manufacturing costs	$8.544 per crate	$8 per crate
Variable marketing and administrative costs	$1.10 per crate	$1 per crate
Fixed manufacturing costs	$37,000	$36,000
Fixed marketing and administrative costs	$44,000	$40,000

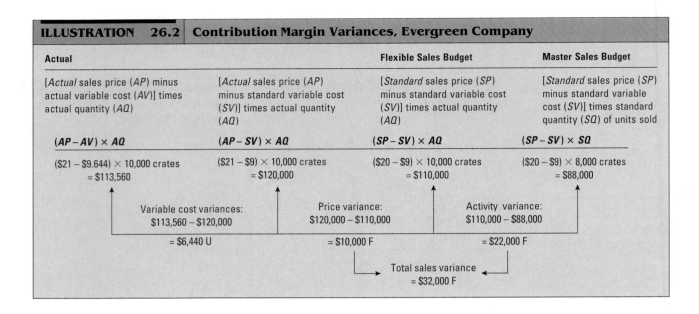

ILLUSTRATION 26.2	Contribution Margin Variances, Evergreen Company

Actual | | **Flexible Sales Budget** | **Master Sales Budget**

[*Actual* sales price (*AP*) minus actual variable cost (*AV*)] times actual quantity (*AQ*)	[*Actual* sales price (*AP*) minus standard variable cost (*SV*)] times actual quantity (*AQ*)	[*Standard* sales price (*SP*) minus standard variable cost (*SV*)] times actual quantity (*AQ*)	[*Standard* sales price (*SP*) minus standard variable cost (*SV*)] times standard quantity (*SQ*) of units sold
(AP − AV) × AQ	**(AP − SV) × AQ**	**(SP − SV) × AQ**	**(SP − SV) × SQ**
($21 − $9.644) × 10,000 crates = $113,560	($21 − $9) × 10,000 crates = $120,000	($20 − $9) × 10,000 crates = $110,000	($20 − $9) × 8,000 crates = $88,000

Variable cost variances:
$113,560 − $120,000
= $6,440 U

Price variance:
$120,000 − $110,000
= $10,000 F

Activity variance:
$110,000 − $88,000
= $22,000 F

Total sales variance
= $32,000 F

The budgeted contribution margin equals the budgeted unit sales price (SP) of $20 minus the budgeted (or standard) variable cost (SV), which is $9 (sum of $8 variable manufacturing and $1 variable marketing and administrative). Consequently, the budgeted contribution margin per unit is

$$\$20 - (\$8 + \$1) = \$20 - \$9 = \$11$$

Illustration 26.2 presents a general model for computing these variances and applies it to the Evergreen Company example. Note that the method is similar to that used to compute cost variances in Chapter 19. To compare with the profit variance analysis in Chapter 18, we also show the actual contribution and the variable cost variances in Illustration 26.2. The actual variable cost (AV) equals $9.644 based on the data given for Evergreen Company in Chapter 18. (The $9.644 is the sum of the actual variable manufacturing cost and the variable marketing and administrative cost.)

Contribution Margin versus Gross Margin

When the contribution margin is used to compute the variances, the variances are called **contribution margin variances.** An alternative is to compute the variances using a budgeted gross margin instead of a budgeted contribution margin. When this method of computing the variances is used, the variance is known as the **gross margin variance.** The basic approach is the same as for contribution margin variances except that the calculation is based on a unit gross margin instead of a unit contribution margin.

contribution margin variance
Variance from changes in revenues and variable costs.

gross margin variance
Variance from changes in revenues and cost of goods sold.

Calculation of the contribution margin variance requires accountants to know which costs are fixed and which are variable. If this information is not available, the gross margin variance is sometimes calculated instead of the contribution margin variance. (Note that computation of the sales price variance is independent of the choice between the gross margin and contribution margin methods of computing sales activity variances.)

Incentive Effects of Commissions Based on Revenue versus Contribution Margins

Sales personnel are often given commissions or bonuses based on sales revenue. Suppose that a salesperson has an opportunity to sell one of the following two products to a customer but not both:

ILLUSTRATION 26.3	Comparison of Actual to Master Budget, Evergreen Company

	(1) Actual (based on actual activity of 10,000 units sold)	(2) Manufacturing Variances	(3) Marketing and Administrative Variances	(4) Sales Price Variances	(5) Flexible Budget (based on actual activity of 10,000 units sold)	(6) Sales Activity (volume) Variance	(7) Master Budget Plan (based on a prediction of 8,000 units sold)
Sales revenue	$210,000	—	—	$10,000 F	$200,000	$40,000 F	$160,000
Less							
Variable manufacturing costs	85,440	$5,440 U	—	—	80,000	16,000 U	64,000
Variable marketing and administrative costs . . .	11,000	—	$1,000 U	—	10,000	2,000 U	8,000
Contribution margin	113,560	5,440 U	1,000 U	10,000 F	110,000	22,000 F	88,000
Less							
Fixed manufacturing costs	37,000	1,000 U	—	—	36,000	—	36,000
Fixed marketing and administrative costs . . .	44,000	—	4,000 U	—	40,000	—	40,000
Operating profits	$ 32,560	$6,440 U	$5,000 U	$10,000 F	$ 34,000	$22,000 F	$ 12,000

Total variance from flexible budget = $1,440 U

Total variance from master budget = $20,560 F

	Revenue	Standard Variable Cost	Contribution Margin
Product A	$100,000	$90,000	$10,000
Product B	50,000	30,000	20,000

If the salesperson's commission is 2 percent of sales, he or she would clearly prefer to sell product A, even though product B provides a greater contribution to profits.

An alternative incentive plan gives the salesperson a commission based on contribution margin. If the salesperson's commission were 10 percent of contribution margin, both the salesperson and the company would benefit from the sale of product B.

In general, it is best to tie employee incentives as closely to organizational goals as possible. If the organizational goal is to maximize current sales, a commission based on revenue makes sense. If the goal is current profit maximization, a commission based on contribution margins may be more appropriate.

Summary

If you recall from previous chapters, the bottom-line objective in variance analysis is to compare the reported income statement amounts with the master budget. To keep in touch with the big picture, in Illustration 26.3 we present the profit variance analysis that compares the master budget to the reported income statement that was first presented in Chapter 18. The sales price and activity variances, which are relevant for our discussion in this chapter, are shown in columns 4 and 6 of Illustration 26.3.

Illustration 26.3 shows that actual revenue exceeds budgeted revenue by $50,000 ($10,000 favorable price variance plus $40,000 difference between the flexible budget revenue and the master budget revenue). It would be incorrect to say that favorable sales results have increased profits by $50,000, however, because the favorable increase in sales volume is partly offset by the variable costs of the additional

2,000 crates produced and sold. Therefore, we say that the favorable sales results have increased profits by $32,000 ($10,000 F sales price variance + $22,000 F sales activity variance).

We next discuss further analysis of these sales variances.

Market Share Variance and Industry Volume Variance

L.O. 2: Use market share variances to evaluate marketing performance.

industry volume variance
The portion of the sales activity variance due to changes in industry volume.

market share variance
The portion of the activity variance due to change in the company's proportion of sales in the markets in which the company operates.

Managers frequently wonder whether the sales activity variance is due to general market conditions or to a change in the company's market share. For example, if sales at The Limited go down, is the decrease due to general market conditions? Or has The Limited's share of the market gone down? The cause may be significant because of promotional strategies and/or pricing policies. At Evergreen Company, for example, the marketing vice president wondered about the cause of the favorable activity variance of 2,000 units: "Our estimated share of the market was 20 percent. We projected industry sales of 40,000 crates, of which we would sell 8,000. We actually sold 10,000 crates. Was that because our share of the market went up from 20 percent to 25 percent (25% × 40,000 crates = 10,000 crates)? Or did we just hold our own at 20 percent, while the market increased to 50,000 crates (20% × 50,000 crates = 10,000 crates)?"

You can find numerous sources of data about industry volume (for example, trade journals, government census data). When these data are available, the activity variance could be divided into an industry volume variance and a market share variance. The **industry volume variance** tells how much of the sales activity variance is due to changes in industry volume. The **market share variance** tells how much of the activity is due to changes in market share. The market share variance is usually more controllable by the marketing department and is a measure of its performance.

Evergreen's marketing vice president learned that the favorable sales activity resulted from an improvement in both industry volume and market share. Industry volume went up from 40,000 units to 41,667; market share went up from 20 percent to 24 percent. Hence, the 2,000-unit favorable activity variance can be broken down into an industry effect and a market share effect, as shown in Illustration 26.4. Of the 2,000-unit increase in company volume, 333 crates, which is 20 percent of 1,667 units, is due to the increase in industry volume (holding market share constant); 1,667 crates, which is 4 percent of 41,667 units, is due to an increased share of the market. Multiplying each figure by the standard contribution margin gives the impact of these variances on operating profits (amounts are rounded):

Industry volume: ($20 − $9) × 333 crates = $3,663 F

Market share: ($20 − $9) × 1,667 crates = $18,337 F

Total activity: ($20 − $9) × 2,000 crates = $22,000 F

Calculation of these variances is also shown in Illustration 26.5.

The use of the industry volume and market share variances enables management to separate that portion of the activity variance that coincides with changes in the overall industry from that which is specific to the company. Favorable market share variances indicate that the company is achieving better than industry average volume changes. This can be very important information to marketing managers who are constantly concerned about their products' market share.

SELF-STUDY QUESTION

1. Insta-Pour Concrete, Inc., produces precast beams for highway and other bridge construction. The company's master budget called for sales of 20,000 beams, which would have been 16 percent of the market in its market area. The contribution margin on each beam is $215. During the year, 21,000 beams were sold. The company's market share had increased to 22 percent of the total market, but the total market was only 95,455 units.

   Compute the industry volume and market share variances.

The solution to this question is at the end of this chapter on page 812.

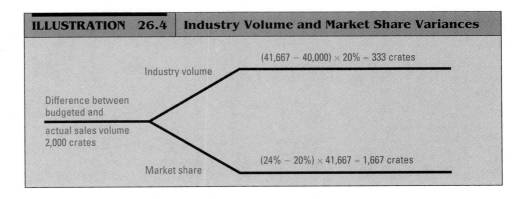

ILLUSTRATION 26.4	Industry Volume and Market Share Variances

Industry volume $(41,667 - 40,000) \times 20\% = 333$ crates

Difference between
budgeted and

actual sales volume
2,000 crates

Market share $(24\% - 20\%) \times 41,667 = 1,667$ crates

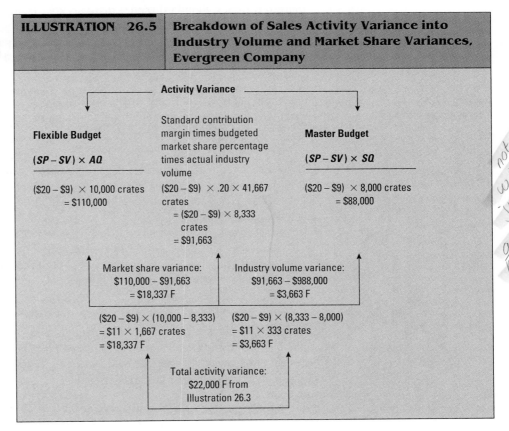

ILLUSTRATION 26.5	Breakdown of Sales Activity Variance into Industry Volume and Market Share Variances, Evergreen Company

Activity Variance

Flexible Budget	Standard contribution margin times budgeted market share percentage times actual industry volume	**Master Budget**
$(SP - SV) \times AQ$		$(SP - SV) \times SQ$
$(\$20 - \$9) \times 10,000$ crates $= \$110,000$	$(\$20 - \$9) \times .20 \times 41,667$ crates $= (\$20 - \$9) \times 8,333$ crates $= \$91,663$	$(\$20 - \$9) \times 8,000$ crates $= \$88,000$

Market share variance:
$\$110,000 - \$91,663$
$= \$18,337$ F

Industry volume variance:
$\$91,663 - \$988,000$
$= \$3,663$ F

$(\$20 - \$9) \times (10,000 - 8,333)$
$= \$11 \times 1,667$ crates
$= \$18,337$ F

$(\$20 - \$9) \times (8,333 - 8,000)$
$= \$11 \times 333$ crates
$= \$3,663$ F

Total activity variance:
$\$22,000$ F from
Illustration 26.3

Note: Your answers may vary slightly due to rounding.

EVALUATING PRODUCT MIX

sales mix variance
Variance arising from the relative proportion of different products sold.

A **sales mix variance** provides useful information when a company sells multiple products, and the products are substitutes for each other. For example, an automobile dealer sells two kinds of cars, Super and Standard. For October, the estimated sales for the company were 1,000 cars, 500 Super models and 500 Standard models. The Super models were expected to have a contribution margin of $3,000 per car, and the Standard models were expected to have a contribution margin of $1,000 per car. Thus, the budgeted total contribution for October was as follows:

Super: 500 at $3,000	$1,500,000
Standard: 500 at $1,000	500,000
Total contribution	$2,000,000

When the October results were tabulated, the company had sold 1,000 cars, and each model had provided the predicted contribution margin per unit. But the total contribution was a disappointing $1,400,000 because instead of the predicted 50–50 mix of cars sold, the mix was 20 percent Super and 80 percent Standard, with the following results:

Super: 200 at $3,000	$ 600,000
Standard: 800 at $1,000	800,000
Total contribution	$1,400,000

The $600,000 decrease from the budgeted contribution margin is the sales mix variance. In this case, it occurred because 300 fewer Super models were sold (for a loss of $300 \times \$3,000 = \$900,000$) while 300 more Standard models were sold (for a gain of $300 \times \$1,000 = \$300,000$). The net effect is a loss of $2,000 in contribution margin for each Standard model that was sold instead of a Super model. (This emphasizes the importance of the substitutability assumption. If a store sells, among other things, jewelry and garden tractors, the mix variance is probably not as useful as when comparing two products that are close substitutes.)

Sales Mix Variances

L.O. 3: Use sales mix variances to evaluate marketing performance.

Assume that Electron Company makes and sells two electronic games, Spacetrack and Earth Evaders. The estimated and actual results for the first quarter of the year were as follows:

	Spacetrack	Earth Evaders	Total
Standard sales price per unit	$20.00	$10.00	—
Actual sales price per unit	22.00	9.00	—
Standard variable cost per unit	10.00	5.00	—
Actual variable cost per unit	11.00	4.50	—
Estimated sales volume (units)	120,000	80,000	200,000
Estimated sales activity percentage	60%	40%	100%
Actual sales volume (units)	140,000	140,000	280,000
Actual sales activity percentage	50%	50%	100%

An analysis of contribution margin variances is shown in Illustration 26.6. This is the analysis that would be presented if the sales mix variance were ignored.

Sales mix variances can be calculated in many ways. Each starts with the same total variance between actual and master budget but then breaks it down in a different manner.

Our computation of the sales mix variances allows us to break down the sales activity variance into two components: sales mix and sales quantity. The *sales mix variance measures the impact of substitution* (it appears that the Earth Evaders model has been substituted for the Spacetrack model), while the **sales quantity variance** *measures the variance in sales quantity, holding the sales mix constant.*

sales quantity variances
In multiproduct companies, a variance arising from the change in volume of sales, independent of any change in mix.

Calculations for this example are presented in Illustration 26.7. The sales price variance is unaffected by our analysis; the sales activity variance is broken down into the mix and quantity variances.

By separating the activity variance into its mix and quantity components, we have isolated the pure mix effect by holding constant the quantity effects, and we have isolated the pure quantity effect by holding constant the mix effect.

Source of the Sales Mix Variance

Although we have calculated each product mix variance to show exact sources, the total mix variance ($140,000 U) is most frequently used. In this example, the unfavorable mix variance is caused by the substitution of the lower contribution Earth Evaders for the higher contribution Spacetrack. To be precise, the substitutions are as follows:

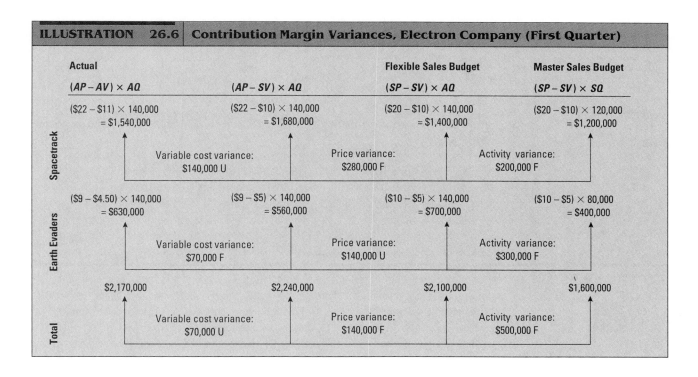

ILLUSTRATION 26.6 | Contribution Margin Variances, Electron Company (First Quarter)

	Actual $(AP - AV) \times AQ$	$(AP - SV) \times AQ$	Flexible Sales Budget $(SP - SV) \times AQ$	Master Sales Budget $(SP - SV) \times SQ$
Spacetrack	($22 − $11) × 140,000 = $1,540,000	($22 − $10) × 140,000 = $1,680,000	($20 − $10) × 140,000 = $1,400,000	($20 − $10) × 120,000 = $1,200,000
	Variable cost variance: $140,000 U	Price variance: $280,000 F	Activity variance: $200,000 F	
Earth Evaders	($9 − $4.50) × 140,000 = $630,000	($9 − $5) × 140,000 = $560,000	($10 − $5) × 140,000 = $700,000	($10 − $5) × 80,000 = $400,000
	Variable cost variance: $70,000 F	Price variance: $140,000 U	Activity variance: $300,000 F	
Total	$2,170,000	$2,240,000	$2,100,000	$1,600,000
	Variable cost variance: $70,000 U	Price variance: $140,000 F	Activity variance: $500,000 F	

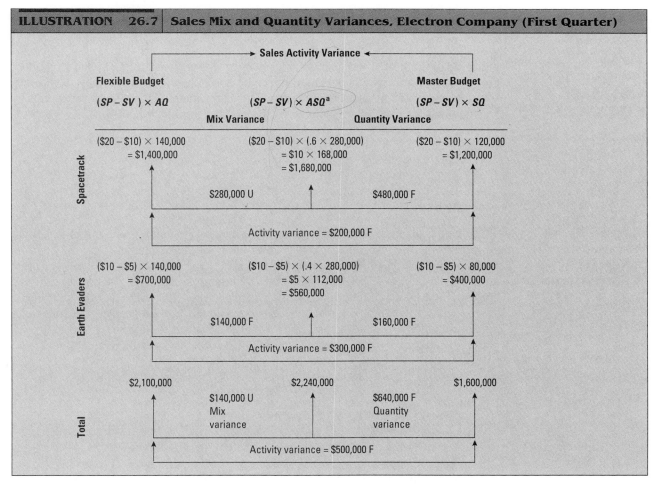

ILLUSTRATION 26.7 | Sales Mix and Quantity Variances, Electron Company (First Quarter)

Sales Activity Variance

	Flexible Budget $(SP - SV) \times AQ$	$(SP - SV) \times ASQ^a$ Mix Variance	Quantity Variance	Master Budget $(SP - SV) \times SQ$
Spacetrack	($20 − $10) × 140,000 = $1,400,000	($20 − $10) × (.6 × 280,000) = $10 × 168,000 = $1,680,000		($20 − $10) × 120,000 = $1,200,000
	$280,000 U	$480,000 F		
	Activity variance = $200,000 F			
Earth Evaders	($10 − $5) × 140,000 = $700,000	($10 − $5) × (.4 × 280,000) = $5 × 112,000 = $560,000		($10 − $5) × 80,000 = $400,000
	$140,000 F	$160,000 F		
	Activity variance = $300,000 F			
Total	$2,100,000	$2,240,000		$1,600,000
	$140,000 U Mix variance	$640,000 F Quantity variance		
	Activity variance = $500,000 F			

$^a ASQ$ = Quantity of units that would have been sold at the standard mix.

Decrease in Spacetrack	28,000 @ $10 =	$280,000 U
Increase in Earth Evaders	28,000 @ $ 5 =	140,000 F
Net effect in units	–0–	
Net effect in dollars		$140,000 U

The quantity variance results from the sale of 80,000 more units than expected or, more precisely,

Spacetrack	(168,000 − 120,000) × $10 =	$480,000 F
Earth Evaders	(112,000 − 80,000) × $ 5 =	160,000 F
Total quantity variance	80,000 units	$640,000 F

SELF-STUDY QUESTION

2. Assume that the master budget has sales of 1,200 units of product A and 800 units of product B. Actual sales volumes were 1,320 of product A and 780 of product B. The expected contribution per unit of product A was $1 ($4 price − $3 standard variable cost), and the expected contribution of product B was $3.50 ($6.50 price − $3 standard variable cost).

Compute the sales activity variances and further break them down into sales mix and quantity components.

The solution to this question is at the end of this chapter on page 812.

PRODUCTION MIX AND YIELD VARIANCES

L.O. 4: Evaluate production performance using production mix and yield variances.

Our analysis of mix and quantity variances for sales also can be applied to production. Often a mix of inputs is used in production. Chemicals, steel, fabrics, plastics, and many other products require a mix of direct materials, some of which can be substituted for each other without greatly affecting product quality.

Mix and Yield Variances in Service Organizations

Companies also substitute different types of labor. Ernst and Young might substitute partner time for staff time on a particular audit job, for example.

Consider a consulting firm that has bid a job for 1,000 hours: 300 hours of partner time at a cost of $60 per hour and 700 hours of staff time at a cost of $20 per hour. Due to scheduling problems, the partner spends 500 hours and the staff member spends 500 hours. If the actual costs are $60 and $20 for partner and staff time, respectively, there is no labor price variance. But even though the 1,000 hours required were exactly what was bid, the job cost is $8,000 over budget, as shown:

$$\text{Actual cost} = (500 \text{ hours} \times \$60) + (500 \text{ hours} \times \$20)$$
$$= \$30,000 + \$10,000$$
$$= \$40,000$$

$$\text{Budgeted cost} = (300 \text{ hours} \times \$60) + (700 \text{ hours} \times \$20)$$
$$= \$18,000 + \$14,000$$
$$= \$32,000$$

production mix variance
A variance that arises from a change in the relative proportion of inputs (a materials or labor mix variance).

The $8,000 over budget results from the substitution of 200 hours of partner time at $60 per hour for 200 hours of staff time at $20 per hour. The **production mix variance** is the difference in labor costs per hour ($60 − $20 = $40) times the number of hours substituted (200): $40 x 200 hours = $8,000.

Two factors are important when considering mix variances. First, there is an assumed *substitutability of inputs,* just as there was an assumed substitutability of sales products to make the sales mix variance meaningful. Although partner time may have been substitutable for staff time, the reverse may not have been true. Second, the input costs must be different for a mix variance to exist. If the hourly costs of both partners and staff were the same, the substitution of hours would have no effect on the total cost of the job.

Mix and Yield Variances in Manufacturing

With the general concept in mind, we proceed with another example, using direct materials, which is a common application of mix variances in a production setting.

Clean Chemical Company makes a product, XZ, that is made up of two direct materials. The standard costs and quantities follow:

Direct Material	Standard Price per Pound	Standard Number of Pounds per Unit of Finished Product
X	$4	5
Z	8	5
		10

The standard cost per unit of finished product is as follows:

X: 5 pounds @ $4 = $20
Z: 5 pounds @ $8 =   40
Total $60

During June, Clean Chemical had the following results:

Units produced	1,000 units of finished product
Materials purchased and used	
X	4,400 pounds at $5
Z	5,800 pounds at $8
	10,200 pounds

production yield variance
Difference between expected output from a given level of inputs and the actual output obtained from those inputs.

Our computation of the mix variance breaks down the direct materials efficiency variance into two components, mix and yield. The mix variance for costs is conceptually the same as the mix variance for sales, and the yield variance is conceptually the same as the sales quantity variance. The mix variance measures the impact of substitution (material Z appears to have been substituted for material X); the **production yield variance** measures the input-output relationship holding the standard mix inputs constant. Standards called for 10,000 pounds of materials to produce 1,000 units of output; however, 10,200 pounds of input were actually used. The overuse of 200 pounds is a physical measure of the yield variance.

To derive mix and yield variances, we use the term *ASQ,* which is the actual amount of input used at the standard mix.

Calculations for the three variances (price, mix, yield) for Clean Chemical are shown in Illustration 26.8. Note that the sum of the mix and yield variances equals the materials efficiency variance, which was discussed in Chapter 19. In examining these calculations, recall that the standard proportions (mix) of direct materials are

| ILLUSTRATION | 26.8 | **Mix and Yield Variances, Clean Chemical** |

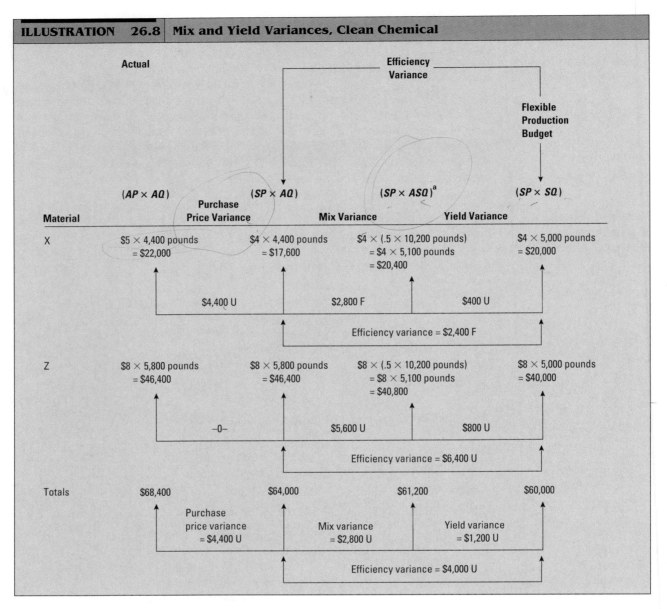

[a]*ASQ* = Actual amount of input used at the standard mix.

X = 50 percent and Z = 50 percent; 10,200 pounds were used in total. Thus, *ASQ* for each material is as follows:

$$X: .5 \times 10{,}200 \text{ pounds} = \underline{\ 5{,}100} \text{ pounds}$$
$$Z: .5 \times 10{,}200 \text{ pounds} = \underline{\ 5{,}100} \text{ pounds}$$
$$\underline{\underline{10{,}200}} \text{ pounds}$$

By separating the efficiency variance into its mix and yield components, we have isolated the pure mix effect by holding constant the yield effect, and we have isolated the pure yield effect by holding constant the mix effect.

We have calculated the mix variance for each direct material to demonstrate its exact source. However, it is the total mix variance ($2,800 U) that is used frequently. In this example, the unfavorable mix is caused by a substitution of the more expensive direct material Z for the less expensive direct material X. To be precise, the substitutions are as follows:

Decrease in X	700 pounds @ $4 = $2,800 decrease
Increase in Z	700 pounds @ $8 = $5,600 increase
Net effect in pounds	–0–
Net effect in dollars	$2,800 increase

As previously indicated, the yield variance results from the overuse of 200 pounds, or more precisely,

Material X: 100 pounds @ $4 =	$ 400 U
Material Z: 100 pounds @ $8 =	800 U
Totals 200 pounds	$1,200 U

SELF-STUDY QUESTION

3. Alexis Company makes a product, AL, from two materials, ST and EE. The standard prices and quantities are as follows:

	ST	EE
Price per pound	$2	$3
Pounds per unit of AL	10 pounds	5 pounds

In May, Alexis produced 7,000 units of AL using the following actual prices and quantities of materials:

	ST	EE
Price per pound	$1.90	$2.80
Pounds used	72,000	38,000

a. Compute materials price and efficiency variances.
b. Compute materials mix and yield variances.

The solution to this question is at the end of this chapter on page 813.

SUMMARY

This chapter covers variances for revenues and nonmanufacturing costs and is an extension of the basic principles presented in Chapters 18 and 19.

The following summarizes the key ideas tied to the chapter's learning objectives.

LO1: Computing and interpreting gross margin and contribution margin variances. Contribution margin variances explain the impact of differences between budgeted and actual sales activity and price. Calculation of the contribution margin variance requires the availability of fixed and variable cost information. If this information is not available, the gross margin variance can be used.

LO2: Using market share variances to evaluate marketing performance. The market share variance tells how much of the sales activity variance is due to changes in market share (rather than general market conditions).

LO3: Using sales mix variances to evaluate marketing performance. The sales mix variance measures the impact of substitution (customers substituting one product for another).

LO4: Evaluate production performance using production mix and yield variances. The production mix variance measures the change in the relative proportion of inputs (materials or labor). The production yield variance measures the difference between expected output from a given level of inputs and the actual output obtained from those inputs.

KEY TERMS

contribution margin variance, 794	production yield variance, 801
gross margin variance, 794	sales activity variance, 793
industry volume variance, 796	sales mix variance, 797
market share variance, 796	sales price variance, 793
production mix variance, 801	sales quantity variance, 798

REVIEW QUESTIONS

26.1 We normally deduct standard costs from the actual revenues when analyzing revenue variances. Why not use actual costs and actual revenues?

26.2 Why is there no efficiency variance for revenues?

26.3 What information does the computation of an industry volume variance provide?

26.4 If the activity variance is zero, could there be any reason to compute a mix variance?

26.5 What are several examples of companies that probably use materials mix and yield variances?

CRITICAL ANALYSIS AND DISCUSSION QUESTIONS

26.6 The marketing manager of a company noted, "We had a favorable revenue variance of $425,000, yet company profits went up by only $114,000. Some part of the organization has dropped the ball; let's find out where the problem is and straighten it out." Comment on this remark.

26.7 A production manager was debating with company management because production had been charged with a large unfavorable production volume variance. The production manager explained: "After all, if marketing had lined up sales for these units we would not have been forced to cut production. Marketing should be charged with the production volume variance, not production." Do you agree with the production manager? Why or why not?

26.8 How could a CPA firm use the mix variance to analyze its revenues?

26.9 How could a CPA firm use the mix variances to analyze salary costs regarding audit services?

26.10 A company has three products that must be purchased in a single package. Is there any benefit to computing a sales mix variance under these circumstances?

EXERCISES

26.11 Sales Price and Activity Variances (L.O. 1)

Creative Towels, Inc., manufactures and sells beach towels. The business is very competitive. The master budget for the last year called for sales of 200,000 units at $9 each. However, as the summer season approached, management realized that they could not sell 200,000 units at the $9 price but would have to offer price concessions. Budgeted variable cost is $3.65 per unit. Actual results showed sales of 190,000 units at an average price of $8.50 each.

Required

Compute sales price and activity variances for Creative Towels.

26.12 Sales Price and Activity Variances (L.O. 1)

Creative Towels, Inc., is trying to decide what to do in the coming year, given the events that transpired last year (see Exercise 26.11). Management conducted a marketing survey, which indicated that the company had two sales alternatives:

1. Sell 220,000 units at $8 each.
2. Sell 185,000 units at $9 each.

The company has actual and standard variable costs of $3.95 per unit.

Required

Compare the two alternatives and show the effect of activity and price differences between the two alternatives. Treat alternative 2 as "master budget" and the other as "actual."

26.13 Industry Volume and Market Share Variances (L.O. 2)

Placer Hills Products budgeted sales of 20,000 units of product B, assuming that the company would have 20 percent of 100,000 units sold in a particular market. The actual results were 18,000 units, based on a 15 percent share of a total market of 120,000 units. The budgeted contribution margin is $3 per unit.

Required

Compute the sales activity variance and break it down into market share and industry volume.

26.14 Sales Price and Activity Variances (L.O. 1)

Sakata, Inc., makes bulk artificial seasonings for use in processed foods. A seasoning was budgeted to sell in 20-liter drums at a price of $48 per drum. The company expected to sell 150,000 drums. Budgeted variable costs are $10 per drum.
During the year, Sakata sold 125,000 drums at a price of $47.

Required

Compute sales price and activity variances.

26.15 Industry Volume and Market Share Variances (L.O. 2)

Refer to the data in Exercise 26.14. Assume that the budgeted sales volume was based on an expected 10 percent of a total market volume of 1.5 million drums, but the actual results were based on a 12.5 percent share of a total market of 1 million drums.

Required

Compute market share and industry volume variances.

26.16 Industry Volume and Market Share Variances—Missing Data (L.O. 2)

The following graph is similar to the one presented in Illustration 26.4 in the chapter. Actual sales volume for the firm exceeds its estimated sales volume.

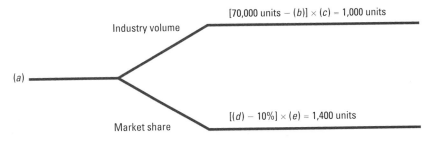

Required

Find the missing amounts:

a. Budgeted minus actual sales volume.
b. Estimated industry volume.
c. Estimated market share percent.
d. Actual market share percent.
e. Actual industry volume.

26.17 Sales Mix and Quantity Variances (L.O. 3)

Fit-Right Gloves Corporation sells two models of golfing gloves. The Basic model has a price of $10.95 per unit, and the Ultra model's price is $24.95 per unit. The master budget called for sales of 400,000 Basics and 180,000 Ultras during the current year. Actual results showed sales of 300,000 Basics, with a price of $11.29 per unit, and 200,000 Ultras, with a price of $25.39 per unit. The standard variable cost is $5 per unit for a Basic and $10 per unit for Ultras.

Required

a. Compute the activity variance for these data.
b. Break down the activity variance into mix and quantity parts.

26.18   Materials Mix and Yield Variances (L.O. 4)

Rosette Industries had the following direct materials data for its product:

> Standard costs for one unit of output
> Material A, 10 units of input at $100
> Material B, 20 units of input at $150

During August, the company had the following results:

Units of output produced	2,000 units
Materials purchased and used	
Material A	22,000 units at $94
Material B	38,000 units at $152

Required

a. Compute materials price and efficiency variances.

b. Compute materials mix and yield variances.

26.19   Sales Price and Activity Variances (L.O. 1)

Chapman, Krueger, and Pollock operate a law firm with partners and staff members. Each billable hour of partner time has a $275 budgeted price and $130 budgeted variable cost. Each billable hour of staff time has a budgeted price of $65 and budgeted variable cost of $35. This month, the partnership budget called for 8,500 billable partner-hours and 34,650 staff-hours. Actual results were as follows:

Partner revenue	$2,150,000	8,000 hours
Staff revenue	2,225,000	34,000 hours

Required   Compute the sales price and activity variances for these data.

26.20   Sales Mix and Quantity Variances (L.O. 3)

Refer to the data in Exercise 26.19. Compute the sales mix and quantity variances.

26.21   Labor Mix and Yield Variances (L.O. 4)

Speedy Burrito has two categories of direct labor, unskilled, which costs $6.50 per hour, and skilled, which costs $10.30 per hour. Management has established standards per "equivalent meal," which has been defined as a typical meal consisting of a burrito, a drink, and a side order. Standards have been set as follows:

Skilled labor	4 minutes per equivalent meal
Unskilled labor	10 minutes per equivalent meal

During May, Speedy Burrito sold 30,000 equivalent meals and incurred the following labor costs:

Skilled labor	1,800 hours	$17,500
Unskilled labor	4,600 hours	33,000

Required

a. Compute labor price and efficiency variances.

b. Compute labor mix and yield variances.

PROBLEMS

26.22   Revenue Analysis Using Industry Data and Multiple Product Lines

In-n-Out Carpet Company makes three grades of indoor-outdoor carpets. Sales volume for the annual budget is determined by estimating the total market volume for indoor-outdoor carpet and then applying the company's prior year market share, adjusted for planned changes due to company programs for the coming year. Volume is apportioned between the three grades based on the prior year's product mix, again adjusted for planned changes due to company programs for the coming year.

The following are the company budget and the results of operations for March.

Budget	Grade 1	Grade 2	Grade 3	Total
Sales—units (in thousands).	1,000 rolls	1,000 rolls	2,000 rolls	4,000 rolls
Sales—dollars (in thousands).	$1,000	$2,000	$3,000	$6,000
Variable costs	700	1,600	2,300	4,600
Contribution margin.	300	400	700	1,400
Manufacturing fixed cost	200	200	300	700
Product margin.	$ 100	$ 200	$ 400	700
Marketing and administrative costs (all fixed).				250
Operating profit.				$ 450

Actual				
Sales—units (in thousands).	800 rolls	1,000 rolls	2,100 rolls	3,900 rolls
Sales—dollars (in thousands).	$ 810	$2,000	$3,000	$5,810
Variable costs	560	1,610	2,320	4,490
Contribution margin.	250	390	680	1,320
Manufacturing fixed cost	210	220	315	745
Product margin.	$ 40	$ 170	$ 365	575
Marketing and administrative costs (all fixed).				275
Operating profit.				$ 300

Industry volume was estimated at 40,000 rolls for budgeting purposes. Actual industry volume for March was 38,000 rolls.

Required

a. Prepare an analysis to show the effects of the sales price and sales activity variances.

b. Break down the sales activity variance into the parts caused by industry volume and market share.

(CMA adapted)

26.23   Sales Mix and Quantity Variances

Refer to the data for the In-n-Out Carpet Company (Problem 26.22). Break down the total activity variance into sales mix and quantity parts.

26.24   Sales Price, Industry Volume, and Mix Variances

SeaAir Airlines plans its budget and subsequently evaluates sales performance based on passenger-miles. A passenger-mile is one paying passenger flying one mile. For this month, the company estimated that its contribution margin would amount to 20 cents per passenger-mile and that 40 million passenger-miles would be flown.

As a result of improvement in the economy, 43 million passenger-miles were flown this month. The price per passenger-mile averaged 30.3 cents. The budgeted variable cost per mile was 10 cents. Subsequent analysis by management indicated that the industry flew 7 percent more passenger-miles this month than expected.

Required

Compute the price, industry volume, and market share effects on company revenues for the month.

26.25   Sales Price, Mix, and Quantity Variances

The following information has been prepared by a member of the controller's staff of Eccentric, Inc.:

ECCENTRIC, INC.
Income Statement
For the Year Ended December 31,
(in thousands)

	Product AR-10		Product ZR-7		Total	
	Budget	Actual	Budget	Actual	Budget	Actual
Unit sales.............	2,000	2,800	6,000	5,600	8,000	8,400
Sales................	$6,000	$7,560	$12,000	$11,760	$18,000	$19,320
Variable costs..........	2,400	2,800	6,000	5,880	8,400	8,680
Fixed costs............	1,800	1,900	2,400	2,400	4,200	4,300
Total costs	4,200	4,700	8,400	8,280	12,600	12,980
Operating profit	$1,800	$2,860	$ 3,600	$ 3,480	$ 5,400	$ 6,340

Required

Analyze the preceding data to show the impact of price, quantity, and sales mix variances on operating profit.

(CMA adapted)

26.26   Materials Mix and Yield Variances

Duo Company manufactures a wide variety of chemical compounds and liquids for industrial uses. The standard mix for producing a single batch of 500 gallons of one liquid is as follows:

Liquid Chemical	Quantity (in gallons)	Cost (per gallon)	Total Cost
Maxan........	100	$2.00	$200
Salex.........	300	.75	225
Cralyn	225	1.00	225
	625		$650

There is a 20 percent loss in liquid volume during processing due to evaporation. The finished liquid is put into 10-gallon bottles for sale. Thus, the standard material cost for a 10-gallon bottle is $13.

The actual quantities of direct materials and the cost of the materials placed in production during November were as follows (materials are purchased and used at the same time):

Liquid Chemical	Quantity (in gallons)	Total Cost
Maxan........	8,480	$17,384
Salex.........	25,200	17,640
Cralyn	18,540	16,686
	52,220	$51,710

 Actual output

A total of 4,000 bottles (40,000 gallons) were produced during November.

Required

Calculate the total direct material variance for the liquid product for the month of November and then further analyze the total variance into

a.   Materials price and efficiency variances.

b.   Materials mix and yield variances.

26.27   Labor Mix and Yield Variances

Rock Solid Engineering Company compares actual results with a flexible budget. The standard direct labor rates used in the flexible budget are established each year at the time the annual plan is formulated and held constant for the entire year.

The standard direct labor rates in effect for the current fiscal year and the standard hours allowed for the actual output of insurance claims for April in a claims department are shown in the following schedule:

	Standard Direct Labor Rate per Hour	Standard Direct Labor-Hours Allowed for Output
Labor class III	$8	500
Labor class II	7	500
Labor class I	5	500

The wage rates for each labor class increased under the terms of a new contract. The standard wage rates were not revised to reflect the new contract.

The actual direct labor-hours worked and the actual direct labor rates per hour experienced for the month of April were as follows:

	Actual Direct Labor Rate per Hour	Actual Direct Labor-Hours
Labor class III	$8.50	550
Labor class II	7.50	650
Labor class I	5.40	375

Required

Calculate the dollar amount of the total direct labor variance for April for Rock Solid Engineering Company and break down the total variance into the following components:

a. Direct labor price and efficiency variances.

b. Direct labor mix and yield variances.

(CMA adapted)

26.28 Contribution Margin Variances

Paulette Division of Outdoor Industries manufactures and sells patio chairs in two versions, a metal model and a lower-quality plastic model. The company uses its own marketing force to sell the chairs.

The chairs are manufactured on two different assembly lines located in adjoining buildings. Division management and the marketing department occupy the third building on the property. Division management includes a division controller responsible for the division's financial activities and preparation of variance reports. The controller structures these reports so that the marketing activities are distinguished from cost factors so that each can be analyzed separately.

The operating results and the related master budget for the first three months of the fiscal year follow on page 810. The budget for the current year assumes that Paulette Division will maintain its present market share of the estimated total patio chair market (plastic and metal combined). A status report was sent to corporate management toward the end of the second month indicating that the division's operating profit for the first quarter would probably be about 45 percent below budget; this estimate was just about on target. The division's operating income was below budget even though industry volume for patio chairs increased by 10 percent more than was expected when the budget was developed.

	Actual	Budget	Favorable (Unfavorable) Relative to the Budget
Sales in units			
Plastic model.	60,000	50,000	10,000
Metal model	20,000	25,000	(5,000)
Sales revenue			
Plastic model.	$630,000	$500,000	$130,000
Metal model	300,000	375,000	(75,000)
Total sales	930,000	875,000	55,000
Less variable costs			
Manufacturing (at standard)			
Plastic model	480,000	400,000	(80,000)
Metal model.	200,000	250,000	50,000
Marketing			
Commissions	46,500	43,750	(2,750)
Bad debt allowance	9,300	8,750	(550)
Total variable costs (except variable manufacturing variances)	735,800	702,500	(33,300)
Contribution margin (except variable manufacturing variances)	194,200	172,500	21,700
Less other costs			
Variable manufacturing cost variances from standards	49,600	—	(49,600)
Fixed manufacturing costs	49,200	48,000	(1,200)
Fixed marketing administrative costs	38,500	36,000	(2,500)
Corporation offices allocation	18,500	17,500	(1,000)
Total other costs	155,800	101,500	(54,300)
Divisional operating profit	$ 38,400	$ 71,000	$ (32,600)

During the quarter, the company produced 55,000 plastic chairs and 22,500 metal chairs. Each manufacturing unit incurred the following costs:

	Quantity	Price	Plastic Model	Metal Model
Direct materials (stated in equivalent finished chairs)				
Purchases				
Plastic	60,000	$5.65	$339,000	
Metal	30,000	6.00		$180,000
Usage				
Plastic	56,000	5.00	280,000	
Metal	23,000	6.00		138,000
Direct labor				
9,300 hours at $6 per hour.			55,800	
5,600 hours at $8 per hour.				44,800
Manufacturing overhead				
Variable				
Supplies.			43,000	18,000
Power			50,000	15,000
Employee benefits			19,000	12,000
Fixed				
Supervision			14,000	11,000
Depreciation.			12,000	9,000
Property taxes and other items.			1,900	1,300

Standard variable manufacturing costs per unit and budgeted monthly fixed manufacturing costs for the current year follow.

	Plastic Model	Metal Model
Direct material.	$ 5.00	$ 6.00
Direct labor		
⅙ hour at $6 per direct labor-hour	1.00	
¼ hour at $8 per direct labor-hour		2.00
Variable overhead		
⅙ hour at $12 per direct labor-hour.	2.00	
¼ hour at $8 per direct labor-hour		2.00
Standard variable manufacturing cost per unit	$ 8.00	$10.00
Budgeted fixed costs per month		
Supervision	$4,500	$3,500
Depreciation	4,000	3,000
Property taxes and other items	600	400
Total budgeted fixed costs for month	$9,100	$6,900

Variable marketing costs are budgeted to be 6 percent of sales-dollars.

Required Compute Paulette Division's sales price, mix, and quantity variances.

(CMA adapted)

26.29 Analyze Industry Effects on Contribution Margins

Refer to the data for Paulette Division (Problem 26.28). Analyze the extent to which the activity variance can be explained in terms of industry and market share effects.

INTEGRATIVE CASE

26.30 Comprehensive Review of Variances, Mix Variances, and Analysis of Differences between Budget and Actual

Sip-Fizz Bottling Company prepared a sales and production budget for the 48-ounce bottle, 12-ounce can, and 10-ounce bottle units that the company produces and sells. Unit variable costs per case of soda are calculated as follows:

	Per Case Costs		
Ingredient	**48 Ounce**	**12 Ounce**	**10 Ounce**
Syrup.	$1.45	$1.00	$ .80
CO₂ gas	.02	.01	.01
Crown	.04	—	.04
Bottle	1.40	—	.30
Can	—	1.64	—
Label	.07	—	—
Total manufacturing cost	2.98	2.65	1.15
Sales commission.	.08	.14	.09
Advertising allowance	.08	.08	.08
Unit variable cost	$3.14	$2.87	$1.32

The advertising allowance is based on the number of cases sold. The selling price for the 48-ounce case is $5.40; for the 12-ounce case, $4.35; and for the 10-ounce case, $2.80. Sales for November were forecasted at 70,000 cases of the 48-ounce bottles, 60,000 cases of 12-ounce cans, and 110,000 cases of 10-ounce bottles. Fixed costs were estimated at $175,000.

During November, actual sales amounted to 80,000 cases of 48-ounce bottles, 50,000 cases of 12-ounce cans, and 120,000 cases of 10-ounce bottles. Actual and budgeted selling prices were equal. Syrup costs were 10 percent higher than expected, but all other costs were at the same per unit amounts as indicated. Total fixed costs, which are all other costs not explicitly identified, amounted to $182,000.

The company uses variable costing for internal reporting purposes. There were no beginning and ending inventories.

Required

a. Determine the budgeted and actual operating profits.

b. Explain the difference between the budgeted and actual net operating profits in as much detail as possible.

SOLUTIONS TO SELF-STUDY QUESTIONS

1.

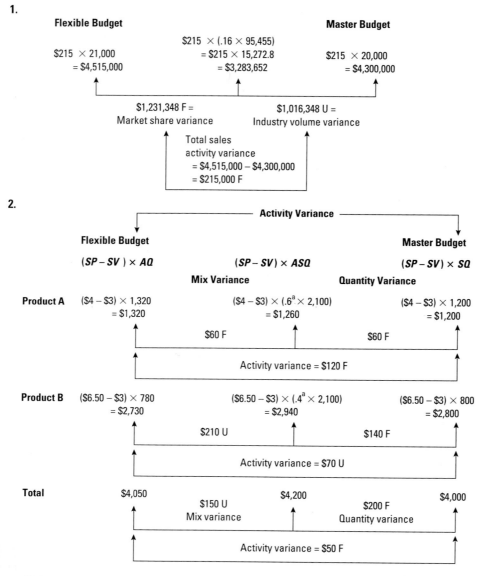

Flexible Budget   **Master Budget**

$215 × (.16 × 95,455)
$215 × 21,000   = $215 × 15,272.8 $215 × 20,000
= \$4,515,000   = \$3,283,652   = \$4,300,000

$1,231,348 F = $1,016,348 U =
Market share variance   Industry volume variance

Total sales
activity variance
= $4,515,000 − $4,300,000
= $215,000 F

2.

────────── **Activity Variance** ──────────

Flexible Budget   **Master Budget**

$(SP − SV) × AQ$ $(SP − SV) × ASQ$ $(SP − SV) × SQ$

Mix Variance   **Quantity Variance**

Product A   ($4 − $3) × 1,320   ($4 − $3) × (.6ᵃ × 2,100)   ($4 − $3) × 1,200
= $1,320   = $1,260   = $1,200

$60 F $60 F

Activity variance = $120 F

Product B   ($6.50 − $3) × 780   ($6.50 − $3) × (.4ᵃ × 2,100)   ($6.50 − $3) × 800
= $2,730   = $2,940   = $2,800

$210 U $140 F

Activity variance = $70 U

Total $4,050 $4,200 $4,000

$150 U $200 F
Mix variance   Quantity variance

Activity variance = $50 F

ᵃBudgeted mix was 60 percent A and 40 percent B.

3. **a.** Price and efficiency variances:

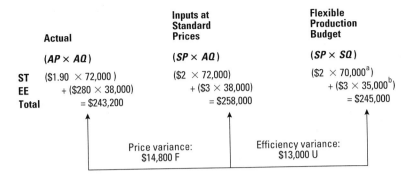

	Actual $(AP \times AQ)$	Inputs at Standard Prices $(SP \times AQ)$	Flexible Production Budget $(SP \times SQ)$
ST EE Total	($1.90 × 72,000) + ($280 × 38,000) = $243,200	($2 × 72,000) + ($3 × 38,000) = $258,000	($2 × 70,000^a) + ($3 × 35,000^b) = $245,000

Price variance:
$14,800 F

Efficiency variance:
$13,000 U

^{a}70,000 pounds = 7,000 units × 10 pounds per unit.

^{b}35,000 pounds = 7,000 units × 5 pounds per unit.

b. Mix and yield variances:

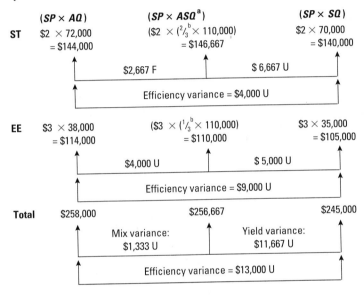

	$(SP \times AQ)$	$(SP \times ASQ^a)$	$(SP \times SQ)$
ST	$2 × 72,000 = $144,000	($2 × ($^2/_3$^{b} × 110,000) = $146,667	$2 × 70,000 = $140,000

$2,667 F $ 6,667 U

Efficiency variance = $4,000 U

EE	$3 × 38,000 = $114,000	($3 × ($^1/_3$^{b} × 110,000) = $110,000	$3 × 35,000 = $105,000

$4,000 U $ 5,000 U

Efficiency variance = $9,000 U

Total	$258,000	$256,667	$245,000

Mix variance:
$1,333 U

Yield variance:
$11,667 U

Efficiency variance = $13,000 U

^{a}*ASQ* = Actual amount of the input used at the standard mix.

^{b}Mix percentage ratio of ST pounds to total and EE pounds to total. For ST, $\dfrac{10}{10 + 5} = {}^2/_3$. For EE, $\dfrac{5}{10 + 5} = {}^1/_3$.

GLOSSARY

The numbers in parentheses after each definition are the chapters in which the term or concept is most extensively discussed.

ABC See activity-based costing.

ABM See activity-based management.

Abnormal Spoilage Spoilage due to reasons other than the usual course of operations of a process. This may include goods spoiled as a result of error or as a result of casualty losses. (6)

Absorption Costing See *Full-Absorption Costing*.

Account Analysis The method of cost estimation that reviews each account making up the total cost being analyzed, and classifies it as fixed or variable. (12)

Acquisition Cost Cost to purchase in investment or inventory item and to get it in place and in condition for use. (23)

Action Set The alternatives available to managers in a given decision-making setting. (26)

Activity-Based Costing (ABC) A costing method that assigns the costs of making a product to the activities that are needed to make a product (which can be either a good or service) and then sums the cost of those activities to determine the cost of making the product. (1, 8, 9, 11, 12, 14, 18, 19)

Activity-Based Management (ABM) The use of activity-based costing and other activity analysis to help management make decisions. (9)

Activity-Based Management Income Statement An income statement that presents the breakdown of the resources supplied, or expenditures, of a traditional income statement into resources used and unused resource capacity for each cost hierarchy. (9)

Activity Center A unit of the organization that performs some activity. (8)

Activity Variance Effect of difference between budgeted and actual sales or production activity levels on profits. (18, 19)

Actual Costing A system of accounting whereby overhead is assigned to products based on actual overhead incurred. (4, 11)

Actual Costs Amounts determined on the basis of actual (historical) costs incurred. See *Actual Costing.*

Adjusted *R*-Square The correlation coefficient in regression squared and adjusted for the number of independent variables used to make the estimate. (12)

Administrative Costs Costs required to manage the organization and provide staff support for organization activities. (2)

Allocation Base A measure related to two or more cost objects used to allocate indirect or common costs shared by two or more objects. For example, direct labor-hours may be related to each unit produced. If direct labor-hours are used to assign manufacturing overhead costs to products, then the direct labor-hours are called the *allocation base*. (3, 7)

Applied Overhead Overhead assigned to a job or other cost object using a predetermined overhead rate. (4)

Appraisal Costs Costs incurred to detect individual units of a product that do not conform to specifications. Also called *detection costs*. (16)

Asset Acquisition Costs involved in purchasing and installing an asset. May involve the disposal of assets currently owned and any gain or loss. (23)

Autocorrelation See *Serial Correlation*.

Backflush Costing A costing method that works backward from output to assign costs to inventories. (3)

Balanced Scorecard A set of performance targets and results that show an organization's performance in meeting its responsibilities to various stakeholders. (22)

Basic Cost Flow Model (Also known as the *basic inventory formula*.) Beginning balance plus transfers-in equals transfers-out plus ending balance. (3)

Batch Orders consisting of identical units that go through the exact same production process. (5)

Batch Production Manufacturing process characterized by the production of product groups that are varied enough to require frequent production line changes. (5)

Behavioral Congruence When individuals behave in the best interest of the organization regardless of their own goals. (20)

Benchmarking The process of measuring one's own products, services, and activities against the best levels of performance. (1, 22)

Bottleneck An operation in which the capacity limits the work flow. (14)

Break-Even Point The volume level where profits equal zero. (13)

Breakeven Time (BET) The length of time it takes to recover the investment made in new product development. (16)

Budget A financial plan of the revenues and resources needed to carry out tasks and meet financial goals. (1, 17)

Budget Plan See *Master Budget*.

Budget Variance See *Spending Variance*.

Budgeted Balance Sheets Statements of financial position that combine estimates of financial position at the beginning and end of the budget period with the estimated results of operations for the period and estimated changes in assets and liabilities. (17)

Budgeted Costing The accounting method that assigns costs to products using a predetermined or budgeted rate for both direct cost (e.g., direct materials) and indirect costs (e.g., overhead). (4)

Budgeting under Uncertainty Making many forecasts, each representing a different possible set of circumstances. (17)

Business-Level Strategy An organization's plan to complete in each of its businesses. (22).

By-Products Outputs of joint production processes that are relatively minor in quantity and/or value. (10)

Carrying Costs Costs that increase with the size of inventory. (24)

Cash Budget Statement of cash on hand at the start of a budget period; expected cash receipts classified by source; expected cash disbursements classified by function, responsibility, and form; and the resulting cash balance at the end of the budget period. (17)

Cause-and-Effect Analysis An analysis that provides diagnostic signals identifying potential causes of defects. (16)

Centralized Refers to those organizations where decisions are made by relatively few individuals at the highest ranks of the organization. (20)

Certified Management Accountant Program A program established to recognize educational achievement and professional competence in management accounting. (Introduction to Student)

CMA Acronym for the certificate issued for the Certified Management Accountant Program. Someone who has received the CMA. (Introduction to Student)

Collusion The cooperative effort of employees to commit fraud or some other unethical act. (25)

Common Costs Costs of shared facilities, products, or services. (7)

Conditional Probabilities Those likelihoods that depend on a specific result. (26)

Constant Gross Margin Percentage Method A method of joint cost allocation that allocates joint costs to products in a way that gross margins are the same for each product. (10)

Constraints Activities, resources, or policies that limit or bound the attainment of an objective. (15)

Continuous-Flow Processing Systems that generally mass-produce a single, homogeneous output in a continuing process. (3, 5)

Contribution Margin The difference between revenues and variable costs. (2, 11, 13)

Contribution Margin Format A financial statement that shows the contribution margin as an intermediate step in computing operating profits or income (2, 11, 13)

Contribution Margin per Unit of Scarce Resource Contribution margin per unit of a particular input with limited availability. (15)

Contribution Margin Ratio Contribution margin as a ratio of sales revenue. (13)

Contribution Margin Variance Variance from changes in revenues minus variable costs. (26)

Control Chart A chart that shows the results of a statistical process control measure—for a sample, batch, or some other unit of measure—designed to provide warning signals that something is wrong. (16)

Controllability Concept The idea that managers should be held responsible for costs or profits over which they have decision-making authority. (20)

Controllability of Variance The extent that a variance can be managed. One rationale used in deciding whether a variance should be calculated, analyzed, or investigated. (19)

Controllable Cost A cost that can be affected by a manager in the short run.

Controller The chief accounting officer in most corporations. (1)

Conversion Costs The sum of direct labor and manufacturing overhead. (2, 5)

Corner Point A corner of the feasible production region in linear programming. (15)

Correlation Coefficient A measure of the linear relationship between two or more variables, such as cost and some activity measure. (12)

Cost A sacrifice of resources. (2)

Cost Accounting The field of accounting that records, measure, and reports information about costs. (1)

Cost Accounting Standards Board The federal government body set up to establish methods of accounting for costs by government defense contractors.

Cost Accumulation The process of adding costs to a cost object, such as a job, department, or inventory account. (3, 4, 5)

Cost Allocation The process of assigning indirect costs to cost objects.

Cost-Benefit Analysis The process of comparing benefits (often measured in savings or increased profits) with costs associated with a particular change in an organization. In this text, cost-benefit analysis usually applies to an analysis of the costs and benefits of alternative costing methods or systems. (1, 5, 8, 12)

Cost-Benefit (2, 7, 8, 10) Test The criterion that an alternative will be chosen if and only if the benefits from it exceed the costs. This criterion is one basis for evaluating cost systems. (3)

Cost Centers Organizational units responsible for costs. (18, 20)

Cost Driver A factor that causes or drives an activity's costs. (1, 8, 19)

Cost Hierarchy Categorization of costs into cost pools based on the relations of costs to cost drivers. Typical hierarchies of costs are capacity-related costs (e.g., building rent), product-related costs (e.g., costs of product design), batch-related costs (e.g., setup costs), and unit-related costs (e.g., direct materials). (9, 11)

Cost Object Any end to which a cost is assigned. Examples include a product, a department, or a product line. (2, 7, 8, 10)

Cost of Capital The weighted-average cost of debt and equity used to finance a project or an operation (e.g., product or product line). (20)

Cost of Goods Finished See *Cost of Goods Manufactured*.

Cost of Goods Manufactured The cost of goods completed and transferred to the finished goods storage area. (2, 3)

Cost of Goods Sold Statement Statement that incorporates and summarizes the information from the direct materials costs schedule and the cost of goods manufactured schedule. (2, 3)

Cost of Goods Sold The cost assigned to products sold during the period. (2, 3)

Cost-Plus Transfer Pricing Transfer pricing policy based on full costing or variable costing plus an allowance for profit. (21)

Cost Pool Groups of individual costs. (8)

Cost Structure The relative proportions of variable costs and fixed costs in an organization's total costs. (13)

Costs for Decision Making Costs that are included in financial analysis by managers. See *Differential Costs*.

Costs for Performance Evaluation Costs that are used in planning and performance evaluation analysis by managers.

Cost Variance Analysis Comparison of actual input quantities and prices with standard input quantities and prices. (19)

Cost-Volume-Profit (CVP) Analysis Study of the interrelationships among costs and volume and how they impact profit. (13)

Critical Probability The probability of different outcomes that equalizes the value of the outcomes.

Critical Success Factors Elements of performance required for success (e.g., service, quality and cost management). (16)

Cross-Department Monitoring A reason for allocating costs where it is hoped that managers of user departments have incentives to monitor the service department's costs. (7)

Current Costs Costs to replace or rebuild an existing asset. (20)

Customer Costing and Profitability Analysis A process of assigning the costs and benefits to each customer to ascertain which customers are generating the most profits to the company. (3, 14)

Customer Response Time The length of time between the time at which the customer places the order for a good or service and the time at which the customer receives the product. (9, 16)

CVP Cost-volume-profit. (13)

CVP under Uncertainty Consideration of the extent of uncertainty and the impact of that uncertainty on decision inputs and outcomes in cost-volume-profit decision analysis.

Decentralized Refers to those organizations where decisions are spread out among relatively many divisional and departmental managers. (20)

Decremental Costs Costs that decrease with a particular course of action. See *Differential Costs*.

Delphi Technique Forecasting method where individual forecasts of group members are submitted anonymously and evaluated by the group as a whole. (17)

Denominator Reason Overhead variance caused by differences between actual activity and the estimated activity used in the denominator of the formula used to compute the predetermined overhead rate. See *Production Volume Variance*.

Department Allocation Method Using this method, companies have a separate overhead cost pool for each department. Each department has its own overhead allocation rate or set of rates. (8)

Dependent Variable In a cost-estimation context, the costs to be estimated from an equation. Also called the *Y-term* or the *left-hand side (LHS)* in regression. (12)

Detection Costs See *appraisal costs*.

Diagnostic Signal A signal identifying the problem and perhaps how to correct it. (16)

Differential Analysis Process of estimating the consequences of alternative actions that decision makers can take. (14, 15)

Differential Costs Costs that change in response to a particular course of action. (1, 14, 15)

Differential Revenues Revenues that change in response to a particular course of action. (1, 14, 15)

Direct Cost Any cost that can be directly related to a cost object. (2)

Direct Costing A synonym for variable costing. (11)

Direct Labor The cost of workers who transform the materials into a finished product during the production process. (2)

Direct Materials Those materials that can feasibly be identified with the product. (2)

Direct Method A method of cost allocation that charges costs of service departments to user departments and ignores any services used by other service departments. (7)

Discount Rate An interest rate used to compute net present values. (23)

Discounted Payback Method A method of assessing investment projects that recognizes the time value of money in a payback context. (16)

Discretionary Cost Center An organization unit where managers are held responsible for costs, but the relationship between costs and outputs is not well established. (20)

Discretionary Costs Costs that are difficult to relate to outputs. Examples include research and development costs, information systems costs, and some advertising costs. (20)

Disinvestment Flows Cash flows that take place at the termination of a capital project. (23)

Dual Rate Method A method of cost allocation that separates a common cost into fixed and variable components and then allocates each component using a different allocation base. (7)

Dual Transfer Pricing Transfer pricing system where the buying department is charged with costs only, and the selling department is credited with the cost plus some profit allowance. (21)

Econometric Models Statistical method of forecasting economic data using regression models. (17)

Economic Order Quantity (EOQ) The number of units to order at one time to minimize total expected annual costs of an inventory system. (24)

Economic Value-Added Annual after-tax operating profit minus the total annual cost of capital. (20)

Efficiency Variance Difference between the inputs that were expected per unit of output and the inputs that were actually used. (19, 26)

Engineering Estimates Cost estimates based on measurement and pricing of the work involved in a task. (12)

EOQ Abbreviation for economic order quantity. (24)

Equivalent Unit The amount of work actually performed on products with varying degrees of completion, translated to that work required to complete an equal number of whole units. (5)

Error Term The unexplained difference between predicted and actual outcomes. Sometimes called *random error*.

Estimate A considered judgment about future events that takes into account past experience and probable changes in circumstances and conditions. (12, 17)

Estimated Net Realizable Value Sales price of final product minus estimated additional processing costs from split-off point necessary to prepare a product for sale. (10)

Expense A cost that is charged against revenue in an accounting period. (2)

External Failure Costs Costs incurred when products and services that do not conform to standards are detected after being delivered to customers. (16)

Factory Burden See *Manufacturing Overhead*.

Factory Overhead See *Manufacturing Overhead*.

Favorable Variances Variances that, taken alone, result in an addition to operating profit. (18)

Feasible Production Region The area in a graph of production opportunities bounded by the limits on production. (15)

Final Cost Center A cost center, such as a production or marketing department, from which costs are not allocated to another cost center. (7)

Financial Accounting The preparation of financial statements and data for outsiders, primarily stockholders and creditors. (1)

Financial Budget Refers to the budget of financial resources; for example, the cash budget and the budgeted balance sheet. (18)

Finished Goods Product that has been completed and is in inventory awaiting sale. (2)

First-in, First-out (FIFO) Costing The first-in, first-out inventory method whereby the first goods received are the first charged out when sold or transferred. (5)

Fixed Costs Costs that are unchanged as volume changes within the relevant range of activity. (2, 12, 13, 14, 15)

Flexible Budget A budget that indicates revenues, costs, and profits for different levels of activity. (18)

Flexible Manufacturing A computer-based manufacturing system that allows companies to make a variety of products with minimal setup time. (3, 25)

Fraudulent Financial Reporting Intentional or reckless conduct that results in materially misleading financial statements. (25)

Freight-in An alternative term for transportation-in.

Full-Absorption Cost The cost used to compute a product's inventory value under generally accepted accounting principles. Variable manufacturing costs plus each unit's share of fixed manufacturing costs. (2)

Full-Absorption Costing A system of accounting for costs in which both fixed and variable manufacturing costs are considered product costs. (2, 11)

Full Cost The sum of all costs of manufacturing and selling a unit of product. (2)

GAAP Acronym for generally accepted accounting principles. (2)

Generally Accepted Accounting Principles (GAAP) The rules, standards, and conventions that guide the preparation of financial accounting statements.

Goal Congruence When all members of a group hold a common set of objectives. (20)

Good Output Units completed and suitable for further processing or for sale at the end of a production process. (6)

Graphic Method Graphic solution of a linear programming problem by selecting the best corner solution visually. (15)

Gross Margin The difference between sales revenues and manufacturing costs; also sales price minus full-absorption cost. (2)

Gross Margin Variance Variance from change in revenues minus cost of goods sold. (25)

Heteroscedasticity In regression analysis, the condition in which the errors are correlated with the magnitude of values of the independent variables. (12)

High-Low Cost Estimation A method of estimating costs based on two cost observations, usually costs at the highest activity level and costs at the lowest activity level. (12)

Hurdle Rate The discount rate required by a company before it will invest in a project. (23)

Hybrid A costing system that incorporates both job and process costing concepts. See *Operation Costing*.

Impact of a Variance The likely effect of a variance. One rationale used in deciding whether a variance is important enough to compute, analyze, and investigate. (19)

Incremental Costs Costs that increase in response to a particular course of action. These are a subset of differential costs. See *Differential Costs.*

Independent Variables The *X*-terms, or predictors, on the right-hand side of a regression equation. In cost accounting, they are cost drivers expected to affect costs. (12)

Indirect Cost Any cost that *cannot* be directly related to a cost object. (2, 7)

Industry Volume Variance The portion of the sales activity variance that is due to changes in industry volume. (25)

Information Cost Cost of obtaining information.

Information Economics A formal system for evaluating whether the cost-benefit test has been met for information.

Information Overload A characteristic of too much data. The intended user is overwhelmed by the quantity of data supplied.

Intercept The point where a line crosses the vertical axis. In regression, this line is the regression line and the intercept is the constant term on the right-hand side of the equation. In cost estimation, the intercept is sometimes used as the fixed cost estimate. (12)

Intermediate Cost Center A cost center whose costs are charged to other departments in the organization. Intermediate cost centers are frequently service departments. (7)

Internal Controls Policies and procedures designed to provide top management with reasonable assurances that organizational goals will be met. (25)

Internal Failure Costs Costs incurred when products and services that do not conform to standards are detected before being delivered to customers. (16)

Internal Rate of Return (IRR) The interest rate that equates the inflows and outflows from an investment project. (23)

Inventoriable Costs Costs added to inventory accounts. (2)

Investment Centers Organizational units responsible for profits and for investment in assets. (20)

Investment Tax Credit A reduction in federal income taxes arising from the purchase of long-term assets. Usually treated as a reduction in investment cost for analytical purposes. (23)

IRR Abbreviation for internal rate of return. (23)

Job Cost Record The source document for entering costs under job costing. This is sometimes referred to as a *job cost sheet, job cost file,* or *job card.* (4)

Job Costing An accounting system that traces costs to individual units for output or specific contracts, batches of goods, or jobs. (3, 4)

Jobs Units that are easily distinguishable from other units. (4)

Joint Cost A cost of production process in which two or more outputs come from the process. (10)

Joint Products Outputs from a common input and common production process. (10)

Just-in-Time Method of production or purchasing designed to obtain goods just in time for use. (1, 3, 16, 24)

***Kaizen* Costing** A costing system that emphasizes continuous improvement in small activities by seeking to reduce production costs continually. (18)

Last-in, First-out (LIFO) Costing The last-in, first-out inventory method whereby the last goods received are charged out first when transferred or sold. See *First-in, First-out.*

Lead Time The time between order placement and order arrival. (24)

Learning Curve The mathematical or graphic representation of the learning phenomenon. (12)

Learning Phenomenon A systematic relationship between the amount of experience in performing a task and the time required to carry out the task. (12)

Linear Programming—Graphic Method Graphic solution of a linear programming problem by selecting the best corner solution. (15)

Lost Units Goods that evaporate or otherwise disappear during a production process. (6)

Make-or-Buy Decision A decision whether to acquire needed goods internally or to purchase them from outside sources. (15)

Management by Exception An approach to management requiring that reports emphasize the deviation from an accepted basing point, such as a standard, a budget, an industry average, or a prior-period experience. (18, 19)

Managerial Accounting The preparation of cost and related data for managers to use in performance evaluation or decision making. (1)

Manufacturing Cycle Efficiency Measure of the efficiency of the total manufacturing cycle. Equals processing time divided by the manufacturing cycle time. (22)

Manufacturing Cycle Time The time involved in processing, moving, storing, and inspecting products and materials. (22)

Manufacturing Department Production departments in organizations that produce goods.

Manufacturing Organization An organization characterized by the conversion of raw inputs into some other output products. (3)

Manufacturing Overhead All manufacturing costs except direct materials and direct labor. (2)

Manufacturing Overhead Variance The difference between applied and actual overhead. (3)

Margin of Safety The excess of projected or actual sales over the break-even volume. (13)

Market-Based Transfer Pricing Transfer pricing policy where the transfer price is set at the market price, or at a small discount from the market price. (21)

Market Share Variance The portion of the sales activity variance due to change in the company's proportion of sales in the markets in which the company operates. (25)

Marketing Costs Costs to obtain customer orders and provide customers with the finished product. (2)

Master Budget The financial plan for the coming year or other planning period. (17)

Materiality Magnitude of financial misstatement such that it is likely to affect the judgment of a reasonable person relying on the information. (25)

Materials Requisition An authorization to obtain materials from a storeroom. It is the source document for recording the transfer of materials to production. (4)

Merchandise Inventory In a merchandising organization, the cost of goods acquired but not yet sold.

Merchandising Organization An organization characterized by marketing goods or services rather than converting raw inputs into outputs. (3)

Mission An organization's purpose. (22)

Mission Statement Description of an organization's values, definition of its responsibilities to stakeholders, and identification of its major strategies. (22)

Mix Variance A variance that arises from a change in the relative proportion of outputs (a sales mix variance) or inputs (a materials or labor mix variance). (26)

Mixed Cost A cost that has both fixed and variable components; also called *semivariable cost*. (2)

Monte Carlo Simultation A method of sampling from the assumed distribution function to obtain simulated observations of costs or other variables.

Multicollinearity Correlation between two or more independent variables in a multiple regression equation. (12)

Multiple-Factor Formula An allocation formula that uses multiple bases for an allocation base when allocating costs. (7)

Multiple Rates of Return Problem arising when computing the internal rate of return for cash flows that change signs more than once in the project's life. It is possible, then, for such a project to have more than one internal rate of return. (23)

Mutually Exclusive Term used in capital investment decisions to describe a situation where selection of one project precludes the selection of another. (23)

Negotiated Transfer Price System whereby the transfer prices are arrived at through negotiation between managers of buying and selling departments. (21)

Net Income Operating profit adjusted for interest, income taxes, extraordinary items, and other items required to comply with GAAP and other regulations. (2)

Net Present Value Difference between the discounted future cash flows from a project and the value of the discounted cash outflows to acquire the project. (23)

Net Present Value Index Ratio of the net present value of a project to the funds invested in the project. (23)

Net Realizable Value Method Joint cost allocation based on the proportional values of the joint products at the split-off point. (10)

New Product Development Time The period between the first consideration of a product and its sale to the customer. (16)

Nominal Discount Rate A rate of interest that includes compensation for inflation. (23)

Nominal Dollars Actual numerical count of money exchanged without adjusting for inflation. (23)

Noncontrollable Cost A cost that cannot be changed or influenced by a given manager.

Nonmanufacturing Costs Administrative and marketing costs. (2)

Nonvalue-Added Activities Activities that do not add value to a good or service. (1, 5, 8, 9)

Normal Costing A system of accounting whereby direct materials and direct labor are charged to cost objects at actual, and manufacturing overhead is applied. (4, 11)

Normal Costs Product cost amounts where actual direct materials and direct labor costs are assigned to products, but where manufacturing overhead is applied using a predetermined rate. (3, 9)

Normal Spoilage Spoiled goods that are a result of the regular operation of the production process. (6)

Numerator Reason A difference between actual and applied overhead caused by differences between estimated overhead costs and actual overhead costs for the period.

Objective Function Mathematical statement of an objective to be maximized or minimized. (13)

On-Time Performance Situations in which the product or service is delivered when it is scheduled to be delivered. (16)

Operating Budgets Refers to the budgeted income statement, the production budget, the budgeted cost of goods sold, and supporting budgets. (18)

Operating Leverage The extent to which an organization's cost structure is made up of fixed costs. (13)

Operating Profit The excess of operating revenues over the operating costs to generate those revenues. (2)

Operation A standardized method or technique that is repetitively performed. (3, 5)

Operating Costing A hybrid costing system often used in manufacturing goods that have some common characteristics plus some individual characteristics. Typically, the production methods are standardized, but materials are different in each product or batch. (3, 5)

Operational Measures of Time Measures that indicate the speed and reliability with which organization's supply products and services to customers. (16)

Opportunity Cost The lost benefit that the best alternative course of action could provide. (2)

Ordering Costs Costs that increase with the number of orders placed for inventory. (24)

Ordinary Least Squares Regression A regression method that minimizes the sum of the squared distances of each observation from the regression line. (12)

Organizational Goals Set of broad objectives established by management that company employees work to achieve. (17)

Outlay Cost A past, present, or future cash outflow. (2)

Outliers Observations of costs of different activity levels (or similar phenomena) that are significantly different from other observations in the data series. (12)

Overapplied Overhead The excess of applied overhead over actual overhead incurred during a period. (4)

Overhead See *Manufacturing Overhead*. It is an ambiguous term when unmodified. Lay people often refer to everything (including administrative costs) but direct materials and direct labor as overhead.

Overhead Variance The difference between actual and applied overhead. (4)

Participative Budgeting The use of input from lower-and middle-management employees; also called *grass roots budgeting*. (17)

Pareto Chart A chart used to display the number of problems or defects in a product over time. (16)

Payback One method of assessing capital investment projects using the rationale that there is a positive relationship between the speed of payback and the rate of return. (23)

Payback Period The time required to recoup an investment from the cash flows from the project. (23)

Payback Reciprocal One divided by the payback period in years. (23)

Period Costs Costs that can be attributed to time intervals. (2, 11)

Periodic Inventory Method A method of inventory accounting whereby inventory balances are determined on specific dates (such as quarterly) by physical count rather than on a continuous basis. (3)

Perpetual Inventory Method A method of accounting whereby inventory records are maintained on a continuously updated basis. (3)

Physical Quantities Method Joint cost allocation based on measurement of the volume, weight, or other physical measure of the joint products at the split-off point. (10)

Planned Variance Variances that are expected to arise if certain conditions affect operations. (19)

Planning Budget Another term for master budget. (17, 18)

Plantwide Allocation Method This method uses one cost pool for the entire plant, and a single allocation rate or set of rates for the entire plant. Contrast this method with *Department Allocation Method*. (8)

Predetermined Overhead Rate An amount obtained by dividing total estimated overhead for the coming period by the total overhead allocation base for the coming period. It is used for applying overhead to cost objects in normal or standard cost systems. (4, 11)

Predictors The variables on the right-hand side of a regression equation (the X-terms) used to predict costs or a similar dependent variable. They are cost drivers that are expected to affect costs. (12)

Present Value The amount of future cash flows discounted to their equivalent worth today. (23)

Price Discrimination Sale of products or services at different prices when the different prices do not reflect differences in marginal costs. (14)

Price Variance Difference between actual and budgeted or standard prices. See *Sales Price Variance* when the price variance applies to sales. (18, 19)

Prime Cost The sum of direct materials and direct labor. (2)

Principal-Agent Relationships The relationship between a superior, referred to as the *principal*, and a subordinate, called the *agent*. (20)

Prior Department Costs Costs incurred in an upstream department and charged to a subsequent department in the production process. (5)

Process Costing An accounting system that is used when identical units are produced through an ongoing series of uniform production steps. Used in continuous processing production settings. (3, 5)

Product Live Cycle The time from initial research and development to the time at which support to the customer ends. (14)

Product-Choice Decisions The product-choice problem arises when there are limited amounts of resources that are being fully used and must be allocated to multiple products. The decision is to choose the optimal product mix. (15)

Product Costs Those costs that can be attributed to products; costs that are part of inventory. For a manufacturer, they include direct materials, direct labor, and manufacturing overhead. The fixed manufacturing costs attributed to products differ under the variable costing and the full-absorption costing systems. (2, 11)

Product Mix A combination of outputs to be produced within the resource constraints of an entity. (15)

Production Budget Production plan of resources needed to meet current sales demand and ensure inventory levels are sufficient for future sales. (17)

Production Cost Report A report that summarizes production and cost results for a period. This report is generally used by managers to monitor production and cost flows. (5)

Production Departments Departments in service, merchandising, or manufacturing organizations that generate goods or services that are ultimately sold to outsiders. (6)

Production Mix Variance A variance arising from a change in the relative proportion of inputs (a materials or labor mix variance). (26)

Production Volume Variance A fixed cost variance caused by a difference between the actual and estimated volume used to estimate unit fixed costs. (19)

Production Yield Variance Difference between expected and actual inputs required to produce a given level of output. (26)

Profit Center An organizational unit responsible for profits; usually responsible for revenues, costs, production, and sales volumes. (18, 20)

Profit Equation Operating profits equal total contribution margin less fixed costs. (13)

Profit Plan The income statement portion of the master budget. (17)

Profit Variance Analysis Analysis of the causes of differences between budgeted profits and the actual profits earned. (18)

Profit-Volume Analysis A version of CVP analysis where the cost and revenue lines are collapsed into a single profit line. See *Cost-Volume-Profit Analysis*. (13)

Project A complex job that often takes months or years to complete and requires the work of many different departments, divisions, or subcontractors. (4)

Prorating Variances Assigning portions of variances to the inventory and cost of goods sold accounts to which the variances are related. (19)

Purchase Price Variance The price variance based on the quantity of materials purchased. (19)

Quality Providing the service (including tangible and intangible features) expected by the customer. (16)

Quantity Discounts Price reductions offered for bulk purchases. (24)

Random Event An occurrence that is beyond the control of the decision maker or manager.

Raw Materials An alternative term for direct materials. (2, 3)

Real Discount Rate The discount rate that compensates only for the use of money, not for inflation. (23)

Real Dollars Monetary measures that are adjusted for the effects of inflation so they have the same purchasing power over time. (23)

Real Return Return on capital after adjustment for the effects of inflation. (23)

Reciprocal Method The method of allocating service department costs that recognizes services provided to and from other service departments. (7)

Regression Statistical procedure to determine the relationship between variables. (12)

Relative Performance Evaluation (RPE) A managerial evaluation method that compares divisional performance with that of peer group divisions (i.e., divisions operating in similar product markets). (20)

Relative Sales Value Method See *Net Realizable Method*. (10)

Relevant Costs Costs that are different under alternative actions. (14, 15)

Relevant Range The activity levels within which a cost projection is valid; in particular, the range within which a given fixed cost or a unit variable cost will be unchanged even though volume changes. (2, 12)

Reorder Point The quantity of inventory on hand that triggers the need to order more inventory. (24)

Repetitive Manufacturing Production process characterized by long production runs, few products, and infrequent production line changes.

Residual Income Investment center profit minus (capital charge times investment center assets). (20)

Resources Supplied In activity-based management, the expenditures or amounts spent on an activity (e.g., for the use of an automobile, the amount of the expenditure on the automobile use). (9)

Resources Used In activity-based management, the resources consumed by the activity as measured by the cost driver rate times the cost driver volume (e.g., for the use of an automobile where the cost driver is miles driven, resources used equals the rate per mile times the number of miles driven). (9)

Responsibility Accounting Reporting financial results for each responsibility center (for example, profits for a profit center, costs for a cost center). (18, 20)

Responsibility Center An organizational unit assigned to a manager who is held accountable for its operations and resources. (1, 18, 20)

Return on Investment (ROI) The ratio of profits to investment in the assets that generate those profits. (20)

Revenue Center An organizational unit responsible for revenues and, typically, also for marketing costs. (20)

Revenue Variances Variances in prices and activity that affect sales or other revenues.

Rework Work performed on products that do not pass inspection and subsequently require additional work (including labor, materials and/or overhead) before being sold. (6)

Risk Premium Additional interest or other compensation required for risks in investments. (23)

Safety Stock Inventory carried to protect against delays in delivery, increased demand, or other similar factors. (24)

Sales Activity Variance Variance due to difference between budgeted and actual volume of sales. (18, 26)

Sales Forecasts Estimates of future sales. (17)

Sales Mix Variance Variance arising from the relative proportion of different products sold. (26)

Sales Price Variance Difference between budgeted and actual sales price. (18, 25)

Sales Quantity Variance In multiproduct companies, a variance arising from the change in volume of sales, independent of any change in mix. (26)

Sales Volume Variance See *Sales Activity Variance*.

Scattergraph A plot of costs against past activity levels; sometimes used as a rough guide for cost estimation. (12)

Scrap An output for which the net realizable value is minimal or even negative because of the costs of disposal. (10)

Semifixed Cost A cost that increases in steps; also called *step cost*. (2, 13)

Semivariable Cost A cost that has both fixed and variable components; also called *mixed cost*. (2)

Sensitivity Analysis The study of the effect of changes in assumptions on the results of a decision model. (17)

Serial Correlation In regression, the condition of a systematic relationship between the residuals in the equation. Sometimes referred to as *autocorrelation*. (12)

Service As used in the context of total quality management, includes the product's tangible and intangible features. Tangible features include how well the product performs; intangible features include the service of the company such as courtesy of sales people. (16)

Service Department An organizational unit whose main job is to provide services to other units in the organization. (7)

Service Organizations Organizations whose output product is a result of the performance of some activity rather than some physical product.

Shadow Price Opportunity cost of an additional unit in a constrained multiple product setting. (15)

Short Run Period of time over which capacity will be unchanged, usually one year. (14)

Simplex Method Solution of a linear programming problem using a mathematical technique. (15)

Simultaneous Solution Method See *Reciprocal Allocation.*

Slope of Cost Line The angle of a line to the horizontal axis. In cost estimation, the slope is usually considered the variable cost estimate. (12)

Source Document A basic record in accounting that initiates the entry of an activity in the accounting system. (4)

Special Order An order that will not affect other sales and is usually a short-run occurrence. (14)

Spending Variance Difference between actual and standard or budgeted overhead costs.

Split-Off Point Stage of processing where two or more products are separated. (10)

Spoilage Goods that are damaged, do not meet specifications, or are otherwise not suitable for further processing or sale as good output. (6)

Staff A corporate group or employee with specialized technical skills, such as accounting or legal staff.

Stakeholders Groups or individuals, such as employees, suppliers, customers, shareholders, and the community, who have a stake in what the organization does. (22)

Standard Cost The anticipated cost of producing and/or selling a unit of output. (18, 19)

Standard Cost Center An organizational unit where managers are held responsible for costs and where the relationship between costs and output is well defined. See *Cost Center.* (18, 20)

Standard Cost System An accounting system in which products are costed using standard costs instead of actual costs. (19)

Standard Costing A method of accounting whereby costs are assigned to cost objects at predetermined amounts. (19)

Standard Deviation A measure or risk based on dispersion. It is computed as the square root of the sum of the squared differences between actual observations and the mean of the data series divided by one less than the number of observations. (12)

Static Budget Budget for a single activity level. Usually the master budget. (18)

Statistical Quality Control A method for evaluating a repetitive process to determine if the process is out of control.

Step Cost A cost that increases in steps. Also called *semi-fixed cost.* (2, 13)

Step Method The method of service department cost allocation that recognizes some interservice department services. (7)

Stockout Running out of inventory. (24)

Strategic Long-Range Plan Statement detailing specific steps to be taken in achieving a company's organizational goals. (17)

Subsidiary Ledger Detailed information used to support the amounts summarized in a general ledger account. (4)

Sunk Cost An expenditure made inthe past that cannot be changed by present or future decisions. (2, 14)

_t_-Statistic t is equal to the coefficient b divided by its standard error. (12)

Target Cost Equals the target price minus the desired profit margin. (14, 18)

Target Costing A market driven method of establishing target costs by starting with a target sales price and subtracting the target margin or profit. (18)

Target Price The price based on customers' perceived value for the product and the price competitors charge. (14)

Tax Basis Remaining tax-depreciable "book value" of an asset for tax purposes. (23)

Tax Credit Recapture Recapture of investment tax credit taken on an asset if the asset is taken out of service before the time required to earn the investment tax credit.

Tax Shield The reduction in tax payment because of depreciation deducted for tax purposes. (23)

Theory of Constraints A management method that focuses on maximizing profits by identifying bottlenecks, or capacity constraints, and by increasing capacity at the bottlenecks. (1, 15, 16)

Throughput Contribution Sales dollars minus costs direct materials and such other variable costs as energy costs and piecework labor. (15)

Time Value of Money The concept that cash received earlier is worth more than cash received later. (23)

Total Cost Variance Difference between total actual costs for the time period and the standard allowed per unit times the number of good units produced. (19)

Total Manufacturing Costs Total costs charged to work in process in a given period. (3)

Total Quality Management A management method by which the organization seeks to excel on all dimensions, with the customer ultimately defining quality. (1, 6, 15, 16)

Transfer Price The price at which goods or services are traded between organizational units. (21)

Transferred-in Costs An alternative term for prior department costs. (5)

Transportation-in Costs The costs incurred by the buyer of goods to ship those goods from the place of sale to the place where the buyer can use the goods.

Treasurer The corporate officer responsible for cash management and financing corporate activities. (1)

Trend Analysis Method of forecasting that ranges from simple visual extrapolation of points on a graph to highly sophisticated computerized time series analysis. (17)

Underapplied Overhead The excess of actual overhead over applied overhead in a period. (4)

Unfavorable Variances Variances that, taken alone, reduce the operating profit or net income. (18)

Unused Resource Capacity The differences between resources used and resources supplied. (See *resources used* and *resources supplied*.) (9)

Upper Control Limit The maximum value that may be observed and still assume that a process is in control. (25)

Usage Variance An alternative term for efficiency variance, usually related to materials used. (19)

User Department A department that uses the services of service departments. (7)

Value of Information Value placed on information one could obtain in a decision-making context.

Value-Added Activities Those activities that customers perceive as adding utility to the goods or services they purchase. (1, 2, 4, 5, 8, 9, 10, 16, 18)

Value-Based Financial Statements Financial statements that break down expenditures into those associated with value-added activities and those associated with nonvalue-added activities. (2)

Value Chain The linked set of activities that increases the usefulness (or value) of the goods or services of an organization. (1, 2, 4, 5, 8, 9, 10, 11, 13, 14, 18)

Value Engineering A systematic evaluation of all aspects of research and development, design of products and processes, production, marketing, distribution, and customer service to reduce costs and satisfy customer needs. (14)

Variable Cost Ratio Variable costs as a percentage of sales-dollars. (13)

Variable Costing A system of accounting for costs that assigns products with only the variable costs of manufacturing. (2, 11)

Variable Costs Costs that change in direct proportion to a change in the volume of activity. (2, 11, 12, 13, 14, 15, 18, 19)

Variance Investigation The expected step taken if managers judge that the benefits of correction exceed the costs of follow-up. (19)

Variances Differences between planned results and actual outcomes. (3, 18, 19)

Warning Signal The signal that a problem needs to be investigated. (16)

Weighted-Average Contribution Margin The contribution margin of more than one product when a constant product mix is assumed. (13)

Weighted-Average Costing The inventory method that combines costs and equivalent units of a period with the costs and equivalent units in beginning inventory for product-costing purposes. (5)

Work in Process Uncompleted work that is in the production process. (2, 3, 4)

Working Capital Cash, accounts receivable, and other short-term assets required to maintain an activity.

X-Terms The terms on the right-hand side of a regression. (12)

NAME INDEX

SUBJECT INDEX